Y0-BVQ-469

ADVANCES IN

NEURAL
INFORMATION
PROCESSING
SYSTEMS 4

OTHER TITLES OF INTEREST
FROM MORGAN KAUFMANN PUBLISHERS

ADVANCES IN

NEURAL INFORMATION PROCESSING SYSTEMS 4

EDITED BY

JOHN E. MOODY
YALE UNIVERSITY

STEVE J. HANSON
SIEMENS RESEARCH CENTER

RICHARD P. LIPPMANN
MIT LINCOLN LABORATORY

MORGAN KAUFMANN PUBLISHERS
2929 CAMPUS DRIVE
SUITE 260
SAN MATEO CALIFORNIA 94403

Editor   *Bruce M. Spatz*
Production Manager   *Yonie Overton*
Project Management   *Professional Book Center*
Composition   *Professional Book Center*
Cover Design   *Jo Jackson*

MORGAN KAUFMANN PUBLISHERS, INC.
   Editorial Office:
   2929 Campus Drive, Suite 260
   San Mateo, CA 94403
   (415)578-9911

Copyright © 1992 by Morgan Kaufmann Publishers, Inc.
All rights reserved
Printed in the United States of America

No part of this publication may be reproduced, stored in a retrieval system, or transmitted in any form or by any means—electronic, mechanical, photocopying, recording,
or otherwise—without the prior written permission of the publisher.

96 95 93 94 92   5 4 3 2 1

Library of Congress Cataloging in Publication Data
is available for this title.

ISSN 1049-5258
ISBN 1-55860-222-4

CONTENTS

Part II NEURO-DYNAMICS

Part III SPEECH

Part VIII OPTICAL CHARACTER RECOGNITION

Part IX CONTROL AND PLANNING

Part XII LEARNING AND GENERALIZATION

Part XIII ARCHITECTURES AND ALGORITHMS

Part XIV PERFORMANCE COMPARISONS

PREFACE

This volume contains 144 papers summarizing the talks and posters presented at the fifth NIPS conference (short for "Neural Information Processing Systems—Natural and Synthetic"), held in Denver, Colorado, from 2–5 December 1991. Since its inception in 1987, the NIPS conference has attracted researchers from many disciplines who are applying their expertise to problems in the field of neural networks. The conference and the following two-day workshop have become a forum for presenting the latest research results and for leading researchers to gather and exchange ideas.

The 1991 conference maintained the high level of excitement of its predecessors. Important new theoretical results were presented concerning the capability and generalization performance of networks. Of particular interest are papers included in this volume by Vapnik, MacKay, Haussler, and others, which describe how to relate the complexity of networks to generalization performance on unseen test data. Many new network architectures were described. Some integrate expert system rules with networks, build hierarchies of networks, use radial basis function hidden nodes, and impose pre-specified invariance on the final solution. Neurobiological papers analyzed and modeled neurons in the hippocampus, in cat striate cortex, and in the blowfly. They also modeled biological networks that control eye movement, form topological maps, and compensate for head movement. Successful applications of neural networks were described in the areas of speech, vision, language, control, medical monitoring, and system diagnostics. Of particular interest was a paper by Tesauro, which demonstrated how a network could be trained to play backgammon at an expert level; papers by Jain, Watrous, and Giles, which described approaches to learning grammars; hybrid hidden-Markov-model/neural-network speech recognizers described by Haffner, Levin, Singer, Renals, and Bengio; papers on optical character recognition; a paper by Jabri, which describes a network to control a wearable heart defibrillator; a paper by Smyth for diagnosis of large-dish antenna pointing systems; and a paper by Röscheisen concerning control of force on rollers in steel rolling mills. Papers also described new analog and digital VLSI chips, systems for neural network implementation, and compared neural network and statistical approaches to pattern classification.

An historical milestone was reached this year, NIPS-91 was the fifth NIPS conference since the first conference was held in 1987. To mark this anniversary, we decided to review the history of events that led to the foundation of the NIPS conference and to discuss the evolution of the conference since its foundation. The following history is based in part on the recollections of Jim Bower, Larry Jackel, and Ed Posner. Some of this history was presented by Larry Jackel at the opening banquet.

While the first NIPS conference met in 1987, its origins can be traced back to the "Hopfest" meetings named in honor of John Hopsfield, held at Caltech. The first few, 1984–1986, were organized by Ed Posner of Caltech. These meetings met in the fall and included researches mainly from the Caltech campus and JPL. In 1985, Larry Jackel of Bell Labs and Demetri Psaltis of Caltech organized the first of what were to become the "Snowbird" meetings. The meetings were intended to be small informal workshops and convened in Santa Barbara. Twenty people were invited, but news of the meeting spread by word of mouth, so that attendance ended up growing to 60. In 1986, the meeting reconvened at Snowbird, which offered better snow conditions. Jackel, Psaltis, and the other organizers intended to keep the attendance down to 100 people, but the interest was so great that many people were turned away even after the attendance was capped at 160. The first Snowbird proceedings was edited by John Denker of Bell Labs and published by the American Institute of Physics (AIP) press.

In 1986, the Snowbird meeting was the only neural network conference, and it clearly could not accommodate the exploding numbers of researchers becoming interested in the field and still maintain the character of a small workshop. To respond to demand, the organizers decided to make Snowbird a more closed meeting, but to set in motion organization of a large meeting that would be open to all interested. The goal was to have a non-commercial meeting, dedicated to scholarship, which would capture some of the flavor of the workshop. The Snowbird organizers nominated a committee with Ed Posner as General Chairman and Yaser Abu Mostafa as Program Chairman (both of Caltech), to organize and run the 1987 NIPS conference, which was officially sponsored by the IEEE Information Theory Society. Denver was chosen as the site due to its central geographical location, ease of access by air, and close proximity to the mountains and the University of Colorado at Boulder.

The 1987 organizers designed the NIPS conference to have many of the advantages of a workshop, while still accommodating a large audience. To maximize scientific interchange, they decided to limit the oral presentations to a single stream, have posters be the majority of presentations, and include poster preview as well as formal poster sessions. Furthermore, a set of post-conference workshops was organized at the Copper Mountain ski resort after the main conference to enable small groups to discuss specific topics. The 1987 conference proved to be a great success, with about 450 attendees and 91 papers making it into the proceedings. Dana Z. Anderson of CU Boulder edited the proceedings, which were published by the AIP press and are now informally known as NIPS Volume 0.

Since 1987, some changes and refinements have been made, but the basic structure of the conference has remained the same. The NIPS 1988 proceedings (NIPS Volume 1, edited by David Tourestzky of Carnegie Mellon) were the first published by Morgan Kaufmann. Also in 1988, the post-conference workshops were moved to Keystone, CO. The refinement processes (three reviewers instead of two), a more cross-disciplinary grouping of presentations, finer presentation catagories, and the addition of five-minute oral poster spotlight presentations. A major and very successful addition to the 1991 conference was the introduction of a day of tutorials preceding the main conference. The 1991 workshops were held at Vail, which proved to ba a popular move.

Finally, 1991 marked the drafting of articles of incorporation for the Neural Information Processing Systems Foundation, which will be responsible for the continuity of the NIPS conference in future years. The initial board of directors of the foundation consists of the 1987 to 1992 NIPS General Chairs (Ed Posner of Cal Tech, Terry Sejnowski of the Salk Institute and UCSD, Scott Kirkpatrick of IBM, Richard Lippmann of MIT Lincoln Labs, John Moody of Yale, and Stephen Hanson of Siemens), a member of the IEEE Information Theory Society (Terry Fine of Cornell), and our legal counsel (Philip Sotel).

The NIPS conference continues to be an exciting, successful meeting due to the efforts of a large group of people. We would first like to thank all the other members of the 1991 program and organizing committees who helped make this conference possible, In particular, we would like to thank Renate Crowley of Siemens for her extensive work throughout the year as the conference secretary and both Renate and Kate Fuqua of CU Boulder for running the conference desk so smoothly. Student contributions are an important part of the NIPS program, and we gratefully thank Tom McKenna of ONR and Steve Suddarth of AFOSR for the student travel funding provided by their agencies. Finally, we thank everyone who attended and submitted papers and the 105 referees who carefully read and reviewed 20 papers each.

John Moody
Stephen Hanson
Richard Lippmann

NIPS-91 ORGANIZING COMMITTEE

General Chair	John Moody, Yale University
Program Chair	Stephen Hanson, Siemens
Workshop CoChair	Gerry Tesauro, IBM
	Scott Kirkpatrick, IBM
Publicity Chair	John Pearson, David Sarnoff Research Lab
Publications Chair	Richard Lippmann, MIT Lincoln Laboratory
Treasurer	Bob Allen, Bellcore
Government/Corporate Liaison	Lee Giles, NEC Research Institute
Local Arrangements Chair	Mike Mozer, University of Colorado
IEEE Liaisons	Rodney Goodman and Ed Posner, Caltech
Tutorials Chair	John Moody, Yale University
APS Liaisons	Eric Baum, NEC Research Institute
	Larry Jackel, AT&T Bell Labs
Neurobiology Liaisons	James Bower, Caltech
	Tom Brown, Yale University
IEEE Liaisons	Rodney Goodman and Ed Posner, Caltech
Overseas Liaison (Japan)	Mitsuo Kawato, ATR Research Laboratories
Overseas Liaison (Australia)	Maran Jabri, University of Sydney
Overseas Liaison (United Kingdom)	John Bridle, RSRE
Overseas Liaison (South America)	Andreas Meier, Simon Bolivar University

NIPS-91 PROGRAM COMMITTEE

Program Chair	Stephen Hanson, Siemens
Program CoChairs	David Ackley, Bellcore
	Pierre Baldi, JPL and Calteh
	William Bialek, NEC Research Institute
	Lee Giles, NEC Research Institute
	Steve Omohundro, ICSI
	Mike Jordan, MIT
	John Platt, Synaptics
	Terry Sejnowski, Salk Institute
	David Stork, Ricoh and Stanford
	Alex Waibel, CMU

NIPS-91 Reviewers

Martin Brady, Penn. State Univ.
Gary Cottrell, UCSD
John Denker, AT&T Lab
John Hertz, NORDITA
James Keeler, Advanced Computing Technology
Alan Lapedes, Los Alamos
David Rogers, RIACS
David G. Stork, Ricoh
Peter Todd, Stanford Univ.
Andreas Weigend, Stanford Univ.
Sue Becker, Univ. of Toronto
David A. Cohn, Univ. of Washington
Michael Littman, Bellcore
David Plaut, CMU
Lori Pratt, Rutgers Univ.
Jürgen Schmidhuber, Technische Univ. Muenchen
Rich Zemel, Univ. of Toronto
Paul Munro, Siemens
Ben Yuhas, Bellcore
Steve Gallant, Northeastern Univ.
Marwen Jabri, Sydney, Univ.
Gary M. Kuhn, CCRP-IDA
Y.C. Lee, Univ. of Maryland
Ken Marko, Ford Motor Company
Michiel Noordewier, Rutgers Univ.
Kevin Lang, NEC
Steven C. Suddarth, AFOSR
Robert Allen, Bellcore
Jonathan Bachrach
Gary Dell, Beckman Institute
Michael G. Dyer, UCLA
Jeff Elman, UCSD
Michael Gasser, UCSD
Lee Giles, NEC
Robert Jacobs, MIT
Stephen Hanson, Siemens
Christopher Atkeson, MIT

Andrew Barto, Univ. of Massachusetts
Judy Franklin, GTE
Vijaykumar Gullipalli, Univ. of Massachusetts
Thomas Martinez, Beckman Institute
Kumpati Narendra, Yale Univ.
Richard Sutton, GTE
Manoel Tenorio, Purdue Univ.
Lyle Ungar, Univ. of Pennsylvania
Josh Alspector, Bellcore
Jim Burr, Stanford Univ.
Federico Faggin, Synaptics
Hans Peter Graf, AT&T
Kristina Johnson, Univ. of Colorado
John Lazzaro, Univ. of Colorado
Dick Lyon, Apple Computer
Dan Schwartz, GTE
Larry Abbott, Brandeis Univ.
Thomas Anastasio, Univ. of Southern California
Joseph Attick, Princeton
William Bialek, Univ. of California at Berkeley
A.B. Bonds, Vanderbilt Univ.
James Bower, California Inst. of Tech.
Thomas Brown, Yale Univ.
Jack Cowan, Univ. of Chicago
Shawn Lockery, Salk Institute
Bartlett Mel, California Inst. of Tech.
Kenneth Miller, California Inst. of Tech.
Eric Schwartz, New York Univ. Medical Center
Terry Sejnowski, Salk Institute
Gordon Shepherd, New Haven
David van Essen, California Inst. of Tech.
Frank Fallside, Univ. of Cambridge
Hervé Bourlard, Phillips
Patrick Haffner, Centre National d'Etudes des Telecommunications

Richard Lippmann, MIT Lincoln Lab
Hong Leung, MIT
John S. Bridle, RSRE
David Burr, Bellcore
Richard Durbin, ICSI
David Hausssler, Univ. of California at
    Santa Cruz
Terry Sanger, MIT
Gerry Tesauro, IBM Watson Lab
Eric Mjolsness, Yale University
Ronny Meir, Bellcore
Sara Solla, Santa Fe Institute
Fernando Pineda, Applied Physics Lab
Steve Omohundro, ICSI

Pierre Baldi, California Inst. of Tech.
Amir Atiya, Texas A&M Univ.
Santosh S. Venkatesh, Univ. of Pennsyl-
    vania
Halbert White, UCSD
Stephen Judd, Siemens
Tom Petsche, Siemens
Subatai Ahmad, ICSI
Joachim Buhmann, Univ. of Southern
    California
Gene Gindi, Yale Univ.
Geoff Hinton, Univ. of Toronto
Nathan Intrator, Brown Univ.

PART I

NEUROBIOLOGY

MODELS WANTED: MUST FIT DIMENSIONS OF SLEEP AND DREAMING*

J. Allan Hobson, Adam N. Mamelak† and Jeffrey P. Sutton‡
Laboratory of Neurophysiology and Department of Psychiatry
Harvard Medical School
74 Fenwood Road, Boston, MA 02115

Abstract

During waking and sleep, the brain and mind undergo a tightly linked and precisely specified set of changes in state. At the level of neurons, this process has been modeled by variations of Volterra-Lotka equations for cyclic fluctuations of brainstem cell populations. However, neural network models based upon rapidly developing knowledge of the specific population connectivities and their differential responses to drugs have not yet been developed. Furthermore, only the most preliminary attempts have been made to model across states. Some of our own attempts to link rapid eye movement (REM) sleep neurophysiology and dream cognition using neural network approaches are summarized in this paper.

1 INTRODUCTION

New models are needed to test the closely linked neurophysiological and cognitive theories that are emerging from recent scientific studies of sleep and dreaming. This section describes four separate but related levels of analysis at which modeling may

---

*Based, in part, upon an invited address by J.A.H. at NIPS, Denver, Dec. 2 1991 and, in part, upon a review paper by J.P.S., A.N.M. and J.A.H. published in the *Psychiatric Annals*.

†Currently in the Department of Neurosurgery, University of California, San Francisco, CA 94143

‡Also in the Center for Biological Information Processing, Whitaker College, E25-201, Massachusetts Institute of Technology, Cambridge, MA 02139

be applied and outlines some of the desirable features of such models in terms of the burgeoning data of sleep and dream science. In the subsequent sections, we review our own preliminary efforts to develop models at some of the levels discussed.

1.1   THE INDIVIDUAL NEURON

Existing models or "neuromines" faithfully represent membrane properties but ignore the dynamic biochemical changes that change neural excitability over the long term. This is particularly important in the modeling of state control where the crucial neurons appear to act more like hormone pumps than like simple electrical transducers. Put succinctly, we need models that consider the biochemical or "wet" aspects of nerve cells, as well as the "dry" or electrical aspects (*cf.* McKenna *et al.*, in press).

1.2   NEURAL POPULATION INTERACTIONS

To mimic the changes in excitability of the modulatory neurons which control sleep and dreaming, new models are needed which incorporate both the engineering principles of oscillators and the biological principles of time-keeping. The latter principle is especially relevant in determining the dramatically variable long period time-constants that are observed within and across species. For example, we need to equip population models borrowed from field biology (McCarley and Hobson, 1975) with specialized properties of "wet" neurons as mentioned in section 1.1.

1.3   COGNITIVE CONSEQUENCES OF MODULATION OF NEURAL NETWORKS

To understand the state-dependent changes in cognition, such as those that distinguish waking and dreaming, a potentially fruitful approach is to mimic the known effects of neuromodulation and examine the information processing properties of neural networks. For example, if the input-output fidelity of networks can be altered by changing their mode (see Sutton *et al.*, this volume), we might be better able to understand the changes in both instantaneous associative properties and long term plasticity alterations that occur in sleep and dreaming. We might thus trap the brain-mind into revealing its rules for making moment-to-moment cross-correlations of its data and for changing the content and status of its storage in memory.

1.4   STATE-DEPENDENT CHANGES IN COGNITION

At the highest level of analysis, psychological data, even that obtained from the introspection of waking and dreaming subjects, need to be more creatively reduced with a view to modeling the dramatic alterations that occur with changes in brain state. As an example, consider the instability of orientation of dreaming, where times, places, persons and actions change without notice. Short of mastering the thorny problem of generating narrative text from a data base, and thus synthesizing an artificial dream, we need to formulate rules and measures of categorizing constancy and transformations (Sutton and Hobson, 1991). Such an approach is a means of further refining the algorithms of cognition itself, an effort which is now limited to simple activation models that cannot change mode.

An important characteristic of the set of new models that are proposed is that each level informs, and is informed by, the other levels. This nested, interlocking feature is represented in figure 1. It should be noted that any erroneous assumptions made at level 1 will have effects at levels 2 and 3 and these will, in turn, impede our capacity to integrate levels 3 and 4. Level 4 models can and should thus proceed with a degree of independence from levels 1, 2 and 3. Proceeding from level 1 upward is the "bottom-up" approach, while proceeding from level 4 downward is the "top-down" approach. We like to think it might be possible to take both approaches in our work while according equal respect to each.

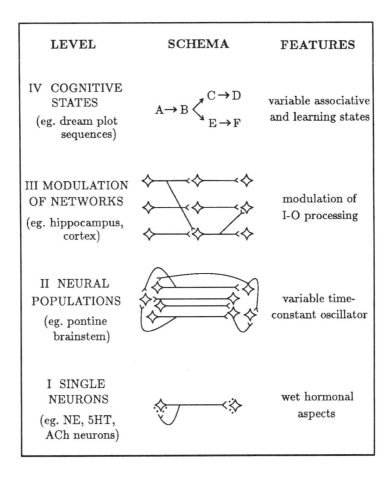

Figure 1: Four levels at which modeling innovations are needed to provide more realistic simulations of brain-mind states such as waking and dreaming. See text for discussion.

2   STATES OF WAKING AND SLEEPING

The states of waking and sleeping, including REM and non-REM (NREM) sleep, have characteristic behavioral, neuronal, polygraphic and psychological features that span all four levels. These properties are summarized in figures 2 and 3. Changes occurring within and between different levels are affected by the sleep-wake or circadian cycle and by the relative shifts in brain chemistry.

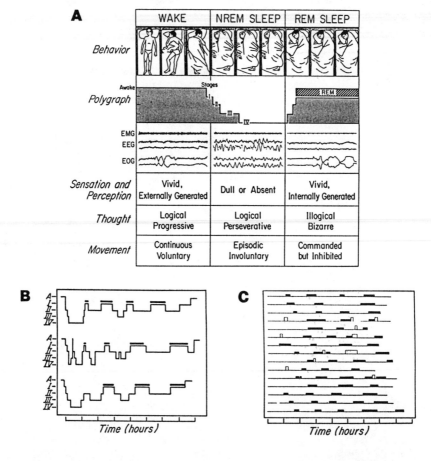

Figure 2: (a) States of waking and NREM and REM sleeping in humans. Characteristic behavioral, polygraphic and psychological features are shown for each state. (b) Ultradian sleep cycle of NREM and REM sleep shown in detailed sleep-stage graphs of 3 subjects. (c) REM sleep periodograms of 15 subjects. From Hobson and Steriade (1986), with permission.

2.1   CIRCADIAN RHYTHMS

The circadian cycle has been studied mathematically using oscillator and other non-linear dynamical models to capture features of sleep-wake rhythms (Moore-Ede and Czeisler, 1984; figure 2). Shorter (infradian) and longer (ultradian) rhythms, relative to the circadian rhythm, have also been examined. In general, oscillators are used to couple neural, endocrine and other pathways important in controlling a variety of functions, such as periods of rest and activity, energy conservation and thermoregulation. The oscillators can be sensitive to external cues or *zeitgebers*, such as light and daily routines, and there is a stong linkage between the circadian clock and the NREM-REM sleep oscillator.

2.2   RECIPROCAL INTERACTION MODEL

In the 1970s, a brainstem oscillator became identified that was central to regulating sleeping and waking. Discrete cell populations in the pons that were most active during waking, less active in NREM sleep and silent during REM sleep were found to contain the monoamines norepinephrine (NE) and serotonin (5HT). Among the many cell populations that became active during REM sleep, but were generally quiescent otherwise, were cells associated with acetylcholine (ACh) release.

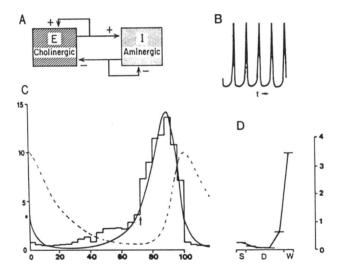

Figure 3: (a) Reciprocal interaction model of REM sleep generation showing the structural interaction between cholinergic and monoaminergic cell populations. Plus sign implies excitatory influences; minus sign implies inhibitory influences. (b) Model output of the cholinergic unit derived from Lotka-Volterra equations. (c) Histogram of the discharge rate from a cholinergic related pontine cell recorded over 12 normalized sleep-wake cycles. Model cholinergic (solid line) and monoaminergic (dotted line) outputs. (d) Noradrenergic discharge rates before (S), during (D) and following (W) a REM sleep episode. From Hobson and Steriade (1986), with permission.

By making a variety of simplifying assumptions, McCarley and Hobson (1975) were able to structurally and mathematically model the oscillations between these monoaminergic and cholinergic cell populations (figure 3). This level 2 model consists of two compartments, one being monoaminergic-inhibitory and the other cholinergic-excitatory. It is based pupon the assumptions of field biology (Volterra-Lotka) and of dry neuromines (level 3). The excitation (inhibition) originating from each compartment influences the other and also feeds back on itself. Numerous predictions generated by the model have been verified experimentally (Hobson and Steriade, 1986).

Because the neural population model shown in figure 3 uses the limited passive membrane type of neuromine discussed in the introduction, the resulting oscillator has a time-constant in the millisecond range, not even close to the real range of minutes to hours that characterize the sleep-dream cycle (figure 2). As such, the model is clearly incapable of realistically representing the long-term dynamic properties that characterize interacting neuromodulatory populations. To surmount this limitation, two modifications are possible: one is to remodel the individual neuromines equipping them with mathematics describing up and down regulation of receptors and intracellular biochemistry that results in long-term changes in synaptic efficacy (*cf.* McKenna *et al.*, in press); another is to model the longer time constants of the sleep cycle in terms of protein transport times between the two populations in brainstems of realistically varying width (*cf.* Hobson and Steriade, 1986).

3   NEUROCOGNITIVE ASPECTS OF WAKING, SLEEPING AND DREAMING

Since the discovery that REM sleep is correlated with dreaming, significant advances have been made in understanding both the neural and cognitive processes occurring in different states of the sleep-wake cycle. During waking, wherein the brain is in a state of relative aminergic dominance, thought content and cognition display consistency and continuity. NREM sleep mentation is typically characterized by ruminative thoughts void of perceptual vividness or emotional tone. Within this state, the aminergic and cholinergic systems are more evenly balanced than in either the wake or REM sleep states. As previously noted, REM sleep is a state associated with relative cholinergic activation. Its mental status manifestations include graphic, emotionally charged and formally bizarre images encompassing visual hallucinations and delusions.

3.1   ACTIVATION-SYNTHESIS MODEL

The activation-synthesis hypothesis (Hobson and McCarley, 1977) was the first account of dream mentation based on the neurophysiological state of REM sleep. It considered factors present at levels 3 and 4, according to the scheme in section 1, and attempted to bridge these two levels. In the model, cholinergic activation and reciprocal monoaminergic disinhibition of neural networks in REM sleep generated the source of dream formation. However, the details of how neural networks might actually synthesize information in the REM sleep state was not specified.

3.2   NEURAL NETWORK MODELS

Several neural network models have subsequently been proposed that also attempt to bridge levels 3 and 4 (for example, Crick and Mitchison, 1983). Recently, Mamelak and Hobson (1989) have suggested a neurocognitive model of dream bizarreness that extends the activation-synthesis hypothesis. In the model, the monoaminergic withdrawal in sleep relative to waking leads to a decrease in the signal-to-noise ratio in neural networks (figure 4). When this is coupled with phasic cholinergic excitation of the cortex, via brainstem ponto-geniculo-occipital (PGO) cell firing (figure 5), cognitive information becomes altered and discontinuous. A central premise of the model is that the monoamines and acetylcholine function as neuromodulators, which modify ongoing activity in networks, without actually supplying afferent input information.

Implementation of the Mamelak and Hobson model as a temporal sequencing network is described by Sutton *et al.* in this volume. Computer simulations demonstrate how changes in modulation similar to some monoaminergic and cholinergic effects can completely alter the way information is collectively sequenced within the same network. This occurs even in the absence of plastic changes in the weights connecting the artificial neurons. Incorporating plasticity, which generally involves neuromodulators such as the monoamines, is a logical next step. This would build important level 1 features into a level 3-4 model and potentially provide useful insight into some state-dependent learning operations.

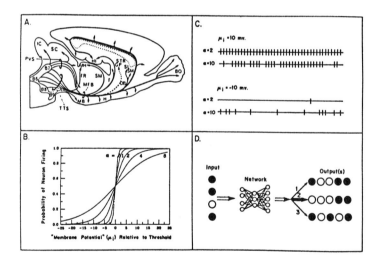

Figure 4: (a) Monoaminergic innervation of the brain is widespread. (b) Plot of the neuron firing probability as a function of the relative membrane potential for various values of monoaminergic modulation (parameterized by α). Higher (lower) modulation is correlated with smaller (larger) α values. (c) Neuron firing when subjected to supra- and sub-threshold inputs of +10 mv and −10 mv, respectively, for $\alpha = 2$ and $\alpha = 10$. (d) For a given input, the repertoire of network outputs generally increases as α increases. From Mamelak and Hobson (1989), with permission.

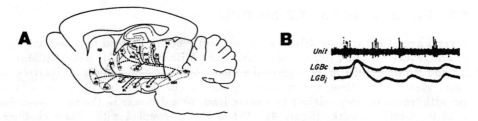

Figure 5: (a) Cholinergic input from the brainstem to the thalamus and cortex is widespread. (b) Unit recordings from PGO burst cells in the pons are correlated with PGO waves recorded in the lateral geniculate bodies (LGB) of the thalamus.

4   CONCLUSION

After discussing four levels at which new models are needed, we have outlined some preliminary efforts at modeling states of waking and sleeping. We suggest that this area of research is ripe for the development of integrative models of brain and mind.

Acknowledgements

Supported by NIH grant MH 13,923, the HMS/MMHC Research & Education Fund, the Livingston, Dupont-Warren and McDonnell-Pew Foundations, DARPA under ONR contract N00014-85-K-0124, the Sloan Foundation and Whitaker College.

References

Crick F, Mitchison G (1983) The function of dream sleep. *Nature* **304** 111-114.

Hobson JA, McCarley RW (1977) The brain as a dream-state generator: An activation-synthesis hypothesis of the dream process. *Am J Psych* **134** 1335-1368.

Hobson JA, Steriade M (1986) Neuronal basis of behavioral state control. In: Mountcastle VB (ed) *Handbook of Physiology - The Nervous System, Vol IV*. Bethesda: Am Physiol Soc, 701-823.

Mamelak AN, Hobson JA (1989) Dream bizarrenes as the cognitive correlate of altered neuronal behavior in REM sleep. *J Cog Neurosci* **1(3)** 201-22.

McCarley RW, Hobson JA (1975) Neuronal excitability over the sleep cycle: A structural and mathematical model. *Science* **189** 58-60.

McKenna T, Davis J, Zornetzer (eds) In press. *Single Neuron Computation*. San Diego, Academic.

Moore-Ede MC, Czeisler CA (eds) (1984) *Mathematical Models of the Circadian Sleep-Wake Cycle*. New York: Raven.

Sutton JP, Hobson (1991) Graph theoretical representation of dream content and discontinuity. *Sleep Research* **20** 164.

Stationarity of Synaptic Coupling Strength Between Neurons with Nonstationary Discharge Properties

Mark R. Sydorenko and Eric D. Young
Dept. of Biomedical Engineering & Center for Hearing Sciences
The Johns Hopkins School of Medicine
720 Rutland Avenue
Baltimore, Maryland 21205

Abstract

Based on a general non-stationary point process model, we computed estimates of the synaptic coupling strength (efficacy) as a function of time after stimulus onset between an inhibitory interneuron and its target postsynaptic cell in the feline dorsal cochlear nucleus. The data consist of spike trains from pairs of neurons responding to brief tone bursts recorded *in vivo*. Our results suggest that the synaptic efficacy is non-stationary. Further, synaptic efficacy is shown to be inversely and approximately linearly related to average presynaptic spike rate. A second-order analysis suggests that the latter result is not due to non-linear interactions. Synaptic efficacy is less strongly correlated with postsynaptic rate and the correlation is not consistent across neural pairs.

1   INTRODUCTION

The aim of this study was to investigate the dynamic properties of the inhibitory effect of type II neurons on type IV neurons in the cat dorsal cochlear nucleus (DCN). Type IV cells are the principal (output) cells of the DCN and type II cells are inhibitory interneurons (Voigt & Young 1990). In particular, we examined the stationarity of the efficacy of inhibition of neural activity in a type IV neuron by individual action potentials (APs) in a type II neuron. Synaptic efficacy, or *effectiveness*, is defined as the average number of postsynaptic (type IV) APs eliminated per presynaptic (type II) AP .

This study was motivated by the observation that post-stimulus time histograms of type IV neurons often show gradual recovery ("buildup") from inhibition (Rhode et al. 1983; Young & Brownell 1976) which could arise through a weakening of inhibitory input over time.

11

Correlograms of pairs of DCN units using long duration stimuli are reported to display inhibitory features (Voigt & Young 1980; Voigt & Young 1990) whereas correlograms using short stimuli are reported to show excitatory features (Gochin et al. 1989). This difference might result from nonstationarity of synaptic coupling. Finally, pharmacological results (Caspary et al. 1984) and current source-density analysis of DCN responses to electrical stimulation (Manis & Brownell 1983) suggest that this synapse may fatigue with activity.

Synaptic efficacy was investigated by analyzing the statistical relationship of spike trains recorded simultaneously from pairs of neurons *in vivo* . We adopt a first order (linear) non-stationary point process model that does not impose *a priori* restrictions on the presynaptic process's distribution. Using this model, estimators of the postsynaptic impulse response to a presynaptic spike were derived using martingale theory and a method of moments approach. To study stationarity of synaptic efficacy, independent estimates of the impulse response were derived over a series of brief time windows spanning the stimulus duration. Average pre- and postsynaptic rate were computed for each window, as well. In this report, we summarize the results of analyzing the dependence of synaptic efficacy (derived from the impulse response estimates) on post-stimulus onset time, presynaptic average rate, postsynaptic average rate, and presynaptic interspike interval.

2   METHODS

2.1   DATA COLLECTION

Data were collected from unanesthetized cats that had been decerebrated at the level of the superior colliculus. We used a posterior approach to expose the DCN that did not require aspiration of brain tissue nor disruption of the local blood supply. Recordings were made using two platinum-iridium electrodes.

The electrodes were advanced independently until a type II unit was isolated on one electrode and a type IV unit was isolated on the other electrode. Only pairs of units with best frequencies (BFs) within 20% were studied. The data consist of responses of the two units to 500-4000 repetitions of a 100-1500 millisecond tone. The frequency of the tone was at the type II BF and the tone level was high enough to elicit activity in the type II unit for the duration of the presentation, but low enough not to inhibit the activity of the type IV unit (usually 5-10 dB above the type II threshold). Driven discharge rates of the two units ranged from 15 to 350 spikes per second. A silent recovery period at least four times longer than the tone burst duration followed each stimulus presentation.

2.3   DATA ANALYSIS

The stimulus duration is divided into 3 to 9 overlapping or non-overlapping time windows ('a' thru 'k' in figure 1). A separate impulse response estimate, presynaptic rate, and postsynaptic rate computation is made using only those type II and type IV spikes that fall within each window. The effectiveness of synaptic coupling during each window is calculated from the area bounded by the impulse response feature and the abscissa (shaded area in figure 1). The effectiveness measure has units of number of spikes.

The synaptic impulse response is estimated using a non-stationary method of moments algorithm. The estimation algorithm is based on the model depicted in figure 2. The thick gray line encircles elements belonging to the postsynaptic (type IV) cell. The neural network surrounding the postsynaptic cell is modelled as a J-dimensional multivariate counting process. Each element of the J-dimensional counting process is an input to the postsynaptic cell. One of these input elements is the presynaptic (type II) cell under observation. The input processes modulate the postsynaptic cell's instantaneous rate function, $\lambda_j(t)$. Roughly speaking, $\lambda_j(t)$ is the conditional firing probability of neuron j given the history of the input events up to time t.

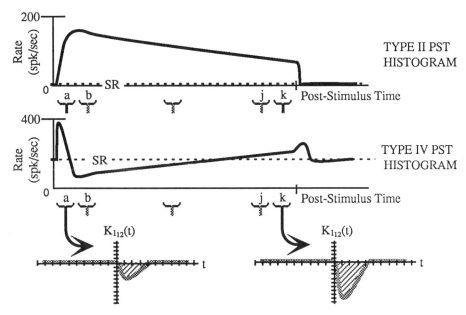

Figure 1: Analysis of Non-stationary Synaptic Coupling

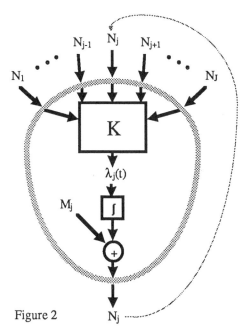

Figure 2

The transformation K describes how the input processes influence $\lambda_j(t)$. We model this transformation as a linear sum of an intrinsic rate component and the contribution of all the presynaptic processes:

$$\lambda_j(t) = K_{0j}(t) + \sum_{k=1}^{J} \int K_{1jk}(t,u)\,dN_k(u) \tag{1}$$

where K_0 describes the intrinsic rate and the K_1 describe the impulse response of the postsynaptic cell in response to an input event. The output of the postsynaptic neuron is modeled as the integral of this rate function plus a mean-zero noise process, the innovation martingale (Bremaud 1981):

$$N_j(t) = \int_{T_0}^{t} \lambda_j(u)\,du + M_j(t). \tag{2}$$

An algorithm for estimating the first order kernel, K_1, was derived without assuming anything about the distribution of the presynaptic process and without assuming stationary first or second order product densities (i.e., without assuming stationary rate or stationary auto-correlation). One or more such assumptions have been made in previous method of moments based algorithms for estimating neural interactions (Chornoboy et al. 1988 describe a maximum likelihood approach that does not require these assumptions).

Since K_1 is assumed to be stationary during the windowed interval (figure 1) while the process product densities are non-stationary (see PSTHs in figure 1), K_1 is an average of separate estimates of K_1 computed at each point in time during the windowed interval:

$$\widehat{K}_{1ij}\left(t^\Delta\right) = \frac{1}{n^\Delta} \sum_{t_i^\Delta - t_j^\Delta = t^\Delta;\ t_j^\Delta \in I} \widehat{K}_{1ij}\left(t_i^\Delta, t_j^\Delta\right)$$

(3)

where K_1 inside the summation is an estimate of the impulse response of neuron i at time t_i^Δ to a spike from neuron j at time t_j^Δ (times are relative to stimulus onset); the digitization bin width Δ (= 0.3 msec in our case) determines the location of the discrete time points as well as the number of separate kernel estimates, n^Δ, within the windowed interval, I. The time dependent kernel, $K_1(\cdot,\cdot)$, is computed by deconvolving the effects of the presynaptic process distribution, described by r_{ii} below, from the estimate of the cross-cumulant density, q_{ij}:

$$\widehat{K}_{1ij}\left(t_i^\Delta, t_j^\Delta\right) = \sum_{v^\Delta} \widehat{q}_{ij}\left(v^\Delta, t_j^\Delta\right) \widehat{r}_{ii}^{-1}\left(t_i^\Delta - v^\Delta, t_j^\Delta\right) \Delta$$

(4)

where:

$$\widehat{q}_{ij}\left(u^\Delta, v^\Delta\right) = \widehat{p}_{ij}\left(u^\Delta, v^\Delta\right) - \widehat{p}_i\left(u^\Delta\right)\widehat{p}_j\left(v^\Delta\right),$$

(5)

$$\widehat{r}_{ii}\left(u^\Delta, v^\Delta\right) = \widehat{q}_{ii}\left(u^\Delta, v^\Delta\right) + \delta\left(u^\Delta - v^\Delta\right)\widehat{p}_i\left(v^\Delta\right),$$

(6)

$$\widehat{r}_{ii}^{-1}\left(u^\Delta, v^\Delta\right) = \mathcal{F}^{-1}\left[\frac{1}{\mathcal{F}\left[\widehat{r}_{ii}\left(u^\Delta, v^\Delta\right)\right]}\right],$$

(7)

$$\widehat{p}_j\left(t_j^\Delta\right) = \#\left\{\text{spike in neuron j during } [t_j^\Delta - \frac{\Delta}{2}, t_j^\Delta + \frac{\Delta}{2})\right\} \Big/ \left(\#\{\text{trials}\}\,\Delta\right),$$

(8)

$$\widehat{p}_{ij}\left(t_i^\Delta, t_j^\Delta\right) = \frac{\#\left\{\text{spike in i during } [t_i^\Delta - \frac{\Delta}{2}, t_i^\Delta + \frac{\Delta}{2}) \text{ and spike in j during } [t_j^\Delta - \frac{\Delta}{2}, t_j^\Delta + \frac{\Delta}{2})\right\}}{\#\{\text{trials}\}\,\Delta^2},$$

(9)

where $\delta(\cdot)$ is the dirac delta function; $\mathcal{F}$ and $\mathcal{F}^{-1}$ are the DFT and inverse DFT, respectively; and $\#\{\cdot\}$ is the number of members in the set described inside the braces. If the presynaptic process is Poisson distributed, expression (4) simplifies to:

$$\widehat{K}_{1ij}\left(t_i^\Delta, t_j^\Delta\right) = \frac{\widehat{q}_{ij}\left(t_i^\Delta, t_j^\Delta\right)}{\widehat{p}_j\left(t_j^\Delta\right)}$$

(10)

Under mild (physiologically justifiable) conditions, the estimator given by (3) converges in quadratic mean and yields an asymptotically unbiased estimate of the true impulse response function (in the general, (4), and Poisson presynaptic process, (10), cases).

3   RESULTS

Figure 3 displays estimates of synaptic impulse response functions computed using traditional cross-correlation analysis and compares them to estimates computed using the method of moments algorithms described above. (We use the definition of cross-correlation given by Voigt & Young 1990; equivalent to the function given by dividing expression (10) by expression (9) after averaging across all t_j.) Figure 3A compares estimates computed from the responses of a real type II and type IV unit during the first 15 milliseconds of stimulation (where nonstationarity is greatest). Note that the cross-correlation estimate is distorted due to the nonstationarity of the underlying processes. This distortion leads to an overestimation of the effectiveness measure (shaded area) as compared to that yielded by the method of moments algorithm below. Figure 3B compares estimates computed using a simulated data set where the presynaptic neuron had regular (non-Poisson) discharge properties. Note the characteristic ringing pattern in the cross-correlation estimate as well as the larger feature amplitude in the non-Poisson method of moments estimate.

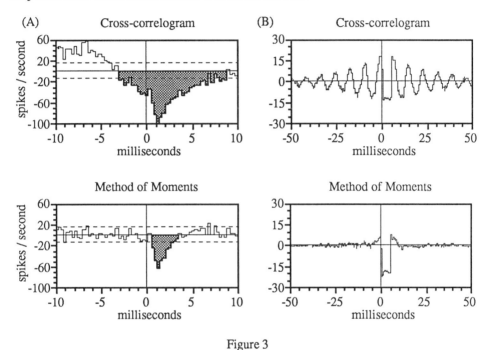

Figure 3

Results from one analysis of eight different type II / type IV pairs are shown in figure 4. For each pair, the effectiveness and the presynaptic (type II) average rate during each window are plotted and fit with a least squares line. Similar analyses were performed for effectiveness versus postsynaptic rate and for effectiveness versus post-stimulus-onset time. The number of pairs showing a positive or negative correlation of effectiveness with each parameter are tallied of table 1. The last column shows the average correlation coefficient of the lines fit to the eight sets of data. Note that: Synaptic efficacy tends to increase with time; there is no consistent relationship between synaptic efficacy and postsynaptic rate; there is a strong inverse and linear correlation between synaptic efficacy and presynaptic rate in 7 out of 8 pairs.

If the data appearing in figure 4 had been plotted as effectiveness versus average interspike interval (reciprocal of average rate) of the presynaptic neuron, the result would suggest that synaptic efficacy increases with average inter-spike interval. This result would be consistent with the interpretation that the effectiveness of an input event is suppressed by the occurrence of an input event immediately before it. The linear model initially used to analyze these data neglects the possibility of such second order effects.

Table 1: Summary of Results

GRAPH	NUMBER OF PAIRS WITH *POSITIVE* SLOPE	NUMBER OF PAIRS WITH *NEGATIVE* SLOPE	AVERAGE LINEAR REGRESSION CORRELATION COEFFICIENT
Effectiveness -vs- Post Stimulus Onset Time	7 / 8	1 / 8	0.83
Effectiveness -vs- Average Postsynaptic Rate	5 / 8	3 / 8	0.72
Effectiveness -vs- Average Presynaptic Rate	1 / 8	7 / 8	**0.89**

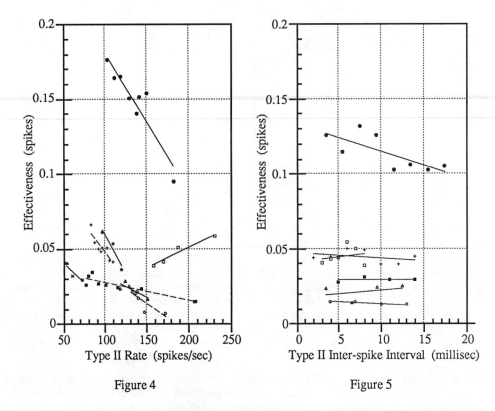

Figure 4   Figure 5

We used a modification of the analysis described in the methods to investigate second order effects. Rather than window small segments of the stimulus duration as in figure 1, the entire duration was used in this analysis. Impulse response estimates were constructed conditional on presynaptic interspike interval. For example, the first estimate was constructed using presynaptic events occurring after a 1 ms interspike interval, the second estimate was based on events after a 2 ms interval, and so on.

The results of the second order analysis are shown in figure 5. Note that there is no systematic relationship between conditioning interspike interval and effectiveness. In fact, lines fitted to these points tend to be horizontal, suggesting that there are no significant second order effects under these experimental conditions.

Our results suggest that synaptic efficacy is inversely and roughly linearly related to average presynaptic rate. We have attempted to understand the mechanism of the observed decrease in efficacy in terms of a model that assumes stationary synaptic coupling mechanisms. The model was designed to address the following hypothesis: Could the decrease in synaptic efficacy at high input rates be due to an increase in the likelihood of driving the stochastic intensity below zero, and, hence decreasing the apparent efficacy of the input due to clipping? The answer was pursued by attempting to reproduce the data collected for the 3 best type II / type IV pairs in our data set. Real data recorded from the presynaptic unit are used as input to these models. The parameters of the models were adjusted so that the first moment of the output process had the same quantitative trajectory as that seen in the real postsynaptic unit. The simulated data were analyzed by the same algorithms used to analyze the real data. Our goal was to compare the simulated results with the real results. If the simulated data showed the same inverse relationship between presynaptic rate and synaptic efficacy as the real data, it would suggest that the phenomenon is due to non-linear clipping by the postsynaptic unit.

The simulation algorithm was based on the model described in figure 2 and equation (1) but with the following modifications:

- The experimentally determined type IV PST profile was substituted for K_0 (this term represents the average combined influence of all extrinsic inputs to the type IV cell plus the intrinsic spontaneous rate).
- An impulse response function estimated from the data was substituted for K_1 (this kernel is stationary in the simulation model).
- The convolution of the experimentally determined type II spikes with the first-order kernel was used to perturb the output cell's stochastic intensity:

$$\lambda_1(t) = \text{MAX} \left[0, \ p_1(t) + \sum_{dN_2(u_i) = \delta} K_{1_{12}}(t - u_i) \right]$$

where: $dN_2(t)$ = Real type II cell spike record, and
    $p_1(t)$ = PST profile of real type IV cell.

- The output process was simulated as a non-homogeneous Poisson process with $\lambda_1(t)$ as its parameter. This process was modified by a 0.5 msec absolute dead time.
- The simulated data were analyzed in the same manner as the real data.

The dependence of synaptic efficacy on presynaptic rate in the simulated data was compared to the corresponding real data. In 1 out of the 3 cases, we observed an inverse relationship between input rate and efficacy despite the use of a stationary first order kernel in the simulation. The similarity between the real and simulated results for this one case suggests that the mechanism may be purely statistical rather than physiological (e.g., not presynaptic depletion or postsynaptic desensitization). The other 2 simulations did not yield a strong dependence of effectiveness on input rate and, hence, failed to mimic the experimental results. In these two cases, the results suggest that the mechanism is not due solely to clipping, but involves some additional, possibly physiological, mechanisms.

4   CONCLUSIONS

1) The amount of inhibition imparted to type IV units by individual presynaptic type II unit action potentials (expressed as the expected number of type IV spikes eliminated per type II spike) is inversely and roughly linearly related to the average rate of the type II unit.

(2) There is no evidence for second order synaptic effects at the type II spike rates tested. In other words, the inhibitory effect of two successive type II spikes is simply the linear sum of the inhibition imparted by each individual spike.

(3) There is no consistent relationship between type II / type IV synaptic efficacy and postsynaptic (type IV) rate.

(4) Simulations, in some cases, suggest that the inverse relationship between presynaptic rate and effectiveness may be reproduced using a simple statistical model of neural interaction.

(5) We found no evidence that would explain the discrepancy between Voigt and Young's results and Gochin's results in the DCN. Gochin observed correlogram features consistent with monosynaptic excitatory connections within the DCN when short tone bursts were used as stimuli. We did not observe excitatory features between any unit pairs using short tone bursts.

Acknowledgements

Dr. Alan Karr assisted in developing Eqns. 1-10. E. Nelken provided helpful comments. Research supported by NIH grant DC00115.

References

Bremaud, P. (1981). Point Processes and Queues: Martingale Dynamics. New York, Springer-Verlag.

Caspary, D.M., Rybak, L.P.et al. (1984). "Baclofen reduces tone-evoked activity of cochlear nucleus neurons." Hear Res. 13: 113-22.

Chornoboy, E.S., Schramm, L.P.et al. (1988). "Maximum likelihood identification of neural point process systems." Biol Cybern. 59: 265-75.

Gochin, P.M., Kaltenbach, J.A.et al. (1989). "Coordinated activity of neuron pairs in anesthetized rat dorsal cochlear nucleus." Brain Res. 497: 1-11.

Manis, P.B. & Brownell, W.E. (1983). "Synaptic organization of eighth nerve afferents to cat dorsal cochlear nucleus." J Neurophysiol. 50: 1156-81.

Rhode, W.S., Smith, P.H.et al. (1983). "Physiological response properties of cells labeled intracellularly with horseradish peroxidase in cat dorsal cochlear nucleus." J Comp Neurol. 213: 426-47.

Voigt, H.F. & Young, E.D. (1980). "Evidence of inhibitory interactions between neurons in dorsal cochlear nucleus." J Neurophys. 44: 76-96.

Voigt, H.F. & Young, E.D. (1990). "Cross-correlation analysis of inhibitory interactions in the Dorsal Cochlear Nucleus." J Neurophys. 54: 1590-1610.

Young, E.D. & Brownell, W.E. (1976). "Responses to tones and noise of single cells in dorsal cochlear nucleus of unanesthetized cats." J Neurophys. 39: 282-300.

Perturbing Hebbian Rules

Peter Dayan
CNL, The Salk Institute
PO Box 85800
San Diego CA 92186-5800, USA
dayan@helmholtz.sdsc.edu

Geoffrey Goodhill
COGS
University of Sussex, Falmer
Brighton BN1 9QN, UK
geoffg@cogs.susx.ac.uk

Abstract

Recently Linsker [2] and MacKay and Miller [3, 4] have analysed Hebbian correlational rules for synaptic development in the visual system, and Miller [5, 8] has studied such rules in the case of two populations of fibres (particularly two eyes). Miller's analysis has so far assumed that each of the two populations has exactly the same correlational structure. Relaxing this constraint by considering the effects of small perturbative correlations within and between eyes permits study of the stability of the solutions. We predict circumstances in which qualitative changes are seen, including the production of binocularly rather than monocularly driven units.

1   INTRODUCTION

Linsker [2] studied how a Hebbian correlational rule could predict the development of certain receptive field structures seen in the visual system. MacKay and Miller [3, 4] pointed out that the form of this learning rule meant that it could be analysed in terms of the eigenvectors of the matrix of time-averaged presynaptic correlations. Miller [5, 8, 7] independently studied a similar correlational rule for the case of two eyes (or more generally two populations), explaining how cells develop in V1 that are ultimately responsive to only one eye, despite starting off as responsive to both. This process is again driven by the eigenvectors and eigenvalues of the developmental equation, and Miller [7] relates Linsker's model to the two population case.

Miller's analysis so far assumes that the correlations of activity within each population are identical. This special case simplifies the analysis enabling the projections from the two eyes to be separated out into sum and difference variables. In general, one would expect the correlations to differ slightly, and for correlations between the eyes to be not exactly zero. We analyse how such perturbations affect the eigenvectors and eigenvalues of the developmental equation, and are able to explain some of the results found empirically by Miller [6].

Further details on this analysis and on the relationship between Hebbian and non-Hebbian models of the development of ocular dominance and orientation selectivity can be found in Goodhill (1991).

2   THE EQUATION

MacKay and Miller [3, 4] study Linsker's [2] developmental equation in the form:
$$\dot{w} = (Q + k_2 J)w + k_1 n$$
where $w = [w_i], i \in [1, n]$ are the weights from the units in one layer $\mathcal{R}$ to a particular unit in the next layer $\mathcal{S}$, Q is the covariance matrix of the activities of the units in layer $\mathcal{R}$, J is the matrix $J_{ij} = 1, \forall\, i, j$, and n is the 'DC' vector $n_i = 1, \forall\, i$.

The equivalent for two populations of cells is:
$$\begin{pmatrix} \dot{w}_1 \\ \dot{w}_2 \end{pmatrix} = \begin{pmatrix} Q_1 + k_2 J & Q_c + k_2 J \\ Q_c + k_2 J & Q_2 + k_2 J \end{pmatrix} \begin{pmatrix} w_1 \\ w_2 \end{pmatrix} + k_1 \begin{pmatrix} n \\ n \end{pmatrix}$$
where Q_1 gives the covariance between cells within the first population, Q_2 gives that between cells within the second, and Q_c (assumed symmetric) gives the covariance between cells in the two populations. Define Q_* as this full, two population, development matrix.

Miller studies the case in which $Q_1 = Q_2 = Q$ and Q_c is generally zero or slightly negative. Then the development of $w_1 - w_2$ (which Miller calls S^D) and $w_1 + w_2$ (S^S) separate; for $Q_c = 0$, these go like:
$$\frac{\delta S^D}{\delta t} = Q S^D \text{ and } \frac{\delta S^S}{\delta t} = (Q + 2k_2 J)S^S + 2k_1 n.$$
and, up to various forms of normalisation and/or weight saturation, the patterns of dominance between the two populations are determined by the initial value and the fastest growing components of S^D. If upper and lower weight saturation limits are reached at roughly the same time (Berns, personal communication), the conventional assumption that the fastest growing eigenvectors of S^D dominate the terminal state is borne out.

The starting condition Miller adopts has $w_1 - w_2 = \epsilon' a$ and $w_1 + w_2 = b$, where ϵ' is small, and a and b are $\mathcal{O}(1)$. Weights are constrained to be positive, and saturate at some upper limit. Also, additive normalisation is applied throughout development, which affects the growth of the S^S (but not the S^D) modes. As discussed by MacKay and Miller [3, 4], this is approximately accommodated in the $k_2 J$ component.

Mackay and Miller analyse the eigendecomposition of $Q + k_2 J$ for general and radially symmetric covariance matrices Q and all values of k_2. It turns out that the eigendecomposition of Q_* for the case $Q_1 = Q_2 = Q$ and $Q_c = 0$ (that studied by Miller) is given in table form by:

E-vector	E-value	Conditions	
(x_i, x_i)	λ_i	$Qx_i = \lambda_i x_i$	$n.x_i = 0$
$(x_i, -x_i)$	λ_i	$Qx_i = \lambda_i x_i$	$n.x_i = 0$
$(y_i, -y_i)$	μ_i	$Qy_i = \mu_i y_i$	$n.y_i \neq 0$
(z_i, z_i)	ν_i	$(Q + 2k_2J)z_i = \nu_i z_i$	$n.z_i \neq 0$

Figure 1 shows the matrix and the two key $(y, -y)$ and $(x, -x)$ eigenvectors.

The details of the decomposition of Q_* in this table are slightly obscured by degeneracy in the eigendecomposition of $Q + k_2J$. Also, for clarity, we write (x_i, x_i) for $(x_i, x_i)^\top$. A consequence of the first two rows in the table is that $(\eta x_i, \theta x_i)$ is an eigenvector for any η and θ; this becomes important later.

That the development of S^D and S^S separates can be seen in the (u, u) and $(u, -u)$ forms of the eigenvectors. In Miller's terms the onset of dominance of one of the two populations is seen in the $(u, -u)$ eigenvectors – dominance requires that μ_j for the eigenvector whose elements are all of the same sign (one such exists for Miller's Q) is larger than the μ_i and the λ_i for all the other such eigenvectors. In particular, on pages 296-300 of [6], he shows various cases for which this does and one in which it does not happen. To understand how this comes about, we can treat the latter as a perturbed version of the former.

3   PERTURBATIONS

Consider the case in which there are small correlations between the projections and/or small differences between the correlations within each projection. For instance, one of Miller's examples indicates that small within-eye anti-correlations can prevent the onset of dominance. This can be perturbatively analysed by setting $Q_1 = Q + \epsilon E_1$, $Q_2 = Q + \epsilon E_2$ and $Q_c = \epsilon E_c$. Call the resulting matrix Q_*^ϵ.

Two questions are relevant. Firstly, are the eigenvectors stable to this perturbation, *ie* are there vectors a_1 and a_2 such that $(u_1 + \epsilon a_1, u_2 + \epsilon a_2)$ is an eigenvector of Q_*^ϵ if (u_1, u_2) is an eigenvector of Q_* with eigenvalue ϕ? Secondly, how do the eigenvalues change?

One way to calculate this is to consider the equation the perturbed eigenvector must satisfy:[1]

$$Q_*^\epsilon \begin{pmatrix} u_1 + \epsilon a_1 \\ u_2 + \epsilon a_2 \end{pmatrix} = (\phi + \epsilon\psi) \begin{pmatrix} u_1 + \epsilon a_1 \\ u_2 + \epsilon a_2 \end{pmatrix}$$

and look for conditions on u_1 and u_2 and the values of a_1, a_2 and ψ by equating the $\mathcal{O}(\epsilon)$ terms. We now consider a specific example. Using the notation of the table above, $(y_i + \epsilon a_1, -y_i + \epsilon a_2)$ is an eigenvector with eigenvalue $\mu_i + \epsilon\psi_i$ if

$$\begin{aligned} (Q - \mu_i I)\, a_1 + k_2J\, (a_1 + a_2) &= -(E_1 - E_c - \psi_i I)\, y_i, \quad \text{and} \\ (Q - \mu_i I)\, a_2 + k_2J\, (a_1 + a_2) &= -(E_c - E_2 + \psi_i I)\, y_i. \end{aligned}$$

Subtracting these two implies that

$$(Q - \mu_i I)\, (a_1 - a_2) = -(E_1 - 2E_c + E_2 - 2\psi_i I)\, y_i.$$

---

[1]This is a standard method for such linear systems, *eg* in quantum mechanics.

However, $y_i^T (Q - \mu_i I) = 0$, since Q is symmetric and y_i is an eigenvector with eigenvalue μ_i, so multiplying on the left by y_i^T, we require that

$$2\psi_i y_i^T y_i = y_i^T (E_1 - 2E_c + E_2) y_i$$

which sets the value of ψ_i. Therefore $(y_i, -y_i)$ *is* stable in the required manner.

Similarly (z_i, z_i) is stable too, with an equivalent perturbation to its eigenvalue. However the pair (x_i, x_i) and $(x_i, -x_i)$ are not stable – the degeneracy from their having the same eigenvalue is broken, and two specific eigenvectors, $(\alpha_i x_i, \beta_i x_i)$ and $(-\beta_i x_i, \alpha_i x_i)$ are stable, for particular values α_i and β_i. This means that to first order, S^D and S^S no longer separate, and the full, two-population, matrix must be solved.

To model Miller's results, call $Q_*^{\epsilon,m}$ the special case of Q_*^ϵ for which $E_1 = E_2 = E$ and $E_c = 0$. Also, assume that the x_i, y_i and z_i are normalised, let $e_1(u) = u^T E_1 u$, *etc*, and define $\gamma(u) = (e_1(u) - e_2(u))/2e_c(u)$, for $e_c(u) \neq 0$, and $\gamma_i = \gamma(x_i)$. Then we have

$$\beta_i/\alpha_i = -\gamma_i \pm \sqrt{1 + \gamma_i^2} \tag{1}$$

and the eigenvalues are:

E-vector	Q_*	$Q_*^{\epsilon,m}$	Q_*^ϵ
			Eigenvalue for case:
$(\alpha_i x_i, \beta_i x_i)$	λ_i	$\lambda_i + \epsilon e_1(x_i)$	$\lambda_i + \epsilon[e_1(x_i) + e_2(x_i) + \Xi_i]/2$
$(-\beta_i x_i, \alpha_i x_i)$	λ_i	$\lambda_i + \epsilon e_1(x_i)$	$\lambda_i - \epsilon[e_1(x_i) + e_2(x_i) + \Xi_i]/2$
$(y_i, -y_i)$	μ_i	$\mu_i + \epsilon e_1(y_i)$	$\mu_i + \epsilon[e_1(y_i) + e_2(y_i) - 2e_c(y_i)]/2$
(z_i, z_i)	ν_i	$\nu_i + \epsilon e_1(z_i)$	$\nu_i + \epsilon[e_1(z_i) + e_2(z_i) + 2e_c(z_i)]/2$

where $\Xi_i = \sqrt{[e_1(x_i) - e_2(x_i)]^2 + 4e_c(x_i)^2}$. For the case Miller treats, since $E_1 = E_2$, the degeneracy in the original solution is preserved, *ie* the perturbed versions of (x_i, x_i) and $(x_i, -x_i)$ have the same eigenvalues. Therefore the S^D and S^S modes still separate.

This perturbed eigendecomposition suffices to show how small additional correlations affect the solutions. We will give three examples. The case mentioned above on page 299 of [6], shows how small same-eye anti-correlations within the radius of the arbor function cause a particular $(y_i, -y_i)$ eigenvector (i.e. one for which all the components of y_i have the same sign) to change from growing faster than a $(x_i, -x_i)$ (for which some components of x_i are positive and some negative to ensure that $n.x_i = 0$) to growing slower than it, converting a monocular solution to a binocular one.

In our terms, this is the $Q_*^{\epsilon,m}$ case, with E_1 a negative matrix. Given the conditions on signs of their components, $e_1(y_i)$ is more negative than $e_1(x_i)$, and so the eigenvalue for the perturbed $(y_i, -y_i)$ would be expected to decrease more than that for the perturbed $(x_i, -x_i)$. This is exactly what is found. Different binocular eigensolutions are affected by different amounts, and it is typically a delicate issue as to which will ultimately prevail. Figure 2 shows a sample perturbed matrix for which dominance will not develop. If the change in the correlations is large $(\mathcal{O}(1))$, then the eigenfunctions can change shape (eg 1s becomes 2s in the notation of [4]). We do not address this here, since we are considering only changes of $\mathcal{O}(\epsilon)$.

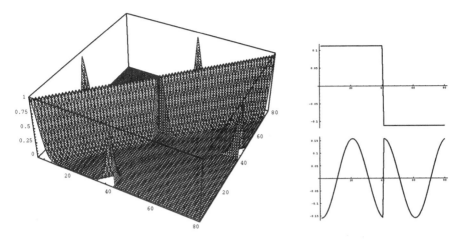

Figure 1: Unperturbed two-eye correlation matrix and $(y, -y)$, $(x, -x)$ eigenvectors. Eigenvalues are 7.1 and 6.4 respectively.

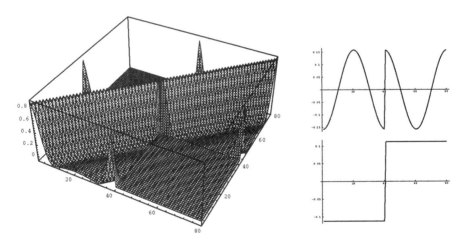

Figure 2: Same-eye anti-correlation matrix and eigenvectors. $(y, -y)$, $(x, -x)$ eigenvalues are 4.8 and 5.4 respectively, and so the order has swapped.

Positive opposite-eye correlations can have exactly the same effect. This time $e_c(y_i)$ is greater than $e_c(x_i)$, and so, again, the eigenvalue for the perturbed $(y_i, -y_i)$ would be expected to decrease more than that for the perturbed $(x_i, -x_i)$. Figure 3 shows an example which is infelicitous for dominance.

The third case is for general perturbations in Q_*^ϵ. Now the mere signs of the components of the eigenvectors are not enough to predict which will be affected more. Figure 4 gives an example for which ocular dominance will still occur. Note that the $(x_i, -x_i)$ eigenvector is no longer stable, and has been replaced by one of the form $(\alpha_i x_i, \beta_i x_i)$.

If general perturbations of the same order of magnitude as the difference between w_1 and w_2 (*ie* $\epsilon' \simeq \epsilon$) are applied, the α_i and β_i terms complicate Miller's S^D analysis to first order. Let $w_1(0) - w_2(0) = \epsilon a$ and apply Q_*^ϵ as an iteration matrix. $w_1(n) - w_2(n)$, the difference between the projections after n iterations has no $\mathcal{O}(1)$ component, but two sets of $\mathcal{O}(\epsilon)$ components; $\{2\mu_i^n (a.y_i) y_i\}$, and

$$\{ \quad \lambda_i^n[1 + \epsilon(\Upsilon_i + \Xi_i)/2\lambda_i]^n (\alpha_i x_i.w_1(0) + \beta_i x_i.w_2(0)) (\alpha_i - \beta_i)x_i - \\ \lambda_i^n[1 + \epsilon(\Upsilon_i - \Xi_i)/2\lambda_i]^n (\alpha_i x_i.w_2(0) - \beta_i x_i.w_1(0)) (\alpha_i + \beta_i)x_i \quad \}$$

where $\Upsilon_i = e_1(x_i) + e_2(x_i)$. Collecting the terms in this expression, and using equation 1, we derive

$$\left\{ \lambda_i^n \left[(\alpha_i^2 + \beta_i^2)x_i.a + 2n\frac{\Xi_i}{\lambda_i}\gamma_i\alpha_i\beta_i x_i.b \right] x_i \right\}$$

where $b = w_1(0) + w_2(0)$. The second part of this expression depends on n, and is substantial because $w_1(0) + w_2(0)$ is $\mathcal{O}(1)$. Such a term does not appear in the unperturbed system, and can bias the competition between the y_i and the x_i eigenvectors, in particular towards the binocular solutions. Again, its precise effects will be sensitive to the unperturbed eigenvalues.

4 CONCLUSIONS

Perturbation analysis applied to simple Hebbian correlational learning rules reveals the following:

- Introducing small anti-correlations within each eye causes a tendency toward binocularity. This agrees with the results of Miller.

- Introducing small positive correlations between the eyes (as will inevitably occur once they experience a natural environment) has the same effect.

- The overall eigensolution is not stable to small perturbations that make the correlational structure of the two eyes unequal. This also produces interesting effects on the growth rates of the eigenvectors concerned, given the initial conditions of approximately equivalent projections from both eyes.

Acknowledgements

We are very grateful to Ken Miller for helpful discussions, and to Christopher Longuet-Higgins for pointing us in the direction of perturbation analysis. Support

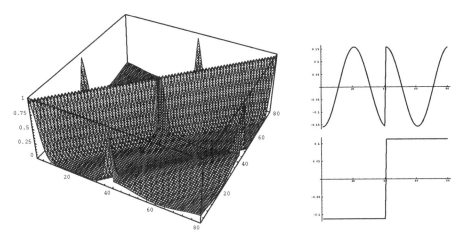

Figure 3: Opposite-eye positive correlation matrix and eigenvectors. Eigenvalues of $(y, -y)$, $(x, -x)$ are 4.8 and 5.4, so ocular dominance is again inhibited.

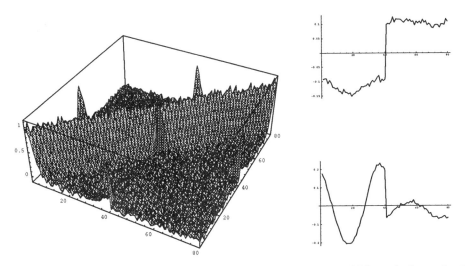

Figure 4: The effect of random perturbations to the matrix. Although the order is restored (eigenvalues are 7.1 and 6.4), note the $(\alpha x, \beta x)$ eigenvector.

was from the SERC and a Nuffield Foundation Science travel grant to GG. GG is grateful to David Willshaw and the Centre for Cognitive Science for their hospitality. GG's current address is The Centre for Cognitive Science, University of Edinburgh, 2 Buccleuch Place, Edinburgh EH8 9LW, Scotland, and correspondence should be directed to him there.

References

[1] Goodhill, GJ (1991). *Correlations, Competition and Optimality: Modelling the Development of Topography and Ocular Dominance.* PhD Thesis, Sussex University.

[2] Linsker, R (1986). From basic network principles to neural architecture (series). *Proc. Nat. Acad. Sci., USA,* **83**, pp 7508-7512, 8390-8394, 8779-8783.

[3] MacKay, DJC & Miller, KD (1990). Analysis of Linsker's simulations of Hebbian rules. *Neural Computation,* **2**, pp 169-182.

[4] MacKay, DJC & Miller, KD (1990). Analysis of Linsker's application of Hebbian rules to linear networks. *Network,* **1**, pp 257-297.

[5] Miller, KD (1989). *Correlation-based Mechanisms in Visual Cortex: Theoretical and Empirical Studies.* PhD Thesis, Stanford University Medical School.

[6] Miller, KD (1990). Correlation-based mechanisms of neural development. In MA Gluck & DE Rumelhart, editors, *Neuroscience and Connectionist Theory.* Hillsborough, NJ: Lawrence Erlbaum.

[7] Miller, KD (1990). Derivation of linear Hebbian equations from a nonlinear Hebbian model of synaptic plasticity. *Neural Computation,* **2**, pp 321-333.

[8] Miller, KD, Keller, JB & Stryker, MP (1989). Ocular dominance column development: Analysis and simulation. *Science,* **245**, pp 605-615.

Statistical Reliability of a Blowfly Movement-Sensitive Neuron

Rob de Ruyter van Steveninck *
Biophysics Group,
Rijksuniversiteit Groningen,
Groningen, The Netherlands

William Bialek
NEC Research Institute
4 Independence Way,
Princeton, NJ 08540

Abstract

We develop a model-independent method for characterizing the reliability of neural responses to brief stimuli. This approach allows us to measure the discriminability of similar stimuli, based on the real-time response of a single neuron. Neurophysiological data were obtained from a movement-sensitive neuron (H1) in the visual system of the blowfly *Calliphora erythrocephala*. Furthermore, recordings were made from blowfly photoreceptor cells to quantify the signal to noise ratios in the peripheral visual system. As photoreceptors form the input to the visual system, the reliability of their signals ultimately determines the reliability of any visual discrimination task. For the case of movement detection, this limit can be computed, and compared to the H1 neuron's reliability. Under favorable conditions, the performance of the H1 neuron closely approaches the theoretical limit, which means that under these conditions the nervous system adds little noise in the process of computing movement from the correlations of signals in the photoreceptor array.

1   INTRODUCTION

In the 1940s and 50s, several investigators realized that understanding the reliability of computation in the nervous system posed significant theoretical challenges. Attempts to perform reliable computations with the available electronic computers

---

*present address: University Hospital Groningen, Dept. of Audiology, POB 30.001, NL 9700RB Groningen, The Netherlands

certainly posed serious practical problems, and the possibility that the problems of natural and artificial computing are related was explored. Guided by the practical problems of electronic computing, von Neumann (1956) formulated the theoretical problem of "reliable computation with unreliable components". Many authors seem to take as self-evident the claim that this is a problem faced by the nervous system as well, and indeed the possibility that the brain may implement novel solutions to this problem has been at least a partial stimulus for much recent research. The qualitative picture adopted in this approach is of the nervous system as a highly interconnected network of rather noisy cells, in which meaningful signals are represented only by large numbers of neural firing events averaged over numerous redundant neurons. Neurophysiological experiments seem to support this view: If the same stimulus is presented repeatedly to a sensory system, the responses of an individual afferent neuron differ for each presentation. This apparently has led to a widespread belief that neurons are inherently noisy, and ideas of redundancy and averaging pervade much of the literature. Significant objections to this view have been raised, however (*cf.* Bullock 1970).

As emphasized by Bullock (*loc.cit*), the issue of reliability of the nervous system is a quantitative one. Thus, the first problem that should be overcome is to find a way for its measurement. This paper focuses on a restricted, but basic question, namely the reliability of a single neuron, much in the spirit of previous work (cf. Barlow and Levick 1969, Levick et al. 1983, Tolhurst at al. 1983, Parker and Hawken 1985). Here the methods of analysis used by these authors are extended in an attempt to describe the neuron's reliability in a way that is as model-independent as possible.

The second–conceptually more difficult–problem, is summarized cogently in Bullock's words, "how reliable is reliable?". Just quantifying reliability is not enough, and the qualitative question of whether redundancy, averaging, multiplexing, or yet more exotic solutions to von Neumann's problem are relevant to the operation of the nervous system hinges on a quantitative comparison of reliability at the level of single cells with the reliability for the whole system. Broadly speaking, there are two ways to make such a comparison: one can compare the performance of the single cell either with the output or with the input of the whole system. As to the first possibility, if a single cell responds to a certain stimulus as reliably as the animal does in a behavioral experiment, it is difficult to imagine why multiple redundant neurons should be used to encode the same stimulus. Alternatively, if the reliability of a single neuron were to approach the limits set by the sensory periphery, there seems to be little purpose for the nervous system to use functional duplicates of such a cell, and the key theoretical problem would be to understand how such optimal processing is implemented. Here we will use the latter approach.

We first quantify the reliability of response of H1, a wide-field movement-sensitive neuron in the blowfly visual system. The method consists essentially of a direct application of signal detection theory to trains of neural impulses generated by brief stimuli, using methods familiar from psychophysics to quantify discriminability. Next we characterize signal transfer and noise in the sensory periphery–the photoreceptor cells of the compound eye–and we compare the reliability of information coded in H1 with the total amount of sensory information available at the input.

2   PREPARATION, STIMULATION AND RECORDING

Experiments were performed on female wild-type blowfly *Calliphora erythrocephala*. Spikes from H1 were recorded extracellularly with a tungsten microelectrode, their arrival times being digitized with 50 μs resolution. The fly watched a binary random-bar pattern (bar width 0.029° visual angle, total size $(30.5°)^2$) displayed on a CRT. Movement steps of 16 different sizes (integer multiples of 0.12°) were generated by custom-built electronics, and presented at 200 ms intervals in the neuron's preferred direction. The effective duration of the experiment was 11 hours, during which time about 10^6 spikes were recorded over 12552 presentations of the 16-step stimulus sequence.

Photoreceptor cells were recorded intracellularly while stimulated by a spatially homogeneous field, generated on the same CRT that was used for the H1 experiments. The CRT's intensity was modulated by a binary pseudo-random waveform, time sampled at 1 ms. The responses to 100 stimulus periods were averaged, and the cell's transfer function was obtained by computing the ratio of the Fourier transform of the averaged response to that of the stimulus signal. The cell's noise power spectrum was obtained by averaging the power spectra of the 100 traces of the individual responses with the average response subtracted.

3   DATA ANALYSIS

3.1   REPRESENTATION OF STIMULUS AND RESPONSE

A single movement stimulus consisted of a sudden small displacement of a wide-field pattern. Steps of varying sizes were presented at regular time-intervals, long enough to ensure that responses to successive stimuli were independent. In the analysis we consider the stimulus to be a point event in time, parametrized by its step size α.

The neuron's signal is treated as a stochastic point process, the parameters of which depend on the stimulus. Its statistical behavior is described by the conditional probability $P(r|\alpha)$ of finding a response r, given that a step of size α was presented. From the experimental data we estimate $P(r|\alpha)$ for each step size separately. To represent a single response r, time is divided in discrete bins of width $\Delta t = 2$ ms. Then r is described by a firing pattern, which is just a vector $\vec{q} = [q_0, q_1, ..]$ of binary digits $q_k(k = 0, n - 1)$, where $q_k = 1$ and $q_k = 0$ respectively signify the presence or the absence of a spike in time bin k (cf. Eckhorn and Pöpel 1974). No response is found within a latency time $t_{lat}=15$ ms after stimulus presentation; spikes fired within this interval are due to spontaneous activity and are excluded from analysis, so $k = 0$ corresponds to 15 ms after stimulus presentation.

The probability distribution of firing patterns, $P(\vec{q}|\alpha)$, is estimated by counting the number of occurrences of each realization of $\vec{q}$ for a large number of presentations of α. This distribution is described by a tree which results from ordering all recorded firing patterns according to their binary representation, earlier times corresponding to more-significant bits. Graphical representations of two such trees are shown in Fig. 1. In constructing a tree we thus perform two operations on the raw spike data: first, individual response patterns are represented in discrete time bins Δt, and second, a permutation is performed on the set of discretized patterns to order them according to their binary representation. No additional assumptions are made about the way the signal is encoded by the neuron. This approach should therefore be quite powerful in revealing any subtle "hidden code" that the neuron might use. As the number of branches in the tree grows exponentially with the number of time bins n, many presentations are needed to describe the tree over a reasonable time interval, and here we use $n = 13$.

3.2   COMPUTATION OF DISCRIMINABILITY

To quantify the performance of the neuron, we compute the discriminability of two nearly equal stimuli α_1 and α_2, based on the difference in neural response statistics described by $P(r|\alpha_1)$ and $P(r|\alpha_2)$. The probability of correct decisions is maximized if one uses a maximum likelihood decision rule, so that in the case of equal prior probabilities the outcome is α_1 if $P(r_{obs}|\alpha_1) > P(r_{obs}|\alpha_2)$, and vice versa. On average, the probability of correctly identifying step α_1 is then:

$$P_c(\alpha_1) = \sum_{\{r\}} P(r|\alpha_1) \cdot H[P(r|\alpha_1) - P(r|\alpha_2)], \qquad (1)$$

where $H(.)$ is the Heaviside step function and the summation is over the set of all possible responses $\{r\}$. An interchange of indices 1 and 2 in this expression yields the formula for correct identification of α_2. The probability of making correct judgements over an entire experiment in which α_1 and α_2 are equiprobable is then simply $P_c(\alpha_1, \alpha_2) = [P_c(\alpha_1) + P_c(\alpha_2)]/2$, which from now on will be referred to as P_c.

This analysis is essentially that for a "two-alternative forced-choice" psychophysical experiment. For convenience we convert P_c into the discriminability parameter d', familiar from psychophysics (Green and Swets 1966), which is the signal-to-noise ratio (difference in mean divided by the standard deviation) in the equivalent equal-variance Gaussian decision problem.

Using the firing-pattern representation, $r = \vec{q}$, and computing d' for successive subvectors of $\vec{q}$ with elements $m = 0, .., k$ and $k = 0, .., n - 1$, we compute P_c for different values of k and from that obtain $d'(k)$, the discriminability as a function of time.

3.3   THEORETICAL LIMITS TO DISCRIMINATION

For the simple stimuli used here it is relatively easy to determine the theoretical limit to discrimination based on the photoreceptor signal quality. For the computation of this limit we use Reichardt's (1957) correlation model of movement detection. This model has been very successful in describing a wide variety of phenomena in biological movement detection, both in fly (Reichardt and Poggio 1976), and in humans (van Santen and Sperling 1984). Also, correlation-like operations can be proved to be optimal for the extraction of movement information at low signal to noise ratio (Bialek 1990). The measured signal transfer of the photoreceptors, combined with the known geometry of the stimulus and the optics of the visual system determine the signal input to the model. The noise input is taken directly

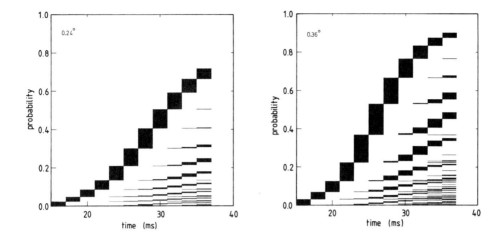

Figure 1: Representation of the firing pattern distributions for steps of 0.24° and 0.36°. Here only 11 time bins are shown.

from the measured photoreceptor noise power spectrum. Details of this computation are given in de Ruyter van Steveninck (1986).

3.4   ERROR ANALYSIS AND DATA REQUIREMENTS

The effects of the approximation due to time-discretization can be assessed by varying the binwidth. It turns out that the results do not change appreciably if the bins are made smaller than 2 ms. Furthermore, if the analysis is to make sense, stationarity is required, i.e. the probability distribution from which responses to a certain stimulus are drawn should be invariant over the course of the experiment. Finally, the distributions, being computed from a finite sample of responses, are subject to statistical error. The statistical error in the final result was estimated by partitioning the data and working out the values of P_c for these partitions separately. The statistical variations in P_c were of the order of 0.01 in the most interesting region of values of P_c, i.e. from 0.6 to 0.9. This results in a typical statistical error of 0.05 in d'. In addition, this analysis revealed no significant trends with time, so we may assume stationarity of the preparation.

4   RESULTS

4.1   STEP SIZE DISCRIMINATION BY THE H1 NEURON

Although 16 different step sizes were used, we limit the presentation here to steps of 0.24° and 0.36°; binary trees representing the two firing-pattern distributions are shown in Fig. 1. The first time bin describes the probabilities of two possible events: either a spike was fired (black) or not (white), and these two probabilities add up to unity. The second time bin describes the four possible combinations of finding

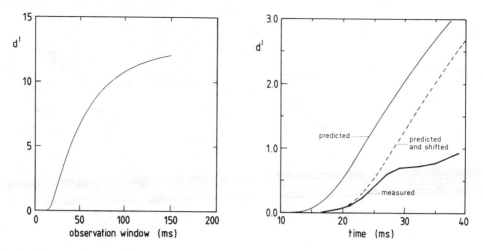

Figure 2: Left: Discrimination performance of an ideal movement detector. See text for further details. Right: comparison of the theoretical and the measured values of $d'(t)$. Fat line: measured performance of H1. Thin solid line: predicted performance, taken from the left figure. Dashed line: the same curve shifted by 5 ms to account for latency time in the pathway from photoreceptor to H1. This time interval was determined independently with powerful movement stimuli.

or not finding a spike in bin 2 combined with finding or not finding a spike in bin 1, and so on. The figure shows that the probability of firing a spike in time bin 1 is slightly higher for the larger step. From above we compute P_c, the probability of correct identification, in a task where the choice is between step sizes of $0.24°$ and $0.36°$ with equal prior probabilities. The decision rule is simple: if a spike is fired in bin 1, choose the larger, otherwise choose the smaller step. In the same fashion we apply this procedure to the following time bin, with four response categories and so on. The value of d' computed from P_c for this step size pair as a function of time is given by the fat line at the right in Fig. 2.

4.2   LIMITS SET BY PHOTORECEPTOR SIGNALS

Figure 2 (left) shows the limit to movement detection computed for an array of 2650 Reichardt correlators stimulated with a step size difference of $0.12°$, conforming to the experimental conditions. Comparing the performance of H1 to this result (the fat and the dashed lines in Fig. 2, right), we see that the neuron follows the limit set by the sensory periphery from about 18 to 28 ms after stimulus presentation. So, for this time window the randomness of H1's response is determined primarily by photoreceptor noise. Up to about 20 Hz, the photoreceptor signal-to-noise ratio closely approached the limit set by the random arrival of photons at the photoreceptors at a rate of about 10^4 effective conversions/s. Hence most of the randomness in the spike train was caused by photon shot noise.

5 DISCUSSION

The approach presented here gives us estimates for the reliability of a single neuron in a well-defined, though restricted experimental context. In addition the theoretical limits to the reliability of movement-detection are computed. Comparing these two results we find that H1 in these conditions uses essentially all of the movement information available over a 10 ms time interval. Further analysis shows that this information is essentially contained in the time of firing of the first spike. The plateau in the measured $d'(t)$ between 28 and 34 ms presumably results from effects of refractoriness, and the subsequent slight rise is due to firing of a second spike.

Thus, a step size difference of 0.12° can be discriminated with d' close to unity, using the timing information of just one spike from one neuron. For the blowfly visual system this angular difference is of the order of one-tenth of the photoreceptor spacing, well within the hyperacuity regime (cf. Parker and Hawken 1985).

It should not be too surprising that the neuron performs well only over a short time interval and does not reach the values for d' computed from the model at large delays (Fig. 2, left): The experimental stimulus is not very natural, and in real-life conditions the fly is likely to see movement changing continuously. (Methods for analyzing responses to continuous movement are treated in de Ruyter van Steveninck and Bialek 1988, and in Bialek et al. 1991.) In such circumstances it might be better not to wait very long to get an accurate estimate of the stimulus at one point in time, but rather to update rough estimates as fast as possible. This would favor a coding principle where successive spikes code independent events, which may explain that the plateau in the measured $d'(t)$ starts at about the point where the computed $d'(t)$ has maximal slope. Such a view is supported by behavioral evidence: A chasing fly tracks the leading fly with a delay of about 30 ms (Land and Collett 1974), corresponding to the time at which the measured $d'(t)$ levels off.

In conclusion we can say that in the experiment, for a limited time window the neuron effectively uses all information available at the sensory periphery. Peripheral noise is in turn determined by photon shot noise so that the reliability of H1's output is set by the physics of its inputs. There is no neuro-anatomical or neuro-physiological evidence for massive redundancy in arthropod nervous systems. More specifically, for the fly visual system, it is known that H1 is unique in its combination of visual field and preferred direction of movement (Hausen 1982), and from the results presented here we may begin to understand why: It just makes little sense to use functional duplicates of any neuron that performs almost perfectly when compared to the noise levels inherently present in the stimulus. It remains to be seen to what extent this conclusion can be generalized, but one should at least be cautious in interpreting the variability of response of a single neuron in terms of noise generated by the nervous system itself.

References

Barlow HB, Levick WR (1969) Three factors limiting the reliable detection of light by retinal ganglion cells of the cat. J Physiol **200**:1-24.

Bialek W (1990) Theoretical physics meets experimental neurobiology. In Jen E (ed.) *1989 Lectures in Complex Systems, SFI Studies in the Sciences of Complexity,*

Lect. Vol. II, pp. 513-595. Addison-Wesley, Menlo Park CA.

Bialek W, Rieke F, de Ruyter van Steveninck RR, Warland D (1991) Reading a neural code. Science **252**:1854-1857.

Bullock TH (1970) The reliability of neurons. J Gen Physiol **55**:565-584.

Eckhorn R, Pöpel B (1974) Rigorous and extended application of information theory to the afferent visual system of the cat. I Basic concepts. Kybernetik **16**:191-200.

Green DM, Swets JA (1966) *Signal detection theory and psychophysics*. Wiley, New York.

Hausen K (1982) Motion sensitive interneurons in the optomotor system of the fly. I. The horizontal cells: Structure and signals. Biol Cybern **45**:143-156.

Land MF, Collett TS (1974) Chasing behaviour of houseflies (*Fannia canicularis*). A description and analysis. J Comp Physiol **89**:331-357.

Levick WR, Thibos LN, Cohn TE, Catanzaro D, Barlow HB (1983) Performance of cat retinal ganglion cells at low light levels. J Gen Physiol **82**:405-426.

Neumann J von (1956) Probabilistic logics and the synthesis of reliable organisms from unreliable components. In Shannon CE and McCarthy J (eds.) *Automata Studies*, Princeton University Press, Princeton NJ, 43-98.

Parker A, Hawken M (1985) Capabilities of monkey cortical cells in spatial-resolution tasks. J Opt Soc Am **A2**:1101-1114.

Reichardt W (1957) Autokorrelations-Auswertung als Funktionsprinzip des Zentral-nervensystems. Z Naturf **12b**:448-457.

Reichardt W, Poggio T (1976) Visual control of orientation behaviour in the fly, Part I. A quantitative analysis. Q Rev Biophys **9**:311-375.

de Ruyter van Steveninck RR (1986) *Real-time performance of a movement-sensitive neuron in the blowfly visual system.* Thesis, Rijksuniversiteit Groningen, the Netherlands.

de Ruyter van Steveninck RR, Bialek W (1988) Real-time performance of a movement-sensitive neuron in the blowfly visual system: coding and information transfer in short spike sequences. Proc R Soc Lond B **234**: 379-414.

van Santen JPH, Sperling G (1984) Temporal covariance model of human motion perception. J Opt Soc Am **A1**:451-473.

Tolhurst DJ, Movshon JA, Dean AF (1983) The statistical reliability of signals in single neurons in cat and monkey visual cortex. Vision Res **23**: 775-785.

The Clusteron: Toward a Simple Abstraction for a Complex Neuron

Bartlett W. Mel
Computation and Neural Systems
Division of Biology
Caltech, 216-76
Pasadena, CA 91125
mel@cns.caltech.edu

Abstract

Are single neocortical neurons as powerful as multi-layered networks? A recent compartmental modeling study has shown that voltage-dependent membrane nonlinearities present in a complex dendritic tree can provide a virtual layer of local nonlinear processing elements between synaptic inputs and the final output at the cell body, analogous to a hidden layer in a multi-layer network. In this paper, an abstract model neuron is introduced, called a *clusteron*, which incorporates aspects of the dendritic "cluster-sensitivity" phenomenon seen in these detailed biophysical modeling studies. It is shown, using a *clusteron*, that a Hebb-type learning rule can be used to extract higher-order statistics from a set of training patterns, by manipulating the spatial ordering of synaptic connections onto the dendritic tree. The potential neurobiological relevance of these higher-order statistics for nonlinear pattern discrimination is then studied within a full compartmental model of a neocortical pyramidal cell, using a training set of 1000 high-dimensional sparse random patterns.

1 INTRODUCTION

The nature of information processing in complex dendritic trees has remained an open question since the origin of the neuron doctrine 100 years ago. With respect to learning, for example, it is not known whether a neuron is best modeled as

35

a pseudo-linear unit, equivalent in power to a simple Perceptron, or as a general nonlinear learning device, equivalent in power to a multi-layered network. In an attempt to characterize the input-output behavior of a whole dendritic tree containing voltage-dependent membrane mechanisms, a recent compartmental modeling study in an anatomically reconstructed neocortical pyramidal cell (anatomical data from Douglas et al., 1991; "NEURON" simulation package provided by Michael Hines and John Moore) showed that a dendritic tree rich in NMDA-type synaptic channels is selectively responsive to spatially clustered, as opposed to diffuse, patterns of synaptic activation (Mel, 1992). For example, 100 synapses which were simultaneously activated at 100 randomly chosen locations about the dendritic arbor were less effective at firing the cell than 100 synapses activated in groups of 5, at each of 20 randomly chosen dendritic locations. The cooperativity among the synapses in each group is due to the voltage dependence of the NMDA channel: Each activated NMDA synapse becomes up to three times more effective at injecting synaptic current when the post-synaptic membrane is locally depolarized by 30-40 mV from the resting potential. When synapses are activated in a group, the depolarizing effects of each helps the others (and itself) to move into this more efficient voltage range.

This work suggested that the spatial *ordering* of afferent synaptic connections onto the dendritic tree may be a crucial determinant of cell responses to specific input patterns. The nonlinear interactions among neighboring synaptic inputs further lent support to the idea that two or more afferents that form closely grouped synaptic connections on a dendritic tree may be viewed as encoding higher-order input-space "features" to which the dendrite is sensitive (Feldman & Ballard, 1982; Mel, 1990; Durbin & Rumelhart, 1990). The more such higher-order features are present in a given input pattern, the more the spatial distribution of active synapses will be clustered, and hence the more the post-synaptic cell will be inclined to fire in response. In a demonstration of this idea through direct manipulation of synaptic ordering, dendritic cluster-sensitivity was shown to allow the model neocortical pyramidal cell to reliably discriminate 50 training images of natural scenes from untrained control images (see Mel, 1992). Since all presented patterns activated the same number of synapses of the same strength, and with no systematic variation in their dendritic locations, the underlying dendritic "discriminant function" was necessarily nonlinear.

A crucial question remains as to whether other, e.g. non-synaptic, membrane non-linearities, such as voltage-dependent calcium channels in the dendritic shaft membrane, could enhance, abolish, or otherwise alter the dendritic cluster-sensitivity phenomenon seen in the NMDA-only case. Some of the simulations presented in the remainder of this paper include voltage-dependent calcium channels and/or an anomalous rectification in the dendritic membrane. However, detailed discussions of these channels and their effects will be presented elsewhere.

2   THE CLUSTERON

2.1   MOTIVATION

This paper deals primarily with an important extension to the compartmental modeling experiments and the hand-tuned demonstrations of nonlinear pattern discrimi-

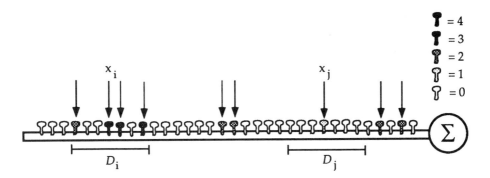

Figure 1: The *Clusteron*. Active inputs lines are designated by arrows; shading of synapses reflects synaptic activation a_i when $x_i \in \{0, 1\}$ and weights are set to 1.

nation capacity presented in (Mel, 1992). If the manipulation of synaptic ordering is necessary for neurons to make effective use of their cluster-sensitive dendrites, then a learning mechanism capable of appropriately manipulating synaptic ordering must also be present in these neurons. An abstract model neuron called a *clusteron* is presented here, whose input-output relation was inspired by the idea of dendritic cluster-sensitivity, and whose learning rule is a variant of simple Hebbian learning. The *clusteron* is a far simpler and more convenient model for the study of cluster-sensitive learning than the full-scale compartmental model described in (Mel, 1992), whose solutions under varying stimulus conditions are computed through numerical integration of a system of several hundred coupled nonlinear differential equations (Hines, 1989). However, once the basic mathematical and algorithmic issues have been better understood, more biophysically detailed models of this type of learning in dendritic trees, as has been reported in (Brown et al., 1990), will be needed.

2.2 INPUT-OUTPUT BEHAVIOR

The *clusteron* is a particular second-order generalization of the thresholded linear unit (TLU), exemplified by the common Perceptron. It consists of a "cell body" where the globally thresholded output of the unit is computed, and a dendritic tree, which for present purposes will be visualized as a single long branch attached to the cell body (fig. 1). The dendritic tree receives a set of N weighted synaptic contacts from a set of afferent "axons". All synaptic contacts are excitatory. The output of the *clusteron* is given by

$$y = g(\sum_{i=1}^{N} a_i), \tag{1}$$

where a_i is the net excitatory input at synapse i and g is a thresholding nonlinearity. Unlike the TLU, in which the net input due to a single input line i is $w_i x_i$, the net input at a *clusteron* synapse i with weight w_i is given by,

$$a_i = w_i x_i (\sum_{j \in \mathcal{D}_i} w_j x_j),\tag{2}$$

where x_i is the direct input stimulus intensity at synapse i, as for the TLU, and $\mathcal{D}_i = \{i - r, \ldots i, \ldots, i + r\}$ represents the neighborhood of radius r around synapse i. It may be noted that the weight on each second-order term is constrained to be the product of elemental weights $w_i w_j$, such that the *clusteron* has only N underlying degrees of freedom as compared to N^2 possible in a full second-order model. For the simplest case of $x_i \in \{0, 1\}$ and all weights set to 1, equation 2 says that the excitatory contribution of each active synapse is equal to the number of coactive synapses within its neighborhood. A synapse that is activated alone in its neighborhood thus provides a net excitatory input of $a_i = 1$; two synapses activated near to each other each provide a net excitatory input of $a_i = a_j = 2$, etc. The biophysical inspiration for the "multiplicative" relation in (2) is that, the net injected current through a region of voltage-dependent dendritic membrane can, under many circumstances, grow faster than linearly with increasing synaptic input to that region. Unlike the dendritic membrane modeled at the biophysical level, however, the *clusteron* in its current definition does not contain any saturating nonlinearities in the dendrites.

2.3   THE LEARNING PROBLEM

The learning problem of present interest is that of two-category classification. A pattern is a sparse N-element vector, where each component is a boolean random variable equal to 1 with probability ρ, and 0 otherwise. Let $T = \{t_1, t_2, \ldots, t_P\}$ be a training set consisting of P randomly chosen patterns. The goal of the classifier is to respond with $y = 1$ to any pattern in T, and $y = 0$ to all other "control" patterns with the same average bit density ρ. Performance at this task is measured by the probability of correct classification on a test set consisting of equal numbers of training and control patterns.

2.4   THE LEARNING RULE

Learning in the *clusteron* is the process by which the ordering of synaptic connections onto the dendrite is manipulated. Second-order features that are statistically prominent in the training set, i.e. pairs of pattern components that are coactivated in the training set more often than average, can become encoded in the *clusteron* as pairs of synaptic connections within the same dendritic neighborhood.

Learning proceeds as follows. Each pattern in T is presented once to the *clusteron* in a random sequence, constituting one training epoch. At the completion of each training epoch, each synapse i whose activation averaged over the training set

$$<a_i> = \frac{1}{P} \sum_{p=1}^{P} a_i^{(p)}$$

falls below threshold θ, is switched with another randomly chosen subthreshold synapse. The threshold can, for example, be chosen as $\theta = \frac{1}{N} \sum_{i=1}^{N} <a_i>$, i.e.

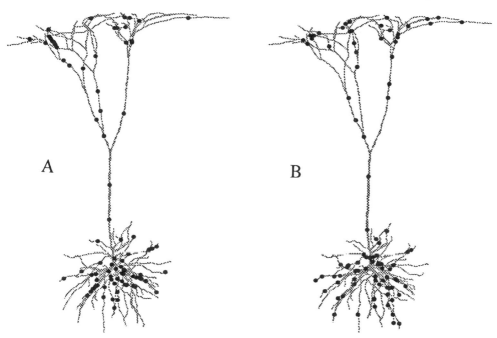

Figure 2: Distribution of 100 active synapses for a trained pattern (A) vs. a random control pattern (B); synapse locations are designated by black dots. Layout A is statistically more "clustery" than B, as evidenced by the presence of several clusters of 5 or more active synapses not found in B. While the total synaptic conductance activated in layout A was 20% less than that in layout B (linked to local variations in input-resistance), layout A generated 5 spikes at the soma, while layout B generated none.

the averaged synaptic activation across all synapses and training patterns. Each synapse whose average activation *exceeds* threshold θ is left undisturbed. Thus, if a synapse is often coactivated with its neighbors during learning, its average activation is high, and its connection is stabilized. If it is only rarely coactivated with its neighbors during learning, it loses its current connection, and is given the opportunity to stabilize a new connection at a new location.

The dynamics of *clusteron* learning may be caricatured as follows. At the start of learning, each "poor performing" synaptic connection improves its average activation level when switched to a new dendritic location where, by definition, it is expected to be an "average performer". The average global response y to training patterns is thus also expected to increase during early training epochs. The average response to random controls remains unchanged, however, since there is no systematic structure in the ordering of synaptic connections relevant to any untrained pattern. This relative shift in the mean responses to training vs. control patterns is the basis for discrimination between them. The learning process approaches its asymptote as each pair of synapses switched, on average, disturbs the optimized *clusteron* neighborhood structure as much as it improves it.

3   RESULTS

The *clusteron* learning rule leads to a permutation of synaptic input connections having the property that the distribution of activated synapses in the dendritic tree associated with the presentation of a typical training pattern is statistically more "clustery" than the distribution of activated synapses associated with the presentation of a random control pattern.

For a given training set size, however, it is crucial to establish that the clustery distributions of active synapses associated with training patterns are in fact of a type that can be reliably discriminated—*within the detailed biophysical model*—from diffuse stimulation of the dendritic tree corresponding to unfamiliar stimulus patterns. In order to investigate this question, a *clusteron* with 17,000 synapses was trained with 1000 training patterns. This number of synapses was chosen in order that a direct map exist between *clusteron* synapses and dendritic spines, which were assumed to lie at 1 μm intervals along the approximately 17,000 μm of total dendritic length of the model neocortical neuron (from Douglas et al., 1991). In these runs, exactly 100 of the 17,000 bits were randomly set in each of the training and control patterns, such that every pattern activated exactly 100 synapses. After 200 training epochs, 100 training patterns and 100 control patterns were selected as a test set. For each test pattern, the locations of its 100 active *clusteron* synapses were mapped onto the dendritic tree in the biophysical model by traversing the latter in depth-first order. For example, training pattern #36 activated synapses as shown in fig. 2A, with synapse locations indicated by black dots. The layout in B was due to a control pattern. It may be perceived that layout A contains several clear groupings of 5 or more synapses that are not observed in layout B.

Within in the biophysical model, the conductance of each synapse, containing both NMDA and non-NMDA components, was scaled inversely with the input resistance measured locally at the dendritic spine head. Membrane parameters were similar to those used in (Mel, 1992); a high-threshold non-inactivating calcium conductance and an anomalous rectifier were used in these experiments as well, and were uniformly distributed over most of the dendritic tree. In the simulation run for each pattern, each of the 100 activated synapses was driven at 100 Hz for 100 ms, asynchronously, and the number of action potentials generated at the soma was counted. The total activated synaptic conductance in fig. 2A was 20% less than that activated by control layout B. However, layout A generated 5 somatic spikes while layout B generated none.

Fig. 3 shows the cell responses averaged over training patterns, four types of degraded training patterns, and control patterns. Most saliently, the average spike count in response to a training pattern was 3 times the average response to a control pattern. Not surprisingly, degraded training patterns gave rise to degraded responses. It is crucial to reiterate that all patterns, regardless of category, activated an identical number of synapses, with no average difference in their synaptic strengths or in dendritic eccentricity. Only the spatial distributions of active synapses were different among categories.

1000 Training Patterns

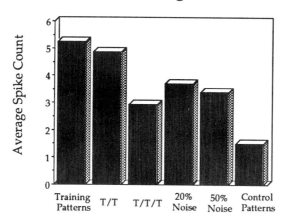

Figure 3: Average cell responses to training patterns, degraded training patterns, and control patterns. Categories designated T/T and T/T/T represented feature composites of 2 or 3 training patterns, respectively. Degraded responses to these categories of stimulus patterns was evidence for the underlying nonlinearity of the dendritic discriminant function.

4   CONCLUSION

These experiments within the *clusteron* model neuron have shown that the assumption of (1) dendritic cluster-sensitivity, (2) a combinatorially rich interface structure that allows every afferent axon potential access to many dendritic loci, and (3) a local Hebb-type learning rule for stabilizing newly formed synapses, are sufficient in principle to allow the learning of nonlinear input-ouput relations with a single dendritic tree. The massive rearrangement of synapses seen in these computational experiments is not strictly necessary; much of the work could be done instead through standard Hebbian synaptic potentiation, if a larger set of post-synaptic neurons is assumed to be available to each afferent instead of a single neuron as used here. Architectural issues relevant to this issue have been discussed at length in (Mel, 1990; Mel & Koch, 1990).

An analysis of the storage capacity of the *clusteron* will be presented elsewhere.

Acknowledgements

This work was supported by the Office of Naval Research, the James McDonnell Foundation, and National Institute of Mental Health. Thanks to Christof Koch for providing an excellent working environment, Ken Miller for helpful discussions, and to Rodney Douglas for discussions and use of his neurons.

References

Brown, T.H., Mainen, Z.F., Zador, A.M., & Claiborne, B.J. Self-organization of hebbian synapses in hippocampal neurons. In *Advances in Neural Information Processing Systems, vol. 3*, R. Lippmann, J. Moody, & D. Touretzky, (Eds.), Palo Alto: Morgan Kauffman, 1991.

Douglas, R.J., Martin, K.A.C., & Whitteridge, D. An intracellular analysis of the visual responses of neurones in striate visual cortex. *J. Physiol.*, 1991, *440*, 659-696.

Durbin, R. & Rumelhart, D.E. Product units: a computationally powerful and biologically plausible extension to backpropagation networks. *Neural Computation*, 1989, *1*, 133.

Feldman, J.A. & Ballard, D.H. Connectionist models and their properties. *Cognitive Science*, 1982, *6*, 205-254.

Hines, M. A program for simulation of nerve equations with branching geometries. *Int. J. Biomed. Comput.*, 1989, *24*, 55-68.

Mel, B.W. The sigma-pi column: a model for associative learning in cerebral neo-cortex. CNS Memo #6, Computation and Neural Systems Program, California Institute of Technology, 1990.

Mel, B.W. NMDA-based pattern classification in a modeled cortical neuron. 1992, *Neural Computation*, in press.

Mel, B.W. & Koch, C. Sigma-pi learning: On radial basis functions and cortical associative learning. In *Advances in neural information processing systems, vol. 2*, D.S. Touretzsky, (Ed.), San Mateo, CA: Morgan Kaufmann, 1990.

Network activity determines
spatio-temporal integration in single cells

Öjvind Bernander, Christof Koch *
Computation and Neural Systems Program,
California Institute of Technology,
Pasadena, Ca 91125, USA.

Rodney J. Douglas
Anatomical Neuropharmacology Unit,
Dept. Pharmacology,
Oxford, UK.

Abstract

Single nerve cells with static properties have traditionally been viewed as the building blocks for networks that show emergent phenomena. In contrast to this approach, we study here how the overall network activity can control single cell parameters such as input resistance, as well as time and space constants, parameters that are crucial for excitability and spatio-temporal integration. Using detailed computer simulations of neocortical pyramidal cells, we show that the spontaneous background firing of the network provides a means for setting these parameters. The mechanism for this control is through the large conductance change of the membrane that is induced by both non-NMDA and NMDA excitatory and inhibitory synapses activated by the spontaneous background activity.

1 INTRODUCTION

Biological neurons display a complexity rarely heeded in abstract network models. Dendritic trees allow for local interactions, attenuation, and delays. Voltage- and

---

*To whom all correspondence should be addressed.

time-dependent conductances can give rise to adaptation, burst-firing, and other non-linear effects. The extent of temporal integration is determined by the time constant, and spatial integration by the "leakiness" of the membrane. It is unclear which cell properties are computationally significant and which are not relevant for information processing, even though they may be important for the proper functioning of the cell. However, it is crucial to understand the function of the component cells in order to make relevant abstractions when modeling biological systems. In this paper we study how the spontaneous background firing of the network as a whole can strongly influence some of the basic integration properties of single cells.

1.1   Controlling parameters via background synaptic activity

The **input resistance**, R_{in}, is defined as $\frac{dV}{dI}$, where dV is the steady state voltage change in response to a small current step of amplitude dI. R_{in} will vary throughout the cell, and is typically much larger in a long, narrow dendrite than in the soma. However, the somatic input resistance is more relevant to the spiking behavior of the neuron, since spikes are initiated at or close to the soma, and hence $R_{in,soma}$ (henceforth simply referred to as R_{in}) will tell us something of the sensitivity of the cell to charge reaching the soma.

The **time constant**, τ_m, for a passive membrane patch is $R_m \cdot C_m$, the membrane resistance times the membrane capacitance. For membranes containing voltage-dependent non-linearities, exponentials are fitted to the step response and the largest time constant is taken to be the membrane time constant. A large time constant implies that any injected charge leaks away very slowly, and hence the cell has a longer "memory" of previous events.

The parameters discussed above (R_{in}, τ_m) clearly have computational significance and it would be convenient to be able to change them dynamically. Both depend directly on the membrane conductance $G_m = \frac{1}{R_m}$, so any change in G_m will change the parameters. Traditionally, however, G_m has been viewed as static, so these parameters have also been considered static. How can we change G_m dynamically?

In traditional models, G_m has two components: active (time- and voltage-dependent) conductances and a passive "leak" conductance. Synapses are modeled as conductance changes, but if only a few are activated, the cable structure of the cell will hardly change at all. However, it is well known that neocortical neurons spike spontaneously, in the absence of sensory stimuli, at rates from 0 to 10 Hz. Since neocortical neurons receive on the order of $5,000$ to $15,000$ excitatory synapses (Larkman, 1991), this spontaneous firing is likely to add up to a large total conductance (Holmes & Woody, 1989). This synaptic conductance becomes crucial if the non-synaptic conductance components are small. Recent evidence show indeed that the non-synaptic conductances are relatively small (when the cell is not spiking) (Anderson et al., 1990). Our model uses a leak $R_m = 100,000\ k\Omega cm^2$, instead of more conventional values in the range of $2,500$–$10,000\ k\Omega cm^2$. These two facts, high R_m and synaptic background activity, allow R_{in} and τ_m to change by more than ten-fold, as described below in this paper.

2   MODEL

A typical layer V pyramidal cell (fig. 2) in striate cortex was filled with HRP during *in vivo* experiments in the anesthetized, adult cat (Douglas et al., 1991). The 3-D coordinates and diameters of the dendritic tree were measured by a computer-assisted method and each branch was replaced by a single equivalent cylinder. This morphological data was fed into a modified version of NEURON, an efficient single cell simulator developed by Hines (1989). The dendrites were passive, while the soma contained seven active conductances, underlying spike generation, adaptation, and slow onset for weak stimuli. The model included two sodium conductances (a fast spiking current and a slower non-inactivating current), one calcium conductance, and four potassium conductances (delayed rectifier, slow 'M' and 'A' type currents, and a calcium-dependent current). The active conductances were modeled using a Hodgkin-Huxley-like formalism.

The model used a total of 5,000 synapses. The synaptic conductance change in time was modeled with an alpha function, $g(t) = \frac{g_{peak}e}{t_{peak}}te^{-t/t_{peak}}$. 4,000 synapses were fast excitatory non-NMDA or AMPA-type ($t_{peak} = 1.5\,msec$, $g_{peak} = 0.5\,nS$, $E_{rev} = 0\,mV$), 500 were medium-slow inhibitory $GABA_A$ ($t_{peak} = 10\,msec$, $g_{peak} = 1.0\,nS$, $E_{rev} = -70\,mV$), and 500 were slow inhibitory $GABA_B$ ($t_{peak} = 40\,msec$, $g_{peak} = 0.1\,nS$, $E_{rev} = -95\,mV$). The excitatory synapses were less concentrated towards the soma, while the inhibitory ones were more so. For a more detailed description of the model, see Bernander et al. (1991).

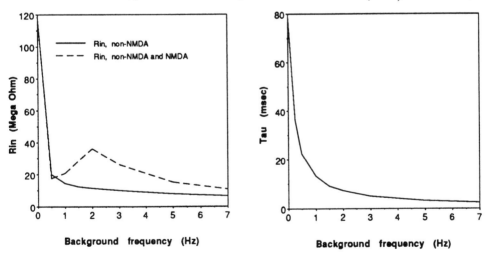

Figure 1: **Input resistance and time constant as a function of background frequency.** In (a), the solid line corresponds to the "standard" model with passive dendrites, while the dashed line includes active NMDA synapses as described in the text.

3   RESULTS

3.1 R_{in} and τ_m change with background frequency

Fig. 1 illustrates what happens to R_{in} and τ_m when the synaptic background activities of all synaptic types are varied simultaneously. In the absence of any synaptic input, $R_{in} = 110 \ M\Omega$ and $\tau_m = 80 \ msec$. At 1 Hz background activity, on average 5 synaptic events are impinging on the cell every $msec$, contributing a total of 24 nS to the somatic input conductance G_{in}. Because of the reversal potential of the excitatory synapses (0 mV), the membrane potential throughout the cell is pulled towards more depolarizing potentials, activating additional active currents. Although these trends continue as f is increased, the largest change can be observed between 0 and 2 Hz.

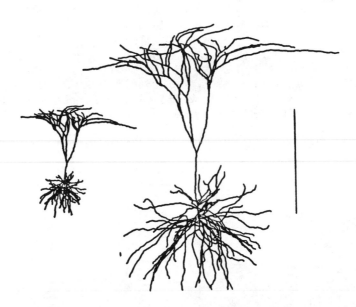

Figure 2: **Spatial integration as a function of background frequency.**
Each dendrite has been "stretched" so that its apparent length corresponds to its electrotonic length. The synaptic background frequency was 0 Hz (left) and 2 Hz (right). The scale bar corresponds to 1 λ (length constant).

Activating synaptic input has two distinct effects: the conductance of the postsynaptic membrane increases and the membrane is depolarized. The system can, at least in principle, independently control these two effects by differentially varying the spontaneous firing frequencies of excitatory versus inhibitory inputs. Thus, increasing f selectively for the $GABA_B$ inhibition will further increase the membrane conductance but move the resting potential towards more hyperpolarizing potentials.

Note that the $0\,Hz$ case corresponds to experiments made with *in vitro* slice preparations or culture. In this case incoming fibers have been cut off and the spontaneous firing rate is very small. Careful studies have shown very large values for R_{in} and τ_m under these circumstances (e.g. Spruston & Johnston, 1991). *In vivo* preparations, on the other hand, leave the cortical circuitry intact and much smaller values of R_{in} and τ_m are usually recorded.

3.2   Spatial integration

Varying synaptic background activity can have a significant impact on the electrotonic structure of the cell (fig. 2). We plot the electrotonic distance of any particular point from the cell body, that is the sum of the electrotonic length's $L_i = \sum_j (l_j/\lambda_j)$ associated with each dendritic segment i, where $\lambda_j = \sqrt{\frac{R_m \cdot d_j}{4 \cdot R_i}}$ is the electrotonic length constant of compartment j, l_j its anatomical length and the sum is taken over all compartments between the soma and compartment i.

Increasing the synaptic background activity from $f = 0$ to $f = 2\,Hz$ has the effect of stretching the "distance" of any particular synapse to the soma by a factor of about 3, on average. Thus, while a distal synapse has an associated L value of about 2.6 at $2\,Hz$ it shrinks to 1.2 if all network activity is shut off, while for a synapse at the tip of a basal dendrite, L shrinks from 0.7 to 0.2. In fact, the EPSP induced by a single excitatory synapse at that location goes from 39 to 151 μV, a decrease of about 4. Thus, when the overall network activity is low, synapses in the superficial layer of cortex could have a significant effect on somatic discharge, while having only a weak modulatory effect on the soma if the overall network activity is high. Note that basal dendrites, which receive a larger number of synapses, stretch more than apical dendrites.

3.3   Temporal integration

That the synaptic background activity can also modify the temporal integration behavior of the cell is demonstrated in fig. 3. At any particular background frequency f, we compute the minimal number of additional excitatory synapses (at $g_{peak} = 0.5\,nS$) necessary to barely generate one action potential. These synapses were chosen randomly from among all excitatory synapses throughout the cell. We compare the case in which all synapses are activated simultaneously (solid line) with the case in which the inputs arrive asynchronously, smeared out over 25 $msec$ (dashed line). If $f = 0$, it requires 115 synapses firing simultaneously to generate a single action potential, while 145 are needed if the input is desynchronized. This small difference between inputs arriving synchronized and at random is due to the long integration period of the cell.

If the background activity increases to $f = 1\,Hz$, 113 synchronized synaptic inputs—spread out all over the cell—are sufficient to fire the cell. If, however, the synaptic input is spread out over 25 $msec$, 202 synapses are now needed in order to trigger a response from the cell. This is mainly due to the much smaller value of τ_m relative to the period over which the synaptic input is spread out. Note that the difference in number of simultaneous synaptic inputs needed to fire the cell for $f = 0$ compared to $f = 1$ is small (i.e. 113 vs. 115), in spite of the more than five-fold decrease in somatic input resistance. The effect of the smaller size of the individual EPSP at higher values of f is compensated for by the fact that the resting potential of the cell has been shifted towards the firing threshold of the cell (about $-49\ mV$).

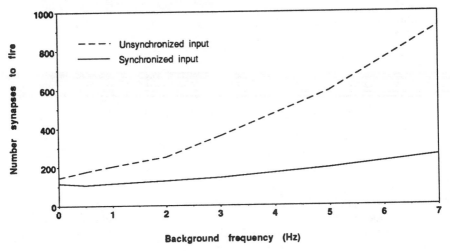

Figure 3: **Phase detection.**

A variable number of excitatory synapses were fired superimposed onto a constant background frequency of 1 Hz. They fired either simultaneously (solid line) or spread out in time uniformly during a 25 msec interval (dashed line). The y axis shows the minimum number of synapses necessary to cause the cell to fire.

3.4   NMDA synapses

Fast excitatory synaptic input in cortex is mediated by both AMPA or non-NMDA as well as NMDA receptors (Miller et al., 1989). As opposed to the AMPA synapse, the NMDA conductance change depends not only on time but also on the post-synaptic voltage:

$$G(V,t) = 1.05 \cdot G_{max} \cdot \frac{e^{-t/\tau_1} - e^{-t/\tau_2}}{1 + \eta \cdot [Mg^{2+}] \cdot e^{-\gamma V}}, \tag{1}$$

where $\tau_1 = 40\ msec$, $\tau_2 = 0.335\ msec$, $\eta = 0.33\ mM^{-1}$, $[Mg^{2+}] = 1\ mM$, $\gamma = 0.06\ mV^{-1}$. During spontaneous background activity many inputs impinge on the cell and we can time-average the equation above. We will then be left with a purely voltage-dependent conductance.

We measured the somatic input resistance, R_{in}, by injecting a small current pulse in the soma (fig. 4) in the standard model. All synapses fired at a 0.5 Hz background frequency. Next we added 4,000 NMDA synapses in addition to the 4,000 non-

NMDA synapses, also at 0.5 Hz, and again injected a current pulse. The voltage response is now *larger* by about 65%, corresponding to a *smaller* input conductance, even though we are adding the positive NMDA conductance. This seeming paradox depends on two effects. First, the input conductance is, by definition, $\frac{dI}{dV} = G(V) + \frac{dG(V)}{dV} \cdot (V - E_{rev})$, where G(V) is the conductance specified in eq. (1). For the NMDA synapse this derivative is negative below about $-35\ mV$. Second, due to the excitation the membrane voltage has drifted towards more depolarized values. This will cause a change in the activation of the other voltage-dependent currents. Even though the summed conductance of these active currents will be larger at the new voltage, the derivative $\frac{dI}{dV}$ will be smaller at that point. In other words, activation of NMDA synapses gives a negative contribution to the *input* conductance, even though more conductances have opened up.

Next we replaced $2,000$ of the $4,000$ non-NMDA synapses in the old model with $2,000$ NMDA synapses and recomputed the input resistance as a function of synaptic background activity. The result is overlaid in figure 1a (dashed line). The curve shifts toward larger values of R_{in} for most values of f. This shift varies between 50 % – 200 %. The cell is more excitable than before.

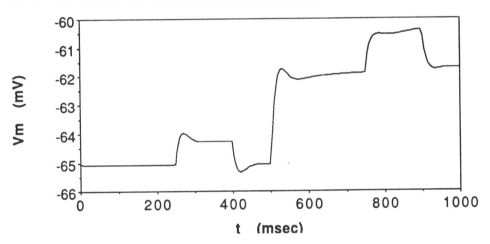

Figure 4: **Negative input conductance from NMDA activation.**
At times $t = 250\ msec$ and $t = 750\ msec$ a 0.05 nA current pulse was injected at the soma and the somatic voltage response was recorded. At $t = 500\ msec$, one NMDA synapse was activated for each non-NMDA synapse, for a total of $8,000$ excitatory synaptic inputs. The background frequency was 0.5 Hz for all synapses.

4   DISCUSSION

We have seen that parameters such as R_{in}, τ_m, and L are not static, but can vary over about one order of magnitude under network control. The potential computational possibilities could be significant.

For example, if a low-contrast stimulus is presented within the receptive field of the cell, the synaptic input rate will be small and the signal-to-noise ratio (SNR) low. In this case, to make the cell more sensitive to the inputs we might want to increase R_{in}. This would automatically be achieved as the total network activation is low. We can improve the SNR by integrating over a longer time period, i.e. by increasing τ_m. This would also be a consequence of the reduced network activity. The converse argument can be made for high-contrast stimuli, associated with high overall network activity and low R_{in} and τ_m values.

Many cortical cells are tuned for various properties of the stimulus, such as orientation, direction, and binocular disparity. As the effective membrane conductance, G_m, changes, the tuning curves are expected to change. Depending on the exact circuitry and implementation of the tuning properties, this change in background frequency could take many forms. One example of phase-tuning was given above. In this case the temporal tuning increases with background frequency.

Acknowledgements

This work was supported by the Office of Naval Research, the National Science Foundation, the James McDonnell Foundation and the International Human Frontier Science Program Organization. Thanks to Tom Tromey for writing the graphic software and to Mike Hines for providing us with NEURON.

References

P. Anderson, M. Raastad & J. F. Storm. (1990) Excitatory synaptic integration in hippocampal pyramids and dentate granule cells. *Symp. Quant. Biol.* **55**, Cold Spring Harbor Press, pp. 81-86.

Ö. Bernander, R. J. Douglas, K. A. C. Martin & C. Koch. (1991) Synaptic background activity influences spatiotemporal integration in single pyramidal cells. *P.N.A.S, USA* **88**: 11569-11573.

R. J. Douglas, K. A. C. Martin & D. Whitteridge. (1991) An intracellular analysis of the visual responses of neurones in cat visual cortex. *J. Physiol.* **440**: 659-696.

M. Hines. (1989) A program for simulation of nerve equations with branching geometries. *Int. J. Biomed. Comput.* **24**: 55-68.

W. R. Holmes & C. D. Woody. (1989) Effects of uniform and non-uniform synaptic activation-distributions on the cable properties of modeled cortical pyramidal neurons. *Brain Research* **505**: 12-22.

A. U. Larkman. (1991) Dendritic morphology of pyramidal neurones of the visual cortex of the rat: III. Spine distributions. *J. Comp. Neurol.* **306**: 332-343.

K. D. Miller, B. Chapman & M. P. Stryker. (1989) Responses of cells in cat visual cortex depend on NMDA receptors. *P.N.A.S.* **86**: 5183-5187.

N. Spruston & D. Johnston. (1992) Perforated patch-clamp analysis of the passive membrane properties of three classes of hippocampal neurons. *J. Neurophysiol.*, in press.

Nonlinear Pattern Separation in Single Hippocampal Neurons with Active Dendritic Membrane

Anthony M. Zador[†] **Brenda J. Claiborne**[§] **Thomas H. Brown**[†]

[†]Depts. of Psychology and Cellular
 & Molecular Physiology
Yale University
New Haven, CT 06511
zador@yale.edu

[§]Division of Life Sciences
University of Texas
San Antonio, TX 78285

ABSTRACT

The dendritic trees of cortical pyramidal neurons seem ideally suited to perform local processing on inputs. To explore some of the implications of this complexity for the computational power of neurons, we simulated a realistic biophysical model of a hippocampal pyramidal cell in which a "cold spot"—a high density patch of inhibitory Ca-dependent K channels and a colocalized patch of Ca channels—was present at a dendritic branch point. The cold spot induced a nonmonotonic relationship between the strength of the synaptic input and the probability of neuronal firing. This effect could also be interpreted as an analog stochastic XOR.

1 INTRODUCTION

Cortical neurons consist of a highly branched dendritic tree that is electrically coupled to the soma. In a typical hippocampal pyramidal cell, over 10,000 excitatory synaptic inputs are distributed across the tree (Brown and Zador, 1990). Synaptic activity results in current flow through a transient conductance increase at the point of synaptic contact with the membrane. Since the primary means of rapid intraneuronal signalling is electrical, information flow can be characterized in terms of the electrical circuit defined by the synapses, the dendritic tree, and the soma.

Over a dozen nonlinear membrane channels have been described in hippocampal pyramidal neurons (Brown and Zador, 1990). There is experimental evidence for a heterogeneous distribution of some of these channels in the dendritic tree (*e.g.* Jones *et al.,* 1989). In the absence of these dendritic channels, the input-output function can sometimes be reasonably approximated by a modified sigmoidal model. Here we report that introducing a cold spot at the junction of two dendritic branches can result in a fundamentally different, nonmonotonic input-output function.

2 MODEL

The biophysical details of the circuit class defined by dendritic trees have been well characterized (*reviewed in* Rall, 1977; Jack *et al.*, 1983). The fundamental circuit consists of a linear and a nonlinear component. The linear component can be approximated by a set of electrical compartments coupled in series (Fig. 1C), each consisting of a resistor and capacitor in parallel (Fig. 1B). The nonlinear component consists of a set of nonlinear resistors in parallel with the capacitance.

The model is summarized in Fig. 1A. Briefly, simulations were performed on a 3000-compartment anatomical reconstruction of a region CA1 hippocampal neuron (Claiborne *et al.*, 1992; Brown *et al.*, 1992). All dendritic membrane was passive, except at the cold spot (Fig. 1A). At the soma, fast K and Na channels (*cf.* Hodgkin-Huxley, 1952) generated action potentials in response to stimuli. The parameters for these channels were modified from Lytton and Sejnowski (1991; *cf.* Borg-Graham, 1991).

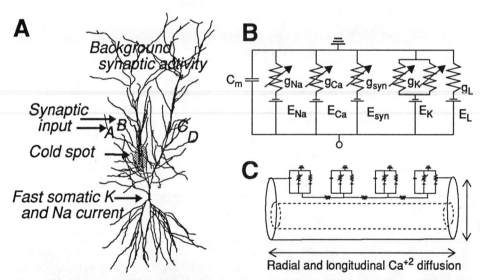

Fig. 1 The model. **(A)** The 3000-compartment electrical model used in these simulations was obtained from a 3-dimensional reconstruction of a hippocampal region CA1 pyramidal neuron (Claiborne et al, 1992). Each synaptic pathway *(A-D)* consisted of an adjustable number of synapses arrayed along the single branch indicated *(see text)*. Random background activity was generated with a spatially uniform distribution of synapses firing according to Poisson statistics. The neuronal membrane was completely passive (linear), except at the indicated cold spot and at the soma. **(B)** In the nonlinear circuit associated with a patch of neuronal membrane containing active channels, each channel is described by a voltage-dependent conductance in series with its ionic battery *(see text)*. In the present model the channels were spatially localized, so no single patch contained all of the nonlinearities depicted in this hypothetical illustration. **(C)** A dendritic segment is illustrated in which both electrical and Ca^{2+} dynamics were modelled. Ca^{2+} buffering, and both radial and longitudinal Ca^{2+} diffusion were simulated.

We distinguished four synaptic pathways *A-D* (*see* Fig. 1A). Each pathway consisted of a population of synapses activated synchronously. The synapses were of the fast *AMPA* type (*see* Brown *et. al.*, 1992). In addition, random background synaptic activity distributed uniformly across the dendritic tree fired according to Poisson statistics.

The cold spot consisted of a high density of a Ca-activated K channel, the *AHP* current (Lancaster and Nicoll, 1987; Lancaster *et. al.*, 1991) colocalized with a low density patch of N-type Ca channels (Lytton and Sejnowski, 1991; *cf.* Borg-Graham, 1991). Upon localized depolarization in the region of the cold spot, influx of Ca^{2+} through the Ca channel resulted in a transient increase in the local $[Ca^{2+}]$. The model included Ca^{2+} buffering, and both radial and longitudinal diffusion in the region of the cold spot. The increased $[Ca^{2+}]$ activated the inhibitory *AHP* current. The interplay between the direct excitatory effect of synaptic input, and its inhibitory effect via the *AHP* channels formed the functional basis of the cold spot.

3   RESULTS

3.1 DYNAMIC BEHAVIOR

Representative behavior of the model is illustrated in Fig. 2. The somatic potential is plotted as a function of time in a series of simulations in which the number of activated synapses in pathway *A/B* was increased from *0* to about *100*. For the first 100 *msec* of each simulation, background synaptic activity generated a noisy baseline. At $t = 100$ *msec*, the indicated number of synapses fired synchronously five times at *100 Hz*. Since the background activity was noisy, the outcome of the each simulation was a random process.

The key effect of the cold spot was to impose a limit on the maximum stimulus amplitude that caused firing, resulting in a window of stimulus strengths that triggered an action potential. In the absence of the cold spot a greater synaptic stimulus invariably increased the likelihood that a spike fired. This limit resulted from the relative magnitude of the *AHP*

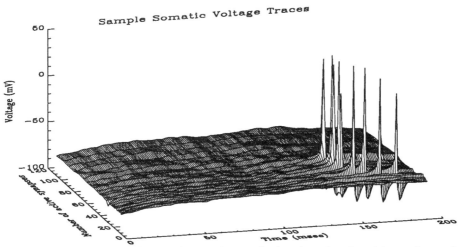

Fig. 2 Sample runs. The membrane voltage at the soma is plotted as a function of time and synaptic stimulus intensity. At $t = 100$ *msec*, a synaptic stimulus consisting of 5 pulses was activitated. The noisy baseline resulted from random synaptic input. A single action potential resulted for input intensities within a range determined by the kinetics of the cold spot.

current "threshold" to the threshold for somatic spiking. The *AHP* current required a relatively high level of activity for its activation. This *AHP* current "threshold" reflected the sigmoidal voltage dependence of N-type Ca current activation ($V_{1/2} = -28\ mV$), since only as the dendritic voltage approached $V_{1/2}$ did dendritic $[Ca^{2+}]$ rise enough to activate the *AHP* current. Because $V_{1/2}$ was much higher than the threshold for somatic spiking (about $-55\ mV$ under current clamp), there was a window of stimulus strengths sufficient to trigger a somatic action potential but insufficient to activate the *AHP* current. Only within this window of between about 20 and 60 synapses (Fig. 2) did an action potential occur.

3.2 LOCAL NON-MONOTONIC RESPONSE FUNCTION

Because the background activity was random, the outcome of each simulation (*e.g.* Fig. 2) represented a sample of a random process. This random process can be used to define many different random variables. One variable of interest is whether a spike fired in response to a stimulus. Although this measure ignores the dynamic nature of neuronal activity, it was still relatively informative because in these simulations no more than one spike fired per experiment.

Fig. 3A shows the dependence of firing probability on stimulus strength. It was obtained by averaging over a population of simulations of the type illustrated in Fig. 2. In the absence of *AHP* current (*dotted line*), the firing probability was a sigmoidal function of activity. In its presence, the firing probability was a smooth nonmonotonic function of the activity (*solid line*). The firing probability was maximum at about 35 synapses, and occurred only in the range between about 10 and 80 synapses. The statistics illustrated in Fig. 3A quantify the nonmonotonicity that is implied by the single sample shown in Fig. 2.

Spikes required the somatic Hodgkin-Huxley-like Na and K channels. To a first approximation, the effect of these channels was to convert a continuous variable—the somatic voltage—into a discrete variable—the presence or absence of a spike. Although this approximation ignores the complex interactions between the soma and the cold spot, it is useful for a qualitative analysis. The nonmonotonic dependence of somatic activity on syn-

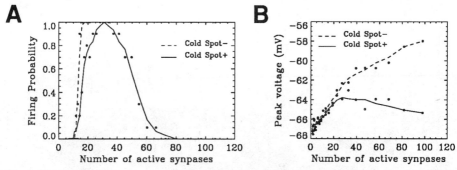

Fig. 3 Nonmonotonic input-output relation. (A) Each point represents the probability that at least one spike was fired at the indicated activity level. In the absence of a cold spot, the firing probability increased sharply and monotonically as the number of synapses in pathway *C/D* increased (*dotted line*). In contrast, the firing probability reached a maximum for pathway *A/B* and then decreased (*solid line*). (B) Each point represents the peak somatic voltage for a single simulation at the indicated activity level in the presence (*pathway A/B; solid line*) and absence (*pathway C/D; dotted line*) of a cold spot. Because each point represents the outcome of a single simulation, in contrast to the average used in *(A)*, the points reflect the variance due to the random background activity.

aptic activity was preserved even when active channels at the soma were eliminated (Fig. 3B). This result emphasizes that the critical nonlinearity was the cold spot itself.

3.3 NONLINEAR PATTERN SEPARATION

So far, we have treated the output as a function of a scalar—the total activity in pathway *A/B* (or *C/D*). In Fig. 3 for example, the total activity was defined as the sum of the activities in pathway *A* and *B*. The spatial organization of the afferents onto 2 pairs of branches—*A* & *B* and *C* & *D* (Fig. 1)—suggested considering the output as a function of the activity in the separate elements of each pair.

The effect of the cold spot can be viewed in terms of the dependence of firing as a function of separate activity in pathways *A* and *B* (Fig. 4). Each filled circle indicates that the neuron fired for the indicated input intensity of pathways *A* and *B*, while a small dot indicates that it did not fire. As suggested by (Fig. 3), the firing probability was highest when the total activity in the two pathways was at some intermediate level. The neuron did not fire when the total activity in the two pathways was too large or too small. In the absence of the cold spot, only a minimum activity level was required.

In our model the probability of firing was a continuous function of the inputs. In the presence of the dendritic cold spot, the corners of this function suggested the logical operation XOR. The probability of firing was high if only one input was activated and low if both or neither was activated.

4   DISCUSSION

4.1 ASSUMPTIONS

Neuronal morphology in the present model was based on a precise reconstruction of a region CA1 pyramidal neuron. The main additional assumptions involved the kinetics and distribution of the four membrane channels, and the dynamics of Ca^{2+} in the neighborhood of influx. The forms assumed for these mechanisms were biophysically plausible, and the kinetic parameters were based on estimates from a collection of experimental studies (*listed in* Lytton and Sejnowski, 1991; Zador *et al.*, 1990). Variation within the range of uncertainty of these parameters did not alter the main conclusions. The chief untested assumption of this model was the existence of cold spots. Although there is experimental evidence

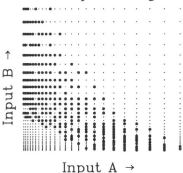

Input A →

Fig. 4 Nonlinear pattern separation Neuronal firing is represented as a joint function of two input pathways (*A/B*). Filled circles indicate that the neuron fired for the indicated stimulus parameters. Some indication of the stochastic nature of this function, resulting form the noisy background, is given by the density of interdigitation of points and circles.

supporting the presence of both Ca and *AHP* channels in the dendrites, there is at present no direct evidence regarding their colocalization.

4.2 COMPUTATIONS IN SINGLE NEURONS

4.2.1 Neurons and Processing Elements

The limitations of the McCulloch and Pitts (1943) PE as a neuron model have long been recognized. Their threshold PE, in which the output is the weighted sum of the inputs passed through a threshold, is static, deterministic and treats all inputs equivalently. This model ignores at least three key complexities of neurons: *temporal, spatial* and *stochastic*. In subsequent years, augmented models have attempted to capture aspects of these complexities. For example, the leaky integrator (Caianiello, 1961; Hopfield, 1984) incorporates the temporal dynamics implied by the linear *RC* component of the circuit element pictured in Fig. 1B. We have demonstrated that the input-output function of a realistic neuron model can have qualitatively different behavior from that of a single processing element (PE).

4.2.2 Interactions Within The Dendritic Tree

The early work of Rall (1964) stressed the spatial complexity of even linear dendritic models. He noted that input from different synapses cannot be considered to arrive at a single point, the soma. Koch *et al.* (1982) extended this observation by exploring the nonlinear interactions between synaptic inputs to different regions of the dendritic tree. They emphasized that these interactions can be local in the sense that they effect subpopulations of synapses and suggested that the entire dendritic tree can be considered in terms of electrically isolated subunits. They proposed a specific role for these subunits in computing a veto— an analog AND-NOT—that might underlie directional selectivity in retinal ganglion cells. The veto was achieved through inhibitory inputs.

The underlying neuron models of Koch *et al.* (1982) and Rall (1964) were time-varying but linear, so it is not surprising that the resulting nonlinearities were monotonic. Much steeper nonlinearities were achieved by Shepherd and Brayton (1987) in a model that assumed excitable spines with fast Hodgkin-Huxley K and Na channels. These channels alone could implement the digital logic operations AND and OR. With the addition of extrinsic inhibitory inputs, they showed that a neuron could implement a full complement of digital logic operations, and concluded that a dendritic tree could in principle implement arbitrarily complex logic operations.

The emphasis of the present model differs from that of both the purely linear and of the digital approaches, although it shares their emphasis on the locality of dendritic computation. Because the cold spot involved strongly nonlinear channels, it implemented a nonmonotonic response function, in contrast to strictly linear dendritic models. At the same time, the present model retained the essentially analog nature of intraneuronal signalling, in contrast to the digital dendritic models. This analog mode seems better suited to processing large numbers of noisy inputs because it preserves the uncertainties rather than making an immediate decision. Focussing on the analog nature of the response eliminated the requirement for operating within the digital range of channel dynamics.

The NMDA receptor-gated channel can give rise to an analog AND with a weaker voltage-dependence than that induced by fast Na and K channels. Mel (1992) described a model in which synapses mediating increases to both the NMDA and AMPA conductances were distributed across the dendritic tree of a cortical neuron. When the synaptic activity was distributed in appropriately sized clusters, the resulting neuronal response function was reminiscent of that of a sigma-pi unit. With suitable preprocessing of inputs, the neuron could perform complex pattern discrimination.

A unique feature of the present model is that functional inhibition arose from purely excitatory inputs. This mechanism underlying this inhibition —the AHP current—was intrinsic to the membrane. In both the Koch *et al.* (1982) and Brayton and Shepherd (1987) models, the veto or NOT operation was achieved through extrinsic synaptic inhibition. This requires additional neuronal circuitry. In the case of a dedicated sensory system like the directionally selective retinal granule cell, it is not unreasonable to imagine that the requisite neuronal circuitry is hardwired. In the limiting case of the digital model, the requisite circuitry would involve a separate inhibitory interneuron for each NOT-gate.

4.2.3 Adaptive Dendritic Computation

What algorithms can harness the computational potential of the dendritic tree? Adaptive dendritic computation is a very new subject. Brown *et al.* (1991, 1992) developed a model in which synapses distributed across the dendritic tree showed interesting forms of spatial self-organization. Synaptic plasticity was governed by a local biophysically-motivated Hebb rule (Zador *et al.*, 1990). When temporally correlated but spatially uncorrelated inputs were presented to the neuron, spatial clusters of strengthened synapses emerged within the dendritic tree. The neuron converted a temporal correlation into a spatial correlation.

The computational role of clusters of strengthened synapses within the dendritic tree becomes important in the presence of nonlinear membrane. If the dendrites are purely passive, then saturation ensures that the current injected per synapse actually *decreases* as the clustering increases. If purely regenerative nonlinearities are present (Brayton and Shepherd, 1987; Mel, 1992), then the response increases. The cold spot extends the range of local dendritic computations.

What might control the formation and distribution of the cold spot itself? Cold spots might arise from the fortuitous colocalization of Ca and K_{AHP} channels. Another possibility is that some specific biophysical mechanism creates cold spots in a use-dependent manner. Candidate mechanisms might involve local changes in second messengers such as $[Ca^{2+}]$ or longitudinal potential gradients (*cf.* Poo, 1985). Bell (1992) has shown that this second mechanism can induce computationally interesting distributions of membrane channels.

4.3 WHY STUDY SINGLE NEURONS?

We have illustrated an important functional difference between a single neuron and a PE. A neuron with cold spots can perform extensive local processing in the dendritic tree, giving rise to a complex mapping between input and output. A neuron may perhaps be likened to a "micronet" of simpler PEs, since any mapping can be approximated by a sufficiently complex network of sigmoidal units (Cybenko, 1989). This raises the objection that since micronets represent just a subset of all neural networks, there may be little to be gained by studying the properties of the special case of neurons.

The intuitive justification for studying single neurons is that they represent a large but highly constrained subset that may have very special properties. Knowledge of the properties general to all sufficiently complex PE networks may provide little insight into the properties specific to single neurons. These properties may have implications for the behavior of circuits of neurons. It is not unreasonable to suppose that adaptive mechanisms in biological circuits will utilize the specific strengths of single neurons.

Acknowledgments

We thank Michael Hines for providing NEURON-MODL assisting with new membrane mechanisms. This research was supported by grants from the Office of Naval Research, the Defense Advanced Research Projects Agency, and the Air Force Office of Scientific Research.

References

Bell, T. (1992) *Neural information processing systems* 4 *(in press)*.

Borg-Graham, L.J. (1991) In H. Wheal and J. Chad (Eds.) *Cellular and Molecular Neurobiology: A Practical Approach*. New York: Oxford University Press.

Brown, T.H. and Zador, A.M. (1990). In G. Shepherd (Ed.) *The synaptic organization of the brain* (Vol. 3, pp. 346-388). New York: Oxford University Press.

Brown, T.H., Mainen, Z.F., Zador, A.M. and Claiborne, B.J. (1991) *Neural information processing systems* 3: 39-45.

Brown, T.H., Zador, A.M., Mainen, Z.F., and Claiborne, B.J. (1992). In: *Single neuron computation.* Eds. T. McKenna, J. Davis, and S.F. Zornetzer. Academic Press *(in press)*.

Caianiello, E.R. (1961) *J. Theor. Biol.* 1: 209-235.

Claiborne, B.J., Zador, A.M., Mainen, Z.F., and Brown, T.H. (1992). In: *Single neuron computation.* Eds. T. McKenna, J. Davis, and S.F. Zornetzer. Academic Press *(in press)*.

Cybenko, G. (1989) *Math. Control, Signals Syst.* 2: 303-314.

Hines, M. (1989). *Int. J. Biomed. Comp*, 24: 55-68.

Hodgkin, A.L. and Huxley, A.F. (1952) *J. Physiol.* 117: 500-544.

Hopfield, J.J. (1984) *Proc. Natl. Acad. Sci. USA* 81: 3088-3092.

Jack, J. Noble, A. and Tsien, R.W. (1975) *Electrical current flow in excitable membranes.* London: Oxford Press.

Jones, O.T., Kunze, D.L. and Angelides, K.J. (1989) *Science.* 244:1189-1193.

Koch, C., Poggio, T. and Torre, V. (1982) *Proc. R. Soc. London B.* 298: 227-264.

Lancaster, B. and Nicoll, R.A. (1987) *J. Physiol.* 389: 187-203.

Lancaster, B., Perkel, D.J., and Nicoll, R.A. (1991) *J. Neurosci.* 11:23-30.

Lytton, W.W. and Sejnowski, T.J. (1991) *J. Neurophys.* 66: 1059-1079.

McCulloch, W.S. and Pitts, W. (1943) *Bull. Math. Biophys.* 5: 115-137.

Mel, B. (1992) *Neural Computation (in press)*.

Poo, M-m. (1985) *Ann. Rev. Neurosci.* 8: 369-406.

Rall, W. (1977) In: *Handbook of physiology.* Eds. E. Kandel and S. Geiger. Washington D.C.: American Physiological Society, pp. 39-97.

Rall, W. (1964) In: *Neural theory and modeling.* Ed. R.F. Reiss. Stanford Univ. Press, pp. 73-79.

Shepherd, G.M. and Brayton, R.K. (1987) *Neuroscience* 21: 151-166.

Zador, A., Koch, C. and Brown, T.H. (1990) *Proc. Natl. Acad. Sci. USA* 87: 6718-6722.

Self-organisation in real neurons:
Anti-Hebb in 'Channel Space'?

Anthony J. Bell
AI-lab,
Vrije Universiteit Brussel
Pleinlaan 2, B-1050 Brussels
BELGIUM, (tony@arti.vub.ac.be)

Abstract

Ion channels are the dynamical systems of the nervous system. Their distribution within the membrane governs not only communication of information between neurons, but also how that information is integrated within the cell. Here, an argument is presented for an 'anti-Hebbian' rule for changing the distribution of *voltage-dependent* ion channels in order to flatten voltage curvatures in dendrites. Simulations show that this rule can account for the self-organisation of dynamical receptive field properties such as resonance and direction selectivity. It also creates the conditions for the faithful conduction within the cell of signals to which the cell has been exposed. Various possible cellular implementations of such a learning rule are proposed, including activity-dependent migration of channel proteins in the plane of the membrane.

1   INTRODUCTION

1.1   NEURAL DYNAMICS

Neural inputs and outputs are temporal, but there are no established ways to think about temporal learning and dynamical receptive fields. The currently popular simple recurrent nets have only one kind of dynamical component: a *capacitor*, or time constant. Though it is *possible* to create any kind of dynamics using capacitors and static non-linearities, it is also *possible* to write any program on a Turing machine.

Biological evolution, it seems, has elected for diversity and complexity over uniformity and simplicity in choosing voltage-dependent ion channels as the 'instruction set' for dynamical computation.

1.2   ION CHANNELS

As more ion channels with varying kinetics are discovered, the question of their computational role has become more pertinent. Figure 1, derived from a model thalamic cell, shows the log time constants of 11 currents, plotted against the voltage ranges over which they activate or inactivate. The variety of available kinetics is probably under-represented here since a combinatorial number of differences can be obtained by combining different protein sub-domains to make a channel [6].

Given the likelihood that channels are inhomogenously distributed throughout the dendrites [7], one way to tackle the question of their computational role is to search for a self-organisational principle for forming this distribution. Such a 'learning rule' could be construed as operating during development or dynamically during the life of an organism, and could be considered complementary to learning involving synaptic changes. The resulting distribution and mix of channels would then be, in some sense, optimal for integrating and communicating the particular high-dimensional spatiotemporal inputs which the cell was accustomed to receiving.

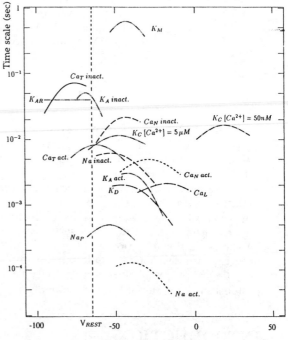

Membrane potential (mV)

Figure 1: Diversity of ion channel kinetics. The voltage-dependent equilibrium log time constants of 11 channels are plotted here for the voltage ranges for which their activation (or inactivation) variables go from $0.1 \to 0.9$ (or $0.9 \to 0.1$). The channel kinetics are taken from a model by W.Lytton [10]. Notice the range of speeds of operation from the spiking Na^+ channel around 0.1ms, to the K_M channel in the 1s (cognitive) range.

2   THE BIOPHYSICAL SUBSTRATE

The substrate for self-organisation is the standard cable model for a dendrite or axon:

$$G_a \frac{\partial^2 V}{\partial x^2} = C \frac{\partial V}{\partial t} + \sum_j \overline{G}_j g_j (V - E_j) + \sum_k \overline{G}_k g_k (V - E_k) \qquad (1)$$

In this G_a represents the conductance along the axis of the cable, C is the capacitance and the two sums represent *synaptic* (indexed by j) and *intrinsic* (indexed by k) currents. $\overline{G}$ is a maximum conductance (a channel density or 'weight'), g is the time-varying fraction of the conductance active, and E is a reversal potential. The system can be summarised by saying that the current flow out of a segment of a neuron is equal to the sum of currents input to that segment, plus the capacitive charging of the membrane.

This leads to a simpler form:

$$i = \sum_j \overline{g}_j i_j + \sum_k \overline{g}_k i_k \qquad (2)$$

Here, $i = \partial^2 V / \partial x^2$, $\overline{g}_j = \overline{G}_j / G_a$, $i_j = g_j(V - E_j)$ and C is considered as an intrinsic conductance whose $\overline{g}_k$ and i_k are C/G_a and $\partial V / \partial t$ respectively. In this form, it is more clear that each part of a neuron can be considered as a 'unit', diffusively coupled to its neighbours, to which it passes its weighted sum of inputs. The weights

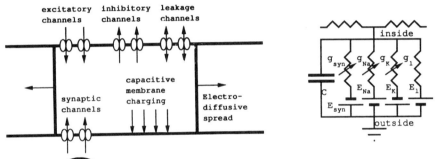

Figure 1: A compartment of a neuron, shown schematically and as a circuit. The cable equation is just Kirchoff's Law: *current in = current out*

$\overline{g}_k$, representing the G_a-normalised densities of channel species k, are considered to span *channel space*, as opposed to the $\overline{g}_j$ weights which are our standard synaptic strength parameters. Parameters determining the dynamics of g_k's specify points in *kinetics space*. Neuromodulation [8], a universally important phenomenon in real nervous systems, consists of specific chemicals inducing short-term changes in the kinetics space co-ordinates of a channel type, resulting, for example, in shifts in the curves in Figure 1.

3   THE ARGUMENT FOR ANTI-HEBB

Learning algorithms, of the type successful in static systems, have not been considered for these low-level dynamical components (though see [2] for approaches to synaptic learning in realistic systems). Here, we address the issue of unsupervised learning for channel densities. In the neural network literature, unsupervised learning consists of Hebbian-type algorithms and information theoretic approaches based on objective functions [1]. In the absence of a good information theoretic framework for continuous time, non-Gaussian analog systems where noise is undefined, we resort to exploring the implications of the effects of simple local rules.

The most obvious rule following from equation 2 would be a correlational one of the following form, with the learning rate ϵ positive or negative:

$$\Delta \bar{g}_k = \epsilon i_k i \qquad (3)$$

While a polarising (or Hebbian) rule (see Figure 3) makes sense for synaptic channels as an a method for amplifying input signals, it makes less sense for intrinsic channels. Were it to operate on such channels, statistical fluctuations from the uniform channel distribution would give rise to self-reinforcing 'hot-spots' with no underlying 'signal' to amplify. For this reason, we investigate the utility of a rectifying (or anti-Hebbian) rule.

Figure 3: A schematic display showing contingent positive and negative voltage curvatures ($\pm i$) above a segment of neuron, and inward and outward currents ($\pm i_k$), through a particular channel type. In situations (a) and (b), a Hebbian version of Equation 3 will raise the channel density ($\bar{g}_k \uparrow$), and in (c) and (d) an anti-Hebbian rule will do this. In the first two cases, the channels are *polarising* the membrane potential, creating high voltage curvature, while in the latter two, they are *rectifying* (or flattening) it. Depending on the sign of ϵ, equation 3 attempts to either maximise or minimise $(\partial^2 V / \partial x^2)^2$.

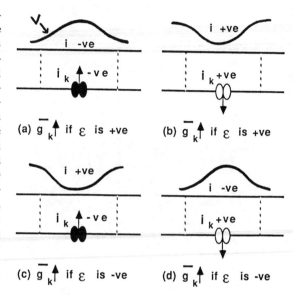

4   EXAMPLES

For the purposes of demonstration, linear RLC electrical components are often used here. These simple 'intrinsic' (non-synaptic) components have the most tractable kinetics of any, and as shown by [11] and [9], the impedances they create capture some of the properties of active membrane. The components are leakage resistances, capacitances and inductances, whose $\bar{g}_k$'s are given by $1/R$, C and $1/L$ respectively. During learning, all $\bar{g}_k$'s were kept above zero for reasons of stability.

4.1   LEARNING RESONANCE

In this experiment, an RLC 'compartment' with no frequency preference was stimulated at a certain frequency and trained according to equation 3 with ϵ negative. After training, the frequency response curve of the circuit had a resonant peak at the training frequency (Figure 4). This result is significant since many auditory and tactile sensory cells are tuned to certain frequencies, and we know that a major component of the tuning is electrical, with resonances created by particular balances of ion channel populations [13].

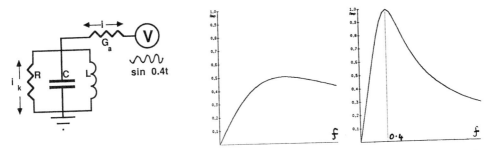

Figure 4: Learning resonance. The curves show the frequency-response curves of the compartment before and after training at a frequency of 0.4.

4.2   LEARNING CONDUCTION

Another role that intrinsic channels must play within a cell is the faithful transmission of information. Any voltage curvatures at a point away from a synapse signify a net cross membrane current which can be seen as distorting the signal in the cable. Thus, by removing voltage curvatures, we preserve the signal. This is demonstrated

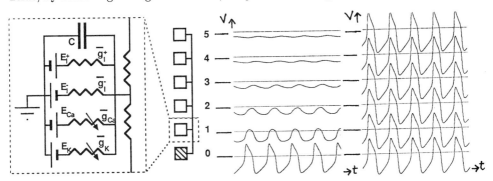

Figure 5: Learning conduction. The cable consists of a chain of compartments, which only conduct the impulse after they acquire active channels.

in the following example: 'learning to be an axon'. A non-linear spiking compartment with Morris-Lecar Ca/K kinetics (see [14]) is coupled to a long passive cable. Before learning, the signal decays passively in the cable (Figure 5). The driving compartment $\bar{g}$-vector, and the capacitances in the cable are then clamped to stop the system from converging on the null solution ($\bar{g} \rightarrow 0$). All other $\bar{g}$'s (including spiking conductances in the cable) can then learn. The first thing learnt was that the inward and outward leakage conductances ($\bar{g}_l^+$ and $\bar{g}_l^-$) adjusted themselves to make the average voltage curvature in each compartment zero (just as bias units in error correction algorithms adjust to make the average error zero). Then the cable filled out with Morris Lecar channels ($\bar{g}_{Ca}$ and $\bar{g}_K$) in *exactly the same ratios* as the driving compartment, resulting in a cable that faithfully propagated the signal.

4.3   LEARNING PHASE-SHIFTING (DIRECTION SELECTIVITY)

The last example involves 4 'sensory' compartments coupled to a 'somatic' compartment as in Figure 6. All are similar to the linear compartments in the resonance example except that the sensory ones receive 'synaptic' input in the form of a sinusoidal current source. The relative phases of the input were shifted to simulate left-to-right motion. After training, the 'dendritic' components had learned, using their capacitors and inductors, to cancel the phase shifts so that the inputs were synchronised in their effect on the 'soma'. This creates a large response in the trained direction, and a small one in the 'null' direction, as the phases cancelled each other.

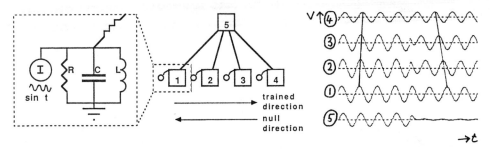

Figure 6: Learning direction selectivity. After training on a drifting sine wave, the output compartment oscillates for the trained direction but not for the null direction (see the trace, where the direction of motion is reversed halfway).

5   DISCUSSION

5.1   CELLULAR MECHANISMS

There is substantial evidence in cell biology for targeting of proteins to specific parts of the membrane, but the fact that equation 3 is dependent on the *correlation* of channel species' activity and local voltages leaves only 4 possible biological implementations:

1. the cellular targeting machinery knows what kind of channel it is delivering, and thus knows where to put it

2. channels in the wrong place are degraded faster than those in the right place

3. channels migrate to the right place while in the membrane

4. the *effective* channel density is altered by activity-dependent neuromodulation or channel-blockage

The third is perhaps the most intriguing. The diffusion of channels in the plane of the membrane, under the influence of induced electric fields has received both theoretical [4, 12] and empirical [7, 3] attention. To a first approximation, the evolution of channel densities can be described by a Smoluchowski equation:

$$\frac{\partial \overline{g}_k}{\partial t} = a \frac{\partial^2 \overline{g}_k}{\partial x^2} + b \frac{\partial}{\partial x} \left(\overline{g}_k \frac{\partial V}{\partial x} \right) \qquad (4)$$

where a is the coefficient of *thermal* diffusion and b is the coefficient of *field induced* motion. This system has been studied previously [4] to explain receptor-clustering in synapse formation, but if the sign of b is reversed, then it fits more closely with the anti-Hebbian rule discussed here. The crucial requirement for true activity-dependence, though, is that b should be different when the channel is open than when it is closed. This may be plausible since channel gating involves movements of charges across the membrane. Coefficients of thermal diffusion have been measured and found not to exceed 10^{-9} cm/sec. This would be enough to fine-tune channel distributions, but not to transport them all the way down dendrites.

The second method in the list is also an attractive possibility. The half-life of membrane proteins can be as low as several hours [3], and it is known that proteins can be differentially labeled for recycling [5].

5.2   ENERGY AND INFORMATION

The anti-Hebbian rule changes $\overline{g}_k$'s in order to minimise the square membrane current density, integrated over the cell in units of axial conductance. This corresponds in two senses to a minimisation of energy. From a circuit perspective, the energy dissipated in the axial resistances is minimised. From a metabolic perspective, the ATP used in pumping ions back across the membrane is minimised. The computation consists of minimising the expected value of this energy, given particular spatiotemporal synaptic input (assuming no change in $\overline{g}_j$'s). More precisely, it searches for:

$$Min_{(\overline{g}_k)} \left(E \left[\int i^2(x,t) \, dG_a(x) \, dt \; \middle| \; g_j(x,t), \; \forall j \right] \right) \qquad (5)$$

This search creates mutual information between input dynamics and intrinsic dynamics. In addition, since the Laplacian ($\nabla_x^2 V = 0$) is what a diffusive system seeks to converge to anyway, the learning rule simply configures the system to speed this convergence on frequently experienced inputs.

Simple zero-energy solutions exist for the above, for example the 'ultra-leaky' compartment ($\overline{g}_l \to \infty$) and the 'point' (or non-existent) compartment ($\overline{g}_k \to 0, \; \forall k$), for compartments with and without synapses respectively. The anti-Hebb rule alone will eventually converge to such solutions, unless, for example, the leakage or capacitance are prevented from learning. Another solution (which has been successfully used for the direction selectivity example) is to make the total available quantity of each $\overline{g}_k$ finite. The $\overline{g}_k$ can then diffuse about between compartments, following the voltage gradients in a manner suggested by equation 4. The resulting behaviour is a finite-resource version of equation 3.

The next goal of this work is to produce a rigorous information theoretic account of single neuron computation. This is seen as a pre-requisite to understanding both neural coding and the computational capabilities of neural circuits, and as a step on the way to properly dynamical neural nets.

Acknowledgements

This work was supported by a Belgian government IMPULS contract and by ES-PRIT Basic Research Action 3234. Thanks to Prof. L. Steels for his support and to Prof T. Sejnowski his hospitality at the Salk Institute where some of this work was done.

References

[1] Becker S. 1990. Unsupervised learning procedures for neural networks, *Int. J. Neur. Sys.*

[2] Brown T., Mainen Z. et al. 1990. in *NIPS 3*, 39-45.   Mel B. 1991. in *Neural Computation*, vol 4 *to appear*.

[3] Darnell J., Lodish H. & Baltimore D. 1990. *Molecular Cell Biology*, Scientific American Books

[4] Fromherz P. 1988. Self-organization of the fluid mosaic of charged channel proteins in membranes, *Proc. Natl. Acad. Sci. USA* 85, 6353-6357

[5] Hare J. 1990. Mechanisms of membrane protein turnover, *Biochim. Biophys. Acta*, 1031, 71-90

[6] Hille B. 1992. *Ionic channels of excitable membranes, 2nd edition*, Sinauer Associates Inc., Sunderland, MA

[7] Jones O. et al. 1989. *Science* 244, 1189-1193.   Lo Y-J. & Poo M-M. 1991. *Science* 254, 1019-1022.   Stollberg J. & Fraser S. 1990. *J. Neurosci.* 10, 1, 247-255.   Angelides K. 1990. *Prog. in Clin. & Biol. Res.* 343, 199-212

[8] Kaczmarek L. & Levitan I. 1987. *Neuromodulation*, Oxford Univ. Press

[9] Koch C. 1984. Cable theory in neurons with active linearized membranes, *Biol. Cybern.* 50, 15-33

[10] Lytton W. 1991. Simulations of cortical pyramidal neurons synchronized by inhibitory interneurons *J. Neurophysiol.* 66, 3, 1059-1079

[11] Mauro A. Conti F. Dodge F. & Schor R. 1970. Subthreshold behaviour and phenomenological impedance of the giant squid axon, *J. Gen. Physiol.* 55, 497-523

[12] Poo M-M. & Young S. 1990. Diffusional and electrokinetic redistribution at the synapse: a physicochemical basis of synaptic competition, *J. Neurobiol.* 21, 1, 157-168

[13] Puil E. et al. *J. Neurophysiol.* 55, 5. . Ashmore J.F. & Attwell D. 1985. *Proc. R. Soc. Lond.* B 226, 325-344.   Hudspeth A. & Lewis R. 1988. *J. Physiol.* 400, 275-297.

[14] Rinzel J. & Ermentrout G. 1989. Analysis of Neural Excitability and Oscillations, in Koch C. & Segev I. (eds) 1989. *Methods in Neuronal Modeling*, MIT Press

SINGLE NEURON MODEL: RESPONSE TO WEAK
MODULATION IN THE PRESENCE OF NOISE

A. R. Bulsara and E. W. Jacobs

Naval Ocean Systems Center, Materials Research Branch, San Diego, CA 92129

F. Moss

Physics Dept., Univ. of Missouri, St. Louis, MO 63121

ABSTRACT

We consider a noisy bistable single neuron model driven by a periodic external modulation. The modulation introduces a correlated switching between states driven by the noise. The information flow through the system from the modulation to the output switching events, leads to a succession of strong peaks in the power spectrum. The signal-to-noise ratio (SNR) obtained from this power spectrum is a measure of the information content in the neuron response. With increasing noise intensity, the SNR passes through a maximum, an effect which has been called *stochastic resonance*. We treat the problem within the framework of a recently developed approximate theory, valid in the limits of weak noise intensity, weak periodic forcing and low forcing frequency. A comparison of the results of this theory with those obtained from a linear system FFT is also presented.

INTRODUCTION

Recently, there has been an upsurge of interest in *single* or few-neuron nonlinear dynamics (see e.g. Li and Hopfield, 1989; Tuckwell, 1988; Paulus, Gass and Mandell, 1990; Aihara, Takake and Toyoda, 1990). However, the precise relationship between the many-neuron connected model and a single effective neuron dynamics has not been examined in detail. Schieve, Bulsara and Davis (1991) have considered a network of N symmetrically interconnected neurons embodied, for example in the "connectionist" models of Hopfield (1982, 1984) or Shamma (1989) (the latter corresponding to a mammalian auditory network). Through an adiabatic elimination procedure, they have obtained, in closed form, the dynamics of a single neuron from the system of coupled differential equations describing the N-neuron problem. The problem has been treated both deterministically and stochastically (through the inclusion of additive and multiplicative noise terms). It is important to point out that the work of Schieve, Bulsara, and Davis does not include *a priori* a self-coupling term, although the inclusion of such a term can be readily implemented in their theory; this has been done by Bulsara and Schieve (1991). Rather, their theory results in an explicit form of the self-coupling term, in terms of the parameters of the remaining neurons in the network. This term, in effect, renormalizes the self-coupling term in the Shamma and Hopfield models. The reduced or "effective" neuron model is expected to reproduce some of the gross features of biological neurons. The fact that simple single neuron models, such as the model to be considered in this work, can indeed reproduce several features observed in biological experiments has been strikingly demonstrated by Longtin, Bulsara and Moss (1991) through their construction of the inter-spike-interval histograms (ISIHs) using a Schmidt trigger to model the neuron. The results of their simple model agree remarkably well with data obtained in two different experiments (on the auditory nerve fiber of squirrel monkey (Rose, Brugge, Andersen and Hind, 1967) and on the cat visual cortex (Siegal, 1990)).

In this work, we consider such a "reduced" neural element subject to a weak periodic external modulation. The modulation introduces a correlated switching between the bistable states, driven by the noise with the signal-to-noise ratio (SNR) obtained from the power spectrum, being taken as a measure of the information content in the neuron response. As the additive noise variance increases, the SNR passes through a maximum. This effect has been called "stochastic resonance" and describes a phenomenon in which the noise actually enhances the information content, i.e., the observability of the signal. Stochastic resonance has been observed in a modulated ring laser experiment (McNamara, Wiesenfeld and Roy, 1988; Vemuri and Roy, 1989) as well as in electron paramagnetic resonance experiments (Gammaitoni, Martinelli, Pardi and Santucci, 1991) and in a modulated magnetoselastic ribbon (Spano and Ditto, 1991). The introduction of multiplicative noise (in the coefficient of the sigmoid transfer function) tends to degrade this effect.

THE MODEL; STOCHASTIC RESONANCE

The reduced neuron model consists of a single Hopfield-type computational element, which may be modeled as a R-C circuit with nonlinear feedback provided by an operational amplifier having a sigmoid transfer function. The equation (which may be rigorously derived from a fully connected network model as outlined in the preceding section) may be cast in the form,

$$\dot{x} + a\, x - b\, \tanh x = x_0 + F(t),\qquad(1)$$

where $F(t)$ is Gaussian delta-correlated noise with zero mean and variance $2D$, x_0 being a dc input (which we set equal to zero for the remainder of this work). An analysis of (1), including multiplicative noise effects, has been given by Bulsara, Boss and Jacobs (1989). For the purposes of the current work, we note that the neuron may be treated as a particle in a one-dimensional potential given by,

$$U(x) = \frac{a\, x^2}{2} - b\, \ln \cosh x,\qquad(2)$$

x being the one-dimensional state variable representing the membrane potential. In general, the coefficients a and b depend on the details of the interaction of our reference neuron to the remaining neurons in the network (Schieve, Bulsara and Davis, 1990). The potential described by (2) is bimodal for $\eta > 1$ with the extrema occurring at (we set $a=1$ throughout the remainder of this work),

$$c = 0,\quad \pm\left[1 - \frac{1 - \tanh b}{1 - b\, \mathrm{sech}^2 b}\right] \approx b\, \tanh b,\qquad(3)$$

the approximation holding for large b. Note that the N-shaped characteristic inherent in the firing dynamics derived from the Hodgkin-Huxley equations (Rinzel and Ermentrout, 1990) is markedly similar to the plot of dU/dx vs. x for the simple bistable system (1). For a stationary potential, and for $D \ll U_0$ where U_0 is the depth of the deterministic potential, the probability that a switching event will occur in unit time, i.e. the switching rate, is given by the Kramers frequency (Kramers, 1940),

$$r_0 = \left\{ D \int_{-c}^{0} dy\, \exp\left(U(y)/D\right) \int_{-\infty}^{y} dz\, \exp\left(-U(z)/D\right) \right\}^{-1},\qquad(4a)$$

which, for small noise, may be cast in the form (the local equilibrium assumption of Kramers),

$$r_0 \approx (2\pi)^{-1}\, |\, |\, U^{(2)}(0)\, |\; U^{(2)}(c)\, |^{1/2}\, \exp\left(-U_0/D\right),\qquad(4b)$$

where $U^{(2)}(x) \equiv d^2 U/dx^2$.

We now include a periodic modulation term $\epsilon \sin \omega t$ on the right-hand-side of (1) (note that for $\epsilon < 2(b-1)^3/(3b)$ one does not observe switching in the noise-free system). This leads to a modulation (i.e. rocking) of the potential (2) with time: an additional term $-x\epsilon\sin\omega t$ is now present on the right-hand-side of (2). In this case, the Kramers rate (4) becomes time-dependent:

$$r(t) \approx r_0 \exp(-x\epsilon\sin\omega t/D),\qquad(5)$$

which is accurate only for $\epsilon \ll U_0$ and $\omega \ll \{U^{(2)}(\pm c)\}^{1/2}$. The latter condition is referred to as the *adiabatic approximation*. It ensures that the probability density corresponding to the time-modulated potential is approximately stationary (the modulation is slow enough that the instantaneous probability density can "adiabatically" relax to a succession of quasi-stationary states).

We now follow the work of McNamara and Wiesenfeld (1989), developing a two-state model by introducing a probability of finding the system in the left or right well of the potential. A rate equation is constructed based on the Kramers rate $r(t)$ given by (5). Within the framework of the adiabatic approximation, this rate equation may be integrated to yield the time-dependent conditional probability density function for finding the system in a given well of the potential. This leads directly to the autocorrelation function $< x(t)\,x(t+\tau) >$ and finally, via the Wiener-Khinchine theorem, to the power spectral density $P(\Omega)$. The details are given by Bulsara, Jacobs, Zhou, Moss and Kiss (1991):

$$P(\Omega) = \left[1 - \frac{2r_0^2\epsilon^2 c^2}{D^2\left(4r_0^2 + \Omega^2\right)} \right] \left[\frac{8c^2 r_0}{4r_0^2 + \Omega^2} \right] + \frac{4\pi c^4 r_0^2 \epsilon^2}{D^2\left(4r_0^2 + \Omega^2\right)} \delta(\omega - \Omega), \qquad (6)$$

where the first term on the right-hand-side represents the noise background, the second term being the signal strength. Taking into account the finite bandwidth of the measuring system, we replace (for the purpose of comparison with experimental results) the delta-function in (6) by the quantity $(\Delta\omega)^{-1}$ where $\Delta\omega$ is the width of a frequency bin in the (experimental) Fourier transformation. We introduce signal-to-noise ratio $SNR = 10\log R$ in decibels, where R is given by

$$R \equiv 1 + \frac{4\pi c^4 r_0^2 \epsilon^2}{D^2\left(4r_0^2 + \omega^2\right)} \left(\Delta\omega\right)^{-1} \left[1 - \frac{2r_0^2\epsilon^2 c^2}{D^2\left(4r_0^2 + \omega^2\right)} \right]^{-1} \left[\frac{4r_0^2 + \omega^2}{8c^2 r_0} \right]. \qquad (7)$$

In writing down the above expressions, the approximate Kramers rate (4b) has been used. However, in what follows, we discuss the effects of replacing it by the exact expression (4a). The location of the maximum of the SNR is found by differentiating the above equation; it depends on the amplitude ϵ and the frequency ω of the modulation, as well as the additive noise variance D and the parameters a and b in the potential.

The SNR computed via the above expression increases as the modulation frequency is lowered relative to the Kramers frequency. Lowering the modulation frequency also sharpens the resonance peak, and shifts it to lower noise values, an effect that has been demonstrated, for example, by Bulsara, Jacobs, Zhou, Moss and Kiss (1991). The above may be readily explained. The effect of the weak modulating signal is to alternately raise and lower the potential well with respect to the barrier height U_0. In the absence of noise and for $\epsilon \ll U_0$, the system cannot switch states, i.e. no information is transferred to the output. In the presence of noise, however, the system can switch states through stochastic activation over the barrier. Although the switching process is statistical, the transition probability is periodically modulated by the external signal. Hence, the output will be correlated, to some degree, with the input signal (the modulation "clocks" the escape events and the whole process will be optimized if the noise by itself produces, on average, two escapes within one modulation cycle).

Figure 1 shows the SNR as a function of the noise variance $2D$. The potential barrier height $U_0 = 2.4$ for the $b = 2.5$ case considered. Curves corresponding to the adiabatic expression (7), as well as the SNR obtained through an exact (numerical) calculation of the Kramers rate, using (4a) are shown, along with the data points obtained via direct numerical simulation of (1). The Kramers rate at the maximum $(2D \approx U_0)$ of the SNR curve is 0.72. This is much greater than the driving frequency $\omega = 0.0393$ used in this plot. The curve computed using the exact expression (4a) fits the numerically obtained data points better than the adiabatic curve at high noise strengths. This is to be expected in light of the approximations used in deriving (4b) from (4a). Also, the expression (6) has been derived from a two-state theory (taking no account of the potential). At low noise, we expect the two-state theory to agree with the actual system more closely. This is reflected in the resonance curves of figure 1 with the adiabatic curve differing (at the maximum) from the data points by approximately 1db. We reiterate that the SNR, as well as the agreement between the data points and the theoretical curves improves as the modulation frequency is lowered relative to the Kramers rate (for a fixed frequency this can be achieved by changing the potential barrier height via the parameters a and b in (2)). On the same plot, we show the SNR obtained by computing directly the Fourier transform of the signal and noise. At very low noise, the "ideal linear filter" yields results that are considerably better than stochastic resonance. However, at moderate-to-high noise, the stochastic resonance, which may be looked upon as a "nonlinear filter", offers at least a 2.5db improvement for the parameters of the figure. As indicated above, the improvement in performance achieved by stochastic resonance over the "ideal linear filter" may be enhanced by raising the Kramers frequency of the nonlinear filter relative to the modulation frequency ω. In fact, as long as the basic conditions of stochastic resonance are realized, the nonlinear filter will outperform the best linear filter except at very low noise.

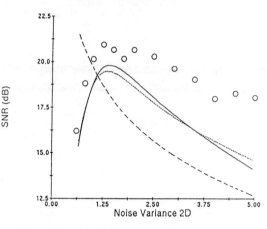

Fig 1. SNR using adiabatic theory, eqn. (7), with $(b,\omega,\epsilon) = (2.5, 0.0393, 0.3)$ and r_0 given by (4b) (solid curve) and (4a) (dotted curve). Data points correspond to SNR obtained via direct simulation of (1) (frequency resolution $= 6.1 \times 10^{-5}$ Hz). Dashed curve corresponds to best possible linear filter (see text).

Multiplicative Noise Effects

We now consider the case when the neuron is exposed to both additive and multiplicative noise. In this case, we set $b(t) = b_0 + \xi(t)$ where

$$<\xi(t)> = 0, \quad <\xi(t)\,\xi(s)> = 2D_m\,\delta(t-s) . \qquad (8)$$

In a real system such fluctuations might arise through the interaction of the neuron with other neurons in the network or with external fluctuations. In fact, Schieve, Bulsara and Davis (1991) have shown that when one derives the "reduced" neuron dynamics in the form (1) from a fully connected N-neuron network with fluctuating synaptic couplings, then the resulting dynamics contain multiplicative noise terms of the kind being discussed here. Even Langevin noise by itself can introduce a pitchfork bifurcation into the long-time dynamics of such a reduced neuron model under the appropriate conditions (Bulsara and Schieve, 1991). In an earlier publication (Bulsara, Boss and Jacobs, 1989), it was shown that these fluctuations can qualitatively alter the behavior of the stationary probability density function that describes the stochastic response of the neuron. In particular, the multiplicative noise may induce additional peaks or erase peaks already present in the density (see for example Horsthemke and Lefever 1984). In this work we maintain D_m sufficiently small that such effects are absent.

In the absence of modulation, one can write down a Fokker Planck equation for the probability density function $p(x,t)$ describing the neuron response:

$$\frac{\partial p}{\partial t} = -\frac{\partial}{\partial x}\left[\alpha(x)p\right] + \frac{1}{2}\frac{\partial^2}{\partial x^2}\left[\beta(x)p\right], \qquad (9)$$

where

$$\alpha(x) \equiv -x + b_0\tanh x + D_m\tanh x\operatorname{sech}^2 x ,$$
$$\beta(x) \equiv 2(D + D_m\tanh^2 x), \qquad (10)$$

D being the additive noise intensity. In the steady state, (9) may be solved to yield a "macroscopic potential" function analogous to the function $U(x)$ defined in (2):

$$U(x) = -2\int^x \frac{\alpha(z)}{\beta(z)}\,dz + \ln\beta(x) . \qquad (11)$$

From (11), one obtains the turning points of the potential through the solution of the transcendental equation

$$x - b_0 \tanh x + D_m \tanh x \operatorname{sech}^2 x = 0 .$$
(12)

The modified Kramers rate, r_{0m}, for this x-dependent diffusion process has been derived by Englund, Snapp and Schieve (1984):

$$r_{0m} = \frac{\beta(0)}{2\pi} [\, |\, U^{(2)}(x_1)\, |\, U^{(2)}(0)\, |\,]^{1/2} \exp[\, U(x_1) - U(0)\,] ,$$
(13)

where the maximum of the potential occurs at $x=0$ and the left minimum occurs at $x=x_1$.

If we now assume that a weak sinusoidal modulation $\epsilon \sin \omega t$ is present, we may once again introduce this term into the potential as in the preceding case, again making the adiabatic approximation. We easily obtain for the modified time-dependent Kramers rate,

$$r_{\pm}(t) = \frac{\beta(0)}{4\pi} [\, |\, U^{(2)}(x_1)\, |\, U^{(2)}(0)\, |\,]^{1/2} \exp\left[\, U(x_1) - U(0) \pm 2 \int_0^{x_1} \frac{\epsilon \sin \omega t}{\beta(z)}\, dz\, \right] .$$
(14)

Following the same procedure as we used in the additive noise case, we can obtain the ratio $R = 1 + S/\Delta\omega\, N$, for the case of both noises being present. The result is,

$$R = 1 + \pi\gamma_0\eta_0^2 (\Delta\omega)^{-1} \left[\, 1 - \frac{2\gamma_0^2\eta_0^2}{\gamma_0^2 + \eta_0^2}\, \right]^{-1} ,$$
(15)

where,

$$\gamma_0 \equiv \frac{\beta(0)}{2\pi} [\, |\, U^{(2)}(x_1)\, |\, U^{(2)}(0)\, |\,]^{1/2} \exp[\, U(x_1) - U(0)\,] ,$$
(16a)

and

$$\eta_0 \equiv \epsilon \int_0^{x_1} \frac{dz}{\beta(z)} = \frac{\epsilon}{2(D + D_m)} \left[\, x_1 + m^{1/2} \tan^{-1}(\, m^{1/2} \tanh x_1)\, \right] ,$$
(16b)

with $m \equiv D_m/D$.

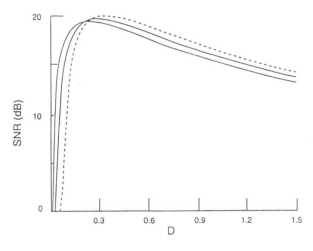

Fig 2. Effect of multiplicative noise, eqn. (15). $(b, \omega, \epsilon) = (2, 0.31, 0.4)$ and $D_m = 0$ (top curve), 0.1 (middle curve) and 0.2 (bottom curve).

In figure 2 we show the effects of both additive and multiplicative noise by plotting the SNR for a fixed external frequency $\omega = 0.31$ with $(b_0, \epsilon) = (2, 0.4)$ as a function of the additive noise intensity D. The curves correspond to different values of D_m, with the uppermost curve corresponding to $D_m = 0$, i.e., for the case of additive noise only. We note that increasing D_m leads to a decrease in the SNR as well as a shift in its maximum to lower values of D. These effects are easily explained using the results of Bulsara, Boss and Jacobs

(1989), wherein it was shown that the effect of multiplicative noise is to decrease, on average, the potential barrier height and to shift the locations of the stable steady states. This leads to a degradation of the stochastic resonance effect at large D_m while shifting the location of the maximum toward lower D.

THE POWER SPECTRUM

We turn now to the power spectrum obtained via direct numerical simulation of the dynamics (1). It is evident that a time series obtained by numerical simulation of (1) would display switching events between the stable states of the potential, the residence time in each state being a random variable. The intrawell motion consists of a random component superimposed on a harmonic component, the latter increasing as the amplitude ϵ of the modulation increases. In the low noise limit, the deterministic motion dominates. However, the adiabatic theory used in deriving the expressions (6) and (7) is a two-state theory that simply follows the switching events between the states but takes no account of this intrawell motion. Accordingly, in what follows, we draw the distinction between the full dynamics obtained via direct simulation of (1) and the "equivalent two-state dynamics" obtained by passing the output through a two-state filter. Such a filter is realized digitally by replacing the time series obtained from a simulation of (1) with a time series wherein the x variable takes on the values $x = \pm c$, depending on which state the system is in. Figure 3 shows the power spectral density obtained from this equivalent two-state system. The top curve represents the signal-free case and the bottom curve shows the effects of turning on the signal. Two features are readily apparent:

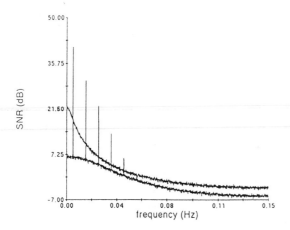

Fig 3. Power spectral density via direct simulation of (1).
$(b, \omega, \epsilon, 2D) = (1.6056, 0.03, 0.65, 0.25)$.
Bottom curve: $\epsilon=0$ case.

1. The power spectrum displays *odd* harmonics of the modulation; this is a hallmark of stochastic resonance (Zhou and Moss, 1990). If one destroys the symmetry of the potential (1) (through the introduction of a small dc driving term, for example), the even harmonics of the modulation appear.
2. The noise floor is lowered when the signal is turned on. This effect is particularly striking in the two-state dynamics. It stems from the fact that the total area under the spectral density curves in figure 3 (i.e. the total power) must be conserved (a consequence of Parseval's theorem). *The power in the signal spikes therefore grows at the expense of the background noise power.* This is a unique feature of weakly modulated bistable noisy systems of the type under consideration in this work, and graphically illustrates the ability of noise to assist information flow to the output (the signal). The effect may be quantified on examining equation (6) above. The noise power spectral density (represented by the first term on the right-hand side) decreases as the term $2r_0^2\epsilon^2c^2\{D^2(4r_0^2 + \Omega^2)\}^{-1}$ approaches unity. This reduction in the noise floor is most pronounced when the signal is of low frequency (compared to the Kramers rate) and large amplitude. A similar effect may be observed in the spectral density corresponding to the full system dynamics. In this case, the total power is only approximately conserved (in a finite bandwidth) and the effect is not so

pronounced.

DISCUSSION

In this paper we have presented the details of a cooperative stochastic process that occurs in *nonlinear* systems subject to weak deterministic modulating signals embedded in a white noise background. The so-called "stochastic resonance" phenomenon may actually be interpreted as a noise-assisted flow of information to the output. The fact that such simple nonlinear dynamic systems (e.g. an electronic Schmidt trigger) are readily realizeable in hardware, points to the possible utility of this technique (far beyond the application to signal processing in simple neural networks) as a nonlinear filter. We have demonstrated that, by suitably adjusting the system parameters (in effect changing the Kramers rate), we can optimize the response to a given modulation frequency and background noise. In a practical system, one can move the location and height of the bell-shaped response curve of figure 1 by changing the potential parameters and, possibly, infusing noise into the system. The noise-enhancement of the SNR improves with decreasing frequency. This is a hallmark of stochastic resonance and provides one with a possible filtering technique at low frequency. It is important to point out that all the effects reported in this work have been reproduced via analog simulations (Bulsara, Jacobs, Zhou, Moss and Kiss, 1991: Zhou and Moss, 1990). Recently a new approach to the processing of information in noisy nonlinear dynamic systems, based on the probability density of residence times in one of the stable states of the potential, has been developed by Zhou, Moss and Jung (1990). This technique, which offers an alternative to the FFT, was applied by Longtin, Moss and Bulsara (1991) in their construction of the inter-spike-interval histograms that describe neuronal spike trains in the central nervous system. Their work points to the important role played by noise in the procesing of information by the central nervous system. The beneficial role of noise has already been recognized by Buhmann and Schulten (1986, 87). They found that noise, deliberately added to the deterministic equations governing individual neurons in a network significantly enhanced the network's performance and concluded that "...*the noise...is an essential feature of the information processing abilities of the neural network and not a mere source of disturbance better suppressed...*"

Acknowledgements

This work was carried out under funding from the Office of Naval Research grant nos. N00014-90-AF-00001 and N000014-90-J-1327.

References

Aihara K., Takake T., and Toyoda M., 1990; "Chaotic Neural Networks", Phys. Lett. A144, 333-340.

Buhmann J., and Schulten K., 1986; "Influence of Noise on the Behavior of an Autoassociative Neural Network", in J. Denker (ed) Neural networks for Computing (AIP conf. procedings, vol 151).

Buhmann J., and Schulten K., 1987; "Influence of Noise on the Function of a "Physiological" Neural Network", Biol. Cyber. 56, 313-327.

Bulsara A., Boss R. and Jacobs E., 1989; "Noise Effects in an Electronic Model of a Single Neuron", Biol. Cyber. 61, 212-222.

Bulsara A., Jacobs E., Zhou T., Moss F. and Kiss L., 1991; "Stochastic Resonance in a Single Neuron Model: Theory and Analog Simulation", J. Theor. Biol. 154, 531-555.

Bulsara A. and Schieve W., 1991; "Single Effective Neuron: Macroscopic Potential and Noise-Induced Bifurcations", Phys. Rev. A, in press.

Englund J., Snapp R., Schieve W., 1984; "Fluctuations, Instabilities and Chaos in the Laser-Driven Nonlinear Ring Cavity", in E. Wolf (ed) Progress in Optics, vol XXI. (North Holland, Amsterdam).

Gammaitoni L., Martinelli M., Pardi L., and Santucci S., 1991; "Observation of Stochastic Resonance in Bistable Electron Paramagnetic Resonance Systems", preprint.

Hopfield J., 1982; "Neural Networks and Physical Systems with Emergent Computational Capabilities", Proc. Natl. Acad. Sci. 79, 2554-2558.

Hopfield J., 1984; "Neurons with Graded Responses have Collective Computational Abilities like those of Two-State Neurons", Proc. Natl. Acad. Sci., 81, 3088-3092.

Horsthemke W., and Lefever R., 1984; Noise-Induced Transitions. (Springer-Verlag, Berlin).

Kramers H., 1940; "Brownian Motion in a Field of Force and the Diffusion Model of Chemical Reactions", Physica 7, 284-304.

Li Z., and Hopfield J., 1989; "Modeling the Olfactory Bulb and its Neural Oscillatoy Processings", Biol. Cyber. 61, 379-392.

Longtin A., Bulsara A., and Moss F., 1991; "Time-Interval Sequences in Bistable Systems and the Noise-Induced Transmission of Information by Sensory Neurons", Phys. Rev. Lett. 67, 656-659.

McNamara B., Wiesenfeld K., and Roy R., 1988; "Observation of Stochastic Resonance in a Ring Laser", Phys. Rev. Lett. 60, 2626-2629.

McNamara B., and Wiesenfeld K., 1989; "Theory of Stochastic Resonance", Phys. Rev. A39, 4854-4869.

Paulus M., Gass S., and Mandell A., 1990; "A Realistic Middle-Layer for Neural Networks", Physica D40, 135-155.

Rinzel J., and Ermentrout B., 1989; "Analysis of Neural Excitability and Oscillations", in Methods in Neuronal Modeling, eds. C. Koch and I. Segev (MIT Press, Cambridge, MA).

Rose J., Brugge J., Anderson D., and Hind J., 1967; "Phase-locked Response to Low-frequency Tones in Single Auditory Nerve Fibers of the Squirrel Monkey", J. Neurophysiol., 30, 769-793.

Schieve W., Bulsara A. and Davis G., 1990; "Single Effective Neuron", Phys. Rev. A43 2613-2623.

Shamma S., 1989; "Spatial and Temporal Processing in Central Auditory Networks", in Methods in Neuronal Modeling, eds. C. Koch and I. Segev (MIT Press, Cambridge, MA).

Siegal R.,1990; "Nonlinear Dynamical System Theory and Primary Visual Cortical Processing", Physica 42D, 385-395.

Spano M., and Ditto W., 1991; "Experimental Observation of Stochastic R Resonance in a Magnetoelastic Ribbon", preprint.

Tuckwell H., 1989; "Stochastic Processes in the Neurosciences", (SIAM, Philadelphia).

Vemuri G., and Roy R., 1990; "Stochastic Resonance in a Bistable Ring Laser", Phys. Rev. A39, 4668-4674.

Zhou T., and Moss F., 1990; "Analog Simulations of Stochastic Resonance", Phys. Rev. A41, 4255-4264.

Zhou T., Moss F., and Jung P., 1991; "Escape-Time Distributions of a Periodically Modulated Bistable System with Noise", Phys. Rev. A42, 3161-3169.

Dual Inhibitory Mechanisms for Definition of Receptive Field Characteristics in Cat Striate Cortex

A. B. Bonds
Dept. of Electrical Engineering
Vanderbilt University
Nashville, TN 37235

Abstract

In single cells of the cat striate cortex, lateral inhibition across orientation and/or spatial frequency is found to enhance pre-existing biases. A contrast-dependent but spatially non-selective inhibitory component is also found. Stimulation with ascending and descending contrasts reveals the latter as a response hysteresis that is sensitive, powerful and rapid, suggesting that it is active in day-to-day vision. Both forms of inhibition are not recurrent but are rather network properties. These findings suggest two fundamental inhibitory mechanisms: a global mechanism that limits dynamic range and creates spatial selectivity through thresholding and a local mechanism that specifically refines spatial filter properties. Analysis of burst patterns in spike trains demonstrates that these two mechanisms have unique physiological origins.

1 INFORMATION PROCESSING IN STRIATE CORTICAL CELLS

The most popular current model of single cells in the striate cortex casts them in terms of spatial and temporal filters. The input to visual cortical cells from lower visual areas, primarily the LGN, is fairly broadband (e.g., Soodak, Shapley & Kaplan, 1987; Maffci & Fiorentini, 1973). Cortical cells perform significant bandwidth restrictions on this information in at least three domains: orientation, spatial frequency and temporal frequency. The most interesting quality of these cells is therefore what they reject from the broadband input signal, rather than what they pass, since the mere passage of the signal adds no information. Visual cortical cells also show contrast-transfer, or amplitude-dependent, nonlinearities which are not seen at lower levels in the visual pathway. The primary focus of our lab is study of the cortical mechanisms that support both the band limitations and nonlinearities that are imposed on the relatively unsullied signals incoming from the LGN. All of our work is done on the cat.

2   THE ROLE OF INHIBITION IN ORIENTATION SELECTIVITY

Orientation selectivity is one of the most dramatic demonstrations of the filtering ability of cortical cells. Cells in the LGN are only mildly biased for stimulus orientation, but cells in cortex are completely unresponsive to orthogonal stimuli and have tuning bandwidths that average only about 40-50° (e.g., Rose & Blakemore, 1974). How this happens remains controversial, but there is general consensus that inhibition helps to define orientation selectivity although the schemes vary. The concept of *cross-orientation inhibition* suggests that the inhibition is itself orientation selective and tuned in a complimentary way to the excitatory tuning of the cell, being smallest at the optimal orientation and greatest at the orthogonal orientation. More recent results, including those from our own lab, suggests that this is not the case.

We studied the orientation dependence of inhibition by presenting two superimposed gratings, a *base* grating at the optimal orientation to provide a steady level of background response activity, and a *mask* grating of varying orientation which yielded either excitation or inhibition that could supplement or suppress the *base*-generated response. There is some confusion when both base and mask generate excitation. In order to separate the response components from each of these stimuli, the two gratings were drifted at differing temporal frequencies. At least in simple cells, the individual contributions to the response from each grating could then be resolved by performing Fourier analysis on the response histograms.

Experiments were done on 52 cells, of which about 2/3 showed organized suppression from the *mask* grating (Bonds, 1989). Fig. 1 shows that while the mask-generated response suppression is somewhat orientation selective, it is by and large much flatter than would be required to account for the tuning of the cell. There is thus *some* orientation dependence of inhibition, but not specifically at the orthogonal orientation as might be expected. Instead, the predominant component of the suppression is constant with mask orientation, or **global**. This suggests that virtually any stimulus can result in inhibition, whether or not the recorded cell actually "sees" it. What orientation-dependent component of inhibition that might appear is expressed in suppressive side-bands near the limits of the excitatory tuning function, which have the effect of enhancing any pre-existing orientation bias.

Thus the concept of cross-orientation inhibition is not particularly correct, since the inhibition is found not just at the "cross" orientation but rather at all orientations. Even without orientation-selective inhibition, a scheme for establishment of true orientation selectivity from orientation-biased LGN input can be derived

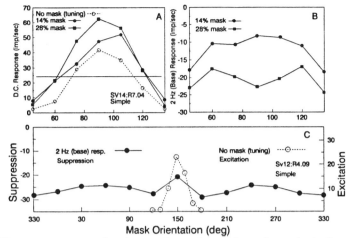

Figure 1: Response suppression by mask gratings of varying orientation. A. Impact of masks of 2 different contrasts on 2 Hz (base-generated) response, expressed by decrease (negative imp/sec) from response level arising from base stimulus alone. B. Similar example for mask orientations spanning a full 360°.

by assuming that the nonselective inhibition is graded and contrast-dependent and that it acts as a thresholding device (Bonds, 1989).

3 THE ROLE OF INHIBITION IN SPATIAL FREQUENCY SELECTIVITY

While most retinal and LGN cells are broadly tuned and predominantly low-pass, cortical cells generally have spatial frequency bandpasses of about 1.5-2 octaves (e.g., Maffei & Fiorentini, 1973). We have examined the influence of inhibition on spatial frequency selectivity using the same strategy as the previous experiment (Bauman & Bonds, 1991). A *base* grating, at the optimal orientation and spatial frequency, drove the cell, and a superimposed *mask* grating, at the optimal orientation but at different spatial and temporal frequencies, provided response facilitation or suppression.

We defined three broad categories of spatial frequency tuning functions: Low pass, with no discernible low-frequency fall-off, band-pass, with a peak between 0.4 and 0.9 c/deg, and high pass, with a peak above 1 c/deg. About 75% of the cells showed response suppression organized with respect to the spatial frequency of mask gratings. For example, Fig. 2A shows a low-pass cells with high-frequency suppression and Fig. 2B shows a band-pass cell with mixed suppression, flanking the tuning curve at both low and high frequencies. In each case response suppression was graded with mask contrast and some suppression was found even at the optimal spatial frequency. Some cells showed no suppression, indicating that the suppression was not merely a stimulus artifact. In all but 2 of 42 cases, the suppression was appropriate to the enhancement of the tuning function (e.g., low-pass cells had high-frequency response suppression), suggesting that the design of the system is more than coincidental. No similar spatial-frequency-dependent suppression was found in LGN cells.

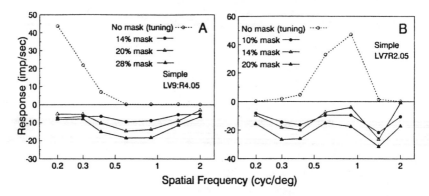

Figure 2: Examples of spatial frequency-dependent response suppression. Upper broken lines show excitatory tuning functions and solid lines below zero indicate response reduction at three different contrasts. A. Low-pass cell with high frequency inhibition. B. Band-pass cell with mixed (low and high frequency) inhibition. Note suppression at optimal spatial frequency in both cases.

4   NON-STATIONARITY OF CONTRAST TRANSFER PROPERTIES

The two experiments described above demonstrate the existence of intrinsic cortical mechanisms that refine the spatial filter properties of the cells. They also reveal a *global* form of inhibition that is spatially non-specific. Since it is found even with spatially optimal stimuli, it can influence the form of the cortical contrast-response function (usually measured with optimal stimuli). This function is essentially logarithmic, with saturation or even super-saturation at higher contrasts (e.g., Albrecht & Hamilton, 1982), as opposed to the more linear response behavior seen in cells earlier in the visual pathway. Cortical cells also show some degree of contrast adaptation; when exposed to high mean contrasts for long periods of time, the response vs contrast curves move rightward (e.g., Ohzawa, Sclar & Freeman, 1985). We addressed the question of whether contrast-response nonlinearity and adaptation might be causally related.

In order to compensate for "intrinsic response variability" in visual cortical cells, experimental stimulation has historically involved presentation of randomized sequences of pattern parameters, the so-called multiple histogram technique (Henry, Bishop, Tupper & Dreher, 1973). Scrambling presentation order distributes time-dependent response variability across all stimulus conditions, but this procedure can be self-defeating by masking any stimulus-dependent response variation. We therefore presented cortical cells with ordered sequences of contrasts, first ascending then descending in a stepwise manner (Bonds, 1991). This revealed a clear and powerful response hysteresis. Fig. 3A shows a solid line representing the contrast-response function measured in the usual way, with randomized parameter presentation, overlaid on an envelope outlining responses to sequentially increasing or decreasing 3-sec contrast epochs; one sequential presentation set required 54 secs. Across 36 cells measured in this same way, the average response hysteresis corresponded to 0.36 log units of contrast. Some hysteresis was found in every cortical cell and in no LGN cells, so this phenomenon is intrinsically cortical.

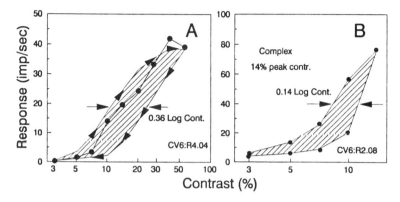

Figure 3: Dynamic response hysteresis. **A.** A response function measured in the usual way, with randomized stimulus sequences (filled circles) is overlaid on the function resulting from stimulation with sequential ascending (upper level) and descending (lower level) contrasts. Each contrast was presented for 3 seconds. **B.** Hysteresis resulting from peak contrast of 14%; 3 secs per datum.

Hysteresis demonstrates a clear dependence of response amplitude on the history of stimulation: at a given contrast, the amplitude is always less if a higher contrast was shown first. This is one manifestation of cortical contrast adaptation, which is well-known. However, adaptation is usually measured after long periods of stimulation with high contrasts, and may not be relevant to normal behavioral vision. Fig. 3B shows hysteresis at a modest response level and low peak contrast (14%), suggesting that it can serve a major function in day-to-day visual processing. The speed of hysteresis also addresses this issue, but it is not so easily measured. Some response histogram waveforms show consistent amplitude loss over a few seconds of stimulation (see also Albrecht, Farrar & Hamilton, 1984), but other histograms can be flat or even show a slight rise over time despite clear contrast adaptation (Bonds, 1991). This suggests the possibility that, in the classical pattern of any well-designed automatic gain control, gain reduction takes place quite rapidly, but its effects linger for some time.

The speed of reaction of gain change is illustrated in the experiment of Fig. 4. A "pedestal" grating of 14% contrast is introduced. After 500 msec, a contrast increment of 14% is added to the pedestal for a variable length of time. The response during the first and last 500 msec of the pedestal presentation is counted and the ratio is taken. In the absence of the increment, this ratio is about 0.8, reflecting the adaptive nature of the pedestal itself. For an increment of even 50 msec duration, this ratio is reduced, and it is reduced monotonically–by up to half the control level–for increments lasting less than a second. The gain control mechanism is thus both sensitive and rapid.

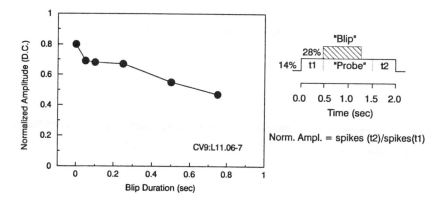

Figure 4: Speed of gain reduction. The ratio of spikes generated during the last and first 500 msec of a 2 sec pedestal presentation can be modified by a brief contrast increment (see text).

5   PHYSIOLOGICAL INDEPENDENCE OF TWO INHIBITORY MECHANISMS

The experimental observations presented above support two basic phenomena: spatially-dependent and spatially-independent inhibition. The question remains whether these two types of inhibition are fundamentally different, or if they stem from the same physiological mechanisms. This question can be addressed by examining the structure of a serial spike train generated by a cortical cell. In general, rather than being distributed continuously, cortical spikes are grouped into discrete packets, or bursts, with some intervening isolated spikes. The burst structure can be fundamentally characterized by two parameters: the burst frequency (*bursts per second*, or BPS) and the burst duration (*spikes per burst*, or SPB).

We have analyzed cortical spike trains for these properties by using an adaptive algorithm to define burst groupings; as a rule of thumb, spike intervals of 8 msec or less were considered to belong to bursts. Both burst frequency (BPS) and structure (SPB) depend strongly on mean firing rate, but once firing rate is corrected for, two basic patterns emerge. Consider two experiments, both yielding firing rate variation about a similar range. In one experiment, firing rate is varied by varying stimulus contrast, while in the other, firing rate is varied by varying stimulus orientation. Burst frequency (BPS) depends only on spike rate, regardless of the type of experiment. In Fig. 5A, no systematic difference is seen between the experiments in which contrast (filled circles) and orientation (open squares) are varied. To quantify the difference between the curves, polynomials were fit to each and the quantity gamma, defined by the (shaded) area bounded by the two polynomials, was calculated; here, it equalled about 0.03.

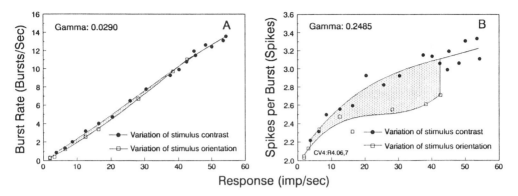

Figure 5: A. Comparison of burst frequency (bursts per second) as function of firing rate resulting from presentations of varying contrast (filled circles) and varying orientation (open squares). B. Comparison of burst length (spikes per burst) under similar conditions. Note that at a given firing rate, burst length is always shorter for experiment parametric on orientation. Shaded area (*gamma*) is quantitative indicator of difference between two curves.

Fig. 5B shows that at similar firing rates, burst length (SPB) is markedly shorter when firing rate is controlled by varying orientation (open squares) rather than contrast (filled circles). In this pair of curves, the gamma (of about 0.25) is nearly ten times that found in the upper curve. This is a clear violation of univariance, since at a given spike rate (output level), the structure of the spike train differs depending on the type of stimulation. Analysis of cortical response merely on the basis of overall firing rate thus does not give the signalling mechanisms the respect they are properly due. This result also implies that the strength of signalling between nerve cells can dynamically vary independent of firing rate. Because of post-synaptic temporal integration, bursts of spikes with short interspike intervals will be much more effective in generating depolarization than spikes at longer intervals. Thus, at a given average firing rate, a cell that generates longer bursts will have more influence on a target cell than a cell that distributes its spikes in shorter bursts, all other factors being equal.

This phenomenon was consistent across a population of 59 cells. Gamma, which reflects the degree of difference between curves measured by variation of contrast and by variation of orientation, averaged zero for curves based on number of bursts (BPS). For both simple and complex cells, gamma for burst duration (SPB) averaged 0.15.

At face value, these results simply mean that when lower spike rates are achieved by use of non-optimal orientations, they result from shorter bursts than when lower spike rates result from reduction of contrast (with the spatial configuration remaining optimal). This means that non-optimal orientations and, from some preliminary results, non-optimal spatial frequencies, result in inhibition that acts specifically to shorten bursts, whereas contrast manipulations for the most part act to modulate both the number and length of bursts.

These results suggest strongly that there are at least two distinct forms of cortical inhibition, with unique physiological bases differentiated by the burst organization in cortical spike trains. Recent results from our laboratory (Bonds, *Unpub. Obs.*) confirm that burst length modulation, which seems to reflect inhibition that depends on the spatial characteristics of the stimulus, is strongly mediated by GABA. Microiontophoretic injection of GABA shortens burst length and injection of bicuculline, a GABA blocker, lengthens bursts. This is wholly consistent with the hypothesis that GABA is central to definition of spatial qualities of the cortical receptive field, and suggests that one can indirectly observe GABA-mediated inhibition by spike train analysis.

Acknowledgements

This work was done in collaboration with Ed DeBruyn, Lisa Bauman and Brian DeBusk. Supported by NIH (RO1-EY03778-09).

References

D. G. Albrecht & D. B. Hamilton. (1982) Striate cortex of monkey and cat: contrast response functions. *Journal of Neurophysiology* **48**, 217-237.

D. G. Albrecht, S. B. Farrar & D. B. Hamilton. (1984) Spatial contrast adaptation characteristics of neurones recorded in the cat's visual cortex. *Journal of Physiology* **347**, 713-739.

A. B. Bonds. (1989) The role of inhibition in the specification of orientation selectivity of cells of the cat striate cortex. *Visual Neuroscience* **2**, 41-55.

A. B. Bonds. (1991) Temporal dynamics of contrast gain control in single cells of the cat striate cortex. *Visual Neuroscience* **6**, 239-255.

L. A. Bauman & A. B. Bonds. (1991) Inhibitory refinement of spatial frequency selectivity in single cells of the cat striate cortex. *Vision Research* **31**, 933-944.

G. Henry, P. O. Bishop, R. M. Tupper & B. Dreher. (1973) Orientation specificity of cells in cat striate cortex. *Vision Research* **13**, 1771-1779.

L. Maffei & A. Fiorentini. (1973) The visual cortex as a spatial frequency analyzer. *Vision Research* **13**, 1255-1267.

I. Ohzawa, G. Sclar & R. D. Freeman. (1985) Contrast gain control in the cat's visual system. *Journal of Neurophysiology* **54**, 651-667.

D. Rose & C. B. Blakemore. (1974) An analysis of orientation selectivity in the cat's visual cortex. *Experimental Brain Research* **20**, 1-17.

R. E. Soodak, R. M. Shapley & E. Kaplan. (1987) Linear mechanism of orientation tuning in the retina and lateral geniculate of the cat. *Journal of Neurophysiology* **58**, 267-275.

A comparison between a neural network model for the formation of brain maps and experimental data

K. Obermayer
Beckman-Institute
University of Illinois
Urbana, IL 61801

K. Schulten
Beckman-Institute
University of Illinois
Urbana, IL 61801

G.G. Blasdel
Harvard Medical School
Harvard University
Boston, MA 02115

Abstract

Recently, high resolution images of the simultaneous representation of orientation preference, orientation selectivity and ocular dominance have been obtained for large areas in monkey striate cortex by optical imaging [1-3]. These data allow for the first time a "local" as well as "global" description of the spatial patterns and provide strong evidence for correlations between orientation selectivity and ocular dominance.

A quantitative analysis reveals that these correlations arise when a five-dimensional feature space (two dimensions for retinotopic space, one each for orientation preference, orientation specificity, and ocular dominance) is mapped into the two available dimensions of cortex while locally preserving topology. These results provide strong evidence for the concept of topology preserving maps which have been suggested as a basic design principle of striate cortex [4-7].

Monkey striate cortex contains a retinotopic map in which are embedded the highly repetitive patterns of orientation selectivity and ocular dominance. The retinotopic projection establishes a "global" order, while maps of variables describing other stimulus features, in particular line orientation and ocularity, dominate cortical organization locally. A large number of pattern models [8-12] as well as models of development [6,7,13-21] have been proposed to describe the spatial structure of these patterns and their development during ontogenesis. However, most models have not been compared with experimental data in detail. There are two reasons for this: (*i*) many model-studies were not elaborated enough to be experimentally testable and (*ii*) a sufficient amount of experimental data obtained from large areas of striate cortex was not available.

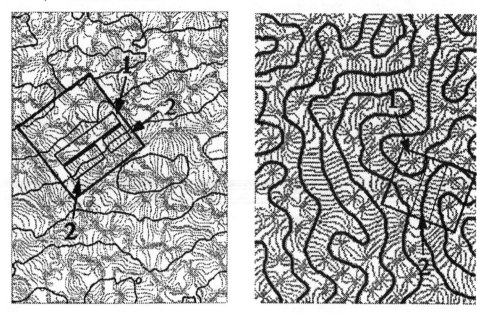

Figure 1: Spatial pattern of orientation preference and ocular dominance in monkey striate cortex (left) compared with predictions of the SOFM-model (right). Isoorientation lines (gray) are drawn in intervals of $11.25°$ (left) and $18.0°$ (right), respectively. Black lines indicate the borders ($w_5(\vec{r}) = 0$) of ocular dominance bands. The areas enclosed by black rectangles mark corresponding elements of organization in monkey striate cortex and in the simulation result (see text). **Left:** Data obtained from a 3.1mm × 4.2mm patch of the striate cortex of an adult macaque (macaca nemestrina) by optical imaging [1-3]. The region is located near the border with area 18, close to midline. **Right:** Model-map generated by the SOFM-algorithm. The figure displays a small section of a network of size $N = d = 512$. The parameters of the simulation were: $\varepsilon = 0.02$, $\sigma_h = 5$, $v_{3,4}^{max} = 20.48$, $v_5^{max} = 15.36$, $9 \cdot 10^7$ iterations, with retinotopic initial conditions and periodic boundary conditions.

1 Orientation and ocular dominance columns in monkey striate cortex

Recent advances in optical imaging [1-3,22,23] now make it possible to obtain high resolution images of the spatial pattern of orientation selectivity and ocular dominance from large cortical areas. Prima vista analysis of data from monkey striate cortex reveals that the spatial pattern of orientation preference and ocular dominance is continuous and highly repetitive across cortex. On a global scale orientation preferences repeat along every direction of cortex with similar periods. Locally, orientation preferences are organized as parallel *slabs* (arrow 1, Fig. 1a) in *linear zones*, which start and end at *singularities* (arrow 2, Fig. 1a), point-like discontinuities, around which orientation preferences change by $\pm 180°$ in a pinwheel-like fashion. Both types of singularities appear in equal numbers (359:354 for maps obtained from four adult macaques) with a density of $5.5/mm^2$ (for regions close to

Fourier transforms	$w_j(\vec{k})$	$= \sum_{\vec{r}} \exp(i\vec{k}\vec{r})\, w_j(\vec{r})$
correlation functions	$C_{ij}(\vec{p})$	$= <w_i(\vec{r})\, w_j(\vec{r}+\vec{p})>_{\vec{r}}$
feature gradients	$\|\nabla_{\vec{r}} w_j(\vec{r})\|$	$= \{(w_j(r_1+1,r_2) - w_j(r_1,r_2))^2$ $+ (w_j(r_1,r_2+1) - w_j(r_1,r_2))^2\}^{1/2}$
Gabor transforms	$g_j(\vec{k},\vec{r})$	$= (2\pi\sigma_g^2)^{-\frac{1}{4}} \int d^2r'\, w_j(\vec{r}')$ $\exp\{-\frac{(\vec{r}-\vec{r}')^2}{4\sigma_g^2} + i\vec{k}(\vec{r}' - \frac{1}{2}\vec{r})\}$

Table 1: Quantitative measures used to characterize cortical maps.

the midline). Figure 1a reveals that the iso–orientation lines cross ocular dominance bands at nearly right angles most of the time (region number 2) and that singularities tend to align with the centers of the ocular dominance bands (region number 1). Where orientation preferences are organized as parallel slabs (region number 2), the iso-orientation contours are often equally spaced and orientation preferences change linearly with distance.

These results are confirmed by a quantitative analysis (see Table 1). For the following we denote cortical location by a two-dimensional vector $\vec{r}$. At each location we denote the (average) position of receptive field centroids in visual space by $(w_1(\vec{r}), w_2(\vec{r}))$. Orientation selectivity is described by a two-dimensional vector $(w_3(\vec{r}), w_4(\vec{r}))$, whose length and direction code for orientation tuning strength and preferred orientation, respectively [1,10]. Ocular dominance is described by a real-valued function $w_5(\vec{r})$, which denotes the difference in response to stimuli presented to the left and right eye. Data acquisition and postprocessing are described in detail in [1-3].

A Fourier transform of the map of orientation preferences reveals a spectrum which is a nearly circular band (Fig. 2a), showing that orientation preferences repeat with similar periods in every direction in cortex. Neglecting the slight anisotropy in the experimental data[1], a power spectrum can be approximated by averaging amplitudes over all directions of the wave-vector (Fig. 2b, dots). The location of the peak corresponds to an average period $\lambda_0 = 710\mu m \pm 50\mu m$[2] and it's width to a *coherence length* of $820\mu m \pm 130\mu m$. The coherence length indicates the typical distance over which orientation preferences can change linearly and corresponds to the average size of linear zones in Fig. 1a. The corresponding autocorrelation functions (Fig. 2c) have a Mexican hat shape. The minimum occurs near $300\mu m$, which indicates that orientation preferences in regions separated by this distance tend to be orthogonal. In summary, the spatial pattern of orientation preference is characterized by local correlation and global "disorder".

---

[1]Along axes parallel to the ocular dominance slabs, orientation preferences repeat on average every $660\mu m \pm 40\mu m$; perpendicular to the stripes every $840\mu m \pm 40\mu m$. The slight horizontal elongation reflects the fact that iso-orientation slabs tend to connect the centers of ocular dominance bands.

[2]All quantities regarding experimental data are averages over four animals, nm1-nm4, unless stated otherwise. Error margins indicate standard deviations.

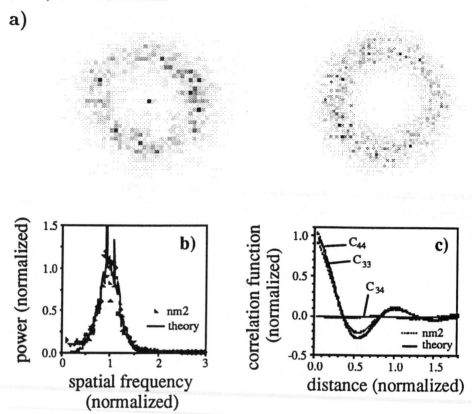

Figure 2: Fourier analysis and correlation functions of the orientation map in monkey striate cortex (animal nm2) compared with the predictions of the SOFM-model. Simulation results were taken from the data set described in Fig. 1, right. **(a)** Fourier spectra of nm2 **(left)** and simulation results **(right)**. Each pixel represents one mode; location and gray value of the pixel indicate wave-vector and energy, respectively. **(b)** Approximate power spectrum (normalized) obtained by averaging the Fourier-spectra in (a) over all directions of the wave-vector. Peak frequency of 1.0 corresponds to 1.4/mm for nm2. **(c)** Correlation functions (normalized). A distance of 1.0 corresponds to $725\mu m$ for nm2.

Local properties of the spatial patterns, as well as correlations between orientation preference and ocular dominance, can be quantitatively characterized using Gabor-Helstrom-transforms (see Table 1). If the radius σ_g of the Gaussian function in the Gabor-filter is smaller than the coherence length the Gabor-transform of any of the quantities $w_3(\vec{r})$, $w_4(\vec{r})$ and $w_5(\vec{r})$ typically consists of two localized regions of high energy located on opposite sides of the origin. The length $|\vec{k}_i|$ of the vectors $\vec{k}_i$, $i \in [3, 4, 5]$, which corresponds to the centroids of these regions, fluctuates around the characteristic wave-number $2\pi/\lambda_0$ of this pattern, and its direction gives the normal to the ocular dominance bands and iso-orientation slabs at the location $\vec{r}$, where the Gabor-transform was performed.

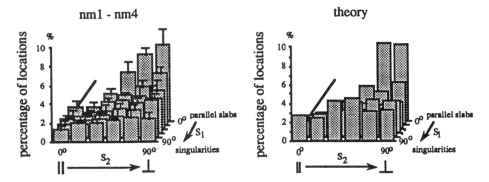

Figure 3: Gabor-analysis of cortical maps. The percentage of map locations is plotted against the parameters s_1 and s_2 (see text) for 3,421 locations randomly selected from the cortical maps of four monkeys, nm1-nm4, (**left**) and for 1,755 locations randomly selected from simulation results (**right**). Error bars indicate standard deviations. Simulation results were taken from the data set described in Fig. 1. σ_g was 150μm for the experimental data and 28 pixels for the SOFM-map.

Results of this analysis are shown in Fig. 3 (left) for 3,434 samples selected randomly from data of four animals. The angle between $\vec{k}_3$ and $\vec{k}_4$ is represented along the s_1 axis. Histograms at the back, where $s_1 = 0°$, represent regions where iso-orientation lines are parallel. Histograms in the front, where $s_1 = 90°$, represent regions containing singularities. The intersection angle of iso-orientation slabs and ocular dominance bands is represented along the s_2 axis. The proportion of sampled regions increases steadily with decreasing s_1. As s_1 approaches zero, values accumulate at the right, where orientation and ocular dominance bands are orthogonal. Thus linear zones *and* singularities are important elements of cortical organization but linear zones (back rows) are the most prominent features in monkey striate cortex[3]. Where iso-orientation regions are organized as parallel slabs, orientation slabs intersect ocular dominance bands at nearly right angles (back and right corner of diagrams).

2   Topology preserving maps

Recently, topology preserving maps have been suggested as a basic design principle underlying these patterns and its was proposed that these maps are generated by simple and biologically plausible pattern formation processes [4,6,7]. In the following we will test these models against the recent experimental data.

We consider a five-dimensional *feature space* V which is spanned by quantities describing the most prominent receptive field properties of cortical cells: position of a receptive field in retinotopic space (v_1, v_2), orientation preference and tuning strength (v_3, v_4), and ocular dominance (v_5). If all combinations of these properties

---

[3]Data from area 17 of the cat indicate that in this species, although both elements are present, singularities are more important [23]

are represented in striate cortex, each point in this five-dimensional feature space is mapped onto one point on the two-dimensional *cortical surface A*.

In order to generate these maps we employ the feature map (SOFM-) algorithm of Kohonen [15,16] which is known to generate topology preserving maps between spaces of different dimensionality [4,5][4]. The algorithm describes the development of these patterns as unsupervised learning, i.e. the features of the input patterns determine the features to be represented in the network [4]. Mathematically, the algorithm assignes *feature vectors* $\vec{w}(\vec{r})$, which are points in the feature space, to cortical *units* $\vec{r}$, which are points on the cortical surface. In our model the surface is divided into $N \times N$ small patches, *units* $\vec{r}$, which are arranged on a two-dimensional lattice (network layer) with periodic boundary conditions (to avoid edge effects). The average receptive field properties of neurons located in each patch are characterized by the feature vector $\vec{w}(\vec{r})$ whose components $(\vec{w}_j(\vec{r})$ are interpreted as receptive field properties of these neurons. The algorithm follows an iterative procedure. At each step an *input vector* $\vec{v}$, which is of the same dimensionality as $\vec{w}(\vec{r})$ is chosen at random according to a probability distribution $P(\vec{v})$. Then the unit $\vec{s}$ whose feature vector $\vec{w}(\vec{s})$ is closest to the input pattern $\vec{v}$ is selected and the components $(\vec{w}_j(\vec{r})$ of its feature vector are changed according to the feature map learning rule [15,16],

$$\Delta\vec{w}(\vec{r}) = \varepsilon \exp\left(-(r_1 - s_1)^2/\sigma_{h1}^2 - (r_2 - s_2)^2/\sigma_{h2}^2\right)(\vec{v} - \vec{w}(\vec{r})), \tag{1}$$

$P(\vec{v})$ was chosen to be constant within a cylindrical manifold in feature space,

$$V = \{\vec{v} \mid w_1(\vec{r}), w_2(\vec{r}) \in [0, d]; \ |(w_3(\vec{r}), w_4(\vec{r}))| < v_{3,4}^{\max}; \ |w_5(\vec{r})| < v_5^{\max}\}, \tag{2}$$

where $v_{3,4}^{\max}$ and $v_5^{\max}$ are some real constants, and zero elsewhere.

Figure 4 shows a typical map, a surface in feature space, generated by the SOFM-algorithm. For the sake of illustration the five-dimensional feature space is projected onto a three-dimensional subspace spanned by the coordinate-axes corresponding to retinotopic location (v_1 and v_2) and ocular dominance (v_5). The locations of feature vectors assigned to the cortical units are indicated by the intersections of a grid in feature space. Preservation of topology requires that the feature vectors assigned to neighboring cortical units must locally have equal distance and must be arranged on a planar square lattice in feature space. Consequently, large changes in one feature, e.g. ocular dominance v_5, along a given direction on the network correlate with small changes of the other features, e.g. retinotopic location v_1 and v_2, along the same direction (crests and troughs of the waves in Fig. 4) and vice versa. Other correlations arise at points where the map exhibits maximal changes in two features. For example for retinotopic location (v_1) and ocular dominance (v_5) to vary at a maximal rate, the surface in Fig. 4 must be parallel to the (v_1, v_5)-plane. Obviously, at such points the directions of maximal change of retinotopic location and ocular dominance are orthogonal on the surface.

In order to compare model predictions with experimental data the surface in the five-dimensional feature space has to be projected into the three-dimensional subspace

---

[4]The exact form of the algorithm is not essential, however. Algorithms based on similar principles, e.g. the elastic net algorithm [6], predict similar patterns.

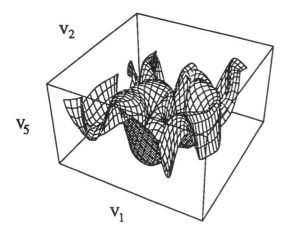

v_2

v_5

v_1

Figure 4: Typical map generated by the SOFM-algorithm. The five-dimensional feature space is projected into the three-dimensional subspace spanned by the three coordinates (v_1, v_2 and v_5). Locations of feature vectors which are mapped to the units in the network are indicated by the intersections of a grid in feature space. Only every fourth vector is shown.

spanned by orientation preferences (v_3 and v_4) and ocular dominance (v_5). This projection cannot be visualized easily because the surface completely fills space, intersecting itself multiple times. However, the same line of reasoning applies: (i) regions where orientation preferences change quickly, correlate with regions where ocular dominance changes slowly, and (ii) in regions where orientation preferences change most rapidly along one direction, ocular dominance has to change most rapidly along the orthogonal direction. Consequently we expect discontinuities of the orientation map to be located in the centers of the ocular dominance bands and iso-orientation slabs to intersect ocular dominance bands at steep angles.

Figures 1, 2 and 3 show simulation results in comparison with experimental data. The algorithm generates all the prominent features of lateral cortical organization: singularities (arrow 1), linear zones (arrow 2), and parallel ocular dominance bands. Singularities are aligned with the centers of ocular dominance bands (region 1) and iso-orientation slabs intersect ocular dominance stripes at nearly right angles (region 2). The shape of Fourier- and power-spectra as well as of the correlation functions agrees quantitatively with the experimental data (see Fig. 2). Isotropic spectra are the result of the invariance of eqs. (1) and (2) under rotation with respect to cortical coordinates $\vec{r}$; global disorder and singularities are a consequence of their invariance under translation. The emergence of singularities can also be understood from an entropy argument. Since dimension reducing maps, which exhibit these features, have increased entropy, they are generated with higher probability. Correlations between orientation preference and ocular dominance, however, follow from geometrical constraints and are inherent properties the topology preserving maps.

3   Conclusions

On the basis of our findings the following picture of orientation and ocular dominance columns in monkey striate cortex emerges. Orientation preferences are organized into linear zones *and* singularities, but areas where iso-orientation regions form parallel slabs are apparent across most of the cortical surface. In linear zones, iso-orientation slabs indeed intersect ocular dominance slabs at right angles as initially suggested by Hubel and Wiesel [8]. Orientation preferences, however, are arranged in an orderly fashion only in regions 0.8mm in size, and the pattern is characterized by local correlation and global disorder.

These patterns can be explained as the result of topology-preserving, dimension reducing maps. Local correlations follow from geometrical constraints and are a direct consequence of the principle of dimension reduction. Global disorder and singularities are consistent with this principle but reflect their generation by a local and stochastic self-organizing process.

Acknowledgements

The authors would like to thank H. Ritter for fruitful discussions and comments and the Boehringer-Ingelheim Fonds for financial support by a scholarship to K. O. This research has been supported by the National Science Foundation (grant numbers DIR 90-17051 and DIR 91-22522). Computer time on the Connection Machine CM-2 has been made available by the National Center for Supercomputer Applications at Urbana-Champaign funded by NSF.

References

[1] Blasdel G.G. and Salama G. (1986), Nature **321**, 579-585.
[2] Blasdel G.G. (1992), J. Neurosci. in press.
[3] Blasdel G.G. (1992), J. Neurosci. in press.
[4] Kohonen T. (1987), Self-Organization and Associative Memory, Springer-Verlag, New York.
[5] Ritter H. and Schulten K. (1988), Biol. Cybern. **60**, 59-71.
[6] Durbin R. and Mitchison M. (1990), Nature **343**, 644-647.
[7] Obermayer K. et al. (1990), Proc. Natl. Acad. Sci. USA **87**, 8345-8349.
[8] Hubel D.H. and Wiesel T.N. (1974), J. Comp. Neurol. **158**, 267-294.
[9] Braitenberg V. and Braitenberg C. (1979), Biol. Cybern. **33**, 179-186.
[10] Swindale N.V. (1982), Proc. R. Soc. Lond. B **215**, 211-230.
[11] Baxter W.T. and Dow B.M. (1989), Biol. Cybern. **61**, 171-182.
[12] Rojer A.S. and Schwartz E.L. (1990), Biol. Cybern. **62**, 381-391.
[13] Malsburg C. (1973), Kybernetik **14**, 85-100.
[14] Takeuchi A. and Amari S. (1979), Biol. Cybern. **35**, 63-72.
[15] Kohonen T. (1982a), Biol. Cybern. **43**, 59-69.
[16] Kohonen T. (1982b), Biol. Cybern. **44**, 135-140.
[17] Linsker R. (1986), Proc. Natl. Acad. Sci. USA **83**, 8779-8783.
[18] Soodak R. (1987), Proc. Natl. Acad. Sci. USA **84**, 3936-3940.
[19] Kammen D.M. and Yuille A.R. (1988), Biol. Cybern. **59**, 23-31.
[20] Miller K.D. et al. (1989), Science **245**, 605-615.
[21] Miller K.D. (1989), Soc. Neurosci. Abs. **15**, 794.
[22] Grinvald A. et al. (1986), Nature **324**, 361-364.
[23] Bonhoeffer T. and Grinvald A. (1991), Nature **353**, 429-431.

Retinogeniculate Development: The Role of Competition and Correlated Retinal Activity

Ron Keesing*
Dept. of Physiology
U.C. San Francisco
San Francisco, CA 94143
keesing@phy.ucsf.edu

David G. Stork
*Ricoh California Research Center
2882 Sand Hill Rd., Suite 115
Menlo Park, CA 94025
stork@crc.ricoh.com

Carla J. Shatz
Dept. of Neurobiology
Stanford University
Stanford, CA
94305

Abstract

During visual development, projections from retinal ganglion cells (RGCs) to the lateral geniculate nucleus (LGN) in cat are refined to produce ocular dominance layering and precise topographic mapping. Normal development depends upon activity in RGCs, suggesting a key role for activity-dependent synaptic plasticity. Recent experiments on prenatal retina show that during early development, "waves" of activity pass across RGCs (Meister, et al., 1991). We provide the first simulations to demonstrate that such retinal waves, in conjunction with Hebbian synaptic competition and early arrival of contralateral axons, can account for observed patterns of retinogeniculate projections in normal and experimentally-treated animals.

1 INTRODUCTION

During the development of the mammalian visual system, initially diffuse axonal inputs are refined to produce the precise and orderly projections seen in the adult. In the lateral geniculate nucleus (LGN) of the cat, projections arriving from retinal ganglion cells (RGCs) of both eyes are initially intermixed, and they gradually segregate before birth to form alternating layers containing axons from only one eye. At the same time, the branching patterns of individual axons are refined, with increased growth in topographically correct locations. Axonal segregation and refinement depends upon presynaptic activity — blocking such activity disrupts normal development (Sretavan, et al., 1988; Shatz & Stryker, 1988). These and findings in other vertebrates (Cline, et al., 1987) suggest that synaptic plasticity may be an essential factor in segregation and modification of RGC axons (Shatz, 1990).

Previous models of visual development based on synaptic plasticity (Miller, et al., 1989; Whitelaw & Cowan, 1981) required an assumption of spatial correlations in RGC activity for normal development. This assumption may have been justified for geniculo*cortical* development, since much of this occurs postnatally: visual stimulation provides the correlations. The assumption was more difficult to justify for retino*geniculate* development, since this occurs *prenatally* — before any optical stimulation.

The first strong evidence for correlated activity before birth has recently emerged in the retinogenculate system: wave-like patterns of synchronized activity pass across the prenatal retina, generating correlations between neighboring cells' activity (Meister, et al., 1991). We believe our model is the first to incorporate these important results.

We propose that during visual development, projections from both eyes compete to innervate LGN neurons. Contralateral projections, which reach the LGN earlier, may have a slight advantage in competing to innervate cells of the LGN located farthest from the optic tract. Retinal waves of activity could reinforce this segregation and improve the precision of topographic mapping by causing weight changes within the same eye — and particularly within the same region of the same eye — to be highly correlated. Unlike similar models of *cortical* development, our model does not require lateral interactions between post-synaptic cells — available evidence suggests that lateral inhibition is not present during early development (Shotwell, et al., 1986). Our model also incorporates axon *growth* — an essential aspect of retinogeniculate development, since the growth and branching of axons toward their ultimate targets occurs simultaneously with synaptic competition. Moreover, synaptic competition may provide cues for growth (Shatz & Stryker, 1988). We consider the possibility that diffusing intracellular signals indicating local synaptic strength guide axon growth.

Below we present simulations which show that this model can account for development in normal and experimentally-treated animals. We also predict the outcomes of novel experiments currently underway.

2 SIMULATIONS

Although the LGN is, of course, three-dimensional, in our model we represent just a single two-dimensional LGN slice, ten cells wide and eight cells high. The retina is then *one*-dimensional: 50 cells long in our simulations. (This ratio of widths, 50/10, is roughly that found in the developing cat.) In order to eliminate edge effects, we "wrap" the retina into a ring; likewise we wrap the LGN into a cylinder.

Development of projections to the LGN is modelled in the following way: projections from all fifty RGCs of the contralateral eye arrive at the base of the LGN before those of the ipsilateral eye. A very rough topographic map is imposed, corresponding to coarse topography which might be supplied by chemical gradients (Wolpert, 1978). Development is then modelled as a series of growth steps, each separated by a period of Hebb-style synaptic competition (Wigstrom & Gustafson, 1985). During competition, synapses are strengthened when pre- and post-synaptic activity are sufficiently correlated, and they are weakened otherwise. More specifically, for a given RGC cell i with activity a_i, the strength of synapse w_{ij} to LGN cell j is changed according to:

$$\Delta w_{ij} = \varepsilon \, (a_i - \alpha)(a_j - \beta) \qquad [1]$$

where α and β are threshholds and ε a learning rate. If a "wave" of retinal activity is present, the activity of RGC cells is determined as a probability of firing based on a Gaussian function of the distance from the center of the wavefront. LGN cell activity is equal to the sum of weighted inputs from RGC cells.

After each wave, the total synaptic weight supported by each RGC cell i is renormalized linearly:

$$w_{ij}(t+1) = \frac{w_{ij}(t)}{\sum\limits_{k} w_{ik}(t)} \qquad [2]$$

The weights supported by each LGN cell are also renormalized, gradually driving them toward some target value T:

$$w_{ij}(t+1) = w_{ij}(t) + [T - \sum\limits_{k} w_{kj}(t)] \qquad [3]$$

Renormalization reflects the notion that there is a limited amount of synaptic weight which can be supported by any neuron.

During growth steps, connections are modified based on the strength of neighboring synapses from the same RGC cell. After normalization, connections grow or retract according to:

$$w_{ij}(t+1) = w_{ij}(t) + \gamma \sum\limits_{neighbors} w_{ik}(t) \qquad [4]$$

where γ is a constant term. Equation 4 shows that weights in areas of high synaptic strength will increase more than those elsewhere.

3 RESULTS

Synaptic competition, in conjunction with waves of pre-synaptic activity and early arrival of contralateral axons, can account for pattens of growth seen in normal and experimentally-treated animals. In the presence of synaptic competition, modelled axons from each eye segregate to occupy discrete layers of the LGN — precisely what is seen in normal development. In the absence of competition, as in treatment with the drug TTX, axons arborize throughout the LGN (Figure 1).

The segregation and refinement of retinal inputs to the LGN is best illustrated by the formation of ocular dominance patterns and topographic ordering. In simulations of normal development, where retinal waves are combined with early arrival of contalateral inputs, strong ocular dominance layers are formed: LGN neurons farthest from the optic tract receive synaptic inputs solely from the contralateral eye and those closer receive only ipsilateral inputs (Figure2, Competition). The development of these ocular dominance patterns is gradual: early in development, a majority of LGN neurons receive inputs from *both* eyes. When synaptic competition is eliminated, there is no segregation into eye-specific layers — LGN neurons receive significant synaptic inputs from both eyes. These results are consistent with labelling studies of cat development (Shatz & Stryker, 1988).

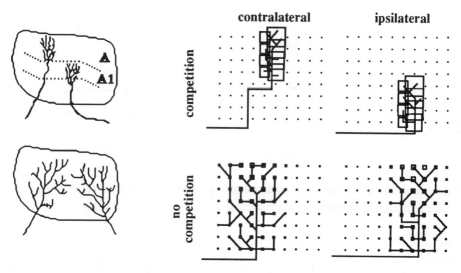

Figure 1: Retinogeniculate projections in vivo (adapted from Sretavan, et al., 1988.) (left), and simulation results (right). In the presence of competition (top), arbors are narrow and spatially localized, confined to the appropriate ocular dominance layer. In the absence of such competition (bottom), contralateral and ipsilateral projections are diffuse; there is no discernible ocular dominance pattern. During simulations, projections are represented by synapses throughout the LGN slice, shown as squares; the particular arborization patterns shown above are inferred from related simulations.

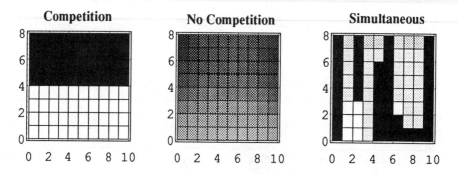

Figure 2: Ocular dominance at the end of development. Dark color indicates strongest synapses from the contralateral eye, light indicates strongest synapses from ipsilateral, and gray indicates significant synapses from both eyes. In the presence of competition, LGN cells segregate into eye-specific layers, with the contralateral eye dominating cells which are farthest from the optic tract (base). When competition is eliminated (No Competition), as in the addition of the drug TTX, there is no segregation into layers and LGN cells receive significant inputs from *both* eyes. These simulations reproduced results from cat development. When inputs from both retinae arrive simultaneously (Simultaneous), ocular dominance "patches" are established, similar to those observed in normal cortical development.

Retinal waves cause the activity of neighboring RGCs to be highly correlated. When combined with synaptic competition, these waves lead to a refinement of topographic ordering of retinogeniculate projections. During development, the coarse topography imposed as RGC axons enter the LGN is refined to produce an accurate, precise mapping of retinal inputs (Figure 3, Competition). Without competition, there is no refinement of topography, and the coarse initial mapping remains.

Competition

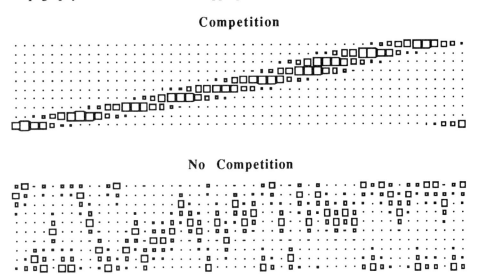

No Competition

Figure 3: Topographic mapping with and without competition. The vertical axis represents ten LGN cells within one section, and the horizontal axis 50 RGC cells. The size of each box indicates strength of the synapse connecting corresponding RGC and LGN cells. If the system is topographically ordered, this connection matrix should contain only connections forming a diagonal from lower left to upper right, as is found in normal development in our model (Competition). When competition is eliminated, the topographic map is coarse and non-contiguous.

4 PREDICTIONS

In addition to replicating current experimental findings, our model makes several interesting predictions about the outcome of novel experiments. If inputs from each eye arrive simultaneously, so that contralateral projections have no advantage in competing to innervate specific regions of the LGN, synaptic competition and retinal waves lead to a pattern of ocular dominance "patches" similar to that observed in visual cortex (Figure 2, Simultaneous). Topography is refined, but in this case a continuous map is formed between the two eyes (Figure 4) — again similar to patterns observed in visual cortex.

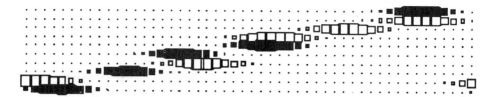

Figure 4: Topographic mapping with synchronous arrival of projections from both eyes. Light boxes represent contralateral inputs, dark boxes represent ipsilateral. Synaptic competition and retinal waves cause ocular segregation and topographic refinement, but in this case the continuous map is formed using both eyes rather than a single eye.

Our model predicts that the width of retinal waves — the distribution of activity around the moving wavefront — is an essential factor in determining both the rate of ocular segregation and topographic refinement. Wide waves, which cause many RGCs within the same eye to be active, will lead to most rapid ocular segregation as a result of competition. However, wide waves can lead to poor topography: RGCs in distant regions of the retina are just as likely to be simultaneously active as neighboring RGCs (Figure 5).

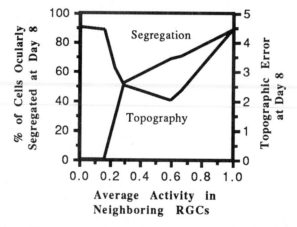

Figure 5: The width of retinal "waves" determines ocular dominance and topography in normal development in our model. Width of retinal waves is represented by the average activity in RGC cells adjacent to the Gaussian wavefront: high activity indicates wide waves. Topographic error (scale at right) represents the average distance from an RGCs target position multiplied by the strength of the synaptic connection. LGN cells are considered ocularly segregated when they receive .9 or more of their total synaptic input from one eye. Wide waves lead to rapid ocular segregation — many RGCs within the same retina are simulaneously active. An intermediate width, however, leads to lower topographic error — wide waves cause spurious correlations, while narrow waves don't provide enough information about neighboring RGCs to significantly refine topography.

5 SUMMARY

Our biological model differs from more developed models of cortical development in its inclusion of 1) differences in the time of arrival of RGC axons from the two eyes, 2) lack of intra-target (LGN) inhibitory connections, 3) absence of visual stimulation, and 4) inclusion of a growth rule. The model can account for the development of topography and ocular dominance layering in studies of normal and experimental-treated cats, and makes predictions concerning the role of retinal waves in both segregation and topography. These neurobiological experiments are currently underway.

Acknowledgements

Thanks to Michael Stryker for helpful suggestions and to Steven Lisberger for his generous support of this work.

References

Cline, H.T., Debski, E.A., & Constantine-Paton, M.. (1987) "N-methyl-D-aspartate receptor antagonist desegregates eye-specific stripes." *PNAS* **84**: 4342-4345.

Meister, M., Wong, R., Baylor, D., & Shatz, C. (1991) "Synchronous Bursts of Action Potentials in Ganglion Cells of the Developing Mammalian Retina." *Science.* **252**: 939-943.

Miller, K.D., Keller, J.B., & Stryker, M.P. (1989) "Ocular Dominance Column Development: Analysis and Simulation." *Science.* **245**: 605-615.

Shatz, C.J. (1990) "Competitive Interactions between Retinal Ganglion Cells during Prenatal Development." *J. Neurobio.* **21**(1): 197-211.

Shatz, C.J., & Stryker, M.P. (1988) "Prenatal Tetrodotoxin Infusion Blocks Segregation of Retinogeniculation Afferents." *Science.* **242**: 87-89.

Shotwell, S.L., Shatz, C.J., & Luskin, M.B. (1986) "Development of Glutamic Acid Decarboxylase Immunoreactivity in the cat's lateral geniculate nucleus." *J. Neurosci.* **6**(5) 1410-1423.

Sretavan, D.W., Shatz, C.J., & Stryker, M.P. (1988) "Modification of Retinal Ganglion Cell Morphology by Prenatal Infusion of Tetrodotoxin." *Nature.* **336**: 468-471.

Whitelaw, V.A., & Cowan, J.D. (1981) "Specificity and plasticity of retinotectal connections: a computational model." *J. Neurosci.* **1**(12) 1369-1387.

Wigstrom, H., & Gustafsson, B. (1985) "Presynaptic and postsynaptic interactions in the control of hippocampal long-term potentiation." in P.W. Landfield & S.A. Deadwyler (Eds.) *Longer-term potentiation: from biophysics to behavior* (pp. 73-107). New York: Alan R. Liss.

Wolpert, L. (1978) "Pattern Formation in Biological Development." *Sci. Amer.* **239**(4): 154-164.

PART II

NEURO-DYNAMICS

Locomotion in a Lower Vertebrate: Studies of the Cellular Basis of Rhythmogenesis and Oscillator Coupling

James T. Buchanan
Department of Biology
Marquette University
Milwaukee, WI 53233

Abstract

To test whether the known connectivies of neurons in the lamprey spinal cord are sufficient to account for locomotor rhythmogenesis, a "connectionist" neural network simulation was done using identical cells connected according to experimentally established patterns. It was demonstrated that the network oscillates in a stable manner with the same phase relationships among the neurons as observed in the lamprey. The model was then used to explore coupling between identical oscillators. It was concluded that the neurons can have a dual role as rhythm generators and as coordinators between oscillators to produce the phase relations observed among segmental oscillators during swimming.

1 INTRODUCTION

One approach to analyzing neurobiological systems is to use simpler preparations that are amenable to techniques which can investigate the cellular, synaptic, and network levels of organization involved in the generation of behavior. This approach has yielded significant progress in the analysis of rhythm pattern generators in several invertebrate preparations (*e.g.*, the stomatogastric ganglion of lobster, Selverston *et al.*, 1983). We have been carrying out similar types of studies of locomotor rhythm generation in a vertebrate preparation, the lamprey spinal cord, which offers many of the same technical advantages of invertebrate nervous systems. To aid our understanding of how identified lamprey interneurons might participate

101

in rhythmogenesis and in the coupling of oscillators, we have used neural network models.

2   FICTIVE SWIMMING

The neuronal correlate of swimming can be induced in the isolated lamprey spinal cord by exposure to glutamate, which is considered to be the principal endogenous excitatory neurotransmitter. As in the intact swimming lamprey, this "fictive" swimming is characterized by periodic bursts of motoneuron action potentials in

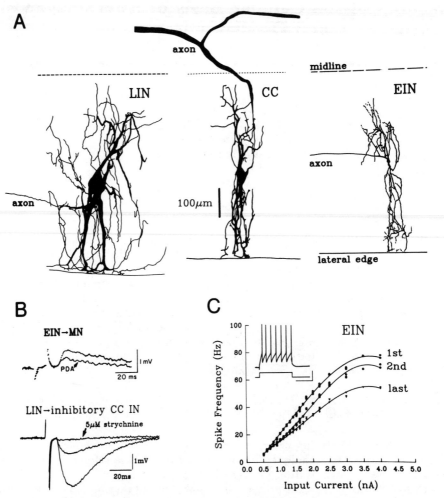

Figure 1: Lamprey spinal interneurons. **A,** drawings of three types of interneurons after intracellular dye injections. **B,** inhibitory and excitatory postsynaptic potentials and the effects of selective antagonists. **C,** firing frequency of the first, second, and last spike intervals during a 400ms current injection.

the ventral roots, and these bursts alternate between sides of the spinal cord and propagate in a head-to-tail direction during forward swimming (Cohen and Wallen, 1980; Wallen and Williams, 1984). Thus, the cellular mechanisms for generating the basic swimming pattern reside within the spinal cord as has been demonstrated for many other vertebrates (Grillner, 1981).

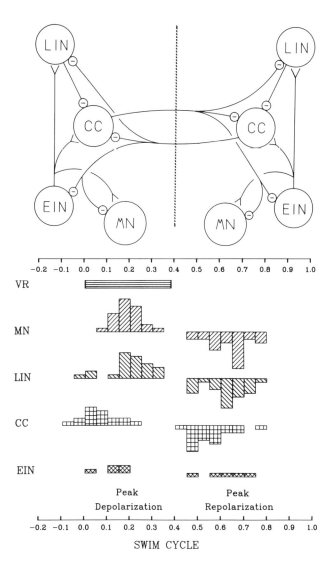

Figure 2: Connectivity and activity patterns. **Top:** synaptic connectivity among the interneurons and motoneurons (MN). **Bottom:** histograms summarizing the activity of cells recorded intracellularly during fictive swimming. Timing of activity of neurons with the onset of the ipsilateral ventral root burst.

The swimming rhythm generator is thought to consist of a chain of coupled oscillators distributed throughout the length of the spinal cord. The isolated spinal cord can be cut into pieces as small as two or three segments in length from any head-to-tail level and still exhibit alternating ventral root bursting upon application of glutamate. The intrinsic swimming frequency in each of these pieces of spinal cord is different by as much as two-fold, and no consistent relationship between intrinsic frequency and the head-to-tail level from which the piece originated has been observed (Cohen, 1986). Thus, coupling among the oscillators must provide some "buffering capacity" to cope with these intrinsic frequency differences. Another feature of the coupling is the constancy of phase lag, such that over a wide range of swimming cycle periods, the delay of ventral root burst onsets between segments is a constant fraction of the cycle period (Wallen and Williams, 1984). Since the cycle period in swimming lamprey can vary over a ten-fold range, axonal conduction time probably is not a factor in the delay between segments.

3 SPINAL INTERNEURONS

In recent years, many classes of spinal neurons have been characterized using a variety of neurobiological techniques, particularly intracellular recording of membrane potential (Rovainen, 1974; Buchanan, 1982; Buchanan et al., 1989). Several of these classes of neurons are active during fictive swimming. These include the lateral interneurons (LIN), cells with axons projecting contralaterally and caudally (CC), and the excitatory interneurons (EIN). The LINs are large neurons with an ipsilaterally and caudally projecting inhibitory axon (Fig. 1A,B). The CC interneurons are medium-sized inhibitory cells (Fig. 1A). The EINs are small interneurons with ipsilaterally and either caudally or rostrally projecting axons (Fig. 1A,B,C). The axons of all these cell types project at least five segments and interact with neurons in multiple segments. The neurons have similar resting and firing properties. They are indistinguishable in their resting potentials, their thresholds, and their action potential amplitudes, durations, and after-spike potentials. Their main differences are size-related parameters such as input resistance and membrane time constant. They fire action potentials throughout the duration of long, depolarizing current pulses, showing some adaptation (a declining frequency with successive action potentials). The plots of spike frequency vs. input current for these various cell types are generally monotonic, with a tendency to saturate at higher levels of input current (Fig. 1C)(Buchanan, 1991).

The synaptic connectivites of these cells have been established with simultaneous intracellular recording of pre- and post-synaptic neurons, and the results are summarized in Fig. 2 along with their activity patterns during fictive swimming. All of the cells exhibit oscillating membrane potentials with depolarizing peaks which tend to occur during the ventral root burst and with repolarizing troughs which occur about one-half cycle later (Buchanan and Cohen 1982). These oscillations appear to be due in large part to two phases of synaptic input: an excitatory depolarizing phase and an inhibitory repolarizing phase (Kahn, 1982; Russell and Wallen, 1983). The excitatory phase of motoneurons comes from EINs and the inhibitory phase from CCs. However, these interneurons not only interact with motoneurons but with other interneurons as well. So the possibility exists that these interneurons provide the synaptic drive for all neurons of the network, not just motoneurons. Additionally, it is possible that rhythmicity itself originates from the pattern of synaptic connectivity because the circuit has a basic alternating network of reciprocal inhibition between CC interneurons on opposite sides of the spinal cord. Reciprocal inhibition as an oscillatory network needs some form of burst-termination, and this could be provided by the feedforward inhibition of ipsilateral CC interneurons by the LINs. This inhibition could also account for the early peak observed in many CC interneurons during fictive swimming (Fig. 2).

4   NEURAL NETWORK MODEL

The ability of the network of Fig. 2 to generate the basic oscillatory pattern of fictive swimming was tested using a "connectionist" neural network simulation (Buchanan, 1992). All of the cells of the neural network had identical S-shaped input-output curves and differed only in their excitatory levels and their synaptic connectivity, which was set according to the scheme of Fig. 2. If the excitation of CCs was made larger than LINs, the network would oscillate (Fig. 3). These oscillations began fairly promptly and could continued for at least thousands of cycles. The phase relations among the units were similar to those in the lamprey: cells on opposite sides of the spinal cord were anti-phasic while most cells on the same side of the cord were co-active. Significantly, both in the model and in the lamprey, the CCs were phase advanced, presumably due to their inhibition by LINs.

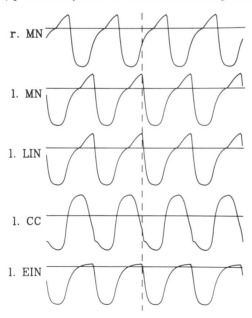

Figure 3: Activity of the neural network model for the lamprey locomotor circuit.

4.1   COUPLING

The neural network model of the lamprey swimming oscillator was further used
to explore how the coupling among locomotor oscillators might be achieved. Two
identical oscillator networks were coupled using the various pairs of cells in one
network connected to pairs of cells in the second network. All nine pairs of possible
connections were tested since all of the interneurons interact with neurons in multiple segments. The coupling was evaluated by several criteria based on observations
of lamprey swimming: 1) the stability of the phase difference between oscillators
and the rate of achieving the steady-state, 2) the ability of the coupling to tolerate
intrinsic frequency differences between oscillators, and 3) the constancy of the phase
lag over a wide range of oscillator frequencies.

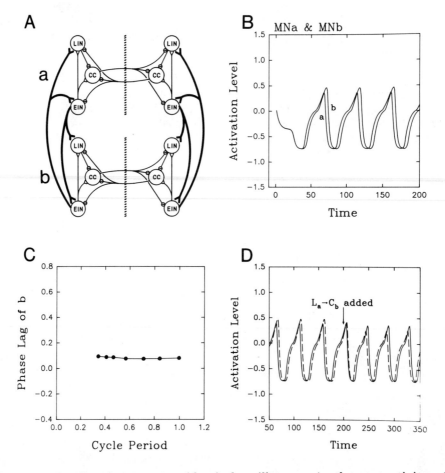

Figure 4: Coupling between two identical oscillators. **A**, the connectivity. **B**,
steady-state coupling within a single cycle. **C**, constancy of phase lag over a range
of oscillator periods. **D**, adding LIN→CC from oscillator a→b, reverses the phase,
simulating backward swimming.

Each of the nine pairs of coupled interneurons between oscillators were capable of producing stable phase locking, although some coupling connections operated over a much wider range of synaptic weights than others. The steady-state phase difference between the oscillators and the rate of reaching it were also dependent on the synaptic weight of the coupling connections. The direction of the phase difference, that is, whether the postsynaptic oscillator was lagging or leading, depended both on the type of postsynaptic cell and the sign of the coupling input to it. If the postsynaptic cell was one which speeds the network (LIN or EIN) then their excitation by the coupling connection produced a lead of the postsynaptic network and their inhibition produced a lag. The opposite pattern held for CCs, which slow the network.

An example of a coupling scheme that satisfied several criteria for lamprey-like coupling is shown in Fig. 4. In this case (Fig. 4A), there was bidirectional, symmetric coupling of EINs in the two oscillators. This gave the network the ability to tolerate intrinsic frequency differences between the oscillators (buffering capacity). To provide a phase lag of oscillator b, EINs were connected to LINs bidirectionally but with greater weight in one direction (b→a). Such coupling reached a steady-state within a single cycle (Fig. 4B), and the phase difference was maintained at the same value over a range of cycle periods (Fig. 4C).

4.2 BACKWARD SWIMMING

It has been shown recently that there is rhythmic presynaptic inhibition of interneuronal axons in the lamprey spinal cord (Alford et al., 1990). This type of cycle-by-cycle modulation of synaptic strength could account for shifts in phase coupling in the lamprey, such as occurs when the animal switches to brief bouts of backward swimming. One mechanism for backward swimming might be the inhibitory connection of LIN→CCs. The LINs have axons which descend up to 50 segments (one-half body length). In the neural network model, this descending inhibition of CC interneurons promotes backward swimming, i.e. a phase lead of the postsynaptic oscillators. Thus, presynaptic inhibition of these connections in nonlocal segments would allow forward swimming, while a removal of this presynaptic inhibition would initiate backward swimming (Fig. 4D).

5 CONCLUSIONS

The modeling described here demonstrates that the identified interneurons in the lamprey spinal cord may be multi-functional. They are known to contribute to the synaptic input to motoneurons during fictive swimming and thus to the shaping of the final motor output, but they may also function as components of the rhythm generating network itself. Finally, by virtue of their multi-segmental connections, they may have the additional role of providing the coupling signals among oscillators. Further experimental work will be required to determine which of these connections are actually used in the lamprey spinal cord for these functions.

References

S. Alford, J. Christenson, & S. Grillner. (1990) Presynaptic $GABA_A$ and $GABA_B$ receptor-mediated phasic modulation in axons of spinal motor interneurons. *Eur. J. Neurosci.*, **3**:107-117.

J.T. Buchanan. (1982) Identification of interneurons with contralateral, caudal axons in the lamprey spinal cord: synaptic interactions and morphology. *J. Neurophysiol.*, **47**:961-975.

J.T. Buchanan. (1991) Electrophysiological properties of lamprey spinal neurons. *Soc. Neurosci. Abstr.*, **17**:1581.

J.T. Buchanan. (1992) Neural network simulations of coupled locomotor oscillators in the lamprey spinal cord. *Biol. Cybern.*, **74**: in press.

J.T. Buchanan & A.H. Cohen. (1982) Activities of identified interneurons, motoneurons, and muscle fibers during fictive swimming in the lamprey and effects of reticulospinal and dorsal cell stimulation. *J. Neurophysiol.*, **47**:948-960.

J.T. Buchanan, S. Grillner, S. Cullheim, & M. Risling. (1989) Identification of excitatory interneurons contributing to generation of locomotion in lamprey: structure, pharmacology, and function. *J. Neurophysiol.*, **62**:59-69.

A.H. Cohen. (1986) The intersegmental coordinating system of the lamprey: experimental and theoretical studies. In S. Grillner, P.S.G. Stein, D.G. Stuart, H. Forssberg, R.M. Herman (eds.), *Neurobiology of Vertebrate Locomotion*, 371-382. London: Macmillan.

A.H. Cohen & P. Wallen. (1980) The neuronal correlate of locomotion in fish: "fictive swimming" induced in an in vitro preparation of the lamprey spinal cord. *Exp. Brain Res.*, **41**:11-18.

S. Grillner. (1981) Control of locomotion in bipeds, tetrapods, and fish. In V.B. Brooks (ed.), *Handbook of Physiology, Sect. 1. The Nervous System Vol. II. Motor Control*, 1179-1236. Maryland: Waverly Press.

J.A. Kahn. (1982) Patterns of synaptic inhibtion in motoneurons and interneurons during fictive swimming in the lamprey, as revealed by Cl^- injections. *J. Comp. Neurol.*, **147**:189-194.

C.M. Rovainen. (1974) Synaptic interactions of identified nerve cells in the spinal cord of the sea lamprey. *J. Comp. Neurol.*, **154**:189-204.

D.F. Russell & P. Wallen. (1983) On the control of myotomal motoneurones during "fictive swimming" in the lamprey spinal cord in vitro. *Acta Physiol. Scand.*, **117**:161-170.

A.I. Selverston, J.P. Miller, & M. Wadepuhl. (1983) Cooperative mechanisms for the production of rhythmic movements. *Sym. Soc. Exp. Biol.*, **37**:55-88.

P. Wallen & T.L. Williams. (1984) Fictive locomotion in the lamprey spinal cord in vitro compared with swimming in the intact and spinal animal. *J. Physiol.*, **64**:862-871.

Adaptive Synchronization of Neural and Physical Oscillators

Kenji Doya
University of California, San Diego
La Jolla, CA 92093-0322, USA

Shuji Yoshizawa
University of Tokyo
Bunkyo-ku, Tokyo 113, Japan

Abstract

Animal locomotion patterns are controlled by recurrent neural networks called central pattern generators (CPGs). Although a CPG can oscillate autonomously, its rhythm and phase must be well coordinated with the state of the physical system using sensory inputs. In this paper we propose a learning algorithm for synchronizing neural and physical oscillators with specific phase relationships. Sensory input connections are modified by the correlation between cellular activities and input signals. Simulations show that the learning rule can be used for setting sensory feedback connections to a CPG as well as coupling connections between CPGs.

1 CENTRAL AND SENSORY MECHANISMS IN LOCOMOTION CONTROL

Patterns of animal locomotion, such as walking, swimming, and flying, are generated by recurrent neural networks that are located in segmental ganglia of invertebrates and spinal cords of vertebrates (Barnes and Gladden, 1985). These networks can produce basic rhythms of locomotion without sensory inputs and are called central pattern generators (CPGs). The physical systems of locomotion, such as legs, fins, and wings combined with physical environments, have their own oscillatory characteristics. Therefore, in order to realize efficient locomotion, the frequency and the phase of oscillation of a CPG must be well coordinated with the state of the physical system. For example, the bursting patterns of motoneurons that drive a leg muscle must be coordinated with the configuration of the leg, its contact with the ground, and the state of other legs.

The oscillation pattern of a CPG is largely affected by proprioceptive inputs. It has been shown in crayfish (Siller et al., 1986) and lamprey (Grillner et al, 1990) that the oscillation of a CPG is entrained by cyclic stimuli to stretch sensory neurons over a wide range of frequency. Both negative and positive feedback pathways are found in those systems. Elucidation of the function of the sensory inputs to CPGs requires computational studies of neural and physical dynamical systems. Algorithms for the learning of rhythmic patterns in recurrent neural networks have been derived by Doya and Yoshizawa (1989), Pearlmutter (1989), and Williams and Zipser (1989). In this paper we propose a learning algorithm for synchronizing a neural oscillator to rhythmic input signals with a specific phase relationship.

It is well known that a coupling between nonlinear oscillators can entrainment their frequencies. The relative phase between oscillators is determined by the parameters of coupling and the difference of their intrinsic frequencies. For example, either in-phase or anti-phase oscillation results from symmetric coupling between neural oscillators with similar intrinsic frequencies (Kawato and Suzuki, 1980). Efficient locomotion involves subtle phase relationships between physical variables and motor commands. Accordingly, our goal is to derive a learning algorithm that can finely tune the sensory input connections by which the relative phase between physical and neural oscillators is kept at a specific value required by the task.

2   LEARNING OF SYNCHRONIZATION

We will deal with the following continuous-time model of a CPG network.

$$\tau_i \frac{d}{dt} x_i(t) = -x_i(t) + \sum_{j=1}^{C} w_{ij} g_j(x_j(t)) + \sum_{k=1}^{S} v_{ik} y_k(t), \tag{1}$$

where $x_i(t)$ and $g_i(x_i(t))$ $(i = 1, \ldots, C)$ represent the states and the outputs of CPG neurons and $y_k(t)$ $(k = 1, \ldots, S)$ represents sensory inputs. We assume that the connection weights $W = \{w_{ij}\}$ are already established so that the network oscillates without sensory inputs. The goal of learning is to find the input connection weights $V = \{v_{ij}\}$ that make the network state $\mathbf{x}(t) = (x_1(t), \ldots, x_C(t))^t$ entrained to the input signal $\mathbf{y}(t) = (y_1(t), \ldots, y_S(t))^t$ with a specific relative phase.

2.1   AN OBJECTIVE FUNCTION FOR PHASE-LOCKING

The standard way to derive a learning algorithm is to find out an objective function to be minimized. If we can approximate the waveforms of $x_i(t)$ and $y_k(t)$ by sine waves, a linear relationship

$$\mathbf{x}(t) = P\,\mathbf{y}(t)$$

specifies a phase-locked oscillation of $\mathbf{x}(t)$ and $\mathbf{y}(t)$. For example, if we have $y_1 = \sin \omega t$ and $y_2 = \cos \omega t$, then a matrix $P = \begin{pmatrix} 1 & 1 \\ 1 & \sqrt{3} \end{pmatrix}$ specifies $x_1 = \sqrt{2} \sin(\omega t + \pi/4)$ and $x_2 = 2\sin(\omega t + \pi/3)$. Even when the waveforms are not sinusoidal, minimization of an objective function

$$E(t) = \frac{1}{2} \|\mathbf{x}(t) - P\mathbf{y}(t)\|^2 = \frac{1}{2} \sum_{i=1}^{C} \{x_i(t) - \sum_{k=1}^{S} p_{ik} y_k(t)\}^2 \tag{2}$$

determines a specific relative phase between $\mathbf{x}(t)$ and $\mathbf{y}(t)$. Thus we call $P = \{p_{ik}\}$ a phase-lock matrix.

2.2 LEARNING PROCEDURE

Using the above objective function, we will derive a learning procedure for phase-locked oscillation of $\mathbf{x}(t)$ and $\mathbf{y}(t)$. First, an appropriate phase-lock matrix P is identified while the relative phase between $\mathbf{x}(t)$ and $\mathbf{y}(t)$ changes gradually in time. Then, a feedback mechanism can be applied so that the network state $\mathbf{x}(t)$ is kept close to the target waveform $P\,\mathbf{y}(t)$.

Suppose we actually have an appropriate phase relationship between $\mathbf{x}(t)$ and $\mathbf{y}(t)$, then the phase-lock matrix P can be obtained by gradient descent of $E(t)$ with respect to p_{ik} as follows (Widrow and Stearns, 1985).

$$\frac{d}{dt}p_{ik} = -\eta\,\frac{\partial E(t)}{\partial p_{ik}} = \eta\,\{x_i(t) - \sum_{j=1}^{S} p_{ij}\,y_j(t)\}\,y_k(t). \tag{3}$$

If the coupling between $\mathbf{x}(t)$ and $\mathbf{y}(t)$ are weak enough, their relative phase changes in time unless their intrinsic frequencies are exactly equal and the systems are completely noiseless. By modulating the learning coefficient η by some performance index of the total system, for example, the speed of locomotion, it is possible to obtain a matrix P that satisfies the requirement of the task.

Once a phase-lock matrix is derived, we can control $\mathbf{x}(t)$ close to $P\,\mathbf{y}(t)$ using the gradient of $E(t)$ with respect to the network state

$$\frac{\partial E(t)}{\partial x_i(t)} = x_i(t) - \sum_{k=1}^{S} p_{ik}\,y_k(t).$$

The simplest feedback algorithm is to add this term to the CPG dynamics as follows.

$$\tau_i\frac{d}{dt}x_i(t) = -x_i(t) + \sum_{j=1}^{C} w_{ij}\,g_j(x_j(t)) - \alpha\{x_i(t) - \sum_{k=1}^{S} p_{ik}\,y_k(t)\}.$$

The feedback gain $\alpha\,(> 0)$ must be set small enough so that the feedback term does not destroy the intrinsic oscillation of the CPG. In that case, by neglecting the small additional decay term $\alpha x_i(t)$, we have

$$\tau_i\frac{d}{dt}x_i(t) = -x_i(t) + \sum_{j=1}^{C} w_{ij}\,g_j(x_j(t)) + \sum_{k=1}^{S} \alpha p_{ik}\,y_k(t), \tag{4}$$

which is equivalent to the equation (1) with input weights $v_{ik} = \alpha p_{ik}$.

3   DELAYED SYNCHRONIZATION

We tested the above learning scheme on a delayed synchronization task; to find coupling weights between neural oscillators so that they synchronize with a specific time delay. We used the following coupled CPG model.

$$\tau \frac{d}{dt} x_i^n(t) = -x_i^n(t) + \sum_{j=1}^{C} w_{ij}^n y_j^n(t) + \alpha \sum_{k=1}^{C} p_{ik}^n y_k^{3-n}(t), \tag{5}$$

$$y_i^n(t) = g(x_i^n(t)), \qquad (i = 1, \ldots, C),$$

where superscripts denote the indices of two CPGs ($n = 1, 2$). The goal of learning was to synchronize the waveforms $y_1^1(t)$ and $y_1^2(t)$ with a time delay ΔT. We used

$$z(t) = -|y_1^1(t - \Delta T) - y_1^2(t)|$$

as the performance index. The learning coefficient η of equation (3) was modulated by the deviation of $z(t)$ from its running average $\bar{z}(t)$ using the following equations.

$$\eta(t) = \eta_0 \{z(t) - \bar{z}(t)\}, \qquad \tau_a \frac{d}{dt} \bar{z}(t) = -\bar{z}(t) + z(t). \tag{6}$$

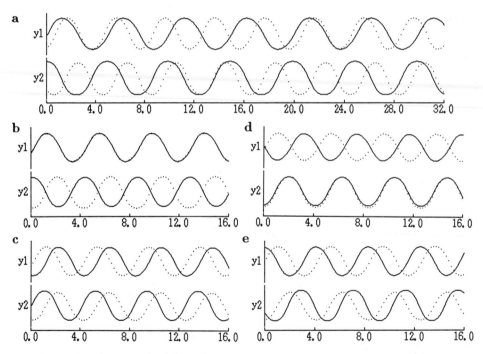

Figure 1: Learning of delayed synchronization of neural oscillators. The dotted and solid curves represent $y_i^1(t)$ and $y_i^2(t)$ respectively. **a**:without coupling. **b**:$\Delta T = 0.0$. **c**:$\Delta T = 1.0$. **c**:$\Delta T = 2.0$. **d**:$\Delta T = 3.0$.

First, two CPGs were trained independently to oscillate with sinusoidal waveforms of period $T_1 = 4.0$ and $T_2 = 5.0$ using continuous-time back-propagation learning (Doya and Yoshizawa, 1989). Each CPG was composed of two neurons ($C = 2$) with time constants $\tau = 1.0$ and output functions $g(\ ) = \tanh(\ )$. Instead of following the two step procedure described in the previous section, the network dynamics (5) and the learning equations (3) and (6) were simulated concurrently with parameters $\alpha = 0.1$, $\eta_0 = 0.2$, and $\tau_a = 20.0$.

Figure 1 **a** shows the oscillation of two CPGs without coupling. Figures 1 **b** through **e** show the phase-locked waveforms after learning for 200 time units with different desired delay times.

4   ZERO-LEGGED LOCOMOTION

Next we applied the learning rule to the simplest locomotion system that involves a critical phase-lock between the state of the physical system and the motor command—a zero-legged locomotion system as shown in Figure 2 **a**.

The physical system is composed of a wheel and a weight that moves back and forth on a track fixed radially in the wheel. It rolls on the ground by changing its balance with the displacement of the weight. In order to move the wheel in a given direction, the weight must be moved at a specific phase with the rotation angle of the wheel. The motion equations are shown in Appendix.

First, a CPG network was trained to oscillate with a sinusoidal waveform of period $T = 1.0$ (Doya and Yoshizawa, 1989). The network consisted of one output and two hidden units ($C = 3$) with time constants $\tau_i = 0.2$ and output functions $g_i(\ ) = \tanh(\ )$. Next, the output of the CPG was used to drive the weight with a force $f = f_{\max} g_1(x_1(t))$. The position r and the velocity $\dot{r}$ of the weight and the rotation angle $(\cos\theta, \sin\theta)$ and the angular velocity of the wheel $\dot{\theta}$ were used as sensory feedback inputs $y_k(t)$ $(k = 1, \ldots, 5)$ after scaling to $[-1, 1]$.

In order to eliminate the effect of biases in $\mathbf{x}(t)$ and $\mathbf{y}(t)$, we used the following learning equations.

$$\frac{d}{dt} p_{ik} = \eta \left\{ (x_i(t) - \bar{x}_i(t)) - \sum_{j=1}^{S} p_{ij}(y_j(t) - \bar{y}_j(t)) \right\} (y_k(t) - \bar{y}_k(t)),$$

$$\tau_x \frac{d}{dt} \bar{x}_i(t) = -\bar{x}_i(t) + x_i(t), \qquad (7)$$

$$\tau_y \frac{d}{dt} \bar{y}_k(t) = -\bar{y}_k(t) + y_k(t).$$

The rotation speed of the wheel was employed as the performance index $z(t)$ after smoothing by the following equation.

$$\tau_s \frac{d}{dt} z(t) = -z(t) + \dot{\theta}(t).$$

The learning coefficient η was modulated by equations (6). The time constants were $\tau_x = 4.0$, $\tau_y = 1.0$, $\tau_s = 1.0$, and $\tau_a = 4.0$. Each training run was started from a random configuration of the wheel and was finished after ten seconds.

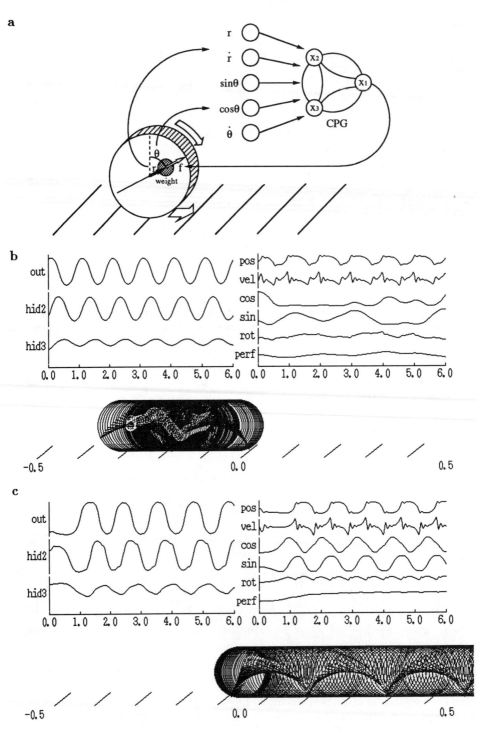

Figure 2: Learning of zero-legged locomotion.

Figure 2 b is an example of the motion of the wheel without sensory feedback. The rhythms of the CPG and the physical system were not entrained to each other and the wheel wandered left and right. Figure 2 c shows an example of the wheel motion after 40 runs of training with parameters $\eta_0 = 0.1$ and $\alpha = 0.2$. At first, the oscillation of the CPG was slowed down by the sensory inputs and then accelerated with the rotation of the wheel in the right direction.

We compared the patterns of sensory input connections made after learning with wheels of different sizes. Table 1 shows the connection weights to the output unit. The positive connection from $\sin \theta$ forces the weight to the right-hand side of the wheel and stabilize clockwise rotation. The negative connection from $\cos \theta$ with smaller radius fastens the rhythm of the CPG when the wheel rotates too fast and the weight is lifted up. The positive input from r with larger radius makes the weight stickier to both ends of the track and slows down the rhythm of the CPG.

Table 1: Sensory input weights to the output unit ($p_{1k}; k = 1, \ldots, 5$).

radius	r	$\dot{r}$	$\cos \theta$	$\sin \theta$	$\dot{\theta}$
2cm	0.15	-0.53	-1.35	1.32	0.07
4cm	0.28	-0.55	-1.09	1.22	0.01
6cm	0.67	-0.21	-0.41	0.98	0.00
8cm	0.70	-0.33	-0.40	0.92	0.03
10cm	0.90	-0.12	-0.30	0.93	-0.02

5   DISCUSSION

The architectures of CPGs in lower vertebrates and invertebrates are supposed to be determined by genetic information. Nevertheless, the way an animal utilizes the sensory inputs must be adaptive to the characteristics of the physical environments and the changing dimensions of its body parts.

Back-propagation through forward models of physical systems can also be applied to the learning of sensory feedback (Jordan and Jacobs, 1990). However, learning of nonlinear dynamics of locomotion systems is a difficult task; moreover, multi-layer back-propagation is not appropriate as a biological model of learning. The learning rule (7) is similar to the covariance learning rule (Sejnowski and Stanton, 1990), which is a biological model of long term potentiation of synapses.

Acknowledgements

The authors thank Allen Selverston, Peter Rowat, and those who gave comments to our poster at NIPS Conference. This work was partly supported by grants from the Ministry of Education, Culture, and Science of Japan.

References

Barnes, W. J. P. & Gladden, M. H. (1985) *Feedback and Motor Control in Invertebrates and Vertebrates*. Beckenham, Britain: Croom Helm.

Doya, K. & Yoshizawa, S. (1989) Adaptive neural oscillator using continuous-time back-propagation learning. *Neural Networks*, **2**, 375–386.

Grillner, S. & Matsushima, T. (1991) The neural network underlying locomotion in Lamprey—Synaptic and cellular mechanisms. *Neuron*, **7**(July), 1-15.

Jordan, M. I. & Jacobs, R. A. (1990) Learning to control an unstable system with forward modeling. In Touretzky, D. S. (ed.), *Advances in Neural Information Processing Systems 2*. San Mateo, CA: Morgan Kaufmann.

Kawato, M. & Suzuki, R. (1980) Two coupled neural oscillators as a model of the circadian pacemaker. *Journal of Theoretical Biology*, **86**, 547–575.

Pearlmutter, B. A. (1989) Learning state space trajectories in recurrent neural networks. *Neural Computation*, **1**, 263–269.

Sejnowski, T. J. & Stanton, P. K. (1990) Covariance storage in the Hippocampus. In Zornetzer, S. F. et al. (eds.), *An Introduction to Neural and Electronic Networks*, 365–377. San Diego, CA: Academic Press.

Siller, K. T., Skorupski, P., Elson, R. C., & Bush, M. H. (1986) Two identified afferent neurones entrain a central locomotor rhythm generator. *Nature*, **323**, 440–443.

Widrow, B. & Stearns, S. D. (1985) *Adaptive Signal Processing*. Englewood Cliffs, NJ: Prentice Hall.

Williams, R. J. & Zipser, D. (1989) A learning algorithm for continually running fully recurrent neural networks. *Neural Computation*, **1**, 270–280.

Appendix

The dynamics of the zero-legged locomotion system:

$$
m\ddot{r} = f_0(1 + \frac{mR^2 \sin^2 \theta}{I_0}) - mg_c(\cos\theta + \frac{mR\sin^2\theta(r + R\cos\theta)}{I_0})
$$
$$
+ mR\sin\theta\frac{\nu + 2m\dot{r}(r + R\cos\theta)}{I_0}\dot{\theta} + mr\dot{\theta}^2,
$$
$$
I_0\ddot{\theta} = -f_0 R\sin\theta + mg_c\sin\theta(r + R\cos\theta) - (\nu + 2m\dot{r}(r + R\cos\theta))\dot{\theta},
$$
$$
f_0 = f_{\max} g(x_1(t)) - \sigma r^3 - \mu\dot{r},
$$
$$
I_0 = I + MR^2 + m(r + R\cos\theta)^2.
$$

Parameters: the masses of the weight $m = 0.2$[kg] and the wheel $M = 0.8$[kg]; the radius of the wheel $R = 0.02$through0.1[m]; the inertial moment of the wheel $I = \frac{1}{2}MR^2$; the maximum force to the weight $f_{\max} = 5$[N]; the stiffness of the limiter of the weight $\sigma = 20/R^3$ [N/m^3]; the damping coefficients of the weight motion $\mu = 0.2/R$ [N/(m/s)] and the wheel rotation $\nu = 0.05(M+m)R$ [N/(rad/s)].

Burst Synchronization Without Frequency-Locking in a Completely Solvable Network Model

Heinz Schuster
Institut für theoretische Physik
Universität Kiel
Olshausenstraße 40
2300 Kiel 1, Germany

Christof Koch
Computation and Neural System Program
California Institute of Technology
Pasadena, California 91125, USA

Abstract

The dynamic behavior of a network model consisting of all-to-all excitatory coupled binary neurons with global inhibition is studied analytically and numerically. We prove that for random input signals, the output of the network consists of synchronized bursts with apparently random intermissions of noisy activity. Our results suggest that synchronous bursts can be generated by a simple neuronal architecture which amplifies incoming coincident signals. This synchronization process is accompanied by dampened oscillations which, by themselves, however, do not play any constructive role in this and can therefore be considered to be an epiphenomenon.

1 INTRODUCTION

Recently synchronization phenomena in neural networks have attracted considerable attention. Gray *et al.* (1989, 1990) as well as Eckhorn *et al.* (1988) provided electrophysiological evidence that neurons in the visual cortex of cats discharge in a semi-synchronous, oscillatory manner in the $40\,Hz$ range and that the firing activity of neurons up to $10\,mm$ away is phase-locked with a mean phase-shift of less than $3\,msec$. It has been proposed that this phase synchronization can solve the binding problem for figure-ground segregation (von der Malsburg and Schneider, 1986) and underly visual attention and awareness (Crick and Koch, 1990).

A number of theoretical explanations based on coupled (relaxation) oscillator models have been proposed for burst synchronization (Sompolinsky *et al.*, 1990). The crucial issue of phase synchronization has also recently been addressed by Bush and Douglas (1991), who simulated the dynamics of a network consisting of bursty, layer V pyramidal cells coupled to a common pool of basket cells inhibiting all pyramidal cells.[1] Bush and Douglas found that excitatory interactions between the pyramidal cells increases the total neural activity as expected and that global inhibition leads to synchronized bursts with random intermissions. These population bursts appear to occur in a random manner in their model. The basic mechanism for the observed burst synchronization is hidden in the numerous anatomical and biophysical details of their model. These, and the related observation that to date no strong oscillations have been recorded in the neuronal activity in visual cortex of awake monkeys, prompted us to investigate how phase synchronization can occur in the absence of frequency locking.

2   A COINCIDENCE NETWORK

We consider n excitatory coupled binary McCulloch-Pitts (1943) neurons whose output $x_i^{t+1} \in [0, 1]$ at time $t + 1$ is given by:

$$x_i^{t+1} = \sigma \left[\frac{\omega}{n} \sum_i x_i^t + \xi_i^t - \theta \right] \tag{1}$$

Here $\omega/n > 1$ is the normalized excitatory all-to-all synaptic coupling, ξ_i^t represents the external binary input and $\sigma[z]$ is the Heaviside step function, such that $\sigma[z] = 1$ for $z > 0$ and 0 elsewhere. Each neuron has the same dynamic threshold $\theta > 0$. Next we introduce the fraction m^t of neurons which fire simultaneously at time t:

$$m^t = \frac{1}{n} \sum_i x_i^t \tag{2}$$

In general, $0 \leq m^t \leq 1$; only if every neuron is active at time t do we have $m^t = 1$. By summing eq. (1) we obtain the following equation of motion for our simple network.

$$m^{t+1} = \frac{1}{n} \sum_i \sigma[\omega m^t + \xi_i^t - \theta] \tag{3}$$

The behavior of this (n+1)-state automata is fully described by the phase-state diagram of Figure 1. If $\theta > 1$ and $\theta/\omega > 1$, the output of the network m^t will vary with the input until at some time t', $m^{t'} = 0$. Since the threshold θ is always larger than the input, the network will remain in this state for all subsequent times. If $\theta < 1$ and $\theta/\omega < 1$, the network will drift until it comes to the state $m^{t'} = 1$. Since subsequent ωm^t is at all times larger than the threshold, the network remains latched at $m^t = 1$. If $\theta > 1$, but $\theta/\omega < 1$, the network can latch in either the $m^t = 0$ or the $m^t = 1$ state and will remain there indefinitely. Lastly, if $\theta < 1$, but $\theta/\omega > 1$, the threshold is by itself not large enough to keep the network latched

---

[1]This model bears similarities to Wilson and Bower's (1992) model describing the origin of phase-locking in olfactory cortex.

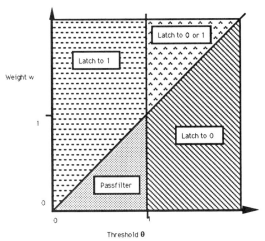

Figure 1: Phase diagram for the network described by eq. (3). Different regions correspond to different stationary output states m^t in the long time limit.

into the $m^t = 1$ state. Defining the normalized input activity as

$$s^t = \frac{1}{n} \sum_i \xi_i^t \tag{4}$$

with $0 \le s^t \le 1$, we see that in this part of phase space $m^{t+1} = s^t$, and the output activity faithfully reflects the input activity at the previous time step.

Let us introduce an adaptive time-dependent threshold, θ^t. We assume that θ^t remains at its value $\theta < 1$ as long as the total activity remains less than 1. If, however, $m^t = 1$, we increase θ^t to a value larger than $\omega + 1$. This has the effect of resetting the activity of the entire network to 0 in the next time step, i.e., $m^{t+1} = (1/n) \sum_i \sigma(\omega + \xi_i - (\omega + 1 + \epsilon)) = 0$. The threshold will then automatically reset itself to its old value:

$$m^{t+1} = \frac{1}{n} \sum_i \sigma[\omega m^t + \xi_i^t - \theta(m^t)] \tag{5}$$

with

$$\theta(m^t) = \begin{cases} \theta < 1 & \text{for } m^t < 1 \\ > \omega + 1 & \text{for } m^t = 1 \end{cases}$$

Therefore, we are operating in the topmost left part of Fig. 1 but preventing the network from latching to $m^t = 1$ by resetting it. Such a dynamic threshold bears some similarities to the models of Horn and Usher (1990) and others, but is much simpler. Note that $\theta(m^t)$ exactly mimics the effect of a common inhibitory neuron which is only excited if all neurons fire simultaneously.

Our network now acts as a coincidence detector, such that all neurons will "fire" at time $t + 2$, i.e., $m_1^{t+2} = 1$ if at least k neurons receive at time t a "1" as input. k is the smallest integer with $k > \theta \cdot n/\omega$. The threshold $\theta(m^t)$ is then transiently increased and the network is reset and the game begins anew. In other words, the

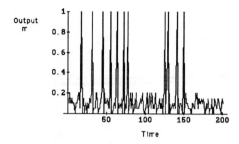

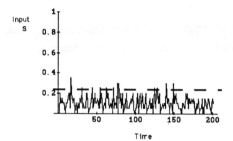

Figure 2: Time dependence of the fraction m^t of output neurons which fire simultaneously compared to the corresponding fraction of input signals s^t for $n = 20$ and $\theta/\omega = 0.225$. The input variables ξ_i^t are independently distributed according to $P(\xi_i^t) = p\delta(\xi_i^t - 1) + (1-p)\delta(\xi_i^t)$ with $p = 0.1$. If more than five input signals with $\xi_i^t = 1$ coincide, the entire population will fire in synchrony two time steps later, i.e. $m^{t+2} = 1$. Note the "random" appearance of the interburst intervals.

network detects coincidences and signals this by a synchronized burst of neuronal activity followed by a brief respite of activity (Figure 2).

The time dependence of m^t given by eq. (5) can be written as:

$$m^{t+1} = \begin{cases} s^t & \text{for } 0 \leq m^t < \frac{\theta}{\omega} \\ 1 & \text{for } \frac{\theta}{\omega} \leq m^t < 1 \\ 0 & \text{for } m^t = 1 \end{cases} \qquad (6)$$

By introducing functions $A(m)$, $B(m)$, $C(m)$ which take on the value 1 in the intervals specified for $m = m^t$ in eq. (6), respectively, and zero elsewhere, m^{t+1} can be written as:

$$m^{t+1} = s^t A(m^t) + 1 \cdot B(m^t) + 0 \cdot C(m^t) \qquad (7)$$

This equation can be iterated, yielding an explicit expression for m^t as a function of the external inputs $s^{t+1}, \ldots s^0$ and the initial value m^0:

$$m^t = (s^{t-1}, 1, 0) M(s^{t-2}) \ldots M(s^0) \begin{pmatrix} A(m^0) \\ B(m^0) \\ C(m^0) \end{pmatrix} \qquad (8)$$

with the matrix

$$M(s) = \begin{pmatrix} A(s) & 0 & 1 \\ B(s) & 0 & 0 \\ C(s) & 1 & 0 \end{pmatrix}$$

Eq. (8) shows that the dynamics of the network can be solved explicitly, by iteratively applying M, $t - 1$ number of times to the initial network configuration.

3   DISTRIBUTION OF BURSTS AND TIME CORRELATIONS

The synchronous activity at time t depends on the specific realization of the input signals at different times (eq. 8). In order to get rid of this ambiguity we resort to averaged quantities where averages are understood over the distribution $\hat{P}\{s^t\}$ of inputs $s^t = \frac{1}{n}\sum_{i=1}^{n}\xi_i^t$. A very useful averaged quantity is the probability $P^t(m)$, describing the fraction m of simultaneously firing neurons at time t. $P^t(m)$ is related to the probability distribution $P\{s^t\}$ via:

$$P^t(m) = \langle\delta[m - m^t\{s^{t-1}, \ldots s^0\}]\rangle) \qquad (9)$$

where $\langle\ldots\rangle$ denotes the average with respect to $\hat{P}\{s^t\}$ and $m^t\{s^{t-1}, \ldots s^0\}$ is given by eq. (8). If the input signals ξ_i^t are uncorrelated in time, m^{t+1} depends according to eq. (7) only on m^t, and the time evolution of $P^t(m)$ can be described by the Chapman-Kolmogorov equation. We then find:

$$P^t(m) = P^\infty(m) + [P^0(m) - P^\infty(m)] \cdot f(t) \qquad (10)$$

where

$$P^\infty(m) = \frac{1}{1 + 2\eta}[\hat{P}(m) + \eta\delta(m - 1) + \eta\delta(m)] \qquad (11)$$

is the limiting distribution which evolves from the initial distribution $P^0(m)$ for large times, because the factor $f(t) = \eta^{\frac{t}{2}}\cos(\Omega t)$, where $\Omega = \pi - \arctan[\sqrt{4\eta - \eta^2}/\eta]$, decays exponentially with time and $\eta = \int_0^1 \hat{P}(s)B(s)ds = \int_{\theta/\omega}^1 \hat{P}(s)ds$. Notice that $0 \leq \eta \leq 1$ holds (for more details, see Koch and Schuster, 1992).

The limiting equilibrium distribution $P^\infty(m)$ evolves from the initial distribution $P^0(m)$ in an oscillatory fashion, with the building up of two delta-functions at $m = 1$ and $m = 0$ at the expense of $P^0(m)$. This signals the emergence of synchronous bursts, i.e., $m^t = 1$, which are always followed at the next time-step by zero activity, i.e., $m^{t+1} = 0$ (see also Fig. 2). The equilibrium value for the mean fraction of synchronized neurons is

$$\langle m^\infty\rangle = \int_0^1 dm P^\infty(m)m = \frac{\langle s\rangle + \eta}{1 + 2\eta} \qquad (12)$$

which is larger than the initial value $\langle s\rangle = \int_0^1 ds P(s)s$, for $\langle s\rangle < \frac{1}{2}$, indicating an increase in synchronized bursting activity.

It is interesting to ask what type of time correlations will develop in the output of our network if it is stimulated with uncorrelated noise, ξ_i^t. The autocovariance function is

$$C(\tau) = \lim_{t\to\infty}[\langle m^{t+\tau}m^t\rangle - \langle m^t\rangle^2], \qquad (13)$$

can be computed directly since m^t and $P^\infty(m)$ are known explicitly. We find

$$C(\tau) = \delta_{\tau,0}C_0 + (1 - \delta_{\tau,0})C_1\eta^{|\tau|/2}\cos(\Omega\tau + \varphi) \qquad (14)$$

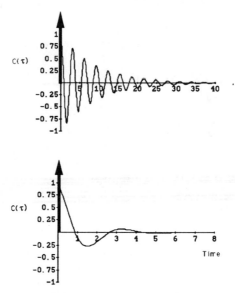

Figure 3: Time dependence of the auto-covariance function $C(\tau)$ for two different values of $\eta = \int_{\theta/\omega}^{1} ds\, \hat{P}(s)$. The top figure corresponds to $\eta = 0.8$ and a period $T = 3.09$, while the bottom correlation function is for $\eta = 0.2$ with an associated $T = 3.50$. Note the different time-scales.

with $\delta_{\tau,0}$ the Kroneker symbol ($\delta_{\tau,0} = 1$ for $\tau = 0$ and 0 else). Figure 3 shows that $C(\tau)$ consists of two parts. A delta peak at $\tau = 0$ which reflects random uncorrelated bursting and an oscillatory decaying part which indicates correlations in the output. The period of the oscillations, $T = 2\pi/\Omega$, varies monotonically between $3 \leq T \leq 4$ as θ/ω moves from zero to one. Since η is given by $\int_{\theta/\omega}^{1} \hat{P}(s)ds$, we see that the strengths of these oscillations increases as the excitatory coupling ω increases. The emergence of periodic correlations can be understood in the limit $\theta/\omega \to 0$, where the period T becomes three (and $\eta = \int_{0}^{1} \hat{P}(s)ds = 1$), because according to eq. (6), $m^t = 0$ is followed by $m^{t+1} = s^t$ which leads for $\theta/\omega \to 0$ always to $m^{t+2} = 1$ followed by $m^{t+3} = 0$. In other words, the temporal dynamics of m^t has the form $0s^110s^410s^710s^{10}10....$ In the opposite case of $\theta/\omega \to 1$, η converges to 0 and the autocovariance function $C(\tau)$ essentially only contains the peak at $\tau = 0$. Thus, the output of the network ranges from completely uncorrelated noise for $\theta/\omega \approx 1$ to correlated periodic bursts for $\frac{\theta}{\omega} \to 0$. The power spectrum of the system is a broad Lorentzian centered at the oscillation frequency, superimposed onto a constant background corresponding to uncorrelated neural activity.

It is important to discuss in this context the effect of the size n of the network. If the input variables ξ_i^t are distributed independently in time and space with probabilities $\tilde{P}_i(\xi_i^t)$, then the distribution $\hat{P}(s)$ has a width which decreases as $1/\sqrt{n}$ as $n \to \infty$. Therefore, in a large system $\eta = \int_{\theta/\omega}^{1} \hat{P}(s)ds$ is either 0 if $\theta/\omega > \langle s \rangle$ or 1 if $\theta/\omega < \langle s \rangle$, where $\langle s \rangle$ is the mean value of s, which coincides for $n \to \infty$ with the maximum of

$\hat{P}(s)$. If $\eta = 0$ the correlation function is a constant according to eq. (14), while the system will exhibit undamped oscillations with period 3 for $\eta = 1$. Therefore, the irregularity of the burst intervals, as shown, for instance, in Fig. 2, is for independent ξ_i^t a finite size effect. Such synchronized dephasing due to finite size has been reported by Sompolinsky *et al.* (1989).

However, for biologically realistic correlated inputs ξ_i^t, the width of $\hat{P}(s)$ can remain finite for $n \gg 1$. For example, if the inputs $\xi_1^t, \ldots, \xi_n^t$ can be grouped into q correlated sets $\xi_1^t \ldots \xi_1^t, \xi_2^t \ldots \xi_2^t, \ldots, \xi_q^t \ldots \xi_q^t$, with finite q, then the width of $\hat{P}(s)$ scales like $1/\sqrt{q}$. Our model, which now effectively corresponds to a situation with a finite number q of inputs, leads in this case to irregular bursts which mirror and amplify the correlations present in the input signals, with an oscillatory component superimposed due to the dynamical threshold.

4   CONCLUSIONS AND DISCUSSION

We here suggest a mechanism for burst synchronization which is based on the fact that excitatory coupled neurons fire in synchrony whenever a sufficient number of input signals coincide. In our model, common inhibition shuts down the activity after each burst, making the whole process repeatable, without entraining any signals. It is rather satisfactory to us that our simple model shows qualitative similar dynamic behavior of the much more detailed biophysical simulations of Bush and Douglas (1991). In both models, all-to-all excitatory coupling leads—together with common inhibition—to burst synchronization without frequency locking. In our analysis we updated all neurons in parallel. The same model has been investigated numerically for serial (asynchronous) updating, leading to qualitatively similar results.

The output of our network develops oscillatory correlations whose range and amplitude increases as the excitatory coupling is strengthened. However, these oscillations do not depend on the presence of any neuronal oscillators, as in our earlier models (e.g., Schuster and Wagner, 1990; Niebur *et al.*,1991). The period of the oscillations reflects essentially the delay between the inhibitory response and the excitatory stimulus and only varies little with the amplitude of the excitatory coupling and the threshold. The crucial role of inhibitory interneurons in controlling the $40\ Hz$ neuronal oscillations has been emphasized by Wilson and Bower (1992) in their simulations of olfactory and visual cortex. Our model shows complete synchronization, in the sense that all neurons fire at the same time. This suggests that the occurrence of tightly synchronized firing activity across neurons is more important for feature linking and binding than the locking of oscillatory frequencies. Since the specific statistics of the input noise is, via coincidence detection, mirrored in the burst statistics, we speculate that our network—acting as an amplifier for the input noise—can play an important role in any mechanism for feature linking that exploits common noise correlations of different input signals.

Acknowledgements

We thank R. Douglas for stimulating discussions and for inspiring us to think about this problem. Our collaboration was supported by the Stiftung Volkswagenwerk. The research of C.K. is supported by the National Science Foundation, the James

McDonnell Foundation, and the Air Force Office of Scientific Research.

References

Bush, P.C. and Douglas, R.J. "Synchronization of bursting action potential discharge in a model network of neocortical neurons." *Neural Computation* **3**: 19–30, 1991.

Crick, F. and Koch, C. "Towards a neurobiological theory of consciousness." *Seminars Neurosci.* **2**: 263-275, 1990.

Eckhorn, R., Bauer, R., Jordan, W., Brosch, M., Kruse, W., Munk, M. and Reitboeck, H.J. "Coherent oscillations: a mechanism of feature linking in the visual cortex?" *Biol. Cybern.* **60**: 121–130, 1988.

Gray, C.M., Engel, A.K., König, P. and Singer, W. "Stimulus-dependent neuronal oscillations in cat visual cortex: Receptive field properties and feature dependence." *Eur. J. Neurosci.* **2**: 607–619, 1990.

Gray, C.M., Konig, P., Engel, A.K. and Singer, W. "Oscillatory response in cat visual cortex exhibits inter-columnar synchronization which reflects global stimulus attributes." *Nature* **338**: 334–337, 1989.

Horn, D. and Usher, M. "Excitatory-inhibitory networks with dynamical thresholds." *Int. J. of Neural Systems* **1**: 249–257, 1990.

Koch, C. and Schuster, H. "A simple network showing burst synchronization without frequency locking." *Neural Computation*, in press.

McCulloch, W.S. and Pitts, W.A. "A logical calculus of the ideas immanent in neural nets." *Bull. Math. Biophys.* **5**: 115-137, 1943.

Niebur, E., Schuster, H.G., Kammen, D.M. and Koch, C. "Oscillator-phase coupling for different two-dimensional network connectivities." *Phys. Rev. A.*, in press.

Schuster, H.G. and Wagner, P. "A model for neuronal oscillations in the visual cortex: I Mean-field theory and the derivation of the phase equations." *Biol. Cybern.* **64**: 77-82, 1990.

Sompolinsky, H., Golomb, D. and Kleinfeld, D. "Global processing of visual stimuli in a neural network of coupled oscillators." *Proc. Natl. Acad. Sci. USA* **87**: 7200–7204, 1989.

von der Malsburg, C. and Schneider, W. "A neural cocktail-party processor." *Biol. Cybern.* **54**: 29–40, 1986.

Wilson, M.A. and Bower, J.M. "Cortical oscillations and temporal interactions in a computer simulation of piriform cortex." *J. Neurophysiol.*, in press.

Oscillatory Model of Short Term Memory

David Horn
School of Physics and Astronomy
Raymond and Beverly Sackler
Faculty of Exact Sciences
Tel-Aviv University
Tel Aviv 69978, Israel

Marius Usher[*]
Dept. of Applied Mathematics
and Computer Science
Weizmann Institute of Science
Rehovot 76100, Israel

Abstract

We investigate a model in which excitatory neurons have dynamical thresholds which display both fatigue and potentiation. The fatigue property leads to oscillatory behavior. It is responsible for the ability of the model to perform segmentation, i.e., decompose a mixed input into staggered oscillations of the activities of the cell-assemblies (memories) affected by it. Potentiation is responsible for sustaining these staggered oscillations after the input is turned off, i.e. the system serves as a model for short term memory. It has a limited STM capacity, reminiscent of the magical number 7 ± 2.

1 Introduction

The limited capacity (7 ± 2) of the short term memory (STM) has been a subject of major interest in the psychological and physiological literature. It seems quite natural to assume that the limited capacity is due to the special dynamical nature of STM. Recently, Crick and Koch (1990) suggested that the working memory is functionally related to the binding process, and is obtained via synchronized oscillations of neural populations. The capacity limitation of STM may then result from the competition between oscillations representing items in STM. In the model which we investigate this is indeed the case.

---

[*]Present address: Division of Biology, 216-76, Caltech, Pasadena CA 91125.

Models of oscillating neural networks can perform various tasks:

1. Phase-locking and synchronization in response to global coherence in the stimuli, such as similarity of orientation and continuity (Kamen et al. 1989; Sompolinsy et al. 1990; Konig & Schillen 1991).

2. Segmentation of incoherent stimuli in low level vision via desynchronization, using oscillator networks with delayed connections (Schillen & Konig 1991).

3. Segmentation according to semantic content, i.e., separate an input of mixed information into its components which are known memories of the system (Wang et al. 1990, Horn and Usher 1991). In these models the memories are represented by competing cell assemblies. The input, which affects a subset of these assemblies, induces staggered oscillations of their activities. This works as long as the number of memories in the input is small, of the order of 5.

4. Binding, i.e., connecting correctly different attributes of the same object which appear in the mixed input (Horn et al. 1991). Binding can be interpreted as matching the phases of oscillations representing attributes of the same object in two different networks which are coupled in a way which does not assume any relation between the attributes.

To these we add here the important task of

5. STM, i.e., keeping information about segmentation or binding after the input is turned off.

In order to qualify as models for STM, the staggered oscillations have to prevail after the input stimuli disappear. Unfortunately, this does not hold for the models quoted above. Once the input disappears, either the network's activity dies out, or oscillations of assemblies not included in the original input are turned on. In other words, the oscillations have no inertia, and thus they do not persist after the disappearance of the sensory input. Our purpose is to present a model of competing neural assemblies which, upon receiving a mixed input develops oscillations which prevail after the stimulus disappears. In order to achieve this, the biological mechanism of post tetanic potentiation will be used.

2   Dynamics of Short Term Potentiation

It was shown that following a tetanus of electrophysiological stimulation temporary modifications in the synaptic strengths, mostly non Hebbian, are observed (Crick and Koch, 1990; Zucker, 1989). The time scale of these synaptic modifications ranges between 50 ms to several minutes. A detailed description of the processes responsible for this mechanism was given by Zucker (1989), exhibiting a rather complex behavior. In the following we will use a simplified version of these mechanisms involving two processes with different time scales. We assume that following a prolonged activation of a synapse, the synaptic strength exhibits depression on a short time scale, but recovers and becomes slightly enhanced on a longer time scale. As illustrated in Fig 1 of Zucker (1989), this captures most of the dynamics of Short Term Potentiation. The fact that these mechanisms are non Hebbian implies that all synapses associated with a presynaptic cell are affected, and thus the unit of change is the presynaptic cell (Crick & Koch 1990).

Our previous oscillatory neural networks were based on the assumption that, in addition to the customary properties of the formal neuron, its threshold increases when the neuron keeps firing, thus exhibiting adaptation or fatigue (Horn & Usher 1989). Motivated by the STP findings we add a new component of facilitaion, which takes place on a longer time scale than fatigue. We denote the dynamical threshold by the continuous variable r which is chosen as a sum of two components, f and p, representing fatigue and potentiation,

$$r = a_1 f - a_2 p. \tag{1}$$

Their dynamics is governed by the equations

$$\gamma df/dt = m + (1/c_1 - 1)f \qquad \gamma dp/dt = m + (1/c_2 - 1)p \tag{2}$$

where m describes the average neuron activity (firing rate) on a time scale which is large compared to the refractory period. The time constants of the fatigue and potentiation components, $\tau_i = \frac{c_i}{c_i - 1}$ are chosen so that $\tau_1 < \tau_2$. As a result the neuron displays fatigue on a short time scale, but recovers and becomes slightly enhanced (potentiated) on a longer time scale. This is clearly seen in Fig. 1, which shows the behavior when the activity m of the corresponding neuron is clamped at 1 for some time (due to sensory input) and quenched to zero afterwards.

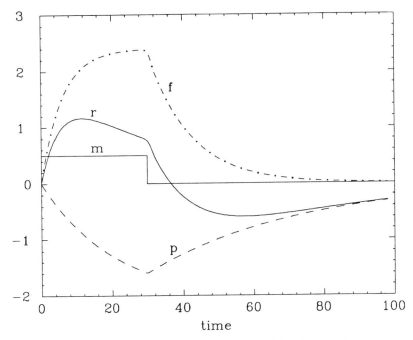

Figure 1: Behavior of the dynamic threshold r and its fatigue f and potentiation p components, when the neuron activity m is clamped as shown. Time scale is arbitrary. The parameters are $c_1 = 1.2$ $c_2 = 1.05$ $a_1 = 4$ $a_2 = 1$.

We observe here that the threshold increases during the cell's activation, being driven to its asymptotic value $a_1 \frac{c_1 - 1}{c_1}$. After the release of the stimulus the dynamic threshold decreases (i.e. the neuron recovers) and turns negative (signifying potentiation). The parameters were chosen so that asymptotically the threshold reaches zero, i.e. no permanent effect is left. In our model we will assume a similar behavior for the excitatory cell-assemblies which carry the memories in our system.

3   The Model

Our basic model (Horn & Usher 1990) is composed of two kinds of neurons which are assumed to have excitatory and inhibitory synapses exclusively. Memory patterns are carried by excitatory neurons only. Furthermore, we make the simplifying assumption that the patterns do not overlap with one another, i.e. the model is composed of disjoint Hebbian cell-assemblies of excitatory neurons which affect one another through their interaction with a single assembly of inhibitory neurons.

Let us denote by $m^\mu(t)$ the fraction of cell-assembly number μ which fires at time t, and by $m^I(t)$ the fraction of active inhibitory neurons. We will refer to m^μ as the activity of the μth memory pattern. There are P different memories in the model, and their activities obey the following differential equations

$$dm^\mu/dt = -m^\mu + F_T(Am^\mu - Bm^I - \theta^\mu + i^\mu) \qquad (3)$$

$$dm^I/dt = -m^I + F_T(CM - Dm^I - \theta^I)$$

where

$$M = \sum_\mu m^\mu \qquad F_T(x) = (1 + e^{-x/T})^{-1}. \qquad (4)$$

θ^μ and θ^I are the thresholds of all excitatory and inhibitory neurons correspondingly and i^μ represents the input into cell assembly μ. The four parameters $A\,B\,C$ and D are all positive and represent the different couplings between the neurons. This system is an attractor neural network. In the absence of input and dynamical thresholds it is a dissipative system which flows into fixed points determined by the memories.

This system is a generalization of the E-I model of Wilson and Cowan (1972) in which we have introduced competing memory patterns. The latter make it into an attractor neural network. Wilson and Cowan have shown that a pair of excitatory and inhibitory assemblies, when properly connected, will form an oscillator. We induce oscillations in a different way, keeping the option of having the network behave either as an attractor neural network or as an oscillating one: we turn the thresholds of the excitatory neurons into dynamic variables, which are defined by

$$\theta^\mu = \theta_0^\mu + br^\mu.$$

The dynamics of the new variables r^μ are chosen to follow equations (1) and (2) where all elements, $r\ f\ p$ and m refer to the same cell-assembly μ. To understand the effects of this change let us first limit ourselves to the fatigue component only, i.e. $a_1 = 1$ and $a_2 = 0$ in Eq. 1. Imagine a situation in which the system would flow into a fixed point $m^\mu = 1$. r^μ will then increase until it reaches the value $c_1/(c_1-1)$. This means that the argument of the F_T function in the equation for m^μ decreases by $g = bc_1/(c_1 - 1)$. If this overcomes the effect of the other terms the amplitude m^μ decreases and the system moves out of the attractor and falls into the basin of a different center of attraction. This process can continue indefinitely creating an oscillatory network which moves from one memory to another. Envisage now turning on a p^μ component leading to an r^μ behavior of the type depicted in Fig. 1. Its effect will evidently be the same as the input i^μ in Eq. (3) during the time in which it is active. In other words, it will help to reactivate the cell-assembly μ, thus carrying the information that this memory was active before. Therefore, its role in our system is to serve as the inertia component necessary for creating the effect of STM.

4   Segmentation and Short Term Memory

In this section we will present results of numerical investigations of our model. The parameters used in the following are $A = C = D = 1$ $B = 1.1$ $\theta_0^\mu = 0.075$ $\theta^I = 0.55$ $T = 0.05$ $b = 0.2$ $\gamma = 2.5$ and the values of a_i and c_i of Fig. 1. We let n of the P memories have a constant input of the form

$$i^\mu = i \quad \mu = 1, \cdots, n \qquad i^\mu = 0 \quad \mu = n+1, \cdots, P. \tag{5}$$

An example of the result of a system with $P = 10$ and $n = 4$ is shown in Fig. 2.

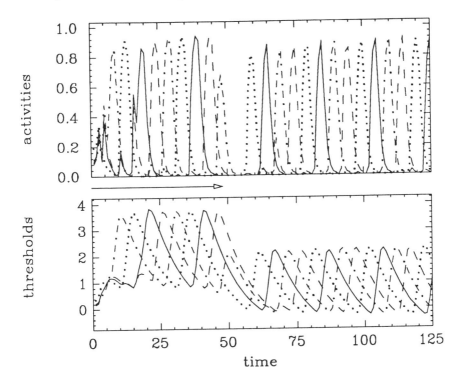

Figure 2: Results of our model for $P = 10$ memories and $n = 4$ inputs. The first frame displays the activities m of the four relevant cell-assemblies, and the second frame represents their r values. The arrow indicates the duration of the mixed input.

Here we display the activities of the cell-assemblies that receive the constant input and their corresponding average thresholds. While the signal of the mixed input is on (denoted by an arrow along the time scale) we see how the phenomenon of segmentation develops. The same staggered oscillation of the four cell-assemblies which received an input is sustained after the signal is turned off. This indicates that the system functions as a STM. Note that no synaptic connections were changed and, once the system will receive a new input its behavior will be revised. However, as long as it is left alone, it will continue to activate the cell-assemblies affected by the original input.

We were able to obtain good results only for low n values, $n \leq 4$. As n is increased we have difficulties with both segmentation and STM. By modifying slightly the paradigm we were able to feed 5 different inputs in a STM, as shown in Fig. 3. This required presenting them at different times, as indicated by the 5 arrows on this figure. In other words, this system does not perform segmentation but it continues to work as a STM. Note, however, that the order of the different activities is no longer maintained after the stimuli are turned off.

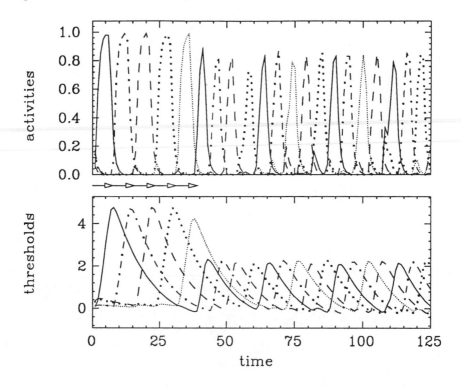

Figure 3: Results for 5 inputs which are fed in consecutively at the times indicated by the short arrows. The model functions as STM without segmentation.

5   Discussion.

Psychological experiments show that subjects can repeat a sequence of verbal items in perfect order as long as their number is small (7 ± 2). The items may be numbers or letters but can also be combinations of the latter such as words or recognizable dates or acronyms. This proves that STM makes use of the encoded material in the long term memory (Miller 1956). This relation between the two different kinds of memory lies in the basis of our model. Long term memory is represented by excitatory cell assemblies. Incorporating threshold fatigue into the model, it acquires the capability of performing temporal segmentation of external input. Adding to the threshold post tetanic potentiation, the model becomes capable of maintaining the segmented information in the form of staggered oscillations. This is the property which we view as responsible for STM.

Both segmentation and STM have very limited capacities. This seems to follow from the oscillatory nature of the system which we use to model these functions. In contrast with long term memory, whose capacity can be increased endlessly by adding neurons and synaptic connections, we find here that only a few items can be stored in the dynamic fashion of staggered oscillations, irrespective of the size of the system. We regard this result as very significant, in view of the fact that the same holds for the limited psychological ability of attention and STM. It may indicate that the oscillatory model contains the key to the understanding of these psychological findings.

In order to validate the hypothesis that STM is based on oscillatory correlations between firing rates of neurons, some more experimental neurobiological and psychophysical research is required. While no conclusive results were yet obtained from recordings of the cortical activity in the monkey, some positive support has been obtained in psychophysical experiments. Preliminary results show that an oscillatory component can be found in the percentage of correct responses in STM matching experiments (Usher & Sagi 1991).

Our mathematical model is based on many specific assumptions. We believe that our main results are characteristic of a class of such models which can be obtained by changing various elements in our system. The main point is that dynamical storage of information can be achieved through staggered oscillations of memory activities. Moreover, to sustain them in the absence of an external input, a potentiation capability has to be present. A model which contains both should be able to accomodate STM in the fashion which we have demonstrated.

Acknowledgements

M. Usher is the recipient of a Dov Biegun post-doctoral fellowship. We wish to thank S. Popescu for helpful discussions.

References

Crick,F. & Koch,C. 1990. Towards a neurobiological theory of consciousness. *Seminars in the Neurosciences 2*, 263–275.

Horn,D., Sagi,D. & Usher,M. 1991. Segmentation, binding and illusory conjunctions. *Neural Comp. 3*, 509–524.

Horn,D. & Usher,M. 1989. Neural networks with dynamical thresholds, *Phys. Rev. A 40*, 1036–1044.

Horn,D. & Usher,M. 1990. Excitatory-inhibitory networks with dynamical thresholds, *Int. J. Neural Syst. 1*, 249–257.

Horn,D. & Usher,M. 1991. Parallel Activation of Memories is an Oscillatory Neural Network. *Neural Comp. 3*, 31–43.

Kammen,D.M., Holmes,P.J. & Koch C. 1990. Origin of oscillations in visual cortex: Feedback versus local coupling. In *Models of Brain Function*, M.Cotterill ed., pp 273–284. Cambridge University Press.

Konig,P. & Schillen,T.B. 1991. Stimulus-dependent assembly formation of oscillatory responses: I. Synchronization, *Neural Comp. 3*, 155–166.

Miller,G. 1956. The magical number seven plus minus two. *Psych. Rev., 63*, 81–97.

Sompolinsky,H., Golomb,D. & Kleinfeld,D. 1990. Global processing of visual stimuli in a neural network of coupled oscillators. *Proc. Natl. Acad. of Sci. USA, 87*, 7200–7204.

Schillen,T.B. & Konig,P. 1991. Stimulus-dependent assembly formation of oscillatory responses: I. Synchronization, *Neural Comp. 3*, 155–166.

Wang,D., Buhmann,J. & von der Malsburg,C. 1990. Pattern segmentation in associative memory. *Neural Comp. 2*, 94–106.

Wilson,H.R. & Cowan,J.D. 1972. Excitatory and inhibitory interactions in localized populations of model neurons. *Biophys. J. 12*, 1–24.

Usher,M. & Sagi D. 1991, in preparation.

Zucker,R.S. 1989. Short-term synaptic plasticity. *Ann. Rev. Neurosci. 12*, 13–31.

PART III

SPEECH

Multi-State Time Delay Neural Networks
for Continuous Speech Recognition

Patrick Haffner
CNET Lannion A TSS/RCP
22301 LANNION, FRANCE
haffner@lannion.cnet.fr

Alex Waibel
Carnegie Mellon University
Pittsburgh, PA 15213
ahw@cs.cmu.edu

Abstract

We present the "Multi-State Time Delay Neural Network" (MS-TDNN) as an extension of the TDNN to robust word recognition. Unlike most other hybrid methods, the MS-TDNN embeds an alignment search procedure into the connectionist architecture, and allows for word level supervision. The resulting system has the ability to manage the sequential order of subword units, while optimizing for the recognizer performance. In this paper we present extensive new evaluations of this approach over speaker-dependent and speaker-independent connected alphabet.

1 INTRODUCTION

Classification based Neural Networks (NN) have been successfully applied to phoneme recognition tasks. Extending those classification capabilities to word recognition is an important research direction in speech recognition. However, connectionist architectures do not model time alignment properly, and they have to be combined with a Dynamic Programming (DP) alignment procedure to be applied to word recognition. Most of these "hybrid" systems (Bourlard, 1989) take advantage of the powerful and well tried probabilistic formalism provided by Hidden Markov Models (HMM) to make use of a reliable alignment procedure. However, the use of this HMM formalism strongly limits one's choice of word models and classification procedures.

MS-TDNNs, which do not use this HMM formalism, suggest new ways to design speech recognition systems in a connectionist framework. Unlike most hybrid systems where connectionist procedures replace some parts of a pre-existing system, MS-TDNNs are designed from scratch as a global Neural Network that performs word recognition. No bootstrapping is required from an HMM, and we can apply learning procedures that correct the recognizer's errors explicitly. These networks have been successfully tested on difficult word recognition tasks, such as speaker-dependent connected alphabet recognition (Haffner et al, 1991a) and speaker-independent telephone digit recognition (Haffner and Waibel, 1991b). Section 2 presents an overview of hybrid Connectionist/HMM architectures and training procedures. Section 3 describes the MS-TDNN architecture. Section 4 presents our novel training procedure. In section 5, MS-TDNNs are tested on speaker-dependent and speaker-independent continuous alphabet recognition.

2   HYBRID SYSTEMS

HMMs are currently the most efficient and commonly used approach for large speech recognition tasks: their modeling capacity, however limited, fits many speech recognition problems fairly well (Lee, 1988). The main limit to the modelling capacity of HMMs is the fact that trainable parameters must be interpretable in a probabilistic framework to be reestimated using the Baum-Welch algorithm with the Maximal Likelihood Estimation training criterion (MLE).

Connectionist learning techniques used in NNs (generally error back-propagation) allow for a much wider variety of architectures and parameterization possibilities. Unlike HMMs, NNs model discrimination surfaces between classes rather than the complete input/output distributions (as in HMMs) : their parameters are only trained to minimize some error criterion. This gain in data modeling capacity, associated with a more discriminant training procedure, has permitted improved performance on a number of speech tasks, especially those in which modeling sequential information is not necessary. For instance, Time Delay Neural Networks have been applied, with high performance, to phoneme classification (Waibel et al, 1989). To extend this performance to word recognition, one has to combine a front-end NN with a procedure performing time alignment, usually based on DP. A variety of alignment procedures and training methods have been proposed for those "hybrid" systems.

2.1 TIME ALIGNMENT

To take into account the time distortions that may appear within its boundaries, a word is generally modeled by a sequence of states *(1,...,s,...,N)* that can have variable durations. The score of a word in the vocabulary accumulates frame-level scores which are a function of the output $\vec{Y}(t) = (Y_1(t), ...,Y_I(t))$ of the front end NN

$$O = Max_{\{T_1, ..., T_{N+1}\}} \sum_{s=1}^{N} \left[\sum_{t \geq T_s}^{t < T_{s+1}} Score_s (\vec{Y}(t)) \right] \qquad (1)$$

The DP algorithm finds the optimal alignment $\{T_1, ..., T_{N+1}\}$ which maximizes this word score. A variety of Score functions have been proposed for Eq.(1). They are most often treated as likelihoods, to apply the probabilistic Viterbi alignment algorithm.

2.1.1 NN outputs probabilities

Outputs of classification based NNs have been shown to approximate Bayes probabilities, provided that they are trained with a proper objective function (Bourlard, 1989). For instance, we can train our front-end NN to output, at each time frame, state probabilities that can be used by a Viterbi alignment procedure (to each state *s* there corresponds a NN output $i(s)$). Eq.(1) gives the resulting word *log (likelihood)* as a sum of frame-level *log(-likelihoods)* which are written[1]:

$$Score_s(\vec{Y}(t)) = \log(Y_{i(s)}(t)) \qquad (2)$$

2.1.2 Comparing NN output to a reference vector

The front end NN can be interpreted as a system remapping the input to a single density continuous HMM (Bengio, 1991). In the case of identity covariance matrices, Eq.(1) gives the *log(likelihood)* for the k-th word (after Viterbi alignment) as a sum of distances between the NN frame-level output and a reference vector associated with the current state[2].

$$Score_s(\vec{Y}(t)) = \left\| \vec{Y}(t) - \vec{Y}^s \right\|^2 \qquad (3)$$

Here, the reference vectors ($\vec{Y}^1, ..., \vec{Y}^s, ..., \vec{Y}^N$) correspond to the means of gaussian PDFs, and can be estimated with the Baum-Welch algorithm.

2.2 TRAINING

The first hybrid models that were proposed (Bourlard, 1989; Franzini, 1991) optimized the state-level NN (with gradient descent) and the word-level HMM (with Baum-Welch) separately. Even though each level of the system may have reached a local optimum of its cost function, training is potentially suboptimal for the given complete system. Global optimization of hybrid connectionist/HMM systems requires a unified training algorithm, which makes use of global gradient descent (Bridle, 1990).

3   THE MS-TDNN ARCHITECTURE

MS-TDNNs have been designed to extend TDNNs classification performance to the word level, within the simplest possible connectionist framework. Unlike the hybrid methods presented in the previous section, the HMM formalism is not taken as the underlying framework here, but many of the models developed within this formalism are applicable to MS-TDNNs.

3.1 FRAME-LEVEL TDNN ARCHITECTURE

All the MS-TDNNs architectures described in this paper use the front-end TDNN architecture (Waibel et al, 1989), shown in Fig.1, at the state level. Each unit of the first hidden layer receives input from a 3-frame window of input coefficients. Similarly, each unit in the second hidden layer receives input from a 5-frame window of outputs of the first hidden layer. At this level of the system (2nd hidden layer), the network produces, at each time frame, the scores for the desired phonetic features. Phoneme recognition TDNNs are trained in a time-shift invariant way by integrating over time the output of a single state.

3.2 BASELINE MS-TDNN

With MS-TDNNs, we have extended the formalism of TDNNs to incorporate time alignment. The front-end TDNN architecture has I output units, whose activations (ranging

---

1. State prior probabilities would add a constant term to Eq.(2)

2. State transition probabilities add an offset to Eq.(3)

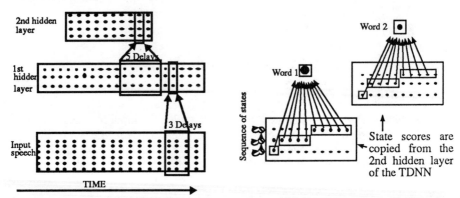

Figure 1: Frame-Level TDNN   Figure 2: MS-TDNN

from 0 to 1) represent the frame-level scores. To each state s corresponds a TDNN output i(s). Different states may share the same output (for instance with phone models). The DP procedure, as described in Eq.(1), determines the sequence of states producing the maximum sum of activations[3]:

$$Score_s(\vec{Y}(t)) = Y_{i(s)} \qquad (4)$$

The frame-level score used in the MS-TDNN combines the advantages of being simple with that of having a formal description as an extension of the TDNN accumulation process to multiple states. It becomes possible to model the accumulation process as a connectionist word unit that sums the activations from the best sequence of incoming state units, as shown in Fig.2. This is mostly useful during the back-propagation phase: at each time frame, we imagine a virtual connection between the active state unit and the word unit, which is used to backpropagate the error at the word level down to the state level.[4]

3.3 EXTENDING MS-TDNNs

In the previous section, we presented the baseline MS-TDNN architecture. We now present extensions to the word-level architecture, which provide additional trainable parameters. Eq.(4) is extended as:

$$Score_s(\vec{Y}(t)) = Weight_i \cdot Y_{i(s)} + Bias_i \qquad (5)$$

---

3. This equation is not very different from Eq.(2) presented in the previous section, however, all attempts to use $log(Y_i(t))$ instead of $Y_i(t)$ have resulted in unstable learning runs, that have never converged properly. During the test phase, the two approaches may be functionally not very different. Outputs that affect the error rate in a critical way are mostly those of the correct word and the best incorrect word, especially when they are close. We have observed that frame level scores which play a key role in discrimination are close to 1.0: the two scores become asymptotically equivalent (less 1): $log(Y_i(t)) \sim Y_i(t) - 1$.

4. The alignment path found by the DP routine during the forward phase is "frozen", so that it can be represented as a connectionist accumulation unit during the backward phase. The problem is that, after modification of the weights, this alignment path may no longer be the optimal one. Practical consequences of this seem minimal.

Weight$_i$ allows to weight differently the importance of each state belonging to the same word. We do not have to assume that each part of a speech pattern contains an equal amount of information.

Bias$_i$ is analog to a transition log(probability) in a HMM.

However, we have observed that a small variation in the value of those parameters may alter recognition performance a lot. The choice of a proper training procedure is critical. Our gradient back-propagation algorithm has been selected for its efficient training of the parameters of the front-end TDNN ; as our training procedure is global, we have also applied it to train *Weight$_i$* and *Bias$_i$*, but with some difficulty.

In section 4.1, we show that they are useful to shift the word scores so that a sigmoid function separates the correct words (output *1*) properly from the incorrect ones (output *0*).

3.4 SEQUENCE MODELS

We design very simple state sequence models by hand that may use phonetic knowledge (phone models) or may not (word models).

Phone Models: The phonetic representation of a word is transcribed as a sequence of states. As an example shown in Fig.3, the letter 'p' combines 3 phone units. P captures the closure and the burst of this stop consonant. P-IY is a co-articulation unit. The phone IY is recognized in a context independent way. This phone is shared with all the other e-set letters. States are duplicated to enforce minimal phone durations.

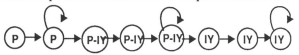

Figure 3 Phone Model for 'p'

Word Models: No specific phonemic meaning is associated with the states of a word. Those states cannot be shared with other words.

Transition States: One can add specialized transition units that are trained to detect this transition more explicitly : the resulting stabilization in segmentation yields an increase in performance. This method is however sensitive to a good bootstrapping of our system on proper phone boundaries, and has so far only been applied to speaker dependent alphabet recognition.

4   TRAINING

In many speech recognition systems, a large discrepancy is found between the training procedure and the testing procedure. The training criterion, generally Maximum Likelihood Estimation, is very far from the word accuracy the system is expected to maximize. Good performance depends on a large quantity of data, and on proper modeling. With MS-TDNNs, we suggest optimization procedures which explicitly attempt to minimize the number of word substitutions ; this approach represents a move towards systems in which the training objective is maximum word accuracy. The same global gradient back-propagation is applied to the whole system, from the output word units down to the input units. Each desired word is associated with a segment of speech with known boundaries, and this association represents a learning sample. The DP alignment procedure is applied between the known word boundaries. We describe now three training procedures we have applied to MS-TDNNs.

4.1 STANDARD BACK-PROPAGATION WITH SIGMOIDAL OUTPUTS

Word outputs $Q_k = f(W_k \cdot O_k + B_k)$ are compared to word targets (*1* for the desired word, *0* for the other words), and the resulting error is back-propagated. O_k is the DP sum given by Eq.(1) for the k-th word in the vocabulary, f is the sigmoid function, W_k gives the slope of the sigmoid and B_k is a bias term, as shown in Fig.4. They are trained so that the sigmoid function separates the correct word (Output *1*) form the incorrect words (Output *0*) properly. When the network is trained with the additional parameters of Eq.(5), *Weight*$_i$ and *Bias*$_i$ can account for these sigmoid slope and bias.

MS-TDNNs are applied to word recognition problems where classes are highly confusable. The score of the best incorrect word may be very close to the score of the correct word: in this case, the slope and the bias are parameters which are difficult to tune, and the learning procedure has problems to attain the 0 and 1 target values. To overcome those difficulties, we have developed new training techniques which do not require the use of a sigmoid function and of fixed word targets.

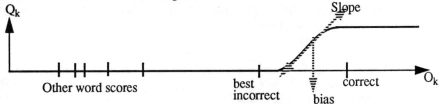

Fig.4. The sigmoid Function

4.2 ON-LINE CORRECTION OF CLASSIFICATION ERRORS

The testing procedure recognizes the word (or the string of words) with the largest output, and there is an error when this is not the correct word. As the goal of the training procedure is to minimize the number of errors, the "ideal" procedure would be, each time a classification error has occurred, to observe where it comes from, and to modify the parameters of the system so that it no longer happens.

The MS-TDNN has to recognize the correct word *CoWo*. There is a *training error* if, for an incorrect word *InWo*, one has $O_{InWo} > O_{CoWo} - m$. No sigmoid function is needed to compare these outputs, m is an additional margin to ensure the robustness of the training procedure. *Only* in the event of a training error do we modify the parameters of the MS-TDNN. The word targets are moving (for instance, the target score for an incorrect word is $O_{CoWo} - m$) instead of fixed (*0* or *1*).

This technique overcomes the difficulties due to the use of an output sigmoid function. Moreover, the number of incorrect words whose output is actually modified is greatly reduced: this is very helpful in training under-represented classes, as the numbers of positive and negative examples become much more balanced.

Compared to the more traditional training technique (with a sigmoid) presented in the previous section, large increases in training speed and word accuracy were observed.

4.3 FUZZY WORD BOUNDARIES

Training procedures we have presented so far do not take into account the fact that the sample words may come from continuous speech. The main difficulty is that their straightforward extension to continuous speech would not be computationally feasible, as the set of possible training classes will consist of all the possible strings of words. We have adopted a staged approach: we modify the training procedure, so that it matches the continuous recognition conditions more and more closely, while remaining computationally feasible.

The first step deals with the problem of word boundaries. During training, known word boundaries give additional information that the system uses to help recognition. But this information is not available when testing. To overcome this problem when learning a correct word (noted *CoWo*), we take as the correct training token the triplet *PreWo-CoWo-NexWo* (*PreWo* is the preceding correct word, *NexWo* is the next correct word in the sentence). All the other triplets *PreWo-InWo-NexWo* are considered as incorrect. These triplets are aligned between the beginning known boundary of *PrevWo* and the ending known boundary of *NexWo*. What is important is that no precise boundary information is given for *CoWo*.

The word classification training criterion presented here only minimizes word substitutions. In connected speech, one has to deal with deletions and insertions errors: procedures to describe them as classification errors are currently being developed.

5   EXPERIMENTS ON CONNECTED ALPHABET

Recognizing spoken letters is considered one of the most challenging small-vocabulary tasks in speech recognition. The vocabulary, consisting of the 26 letters of the American English alphabet, is highly confusable, especially among subsets like the E-set ('B','C','D','E','G','P','T','V','Z') or ('M','N'). In all experiments, as input parameters, 16 filterbank melscale spectrum coefficients are computed at a 10msec frame rate. Phone models are used.

5.1 SPEAKER DEPENDENT ALPHABET

Our database consists of 1000 connected strings of letters, some corresponding to grammatical words and proper names, others simply random. There is an average of five letters per string. The learning procedure is described in §4.1 and applied to the extended MS-TDNN (§3.3), with a bootstrapping phase where phone labels are used to give the alignment of the desired word. During testing, time alignment is performed over the whole sentence. A one-stage DP algorithm (Ney, 1984) for connected words (with no grammar) is used in place of the isolated word DP algorithm used in the training phase. The additional use of minimal word durations, word entrance penalties and word boundary detectors has reduced the number of word insertions and deletions (in the DP algorithm) to an acceptable level. On two speakers, the word error rates are respectively 2.4% and 10.3%. By comparison, SPHINX, achieved error rates of 6% and 21.7%, respectively, when context-independent (as in our MS-TDNN) phone models were used. Using context-dependent models (as described in Lee, 1988), SPHINX performance achieves 4% and 16.1% error rates, respectively. No comparable results yet exist for the MS-TDNN for this case.

5.2 SPEAKER INDEPENDENT ALPHABET (RMspell)

Our database, a part of the DARPA Resource Management database (RM), consists of 120 speakers, spelling about 15 words each. 109 speakers (about 10,000 spelled letters) are used for training. 11 speakers (about 1000 spelled letters) are used for testing. 57 phone units, in the second hidden layer, account for the phonemes and the co-articulation units. We apply the training algorithms described in §4.2 and §4.3 to our baseline MS-

TDNN architecture (§3.2), without any additional procedure (for instance, no phonetic bootstrapping). An important difference from the experimental conditions described in the previous section is that we have kept training and testing conditions exactly similar (for instance, the same knowledge of the boundaries is used during training and testing).

Table 1: Alphabet classification errors (we do not allow for insertions or deletions errors).

Algorithm	%Error
Known Word Boundaries (§4.2)	5.7%
Fuzzy Word Boundaries (§4.3)	6.5%

6   SUMMARY

We presented in this paper MS-TDNNs, which extend TDNNs classification performance to the sequence level. They integrate the DP alignment procedure within a straightforward connectionist framework. We developed training procedures which are computationally reasonable and train the MS-TDNN in a global way. Their only supervision is the minimization of the recognizer's error rate. Experiments were conducted on speaker independent continuous alphabet recognition. The word error rates are 5.7% with known word boundaries and 6.5% with fuzzy word boundaries.

Acknowledgments

The authors would like to express their gratitude to Denis Jouvet and Michael Witbrock, for their help writing this paper, and to Cindy Wood, for gathering the databases. This work was partially performed at CNET laboratories, and at Carnegie Mellon University, under DARPA support.

References

Bengio, Y "Artificial Neural Networks and their Application to Sequence Recognition" Ph.D. Thesis, McGill University, Montreal, June 1991.

Bourlard, H and Morgan, N. "Merging Multilayer Perceptrons and Hidden Markov Models: Some Experiments in Continuous Speech Recognition", TR-89-033, ICSI, Berkeley, CA, July 1989

Bridle, J.S. "Alphanets: a recurrent 'neural' network architecture with a hidden Markov model interpretation." Speech Communication, "Neurospeech" issue, Feb 1990.

Franzini, M.A., Lee, K.F., and Waibel, A.H.,"Connectionist Viterbi Training: A New Hybrid Method for Continuous Speech Recognition," ICASSP, Albuquerque 1990

Haffner, P., Franzini.M. and Waibel A., " Integrating Time Alignment and Neural Networks for High Performance Continuous Speech Recognition " ICASSP, Toronto 1991a.

Haffner, P and Waibel A. "Time-Delay Neural Networks Embedding Time Alignment: a Performance Analysis" Europseech'91, Genova, September 1991b.

Lee, K.F. "Large-Vocabulary Speaker-Independent Continuous Speech Recognition: the SPHINX system", PhD Thesis, Carnegie Mellon University, 1988.

Ney, H. "The Use of a One-Stage Dynamic Programming Algorithm for Connected Word Recognition" in IEEE Trans. on Acoustics, Speech and Signal Processing. April 1984.

Waibel, A.H., Hanazawa, T., Hinton, G., Shikano, K., and Lang, K., " Phoneme Recognition using Time-Delay Neural Networks " in IEEE Transactions on Acoustics, Speech and Signal Processing 37(3):328-339, 1989.

Modeling Applications with the Focused Gamma Net

Jose C. Principe, Bert de Vries, Jyh-Ming Kuo and Pedro Guedes de Oliveira*

Department of Electrical Engineering
University of Florida, CSE 447
Gainesville, FL 32611
principe@synapse.ee.ufl.edu

*Departamento Eletronica/INESC
Universidade de Aveiro
Aveiro, Portugal

Abstract

The focused gamma network is proposed as one of the possible implementations of the gamma neural model. The focused gamma network is compared with the focused backpropagation network and TDNN for a time series prediction problem, and with ADALINE in a system identification problem.

1   INTRODUCTION

At NIPS-90 we introduced the *gamma neural model*, a real time neural net for temporal processing (de Vries and Principe, 1991). This model is characterized by a neural short term memory mechanism, the gamma memory structure, which is implemented as a tapped delay line of adaptive dispersive elements. The gamma model seems to provide an integrative framework to study the neural processing of time varying patterns (de Vries and Principe, 1992). In fact both the memory by delays as implemented in TDNN (Lang et al, 1990) and memory by local feedback (self-recurrent loops) as proposed by Jordan (1986), and Elman (1990) are special cases of the gamma memory structure. The preprocessor utilized in Tank's and Hopfield concentration in time (CIT) network (Tank and Hopfield, 1989) can be shown to be very similar to the dispersive structure utilized in the gamma memory (deVries, 1991). We studied the gamma memory as an independent adaptive filter structure (Principe et al, 1992), and concluded that it is a special case of a class of IIR (infinite impulse response) adaptive filters, which we called the generalized feedforward structures. For these structures, the well known Wiener-Hopf solution to find the optimal filter weights can be analytically computed. One of the advantages of the gamma memory as an adaptive filter is that, although being a recursive structure, stability is easily ensured. Moreover, the LMS algorithm can be easily extended to adapt all the filter weights, including the parameter that controls the depth of memory, with the same complexity as the conventional LMS algorithm (i.e. the algorithm complexity is linear in the number of weights). Therefore, we achieved a theoretical framework to study memory mechanisms in neural networks.

In this paper we compare the gamma neural model with other well established neural networks that process time varying signals. Therefore the first step is to establish a topology for the gamma model. To make the comparison easier with respect to TDNN and Jordan's networks, we will present our results based on the focused gamma network. The focused gamma network is a multilayer feedforward structure with a gamma memory plane in the first layer (Figure 1). The learning equations for the focused gamma network and its memory characteristics will be addressed in detail. Examples will be presented for prediction of complex biological signals (electroencephalogram-EEG) and chaotic time series, as well as a system identification example.

2   THE FOCUSED GAMMA NET

The focused neural architecture was introduced by Mozer (1988) and Stornetta et al (1988). It is characterized by a a two stage topology where the input stage stores traces of the input signal, followed by a nonlinear continuous feedforward mapper network (Figure 1). The gamma memory plane represents the input signal in a time-space plane (spatial dimension M, temporal dimension K). The activations in the memory layer are $I_{ik}(t)$, and the activations in the feedforward network are represented by $x_i(t)$. Therefore the following equations apply respectively for the input memory plane and for the feedforward network,

$$I_0(t) = I_i(t)$$
$$I_{ik}(t) = (1 - \mu_i) I_{ik}(t-1) + \mu_i I_{i, k-1}(t-1) , \text{ i=1,...,M; k=1,...,K.} \qquad (1)$$

$$x_i(t) = \sigma \left(\sum_{j < i} w_{ij} x_j(t) + \sum_{j, k} w_{ijk} I_{jk}(t) \right) \qquad , \text{ i=1,...,N.} \qquad (2)$$

where μ_i is an adaptive parameter that controls the depth of memory (Principe et al, 1992), and w_{ijk} are the spatial weights. Notice that the focused gamma network for K=1 is very similar to the focused-backpropagation network of Mozer and Stornetta. Moreover, when $\mu=1$ the gamma memory becomes a tapped delay line which is the configuration utilized in TDNN, with the time-to-space conversion restricted to the first layer (Lang et al, 1990). Notice also that if the nonlinear feedforward mapper is restricted to one layer of linear elements, and $\mu=1$, the focused gamma memory becomes the adaptive linear combiner - ADALINE (Widrow et al,1960).

In order to better understand the computational properties of the gamma memory we defined two parameters, the mean memory depth D and memory resolution R as

$$D = \frac{K}{\mu} \qquad\qquad R = \frac{K}{D} = \mu \qquad\qquad (3)$$

(de Vries, 1991). Memory depth measures how far into the past the signal conveys information for the processing task, while resolution quantifies the temporal proximity of the memory traces.

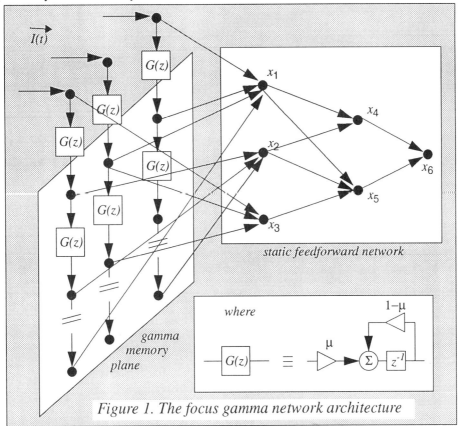

Figure 1. The focus gamma network architecture

The important aspect in the gamma memory formalism is that μ, which controls both the memory resolution and depth, is an adaptive parameter that is learned from the signal according to the optimization of a performance measure. Therefore the focused gamma network always works with the optimal memory depth/ resolution for the processing problem. The gamma memory is an adaptive recursive structure, and as such can go unstable during adaptation. But due to the local feedback nature of $G(z)$, stability is easily ensured by keeping $0 < \mu < 2$.

The focused gamma network is a recurrent neural model, but due to the topology selected, the spatial weights can be learned using regular backpropagation (Rumelhart et al, 1986). However for the adaptation of μ, a recurrent learning procedure is necessary. Since most of the times the order of the gamma memory is small, we recommend adapting μ with direct differentiation using the real time recurrent learning (RTRL) algorithm (Williams and Zipzer,1989), which when applied to the gamma memory yields,

$$\frac{\partial}{\partial \mu_i} E(t) = \sum_m \frac{\partial E}{\partial x_m(t)} x \left(\frac{\partial x_m(t)}{\partial I_{ik}(t)} \; x \; \frac{\partial I_{ik}(t)}{\partial \mu_i} \right)$$

$$= - \sum_m e_m(t) \sigma' [net_m(t)] \sum_k w_{mik} \alpha_i^k(t)$$

where by definition $\alpha_i^k(t) = \frac{\partial}{\partial \mu_i} I_{ik}(t)$, and

$$\frac{\partial}{\partial \mu_i} I_{ik}(t) = (1 - \mu_i) \alpha_i^k(t-1) + \mu_i \alpha_i^{k-1}(t-1) + [I_{i,k-1}(t-1) - I_{i,k}(t-1)]$$

However, backpropagation through time (BPTT) (Werbos, 1990) can also be utilized, and will be more efficient when the temporal patterns are short.

3   EXPERIMENTAL RESULTS

The results for prediction that will be presented here utilized the focused gamma network as depicted in Figure 2a, while for the case of system identification, the block diagram is presented in Figure 2b.

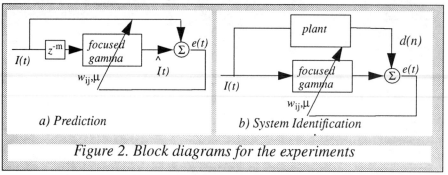

a) Prediction   *b) System Identification*

Figure 2. Block diagrams for the experiments

Prediction of EEG

We selected an EEG signal segment for our first comparison, because the EEG is notorious for its complexity. The problem was to predict the signal five steps ahead (feedforward prediction). Figure 3 shows a four second segment of sleep stage 2. The topology utilized was K gamma units, a one-hidden layer configuration with 5 units (nonlinear) and one linear output unit. The performance criterion is the mean square error signal. We utilized backpropagation to adapt the spatial weights (w_{ijk}), and parametrized μ between 0 and 1 in steps of 0.1. Figure 3b displays the curves of minimal mean square error versus μ.

One can immediately see that the minimum mean square error is obtained for values of μ different from one, therefore for the same memory order the gamma memory outperforms the tapped delay line as utilized in TDNN (which once again is equivalent to the gamma memory for $\mu=1$). For the case of the EEG it seems that the advantage of the gamma memory diminishes when the order of the memory is increased. However, the case of K=2, μ=0.6 produces equivalent performance of a TDNN with 4 memory taps (K=4). Since in experimental conditions there is always noise, experience has shown that the fewer number of adaptive parameters yield better signal fitting and simplifies training, so the focused gamma network is preferable.

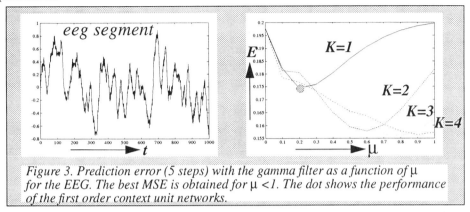

Figure 3. Prediction error (5 steps) with the gamma filter as a function of μ for the EEG. The best MSE is obtained for μ <1. The dot shows the performance of the first order context unit networks.

Notice also that the case of networks with first order context unit is obtained for K=1, so even if the time constant is chosen right (μ=0.2 in this case), the performance can be improved if higher order memory kernels are utilized. It is also interesting to note that the optimal memory depth for the EEG prediction problem seems to be around 4, as this is the value of K/μ $_{optimal}$. The information regarding the "optimal memory depth" is not obtainable with conventional models.

Prediction of Mackey-Glass time series

The Mackey-Glass system is a delay differential equation that becomes chaotic for some values of the parameters and delays (Mackey-Glass, 1977). The results that will be presented here regard the Mackey-Glass system with delay D=30. The time series was generated using a fourth order Runge-Kutta algorithm. The table in Figure 4 shows the performance of TDNN and the focused gamma network with the same number of free parameters. The number of hidden units was kept the same in both networks, but TDNN utilized 5 input units, while the focused gamma network had 4 input units, and the adaptive memory depth parameter μ. The two systems were trained with the same number of samples, and training epochs. For TDNN this was the value that gave the best training when cross validation was utilized (the error in the test set increased after 100 epochs). For this example μ was adapted on-line using RTRL, with the initial value set at μ=1, and with the same step size as for the spatial weights. As the Table shows, the MSE in the training for the gamma network is substantially lower than for TDNN. Figure 4 shows the behavior of μ during the training epochs. It is interesting to see that the value of μ changes during training and settles around a value of 0.92. In terms of learning curve (the MSE as a function of epoch) notice that there is an intersection of the learning curves for the TDNN and gamma network around epoch 42 when the value of μ=1, as we could expect from our analysis. The gamma network starts outperforming TDNN when the correct value of μ is approached.

This example shows that μ can be learned on line, and that once again having the freedom to select the right value of memory depth helps in terms of prediction performance. For both these cases the required memory depth is relatively shallow, what we can expect since a chaotic time series has positive Lyapunov exponents, so the important information to predict the next point is in the short-term past. The same argument applies to the EEG, that can also be modeled as a chaotic time series (Lo and Principe, 1989). Cases where the long-term past is important for the task should enhance the advantage of the gamma memory.

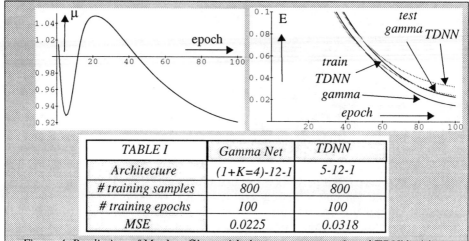

TABLE I	Gamma Net	TDNN
Architecture	(1+K=4)-12-1	5-12-1
# training samples	800	800
# training epochs	100	100
MSE	0.0225	0.0318

Figure 4. Prediction of Mackey-Glass with the gamma network and TDNN with same number of free parameters. Notice that the learning curves intersect around epoch 42, exactly when the m of the gamma was 1. The Figure 4b also shows that the gamma network is able to achieve a smaller error in this problem.

Linear System Identification

The last example is the identification of a third order linear lowpass elliptic transfer function with poles and zeros, given by

$$H(z) = \frac{1 - 0.8731z^{-1} - 0.8731z^{-2} + z^{-3}}{1 - 2.8653z^{-1} + 2.7505z^{-2} - 0.8843z^{-3}}$$

The cutoff frequency of this filter was selected such that the impulse response was long, effectively creating the need for a deep memory for good identification. For this case the focused gamma network was reduced to an ADALINE(μ) (deVries et al, 1991), i.e. the feedforward mapper was a one layer linear network. The block diagram of Figure 2b was utilized to train the gamma network, and I(t) was chosen to be white gaussian noise. Figure 5 shows the MSE as a function of μ for gamma memory orders up to k=3. Notice that the information gained from the Figure 5 agrees with our speculations. The optimal value of the memory is K/μ ~ 17 samples. For this value the third order ADALINE performs very poorly because there is not enough information in 3 delays to identify the transfer function with small error. The gamma memory, on the other hand can choose μ small to encompass the required length, even for a third order memory. The price paid is reduced resolution, but the performance is still much better than the ADALINE of the same order (a factor of 10 improvement).

4   CONCLUSIONS

In this paper we propose a specific topology of the gamma neural model, the focused gamma network. Several important neural networks become special cases of the focused gamma network. This allowed us to compare the advantages of having a more versatile memory structure than any of the networks under comparison.

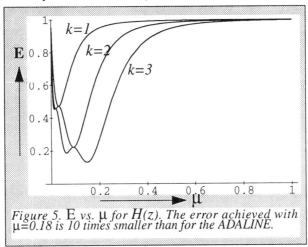

Figure 5. E *vs.* μ *for H(z). The error achieved with μ=0.18 is 10 times smaller than for the ADALINE.*

The conclusion is that the gamma memory is computationally more powerful than fixed delays or first order context units. The major advantage is that the gamma model formalism allows the memory depth to be optimally set for the problem at hand. In the case of the chaotic time series, where the information to predict the future is concentrated in the neighborhood of the present sample, the gamma memory selected the most appropriate value, but its performance is similar to TDNN. However, in cases where the required depth of memory is much larger than the size of the tapped delay line, the gamma memory outperforms the fixed depth topologies with the same number of free parameters.

The price paid for this optimal performance is insignificant. As a matter of fact, μ can be adapted in real-time with RTRL (or BPTT), and since it is a single global parameter the complexity of the algorithm is still O(K) with RTRL. The other possible problem, instability, is easily controlled by requiring that the value of μ be limited to 0<μ<2.

The focused gamma memory is just one of the possible neural networks that can be implemented with the gamma model. The use of gamma memory planes in the hidden or output processing elements will enhance the computational power of the neural network. Notice that in these cases the short term mechanism is not only utilized to store information of the signal past, but will also be utilized to store the past values of the neural states. We can expect great savings in terms of network size with these other structures, mainly in cases where the information of the long-term past is important for the processing task.

Acknowledgments

This work has been partially supported by NSF grant DDM-8914084.

References

De Vries B. and Principe J.C. (1991). A Theory for Neural Nets with Time Delays. In Lippmann R., Moody J., and Touretzky D. (eds.), *NIPS90 proceedings*, San Mateo, CA, Morgan Kaufmann.

DeVries B., Principe J., Oliveira P. (1991). Adaline with Adaptive Recursive Memory, *Proc. IEEE Work. Neural Nets for Sig. Proc.*, Princeton, 101-110, IEEE Press.

DeVries and Principe, (1992). The gamma neural net - A new model for temporal processing. Accepted for publication, *Neural Networks*.

DeVries B.(1991). Temporal Processing with Neural Networks- The Development of the Gamma Model, Ph.D. Dissertation, *University of Florida*.

Elman, (1988). Finding structure in time. *CRL technical report 8801*, 1988.

Jordan, (1986). Attractor dynamics and parallelism in a connectionist sequential machine. *Proc. Cognitive Science* 1986.

Lang et. al. (1990). A time-delay neural network architecture for isolated word recognition. *Neural Networks, vol.3 (1)*, 1990.

Lo P.C. and Principe, J.C. (1989). Dimensionality analysis of EEG Segments: experimental considerations, *Proc. IJCNN 89*, vol I, 693-698.

Mackey D., Glass L. (1977). Oscillation and Chaos in Physiological Control Systems, *Science 197*, 287.

Mozer M.C. (1989). A Focused Backpropagation Algorithm for Temporal Pattern Recognition. *Complex Systems* 3, 349-381.

Principe J.C., De Vries B., Oliveira, P.(1992). The Gamma Filter - A New Class of Adaptive IIR Filters with Restricted Feedback. Accepted for publication in *IEEE Transactions on Signal Processing*.

Rumelhart D.E., Hinton G.E. and Williams R.J. (1986). Learning Internal Representations by Error Back-propagation. In Rumelhart D.E., McClelland J.L. (eds.) , *Parallel Distributed Processing*, vol. 1, ch. 8, MIT Press.

Stornetta W.S., Hogg T. and Huberman B.A. (1988). A Dynamical Approach to Temporal Pattern Processing. In Anderson D.Z. (ed.), *Neural Information Processing Systems*, 750-759.

Tank and Hopfield, (1987). Concentrating information in time: analog neural networks with applications to speech recognition problems. *1st int. conf. on neural networks*, IEEE, 1987.

Werbos P. (1990). Backpropagation through time:what it does and how to do it., *Proc. IEEE*, vol 78, no 10, 1550-1560.

Widrow B., Hoff M. (1960). Adaptive Switching Circuits, *IRE Wescon Conf. Rep.*, pt 4.

Williams J., and Zipzer D (1989). A learning algorithm for continually tunning fiully recurrent neural networks, *Neural Computation*, vol 1 no 2, pp 270-281, MIT Press.

Time-Warping Network :
A Hybrid Framework for Speech Recognition

Esther Levin   Roberto Pieraccini   Enrico Bocchieri

AT&T Bell Laboratories
Speech Research Department
Murray Hill, NJ 07974 USA

ABSTRACT

Recently, much interest has been generated regarding speech recognition systems based on Hidden Markov Models (HMMs) and neural network (NN) hybrids. Such systems attempt to combine the best features of both models: the temporal structure of HMMs and the discriminative power of neural networks. In this work we define a time-warping (TW) neuron that extends the operation of the formal neuron of a back-propagation network by warping the input pattern to match it optimally to its weights. We show that a single-layer network of TW neurons is equivalent to a Gaussian density HMM-based recognition system, and we propose to improve the discriminative power of this system by using back-propagation discriminative training, and/or by generalizing the structure of the recognizer to a multi-layered net. The performance of the proposed network was evaluated on a highly confusable, isolated word, multi speaker recognition task. The results indicate that not only does the recognition performance improve, but the separation between classes is enhanced also, allowing us to set up a rejection criterion to improve the confidence of the system.

I. INTRODUCTION

Since their first application in speech recognition systems in the late seventies, hidden Markov models have been established as a most useful tool, mainly due to their ability to handle the sequential dynamical nature of the speech signal. With the revival of connectionism in the mid-eighties, considerable interest arose in applying artificial neural networks for speech recognition. This interest was based on the discriminative power of NNs and their ability to deal with non-explicit knowledge. These two paradigms, namely HMM and NN, inspired by different philosophies, were seen at first as different and competing tools. Recently, links have been established between these two paradigms, aiming at a hybrid framework in which the advantages of the two models can be combined. For example, Bourlard and Wellekens [1] showed that neural networks with proper architecture can be regarded as non-parametric models for computing "discriminant probabilities" related to HMM. Bridle [2] introduced "Alpha-nets", a recurrent neural architecture that implements the alpha computation of HMM, and found connections between back-propagation [3] training and discriminative HMM parameter estimation. Predictive neural nets were shown to have a statistical interpretation [4], generalizing the conventional hidden Markov model by assuming that the speech signal is generated by nonlinear dynamics contaminated by noise.

In this work we establish one more link between the two paradigms by introducing the time-warping network (TWN) that is a generalization of both an HMM-based recognizer and a back-propagation net. The basic element of such a network, a *time-warping neuron*, generalizes the function of a formal neuron by warping the input signal in order maximize its activation. In the special case of network parameter values, a single-layered network of time-warping (TW) neurons is equivalent to a recognizer based on Gaussian HMMs. This equivalence of the HMM-based recognizer and single-layer TWN suggests ways of using discriminative neural tools to enhance the performance of the recognizer. For instance, a training algorithm, like back-propagation, that minimizes a quantity related to the recognition performance, can be used to train the recognizer instead of the standard non-discriminative maximum likelihood training. Then, the architecture of the recognizer can be expanded to contain more than one layer of units, enabling the network to form discriminant feature detectors in the hidden layers.

This paper is organized as follows: in the first part of Section 2 we describe a simple HMM-based recognizer. Then we define the time-warping neuron and show that a single-layer network built with such neurons is equivalent to the HMM recognizer. In Section 3 two methods are proposed to improve the discriminative power of the recognizer, namely, adopting neural training algorithms and extending the structure of the recognizer to a multi-layer net. For special cases of such multi-layer architecture such net can implement a conventional or weighted [5] HMM recognizer. Results of experiments using a TW network for recognition of the English E-set are presented in Section 4. The results indicate that not only does the recognition performance improve, but the separation between classes is enhanced also, allowing us to set up a rejection criterion to improve the confidence of the system. A summary and discussion of this work are included in Section 5.

II. THE MODEL

In this section first we describe the basic HMM-based speech recognition system that is used in many applications, including isolated and connected word recognition [6] and large vocabulary subword-based recognition [7]. Though in this paper we treat the case of isolated word recognition, generalization to connected speech can be made like in [6,7]. In the second part of this section we define a single-layered time-warping network and show that it is equivalent to the HMM based recognizer when certain conditions constraining the network parameter values apply.

II.1 THE HIDDEN MARKOV MODEL-BASED RECOGNITION SYSTEM

A HMM-based recognition system consists of K N-state HMMs, where K is the vocabulary size (number of words or subword units in the defined task). The k-th HMM, Ω^k, is associated with the k-th word in the vocabulary and is characterized by a matrix $\mathbf{A}^k = \{a_{ij}^k\}$ of transition probabilities between states,

$$a_{ij}^k = Pr(s_t = j \mid s_{t-1} = i) \ , \ 0 \leq i \leq N \ , \ 1 \leq j \leq N, \tag{1}$$

where s_t denotes the active state at time t ($s_0 = 0$ is a dummy initial state) and by a set of emission probabilities (one per state):

$$Pr(X_t \mid s_t=i)=\frac{1}{\sqrt{2\pi \parallel \Sigma_i^k \parallel^2}} \exp[-\frac{1}{2}(X_t-\mu_i^k)^* (\Sigma_i^k)^{-1} (X_t-\mu_i^k)] , \; i=1, \cdots, N , \quad (2)$$

where X_t is the d-dimensional observation vector describing some parametric representation of the t-th frame of the spoken token, and $()^*$ denotes the transpose operation.

For the case discussed here, we concentrate on *strictly left-to-right* HMMs, where $a_{ij}^k \neq 0$ only if $j=i$ or $j=i+1$, and a simplified case of (2) where all $\Sigma_i^k=I_d$, the d=dimensional unit matrix.

The system recognizes a speech token of duration T, $X=\{X_1,X_2, \cdots, X_T\}$, by classifying the token into the class k_0 with the highest likelihood $L^{k_0}(X)$,

$$k_0=arg\max_{1\leq k\leq K} L^k(X). \quad (3)$$

The likelihood $L^k(X)$ is computed for the k-th HMM as

$$L^k(X)=\max_{\{i_1, \cdots, i_T\}} \log[Pr(X \mid \Omega^k, s_i=i_1, \cdots, s_T=i_t)] \quad (4)$$

$$= \max_{\{i_1, \cdots, i_T\}} \sum_{t=1}^{T} \frac{-1}{2} \parallel X_t-\mu_{i_t}^k \parallel^2 +\log a_{i_{t-1}i_t}^k - \log 2\pi .$$

The state sequence that maximizes (4) is found by using the Viterbi [8] algorithm.

II.2 THE EQUIVALENT SINGLE-LAYER TIME-WARPING NETWORK

A single-layer TW network is composed of K TW neurons, one for each word in the vocabulary. The TW neuron is an extension of a formal neuron that can handle dynamic and temporally distorted patterns. The k-th TW neuron, associated with the k-th vocabulary word, is characterized by a bias w_0^k and a set of weights, $W = \{W_1,W_2, \cdots, W_N\}$, where W_i is a column vector of dimensionality $d+2$. Given an input speech token of duration T, $X=\{X_1,X_2, \cdots, X_T\}$, the output activation y^k of the k-th unit is computed as

$$y^k=g(\sum_{t=1}^{T} \hat{X}_t^* \cdot \hat{W}_{i_t}^k +w_0^k)=g(\sum_{j=1}^{N} (\sum_{t:i_t=j} \hat{X}_t^*)\cdot\hat{W}_j^k +w_0^k), \quad (5)$$

where $g(\cdot)$ is a sigmoidal, smooth, strictly increasing nonlinearity, and $\hat{X}_t^* =[X_t^*, 1, 1]$ is an $d+2$ - dimensional augmented input vector. The corresponding indices i_t, $t=1, \cdots, T$ are determined by the following condition:

$$\{ i_1, \cdots, i_T \} = argmax \sum_{t=1}^{T} \hat{X}_t^* \cdot \hat{W}_{i_t}^k +w_0^k . \quad (6)$$

In other words, a TW neuron warps the input pattern to match it optimally to its weights (6) and computes its output using this warped version of the input (5). The time-warping process of (6) is a distinguishing feature of this neural model, enabling it to deal with the dynamic nature of a speech signal and to handle temporal distortions.

All TW neurons in this single-layer net recognizer receive the same input speech token X. Recognition is performed by selecting the word class corresponding to the neuron with the maximal output activation.

It is easy to show that when

$$[\hat{W}_j^k]^* =[[\mu_j^k]^* , -\frac{1}{2} \parallel \mu_j^k \parallel^2 , \log a_{j,j}^k], \quad (7a)$$

and

$$w_0^k = \sum_{j=1}^{N} \log a_{j,j-1}^k - \log a_{j,j}^k \qquad (7b)$$

this network is equivalent to an HMM-based recognition system, with K N-state HMMs, as described above.[1]

This equivalent neural representation of an HMM-based system suggests ways of improving the discriminative power of the recognizer, while preserving the temporal structure of the HMM, thus allowing generalization to more complicated tasks (e.g., continuous speech, subword units, etc.).

III. IMPROVING DISCRIMINATION

There are two important differences between the HMM-based system and a neural net approach to speech recognition that contribute to the improved discrimination power of the latter, namely, training and structure.

III.1 DISCRIMINATIVE TRAINING

The HMM parameters are usually estimated by applying the maximum likelihood approach, using only the examples of the word represented by the model and disregarding the rival classes completely. This is a non-discriminative approach: the learning criterion is not directly connected to the improvement of recognition accuracy. Here we propose to enhance the discriminative power of the system by adopting a neural training approach.

NN training algorithms are based on minimizing an error function E, which is related to the performance of the network on the training set of labeled examples, $\{X^l, Z^l\}$, $l=1, \cdots, L$, where $Z^l=[z_1^l, \cdots, z_K^l]^*$ denotes the vector of target neural outputs for the l-th input token. Z^l has $+1$ only in the entry corresponding to the right word class, and -1 elsewhere. Then,

$$E = \sum_{l=1}^{L} E^l(Z^l, Y^l), \qquad (8)$$

where $Y^l=[y_1^l, \cdots, y_K^l]^*$ is a vector of neural output activations for the l-th input token, and $E^l(Z^l, Y^l)$ measures the distortion between the two vectors. One choice for $E^l(Z^l, Y^l)$ is a quadratic error measure, i.e., $E^l(Z^l, Y^l) = \| Z^l - Y^l \|^2$. Other choices include the cross-entropy error [9] and the recently proposed discriminative error functions, which measure the misclassification rate more directly [10].

The gradient based training algorithms (such as back-propagation) modify the parameters of the network after presentation of each training token to minimize the error (8). The change in the j-th weight subvector of the k-th model after presentation of the l-th training token, $\Delta^l W_j^k$ is inversely proportional to the derivative of the error E^l with respect to this weight subvector,

$$\Delta^l W_j^k = -\alpha \frac{\partial E^l}{\partial W_j^k} = -\alpha \sum_{m=1}^{K} \frac{\partial E^l}{\partial y_m^l} \frac{\partial y_m^l}{\partial W_j^k} , \; 1 \le j \le N , \; 1 \le k \le K , \qquad (9)$$

where $\alpha > 0$ is a step-size, resulting in an updated weight vector $[\hat{W}_j^k]^* = [[W_j^k + \Delta W_j^k]^* , -\frac{1}{2} \| W_j^k + \Delta W_j^k \|^2 , \log a_{j,j}^k]$. To compute the terms $\frac{\partial y_m^l}{\partial W_j^k}$

---

1. With minor changes we can show equivalence to a general Gaussian HMM, where the covariance matrices are not restricted to be the unit matrix.

we have to consider (5) and (6) that define the operation of the neuron. Equation (6) expresses the dependence of the warping indices $i_1, \cdots, i_T$ on W_j^k. In the proposed learning rule we compute the gradient for the quadratic error criterion using only (5).

$$\Delta^l W_j^k = \alpha (z_k - y_k) g'(\cdot) \sum_{t : i_t = j} X_t^l - W_j^k \,, \qquad (10)$$

where the values of i_t fulfill condition (6). Although the weights do not change according to the exact gradient descent rule (since (6) is not taken into account for back-propagation) we found experimentally that the error made by the network always decreases after the weight update. This fact also can be proved when certain conditions restricting the step-size α hold, and we conjecture that it is always true for $\alpha > 0$.

III.2 THE STRUCTURE OF THE RECOGNIZER

When the equivalent neural representation of the HMM-based recognizer is used, there exists a natural way of adaptively increasing the complexity of the decision boundaries and developing discriminative feature detectors. This can be done by extending the structure of the recognizer to a multi-layered net. There are many possible architectures that result from such an extension by changing the number of hidden layers, as well as the number and the type (i.e., standard or TW) of neurons in the hidden layers. Moreover, the role of the TW neurons in the first hidden layer is different now: they are no longer class representatives, as in a single-layered net, but just abstract computing elements with built-in time scale normalization. In this work we investigate only a simple special case of such multi-layered architecture. The multi-layered network we use has a single hidden layer, with $N \times K$ TW neurons. Each hidden neuron corresponds to one state of one of the original HMMs, and is characterized by a weight vector $\hat{W}_j$ and a bias w_j^k. The output activation h_j^k of the neuron is given as

$$h_j^k = g(u_j^k), \qquad (11)$$

where

$$u_j^k = \sum_{t : i_t = j} \hat{X}_t^* \hat{W}_j^k + w_j^k \,, $$

and

$$\{ i_1, \cdots, i_T \} = argmax \sum_{j=1}^{N} u_j^k \,.$$

The output layer is composed of K standard neurons. The activation of output neurons $y^k, k = 1, \ldots, K$, is determined by the hidden layer neurons activations as

$$y^k = g(H^* V^k + v_k), \qquad (12)$$

where V^k is a $N \times K$ dimensional weight vector, H is the vector of hidden neurons activation, and v_k is a bias term.

In a special case of parameter values, when $\hat{W}_j^k$ satisfy the conditions (7a,b) and

$$w_j^k = \log a_{j,j-1}^k - \log a_{j,j}^k \,, \qquad (13)$$

the activation h_j^k corresponds to an accumulated j-th state likelihood of the k-th HMM and the network implements a weighted [5] HMM recognizer where the connection weight vectors V^k determine the relative weights assigned to each state likelihood in the final classification. Such network can learn to adopt these weights to enhance discrimination by giving large positive weights to states that contain information important for discrimination and ignoring (by forming zero or close to zero weights) those states that do not contribute to discrimination. A back-propagation algorithm can be used for training this net.

IV. EXPERIMENTAL RESULTS

To evaluate the effectiveness of the proposed TWN, we conducted several experiments that involved recognition of the highly confusable English E-set (i.e., /b, c, d, e, g, p, t, v, z/). The utterances were collected from 100 speakers, 50 males and 50 females, each speaking every word in the E-set twice, once for training and once for testing. The signal was sampled at 6.67 kHz. We used 12 cepstral and 12 delta-cepstral LPC-derived [11] coefficients to represent each 45 msec frame of the sampled signal.

We used a baseline conventional HMM-based recognizer to initialize the TW network, and to get a benchmark performance. Each strictly left-to-right HMM in this system has five states, and the observation densities are modeled by four Gaussian mixture components. The recognition rates of this system are 61.7% on the test data, and 80.2% on the training data.

Experiment with single-layer TWN: In this experiment the single-layer TW network was initialized according to (7), using the parameters of the baseline HMMs. The four mixture components of each state were treated as a fully connected set of four states, with transition probabilities that reflect the original transition probabilities and the relative weights of the mixtures. This corresponds to the case in which the local likelihood is computed using the dominant mixture component only. The network was trained using the suggested training algorithm (10), with quadratic error function. The recognition rate of the trained network increased to 69.4% on the test set and 93.6% on the training set.

Experiment with multi-layer TWN: In this experiment we used the multi-layer network architecture described in the previous section. The recognition performance of this network after training was 74.4% on the test set and 91% on the training set.

Figures 1, 2, and 3 show the recognition performance of a single-layer TWN, initialized by a baseline HMM, the trained single-layer TWN, and the trained multi-layer TWN, respectively. In these figures the activation of the unit representing the correct class is plotted against the activation of the *best wrong* unit (i.e., the incorrect class with the highest score) for each input utterance. Therefore, the utterances that correspond to the marks above the diagonal line are correctly recognized, and those under it are misclassified. The most interesting observation that can be made from these plots is the striking difference between the multi-layer and the single-layer TWNs. The single-layer TWNs in Figures 1 and 2 (the baseline and the trained) exhibit the same typical behavior when the utterances are concentrated around the diagonal line. For the multi-layer net, the utterances that were recognized correctly tend to concentrate in the upper part of the graph, having the correct unit activation close to 1.0. This property of a multi-layer net can be used for introducing error rejection criterions: utterances for which the difference between the highest activation and second high activation is less than a prescribed threshold are rejected. In Figure 4 we compare the test performance of the multi-layer net and the baseline system, both with such rejection mechanism, for different values of rejection threshold. As expected, the multi-layer net outperforms the baseline recognizer, by showing much smaller misclassification rate for the same number of rejections.

V. SUMMARY AND DISCUSSION

In this paper we established a hybrid framework for speech recognition, combining the characteristics of hidden Markov models and neural networks. We showed that a HMM-based recognizer has an equivalent representation as a single-layer network composed of time-warping neurons, and proposed to improve the discriminative power of the recognizer by using back-propagation training and by generalizing the structure of the recognizer to a multi-layer net. Several experiments were conducted for testing the performance of the proposed network on a highly confusable vocabulary (the English E-set). The recognition performance on the test set of a single-layer TW net improved from 61% (when initialized with a baseline HMMs) to 69% after training. Expending the structure of the recognizer by one more layer of neurons, we obtained further improvement of recognition accuracy up to 74.4%. Scatter plots of the results indicate that in the multi-layer case, there is a qualitative change in the performance of the recognizer, allowing us to set up a rejection criterion to improve the confidence of the system.

References

1. H. Bourlard, C.J. Wellekens, "Links between Markov models and multilayer perceptrons," *Advances in Neural Information Processing Systems*, pp.502-510, Morgan Kauffman, 1989.
2. J.S. Bridle, "Alphanets: a recurrent 'neural' network architecture with a hidden Markov model interpretation," *Speech*Communication, April 1990.
3. D.E. Rumelhart, G.E. Hinton and R.J. Williams, "Learning internal representation by error propagation," *Parallel Distributed Processing: Exploration in the Microstructure of Cognition*, MIT Press, 1986.
4. E. Levin, "Word recognition using hidden control neural architecture," *Proc. of ICASSP*, Albuquerque, April 1990.
5. K.-Y. Su, C.-H. Lee, "Speech Recognition Using Weighted HMM and Subspace Projection Approaches," *Proc of ICASSP*, Toronto, 1991.
6. L. R. Rabiner, "A tutorial on hidden Markov models and selected applications in speech recognition," *Proc. of IEEE*, vol. 77, No. 2, pp. 257-286, February 1989.
7. C.-H. Lee, L. R. Rabiner, R. Pieraccini, J. G. Wilpon, "Acoustic Modeling for Large Vocabulary Speech Recognition," *Computer Speech and Language*, 1990, No. 4, pp. 127-165.
8. G.D. Forney, "The Viterbi algorithm," *Proc. IEEE*, vol. 61, pp. 268-278, Mar. 1973.
9. S.A. Solla, E. Levin, M. Fleisher, "Improved targets for multilayer perceptron learning," *Neural Networks Journal*, 1988.
10. B.-H. Juang, S. Katagiri, "Discriminative Learning for Minimum Error Classification," *IEEE Trans. on SP*, to be published.
11. B.S. Atal, "Effectiveness of linear prediction characteristics of the speech wave for automatic speaker identification and verification," *J. Acoust. Soc. Am.*, vol. 55, No. 6, pp. 1304-1312, June 1974.

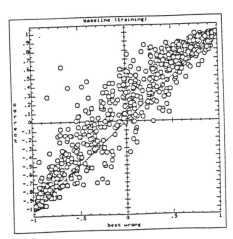 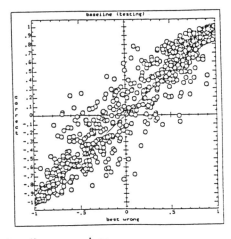

Figure 1: Scatter plot for baseline recognizer

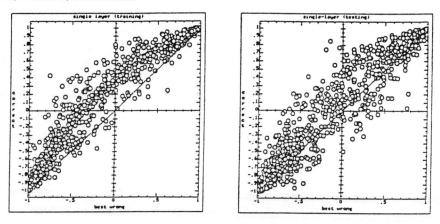

Figure 2: Scatter plot for trained single-layer TWN

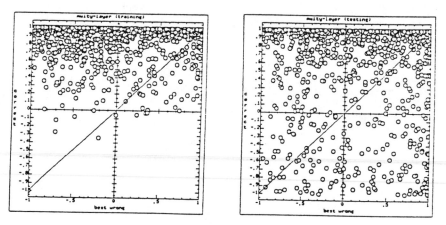

Figure 3: Scatter plot for multi-layer TWN

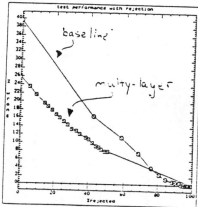

Figure 4: Rejection performance of baseline recognizer and the multi-layer TWN

Improved Hidden Markov Model Speech Recognition Using Radial Basis Function Networks

Elliot Singer and Richard P. Lippmann
Lincoln Laboratory, MIT
Lexington, MA 02173-9108, USA

Abstract

A high performance speaker-independent isolated-word hybrid speech recognizer was developed which combines Hidden Markov Models (HMMs) and Radial Basis Function (RBF) neural networks. In recognition experiments using a speaker-independent E-set database, the hybrid recognizer had an error rate of 11.5% compared to 15.7% for the robust unimodal Gaussian HMM recognizer upon which the hybrid system was based. These results and additional experiments demonstrate that RBF networks can be successfully incorporated in hybrid recognizers and suggest that they may be capable of good performance with fewer parameters than required by Gaussian mixture classifiers. A global parameter optimization method designed to minimize the overall word error rather than the frame recognition error failed to reduce the error rate.

1 HMM/RBF HYBRID RECOGNIZER

A hybrid isolated-word speech recognizer was developed which combines neural network and Hidden Markov Model (HMM) approaches. The hybrid approach is an attempt to capitalize on the superior static pattern classification performance of neural network classifiers [6] while preserving the temporal alignment properties of HMM Viterbi decoding. Our approach is unique when compared to other studies [2, 5] in that we use Radial Basis Function (RBF) rather than multilayer sigmoidal networks. RBF networks were chosen because their static pattern classification performance is comparable to that of other networks and they can be trained rapidly using a one-pass matrix inversion technique [8].

The hybrid HMM/RBF isolated-word recognizer is shown in Figure 1. For each

159

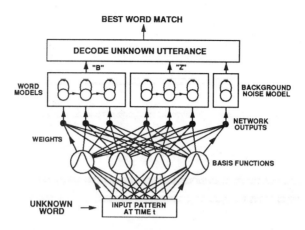

Figure 1: Block diagram of the hybrid recognizer for a two word vocabulary.

pattern presented at the input layer, the RBF network produces nodal outputs which are estimates of Bayesian probabilities [9]. The RBF network consists of an input layer, a hidden layer composed of Gaussian basis functions, and an output layer. Connections from the input layer to the hidden layer are fixed at unity while those from the hidden layer to the output layer are trained by minimizing the overall mean-square error between actual and desired output values. Each RBF output node has a corresponding state in a set of HMM word models which represent the words in the vocabulary. HMM word models are left-to-right with no skip states and have a one-state background noise model at either end. The background noise models are identical for all words. In the simplified diagram of Figure 1, the vocabulary consists of 2 E-set words and the HMMs contain 3 states per word model. The number of RBF output nodes (classes) is thus equal to the total number of HMM non-background states plus one to account for background noise. In recognition, Viterbi decoders use the nodal outputs of the RBF network as observation probabilities to produce word likelihood scores. Since the outputs of the RBF network can take on any value, they were initially hard limited to 0.0 and 1.0. The transition probabilities estimated as part of HMM training are retained. The final response of the recognizer corresponds to that word model which produces the highest Viterbi likelihood. Note that the structure of the HMM/RBF hybrid recognizer is identical to that of a tied-mixture HMM recognizer. For a discussion and comparison of the two recognizers, see [10].

Training of the hybrid recognizer begins with the preliminary step of training an HMM isolated-word recognizer. The robust HMM recognizer used provides good recognition performance on many standard difficult isolated-word speech databases [7]. It uses continuous density, unimodal diagonal-covariance Gaussian classifiers for each word state. Variances of all states are equal to the grand variance averaged over all words and states. The trained HMM recognizer is used to force an alignment of every training token and assign a label to each frame. Labels correspond to both states of HMM word models and output nodes of the RBF network.

The Gaussian centers in the RBF hidden layer are obtained by performing k-means clustering on speech frames and separate clustering on noise frames, where speech and noise frames are distinguished on the basis of the initial Viterbi alignment. The RBF weights from the hidden layer to the output layer are computed by presenting input frames to the RBF network and setting the desired network outputs to 1.0 for the output node corresponding to the frame label and 0.0 for all other nodes. The RBF hidden node outputs and their correlations are accumulated across all training tokens and are used to estimate weights to the RBF output nodes using a fast one-pass algorithm [8]. Unlike the performance of the system reported in [5], additional training iterations using the hybrid recognizer to label frames did not improve performance.

2   DATABASE

All experiments were performed using a large, speaker-independent E-set (9 word) database derived from the ISOLET Spoken Letter Database [4]. The training set consisted of 1,080 tokens (120 tokens per word) spoken by 60 female and 60 male speakers for a total of 61,466 frames. The test set consisted of 540 tokens (60 tokens per word) spoken by a different set of 30 female and 30 male speakers for a total of 30,406 frames. Speech was sampled at 16 kHz and had an average SNR of 31.5 dB. Input vectors were based on a mel-cepstrum analysis of the speech waveform as described in [7]. The input analysis window was 20ms wide and was advanced at 10ms intervals. Input vectors were created by adjoining the first 12 non-energy cepstral coefficients, the first 13 first-difference cepstral coefficients, and the first 13 second-difference cepstral coefficients. Since the hybrid was based on an 8 state-per-word robust HMM recognizer, the RBF network contained a total of 73 output nodes (72 speech nodes and 1 background node). The error rate of the 8 state-per-word robust HMM recognizer on the speaker-independent E-set task was 15.7%.

3   MODIFICATIONS TO THE HYBRID RECOGNIZER

The performance of the baseline HMM/RBF hybrid recognizer described in Section 1 is quite poor. We found it necessary to select the recognizer structure carefully and utilize intermediate outputs properly to achieve a higher level of performance. A full description of these modifications is presented in [10]. Briefly, they include normalizing the hidden node outputs to sum to 1.0, normalizing the RBF outputs by the corresponding *a priori* class probabilities as estimated from the initial Viterbi alignment, expanding the RBF network into three individually trained subnetworks corresponding to the ceptrum, first difference cepstrum, and second difference cepstrum data streams, setting a lower limit of 10^{-5} on the values produced at the RBF output nodes, adjusting a global scaling factor applied to the variances of the RBF centers, and setting the number of centers to 33, 33, and 65 for the first, second, and third subnets, respectively. The structure of the final hybrid recognizer is shown in Figure 2. This recognizer has an error rate of 11.5% (binomial standard deviation = ±1.4) on the E-set test data compared to 15.7% (±1.6) for the 8 state-per-word unimodal Gaussian HMM recognizer, and 9.6% (±1.3) for a considerably more complex tied-mixture HMM recognizer [10]. The final hybrid system contained a total of 131 Gaussians and 9,563 weights. On a SUN SPARCstation 2, training time for the final hybrid recognizer was about 1 hour and testing time was about 10 minutes.

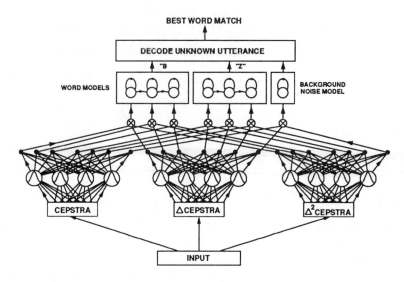

Figure 2: Block diagram of multiple subnet hybrid recognizer.

4   GLOBAL OPTIMIZATION

In the hybrid recognizer described above, discriminative training is performed at the frame level. A preliminary segmentation by the HMM recognizer assigns each speech frame to a specific RBF output node or, equivalently, an HMM word state. The RBF network weights are then computed to minimize the squared error between the network output and the desired output over all input frames. The goal of the recognizer, however, is to classify words. To meet this goal, discriminant training should be performed on word-level rather than frame-level outputs. Recently, several investigators have described techniques that optimize parameters based on word-level discriminant criteria [1, 3]. These techniques seek to maximize a mutual information type of criterion:

$$C = log\frac{L_c}{L},$$

where L_c is the likelihood score of the word model corresponding to the correct result and $L = \sum_w L_w$ is the sum of the word likelihood scores for all models. By computing $\partial C/\partial \theta$, the gradient of C with respect to parameter θ, we can optimize any parameter in the hybrid recognizer using the update equation

$$\hat{\theta} = \theta + \eta\frac{\partial C}{\partial \theta},$$

where $\hat{\theta}$ is the new value of parameter θ, θ is the previous value, and η is a gain term proportional to the learning rate. Following [1], we refer to the word-level optimization technique as "global optimization."

To apply global optimization to the HMM/RBF hybrid recognizer, we derived the formulas for the gradient of C with respect to w_{ij}^k, the weight connecting RBF center i to RBF output node j in subnet k; p_j^k, the RBF output normalization factor for RBF output node j in subnet k; and m_{il}^k, the lth element of the mean of center i of subnet k. For each token of length T frames, these are given by

$$\frac{\partial C}{\partial w_{ij}^k} = \left(\frac{\delta_{cj} - P_w}{L_w} \right) \sum_{t=1}^{T} \frac{\alpha_{jt} \beta_{jt}}{r_{jt}^k} \Phi_{it}^k,$$

$$\frac{\partial C}{\partial p_j^k} = \left(\frac{\delta_{cj} - P_w}{L_w} \right) \left(\frac{-1}{p_j^k} \right) \sum_{t=1}^{T} \alpha_{jt} \beta_{jt},$$

and

$$\frac{\partial C}{\partial m_{il}^k} = \sum_{j=1}^{N_k} \left(\frac{\delta_{cj} - P_w}{L_w} \right) w_{ij}^k \sum_{t=1}^{T} \frac{\alpha_{jt} \beta_{jt}}{r_{jt}^k} \left(\frac{x_{lt}^k - m_{il}^k}{h^k \sigma_{il}^k} \right) \Phi_{it}^k (1 - \Phi_{it}^k),$$

where

$$
\begin{aligned}
L_w &= \text{likelihood score for word model } w, \\
P_w &= L_w / \sum_w L_w \text{ is the normalized word likelihood}, \\
\delta_{cj} &= \begin{cases} 1 \text{ if RBF output node } j \text{ is a member of the correct word model} \\ 0 \text{ otherwise}, \end{cases} \\
\alpha_{jt} &= \text{forward partial probability of HMM state } j \text{ at time t}, \\
\beta_{jt} &= \text{backward partial probability of HMM state } j \text{ at time } t, \\
r_{jt}^k &= \text{unnormalized output of RBF node } j \text{ of subnet } k \text{ at time } t, \\
\Phi_{it}^k &= \text{normalized output of } i^{th} \text{ Gaussian center of subnet } k \text{ at time } t, \\
&\quad \sum_i \Phi_{it}^k = 1, \\
x_{lt}^k &= l^{th} \text{ element of the input vector for subnet } k \text{ at time } t, \\
h^k &= \text{global scaling factor for the variances of subnet } k, \\
\sigma_{il}^k &= l^{th} \text{ component of the standard deviation of the } i^{th} \text{ Gaussian center} \\
&\quad \text{of subnet } k, \\
N_k &= \text{number of RBF output nodes in subnet } k.
\end{aligned}
$$

In implementing global optimization, the frame-level training procedure described earlier serves to initialize system parameters and hill climbing methods are used to reestimate parameters iteratively. Thus, weights are initialized to the values derived using the one-pass matrix inversion procedure, RBF output normalization factors are initialized to the class priors, and Gaussian means are initialized to the k-means clustering values. Note that while the priors sum to one, no such constraint was placed on the RBF output normalization factors during global optimization.

It is worth noting that since the RBF network outputs in the hybrid recognizer are *a posteriori* probabilities normalized by *a priori* class probabilities, their values may exceed 1. The accumulation of these quantities in the Viterbi decoders often leads to values of $\alpha_{jt}\beta_{jt}$ and L_w in the range of 10^{80} or greater. Numerical problems with the implementation of the global optimization equations were avoided by using log arithmetic for intermediate operations and working with the quantity β_{jt}/L_w throughout. Values of η which produced reasonable results were generally in the range of 10^{-10} to 10^{-6}

The results of using the global optimization technique to estimate the RBF weights are shown in Figure 3. Figure 3(a) shows the recognition performance on the training and test sets versus the number of training iterations and Figure 3(b) tracks the value of the criterion $C = L_c/L$ on the training and test set under the same conditions. It is apparent that the method succeeds in iteratively increasing the value of the criterion and in significantly lowering the error rate on the training data. Unfortunately, this behavior does not extend to improved performance on the test data. This suggests that global optimization is overfitting the hybrid word models to the training data. Results using global optimization to estimate RBF output normalization factors and the Gaussian means produced similar results.

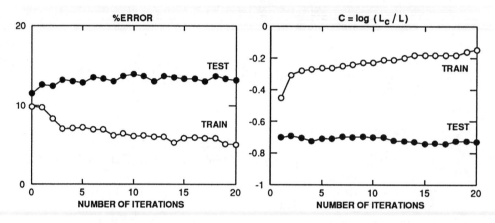

Figure 3: (a) Error rates for training and test data. (b) Criterion C for training and test data.

5   ACCURACY OF BAYES PROBABILITY ESTIMATION

Three methods were used to determine how well RBF outputs estimate Bayes probabilities. First, since network outputs must sum to one if they are probabilities, we computed the RMS error between the sum of the RBF outputs and unity for all frames of the test data. The average RMS error was low (10^{-4} or less for each subnet). Second, the average output of each RBF node was computed because this should equal the *a priori* probability of the class associated with the node [9]. This condition was true for each subnet with an average RMS error on the order of 10^{-5}.

For the final method, we partitioned the outputs into 100 equal size bins between 0.0 and 1.0. For each input pattern, we used the output values to select the appropriate bins and incremented the corresponding bin counts by one. In addition, we incremented the correct-class bin count for the one bin which corresponded to the class of the input pattern. For example, data indicated that for the 61,466 frames of training tokens, nodal outputs of the cepstra subnet in the range 0.095-0.105 occurred 29,698 times and were correct classifications (regardless of class) 3,067 times. If the outputs of the network were true Bayesian probabilities, we would expect the relative frequency of correct labeling to be close to 0.1. Similarly, relative frequencies measured in other intervals would also be expected to be close to the value of the corresponding center of the interval. Thus, a plot of the relative frequencies for each bin versus the bin centers should show the measured values lying close to the diagonal.

The measured relative frequency data for the cepstra subnet and $\pm 2\sigma$ bounds for the binomial standard deviations of the relative frequencies are shown in Figure 4. Outputs below 0.0 and above 1.0 are fixed at 0.0 and 1.0, respectively. Although the relative frequencies tend to be clustered around the diagonal, many values lie outside the bounds. Furthermore, goodness-of-fit measurements using the χ^2 test indicate that fits fail at significance levels well below .01. We conclude that although the system provides good recognition accuracy, better performance may be obtained with improved estimation of Bayesian probabilities.

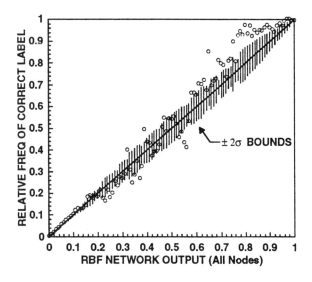

Figure 4: Relative frequency of correct class labeling and $\pm 2\sigma$ bounds for the binomial standard deviation, cepstra subnet.

6   SUMMARY AND CONCLUSIONS

This paper describes a hybrid isolated-word speech recognizer which successfully integrates Radial Basis Function neural networks and Hidden Markov Models. The hybrid's performance is better than that of a tied-mixture recognizer of comparable complexity and near that of a tied-mixture recognizer of considerably greater complexity. The structure of the RBF networks and the processing of network outputs had to be carefully selected to provide this level of performance. A global optimization technique designed to maximize a word discrimination criterion did not succeed in improving performance further. Statistical tests indicated that the accuracy of the Bayesian probability estimation performed by the RBF networks could be improved. We conclude that RBF networks can be used to provide good performance and short training times in hybrid recognizers and that these systems may require fewer parameters than Gaussian-mixture-based recognizers at comparable performance levels.

Acknowledgements

This work was sponsored by the Defense Advanced Research Projects Agency. The views expressed are those of the authors and do not reflect the official policy or position of the U.S. Government.

References

[1] Yoshua Bengio, Renato De Mori, Giovanni Flammia, and Ralf Kompe. Global optimization of a neural network – Hidden Markov model hybrid. Technical Report TR-SOCS-90.22, MgGill University School of Computer Science, Montreal, Qc., Canada, December 1990.

[2] Herve Bourlard and Nelson Morgan. A continuous speech recognition system embedding MLP into HMM. In D. Touretzky, editor, *Advances in Neural Information Processing 2*, pages 186–193. Morgan Kaufmann, San Mateo, CA, 1990.

[3] John S. Bridle. Alpha-nets: A recurrent neural network architecture with a hidden Markov model interpretation. *Speech Communication*, 9:83–92, 1990.

[4] Ron Cole, Yeshwant Muthusamy, and Mark Fanty. The Isolet spoken letter database. Technical Report CSE 90-004, Oregon Graduate Institute of Science and Technology, Beverton, OR, March 1990.

[5] Michael Franzini, Kai-Fu Lee, and Alex Waibel. Connectionist viterbi training: A new hybrid method for continuous speech recognition. In *Proceedings of IEEE International Conference on Acoustics Speech and Signal Processing*. IEEE, April 1990.

[6] Richard P. Lippmann. Pattern classification using neural networks. *IEEE Communications Magazine*, 27(11):47–54, November 1989.

[7] Richard P. Lippmann and Ed A. Martin. Multi-style training for robust isolated-word speech recognition. In *Proceedings International Conference on Acoustics Speech and Signal Processing*, pages 705–708. IEEE, April 1987.

[8] Kenney Ng and Richard P. Lippmann. A comparative study of the practical characteristics of neural network and conventional pattern classifiers. In R. P. Lippmann, J. Moody, and D. S. Touretzky, editors, *Advances in Neural Information Processing 3*. Morgan Kaufmann, San Mateo, CA, 1991.

[9] Mike D. Richard and Richard P. Lippmann. Neural network classifiers estimate Bayesian a posteriori probabilities. *Neural Computation*, In Press.

[10] Elliot Singer and Richard P. Lippmann. A speech recognizer using radial basis function neural networks in an HMM framework. In *Proceedings of the International Conference on Acoustics, Speech, and Signal Processing*. IEEE, 1992.

Connectionist Optimisation of Tied Mixture Hidden Markov Models

Steve Renals
Nelson Morgan
ICSI
Berkeley CA 94704
USA

Hervé Bourlard

L&H Speechproducts
Ieper B-9800
Belgium

Horacio Franco
Michael Cohen
SRI International
Menlo Park CA 94025
USA

Abstract

Issues relating to the estimation of hidden Markov model (HMM) local probabilities are discussed. In particular we note the isomorphism of radial basis functions (RBF) networks to tied mixture density modelling; additionally we highlight the differences between these methods arising from the different training criteria employed. We present a method in which connectionist training can be modified to resolve these differences and discuss some preliminary experiments. Finally, we discuss some outstanding problems with discriminative training.

1 INTRODUCTION

In a statistical approach to continuous speech recognition the desired quantity is the posterior probability $P(\mathbf{W}_1^W|\mathbf{X}_1^T, \Theta)$ of a word sequence $\mathbf{W}_1^W = \mathbf{w}_1, ..., \mathbf{w}_W$ given the acoustic evidence $\mathbf{X}_1^T = \mathbf{x}_1, ..., \mathbf{x}_T$ and the parameters of the speech model used Θ. Typically a set of models is used, to separately model different units of speech. This probability may be re-expressed using Bayes' rule:

$$(1) \quad P(\mathbf{W}_1^W|\mathbf{X}_1^T, \Theta) = \frac{P(\mathbf{X}_1^T|\mathbf{W}_1^W, \Theta)P(\mathbf{W}_1^W|\Theta)}{P(\mathbf{X}_1^T|\Theta)}$$

$$= \frac{P(\mathbf{X}_1^T|\mathbf{W}_1^W, \Theta)P(\mathbf{W}_1^W|\Theta)}{\sum_{\mathbf{W}'} P(\mathbf{X}_1^T|\mathbf{W}', \Theta)P(\mathbf{W}'|\Theta)}.$$

$P(\mathbf{X}_1^T|\mathbf{W}_1^W, \Theta)/P(\mathbf{X}_1^T|\Theta)$ is the acoustic model. This is the ratio of the likelihood of the acoustic evidence given the sequence of word models, to the probability of the acoustic data being generated by the complete set of models. $P(\mathbf{X}_1^T|\Theta)$ may be regarded as a normalising term that is constant (across models) at recognition time. However at training time the parameters Θ are being adapted, thus $P(\mathbf{X}_1^T|\Theta)$ is no longer constant. The prior, $P(\mathbf{W}_1^W|\Theta)$, is obtained from a language model.

The basic unit of speech, typically smaller than a word (here we use phones), is modelled by a hidden Markov model (HMM). Word models consist of concatenations of phone HMMs (constrained by pronunciations stored in a lexicon), and sentence models consist of concatenations of word HMMs (constrained by a grammar). The lexicon and grammar together make up a language model, specifying prior probabilities for sentences, words and phones.

A HMM is a stochastic automaton defined by a set of states q_i, a topology specifying allowed state transitions and a set of local probability density functions (PDFs) $P(\mathbf{x}_t, q_i|q_j, \mathbf{X}_1^{t-1})$. Making the further assumptions that the output at time t is independent of previous outputs and depends only on the current state, we may separate the local probabilities into state transition probabilities $P(q_i|q_j)$ and output PDFs $P(\mathbf{x}_t|q_i)$. A set of initial state probabilities must also be specified.

The parameters of a HMM are usually set via a maximum likelihood procedure that optimally estimates the joint density $P(q, \mathbf{x}|\Theta)$. The forward-backward algorithm, a provably convergent algorithm for this task, is extremely efficient in practice. However, in speech recognition we do not wish to make the best model of the data $\{\mathbf{x}, \mathbf{q}\}$ given the model parameters; we want to make the optimal discrimination between classes at each time. This can be better achieved by computing a discriminant $P(q|\mathbf{x}, \Theta)$. Note that in this case we do not model the input density $P(\mathbf{x}|\Theta)$.

We may estimate $P(q|\mathbf{x}, \Theta)$ using a feed-forward network trained to an entropy criterion (Bourlard & Wellekens, 1989). However, we require likelihoods of the form $P(\mathbf{x}|q, \Theta)$, as HMM output probabilities. We may convert posterior probabilities to scaled likelihoods $P(\mathbf{x}|q, \Theta)/P(\mathbf{x}|\Theta)$, by dividing the network outputs by the relative frequencies of each class[1]. Note that we are not using connectionist training to obtain density estimates here; we are obtaining a ratio and not modelling $P(\mathbf{x}|\Theta)$. This ratio is the quantity that we wish to maximise: this corresponds to maximising $P(\mathbf{x}|q_c, \Theta)$ and minimising $P(\mathbf{x}|q_i, \Theta)$, $i \neq c$, where q_c is the correct class. We have used discriminatively trained networks to estimate the output PDFs (Bourlard & Morgan, 1991; Renals et al., 1991, 1992), and have obtained superior results to maximum likelihood training on continuous speech recognition tasks.

In this paper, we are mainly concerned with radial basis function (RBF) networks. A RBF network generally has a single hidden layer, whose units may be regarded as computing local (or approximately local) densities, rather than global decision surfaces. The resultant posteriors are obtained by output units that combine these local densities. We are interested in using RBF networks for various reasons:

- A RBF network is isomorphic to a tied mixture density model, although the training criterion is typically different. The relationship between the two is explored in this paper.

- The locality of RBFs makes them suitable for situations in which the input

---

[1]These are the estimates of $P(q_i)$ implicitly used during classifier training.

distribution may change (e.g. speaker adaptation). Surplus RBFs in a region of the input space where data no longer occurs will not effect the final classification. This is not so for sigmoidal hidden units in a multi-layer perceptron (MLP), which have a global effect.

- RBFs are potentially more computationally efficient than MLPs at both training and recognition time.

2 TIED MIXTURE HMM

Tied mixtures of Gaussians have proven to be powerful PDF estimators in HMM speech recognition systems (Huang & Jack, 1989; Bellegarda & Nahamoo, 1990). The resulting systems are also known as semi-continuous HMMs. Tied mixture density estimation may be regarded as an interpolation between discrete and continuous density modelling Essentially, tied mixture modelling has a single "codebook" of Gaussians shared by all output PDFs. Each of these PDFs has its own set of mixture coefficients used to combine the individual Gaussians. If $f_k(\mathbf{x}|q_k)$ is the output PDF of state q_k, and $N_j(\mathbf{x}|\mu_j, \Sigma_j)$ are the component Gaussians, then:

$$(2) \qquad f_k(\mathbf{x}|q_k, \Theta) = \sum_j a_{kj} N_j(\mathbf{x}|\mu_j, \Sigma_j)$$

$$\sum_j a_{kj} = 1 \qquad 0 \le a_{kj} \le 1,$$

where a_{kj} is an element of the matrix of mixture coefficients (which may be interpreted as the prior probability $P(\mu_j, \Sigma_j|q_k)$) defining how much component density $N_j(\mathbf{x}|\mu_j, \Sigma_j)$ contributes to output PDF $f_k(\mathbf{x}|q_k, \Theta)$. Alternatively this may be regarded as "fuzzy" vector quantisation.

3 RADIAL BASIS FUNCTIONS

The radial basis functions (RBF) network was originally introduced as a means of function interpolation (Powell, 1985; Broomhead & Lowe, 1988). A set of K approximating functions, $f_k(\mathbf{x})$ is constructed from a set of J basis functions $\phi(\mathbf{x})$:

$$(3) \qquad f_k(\mathbf{x}) = \sum_{j=1}^{J} a_{kj} \phi_j(\mathbf{x}) \qquad 1 \le k \le K$$

This equation defines a RBF network with J RBFs (hidden units) and K outputs. The output units here are linear, with weights a_{kj}. The RBFs are typically Gaussians, with means μ_j and covariance matrices Σ_j:

$$(4) \qquad \phi_j(\mathbf{x}) = R \exp\left(-\frac{1}{2}(\mathbf{x} - \mu_j)^T \Sigma_j^{-1} (\mathbf{x} - \mu_j) \right),$$

where R is a normalising constant. The covariance matrix is frequently assumed to be diagonal[2].

---

[2]This is often reasonable for speech applications, since mel or PLP cepstral coefficients are orthogonal.

Such a network has been used for HMM output probability estimation in continuous speech recognition (Renals et al., 1991) and an isomorphism to tied-mixture HMMs was noted. However, there is a mismatch between the posterior probabilities estimated by the network and the likelihoods required for the HMM decoding. Previously this was resolved by dividing the outputs by the relative frequencies of each state. It would be desirable, though, to retain the isomorphism to tied mixtures: specifically we wish to interpret the hidden-to-output weights of an RBF network as the mixture coefficients of a tied mixture likelihood function. This can be achieved by defining the transfer units of the output units to implement Bayes' rule, which relates the posterior $g_k(\mathbf{x})$ to the likelihood $f_k(\mathbf{x})$:

$$(5) \qquad g_k(\mathbf{x}) = \frac{f_k(\mathbf{x})P(q_k)}{\sum_{l=1}^{K} f_l(\mathbf{x})P(q_l)} .$$

Such a transfer function ensures the output units sum to 1; if $f_k(\mathbf{x})$ is guaranteed non-negative, then the outputs are formally probabilities. The output of such a network is a probability distribution and we are using '1-from-K' training: thus the relative entropy E is simply:

$$(6) \qquad E = -\log g_c(\mathbf{x}),$$

where q_c is the desired output class (HMM distribution). Bridle (1990) has demonstrated that minimising this error function is equivalent to maximising the mutual information between the acoustic evidence and HMM state sequence.

If we wish to interpret the weights as mixture coefficients, then we must ensure that they are non-negative and sum to 1. This may be achieved using a normalised exponential (softmax) transformation:

$$(7) \qquad a_{kj} = \frac{\exp(w_{kj})}{\sum_h \exp(w_{kh})} .$$

The mixture coefficients a_{kj} are used to compute the likelihood estimates, but it is the derived variables w_{kj} that are used in the unconstrained optimisation.

3.1   TRAINING

Steepest descent training specifies that:

$$(8) \qquad \frac{\partial w_{kj}}{\partial t} = -\frac{\partial E}{\partial w_{kj}} .$$

Here E is the relative entropy objective function (6). We may decompose the right hand side of this by a careful application of the chain rule of differentiation:

$$(9) \qquad \frac{\partial E}{\partial w_{kj}} = \sum_{l=1}^{K} \frac{\partial E}{\partial g_l(\mathbf{x})} \frac{\partial g_l(\mathbf{x})}{\partial f_k(\mathbf{x})} \sum_{h=1}^{J} \frac{\partial f_k(\mathbf{x})}{\partial a_{kh}} \frac{\partial a_{kh}}{\partial w_{kj}} .$$

We may write down expressions for each of these partials (where δ_{ab} is the Kronecker delta and q_c is the desired state):

$$(10) \qquad \frac{\partial E}{\partial g_l(\mathbf{x})} = -\frac{\delta_{cl}}{g_c}$$

$$(11) \qquad \frac{\partial g_l(\mathbf{x})}{\partial f_k(\mathbf{x})} = \frac{g_k(\mathbf{x})}{f_k(\mathbf{x})}(\delta_{kl} - g_l)$$

$$(12) \qquad \frac{\partial f_k(\mathbf{x})}{\partial a_{kh}} = \phi_h(\mathbf{x})$$

$$(13) \qquad \frac{\partial a_{kh}}{\partial w_{kj}} = a_{kh}(\delta_{hj} - a_{kj}).$$

Substituting (10), (11), (12) and (13) into (9) we obtain:

$$(14) \qquad \frac{\partial E}{\partial w_{kj}} = \frac{1}{f_k(\mathbf{x})}(g_k(\mathbf{x}) - \delta_{kc})\,a_{kj}\left(\phi_j(\mathbf{x}) - f_k(\mathbf{x})\right).$$

Apart from the added terms due to the normalisation of the weights, the major difference in the gradient compared with using a sigmoid or softmax transfer function is the $1/f_k(\mathbf{x})$ factor. To some extent we may regard this as a dimensional term.

The required gradient is simpler if we construct the network to estimate log likelihoods, replacing $f_k(\mathbf{x})$ with $z_k(\mathbf{x}) = \log f_k(\mathbf{x})$:

$$(15) \qquad z_k(\mathbf{x}) = \sum_j w_{kj}\phi_j(\mathbf{x})$$

$$(16) \qquad g_k(\mathbf{x}) = \frac{p(q_k)\exp(z_k(\mathbf{x}))}{\sum_l p(q_l)\exp(z_l(\mathbf{x}))}.$$

Since this is in the log domain, no constraints on the weights are required. The new gradient we need is:

$$(17) \qquad \frac{\partial g_l(\mathbf{x})}{\partial f_k(\mathbf{x})} = g_k(\delta_{kl} - g_l).$$

Thus the gradient of the error is:

$$(18) \qquad \frac{\partial E}{\partial w_{kj}} = (g_k(\mathbf{x}) - \delta_{ck})\,\phi_j(\mathbf{x}).$$

Since we are in log domain, the $1/f_k(\mathbf{x})$ factor is additive and thus disappears from the gradient. This network is similar to Bridle's softmax, except here uniform priors are not assumed; the gradient is of identical form, though. In this case the weights do not have a simple relationship with the mixture coefficients obtained in tied mixture density modelling.

We may also train the means and variances of the RBFs by back-propagation of error; the gradients are straightforward.

3.2 PRELIMINARY EXPERIMENTS

We have experimented with both the Bayes' rule transfer function (5) and the variant in the log domain (16). We used a phoneme classification task, with a database consisting of 160,000 frames of continuous speech. We typically computed the parameters of the RBFs by a k-means clustering process. We found that the gradient resulting from the first transfer function (14) had a tendency to numerical instability, due to the $1/f$ term; thus most of our experiments have used the log domain transfer function.

In experiments using a 1000 RBFs, we have obtained frame classification rates of 52%. This is somewhat poorer than the frame classification we obtain using a 512 hidden unit MLP (59%). We are investigating improvements to our procedure, including variations to the learning schedule, the use of the EM algorithm to set RBF parameters and the use of priors on the weight matrix.

4   PROBLEMS WITH DISCRIMINATIVE TRAINING

4.1   UNLABELLED DATA

A problem arises from the use of unlabelled or partially labelled data. When training a speech recogniser, we typically know the word sequence for an utterance, but we do not have a time-aligned phonetic transcription. This is a case of partially labelled data: a training set of data pairs $\{x_t, q_t\}$ is unavailable, but we do not have purely unlabelled data $\{x_t\}$. Instead, we have the constraining information of the word sequence $\mathbf{W}$. Thus $P(q_i|x_t)$ may be decomposed as:

$$(19) \qquad P(q_i|x_t) = P(q_i|x_t, \mathbf{W})P(\mathbf{W}|x_t) \,.$$

We usually make the further approximation that the optimal state sequence is much more likely than any competing state sequence. Thus, $P(q_c|x_t) = 1$, and the probabilities of all other states at time t are 0. This most likely state sequence (which may be computed using a forced Viterbi alignment) is often used as the desired outputs for a discriminatively trained network. Using this alignment implicitly assumes model correctness; however, we use discriminative training because we believe the HMMs are an inadequate speech model. Hence there is a mismatch between the maximum likelihood labelling and alignment, and the discriminative training used for the networks.

It may be that this mismatch is responsible for the lack of robustness of discriminative training (compared with pure maximum likelihood training) in vocabulary independent speech recognition tasks (Paul et al., 1991). The assumption of model correctness used to generate the labels may have the effect of further embedding specifics of the training data into the final models. A solution to this problem may be to use a probabilistic alignment, with a distribution over labels at each timestep. This could be computed using the forward-backward algorithm, rather than the Viterbi approximation. This maximum likelihood approach still assumes model correctness of course. A discriminative approach to this problem would also attempt to infer distributions over labels. A basic goal might be to sharpen the distribution toward the maximum likelihood estimate. An example of such a method is the 'phantom targets' algorithm introduced by Bridle & Cox (1991).

These optimisations are local: the error is not propagated through time. Algorithms for globally optimising discriminative training have been proposed (e.g. Bengio et al., these proceedings), but are not without problems, when used with a constraining language model. The problem is that to compute the posterior, the ratio of the probabilities of generating the correct utterance and generating all allowable utterances must be computed.

4.2 THE PRIORS

It has been shown, both theoretically and in practice, that the training and recognition procedures used with standard HMMs remain valid for posterior probabilities (Bourlard & Wellekens, 1989). Why then do we replace these posterior probabilities with likelihoods?

The answer to this problem lies in a mismatch between the prior probabilities given by the training data and those imposed by the topology of the HMMs. Choosing the HMM topology also amounts to fixing the priors. For instance, if classes q_k represent phones, prior probabilities $P(q_k)$ are fixed when word models are defined as particular sequences of phone models. This discussion can be extended to different levels of processing: if q_k represents sub-phonemic states and recognition is constrained by a language model, prior probabilities q_k are fixed by (and can be calculated from) the phone models, word models and the language model. Ideally, the topologies of these models would be inferred directly from the training data, by using a discriminative criterion which implicitly contains the priors. Here, at least in theory, it would be possible to start from fully-connected models and to determine their topology according to the priors observed on the training data. Unfortunately this results in a huge number of parameters that would require an unrealistic amount of training data to estimate them significantly. This problem has also been raised in the context of language modelling (Paul et al., 1991).

Since the ideal theoretical solution is not accessible in practice, it is usually better to dispose of the poor estimate of the priors obtained using the training data, replacing them with "prior" phonological or syntactic knowledge.

5 CONCLUSION

Having discussed the similarities and differences between RBF networks and tied mixture density estimators, we present a method that attempts to resolve a mismatch between discriminative training and density estimation. Some preliminary experiments relating to this approach were discussed; we are currently performing further speech recognition experiments using these methods. Finally we raised some important issues pertaining to discriminative training.

Acknowledgement

This work was partially funded by DARPA contract MDA904-90-C-5253.

References

Bellegarda, J. R. & Nahamoo, D. (1990). Tied mixture continuous parameter modeling for speech recognition. *IEEE Transactions on Acoustics, Speech and Signal Processing, 38*, 2033–2045.

Bourlard, H. & Morgan, N. (1991). Conectionist approaches to the use of Markov models for continuous speech recognition. In Lippmann, R. P., Moody, J. E., & Touretzky, D. S. (Eds.), *Advances in Neural Information Processing Systems*, Vol. 3, pp. 213–219. Morgan Kaufmann, San Mateo CA.

Bourlard, H. & Wellekens, C. J. (1989). Links between Markov models and multi-layer perceptrons. In Touretzky, D. S. (Ed.), *Advances in Neural Information Processing Systems*, Vol. 1, pp. 502–510. Morgan Kaufmann, San Mateo CA.

Bridle, J. S. & Cox, S. J. (1991). RecNorm: Simultaneous normalisation and classification applied to speech recognition. In Lippmann, R. P., Moody, J. E., & Touretzky, D. S. (Eds.), *Advances in Neural Information Processing Systems*, Vol. 3, pp. 234–240. Morgan Kaufmann, San Mateo CA.

Bridle, J. S. (1990). Training stochastic model recognition algorithms as networks can lead to maximum mutual information estimation of parameters. In Touretzky, D. S. (Ed.), *Advances in Neural Information Processing Systems*, Vol. 2, pp. 211–217. Morgan Kaufmann, San Mateo CA.

Broomhead, D. S. & Lowe, D. (1988). Multi-variable functional interpolation and adaptive networks. *Complex Systems*, *2*, 321–355.

Huang, X. D. & Jack, M. A. (1989). Semi-continuous hidden Markov models for speech signals. *Computer Speech and Language*, *3*, 239–251.

Paul, D. B., Baker, J. K., & Baker, J. M. (1991). On the interaction between true source, training and testing language models. In *Proceedings IEEE International Conference on Acoustics, Speech and Signal Processing*, pp. 569–572 Toronto.

Powell, M. J. D. (1985). Radial basis functions for multi-variable interpolation: a review. Tech. rep. DAMPT/NA12, Dept. of Applied Mathematics and Theoretical Physics, University of Cambridge.

Renals, S., McKelvie, D., & McInnes, F. (1991). A comparative study of continuous speech recognition using neural networks and hidden Markov models. In *Proceedings IEEE International Conference on Acoustics, Speech and Signal Processing*, pp. 369–372 Toronto.

Renals, S., Morgan, N., Cohen, M., & Franco, H. (1992). Connectionist probability estimation in the DECIPHER speech recognition system. In *Proceedings IEEE International Conference on Acoustics, Speech and Signal Processing* San Francisco. In press.

Neural Network - Gaussian Mixture Hybrid for Speech Recognition or Density Estimation

Yoshua Bengio
Dept. Brain and Cognitive Sciences
Massachusetts Institute of Technology
Cambridge, MA 02139

Renato De Mori
School of Computer Science
McGill University
Canada

Giovanni Flammia
Speech Technology Center,
Aalborg University, Denmark

Ralf Kompe
Erlangen University, Computer Science
Erlangen, Germany

Abstract

The subject of this paper is the integration of multi-layered Artificial Neural Networks (ANN) with probability density functions such as Gaussian mixtures found in continuous density Hidden Markov Models (HMM). In the first part of this paper we present an ANN/HMM hybrid in which all the parameters of the the system are simultaneously optimized with respect to a single criterion. In the second part of this paper, we study the relationship between the density of the inputs of the network and the density of the outputs of the networks. A few experiments are presented to explore how to perform density estimation with ANNs.

1   INTRODUCTION

This paper studies the integration of Artificial Neural Networks (ANN) with probability density functions (pdf) such as the Gaussian mixtures often used in continuous density Hidden Markov Models. The ANNs considered here are multi-layered or recurrent networks with hyperbolic tangent hidden units. Raw or preprocessed data is fed to the ANN, and the outputs of the ANN are used as observations for a parametric probability density function such as a Gaussian mixture. One may view either the ANN as an adaptive preprocessor for the Gaussian mixture, or the Gaussian mixture as a statistical postprocessor for the ANN. A useful role for the ANN would be to transform the input data so that it can be more efficiently modeled by a Gaussian mixture. An interesting situation is one in which most of the input data points can be described in a lower dimensional space. In this case, it is desired that the ANN learns the possibly non-linear transformation to a more compact representation.

175

In the first part of this paper, we briefly describe a hybrid of ANNs and Hidden Markov Models (HMM) for continuous speech recognition. More details on this system can be found in (Bengio 91). In this hybrid, all the free parameters are simultaneously optimized with respect to a single criterion. In recent years, many related combinations have been studied (e.g., Levin 90, Bridle 90, Bourlard & Wellekens 90). These approaches are often motivated by observed advantages and disadvantages of ANNs and HMMs in speech recognition (Bourlard & Wellekens 89, Bridle 90). Experiments of phoneme recognition on the TIMIT database with the proposed ANN/HMM hybrid are reported. The task under study is the recognition (or spotting) of plosive sounds in continuous speech. Comparative results on this task show that the hybrid performs better than the ANN alone, better than the ANN followed by a dynamic programming based postprocessor using duration constraints, and better than the HMM alone. Furthermore, a global optimization of all the parameters of the system also yielded better performance than a separate optimization.

In the second part of this paper, we attempt to extend some of the findings of the first part, in order to use the same basic architecture (ANNs followed by Gaussian mixtures) to perform density estimation. We establish the relationship between the network input and output densities, and we then describe a few experiments exploring how to perform density estimation with this system.

2   ANN/HMM HYBRID

In a HMM, the likelihood of the observations, given the model, depends in a simple continuous way on the observations. It is therefore possible to compute the derivative of an optimization criterion C, with respect to the observations of the HMM. For example, one may use the criterion of the Maximum Likelihood (ML) of the observations, or of the Maximum Mutual Information (MMI) between the observations and the correct sequence. If the observation at each instant is the vector output, Y_t, of an ANN, then one can use this gradient, $\frac{\partial C}{\partial Y_t}$, to optimize the parameters of the ANN with back-propagation. See (Bridle 90, Bottou 91, Bengio 91, Bengio et al 92) on ways to compute this gradient.

2.1   EXPERIMENTS

A preliminary experiment has been performed using a prototype system based on the integration of ANNs with HMMs. The ANN was initially trained based on a prior task decomposition. The task is the recognition of plosive phonemes pronounced by a large speaker population. The 1988 version of the TIMIT continuous speech database has been used for this purpose. SI and SX sentences from regions 2, 3 and 6 were used, with 1080 training sentences and 224 test sentences, 135 training speakers and 28 test speakers. The following 8 classes have been considered: /p/,/t/,/k/,/b/,/d/,/g/,/dx/,/all other phones/. Speaker-independent recognition of plosive phonemes in continuous speech is a particularly difficult task because these phonemes are made of short and non-stationary events that are often confused with other acoustically similar consonants or may be merged with other unit segments by a recognition system.

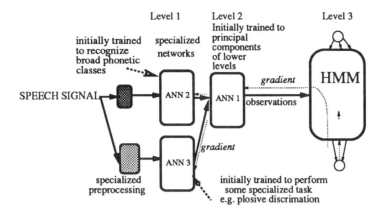

Figure 1: *Architecture of the ANN/HMM Hybrid for the Experiments.*

The ANNs were trained with back-propagation and on-line weight update. As discussed in (Bengio 91), speech knowledge is used to design the input, output, and architecture of the system and of each one of the networks. The experimental system is based on the scheme shown in Figure 1. The architecture is built on three levels. The approach that we have taken is to select different input parameters and different ANN architectures depending on the phonetic features to be recognized. At level 1, two ANNs are initially trained to perform respectively plosive recognition (ANN3) and broad classification of phonemes (ANN2). ANN3 has delays and recurrent connections and is trained to recognize static articulatory features of plosives in a way that depends of the place of articulation of the right context phoneme. ANN2 has delays but no recurrent connections. The design of ANN2 and ANN3 is described in more details in (Bengio 91). At level 2, ANN1 acts as an integrator of parameters generated by the specialized ANNs of level 1. ANN1 is a linear network that initially computes the 8 principal components of the concatenated output vectors of the lower level networks (ANN2 and ANN3). In the experiment described below, the combined network (ANN1+ANN2+ANN3) has 23578 weights. Level 3 contains the HMMs, in which each distribution is modeled by a Gaussian mixture with 5 densities. See (Bengio et al 92) for more details on the topology of the HMM. The covariance matrix is assumed to be diagonal since the observations are initially principal components and this assumption reduces significantly the number of parameters to be estimated. After one iteration of ML re-estimation of the HMM parameters only, all the parameters of the hybrid system were simultaneously tuned to maximize the ML criterion for the next 2 iterations. Because of the simplicity of the implementation of the hybrid trained with ML, this criterion was used in these experiments. Although such an optimization may theoretically worsen performance[1], we observed an marked improvement in performance after the final global tuning. This may be explained by the fact that a nearby local maximum of

---

[1]In section 3, we consider maximization of the likelihood of the inputs of the network,

the likelihood is attained from the initial starting point based on prior and separate training of the ANN and the HMM.

Table 1: *Comparative Recognition Results. % recognized = 100 - % substitutions - % deletions. % accuracy = 100 - % substitutions - % deletions -% insertions.*

	% rec	% ins	% del	% subs	% acc
ANNs alone	85	32	0.04	15	53
HMMs alone	76	6.3	2.2	22.3	69
ANNs+DP	88	16	0.01	11	72
ANNs+HMM	87	6.8	0.9	12	81
ANNs+HMM+global opt.	90	3.8	1.4	9.0	86

In order to assess the value of the proposed approach as well as the improvements brought by the HMM as a post-processor for time alignment, the performance of the hybrid system was evaluated and compared with that of a simple post-processor applied to the outputs of the ANNs and with that of a standard dynamic programming postprocessor that models duration probabilities for each phoneme. The simple post-processor assigns a symbol to each output frame of the ANNs by comparing the target output vectors with actual output vectors. It then smoothes the resulting string to remove very short segments and merges consecutive segments that have the same symbol. The dynamic programming (DP) postprocessor finds the sequence of phones that minimizes a cost that imposes durational constraints for each phoneme. In the HMM alone system, the observations are the cepstrum and the energy of the signal, as well as their derivatives. Comparative results for the three systems are summarized in Table 1.

3   DENSITY ESTIMATION WITH AN ANN

In this section, we consider an extension of the system of the previous section. The objective is to perform density estimation of the inputs of the ANN. Instead of maximizing a criterion that depends on the density of the outputs of an ANN, we maximize the likelihood of inputs of the ANN. Hence the ANN is more than a preprocessor for the gaussian mixtures, it is part of the probability density function that is to be estimated. Instead of representing a pdf only with a set of spatially local functions or kernels such as gaussians (Silverman 86), we explore how to use a global transformation such as one performed by an ANN in order to represent a pdf. Let us first define some notation: $f_X(x) \overset{\text{def}}{=} p(X = x)$, $f_Y(y) \overset{\text{def}}{=} p(Y = y)$, and $f_{X|Y(X)}(x) \overset{\text{def}}{=} p(X = x \mid Y = y(x))$.

3.1   RELATION BETWEEN INPUT PDF AND OUTPUT PDF

Theorem *Suppose a random variable Y (e.g., the outputs of an ANN) is a deterministic parametric function $y(X)$ of a random variable X (here, the inputs of the ANN), where y and x are vectors of dimension n_y and n_x. Let $J = \frac{\partial(y_1, y_2, \ldots y_{n_y})}{\partial(x_1, x_2, \ldots x_{n_x})}$*

---

not the outputs of the network.

be the Jacobian of the transformation from X to Y, and assume $J = UDV^t$ be a singular value decomposition of J, with $s(x) = | \prod_i^{n_y} D_{ii} |$ the product of the singular values. Suppose Y is modeled by a probability density function $f_Y(y)$. Then, for $n_x >= n_y$ and $s(x) > 0$

$$f_X(x) \;\; = \;\; f_Y(y(x)) \;\; f_{X|Y(X)}(x) \;\; s(x) \tag{1}$$

Proof. In the case in which $n_x = n_y$, by change of variable $y \to x$ in the following integral,

$$\int_{\Omega_y} f_Y(y) \, dy \;\; = \;\; 1 \tag{2}$$

we obtain the following result[2]:

$$f_X(x) = f_Y(y(x)) \; | \, \mathrm{Determinant}(J) \, | \tag{3}$$

Let us now consider the case $n_y < n_x$, i.e., the network has less outputs than inputs. In order to do so we will introduce an intermediate transformation to a space Z of dimension n_x in which some dimensions directly correspond to Y. Define Z such that $\frac{\partial(z_1, z_2, \ldots, z_{n_x})}{\partial(x_1, x_2, \ldots, x_{n_x})} = V^t$. Decompose Z into Z' and Z'':

$$z' = (z_1, \ldots, z_{n_y}) \, , \;\; z'' = (z_{n_y+1}, \ldots, z_{n_x}) \tag{4}$$

There is a one-to-one mapping $y_z(z')$ between Z' and Y, and its Jacobian is UD', where D' is the matrix composed of the first n_y columns of D. Perform a change of variables $y \to z'$ in the integral of equation 2:

$$\int_{\Omega_{z'}} f_Y(y_z(z')) \, s \, dz' \;\; = \;\; 1 \tag{5}$$

In order to make a change of variable to the variable x, we have to specify the conditional pdf $f_{X|Y(X)}(x)$ and the corresponding pdf $p(z'' \mid z') = p(z'', z' \mid z') =^3 p(z \mid y) =^4 f_{X|Y(X)}(x)$. Hence we can write

$$\int_{\Omega_{z''}} p(z'' \mid z') \, dz'' \;\; = 1 \tag{6}$$

Multiplying the two integrals in equations 5 and 6, we obtain the following:

$$1 = \int_{\Omega_{z''}} p(z'' \mid z') \, dz'' \int_{\Omega_{z'}} f_Y(y_z(z')) \, s \, dz' = \int_{\Omega_z} f_Y(y_z(z')) \, p(z'' \mid z') s \, dz \tag{7}$$

and substituting $z \to V^t x$:

$$\int_{\Omega_x} f_Y(y(x)) \, f_{X|Y(X)}(x) \, s(x) \, dx \;\; = \;\; 1, \tag{8}$$

which yields to the general result of equation 1 □.

Unfortunately, it is not clear how to efficiently evaluate $f_{X|Y(X)}(x)$ and then compute its derivative with respect to the network weights. In the experiments described in the next section we first study empirically the simpler case in which $n_x = n_y$.

---

[2]in that case, $| \, \mathrm{Determinant}(J) \, | = s$ and $f_{X|Y(X)}(x) = 1$.

[3]knowing z' is equivalent to knowing y.

[4]because $z = V^t x$ and $\mathrm{Determinant}(V) = 1$.

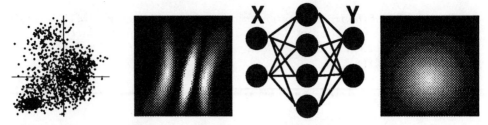

Figure 2: *First Series of Experiments on Density Estimation with an ANN, for data generated on a non-linear input curve. From left to right: Input samples, density of the input, X, estimated with ANN+Gaussian, ANN that maps X to Y, density of the output, Y, as estimated by a Gaussian.*

3.2   ESTIMATION OF THE PARAMETERS

When estimating a pdf, one can approximate the functions $f_Y(y)$ and $y(x)$ by parameterized functions. For example, we consider for the output pdf the class of densities $f_Y(y;\theta)$ modeled by a Gaussian mixture of a certain number of components, where θ is a set of means, variances and mixing proportions. For the non-linear transformation $y(x;\omega)$ from X to Y, we choose an ANN, defined by its architecture and the values of its weights ω. In order to choose values for the Gaussian and ANN parameters one can maximize the a-posteriori (MAP) probability of these parameters given the data, or if no prior is known or assumed, maximize the likelihood (ML) of the input data given the parameters. In the preliminary experiments described here, the logarithm of the likelihood of the data was maximized, i.e., the optimal parameters are defined as follows:

$$(\hat{\theta}, \hat{\omega}) = \underset{(\theta,\omega)}{\operatorname{argmax}} \sum_{x \in \Xi} \log(f_X(x)) \tag{9}$$

where Ξ is the set of inputs samples.

In order to estimate a density with the above described system, one computes the derivative of $p(X = x \mid \theta, \omega)$ with respect to ω. If the output pdf is a Gaussian mixture, we reestimate its parameters θ with the EM algorithm (only $f_Y(y)$ depends on θ in the expression for $f_X(x)$ in equations 3 or 1). Differentiating equation 3 with respect to ω yields:

$$\frac{\partial}{\partial \omega}(\log f_X(x)) = \frac{\partial}{\partial \omega}(\log f_Y(y(x;\omega);\theta)) + \sum_{i,j} \frac{\partial}{\partial J_{ij}}(\log(\text{Determinant}(J)))\frac{\partial J_{ij}}{\partial \omega}$$

$$\tag{10}$$

The derivative of the logarithm of the determinant can be computed simply as follows (Bottou 91):

$$\frac{\partial}{\partial J_{ij}}(\log(\text{Determinant}(J))) = (J^{-1})_{ji}, \tag{11}$$

since $\forall A$, $\text{Determinant}(A) = \sum_j A_{ij}\text{Cofactor}_{ij}(A)$, and $(A^{-1})_{ij} = \frac{\text{Cofactor}_{ji}(A)}{\text{Determinant}(A)}$.

Figure 3: *Second Series of Experiments on Density Estimation with an ANN. From left to right: Input samples, density with non-linear net + Gaussian, output samples after network transformation.*

3.3   EXPERIMENTS

The first series of experiments verified that a transformation of the inputs with an ANN could improve the likelihood of the inputs and that gradient ascent in the ML criterion could find a good solution. In these experiments, we attempt to model some two-dimensional data extracted from a speech database. The 1691 training data points are shown in the left of Figure 2. In the first experiment, a diagonal Gaussian is used, with no ANN. In the second experiment a linear network and a diagonal Gaussian are used. In the third experiment, a non-linear network with 4 hidden units and a diagonal Gaussian are used. The average log likelihoods obtained on a test set of 617 points were -3.00, -2.95 and -2.39 respectively for the three experiments. The estimated input and output pdfs for the last experiment are depicted in Figure 2, with white indicating high density and black low density.

The second series of experiments addresses the following question: if we use a Gaussian mixture with diagonal covariance matrix and most of the data is on a non-linear hypersurface Φ of dimension less than n_x, can the ANN's outputs separate the dimensions in which the data varies greatly (along Φ) from those in which it almost doesn't (orthogonal to Φ)? Intuitively, it appears that this will be the case, because the variance of outputs which don't vary with the data will be close to zero, while the determinant of the Jacobian is non-zero. The likelihood will correspondingly tend to infinity. The first experiment in this series verified that this was the case for linear networks. For data generated on a diagonal line in 2-dimensional space, the resulting network separated the "variant" dimension from the "invariant" dimension, with one of the output dimensions having near zero variance, and the transformed data lying on a line parallel to the other output dimension.

Experiments with non-linear networks suggest that with such networks, a solution that separates the variant dimensions from the invariant ones is not easily found by gradient ascent. However, it was possible to show that such a solution was at a maximum (possibly local) of the likelihood. A last experiment was designed to demonstrate this. The input data, shown in Figure 3, was artificially generated to make sure that a solution existed. The network had 2 inputs, 3 hidden units and 2 outputs. The input samples and the input density corresponding to the weights in a maximum of the likelihood are displayed in Figure 3, along with the transformed input data for those weights. The points are projected by the ANN to a line parallel to the first output dimension. Any variation of the weights from that solution, in the direction of the gradient, even with a learning rate as small as 10^{-14}, yielded either no perceptible improvement or a decrease in likelihood.

4   CONCLUSION

This paper has studied an architecture in which an ANN performs a non-linear transformation of the data to be analyzed, and the output of the ANN is modeled by a Gaussian mixture. The design of the ANN can incorporate prior knowledge about the problem, for example to modularize the task and perform an initial training of the sub-networks. In phoneme recognition experiments, an ANN/HMM hybrid based on this architecture performed better than the ANN alone or the HMM alone. In the second part of th paper, we have shown how the pdf of the input of the network relates to the pdf of the outputs of the network. The objective of this work is to perform density estimation with a non-local non-linear transformation of the data. Preliminary experiments showed that such estimation was possible and that it did improve the likelihood of the resulting pdf with respect to using only a Gaussian pdf. We also studied how this system could perform a non-linear analogue to principal components analysis.

References

Bengio Y. 1991. Artificial Neural Networks and their Application to Sequence Recognition. PhD Thesis, School of Computer Science, McGill University, Montreal, Canada.

Bengio Y., De Mori R., Flammia G., and Kompe R. 1992. Phonetically motivated acoustic parameters for continuous speech recognition using artificial neural networks. To appear in *Speech Communication*.

Bottou L. 1991. Une approche théorique à l'apprentissage connexioniste; applications à la reconnaissance de la parole. Doctoral Thesis, Université de Paris Sud, France.

Bourlard, H. and Wellekens, C.J. (1989). Speech pattern discrimination and multilayer perceptrons. *Computer, Speech and Language*, vol. 3, pp. 1-19.

Bridle J.S. 1990. Training stochastic model recognition algorithms as networks can lead to maximum mutual information estimation of parameters. *Advances in Neural Information Processing Systems 2*, (ed. D.S. Touretzky) Morgan Kauffman Publ., pp. 211-217.

Levin E. 1990. Word recognition using hidden control neural architecture. *Proceedings of the International Conference on Acoustics, Speech and Signal Processing*, Albuquerque, NM, April 90, pp. 433-436.

Silverman B.W. 1986. Density Estimation for Statistics and Data Analysis. Chapman and Hall, New York, NY.

JANUS: Speech-to-Speech Translation Using Connectionist and Non-Connectionist Techniques

Alex Waibel[*] Ajay N. Jain[†]
Arthur McNair   Joe Tebelskis
School of Computer Science
Carnegie Mellon University
Pittsburgh, PA 15213

Louise Osterholtz
Computational Linguistics Program
Carnegie Mellon University

Hiroaki Saito
Keio University
Tokyo, Japan

Otto Schmidbauer
Siemens Corporation
Munich, Germany

Tilo Sloboda   Monika Woszczyna
University of Karlsruhe
Karlsruhe, Germany

ABSTRACT

We present JANUS, a speech-to-speech translation system that utilizes diverse processing strategies, including connectionist learning, traditional AI knowledge representation approaches, dynamic programming, and stochastic techniques. JANUS translates continuously spoken English and German into German, English, and Japanese. JANUS currently achieves 87% translation fidelity from English speech and 97% from German speech. We present the JANUS system along with comparative evaluations of its interchangeable processing components, with special emphasis on the connectionist modules.

[*]Also with University of Karlsruhe, Karlsruhe, Germany.
[†]Now with Alliant Techsystems Research and Technology Center, Hopkins, Minnesota.

1 INTRODUCTION

In an age of increasing globalization of our economies and ever more efficient communication media, one important challenge is the need for effective ways of overcoming language barriers. Human translation efforts are generally expensive and slow, thus eliminating this possibility between individuals and around rapidly changing material (e.g. newscasts, newspapers). This need has recently lead to a resurgence of effort in machine translation—mostly of written language.

Much of human communication, however, is spoken, and the problem of spoken language translation must also be addressed. If successful, speech-to-text translation systems could lead to automatic subtitles in TV-broadcasts and cross-linguistic dictation. Speech-to-speech translation could be deployed as interpreting telephone service in restricted domains such as cross-linguistic hotel/conference reservations, catalog purchasing, travel planning, etc., and eventually in general domains, such as person-to-person telephone calls. Apart from telephone service, speech translation could facilitate multilingual negotiations and collaboration in face-to-face or video-conferencing settings.

With the potential applications so promising, what are the scientific challenges? Speech translation systems will need to address three distinct problems:

- *Speech Recognition and Understanding*: A naturally spoken utterance must be recognized and understood in the context of ongoing dialog.
- *Machine Translation*: A recognized message must be translated from one language into another (or several others).
- *Speech Synthesis*: A translated message must be synthesized in the target language.

Considerable challenges still face the development of each of the components, let alone the combination of the three. Among them only speech synthesis is mature enough for commercial systems to exist that can synthesize intelligible speech in several languages from text. But even here, to guarantee acceptance of the translation system, research is needed to improve naturalness and to allow for adaptation of the output speech (in the target language) to the voice characteristics of the input speaker. Speech recognition systems to date are generally limited in vocabulary size, and can only accept grammatically well-formed utterances. They require improvement to handle spontaneous unrestricted dialogs. Machine Translation systems require considerable development effort to work in a given language pair and domain reasonably well, and generally require syntactically well-formed input sentences. Improvements are needed to handle ill-formed sentences well and to allow for flexibility in the face of changes in domain and language pairs.

Beyond the challenges facing each system component, the combination of the three also introduces extra difficulties. Both the speech recognition and machine translation components, must deal with *spoken* language—ill-formed noisy input, both acoustically as well as syntactically. Therefore, the speech recognition component must be concerned less with *transcription* fidelity than *semantic* fidelity, while the MT-component must try to capture the meaning or intent of the input sentence without being guaranteed a syntactically legal sequence of words. In addition, non-symbolic prosodic information (intonation, rhythm, etc.) and dialog state must be taken into consideration to properly translate an input utterance. A closer cooperation between traditional signal processing and language level processing must be achieved.

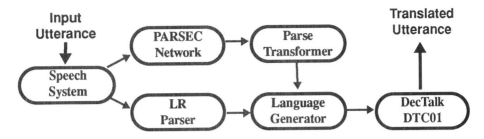

Figure 1: High-level JANUS architecture

JANUS is our first attempt at multilingual speech translation. It is the result of a collaborative effort between ATR Interpreting Telephony Research Laboratories, Carnegie Mellon University, Siemens Corporation, and the University of Karlsruhe. JANUS currently accepts continuously spoken sentences from a conference registration scenario, where a fictitious caller attempts to register to an international conference. The dialogs are read aloud from dialog scripts that make use of a vocabulary of approximately 400 words. Speaker-dependent and independent versions of the input recognition systems have been developed. JANUS currently accepts continuously spoken English and German input and produces spoken German, English, and Japanese output as a result.

While JANUS has some of the limitations mentioned above, it is the first tri-lingual continuous large vocabulary speech translation system to-date. It is a vehicle toward overcoming some of the limitations described. A particular focus is the trainability of system components, so that flexible, adaptive, and robust systems may result. JANUS is a hybrid system that uses a blend of computational strategies: connectionist, statistical and knowledge based techniques. This paper will describe each of JANUS's processing components separately and particularly highlight the relative contributions of connectionist techniques within this ensemble. Figure 1 shows a high-level diagram of JANUS's components.

2 SPEECH RECOGNITION

Two alternative speech recognition systems are currently used in JANUS: Linked Predictive Neural Networks (LPNNs) and Learned Vector Quantization networks (LVQ) (Tebelskis *et al.* 1991; Schmidbauer and Tebelskis 1992). They are both connectionist, continuous-speech recognition systems, and both have vocabularies of approximately 400 English and 400 German words. Each use statistical bigram or word-pair grammars derived from the conference registration database. The systems are based on canonical phoneme models (states) that can be logically concatenated in any order to create models for different words. The need for training data with labeled phonemes can be reduced by first bootstrapping the networks on a small amount of speech with forced *phoneme* boundaries, then training on the whole database using only forced *word* boundaries.

In the LPNN system, each phoneme model is implemented by a predictive neural network. Each network is trained to accurately predict the next frame of speech within segments of speech corresponding to its phoneme model. Continuous scores (prediction errors) are accumulated for various word candidates. The LPNN module produces either a single hypothesized sentence or the first N best hypotheses using a modified dynamic-programming beam-search algorithm (Steinbiss 1989). The LPNN system has speaker-dependent word accuracy rates of 93% with first-best recognition, and sentence accuracy of 69%.

LVQ is a vector clustering technique based on neural networks. We have used LVQ to automatically cluster speech frames into a set of acoustic features; these features are fed into a set of output units that compute the emission probability for HMM states. This technique gives speaker-dependent word accuracy rates of 98%, 86%, and 82% for English conference registration tasks of perplexity 7, 61, and 111, respectively. The sentence recognition rate at perplexity 7 is 80%.

We are also evaluating other approaches to speech recognition, such as the Multi-State TDNN for continuous-speech (Haffner, Franzini, and Waibel 1991) and a neural-network based word spotting system that may be useful for modeling spontaneous speech effects (Zeppenfield and Waibel 1992). The recognitions systems' text output serves as input to the alternative parsing modules of JANUS.

3 LANGUAGE UNDERSTANDING AND TRANSLATION

3.1 LANGUAGE ANALYSIS

The translation module of JANUS is based on the Universal Parser Architecture (UPA) developed at Carnegie Mellon (Tomita and Carbonell 1987; Tomita and Nyberg 1988). It is designed for efficient multi-lingual translation. Text in a source language is parsed into a language independent frame-based *interlingual* representation. From the interlingua, text can be generated in different languages.

The system requires hand-written parsing and generation grammars for each language to be processed. The parsing grammars are based on a Lexical Functional Grammar formalism, and are implemented using Tomita's Generalized LR parsing Algorithm (Tomita 1991). The generation grammars are compiled into LISP functions. Both parsing and generation with UPA approach real-time. Figure 2 shows an example of the input, interlingual representation, and the output of the JANUS system

3.2 PARSEC: CONNECTIONIST PARSING

JANUS can use a connectionist parser in place of the LR parser to process the output of the speech system. PARSEC is a structured connectionist parsing architecture that is geared toward the problems found in spoken language (for details, see Jain 1992 (in this volume) and Jain's PhD thesis, in preparation). PARSEC networks exhibit three strengths:

- They automatically learn to parse, and generalize well compared to hand-coded grammars.
- They tolerate several types of noise without any explicit noise modeling.
- They can learn to use multi-modal input such as pitch in conjunction with syntax and semantics.

The PARSEC network architecture relies on a variation of supervised back-propagation learning. The architecture differs from some other connectionist approaches in that it is highly structured, both at the macroscopic level of modules, and at the microscopic level of connections.

Input

Hello is this the office for the conference.

Interlingual Representation

```
((CFNAME *is-this-phone)
 (MOOD *interrogative)
 (OBJECT ((NUMBER sg) (DET the)
          (CFNAME *conf-office)))
 (SADJUNCT1 ((CFNAME *hello))))
```

Output

Japanese: MOSHI MOSHI KAIGI JIMUKYOKU DESUKA
German: HALLO IST DIES DAS KONFERENZBUERO

Figure 2: Example of input, interlingua, and output of JANUS

3.2.1 Learning and Generalization

Through exposure to example output parses, PARSEC networks learn parsing behavior. Trained networks generalize well compared to hand-written grammars. In direct tests of coverage for the conference registration domain, PARSEC achieved 67% correct parsing of novel sentences, whereas hand-written grammars achieved just 5%, 25%, and 38% correct. Two of the grammars were written as part of a contest with a large cash prize for best coverage.

The process of training PARSEC networks is highly automated, and is made possible through the use of constructive learning coupled with a robust control procedure that dynamically adjusts learning parameters during training. Novice users of the PARSEC system were able to train networks for parsing a German-language version of the conference registration task and a novel English air-travel reservation task.

3.2.2 Noise Tolerance

We have compared PARSEC's performance on noisy input with that of hand-written grammars. On synthetic ungrammatical conference registration sentences, PARSEC produced acceptable interpretations 66% of the time, with the three hand-coded grammars mentioned above performing at 2%, 38%, and 34%, respectively. We have also evaluated PARSEC in the context of noisy speech recognition in JANUS, and this is discussed later.

3.2.3 Multi-Modal Input

A somewhat elusive goal of spoken language processing has been to utilize information from the speech signal beyond just word sequences in higher-level processing. It is well known that humans use such information extensively in conversation. Consider the utterances "Okay." and "Okay?" Although semantically distinct, they cannot be distinguished based on word sequence, but pitch contours contain the necessary information (Figure 3).

```
FILE: s.0.0  "Okay."    duration = 409.1 msec, mean freq = 113.2
0.1 **********                        *         *           *************
0.0            **********************  ********  *****************


FILE: q.0.0  "Okay?"    duration = 377.0 msec, mean freq = 137.3
0.6                                                             *
0.5                                                    ****** *
0.4                                              ****
0.3                                          ****
0.2                                   ******
0.1 ********                 *****************
0.0            **************************
```

Figure 3: Smoothed pitch contours.

In a grammar-based system, it is difficult to incorporate real-valued vector input in a useful way. In a PARSEC network, the vector is just another set of input units. A module of a PARSEC network was augmented to contain an additional set of units that contained pitch information. The pitch contours were smoothed output from the OGI Neural Network Pitch Tracker (Barnard *et al*. 1991).

Within the JANUS system, the augmented PARSEC network brings new functionality. Intonation affects translation in JANUS when using the augmented PARSEC network. The sentence, "This is the conference office." is translated to "Kaigi jimukyoku desu." "This is the conference office?" is translated to "Kaigi jimukyoku desuka?" This required no changes in the other modules of the JANUS system. It also should be possible to use other types of information from the speech signal to aid in robust parsing (e.g. energy patterns to disambiguate clausal structure).

4   SPEECH SYNTHESIS

To generate intelligible speech in the respective target languages, we have predominantly used commercial devices. Most notably, DEC-talk has provided unrestricted English text-to-speech synthesis. DEC-talk has also been used for Japanese and German synthesis. The internal English text-to-phoneme conversion rules and tables of DEC-talk were bypassed by external German and Japanese text-to-phoneme look-up tables that convert the German/Japanese target sentences into phonemic strings for DEC-talk synthesis. The resulting synthesis is limited to the task vocabulary, but the external tables result in intelligible German and Japanese speech—albeit with a pronounced American accent.

To allow for greater flexibility in vocabulary and more language specific synthesis, several alternate devices are currently being integrated. For Japanese, in particular, two high quality speech synthesizers developed separately by NEC and ATR will be used to provide more satisfactory results. In JANUS, no attempt has so far been made to adapt the output speech to the input speaker's voice characteristics. However, this has recently been demonstrated by work with code book mapping (Abe, Shikano, and Kuwabara 1990) and connectionist mapping techniques (Huang, Lee, and Waibel 1991).

5 IMPLEMENTATION ISSUES AND PERFORMANCE

5.1 Parallel Hardware

Neural network forward passes for the speech recognizer were programmed on two general purpose parallel machines, a MasPar computer at the University of Karlsruhe, Germany and an Intel iWarp at Carnegie Mellon. The MasPar is a parallel SIMD machine with 4096 processing elements. The iWarp is a MIMD machine, and a 16MHz, 64 cell experimental version was used for testing.

The use of parallel hardware and algorithms has significantly decreased JANUS's processing time. Compared to forward pass calculations performed by a DecStation 5000, the iWarp is 9 times faster (41.4 million connections per second). The MasPar does the forward pass calculations for a two second utterance in less than 500 milliseconds. Both the iWarp and MasPar are scalable. Efforts are underway to implement other parts of JANUS on parallel hardware with the goal of near real-time performance.

5.2 Performance

Currently, English JANUS using the LR parsing module (JANUS-LR) performs at 87% correct translation using the LPNN speech system with the N-best sentence hypotheses. German JANUS performs at 97% correct translation (on a subset of the conference registration database) using German versions of the LPNN system and LR parsing grammar.

English JANUS using PARSEC (JANUS-NN) does not perform as well as the LR parser version in N-best mode, with 80% correct translation. PARSEC is not able to select from a list of ranked candidate utterance hypotheses as robustly as is the LR parser using a very tight grammar. However, the grammar used for this comparison only achieves 5% coverage of novel test sentences, compared with PARSEC's 67%. This vast difference in coverage explains some of the N-best performance difference.

In First-best mode, however, JANUS-NN does *better* than JANUS-LR (77% versus 70%). The PARSEC network is able to produce acceptable parses for a number of noisy speech recognition hypotheses, but JANUS-LR tends to reject those hypotheses as unparsable. PARSEC's flexibility, which hurt its N-best performance, enhances its F-best performance. No performance evaluations were carried out using German PARSEC in German JANUS.

6 CONCLUSION

In this paper we have described JANUS, a multi-lingual speech-to-speech translation system. JANUS uses a mixture of connectionist, statistical and rule based strategies to achieve this goal. Connectionist models have contributed in providing high performance recognition and parsing performance as well as greater robustness in the light of task variations and syntactically ill-formed sentences. Connectionist models also provide a mechanism for merging traditionally distinct symbolic (syntax) and signal-level (intonation) information gracefully and achieve successful disambiguation between grammatical statements whose mood can be affected by intonation. Finally, connectionist sentence analysis appears to offer high flexibility as the relevant modules can be retrained automatically for new tasks, domains and even languages without laborious recoding. We plan to continue exploring different mixtures of computing paradigms to achieve higher performance.

Acknowledgements

The authors gratefully acknowledge the support of ATR Interpreting Telephony Laboratories, Siemens Corporation, NEC Corporation, and the National Science Foundation.

References

Abe, M., K. Shikano, H. Kuwabara. 1990. Cross Language Voice Conversion. In *IEEE Proceedings of the International Conference on Acoustics, Speech, and Signal Processing*.

Barnard, E., R. A. Cole, M. P. Vea, F. A. Alleva. 1991. Pitch Detection with a Neural-Net Classifier. *IEEE Transactions on Signal Processing* 39(2): 298–307.

Haffner, P., M. Franzini, and A. Waibel. 1991. Integrating time alignment and neural networks for high performance speech recognition. In *IEEE Proceedings of the International Conference on Acoustics, Speech, and Signal Processing*.

Huang, X. D., K. F. Lee, A. Waibel. 1991. In *Proceedings of the IEEE-SP Workshop on Neural Networks for Signal Processing*.

Jain, A. N. 1992. Generalization performance in PARSEC—A structured connectionist learning architecture. In *Advances in Neural Information Processing Systems 4*, ed. J. E. Moody, S. J. Hanson, and R. P. Lippmann. San Mateo, CA: Morgan Kaufmann Publishers.

Jain, A. N. In preparation. PARSEC: A Connectionist Learning Architecture for Parsing Spoken Language. PhD Thesis, School of Computer Science, Carnegie Mellon University.

Schmidbauer, O. and J. Tebelskis. 1992. An LVQ based reference model for speaker-adaptive speech recognition. In *IEEE Proceedings of the International Conference on Acoustics, Speech, and Signal Processing*.

Steinbiss, V. 1989. Sentence-hypothesis generation in a continuous-speech recognition system. In *Proceedings of the 1989 European Conference on Speech Communication and Technology*, Vol. 2, 51–54.

Tebelskis, J., A. Waibel, B. Petek, O. Schmidbauer. 1991. Continuous speech recognition by Linked Predictive Neural Networks. In *Advances in Neural Information Processing System 3*, ed. R. Lippmann, J. Moody, and D. Touretzky. San Mateo, CA: Morgan Kaufmann Publishers.

Tomita, M. (ed.). 1991. *Generalized LR Parsing*. Norwell, MA: Kluwer Academic Publishers.

Tomita, M. and J. G. Carbonell. 1987. *The Universal Parser Architecture for Knowledge-Based Machine Translation*. Technical Report CMU-CMT-87-01, Center for Machine Translation, Carnegie Mellon University.

Tomita, M. and E. Nyberg. 1988. *Generation Kit and Transformation Kit*. Technical Report CMU-CMT-88-MEMO, Center for Machine Translation, Carnegie Mellon University.

Zeppenfield, T. and A. Waibel. 1992. A hybrid neural network, dynamic programming word spotter. In *IEEE Proceedings of the International Conference on Acoustics, Speech, and Signal Processing*.

Forward Dynamics Modeling of Speech Motor Control Using Physiological Data

Makoto Hirayama   Eric Vatikiotis-Bateson   Mitsuo Kawato
ATR Auditory and Visual Perception Research Laboratories
2 - 2, Hikaridai, Seika-cho, Soraku-gun, Kyoto 619-02, JAPAN

Michael I. Jordan
Department of Brain and Cognitive Sciences
Massachusetts Institute of Technology
Cambridge, MA 02139

Abstract

We propose a paradigm for modeling speech production based on neural networks. We focus on characteristics of the musculoskeletal system. Using real physiological data – articulator movements and EMG from muscle activity – a neural network learns the forward dynamics relating motor commands to muscles and the ensuing articulator behavior. After learning, simulated perturbations, were used to asses properties of the acquired model, such as natural frequency, damping, and interarticulator couplings. Finally, a cascade neural network is used to generate continuous motor commands from a sequence of discrete articulatory targets.

1   INTRODUCTION

A key problem in the formal study of human language is to understand the process by which linguistic intentions become speech. Speech production entails extraordinary coordination among diverse neurophysiological and anatomical structures from which unfolds through time a complex acoustic signal that conveys to listeners something of the speaker's intention. Analysis of the speech acoustics has not revealed the encoding of these intentions, generally conceived to be ordered strings of some basic unit, e.g., the phoneme. Nor has analysis of the articulatory system provided an answer, although recent pioneering work by Jordan (1986), Saltzman (1986), Laboissière (1990) and others

191

has brought us closer to an understanding of the articulatory-to-acoustic transform and has demonstrated the importance of modeling the articulatory system's temporal properties. However, these efforts have been limited to kinematic modeling because they have not had access to the neuromuscular activity of the articulatory structures.

In this study, we are using neural networks to model speech production. The principle steps of this endeavor are shown in Figure 1. In this paper, we focus on characteristics of the musculoskeletal system. Using real physiological data – articulator movements and EMG from muscle activity – a neural network learns the forward dynamics relating motor commands to muscles and the ensuing articulator behavior. After learning, a cascade neural network model (Kawato, Maeda, Uno, & Suzuki, 1990) is used to generate continuous motor commands.

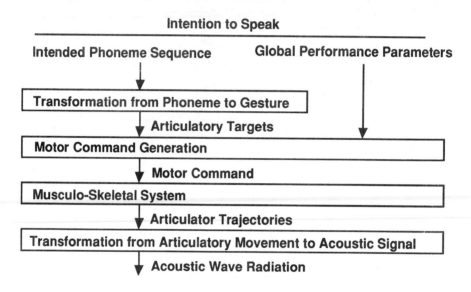

Figure 1: Forward Model of Speech Production

2   EXPERIMENT

Movement, EMG, and acoustic data were recorded for one speaker who produced reiterant versions of two sentences. Speaking rate was fast and the reiterant syllables were ba, bo. Figure 2 shows approximate marker positions for tracking positions of the jaw (horizontal and vertical) and lips (vertical only) and muscle insertion points for hooked-wire, bipolar EMG recording from four muscles: ABD (anterior belly of the digastric) for jaw lowering, OOI(orbicularis oris inferior) and MTL (mentalis) for lower lip raising and protrusion, and GGA (genioglossus anterior) for tongue tip lowering.

All movement and EMG (rectified and integrated) signals were digitized (12 bit) at 200 Hz and then numerically smoothed at 40 Hz. Position signals were differentiated to obtain velocity and then, after smoothing at 22 Hz, differentiated again to get acceleration. Figure 3 shows data for one reiterant utterance using ba.

Articulator
UL : upper lip (vertical)
LL : lower lip (vertical)
JX : jaw (horizontal)
JY : jaw (vertical)

Muscle
ABD : anterior belly of the digastric
OOI : orbicularis oris inferior
MTL : mentalis
GGA : genioglossus anterior

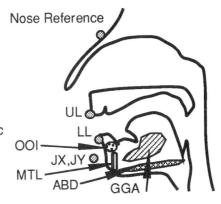

Nose Reference

UL
LL
OOI
JX,JY
MTL
ABD   GGA

Figure 2: Approximate Positions of Markers and Muscle Insertion
for Recording Movement and EMG

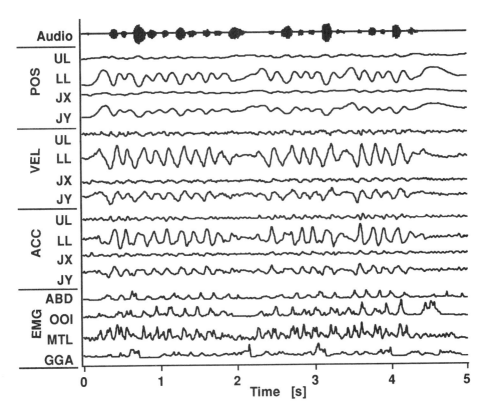

Figure 3: Time Series Representations for All Channels
of One Reiterant Rendition Using *ba*

3 FORWARD DYNAMICS MODELING OF THE MUSCULO-SKELETAL SYSTEM AND TRAJECTORY PREDICTION FROM MUSCLE EMG

The forward dynamics model (FDM) for *ba*, *bo* production was obtained using a three-layer perceptron with back propagation (Rumelhart, Hinton, & Williams, 1986). The network learns the correlations between position, velocity, EMG at time *t* and the changes of position and velocity for all articulators at the next time sample *t+1*.

After learning, the forward dynamics model is connected recurrently as shown in Figure 4. The network uses only the initial articulator position and velocity values and the continuous EMG "motor command" input to generate predicted trajectories. The FDM estimates the changes of position and velocity and sums them with position and velocity values of the previous sample *t* to obtain estimated values at the next sample *t+1*.

Figure 5 compares experimentally observed trajectories with trajectories predicted by this network. Spatiotemporal characteristics are very similar, e.g., amplitude, frequency, and phase, and demonstrate the generally good performance of the model. There is, however, a tendency towards negative offset in the predicted positions. There are two important limitations that reduce the current model's ability to compensate for position shifts in the test utterance. First, there is no specified equilibrium or rest position in articulator space, towards which articulators might tend in the absence of EMG activity. Second, the acquired FDM is based on limited EMG; at most there is correlated EMG for only one direction of motion per articulator. Addition of antagonist EMG and/or an estimate of equilibrium position in articulator or, eventually, task coordinates should increase the model's generalization capability.

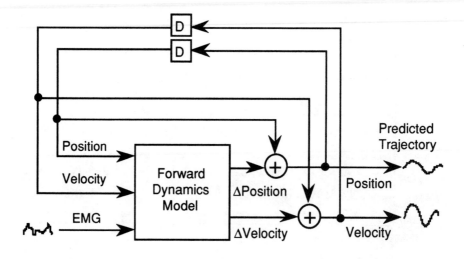

Figure 4: Recurrent Network for Trajectory Prediction from Muscle EMG

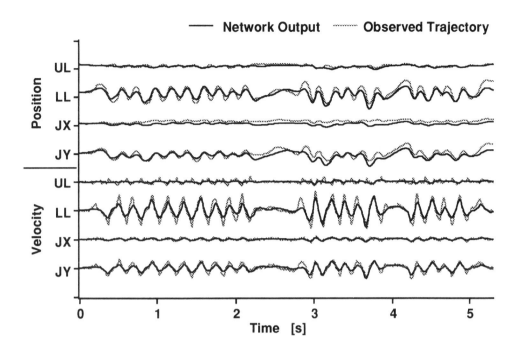

Figure 5: Experimentally Observed *vs.* Predicted Trajectories

4   ESTIMATION OF DYNAMIC PARAMETER

To investigate quantitative characteristics of the obtained forward dynamics model, the model system's response to two types of simulated perturbation were examined.

The first simulated perturbation confirmed that the model system indeed learned an appropriate nonlinear dynamics and affords a rough estimation of the its visco-elastic properties, such as natural frequency (1.0 Hz) and damping ratio (0.24). Simulated release of the lower lip at various distances from rest revealed underdamped though stable behavior, as shown in Figure 6a.

The second perturbation entailed observing articulator response to a step increase (50 % of full-scale) in EMG activity for each muscle. Figure 6b demonstrates that the learned relation between EMG input and articulator movement output is dynamical rather than kinematic because articulator responses are not instantaneous. Learned responses to each muscle's activation also show some interesting and reasonable (though not always correct) couplings between different articulators.

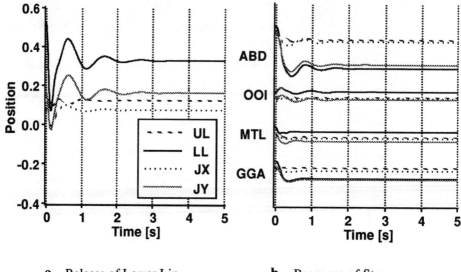

a. Release of Lower Lip
from Rest Position + 0.2

b. Response of Step
Increase (+0.5) in EMG

Figure 6: Visco-Elastic Property of the FDM Observed by Simulated Perturbations

5   MOTOR COMMAND GENERATION USING CASCADE NEURAL NETWORK MODEL

Observed articulator movements are smooth. Their smoothness is due partly to physical dynamic properties (inertia, viscosity). Furthermore, smoothness may be an attribute of the motor command itself, thereby resolving the ill-posed computational problem of generating continuous motor commands from a small number of discrete articulatory targets.

To test this, we incorporated a smoothness constraint on the motor command (rectified EMG, in this case), which is conceptually similar to previously proposed constraints on change of torque (Uno, Kawato, & Suzuki, 1989) and muscle-tension (Uno, Suzuki, & Kawato, 1989). Two articulatory target (via-point) constraints were specified spatially, one for consonant closure and the other for vowel opening, and assigned to each of the 21 consonant + vowel syllables. The alternating sequence of via-points was isochronous (temporally equidistant) except for initial, medial and final pauses. The cascade neural network (Figure 7) then generated smooth EMG and articulator trajectories whose spatiotemporal asymmetry approximated the prosodic patterning of the natural test utterances (Figure 8). Although this is only a preliminary implementation of via-point and smoothness constraints, the model's ability to generate trajectories of appropriate spatiotemporal complexity from a series of alternating via-point inputs is encouraging.

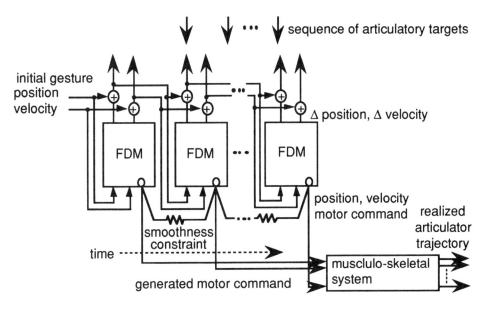

Figure 7: Cascade Neural Network Model for Motor Command Generation

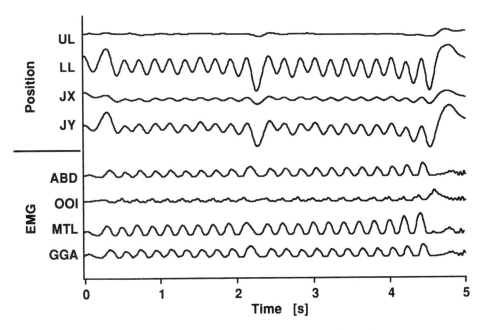

Figure 8: Generated Motor Command (EMG) with Trajectory
To Satisfy Articulatory Targets

6 CONCLUSION AND FUTURE WORK

Our intent here has been to provide a preliminary model of speech production based on the articulatory system's dynamical properties. We used real physiological data — EMG — to obtain the forward dynamics model of the articulators from a multilayer perceptron. After training, a recurrent network predicted articulator trajectories using the EMG signals as the motor command input. Simulated perturbations were used to examine the model system's response to isolated inputs and to assess its visco-elastic properties and interarticulator couplings. Then, we incorporated a reasonable smoothness criterion — minimum-motor-command-change — into a cascade neural network that generated realistic trajectories from a bead-like string of via-points.

We are now attempting to model various styles of real speech using data from more muscles and articulators such as the tongue. Also, the scope of the model is being expanded to incorporate global performance parameters for motor command generation, and the transformations from phoneme to articulatory gesture and from articulatory movement to acoustic signal.

Finally, a main goal of our work is to develop engineering applications for speech synthesis and recognition. Although our model is still preliminary, we believe resolving the difficulties posed by coarticulation, segmentation, prosody, and speaking style ultimately depends on understanding physiological and computational aspects of speech motor control.

Acknowledgement

We thank Vincent Gracco and Kiyoshi Oshima for muscle insertions; Haskins Laboratories for use of their facilities (NIH grant DC-00121); Kiyoshi Honda, Philip Rubin, Elliot Saltzman and Yoh'ichi Toh'kura for insightful discussion; and Kazunari Nakane and Eiji Yodogawa for continuous encouragement. Further support was provided by HFSP grants to M. Kawato and M. I. Jordan.

References

Jordan, M. I. (1986) Serial order: a parallel distributed processing approach, *ICS (Institute for Cognitive Science, University of California) Report*, **8604**.

Kawato, M., Maeda, M., Uno, Y. & Suzuki, R. (1990) Trajectory Formation of Arm Movement by Cascade Neural Network Model Based on Minimum Torque-change Criterion, *Biol. Cybern.* **62**, 275-288.

Laboissière, R., Schwarz, J. L. & Bailly, G. (1990) Motor Control for Speech Skills: a Connectionist Approach, *Proceeding of the 1990 Summer School*, Morgan Kaufmann Publishers, 319-327.

Rumelhart, D.E., Hinton, G.E. & Williams, R.J.(1986) Learning Internal Representation by Error Propagation, *Parallel Distributed Processing* Chap. 8, MIT Press.

Saltzman, E.L. (1986) Task dynamics coordination of the speech articulators: A preliminary model, *Experimental Brain Research*, Series 15, 129-144.

Uno, Y., Kawato, M., & Suzuki, R. (1989) Formation and Control of Optimal Trajectory in Human Multijoint Arm Movement, *Biol. Cybern.* **61**, 89-101.

Uno, Y., Suzuki, R. & Kawato, M. (1989) Minimum muscle-tension-change model which reproduces human arm movement, *Proceedings of the 4th symposium on Biological and Physiological Engineering*, 299-302, in Japanese.

English Alphabet Recognition with Telephone Speech

Mark Fanty, Ronald A. Cole and Krist Roginski
Center for Spoken Language Understanding
Oregon Graduate Institute of Science and Technology
19600 N.W. Von Neumann Dr., Beaverton, OR 97006

Abstract

A recognition system is reported which recognizes names spelled over the telephone with brief pauses between letters. The system uses separate neural networks to locate segment boundaries and classify letters. The letter scores are then used to search a database of names to find the best scoring name. The speaker-independent classification rate for spoken letters is 89%. The system retrieves the correct name, spelled with pauses between letters, 91% of the time from a database of 50,000 names.

1 INTRODUCTION

The English alphabet is difficult to recognize automatically because many letters sound alike; e.g., B/D, P/T, V/Z and F/S. When spoken over the telephone, the information needed to discriminate among several of these pairs, such as F/S, P/T, B/D and V/Z, is further reduced due to the limited bandwidth of the channel

Speaker-independent recognition of spelled names over the telephone is difficult due to variability caused by channel distortions, different handsets, and a variety of background noises. Finally, when dealing with a large population of speakers, dialect and foreign accents alter letter pronunciations. An R from a Boston speaker may not contain an [r].

Human classification performance on telephone speech underscores the difficulty of the problem. We presented each of ten listeners with 3,197 spoken letters in random order for identification. The letters were taken from 100 telephone calls in which the English alphabet was recited with pauses between letters, and 100 different telephone calls with first or last names spelled with pauses between letters. Our subjects averaged 93% correct classification of the letters, with performance ranging from 90% to 95%. This compares to error rates of about 1% for high quality microphone speech [DALY 87].

Over the past three years, our group at OGI has produced a series of letter classification and name retrieval systems. These systems combine speech knowledge and neural network classification to achieve accurate spoken letter recognition [COLE 90, FANTY 91]. Our initial work focused on speaker-independent recognition of isolated letters using high quality microphone speech. By accurately locating segment boundaries and carefully designing feature measurements to discriminate among letters, we achieved 96% classification of letters.

We extended isolated letter recognition to recognition of words spelled with brief pauses between the letters, again using high quality speech [FANTY 91, COLE 91]. This task is more difficult than recognition of isolated letters because there are "pauses" within letters, such as the closures in "X," "H" and "W," which must be distinguished from the pauses that separate letters, and because speakers do not always pause between letters when asked to do so. In the system, a neural network segments speech into a sequence of broad phonetic categories. Rules are applied to the segmentation to locate letter boundaries, and the hypothesized letters are re-classified using a second neural network. The letter scores from this network are used to retrieve the best scoring name from a database of 50,000 last names. First choice name retrieval was 95.3%, with 99% of the spelled names in the top three choices. Letter recognition accuracy was 90%.

During the past year, with support from US WEST Advanced Technologies, we have extended our approach to recognition of names spelled over the telephone. This report describes the recognition system, some experiments that motivated its design, and its current performance.

1.1   SYSTEM OVERVIEW

Data Capture and Signal Processing.   Telephone speech is sampled at 8 kHz at 14-bit resolution. Signal processing routines perform a seventh order PLP (Perceptual Linear Predictive) analysis [HERMANSKY 90] every 3 msec using a 10 msec window. This analysis yields eight coefficients per frame, including energy.

Phonetic Classification.   Frame-based phonetic classification provides a sequence of phonetic labels that can be used to locate and classify letters. Classification is performed by a fully-connected three-layer feed-forward network that assigns 22 phonetic category scores to each 3 msec time frame. The 22 labels provide an intermediate level of description, in which some phonetic categories, such as [b]-[d], [p]-[t]-[k] and [m]-[n] are combined; these fine phonetic distinctions are performed during letter classification, described below. The input to the network consists of 120 features representing PLP coefficients in a 432 msec window centered on the frame to be classified.

The frame-by-frame outputs of the phonetic classifier are converted to a sequence of phonetic segments corresponding to a sequence of hypothesized letters. This is done with a Viterbi search that uses duration and phoneme sequence constraints provided by letter models. For example, the letter model for MN consists of optional glottalization (MN-q), followed by the vowel [eh] (MN-eh), followed by the nasal murmur (MN-mn). Because background noise is often classified as [f]-[s] or [m]-[n], a noise "letter" model was added which consists of either of these phonemes.

Letter Classification. Once letter segmentation is performed, a set of 178 features is computed for each letter and used by a fully-connected feed-forward network with one hidden layer to reclassify the letter. Feature measurements are based on the phonetic boundaries provided by the segmentation. At present, the features consist of segment durations, PLP coefficients for thirds of the consonant (fricative or stop) before the first sonorant, PLP for sevenths of the first sonorant, PLP for the 200 msecs after the sonorant, PLP slices 6 and 10 msec after the sonorant onset, PLP slices 6 and 30 msec before any internal sonorant boundary (e.g. [eh]/[m]), zero crossing and amplitude profiles from 180 msec before the sonorant to 180 msec after the sonorant. The outputs of the classifier are the 26 letters plus the category "not a letter."

Name Retrieval. The output of the classifier is a score between 0 and 1 for each letter. These scores are treated as probabilities and the most likely name is retrieved from the database of 50,000 last names. The database is stored in an efficient tree structure. Letter deletions and insertions are allowed with a penalty.

2 SYSTEM DEVELOPMENT

2.1 DATA COLLECTION

Callers were solicited through local newspaper and television coverage, and notices on computer bulletin boards and news groups. Callers had the choice of using a local phone number or toll-free 800-number.

A Gradient Technology Desklab attached to a UNIX workstation was programmed to answer the phone and record the answers to pre-recorded questions. The first three thousand callers were given the following instructions, designed to generate spoken and spelled names, city names, and yes/no responses: (1) What city are you calling from? (2) What is your last name? (3) Please spell your last name. (4) Please spell your last name with short pauses between letters. (5) Does your last name contain the letter "A" as in apple? (6) What is your first name? (7) Please spell your first name with short pauses between letters. (8) What city and state did you grow up in? (9) Would you like to receive more information about the results of this project?

In order to achieve sufficient coverage of rare letters, the final 1000 speakers were asked to recite the entire English alphabet with brief pauses between letters.

The system described here was trained on 800 speakers and tested on 400 speakers. The training set contains 400 English alphabets and 800 first and last names spelled with pauses between letters. The test set consists of 100 alphabets and 300 last names spelled with pauses between letters.

A subset of the data was phonetically labeled to train and evaluate the neural network segmenter. Time-aligned phonetic labels were assigned to 300 first and last names and 100 alphabets, using the following labels: cl bcl dcl kcl pcl tcl q aa ax ay b ch d ah eh ey f iy jh k l m n ow p r s t uw v w y z h#. This label set represents a subset of the TIMIT [LAMEL 86] labels sufficient to describe the English alphabet.

2.2   FRAME-BASED CLASSIFICATION

Explicit location of segment boundaries is an important feature of our approach. Consider, for example, the letters B and D. They are distinguished by information at the onset of the letter; the spectrum of the release burst of [b] and [d], and the formant transitions during the first 10 or 15 msec of the vowel [iy]. By precisely locating the burst onset and vowel onset, feature measurements can be designed to optimize discrimination. Moreover, the duration of the initial consonant segment can be used to discriminate B from P, and D from T.

A large number of experiments were performed to improve segmentation accuracy. [ROGINSKI 91]. These experiments focused on (a) determining the appropriate set of phonetic categories, (b) determining the set of features that yield the most accurate classification of these categories, and (c) determining the best strategy for sampling speech frames within the phonetic categories.

Phonetic Categories.   Given our recognition strategy of first locating segment boundaries and then classifying letters, it makes little sense to attempt to discriminate [b]-[d], [p]-[t]-[k] or [m]-[n] at this stage. Experiments confirmed that using the complete set of phonetic categories found in the English alphabet did not produce the most accurate frame-based phonetic classification. The actual choice of categories was guided initially by perceptual confusions in the listening experiment, and was refined through a series of experiments in which different combinations of acoustically similar categories were merged.

Features Used for Classification.   A series of experiments was performed which covaried the amount of acoustic context provided to the network and the number of hidden units in the network. The results are shown in Figure 1. A network with 432 msec of spectral information, centered on the frame to be classified, and 40 hidden units was chosen as the best compromise.

Sampling of Speech Frames.   The training and test sets contained about 1.7 million 3 msec frames of speech; too many to train on all of them The manner in which speech frames were sampled was found to have a large effect of performance. It was necessary to sample more speech frames from less frequently occurring categories and those with short durations (e.g., [b]).

The *location* within segments of the speech frames selected was found to have a profound effect on the accuracy of boundary location. Accurate boundary placement required the correct proportion of speech frames sampled near segment boundaries. For example, in order to achieve accurate location of stop bursts, it was necessary to sample a high proportion of speech frames just prior to the burst (within the

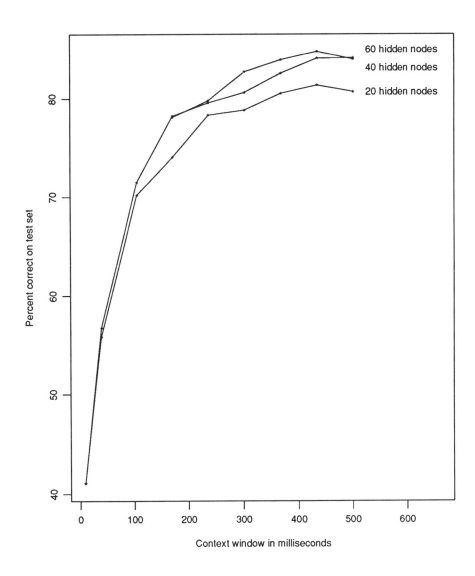

Figure 1: Performance of the phonetic classifier as a function of PLP context and number of hidden units.

closure category). Figure 2 shows the improvement in the placement of the [b]/[iy] boundary after sampling more training frames near that boundary.

2.3 LETTER CLASSIFICATION

In order to avoid segmenting training data for letter classification by hand, an automatic procedure was used. Each utterance was listened to and the letter names were transcribed manually. Segmentation was performed as described above, except the Viterbi search was forced to match the transcribed letter sequence. This resulted in very accurate segmentation.

One concern with this procedure was that artificially good segmentation for the training data could hurt performance on the test set, where there are bound to be more segmentation errors (since the letter sequence is not known). The letter classifier should be able to recover from segmentation errors (e.g. a B being segmented as V with a long [v] before the burst). To do so, the network must be trained with errorful segmentation.

The solution is to perform two segmentations. The forced segmentation finds the letter boundaries so the correct identity is known. A second, unforced, segmentation is performed and these phonetic boundaries are used to generate features used to train the classifier.

Any "letters" found by the unforced search which correspond to noise or silence from the forced search are used as training data for the "not a letter" category. So there are two ways noise can be eliminated: It can match the noise model of the segmenter during the Viterbi search, or it can match a letter during segmentation, but be reclassified as "not a letter" by the letter classifier. Both are necessary in the current system.

3 PERFORMANCE

Frame-Based Phonetic Classification. The phonetic classifier was trained on selected speech frames from 200 speakers. About 450 speech frames were selected from 50 different occurrences of each phonetic category. Phonetic segmentation performance on 50 alphabets and 150 last names was evaluated by comparing the first-choice of the classifier at each time frame to the label provided by a human expert. The frame-by-frame agreement was 80% before the Viterbi search and 90% after the Viterbi search.

Letter Classification and Name Retrieval. The training set consists of 400 alphabets spelled by 400 callers plus first and last names spelled by 400 callers, all with pauses between the letters.

When tested on 100 alphabets from new speakers, the letter classification was 89% with less than 1% insertions. When tested on 300 last names from new speakers, the letter classification was 87% with 1.5% insertions.

For the 300 callers spelling their last name, 90.7% of the names were correctly retrieved from a list of 50,000 common last names. 95.7% of the names were in the

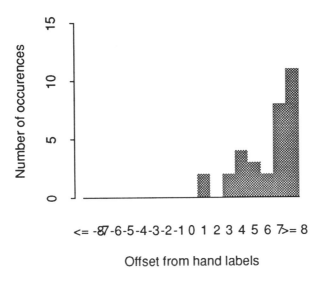

Offset from hand labels

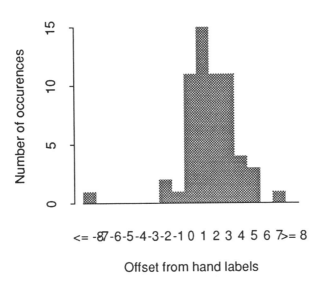

Offset from hand labels

Figure 2: Test set improvement in the placement of the [b]/[iy] boundary after sampling more training frames near that boundary. The top histogram shows the difference between hand-labeled boundaries and the system's boundaries in 3 msec frames before adding extra boundary frames. The bottom histogram shows the difference after adding the boundary frames.

top three.

4   DISCUSSION

The recognition system described in this paper classifies letters of the English alphabet produced by any speaker over telephone lines at 89% accuracy for spelled alphabets and retrieves names from a list of 50,000 with 91% first choice accuracy.

The system has a number of characteristic features. We represent speech using an auditory model—Perceptual Linear Predictive (PLP) analysis. We perform explicit segmentation of the speech signal into phonetic categories. Explicit segmentation allows us to use segment durations to discriminate letters, and to extract features from specific regions of the signal. Finally, speech knowledge is used to design a set of features that work best for English letters. We are currently analyzing errors made by our system. The great advantage of our approach is that individual errors can be analyzed, and individual features can be added to improve performance.

Acknowledgements

Research supported by US WEST Advanced Technologies, APPLE Computer Inc., NSF, ONR, Digital Equipment Corporation and Oregon Advanced Computing Institute.

References

[COLE 91] R. A. Cole, M. Fanty, M. Gopalakrishnan, and R. D. T. Janssen. Speaker-independent name retrieval from spellings using a database of 50,000 names. In *Proceedings of the IEEE International Conference on Acoustics, Speech, and Signal Processing*, 1991.

[COLE 90] R. A. Cole, M. Fanty, Y. Muthusamy, and M. Gopalakrishnan. Speaker-independent recognition of spoken English letters. In *Proceedings of the International Joint Conference on Neural Networks*, San Diego, CA, 1990.

[DALY 87] N. Daly. Recognition of words from their spellings: Integration of multiple knowledge sources. Master's thesis, Massachusetts Institute of Technology, May, 1987.

[FANTY 91] M. Fanty and R. A. Cole. Spoken letter recognition. In R. P. Lippman, J. Moody, and D. S. Touretzky, editors, *Advances in Neural Information Processing Systems 3*. San Mateo, CA: Morgan Kaufmann, 1991.

[HERMANSKY 90] H. Hermansky. Perceptual Linear Predictive (PLP) analysis of speech. *J. Acoust. Soc. Am.*, 87(4):1738–1752, 1990.

[LAMEL 86] L. Lamel, R. Kassel, and S. Seneff. Speech database development: Design and analysis of the acoustic-phonetic corpus. In *Proceedings of the DARPA Speech Recognition Workshop*, pages 100–110, 1986.

[ROGINSKI 91] Krist Roginski. A neural network phonetic classifier for telephone spoken letter recognition. Master's thesis, Oregon Graduate Institute, 1991.

PART IV

LANGUAGE

Generalization Performance in PARSEC—A Structured Connectionist Parsing Architecture

Ajay N. Jain[*]
School of Computer Science
Carnegie Mellon University
Pittsburgh, PA 15213-3890

ABSTRACT

This paper presents PARSEC—a system for generating connectionist parsing networks from example parses. PARSEC is not based on formal grammar systems and is geared toward spoken language tasks. PARSEC networks exhibit three strengths important for application to speech processing: 1) they *learn* to parse, and generalize well compared to hand-coded grammars; 2) they tolerate several types of noise; 3) they can learn to use multi-modal input. Presented are the PARSEC architecture and performance analyses along several dimensions that demonstrate PARSEC's features. PARSEC's performance is compared to that of traditional grammar-based parsing systems.

1 INTRODUCTION

While a great deal of research has been done developing parsers for natural language, adequate solutions for some of the particular problems involved in spoken language have not been found. Among the unsolved problems are the difficulty in constructing task-specific grammars, lack of tolerance to noisy input, and inability to effectively utilize non-symbolic information. This paper describes PARSEC—a system for generating connectionist parsing networks from example parses.

---

[*]Now with Alliant Techsystems Research and Technology Center (jain@rtc.atk.com).

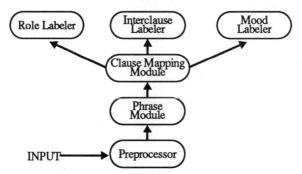

Figure 1: PARSEC's high-level architecture

PARSEC networks exhibit three strengths:

- They automatically learn to parse, and generalize well compared to hand-coded grammars.
- They tolerate several types of noise without any explicit noise modeling.
- They can learn to use multi-modal input such as pitch in conjunction with syntax and semantics.

The PARSEC network architecture relies on a variation of supervised back-propagation learning. The architecture differs from some other connectionist approaches in that it is highly structured, both at the macroscopic level of modules, and at the microscopic level of connections. Structure is exploited to enhance system performance.[1]

Conference registration dialogs formed the primary development testbed for PARSEC. A separate speech recognition effort in conference registration provided data for evaluating noise-tolerance and also provided an application for PARSEC in speech-to-speech translation (Waibel *et al.* 1991).

PARSEC differs from early connectionist work in parsing (e.g. Fanty 1985; Selman 1985) in its emphasis on learning. It differs from recent connectionist approaches (e.g. Elman 1990; Miikkulainen 1990) in its emphasis on performance issues such as generalization and noise tolerance in real tasks. This papers presents the PARSEC architecture, its training algorithms, and performance analyses that demonstrate PARSEC's features.

2 PARSEC ARCHITECTURE

The PARSEC architecture is modular and hierarchical. Figure 1 shows the high-level architecture. PARSEC can learn to parse complex English sentences including multiple clauses, passive constructions, center-embedded constructions, etc. The input to PARSEC is presented sequentially, one word at a time. PARSEC produces a case-based representation of a parse as the input sentence develops.

---

[1]PARSEC is a generalization of a previous connectionist parsing architecture (Jain 1991). For a detailed exposition of PARSEC, please refer to Jain's PhD thesis (in preparation).

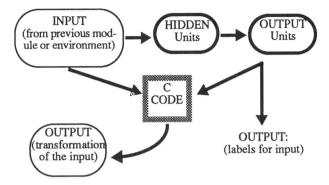

Figure 2: Basic structure of a PARSEC module

The parse for the sentence, "I will send you a form immediately," is:

```
([statement]
    ([clause]
        ([agent]        I)
        ([action]       will send)
        ([recipient]    you)
        ([patient]      a form)
        ([time]         immediately)))
```

Input words are represented as binary feature patterns (primarily syntactic with some semantic features). These feature representations are hand-crafted.

Each module of PARSEC can perform either a transformation or a labeling of its input. The output function of each module is represented across localist connectionist units. The actual transformations are made using non-connectionist subroutines.[2] Figure 2 shows the basic structure of a PARSEC module. The bold ovals contain units that learn via back-propagation.

There are four steps in generating a PARSEC network: 1) create an example parse file; 2) define a lexicon; 3) train the six modules; 4) assemble the full network. Of these, only the first two steps require substantial human effort, and this effort is small relative to that required for writing a grammar by hand. Training and assembly are automatic.

2.1 PREPROCESSING MODULE

This module marks alphanumeric sequences, which are replaced by a single special marker word. This prevents long alphanumeric strings from overwhelming the length constraint on phrases. Note that this is not always a trivial task since words such as "a" and "one" are lexically ambiguous.

INPUT: "It costs three hundred twenty one dollars."
OUTPUT: "It costs ALPHANUM dollars."

---

[2]These transformations could be carried out by connectionist networks, but at a substantial computational cost for training and a risk of undergeneralization.

2.2 PHRASE MODULE

The Phrase module processes the evolving output of the Prep module into *phrase blocks*. Phrase blocks are non-recursive contiguous pieces of a sentence. They correspond to simple noun phrases and verb groups.[3] Phrase blocks are represented as grouped sets of units in the network. Phrase blocks are denoted by brackets in the following:

INPUT: "I will send you a new form in the morning."
OUTPUT: "[I] [will send] [you] [a new form] [in the morning]."

2.3 CLAUSE MAPPING MODULE

The Clause module uses the output of the Phrase module as input and assigns the clausal structure. The result is an unambiguous bracketing of the phrase blocks that is used to transform the phrase block representation into representations for each clause:

INPUT: "[I] [would like] [to register] [for the conference]."
OUTPUT: "{[I] [would like]} {[to register] [for the conference]}."

2.4 ROLE LABELING MODULE

The Roles module associates case-role labels with each phrase block in each clause. It also denotes attachment structure for prepositional phrases ("MOD-1" indicates that the current phrase block modifies the previous one):

INPUT: "{[The titles] [of papers] [are printed] [in the forms]}"
OUTPUT: "{[The titles] [of papers] [are printed] [in the forms]}"
                PATIENT   MOD-1   ACTION   LOCATION

2.5 INTERCLAUSE AND MOOD MODULES

The Interclause and Mood modules are similar to the Roles module. They both assign labels to constituents, except they operate at higher levels. The Interclause module indicates, for example, subordinate and relative clause relationships. The Mood module indicates the overall sentence mood (declarative or interrogative in the networks discussed here).

3 GENERALIZATION

Generalization in large connectionist networks is a critical issue. This is especially the case when training data is limited. For the experiments reported here, the training data was limited to twelve conference registration dialogs containing approximately 240 sentences with a vocabulary of about 400 words. Despite the small corpus, a large number of English constructs were covered (including passives, conditional constructions, center-embedded relative clauses, etc.).

A set of 117 disjoint sentences was obtained to test coverage. The sentences were generated by a group of people different from those that developed the 12 dialogs. These sentences used the same vocabulary as the 12 dialogs.

---

[3]Abney has described a similar linguistic unit called a *chunk* (Abney 1991).

3.1 EARLY PARSEC VERSIONS

Straightforward training of a PARSEC network resulted in poor generalization performance, with only 16% of the test sentences being parsed correctly. One of the primary sources for error was positional sensitivity acquired during training of the three transformational modules. In the Phrase module, for example, each of the phrase boundary detector units was supposed to learn to indicate a boundary between words in specific positions.

Each of the units of the Phrase module is performing essentially the same job, but the network doesn't "know" this and cannot learn this from a small sample set. By sharing the connection weights across positions, the network is forced to be position insensitive (similar to TDNN's as in Waibel *et al.* 1989). After modifying PARSEC to use shared weights and localized connectivity in the lower three modules, generalization performance increased to 27%. The primary source of error shifted to the Roles module.

Part of the problem could be ascribed to the representation of phrase blocks. They were represented across rows of units that each define a word. In the phrase block "the big dog," "dog" would have appeared in row 3. This changes to row 2 if the phrase block is just "the dog." A network had to learn to respond to the heads of phrase blocks even though they moved around. An augmented phrase block representation in which the last word of the phrase block was copied to position 0 solved this problem. With the augmented phrase block representation coupled with the previous improvements, PARSEC achieved 44% coverage.

3.2 PARSEC: FINAL VERSION

The final version of PARSEC uses all of the previous enhancements plus a technique called *Programmed Constructive Learning* (PCL). In PCL, hidden units are added to a network one at a time as they are needed. Also, there is a specific series of hidden unit types for each module of a PARSEC network. The hidden unit types progress from being highly local in input connectivity to being more broad. This forces the networks to learn general predicates before specializing and using possibly unreliable information.

The final version of PARSEC was used to generate another parsing network.[4] Its performance was 67% (78% including near-misses). Table 1 summarizes these results.

3.3 COMPARISON TO HAND-CODED GRAMMARS

PARSEC's performance was compared to that of three independently constructed grammars. Two of the grammars were commissioned as part of a contest where the first prize ($700) went to the grammar-writer with best coverage of the test set and the second prize ($300) went to the other grammar writer.[5] The third grammar was independently constructed as part of the JANUS system (described later). The contest grammars achieved 25% and 38% coverage, and the other grammar achieved just 5% coverage of the test set

---

[4]This final parsing network was not trained all the way to completion. Training to completion hurts generalization performance.

[5]The contest participants had 8 weeks to complete their grammars, and they both spent over 60 hours doing so. The grammar writers work in Machine Translation and Computational Linguistics and were quite experienced.

Table 1: PARSEC's comparative performance

	Coverage	Noise	Ungram.
PARSEC V4	67% (78%)	77%	66%
Grammar 1	38% (39%)	–	34%
Grammar 2	25% (26%)	–	38%
Grammar 3	5% (5%)	70%	2%

(see Table 1). All of the hand-coded grammars produced NIL parses for the majority of test sentences. In the table, numbers in parentheses include near-misses.

PARSEC's performance was substantially better than the best of the hand-coded grammars. PARSEC has a systematic advantage in that it is trained on the *incremental* parsing task and is exposed to partial sentences during training. Also, PARSEC's constructive learning approach coupled with weight sharing emphasizes local constraints wherever possible, and distant variations in input structure do not adversely affect parsing.

4   NOISE TOLERANCE

The second area of performance analysis for PARSEC was noise tolerance. Preliminary comparisons between PARSEC and a rule-based parser in the JANUS speech-to-speech translation system were promising (Waibel *et al.* 1991). More extensive evaluations corroborated the early observations. In addition, PARSEC was evaluated on synthetic ungrammatical sentences. Experiments on spontaneous speech using DARPA's ATIS task are ongoing.

4.1   NOISE IN SPEECH-TO-SPEECH TRANSLATION

In the JANUS system, speech recognition is provided by an LPNN (Tebelskis *et al.* 1991), parsing can be done by a PARSEC network or an LR parser, translation is accomplished by processing the interlingual output of the parser using a standard language generation module, and speech generation is provided by off-the-shelf devices. The system can be run using a single (often noisy) hypothesis from the LPNN or a ranked list of hypotheses.

When run in single-hypothesis mode, JANUS using PARSEC correctly translated 77% of the input utterances, and JANUS using the LR parser (Grammar 3 in the table) achieved 70%. The PARSEC network was able to parse a number of incorrect recognitions well enough that a successful translation resulted. However, when run in multi-hypothesis mode, the LR parser achieved 86% compared to PARSEC's 80%. The LR parser utilized a very tight grammar and was able to robustly reject hypotheses that deviated from expectations. This allowed the LR parser to "choose" the correct hypothesis more often than PARSEC. PARSEC tended to accept noisy utterances that produced incorrect translations. Of course, given that the PARSEC network's coverage was so much higher than that of the grammar used by the LR parser, this result is not surprising.

4.2   SYNTHETIC UNGRAMMATICALITY

Using the same set of grammars for comparison, the parsers were tested on ungrammatical input from the CR task. These sentences were corrupted versions of sentences used for

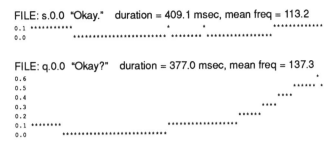

FILE: s.0.0 "Okay."   duration = 409.1 msec, mean freq = 113.2

FILE: q.0.0 "Okay?"   duration = 377.0 msec, mean freq = 137.3

Figure 3: Smoothed pitch contours.

training. Training sentences were used to decouple the effects of noise from coverage. Table 1 shows the results. They essentially mirror those of the coverage tests. PARSEC is substantially less sensitive to such effects as subject/verb disagreement, missing determiners, and other non-catastrophic irregularities.

Some researchers have augmented grammar-based systems to be more tolerant of noise (e.g. Saito and Tomita 1988). However, the PARSEC network in the test reported here was trained only on grammatical input and still produced a degree of noise tolerance for free. In the same way that one can explicitly build noise tolerance into a grammar-based system, one can train a PARSEC network on input that includes specific types of noise. The result should be some noise tolerance beyond what was explicitly trained.

5 MULTI-MODAL INPUT

A somewhat elusive goal of spoken language processing has been to utilize information from the speech signal beyond just word sequences in higher-level processing. It is well known that humans use such information extensively in conversation. Consider the utterances "Okay." and "Okay?" Although semantically distinct, they cannot be distinguished based on word sequence, but pitch contours contain the necessary information (Figure 3).

In a grammar-based system, it is difficult to incorporate real-valued vector input in a useful way. In a PARSEC network, the vector is just another set of input units. The Mood module of a PARSEC network was augmented to contain an additional set of units that contained pitch information. The pitch contours were smoothed output from the OGI Neural Network Pitch Tracker (Barnard *et al.* 1991). PARSEC added another hidden unit to utilize the new information.

The trained PARSEC network was tolerant of speaker variation, gender variation, utterance variation (length and content), and a combination of these factors. Although not explicitly trained to do so, the network correctly processed sentences that were grammatical questions but had been pronounced with the declining pitch of a typical statement.

Within the JANUS system, the augmented PARSEC network brings new functionality. Intonation affects translation in JANUS when using the augmented PARSEC network. The sentence, "This is the conference office." is translated to "Kaigi jimukyoku desu." "This is the conference office?" is translated to "Kaigi jimukyoku desuka?" This required no changes in the other modules of the JANUS system. It also should be possible to use other types of information from the speech signal to aid in robust parsing (e.g. energy patterns to disambiguate clausal structure).

6 CONCLUSION

PARSEC is a system for generating connectionist parsing networks from training examples. Experiments using a conference registration conversational task showed that PARSEC: 1) learns and generalizes well compared to hand-coded grammars; 2) tolerates noise: recognition errors and ungrammaticality; 3) successfully learns to combine intonational information with syntactic/semantic information. Future work with PARSEC will be continued by extending it to new languages, larger English tasks, and speech tasks that involve tighter coupling between speech recognition and parsing. There are numerous issues in NLP that will be addressed in the context of these research directions.

Acknowledgements

The author gratefully acknowledges the support of DARPA, the National Science Foundation, ATR Interpreting Telephony Laboratories, NEC Corp., and Siemens Corp.

References

Abney, S. P. 1991. Parsing by chunks. In *Principle-Based Parsing*, ed. R. Berwick, S. P. Abney, C. Tenny. Kluwer Academic Publishers.

Barnard, E., R. A. Cole, M. P. Vea, F. A. Alleva. 1991. Pitch Detection with a Neural-Net Classifier. *IEEE Transactions on Signal Processing* 39(2): 298–307.

Elman, J. L. 1989. *Representation and Structure in Connectionist Networks*. Tech. Rep. CRL 8903. Center for Research in Language, University of California, San Diego.

Fanty, M. 1985. *Context Free Parsing in Connectionist Networks*. Tech. Rep. TR174, Computer Science Department, University of Rochester.

Jain, A. N. and A. H. Waibel. 1990. Robust connectionist parsing of spoken language. In *Proceedings of the 1990 IEEE International Conference on Acoustics, Speech, and Signal Processing*

Jain, A. N. In preparation. *PARSEC: A Connectionist Learning Architecture for Parsing Speech*. PhD Thesis. School of Computer Science, Carnegie Mellon University.

Miikkulainen, R. 1990. A PDP architecture for processing sentences with relative clauses. In *Proceedings of the 13th Annual Conference of the Cognitive Science Society.*

Saito, H., and M. Tomita. 1988. Parsing noisy sentences. In *Proceedings of INFO JAPAN '88: International Conference of the Information Processing Society of Japan*, 553–59.

Selman, B. 1985. *Rule-Based Processing in a Connectionist System for Natural Language Understanding*. Ph.D. Thesis, University of Toronto. Available as Tech. Rep. CSRI-168.

Tebelskis, J., A. Waibel, B. Petek, and O. Schmidbauer. 1991. Continuous speech recognition using linked predictive neural networks. In *Proceedings of the 1991 IEEE International Conference on Acoustics, Speech, and Signal Processing.*

Waibel, A., T. Hanazawa, G. Hinton, K. Shikano, and K. Lang. 1989. Phoneme recognition using time-delay neural networks. *IEEE Transactions on Acoustics, Speech, and Signal Processing* 37(3):328–339.

Waibel, A., A. N. Jain, A. E. McNair, H. Saito, A. G. Hauptmann, and J. Tebelskis. 1991. JANUS: A speech-to-speech translation system using connectionist and symbolic processing strategies. In *IEEE Proceedings of the International Conference on Acoustics, Speech, and Signal Processing.*

Constructing Proofs in Symmetric Networks

Gadi Pinkas
Computer Science Department
Washington University
Campus Box 1045
St. Louis, MO 63130

Abstract

This paper considers the problem of expressing predicate calculus in connectionist networks that are based on energy minimization. Given a first-order-logic knowledge base and a bound k, a symmetric network is constructed (like a Boltzman machine or a Hopfield network) that searches for a proof for a given query. If a resolution-based proof of length no longer than k exists, then the global minima of the energy function that is associated with the network represent such proofs. The network that is generated is of size cubic in the bound k and linear in the knowledge size. There are no restrictions on the type of logic formulas that can be represented. The network is inherently fault tolerant and can cope with inconsistency and nonmonotonicity.

1 Introduction

The ability to reason from acquired knowledge is undoubtedly one of the basic and most important components of human intelligence. Among the major tools for reasoning in the area of AI are deductive proof techniques. However, traditional methods are plagued by intractability, inability to learn and adjust, as well as by inability to cope with noise and inconsistency. A connectionist approach may be the missing link: fine grain, massively parallel architecture may give us real-time approximation; networks are potentially trainable and adjustable; and they may be made tolerant to noise as a result of their collective computation.

Most connectionist reasoning systems that implement parts of first-order logic (see for examples: [Hölldobler 90], [Shastri et al. 90]) use the spreading activation paradigm and usually trade expressiveness with time efficiency. In contrast, this paper uses the energy minimization paradigm (like [Derthick 88], [Ballard 86] and [Pinkas 91c]), representing an intractable problem, but trading time with correctness; i.e., as more time is given, the probability of converging to a correct answer increases.

Symmetric connectionist networks used for constraint satisfaction are the target platform [Hopfield 84b], [Hinton, Sejnowski 86], [Peterson, Hartman 89], [Smolensky 86]. They are characterized by a quadratic energy function that should be minimized. Some of the models in the family may be seen as performing a search for a *global* minimum of their energy function. The task is therefore to represent logic deduction that is bound by a *finite* proof length as energy minimization (without a bound on the proof length, the problem is undecidable). When a query is clamped, the network should search for a proof that supports the query. If a proof to the query exists, then every global minimum of the energy function associated with the network represents a proof. If no proof exists, the global minima represent the lack of a proof.

The paper elaborates the propositional case; however, due to space limitations, the first-order (FOL) case is only sketched. For more details and full treatment of FOL see [Pinkas 91j].

2   Representing proofs of propositional logic

I'll start by assuming that the knowledge base is propositional.

The proof area:
A proof is a list of clauses ending with the query such that every clause used is either an original clause, a copy (or weakening) of a clause that appears earlier in the proof, or a result of a resolution step of the two clauses that appeared just earlier. The proof emerges as an activation pattern on special unit structures called the proof area, and is represented in reverse to the common practice (the query appears first). For example: given a knowledge base of the following clauses:
1) A
2) $\neg A \lor B \lor C$
3) $\neg B \lor D$
4) $\neg C \lor D$
we would like to prove the query D, by generating the following list of clauses:

1) D (obtained by resolution of clauses 2 and 3 by canceling A).
2) A (original clause no. 1).
3) $\neg A \lor D$ (obtained by resolution of clauses 4 and 5 by canceling C).
4) $\neg C \lor D$ (original clause no. 4).
5) $\neg A \lor C \lor D$ (obtained by resolution of clauses 6 and 7 by canceling B).
6) $\neg B \lor D$ (original clause no. 3).
7) $\neg A \lor B \lor C$ (original clause no. 2).

Each clause in the proof is either an original clause, a copy of a clause from earlier in the proof, or a resolution step.

The matrix C in figure 1, functions as a clause list. This list represents an ordered set of clauses that form the proof. The query clauses are clamped onto this area and activate hard constraints that force the rest of the units of the matrix to form a valid proof (if it exists).

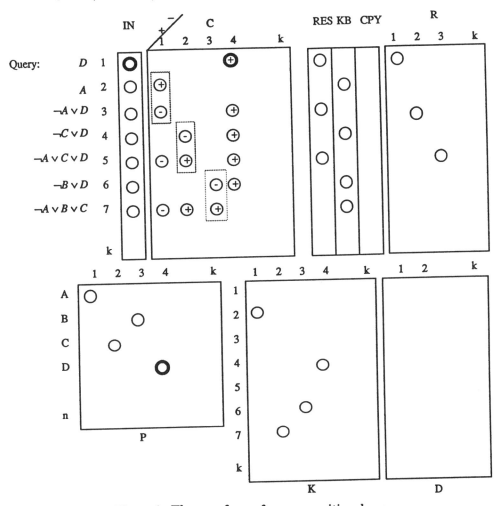

Figure 1: The proof area for a propositional case

Variable binding is performed by dynamic allocation of instances using a technique similar to [Anandan et al. 89] and [Barnden 91]. In this technique, if two symbols need to be bound together, an instance is allocated from a pool of general purpose instances, and is connected to both symbols. An instance can be connected to a literal in a clause, to a predicate type, to a constant, to a function or to a slot of another instance (for example, a constant that is bound to the first slot of a predicate).

The clauses that participate in the proof are represented using a 3-dimensional matrix $(C_{s,i,j})$ and a 2-dimensional matrix $(P_{i,j})$ as illustrated in figure 1. The rows of C represent clauses of the proof, while the rows of P represent atomic propositions. The columns of both matrices represent the pool of instances used for binding propositions to clauses.

A clause is a list of negative and positive instances that represent literals. The instance thus behaves as a two-way pointer that binds composite structures like clauses with their constituents (the atomic propositions). A row i in the matrix C represents a clause which is composed of pairs of instances. If the unit $C_{+,i,j}$ is set, then the matrix represents a positive literal in clause i. If $P_{A,j}$ is also set, then $C_{+,i,j}$ represents a *positive* literal of clause i that is bound to the atomic proposition A. Similarly $C_{-,i,j}$ represents a *negative* literal.

The first row of matrix C in the figure is the query clause D. It contains only one positive literal that is bound to atomic proposition D via instance 4. For another example consider the third row of the C which represents a clause of two literals: a positive one that is bound to D via instance 4, and a negative one bound to A via instance 1 (it is the clause $\neg A \lor D$, generated as a result of a resolution step).

Participation in the proof: The vector IN represents whether clauses in C participate in the proof. In our example, all the clauses are in the proof; however, in the general case some of the rows of C may be meaningless. When IN_i is on, it means that the clause i is in the proof and must be proved as well. Every clause that participates in the proof is either a result of a resolution step (RES_i is set), a copy of a some clause (CPY_i is set), or it is an original clause from the knowledge base (KB_i is set). The second clause of C in figure 1 for example is an original clause of the knowledge base. If a clause j is copied, it must be in the proof itself and therefore IN_j is set. Similarly, if clause i is a result of a resolution step, then the two resolved clauses must also be in the proof ($IN_{i+1,j}$ and $IN_{i+2,j}$) and therefore must be themselves resolvents, copies or originals. This chain of constraints continues until all constraints are satisfied and a valid proof is generated.

Posting a query: The user posts a query clamping its clauses onto the first rows of C and setting the appropriate IN units. This indicates that the query clauses participate in the proof and should be proved by either a resolution step, a copy step or by an original clause. Figure 1 represents the complete proof for the query D. We start by allocating an instance (4) for D in the P matrix, and clamping a positive literal D in the first row of C ($C_{+,1,4}$); the rest of the first row's units are clamped zero. The unit IN_1 is biased (to have the value of one), indicating that the query is in the proof; this cause a chain of constraints to be activated that are satisfied only by a valid proof. If no proof exists, the IN_1 unit will become zero; i.e., the global minima is obtained by setting IN_1 to zero despite the bias.

Representing resolutions steps: The vector RES is a structure of units that indicates which are the clauses in C that are obtained by a resolution step. If RES_i is set, then the ith row is obtained by resolving row $i+1$ of C with row $i+2$. Thus, the unit RES_1 in figure 1 indicates that the clause D of the first row of C is a resolvent of the second and the third rows of C representing $\neg A \lor D$ and A respectfully. Two literals cancel each other if they have opposite signs and are represented by the same instance. In figure 1, literal A of the third row of C and literal $\neg A$ of the second row cancel each other, generating the clause of the first row.

The rows of matrix R represent literals canceled by resolution steps. If row i of

C is the result of a resolution step, there must be one and only one instance j such that both clause $i+1$ and clause $i+2$ include it with opposite signs. For example (figure 1): clause D in the first row of C is the result of resolving clause A with clause $\neg A \vee D$ which are in the second and third rows of C respectfully. Instance 1, representing atomic proposition A, is the one that is canceled; $R_{1,1}$ is set therefore, indicating that clause 1 is obtained by a resolution step that cancels the literals of instance 1.

Copied and original clauses: The matrix D indicates which clauses are copied to other clauses in the proof area. Setting $D_{i,j}$ means that clause i is obtained by copying (or weakening) clause j into clause i (the example does not use copy steps).

The matrix K indicates which original knowledge-base clauses participate in the proof. The unit $K_{i,j}$ indicates that a clause i in the proof area is an original clause, and the syntax of the j-th clause in the knowledge base must be imposed on the units of clause i. In figure 1 for example, clause 2 in the proof (the second row in C), assumes the identity of clause number 1 in the knowledge base and therefore $K_{1,2}$ is set.

3   Constraints

We are now ready to specify the constraints that must be satisfied by the units so that a proof is found. The constraints are specified as well formed logic formulas. For example the formula $(A \vee B) \wedge C$ imposes a constraint over the units (A, B, C) such that the only possible valid assignments to those units are $(011), (101), (111)$. A general method to implement an arbitrary logical constraint on connectionist networks is shown in [Pinkas 90b]. Most of the constraints specified in this section are hard constraints; i.e., must be satisfied for a valid proof to emerge. Towards the end of this section, some soft constraints are presented.

In-proof constraints: If a clause participates in the proof, it must be either a result of a resolution step, a copy step or an original clause. In logic, the constraints may be expressed as: $\forall i : IN_i \to RES_i \vee CPY_i \vee KB_i$. The three units (per clause i) consist a winner takes all subnetwork (WTA). This means that only one of the three units is actually set. The WTA constraints may be expressed as:
$$RES_i \to \neg CPY_i \wedge \neg KB_i$$
$$CPY_i \to \neg RES_i \wedge \neg KB_i$$
$$KB_i \to \neg RES_i \wedge \neg CPY_i$$
The WTA property may be enforced by inhibitory connections between every pair of the three units.

Copy constraints: If CPY_i is set then clause i must be a copy of another clause j in the proof. This can be expressed as $\forall i : CPY_i \to \bigvee_j (D_{i,j} \wedge IN_j)$. The rows of D are WTAs allowing i to be a copy of only one j. In addition, if clause j is copied or weakened into clause i then every unit set in clause j must also be set in clause i. This may be specified as: $\forall i, j, l : D_{i,j} \to ((C_{+,i,l} \leftarrow C_{+,j,l}) \wedge (C_{-,i,l} \leftarrow C_{-,j,l}))$.

Resolution constraints: If a clause i is a result of resolving the two clauses $i+1$ and $i+2$, then there must be one and only one instance (j) that is canceled (represented by $R_{i,j}$), and C_i is obtained by copying both the instances of C_{i+1} and C_{i+2}, without the instance j. These constraints may be expressed as:

$\forall i : RES_i \rightarrow \bigvee_j R_{i,j}$ at least one instance is canceled

$\forall i, j, j', j' \neq j : R_{i,j} \rightarrow \neg R_{i,j'}$ only one instance is canceled (WT

$\forall i, j : R_{i,j} \rightarrow (C_{+,i+1,j} \wedge C_{-,i+2,j}) \vee (C_{-,i+1,j} \wedge C_{+,i+2,j})$ cancel literals with opposite signs.

$\forall i : RES_i \rightarrow IN_{i+1} \wedge IN_{i+2}$ the two resolvents are also in proo

$\forall i : RES_i \rightarrow (C_{+,i,j} \leftrightarrow (C_{+,i+1,j} \vee C_{+,i+2,j}) \wedge \neg R_{i,j}$ copy positive literals

$\forall i : RES_i \rightarrow (C_{-,i,j} \leftrightarrow (C_{-,i+1,j} \vee C_{-,i+2,j}) \wedge \neg R_{i,j}$ copy negative literals

Clause-instance constraints: The sign of an instance in a clause should be unique; therefore, any instance pair in the matrix C is WTA: $\forall i, j : C_{+,i,j} \rightarrow \neg C_{-,i,j}$. The columns of matrix P are WTAs since an instance is allowed to represent only one atomic proposition: $\forall A, i, B \neq A : P_{A,i} \rightarrow \neg P_{B,i}$. The rows of P may be also WTAs: $\forall A, i, j \neq i : P_{A,i} \rightarrow \neg P_{A,j}$ (this constraint is not imposed in the FOL case).

Knowledge base constraints: If a clause i is an original knowledge base clause, then there must be a clause j (out of the m original clauses) whose syntax is forced upon the units of the i-th row of matrix C. This constraint can be expressed as: $\forall i : KB_i \rightarrow \bigvee_j^m K_{i,j}$. The rows of K are WTA networks so that only one original clause is forced on the units of clause i: $\forall i, j, j' \neq j : K_{i,j} \rightarrow \neg K_{i,j'}$.

The only hard constraints that are left are those that force the syntax of a particular clause from the knowledge base. Assume for example that $K_{i,4}$ is set, meaning that clause i in C must have the syntax of the fourth clause in the knowledge base of our example ($\neg C \vee D$). Instances j and j' must be allocated to the atomic propositions C and D respectfully, and must appear also in clause i as the literals $C_{-,i,j}$ and $C_{+,i,j'}$. The following constraints capture the syntax of ($\neg C \vee D$):

$\forall i : K_{i,4} \rightarrow \bigvee_j (C_{-,i,j} \wedge P_{C,j})$ there exists a negative literal that is bound to C;

$\forall i : K_{i,4} \rightarrow \bigvee_j (D_{+,i,j} \wedge P_{C,j})$ there exists a positive literal that is bound to D.

FOL extension:

In first-order predicate logic (FOL) instead of atomic propositions we must deal with predicates (see [Pinkas 91j] for details). As in the propositional case, a literal in a clause is represented by a positive or negative instance; however, the instance must be allocated now to a predicate name and may have slots to be filled by other instances (representing functions and constants). To accommodate such complexity a new matrix ($NEST$) is added, and the role of matrix P is revised.

The matrix P must accommodate now function names, predicate names and constant names instead of just atomic propositions. Each row of P represents a name, and the columns represent instances that are allocated to those names. The rows of P that are associated with predicates and functions may contain several different instances of the same predicate or function, thus, they are not WTA anymore. In order to represent compound terms and predicates, instances may be bound to slots of other instances. The new matrix ($NEST_{i,j,p}$) is capable of representing such bindings. If $NEST_{i,j,p}$ is set, then instance i is bound to the p slot of instance j. The columns of $NEST$ are WTA, allowing only one instance to be bound to a certain slot of another instance. When a clause i is forced to have the syntax of some original clause l, syntactic constraints are triggered so that the literals of clause i become instantiated by the relevant predicates, functions, constants and variables imposed by clause l.

Unification is implicitly obtained if two predicates are representing by the same instance while still satisfying all the constraints (imposed by the syntax of the two clauses). When a resolution step is needed, the network tries to allocate the same instance to the two literals that need to cancel each other. If the syntactic constraints on the literals permit such sharing of an instance, then the attempt to share the instance is successful and a unification occurs (occur check is done implicitly since the matrix $NEST$ allows the only finite trees to be represented).

Minimizing the violation of soft constraints: Among the valid proofs some are preferable to others. By means of soft constraints and optimization it is possible to encourage the network to search for preferred proofs. Theorem-proving thus is viewed as a constraint optimization problem. A weight may be assigned to each of the constraints [Pinkas 91c] and the network tries to minimize the weighted sum of the violated constraints, so that the set of the optimized solutions is exactly the set of the preferred proofs. For example, preference of proofs with most general unification is obtained by assignment of small penalties (negative bias) to every binding of a function to a position of another instance (in $NEST$). Using similar techniques, the network can be made to prefer shorter, more parsimonious or more reliable proofs, low-cost plans or even more specific arguments as in nonmonotonic reasoning.

4   Summary

Given a finite set T of m clauses, where n is the number of different predicates, functions and constants, and given also a bound k over the proof length, we can generate a network that searches for a proof with length not longer then k, for a clamped query Q. If a global minimum is found then an answer is given as to whether there exists such a proof, and the proof (with MGU's) may be extracted from the state of the visible units. Among the possible valid proofs the system prefers some "better" proofs by minimizing the violation of soft constraints. The concept of "better" proofs may apply to applications like planning (minimize the cost), abduction (parsimony) and nonmonotonic reasoning (specificity).

In the propositional case the generated network is of $O(k^2 + km + kn)$ units and $O(k^3 + km + kn)$ connections. For predicate logic there are $O(k^3 + km + kn)$ units and connections, and we need to add $O(k^i m)$ connections and hidden units, where i is the complexity-level of the syntactic constraints [Pinkas 91j].

The results improve an earlier approach [Ballard 86]: There are no restrictions on the rules allowed; every proof no longer than the bound is allowed; the network is compact and the representation of bindings (unifications) is efficient; nesting of functions and multiple uses of rules are allowed; only one relaxation phase is needed; inconsistency is allowed in the knowledge base, and the query does not need to be negated and pre-wired (it can be clamped during query time).

The architecture discussed has a natural fault-tolerance capability: When a unit becomes faulty, it simply cannot assume a role in the proof, and other units are allocated instead.

Acknowledgment: I wish to thank Dana Ballard, Bill Ball, Rina Dechter, Peter Haddawy, Dan Kimura, Stan Kwasny, Ron Loui and Dave Touretzky for helpful comments.

References

[Anandan et al. 89] P. Anandan, S. Letovsky, E. Mjolsness, "Connectionist variable binding by optimization," *Proceedings of the 11th Cognitive Science Society* 1989.

[Ballard 86] D. H. Ballard "Parallel Logical Inference and Energy Minimization," *Proceedings of the 5th National Conference on Artificial Intelligence*, Philadelphia, pp. 203-208, 1986.

[Barnden 91] J.A. Barnden, "Encoding complex symbolic data structures with some unusual connectionist techniques," in J.A Barnden and J.B. Pollack, *Advances in Connectionist and Neural Computation Theory 1*, High-level connectionist models, Ablex Publishing Corporation, 1991.

[Derthick 88] M. Derthick "Mundane reasoning by parallel constraint satisfaction," PhD thesis, CMU-CS-88-182 Carnegie Mellon University, Sept. 1988

[Hinton, Sejnowski 86] G.E Hinton and T.J. Sejnowski, "Learning and re-learning in Boltzman Machines," in J. L. McClelland and D. E. Rumelhart, *Parallel Distributed Processing: Explorations in The Microstructure of Cognition I*, pp. 282 - 317, MIT Press, 1986.

[Hölldobler 90] S. Hölldobler, "CHCL, a connectionist inference system for Horn logic based on connection method and using limited resources," International Computer Science Institute TR-90-042, 1990.

[Hopfield 84b] J. J. Hopfield "Neurons with graded response have collective computational properties like those of two-state neurons," *Proceedings of the National Academy of Sciences 81*, pp. 3088-3092, 1984.

[Peterson, Hartman 89] C. Peterson, E. Hartman, "Explorations of mean field theory learning algorithm," *Neural Networks 2*, no. 6, 1989.

[Pinkas 90b] G. Pinkas, "Energy minimization and the satisfiability of propositional calculus," *Neural Computation 3*, no. 2, 1991.

[Pinkas 91c] G. Pinkas, "Propositional Non-Monotonic Reasoning and Inconsistency in Symmetric Neural Networks," *Proceedings of IJCAI*, Sydney, 1991.

[Pinkas 91j] G. Pinkas, "First-order logic proofs using connectionist constraint relaxation," technical report, Department of Computer Science, Washington University, WUCS-91-54, 1991.

[Shastri et al. 90] L. Shastri, V. Ajjanagadde, "From simple associations to systematic reasoning: A connectionist representation of rules, variables and dynamic bindings," technical report, University of Pennsylvania, Philadelphia, MS-CIS-90-05, 1990.

[Smolensky 86] P. Smolensky, "Information processing in dynamic systems: Foundations of harmony theory," in J.L.McClelland and D.E.Rumelhart, *Parallel Distributed Processing: Explorations in The Microstructure of Cognition I*, MIT Press, 1986.

A Connectionist Learning Approach to Analyzing Linguistic Stress

Prahlad Gupta
Department of Psychology
Carnegie Mellon University
Pittsburgh, PA 15213

David S. Touretzky
School of Computer Science
Carnegie Mellon University
Pittsburgh, PA 15213

Abstract

We use connectionist modeling to develop an analysis of stress systems in terms of ease of learnability. In traditional linguistic analyses, learnability arguments determine default parameter settings based on the feasibilty of logically deducing correct settings from an initial state. Our approach provides an empirical alternative to such arguments. Based on perceptron learning experiments using data from nineteen human languages, we develop a novel characterization of stress patterns in terms of six parameters. These provide both a partial description of the stress pattern itself and a prediction of its learnability, without invoking abstract theoretical constructs such as metrical feet. This work demonstrates that machine learning methods can provide a fresh approach to understanding linguistic phenomena.

1 LINGUISTIC STRESS

The domain of stress systems in language is considered to have a relatively good linguistic theory, called *metrical phonology*[1]. In this theory, the stress patterns of many languages can be described concisely, and characterized in terms of a set of linguistic "parameters," such as bounded vs. unbounded metrical feet, left vs. right dominant feet, etc.[2] In many languages, stress tends to be placed on certain kinds of syllables rather than on others; the former are termed *heavy* syllables, and the latter *light* syllables. Languages that distinguish

---

[1]For an overview of the theory, see [Goldsmith 90, chapter 4].

[2]See [Dresher 90] for one such parameter scheme.

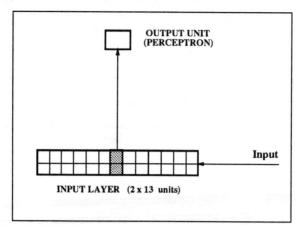

Figure 1: Perceptron model used in simulations.

between heavy and light syllables are termed *quantity-sensitive* (QS), while languages that do not make this distinction are termed *quantity-insensitive* (QI). In some QS languages, what counts as a heavy syllable is a closed syllable (a syllable that ends in a consonant), while in others it is a syllable with a long vowel. We examined the stress patterns of nineteen QI and QS systems, summarized and exemplified in Table 1. The data were drawn primarily from descriptions in [Hayes 80].

2   PERCEPTRON SIMULATIONS

In separate experiments, we trained a perceptron to produce the stress pattern of each of these languages. Two input representations were used. In the *syllabic* representation, used for QI patterns only, a syllable was represented as a [1 1] vector, and [0 0] represented no syllable. In the *weight-string* representation, which was necessary for QS languages, the input patterns used were [1 0] for a heavy syllable, [0 1] for a light syllable, and [0 0] for no syllable. For stress systems with up to two levels of stress, the output targets used in training were 1.0 for primary stress, 0.5 for secondary stress, and 0 for no stress. For stress systems with three levels of stress, the output targets were 0.6 for secondary stress, 0.35 for tertiary stress, and 1.0 and 0 respectively for primary stress and no stress. The input data set for all stress systems consisted of all word-forms of up to seven syllables. With the syllabic input representation there are 7 of these, and with the weight-string representation, there are 255. The perceptron's input array was a buffer of 13 syllables; each word was processed one syllable at a time by sliding it through the buffer (see Figure 1). The desired output at each step was the stress level of the middle syllable of the buffer. Connection weights were adjusted at each step using the back-propagation learning algorithm [Rumelhart 86]. One *epoch* consisted of one presentation of the entire training set. The network was trained for as many epochs as necessary to ensure that the stress value produced by the perceptron was within 0.1 of the target value, for each syllable of the word, for all words in the training set. A *learning rate* of 0.05 and *momentum* of 0.90 was used in all simulations. Initial weights were uniformly distributed random values in the range ±0.5. Each simulation was run at least three times, and the learning times averaged.

Ref	Language	Description of stress pattern	Examples
Quantity-Insensitive Languages:			
L1	Latvian	Fixed word-initial stress.	$S^1 S^0 S^0 S^0 S^0 S^0 S^0$
L2	French	Fixed word-final stress.	$S^0 S^0 S^0 S^0 S^0 S^0 S^1$
L3	Maranungku	Primary stress on first syllable, secondary stress on alternate succeeding syllables.	$S^1 S^0 S^2 S^0 S^2 S^0 S^2$
L4	Weri	Primary stress on last syllable, secondary stress on alternate preceding syllables.	$S^2 S^0 S^2 S^0 S^2 S^0 S^1$
L5	Garawa	Primary stress on first syllable, secondary stress on penultimate syllable, tertiary stress on alternate syllables preceding the penult, no stress on second syllable.	$S^1 S^0 S^0 S^3 S^0 S^2 S^0$
L6	Lakota	Primary stress on second syllable.	$S^0 S^1 S^0 S^0 S^0 S^0 S^0$
L7	Swahili	Primary stress on penultimate syllable.	$S^0 S^0 S^0 S^0 S^0 S^1 S^0$
L8	Paiute	Primary stress on second syllable, secondary stress on alternate succeeding syllables.	$S^0 S^1 S^0 S^2 S^0 S^2 S^0$
L9	Warao	Primary stress on penultimate syllable, secondary stress on alternate preceding syllables.	$S^0 S^2 S^0 S^2 S^0 S^1 S^0$
Quantity-Sensitive Languages:			
L10	Koya	Primary stress on first syllable, secondary stress on heavy syllables. (Heavy = closed syllable or syllable with long vowel.)	$L^1 L^0 L^0 H^2 L^0 L^0 L^0$ $L^1 L^0 L^0 L^0 L^0 L^0 L^0$
L11	Eskimo	(Primary) stress on final and heavy syllables. (Heavy = closed syllable.)	$L^0 L^0 L^0 H^1 L^0 L^0 L^1$ $L^0 L^0 L^0 L^0 L^0 L^0 L^1$
L12	Gurkhali	Primary stress on first syllable except when first syllable light and second syllable heavy. (Heavy = long vowel.)	$L^1 L^0 L^0 H^0 L^0 L^0 L^0$ $L^0 H^1 L^0 H^0 L^0 L^0 L^0$
L13	Yapese	Primary stress on last syllable except when last is light and penultimate heavy. (Heavy = long vowel.)	$L^0 L^0 L^0 H^0 L^0 L^0 L^1$ $L^0 H^0 L^0 H^0 L^0 H^1 L^0$
L14	Ossetic	Primary stress on first syllable if heavy, else on second syllable. (Heavy = long vowel.)	$H^1 L^0 L^0 H^0 L^0 L^0 L^0$ $L^0 L^1 L^0 L^0 L^0 L^0 L^0$
L15	Rotuman	Primary stress on last syllable if heavy, else on penultimate syllable. (Heavy = long vowel.)	$L^0 L^0 L^0 H^0 L^0 L^0 H^1$ $L^0 L^0 L^0 L^0 L^0 L^1 L^0$
L16	Komi	Primary stress on first heavy syllable, or on last syllable if none heavy. (Heavy = long vowel.)	$L^0 L^0 H^1 L^0 L^0 H^0 L^0$ $L^0 L^0 L^0 L^0 L^0 L^0 L^1$
L17	Cheremis	Primary stress on last heavy syllable, or on first syllable if none heavy. (Heavy = long vowel.)	$L^0 L^0 H^0 L^0 L^0 H^1 L^0$ $L^1 L^0 L^0 L^0 L^0 L^0 L^0$
L18	Mongolian	Primary stress on first heavy syllable, or on first syllable if none heavy. (Heavy = long vowel.)	$L^0 L^0 H^1 L^0 L^0 H^0 L^0$ $L^1 L^0 L^0 L^0 L^0 L^0 L^0$
L19	Mayan	Primary stress on last heavy syllable, or on last syllable if none heavy. (Heavy = long vowel.)	$L^0 L^0 H^0 L^0 L^0 H^1 L^0$ $L^0 L^0 L^0 L^0 L^0 L^0 L^1$

Table 1: Stress patterns: description and example stress assignment. Examples are of stress assignment in seven-syllable words. Primary stress is denoted by the superscript 1 (e.g., S^1), secondary stress by the superscript 2, tertiary stress by the superscript 3, and no stress by the superscript 0. "S" indicates an arbitrary syllable, and is used for the QI stress patterns. For QS stress patterns, "H" and "L" are used to denote Heavy and Light syllables, respectively.

3   PRELIMINARY ANALYSIS OF LEARNABILITY OF STRESS

The learning times differ considerably for {Latvian, French}, {Maranungku, Weri}, {Lakota, Polish} and Garawa, as shown in the last column of Table 2. Moreover, Paiute and Warao were unlearnable with this model.[3] Differences in learning times for the various stress patterns suggested that the factors ("parameters") listed below are relevant in determining learnability.

1. **Inconsistent Primary Stress (IPS):** it is computationally expensive to learn the pattern if neither edge receives primary stress except in mono- and di-syllables; this can be regarded as an index of computational complexity that takes the values {0, 1}: 1 if an edge receives primary stress inconsistently, and 0, otherwise.

2. **Stress clash avoidance (SCA):** if the components of a stress pattern can potentially lead to *stress clash*[4], then the language may either actually permit such stress clash, or it may avoid it. This index takes the values {0, 1}: 0 if stress clash is permitted, and 1 if stress clash is avoided.

3. **Alternation (Alt):** an index of learnability with value 0 if there is no alternation, and value 1 if there is. Alternation refers to a stress pattern that repeats on alternate syllables.

4. **Multiple Primary Stresses (MPS):** has value 0 if there is exactly one primary stress, and value 1 if there is more then one primary stress. It has been assumed that a repeating pattern of primary stresses will be on alternate, rather than adjacent syllables. Thus, [Alternation=0] implies [MPS=0]. Some of the hypothetical stress patterns examined below include ones with more than one primary stress; however, as far as is known, no actually occurring QI stress pattern has more than one primary stress.

5. **Multiple Stress Levels (MSL):** has value 0 if there is a single level of stress (primary stress only), and value 1 otherwise.

Note that it is possible to order these factors with respect to each other to form a five-digit binary string characterizing the ease/difficulty of learning. That is, the computational complexity of learning a stress pattern can be characterized as a 5-bit binary number whose bits represent the five factors above, in decreasing order of significance. Table 2 shows that this characterization captures the learning times of the QI patterns quite accurately. As an example of how to read Table 2, note that Garawa takes longer to learn than Latvian (165 vs. 17 epochs). This is reflected in the parameter setting for Garawa, "01101", being lexicographically greater than that for Latvian, "00000". A further noteworthy point is that this framework provides an account of the non-learnability of Paiute and Warao, viz,. that stress patterns whose parameter string is lexicographically greater than "10000" are unlearnable by the perceptron.

4   TESTING THE QI LEARNABILITY PREDICTIONS

We devised a series of thirty artificial QI stress patterns (each a variation on some language in Table 1) to examine our parameter scheme in more detail. The details of the patterns

---

[3]They were learnable in a three-layer model, which exhibited a similar ordering of learning times [Gupta 92].

[4]Placement of stress on adjacent syllables.

IPS	SCA	Alt	MPS	MSL	QI LANGUAGES	REF	EPOCHS (syllabic)
0	0	0	0	0	Latvian	L1	17
					French	L2	16
0	0	1	0	1	Maranungku	L3	37
					Weri	L4	34
0	1	1	0	1	Garawa	L5	165
1	0	0	0	0	Lakota	L6	255
					Swahili	L7	254
1	0	1	0	1	Paiute	L8	**
					Warao	L9	**

Table 2: Preliminary analysis of learning times for QI stress systems, using the *syllabic* input representation. IPS=Inconsistent Primary Stress; SCA=Stress Clash Avoidance; Alt=Alternation; MPS=Multiple Primary Stresses; MSL=Multiple Stress Levels. References L1-L9 refer to Table 1.

Agg	IPS	SCA	Alt	MPS	MSL	QI LANGS	REF	TIME	QS LANGS	REF	TIME
0	0	0	0	0	0	Latvian	L1	2			
						French	L2	2			
0	0	0	0	0	1				Koya	L10	2
0	0	0	0	1	0				Eskimo	L11	3
0	0	0	1	0	1	Maranungku	L3	3			
						Weri	L4	3			
0	0	1	1	0	1	Garawa	L5	7			
0	0.25	0	0	0	0				Gurkhali	L12	19
									Yapese	L13	19
0	0.50	0	0	0	0				Ossetic	L14	30
									Rotuman	L15	29
0	1	0	0	0	0	Lakota	L6	10			
						Swahili	L7	10			
0	1	0	1	0	1	Paiute	L8	**			
						Warao	L9	**			
1	0	0	0	0	0				Komi	L16	216
									Cheremis	L17	212
2	0	0	0	0	0				Mongolian	L18	2306
									Mayan	L19	2298

Table 3: Summary of results and analysis of QI and QS learning (using *weight-string* input representations). Agg=Aggregative Information; IPS=Inconsistent Primary Stress; SCA=Stress Clash Avoidance; Alt=Alternation; MPS=Multiple Primary Stresses; MSL=Multiple Stress Levels. References index into Table 1. Time is learning time in *epochs*.

are not crucial for present purposes (see [Gupta 92] for details). What is important to note is that the learnability predictions generated by the analytical scheme described in the previous section show good agreement with actual perceptron learning experiments on these patterns.

The learning results are summarized in Table 4. It can be seen that the 5-bit characterization fits the learning times of various actual and hypothetical patterns reasonably well (although there are exceptions – for example, the hypothetical stress patterns with reference numbers h21 through h25 have a higher 5-bit characterization than other stress patterns, but lower learning times.) Thus, the "complexity measure" suggested here appears to identify a number of factors relevant to the learnability of QI stress patterns within a minimal two-layer connectionist architecture. It also assesses their relative impacts. The analysis is undoubtedly a simplification, but it provides a completely novel framework within which to relate the various learning results. The important point to note is that this analytical framework arises from a consideration of (a) the nature of the stress systems, and (b) the learning results from simulations. That is, this framework is empirically based, and makes no reference to abstract constructs of the kind that linguistic theory employs. Nevertheless, it provides a descriptive framework, much as the linguistic theory does.

5   INCORPORATING QS SYSTEMS INTO THE ANALYSIS

Consideration of the QS stress patterns led to *refinement* of the IPS parameter without changing its setting for the QI patterns. This parameter is modified so that its value indicates *the proportion of cases in which primary stress is not assigned at the edge of a word*. Additionally, through analysis of connection weights for QS patterns, a sixth parameter, *Aggregative Information*, is added as a further index of computational complexity.

6. Aggregative Information (Agg) : has value 0 if no aggregative information is required (*single-positional* information suffices); 1 if one kind of aggregative information is required; and 2 if two kinds of aggregative information are required.

Detailed discussion of the analysis leading to these refinements is beyond the scope of this paper; the interested reader is referred to [Gupta 92]. The point we wish to make here is that, with these modifications, the same parameter scheme can be used for both the QI and QS language classes, with good learnability predictions *within* each class, as shown in Table 3. Note that in this table, learning times for all languages are reported in terms of the weight-string representation (255 input patterns) rather than the unweighted syllabic representation (7 input patterns) used for the initial QI studies. Both the QI and QS results fall into a single analysis within this generalized parameter scheme and weight-string representation, but with a less perfect fit than the within-class results.

6   DISCUSSION

Traditional linguistic analysis has devised abstract theoretical constructs such as "metrical foot" to *describe* linguistic stress systems. Learnability arguments were then used to determine default parameter settings (e.g., whether feet should by default be assumed to be bounded or unbounded, left or right dominant, etc.) based on the feasibility of logically deducing correct settings from an initial state. As an example, in one analysis

IPS	SCA	Alt	MPS	MSL	LANGUAGE	REF	EPOCHS (syllabic)
		0	0	0	Latvian	*L1*	17
					French	*L2*	16
		0	0	1	Latvian2stress	h1	21
					Latvian3stress	h2	11
					French2stress	h3	23
					French3stress	h4	14
		0	1	0	Latvian2edge	h5	30
		0	1	1	Latvian2edge2stress	h6	37
		1	0	0	*impossible*		
		1	0	1	Maranungku	*L3*	37
					Weri	*L4*	34
					Maranungku3stress	h7	43
					Weri3stress	h8	41
					Latvian2edge2stress-alt	h9	58
					Garawa-SC	h10	38
					Garawa2stress-SC	h11	50
		1	1	0	Maranungku1stress	h12	61
					Weri1stress	h13	65
					Latvian2edge-alt	h14	78
					Garawa1stress-SC	h15	88
		1	1	1	Latvian2edge2stress-1alt	h16	85
	1	0	0	0	*impossible*		
	1	0	0	1	Garawa-non-alt	h17	164
					Latvian3stress2edge-SCA	h18	163
	1	0	1	0	Latvian2edge-SCA	h19	194
	1	0	1	1	Latvian2edge2stress-SCA	h20	206
	1	1	0	1	Garawa	*L5*	165
					Garawa2stress	h21	71
					Latvian2edge2stress-alt-SCA	h22	91
	1	1	1	0	Garawa1stress	h23	121
					Latvian2edge-alt-SCA	h24	126
	1	1	1	1	Latvian2edge2stress-1alt-SCA	h25	129
1		0	0	0	Lakota	*L6*	255
					Swahili	*L7*	254
1		0	0	1	Lakota2stress	h26	**
1		0	1	0	Lakota2edge	h27	**
1		0	1	1	Lakota2edge2stress	h28	**
1		1	0	1	Paiute	*L8*	**
					Warao	*L9*	**
1		1	1	0	Lakota-alt	h29	**
1		1	1	1	Lakota2stress-alt	h30	**

Table 4: Analysis of Quantity-Insensitive learning using the *syllabic* input representation. IPS=Inconsistent Primary Stress; SCA=Stress Clash Avoidance; Alt=Alternation; MPS=Multiple Primary Stresses; MSL=Multiple Stress Levels. References L1-L9 index into Table 1.

[Dresher 90, p. 191], "metrical feet" are taken to be "iterative" by default, since there is evidence that can cause revision of this default if it turns out to be the incorrect setting, but there might not be such disconfirming evidence if the feet were by default taken to be "non-iterative". We provide an alternative to logical deduction arguments for determining "markedness" of parameter values, by measuring learnability (and hence markedness) empirically. The parameters of our novel analysis generate both a partial description of each stress pattern and a prediction of its learnability. Furthermore, our parameters encode linguistically salient concepts (e.g., *stress clash avoidance*) as well as concepts that have computational significance (*single-positional* vs. *aggregative* information.) Although our analyses do not explicitly invoke theoretical linguistic constructs such as metrical feet, there are suggestive similarities between such constructs and the weight patterns the perceptron develops [Gupta 91].

In conclusion, this work offers a fresh perspective on a well-studied linguistic domain, and suggests that machine learning techniques in conjunction with more traditional tools might provide the basis for a new approach to the investigation of language.

Acknowledgements

We would like to acknowledge the feedback provided by Deirdre Wheeler throughout the course of this work. The first author would like to thank David Evans for access to exceptional computing facilities at Carnegie Mellon's Laboratory for Computational Linguistics, and Dan Everett, Brian MacWhinney, Jay McClelland, Eric Nyberg, Brad Pritchett and Steve Small for helpful discussion of earlier versions of this paper. Of course, none of them is responsible for any errors.

The second author was supported by a grant from Hughes Aircraft Corporation, and by the Office of Naval Research under contract number N00014-86-K-0678.

References

[Dresher 90] Dresher, B., & Kaye, J., A Computational Learning Model for Metrical Phonology, *Cognition* 34, 137-195.

[Goldsmith 90] Goldsmith, J., *Autosegmental and Metrical Phonology*, Basil Blackwell, Oxford, England, 1990.

[Gupta 91] Gupta, P. & Touretzky, D., What a perceptron reveals about metrical phonology. *Proceedings of the Thirteenth Annual Conference of the Cognitive Science Society*, 334-339. Lawrence Erlbaum, Hillsdale, NJ, 1991.

[Gupta 92] Gupta, P. & Touretzky, D., Connectionist Models and Linguistic Theory: Investigations of Stress Systems in Language. Manuscript.

[Hayes 80] Hayes, B., *A Metrical Theory of Stress Rules*, doctoral dissertation, Massachusetts Institute of Technology, Cambridge, MA, 1980. Circulated by the Indiana University Linguistics Club, 1981.

[Rumelhart 86] Rumelhart, D., Hinton, G., & Williams, R, Learning Internal Representations by Error Propagation, in D. Rumelhart, J. McClelland & the PDP Research Group. *Parallel Distributed Processing, Volume 1: Foundations*, MIT Press, Cambridge, MA, 1986.

Propagation Filters in PDS Networks for Sequencing and Ambiguity Resolution

Ronald A. Sumida
Michael G. Dyer
Artificial Intelligence Laboratory
Computer Science Department
University of California
Los Angeles, CA, 90024
sumida@cs.ucla.edu

Abstract

We present a Parallel Distributed Semantic (PDS) Network architecture that addresses the problems of sequencing and ambiguity resolution in natural language understanding. A PDS Network stores phrases and their meanings using multiple PDP networks, structured in the form of a semantic net. A mechanism called Propagation Filters is employed: (1) to control communication between networks, (2) to properly sequence the components of a phrase, and (3) to resolve ambiguities. Simulation results indicate that PDS Networks and Propagation Filters can successfully represent high-level knowledge, can be trained relatively quickly, and provide for parallel inferencing at the knowledge level.

1   INTRODUCTION

Backpropagation has shown considerable potential for addressing problems in natural language processing (NLP). However, the traditional PDP [Rumelhart and McClelland, 1986] approach of using one (or a small number) of backprop networks for NLP has been plagued by a number of problems: (1) it has been largely unsuccessful at representing high-level knowledge, (2) the networks are slow to train, and (3) they are sequential at the knowledge level. A solution to these problems is to represent high-level knowledge structures over a large number of smaller PDP networks. Reducing the size of each network allows for much faster training, and since the different networks can operate in parallel, more than one knowledge structure can be stored or accessed at a time.

In using multiple networks, however, a number of important issues must be addressed: how the individual networks communicate with one another, how patterns are routed from one network to another, and how sequencing is accomplished as patterns are propagated. In previous papers [Sumida and Dyer, 1989] [Sumida, 1991], we have demonstrated how to represent high-level semantic knowledge and generate dynamic inferences using Parallel Distributed Semantic (PDS) Networks, which structure multiple PDP networks in the form of a semantic network. This paper discusses how Propagation Filters address communication and sequencing issues in using multiple PDP networks for NLP.

2   PROPAGATION FILTERS

Propagation Filters are inspired by the idea of skeleton filters, proposed by [Sejnowski, 1981, Hinton, 1981]. They are composed of: (1) sets of filter ensembles that gate the connection from a source to a destination and (2) a selector ensemble that decides which filter group to enable. Each filter group is sensitive to a particular pattern over the selector. When the particular pattern occurs, the source pattern is propagated to its destination. Figure 1 is an example of a propagation filter where the "01" pattern over units 2 and 3 of the selector opens up filter group1, thus permitting the pattern to be copied from source1 to destination1. The units of filter group2 do not respond to the "01" pattern and remain well below thresold, so the activation pattern over the source2 ensemble is not propagated.

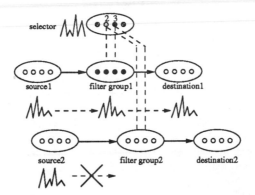

Figure 1: A Propagation Filter architecture. The small circles indicate PDP units within an ensemble (oval), the black arrows represent full connectivity between two ensembles, and the dotted lines connecting units 2 and 3 of the selector to each filter group oval indicate total connectivity from selector units to filter units. The jagged lines are suggestive of temporary patterns of activation over an ensemble.

The units in a filter group receive input from units in the selector. The weights on these input connections are set so that when a specific pattern occurs over the selector, every unit in the filter group is driven above threshold. The filter units also receive input from the source units and provide output to the destination units. The weights on both these i/o connections can be set so that the filter merely *copies* the pattern from the source to the destination when its units exceed threshold (as in Figure 1). Alternatively, these weights can be set (e.g. using backpropagation) so that the filter *transforms* the source pattern to a desired destination pattern.

3   PDS NETWORKS

PDS Networks store syntactic and semantic information over multiple PDP networks, with each network representing a class of concepts and with related networks connected in the general manner of a semantic net. For example, Figure 2 shows a network for encoding a basic sentence consisting of a subject, verb and direct object. The network is connected to other PDP networks, such as HUMAN, VERB and ANIMAL, that store information about the content of the subject role (s-content), the filler for the verb role, and the content of the direct-object role (do-content). Each network functions as a type of *encoder net*, where: (1) the input and output layers have the same number of units and are presented with exactly the same pattern, (2) the weights of the network are modified so that the input pattern will recreate itself as output, and (3) the resulting hidden unit pattern represents a *reduced description* of the input. In the networks that we use, a single set of units is used for both the input and output layers. The net can thus be viewed as an encoder with the output layer folded back onto the input layer and with two sets of connections: one from the single input/output layer to the hidden layer, and one from the hidden layer back to the i/o layer. In Figure 2 for example, the subject-content, verb, and direct-object-content role-groups collectively represent the input/output layer, and the BASIC-S ensemble represents the hidden layer.

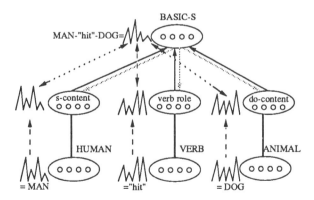

Figure 2: The network that stores information about a basic sentence. The black arrows represent links from the input layer to the hidden layer and the grey arrows indicate links from the hidden layer to the output layer. The thick lines represent links between networks that propagate a pattern without changing it.

A network stores information by learning to encode the items in its training set.

For each item, the patterns that represent its features are presented to the input role groups, and the weights are modified so that the patterns recreate themselves as output. For example, in Figure 2, the MAN-"hit"-DOG pattern is presented to the BASIC-S network by propagating the MAN pattern from the HUMAN network to the s-content role, the "hit" pattern from the VERB network to the verb-content role, and the DOG pattern from the ANIMAL network to the do-content role. The BASIC-S network is then trained on this pattern by modifying the weights between the input/output role groups and the BASIC-S hidden units so that the MAN-"hit"-DOG pattern recreates itself as output. The network automatically generalizes by having the hidden units become sensitive to common features of the training patterns. When the network is tested on a new concept (i.e., one that is not in the training set), the pattern over the hidden units reflects its similarity to the items seen during training.

3.1   SEQUENCING PHRASES

To illustrate how Propagation Filters sequence the components of a phrase, consider the following sentence, whose constituents occur in the standard subject-verb-object order: *S1. The man hit the dog.* We would like to recognize that the BASIC-S network of Figure 2 is applicable to the input by binding the roles of the network to the correct components. In order to generate the proper role bindings, the system must: (1) recognize the components of the sentence in the correct order (e.g. "the man" should be recognized as the subject, "hit" as the verb, and "the dog" as the direct object), and (2) associate each phrase of the input with its meaning (e.g. reading the phrase "the man" should cause the pattern for the concept MAN to appear over the HUMAN units). Figure 3 illustrates how Propagation Filters properly sequence the components of the sentence.

First, the phrase "the man" is read by placing the pattern for "the" over the determiner network (Step 1) and the pattern for "man" over the noun network (Step 2). The "the" pattern is then propagated to the np-determiner input role units of the NP network (Step 3) and the "man" pattern to the np-noun role input units (Step 4). The pattern that results over the hidden NP units is then used to represent the entire phrase "the man" (Step 5). The filters connecting the NP units with the subject and direct object roles are not enabled, so the pattern is not yet bound to any role. Next, the word "hit" is read and a pattern for it is generated over the VERB units (Step 6). The BASIC-S network is now applicable to the input (for simplicity of exposition, we ignore passive constructions here). Since there are no restrictions (i.e., no filter) on the connection between the VERB units and the verb role of BASIC-S, the "hit" pattern is bound to the verb role (Step 7). The verb role units act as the selector of the Propagation Filter that connects the NP units to the subject units. The filter is constructed so that whenever any of the verb role units receive non-zero input (i.e., whenever the role is bound) it opens up the filter group connecting NP with the subject role (Step 8). Thus, the pattern for "the man" is copied from NP to the subject (Step 9) and deleted from the NP units. Similarly, the subject units act as the selector of a filter that connects NP with the direct object. Since the subject was just bound, the connection from the NP to direct object is enabled (Step 10). At this point, the system has generated the *expectation* that a NP will occur next. The phrase "the dog" is now read and

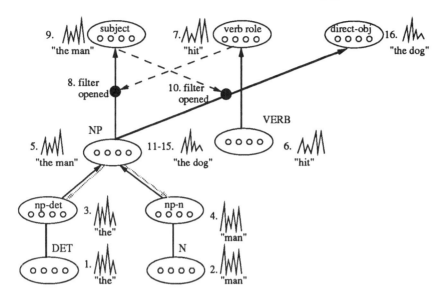

Figure 3: The figure shows how Propagation Filters sequence the components of the sentence "The man hit the dog". The numbers indicate the order of events. The dotted arrows indicate Propagation Filter connections from a selector to an open filter group (indicated by a black circle) and the dark arrows represent the connections from a source to a destination.

its pattern is generated over the NP units (Steps 11-15). Finally, the pattern for "the dog" is copied across the open connection from NP to direct-object (Step 16).

3.2   ASSOCIATING PHRASES WITH MEANINGS

The next task is to associate lexical patterns with their corresponding semantic patterns and bind semantic patterns to the appropriate roles in the BASIC-S network. Figure 4 indicates how Propagation Filters: (1) transform the phrase "the man" into its meaning (i.e., MAN), and (2) bind MAN to the s-content role of BASIC-S.

Reading the word "man", by placing the "man" pattern into the noun units (Step 2), opens the filter connecting N to HUMAN (Step 5), while leaving the filters connecting N to other networks (e.g. ANIMAL) closed. The opened filter transforms the lexical pattern "man" over N into the semantic pattern MAN over HUMAN (Step 7). Binding "the man" to subject (Step 8) by the procedure shown in the Figure 3 opens the filter connecting HUMAN to the s-content role of BASIC-S (Step 9). The s-content role is then bound to MAN (Step 10).

The do-content role is bound by a procedure similar to that shown in Figure 4. When "dog" is read, the filter connecting N with ANIMAL is opened while filters to other networks (e.g. HUMAN) remain closed. The "dog" pattern is then transformed into the semantic pattern DOG over the ANIMAL units. When "the dog"

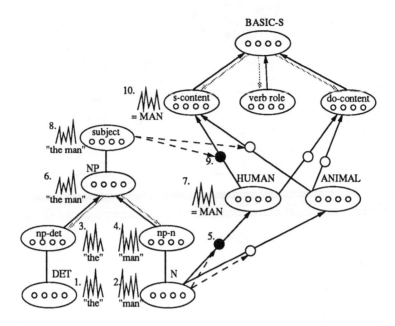

Figure 4: The figure illustrates how the concept MAN is bound to the s-content role of BASIC-S, given the phrase "the man" as input. Black (white) circles indicate open (closed) filters.

is bound to direct-object as in Figure 3, the filter from ANIMAL to do-content is opened, and DOG is propagated from ANIMAL to the do-content role of BASIC-S.

3.3 AMBIGUITY RESOLUTION AND INFERENCING

There are two forms that inference and ambiguity resolution can take: (1) routing patterns (e.g. propagation of role bindings) to the appropriate subnets and (2) pattern reconstruction from items seen during training.

(1) *Pattern Routing*: Propagation Filters help resolve ambiguities by having the selector only open connections to the network containing the correct interpretation. As an example, consider the following sentence: *S2. The singer hit the note.* Both S2 and S1 (Sec. 3.1) have the same syntactic structure and are therefore represented over the BASIC-S ensemble of Figure 2. However, the meaning of the word "hit" in S1 refers to physically striking an object while in S2 it refers to singing a musical note. The pattern over the BASIC-S units that represents S1 differs significantly from the pattern that represents S2, due to the differences in the s-content and do-content roles. A Propagation Filter with the BASIC-S units as its selector uses the differences in the two patterns to determine whether to open connections to the HIT network or to the PERFORM-MUSIC network (Figure 5).

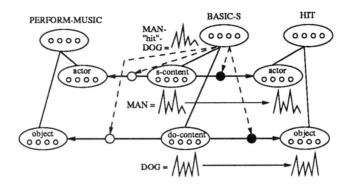

Figure 5: The pattern over BASIC-S acts as a selector that determines whether to open the connections to HIT or to PERFORM-MUSIC. Since the input here is MAN-"hit"-DOG, the filters to HIT are opened while the filters to PERFORM-MUSIC remain closed. The black and grey arrows indicating connections between the input/output and hidden layers have been replaced by a single thin line.

During training, the BASIC-S network was presented with sentences of the general form <MUSIC-PERFORMER "hit" MUSICAL-NOTE> and <ANIMATE "hit" OBJECT>. The BASIC-S hidden units generalize from the training sentences by developing a distinct pattern for each of the two types of "hit" sentences. The Propagation Filter is then constructed so that the hidden unit pattern for <MUSIC-PERFORMER "hit" MUSICAL-NOTE> opens up connections to PERFORM-MUSIC, while the pattern for <ANIMATE "hit" OBJECT> opens up connections to HIT. Thus, when S1 is presented, the BASIC-S hidden units develop the pattern classifying it as <ANIMATE "hit" OBJECT>, which enables connections to HIT. For example, Figure 5 shows how the MAN pattern is routed from the s-content role of BASIC-S to the actor role of HIT and the DOG pattern is routed from the do-content role of BASIC-S to the object role of HIT. If S2 is presented instead, the hidden units will classify it as <MUSIC-PERFORMER "hit" MUSICAL-NOTE> and open the connections to PERFORM-MUSIC.

The technique of using propagation filters to control pattern routing can also be applied to generate inferences. Consider the sentence, "Douglas hit Tyson". Since both are boxers, it is plausible they are involved in a competitive activity. In S1, however, punishing the dog is a more plausible motivation for HIT. The proper inference is generated in each case by training the HIT network (Figure 5) on a number of instances of boxers hitting one another and of people hitting dogs. The network learns two distinct sets of hidden unit patterns: <BOXER-HIT-BOXER> and <HUMAN-HIT-DOG>. A Propagation Filter, (like that shown in Figure 5) with the HIT units as its selector, uses the differences in the two classes of patterns to route to either the network that stores competitive activities or to the network that stores punishment acts.

(2) *Pattern Reconstruction*: The system also resolves ambiguities by reconstructing patterns that were seen during training. For example, the word "note" in sentence

S2 is ambiguous and could refer to a message, as in "The singer left the note". Thus, when the word "note" is read in S2, the do-content role of BASIC-S can be bound to MESSAGE or to MUSICAL-NOTE. To resolve the ambiguity, the BASIC-S network uses the information that SINGER is bound to the s-content role and "hit" to the verb role to: (1) reconstruct the <MUSIC-PERFORMER "hit" MUSICAL-NOTE> pattern that it learned during training and (2) predict that the do-content will be MUSICAL-NOTE. Since the prediction is consistent with one of the possible meanings for the do-content role, the ambiguity is resolved. Similarly, if the input had been "The singer left the note", BASIC-S would use the binding of a human to the s-content role and the binding of "left" to the verb role to reconstruct the pattern <HUMAN "left" MESSAGE> and thus resolve the ambiguity.

4   CURRENT STATUS AND CONCLUSIONS

PDS Networks and Propagation Filters are implemented in DCAIN, a natural language understanding system that: (1) takes each word of the input sequentially, (2) binds the roles of the corresponding syntactic and semantic structures in the proper order, and (3) resolves ambiguities. In our simulations with DCAIN, we successfully represented high-level knowledge by structuring individual PDP networks in the form of a semantic net. Because the system's knowledge is spread over multiple subnetworks, each one is relatively small and can therefore be trained quickly. Since the subnetworks can operate in parallel, DCAIN is able to store and retrieve more than one knowledge structure simultaneously, thus achieving knowlege-level parallelism. Because PDP ensembles (versus single localist units) are used, the generalization, noise and fault-tolerance properties of the PDP approach are retained. At the same time, Propagation Filters provide control over the way patterns are routed (and transformed) between subnetworks. The PDS architecture, with its Propagation Filters, thus provides significant advantages over traditional PDP models for natural language understanding.

References

[Hinton, 1981] G. E. Hinton. Implementing Semantic Networks in Parallel Hardware. In *Parallel Models of Associative Memory*, Lawrence Erlbaum, Hillsdale, NJ, 1981.

[Rumelhart and McClelland, 1986] D. E. Rumelhart and J. L. McClelland. *Parallel Distributed Processing*, Volume 1. MIT Press, Cambridge, Massachusetts, 1986.

[Sejnowski, 1981] T. J. Sejnowski. Skeleton Filters in the Brain. In *Parallel Models of Associative Memory*, Lawrence Erlbaum, Hillsdale, NJ, 1981.

[Sumida and Dyer, 1989] R. A. Sumida and M. G. Dyer. Storing and Generalizing Multiple Instances while Maintaining Knowledge-Level Parallelism. In *Proceedings of the Eleventh International Joint Conference on Artificial Intelligence*, Detroit, MI, 1989.

[Sumida, 1991] R. A. Sumida. Dynamic Inferencing in Parallel Distributed Semantic Networks. In *Proceedings of the Thirteenth Annual Conference of the Cognitive Science Society*, Chicago, IL, 1991.

A Segment-based Automatic Language Identification System

Yeshwant K. Muthusamy & Ronald A. Cole
Center for Spoken Language Understanding
Oregon Graduate Institute of Science and Technology
Beaverton OR 97006-1999

Abstract

We have developed a four-language automatic language identification system for high-quality speech. The system uses a neural network-based segmentation algorithm to segment speech into seven broad phonetic categories. Phonetic and prosodic features computed on these categories are then input to a second network that performs the language classification. The system was trained and tested on separate sets of speakers of American English, Japanese, Mandarin Chinese and Tamil. It currently performs with an accuracy of 89.5% on the utterances of the test set.

1   INTRODUCTION

Automatic language identification is the rapid automatic determination of the language being spoken, by any speaker, saying anything. Despite several important applications of automatic language identification, this area has suffered from a lack of basic research and the absence of a standardized, public-domain database of languages.

It is well known that languages have characteristic sound patterns. Languages have been described subjectively as "singsong", "rhythmic", "guttural", "nasal" etc. The key to solving the problem of automatic language identification is the detection and exploitation of such differences between languages.

We assume that each language in the world has a unique acoustic structure, and that this structure can be defined in terms of phonetic and prosodic features of speech.

Phonetic, or segmental features, include the the inventory of phonetic segments and their frequency of occurrence in speech. Prosodic information consists of the relative durations and amplitudes of sonorant (vowel-like) segments, their spacing in time, and patterns of pitch change within and across these segments.

To the extent that these assumptions are valid, languages can be identified automatically by segmenting speech into broad phonetic categories, computing segment-based features that capture the relevant phonetic and prosodic structure, and training a classifier to associate the feature measurements with the spoken language.

We have developed a language identification system that uses a neural network to segment speech into a sequence of seven broad phonetic categories. Information about these categories is then used to train a second neural network to discriminate among utterances spoken by native speakers of American English, Japanese, Mandarin Chinese and Tamil. When tested on utterances produced by six new speakers from each language, the system correctly identifies the language being spoken 89.5% of the time.

2   SYSTEM OVERVIEW

The following steps transform an input utterance into a decision about what language was spoken.

Data Capture

The speech is recorded using a Sennheiser HMD 224 noise-canceling microphone, low-pass filtered at 7.6 kHz and sampled at 16 kHz.

Signal Representations

A number of waveform and spectral parameters are computed in preparation for further processing. The spectral parameters are generated from a 128-point discrete Fourier transform computed on a 10 ms Hanning window. All parameters are computed every 3 ms.

The waveform parameters consist of estimates of (i) $zc8000$: the zero-crossing rate of the waveform in a 10 ms window, (ii) $ptp700$ and $ptp8000$: the peak-to-peak amplitude of the waveform in a 10 ms window in two frequency bands (0–700 Hz and 0–8000 Hz), and (iii) $pitch$: the presence or absence of pitch in each 3 ms frame. The pitch estimate is derived from a neural network pitch tracker that locates pitch periods in the filtered (0–700 Hz) waveform [2]. The spectral parameters consist of (i) DFT coefficients, (ii) $sda700$ and $sda8000$: estimates of averaged spectral difference in two frequency bands, (iii) sdf: spectral difference in adjacent 9 ms intervals, and (iv) $cm1000$: the center-of-mass of the spectrum in the region of the first formant.

Broad Category Segmentation

Segmentation is performed by a fully-connected, feedforward, three-layer neural network that assigns 7 broad phonetic category scores to each 3 ms time frame of the utterance. The broad phonetic categories are: VOC (vowel), FRIC (fricative),

STOP (pre-vocalic stop), PRVS (pre-vocalic sonorant), INVS (inter-vocalic sonorant), POVS (post-vocalic sonorant), and CLOS (silence or background noise). A Viterbi search, which incorporates duration and bigram probabilities, uses these frame-based output activations to find the best scoring sequence of broad phonetic category labels spanning the utterance. The segmentation algorithm is described in greater detail in [3].

Language Classification

Language classification is performed by a second fully-connected feedforward network that uses phonetic and prosodic features derived from the time-aligned broad category sequence. These features, described below, are designed to capture the phonetic and prosodic differences between the four languages.

3   FOUR-LANGUAGE HIGH-QUALITY SPEECH DATABASE

The data for this research consisted of natural continuous speech recorded in a laboratory by 20 native speakers (10 male and 10 female) of each of American English, Mandarin Chinese, Japanese and Tamil. The speakers were asked to speak a total of 20 utterances[1] : 15 conversational sentences of their choice, two questions of their choice, the days of the week, the months of the year and the numbers 0 through 10. The objective was to have a mix of unconstrained- and restricted-vocabulary speech. The segmentation algorithm was trained on just the conversational sentences, while the language classifier used all utterances from each speaker.

4   NEURAL NETWORK SEGMENTATION

4.1   SEGMENTER TRAINING

4.1.1   Training and Test Sets

Five utterances from each of 16 speakers per language were used to train and test the segmenter. The training set had 50 utterances from 10 speakers (5 male and 5 female) from each of the 4 languages, for a total of 200 utterances. The development test set had 10 utterances from a different set of 2 speakers (1 male and 1 female) from each language, for a total of 40 utterances. The final test set had 20 utterances from yet another set of 4 speakers (2 male and 2 female) from each language for a total of 80 utterances. The average duration of the utterances in the training set was 4.7 secs and that of the test sets was 5.7 secs.

4.1.2   Network Architecture

The segmentation network was a fully-connected, feed-forward network with 304 input units, 18 hidden units and 7 output units. The number of hidden units was determined experimentally. Figure 1 shows the network configuration and the input features.

---

[1]Five speakers in Japanese and one in Tamil provided only 10 utterances each.

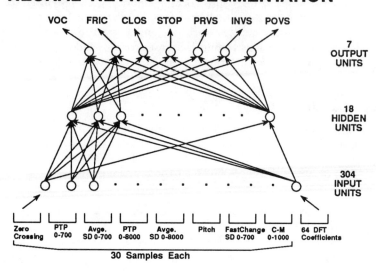

Figure 1: Segmentation Network

4.1.3   Feature Measurements

The feature measurements used to train the network include the 64 DFT coefficients at the frame to be classified and 30 samples each of *zc8000*, *ptp700*, *ptp8000*, *sda700*, *sda8000*, *sdf*, *pitch* and *cm1000*, for a total of 304 features. These samples were taken from a 330 ms window centered on the frame, with more samples being taken in the immediate vicinity of the frame than near the ends of the window.

4.1.4   Hand-labeling

Both the training and test utterances were hand-labeled with 7 broad phonetic category labels and checked by a second labeler for correctness and consistency.

4.1.5   Coarse Sampling of Frames

As it was not computationally feasible to train on every 3 ms frame in each utterance, only a few frames were chosen at random from each segment. To ensure approximately equal number of frames from each category, fewer frames were sampled from the more frequent categories such as vowels and closures.

4.1.6   Network Training

The networks were trained using backpropagation with conjugate gradient optimization [1]. Training was continued until the performance of the network on the development test set leveled off.

4.2 SEGMENTER EVALUATION

Segmentation performance was evaluated on the 80-utterance final test set. The segmenter output was compared to the hand-labels for each 3 ms time frame. First choice accuracy was 85.1% across the four languages. When scored on the middle 80% and middle 60% of each segment, the accuracy rose to 86.9% and 88.0% respectively, pointing to the presence of boundary errors.

5 LANGUAGE IDENTIFICATION

5.1 CLASSIFIER TRAINING

5.1.1 Training and Test Sets

The training set contained 12 speakers from each language, with 10 or 20 utterances per speaker, for a total of 930 utterances. The development test set contained a different group of 2 speakers per language with 20 utterances from each speaker, for a total of 160 utterances. The final test set had 6 speakers per language, with 10 or 20 utterances per speaker, for a total of 440 utterances. The average duration of the utterances in the training set was 5.1 seconds and that of the test sets was 5.5 seconds.

5.1.2 Feature Development

Several passes were needed through the iterative process of feature development and network training before a satisfactory feature set was obtained. Much of the effort was concentrated on statistical and linguistic analysis of the languages with the objective of determining the distinguishing characteristics among them. For example, the knowledge that Mandarin Chinese was the only monosyllabic tonal language in the set (the other three being stress languages), led us to design features that attempted to capture the large variation in pitch within and across segments for Mandarin Chinese utterances. Similarly, the presence of sequences of equal-length broad category segments in Japanese utterances led us to design an "inter-segment duration difference" feature. The final set of 80 features is described below. All the features are computed over the entire length of an utterance and use the time-aligned broad category sequence provided by the segmentation algorithm. The numbers in parentheses refer to the number of values generated.

- Intra-segment pitch variation: Average of the standard deviations of the pitch within all sonorant segments—VOC, PRVS, INVS, POVS (4 values)

- Inter-segment pitch variation: Standard deviation of the average pitch in all sonorant segments (4 values)

- Frequency of occurrence (number of occurrences per second of speech) of triples of segments. The following triples were chosen based on statistical analyses of the training data: VOC-INVS-VOC, CLOS-PRVS-VOC, VOC-POVS-CLOS, STOP-VOC-FRIC, STOP-VOC-CLOS, and FRIC-VOC-CLOS (6 values)

- Frequency of occurrence of each of the seven broad phonetic labels (7 values)

- Frequency of occurrence of all segments (number of segments per second) (1 value)

- Frequency of occurrence of all consonants (STOPs and FRICs) (1 value)

- Frequency of occurrence of all sonorants (4 values)

- Ratio of number of sonorant segments to total number of segments (1 value)

- Fraction of the total duration of the utterance devoted to each of the seven broad phonetic labels (7 values)

- Fraction of the total duration of the utterance devoted to all sonorants (1 value)

- Frequency of occurrence of voiced consonants (1 value)

- Ratio of voiced consonants to total number of consonants (1 value)

- Average duration of the seven broad phonetic labels (7 values)

- Standard deviation of the duration of the seven broad phonetic labels (7 values)

- Segment-pair ratios: conditional probability of occurrence of selected pairs of segments. The segment-pairs were selected based on histogram plots generated on the training set. Examples of selected pairs: POVS-FRIC, VOC-FRIC, INVS-VOC, etc. (27 values)

- Inter-segment duration difference: Average absolute difference in durations between successive segments (1 value)

- Standard deviation of the inter-segment duration differences (1 value)

- Average distance between the centers of successive vowels (1 value)

- Standard deviation of the distances between centers of successive vowels (1 value)

5.2   LANGUAGE IDENTIFICATION PERFORMANCE

5.2.1   Single Utterances

During the feature development phase, the 2 speakers-per-language development test set was used. The classifier performed at an accuracy of 90.0% on this small test set. For final evaluation, the development test set was combined with the original training set to form a 14 speakers-per-language training set. The performance of the classifier on the 6 speakers-per-language final test set was 79.6%. The individual language performances were English 75.8%, Japanese 77.0%, Mandarin Chinese 78.3%, and Tamil 88.0%. This result was obtained with training and test set utterances that were approximately 5.4 seconds long on the average.

5.2.2   Concatenated Utterances

To observe the effect of training and testing with longer durations of speech per utterance, a series of experiments were conducted in which pairs and triples of utterances from each speaker were concatenated end-to-end (with 350 ms of silence in between to simulate natural pauses) in both the training and test sets. It is to be noted that the total duration of speech used in training and testing remained unchanged for all these experiments. Table 1 summarizes the performance of the

Table 1: Percentage Accuracy on Varying Durations of Speech Per Utterance

	Avge. Duration of Test Utts. (sec)		
Avge. Duration of Training Utts. (sec)	5.7	11.8	17.1
5.3	79.6	73.6	71.2
10.6	71.8	86.8	85.0
15.2	67.9	85.5	89.5

classifier when trained and tested on different durations of speech per utterance. The rows of the table show the effect of testing on progressively longer utterances for a given training set, while the columns of the table show the effect of training on progressively longer utterances for a given test set. Not surprisingly, the best performance is obtained when the classifier is trained and tested on three utterances concatenated together.

6 DISCUSSION

The results indicate that the system performs better on longer utterances. This is to be expected given the feature set, since the segment-based statistical features tend to be more reliable with a larger number of segments. Also, it is interesting to note that we have obtained an accuracy of 89.5% without using any spectral information in the classifier feature set. All of the features are based on the broad phonetic category segment sequences provided by the segmenter.

It should be noted that approximately 15% of the utterances in the training and test sets consisted of a fixed vocabulary: the days of the week, the months of the year and the numbers zero through ten. It is likely that the inclusion of these utterances inflated classification performance. Nevertheless, we are encouraged by the 10.5% error rate, given the small number of speakers and utterances used to train the system.

Acknowledgements

This research was supported in part by NSF grant No. IRI-9003110, a grant from Apple Computer, Inc., and by a grant from DARPA to the Department of Computer Science & Engineering at the Oregon Graduate Institute. We thank Mark Fanty for his many useful comments.

References

[1] E. Barnard and R. A. Cole. A neural-net training program based on conjugate-gradient optimization. Technical Report CSE 89-014, Department of Computer Science, Oregon Graduate Institute of Science and Technology, 1989.

[2] E. Barnard, R. A. Cole, M. P. Vea, and F. A. Alleva. Pitch detection with a neural-net classifier. *IEEE Transactions on Signal Processing*, 39(2):298–307, February 1991.

[3] Y. K. Muthusamy, R. A. Cole, and M. Gopalakrishnan. A segment-based approach to automatic language identification. In *Proceedings 1991 IEEE International Conference on Acoustics, Speech, and Signal Processing*, Toronto, Canada, May 1991.

PART V

TEMPORAL SEQUENCES

The Efficient Learning of Multiple Task Sequences

Satinder P. Singh
Department of Computer Science
University of Massachusetts
Amherst, MA 01003

Abstract

I present a modular network architecture and a learning algorithm based on incremental dynamic programming that allows a single learning agent to learn to solve multiple Markovian decision tasks (MDTs) with significant transfer of learning across the tasks. I consider a class of MDTs, called composite tasks, formed by temporally concatenating a number of simpler, elemental MDTs. The architecture is trained on a set of composite and elemental MDTs. The temporal structure of a composite task is assumed to be unknown and the architecture learns to produce a temporal decomposition. It is shown that under certain conditions the solution of a composite MDT can be constructed by computationally inexpensive modifications of the solutions of its constituent elemental MDTs.

1 INTRODUCTION

Most applications of domain independent learning algorithms have focussed on learning single tasks. Building more sophisticated learning agents that operate in complex environments will require handling multiple tasks/goals (Singh, 1992). Research effort on the scaling problem has concentrated on discovering faster learning algorithms, and while that will certainly help, techniques that allow transfer of learning across tasks will be indispensable for building autonomous learning agents that have to learn to solve multiple tasks. In this paper I consider a learning agent that interacts with an external, finite-state, discrete-time, stochastic dynamical environment and faces multiple sequences of Markovian decision tasks (MDTs).

251

Each MDT requires the agent to execute a sequence of actions to control the environment, either to bring it to a desired state or to traverse a desired state trajectory over time. Let S be the finite set of states and A be the finite set of actions available to the agent.[1] At each time step t, the agent observes the system's current state $x_t \in S$ and executes action $a_t \in A$. As a result, the agent receives a payoff with expected value $R(x_t, a_t) \in \mathbb{R}$ and the system makes a transition to state $x_{t+1} \in S$ with probability $P_{x_t x_{t+1}}(a_t)$. The agent's goal is to learn an optimal closed loop control policy, i.e., a function assigning actions to states, that maximizes the agent's objective. The objective used in this paper is $J = \sum_{t=0}^{\infty} \gamma^t R(x_t, a_t)$, i.e., the sum of the payoffs over an infinite horizon. The discount factor, $0 \leq \gamma \leq 1$, allows future payoff to be weighted less than more immediate payoff. Throughout this paper, I will assume that the learning agent does not have access to a model of the environment. Reinforcement learning algorithms such as Sutton's (1988) temporal difference algorithm and Watkins's (1989) Q-learning algorithm can be used to learn to solve single MDTs (also see Barto et al., 1991).

I consider compositionally-structured MDTs because they allow the possibility of sharing knowledge across the many tasks that have common subtasks. In general, there may be n elemental MDTs labeled $T_1, T_2, \ldots, T_n$. Elemental MDTs cannot be decomposed into simpler subtasks. Composite MDTs, labeled $C_1, C_2, \ldots, C_m$, are produced by temporally concatenating a number of elemental MDTs. For example, $C_j = [T(j, 1)T(j, 2) \cdots T(j, k)]$ is composite task j made up of k elemental tasks that have to be performed in the order listed. For $1 \leq i \leq k$, $T(j, i) \in \{T_1, T_2, \ldots, T_n\}$ is the ith elemental task in the list for task C_j. The sequence of elemental tasks in a composite task will be referred to as the decomposition of the composite task; the decomposition is assumed to be unknown to the learning agent.

Compositional learning involves solving a composite task by learning to compose the solutions of the elemental tasks in its decomposition. It is to be emphasized that given the short-term, evaluative nature of the payoff from the environment (often the agent gets informative payoff only at the completion of the composite task), the task of discovering the decomposition of a composite task is formidable. In this paper I propose a compositional learning scheme in which separate modules learn to solve the elemental tasks, and a task-sensitive gating module solves composite tasks by learning to compose the appropriate elemental modules over time.

2   ELEMENTAL AND COMPOSITE TASKS

All elemental tasks are MDTs that share the the same state set S, action set A, and have the same environment dynamics. The payoff function for each elemental task T_i, $1 \leq i \leq n$, is $R_i(x, a) = \sum_{y \in S} P_{xy}(a) r_i(y) - c(x, a)$, where $r_i(y)$ is a positive reward associated with the state y resulting from executing action a in state x for task T_i, and $c(x, a)$ is the positive cost of executing action a in state x. I assume that $r_i(x) = 0$ if x is not the desired final state for T_i. Thus, the elemental tasks share the same cost function but have their own reward functions.

A composite task is not itself an MDT because the payoff is a function of both

---

[1]The extension to the case where different sets of actions are available in different states is straightforward.

the state and the current elemental task, instead of the state alone. Formally, the new state set[2] for a composite task, S', is formed by augmenting the elements of set S by n bits, one for each elemental task. For each $x' \in S'$, the *projected state* $x \in S$ is defined as the state obtained by removing the augmenting bits from x'. The environment dynamics and cost function, c, for a composite task is defined by assigning to each $x' \in S'$ and $a \in A$ the transition probabilities and cost assigned to the projected state $x \in S$ and $a \in A$. The reward function for composite task C_j, r_j^c, is defined as follows. $r_j^c(x') \geq 0$ if the following are all true: i) the projected state x is the final state for some elemental task in the decomposition of C_j, say task T_i, ii) the augmenting bits of x' corresponding to elemental tasks appearing before and including subtask T_i in the decomposition of C_j are one, and iii) the rest of the augmenting bits are zero; $r_j^c(x') = 0$ everywhere else.

3   COMPOSITIONAL Q-LEARNING

Following Watkins (1989), I define the Q-value, $Q(x, a)$, for $x \in S$ and $a \in A$, as the expected return on taking action a in state x under the condition that an optimal policy is followed thereafter. Given the Q-values, a greedy policy that in each state selects an action with the highest associated Q-value, is optimal. Q-learning works as follows. On executing action a in state x at time t, the resulting payoff and next state are used to update the estimate of the Q-value at time t, $\hat{Q}_t(x, a)$:

$$\hat{Q}_{t+1}(x, a) \quad = \quad (1.0 - \alpha_t)\hat{Q}_t(x, a) + \alpha_t[R(x, a) + \gamma \max_{a' \in A} \hat{Q}_t(y, a')], \qquad (1)$$

where y is the state at time $t + 1$, and α_t is the value of a positive learning rate parameter at time t. Watkins and Dayan (1992) prove that under certain conditions on the sequence $\{\alpha_t\}$, if every state-action pair is updated infinitely often using Equation 1, $\hat{Q}_t$ converges to the true Q-values asymptotically.

Compositional Q-learning (CQ-learning) is a method for constructing the Q-values of a composite task from the Q-values of the elemental tasks in its decomposition. Let $Q_{T_i}(x, a)$ be the Q-value of (x, a), $x \in S$ and $a \in A$, for elemental task T_i, and let $Q_{T_i}^{C_j}(x', a)$ be the Q-value of (x', a), for $x' \in S'$ and $a \in A$, for task T_i when performed as part of the composite task $C_j = [T(j, 1) \cdots T(j, k)]$. Assume $T_i = T(j, l)$. Note that the superscript on Q refers to the task and the subscript refers to the elemental task currently being performed. The absence of a superscript implies that the task is elemental.

Consider a set of undiscounted ($\gamma = 1$) MDTs that have compositional structure and satisfy the following conditions:
(A1) Each elemental task has a single desired final state.
(A2) For all elemental and composite tasks, the expected value of undiscounted return for an optimal policy is bounded both from above and below for all states.
(A3) The cost associated with each state-action pair is independent of the task being accomplished.

---

[2]The theory developed in this paper does not depend on the particular extension of S chosen, as long as the appropriate connection between the new states and the elements of S can be made.

(A4) For each elemental task T_i, the reward function r_i is zero for all states except the desired final state for that task. For each composite task C_j, the reward function r_j^c is zero for all states except *possibly* the final states of the elemental tasks in its decomposition (Section 2).

Then, for any elemental task T_i and for all composite tasks C_j containing elemental task T_i, the following holds:

$$Q_{T_i}^{C_j}(x', a) = Q_{T_i}(x, a) + K(C_j, T(j, l)), \tag{2}$$

for all $x' \in S'$ and $a \in A$, where $x \in S$ is the projected state, and $K(C_j, T(j, l))$ is a function of the composite task C_j and subtask $T(j, l)$, where $T_i = T(j, l)$. Note that $K(C_j, T(j, l))$ is independent of the state and the action. Thus, given solutions of the elemental tasks, learning the solution of a composite task with n elemental tasks requires learning only the values of the function K for the n different subtasks. A proof of Equation 2 is given in Singh (1992).

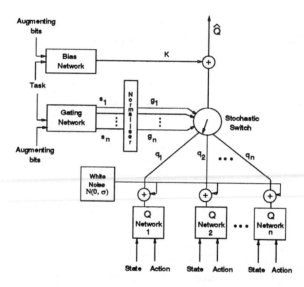

Figure 1: The CQ-Learning Architecture (CQ-L). This figure is adapted from Jacobs et al. (1991). See text for details.

Equation 2 is based on the assumption that the decomposition of the composite tasks is known. In the next Section, I present a modular architecture and learning algorithm that simultaneously discovers the decomposition of a composite task and implements Equation 2.

4   CQ-L: CQ-LEARNING ARCHITECTURE

Jacobs (1991) developed a modular connectionist architecture that performs task decomposition. Jacobs's gating architecture consists of several expert networks and a gating network that has an output for each expert network. The architecture has been used to learn multiple non-sequential tasks within the supervised learning

Table 1: Tasks. Tasks T_1, T_2, and T_3 are elemental tasks; tasks C_1, C_2, and C_3 are composite tasks. The last column describes the compositional structure of the tasks.

Label	Command	Description	Decomposition
T_1	000001	visit A	T_1
T_2	000010	visit B	T_2
T_3	000100	visit C	T_3
C_1	001000	visit A and then C	$T_1 T_3$
C_2	010000	visit B and then C	$T_2 T_3$
C_3	100000	visit A, then B and then C	$T_1 T_2 T_3$

paradigm. I extend the modular network architecture to a CQ-Learning architecture (Figure 1), called CQ-L, that can learn multiple compositionally-structured sequential tasks even when training information required for supervised learning is not available. CQ-L combines CQ-learning and the gating architecture to achieve transfer of learning by "sharing" the solutions of elemental tasks across multiple composite tasks. Only a very brief description of the CQ-L is provided in this paper; details are given in Singh (1992).

In CQ-L the expert networks are Q-learning networks that learn to approximate the Q-values for the elemental tasks. The Q-networks receive as input both the current state and the current action. The gating and bias networks (Figure 1) receive as input the augmenting bits and the task command used to encode the current task being performed by the architecture. The stochastic switch in Figure 1 selects one Q-network at each time step. CQ-L's output, $\hat{Q}$, is the output of the selected Q-network added to the output of the bias network.

The learning rules used to train the network perform gradient descent in the log likelihood, $L(t)$, of generating the estimate of the desired Q-value at time t, denoted $D(t)$, and are given below:

$$q_j(t+1) = q_j(t) + \alpha_Q \frac{\partial \log L(t)}{\partial q_j(t)},$$

$$s_i(t+1) = s_i(t) + \alpha_g \frac{\partial \log L(t)}{\partial s_i(t)}, \text{and}$$

$$b(t+1) = b(t) + \alpha_b(D(t) - \hat{Q}(t)),$$

where q_j is the output of the jth Q-network, s_i is the ith output of the gating network, b is the output of the bias network, and α_Q, α_b and α_g are learning rate parameters. The backpropagation algorithm (e.g., Rumelhart et al., 1986) was used to update the weights in the networks. See Singh (1992) for details.

5   NAVIGATION TASK

To illustrate the utility of CQ-L, I use a navigational test bed similar to the one used by Bachrach (1991) that simulates a planar robot that can translate simultaneously

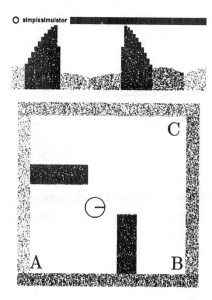

Figure 2: Navigation Testbed. See text for details.

and independently in both x and y directions. It can move one radius in any direction on each time step. The robot has 8 distance sensors and 8 gray-scale sensors evenly placed around its perimeter. These 16 values constitute the state vector. Figure 2 shows a display created by the navigation simulator. The bottom portion of the figure shows the robot's environment as seen from above. The upper panel shows the robot's state vector. Three different goal locations, A, B, and C, are marked on the test bed. The set of tasks on which the robot is trained are shown in Table 1. The elemental tasks require the robot to go to the given goal location from a random starting location in minimum time. The composite tasks require the robot to go to a goal location via a designated sequence of subgoal locations.

Task commands were represented by standard unit basis vectors (Table 1), and thus the architecture could not "parse" the task command to determine the decomposition of a composite task. Each Q-network was a feedforward connectionist network with a single hidden layer containing 128 radial basis units. The bias and gating networks were also feedforward nets with a single hidden layer containing sigmoid units. For all $x \in S \cup S'$ and $a \in A$, $c(x, a) = -0.05$. $r_i(x) = 1.0$ only if x is the desired final state of elemental task T_i, or if $x \in S'$ is the final state of composite task C_i; $r_i(x) = 0.0$ in all other states. Thus, for composite tasks no intermediate payoff for successful completion of subtasks was provided.

6   SIMULATION RESULTS

In the simulation described below, the performance of CQ-L is compared to the performance of a "one-for-one" architecture that implements the "learn-each-task-separately" strategy. The one-for-one architecture has a pre-assigned distinct network for each task, which prevents transfer of learning. Each network of the one-for-one architecture was provided with the augmented state.

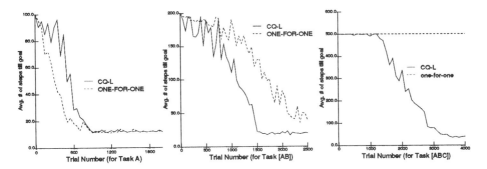

Figure 3: Learning Curves for Multiple tasks.

Both CQ-L and the one-for-one architecture were separately trained on the six tasks T_1, T_2, T_3, C_1, C_2, and C_3 until they could perform the six tasks optimally. CQ-L contained three Q-networks, and the one-for-one architecture contained six Q-networks. For each trial, the starting state of the robot and the task identity were chosen randomly. A trial ended when the robot reached the desired final state or when there was a time-out. The time-out period was 100 for the elemental tasks, 200 for C_1 and C_2, and 500 for task C_3. The graphs in Figure 3 show the number of actions executed per trial. Separate statistics were accumulated for each task.

The rightmost graph shows the performance of the two architectures on elemental task T_1. Not surprisingly, the one-for-one architecture performs better because it does not have the overhead of figuring out which Q-network to train for task T_1. The middle graph shows the performance on task C_1 and shows that the CQ-L architecture is able to perform better than the one-for-one architecture for a composite task containing just two elemental tasks. The leftmost graph shows the results for composite task C_3 and illustrates the main point of this paper. The one-for-one architecture is unable to learn the task, in fact it is unable to perform the task more than a couple of times due to the low probability of randomly performing the correct task sequence.

This simulation shows that CQ-L is able to learn the decomposition of a composite task and that compositional learning, due to transfer of training across tasks, can be faster than learning each composite task separately. More importantly, CQ-L is able to learn to solve composite tasks that cannot be solved using traditional schemes.

7   DISCUSSION

Learning to solve MDTs with large state sets is difficult due to the sparseness of the evaluative information and the low probability that a randomly selected sequence of actions will be optimal. Learning the long sequences of actions required to solve such tasks can be accelerated considerably if the agent has prior knowledge of useful subsequences. Such subsequences can be learned through experience in learning to solve other tasks. In this paper, I define a class of MDTs, called composite MDTs, that are structured as the temporal concatenation of simpler MDTs, called elemental MDTs. I present CQ-L, an architecture that combines the Q-learning algorithm of Watkins (1989) and the modular architecture of Jacobs et al. (1991) to achieve transfer of learning by sharing the solutions of elemental tasks across multiple composite tasks. Given a set of composite and elemental MDTs, the sequence in which the learning agent receives training experiences on the different tasks determines the relative advantage of CQ-L over other architectures that learn the tasks separately. The simulation reported in Section 6 demonstrates that it is possible to train CQ-L on intermixed trials of elemental and composite tasks. Nevertheless, the ability of CQ-L to scale well to complex sets of tasks will depend on the choice of the training sequence.

Acknowledgements

This work was supported by the Air Force Office of Scientific Research, Bolling AFB, under Grant AFOSR-89-0526 and by the National Science Foundation under Grant ECS-8912623. I am very grateful to Andrew Barto for his extensive help in formulating these ideas and preparing this paper.

References

J. R. Bachrach. (1991) A connectionist learning control architecture for navigation. In R. P. Lippmann, J. E. Moody, and D. S. Touretzky, editors, *Advances in Neural Information Processing Systems 3*, pages 457–463, San Mateo, CA. Morgan Kaufmann.

A. G. Barto, S. J. Bradtke, and S. P. Singh. (1991) Real-time learning and control using asynchronous dynamic programming. Technical Report 91-57, University of Massachusetts, Amherst, MA. Submitted to *AI Journal.*

R. A. Jacobs. (1990) *Task decomposition through competition in a modular connectionist architecture.* PhD thesis, COINS dept, Univ. of Massachusetts, Amherst, Mass. U.S.A.

R. A. Jacobs, M. I. Jordan, S. J. Nowlan, and G. E. Hinton. (1991) Adaptive mixtures of local experts. *Neural Computation,* 3(1).

D. E. Rumelhart, G. E. Hinton, and R. J. Williams. (1986) Learning internal representations by error propagation. In D. E. Rumelhart and J. L. McClelland, editors, *Parallel Distributed Processing: Explorations in the Microstructure of Cognition, vol.1: Foundations.* Bradford Books/MIT Press, Cambridge, MA.

S. P. Singh. (1992) Transfer of learning by composing solutions for elemental sequential tasks. *Machine Learning.*

R. S. Sutton. (1988) Learning to predict by the methods of temporal differences. *Machine Learning,* 3:9–44.

C. J. C. H. Watkins. (1989) *Learning from Delayed Rewards.* PhD thesis, Cambridge Univ., Cambridge, England.

C. J. C. H. Watkins and P. Dayan. (1992) Q-learning. *Machine Learning.*

Practical Issues in Temporal Difference Learning

Gerald Tesauro
IBM Thomas J. Watson Research Center
P. O. Box 704
Yorktown Heights, NY 10598
tesauro@watson.ibm.com

Abstract

This paper examines whether temporal difference methods for training connectionist networks, such as Suttons's TD(λ) algorithm, can be successfully applied to complex real-world problems. A number of important practical issues are identified and discussed from a general theoretical perspective. These practical issues are then examined in the context of a case study in which TD(λ) is applied to learning the game of backgammon from the outcome of self-play. This is apparently the first application of this algorithm to a complex nontrivial task. It is found that, with zero knowledge built in, the network is able to learn from scratch to play the entire game at a fairly strong intermediate level of performance, which is clearly better than conventional commercial programs, and which in fact surpasses comparable networks trained on a massive human expert data set. The hidden units in these network have apparently discovered useful features, a longstanding goal of computer games research. Furthermore, when a set of hand-crafted features is added to the input representation, the resulting networks reach a near-expert level of performance, and have achieved good results against world-class human play.

1 INTRODUCTION

We consider the prospects for applications of the TD(λ) algorithm for delayed reinforcement learning, proposed in (Sutton, 1988), to complex real-world problems. TD(λ) is an algorithm for adjusting the weights in a connectionist network which has the following form:

$$\Delta w_t = \alpha(P_{t+1} - P_t) \sum_{k=1}^{t} \lambda^{t-k} \nabla_w P_k \tag{1}$$

where P_t is the network's output upon observation of input pattern x_t at time t, w is the vector of weights that parameterizes the network, and $\nabla_w P_k$ is the gradient of network output with respect to weights. Equation 1 basically couples a temporal difference method for temporal credit assignment with a gradient-descent method for structural credit assigment; thus it provides a way to adapt supervised learning procedures such as back-propagation to solve temporal credit assignment problems. The λ parameter interpolates between two limiting cases: $\lambda = 1$ corresponds to an explicit supervised pairing of each input pattern x_t with the final reward signal, while $\lambda = 0$ corresponds to an explicit pairing of x_t with the next prediction P_{t+1}.

Little theoretical guidance is available for practical uses of this algorithm. For example, one of the most important issues in applications of network learning procedures is the choice of a good representation scheme. However, the existing theoretical analysis of TD(λ) applies primarily to look-up table representations in which the network has enough adjustable parameters to explicitly store the value of every possible state in the state space. This will clearly be intractable for real-world problems, and the theoretical results may be completely inappropriate, as they indicate, for example, that every possible state in the state space has to be visited infinitely many times in order to guarantee convergence.

Another important class of practical issues has to do with the nature of the task being learned, e.g., whether it is noisy or deterministic. In volatile environments with a high step-to-step variance in expected reward, TD learning is likely to be difficult. This is because the value of P_{t+1}, which is used as a heuristic teacher signal for P_t, may have nothing to do with the true value of the state x_t. In such cases it may be necessary to modify TD(λ) by including a lookahead process which averages over the step-to-step noise.

Additional difficulties must also be expected if the task is a combined prediction-control task, in which the predictor network is used to make control decisions, as opposed to a prediction only task. As the network's predictions change, its control strategies also change, and this changes the target predictions that the network is trying to learn. In this case, theory does not say whether the combined learning system would converge at all, and if so, whether it would converge to the optimal predictor-controller. It might be possible for the system to get stuck in a self-consistent but non-optimal predictor-controller.

A final set of practical issues are algorithmic in nature, such as convergence, scaling, and the possibility of overtraining or overfitting. TD(λ) has been proven to converge only for a linear network and a linearly independent set of input patterns (Sutton, 1988; Dayan, 1992). In the more general case, the algorithm may not converge even to a locally optimal solution, let alone to a globally optimal solution.

Regarding scaling, no results are available to indicate how the speed and quality of TD learning will scale with the temporal length of sequences to be learned, the dimensionality of the input space, the complexity of the task, or the size of the network. Intuitively it seems likely that the required training time might increase dramatically with the sequence length. The training time might also scale poorly with the network or input space dimension, e.g., due to increased sensitivity to noise in the teacher signal. Another potential problem is that the quality of solution found by gradient-descent learning relative to the globally optimal solution might get progressively worse with increasing network size.

Overtraining occurs when continued training of the network results in poorer performance. Overfitting occurs when a larger network does not do as well on a task as a smaller network. In supervised learning, both of these problems are believed to be due to a limited data set. In the TD approach, training takes place on-line using patterns generated *de novo*, thus one might hope that these problems would not occur. But both overtraining and overfitting may occur if the error function minimized during training does not correspond to the performance function that the user cares about. For example, in a combined prediction-control task, the user may care only about the quality of control signals, not the absolute accuracy of the predictions.

2   A CASE STUDY: TD LEARNING OF BACKGAMMON STRATEGY

We have seen that existing theory provides little indication of how $TD(\lambda)$ will behave in practical applications. In the absence of theory, we now examine empirically the above-mentioned issues in the context of a specific application: learning to play the game of backgammon from the outcome of self-play. This application was selected because of its complexity and stochastic nature, and because a detailed comparison can be made with the alternative approach of supervised learning from human expert examples (Tesauro, 1989; Tesauro, 1990).

It seems reasonable that, by watching two fixed opponents play out a large number of games, a network could learn by TD methods to predict the expected outcome of any given board position. However, the experiments presented here study the more interesting question of whether a network can learn from its own play. The learning system is set up as follows: the network observes a sequence of board positions $x_1, x_2, ..., x_f$ leading to a final reward signal z. In the simplest case, $z = 1$ if White wins and $z = 0$ if Black wins. In this case the network's output P_t is an estimate of White's probability of winning from board position x_t. The sequence of board positions is generated by setting up an initial configuration, and making plays for both sides using the network's output as an evaluation function. In other words, the move which is selected at each time step is the move which maximizes P_t when White is to play and minimizes P_t when Black is to play.

The representation scheme used here contained only a simple encoding of the "raw" board description (explained in detail in figure 2), and did not utilize any additional pre-computed "features" relevant to good play. Since the input encoding scheme contains no built-in knowledge about useful features, and since the network only observes its own play, we may say that this is a "knowledge-free" approach to learning backgammon. While it's not clear that this approach can make any progress beyond a random starting state, it at least provides a baseline for judging other approaches using various forms of built-in knowledge.

The approach described above is similar in spirit to Samuel's scheme for learning checkers from self-play (Samuel, 1959), but in several ways it is a more challenging learning task. Unlike the raw board description used here, Samuel's board description used a number of hand-crafted features which were designed in consultation with human checkers experts. The evaluation function learned in Samuel's study was a linear function of the input variables, whereas multilayer networks learn more complex nonlinear functions. Finally, Samuel found that it was necessary to give the learning system at least one fixed intermediate goal, material advantage, as well as the ultimate goal of the game. The proposed backgammon learning system has no such intermediate goals.

The networks had a feedforward fully-connected architecture with either no hidden units, or a single hidden layer with between 10 and 40 hidden units. The learning algorithm parameters were set, after a certain amount of parameter tuning, at $\alpha = 0.1$ and $\lambda = 0.7$.

The average sequence length appeared to depend strongly on the quality of play. With decent play on both sides, the average game length is about 50-60 time steps, whereas for the random initial networks, games often last several hundred or even several thousand time steps. This is one of the reasons why the proposed self-learning scheme appeared unlikely to work.

Learning was assessed primarily by testing the networks in actual game play against Sun Microsystems' Gammontool program. Gammontool is representative of the playing ability of typical commercial programs, and provides a decent benchmark for measuring game-playing strength: human beginners can win about 40% of the time against it, decent intermediate-level humans would win about 60%, and human experts would win about 75%. (The random initial networks before training win only about 1%.)

Networks were trained on the entire game, starting from the opening position and going all the way to the end. This is an admittedly naive approach which was not expected to yield any useful results other than a reference point for judging more sensible approaches. However, the rather surprising result was that a significant amount of learning actually took place. Results are shown in figure 1. For comparison purposes, networks with the same input coding scheme were also trained on a massive human expert data base of over 15,000 engaged positions, following the training procedure described in (Tesauro, 1989). These networks were also tested in game play against Gammontool.

Given the complexity of the task, size of input space and length of typical sequences, it seems remarkable that the TD nets can learn on their own to play at a level substantially better than Gammontool. Perhaps even more remarkable is that the TD nets surpass the EP nets trained on a massive human expert data base: the best TD net won 66.2% against Gammontool, whereas the best EP net could only manage 59.4%. This was confirmed in a head-to-head test in which the best TD net played 10,000 games against the best EP net. The result was 55% to 45% in favor of the TD net. This confirms that the Gammontool benchmark gives a reasonably accurate measure of relative game-playing strength, and that the TD net really is better than the EP net. In fact, the TD net with no features appears to be as good as Neurogammon 1.0, backgammon champion of the 1989 Computer

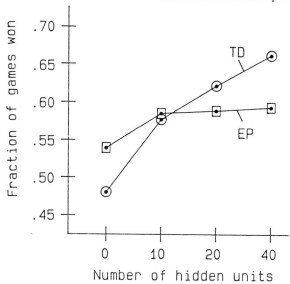

Figure 1: Plot of game performance against Gammontool vs. number of hidden units for networks trained using TD learning from self-play (TD), and supervised training on human expert preferences (EP). Each data point represents the result of a 10,000 game test, and should be accurate to within one percentage point.

Olympiad, which does have features, and which wins 65% against Gammontool. A 10,000 game test of the best TD net against Neurogammon 1.0 yielded statistical equality: 50% for the TD net and 50% for Neurogammon.

It is also of interest to examine the weights learned by the TD nets, shown in figure 2. One can see a great deal of spatially organized structure in the pattern of weights, and some of this structure can be interpreted as useful features by a knowledgable backgammon player. For example, the first hidden unit in figure 2 appears to be a race-oriented feature detector, while the second hidden unit appears to be an attack-oriented feature detector. The TD net has apparently solved the long-standing "feature discovery" problem, which was recently stated in (Frey, 1986) as follows: "Samuel was disappointed in his inability to develop a mechanical strategy for defining features. He thought that true machine learning should include the discovery and definition of features. Unfortunately, no one has found a practical way to do this even though more than two and a half decades have passed."

The training times needed to reach the levels of performance shown in figure 1 were on the order of 50,000 training games for the networks with 0 and 10 hidden units, 100,000 games for the 20-hidden unit net, and 200,000 games for the 40-hidden unit net. Since the number of training games appears to scale roughly linearly with the number of weights in the network, and the CPU simulation time per game on a serial computer also scales linearly with the number of weights, the total CPU time thus scales quadratically with the number of weights: on an IBM RS/6000 workstation, the smallest network was trained in several hours, while the largest net required two weeks of simulation time.

In qualitative terms, the TD nets have developed a style of play emphasizing run-

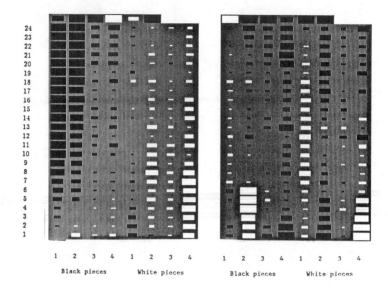

Figure 2: Weights from the input units to two hidden units in the best TD net. Black squares represent negative weights; white squares represent positive weights; size indicates magnitude of weights. Rows represent spatial locations 1-24, top row represents no. of barmen, men off, and side to move. Columns represent number of Black and White men as indicated. The first hidden unit has two noteworthy features: a linearly increasing pattern of negative weights for Black blots and Black points, and a negative weighting of White men off and a positive weighting of Black men off. These contribute to an estimate of Black's probability of winning based on his racing lead. The second hidden unit has the following noteworthy features: strong positive weights for Black home board points, strong positive weights for White men on bar, positive weights for White blots, and negative weights for White points in Black's home board. These factors all contribute to the probability of a successful Black attacking strategy.

ning and tactical play, whereas the EP nets favor more quiescent positional play emphasizing blocking rather than racing. This is more in line with human expert play, but it often leads to complex prime vs. prime and back-game situations that are hard for the network to evaluate properly. This suggests one possible advantage of the TD approach over the EP approach: by imitating an expert teacher, the learner may get itself into situations that it can't handle. With the alternative approach of learning from experience, the learner may not reproduce the expert strategies, but at least it will learn to handle whatever situations are brought about by its own strategy.

It's also interesting that TD net plays well in early phases of play, whereas its play becomes worse in the late phases of the game. This is contrary to the intuitive notion that states far from the end of the sequence should be harder to learn than states near the end. Apparently the inductive bias due to the representation scheme and network architecture is more important than temporal distance to the final outcome.

3 TD LEARNING WITH BUILT-IN FEATURES

We have seen that TD networks with no built-in knowledge are able to reach computer championship levels of performance for this particular application. It is then natural to wonder whether even greater levels of performance might be obtained by adding hand-crafted features to the input representation. In a separate series of experiments, TD nets containing all of Neurogammon's features were trained from self-play as described in the previous section. Once again it was found that the performance improved monotonically by adding more hidden units to the network, and training for longer training times. The best performance was obtained with a network containing 80 hidden units and over 25,000 weights. This network was trained for over 300,000 training games, taking over a month of CPU time on an RS/6000 workstation. The resulting level of performance was 73% against Gammontool and nearly 60% against Neurogammon. This is very close to a human expert level of performance, and is the strongest program ever seen by this author.

The level of play of this network was also tested in an all-day match against two-time World Champion Bill Robertie, one of the world's best backgammon players. At the end of the match, a total of 31 games had been played, of which Robertie won 18 and the TD net 13. This showed that the TD net was capable of a respectable showing against world-class human play. In fact, Robertie thinks that the network's level of play is equal to the average good human tournament player.

It's interesting to speculate about how far this approach can be carried. Further substantial improvements might be obtained by training much larger networks on a supercomputer or special-purpose hardware. On such a machine one could also search beyond one ply, and there is some evidence that small-to-moderate improvements could be obtained by running the network in two-ply search mode. Finally, the features in Berliner's BKG program (Berliner, 1980) or in some of the top commercial programs are probably more sophisticated than Neurogammon's relatively simple features, and hence might give better performance. The combination of all three improvements (bigger nets, two-ply search, better features) could conceivably result in a network capable of playing at world-class level.

4 CONCLUSIONS

The experiments in this paper were designed to test whether TD(λ) could be successfully applied to complex, stochastic, nonlinear, real-world prediction and control problems. This cannot be addressed within current theory because it cannot answer such basic questions as whether the algorithm converges or how it would scale.

Given the lack of any theoretical guarantees, the results of these experiments are very encouraging. Empirically the algorithm always converges to at least a local minimum, and the quality of solution generally improves with increasing network size. Furthermore, the scaling of training time with the length of input sequences, and with the size and complexity of the task, does not appear to be a serious problem. This was ascertained through studies of simplified endgame situations, which took about as many training games to learn as the full-game situation (Tesauro, 1992). Finally, the network's move selection ability is better than one would expect based on its prediction accuracy. The absolute prediction accuracy is only at the 10% level, whereas the difference in expected outcome between optimal and non-optimal moves is usually at the level of 1% or less.

The most encouraging finding, however, is a clear demonstration that TD nets with zero built-in knowledge can outperform identical networks trained on a massive data base of expert examples. It would be nice to understand exactly how this is possible. The ability of TD nets to discover features on their own may also be of some general importance in computer games research, and thus worthy of further analysis.

Beyond this particular application area, however, the larger and more important issue is whether learning from experience can be useful and practical for more general complex problems. The quality of results obtained in this study indicates that the approach may work well in practice. There may also be some intrinsic advantages over supervised training on a fixed data set. At the very least, for tasks in which the exemplars are hand-labeled by humans, it eliminates the laborious and time-consuming process of labeling the data. Furthermore, the learning system would not be fundamentally limited by the quantity of labeled data, or by errors in the labeling process. Finally, preserving the intrinsic temporal nature of the task, and informing the system of the consequences of its actions, may convey important information about the task which is not necessarily contained in the labeled exemplars. More theoretical and empirical work will be needed to establish the relative advantages and disadvantages of the two approaches; this could result in the development of hybrid algorithms combining the best of both approaches.

References

H. Berliner, "Computer backgammon." *Sci. Am.* **243:1**, 64-72 (1980).

P. Dayan, "Temporal differences: TD(λ) for general λ." *Machine Learning*, in press (1992).

P. W. Frey, "Algorithmic strategies for improving the performance of game playing programs." In: D. Farmer et al. (Eds.), *Evolution, Games and Learning*. Amsterdam: North Holland (1986).

A. Samuel, "Some studies in machine learning using the game of checkers." *IBM J. of Research and Development* **3**, 210-229 (1959).

R. S. Sutton, "Learning to predict by the methods of temporal differences." *Machine Learning* **3**, 9-44 (1988).

G. Tesauro and T. J. Sejnowski, "A parallel network that learns to play backgammon." *Artificial Intelligence* **39**, 357-390 (1989).

G. Tesauro, "Connectionist learning of expert preferences by comparison training." In D. Touretzky (Ed.), *Advances in Neural Information Processing* **1**, 99-106 (1989).

G. Tesauro, "Neurogammon: a neural network backgammon program." *IJCNN Proceedings* **III**, 33-39 (1990).

G. Tesauro, "Practical issues in temporal difference learning." *Machine Learning*, in press (1992).

HARMONET: A Neural Net for Harmonizing Chorales in the Style of J.S.Bach

Hermann Hild
hhild@ira.uka.de

Johannes Feulner
johannes@ira.uka.de

Wolfram Menzel
menzel@ira.uka.de

Institut für Logik, Komplexität und Deduktionssysteme
Am Fasanengarten 5
Universität Karlsruhe
W-7500 Karlsruhe 1, Germany

Abstract

HARMONET, a system employing connectionist networks for music processing, is presented. After being trained on some dozen Bach chorales using error backpropagation, the system is capable of producing four-part chorales in the style of J.S.Bach, given a one-part melody. Our system solves a musical real-world problem on a performance level appropriate for musical practice. HARMONET's power is based on (a) a new coding scheme capturing musically relevant information and (b) the integration of backpropagation and symbolic algorithms in a hierarchical system, combining the advantages of both.

1 INTRODUCTION

Neural approaches to music processing have been previously proposed (Lischka, 1989) and implemented (Mozer, 1991)(Todd, 1989). The promise neural networks offer is that they may shed some light on an aspect of human creativity that doesn't seem to be describable in terms of symbols and rules. Ultimately what music is (or isn't) lies in the eye (or ear) of the beholder. The great composers, such as Bach or Mozart, learned and obeyed quite a number of rules, e.g. the famous prohibition of parallel fifths. But these rules alone do not suffice to characterize a personal or even historic style. An easy test is to generate music at random, using only

267

A Chorale Melody

Bach's Chorale Harmonization

Figure 1: The beginning of the chorale melody "Jesu, meine Zuversicht" and its harmonization by J.S.Bach

schoolbook rules as constraints. The result is "error free" but aesthetically offensive. To overcome this gap between obeying rules and producing music adhering to an accepted aesthetic standard, we propose HARMONET, which integrates symbolic algorithms and neural networks to compose four part chorales in the style of J.S. Bach (1685 - 1750), given the one part melody. The neural nets concentrate on the creative part of the task, being responsible for aesthetic conformance to the standard set by Bach in nearly 400 examples. Original Bach Chorales are used as training data. Conventional algorithms do the bookkeeping tasks like observing pitch ranges, or preventing parallel fifths. HARMONET's level of performance approaches that of improvising church organists, making it applicable to musical practice.

2   TASK DEFINITION

The process of composing an accompaniment for a given chorale melody is called **chorale harmonization**. Typically, a chorale melody is a plain melody often harmonized to be sung by a choir. Correspondingly, the four voices of a chorale harmonization are called soprano (the melody part), alto, tenor and bass. Figure 1 depicts an example of a chorale melody and its harmonization by J.S.Bach. For centuries, music students have been routinely taught to solve the task of chorale harmonization. Many theories and rules about "dos" and "don'ts" have been developed. However, the task of HARMONET is to learn to harmonize chorales *from example*. Neural nets are used to find stylisticly characteristic harmonic sequences and ornamentations.

3   SYSTEM OVERVIEW

Given a set of Bach chorales, our goal is to find an approximation $\hat{f}$ of the quite complex function[1] f which maps chorale melodies into their harmonization as demonstrated by J.S.Bach on almost 400 examples. In the following sections we propose a decomposition of f into manageable subfunctions.

3.1   TASK DECOMPOSITION

The learning task is decomposed along two dimensions:

Different levels of abstractions. The **chord skeleton** is obtained if eighth and sixteenth notes are viewed as omitable ornamentations. Furthermore, if the chords are conceived as harmonies with certain attributes such as "inversion" or "characteristic dissonances", the chorale is reducible to its **harmonic skeleton**, a thoroughbass-like representation (Figure 2).

Locality in time. The accompaniment is divided into smaller parts, each of which is learned independently by looking at some local context, a window. Treating small parts independently certainly hurts global consistency. Some of the dependencies lost can be regained if the current decision window additionally considers the outcome of its predecessors (external feedback). Figure 3 shows two consecutive windows cut out from the harmonic skeleton.

To harmonize a chorale, HARMONET starts by learning the harmonic skeleton, which then is refined to the chord skeleton and finally augmented with ornamenting quavers (Figure 4, left side).

3.2   THE HARMONIC SKELETON

Chorales have a rich harmonic structure, which is mainly responsible for their "musical appearance". Thus generating a good harmonic skeleton is the most important of HARMONET's subtasks. HARMONET creates a harmonic sequence by sweeping through the chorale melody and determining a harmony for each quarter note, considering its local context and the previously found harmonies as input.
At each quarterbeat position t, the following information is extracted to form one training example:

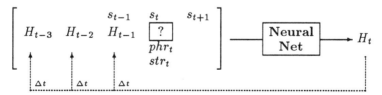

The target to be learned (the harmony H_t at position t) is marked by the box. The input consists of the harmonic context to the left (the external feedback H_{t-3}, H_{t-2} and H_{t-1}) and the melodic context (pitches s_{t-1}, s_t and s_{t+1}). phr_t contains

---

[1]To be sure, f is not a function but a relation, since there are many "legal" accompaniments for one melody. For simplicity, we view f as a function.

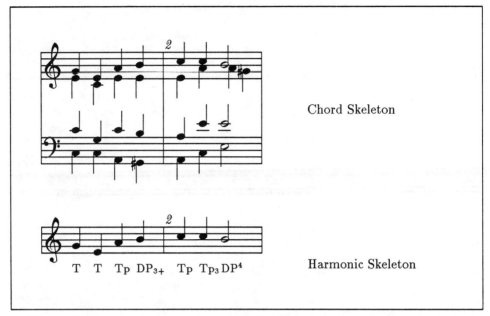

Figure 2: The chord and the harmonic skeleton of the chorale from figure 1.

information about the relative position of t to the beginning or end of a musical phrase. str_t is a boolean value indicating whether s_t is a stressed quarter. A harmony H_t has three components: Most importantly, the *harmonic function* relates the key of the harmony to the key of the piece. The *inversion* indicates the bass note of the harmony. The *characteristic dissonances* are notes which do not directly belong to the harmony, thus giving it additional tension.

The **coding of pitch** is decisive for recognizing musically relevant regularities in the training examples. This problem is discussed in many places (Shepard, 1982) (Mozer, 1991). We developed a new coding scheme guided by the harmonic necessities of homophonic music pieces: A note s is represented as the set of harmonic functions that contain s, as shown below:

Fct.	T	D	S	Tp	Sp	Dp	DD	DP	TP	d	Vtp	SS
C	1	0	1	1	0	0	0	0	0	0	0	0
D	0	1	0	0	1	0	1	0	0	1	1	1
E	..											

T, D, S, Tp etc. are standard musical abbreviations to denote harmonic functions. The resulting representation is distributed with respect to pitch. However, it is local with respect to harmonic functions. This allows the network to anticipate future harmonic developments even though there cannot be a lookahead for harmonies yet uncomposed.

Besides the 12 input units for each of the pitches s_{t-1}, s_t, s_{t+1}, we need $12+5+3 =$

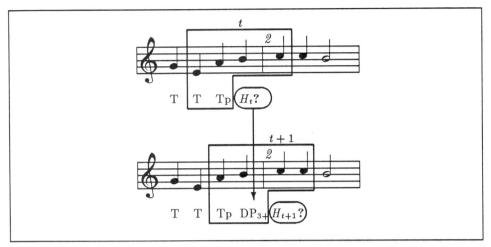

Figure 3: The harmonic skeleton broken into local windows. The harmony H_t, determined at quarterbeat position t, becomes part of the input of the window at position $t + 1$.

20 input units for each of the 3 components of the harmonies H_{t-3}, H_{t-2} and H_{t-1}, 9 units to code the phrase information phr_t and 1 unit for the stress str_t. Thus our net has a total of $3 * 12 + 3 * 20 + 9 + 1 = 106$ input units and 20 output units. We used one hidden layer with 70 units.

In a more advanced version (Figure 4, right side), we use three nets (N1, N2, N3) in parallel, each of which was trained on windows of different size. The harmonic function for which the majority of these three nets votes is passed to two subsequent nets (N4, N5) determining the chord inversion and characteristic dissonances of the harmony. Using windows of different sizes in parallel employs statistical information to solve the problem of chosing an appropriate window size.

3.3   THE CHORD SKELETON

The task on this level is to find the two middle parts (alto and tenor) given the soprano S of the chorale melody and the harmony H determined by the neural nets. Since H includes information about the chord inversion, the pitch of the bass (modulo its octave) is already given. The problem is tackled with a "generate and test" approach: Symbolic algorithms select a "best" chord out of the set of all chords consistent with the given harmony H and common chorale constraints.

3.4   QUAVER ORNAMENTATIONS

In the last subtask, another net is taught how to add ornamenting eighths to the chord skeleton. The output of this network is the set of eighth notes (if any) by which a particular chord C_t can be augmented. The network's input describes the local context of C_t in terms of attributes such as the intervals between C_t and C_{t+1}, voice leading characteristics, or the presence of eighths in previous chords.

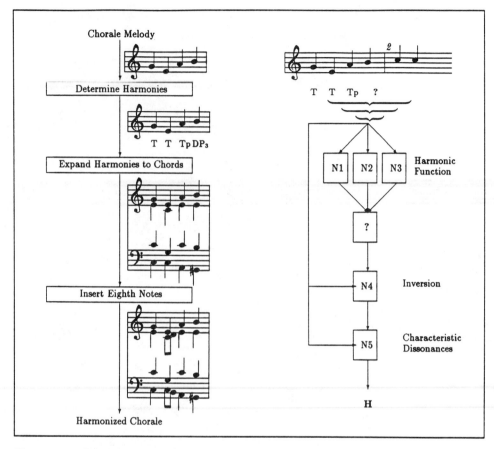

Figure 4: Left side: Overall structure of HARMONET. Right side: A more special-ized architecture with parallel and sequential nets (see text).

4 PERFORMANCE

HARMONET was trained separately on two sets of Bach chorales, each containing 20 chorales in major and minor keys, respectively. By passing the chorales through a window as explained above, each set amounted to approx. 1000 training examples. All nets were trained with the error backpropagation algorithm, needing 50 to 100 epochs to achieve reasonable convergence.

Figures 5 and 6 show two harmonizations produced by HARMONET, given melodies which were not in the training set. An audience of music professionals judged the quality of these and other chorales produced by HARMONET to be on the level on an improvising organist. HARMONET also compares well to non-neural approaches. In figure 6 HARMONET's accompaniment is shown on a chorale melody also used in the Ph.D. thesis of (Ebcioglu, 1986) to demonstrate the expert system "CHORAL".

Figure 5: A chorale in a major key harmonized by HARMONET.

Figure 6: "Happy Birthday" harmonized by HARMONET.

5   CONCLUSIONS

The music processing system HARMONET presented in this paper clearly shows that musical real-world applications are well within the reach of connectionist approaches. We believe that HARMONET owes much of its success to a clean task decomposition and a meaningful selection and representation of musically relevant features. By using a hybrid approach we allow the networks to concentrate on musical essentials instead of on structural constraints which may be hard for a network to learn but easy to code symbolically. The abstraction of chords to harmonies reduces the problem space and resembles a musician's problem approach. The "harmonic representation" of pitch shows the harmonic character of the given melody more explicitly.

We have also experimented to replace the neural nets in HARMONET by other learning techniques such as decision trees (ID3) or nearest neighbor classification. However, as also reported on other tasks (Dietterich et al., 1990), they were outperformed by the neural nets.

HARMONET is not a general music processing system, its architecture is designed to solve a quite difficult but also quite specific task. However, due to HARMONET's neural learning component, only a comparatively small amount of musical expert knowledge was necessary to design the system, making it easier to build and more flexible than a pure rule based system.

Acknowledgements

We thank Heinz Braun, Heiko Harms and Gudrun Socher for many fruitful discussions and contributions to this research and our music lab.

References

J.S.Bach (Ed.: Bernhard Friedrich Fischer) **389 Choralgesänge für vierstimmigen Chor**. Edition Breitkopf, Nr. 3765.

Dietterich,T.G., Hild,H., & Bakiri,G. **A comparative study of ID3 and Backpropagation for English Text-to-Speech Mapping**. Proc. of the Seventh International Conference on Machine Learning (pp. 24-31). Kaufmann, 1990.

Ebcioğlu,K. **An Expert System for Harmonization of Chorales in the Style of J.S.Bach**. Ph.D. Dissertation, Department of C.S., State University of New York at Buffalo, New York, 1986.

Lischka,C. **Understanding Music Cognition**. GMD St.Augustin, FRG, 1989.

Mozer,M.C., Soukup,T. **Connectionist Music Composition Based on Melodic and Stylistic Constraints**. Advances in Neural Information Processing 3 (NIPS 3), R.P. Lippmann, J. E. Moody, D.S. Touretzky (eds.), Kaufmann 1991.

Shepard, Roger N. **Geometrical Approximations to the Structure of Musical Pitch**. Psychological Review, Vol. 89, Nr. 4, July 1982.

Todd, Peter M. **A Connectionist Approach To Algorithmic Composition**. Computer Music Journal, Vol. 13, No. 4, Winter 1989.

Induction of Multiscale Temporal Structure

Michael C. Mozer
Department of Computer Science &
Institute of Cognitive Science
University of Colorado
Boulder, CO 80309–0430

Abstract

Learning structure in temporally-extended sequences is a difficult computational problem because only a fraction of the relevant information is available at any instant. Although variants of back propagation can in principle be used to find structure in sequences, in practice they are not sufficiently powerful to discover arbitrary contingencies, especially those spanning long temporal intervals or involving high order statistics. For example, in designing a connectionist network for music composition, we have encountered the problem that the net is able to learn musical structure that occurs locally in time—e.g., relations among notes within a musical phrase—but not structure that occurs over longer time periods—e.g., relations among phrases. To address this problem, we require a means of constructing a *reduced description* of the sequence that makes global aspects more explicit or more readily detectable. I propose to achieve this using hidden units that operate with different time constants. Simulation experiments indicate that slower time-scale hidden units are able to pick up global structure, structure that simply can not be learned by standard back propagation.

Many patterns in the world are intrinsically temporal, e.g., speech, music, the unfolding of events. Recurrent neural net architectures have been devised to accommodate time-varying sequences. For example, the architecture shown in Figure 1 can map a sequence of inputs to a sequence of outputs. Learning structure in temporally-extended sequences is a difficult computational problem because the input pattern may not contain all the task-relevant information at any instant. Thus,

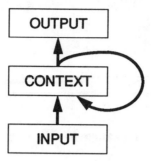

Figure 1: A generic recurrent network architecture for processing input and output sequences. Each box corresponds to a layer of units, each line to full connectivity between layers.

the context layer must hold on to relevant aspects of the input history until a later point in time at which they can be used.

In principle, variants of back propagation for recurrent networks (Rumelhart, Hinton, & Williams, 1986; Williams & Zipser, 1989) can discover an appropriate representation in the context layer for a particular task. In practice, however, back propagation is not sufficiently powerful to discover arbitrary contingencies, especially those that span long temporal intervals or that involve high order statistics (e.g., Mozer, 1989; Rohwer, 1990; Schmidhuber, 1991).

Let me present a simple situation where back propagation fails. It involves remembering an event over an interval of time. A variant of this task was first studied by Schmidhuber (1991). The input is a sequence of discrete symbols: A, B, C, D, $\cdots$, X, Y. The task is to predict the next symbol in the sequence. Each sequence begins with either an X or a Y—call this the *trigger symbol*—and is followed by a fixed sequence such as ABCDE, which in turn is followed by a second instance of the trigger symbol, i.e., XABCDEX or or YABCDEY. To perform the prediction task, it is necessary to store the trigger symbol when it is first presented, and then to recall the same symbol five time steps later.

The number of symbols intervening between the two triggers—call this the *gap*—can be varied. By training different networks on different gaps, we can examine how difficult the learning task is as a function of gap. To better control the experiments, all input sequences had the same length and consisted of either X or Y followed by ABCDEFGHIJK. The second instance of the trigger symbol was inserted at various points in the sequence. For example, XABCDXEFGHIJK represents a gap of 4, YABCDEFGHYIJK a gap of 8.

Each training set consisted of two sequences, one with X and one with Y. Different networks were trained on different gaps. The network architecture consisted of one input and output unit per symbol, and ten context units. Twenty-five replications of each network were run with different random initial weights. If the training set was not learned within 10000 epochs, the replication was counted as a "failure." The primary result was that training sets with gaps of 4 or more could not be learned reliably, as shown in Table 1.

Table 1: Learning contingencies across gaps

gap	% failures	mean # epochs to learn
2	0	468
4	36	7406
6	92	9830
8	100	10000
10	100	10000

The results are suprisingly poor. My general impression is that back propagation is powerful enough to learn only structure that is fairly *local* in time. For instance, in earlier work on neural net music composition (Mozer & Soukup, 1991), we found that our network could master the rules of composition for notes within a musical phrase, but not rules operating at a more global level—rules for how phrases are interrelated.

The focus of the present work is on devising learning algorithms and architectures for better handling temporal structure at more *global* scales, as well as multiscale or hierarchical structure. This difficult problem has been identified and studied by several other researchers, including Miyata and Burr (1990), Rohwer (1990), and Schmidhuber (1991).

1   BUILDING A REDUCED DESCRIPTION

The basic idea behind my work involves building a *reduced description* (Hinton, 1988) of the sequence that makes global aspects more explicit or more readily detectable. The challenge of this approach is to devise an appropriate reduced description. I've experimented with a scheme that constructs a reduced description that is essentially a bird's eye view of the sequence, sacrificing a representation of individual elements for the overall contour of the sequence. Imagine a musical tape played at double the regular speed. Individual sounds are blended together and become indistinguishable. However, coarser time-scale events become more explicit, such as an ascending trend in pitch or a repeated progression of notes. Figure 2 illustrates the idea. The curve in the left graph, depicting a sequence of individual pitches, has been smoothed and compressed to produce the right graph. Mathematically, "smoothed and compressed" means that the waveform has been low-pass filtered and sampled at a lower rate. The result is a waveform in which the alternating upwards and downwards flow is unmistakable.

Multiple views of the sequence are realized using context units that operate with different *time constants*:

$$c_i(t) = \tau_i c_i(t-1) + (1 - \tau_i) \tanh[net_i(t)], \tag{1}$$

where $c_i(t)$ is the activity of context unit i at time t, $net_i(t)$ is the net input to unit i at time t, including activity both from the input layer and the recurrent context connections, and τ_i is a time constant associated with each unit that has the range $(0, 1)$ and determines the responsiveness of the unit—the rate at which

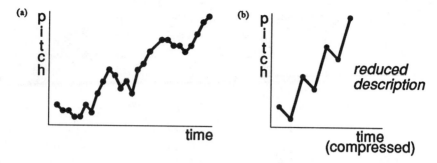

Figure 2: (a) A sequence of musical notes. The vertical axis indicates the pitch, the horizontal axis time. Each point corresponds to a particular note. (b) A smoothed, compact view of the sequence.

its activity changes. With $\tau_i = 0$, the activation rule reduces to the standard one and the unit can sharply change its response based on a new input. With large τ_i, the unit is sluggish, holding on to much of its previous value and thereby averaging the response to the net input over time. At the extreme of $\tau_i = 1$, the second term drops out and the unit's activity becomes fixed. Thus, large τ_i smooth out the response of a context unit over time. Note, however, that what is smoothed is the activity of the context units, not the input itself as Figure 2 might suggest.

Smoothing is one property that distinguishes the waveform in Figure 2b from the original. The other property, compactness, is also achieved by a large τ_i, although somewhat indirectly. The key benefit of the compact waveform in Figure 2b is that it allows a longer period of time to be viewed in a single glance, thereby explicating contingencies occurring in this interval during learning. The context unit activation rule (Equation 1) permits this. To see why this is the case, consider the relation between the error derivative with respect to the context units at time t, $\partial E / \partial c(t)$, and the error back propagated to the previous step, $t - 1$. One contribution to $\partial E / \partial c_i(t - 1)$, from the first term in Equation 1, is

$$\frac{\partial E}{\partial c_i(t)} \frac{\partial}{\partial c_i(t-1)} [\tau_i c_i(t-1)] = \tau_i \frac{\partial E}{\partial c_i(t)}. \tag{2}$$

This means that when τ_i is large, most of the error signal in context unit i at time t is carried back to time $t - 1$. Intuitively, just as the activation of units with large τ_i changes slowly forward in time, the error propagated back through these units changes slowly too. Thus, the back propagated error signal can make contact with points further back in time, facilitating the learning of more global structure in the input sequence.

Time constants have been incorporated into the activation rules of other connectionist architectures (Jordan, 1987; McClelland, 1979; Mozer, 1989; Pearlmutter, 1989; Pineda, 1987). However, none of this work has exploited time constants to control the temporal responsivity of individual units.

2   LEARNING AABA PHRASE PATTERNS

A simple simulation illustrates the benefits of temporal reduced descriptions. I generated pseudo musical phrases consisting of five notes in ascending chromatic order, e.g., $F\#_2$ G_2 $G\#_2$ A_2 $A\#_2$ or C_4 $C\#_4$ D_4 $D\#_4$ E_4, where the first pitch was selected at random.[1] Pairs of phrases—call them A and B—were concatenated to form an AABA pattern, terminated by a special END marker. The complete melody then consisted of 21 elements—four phrases of five notes followed by the END marker—an example of which is:

$F\#_2$ G_2 $G\#_2$ A_2 $A\#_2$ $F\#_2$ G_2 $G\#_2$ A_2 $A\#_2$ C_4 $C\#_4$ D_4 $D\#_4$ E_4 $F\#_2$ G_2 $G\#_2$ A_2 $A\#_2$ END.

Two versions of CONCERT were tested, each with 35 context units. In the *standard* version, all 35 units had $\tau = 0$; in the *reduced description* or *RD* version, 30 had $\tau = 0$ and 5 had $\tau = 0.8$. The training set consisted of 200 examples and the test set another 100 examples. Ten replications of each simulation were run for 300 passes through the training set. See Mozer and Soukup (1991) for details of the network architecture and note representations.

Because of the way that the sequences are organized, certain pitches can be predicted based on local structure whereas other pitches require a more global memory of the sequence. In particular, the second through fifth pitches within a phrase can be predicted based on knowledge of the immediately preceding pitch. To predict the first pitch in the repeated A phrases and to predict the END marker, more global information is necessary. Thus, the analysis was split to distinguish between pitches requiring only local structure and pitches requiring more global structure. As Table 2 shows, performance requiring global structure was significantly better for the RD version ($F(1,9)=179.8$, $p < .001$), but there was only a marginally reliable difference for performance involving local structure ($F(1,9)=3.82$, $p=.08$). The global structure can be further broken down to prediction of the END marker and prediction of the first pitch of the repeated A phrases. In both cases, the performance improvement for the RD version was significant: 88.0% versus 52.9% for the end of sequence ($F(1,9)=220$, $p < .001$); 69.4% versus 61.2% for the first pitch ($F(1,9)=77.6$, $p < .001$).

Experiments with different values of τ in the range .7–.95 yielded qualitatively similar results, as did experiments in which the A and B phrases were formed by random walks in the key of C major.

---

[1]One need not understand the musical notation to make sense of this example. Simply consider each note to be a unique symbol in a set of symbols having a fixed ordering. The example is framed in terms of music because my original work involved music composition.

Table 2: Performance on AABA phrases

structure	standard version	RD version
local	97.3%	96.7%
global	58.4%	75.6%

3   DETECTING CONTINGENCIES ACROSS GAPS— REVISITED

I now return to the prediction task involving sequences containing two X's or Y's separated by a stream of intervening symbols. A reduced description network had no problem learning the contingency across wide gaps. Table 3 compares the results presented earlier for a standard net with ten context units and the results for an RD net having six standard context units ($\tau = 0$) and four units having identical nonzero τ, in the range of .75–.95. More on the choice of τ below, but first observe that the reduced description net had a 100% success rate. Indeed, it had no difficulty with much wider gaps: I tested gaps of up to 25 symbols. The number of epochs to learn scales roughly linearly with the gap.

When the task was modified slightly such that the intervening symbols were randomly selected from the set {A,B,C,D}, the RD net still had no difficulty with the prediction task.

The bad news here is that the choice of τ can be important. In the results reported above, τ was selected to optimize performance. In general, a larger τ was needed to span larger gaps. For small gaps, performance was insensitive to the particular τ chosen. However, the larger the temporal gap that had to be spanned, the smaller the range of τ values that gave acceptable results. This would appear to be a serious limitation of the approach. However, there are several potential solutions.

1. One might try using back propagation to train the time constants directly. This does not work particularly well on the problems I've examined, apparently because the path to an appropriate τ is fraught with local optima. Using gradient descent to fine tune τ, once it's in the right neighborhood, is somewhat more successful.

2. One might include a complete range of τ values in the context layer. It is not difficult to determine a rough correspondence between the choice of τ and the temporal interval to which a unit is optimally tuned. If sufficient units are used to span a range of intervals, the network should perform well. The down side, of course, is that this gives the network an excess of weight parameters with which it could potentially overfit the training data. However, because the different τ correspond to different temporal scales, there is much less freedom to abuse the weights here than, say, in a situation where additional hidden units are added to a feedforward network.

Table 3: Learning contingencies across gaps (revisited)

gap	standard net		reduced description net	
	% failures	mean # epochs to learn	% failures	mean # epochs to learn
2	0	468	0	328
4	36	7406	0	584
6	92	9830	0	992
8	100	10000	0	1312
10	100	10000	0	1630

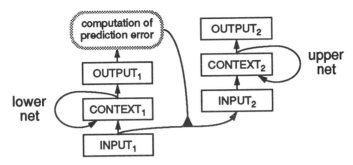

Figure 3: A sketch of the Schmidhuber (1991) architecture

3. One might dynamically adjust τ as a sequence is presented based on external criteria. In Section 5, I discuss one such criterion.

4   MUSIC COMPOSITION

I have used music composition as a domain for testing and evaluating different approaches to learning multiscale temporal structure. In previous work (Mozer & Soukup, 1991), we designed a sequential prediction network, called CONCERT, that learns to reproduce a set of pieces of a particular musical style. CONCERT also learns structural regularities of the musical style, and can be used to compose new pieces in the same style. CONCERT was trained on a set of Bach pieces and a set of traditional European folk melodies. The compositions it produces were reasonably pleasant, but were lacking in global coherence. The compositions tended to wander randomly with little direction, modulating haphazardly from major to minor keys, flip-flopping from the style of a march to that of a minuet. I attribute these problems to the fact that CONCERT had learned only local temporal structure.

I have recently trained CONCERT on a third set of examples—waltzes—and have included context units that operate with a range of time constants. There is a consensus among listeners that the new compositions are more coherent. I am presently running more controlled simulations using the same musical training set and versions of CONCERT with and without reduced descriptions, and am attempting to quantify CONCERT's abilities at various temporal scales.

5   A HYBRID APPROACH

Schmidhuber (1991; this volume) has proposed an alternative approach to learning multiscale temporal structure in sequences. His approach, the *chunking architecture*, basically involves two (or more) sequential prediction networks cascaded together (Figure 3). The lower net receives each input and attempts to predict the next input. When it fails to predict reliably, the next input is passed to the upper net. Thus, once the lower net has been trained to predict local temporal structure, such structure is removed from the input to the upper net. This simplifies the task of learning global structure in the upper net.

Schmidhuber's approach has some serious limitations, as does the approach I've described. We have thus merged the two in a scheme that incorporates the strengths of each approach (Schmidhuber, Prelinger, Mozer, Blumenthal, & Mathis, in preparation). The architecture is the same as depicted in Figure 3, except that all units in the upper net have associated with them a time constant τ_u, and the prediction error in the lower net determines τ_u. In effect, this allows the upper net to kick in only when the lower net fails to predict. This avoid the problem of selecting time constants, which my approach suffers. This also avoids the drawback of Schmidhuber's approach that yes-or-no decisions must be made about whether the lower net was successful. Initial simulation experiments indicate robust performance of the hybrid algorithm.

Acknowledgements

This research was supported by NSF Presidential Young Investigator award IRI-9058450, grant 90-21 from the James S. McDonnell Foundation, and DEC external research grant 1250. Thanks to Jürgen Schmidhuber and Paul Smolensky for helpful comments regarding this work, and to Darren Hardy for technical assistance.

References

Hinton, G. E. (1988). Representing part–whole hierarchies in connectionist networks. *Proceedings of the Eighth Annual Conference of the Cognitive Science Society.*

Jordan, M. I. (1987). Attractor dynamics and parallelism in a connectionist sequential machine. In *Proceedings of the Eighth Annual Conference of the Cognitive Science Society* (pp. 531–546). Hillsdale, NJ: Erlbaum.

McClelland, J. L. (1979). On the time relations of mental processes: An examination of systems of processes in cascade. *Psychological Review, 86*, 287–330.

Miyata, Y., & Burr, D. (1990). Hierarchical recurrent networks for learning musical structure. Unpublished Manuscript.

Mozer, M. C. (1989). A focused back-propagation algorithm for temporal pattern recognition. *Complex Systems, 3*, 349–381.

Mozer, M. C., & Soukup, T. (1991). CONCERT: A connectionist composer of erudite tunes. In R. P. Lippmann, J. Moody, & D. S. Touretzky (Eds.), *Advances in neural information processing systems 3* (pp. 789–796). San Mateo, CA: Morgan Kaufmann.

Pearlmutter, B. A. (1989). Learning state space trajectories in recurrent neural networks. *Neural Computation, 1*, 263–269.

Pineda, F. (1987). Generalization of back propagation to recurrent neural networks. *Physical Review Letters, 19*, 2229–2232.

Rohwer, R. (1990). The 'moving targets' training algorithm. In D. S. Touretzky (Ed.), *Advances in neural information processing systems 2* (pp. 558–565). San Mateo, CA: Morgan Kaufmann.

Rumelhart, D. E., Hinton, G. E., & Williams, R. J. (1986). Learning internal representations by error propagation. In D. E. Rumelhart & J. L. McClelland (Eds.), *Parallel distributed processing: Explorations in the microstructure of cognition. Volume I: Foundations* (pp. 318–362). Cambridge, MA: MIT Press/Bradford Books.

Schmidhuber, J. (1991). *Neural sequence chunkers* (Report FKI-148-91). Munich, Germany: Technische Universitaet Muenchen, Institut fuer Informatik.

Williams, R. J., & Zipser, D. (1989). A learning algorithm for continually running fully recurrent neural networks. *Neural Computation, 1*, 270–280.

NETWORK MODEL OF STATE-DEPENDENT SEQUENCING

Jeffrey P. Sutton,[*] **Adam N. Mamelak**[†] **and J. Allan Hobson**
Laboratory of Neurophysiology and Department of Psychiatry
Harvard Medical School
74 Fenwood Road, Boston, MA 02115

Abstract

A network model with temporal sequencing and state-dependent modulatory features is described. The model is motivated by neurocognitive data characterizing different states of waking and sleeping. Computer studies demonstrate how unique states of sequencing can exist within the same network under different aminergic and cholinergic modulatory influences. Relationships between state-dependent modulation, memory, sequencing and learning are discussed.

1 INTRODUCTION

Models of biological information processing often assume only one mode or state of operation. In general, this state depends upon a high degree of fidelity or modulation among the neural elements. In contrast, real neural networks often have a repertoire of processing states that is greatly affected by the relative balances of various neuromodulators (Selverston, 1988; Harris-Warrick and Marder, 1991). One area where changes in neuromodulation and network behavior are tightly and dramatically coupled is in the sleep-wake cycle (Hobson and Steriade, 1986; Mamelak and Hobson, 1989). This cycle consists of three main states: wake, non-rapid eye

---

[*]Also in the Center for Biological Information Processing, Whitaker College, E25-201, Massachusetts Institute of Technology, Cambridge, MA 02139

[†]Currently in the Department of Neurosurgery, University of California, San Francisco, CA 94143

movement (NREM) sleep and rapid eye movement (REM) sleep. Each state is characterized by a unique balance of monoaminergic and cholinergic neuromodulation (Hobson and Steriade, 1986; figure 1). In humans, each state also has characteristic cognitive sequencing properties (Foulkes, 1985; Hobson, 1988; figure 1). An integration and better understanding of the complex relationships between neuromodulation and information sequencing are desirable from both a computational and a neurophysiological perspective. In this paper, we present an initial approach to this difficult neurocognitive problem using a network model.

STATE	MODULATION		SEQUENCING
	tonic aminergic (β)	phasic cholinergic (δ)	
WAKE	high	low	progressive A1 $\rightarrow$ A2 $\dashrightarrow$ A3 $\downarrow$ $\leftarrow$ input B1 $\rightarrow$ B2
NREM SLEEP	inter-mediate	low	perseverative A1 $\nearrow$ $\searrow$ A3 $\leftarrow$ A2
REM SLEEP	low	high	bizarre A1 $\rightarrow$ A2 $\downarrow$ $\leftarrow$ PGO A2/B1 PGO $\rightarrow$ $\downarrow$ B2 $\rightarrow$ B3

Figure 1: Overview of the three state model which attempts to integrate aspects of neuromodulation and cognitive sequencing. The aminergic and cholinergic systems are important neuromodulators that filter and amplify, as opposed to initiating or carrying, distributed information embedded as memories (eg. $A1$, $A2$, $A3$) in neural networks. In the wake state, a relative aminergic dominance exists and the associated network sequencing is logical and progressive. For example, the sequence $A1 \rightarrow A2$ transitions to $B1 \rightarrow B2$ when an appropriate input (eg. $B1$) is present at a certain time. The NREM state is characterized by an intermediate aminergic-to-cholinergic ratio correlated with ruminative and perseverative sequences. Unexpected or "bizarre" sequences are found in the REM state, wherein phasic cholinergic inputs dominate and are prominent in the ponto-geniculo-occipital (PGO) brain areas. Bizarreness is manifest by incongruous or mixed memories, such as $A2/B1$, and sequence discontinuities, such as $A2 \rightarrow A2/B1 \rightarrow B2$, which may be associated with PGO bursting in the absence of other external input.

2 AMINERGIC AND CHOLINERGIC NEUROMODULATION

As outlined in figure 1, there are unique correlations among the aminergic and cholinergic systems and the forms of information sequencing that exist in the states of waking and NREM and REM sleep. The following brief discussion, which undoubtably oversimplifies the complicated and widespread actions of these systems, highlights some basic and relevant principles. Interested readers are referred to the review by Hobson and Steriade (1986) and the article by Hobson *et al.* in this volume for a more detailed presentation.

The biogenic amines, including norepinephrine, serotonin and dopamine, have been implicated as tonic regulators of the signal-to-noise ratio in neural networks (*eg.* Mamelak and Hobson, 1989). Increasing (decreasing) the amount of aminergic modulation improves (worsens) network fidelity (figure 2a). A standard means of modeling this property is by a stochastic or gain factor, analogous to the well-known Boltzmann factor $\beta = 1/kT$, which is present in the network updating rule.

Complex neuromodulatory effects of acetylcholine depend upon the location and types of receptors and channels present in different neurons. One main effect is facilitatory excitation (figure 2b). Mamelak and Hobson (1989) have suggested how the phasic release of acetylcholine, involving the bursting of PGO cells in the brainstem, coupled with tonic aminergic demodulation, could induce bifurcations in information sequencing at the network level. The model described in the next section sets out to test this notion.

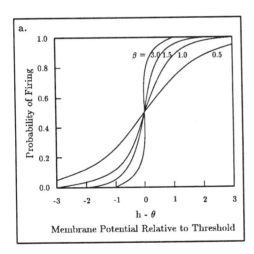
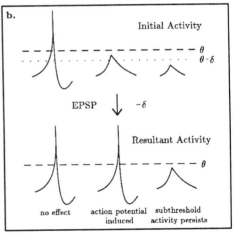

Figure 2: (a) Plot of neural firing probability as a function of the membrane potential, h, relative to threshold, θ, for values of aminergic modulation β of 0.5, 1.0, 1.5 and 3.0. (b) Schematic diagram of cholinergic facilitation, where EPSPs of magnitude δ only induce a change in firing activity if h is initially in the range $(\theta - \delta, \theta)$. Modified from Mamelak and Hobson (1989).

3   ASSOCIATIVE SEQUENCING NETWORK

There are several ways to approach the problem of modeling modulatory effects on temporal sequencing. We have chosen to commence with an associative network that is an extension of the work on models resembling elementary motor pattern generators (Kleinfeld, 1986; Sompolinsky and Kanter, 1986; Gutfreund and Mezard, 1988). We consider it to be significant that recent data on brainstem control systems show an overlap between sleep-wake regulators and locomotor pattern generators (Garcia-Rill *et al.*, 1990).

The network consists of N neural elements with binary values $S_i = \pm 1$, $i = 1, ..., N$, corresponding to whether they are firing or not firing. The elements are linked together by two kinds of *a priori* learned synaptic connections. One kind,

$$J_{ij}^{(1)} = \frac{1}{N} \sum_{\mu=1}^{p} \xi_i^{\mu} \xi_j^{\mu}, \qquad i \neq j, \tag{1}$$

encodes a set of p uncorrelated patterns $\{\xi_i^{\mu}\}_{i=1}^{N}$, $\mu = 1, ..., p$, where each ξ_i^{μ} takes the value ± 1 with equal probabilities. These patterns correspond to memories that are stable until a transition to another memory is made. Transitions in a sequence of memories $\mu = 1 \to 2 \to \cdots \to q < p$ are induced by a second type of connection

$$J_{ij}^{(2)} = \frac{\lambda}{N} \sum_{\mu=1}^{q-1} \xi_i^{\mu+1} \xi_j^{\mu}. \tag{2}$$

Here, λ is a relative weight of the connection types. The average time spent in a memory pattern before transitioning to the next one in a sequence is τ. At time t, the membrane potential is given by

$$h_i(t) = \sum_{j=1}^{N} \left[J_{ij}^{(1)} S_j(t) + J_{ij}^{(2)} S_j(t - \tau) \right] + \delta_i(t) + I_i(t). \tag{3}$$

The two terms contained in the brackets reflect intrinsic network interactions, while phasic PGO effects are represented by the $\delta_i(t)$. External inputs, other than PGO inputs, to $h_i(t)$ are denoted by $I_i(t)$. Dynamic evolution of the network follows the updating rule

$$S_i(t+1) = \pm 1, \qquad \text{with probability} \qquad \left\{ 1 + e^{\mp 2\beta[h_i(t) - \theta_i(t)]} \right\}^{-1}. \tag{4}$$

In this equation, the amount of aminergic-like modulation is parameterized by β. While updating could be done serially, a parallel dynamic process is chosen here for convenience. In the absence of external and PGO-like inputs, and with $\beta > 1.0$, the dynamics have the effect of generating trajectories on an adiabatically varying hypersurface that molds in time to produce a path from one basin of attraction to another. For $\beta < 1.0$, the network begins to lose this property. Lowering β mostly affects neural elements close to threshold, since the decision to change firing activity centers around the threshold value. However, as β decreases, fluctuations in the membrane potentials increase and a larger fraction of the neural elements remain, on average, near threshold.

4   SIMULATION RESULTS

A network consisting of $N = 50$ neural elements was examined wherein $p = 6$ memory patterns ($A1$, $A2$, $A3$, $B1$, $B2$ and $B3$) were chosen at random ($p/N = 0.12$). These memories were arranged into two loops, **A** and **B**, according to equation (2) such that the cyclic sequences $A1 \rightarrow A2 \rightarrow A3 \rightarrow A1 \rightarrow \cdots$ and $B1 \rightarrow B2 \rightarrow B3 \rightarrow B1 \rightarrow \cdots$ were stored in loops **A** and **B**, respectively. For simplicity, $\delta_i(t) = \delta(t)$ and $\theta_i(t) = 0$, $\forall i$. The transition parameters were set to $\lambda = 2.5$ and $\tau = 8$ for all the simulations to ensure reliable pattern generation under fully modulated conditions (large β, $\delta = 0$; Somplinsky and Kanter, 1986). Variations in β, $\delta(t)$ and $I_i(t)$ delineated the individual states that were examined.

In the model wake state, where there was a high degree of aminergic-like modulation (*eg.* $\beta = 2.0$), the network generated loops of sequential memories. Once cued into one of the two loops, the network would remain in that loop until an external input caused a transition into the other loop (figure 3).

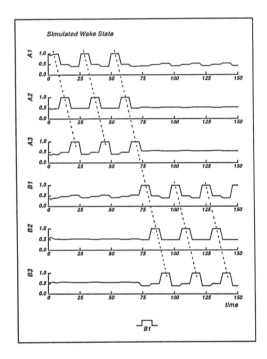

Figure 3: Plot of overlap as a function of time for each of the six memories $A1$, $A2$, $A3$, $B1$, $B2$, $B3$ in the simulated wake state. The overlap is a measure of the normalized Hamming distance between the instantaneous pattern of the network and a given memory. $\beta = 2.0$, $\delta = 0$, $\lambda = 2.5$, $\tau = 8$. The network is cued in pattern $A1$ and then sequences through loop **A**. At $t = 75$, pattern $B1$ is inputted to the network and loop **B** ensues. The dotted lines highlight the transitions between different memory patterns.

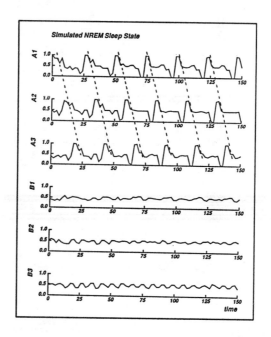

Figure 4: Graph of overlap *vs.* time for each of the six memories in the simulated NREM sleep state. $\beta = 1.1$, $\delta = 0$, $\lambda = 2.5$, $\tau = 8$. Initially, the network is cued in pattern $A1$ and remains in loop **A**. Considerable fluctuations in the overlaps are present and external inputs are absent.

As β was decreased (*eg.* $\beta = 1.1$), partially characterizing conditions of a model NREM state, sequencing within a loop was observed to persist (figure 4). However, decreased stability relative to the wake state was observed and small perturbations could cause disruptions within a loop and occasional bifurcations between loops. Nevertheless, in the absence of an effective mechanism to induce inter-loop transitions, the sequences were basically repetitive in this state.

For small β (*eg.* $0.8 < \beta < 1.0$) and various PGO-like activities within the simulated REM state, a diverse and rich set of dynamic behaviors was observed, only some of which are reported here. The network was remarkably sensitive to the timing of the PGO type bursts. With $\beta = 1.0$, inputs of $\delta = 2.5$ units in clusters of 20 time steps occurring with a frequency of approximately one cluster per 50 time steps could induce the following: (a) no or little effect on identifiable intra-loop sequencing; (b) bifurcations between loops; (c) a change from orderly intra-loop sequencing to apparent disorder;[1] (d) a change from apparent disorder to orderly progression within a single loop ("defibrillation" effect); (e) a change from a disorderly pattern to another disorderly pattern. An example of transition types (c) and (d), with the overall effect of inducing a bifurcation between the loops, is shown in figure 5.

---

[1] On detailed inspection, the apparent disorder actually revealed several sequences in loops **A** and/or **B** running out of phase with relative delays generally less than τ.

In general, lower intensity (*eg.* 2.0 to 2.5 units), longer duration (*eg.* >20 time steps) PGO-like bursting was more effective in inducing bifurcations than higher intensity (*eg.* 4.0 units), shorter duration (*eg.* 2 time steps) bursts. PGO induced bifurcations were possible in all states and were associated with significant populations of neural elements that were below, but within δ units of threshold.

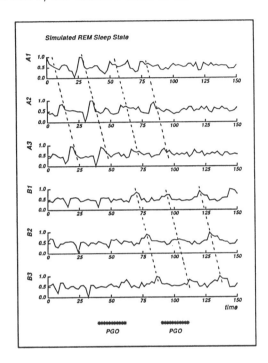

Figure 5: REM sleep state plot of overlap *vs.* time for each of the six memories. $\beta = 1.0$, $\delta = 2.5$, $\lambda = 2.5$, $\tau = 8$. The network sequences progressively in loop **A** until a cluster of simulated PGO bursts (asterisks) occurs lasting $40 < t < 60$. A complex output involving alternating sequences from loop **A** and loop **B** results (note dotted lines). A second PGO burst cluster during the interval $90 < t < 110$ yields an output consisting of a single loop **B** sequence. Over the time span of the simulation, a bifurcation from loop **A** to loop **B** has been induced.

5   STATE-DEPENDENT LEARNING

The connections set up by equations (1) and (2) are determined *a priori* using a standard Hebbian learning algorithm and are not altered during the network simulations. Since neuromodulators, including the monoamines norepinephrine and serotonin, have been implicated as essential factors in synaptic plasticity (Kandel *et al.*, 1987), it seems reasonable that state changes in modulation may also affect changes in plasticity. This property, when superimposed on the various sequencing features of a network, may yield possibly novel memory and sequence formations, associations and perhaps other unexamined global processes.

6   CONCLUSIONS

The main finding of this paper is that unique states of information sequencing can exist within the same network under different modulatory conditions. This result holds even though the model makes significant simplifying assumptions about the neurophysiological and cognitive processes motivating its construction. Several observations from the model also suggest mechanisms whereby interactions between the aminergic and cholinergic systems can give rise to sequencing properties, such as discontinuities, in different states, especially REM sleep. Finally, the model provides a means of investigating some of the complex and interesting relationships between modulation, memory, sequencing and learning within and between different states.

Acknowledgements

Supported by NIH grant MH 13,923, the HMS/MMHC Research & Education Fund, the Livingston, Dupont-Warren and McDonnell-Pew Foundations, DARPA under ONR contract N00014-85-K-0124, the Sloan Foundation and Whitaker College.

References

Foulkes D (1985) *Dreaming: A Cognitive-Psychological Analysis.* Hillsdale: Erlbaum.

Garcia-Rill E, Atsuta Y, Iwahara T, Skinner RD (1990) Development of brainstem modulation of locomotion. *Somatosensory Motor Research* **7** 238-239.

Gutfreund H, Mezard M (1988) Processing of temporal sequences in neural networks. *Phys Rev Lett* **61** 235-238.

Harris-Warrick RM, Marder E (1991) Modulation of neural networks for behavior. *Annu Rev Neurosci* **14** 39-57.

Hobson JA (1988) *The Dreaming Brain.* New York: Basic.

Hobson JA, Steriade M (1986) Neuronal basis of behavioral state control. In: Mountcastle VB (ed) *Handbook of Physiology - The Nervous System, Vol IV.* Bethesda: Am Physiol Soc, 701-823.

Kandel ER, Klein M, Hochner B, Shuster M, Siegelbaum S, Hawkins R, *et al.* (1987) Synaptic modulation and learning: New insights into synaptic transmission from the study of behavior. In: Edelman GM, Gall WE, Cowan WM (eds) *Synaptic Function.* New York: Wiley, 471-518.

Kleinfeld D (1986) Sequential state generation by model neural networks. *Proc Natl Acad Sci USA* **83** 9469-9473.

Mamelak AN, Hobson JA (1989) Dream bizarreness as the cognitive correlate of altered neuronal behavior in REM sleep. *J Cog Neurosci* **1(3)** 201-22.

Selverston AI (1988) A consideration of invertebrate central pattern generators as computational data bases. *Neural Networks* **1** 109-117.

Sompolinsky H, Kanter I (1986) Temporal association in asymmetric neural networks. *Phys Rev Lett* **57** 2861-2864.

LEARNING UNAMBIGUOUS REDUCED SEQUENCE DESCRIPTIONS

Jürgen Schmidhuber
Dept. of Computer Science
University of Colorado
Campus Box 430
Boulder, CO 80309, USA
yirgan@cs.colorado.edu

Abstract

Do you want your neural net algorithm to learn sequences? Do not limit yourself to conventional gradient descent (or approximations thereof). Instead, use your sequence learning algorithm (any will do) to implement the following method for history compression. No matter what your final goals are, train a network to predict its next input from the previous ones. Since only unpredictable inputs convey new information, ignore all predictable inputs but let all unexpected inputs (plus information about the time step at which they occurred) become inputs to a higher-level network of the same kind (working on a slower, self-adjusting time scale). Go on building a hierarchy of such networks. This principle reduces the descriptions of event sequences *without loss of information*, thus easing supervised or reinforcement learning tasks. Alternatively, you may use two recurrent networks to collapse a multi-level predictor hierarchy into a single recurrent net. Experiments show that systems based on these principles can require less computation per time step *and* many fewer training sequences than conventional training algorithms for recurrent nets. Finally you can modify the above method such that predictability is not defined in a yes-or-no fashion but in a continuous fashion.

1   INTRODUCTION

The following methods for supervised sequence learning have been proposed: Simple recurrent nets [7][3], time-delay nets (e.g. [2]), sequential recursive auto-associative memories [16], back-propagation through time or BPTT [21] [30] [33], Mozer's 'focused back-prop' algorithm [10], the IID- or RTRL-algorithm [19][1][34], its accelerated versions [32][35][25], the recent fast-weight algorithm [27], higher-order networks [5], as well as continuous time methods equivalent to some of the above [14][15][4]. The following methods for sequence learning by reinforcement learning have been proposed: Extended REINFORCE algorithms [31], the neural bucket brigade algorithm [22], recurrent networks adjusted by adaptive critics [23](see also [8]), buffer-based systems [13], and networks of hierarchically organized neuron-like "bions" [18].

With the exception of [18] and [13], these approaches waste resources and limit efficiency by focusing on *every* input instead of focusing only on *relevant* inputs. Many of these methods have a second drawback as well: The longer the time lag between an event and the occurrence of a related error the less information is carried by the corresponding error information wandering 'back into time' (see [6] for a more detailed analysis). [11], [12] and [20] have addressed the latter problem but not the former. The system described by [18] on the other hand addresses both problems, but in a manner much different from that presented here.

2   HISTORY COMPRESSION

A major contribution of this work is an adaptive method for removing redundant information from sequences. This principle can be implemented with the help of any of the methods mentioned in the introduction.

Consider a deterministic discrete time predictor (not necessarily a neural network) whose state at time t of sequence p is described by an environmental input vector $x^p(t)$, an internal state vector $h^p(t)$, and an output vector $z^p(t)$. The environment may be non-deterministic. At time 0, the predictor starts with $x^p(0)$ and an internal start state $h^p(0)$. At time $t \geq 0$, the predictor computes

$$z^p(t) = f(x^p(t), h^p(t)).$$

At time $t > 0$, the predictor furthermore computes

$$h^p(t) = g(x^p(t-1), h^p(t-1)).$$

All information about the input at a given time t_x can be reconstructed from $t_x, f, g, x^p(0), h^p(0)$, and the pairs $(t_s, x^p(t_s))$ for which $0 < t_s \leq t_x$ and $z^p(t_s - 1) \neq x^p(t_s)$. This is because if $z^p(t) = x^p(t+1)$ at a given time t, then the predictor is able to predict the next input from the previous ones. The new input is *derivable* by means of f and g.

Information about the observed input sequence can be even further compressed beyond just the unpredicted input vectors $x^p(t_s)$. It suffices to know only those *elements* of the vectors $x^p(t_s)$ that were not correctly predicted.

This observation implies that we can discriminate one sequence from another by knowing *just the unpredicted inputs and the corresponding time steps at which they occurred.* No information is lost if we ignore the expected inputs. We do not even have to know f and g. I call this *the principle of history compression.*

From a theoretical point of view it is important to know at what time an unexpected input occurs; otherwise there will be a potential for ambiguities: Two different input sequences may lead to the same shorter sequence of unpredicted inputs. With many practical tasks, however, there is no need for knowing the critical time steps (see section 5).

3   SELF-ORGANIZING PREDICTOR HIERARCHY

Using the principle of history compression we can build a self-organizing hierarchical neural 'chunking' system[1]. The basic task can be formulated as a prediction task. At a given time step the goal is to predict the next input from previous inputs. If there are external target vectors at certain time steps then they are simply treated as another part of the input to be predicted.

The architecture is a hierarchy of predictors, the input to each level of the hierarchy is coming from the previous level. P_i denotes the ith level network which is trained to *predict its own next input from its previous inputs*[2]. We take P_i to be one of the conventional dynamic recurrent neural networks mentioned in the introduction; however, it might be some other adaptive sequence processing device as well[3].

At each time step the input of the lowest-level recurrent predictor P_0 is the current external input. We create a new higher-level adaptive predictor P_{s+1} whenever the adaptive predictor at the previous level, P_s, stops improving its predictions. When this happens the weight-changing mechanism of P_s is switched off (to exclude potential instabilities caused by ongoing modifications of the lower-level predictors). If at a given time step P_s ($s \geq 0$) fails to predict its next input (or if we are at the beginning of a training sequence which usually is not predictable either) then P_{s+1} will receive as input the concatenation of this next input of P_s *plus a unique representation of the corresponding time step*[4]; the activations of P_{s+1}'s hidden and output units will be updated. Otherwise P_{s+1} will not perform an activation update. This procedure ensures that P_{s+1} is fed with an *unambiguous* reduced description[5] of the input sequence observed by P_s. This is theoretically justified by the principle of history compression.

In general, P_{s+1} will receive fewer inputs over time than P_s. With existing learning

---

[1]See also [18] for a different hierarchical connectionist chunking system based on similar principles.

[2]Recently I became aware that Don Mathis had some related ideas (personal communication). A hierarchical approach to sequence *generation* was pursued by [9].

[3]For instance, we might employ the more limited feed-forward networks and a 'time window' approach. In this case, the number of previous inputs to be considered as a basis for the next prediction will remain fixed.

[4]A unique time representation is theoretically necessary to provide P_{s+1} with unambiguous information about when the failure occurred (see also the last paragraph of section 2). A unique representation of the time that went by since the *last* unpredicted input occurred will do as well.

[5]In contrast, the reduced descriptions referred to by [11] are not unambiguous.

algorithms, the higher-level predictor should have less difficulties in learning to predict the critical inputs than the lower-level predictor. This is because P_{s+1}'s 'credit assignment paths' will often be short compared to those of P_s. This will happen if the incoming inputs carry global temporal structure which has not yet been discovered by P_s. (See also [18] for a related approach to the problem of credit assignment in reinforcement learning.)

This method is a simplification and an improvement of the recent chunking method described by [24].

A multi-level predictor hierarchy is a rather safe way of learning to deal with sequences with multi-level temporal structure (e.g speech). Experiments have shown that multi-level predictors can quickly learn tasks which are practically unlearnable by conventional recurrent networks, e.g. [6].

4   COLLAPSING THE HIERARCHY

One disadvantage of a predictor hierarchy as above is that it is not known in advance how many levels will be needed. Another disadvantage is that levels are explicitly separated from each other. It may be possible, however, to collapse the hierarchy into a single network as outlined in this section. See details in [26].

We need two conventional recurrent networks: The *automatizer* A and the *chunker* C, which correspond to a distinction between automatic and attended events. (See also [13] and [17] which describe a similar distinction in the context of reinforcement learning). At each time step A receives the current external input. A's error function is threefold: One term forces it to emit certain desired target outputs at certain times. If there is a target, then it becomes part of the next input. The second term forces A at every time step to predict its own next non-target input. The third (crucial) term will be explained below.

If and only if A makes an error concerning the first and second term of its error function, the unpredicted input (including a potentially available teaching vector) *along with a unique representation of the current time step* will become the new input to C. Before this new input can be processed, C (whose last input may have occurred many time steps earlier) is trained to predict this higher-level input from its current internal state and its last input (employing a conventional recurrent net algorithm). After this, C performs an activation update which contributes to a higher level internal representation of the input history. Note that according to the principle of history compression C is fed with an *unambiguous reduced description of the input history.* The information deducible by means of A's predictions can be considered as *redundant.* (The beginning of an episode usually is not predictable, therefore it has to be fed to the chunking level, too.)

Since C's 'credit assignment paths' will often be short compared to those of A, C will often be able to develop useful internal representations of previous unexpected input events. Due to the final term of its error function, A will be forced to reproduce these internal representations, *by predicting C's state.* Therefore A will be able to create useful internal representations by itself in an *early* stage of processing a given sequence; it will often receive meaningful error signals long before errors of the first or second kind occur. These internal representations in turn must carry the discriminating information for enabling A to improve its low-level predictions. Therefore the chunker will receive fewer and fewer inputs, since more and more inputs become predictable by the automatizer. This is the *collapsing operation*. Ideally, the chunker will become obsolete after some time.

It must be emphasized that unlike with the incremental creation of a multi-level predictor hierarchy described in section 3, there is no formal proof that the 2-net *on-line* version is free of instabilities. One can imagine situations where A unlearns previously learned predictions because of the third term of its error function. Relative weighting of the different terms in A's error function represents an ad-hoc remedy for this potential problem. In the experiments below, relative weighting was not necessary.

5   EXPERIMENTS

One experiment with a multi-level chunking architecture involved a grammar which produced strings of many a's and b's such that there was local temporal structure within the training strings (see [6] for details). The task was to differentiate between strings with long overlapping suffixes. The conventional algorithm completely failed to solve the task; it became confused by the great numbers of input sequences with similar endings. Not so the chunking system: It soon discovered certain hierarchical temporal structures in the input sequences and decomposed the problem such that it was able to solve it within a few hundred-thousand training sequences.

The 2-net chunking system (the one with the potential for collapsing levels) was also tested against the conventional recurrent net algorithms. (See details in [26].) With the conventional algorithms, with various learning rates, and with more than 1,000,000 training sequences *performance did not improve in prediction tasks involving even as few as 20 time steps between relevant events.*

But, the 2-net chunking system was able to solve the task rather quickly. An efficient approximation of the BPTT-method was applied to both the chunker and the automatizer: *Only 3 iterations of error propagation 'back into the past' were performed at each time step.* Most of the test runs required less than 5000 training sequences. *Still the final weight matrix of the automatizer often resembled what one would hope to get from the conventional algorithm.* There were hidden units which learned to bridge the 20-step time lags by means of strong self-connections. The chunking system needed *less computation per time step than the conventional method and required many fewer training sequences.*

6   CONTINUOUS HISTORY COMPRESSION

The history compression technique formulated above defines expectation-mismatches in a yes-or-no fashion: Each input unit whose activation is not predictable at a certain time gives rise to an unexpected event. Each unexpected event provokes an update of the internal state of a higher-level predictor. The updates always take place according to the conventional activation spreading rules for recurrent neural nets. There is no concept of a partial mismatch or of a 'near-miss'. There is no possibility of updating the higher-level net 'just a little bit' in response to a 'nearly expected input'. In practical applications, some 'epsilon' has to be used to define an acceptable mismatch.

In reply to the above criticism, *continuous history compression* is based on the following ideas. In what follows, $v_i(t)$ denotes the i-th component of vector $v(t)$.

We use a local input representation. The components of $z^p(t)$ are forced to sum up to 1 and are interpreted as a prediction of the probability distribution of the possible $x^p(t+1)$. $z_j^p(t)$ is interpreted as the prediction of the probability that $x_j^p(t+1)$ is 1.

The output entropy

$$-\sum_j z_j^p(t) log \ z_j^p(t)$$

can be interpreted as a measure of the predictor's confidence. In the worst case, the predictor will expect every possible event with equal probability.

How much information (relative to the current predictor) is conveyed by the event $x_j^p(t+1) = 1$, once it is observed? According to [29] it is

$$-log \ z_j^p(t).$$

[28] defines update procedures based on Mozer's recent update function [12] that let highly informative events have a stronger influence on the history representation than less informative (more likely) events. The 'strength' of an update in response to a more or less unexpected event is a monotonically increasing function of the information the event conveys. One of the update procedures uses Pollack's recursive auto-associative memories [16] for storing unexpected events, thus yielding an entirely local learning algorithm for learning extended sequences.

7   ACKNOWLEDGEMENTS

Thanks to Josef Hochreiter for conducting the experiments. Thanks to Mike Mozer and Mark Ring for useful comments on an earlier draft of this paper. This research was supported in part by NSF PYI award IRI–9058450, grant 90–21 from the James S. McDonnell Foundation, and DEC external research grant 1250 to Michael C. Mozer.

References

[1] J. Bachrach. Learning to represent state, 1988. Unpublished master's thesis, University of Massachusetts, Amherst.

[2] U. Bodenhausen and A. Waibel. The tempo 2 algorithm: Adjusting time-delays by supervised learning. In D. S. Lippman, J. E. Moody, and D. S. Touretzky, editors, *Advances in Neural Information Processing Systems 3*, pages 155–161. San Mateo, CA: Morgan Kaufmann, 1991.

[3] J. L. Elman. Finding structure in time. Technical Report CRL Technical Report 8801, Center for Research in Language, University of California, San Diego, 1988.

[4] M. Gherrity. A learning algorithm for analog fully recurrent neural networks. In *IEEE/INNS International Joint Conference on Neural Networks, San Diego*, volume 1, pages 643–644, 1989.

[5] C. L. Giles and C. B. Miller. Learning and extracting finite state automata. Accepted for publication in *Neural Computation*, 1992.

[6] Josef Hochreiter. Diploma thesis, 1991. Institut für Informatik, Technische Universität München.

[7] M. I. Jordan. Serial order: A parallel distributed processing approach. Technical Report ICS Report 8604, Institute for Cognitive Science, University of California, San Diego, 1986.

[8] G. Lukes. Review of Schmidhuber's paper 'Recurrent networks adjusted by adaptive critics'. *Neural Network Reviews*, 4(1):41–42, 1990.

[9] Y. Miyata. An unsupervised PDP learning model for action planning. In *Proc. of the Tenth Annual Conference of the Cognitive Science Society, Hillsdale, NJ*, pages 223–229. Erlbaum, 1988.

[10] M. C. Mozer. A focused back-propagation algorithm for temporal sequence recognition. *Complex Systems*, 3:349–381, 1989.

[11] M. C. Mozer. Connectionist music composition based on melodic, stylistic, and psychophysical constraints. Technical Report CU-CS-495-90, University of Colorado at Boulder, 1990.

[12] M. C. Mozer. Induction of multiscale temporal structure. In D. S. Lippman, J. E. Moody, and D. S. Touretzky, editors, *Advances in Neural Information Processing Systems 4*, to appear. San Mateo, CA: Morgan Kaufmann, 1992.

[13] C. Myers. Learning with delayed reinforcement through attention-driven buffering. TR, Imperial College of Science, Technology and Medicine, 1990.

[14] B. A. Pearlmutter. Learning state space trajectories in recurrent neural networks. *Neural Computation*, 1:263–269, 1989.

[15] F. J. Pineda. Time dependent adaptive neural networks. In D. S. Touretzky, editor, *Advances in Neural Information Processing Systems 2*, pages 710–718. San Mateo, CA: Morgan Kaufmann, 1990.

[16] J. B. Pollack. Recursive distributed representation. *Artificial Intelligence*, 46:77–105, 1990.

[17] M. A. Ring. PhD Proposal: Autonomous construction of sensorimotor hierarchies in neural networks. Technical report, Univ. of Texas at Austin, 1990.

[18] M. A. Ring. Incremental development of complex behaviors through automatic construction of sensory-motor hierarchies. In L. Birnbaum and G. Collins, editors, *Machine Learning: Proceedings of the Eighth International Workshop*, pages 343–347. Morgan Kaufmann, 1991.

[19] A. J. Robinson and F. Fallside. The utility driven dynamic error propagation network. Technical Report CUED/F-INFENG/TR.1, Cambridge University Engineering Department, 1987.

[20] R. Rohwer. The 'moving targets' training method. In J. Kindermann and A. Linden, editors, *Proceedings of 'Distributed Adaptive Neural Information Processing', St.Augustin, 24.-25.5,*. Oldenbourg, 1989.

[21] D. E. Rumelhart, G. E. Hinton, and R. J. Williams. Learning internal representations by error propagation. In D. E. Rumelhart and J. L. McClelland, editors, *Parallel Distributed Processing*, volume 1, pages 318–362. MIT Press, 1986.

[22] J. H. Schmidhuber. A local learning algorithm for dynamic feedforward and recurrent networks. *Connection Science*, 1(4):403–412, 1989.

[23] J. H. Schmidhuber. Recurrent networks adjusted by adaptive critics. In *Proc. IEEE/INNS International Joint Conference on Neural Networks, Washington, D. C.*, volume 1, pages 719–722, 1990.

[24] J. H. Schmidhuber. Adaptive decomposition of time. In T. Kohonen, K. Mäkisara, O. Simula, and J. Kangas, editors, *Artificial Neural Networks*, pages 909–914. Elsevier Science Publishers B.V., North-Holland, 1991.

[25] J. H. Schmidhuber. A fixed size storage $O(n^3)$ time complexity learning algorithm for fully recurrent continually running networks. Accepted for publication in *Neural Computation*, 1992.

[26] J. H. Schmidhuber. Learning complex, extended sequences using the principle of history compression. Accepted for publication in *Neural Computation*, 1992.

[27] J. H. Schmidhuber. Learning to control fast-weight memories: An alternative to recurrent nets. Accepted for publication in *Neural Computation*, 1992.

[28] J. H. Schmidhuber, M. C. Mozer, and D. Prelinger. Continuous history compression. Technical report, Dept. of Comp. Sci., University of Colorado at Boulder, 1992.

[29] C. E. Shannon. A mathematical theory of communication (parts I and II). *Bell System Technical Journal*, XXVII:379–423, 1948.

[30] P. J. Werbos. Generalization of backpropagation with application to a recurrent gas market model. *Neural Networks*, 1, 1988.

[31] R. J. Williams. Toward a theory of reinforcement-learning connectionist systems. Technical Report NU-CCS-88-3, College of Comp. Sci., Northeastern University, Boston, MA, 1988.

[32] R. J. Williams. Complexity of exact gradient computation algorithms for recurrent neural networks. Technical Report Technical Report NU-CCS-89-27, Boston: Northeastern University, College of Computer Science, 1989.

[33] R. J. Williams and J. Peng. An efficient gradient-based algorithm for on-line training of recurrent network trajectories. *Neural Computation*, 4:491–501, 1990.

[34] R. J. Williams and D. Zipser. Experimental analysis of the real-time recurrent learning algorithm. *Connection Science*, 1(1):87–111, 1989.

[35] R. J. Williams and D. Zipser. Gradient-based learning algorithms for recurrent networks and their computational complexity. In *Back-propagation: Theory, Architectures and Applications*. Hillsdale, NJ: Erlbaum, 1992, in press.

PART VI

RECURRENT NETWORKS

Recurrent Networks and NARMA Modeling

Jerome Connor   **Les E. Atlas**
FT-10
Interactive Systems Design Laboratory
Dept. of Electrical Engineering
University of Washington
Seattle, Washington 98195

Douglas R. Martin
B-317
Dept. of Statistics
University of Washington
Seattle, Washington 98195

Abstract

There exist large classes of time series, such as those with nonlinear moving average components, that are not well modeled by feedforward networks or linear models, but can be modeled by recurrent networks. We show that recurrent neural networks are a type of nonlinear autoregressive-moving average (NARMA) model. Practical ability will be shown in the results of a competition sponsored by the Puget Sound Power and Light Company, where the recurrent networks gave the best performance on electric load forecasting.

1 Introduction

This paper will concentrate on identifying types of time series for which a recurrent network provides a significantly better model, and corresponding prediction, than a feedforward network. Our main interest is in discrete time series that are parsimoniously modeled by a simple recurrent network, but for which, a feedforward neural network is highly non-parsimonious by virtue of requiring an infinite amount of past observations as input to achieve the same accuracy in prediction.

Our approach is to consider predictive neural networks as stochastic models. Section 2 will be devoted to a brief summary of time series theory that will be used to illustrate the the differences between feedforward and recurrent networks. Section 3 will investigate some of the problems associated with nonlinear moving average and state space models of time series. In particular, neural networks will be analyzed as

301

nonlinear extensions of traditional linear models. From the preceding sections, it will become apparent that the recurrent network will have advantages over feedforward neural networks in much the same way that ARMA models have over autoregressive models for some types of time series.

Finally in section 4, the results of a competition in electric load forecasting sponsored by the Puget Sound Power and Light Company will discussed. In this competition, a recurrent network model gave superior results to feedforward networks and various types of linear models. The advantages of a state space model for multivariate time series will be shown on the Puget Power time series.

2   Traditional Approaches to Time Series Analysis

The statistical approach to forecasting involves the construction of stochastic models to predict the value of an observation x_t using previous observations. This is often accomplished using linear stochastic difference equation models, with random inputs.

A very general class of linear models used for forecasting purposes is the class of ARMA(p,q) models

$$x_t = \sum_{i=1}^{p} \phi x_{t-i} + \sum_{j=1}^{q} \theta e_{t-j} + e_t$$

where e_t denotes random noise, independent of past x_t. The conditional mean (minimum mean square error) predictor $\hat{x}_t$ of x_t can be expressed in the recurrent form

$$\hat{x}_t = \sum_{i=1}^{p} \phi x_{t-i} + \sum_{j=1}^{q} \theta e_{t-j}.$$

where e_k is approximated by

$$\hat{e}_k = x_k - \hat{x}_k, \quad k = t-1, ..., t-q$$

The key properties of interest for an ARMA(p,q) model are stationarity and invertibility. If the process x_t is stationary, its statistical properties are independent of time. Any stationary ARMA(p,q) process can be written as a moving average

$$x_t = \sum_{k=1}^{\infty} h_k e_{t-k} + e_t.$$

An invertible process can be equivalently expressed in terms of previous observations or residuals. For a process to be invertible, all the poles of the z-transform must lie inside the unit circle of the z plane. An invertible ARMA(p,q) process can be written as an infinite autoregression

$$x_t = \sum_{k=1}^{\infty} \phi_k x_{t-k} + e_t.$$

As an example of how the inverse process occurs, let e_t be solved for in terms of x_t and then substitute previous e_t's into the original process. This can be illustrated with an MA(1) process

$$x_t = e_t + \theta e_{t-1}$$
$$e_{t-i} = x_{t-i} - \theta e_{t-i-1}$$
$$x_t = e_t + \theta(x_{t-1} - \theta e_{t-2})$$
$$x_t = e_t + \sum_i (-1)^{i-1} \theta^i x_{t-i}$$

Looking at this example, it can be seen that an MA(1) processes with $|\theta| \geq 1$ will depend significantly on observations in the distant past. However, if $|\theta| < 1$, then the effect of the distant past is negligible.

In the nonlinear case, it will be shown that it is not always possible to go back and forth between descriptions in terms of observables (e.g. x_i) and descriptions in terms of unobservables (e.g. e_i) even when $s_t = 0$. For a review of time series prediction in greater depth see the works of Box [1] or Harvey [2].

3   Nonlinear ARMA Models

Many types of nonlinear models have been proposed in the literature. Here we focus on feedforward and recurrent neural networks and how they relate to nonlinear ARMA models.

3.1   Nonlinear Autoregressive Models

The simplest generalization to the nonlinear case would be the nonlinear autoregressive (NAR) model

$$x_t = h(x_{t-1}, x_{t-2}, ..., x_{t-p}) + e_t,$$

where $h()$ is an unknown smooth function with the assumption the best (i.e., minimum mean square error) prediction of x_t given $x_{t-1}, ..., x_{t-p}$ is its conditional mean

$$\hat{x}_t = E(x_t | x_{t-1}, ..., x_{t-p}) = h(x_{t-1}, ..., x_{t-p}).$$

Feedforward networks were first proposed as an NAR model for time series prediction by Lapedes and Farber [3]. A feedforward network is a nonlinear approximation to h given by

$$\hat{x}_t = h(x_{t-1}, ..., x_{t-p}) = \sum_{i=1}^{I} W_i f(\sum_{j=1}^{p} w_{ij} x_{t-j}).$$

The weight matrix w is lower diagonal and will allow no feedback. Thus the feedforward network is a nonlinear mapping from previous observation onto predictions of future observations. The function $f(x)$ is a smooth bounded monotonic function, typically a sigmoid.

The parameters W_i and w_{ij} are estimates from a training sample $x_1^0, ..., x_N^0$, thereby obtaining an estimate of $\hat{h}$ of h. Estimates are obtained by minimizing the sum of the square residuals $\sum_{t=1}^{n}(x_t - \hat{x}_t)^2$ by gradient descent procedure known as "backpropagation"[4].

3.2   NARMA or NMA

A simple nonlinear generalization of ARMA models is

$$x_t = h(x_{t-1}, x_{t-2}, ..., x_{t-p}, e_{t-1}, ..., e_{t-q}) + e_t.$$

It is natural to predict

$$\hat{x}_t = \hat{h}(x_{t-1}, x_{t-2}, ..., x_{t-p}, \hat{e}_{t-1}, ..., \hat{e}_{t-q}).$$

If the model $\hat{h}(x_{t-1}, x_{t-2}, ..., x_{t-p}, \hat{e}_{t-1}, ..., \hat{e}_{t-q})$ is chosen, then a recurrent network can approximate it as

$$\hat{x}_t = h(x_{t-1}, ..., x_{t-p}) = \sum_{i=1}^{I} W_i f(\sum_{j=1}^{p} w_{ij} x_{t-j} + \sum_{j=1}^{q} w'_{ij}(x_{t-j} - \hat{x}_{t-j})).$$

This model is a special case of the fully interconnected recurrent network

$$\hat{x}_t = \sum_{i=1}^{I} W_i f(\sum_{j=1}^{n} w''_{ij} x_{t-j})$$

where w''_{ij} are coefficients of a full matrix.

Nonlinear autoregressive models and nonlinear moving average models are not always equivalent for nondeterministic processes as in the linear case. If the probability of the next observation depends on the previous state of the process, a representation built on e_t may not be complete unless some information on the previous state is added[8]. The problem is that if $e_t, ..., e_{t-m}$ are known, there is still not enough information to determine which state the series is in at $t - m$. Given the lack of knowledge of the initial state, it is impossible to predict future states and without the state information, the best predictions cannot be made.

If the moving average representation cannot be made with e_t alone, it still may be possible to express a model in terms of past e_t and state information.

$$X_t = h(s_t, s_{t-1}, ..., e_t, e_{t-1}, ...).$$

It has been shown that for a large class of nondeterministic Markov processes, a model of this form can be constructed[8]. This link is important, because a recurrent network is this type of model. For further details on using recurrent networks to NARMA modeling see Connor et al[9].

4   Competition on Load Forecasting Data

A fully interconnected recurrent network trained with the Williams and Zipser algorithm [10] was part of a competition to predict the loads of the Puget Sound Power and Light Company from November 11, 1990 to March 31, 1991. The object was to predict the demand for the electric power, known as the load, profile of each day on the previous working day. Because the forecast is made on Friday morning, the Monday prediction is the most difficult. Actual loads and temperatures of the past are available as well as forecasted temperatures for the day of the prediction.

Neural networks are not parsimonious and many parameters need to be determined. Seasonality limits the amount of useful data for the load forecasting problem. For example, the load profile in August is not useful for predicting the load profile in January. This limited amount of data severely constrains the number of parameters a model can accurately determine. We avoided seasonality, while increasing the size of the training set by including data form the last four winters. In total 26976 vectors were available when data from August 1 to March 31 for 1986 to 1990 were included. The larger training set enables neural network models be trained with less danger of overfitting the data. If the network can accurately model load growth over the years, then the network will have the added advantage of being exposed to a larger temperature spectrum on which to base future predictions. The larger temperature spectrum is hypothetically useful for predicting phenomenon such as cold snaps which can result in larger loads than normal. It should be noted that neural networks have been applied to this model in the past[6].

Initially five recurrent models were constructed, one for each day of the week, with Wednesday, Thursday and Friday in a single network. Each network has temperature and load values from a week previous at that hour, the forecasted temperature of the hour to be predicted, the hour year and the week of the forecast. The week of the forecast was included to allow the network to model the seasonality of the data. Some models have added load and temperature from earlier in the week, depending on the availability of the data. The networks themselves consisted of three to four neurons in the hidden layer. This predictor is of the form

$$l_t(k) = \xi_t(k-7) + f(l_t(k-7), \xi_t(k-7), \hat{T}_t(k), T_8(k-1), t, d, y),$$

where $f()$ is a nonlinear function, $l_t(k)$ is the load at time t and day k, ξ_t is the noise, T is the temperature, $\hat{T}$ is the forecasted temperature, d is the day of the week, and y is the year of the data.

After comparing its performance to the winner of the competition, the linear model in Fig. 1, the poor performance could be attributed to the choice of model, rather than a problem with recurrent networks. It should be mentioned that the linear model took as one of its inputs, the square of the last available load. This is a parsimonious way of modeling nonlinearities. A second recurrent predictor was then built with the same input and output configuration as the linear model, save the square of the previous load term which the nets nonlinearities can handle. This net, denoted as the Recurrent Network, had a different recurrent model for each hour of the day. Each hour of the day had a different model, this yielded the best predictions. This predictor is of the form

$$l_t(k) = \xi_t(k) + f_t(l_t(k-1), \xi_t(k-1), \hat{T}_t(k), T_8(k-1), d, y).$$

All of the models in the figure use the last available load, forecasted temperature at the hour to be predicted, maximum forecasted temperature of the day to be predicted, the previous midnight temperatures, and the hour and year of the prediction. A second recurrent network was also trained with the last available load at that hour, this enabled e_{t-1} to be modeled. The availability of e_{t-1} turned out to be the difference between making superior and average predictions. It should be noted that the use of e_{t-1} did not improve the results of linear models.

The three most important error measures are the weekly morning, afternoon, and total loads and are listed in the table below. The A.M. peak is the mean average

	83-84	84-85	85-86	90-91
Feedforward	.0180	.0317	.0175	.0331
Recurrent	.0275	.0355	.0218	.0311

Table 1: Mean Square Error

percent error (MAPE) of the summed predictions of 7 A.M. to 9 A.M., the P.M. peak is the MAPE of the summed predictions of 5 P.M. to 7 P.M, and the total is the MAPE of the summed predictions over the entire day. Results, of the total power for the day prediction, of the recurrent network and other predictors are shown in Fig. 1. The performance on the A.M. and P.M. peaks were similar[9].

The failure of the daily recurrent network to accurately predict is a product of trying to model to complex a problem. When the complexity of the problem was reduced to that of predicting a single hour of the day, results improved significantly[7].

The superior performance of the recurrent network over the feedforward network is time series dependent. A feedforward and a recurrent network with the same input representation was trained to predict the 5 P.M. load on the previous work day. The feedforward network succeeded in modeling the training set with a mean square error of .0153 compared to the recurrent networks .0179. However, when the tested on several winter outside the training set the results, listed in the table below, varied. For the 1990-91 winter, the recurrent network did better with a mean square error of .0311 compared to the feedforward networks .0331. For the other winter of the years before the training set, the results were quite different, the feedforward network won in all cases. The differences in prediction performance can be explained by the inability of the feedforward network to model load growth in the future. The loads experience in the 1990-91 winter were outside the range of the entire training set. The earlier winters range of loads were not as far form the training set and the feedforward network modeled them well.

The effect of the nonlinear nature of neural networks was apparent in the error residuals of the training and test sets. Figs. 2 and 3 are plots of the residuals against the predicted load for the training and test sets respectively. In Fig. 2, the mean and variance of the residuals is roughly constant as a function of the predicted load, this is indicative of a good fit to the data. However, in Fig. 3, the errors tend to be positive for larger loads and negative for lesser loads. This is a product of the squashing effect of the sigmoidal nonlinearities. The squashing effect becomes acute during the prediction of the peak loads of the winter. These peak loads are caused when a cold spell occurs and the power demand reaches record levels. This is the only measure on which the performance of the recurrent networks is surpassed, human experts outperformed the recurrent network for predictions during cold spells. The recurrent network did outperform all other statistical models on this measure.

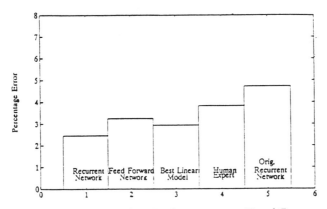

Figure 1: Competition Performance on Total Power

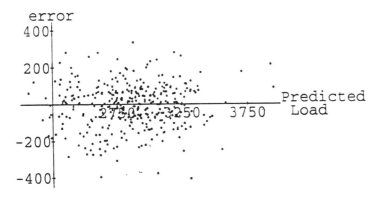

Figure 2: Prediction vs. Residual on Training Set

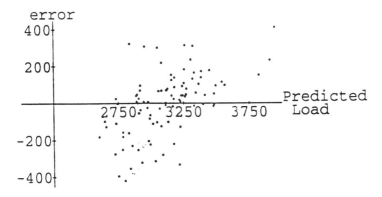

Figure 3: Prediction vs. Residual on Testing Set

5   Conclusion

Recurrent networks are the nonlinear neural network analog of linear ARMA models. As such, they are well-suited for time series that possess moving average components, are state dependent, or have trends. Recurrent neural networks can give superior results for load forecasting, but as with linear models, the choice of model is critical to good prediction performance.

6   Acknowledgements

We would like to than Milan Casey Brace of the Puget Power Corporation, Dr. Seho Oh, Dr. Mohammed El-Sharkawi, Dr. Robert Marks, and Dr. Mark Damborg for helpful discussions. We would also like to thank the National Science Foundation for partially supporting this work.

References

[1] G. Box, *Time series analysis: forecasting and control*, Holden-Day, 1976.

[2] A. C. Harvey, *The econometric analysis of time series*, MIT Press, 1990.

[3] A. Lapedes and R. Farber, "Nonlinear Signal Processing Using Neural Networks: Prediction and System Modeling", Technical Report, LA-UR87-2662, Los Alamos National Laboratory, Los Alamos, New Mexico, 1987.

[4] D.E. Rumelhart, G.E. Hinton, and R.J. Williams, "Learning internal representations by error propagation", in *Parallel Distributed Processing*, vol. 1, D.E. Rumelhart, and J.L. NcCelland, eds. Cambridge:M.I.T. Press, 1986, pp. 318-362.

[5] M.C. Brace , *A Comparison of the Forecasting Accuracy of Neural Networks with Other Established Techniques*, Proc. of the 1st Int. Forum on Applications of Neural Networks to Power Systems, Seattle, July 23-26, 1991.

[6] L. Atlas, J. Connor, et al., "Performance Comparisons Between Backpropagation Networks and Classification Trees on Three Real-World Applications", *Advances in Neural Information Processing Systems 2*, pp. 622-629, ed. D. Touretzky, 1989.

[7] S. Oh et al., *Electric Load Forecasting Using an Adaptively Trained Layered Perceptron*, Proc. of the 1st Int. Forum on Applications of Neural Networks to Power Systems, Seattle, July 23-26, 1991.

[8] M. Rosenblatt, *Markov Processes. Structure and Asymptotic Behavior*, Springer-Verlag, 1971, 160-182.

[9] J. Connor, L. E. Atlas, and R. D. Martin, "Recurrent Neural Networks and Time Series Prediction", to be submitted to *IEEE Trans. on Neural Networks*, 1992.

[10] R. Williams and D. Zipser. *A Learning Algorithm for Continually Running Fully Recurrent Neural Networks*, Neural Computation, 1, 1989, 270-280.

Induction of Finite-State Automata Using Second-Order Recurrent Networks

Raymond L. Watrous
Siemens Corporate Research
755 College Road East, Princeton, NJ 08540

Gary M. Kuhn
Center for Communications Research, IDA
Thanet Road, Princeton, NJ 08540

Abstract

Second-order recurrent networks that recognize simple finite state languages over {0,1}* are induced from positive and negative examples. Using the complete gradient of the recurrent network and sufficient training examples to constrain the definition of the language to be induced, solutions are obtained that correctly recognize strings of arbitrary length. A method for extracting a finite state automaton corresponding to an optimized network is demonstrated.

1 Introduction

We address the problem of inducing languages from examples by considering a set of finite state languages over {0, 1}* that were selected for study by Tomita (Tomita, 1982):

L1. 1*

L2. (10)*

L3. no odd-length 0-string anywhere after an odd-length 1-string

L4. not more than 2 0's in a row

L5. bit pairs, #01's + #10's = 0 mod 2

L6. abs(#1's - #0's) = 0 mod 3

L7. 0*1*0*1*

Tomita also selected for each language a set of positive and negative examples (summarized in Table 1) to be used as a training set. By a method of heuristic search over the space of finite state automata with up to eight states, he was able to induce a recognizer for each of these languages (Tomita, 1982).

Recognizers of finite-state languages have also been induced using first-order recurrent connectionist networks (Elman, 1990; Williams and Zipser, 1988; Cleeremans, Servan-Schreiber and McClelland, 1989). Generally speaking, these results were obtained by training the network to predict the next symbol (Cleeremans, Servan-Schreiber and McClelland, 1989; Williams and Zipser, 1988), rather than by training the network to accept or reject strings of different lengths. Several training algorithms used an approximation to the gradient (Elman, 1990; Cleeremans, Servan-Schreiber and McClelland, 1989) by truncating the computation of the backward recurrence.

The problem of inducing languages from examples has also been approached using second-order recurrent networks (Pollack, 1990; Giles et al., 1990). Using a truncated approximation to the gradient, and Tomita's training sets, Pollack reported that "none of the ideal languages were induced" (Pollack, 1990). On the other hand, a Tomita language has been induced using the complete gradient (Giles et al., 1991). This paper reports the induction of several Tomita languages and the extraction of the corresponding automata with certain differences in method from (Giles et al., 1991).

2   Method

2.1   Architecture

The network model consists of one input unit, one threshold unit, N state units and one output unit. The output unit and each state unit receive a first order connection from the input unit and the threshold unit. In addition, each of the output and state units receives a second-order connection for each pairing of the input and threshold unit with each of the state units. For $N = 3$, the model is mathematically identical to that used by Pollack (Pollack, 1990); it has 32 free parameters.

2.2   Data Representation

The symbols of the language are represented by byte values, that are mapped into real values between 0 and 1 by dividing by 255. Thus, the ZERO symbol is represented by octal 040 (0.1255). This value was chosen to be different from 0.0, which is used as the initial condition for all units except the threshold unit, which is set to 1.0. The ONE symbol was chosen as octal 370 (0.97255). All strings are terminated by two occurrences of a termination symbol that has the value 0.0.

Language	Grammatical Strings			Ungrammatical Strings		
	Length ≤ 10		Longer Strings	Length ≤ 10		Longer Strings
	Total	Training	In Training Set	Total	Training	In Training Set
1	11	9		2036	8	
2	6	5	1	2041	10	
3	652	11	2	1395	11	1
4	1103	10	1	944	7	2
5	683	9		1364	11	1
6	683	10		1364	11	1
7	561	11	2	1486	6	2

Table 1: Number of grammatical and ungrammatical strings of length 10 or less for Tomita languages and number of those included in the Tomita training sets.

2.3   Training

The Tomita languages are characterized in Table 1 by the number of grammatical strings of length 10 or less (out of a total of 2047 strings). The Tomita training sets are also characterized by the number of grammatical strings of length 10 or less included in the training data. For completeness, the Table also shows the number of grammatical strings in the training set of length greater than 10. A comparison of the number of grammatical strings with the number included in the training set shows that while Languages 1 and 2 are very sparse, they are almost completely covered by the training data, whereas Languages 3-7 are more dense, and are sparsely covered by the training sets. Possible consequences of these differences are considered in discussing the experimental results.

A mean-squared error measure was defined with target values of 0.9 and 0.1 for accept and reject, respectively. The target function was weighted so that error was injected only at the end of the string.

The complete gradient of this error measure for the recurrent network was computed by a method of accumulating the weight dependencies backward in time (Watrous, Ladendorf and Kuhn, 1990). This is in contrast to the truncated gradient used by Pollack (Pollack, 1990) and to the forward-propagation algorithm used by Giles (Giles et al., 1991).

The networks were optimized by gradient descent using the BFGS algorithm. A termination criterion of 10^{-10} was set; it was believed that such a strict tolerance might lead to smaller loss of accuracy on very long strings. No constraints were set on the number of iterations.

Five networks with different sets of random initial weights were trained separately on each of the seven languages described by Tomita using exactly his training sets (Tomita, 1982), including the null string. The training set used by Pollack (Pollack, 1990) differs only in not including the null string.

2.4   Testing

The networks were tested on the complete set of strings up to length 10. Acceptance of a string was defined as the network having a final output value of greater than

$0.9 - T$ and rejection as a final value of less than $0.1 + T$, where $0 \leq T < 0.4$ is the tolerance. The decision was considered ambiguous otherwise.

3   Results

The results of the first experiment are summarized in Table 2. For each language, each network is listed by the seed value used to initialize the random weights. For each network, the iterations to termination are listed, followed by the minimum MSE value reached. Also listed is the percentage of strings of length 10 or less that were correctly recognized by the network, and the percentage of strings for which the decision was uncertain at a tolerance of 0.0.

The number of iterations until termination varied widely, from 28 to 37909. There is no obvious correlation between number of iterations and minimum MSE.

3.1   Language 1

It may be observed that Language 1 is recognized correctly by two of the networks (seeds 72 and 987235) and nearly correctly by a third (seed 239). This latter network failed on the strings 1^9 and 1^{10}, both of which were not in the training set.

The network of seed 72 was further tested on all strings of length 15 or less and made no errors. This network was also tested on a string of 100 ones and showed no diminution of output value over the length of the string. When tested on strings of 99 ones plus either an initial zero or a final zero, the network also made no errors. Another network, seed 987235, made no errors on strings of length 15 or less but failed on the string of 100 ones. The hidden units broke into oscillation after about the 30th input symbol and the output fell into a low amplitude oscillation near zero.

3.2   Language 2

Similarly, Language 2 was recognized correctly by two networks (seeds 89340 and 987235) and nearly correctly by a third network (seed 104). The latter network failed only on strings of the form (10)*010, none of which were included in the training data.

The networks that performed perfectly on strings up to length 10 were tested further on all strings up to length 15 and made no errors. These networks were also tested on a string of 100 alternations of 1 and 0, and responded correctly. Changing the first or final zero to a one caused both networks correctly to reject the string.

3.3   The Other Languages

For most of the other languages, at least one network converged to a very low MSE value. However, networks that performed perfectly on the training set did not generalize well to a definition of the language. For example, for Language 3, the network with seed 104 reached a MSE of 8×10^{-10} at termination, yet the performance on the test set was only 78.31%. One interpretation of this outcome is that the intended language was not sufficiently constrained by the training set.

Language	Seed	Iterations	MSE	Accuracy	Uncertainty
	72	28	0.0012500000	100.00	0.00
	104	95	0.0215882357	78.07	20.76
1	239	8707	0.0005882353	99.90	0.00
	89340	5345	0.0266176471	66.93	0.00
	987235	994	0.0000000001	100.00	0.00
	72	5935	0.0005468750	93.36	4.93
	104	4081	0.0003906250	99.80	0.20
2	239	807	0.0476171875	62.73	37.27
	89340	1084	0.0005468750	100.00	0.00
	987235	10706	0.0001562500	100.00	0.00
	72	442	0.0149000000	47.09	33.27
	104	37909	0.0000000008	78.31	0.15
3	239	9264	0.0087000000	74.60	11.87
	89340	8250	0.0005000000	73.57	0.00
	987235	5769	0.0136136712	50.76	23.94
	72	8630	0.0004375001	52.71	6.45
	104	60	0.0624326924	20.86	50.02
4	239	2272	0.0005000004	55.40	9.38
	89340	10680	0.0003750001	60.92	15.53
	987235	324	0.0459375000	22.62	77.38
	72	890	0.0526912920	34.39	63.80
	104	368	0.0464772727	45.92	41.62
5	239	1422	0.0487500000	31.46	36.93
	89340	2775	0.0271525856	46.12	22.52
	987235	2481	0.0209090867	66.83	2.49
	72	524	0.0788760972	0.05	99.95
	104	332	0.0789530751	0.05	99.95
6	239	1355	0.0229551248	31.95	47.04
	89340	8171	0.0001733280	46.21	5.32
	987235	306	0.0577867426	37.71	24.87
	72	373	0.0588385157	9.38	86.08
	104	8578	0.0104224185	55.74	17.00
7	239	969	0.0211073814	52.76	26.58
	89340	4259	0.0007684520	54.42	0.49
	987235	666	0.0688690476	12.55	74.94

Table 2: Results of Training Three State-Unit Network from 5 Random Starts on Tomita.Languages Using Tomita Training Data

In the case of Language 5, in *no* case was the MSE reduced below 0.02. We believe that the model is sufficiently powerful to compute the language. It is possible, however, that the power of the model is marginally sufficient, so that finding a solution depends critically upon the initial conditions.

Seed	Iterations	MSE	Accuracy	Uncertainty
72	215	0.0000001022	100.00	0.00
104	665	0.0000000001	99.85	0.05
239	205	0.0000000001	99.90	0.10
89340	5244	0.0005731708	99.32	0.10
987235	2589	0.0004624581	92.13	6.55

Table 3: Results of Training Three State-Unit Network from 5 Random Starts on Tomita Language 4 Using Probabilistic Training Data (p=0.1)

4   Further Experiments

The effect of additional training data was investigated by creating training sets in which each string of length 10 or less is randomly included with a fixed probability p. Thus, for $p = 0.1$ approximately 10% of 2047 strings are included in the training set. A flat random sampling of the lexicographic domain may not be the best approach, however, since grammaticality can vary non-uniformly.

The same networks as before were trained on the larger training set for Language 4, with the results listed in Table 3.

Under these conditions, a network solution was obtained that generalizes perfectly to the test set (seed 72). This network also made no errors on strings up to length 15. However, very low MSE values were again obtained for networks that do not perform perfectly on the test data (seeds 104 and 239). Network 239 made two ambiguous decisions that would have been correct at a tolerance value of 0.23. Network 104 incorrectly accepted the strings 000 and 1000 and would have correctly accepted the string 0100 at a tolerance of 0.25. Both networks made no additional errors on strings up to length 15. The training data may still be slightly indeterminate. Moreover, the few errors made were on short strings, that are not included in the training data.

Since this network model is continuous, and thus potentially infinite state, it is perhaps not surprising that the successful induction of a finite state language seems to require more training data than was needed for Tomita's finite state model (Tomita, 1982).

The effect of more complex models was investigated for Language 5 using a network with 11 state units; this increases the number of weights from 32 to 288. Networks of this type were optimized from 5 random initial conditions on the original training data. The results of this experiment are summarized in Table 4. By increasing the complexity of the model, convergence to low MSE values was obtained in every case, although none of these networks generalized to the desired language. Once again, it is possible that more data is required to constrain the language sufficiently.

5   FSA Extraction

The following method for extracting a deterministic finite-state automaton corresponding to an optimized network was developed:

Seed	Iterations	MSE	Accuracy	Uncertainty
72	1327	0.0002840909	53.00	11.87
104	680	0.0001136364	39.47	16.32
239	357	0.0006818145	61.31	3.32
89340	122	0.0068189264	63.36	6.64
987235	4502	0.0001704545	48.41	16.95

Table 4: Results of Training Network with 11 State-Units from 5 Random Starts on Tomita Language 5 Using Tomita Training Data

1. Record the response of the network to a set of strings.

2. Compute a zero bin-width histogram for each hidden unit and partition each histogram so that the intervals between adjacent peaks are bisected.

3. Initialize a state-transition table which is indexed by the current state and input symbol; then, for each string:

   (a) Starting from the NULL state, for each hidden unit activation vector:

       i. Obtain the next state label from the concatenation of the histogram interval number of each hidden unit value.

       ii. Record the next state in the state-transition table. If a transition is recorded from the same state on the same input symbol to two different states, move or remove hidden unit histogram partitions so that the two states are collapsed and go to 3; otherwise, update the current state.

   (b) At the end of the string, mark the current state as accept, reject or uncertain according as the output unit is ≥ 0.9, ≤ 0.1 or otherwise. If the current state has already received a different marking, move or insert histogram partitions so that the offending state is subdivided and go to 3.

If the recorded strings are processed successfully, then the resulting state-transition table may be taken as an FSA interpretation of the optimized network. The FSA may then be minimized by standard methods (Giles et al., 1991). If no histogram partition can be found such that the process succeeds, the network may not have a finite-state interpretation.

As an approximation to Step 3, the hidden unit vector was labeled by the index of that vector in an initially empty set of reference vectors for which each component value was within some global threshold (θ) of the hidden unit value. If no such reference vector was found, the observed vector was added to the reference set. The threshold θ could be raised or lowered as states needed to be collapsed or subdivided.

Using the approximate method, for Language 1, the correct and minimal FSA was extracted from one network (seed 72, $\theta = 0.1$). The correct FSA was also extracted from another network (seed 987235, $\theta = 0.06$), although for no partition of the hidden unit activation values could the minimal FSA be extracted. Interestingly, the FSA extracted from the network with seed 239 corresponded to 1^n for $n \leq 8$. Also, the FSA for another network (seed 89340, $\theta = 0.0003$) was nearly correct, although the string accuracy was only 67%; one state was wrongly labeled "accept".

For Language 2, the correct and minimal FSA was extracted from one network (seed 987235, $\theta = 0.00001$). A correct FSA was also extracted from another network (seed

89340, $\theta = 0.0022$), although this FSA was not minimal.

For Language 4, a histogram partition was found for one network (seed 72) that led to the correct and minimal FSA; for the zero-width histogram, the FSA was correct, but not minimal.

Thus, a correct FSA was extracted from every optimized network that correctly recognized strings of length 10 or less from the language for which it was trained. However, in some cases, no histogram partition was found for which the extracted FSA was minimal. It also appears that an almost-correct FSA can be extracted, which might perhaps be corrected externally. And, finally, the extracted FSA may be correct, even though the network might fail on very long strings.

6   Conclusions

We have succeeded in recognizing several simple finite state languages using second-order recurrent networks and extracting corresponding finite-state automata. We consider the computation of the complete gradient a key element in this result.

Acknowledgements

We thank Lee Giles for sharing with us their results (Giles et al., 1991).

References

Cleeremans, A., Servan-Schreiber, D., and McClelland, J. (1989). Finite state automata and simple recurrent networks. *Neural Computation*, 1(3):372–381.

Elman, J. L. (1990). Finding structure in time. *Cognitive Science*, 14:179–212.

Giles, C. L., Chen, D., Miller, C. B., Chen, H. H., Sun, G. Z., and Lee, Y. C. (1991). Second-order recurrent neural networks for grammatical inference. In *Proceedings of the International Joint Conference on Neural Networks*, volume II, pages 273–281.

Giles, C. L., Sun, G. Z., Chen, H. H., Lee, Y. C., and Chen, D. (1990). Higher order recurrent networks and grammatical inference. In Touretzky, D. S., editor, *Advances in Neural Information Systems 2*, pages 380–387. Morgan Kaufmann.

Pollack, J. B. (1990). The induction of dynamical recognizers. Technical Report 90-JP-AUTOMATA, Ohio State University.

Tomita, M. (1982). Dynamic construction of finite automata from examples using hill-climbing. In *Proceedings of the Fourth International Cognitive Science Conference*, pages 105–108.

Watrous, R. L., Ladendorf, B., and Kuhn, G. M. (1990). Complete gradient optimization of a recurrent network applied to /b/, /d/, /g/ discrimination. *Journal of the Acoustical Society of America*, 87(3):1301–1309.

Williams, R. J. and Zipser, D. (1988). A learning algorithm for continually running fully recurrent neural networks. Technical Report ICS Report 8805, UCSD Institute for Cognitive Science.

Extracting and Learning an Unknown Grammar with Recurrent Neural Networks

C.L.Giles*, C.B. Miller
NEC Research Institute
4 Independence Way
Princeton, N.J. 08540
giles@research.nj.nec.com

D. Chen, G.Z. Sun, H.H. Chen, Y.C. Lee
*Institute for Advanced Computer Studies
Dept. of Physics and Astronomy
University of Maryland
College Park, Md 20742

Abstract

Simple second-order recurrent networks are shown to readily learn small *known* regular grammars when trained with positive and negative strings examples. We show that similar methods are appropriate for learning *unknown* grammars from examples of their strings. The training algorithm is an *incremental* real-time, recurrent learning (RTRL) method that computes the complete gradient and updates the weights at the end of each string. After or *during* training, a dynamic clustering algorithm extracts the production rules that the neural network has learned. The methods are illustrated by *extracting* rules from *unknown* deterministic regular grammars. For many cases the *extracted* grammar outperforms the neural net from which it was extracted in correctly classifying unseen strings.

1   INTRODUCTION

For many reasons, there has been a long interest in "language" models of neural networks; see [Elman 1991] for an excellent discussion. The orientation of this work is somewhat different. The focus here is on what are good measures of the computational capabilities of recurrent neural networks. Since currently there is little theoretical knowledge, what problems would be "good" experimental benchmarks? For discrete inputs, a natural choice would be the problem of learning formal grammars - a "hard" problem even for regular grammars [Angluin, Smith 1982]. Strings of grammars can be presented one character at a time and strings can be of arbitrary length. However, the strings themselves would be, for the most part, feature independent. Thus, the learning capabilities would be, for the most part, feature independent and, therefore insensitive to feature extraction choice.

The learning of *known* grammars by recurrent neural networks has shown promise, for example [Cleeresman, et al 1989], [Giles, et al 1990, 1991, 1992], [Pollack 1991], [Sun, et al 1990], [Watrous, Kuhn 1992a,b], [Williams, Zipser 1988]. But what about learning *unknown* grammars? We demonstrate in this paper that not only can *unknown* grammars be learned, but it is possible to *extract* the grammar from the neural network, both during and after training. Furthermore, the extraction process requires no a priori knowledge about the grammar, except that the grammar's representation can be *regular*, which is always true for a grammar of bounded string length; which is the grammatical "training sample."

2   FORMAL GRAMMARS

We give a brief introduction to grammars; for a more detailed explanation see [Hopcroft & Ullman, 1979]. We define a grammar as a 4-tuple (**N, V, P, S**) where **N** and **V** are nonterminal and terminal vocabularies, **P** is a finite set of production rules and **S** is the start symbol. All grammars we discuss are deterministic and regular. For every grammar there exists a language - the set of strings the grammar generates - and an automaton - the machine that recognizes (classifies) the grammar's strings. For regular grammars, the recognizing machine is a deterministic finite automaton (DFA). There exists a one-to-one mapping between a DFA and its grammar. Once the DFA is known, the production rules are the ordered triples *(node, arc, node)*.

Grammatical inference [Fu 1982] is defined as the problem of finding (learning) a grammar from a finite set of strings, often called the training sample. One can interpret this problem as devising an inference engine that learns and extracts the grammar, see Figure 1.

Figure 1: Grammatical inference

For a training sample of positive and negative strings and no knowledge of the unknown regular grammar, the problem is NP-complete (for a summary, see [Angluin, Smith 1982]). It is possible to construct an inference engine that consists of a recurrent neural network and a rule extraction process that yields an inferred grammar.

3   RECURRENT NEURAL NETWORK

3.1   ARCHITECTURE

Our recurrent neural network is quite simple and can be considered as a simplified version of the model by [Elman 1991]. For an excellent discussion of recurrent networks full of references that we don't have room for here, see [Hertz, et al 1991].

A fairly general expression for a recurrent network (which has the same computational power as a DFA) is:

$$S_i^{t+1} = F(S_j^t, I^t; W)$$

where F is a nonlinearity that maps the state neuron S^t and the input neuron I^t at time t to the next state S^{t+1} at time $t+1$. The weight matrix W parameterizes the mapping and is usually learned (however, it can be totally or partially programmed). A DFA has an analogous mapping but does not use W. For a recurrent neural network we define the mapping F and order of the mapping in the following manner [Lee, et al 1986]. For a **first-order** recurrent net:

where N is the number of hidden state neurons and L the number of input neurons; W_{ij} and Y_{ij} are the real-valued weights for respectively the state and input neurons; and σ is a stan-

$$S_i^{t+1} = \sigma\left(\sum_j^N W_{ij}S_j^t + \sum_k^L Y_{ik}I_k^t\right)$$

dard sigmoid discriminant function. The values of the hidden state neurons S^t are defined in the finite N-dimensional space $[0,1]^N$. Assuming all weights are connected and the net is fully recurrent, the weight space complexity is bounded by $O(N^2+NL)$. *Note that the input and state neurons are not the same neurons.* This representation has the capability, assuming sufficiently large N and L, to represent any state machine. Note that there are non-trainable unit weights on the recurrent feedback connections.

The natural **second-order** extension of this recurrent net is:

$$S_i^{t+1} = \sigma\left(\sum_{j,k}^{N,L} W_{ijk}S_j^t S_k^t\right) \Rightarrow \sigma\left(\sum_{j,k}^{N,L} W_{ijk}S_j^t I_k^t\right)$$

where certain state neurons become input neurons. Note that the weights W_{ijk} modify a product of the hidden S_j and input I_k neurons. This quadratic form <u>directly represents</u> the state transition diagrams of a state automata process -- *(input, state)* $\Rightarrow$ *(next-state)* and thus makes the state transition mapping very easy to learn. It also permits the net to be *directly programmed* to be a particular DFA. Unpublished experiments comparing first and second order recurrent nets confirm this ease-in-learning hypothesis. The space complexity (number of weights) is $O(LN^2)$. For L«N, both first- and second-order are of the same complexity, $O(N^2)$.

3.2   SUPERVISED TRAINING & ERROR FUNCTION

The error function is defined by a special recurrent *output neuron* which is checked at the end of each string presentation to see if it is on or off. By convention this *output neuron* should be on if the string is a positive example of the grammar and off if negative. In practice an error tolerance decides the on and off criteria; see [Giles, et al 1991] for detail. [If a multiclass recognition is desired, another error scheme using many output neurons can be constructed.] We define two error cases: (1) the network fails to reject a negative string (the output neuron is on); (2) the network fails to accept a positive string (the output neuron is off). This accept or reject occurs at the *end of each string* - we define this problem as *inference* versus *prediction*.There is no prediction of the next character in the string sequence. As such, *inference* is a more difficult problem than *prediction*. If knowledge of the classification of every substring of every string exists and alphabetical training order is preserved, then the *prediction* and *inference* problems are equivalent.

The training method is real-time recurrent training (RTRL). For more details see [Williams, Zipser 1988]. The error function is defined as:

$$E = (1/2)\left(Target - S_o^f\right)^2$$

where S_o^f is the output neuron value at the final time step $t=f$ when the final character is presented and *Target* is the desired value of $(1,0)$ for (positive, negative) examples. Using gradient descent training, the weight update rule for a second-order recurrent net becomes:

$$W_{lmn} = -\alpha\nabla E = \alpha\left(Target - S_o^f\right)\cdot\frac{\partial S_o^f}{\partial W_{lmn}}$$

where α is the learning rate. From the recursive network state equation we obtain the relationship between the derivatives of S^t and S^{t+1}:

$$\frac{\partial S_i^t}{\partial W_{lmn}} = \sigma' \cdot \left[\delta_{il} S_m^{t-1} I_n^{t-1} + \sum_{jk}^{NL} W_{ijk} I_k^{t-1} \frac{\partial S_j^{t-1}}{\partial W_{lmn}} \right]$$

where σ' is the derivative of the discriminant function. This permits on-line learning with partial derivatives calculated iteratively at each time step. Let $\partial S^{t=0}/\partial W_{lmn} = 0$. Note that the space complexity is $O(L^2 N^4)$ which can be prohibitive for large N and full connectivity. It is important to note that for all training discussed here, the full gradient is calculated as given above.

3.3   PRESENTATION OF TRAINING SAMPLES

The training data consists of a series of stimulus-response pairs, where the stimulus is a string of 0's and 1's, and the response is either "1" for positive examples or "0" for negative examples. The positive and negative strings are generated by an *unknown* source grammar (created by a program that creates random grammars) prior to training. At each discrete time step, *one symbol* from the string activates *one input neuron*, the other input neurons are zero (one-hot encoding). *Training is on-line and occurs after each string presentation; there is no total error accumulation as in batch learning;* contrast this to the batch method of [Watrous, Kuhn 1992]. An extra *end symbol* is added to the string alphabet to give the network more power in deciding the best final neuron state configuration. This requires another input neuron and does not increase the complexity of the DFA (only N^2 more weights). The sequence of strings presented during training is very important and certainly gives a bias in learning. We have performed many experiments that indicate that training with alphabetical order with an equal distribution of positive and negative examples is much faster and converges more often than random order presentation.

The *training algorithm is on-line, incremental*. A small portion of the training set is pre-selected and presented to the network. The net is trained at the end of each string presentation. Once the net has learned this small set or reaches a maximum number of epochs (set before training, 1000 for experiments reported), a small number of strings (10) classified incorrectly are chosen from the rest of the training set and added to the pre-selected set. This small string increment prevents the training procedure from driving the network too far towards any local minima that the misclassified strings may represent. Another cycle of epoch training begins with the augmented training set. If the net correctly classifies all the training data, the net is said to *converge*. The total number of cycles that the network is permitted to run is also limited, usually to about 20.

4   RULE EXTRACTION (DFA GENERATION)

As the network is training (or after training), we apply a procedure we call d*ynamic state partitioning (dsp)* for extracting *the network's current conception of the DFA it is learning or has learned*. The rule extraction process has the following steps: 1) clustering of DFA states, 2) constructing a transition diagram by connecting these states together with the alphabet-labelled transitions, 3) putting these transitions together to make the full digraph - forming cycles, and 4) reducing the digraph to a minimal representation. The hypothesis is that during training, the network begins to partition (or quantize) its state space into fairly well-separated, distinct regions or clusters, which represent corresponding states in some DFA. See [Cleeremans, et al 1989] and [Watrous and Kuhn 1992a] for other clustering methods. A simple way of finding these clusters is to divide each neuron's range [0,1] into q partitions of equal size. For N state neurons, qN partitions. For example, for $q=2$, the values of $S^t \geq 0.5$ are 1 and $S^t < 0.5$ are 0, and there are $2N$ regions with 2^N possible values. Thus for N hidden neurons, there exist q^N possible *regions*. The DFA is constructed by generating a state transition diagram -- associating an input symbol with a set of hidden neuron *partitions* that it is currently in and the set of neuron *partitions* it activates. This ordered triple is also a **production rule**.The initial *partition*, or start state of the DFA, is determined from the initial value of $S^{t=0}$. If the next input symbol maps to the same *partition* we assume a loop in the DFA. Otherwise, a new state in the DFA is formed.This constructed DFA may contain a maximum of q^N states; in practice it is usually much less, since not all neuron partition sets are ever reached. This is basically a tree pruning method and different DFA could be generated based on the choice of branching order. The *extracted* DFA can then be reduced to its minimal size using standard minimization algorithms (an $O(N^2)$ algorithm where N is the number of DFA states) [Hopcroft, Ullman 1979]. [This minimization procedure does not change the grammar of the DFA; the unminimized DFA has same time complexity as the minimized DFA. The process just rids the DFA of redundant, unnecessary states and reduces the space complexity.] *Once the DFA is known, the production rules are easily extracted.*

Since many partition values of q are available, *many DFA can be extracted*. How is the q that gives the best DFA chosen? Or viewed in another way, using different q, what DFA gives the best representation of the grammar of the training set? One approach is to use different q's (starting with q=2), different branching order, different runs with different numbers of neurons and different initial conditions, and see if any similar sets of DFA emerge. Choose the DFA whose similarity set has the smallest number of states and appears most often - an Occam's razor assumption. Define the guess of the DFA as DFA$_g$.This method seems to work fairly well. Another is to see which of the DFA give the best performance on the training set, assuming that the training set is not perfectly learned. We have little experience with this method since we usually train to perfection on the training set. *It should be noted that this DFA extraction method may be applied to any discrete-time recurrent net, regardless of network order or number of hidden layers.* Preliminary results on first-order recurrent networks show that the same DFA are extracted as second-order, but the first-order nets are less likely to converge and take longer to converge than second-order.

5   SIMULATIONS - GRAMMARS LEARNED

Many different small (< 15 states) regular *__known__* grammars have been learned successfully with both first-order [Cleeremans, et al 1989] and second-order recurrent models [Giles, et al 91] and [Watrous, Kuhn 1992a]. In addition [Giles, et al 1990 & 1991] and [Watrous, Kuhn 1992b] show how corresponding DFA and production rules can be extracted. *However for all of the above work, the grammars to be learned were __already__ known.* What is more interesting is the learning of *unknown grammars*.

In figure 2b is a randomly generated minimal 10-state regular grammar created by a program in which the only inputs are the number of states of the unminimized DFA and the alphabet size *p*. (A good estimate of the number of possible unique DFA is $(n2^n n^{pn}/n!)$ [Alon, et al 1991] where n is number of DFA states) The shaded state is the start state, filled and dashed arcs represent 1 and 0 transitions and all final states have a shaded outer circle. This *unknown* (honestly, we didn't look) DFA was learned with both 6 and 10 hidden state neuron second-order recurrent nets using the first 1000 strings in alphabetical training order (we could ask the *unknown* grammar for strings). Of two runs for both 10 and 6 neurons, both of the 10 and one of the 6 converged in less than 1000 epochs. (The initial weights were all randomly chosen between [1,-1] and the learning rate and momentum were both 0.5.) Figure 2a shows one of the unminimized DFA that was extracted for a partition parameter of q=2. The minimized 10-state DFA, figure 3b, appeared for q=2 for one 10 neuron net and for q=2,3,4 of the converged 6 neuron net. Consequently, using our previous criteria, we chose this DFA as DFA$_g$, our guess at the unknown grammar. We then asked

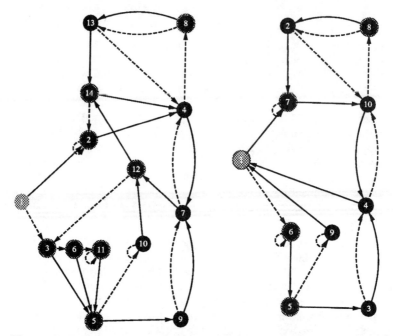

Figures 2a & 2b. Unminimized and minimized 10-state random grammar.

the program what the grammar was and discovered we were correct in our guess. The other minimized DFA for different q's were all unique and usually very large (number of states > 100).

The *trained* recurrent nets were then checked for generalization errors on all strings up to length 15. All made a small number of errors, usually less than 1% of the total of 65,535 strings. However, the correct extracted DFA was perfect and, of course, makes no errors on strings of any length. *Again, [Giles, et al 1991, 1992], the extracted DFA outperforms the trained neural net from which the DFA was extracted.*

Figures 3a and 3b, we see the dynamics of DFA extraction as a 4 hidden neuron neural network is learning as a function of epoch and partition size. This is for grammar Tomita-4 [Giles, et al 1991, 1992]] - a 4-state grammar that rejects any string which has more than three 0's in a row. The number of states of the extracted DFA starts out small, then increases, and finally decreases to a constant value as the grammar is learned. As the partition q of the neuron space increases, the number of minimized and unminimized states increases. When the grammar is learned, the number of minimized states becomes constant and, as expected, the number of minimized states, independent of q, becomes the number of states in the grammar's DFA - 4.

6 CONCLUSIONS

Simple recurrent neural networks are capable of learning small regular *unknown* grammars rather easily and generalize fairly well on unseen grammatical strings. The training results are fairly independent of the initial values of the weights and numbers of neurons. For a well-trained neural net, the generalization performance on long unseen strings can be perfect.

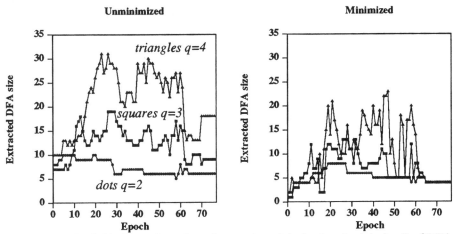

Figures 3a & 3b. Size of number of states (unminimized and minimized) of DFA versus training epoch for different partition parameter q. The correct state size is 4.

A heuristic algorithm called dynamic state partitioning was created to *extract* deterministic finite state automata (DFA) from the neural network, both *during* and *after* training. Using a standard DFA minimization algorithm, the extracted DFA can be reduced to an *equivalent* minimal-state DFA which has reduced space (not time) complexity. When the source or generating grammar is unknown, a good guess of the unknown grammar DFA_g can be obtained from the minimal DFA that is most often extracted from different runs with different numbers of neurons and initial conditions. *From the extracted DFA, minimal or not, the production rules of the learned grammar are evident.*

There are some interesting aspects of the extracted DFA. Each of the unminimized DFA seems to be <u>unique</u>, even those with the same number of states. For recurrent nets that converge, it is often possible to *extract* DFA that are perfect, i.e. the grammar of the unknown source grammar. For these cases all unminimized DFA whose minimal sizes have the same number of states constitute a large *equivalence class* of neural-net-generated DFA, and have the *same performance* on string classification. This *equivalence class* extends across neural networks which vary both in size (number of neurons) and initial conditions. Thus, the *extracted DFA* gives a good indication of how well the neural network learns the grammar.

In fact, for most of the trained neural nets, the extracted DFA_g outperforms the trained neural networks in classification of unseen strings. (By definition, a perfect DFA will correctly classify all unseen strings). This is not surprising due to the possibility of error accumulation as the neural network classifies *long* unseen strings [Pollack 1991]. However, when the neural network has learned the grammar well, its generalization performance can be perfect on all strings tested [Giles, et al 1991, 1992]. Thus, the neural network can be considered as a tool for extracting a DFA that is representative of the unknown grammar. Once the DFA_g is obtained, it can be used independently of the trained neural network.

The learning of small DFA using second-order techniques and the full gradient computation reported here and elsewhere [Giles, et al 1991, 1992], [Watrous, Kuhn 1992a, 1992b] give a strong impetus to using these techniques for learning DFA. The question of DFA state capacity and scalability is unresolved. Further work must show how well these approaches can model grammars with large numbers of states and establish a theoretical and experimental relationship between DFA state capacity and neural net size.

Acknowledgments

The authors acknowledge useful and helpful discussions with E. Baum, M. Goudreau, G. Kuhn, K. Lang, L. Valiant, and R. Watrous. The University of Maryland authors gratefully acknowledge partial support from AFOSR and DARPA.

References

N. Alon, A.K. Dewdney, and T.J.Ott, 'Efficient Simulation of Finite Automata by Neural Nets, *Journal of the ACM*, Vol 38, p. 495 (1991).

D. Angluin, C.H. Smith, Inductive Inference: Theory and Methods, *ACM Computing Surveys,* Vol 15, No 3, p. 237, (1983).

A. Cleeremans, D. Servan-Schreiber, J. McClelland, Finite State Automata and Simple Recurrent Recurrent Networks, *Neural Computation*, Vol 1, No 3, p. 372 (1989).

J.L. Elman, Distributed Representations, Simple Recurrent Networks, and Grammatical Structure, *Machine Learning*, Vol 7, No 2/3, p. 91 (1991).

K.S. Fu, *Syntactic Pattern Recognition and Applications,* Prentice-Hall, Englewood Cliffs, N.J. Ch.10 (1982).

C.L. Giles, G.Z. Sun, H.H. Chen, Y.C. Lee, D. Chen, Higher Order Recurrent Networks & Grammatical Inference, *Advances in Neural Information Systems 2*, D.S. Touretzky (ed), Morgan Kaufmann, San Mateo, Ca, p.380 (1990).

C.L. Giles, D. Chen, C.B. Miller, H.H. Chen, G.Z. Sun, Y.C. Lee, Grammatical Inference Using Second-Order Recurrent Neural Networks, *Proceedings of the International Joint Conference on Neural Networks*, IEEE91CH3049-4, Vol 2, p.357 (1991).

C.L. Giles, C.B. Miller, D. Chen, H.H. Chen, G.Z. Sun, Y.C. Lee, Learning and Extracting Finite State Automata with Second-Order Recurrent Neural Networks, *Neural Computation*, accepted for publication (1992).

J. Hertz, A. Krogh, R.G. Palmer, *Introduction to the Theory of Neural Computation*, Addison-Wesley, Redwood City, Ca., Ch. 7 (1991).

J.E. Hopcroft, J.D. Ullman, *Introduction to Automata Theory, Languages, and Computation,* Addison Wesley, Reading, Ma. (1979).

Y.C. Lee, G. Doolen, H.H. Chen, G.Z. Sun, T. Maxwell, H.Y. Lee, C.L. Giles, Machine Learning Using a Higher Order Correlational Network, *Physica D*, Vol 22-D, No1-3, p. 276 (1986).

J.B. Pollack, The Induction of Dynamical Recognizers, *Machine Learning*, Vol 7, No 2/3, p. 227 (1991).

G.Z. Sun, H.H. Chen, C.L. Giles, Y.C. Lee, D. Chen, Connectionist Pushdown Automata that Learn Context-Free Grammars, *Proceedings of the International Joint Conference on Neural*, Washington D.C., Lawrence Erlbaum Pub., Vol I, p. 577 (1990).

R.L. Watrous, G.M. Kuhn, Induction of Finite-State Languages Using Second-Order Recurrent Networks, *Neural Computation*, accepted for publication (1992a) and *these proceedings,* (1992b).

R.J. Williams, D. Zipser, A Learning Algorithm for Continually Running Fully Recurrent Neural Networks, *Neural Computation*, Vol 1, No 2, p. 270, (1989).

Operators and curried functions:
Training and analysis of simple recurrent networks

Janet Wiles
Depts of Psychology and Computer Science,
University of Queensland
QLD 4072 Australia.
janetw@cs.uq.oz.au

Anthony Bloesch,
Dept of Computer Science,
University of Queensland,
QLD 4072 Australia
anthonyb@cs.uq.oz.au

Abstract

We present a framework for programming the hidden unit representations of simple recurrent networks based on the use of *hint* units (additional targets at the output layer). We present two ways of analysing a network trained within this framework: Input patterns act as *operators* on the information encoded by the context units; symmetrically, patterns of activation over the context units act as *curried functions* of the input sequences. Simulations demonstrate that a network can learn to represent three different functions simultaneously and canonical discriminant analysis is used to investigate how operators and curried functions are represented in the space of hidden unit activations.

1 INTRODUCTION

Many recent papers have contributed to the understanding of recurrent networks and their potential for modelling sequential phenomena (see for example Giles, Sun, Chen, Lee, & Chen, 1990; Elman, 1989; 1990; Jordan, 1986; Cleeremans, Servan-Schreiber & McClelland, 1989; Williams & Zipser, 1988). Of particular interest in these papers is the development of recurrent architectures and learning algorithms able to solve complex problems. The perspective of the work we present here has many similarities with these studies, however, we focus on *programming* a recurrent network for a specific task, and hence provide appropriate sequences of inputs to learn the temporal component.

The function computed by a neural network is conventionally represented by its weights. During training, the task of a network is to learn a set of weights that causes the appropriate action (or set of context–specific actions) for each input pattern. However, in

325

a network with recurrent connections, patterns of activation are also part of the function computed by a network. After training (when the weights have been fixed) each input pattern has a specific effect on the pattern of activation across the hidden and output units which is modulated by the current state of those units. That is, each input pattern is a context sensitive *operator* on the state of the system.

To illustrate this idea, we present a task in which many sequences of the form, {F, arg1, ..., arg*n*} are input to a network, which is required to output the value of each function, F(arg1, ..., arg*n*). The task is interesting since it illustrates how more than one function can be computed by the same network and how the function selected can be specified by the inputs. Viewing all the inputs (both function patterns, F, and argument patterns, arg*i*) as operators allows us to analyse the effect of each input on the state of the network (the pattern of activation in the hidden and context units). From this perspective, the weights in the network can be viewed as an interpreter which has been programmed to carry out the operations specified by each input pattern.

We use the term *programming* intentionally, to convey the idea that the actions of each input pattern play a specific role in the processing of a sequence. In the simulations described in this paper, we use the simple recurrent network (*SRN*) proposed by Elman (1990). The art of programming enters the simulations in the use of extra target units, called *hints*, that are provided at the output layer. At each step in learning a sequence, hints specify all the information that the network must preserve in the hidden unit representation (the state of the system) in order to calculate outputs later in the sequence (for a discussion of the use of hints in training a recurrent network see Rumelhart, Hinton & Williams, 1986).

2 SIMULATIONS

Three different boolean functions and their arguments were specified as sub–sequences of patterns over the inputs to an *SRN*. The network was required to apply the function specified by the first pattern in each sequence to each of the subsequent arguments in turn. The functions provided were boolean functions of the current input and previous output, AND, OR and XOR (i.e., *exclusive-or*) and the arguments were arbitrary length strings of 0's and 1's. The context units were not reset between sub-sequences. An *SRN* with 3 input, 5 hidden, 5 context, 1 output and 5 hint units was trained using backpropagation with a momentum term. The 5 hint units at the output layer provided information about the boolean functions during training (via the backpropagation of errors), but not during testing. The network was trained on three data sets each containing 700 (ten times the number of weights in the network) randomly generated patterns, forming function and arguments sequences of average length 0.5, 2 and 4 arguments respectively. The network was trained for one thousand iterations on each training set.

2.1 RESULTS AND GENERALISATION

After training, the network correctly computed every pattern in the three training sets (using a closest match criterion for scoring the output) and also in a test set of sequences generated using the same statistics. Generalisation test data consisting of all possible sequences composed of each function and eight arguments, and long sequences each of 50 arguments also produced the correct output for every pattern in every sequence. To test

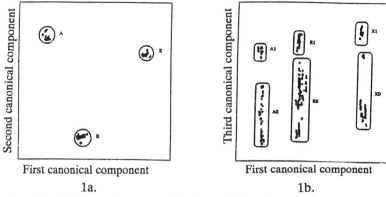

Figure 1a. The hidden unit patterns for the training data, projected onto the first two canonical components. These components separate the patterns into 3 distinct regions corresponding to the initial pattern (AND, OR or XOR) in each sequence. 1b. The first and third canonical components further separate the hidden unit patterns into 6 regions which have been marked in the diagrams above by the corresponding output classes A1, A0, R1, R0, X1 and X0. These regions are effectively the computational states of the network.

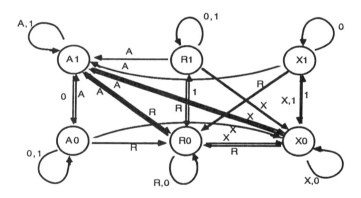

Figure 2. Finite state machine to compute the three-function task.

Another way of considering sub–sequences in the input stream is to describe all the inputs as functions, not over the other inputs, as above, but as functions of the state (for which we use the term *operators*). Using this terminology, a sub–sequence is a composition of operators which act on the current state,

$$G(S(t)) = argt \circ \ldots \circ arg2 \circ arg1 \circ S(0),$$

where $(f \circ g)(x) = f(g(x))$, and $S(0)$ is the initial state of the network. A consequence of describing the input patterns as operators is that even the 0 and 1 data bits can be seen as operators that transform the internal state (see Box 1).

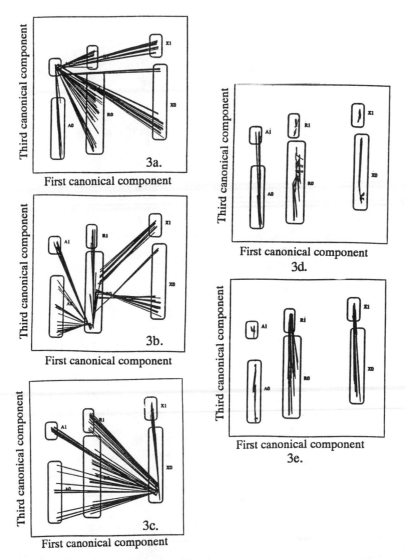

Figure 3. State transitions caused by each input pattern, projected onto the first and third canonical components of the hidden unit patterns (generated by the training data as in Figure 1). 3a-c. Transitions caused by the AND, OR and XOR input patterns respectively. From every point in the hidden unit space, the input patterns for AND, OR and XOR transform the hidden units to values corresponding to a point in the regions marked A1, R0 and X0 respectively. 3d-e. Transitions caused by the 0 and 1 input patterns respectively. The 0 and 1 inputs are context sensitive operators. The 0 input causes changes in the hidden unit patterns corresponding to transitions from the state A1 to A0, but does not cause transitions from the other 5 regions. Conversely, a 1 input does not cause the hidden unit patterns to change from the regions A1, A0 or R1, but causes transitions from the regions R0, X1 and X0.

Input operators	*Patterns on the input units*	*Effect on information encoded in the state*
AND	0 1 1	$cf \rightarrow$ AND
OR	1 1 0	$cf \rightarrow$ OR
XOR	1 0 1	$cf \rightarrow$ XOR
1	1 1 1	$x(t) \rightarrow x(t\text{-}1)$ if $cf =$ AND
		1 if $cf =$ OR
		NOT($x(t\text{-}1)$) if $cf =$ XOR
0	0 0 0	$x(t) \rightarrow$ 0 if $cf =$ AND
		$x(t\text{-}1)$ if $cf =$ OR
		$x(t\text{-}1)$ if $cf =$ XOR

Box 1. Operators for the 5 input patterns. The operation performed by each input pattern is described in terms of the effect it has on information encoded by the hidden unit patterns. The first and second columns specify the input operators and their corresponding input patterns. The third column specifies the effect that each input in a sub–sequence has on information encoded in the state, represented as cf, for current function, and $x(t)$ for the last output.

For each input pattern, we plotted all the transitions in hidden unit space resulting from that input projected onto the canonical components used in Figure 1. Figures 3a to 3e show transitions for each of the five input operators. For the three "function" inputs, OR, AND, and XOR, the effect is to collapse the hidden unit patterns to a single region – a particular state. These are relatively context insensitive operations. For the two "argument" inputs, 0 and 1, the effect is sensitive to the context in which the input occurs (i.e., the previous state of the hidden units). A similar analysis of the states themselves focuses on the hidden unit patterns and the information that they must encode in order to compute the three-function task. At each timestep the weights in the network construct a pattern of activation over the hidden units that reduces the structured arguments of a complex function of several arguments by a simpler function of one less argument. This can be represented as follows:

$$G(F, arg1, \dots argn) \rightarrow F(arg1, \dots argn)$$
$$\rightarrow F_{arg1}(arg2, \dots argn)$$
$$\rightarrow F_{arg1arg2}(arg3, \dots argn).$$

This process of replacing structured arguments by a corresponding sequence of simple ones is known as *currying* the input sequence (for a review of curried functions, see Bird and Wadler, 1988). Using this terminology, the pattern of activation in the hidden units is a *curried function* of the entire input sequence up to that time step. The network combines the previous hidden unit patterns (preserved in the context units) with the current input patterns to compute the next curried function in the sequence. Since there are 6 states required by the network, there are 6 classes of equivalent curried functions. Figure 4 shows the transition diagrams for each of the 6 equivalence classes of curried functions from the same simulation shown in Figures 1 and 3.

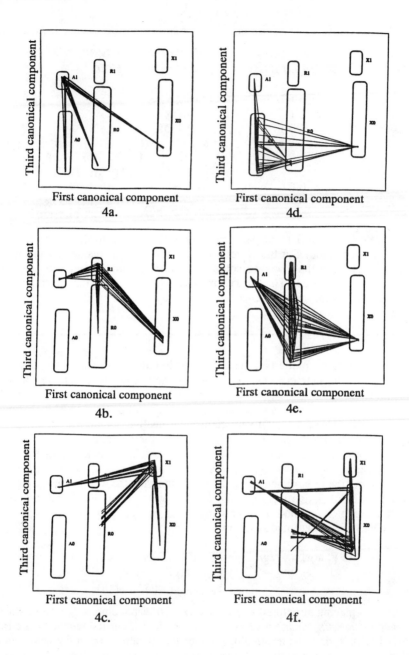

Figure 4. State transitions for each hidden unit pattern, grouped into classes of curried functions, projected onto the first and third canonical components. 4a-f. Transitions from A1, R1, X1, A0, R0 and X0 respectively. Each pattern of activation corresponds to a curried function of the input sequence up to that item in the sequence.

how often the network finds a good solution, five simulations were completed with the above parameters, all started with different sets of random weights, and randomly generated training patterns. Three simulations learnt the training set perfectly (the other two simulations appeared to be converging, but slowly: worst case error less than 1%). On the test data, the results were also good (worst case 7% error).

2.2 ANALYSIS

The hidden unit patterns generated by the training data in the simulations described above were analysed using canonical discriminant analysis (*CDA*, Kotz & Johnson, 1982). Six output classes were specified, corresponding to one class for each output for each function. The output classes were used to compute the first three canonical components of the hidden unit patterns (which are 5–dimensional patterns corresponding to the 5 hidden units). The graph of the first two canonical components (see Figure 1a) shows the hidden unit patterns separated into three tight clusters, corresponding to the sequence type (OR, AND and XOR). The first and third canonical components (see Figure 1b) reveals more of the structure within each class. The six classes of hidden unit patterns are spread across six distinct regions (these correspond to the 6 states of the minimal finite state machine, as shown in Figure 2). The first canonical component separates the hidden unit patterns into sequence type (OR, AND, or XOR, separated across the page). Within each region, the third canonical component separates the outputs into 0's and 1's (separated down the page). Cluster analysis followed by *CDA* on the clusters gave similar results.

3 DISCUSSION

In a network that is dedicated to computing a boolean function such as XOR, it seems obvious that the information for computing the function is in the weights. The simulations described in this paper show that this intuition does not necessarily generalise to other networks. The three-function task requires that the network use the first input in a sequence to select a function which is then applied to subsequent arguments. In general, for any given network, the function that is computed over a given sub–sequence will be specified by the interaction between the weights and the activation pattern.

The function computed by the networks in these simulations can be described in terms of the output of the global function, $O(t) = G(arg1, ..., argt)$, computed by the weights of the network, which is a function of the whole input sequence. An equivalent description can be given in terms of sub–sequences of the input stream, which specify a boolean function over subsequent arguments, $G(F, arg1, ..., argt) = F(arg1, ..., argt)$. Both these levels of description follow the traditional approach of separating functions and data, where the patterns of activity can be described as *either* one or the other.

It appears to us that descriptions based on operators and curried functions provide a promising approach for the integration of representation and process within recurrent networks. For example, in the simulations described by Elman (1990), words can be understood as denoting operators which act on the state of the recurrent network, rather than denoting objects as they do in traditional linguistic theory. The idea of currying can also be applied to feedback from the output layer, for example in the networks developed by Jordan (1986), or to the product units used by Giles et al. (1990).

Acknowledgements

We thank Jeff Elman, Ian Hayes, Julie Stewart and Bill Wilson for many discussions on these ideas, and Simon Dennis and Steven Phillips for developing the canonical discriminant program. This work was supported by grants from the Australian Research Council and A. Bloesch was supported by an Australian Postgraduate Research Award.

References

Bird, R., and Wadler P. (1988). *Introduction to Functional Programming*, Prentice Hall, NY.

Cleeremans, A., Servan-Schreiber, D., and McClelland, J.L. (1989). Finite state automata and simple recurrent networks, *Neural Computation*, 1, 372-381.

Elman, J. (1989). Representation and structure in connectionist models. UCSD CRL Technical Report 8903, August 1989.

Elman, J. (1990). Finding structure in time. *Cognitive Science*, 14, 179-211.

Giles, C. L., Sun, G. Z., Chen, H. H., Lee, Y. C., and Chen, D. (1990). Higher Order Recurrent Networks. In D.S. Touretzky (ed.) Advances in Neural Information Processing Systems 2, Morgan-Kaufmann, San Mateo, Ca., 380-387.

Jordan, M. I. (1986). Serial order: A parallel distributed processing approach. Institute for Cognitive Science, Technical Report 8604. UCSD.

Kotz, S., and Johnson, N.L. (1982). *Encyclopedia of Statistical Sciences*. John Wiley and Sons, NY.

Rumelhart, D.E., Hinton, G.E., and Williams, R.J. (1986). Learning internal representations by error propagation. In D.E. Rumelhart & J.L. McClelland (eds.), *Parallel distributed processing: Explorations in the microstructure of cognition* (Vol. 1, pp. 318-362). Cambridge, MA: MIT Press.

Williams, R. J., and Zipser, D. (1988). A Learning Algorithm for Continually Running Fully Recurrent Neural Networks, Institute for Cognitive Science, Technical Report 8805. UCSD.

Green's Function Method for Fast On-line Learning Algorithm of Recurrent Neural Networks

Guo-Zheng Sun, Hsing-Hen Chen and Yee-Chun Lee
Institute for Advanced Computer Studies
and
Laboratory for Plasma Research,
University of Maryland
College Park, MD 20742

Abstract

The two well known learning algorithms of recurrent neural networks are the back-propagation (Rumelhart & et. al., Werbos) and the forward propagation (Williams and Zipser). The main drawback of back-propagation is its off-line backward path in time for error cumulation. This violates the on-line requirement in many practical applications. Although the forward propagation algorithm can be used in an on-line manner, the annoying drawback is the heavy computation load required to update the high dimensional sensitivity matrix ($O(N^4)$ operations for each time step). Therefore, to develop a fast forward algorithm is a challenging task. In this paper we proposed a forward learning algorithm which is one order faster (only $O(N^3)$ operations for each time step) than the sensitivity matrix algorithm. The basic idea is that instead of integrating the high dimensional sensitivity dynamic equation we solve forward in time for its Green's function to avoid the redundant computations, and then update the weights whenever the error is to be corrected.

A Numerical example for classifying state trajectories using a recurrent network is presented. It substantiated the faster speed of the proposed algorithm than the Williams and Zipser's algorithm.

I. Introduction.

In order to deal with sequential signals, recurrent neural networks are often put forward as a useful model. A particularly pressing issue concerning recurrent networks is the search for an efficient on-line training algorithm. Error back-propagation method (Rumelhart, Hinton, and Williams[1]) was originally proposed to handle feedforward networks. This method can be applied to train recurrent networks if one unfolds the time sequence of mappings into a multilayer feed-forward net, each layer with identical weights. Due to the nature of backward path, it is basically an off-line method. Pineda [2] generalized it to recurrent networks with hidden neurons. However, he is mostly interested in time-independent fixed point type of behaviors. Pearlmutter [3] proposed a scheme to learn temporal trajectories which involves equations to be solved backward in time. It is essentially a generalized version of error back-propagation to the problem of learning a target state trajectory. The viable on-line method to date is the RTRL (Real Time Recurrent Learning) algorithm (Williams and Zipser [4]), which propagates a sen-

333

sitivity matrix forward in time. The main drawback of this algorithm is its high cost of computation. It needs $O(N^4)$ number of operations per time step. Therefore, a faster (less than $O(N^4)$) operations) on-line algorithm appears to be desirable.

Toomarian and Barhen [5] proposed an $O(N^2)$ on-line algorithm. They derived the same equations as Pearlmutter's back-propagation using adjoint-operator approach. They then tried to convert the backward path into a forward path by adding a *Delta* function to its source term. But this is not correct. The problem is not merely because it "precludes straightforward numerical implementation" as they acknowledged later [6]. Even in theory, the result is not correct. The mistake is in their using a not well defined equity of the *Delta* function integration. Briefly speaking, the equity $\int_{t_0}^{t_f} \delta(t - t_f) f(t)\, dt = f(t_f)$ is not right if the function $f(t)$ is discontinuous at $t = t_f$. The value of the left-side integral depends on the distribution of function $f(t)$ and therefore is not uniquely defined. If we deal with the discontinuity carefully by splitting time interval from t_0 to t_f into two segments: t_0 to t_f-ε and t_f-ε to t_f and let $\varepsilon \to 0$, we will find out that adding a *Delta* function to the source term does not affect the basic property of the adjoint equation. Namely, it still has to be solved backward in time.

Recently, Toomarian and Barhen [6] modified their adjoint-operator approach and proposed an alternative $O(N^3)$ on-line training algorithm. Although, in nature, their result is very similar to what we presented in this paper, it will be seen that our approach is more straightforward and can be easily implemented numerically.

Schmidhuber[7] proposed an $O(N^3)$ algorithm which is a combination of back propagation (within each data block of size N) and forward propagation (between blocks). It is therefore not truly an on-line algorithm.

Sun, Chen and Lee [8] studied this problem, using a more general approach - variational approach, in which a constrained optimization problem with Lagrangian multipliers was considered. The dynamic equation of the Lagrangian multiplier was derived, which is exactly the same as adjoint equation[5]. By taking advantage of linearity of this equation an $O(N^3)$ on-line algorithm was derived. But, the numerical implementation of the algorithm, especially the numerical instabilities are not addressed in the paper.

In this paper we will present a new approach to this problem - the Green's function method. The advantages of the this method are the simple mathematical formulation and easy numerical implementation. One numerical example of trajectory classification is presented to substantiate the faster speed of the proposed algorithm. The numerical results are benchmarked with Williams and Zipser's algorithm.

II. Green's Function Approach.

(a) Definition of the Problem

Consider a fully recurrent network with neural activity represented by an N-dimensional vector $\mathbf{x}(t)$. The dynamic equations can be written in general as a set of first order differential equations:

$$\dot{x}(t) = F(x(t), w, I(t)) \tag{1}$$

where w is a matrix representing the set of weights and all other adjustable parameters, $I(t)$ is a vector representing the neuron units clamped by external input signals at time t. For a simple network connected by first order weights the nonlinear function F may look like

$$F(x(t), w, I(t)) = -x(t) + g(w \cdot x) + I(t) \tag{2}$$

where the scaler function $g(u)$ could be, for instance, the *Sigmoid* function $g(u) = 1/(1+e^{-u})$. Suppose that part of the state neurons $\{x_i \mid i \in M\}$ are measurable and part of neurons $\{x_i \mid i \in$

H} are hidden. For the measurable units we may have desired output $\hat{x}(t)$. In order to train the network, an objective functional (or an error measure functional) is often given to be

$$E(x, \hat{x}) = \int_{t_o}^{t_f} e(x(t), \hat{x}(t)) dt \tag{3}$$

where functional E depends on weights w implicitly through the measurable neurons $\{x_i \mid i \in M\}$. A typical error function *is*

$$e(x(t), \hat{x}(t)) = (x(t) - \hat{x}(t))^2 \tag{4}$$

The gradient descent learning is to modify the weights according to

$$\Delta w \propto -\frac{\partial E}{\partial w} = -\int_{t_o}^{t_f} \frac{\partial e}{\partial x} \cdot \frac{\partial x}{\partial w} dt. \tag{5}$$

In order o evaluate the integral in Eq. (5) one needs to know both $\partial e/\partial w$ and $\partial x/\partial w$. The first term can be easily obtained by taking derivative of the given error function $e(x(t), \hat{x}(t))$. For the second term one needs to solve the differential equation

$$\frac{d}{dt}\left(\frac{\partial x}{\partial w}\right) = \frac{\partial F}{\partial x} \cdot \frac{\partial x}{\partial w} + \frac{\partial F}{\partial w} \tag{6}$$

which is easily derived by taking derivative of Eq.(1) with respect to w. The well known forward algorithm of recurrent networks [4] is to solve Equation (6) forward in time and make the weight correction at the end ($t = t_f$) of the input sequence. (This algorithm was developed independently by several researchers, but due to the page limitation we could not refer all related papers and now simply call it Williams and Zipser's algorithm) The on-line learning is to make weight correction whenever an error is to be corrected during the input sequence

$$\Delta w(t) = -\eta \left(\frac{\partial e}{\partial x} \cdot \frac{\partial x}{\partial w}\right) \tag{7}$$

The proof of convergence of on-line learning algorithm will be addressed elsewhere.

The main drawback of this forward algorithm is that it requires $O(N^4)$ operations per time step to update the matrix $\partial x/\partial w$. Our goal of the Green's function approach is to find an on-line algorithm which requires less computation load.

(b). Green's Function Solution

First let us analyze the computational complexity when integrating Eq. (6) directly. Rewrite Eq. (6) as

$$L \cdot \frac{\partial x}{\partial w} = \frac{\partial F}{\partial w} \tag{8}$$

where the linear operator L is defined as $L = \frac{d}{dt} - \frac{\partial F}{\partial x}$

Two types of redundancy will be seen from Eq. (8). First, the operator L does not depend on w explicitly, which means that what we did in solving for $\partial x/\partial w$ is to repeatedly solve the identical differential equation for each components of w. This is redundant. It is especially wasteful when higher order connection weights are used. The second redundancy is in the special form of $\partial F/\partial w$ for neural computations where the same activity function (say, *Sigmoid* function) is used for every neuron, so that

$$\frac{\partial F_k}{\partial w_{ij}} = g'(\sum_l w_{kl} \cdot x_l)\, \delta_{ki}\, x_j \tag{9}$$

where δ_{ki} is the Kronecker delta function. It is seen from Eq. (9) that among N^3 components of this third order tensor most of them, $N^2(N\text{-}1)$, are zero (when $k \neq i$) and need not to be computed repeatedly. In the original forward learning scheme, we did not pay attention to this redundancy.

Our Green's function approach is able to avoid the redundancy by solving for the low dimensional Green's function. And then we construct the solution of Eq. (8) by the dot product of $\partial F/\partial w$ with the Green's function, which can in turn be reduced to a scaler product due to Eq. (9).

The Green's function of the operator L is defined as a dual time tensor function $G(t\text{-}\tau)$ which satisfies the following equation

$$\frac{d}{dt} G(t-\tau) - \frac{\partial F}{\partial x} \cdot G(t-\tau) = \delta(t-\tau) \tag{10}$$

It is well known that, if the solution of Eq. (10) is known, the solution of the original equation Eq. (6) (or (8)) can be constructed using the source term $\partial F/\partial w$ through the integral

$$\frac{\partial x}{\partial w}(t) = \int_{t_o}^{t_f} (G(t-\tau) \cdot \frac{\partial F}{\partial w}(\tau))\, d\tau \tag{11}$$

To find the Green's function solution we first introduce a tensor function $V(t)$ that satisfies the homogeneous form of Eq. (10)

$$\begin{cases} \frac{d}{dt} V(t) - \frac{\partial F}{\partial x} \cdot V(t) = 0 \\ V(t_0) = 1 \end{cases} \tag{12}$$

The solution of Eq. (10) or the Green's function can then be constructed as

$$G(t-\tau) = V(t) \cdot V^1(\tau) H(t-\tau) \tag{13}$$

where $H(t\text{-}\tau)$ is the *Heaviside* function defined as

$$H(t-\tau) = \begin{cases} 1 & t \geq \tau \\ 0 & t < \tau \end{cases}$$

Using the well known equalities

$$\frac{d}{dt} H(t-\tau) = \delta(t-\tau)$$

and $f(t,\tau)\, \delta(t-\tau) = f(t,t)\, \delta(t-\tau)$,

one can easily verify that the constructed Green's function shown in Eq. (13) is correct, that is, it satisfies Eq. (10). Substituting $G(t\text{-}\tau)$ from Eq. (13) into Eq. (11) we obtain the solution of Eq. (6) as,

$$\frac{\partial x}{\partial w}(t) = V(t) \cdot \int_{t_o}^{t} ((V(\tau))^{-1} \cdot \frac{\partial F}{\partial w}(\tau))\, d\tau \tag{14}$$

We note that this formal solution not only satisfies Eq. (6) but also satisfies the required initial condition

$$\frac{\partial x}{\partial w}(t_0) = 0 \, . \tag{15}$$

The "on-line" weight correction at time t is obtained easily from Eq. (5)

$$\delta w = -\eta \frac{\partial e}{\partial x} \cdot \frac{\partial x}{\partial w} = -\eta \left(\frac{\partial e}{\partial x} \cdot V(t) \int_{t_o}^{t} ((V(\tau))^{-1} \cdot \frac{\partial F}{\partial w}(\tau)) \, d\tau \right) \tag{16}$$

(c) Implementation

To implement Eq. (16) numerically we will introduce two auxiliary memories. First, we define $U(t)$ to be the inverse of matrix $V(t)$, i.e. $U(t) = V^{-1}(t)$. It is easy to see that the dynamic equation of $U(t)$ is

$$\begin{cases} \frac{d}{dt} U(t) + U(t) \cdot \frac{\partial F}{\partial x} = 0 \\ U(t_0) = 1 \end{cases} \tag{17}$$

Secondly, we define a third order tensor Π_{ijk} that satisfies

$$\begin{cases} \frac{d\Pi}{dt} = U(t) \cdot \frac{\partial F}{\partial w} \\ \Pi(t_0) = 0 \end{cases} \tag{18}$$

then the weight correction in Eq. (16) becomes

$$\delta w = -\eta (v(t) \cdot \Pi(t)) \tag{19}$$

where the vector $v(t)$ is the solution of the linear equation

$$v(t) \cdot U(t) = \frac{\partial e}{\partial x} \tag{20}$$

In discrete time, Eqs. (17) - (20) become:

$$\begin{cases} U_{ij}(t) = U_{ij}(t-1) + \Delta t \sum_k U_{ik}(t-1) \frac{\partial F_k}{\partial x_j} \\ U_{ij}(0) = \delta_{ij} \end{cases} \tag{21}$$

$$\begin{cases} \Pi_{ijk}(t) = \Pi_{ijk}(t-1) + (\Delta t) U_{ij}(t-1) \frac{\partial F_j}{\partial w_{jk}} \\ \Pi_{ijk}(0) = 0 \end{cases} \tag{22}$$

$$\sum_i v_i(t) \cdot U_{ij}(t) = \frac{\partial e}{\partial x_j} \tag{23}$$

$$\Delta w_{ij} = -\eta \left(\sum_k v_k(t) \Pi_{kij}(t) \right) \tag{24}$$

To summarize the procedure of the Green's function method, we need to simultaneously integrate Eq. (21) and Eq. (22) for $U(t)$ and Π forward in time starting from $U_{ij}(0) = \delta_{ij}$ and $\Pi_{ijk}(0) = 0$. Whenever error message are generated, we shall solve Eq. (23) for $v(t)$ and update weights according to Eq. (24).

The memory size required by this algorithm is simply $N^3 + N^2$ for storing $U(t)$ and $\Pi(t)$.

The speed of the algorithm is analyzed as follows. From Eq. (21) and Eq. (22) we see that the update of $U(t)$ and Π both need N^3 operations per time step. To solve for $v(t)$ and update w, we need also N^3 operations per time step. So, the on-line updating of weights needs totally $4N^3$ operations per time step. This is one order of magnitude faster than the current forward learning scheme.

III Numerical Simulation

We present in this section numerical examples to demonstrate the proposed learning algorithm and benchmark it against Williams&Zipser's algorithm.

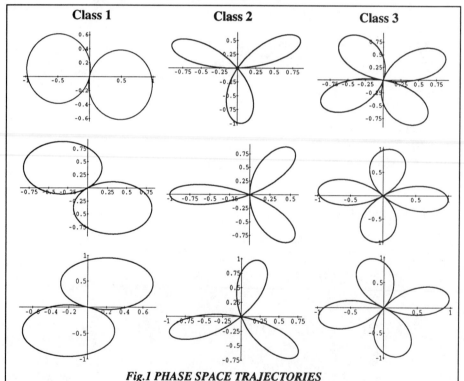

Fig.1 PHASE SPACE TRAJECTORIES
Three different shapes of 2-D trajectory, each is shown in one column with three examples. Recurrent neural networks are trained to recognize the different shapes of trajectory.

We consider the trajectory classification problem. The input data are the time series of two dimensional coordinate pairs $\{x(t), y(t)\}$ sampled along three different types of trajectories in the phase space. The sampling is taken uniformly with $\Delta t = 2\pi/60$. The trajectory equations are

$$\begin{aligned}
x(t) &= \sin(t + \beta)\,|\sin(t)| & x(t) &= \sin(0.5t + \beta)\sin(1.5t) & x(t) &= \sin(t + \beta)\sin(2t) \\
y(t) &= \cos(t + \beta)\,|\sin(t)| & y(t) &= \cos(0.5t + \beta)\sin(1.5t) & y(t) &= \cos(t + \beta)\sin(2t)
\end{aligned}$$

where β is a uniformly distributed random parameter. When β is changed, these trajectories are distorted accordingly. Nine examples (three for each class) are shown in Fig.1. The neural net used here is a fully recurrent first-order network with dynamics

$$S_i(t+1) = S_i(t) + \left(Tanh\left(\sum_{j=1}^{N+6} W_{ij}(S \oplus I)_j \right) \right) \tag{25}$$

where S and I are vectors of state and input neurons, the symbol $\oplus$ represents concatenation, and N is the number of state. Six input neurons are used to represent the normalized vector $\{1, x(t), y(t), x(t)^2, y(t)^2, x(t)y(t)\}$. The neural network structure is shown in Fig. 2.

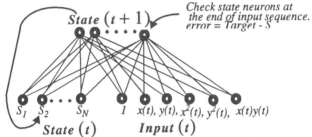

Fig.2 Recurrent Neural Network for Trajectory Classification

For recognition, each trajectory data sequence needs to be fed to the input neurons and the state neurons evolve according to the dynamics in Eq. (25). At the end of input series we check the last three state neurons and classify the input trajectory according to the "winner-take-all" rule. For training, we assign the desired final output for the three trajectory classes to $(1,0,0)$, $(0,1,0)$ and $(0,0,1)$ respectively. Meanwhile, we need to simultaneously integrate Eq. (21) for $U(t)$ and Eq. (22) for Π. At the end, we calculated the error from Eq. (4) and solve Eq. (23) for $v(t)$ using LU decomposition algorithm. Finally, we update weights according to Eq. (24). Since the classification error is generated at the end of input sequence, this learning does not have to be on-line. We present this example only to compare the speeds of the proposed fast algorithm against the Williams and Zipser's. We run the two algorithms for the same number of iterations and compare the CPU time used. The results are shown in Table.1, where in each one iteration we present 150 training patterns, 50 for each class. These patterns are chosen by randomly selecting β values. It is seen that the CPU time ratio is $O(1/N)$, indicating the Green's. function algorithm is one order faster in N.

Another issue to be considered is the error convergent rate (or learning rate, as usually called). Although the two algorithms calculate the same weight correction as in Eq. (7), due to different numerical schemes the outcomes may be different. As the result, the error convergent rates are slightly different even if the same learning rate η is used. In all numerical simulations we have conducted the learning results are very good (in testing, the recognition is perfect, no single misclassification was found). But, during training the error convergence rates are different. The numerical experiments show that the proposed fast algorithm converges slower than the Williams and Zipser's for the small size neural nets but faster for the large size neural net.

Simulation \ Algorithm	Fast Algorithm	Williams&Zipser's	ratio
N = 4 (Number of Iterations = 200)	1607.4	5020.8	1 : 3
N = 8 (Number of Iterations = 50)	1981.7	10807.0	1 : 5
N = 12 (Number of Iterations = 50)	5947.6	45503.0	1 : 8

Table 1. The CPU time (in seconds) comparison, implemented in DEC3100 Workstation, for learning the trajectory classification example.

IV. Conclusion

The Green's function has been used to develop a faster on-line learning algorithm for recurrent neural networks. This algorithm requires $O(N^3)$ operations for each time step, which is one order faster than the Williams and Zipser's algorithm. The memory required is $O(N^3)$.

One feature of this algorithm is its straightforward formula, which can be easily implemented numerically. A numerical example of trajectory classification has been used to demonstrate the speed of this fast algorithm compared to Williams and Zipser's algorithm.

References

[1] D.Rumelhart, G. Hinton, and R. Williams. Learning internal representations by error propagation. In Parallel distributed processing: Vol.I MIT press 1986. P. Werbos, Beyond Regression: New tools for prediction and analysis in the behavior sciences. Ph.D. thesis, Harvard university, 1974.

[2] F. Pineda, Generalization of back-propagation to recurrent neural networks. *Phys. Rev. Letters, 19(59):2229*, 1987.

[3] B. Pearlmutter, Learning state space trajectories in recurrent neural networks. *Neural Computation,1(2):263*, 1989.

[4] R. Williams and D. Zipser, A learning algorithm for continually running fully recurrent neural networks. Tech. Report ICS Report 8805, UCSD, La Jolla, CA 92093, November 1988.

[5] N. Toomarian, J. Barhen and S. Gulati, "Application of Adjoint Operators to Neural Learning", *Appl. Math. Lett., 3(3), 13-18*, 1990.

[6] N. Toomarian and J. Barhen, "Adjoint-Functions and Temporal Learning Algorithms in Neural Networks", *Advances in Neural Information Processing Systems 3*, p. 113-120, Ed. by R. Lippmann, J. Moody and D. Touretzky, Morgan Kaufmann, 1991.

[7] J. H. Schmidhuber, "An $O(N^3)$ Learning Algorithm for Fully Recurrent Networks", Tech Report FKI-151-91, Institut für Informatik, Technische Universität München, May 1991.

[8] Guo-Zheng Sun, Hsing-Hen Chen and Yee-Chun Lee, "A Fast On-line Learning Algorithm for Recurrent Neural Networks", *Proceedings of International Joint Conference on Neural Networks, Seattle, Washington, page II-13*, June 1991.

Dynamically-Adaptive Winner-Take-All Networks

Trent E. Lange
Artificial Intelligence Laboratory
Computer Science Department
University of California, Los Angeles, CA 90024

Abstract

Winner-Take-All (WTA) networks, in which inhibitory interconnections are used to determine the most highly-activated of a pool of units, are an important part of many neural network models. Unfortunately, convergence of normal WTA networks is extremely sensitive to the magnitudes of their weights, which must be hand-tuned and which generally only provide the right amount of inhibition across a relatively small range of initial conditions. This paper presents *Dynamically-Adaptive Winner-Take-All (DAWTA)* networks, which use a regulatory unit to provide the competitive inhibition to the units in the network. The DAWTA regulatory unit dynamically adjusts its level of activation during competition to provide the right amount of inhibition to differentiate between competitors and drive a single winner. This dynamic adaptation allows DAWTA networks to perform the winner-take-all function for nearly any network size or initial condition, using $O(N)$ connections. In addition, the DAWTA regulatory unit can be biased to find the level of inhibition necessary to settle upon the K most highly-activated units, and therefore serve as a K-Winners-Take-All network.

1. INTRODUCTION

Winner-Take-All networks are fixed group of units which compete by mutual inhibition until the unit with the highest initial activation or input level suppresses the activation of all the others. Winner-take-all selection of the most highly-activated unit is an important part of many neural network models (e.g. McClelland and Rumelhart, 1981; Feldman and Ballard, 1982; Kohonen, 1984; Touretzky, 1989; Lange and Dyer, 1989a,b).

Unfortunately, successful convergence in winner-take-all networks is extremely sensitive to the magnitudes of the inhibitory weights between units and other network parameters. For example, a weight value for the mutually-inhibitory connections allowing the most highly-activated unit to suppress the other units in one initial condition (e.g. Figure 1a) may not provide enough inhibition to select a single winner if the initial input activation levels are closer together and/or higher (e.g. Figure 1b). On the other hand, if the compe-

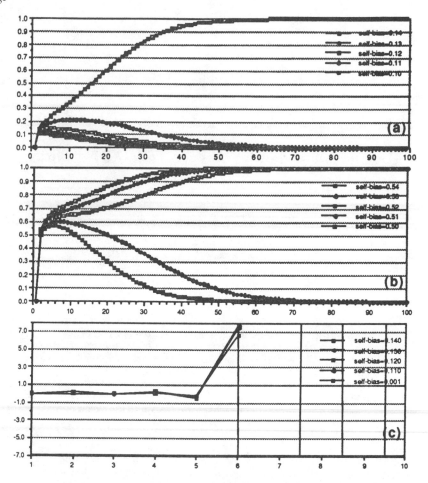

Figure 1. Several plots of activation versus time for different initial conditions in a winner-take-all network in which there is a bidirectional inhibitory connection of weight -0.2 between every pair of units. Unit activation function is that from the interactive activation model of McClelland and Rumelhart (1981). (a) Network in which five units are given an input self bias ranging from 0.10 to 0.14. (b) Network in which five units are given an input self bias ranging from 0.50 to 0.54. Note that the network ended up with three winners because the inhibitory connections of weight -0.2 did not provide enough inhibition to suppress the second and third most-active nodes. (c) Network in which 100 units are given an input self bias ranging from 0.01 to 0.14. The combined activation of all 100 nodes through the inhibitory weight of -0.2 provides far too much inhibition, causing the network to overreact and oscillate wildly

tition involves a larger number of active units, then the same inhibitory weights may provide too much inhibition and either suppress the activations of all units or lead to oscillations (e.g. Figure 1c).

Because of these problems, it is generally necessary to hand-tune network parameters to allow for successful winner-take-all performance in a given neural network architecture having certain expected levels of incoming activations. For complex networks, this can require a detailed mathematical analysis of the model (cf. Touretzky & Hinton, 1988) or a heuristic, computer-assisted trial-and-error search process (cf. Reggia, 1989) to find the values of inhibitory weights, unit thresholds, and other network parameters necessary for clear-cut winner-take-all performance in a given model's input space. In some cases, however, no set of network constant network parameters can be found to handle the range of possible initial conditions a model may be faced with (Barnden, Kankanahalli, and Dharmavaratha, 1990), such as when the numbers of units actually competing in a given network may be two at one time and thousands at another (e.g. Barnden, 1990; Lange, in press).

This paper presents a new variant of winner-take-all networks, the *Dynamically-Adaptive Winner-Take-All (DAWTA)* network. DAWTA networks, using $O(N)$ connections, are able to robustly act as winner-take-all networks for nearly any network initial condition without any hand-tuning of network parameters. In essence, the DAWTA network dynamically "tunes" itself by adjusting the level of inhibition sent to each unit in the network depending upon feedback from the current conditions of the competition. In addition, a biasing activation can be added to the network to allow it to act as a K-Winners-Take-All network (cf. Majani, Erlanson, and Abu-Mostafa, 1989), in which the K most highly-activated units end up active.

2. DYNAMICALLY-ADAPTIVE WTA NETWORKS

The basic idea behind the Dynamically-Adaptive Winner-Take-All mechanism can be described by looking at a version of a winner-take-all network that is functionally equivalent to a normal winner-take-all network but which uses only $O(N)$ connections. Several researchers have pointed out that the $(N^2-N)/2$ bidirectional inhibitory connections (each of weight $-w_I$) normally needed in a winner-take-all network can be replaced by an excitatory self-connection of weight w_I for each unit and a single regulatory unit that sums up the activations of all N units and inhibits them each by that $-w_I$ times that amount (Touretzky & Hinton, 1988; Majani *et al.*, 1989) (see Figure 2).

When viewed in this fashion, the mutually inhibitory connections of winner-take-all networks can be seen as a regulator (i.e. the regulatory unit) that is attempting to provide the right amount of inhibition to the network to allow the winner-to-be unit's activation to grow while suppressing the activations of all others. This is exactly what happens when w_I has been chosen correctly for the activations of the network (as in Figure 1a). However, because the amount of this regulatory inhibition is fixed precisely by that inhibitory weight (i.e. always equal to that weight times the sum of the network activations), there is no way for it to increase when it is not enough (as in Figure 1b) or decrease when it is too much (as in Figure 1c).

2.1. THE DAWTA REGULATORY UNIT

From the point of view of the competing units' inputs, the Dynamically-Adaptive Winner-Take-All network is equivalent to the regulatory-unit simplification of a normal winner-take-all network. Each unit has an excitatory connection to itself and an inhibitory connection from a regulatory unit whose function is to suppress the activations

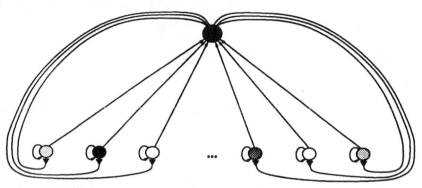

Figure 2. Simplification of a standard WTA network using $O(n)$ connections by introduction of a regulatory unit (top node) that sums up the activations of all network units. Each unit has an excitatory connection to itself and an inhibitory connection of weight $-w_l$ from the regulatory unit. Shading of units (darker = higher) represents their levels of activation at a hypothetical time in the middle of network cycling.

of all but the winning unit[1]. However, the regulatory unit itself, and how it calculates the inhibition it provides to the network, is different.

Whereas the connections to the regulatory unit in a normal winner-take-all network cause it to produce an inhibitory activation (i.e. the sum of the units' activations) that happens to work if its inhibitory weights were set correctly, the structure of connections to the regulatory unit in a dynamically-adaptive winner-take-all network cause it to continually adjust its level of activation until the right amount of inhibition is found, regardless of the network's initial conditions. As the network cycles and the winner-take-all is being performed, the DAWTA regulatory unit's activation inhibits the networks' units, which results in feedback to the regulatory unit that causes it to increase its activation if more inhibition is required to induce a single winner, or decrease its activation if less is required. Accordingly, the DAWTA regulatory unit's activation ($a_R(t)$) now includes its previous activation, and is the following:

$$a_R(t+1) = a_R(t) + \begin{cases} -\Theta & net_R(t+1) \leq -\Theta \\ net_R(t+1) & -\Theta < net_R(t+1) < \Theta \\ \Theta & net_R(t+1) \geq \Theta \end{cases}$$

where $net_R(t+1)$ is the total net input to the regulator at time $t+1$, and Θ is a small constant (typically 0.05) whose purpose is to stop the regulatory unit's activation from rising or falling too rapidly on any given cycle. Figure 3 shows the actual Dynamically-Adaptive Winner-Take-All network. As in Figure 2, the regulatory unit is the unit at the top and the competing units are the the the circular units at the bottom that are inhibited by it and which have connections (of weight w_s) to themselves. However, there are now two

---

[1]As in all winner-take-all networks, the competing units may also have inputs from outside the network that provide the initial activations driving the competition.

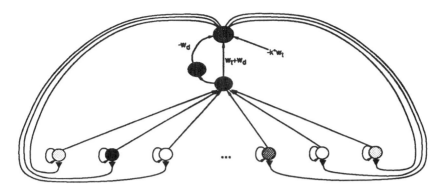

Figure 3. Dynamically-Adaptive Winner-Take-All Network at a hypothetical time in the middle of network cycling. The topmost unit is the DAWTA regulatory unit, whose outgoing connections to all of the competing units at the bottom all have weight -1. The input $-k^*w_d$ is a constant self biasing activation to the regulatory unit whose value determines how many winners it will try to drive. The two middle units are simple linear summation units each having inputs of unit weight that calculate the total activation of the competing units at time t and time t-1, respectively.

intermediate units that calculate the net inputs that increase or decrease the regulatory unit's inhibitory activation depending on the state of the competition. These inputs cause the regulatory unit to receive a net input net_R (t+1) of:

$$net_R(t+1) = (w_t+w_d)o_t(t-1) - w_d o_t(t-2) - kw_t$$

which simplifies to:

$$net_R(t+1) = w_t(o_t(t-1) - k) + w_d(o_t(t-1) - o_t(t-2))$$

where $o_t(t)$ is the total summed output of all of the competing units (calculated by the intermediate units shown), w_t and w_d are constant weights, and k is the number of winners the network is attempting to seek (1 to perform a normal winner-take-all).

The effect of the above activation function and the connections shown in Figure 3 is to apply two different activation pressures on the regulatory unit, each of which combined over time drive the DAWTA regulatory unit's activation to find the right level of inhibition to suppress all but the winning unit. The most important pressure, and the key to the DAWTA regulatory unit's success, is that the regulatory unit's activation increases by a factor of w_t if there is too much activation in the network, and decreases by a corresponding factor if there is not enough activation in the network. This is the result of the term $w_t(o_t(t-1) - k)$ in its net input function, which simplifies to $w_t(o_t(t-1) - 1)$ when k equals 1. The "right amount" of total activation in the network is simply the total summed activation of the goal state, i.e. the winner-take-all network state in which there is one active unit (having activation 1) and in which all other competing units have been driven down to an activation of 0, leaving the total network activation $o_t(t)$ equal to 1. The factor $w_t(o_t(t-1) - 1)$ of the regulatory input's net input will therefore tend to increase the regulatory unit's activation if there are too many units active in the network (e.g. if there are three units with activity 0.7, 0.5, and 0.3, since the total output $o_t(t)$ will be 1.5), to decrease its activation if there is not enough totally active units in the network (e.g. one unit with activation 0.2 and the rest with activation 0.0), and to leave its activation unchanged if the activation is the same as the final goal activation. Note that any temporary coincidences in which the total network activation sums to 1 but which is not the final winner-take-all state (e.g. when one unit has activation 0.6 and another has activation 0.4) will be broken by the competing units themselves, since the winning unit's activation will always rise more quickly than the loser's just by its own activation function (e.g. that of McClelland and Rumelhart, 1981).

The other pressure on the DAWTA regulatory unit, from the $w_d(o_t(t-1) - o_t(t-2))$ term of $net_R(t+1)$, is to tend to decrease the regulator's activation if the overall network activation is falling too rapidly, or to increase it if the overall network activation is rising too rapidly. This is essentially a dampening term to avoid oscillations in the network in the early stages of the winner-take-all, in which there may be many active units whose activations are falling rapidly (due inhibition from the regulatory unit), but in which the total network activation is still above the final goal activation. As can be seen, this second term of the regulatory unit's net input will also sum to 0 and therefore leave the regulatory unit's activation unchanged when the goal state of the network has been reached, since the total activation of the network in the winner-take-all state will remain constant.

All of the weights and connections of the DAWTA network are constant parameters that are the same for any size network or set of initial network conditions. Typically we have used $w_t = 0.025$ and $w_d = 0.5$. The actual values are not critical, as long as $w_d \gg w_s$, which assures that w_d is high enough to dampen the rapid rise or fall in total network activation sometimes caused by the direct pressure of w_t. The value of the regulatory unit's self bias term kw_t that sets the goal total network activation that the regulatory unit attempts to reach is simply determined simply by k, the number of winners desired (1 for a normal winner-take-all network), and w_t.

3. RESULTS

Dynamically-adaptive winner-take-all networks have been tested in the DESCARTES connectionist simulator (Lange, 1990) and used in our connectionist model of short-term sequential memory (Lange, in press). Figures 4a-c show the plots of activation versus time in networks given the same initial conditions as those of the normal winner-take-all network shown in Figures 1a-c. Note that in each case the regulatory unit's activation starts off at zero and increases until it reaches a level that provides sufficient inhibition to start driving the winner-take-all. So whereas the inhibitory weights of -0.2 that worked for inputs ranging from 0.10 to 0.14 in the winner-take-all network in Figure 1a could not provide enough inhibition to drive a single winner when the inputs were over 0.5 (Figure 1b), the DAWTA regulatory unit simply increases its activation level until the inhibition it provides is sufficient to start suppressing the eventual losers (Figures 4a and 4b). As can also be seen in the figures, the activation of the regulatory unit tends to vary over time with different feedback from the network in a process that maximizes differentiation between units while assuring that the group of remaining potential winners stays active and are not over-inhibited.

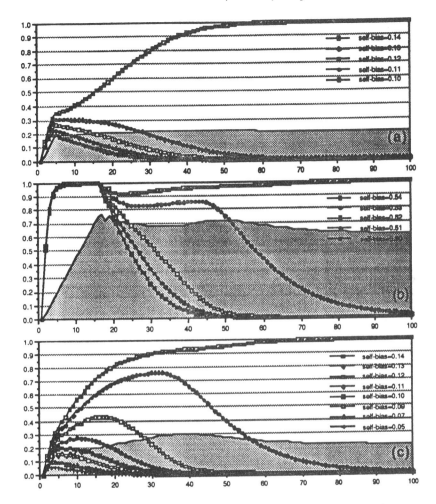

Figure 4. Plots of activation versus time in a dynamically-adaptive winner-take-all network given the same activation functions and initial conditions of the winner-take-all plots in Figure 1. The grey background plot shows the activation level of the regulatory unit. (a) With five units activated with self-biases from 0.10 to 0.14. (b) With five units activated with self-biases from 0.50 to 0.54. (c) With 100 units activated with self-biases from 0.01 to 0.14

Finally, though there is not space to show the graphic results here, the same DAWTA networks have been simulated to drive a successful winner-take-all within 200 cycles on networks ranging in size from 2 to 10,000 units and on initial conditions where the winning unit has an input of 0.000001 to initial conditions where the winning unit has an input of 0.999, without tuning the network in any way. The same networks have also been successfully simulated to act as K-winner-take-all networks (i.e. to select the K most active units) by simply setting the desired value for k in the DAWTA's self bias term kw_d.

4. CONCLUSIONS

We have presented Dynamically-Adaptive Winner-Take-All networks, which use $O(N)$ connections to perform the winner-take-all function. Unlike normal winner-take-all networks, DAWTA networks are able to select the most highly-activated unit out of a group of units for nearly any network size and initial condition without tuning any network parameters. They are able to do so because the inhibition that drives the winner-take-all network is provided by a regulatory-unit that is constantly getting feedback from the state of the network and dynamically adjusting its level to provide the right amount of inhibition to differentiate the winning unit from the losers. An important side-feature of this dynamically-adaptive inhibition approach is that it can be biased to select the K most highly-activated units, and therefore serve as a K-winners-take-all network.

References

Barnden, J. (1990). The power of some unusual connectionist data-structuring techniques. In J. A. Barnden and J. B. Pollack (Eds.), *Advances in connectionist and neural computation theory*, Norwood, NJ: Ablex.

Barnden, J., Kankanahalli, S., Dharmavaratha, D. (1990). Winner-take-all networks: Time-based versus activation-based mechanisms for various selection tasks. *Proceedings of the IEEE International Symposium on Circuits and Systems*, New Orleans, LA.

Feldman, J. A. & Ballard, D. H. (1982). Connectionist models and their properties. *Cognitive Science, 6*, 205-254.

Kohonen, T. (1984). *Self-organization and associative memory*. New York: Springer-Verlag, Berlin.

Lange, T. (1990). Simulation of heterogeneous neural networks on serial and parallel machines. *Parallel Computing, 14*, 287-303.

Lange, T. (in press). Hybrid connectionist models: Temporary bridges over the gap between the symbolic and the subsymbolic. To appear in J. Dinsmore (ed.), *Closing the Gap: Symbolic vs. Subsymbolic Processing*. Hillsdale, NJ: Lawrence Erlbaum Associates.

Lange, T. & Dyer, M. G. (1989a). Dynamic, non-local role-bindings and inferencing in a localist network for natural language understanding. In David S. Touretzky, editor, *Advances in Neural Information Processing Systems I*, p. 545-552, Morgan Kaufmann, San Mateo, CA.

Lange, T. & Dyer, M. G. (1989b). High-level inferencing in a connectionist network. *Connection Science, 1 (2)*, 181-217.

Majani, E., Erlanson, R. & Abu-Mostafa, Y. (1989). On the k-winners-take-all network. In David S. Touretzky, editor, *Advances in Neural Information Processing Systems I*, p. 634-642, Morgan Kaufmann, San Mateo, CA.

McClelland, J. L., & Rumelhart, D. E. (1981). An interactive activation model of context effects in letter perception: Part 1. An account of basic findings. *Psychological Review, 88*, 375-407.

Reggia, J. A. (1989). Methods for deriving competitive activation mechanisms. *Proceedings of the First Annual International Joint Conference on Neural Networks*.

Touretzky, D. (1989). Analyzing the energy landscapes of distributed winner-take-all networks (1989). In David S. Touretzky, editor, *Advances in Neural Information Processing Systems I*, p. 626-633, Morgan Kaufmann, San Mateo, CA.

Touretzky, D., & Hinton, G. (1988). A distributed connectionist production system. *Cognitive Science, 12*, 423-466.

PART VII

VISION

Information Processing to Create Eye Movements

David A. Robinson
Departments of Ophthalmology
and Biomedical Engineering
The Johns Hopkins University
School of Medicine
Baltimore, MD 21205

ABSTRACT

Because eye muscles never cocontract and do not deal with external loads, one can write an equation that relates motoneuron firing rate to eye position and velocity - a very uncommon situation in the CNS. The semicircular canals transduce head velocity in a linear manner by using a high background discharge rate, imparting linearity to the premotor circuits that generate eye movements. This has allowed deducing some of the signal processing involved, including a neural network that integrates. These ideas are often summarized by block diagrams. Unfortunately, they are of little value in describing the behavior of single neurons - a finding supported by neural network models.

1 INTRODUCTION

The neural networks in our studies are quite simple. They differ from other applications in that they attempt to model real neural subdivisions of the oculomotor system which have been extensively studied with microelectrodes. Thus, we can ask the extent to which neural networks succeed in describing the behavior of hidden units that is already known. A major benefit of using neural networks in the oculomotor system is to illustrate clearly the shortcomings of block diagram models which tell one very little about what one may expect if one pokes a microelectrode inside one of its boxes. Conversely, single unit behavior is so loosely coupled to system behavior that, although the simplicity of the oculomotor system allows the relationships to be understood, one fears that, in a more complicated system, the behavior of single (hidden) units will give

351

little information about what a system is trying to do, never mind how.

2 SIMPLIFICATIONS IN OCULOMOTOR CONTROL

Because it is impossible to cocontract our eye muscles and because their viscoelastic load never varies, it is possible to write an equation that uniquely relates the discharge rates of their motoneurons and the position of the load (eye position). This cannot be done in the case of, for example, limb muscles. Moreover, this system is well-approximated by a first-order, linear differential equation. Linearity comes about from the design of the semicircular canals, the origin of the vestibulo-ocular reflex (VOR). This reflex creates eye movements that compensate for head movements to stabilize the eyes in space for clear vision. The canals primarily transduce head velocity, neurally encoded into the discharge rates of its afferents. These rates modulate above and below a high background rate (typically 100 spikes/sec) that keeps them well away from cutoff and provides a wide linear range. The core of this reflex is only three neurons long and the canals impose their properties - linear modulation around a high background rate - onto all down-stream neurons including the motoneurons.

In addition to linearity, the functions of the various oculomotor subsystems are clear. There is no messy stretch reflex, the muscle fibers are straight and parallel, and there is only one "joint." All these features combine to help us understand the premotor organization of oculomotor signals in the caudal pons, a system that has enjoyed much block-diagram modelling and now, neural network modelling.

3 DISTRIBUTION OF OCULOMOTOR SIGNALS

The first application of neural networks to the oculomotor system was a study of Anastasio and Robinson (1989). The problem addressed concerned the convergence of diverse oculomotor signals in the caudal pons. There are three major oculomotor subsystems: the VOR; the saccadic system that causes the eyes to jump rapidly from one target to another; and the smooth pursuit system that allows the eyes to track a moving target. Each appears in the caudal pons as a velocity command. The canals, via the vestibular nuclei, provide an eye-velocity command, E_v, for compensatory vestibular eye movements. Burst neurons in the nearby pontine reticular formation provide a signal, E_s, for the desired eye velocity for a saccade. Purkinje cells in the cerebellum carry an eye-velocity signal, E_p, for pursuit eye movements. Thus, three eye-velocity commands converge in the region of the motoneurons.

When one records from cells in this region one finds a discharge rate R of:

$$R \simeq R_o + r_p \dot{E}_p + r_v \dot{E}_v + r_s \dot{E}_s \qquad (1)$$

where R_o is the high background rate previously described and r_p, r_v and r_s are coefficients that can assume any values, in a seemingly random way, for any one neuron (e.g. Tomlinson and Robinson, 1984). Now a block-diagram model need show only the three velocity commands converging on the motoneurons and would not suggest the existence of neurons carrying complicated signals like that of Equ. (1). On the other hand, such behavior has a nice, messy, biological flavor. Somehow, it would seem odd if such signals did not exist. What is clearly happening is that the signals E_p, E_v and E_s

are being distributed over the interneurons and then reassembled in the correct amount on the motoneurons. This is just a simple, specific example of distributed parallel processing in the nervous system.

A neural network model is merely an explicit statement of such a distribution. Initial randomization of the synaptic weights followed by error-driven learning creates hidden units that conform to Equ. (1). We concluded that a neural network model was entirely appropriate for this neural system. This exercise also brought home, although in a simple way, the obvious, but often overlooked, message that block-diagram models can be misleading about how their conceptual functions are realized by neurons.

We next examined distribution of the spatial properties of the interneurons of the VOR (Anastasio and Robinson, 1990). We used only the vertical VOR to keep things simple. The inputs were the primary afferents of the four vertical semicircular canals that sense head rotations in all combinations of pitch and roll. The output layer was the four motoneurons of the vertical recti and oblique muscles that move the eye vertically and in cyclotorsion. The model was trained to perform compensatory eye movements in all combinations of pitch and roll.

The sensitivity axis is that axis around which rotation of the head or eye produces maximum modulation in discharge rate. The sensitivity axis of a canal unit is perpendicular to the plane in which the canal lies. That of a motoneuron is that axis around which its muscle will rotate the eye. What were the sensitivity axes of the hidden units?

A block diagram of the spatial manipulations of the VOR consists of matrices. The geometry of the canals can be described by a 3 x 3 matrix that converts a head-velocity vector into its neurally encoded representation on canal nerves. The geometry of the muscles can be described as another matrix that converts the neurally-encoded motoneuron vector into a physical eye-rotation vector. The brain-stem matrix describes how the canal neurons must project to the motoneurons (Robinson, 1982). In this scheme, interneurons would have only fixed sensitivity axes laying somewhere between that of a canal unit and a motoneuron. In our model, however, sensitivity axes are distributed in the network; those of the hidden units point in a variety of directions. This has also been confirmed by microelectrode recordings (Fukushima et al., 1990). Thus, spatial aspects of transformations, just like temporal aspects, are distributed over the interneurons.

Again, block-diagrams, in this case in the form of a matrix, are misleading about what one will find with a microelectrode. Again, recording from single units tells one little about what a network is trying to do. There is much talk in motor physiology about coordinate systems and transformations from one to another. The question is asked "What coordinate system is this neuron working in?" In this example, individual hidden units do not behave as if they belonged to any coordinate system and this raises the problem of whether this is really a meaningful question.

4 THE NEURAL INTEGRATOR

Muscles are largely position actuators; against a constant load, position is proportional to innervation.   The motoneurons of the extraocular muscles also need a signal proportional to desired eye position as well as velocity. Since eye-movement commands enter the caudal pons as eye-velocity commands, the necessary eye-position command is obtained by integrating the velocity signals (see Robinson, 1989, for a review). The location of the neural network has been discovered in the caudal pons and it is intriguing to speculate how it might work. Hardwired networks, based on positive feedback, have been proposed utilizing lateral inhibition (Cannon et al., 1983) and more recently a learning neural network (dynamic) has been proposed for the VOR (Arnold and Robinson, 1991). The hidden units are freely connected, the input is from two canal units in push-pull, the output is two motoneurons also in push-pull, which operate on the plant transfer function, $1/(sT_e + 1)$, (T_e is the plant time constant), to create an eye position which should be the time integral of the input head velocity. The error is retinal image slip (the difference between actual and ideal eye velocity). Its rms value over a trial interval is used to change synaptic weights in a steepest descent method until the error is negligible.   To compensate the plant lag, the network must produce a combination output of eye velocity plus its integral, eye position, and these two signals, with various weights, are seen on all hidden units which, thus, look remarkably like the integrator neurons that we record from.

This exercise raises several issues. The block-diagram model of this network is a box marked $1/s$ in parallel with the direct velocity feedforward path given the gain T_e. The parallel combination is $(sT_e + 1)/s$. The zero cancels the pole of the plant leaving $1/s$, so that eye position is the perfect integral of head velocity. While such a diagram is conceptually very useful in diagnosing disorders (Zee and Robinson, 1979), it contains no hint of how neurons might effect integration and so is useless in this regard. Moreover, Galiana and Outerbridge (1984) have pointed out, although in a more complex context, that a direct feedforward path of gain T_e with a positive feedback path around it containing a model of the plant, produces exactly the same transfer function.   Should we worry about which is correct - feedforward or feedback? Perhaps we should, but note that the neural network model of the integrator just described contains both feedback and feedforward pathways and relies on positive feedback.   There is a suspicion that the latter network may subsume both block diagrams making questions about which is correct irrelevant. One thing is certain, at this level of organization, so close to the neuron level, block-diagrams, while having conceptual value, are not only useless but can be misleading if one is interested in describing real neural networks.

Finally, how does one test a model network such as that proposed for the neural integrator? It involves the microcircuitry with which small sets of circumscribed cells talk to each other and process signals. The technology is not yet available to allow us to answer this question. I know of no real, successful examples. This, I believe, is a true roadblock in neurophysiology. If we cannot solve it, we must forever be content to describe what cell groups do but not how they do it.

Acknowledgements
This research is supported by Grant 5 R37 EY00598 from the National Eye Institute of the National Institutes of Health.

References

T.J. Anastasio & D.A. Robinson. (1989) The distributed representation of vestibulo-ocular signals by brain-stem neurons. *Biol. Cybern.*, **61**:79-88.

T.J. Anastasio & D.A. Robinson. (1990) Distributed parallel processing in the vertical vestibulo-ocular reflex: Learning networks compared to tensor theory. *Biol. Cybern.*, **63**:161-167.

D.B. Arnold & D.A. Robinson. (1991) A learning network model of the neural integrator of the oculomotor system. *Biol. Cybern.*, **64**:447-454.

S.C. Cannon, D.A. Robinson & S. Shamma. (1983) A proposed neural network for the integrator of the oculomotor system. *Biol. Cybern.*, **49**:127-136.

K. Fukushima, S.I. Perlmutter, J.F. Baker & B.W. Peterson. (1990) Spatial properties of second-order vestibulo-ocular relay neurons in the alert cat. *Exp. Brain Res.*, **81**:462-478.

H.L. Galiana & J.S. Outerbridge. (1984) A bilateral model for central neural pathways in vestibuloocular reflex. *J. Neurophysiol.*, **51**:210-241.

D.A. Robinson. (1982) The use of matrices in analyzing the three-dimensional behavior of the vestibulo-ocular reflex. *Biol. Cybern.*, **46**:53-66.

D.A. Robinson. (1989) Integrating with neurons. *Ann. Rev. Neurosci.*, **12**:33-45.

R.D. Tomlinson & D.A. Robinson. (1984) Signals in vestibular nucleus mediating vertical eye movements in the monkey. *J. Neurophysiol.*, **51**:1121-1136.

D.S. Zee & D.A. Robinson. (1979) Clinical applications of oculomotor models. In H.S. Thompson (ed.), *Topics in Neuro-Ophthalmology*, 266-285. Baltimore, MD: Williams & Wilkins.

Decoding of Neuronal Signals in Visual Pattern Recognition

Emad N Eskandar
Laboratory of Neuropsychology
National Institute of Mental Health
Bethesda MD 20892 USA

Barry J Richmond
Laboratory of Neuropsychology
National Institute of Mental Health
Bethesda MD 20892 USA

John A Hertz
NORDITA
Blegdamsvej 17
DK-2100 Copenhagen Ø, Denmark

Lance M Optican
Laboratory of Sensorimotor Research
National Eye Institute
Bethesda MD 20892 USA

Troels Kjær
NORDITA
Blegdamsvej 17
DK-2100 Copenhagen Ø, Denmark

Abstract

We have investigated the properties of neurons in inferior temporal (IT) cortex in monkeys performing a pattern matching task. Simple back-propagation networks were trained to discriminate the various stimulus conditions on the basis of the measured neuronal signal. We also trained networks to predict the neuronal response waveforms from the spatial patterns of the stimuli. The results indicate that IT neurons convey temporally encoded information about both current and remembered patterns, as well as about their behavioral context.

1   INTRODUCTION

Anatomical and neurophysiological studies suggest that there is a cortical pathway specialized for visual object recognition, beginning in the primary visual cortex and ending in the inferior temporal (IT) cortex (Ungerleider and Mishkin, 1982). Studies of IT neurons in awake behaving monkeys have found that visually elicited responses depend on the pattern of the stimulus and on the behavioral context of the stimulus presentation (Richmond and Sato, 1987; Miller et al, 1991). Until now, however, no attempt had been made to quantify the temporal pattern of firing in the context of a behaviorally complex task such as pattern recognition.

Our goal was to examine the information present in IT neurons about visual stimuli and their behavioral context. We explicitly allowed for the possibility that this information was encoded in the temporal pattern of the response. To decode the responses, we used simple feed-forward networks trained by back propagation.

In work reported elsewhere (Eskandar et al, 1991) this information is calculated another way, with similar results.

2   THE EXPERIMENT

Two monkeys were trained to perform a sequential nonmatch to sample task using a complete set of 32 black-and-white patterns based on 2-D Walsh functions. While the monkey fixated and grasped a bar, a sample pattern appeared for 352 msecs; after a pause of 500 msecs a test stimulus appeared for 352 msecs. The monkey indicated whether the test stimulus failed to match the sample stimulus by releasing the bar. (If the test matched the stimulus, the monkey waited for a third stimulus, different from the sample, before releasing the bar; see Fig. 1.)

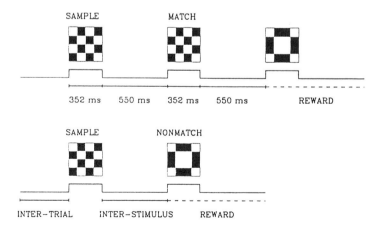

Figure 1: The nonmatch–to–sample task.

The type of trial (match or nonmatch) and the pairings of sample stimuli with nonmatch stimuli were selected randomly. A single experiment usually contained several thousand trials; thus each of the 32 patterns appeared repeatedly under the three conditions (sample, match, and nonmatch). Single neuron recordings from IT cortex were carried out while the monkeys were performing the task.

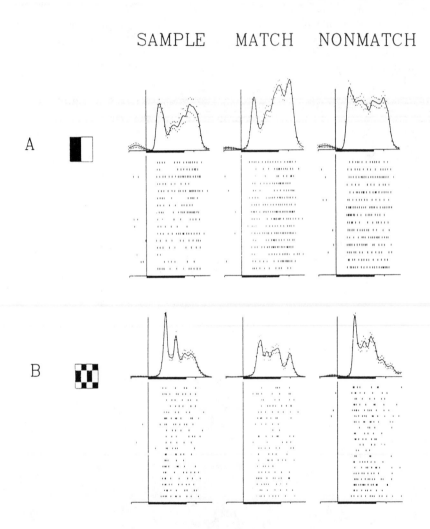

Figure 2: Responses produced by 2 stimuli under 3 behavioural conditions.

Fig. 2 shows the neuronal signals produced by two different stimulus patterns in the three behavioural conditions: sample, match and nonmatch. The lower parts of the figure show single-trial spike trains, while the upper parts show the effective time-dependent firing probabilities, inferred from the spike trains by convolving each spike with a Gaussian kernel, adding these up for each trial and averaging the resulting continuous signals over trials. It is evident that for a given stimulus pattern the average signals produced in different behavioural conditions are different. In what follows, we proceed further to show that there is information about behavioural condition in the signal produced *in a single trial*. We will compute its average value explicitly.

3   DECODING NETWORKS

To compute this information we trained networks to decode the measured signal. The form of the network is shown in Fig. 3.

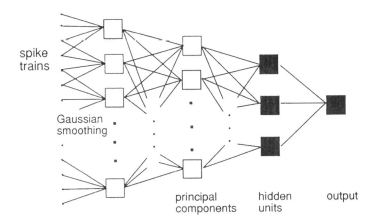

Figure 3: Network to decode neuronal signals for information about behavioural condition.

The first two layers of the network shown preprocess the spike trains as follows: We begin with the spikes measured in an interval starting 90 msec after the stimulus onset and lasting 256 msec. First each spike is convolved with a Gaussian kernel to produce a continuous signal. This signal is sampled at 4-msec intervals, giving a 64-dimensional input vector. In the second step this input vector is compressed by throwing out all but a small number of its principal components (PC's). The PC basis was obtained by diagonalizing the 64×64 covariance matrix of the inputs computed over all trials in the experiment. The remaining PC's are then the input to the rest of the network, which is a standard one with one further hidden layer. Earlier work showed that the first five PC's transmit most of the pattern information in a neuronal response (Richmond et al, 1987). Furthermore, the first PC is highly correlated with the spike count. Thus, our subsequent analysis was either on the first PC alone, as a measure of spike count, or on the first five PC's, as a measure that incorporates temporal modulation.

We trained the networks to make pairwise discriminations between responses measured under different conditions (sample-match, sample-nonmatch, or match-nonmatch). Thus there is a single output unit, and the target is a 1 or 0 according to the behavioural condition under which that spike train was measured.

The final two layers of the network were trained by standard backpropagation of errors for the cross-entropy cost function

$$E = \sum_{\mu} \left\{ T^{\mu} \log \left[\frac{T^{\mu}}{O(\mathbf{x}^{\mu})} \right] + (1 - T^{\mu}) \log \left[\frac{1 - T^{\mu}}{1 - O(\mathbf{x}^{\mu})} \right] \right\}, \tag{1}$$

where T^{μ} is the target and O^{μ} the network output produced by the input vector $\mathbf{x}^{\mu}$ for training example μ. The output of the network with the weights that result from this training is then the optimal estimate (given the chosen architecture) of the probability of a behavioural condition, given the measured neuronal signal used as input. The number of hidden units was adjusted to minimize the generalization error, which was computed on one quarter of the data that was reserved for this purpose.

We then calculated the mean equivocation,

$$\epsilon = -\langle O(\mathbf{x}) \log(O(\mathbf{x}) + [1 - O(\mathbf{x})] \log[1 - O(\mathbf{x})] \rangle_{\mathbf{x}}, \tag{2}$$

where $O(\mathbf{x})$ is the value of the output unit for input $\mathbf{x}$ and the average is over all inputs. (We calculated this by averagng over the test or training sets; the results were not sensitive to which one we chose.) The equivocation is a measure of the neuron's uncertainty with respect to a given discrimination. From it we can compute the transmitted information

$$I = I_{a\ priori} - \epsilon = 1 - \epsilon. \tag{3}$$

The last equality follows because in our data sets the two conditions always occur equally often.

It is evident from Fig. 2 that if we already know that our signal is produced by a particular stimulus pattern, the discrimination of the behavioural condition will be easier than if we do not possess this *a priori* knowledge. This is because the signal varies with stimulus as well as behavioural condition (more strongly, in fact), and the dependence on the latter has to be sorted out from that on the former. To get an idea of the effect of this "distraction", we performed 4 separate calculations for each of the 3 behavioural-condition discriminations, using 1, 4, 8, and all 32 stimulus patterns, respectively.

The results are summarized in Fig. 4, which shows the transmitted information about the 3 different behavioural-condition discriminations at the various levels of distraction, averaged over 5 cells. It also indicates how much of the transmitted information in each case is contained in the spike count alone (i.e. the first PC of the signal).

It is apparent that measurable information about behavioural condition is present in a single neuronal response, even in the total absence of *a priori* information about the stimulus pattern. It is also evident that most of this information is contained in

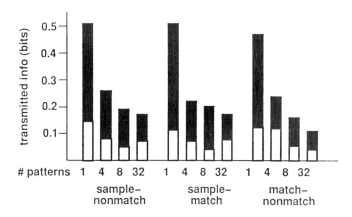

Figure 4: Transmitted information for the three behavioural discriminations with different numbers of patterns. The lower white region on each bar shows the information transmitted in the first PC alone.

the time-dependence of the firing: the information contained in the first PC of the signal is significantly less (paired t-test $p < 0.001$) and was barely out of the noise.

A finite data set can lead to a biased estimate of the transmitted information (Optican et al, 1991). In order to control for this we made a preliminary study of the dependence of the calculated equivocation on training set size. We varied the number of trials available to the network in a range (64 - 1024) for one pair of discriminations (sample vs. nonmatch). The calculated apparent equivocation increased with the sample size N, indicating a small-sample bias. The best correlation (Pearson $r = -0.86$) was obtained with a fit of the form:

$$\epsilon(N) = \epsilon_\infty - cN^{-1/2} \quad (c > 0). \tag{4}$$

This gives us a systematic way to estimate the small-sample bias and thus provide an improved estimate ϵ_∞ of the true equivocation. Details will be reported elsewhere.

4   PREDICTING NEURONAL RESPONSES

In a second set of analyses, we examined the neuronal encoding of both current and recalled patterns. The networks were trained to predict the neuronal response (as represented by its first 5 PC's) from the spatial pattern of the current nonmatch stimulus, that of the immediately preceding sample stimulus, or both. The inputs were the pixel values of the patterns.

The network is shown in Fig. 5. In order to avoid having different architectures for predictions from one and two input patterns, we always used a number of input units equal to twice the number of pixels in the input. In the case where the prediction was to be made on the basis of both previous and current patterns, each pattern was fed into half the input units. For prediction from just one pattern (either the current or previous one), the single input pixel array was loaded separately onto both halves of the input array. As in the previous analyses, the number of hidden units was fixed by testing on a quarter of the data held out of the training set for this purpose.

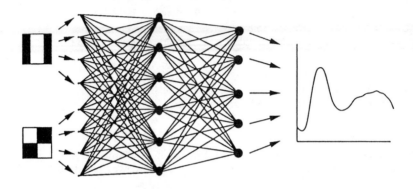

Figure 5: Network for predicting neuronal responses from the stimulus. The inputs are pixel values of the stimuli (see text), and the targets are the first 5 PC's of the measured response.

We performed this analysis on data from 6 neurons. Not surprisingly, the predicted waveforms were better when the input was the current pattern (normalized mean square error (mse) = 0.482) than when it was the previous pattern (mse = 0.589). However, the best prediction was obtained when the input reflected both the current and previous patterns (mse = 0.422). Thus the neurons we analyzed conveyed information about both remembered and current stimuli.

5   CONCLUSION

The results presented here demonstrate the utility of connectionist networks in analyzing neuronal information processing. We have shown that temporally modulated responses in IT cortical neurons convey information about both spatial patterns and behavioral context. The responses also convey information about the patterns of remembered stimuli. Based on these results, we hypothesize that inferior temporal neurons play a role in comparing visual patterns with those presented at an earlier time.

Acknowledgements

This work was supported by NATO through Collaborative Research Grant CRG 900189. EE received support from the Howard Hughes Medical Institute as an NIH Research Scholar.

References

E N Eskandar et al (1991): Inferior temporal neurons convey information about stimulus patterns and their behavioral relevance, *Soc Neurosci Abstr* **17** 443; Role of inferior temporal neurons in visual memory, submitted to *J Neurophysiol.*

E K Miller et al (1991): A neural mechanism for working and recognition memory in inferior temporal cortex, *Science* **253**

L M Optican et al (1991): Unbiased measures of transmitted information and channel capacity from multivariate neuronal data, *Biol Cybernetics* **65** 305-310.

B J Richmond and T Sato (1987): Enhancement of inferior temporal neurons during visual discrimination, *J NeurophysioL* **56** 1292-1306.

B J Richmond et al (1987): Temporal encoding of two-dimensional patterns by single units in primate inferior temporal cortex, *J Neurophysiol* **57** 132-178.

L G Ungerleider and M Mishkin (1982): Two cortical visual systems, in *Analysis of Visual Behavior*, ed. D J Ingle, M A Goodale and R J W Mansfield, pp 549-586. Cambridge: MIT Press.

Learning How To Teach
or
Selecting Minimal Surface Data

Davi Geiger
Siemens Corporate Research, Inc
755 College Rd. East
Princeton, NJ 08540
USA

Ricardo A. Marques Pereira
Dipartimento di Informatica
Universita di Trento
Via Inama 7, Trento, TN 38100
ITALY

Abstract

Learning a map from an input set to an output set is similar to the problem of reconstructing hypersurfaces from sparse data (Poggio and Girosi, 1990). In this framework, we discuss the problem of automatically selecting "minimal" surface data. The objective is to be able to approximately reconstruct the surface from the selected sparse data. We show that this problem is equivalent to the one of compressing information by data removal and the one of learning how to teach. Our key step is to introduce a process that statistically selects the data according to the model. During the process of data selection (learning how to teach) our system (teacher) is capable of predicting the new surface, the approximated one provided by the selected data. We concentrate on piecewise smooth surfaces, e.g. images, and use mean field techniques to obtain a deterministic network that is shown to compress image data.

1 Learning and surface reconstruction

Given a dense input data that represents a hypersurface, how could we automatically select *very* few data points such as to be able to use these fewer data points (sparse data) to approximately reconstruct the hypersurface ?

We will be using the term surface to refer to hypersurface (surface in multidimen-

364

sions) throughout the paper.

It has been shown (Poggio and Girosi, 1990) that the problem of reconstructing a surface from sparse and noisy data is equivalent to the problem of learning from examples. For instance, to learn how to add numbers can be cast as finding the map from $X = \{pair\ of\ numbers\}$ to $F = \{sum\}$ from a set of noisy examples. The surface is $F(X)$ and the sparse and noisy data are the set of N examples $\{(x_i, d_i)\}$, where $i = 0, 1, ..., N$ and $x_i = (a_i, b_i) \in X$, such that $a_i + b_i = d_i + \eta_i$ (η_i being the noise term). Some *a priori* information about the surface, e.g. the smoothness one, is necessary for reconstruction.

Consider a set of N input-output examples, $\{(x_i, d_i)\}$, and a form $\parallel Pf \parallel^2$ for the cost of the deviation of f, the approximated surface, from smoothness. P is a differential operator and $\parallel \cdot \parallel$ is a norm (usually L^2). To find the surface f, that best fits (i) the data and (ii) the smoothness criteria, is to solve the problem of minimizing the functional

$$V(f) = \sum_{i=0}^{N-1} (d_i - f(x_i))^2 + \mu \parallel Pf \parallel^2 \ .$$

Different methods of solving the function can yield different types of network. In particular using the Green's method gives supervised backprop type of networks (Poggio and Girosi, 1990) and using optimization techniques (like gradient descent) we obtain unsupervised (with feedback) type of networks.

2   Learning how to teach arithmetic operations

The problem of learning how to *add* and *multiply* is a simple one and yet provide insights to our approach of selecting the minimum set of examples.

Learning arithmetic operations   The surface given by the addition of two numbers, namely $f(x, y) = x + y$, is a plane passing through the origin. The multiplication surface, $f(x, y) = xy$, is hyperbolic. The *a priori* knowledge of the *addition* and *multiplication* surface can be expressed as a minimum of the functional

$$V(f) = \int_{-\infty}^{\infty} \int_{-\infty}^{\infty} \parallel \nabla^2 f(x, y) \parallel dx\, dy$$

where

$$\nabla^2 f(x, y) = (\frac{\partial^2}{\partial x^2} + \frac{\partial^2}{\partial y^2}) f(x, y) \quad .$$

Other functions also minimize $V(f)$, like $f(x, y) = x^2 - y^2$, and so a few examples are necessary to learn how to add and multiply given the above prior knowledge. If the prior assumption consider a larger class of basis functions, then more examples will be required. Given p input-output examples, $\{(x_i, y_i); d_i\}$, the learning problem of adding and multiplying can be cast as the optimization of

$$V(f) = \sum_{i=0}^{p-1} (f(x_i, y_i) - d_i)^2 + \mu \int_{-\infty}^{\infty} \int_{-\infty}^{\infty} \| \nabla^2 f(x, y) \| \, dx \, dy \quad .$$

We now consider the problem of selecting the examples from the full surface data.

A sparse process for selecting data   Let us assume that the full set of data is given in a 2-Dimensional lattice. So we have a finite amount of data (N^2 data points), with the input-output set being $\{(x_i, y_j); d_{ij}\}$, where $i, j = 0, 1, ..., N-1$. To select p examples we introduce a sparse process that selects out data by modifying the cost function according to

$$V = \sum_{i,j=0}^{N-1} (1 - s_{ij})(f(x_i, y_j) - d_{ij})^2 + \mu \int_{-\infty}^{\infty} \int_{-\infty}^{\infty} \| \nabla^2 f(x, y) \| + \lambda (p - \sum_{i,j=0}^{N-1} (1 - s_{ij}))^2$$

where $s_{ij} = 1$ selects out the data and we have added the last term to assure that p examples are selected. The data term forces noisy data to be thrown out first, the second order smoothness of f reduces the need for many examples ($p \approx 10$) to learn these arithmetic operations. Learning s is equivalent to learn how to select the examples, or to learn how to teach. The system (teacher) has to learn a set of examples (sparse data) that contains all the "relevant" information. The redundant information can be "filled in" by the prior knowledge. Once the teacher has learned these selected examples, he, she or it (machine) presents them to the student that with the *a priori* knowledge about surfaces is able to approximately learn the full input-output map (surface).

3   Teaching piecewise smooth surfaces

We first briefly introduce the weak membrane model, a coupled Markov random field for modeling piecewise smooth surfaces. Then we lay down the framework for learning to teach this surface.

3.1   Weak membrane model

Within the Bayes approach the *a priori* knowledge that surfaces are smooth (first order smoothness) but not at the discontinuities has been analyzed by (Geman and Geman, 1984) (Blake and Zisserman, 1987) (Mumford and Shah, 1985) (Geiger and Girosi, 1991). If we consider the noise to be white Gaussian, the final posterior probability becomes $P(f, l|g) = \frac{1}{Z} e^{-\beta V(f,l)}$, where

$$V(f, l) = \sum_{i,j} [(f_{ij} - g_{ij})^2 + \mu \| \nabla f \|_{ij}^2 (1 - l_{ij}) + \gamma_{ij} l_{ij}], \tag{1}$$

We represented surfaces by f_{ij} at pixel (i, j), and discontinuities by l_{ij}. The input data is g_{ij}, $\| \nabla f \|_{ij}$ is the norm of the gradient at pixel (i, j). Z is a normalization constant, known as the partition function. β is a global parameter of the model and is inspired on thermodynamics, and μ and γ_{ij} are parameters to be estimated. This model, when used for image segmentation, has been shown to give a good pattern of discontinuities and eliminate the noise. Thus, suggesting that the piecewise assumption is valid for images.

3.2   Redundant data

We have assumed the surface to be smooth and therefore there is redundant information within smooth regions. We then propose a model that selects the "relevant" information according to two criteria

1.   Discontinuity data: Discontinuities usually capture relevant information, and it is possible to roughly approximate surfaces just using edge data (see Geiger and Pereira, 1990). A limitation of just using edge data is that an oversmoothed surface is represented.

2. Texture data: Data points that have significant gradients (not enough to be a discontinuity) are here considered texture data. Keeping texture data allows us to distinguish between flat surfaces, as for example a clean sky in an image, and texture surfaces, as for example the leaves in the tree (see figure 2).

3.3   The sparse process

Again, our proposal is first to extend the weak membrane model by including an additional binary field - the *sparse process* s- that is 1 when data is selected out and 0 otherwise. There are natural connections between the process s and robust statistics (Huber, 1988) as discussed in (Geiger and Yuille, 1990) and (Geiger and Pereira, 1991). We modify (1) by considering (see also Geiger and Pereira, 1990)

$$V(f,l,s) = \sum_{i,j}[(1 - s_{ij})(f_{ij} - g_{ij})^2 + \mu \parallel \nabla f \parallel_{ij}^2 (1 - l_{ij}) + \eta_{ij}s_{ij} + \gamma_{ij}l_{ij}]. \quad (2)$$

where we have introduced the term $\eta_{ij}s_{ij}$ to keep some data otherwise $s_{ij} = 1$ everywhere. If the data term is too large, the process $s = 1$ can suppress it. We will now assume that the data is noise-free, or that the noise has already been smoothed out. We then want to find which data points ($s = 0$) are necessary to keep to reconstruct f.

3.4   Mean field equations and unsupervised networks

To impose the **discontinuity data** constraint we use the hard constraint technique (Geiger and Yuille, 1990 and its references). We do *not allow* states that throw out data ($s_{ij} = 1$) at the edge location ($l_{ij} = 1$). More precisely, within the statistical framework we reduce the possible states for the processes s and l to $s_{ij}l_{ij} = 0$. Therefore, excluding the state ($s_{ij} = 1, l_{ij} = 1$). Applying the saddle point approximation, a well known mean field technique (Geiger and Girosi, 1989 and its references), on the field f, we can compute the partition function

$$Z = \sum_{f=(0,..,255)^{N^2}} \sum_{s,l=(0,1)^{N^2}}^{s.l=0} e^{-\beta V(f,l,s)} \approx \sum_{s,l=(0,1)^{N^2}}^{s.l=0} e^{-\beta V(\bar{f},l,s)} \approx \prod_{ij} Z_{ij}$$

$$Z_{ij} = \left(e^{-\beta[\gamma_{ij}+(\bar{f}_{ij}-g_{ij})^2]} + e^{-\beta[\mu\|\nabla f\|_{ij}^2+\eta_{ij}]} + e^{-\beta[\mu\|\nabla f\|_{ij}^2+(f_{ij}-g_{ij})^2]} \right) \qquad (3)$$

where $\bar{f}$ maximizes Z. After applying mean field techniques we obtain the following equations for the processes l and s

$$\bar{l}_{ij} = e^{-\beta[\gamma_{ij}+(f_{ij}-g_{ij})^2]}/Z_{ij} \qquad , \qquad \bar{s}_{ij} = e^{-\beta[\mu\|\nabla f\|_{ij}^2+\eta_{ij}]}/Z_{ij} \qquad (4)$$

and, using the definition $\| \nabla f \|_{ij}^2 = [(f_{i,j+1} - f_{i+1,j})^2 + (f_{i+1,j+1} - f_{i,j})^2$, the mean field self consistent equation (Geiger and Pereira, 1991) becomes

$$(1 - \bar{s}_{ij})(\bar{f}_{ij} - g_{ij}) = -\mu \Big\{ K_{ij}(1 - \bar{l}_{ij}) + K_{i-1,j-1}(1 - \bar{l}_{i-1,j-1}) +$$

$$M_{i-1,j}(1 - \bar{l}_{i-1,j}) + M_{i,j-1}(1 - \bar{l}_{i,j-1}) \Big\} \qquad (5)$$

where $K_{ij} = (f_{i+1,j+1} - f_{i,j})^2$ and $M_{ij} = (f_{i+1,j} - f_{i,j+1})^2$. The set of coupled equations (5) (4) can be mapped to an unsupervised network, we call a minimal surface representation network (MSRN), and can efficiently be solved in a massively parallel machine. Notice that $s_{ij} + l_{ij} \geq 1$, because of the hard constraint, and in the limit of $\beta \to \infty$ the processes s and l becomes either 0 or 1. In order to throw away redundant (smooth) data keeping some of the texture we adapt the cost η_{ij} according to the gradient of the surface. More precisely, we set

$$\eta_{ij} = \eta[(\Delta_{ij}^h g)^2 + (\Delta_{ij}^v g)^2] \qquad (6)$$

where $(\Delta_{ij}^h g)^2 = (g_{i+1,j} - g_{i-1,j})^2$ and $(\Delta_{ij}^v g)^2 = (g_{i,j+1} - g_{i,j-1})^2$. The smoother is the data the lower is the cost to discard the data ($s_{ij} = 1$). In the limit of $\eta \to 0$ only edge data ($l_{ij} = 1$) is kept, since from (4) $lim_{\eta \to 0} s_{ij} = 1 - l_{ij}$.

3.5   Learning how to teach and the approximated surface

With the mean field equations we compute the approximated surface f simultaneously to s and to l. Thus, while learning the process s (the selected data) the system also predict the approximated surface f that the student will learn from the selected examples. By changing the parameters, say μ and η, the teacher can choose the optimal parameters such as to select less data and preserve the quality of the approximated surface. Once s has been learned the system only feeds the selected data points to the learner machinery. We actually relax the condition and feed the learner with the selected data and the corresponding discontinuity map (l). Notice that in the limit of $\eta \to 0$ the selected data points are coincident with the discontinuities ($l = 1$).

4   Results: Image compression

We show the results of the algorithm to learn the minimal representation of images. The algorithm is capable of image compression and one advantage over the cosine transform (traditional method) is that it does not have the problem of breaking the images into blocks. However, a more careful comparison is needed.

4.1   Learning s, f, and l

To analyze the quality of the surface approximation, we show in figure 1 the performance of the network as we vary the threshold η. We first show a face image and the line process and then the predicted approximated surfaces together with the correspondent sparse process s.

4.2   Reconstruction, Generalization or "The student performance"

We can now test how the student learns from the selected examples, or how good is the surface reconstruction from the selected data. We reconstruct the approximate surfaces by running (5) again, but with the selected surface data points ($s_{ij} = 0$) and the discontinuities ($l_{ij} = 1$) given from the previous step. We show in figure 2f that indeed we obtain the predicted surfaces (the student has learned).

References :

E. B. Baum and Y. Lyuu. 1991. The transition to perfect generalization in perceptrons, *Neural Computation*, vol.3, no.3. pp.386-401.

A. Blake and A. Zisserman. 1987. Visual Reconstruction, *MIT Press*, Cambridge, Mass.

D. Geiger and F. Girosi. 1989. Coupled Markov random fields and mean field theory, Advances in Neural Information Processing Systems 2, Morgan Kaufmann, D. Touretzky.

D. Geiger and A. Yuille. 1991. A common framework for image segmentation, *Int. Jour. Comp. Vis.*,vol.6:3, pp. 227-243.

D. Geiger and F. Girosi. 1991. Parallel and deterministic algorithms for MRFs: surface reconstruction, *PAMI*, May 1991, vol.PAMI-13, 5, pp.401-412 .

D. Geiger and R. M. Pereira. 1991. The outlier process, *IEEE Workshop on Neural Networks for signal Processing*, Princeton, NJ.

S. Geman and D. Geman. 1984. Stochastic Relaxation, Gibbs Distributions, and the Bayesian Restoration of Images,*PAMI*, vol.PAMI-6, pp.721–741K.

J.J. Hopfield. 1984. Neural networks and physical systems with emergent collective computational abilities, *Proc. Nat. Acad. Sci.*,79 , pp. 2554-2558.

P.J. Huber. 1981. Robust Statistics, *John Wiley and Sons*, New York.

D. Mumford and J. Shah. 1985. Boundary detection by minimizing functionals, I , *Proc. IEEE Conf. on Computer Vision & Pattern Recognition*, San Francisco, CA .

T. Poggio and F. Girosi. 1990. Regularization algorithms for learning that are equivalent to multilayer network, *Science*,vol-247, pp. 978-982.

D. E. Rumelhart, G. Hinton and R. J. Williams. 1986. Learning internal representations by error backpropagation. *Nature*, 323, 533.

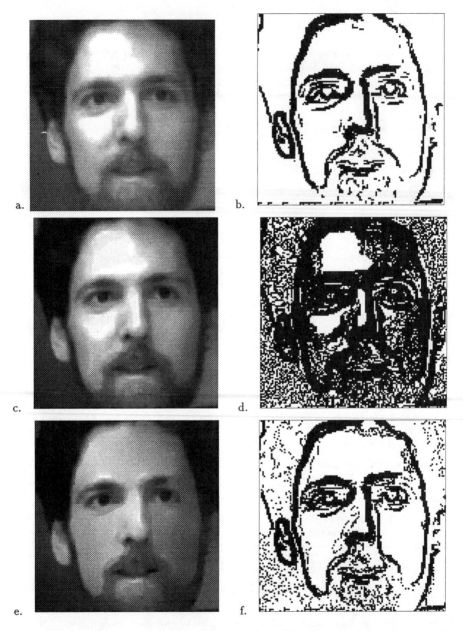

Figure 1: *(a) 8-bit image of 128 X 128 pixels. (b) The edge map for $\mu = 1.0$, $\gamma_{ij} = 100.0$. After 200 iterations and final $\beta = 25 \approx \infty$ (c) the approximated image for $\mu = 0.01$, $\gamma_{ij} = 1.0$ and $\eta = 0.0009$. (d) the corresponding sparse process (e) approximated image $\mu = 0.01$, $\gamma_{ij} = 1.0$ and $\eta = 0.0001$. (f) the corresponding sparse process.*

Figure 2: *(a) 8-bit image of 256 X 256 pixels. (b) The final image after data has been selected out. Final values for the parameters:* $\mu = 0.02$, $\gamma_{ij} = 2.8$, $\eta = 0.005$, *final* $\beta = 25 \approx \infty$, *400 iterations. (c) The sparse process, where black dots represent* $s_{ij} = 0$ *(data kept). (d) The initial selected data from (a) using the process s (c) (e) The reconstruction of the image after 4 iterations. (f) After 80 iterations. As predicted, it is very close to (b).*

Learning to Make Coherent Predictions in Domains with Discontinuities

Suzanna Becker and Geoffrey E. Hinton
Department of Computer Science, University of Toronto
Toronto, Ontario, Canada M5S 1A4

Abstract

We have previously described an unsupervised learning procedure that discovers spatially coherent properties of the world by maximizing the information that parameters extracted from different parts of the sensory input convey about some common underlying cause. When given random dot stereograms of curved surfaces, this procedure learns to extract surface depth because that is the property that is coherent across space. It also learns how to interpolate the depth at one location from the depths at nearby locations (Becker and Hinton, 1992). In this paper, we propose two new models which handle surfaces with discontinuities. The first model attempts to detect cases of discontinuities and reject them. The second model develops a mixture of expert interpolators. It learns to detect the locations of discontinuities and to invoke specialized, asymmetric interpolators that do not cross the discontinuities.

1 Introduction

Standard backpropagation is implausible as a model of perceptual learning because it requires an external teacher to specify the desired output of the network. We have shown (Becker and Hinton, 1992) how the external teacher can be replaced by internally derived teaching signals. These signals are generated by using the assumption that different parts of the perceptual input have common causes in the external world. Small modules that look at separate but related parts of the perceptual input discover these common causes by striving to produce outputs that agree with each other (see Figure 1 a). The modules may look at different modalities (e.g. vision and touch), or the same modality at different times (e.g. the consecutive 2-D views of a rotating 3-D object), or even spatially adjacent parts of the same image. In previous work, we showed that when our learning procedure is applied to adjacent patches of 2-dimensional images, it allows a neural network that has no prior knowledge of the third dimension to discover depth in random dot stereograms of curved surfaces. A more general version of the method allows the network to discover the best way of interpolating the depth at one location from the depths at nearby locations. We first summarize this earlier work, and then introduce two new models which allow coherent predictions to be made in the presence of discontinuities.

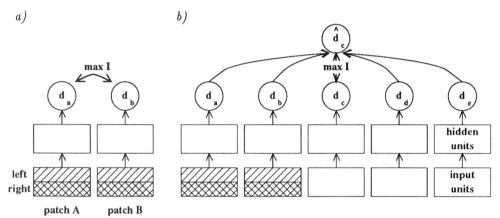

Figure 1: *a) Two modules that receive input from corresponding parts of stereo images. The first module receives input from stereo patch A, consisting of a horizontal strip from the left image (striped) and a corresponding strip from the right image (hatched). The second module receives input from an adjacent stereo patch B. The modules try to make their outputs, d_a and d_b, convey as much information as possible about some underlying signal (i.e., the depth) which is common to both patches. b) The architecture of the interpolating network, consisting of multiple copies of modules like those in a) plus a layer of interpolating units. The network tries to maximize the information that the locally extracted parameter d_c and the contextually predicted parameter $\hat{d}_c$ convey about some common underlying signal. We actually used 10 modules and the central 6 modules tried to maximize agreement between their outputs and contextually predicted values. We used weight averaging to constrain the interpolating function to be identical for all modules.*

2   Learning spatially coherent features in images

The simplest way to get the outputs of two modules to agree is to use the squared difference between the outputs as a cost function, and to adjust the weights in each module so as to minimize this cost. Unfortunately, this usually causes each module to produce the same constant output that is unaffected by the input to the module and therefore conveys no information about it. What we want is for the outputs of two modules to agree closely (i.e. to have a small expected squared difference) *relative* to how much they both vary as the input is varied. When this happens, the two modules must be responding to something that is common to their two inputs. In the special case when the outputs, d_a, d_b, of the two modules are scalars, a good measure of agreement is:

$$I = 0.5 \log \frac{V(d_a + d_b)}{V(d_a - d_b)} \tag{1}$$

where V is the variance over the training cases. If d_a and d_b are both versions of the same underlying Gaussian signal that have been corrupted by independent Gaussian noise, it can be shown that I is the mutual information between the underlying signal and the average of d_a and d_b. By maximizing I we force the two modules to extract as pure a version as possible of the underlying common signal.

2.1   The basic stereo net

We have shown how this principle can be applied to a multi-layer network that learns to extract depth from random dot stereograms (Becker and Hinton, 1992). Each network module received input from a patch of a left image and a corresponding patch of a right image, as shown in Figure 1 a). Adjacent modules received input from adjacent stereo image patches, and learned to extract depth by trying to maximize agreement between their outputs. The real-valued depth (relative to the plane of fixation) of each patch of the surface gives rise to a disparity between features in the left and right images; since that disparity is the only property that is coherent across each stereo image, the output units of modules were able to learn to accurately detect relative depth.

2.2   The interpolating net

The basic stereo net uses a very simple model of coherence in which an underlying parameter at one location is assumed to be approximately equal to the parameter at a neighbouring location. This model is fine for the depth of fronto-parallel surfaces but it is far from the best model of slanted or curved surfaces. Fortunately, we can use a far more general model of coherence in which the parameter at one location is assumed to be an unknown linear function of the parameters at nearby locations. The particular linear function that is appropriate can be learned by the network.

We used a network of the type shown in Figure 1 b). The depth computed locally by a module, d_c, was compared with the depth predicted by a linear combination $\hat{d}_c$ of the outputs of nearby modules, and the network tried to maximize the agreement between d_c and $\hat{d}_c$.

The contextual prediction, $\hat{d}_c$, was produced by computing a weighted sum of the outputs of *two* adjacent modules on either side. The interpolating weights used in this sum, and all other weights in the network, were adjusted so as to maximize agreement between locally computed and contextually predicted depths. To speed the learning, we first trained the lower layers of the network as before, so that agreement was maximized between neighbouring locally computed outputs. This made it easier to learn good interpolating weights. When the network was trained on stereograms of cubic surfaces, it learned interpolating weights of $-0.147, 0.675, 0.656, -0.131$ (Becker and Hinton, 1992). Given noise free estimates of local depth, the optimal linear interpolator for a cubic surface is $-0.167, 0.667, 0.667, -0.167$.

3 Throwing out discontinuities

If the surface is continuous, the depth at one patch can be accurately predicted from the depths of two patches on either side. If, however, the training data contains cases in which there are depth discontinuities (see figure 2) the interpolator will also try to model these cases and this will contribute considerable noise to the interpolating weights and to the depth estimates. One way of reducing this noise is to treat the discontinuity cases as outliers and to throw them out. Rather than making a hard decision about whether a case is an outlier, we make a soft decision by using a mixture model. For each training case, the network compares the locally extracted depth, d_c, with the depth predicted from the nearby context, $\hat{d}_c$. It assumes that $d_c - \hat{d}_c$ is drawn from a zero-mean Gaussian if it is a continuity case and from a uniform distribution if it is a discontinuity case. It can then estimate the probability of a continuity case:

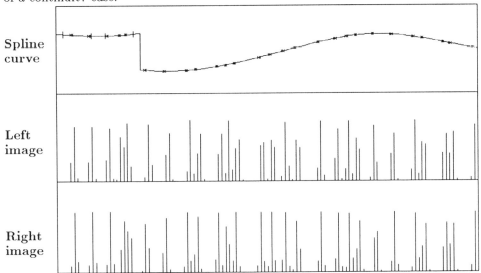

Figure 2: **Top:** *A curved surface strip with a discontinuity created by fitting 2 cubic splines through randomly chosen control points, 25 pixels apart, separated by a depth discontinuity. Feature points are randomly scattered on each spline with an average of 0.22 features per pixel.* **Bottom:** *A stereo pair of "intensity" images of the surface strip formed by taking two different projections of the feature points, filtering them through a gaussian, and sampling the filtered projections at evenly spaced sample points. The sample values in corresponding patches of the two images are used as the inputs to a module. The depth of the surface for a particular image region is directly related to the disparity between corresponding features in the left and right patch. Disparity ranges continuously from −1 to +1 image pixels. Each stereo image was 120 pixels wide and divided into 10 receptive fields 10 pixels wide and separated by 2 pixel gaps, as input for the networks shown in figure 1. The receptive field of an interpolating unit spanned 58 image pixels, and discontinuities were randomly located a minimum of 40 pixels apart, so only rarely would more than one discontinuity lie within an interpolator's receptive field.*

$$p_{cont}(d_c - \hat{d}_c) = \frac{N(d_c - \hat{d}_c, 0, \hat{V}_{cont}(d_c - \hat{d}_c))}{N(d_c - \hat{d}_c, 0, \hat{V}_{cont}(d_c - \hat{d}_c)) + k_{discont}} \qquad (2)$$

where N is a gaussian, and $k_{discont}$ is a constant representing a uniform density. [1]

We can now optimize the *average* information d_c and $\hat{d}_c$ transmit about their common cause. We assume that no information is transmitted in discontinuity cases, so the average information depends on the probability of continuity and on the variance of $d_c + \hat{d}_c$ and $d_c - \hat{d}_c$ measured only in the continuity cases.

$$I^* = 0.5 \; P_{cont} \; \log \frac{V_{cont}(d_c + \hat{d}_c)}{V_{cont}(d_c - \hat{d}_c)} \qquad (3)$$

We tried several variations of this mixture approach. The network is quite good at rejecting the discontinuity cases, but this leads to only a modest improvement in the performance of the interpolator. In cases where there is a depth discontinuity between d_a and d_b or between d_d and d_e the interpolator works moderately well because the weights on d_a or d_e are small. Because of the term P_{cont} in equation 3 there is pressure to include these cases as continuity cases, so they probably contribute noise to the interpolating weights. In the next section we show how to avoid making a forced choice between rejecting these cases or treating them just like all the other continuity cases.

4   Learning a mixture of expert interpolators

The presence of a depth discontinuity somewhere within a strip of five adjacent patches does not entirely eliminate the coherence of depth across these patches. It just restricts the range over which this coherence operates. So instead of throwing out cases that contain a discontinuity, the network could try to develop a number of different, specialized interpolators each of which captures the particular type of coherence that remains in the presence of a discontinuity at a particular location. If, for example, there is a depth discontinuity between d_c and d_e, an extrapolator with weights of $-1.0, +2.0, 0, 0$ would be an appropriate predictor of d_c.

Figure 3 shows the system of five expert interpolators that we used for predicting d_c from the neighboring depths. To allow the system to invoke the appropriate interpolator, each expert has its own "controller" which must learn to detect the presence of a discontinuity at a particular location (or the absence of a discontinuity in the case of the interpolator for pure continuity cases). The outputs of the controllers are normalized, as shown in figure 3, so that they form a probability distribution. We can think of these normalized outputs as the probability with which the system selects a particular expert. The controllers get to see all five local depth estimates and most of them learn to detect particular depth discontinuities by using large weights of opposite sign on the local depth estimates of neighboring patches.

---

[1]We empirically select a good (fixed) value of $k_{discont}$, and we choose a starting value of $\hat{V}_{cont}(d_c - \hat{d}_c)$ (some proportion of the initial variance of $d_c - \hat{d}_c$), and gradually shrink it during learning.

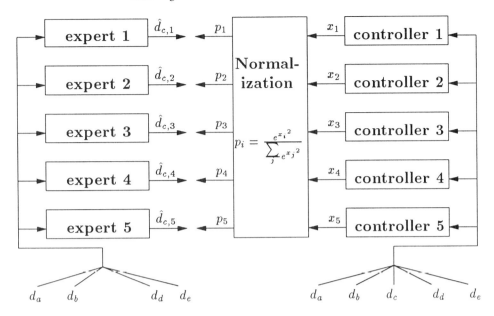

Figure 3: *The architecture of the mixture of interpolators and discontinuity detectors. We actually used a larger modular network and equality constraints between modules, as described in figure 1 b), with 6 copies of the architecture shown here. Each copy received input from different but overlapping parts of the input.*

Figure 4 shows the weights learned by the experts and by their controllers. As expected, there is one interpolator (the top one) that is appropriate for continuity cases and four other interpolators that are appropriate for the four different locations of a discontinuity. In interpreting the weights of the controllers it is important to remember that a controller which produces a small x value for a particular case may nevertheless assign high probability to its expert if all the other controllers produce even smaller x values.

4.1 The learning procedure

In the example presented here, we first trained the network shown in figure 1b) on images with discontinuities. We then used the outputs of the depth extracting layer, $d_a, \ldots, d_e$ as the inputs to the expert interpolators and their controllers. The system learned a set of expert interpolators without backpropagating derivatives all the way down to the weights of the local depth extracting modules. So the local depth estimates $d_a, \ldots, d_e$ did not change as the interpolators were learned.

To train the system we used an unsupervised version of the competing experts algorithm described by Jacobs, Jordan, Nowlan and Hinton (1991). The output of the ith expert, $\hat{d}_{c,i}$, is treated as the mean of a Gaussian distribution with variance σ^2 and the normalized output of each controller, p_i, is treated as the mixing proportion of that Gaussian. So, for each training case, the outputs of the experts and their controllers define a probability distribution that is a mixture of Gaussians. The aim

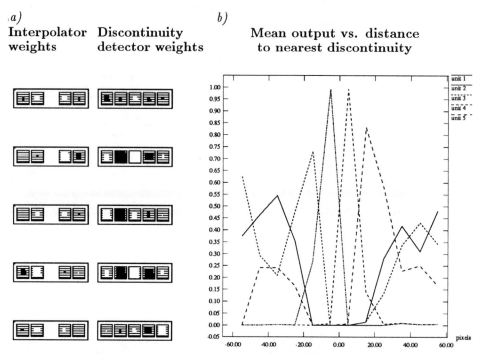

a)
Interpolator Discontinuity
weights   detector weights

b)
Mean output vs. distance
to nearest discontinuity

Figure 4: *a) Typical weights learned by the five competing interpolators and cor-responding five discontinuity detectors. Positive weights are shown in white, and negative weights in black. b)The mean probabilities computed by each discontinuity detector are plotted against the the distance from the center of the units' receptive field to the nearest discontinuity. The probabilistic outputs are averaged over an ensemble of 1000 test cases. If the nearest discontinuity is beyond ± thirty pixels, it is outside the units' receptive field and the case is therefore a continuity example.*

of the learning is to maximize the log probability density of the desired output, d_c, under this mixture of Gaussians distribution. For a particular training case this log probability is given by:

$$\log P(d_c) = \log \sum_i p_i \frac{1}{\sqrt{2\pi}\sigma} \exp\left(-\frac{(d_c - \hat{d}_{c,i})^2}{2\sigma^2}\right) \tag{4}$$

By taking derivatives of this objective function we can simultaneously learn the weights in the experts and in the controllers. For the results shown here, the nework was trained for 30 conjugate gradient iterations on a set of 1000 random dot stereograms with discontinuities.

The rationale for the use of a variance ratio in equation 1 is to prevent the variances of d_a and d_b collapsing to zero. Because the local estimates $d_1, \ldots, d_5$ did not change as the system learned the expert interpolators, it was possible to use $(d_c - \hat{d}_{c,i})^2$ in the objective function without worrying about the possibility that the variance of d_c across cases would collapse to zero during the learning. Ideally we would like to refine the weights of the local depth estimators to maximize their agreement with the contextually predicted depths produced by the mixture of expert interpolators. One way to do this would be to generalize equation 3 to handle a mixture of expert interpolators:

$$I^* = 0.5 \sum_i P_i \ \log \frac{V_i(d_c + \hat{d}_{c,i})}{V_i(d_c - \hat{d}_{c,i})} \tag{5}$$

Alternatively we could modify equation 4 by normalizing the difference $(d_c - \hat{d}_{c,i})^2$ by the actual variance of d_c, though this makes the derivatives considerably more complicated.

5   Discussion

The competing controllers in figure 3 explicitly represent which regularity applies in a particular region. The outputs of the controllers for nearby regions may themselves exhibit coherence at a larger spatial scale, so the same learning technique could be applied recursively. In 2-D images this should allow the continuity of depth edges to be discovered.

The approach presented here should be applicable to other domains which contain a mixture of alternative local regularities across space or time. For example, a rigid shape causes a linear constraint between the locations of its parts in an image, so if there are many possible shapes, there are many alternative local regularities (Zemel and Hinton, 1991).

Our learning procedure differs from methods that try to capture as much information as possible about the input (Linsker, 1988; Atick and Redlich, 1990) because we ignore information in the input that is not coherent across space.

Acknowledgements

This research was funded by grants from NSERC and the Ontario Information Technology Research Centre. Hinton is Noranda fellow of the Canadian Institute for Advanced Research. Thanks to John Bridle and Steve Nowlan for helpful discussions.

References

Atick, J. J. and Redlich, A. N. (1990).   Towards a theory of early visual processing. Technical Report IASSNS-HEP-90/10, Institute for Advanced Study, Princeton.

Becker, S. and Hinton, G. E. (1992).   A self-organizing neural network that discovers surfaces in random-dot stereograms. January 1992 *Nature*.

Jacobs, R. A., Jordan, M. I., Nowlan, S. J., and Hinton, G. E. (1991). Adaptive mixtures of local experts. *Neural Computation*, 3(1).

Linsker, R. (1988). Self-organization in a perceptual network. *IEEE Computer,* March, 21:105–117.

Zemel, R. S. and Hinton, G. E. (1991). Discovering viewpoint-invariant relationships that characterize objects. In *Advances In Neural Information Processing Systems 3*, pages 299–305. Morgan Kaufmann Publishers.

Recurrent Eye Tracking Network Using a Distributed Representation of Image Motion

P. A. Viola
Artificial Intelligence Laboratory
Massachusetts Institute of Technology

S. G. Lisberger
Department of Physiology
W.M. Keck Foundation Center for Integrative Neuroscience
Neuroscience Graduate Program
University of California, San Francisco

T. J. Sejnowski
Salk Institute, Howard Hughes Medical Institute
Department of Biology
University of California, San Diego

Abstract

We have constructed a recurrent network that stabilizes images of a moving object on the retina of a simulated eye. The structure of the network was motivated by the organization of the primate visual target tracking system. The basic components of a complete target tracking system were simulated, including visual processing, sensory-motor interface, and motor control. Our model is simpler in structure, function and performance than the primate system, but many of the complexities inherent in a complete system are present.

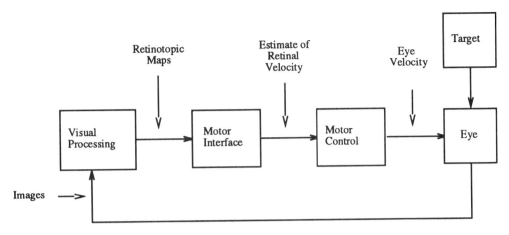

Figure 1: The overall structure of the visual tracking model.

1 Introduction

The fovea of the primate eye has a high density of photoreceptors. Images that fall within the fovea are perceived with high resolution. Perception of moving objects poses a particular problem for the visual system. If the eyes are fixed a moving image will be blurred. When the image moves out the of the fovea, resolution decreases. By moving their eyes to foveate and stabilize targets, primates ensure maximum perceptual resolution. In addition, active target tracking simplifies other tasks, such as spatial localization and spatial coordinate transformations (Ballard, 1991).

Visual tracking is a feedback process, in which the eyes are moved to stabilize and foveate the image of a target. Good visual tracking performance depends on accurate estimates of target velocity and a stable feedback controller. Although many visual tracking systems have been designed by engineers, the primate visual tracking system has yet to be matched in its ability to perform in complicated environments, with unrestricted targets, and over a wide variety of target trajectories. The study of the primate oculomotor system is an important step toward building a system that can attain primate levels of performance. The model presented here can accurately and stably track a variety of targets over a wide range of trajectories and is a first step toward achieving this goal.

Our model has four primary components: a model eye, a visual processing network, a motor interface network, and a motor control network (see Figure 1). The model eye receives a sequence of images from a changing visual world, synthetically rendered, and generates a time-varying output signal. The retinal signal is sent to the visual processing network which is similar in function to the motion processing areas of the visual cortex. The visual processing network constructs a distributed representation of image velocity. This representation is then used to estimate the velocity of the target on the retina. The retinal velocity of the target forms the input to the motor control network that drives the eye. The eye responds by rotating,

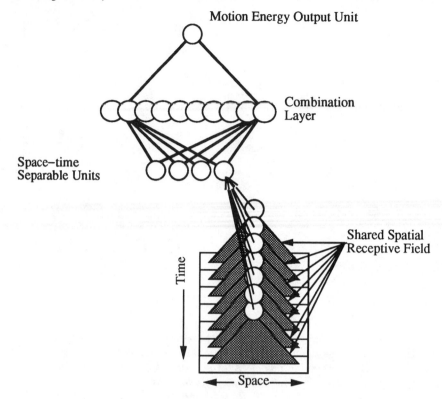

Figure 2: The structure of a motion energy unit. Each space-time separable unit has a receptive field that covers 16 pixels in space and 16 steps in time (for a total of 256 inputs). The shaded triangles denote complete projections.

which in turn affects incoming retinal signals.

If these networks function perfectly, eye velocity will match target velocity. Our model generates smooth eye motions to stabilize smoothly moving targets. It makes no attempt to foveate the image of a target. In primates, eye motions that foveate targets are called saccades. Saccadic mechanisms are largely separate from the smooth eye motion system (Lisberger et. al. 1987). We do not address them here.

In contrast with most engineered systems, our model is adaptive. The networks used in the model were trained using gradient descent[1]. This training process circumvented the need for a separate calibration of the visual tracking system.

2   Visual Processing

---

[1] Network simulations were carried out with the SN2 neural network simulator.

The middle temporal cortex (area MT) contains cells that are selective for the direction of visual motion. The neurons in MT are organized into a retinotopic map and small lesions in this area lead to selective impairment of visual tracking in the corresponding regions of the visual field (Newsome and Pare, 1988). The visual processing networks in our model contain directionally-selective processing units that are arranged in a retinotopic map. The spatio-temporal motion energy filter of Adelson and Bergen (Adelson and Bergen, 1985) has many of the properties of directionally-selective cortical neurons; it is used as the basis for our visual processing network. We constructed a four layer time-delay neural network that implements a motion energy calculation.

A single motion-energy unit can be constructed from four intermediate units having separable spatial and temporal filters. Adelson and Bergen demonstrate that two spatial filters (of even and odd symmetry) and two temporal filters (temporal derivatives for fast and slow speeds) are sufficient to detect motion. The filters are combined to construct 4 intermediate units which project to a single motion energy unit. Because the spatial and temporal properties of the receptive field are separable, they can be computed separately and convolved together to produce the final output. The temporal response is therefore the same throughout the extent of the spatial receptive field.

In our model, motion energy units are implemented as backpropagation networks. These units have a receptive field 16 pixels wide over a 16 time step window. Because the input weights are shared, only 32 parameters were needed for each space-time separable unit. Four space-time separable units project through a 16 unit combination layer to the output unit (see Figure 2). The entire network can be trained to approximate a variety of motion-energy filters.

We trained the motion energy network in two different ways: as a single multilayered network and in stages. Staged training proceded first by training intermediate units, then, with the intermediate units fixed, by training the three layer network that combines the intermediate units to produce a single motion energy output. The output unit is active when a pattern in the appropriate range of spatial frequencies moves through the receptive field with appropriate velocity. Many such units are required for a range of velocities, spatial frequencies, and spatial locations. We use six different types of motion energy units – each tuned to a different temporal frequency – at each of the central 48 positions of a 64 pixel linear retina. The 6 populations form a distributed, velocity-tuned representation of image motion for a total of 288 motion energy units.

In addition to the motion energy filters, static spatial frequency filters are also computed and used in the interface network, one for each band and each position for a total of 288 units.

We chose an adaptive network rather than a direct motion energy calculation because it allows us to model the dynamic nature of the visual signal with greater flexibility. However, this raises complications regarding the set of training images. Assuming 5 bits of information at each retinal position, there are well over 10 to the 100th possible input patterns. We explored sine waves, random spots and a variety of spatial pre-filters, and found low-pass filtered images of moving random spots worked best. Typically we began the training process from a plausible set of weights, rather than from random values, to prevent the network from settling into an initial local minima. Training proceeded for days until good performance was obtained on a testing set.

Krauzlis and Lisberger (1989) have predicted that the visual stimulus to the visual tracking system in the brain contains information about the acceleration and impulse of the target as well as the velocity. Our motion energy networks are sensitive to target acceleration, producing transients for accelerating stimuli.

3   The Interface Network

The function of the interface is to take the distributed representation of the image motion and extract a single velocity estimate for the moving object. We use a relatively simple method that was adequate for tracking single objects without other moving distractors. The activity level of a single motion energy unit is ambiguous. First, it is necessary for the object to have a feature that is matched to the spatial frequency bandpass of the motion energy unit. Second, there is an array of units for each spatial frequency and the object will stimulate only a few of these at any given time. For instance, a large white object will have no features in its interior; a unit with its receptive field located in the interior can detect no motion. Conversely, detectors with receptive fields on the border between the object and the background will be strongly stimulated.

We use two stages of processing to extract a velocity. In the first stage, the motion energy in each spatial frequency band is estimated by summing the outputs of the motion energy filters across the retina weighted by the spatial frequency filter at each location. The six populations of spatial frequency units each yield one value. Next, a 6-6-1 feedforward network, trained using backpropagation, predicts target velocity from these values.

4   The Motor Control Network

In comparison with the visual processing network, the motor control network is quite small (see Figure 3). The goal of the network is to move the eye to stabilize the image of the object. The visual processing and interface networks convert images of the moving target into an estimate for the retinal velocity of the target. This retinal velocity can be considered a motor error. One approach to reducing this error is a simple proportional feedback controller, which drives the eye at a velocity proportional to the error. There is a large, 50-100 ms delay that occurs during visual processing in the primate visual system. In the presence of a large delay a proportional controller will either be inaccurate or unstable. For this reason simple proportional feedback is not sufficient to control tracking in the primate. Tracking can be made stable and accurate by including an internal positive feedback pathway to prevent instability while preserving accuracy (Robinson, 1971).

The motor control network was based on a model of the primate visual tracking motor control system by Lisberger and Sejnowski (1992). This recurrent artificial neural network includes both the smooth visual tracking system and the vestibulo-ocular system, which is important for compensating head movements. We use a

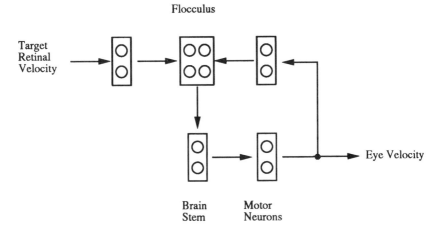

Figure 3: The structure of the recurrent network. Each circle is a unit. Units within a box are not interconnected and all units between boxes were fully interconnected as indicated by the arrows.

simpler version of that model that does not have vestibular inputs. The network is constructed from units with continuous smooth temporal responses. The state of a unit is a function of previous inputs and previous state:

$$s_j(t + \Delta t) = (1 - \tau \Delta t)s_j(t) + I\tau \Delta t$$

where $s_j(t)$ is the state of unit j at time t, τ is a time constant and I is the sigmoided sum of the weighted pre-synaptic activities. The resulting network is capable of smooth responses to inputs.

The motor control network has 12 units, each with a time constant of 5 ms (except for a few units with longer delay). There is a time delay of 50 ms between the interface network and control network. (see Figure 3). The input to the network is retinal target velocity, the output is eye velocity. The motor control network is trained to track a target in the presence of the visual delay.

The motor control network contains a positive feedback loop that is necessary to maintain accurate tracking even when the error signal falls to zero. The overall control network also contains a negative feedback loop since the output of the network affects subsequent inputs. The gradient descent optimization procedure uses the relationship between the output and the input during training—this relationship can be considered a model of the plant. It should be possible to use the same approach with more complex plants.

The control network was trained with the visual processing network frozen. A training example consists of an object trajectory and the goal trajectory for the eye. A standard recurrent network training paradigm is used to adjust the weights to minimize the error between actual outputs and desired outputs for step changes in target velocity.

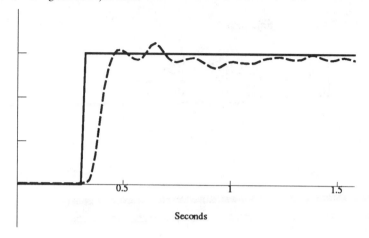

Seconds

Figure 4: Response of the eye to a step in target velocity of 30 degrees per second. The solid line is target velocity, the dashed line is eye velocity. This experiment was performed with a target that did not appear in the training set.

5   Performance

After training the network on a set of trajectories for a single target, the tracking performance was equally good on new targets. Tracking is accurate and stable - with little tendency to ring (see Figure 4). This good performance is surprising in the presence of a 50 millisecond delay in the visual feedback signal[2]. Stable tracking is not possible without the positive internal feedback loop in the model (eye velocity signal to the flocculus in Figure 3).

6   Limitations

The system that we have designed is a relatively small one having a one-dimensional retina only 64 pixels wide. The eye and the target can only move in one dimension—along the length of the retina. The visual analysis that is performed is not, however, limited to one dimension. Motion energy filters are easily generalized to a two-dimensional retina. Our approach should be extendable to the two-dimensional tracking problem.

The backgrounds of images that we used for tracking were featureless. The current system cannot distinguish target features from background features. Also, the interface network was designed to track a single object in the absence of moving distractors. The next step is to expand this interface to model the attentional phenomena observed in primate tracking, especially the process of initial target

---

[2]We selected time constants, delays, and sampling rates throughout the model to roughly approximate the time course of the primate visual tracking response. The model runs on a workstation taking approximately thirty times real-time to complete a processing step.

acquisition.

7 Conclusion

In simulations, our eye tracking model performed well. Many additional difficulties must be addressed, but we feel this system can perform well under real-world real-time constraints. Previous work by Lisberger and Sejnowski (1992) demonstrates that this visual tracking model can be integrated with inertial eye stabilization—the vestibulo-ocular reflex. Ultimately, it should be possible to build a physical system using these design principles.

Every component of the system was designed using network learning techniques. The visual processing, for example, had a variety of components that were trained separately and in combinations. The architecture of the networks were based on the anatomy and physiology of the visual and oculomotor systems. This approach to reverse engineering is based on the existing knowledge of the flow of information through the relevant brain pathways.

It should also be possible to use the model to develop and test theories about the nature of biological visual tracking. This is just a first step toward developing a realistic model of the primate oculomotor system, but it has already provided useful predictions for the possible sites of plasticity during gain changes of the vestibulo-ocular reflex (Lisberger and Sejnowski, 1992).

References

[1] E. H. Adelson and J. R. Bergen. Spatiotemporal energy models of the perception of motion. *Journal of the Optical Society of America*, 2(2):284–299, 1985.

[2] D. H. Ballard. Animate vision. *Artificial Intelligence*, 48:57–86, 1991.

[3] R.J. Krauzlis and S. G. Lisberger. A control systems model of smooth pursuit eye movements with realistic emergent properties. *Neural Computation*, 1:116–122, 1992.

[4] S. G. Lisberger, E. J. Morris, and L. Tychsen. *Ann. Rev. Neurosci.*, 10:97–129, 1987.

[5] S.G. Lisberger and T.J. Sejnowski. Computational analysis suggests a new hypothesis for motor learning in the vestibulo-ocular reflex. Submitted for publication., 1992.

[6] W.T. Newsome and E. B. Pare. A selective impairment of motion perception following lesions of the middle temporal visual area (MT). *J. Neuroscience*, 8:2201–2211, 1988.

[7] D. A. Robinson. Models of oculomotor neural organization. In P. Bach y Rita and C. C. Collins, editors, *The Control of Eye Movements*, page 519. Academic, New York, 1971.

Against Edges: Function Approximation with Multiple Support Maps

Trevor Darrell and Alex Pentland
Vision and Modeling Group, The Media Lab
Massachusetts Institute of Technology
E15-388, 20 Ames Street
Cambridge MA, 02139

Abstract

Networks for reconstructing a sparse or noisy function often use an edge field to segment the function into homogeneous regions, This approach assumes that these regions do not overlap or have disjoint parts, which is often false. For example, images which contain regions split by an occluding object can't be properly reconstructed using this type of network. We have developed a network that overcomes these limitations, using support maps to represent the segmentation of a signal. In our approach, the support of each region in the signal is explicitly represented. Results from an initial implementation demonstrate that this method can reconstruct images and motion sequences which contain complicated occlusion.

1   Introduction

The task of efficiently approximating a function is central to the solution of many important problems in perception and cognition. Many vision algorithms, for instance, integrate depth or other scene attributes into a dense map useful for robotic tasks such as grasping and collision avoidance. Similarly, learning and memory are often posed as a problem of generalizing from stored observations to predict future behavior, and are solved by interpolating a surface through the observations in an appropriate abstract space. Many control and planning problems can also be solved by finding an optimal trajectory given certain control points and optimization constraints.

In general, of course, finding solutions to these approximation problems is an ill-posed problem, and no exact answer can be found without the application of some prior knowledge or assumptions. Typically, one assumes the surface to be fit is either locally smooth or has some particular parametric form or basis function description. Many successful systems have been built to solve such problems in the cases where these assumptions are valid. However in a wide range of interesting cases where there is no single global model or universal smoothness constraint, such systems have difficulty. These cases typically involve the approximation or estimation of a heterogeneous function whose typical local structure is known, but which also includes an unknown number of abrupt changes or discontinuities in shape.

2   Approximation of Heterogeneous Functions

In order to accurately approximate a heterogeneous function with a minimum number of parameters or interpolation units, it is necessary to divide the function into homogeneous chunks which can be approximated parsimoniously. When there is more than one homogeneous chunk in the signal/function, the data must be segmented so that observations of one object do not intermingle with and corrupt the approximation of another region.

One simple approach is to estimate an edge map to denote the boundaries of homogeneous regions in the function, and then to regularize the function within such boundaries. This method was formalized by Geman and Geman (1984), who developed the "line-process" to insert discontinuities in a regularization network. A regularized solution can be efficiently computed by a neural network, either using discrete computational elements or analog circuitry (Poggio et al. 1985; Terzopoulos 1988). In this context, the line-process can be thought of as an array of switches placed between interpolation nodes (Figure 1a). As the regularization proceeds in this type of network, the switches of the line process open and prevent smoothing across suspected discontinuities. Essentially, these switches are opened when the squared difference between neighboring interpolated values exceeds some threshold (Blake and Zisserman 1987; Geiger and Girosi 1991). In practice a continuation method is used to avoid problems with local minima, and a continuous non-linearity is used in place of a boolean discontinuity. The term "resistive fuse" is often used to describe these connections between interpolation sites (Harris et al. 1990).

3   Limitations of Edge-based Segmentation

An edge-based representation assumes that homogeneous chunks of a function are completely connected, and have no disjoint subregions. For the visual reconstruction task, this implies that the projection of an object onto the image plane will always yield a single connected region. While this may be a reasonable assumption for certain classes of synthetic images, it is not valid for realistic natural images which contain occlusion and/or transparent phenomena.

While a human observer can integrate over gaps in a region split by occlusion, the line process will prevent any such smoothing, no matter how close the subregions are in the image plane. When these disjoint regions are small (as when viewing an object through branches or leaves), the interpolated values provided by such a

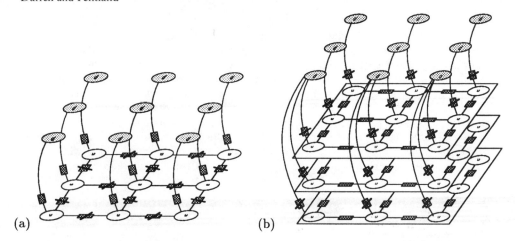

(a)   (b)

Figure 1: (a) Regularization network with line-process. Shaded circles represent data nodes, while open circles represent interpolation nodes. Solid rectangles indicate resistors; slashed rectangles indicate "resistive fuses". (b) Regularization network with explicit support maps; support process can be implemented by placing resistive fuses between data and interpolation nodes (other constraints on support are described in text).

network will not be reliable, since observation noise can not be averaged over a large number of samples.

Similarly, an edge-based approach cannot account for the perception of motion transparency, since these stimuli have no coherent local neighborhoods. Human observers can easily interpolate 3-D surfaces in transparent random-dot motion displays (Husain et al. 1989). In this type of display, points only last a few frames, and points from different surfaces are transparently intermingled. With a line-process, no smoothing or integration would be possible, since neighboring points in the image belong to different 3-D surfaces. To represent and process images containing this kind of transparent phenomena, we need a framework that does not rely on a global 2D edge map to make segmentation decisions. By generalizing the regularization/surface interpolation paradigm to use support maps rather than a line-process, we can overcome limitations the discontinuity approach has with respect to transparency.

4   Using Support Maps for Segmentation

Our approach decomposes a heterogeneous function into a set of individual approximations corresponding to the homogeneous regions of the function. Each approximation covers a specific region, and ues a support map to indicate which points belong to that region. Unlike an edge-based representation, the support of an approximation need not be a connected region — in fact, the support can consist of a scattered collection of independent points!

For a single approximation, it is relatively straight-forward to compute a support map. Given an approximation, we can find the support it has in the function by thresholding the residual error of that approximation. In terms of analog regularization, the support map (or support "process") can be implemented by placing a resistive fuse between the data and the interpolating units (Figure 1b).

A single support map is limited in usefulness, since only one region can be approximated. In fact, it reduces to the "outlier" rejection paradigm of certain robust estimation methods, which are known to have severe theoretical limits on the amount of outlier contamination they can handle (Meer et al. 1991; Li 1985). To represent true heterogeneous stimuli, multiple support maps are needed, with one support map corresponding to each homogeneous (but not necessarily connected) region.

We have developed a method to estimate a set of these support maps, based on finding a minimal length description of the function. We adopt a three-step approach: first, we generate a set of candidate support maps using simple thresholding techniques. Second, we find the subset of these maps which minimally describes the function, using a network optimization to find the smallest set of maps that covers all the observations. Finally, we re-allocate the support in this subset, such that only the approximation with the lowest residual error supports a particular point.

4.1   Estimating Initial Support Fields

Ideally, we would like to consider all possible support patterns of a given dimension as candidate support maps. Unfortunately, the combinatorics of the problem makes this impossible; instead, we attempt to find a manageable number of initial maps which will serve as a useful starting point.

A set of candidate approximations can be obtained in many ways. In our work we have initialized their surfaces either using a table of typical values or by fitting a small fixed regions of the function. We denote each approximation of a homogeneous region as a tuple, $(a_i, \vec{s_i}, \vec{u_i}, \vec{r_i})$, where $\vec{s_i} = \{s_{ij}\}$ is a support map, $\vec{u_i} = \{u_{ij}\}$ is the approximated surface, and $\vec{r_i} = \{r_{ij}\}$ is the residual error computed by taking the difference of $\vec{u_i}$ with the observed data. (The scalar a_i is used in deciding which subset of approximations are used in the final representation.) The support fields are set by thresholding the residual field based on our expected (or assumed) observation variance θ.

$$s_{ij} = \left\{ \begin{array}{ll} 1 & if\ (r_{ij})^2\ <\ \theta \\ 0 & otherwise \end{array} \right\}$$

4.2   Estimating the Number of Regions

Perhaps the most critical problem in recovering a good heterogeneous description is estimating how many regions are in the function. Our approach to this problem is based on finding a small set of approximations which constitutes a parsimonious description of the function. We attempt to find a subset of the candidate approximations whose support maps are a *minimal covering* of the function, e.g. the smallest subset whose combined support covers the entire function. In non-degenerate cases this will consist of one approximation for each real region in the function.

The quantity a_i indicates if approximation i is included in the final representation. A positive value indicates it is "active" in the representation; a negative value indicates it is excluded from the representation. Initially a_i is set to zero for each approximation; to find a minimal covering, this quantity is dynamically updated as a function of the number of points uniquely supported by a particular support map.

A point is uniquely supported in a support map if it is supported by that map and no other. Essentially, we find these points by modulating the support values of a particular approximation with shunting inhibition from all other active approximations. To compute c_{ij}, a flag that indicates whether or not point j of map i is uniquely supported, we multiply each support map with the product of the inverse of all other maps whose a_i value indicates it is active:

$$c_{ij} = s_{ij} \prod_{k \neq i}(1 - s_{kj}\sigma(a_k))$$

where $\sigma()$ is a sigmoid function which converts the real-valued a_i into a multiplicative factor in the range $(0, 1)$. The quantity c_{ij} is close to one at uniquely supported points, and close to zero for all other points.

If there are a sufficient number of uniquely supported points in an approximation, we increase a_i, otherwise it is decreased:

$$\frac{d}{dt}a_i = \sum_j c_{ij} - \alpha. \tag{1}$$

where α specifies the penalty for adding another approximation region to the representation. This constant determines the smallest number of points we are willing to have constitute a distinct region in the function. The network defined by these equations has a corresponding Lyoponov function:

$$E = \sum_i^N a_i(-\sum_j^M(\sigma(s_{ij})\prod_{k \neq i}(1 - \sigma(s_{kj})\sigma(a_k))) + \alpha)$$

so it will be guaranteed to converge to a local minima if we bound the values of a_i (for fixed s_{ij} and α). After convergence, those approximations with positive a_i are kept, and the rest are discarded. Empirically we have found the local minima found by our network correspond to perceptually salient segmentations.

4.3   Refining Support Fields

Once we have a set of approximations whose support maps minimally cover the function (and presumably correspond to the actual regions of the function), we can refine the support using a more powerful criteria than a local threshold. First, we interpolate the residual error values through unsampled points, so that support can be computed even where there are no observations. Then we update the support maps based on which approximation has the lowest residual error for a given point:

$$s_{ij} = \begin{cases} 1 & if \ (r_{ij})^2 < \theta \\ & and \ (r_{ij})^2 = \min_{\{k|a_k>0\}}(r_{kj})^2 \\ 0 & otherwise \end{cases}$$

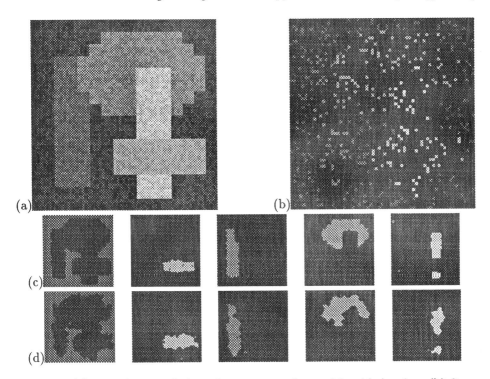

Figure 2: (a) Function consisting of constant regions with added noise. (b) Same function sparsely sampled. (c) Support maps found to approximate uniformly sampled function. (d) Support maps found for sparsely sampled function.

5   Results

We tested how well our network could reconstruct functions consisting of piecewise constant patches corrupted with random noise of known variance. Figure 2(a) shows the image containing the function the used in this experiment. We initialized 256 candidate approximations, each with a different constant surface. Since the image consisted of piecewise constant regions, the interpolation performed by each approximation was to compute a weighted average of the data over the supported points. Other experiments have used more powerful shape models, such as thin-plate or membrane Markov random fields, as well as piecewise-quadratic polynomials (Darrell et al. 1990).

Using a penalty term which prevented approximations with 10 or fewer support points to be considered ($\alpha = 10.0$), the network found 5 approximations which covered the entire image; their support maps are shown in Figure 2(c). The estimated surfaces corresponded closely to the values in the constant patches before noise was added. We ran a the same experiment on a sparsely sampled version of this function, as shown in Figure 2(b) and (d), with similar results and only slightly reduced accuracy in the recovered shape of the support maps.

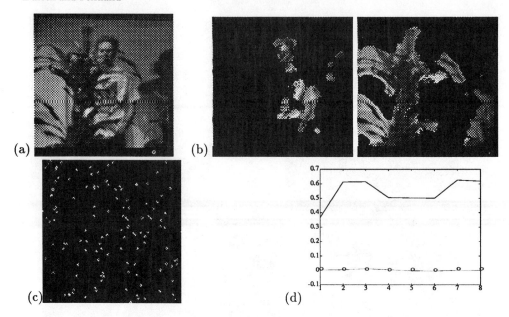

(a) (b)

(c) (d)

Figure 3: (a) First frame from image sequence and (b) recovered regions. (c) First frame from random dot sequence described in text. (d) Recovered parameter values across frames for dots undergoing looming motion; solid line plots T_z, dotted line plots T_x, and circles plot T_y for each frame.

We have also applied our framework to the problem of motion segmentation. For homogeneous data, a simple "direct" method can be used to model image motion (Horn and Weldon 1988). Under this assumption, the image intensities for a region centered at the origin undergoing a translation (T_x, T_y, T_z) satisfy at each point

$$0 = \frac{dI}{dt} + T_x \frac{dI}{dx} + T_y \frac{dI}{dy} + T_z \left(x \frac{dI}{dx} + y \frac{dI}{dy} \right)$$

where I is the image function. Each approximation computes a motion estimate by selecting a T vector which minimizes the square of the right hand side of this equation over its support map, using a weighted least-squares algorithm. The residual error at each point is then simply this constraint equation evaluated with the particular translation estimate.

Figure 3(a) shows the first frame of one sequence, containing a person moving behind a stationary plant. Our network began with 64 candidate approximations, with the initial motion parameters in each distributed uniformly along the parameter axes. Figure 3(b) shows the segmentation provided by our method. Two regions were found to be needed, one for the person and one for the plant. Most of the person has been correctly grouped together despite the occlusion caused by the plant's leaves. Points that have no spatial or temporal variation in the image sequence are not attributed to any approximation, since they are invisible to our motion model. Note that there is a cast shadow moving in synchrony with the person in the scene, and is thus grouped with that approximation.

Finally, we ran our system on the finite-lifetime, transparent random dot stimulus described in Section 2. Since our approach recovers a global motion estimate for each region in each frame, we do not need to build explicit pixel-to-pixel correspondences over long sequences. We used two populations of random dots, one undergoing a looming motion and one a rightward shift. After each frame 10% of the dots died off and randomly moved to a new point on the 3-D surface. Ten 128x128 frames were rendered using perspective projection; the first is shown in Figure 3(c)

We applied our method independently to each trio of successive frames, and in each case two approximations were found to account for the motion information in the scene. Figure 3(d) shows the parameters recovered for the looming motion. Similar results were found for the translating motion, except that the T_x parameter was nonzero rather than T_z. Since the recovered estimates were consistent, we would be able to decrease the overall uncertainty by averaging the parameter values over successive frames.

References

Geman, S., and Geman, D. (1984) Stochastic relaxation, Gibbs distribution, and Bayesian restoration of images. *Trans. Pattern Anal. Machine Intell.* 6:721-741.

Poggio, T., Torre, V., and Koch, C. (1985) Computational vision and regularization theory. *Nature* 317(26).

Terzopoulos, D. (1988) The computation of visible surface representations. *IEEE Trans. Pattern Anal. Machine Intell.* 10:4.

Geiger, D., and Girosi, F. (1991) Parallel and deterministic algorithms from MRF's: surface reconstruction. *Trans. Pattern Anal. Machine Intell.* 13:401-412.

Blake, A. and Zisserman, A. (1987) *Visual Reconstruction*; MIT Press, Cambridge, MA.

Harris J., Koch, C., Staats, E., and Luo, J. (1990) Analog hardware for detecting discontinuities in early vision *Intl. J. Computer Vision* 4:211-233.

Husain, M., Treue, S., and Andersen, R. A. (1989) Surface interpolation in three-dimensional structure-from-motion perception. *Neural Computation* 1:324-333.

Meer, P., Mintz, D., and Rosenfeld, A. (1991) Robust regression methods for computer vision: A review. *Intl. J. Computer Vision*; 6:60-70.

Li, G. (1985) Robust Regression. In D.C. Hoaglin, F. Mosteller and J.W. Tukey (Eds.) *Exploring Data, Tables, Trends and Shapes*: John Wiley & Sons, N.Y.

Darrell, T., Sclaroff, S., and Pentland, A. P. (1990) Segmentation by minimal description. *Proc. IEEE 3nd Intl. Conf. Computer Vision*; Osaka, Japan.

Horn, B.K.P., and Weldon, E.J. (1988) Direct methods for recovering motion. *Intl. J. Computer Vision* 2:51-76.

Markov Random Fields Can Bridge Levels of Abstraction

Paul R. Cooper
Institute for the Learning Sciences
Northwestern University
Evanston, IL
cooper@ils.nwu.edu

Peter N. Prokopowicz
Institute for the Learning Sciences
Northwestern University
Evanston, IL
prokopowicz@ils.nwu.edu

Abstract

Network vision systems must make inferences from evidential information across levels of representational abstraction, from low level invariants, through intermediate scene segments, to high level behaviorally relevant object descriptions. This paper shows that such networks can be realized as Markov Random Fields (MRFs). We show first how to construct an MRF functionally equivalent to a Hough transform parameter network, thus establishing a principled probabilistic basis for visual networks. Second, we show that these MRF parameter networks are more capable and flexible than traditional methods. In particular, they have a well-defined probabilistic interpretation, intrinsically incorporate feedback, and offer richer representations and decision capabilities.

1 INTRODUCTION

The nature of the vision problem dictates that neural networks for vision must make inferences from evidential information across levels of representational abstraction. For example, local image evidence about edges might be used to determine the occluding boundary of an object in a scene. This paper demonstrates that parameter networks [Ballard, 1984], which use voting to bridge levels of abstraction, can be realized with Markov Random Fields (MRFs).

We show two main results. First, an MRF is constructed with functionality formally equivalent to that of a parameter net based on the Hough transform. Establishing

396

this equivalence provides a sound probabilistic foundation for neural networks for vision. This is particularly important given the fundamentally evidential nature of the vision problem.

Second, we show that parameter networks constructed from MRFs offer a more flexible and capable framework for intermediate vision than traditional feedforward parameter networks with threshold decision making. In particular, MRF parameter nets offer a richer representational framework, the potential for more complex decision surfaces, an integral treatment of feedback, and probabilistically justified decision and training procedures. Implementation experiments demonstrate these features.

Together, these results establish a basis for the construction of integrated network vision systems with a single well-defined representation and control structure that intrinsically incorporates feedback.

2 BACKGROUND

2.1 HOUGH TRANSFORM AND PARAMETER NETS

One approach to bridging levels of abstraction in vision is to combine local, highly variable evidence into segments which can be described compactly by their parameters. The Hough transform offers one method for obtaining these high-level parameters. Parameter networks implement the Hough transform in a parallel feedforward network. The central idea is voting: local low-level evidence cast votes via the network for compatible higher-level parameterized hypotheses. The classic Hough example finds lines from edges. Here local evidence about the direction and magnitude of image contrast is combined to extract the parameters of lines (e.g. slope-intercept), which are more useful scene segments. The Hough transform is widely used in computer vision (e.g. [Bolle *et al.*, 1988]) to bridge levels of abstraction.

2.2 MARKOV RANDOM FIELDS

Markov Random Fields offer a formal foundation for networks [Geman and Geman, 1984] similar to that of the Boltzmann machine. MRFs define a prior joint probability distribution over a set $\mathbf{X}$ of discrete random variables. The possible values for the variables can be interpreted as possible local features or hypotheses. Each variable is associated with a node S in an undirected graph (or network), and can be written as X_s. An assignment of values to all the variables in the field is called a configuration, and is denoted ω; an assignment of a single variable is denoted ω_s. Each fully-connected neighborhood C in a configuration of the field has a weight, or clique potential, V_c.

We are interested in the probability distributions P over the random field $\mathbf{X}$. Markov Random Fields have a locality property:

$$P(X_s = \omega_s | X_r = \omega_r, r \in S, r \neq s) = P(X_s = \omega_s | X_r = \omega_r, r \in N_s) \qquad (1)$$

that says roughly that the state of site is dependent only upon the state of its neighbors (N_s). MRFs can also be characterized in terms of an energy function U

with a Gibb's distribution:

$$P(\omega) = \frac{e^{-U(\omega)/T}}{Z} \tag{2}$$

where T is the temperature, and Z is a normalizing constant.

If we are interested only in the prior distribution $P(\omega)$, the energy function U is defined as:

$$U(\omega) = \sum_{c \in C} V_c(\omega) \tag{3}$$

where C is the set of cliques defined by the neighborhood graph, and the V_c are the clique potentials. Specifying the clique potentials thus provides a convenient way to specify the global joint prior probability distribution P, i.e. to encode prior domain knowledge about plausible structures.

Suppose we are instead interested in the distribution $P(\omega|O)$ on the field after an observation O, where an observation constitutes a combination of spatially distinct observations at each local site. The evidence from an observation at a site is denoted $P(O_s|\omega_s)$ and is called a likelihood. Assuming likelihoods are local and spatially distinct, it is reasonable to assume that they are conditionally independent. Then, with Bayes' Rule we can derive:

$$U(\omega|O) = \sum_{c \in C} V_c(\omega) - T \sum_{s \in S} \log P(O_s|\omega_s) \tag{4}$$

The MRF definition, together with evidence from the current problem, leaves a probability distribution over all possible configurations. An algorithm is then used to find a solution, normally the configuration of maximal probability, or equivalently, minimal energy as expressed in equation 4. The problem of minimizing non-convex energy functions, especially those with many local minima, has been the subject of intense scrutiny recently (e.g. [Kirkpatrick *et al.*, 1983; Hopfield and Tank, 1985]). In this paper we focus on developing MRF representations wherein the minimum energy configuration defines a desirable goal, not on methods of finding the minimum. In our experiments have have used the deterministic Highest Confidence First (HCF) algorithm [Chou and Brown, 1990].

MRFs have been widely used in computer vision applications, including image restoration, segmentation, and depth reconstruction [Geman and Geman, 1984; Marroquin, 1985; Chellapa and Jain, 1991]. All these applications involve flat representations at a single level of abstraction. A novel aspect of our work is the hierarchical framework which explicitly represents visual entities at different levels of abstraction, so that these higher-order entities can serve as an interpretation of the data as well as play a role in further constraint satisfaction at even higher levels.

3   CONSTRUCTING MRFS EQUIVALENT TO PARAMETER NETWORKS

Here we define a Markov Random Field that computes a Hough transform; i.e. it detects higher-order features by tallying weighted votes from low-level image components and thresholding the sum. The MRF has one discrete variable for

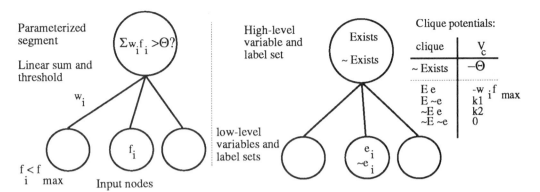

Figure 1: Left: Hough-transform parameter net. Input determines confidence f_i in each low-level feature; these confidences are weighted (w_i), summed, and thresholded. Right: Equivalent MRF. Circles show variables with possible labels and non-zero unary clique potentials; lines show neighborhoods; potentials are for the four labellings of the binary cliques.

the higher-order feature, whose possible values are *exists* and *doesn't exist* and one discrete variable for each voting element, with the same two possible values. Such a field could be replicated in space to compute many features simultaneously.

The construction follows from two ideas: first, the clique potentials of the network are defined such that only two of the many configurations need be considered, the other configurations being penalized by high clique potentials (i.e. low a priori probability). One configuration encodes the decision that the higher-order feature exists, the other that it doesn't exist. The second point is that the energy of the "doesn't exist" configuration is independent of the observation, while the energy of the "exists" configurations improves with the strength of the evidence.

Consider a parameter net for the Hough transform that represents only a single parameterized image segment (e.g. a line segment) and a set of low-level features, (e.g. edges) which vote for it (Figure 1 left). The variables, labels, and neighborhoods, of the equivalent MRF are defined in the right side of Figure 1 The clique potentials, which depend on the Hough parameters, are shown in the right side of the figure for a single neighborhood of the graph (There are four ways to label this clique.) Unspecified unary potentials are zero. Evidence applies only to the labels e_i; it is the likelihood of making a local observation O_i:

$$P(O_i \mid e_i) = e^{w_i(f_i - f_{max})} \tag{5}$$

In lemma 1, we show that the configuration $\omega_E = E e_1 e_2 \ldots e_n$, has an energy equal to the negated weighted sum of the feature inputs, and configuration $\omega_\theta = \neg E \neg e_1 \neg e_2 \ldots \neg e_n$ has a constant energy equal to the negated Hough threshold. Then, in lemma 2, we show that the clique potentials restrict the possible configurations to only these two, so that the network must have its minimum energy in a configuration whose high-level feature has the correct label.

Lemma 1:

$U(\omega_E \mid O) = -\sum_{i=1}^{n} w_i f_i$

$U(\omega_\theta \mid O) = -\theta$

Proof: The energy contributed by the clique potentials in ω_E is $\sum_{i=1}^{n} -w_i f_{max}$. Defining $W \equiv \sum_{i=1}^{n} w_i$, this simplifies to $-W f_{max}$.

The evidence also contributes to the energy of ω_E, in the form: $-\sum_{i=1}^{n} \log e_i$. Substituting from 5 into 4 and simplifying gives the total posterior energy of ω_E:

$$U(\omega_E \mid O) = -W f_{max} + W f_{max} - \sum_{i=1}^{n} w_i f_i = -\sum_{i=1}^{n} w_i f_i \qquad (6)$$

The energy of the configuration ω_θ does not depend on evidence derived from the Hough features. It has only one clique with a non-zero potential, the unary clique of label $\neg E$. Hence $U(\omega_\theta \mid O) = -\theta$. $\square$

Lemma 2:

$(\forall \omega)(\omega = E \ldots \neg e_k \ldots) \Rightarrow U(\omega \mid O) > U(\omega_E \mid O)$

$(\forall \omega)(\omega = \neg E \ldots e_k \ldots) \Rightarrow U(\omega \mid O) > U(\omega_\theta \mid O)$

Proof: For a mixed configuration $\omega = E \ldots \neg e_k \ldots$, changing label $\neg e_k$ to e_k adds energy because of the evidence associated with e_k. This is at most $w_i f_{max}$. It also removes energy because of the potential of the clique $E e_k$, which is $-w_i f_{max}$. Because the clique potential K_2 from $E \neg e_k$ is also removed, if $K_2 > 0$, then changing this label always reduces the energy.

For a mixed configuration $\omega = \neg E \ldots e_k \ldots$, changing the low-level label e_k to $\neg e_k$ cannot add to the energy contributed by evidence, since $\neg e_k$ has no evidence associated with it. There is no binary clique potential for $\neg E \neg e$, but the potential K_1 for clique $\neg E e_k$ is removed. Therefore, again, choosing any $K_1 > 0$ reduces energy and ensures that compatible labels are preferred. $\square$

From lemma 2, there are two configurations that could possibly have minimal posterior energy. From lemma 1, the configuration which represents the existence of the higher-order feature is preferred if and only if the weighted sum of the evidence exceeds threshold, as in the Hough transform.

Often it is desirable to find the mode in a high-level parameter space rather than those elements which surpass a fixed threshold. Finding a single mode is easy to do in a Hough-like MRF; add lateral connections between the *exists* labels of the high-level features to form a winner-take-all network. If the potentials for these cliques are large enough, it is not possible for more than one variable corresponding to a high-level feature to be labeled *exists*.

4   BEYOND HOUGH TRANSFORMS: MRF PARAMETER NETS

The essentials of a parameter network are a set of variables representing low-order features, a set of variables representing high-order features, and the appropriate

Figure 2: Noisy image data

Figure 3: Three parameter-net MRF experiments: white dots in the lower images indicate the decision that a horizontal or vertical local edge is present. Upper images show the horizontal and vertical lines found. The left net is a feedforward Hough transform; the middle net uses positive feedback from lines to edges; the right net uses negative feedback, from non-existing lines to non-existing edges

weighted connections between them. This section explores the characteristics of more "natural" MRF parameter networks, still based on the same variables and connections, but not limited to binary label sets and sum/threshold decision procedures.

4.1   EXPERIMENTS WITH FEEDBACK

The Hough transform and its parameter net instantiation are inherently feed-forward. In contrast, all MRFs intrinsically incorporate feedback. We experimented with a network designed to find lines from edges. Horizontal and vertical edge inputs are represented at the low level, and horizontal and vertical lines which span the image at the high level. The input data look like Figure 2. Probabilistic evidence for the low-level edges is generated from pixel data using a model of edge-image formation [Sher, 1987]. The edges vote for compatible lines. In Figure 3, the decision of the feed-forward, Hough transform MRF is shown at the left: edges exist where the local evidence is sufficient; lines exist where enough votes are received.

Keeping the same topology, inputs, and representations in the MRF, we added top-down feedback by changing binary clique potentials so that the existence of a line at the high level is more strongly compatible with the existence of its edges. Missing edges are filled in (middle). By making non-existent lines strongly incompatible with the existence of edges, noisy edges are substantially removed (right). Other MRFs for segmentation [Chou and Brown, 1990; Marroquin, 1985] find collinear edges, but cannot reason about lines and therefore cannot exploit top-down feedback.

4.2   REPRESENTATION AND DECISION MAKING

Both parameter nets and MRFs represent confidence in local hypotheses, but here the MRF framework has intrinsic advantages. MRFs can simultaneously represent independent beliefs for and against the same hypotheses. In an active vision system, which must reason about gathering as well as interpreting evidence, one could extend this to include the label *don't know*, allowing explicit reasoning about the condition in which the local evidence insufficiently supports any decision. MRFs can also express higher-order constraints as more than a set of pairs. The exploitation of appropriate 3-cliques, for example, has been shown to be very useful [Cooper, 1990].

Since the potentials in an MRF are related to local conditional probabilities, there is a principled way to obtain them. Observations can be used to estimate local joint probabilities, which can be converted to the clique potentials defining the prior distribution on the field [Pearl, 1988; Swain, 1990].

Most evidence integration schemes require, in addition to the network topology and parameters, the definition of a decision making process (e.g. thresholding) and a theory of parameter acquisition for that process, which is often ad hoc. To estimate the maximum posterior probability of a MRF, on the other hand, is intrinsically to make a decision among the possibilities embedded in the chosen variables and labels.

The space of possible decisions (interpretations of problem input) is also much richer for MRFs than for parameter networks. For both nets, the nodes for which evidence is available define a n-dimensional problem input space. The weights divide this space into regions defined by the one best interpretation (configuration) for all problems in that region. With parameter nets, these regions are separated by planes, since only the sum of the inputs matters. In MRFs, the energy depends on the log-product of the evidence and the sum of the potentials, allowing more general decision surfaces. Non-linear decisions such as AND or XOR are easy to encode, whereas they are impossible for the linear Hough transform.

5   CONCLUSION

This paper has shown that parameter networks can be constructed with Markov Random Fields. MRFs can thus bridge representational levels of abstraction in network vision systems. Furthermore, it has been demonstrated that MRFs offer the potential for a significantly more powerful implementation of parameter nets, even if their topological architecture is identical to traditional Hough networks. In short, at least one method is now available for constructing intermediate vision solutions with Markov Random Fields.

It may thus be possible to build entire integrated vision systems with a single well-justified formal framework - Markov Random Fields. Such systems would have a unified representational scheme, constraints and evidence with well-defined semantics, and a single control structure. Furthermore, feedback and feedforward flow of information, crucial in any complete vision system, is intrinsic to MRFs.

Of course, the task still remains to build a functioning vision system for some domain. In this paper we have said nothing about the definition of specific "features" and the constraints between them that would constitute a useful system. But providing essential tools implemented in a well-defined formal framework is an important step toward building robust, functioning systems.

Acknowledgements

Support for this research was provided by NSF grant #IRI-9110492 and by Andersen Consulting, through their founding grant to the Institute for the Learning Sciences. Patrick Yuen wrote the MRF simulator that was used in the experiments.

References

[Ballard, 1984] D.H. Ballard, "Parameter Networks," *Artificial Intelligence*, 22(3):235–267, 1984.

[Bolle *et al.*, 1988] Ruud M. Bolle, Andrea Califano, Rick Kjeldsen, and R.W. Taylor, "Visual Recognition Using Concurrent and Layered Parameter Networks," Technical Report RC-14249, IBM Research Division, T.J. Watson Research Center, Dec 1988.

[Chellapa and Jain, 1991] Rama Chellapa and Anil Jain, editors, *Markov Random Fields: Theory and Application*, Academic Press, 1991.

[Chou and Brown, 1990] Paul B. Chou and Christopher M. Brown, "The Theory and Practice of Bayesian Image Labeling," *International Journal of Computer Vision*, 4:185–210, 1990.

[Cooper, 1990] Paul R. Cooper, "Parallel Structure Recognition with Uncertainty: Coupled Segmentation and Matching," In *Proceedings of the Third International Conference on Computer Vision ICCV '90*, Osaka, Japan, December 1990.

[Geman and Geman, 1984] Stuart Geman and Donald Geman, "Stochastic Relaxation, Gibbs Distributions, and the Bayesian Restoration of Images," *PAMI*, 6(6):721–741, November 1984.

[Hopfield and Tank, 1985] J. J. Hopfield and D. W. Tank, ""Neural" Computation of Decisions in Optimization Problems," *Biological Cybernetics*, 52:141–152, 1985.

[Kirkpatrick *et al.*, 1983] S. Kirkpatrick, C.D. Gelatt, and M.P. Vecchi, "Optimization by Simulated Annealing," *Science*, 220:671–680, 1983.

[Marroquin, 1985] Jose Luis Marroquin, "Probabilistic Solution of Inverse Problems," Technical report, MIT Artificial Intelligence Laboratory, September, 1985.

[Pearl, 1988] Judea Pearl, *Probabilistic Reasoning in Intelligent Systems*, Morgan Kaufman, 1988.

[Sher, 1987] David B. Sher, "A Probabilistic Approach to Low-Level Vision," Technical Report 232, Department of Computer Science, University of Rochester, October 1987.

[Swain, 1990] Michael J. Swain, "Parameter Learning for Markov Random Fields with Highest Confidence First Estimation," Technical Report 350, Dept. of Computer Science, University of Rochester, August 1990.

Illumination and View Position in 3D Visual Recognition

Amnon Shashua
M.I.T. Artificial Intelligence Lab., NE43-737
and Department of Brain and Cognitive Science
Cambridge, MA 02139

Abstract

It is shown that both changes in viewing position and illumination conditions can be compensated for, prior to recognition, using combinations of images taken from different viewing positions and different illumination conditions. It is also shown that, in agreement with psychophysical findings, the computation requires at least a sign–bit image as input — contours alone are not sufficient.

1 Introduction

The task of visual recognition is natural and effortless for biological systems, yet the problem of recognition has been proven to be very difficult to analyze from a computational point of view. The fundamental reason is that novel images of familiar objects are often not sufficiently similar to previously seen images of that object. Assuming a rigid and isolated object in the scene, there are two major sources for this variability: geometric and photometric. The geometric source of variability comes from changes of view position. A 3D object can be viewed from a variety of directions, each resulting with a different 2D projection. The difference is significant, even for modest changes in viewing positions, and can be demonstrated by superimposing those projections (see Fig. 4, first row second image). Much attention has been given to this problem in the visual recognition literature ([9], and references therein), and recent results show that one can compensate for changes in viewing position by generating novel views from a small number of model views of the object [10, 4, 8].

Figure 1: A 'Mooney' image. See text for details.

The photometric source of variability comes from changing illumination conditions (positions and distribution of light sources in the scene). This has the effect of changing the brightness distribution in the image, and the location of shadows and specular reflections. The traditional approach to this problem is based on the notion of edge detection. The idea is that discontinuities in image brightness remain stable under changes of illumination conditions. This invariance is not complete and furthermore it is an open question whether this kind of contour information is sufficient, or even relevant, for purposes of visual recognition.

Consider the image in Fig. 1, adopted from Mooney's Closure Faces Test [6]. Most observers show no difficulty in interpreting the shape of the object from the right-hand image, but cannot identify the object when presented with only the contours. Also, many of the contours are shadow contours and therefore critically rely on the direction of light source. In Fig. 2 four frontal images of a doll from four different illumination conditions are shown together with their intensity step edges. The change in the contour image is significant and is not limited to shadow contours — some object edges appear or disappear as a result of the change in brightness distribution. Also shown in Fig. 4 is a sign–bit image of the intensity image followed by a convolution with a Difference of Gaussians. As with the Mooney image, it is considerably more difficult to interpret the image of a complex object with only the zero–crossing (or level–crossing) contours than when the sign–bits are added.

It seems, therefore, that a successful recognition scheme should be able to cope with changes in illumination conditions, as well as changes in viewing positions, by working with a richer source of information than just contours (for a different point of view, see [1]). The minimal information that seems to be sufficient, at least for coping with the photometric problem, is the sign–bit image.

The approach to visual recognition in this study is in line with the 'alignment' approach [9] and is also inspired by the work of Ullman and Basri [10] who show that the geometric source of variability can be handled by matching the novel projection to a linear combination of a small number of previously seen projections of that object. A recognition scheme that can handle both the geometric and photometric sources of variability is suggested by introducing three new results: (i) any image of a surface with a linear reflectance function (including Lambertian and Phong's model without point specularities) can be expressed as a linear combination of a fixed set of three images of that surface taken under different illumination conditions, (ii) from a computational standpoint, the coefficients are better recovered using the sign–bit image rather than the contour image, and (iii) one can compensate for both changes in viewing position and illumination conditions by using combinations of images taken from different viewing positions and different illumination conditions.

2   Linear Combination of Images

We start by assuming that view position is fixed and the only parameter that is allowed to change is the positions and distribution of light sources. The more general result that includes changes in viewing positions will be discussed in section 4.

Proposition 1 *All possible images of a surface, with a linear reflectance function, generated by all possible illumination conditions (positions and distribution of light sources) are spanned by a linear combination of images of the surface taken from independent illumination conditions.*

Proof: Follows directly from the general result that if $f_j(x)$, $x \in R^k$, $j = 1, ..., k$, are k linear functions, which are also linearly independent, then for any linear function $f(x)$, we have that $f(x) = \sum_j a_j f_j(x)$, for some constants a_j. []

The simplest case for which this result holds is the Lambertian reflectance model under a point light source (observed independently by Yael Moses, personal communication). Let r be an object point projecting to p. Let n_r represent the normal and albedo at r (direction and magnitude), and s represent the light source and its intensity. The brightness at p under the Lambertian model is $I(p) = n_r \cdot s$, and because s is fixed for all point p, we have $I(p) = a_1 I_1(p) + a_2 I_2(p) + a_3 I_3(p)$ where $I_j(p)$ is the brightness under light source s_j and where s_1, s_2, s_3 are linearly independent. This result generalizes, in a straightforward manner, to the case of multiple light sources as well.

The Lambertian model is suitable for matte surfaces, i.e. surfaces that diffusely reflect incoming light rays. One can add a 'shininess' component to account for the fact that for non-ideal Lambertian surfaces, more light is reflected in a direction making an equal angle of incidence with reflectance. In Phong's model of reflectance [7] this takes the form of $(n_r \cdot h)^c$ where h is the bisector of s and the viewer's direction v. The power constant c controls the degree of sharpness of the point specularity, therefore outside that region one can use a linear version of Phong's model by replacing the power constant with a multiplicative constant, to get the following function: $I(p) = n_r \cdot [s + \rho(v + s)]$. As before, the bracketed vector is fixed for all image points and therefore the linear combination result holds.

The linear combination result suggests therefore that changes in illumination can be compensated for, prior to recognition, by selecting three points (that are visible to s, s_1, s_2, s_3) to solve for a_1, a_2, a_3 and then match the novel image I with $I' = \sum_j a_j I_j$. The two images should match along all points p whose object points r are visible to s_1, s_2, s_3 (even if $n_r \cdot s < 0$, i.e. p is attached–shadowed); approximately match along points for which $n_r \cdot s_j < 0$, for some j ($I_j(p)$ is truncated to zero, geometrically s is projected onto the subspace spanned by the remaining basis light sources) and not match along points that are cast–shadowed in I ($n_r \cdot s > 0$ but r is not visible to s because of self occlusion). Coping with cast–shadows is an important task, but is not in the scope of this paper.

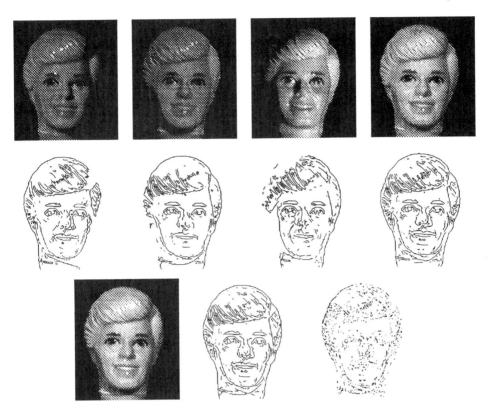

Figure 2: Linear combination of model images taken from the same viewing position and under different illumination conditions. *Row 1,2:* Three model images taken under a varying point light source, and the input image, and their brightness edges. *Row 3:* The image generated by the linear combination of the model images, its edges, and the difference edge image between the input and generated image.

The linear combination result also implies that, for the purposes of recognition, one does not need to recover shape or light source direction in order to compensate for changes in brightness distribution and attached shadows. Experimental results, on a non-ideal Lambertian surface, are shown in Fig. 2.

3   Coefficients from Contours and Sign–bits

Mooney pictures, such as in Fig. 1, demonstrate that humans can cope well with situations of varying illumination by using only limited information from the input image, namely the sign–bits, yet are not able to do so from contours alone. This observation can be predicted from a computational standpoint, as shown below.

Proposition 2 *The coefficients that span an image I by the basis of three other images, as described in proposition 1, can be solved, up to a common scale factor,*

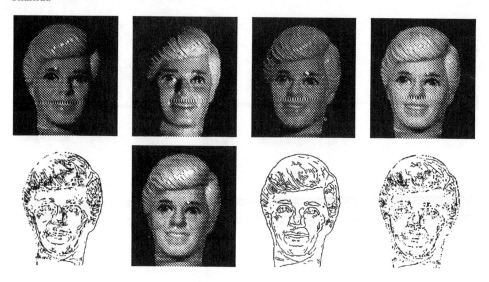

Figure 3: Compensating for both changes in view and illumination. *Row 1:* Three model images, one of which is taken from a different viewing direction (23° apart), and the input image from a novel viewing direction (in between the model images) and illumination condition. *Row 2:* difference image between the edges of the input image (shown separately in Fig. 4) and the edges of the view transformed first model image (first row, lefthand), the final generated image (linear combination of the three transformed model images), its edges, and the difference image between edges of input and generated image.

from just the contours of I — zero-crossings or level-crossings.

Proof: Let a_j be the coefficients that span I by the basis images I_j, $j = 1, 2, 3$, i.e. $I = \sum_j a_j I_j$. Let f, f_j be the result of applying a Difference of Gaussians (DOG) operator, with the same scale, on images I, I_j, $j = 1, 2, 3$. Since DOG is a linear operator we have that $f = \sum_j a_j f_j$. Since $f(p) = 0$ along zero-crossing points p of I, then by taking any three zero-crossing points, which are not on a cast–shadow border, we get a homogeneous set of equations from which a_j can be solved up to a common scale factor.

Similarly, let k be an unknown threshold applied to I. Therefore, along level crossings of I we have $k = \sum_j a_j I_j$, hence 4 level-crossing points, that are visible to all four light sources, are sufficient to solve for a_j and k. $\square$

This result is in accordance with what is known from image compression literature of reconstructing an image, up to a scale factor, from contours alone [2]. In both cases, here and in image compression, this result may be difficult to apply in practice because the contours are required to be given at sub-pixel accuracy. One can relax the accuracy requirement by using the gradients along the contours — a technique that works well in practice. Nevertheless, neither gradients nor contours at sub-pixel accuracy are provided by Mooney pictures, which leaves us with the sign–bits as the source of information for solving for the coefficients.

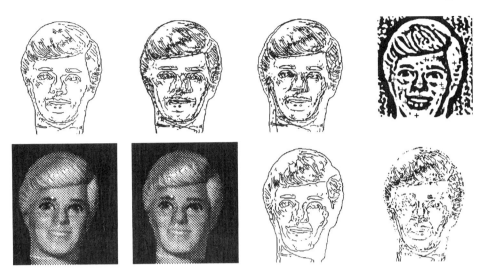

Figure 4: Compensating for changes in viewing position and illumination from a single view (model images are all from a single viewing position). Model images are the same as in Fig. 2, input image the same as in Fig. 3. *Row 1:* edges of input image, overlay of input edge image and edges of first model image, overlay with edges of the 2D affine transformed first model image, sign–bit input image with marked 'example' locations (16 of them). *Row 2:* linear combination image of the 2D affine transformed model images, the final generated image, its edges, overlay with edges of the input image.

Proposition 3 *Solving for the coefficients from the sign–bit image of I is equivalent to solving for a separating hyperplane in 3D in which image points serve as 'examples'.*

Proof: Let $z(p) = (f_1, f_2, f_3)^T$ be a vector function and $\omega = (a_1, a_2, a_3)^T$ be the unknown weight vector. Given the sign-bit image $\hat{f}$ of I, we have that for every point p, excluding zero-crossings, the scalar product $\omega^T z(p)$ is either positive or negative. In this respect, one can consider points in $\hat{f}$ as 'examples' in 3D space and the coefficients a_j as a vector normal to the separating hyperplane. $\Box$

A similar result can be obtained for the case of a thresholded image. The separating hyperplane in that case is defined in 4D, rather than 3D. Many schemes for finding a separating hyperplane have been described in Neural Network literature (see [5] for review) and in Discriminant Analysis literature ([3], for example). Experimental results shown in the next section show that 10—20 points, distributed over the entire object, are sufficient to produce results that are indistinguishable from those obtained from an exact solution.

By using the sign-bits instead of the zero-crossing contours we are trading a unique (up to a scale factor), but unstable, solution for an approximate, but stable, one. Also, by taking the sample points relatively far away from the contours (in order to minimize the chance of error) the scheme can tolerate a certain degree of misalignment between the basis images and the novel image. This property will be used in one of the schemes, described below, for combining changes of viewing positions and illumination conditions.

4   Changing Illumination and Viewing Positions

In this section, the recognition scheme is generalized to cope with both changes in illumination and viewing positions. Namely, given a set of images of an object as a model and an input image viewed from a novel viewing position and taken under a novel illumination condition we would like to generate an image, from the model, that is similar to the input image.

Proposition 4 *Any set of three images, satisfying conditions of proposition 1, of an object can be used to compensate for both changes in view and illumination.*

Proof: Any change in viewing position will induce both a change in the location of points in the image, and a change in their brightness (because of change in viewing angle and change in angle between light source and surface normal). From proposition 1, the change in brightness can be compensated for provided all the images are in alignment. What remains, therefore, is to bring the model images and the input image into alignment.

Case 1: If each of the three model images is viewed from a different position, then the remaining proof follows directly from the result of Ullman and Basri [10] who show that any view of an object with smooth boundaries, undergoing any affine transformation in space, is spanned by three views of the object.

Case 2: If only two of the model images are viewed from different positions, then given full correspondence between all points in the two model views and 4 corresponding points with the input image, we can transform all three model images to align with the input image in the following way. The 4 corresponding points between the input image and one of the model images define three corresponding vectors (taking one of the corresponding points, say o, as an origin) from which a 2D affine transformation, matrix A and vector w, can be recovered. The result, proved in [8], is that for every point p' in the input image who is in correspondence with p in the model image we have that $p' = [Ap + o' - Ao] + \alpha_p w$. The parameter α_p is invariant to any affine transformation in space, therefore is also invariant to changes in viewing position. One can, therefore, recover α_p from the known correspondence between two model images and use that to predict the location p'. It can be shown that this scheme provides also a good approximation in the case of objects with smooth boundaries (like an egg or a human head, for details see [8]).

Case 3: All three model images are from the same viewing position. The model images are first brought into 'rough alignment' (term adopted from [10]) with the input image by applying the transformation $Ap + o' - Ao + w$ to all points p in each model image. The remaining displacement between the transformed model images and the input image is $(\alpha_p - 1)w$ which can be shown to be bounded by the depth variation of the surface [8]. (In case the object is not sufficiently flat, more than 4 points may be used to define local transformations via a triangulation of those points). The linear combination coefficients are then recovered using the sign–bit scheme described in the previous section. The three transformed images are then linearly combined to create a new image that is compensated for illumination but is still displaced from the input image. The displacement can be recovered by using a brightness correlation scheme along the direction w to find $\alpha_p - 1$ for each point p. (for details, see [8]). $\square$

Experimental results of the last two schemes are shown in Figs. 3 and 4. The four corresponding points, required for view compensation, were chosen manually along the tip of eyes, eye-brow and mouth of the doll. The full correspondence that is required between the third model view and the other two in scheme 2 above, was established by first taking two pictures of the third view, one from a novel illumination condition and the other from a similar illumination condition to one of the other model images. Correspondence was then determined by using the scheme described in [8]. The extra picture was then discarded. The sample points for the linear combination were chosen automatically by selecting 10 points in smooth brightness regions. The sample points using the sign–bit scheme were chosen manually.

5 Summary

It has been shown that the effects photometry and geometry in visual recognition can be decoupled and compensated for prior to recognition. Three new results were shown: (i) photometric effects can be compensated for using a linear combination of images, (ii) from a computational standpoint, contours alone are not sufficient for recognition, and (iii) geometrical effects can be compensated for from any set of three images, from different illuminations, of the object.

Acknowledgments

I thank Shimon Ullman for his advice and support. Thanks to Ronen Basri, Tomaso Poggio, Whitman Richards and Daphna Weinshall for many discussions. A.S. is supported by NSF grant IRI-8900267.

References

[1] Cavanagh,P. *Proc. 13th ECVP, Andrei,G. (Ed.), 1990.*

[2] Curtis,S.R and Oppenheim,A.V. in Whitman,R. and Ullman,S. (eds.) *Image Understanding 1989.* pp.92–110, Ablex, NJ 1990.

[3] Duda,R.O. and Hart,P.E. *pattern classification and scene analysis.* NY, Wiley 1973.

[4] Edelman,S. and Poggio,T. *Massachusetts Institute of Technology, A.I. Memo 1181, 1990*

[5] Lippmann,R.P. *IEEE ASSP Magazine,* pp.4–22, 1987.

[6] Mooney,C.M. *Can. J. Psychol.* 11:219–226, 1957.

[7] Phong,B.T. *Comm. ACM,* 18, 6:311-317, 1975.

[8] Shashua,A. *Massachusetts Institute of Technology, A.I. Memo 1327, 1991*

[9] Ullman,S. *Cognition,* 32:193–254, 1989.

[10] Ullman,S. and Basri,R. *Massachusetts Institute of Technology, A.I. Memo 1052, 1989*

Hierarchical Transformation of Space in the Visual System

Alexandre Pouget   Stephen A. Fisher

Terrence J. Sejnowski
Computational Neurobiology Laboratory
The Salk Institute
La Jolla, CA 92037

Abstract

Neurons encoding simple visual features in area V1 such as orientation, direction of motion and color are organized in retinotopic maps. However, recent physiological experiments have shown that the responses of many neurons in V1 and other cortical areas are modulated by the direction of gaze. We have developed a neural network model of the visual cortex to explore the hypothesis that visual features are encoded in head-centered coordinates at early stages of visual processing. New experiments are suggested for testing this hypothesis using electrical stimulations and psychophysical observations.

1   Introduction

Early visual processing in cortical areas V1, V2 and MT appear to encode visual features in eye-centered coordinates. This is based primarily on anatomical data and recordings from neurons in these areas, which are arranged in retinotopic maps. In addition, when neurons in the visual cortex are electrically stimulated [9], the direction of the evoked eye movement depends only on the retinotopic position of the stimulation site, as shown in figure 1. Thus, when a position corresponding to the left part of the visual field is stimulated, the eyes move toward the left (left figure), and eye movements in the opposite direction are induced if neurons on the right side are stimulated (right figure).

412

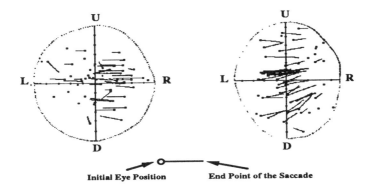

Figure 1: Eye Movements Evoked by Electrical Stimulations in V1

A variety of psychophysical experiments provide further evidence that simple visual features are organized according to retinal coordinates rather than spatiotopic coordinates [10, 5].

At later stages of visual processing the receptive fields of neurons become very large and in the posterior parietal cortex, containing areas believed to be important for sensory-motor coordination (LIP, VIP and 7a), the visual responses of neurons are modulated by both eye and head position [1, 2]. A previous model of the parietal cortex showed that the gain fields of the neurons observed there are consistent with a distributed spatial transformation from retinal to head-centered coordinates [14].

Recently, several investigators have found that static eye position also modulates the visual response of many neurons at early stages of visual processing, including the LGN, V1 and V3a [3, 6, 13, 12]. Furthermore, the modulation appears to be qualitatively similar to that previously reported in the parietal cortex and could contribute to those responses. These new findings suggest that coordinate transformations from retinal to spatial representations could be initiated much earlier than previously thought.

We have used network optimization techniques to study the spatial transformations in a feedforward hierarchy of cortical maps. The goals of the model were 1) to determine whether the modulation of neural responses with eye position as observed in V1 or V3a is sufficient to provide a head-centered coordinate frame, 2) to help interpret data based on the electrical stimulation of early visual areas, and 3) to provide a framework for designing experiments and testing predictions.

2   Methods

2.1   Network Task

The task of the network was to compute the head-centered coordinates of objects. If $\vec{E}$ is the eye position vector and $\vec{R}$ is the vector for the retinal position of the

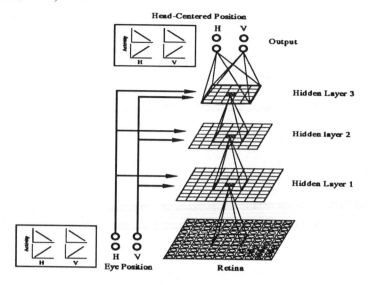

Figure 2: Network Architecture

object, then the head-centered position $\vec{P}$ is given by:

$$\vec{P} = \vec{R} + \vec{E} \qquad (1)$$

A two layer network with linear units can solve this problem. However, the goal of our study was not to find the optimal architecture for this task, but to explore the types of intermediate representation developed in a multilayer network of non-linear units and to compare these results with physiological recordings.

2.2   Network Architecture

We trained a partially-connected multilayer network to compute the head-centered position of objects from retinal and eye position signals available at the input layer. Weights were shared within each hidden layer [7] and adjusted with the backprop-agation algorithm [11]. All simulations were performed with the SN2 simulator developed by Botou and LeCun.

In the hierarchical architecture illustrated in figure 2, the sizes of the receptive fields were restricted in each layer and several hidden units were dedicated to each location, typically 3 to 5 units, depending on the layer. Although weights were shared between locations within a layer, each type of hidden unit was allowed to develop its own receptive field properties. This architecture preserves two essential aspects of the visual cortex: 1) restricted receptive fields organized in retinotopic maps and 2) the sizes of the receptive fields increase with distance from the retina.

Training examples consisted of an eye position vector and a gaussian pattern of activity placed at a particular location on the input layer and these were system-

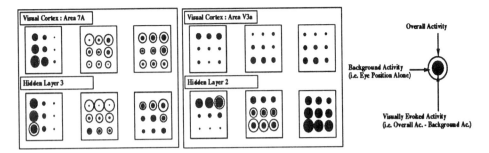

Figure 3: Spatial Gain Fields: Comparison Between Hidden Units and Cortical Neurons (background activity not shown for V3a neurons)

atically varied throughout the training. For some trials there were no visual inputs and the output layer was trained to reproduce the eye position.

2.3   Electrical Stimulation Experiments

Determining the head-centered position of an object is equivalent to computing the position of the eye required to foveate the object (i.e. for a foveated object $\vec{R} = 0$, which, according to equation 1, implies that $\vec{P} = \vec{E}$). Thus, the output of our network can be interpreted as the eye position for an intended saccadic eye movement to acquire the object.

For the electrical stimulation experiments we followed the protocol suggested by Goodman and Andersen [4] in an earlier study of the Zipser-Andersen model of parietal cortex [14]. The cortical model was stimulated by clamping the activity of a set of hidden units at a location in one of the layers to 1, their maximum values, and setting all visual inputs to 0. The changes in the activity of the output units were computed and interpreted as an intended saccade.

3   Results

We trained several networks with various numbers of hidden units per layer and found that they all converged to a nearly perfect solution in a few thousand sweeps through the training set.

3.1   Comparison Between Hidden Units and Cortical Neurons

The influence of eye position on the visual response of a cortical neuron is typically assessed by finding the visual stimulus eliciting the best response and measuring the gain of this response at nine different eye fixations [1]. The responses are plotted as circles with diameters proportional to activity and the set of nine circles is called the spatial gain field of a unit. We adopted the same procedure for studying the hidden units in the model.

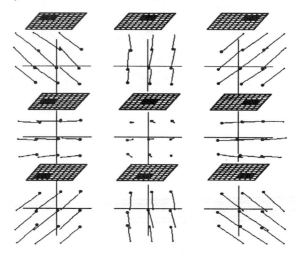

Figure 4: Eye Movements Evoked by Stimulating the Retina

The units in a fully-developed network have properties that are similar to those observed in cortical neurons (figure 3). Despite having restricted receptive fields, the overall activity of most units increased monotonically in one direction of eye position, each unit having a different preferred direction in head-centered space. Also, the inner and outer circles, corresponding to the visual activity and the overall activity (visual plus background) did not always increase along the same direction due to the nonlinear sigmoid squashing function of the unit.

3.2   Significance of the Spatial Gains Fields

Each hidden layer of the network has a retinotopic map but also contains spatiotopic (i.e. head-centered) information through the spatial gain fields. We call these retinospatiotopic maps.

At each location on a map, $\vec{R}$ is implicitly encoded by the position of a unit on the map, and $\vec{E}$ is provided by the inputs from the eye position units. Thus, each location contains all the information needed to recover $\vec{P}$, the head-centered coordinate. Therefore, all of the visual features in the map, such as orientation or color, are encoded in head-centered coordinates. This suggests that some visual representations in V1 and V3a may be retinospatiotopic.

3.3   Electrical Stimulation Experiments

Can electrical stimulation experiments distinguish between a purely retinotopic map, like the retina, and retinospatiotopic maps, like each of the hidden layers?

When input units in the retina are stimulated, the direction of the evoked movement is determined by the location of the stimulation site on the map (figure 4), as expected from a purely retinotopic map. For example, stimulating units in the upper

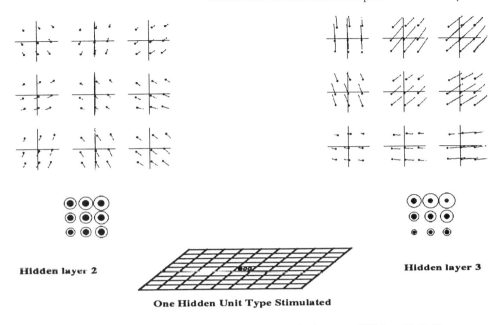

Hidden layer 2   **Hidden layer 3**

One Hidden Unit Type Stimulated

Figure 5: Eye Movements Evoked by Stimulating one Hidden Unit Type

left corner of the map produces an output in the upper left direction, regardless of initial eye position.

There were several types of hidden units at each spatial position of a hidden layer. When the hidden units were stimulated independently, the pattern of induced eye movements was no longer a function solely of the location of the stimulation (figure 5). Other factors, such as the preferred head-centered direction of the stimulated cell, were also important. Hence, the intermediate maps were not purely retinotopic.

If all the hidden units present at one location in a hidden layer were activated together, the pattern of outputs resembled the one obtained by stimulating the input layer (figure 6). Even though each hidden unit has a different preferred head-centered direction, when simultaneously activated, these directions balanced out and the dominant factor became the location of the stimulation.

Strong electrical stimulation in area V1 of the visual cortex is likely to recruit many neurons whose receptive fields share the same retinal location. This might explain why McIlwain [9] observed eye movements in directions that depended only on the position of the stimulation site. In higher visual areas with weaker retinotopy, it might be possible to obtain patterns closer to those produced by stimulating only one type of hidden unit. Such patterns of eye movements have already been observed in parietal area LIP [4].

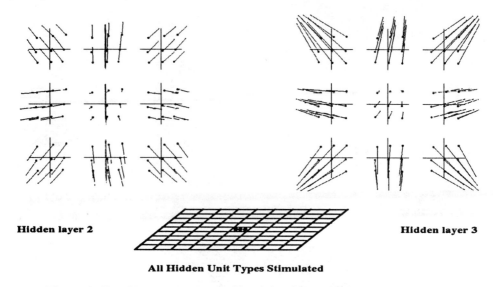

Hidden layer 2   **Hidden layer 3**

All Hidden Unit Types Stimulated

Figure 6: Eye Movements Evoked by Stimulating all Hidden Unit Types

4   Discussion and Predictions

The analysis of our hierarchical model shows that the gain modulation of visual responses observed at early stages of visual processing are consistent with the hypothesis that low-level visual features are encoded in head-centered coordinates. What experiments could confirm this hypothesis?

Electrical stimulation cannot distinguish between a retinotopic and a retinospatiotopic representation unless the number of neurons stimulated is small or restricted to those with similar gain fields. This might be possible in an intermediate level of processing, such as area V3a.

Most psychophysical experiments have been designed to test for purely head-centered maps [10, 5] and not for retinotopic maps receiving a static eye position signal. New experiments are needed that look for interactions between eye position and visual features. For example, it should be possible to obtain motion aftereffects that are dependent on eye position; that is, an aftereffect in which the direction of motion depends on the gaze direction. John Mayhew [8] has already reported this type of gaze-dependent aftereffect for rotation, which is probably represented at later stages of visual processing. Similar experiments with translational motion could probe earlier levels of visual processing.

If information on spatial location is already present in area V1, the primary visual area that projects to other areas of the visual cortex in primates, then we need to re-evaluate the representation of objects in visual cortex. In the model presented here, the spatial location of an object was encoded along with its other features in a distributed fashion; hence spatial location should be considered on equal footing with other features of an object. Such early spatial transformations would affect other aspects of visual processing, such as visual attention and object recognition, and may also be important for nonspatial tasks, such as shape constancy (John Mayhew, personal communication).

References

[1] R.A. Andersen, G.K. Essick, and R.M. Siegel. Encoding of spatial location by posterior parietal neurons. *Science*, 230:456–458, 1985.

[2] P.R. Brotchie and R.A. Andersen. A body-centered coordinate system in posterior parietal cortex. In *Neurosc. Abst.*, page 1281, New Orleans, 1991.

[3] C. Galleti and P.P. Battaglini. Gaze-dependent visual neurons in area v3a of monkey prestriate cortex. *J. Neurosc.*, 9:1112–1125, 1989.

[4] S.J. Goodman and R.A. Andersen. Microstimulations of a neural network model for visually guided saccades. *J. Cog. Neurosc.*, 1:317–326, 1989.

[5] D.E. Irwin, J.L. Zacks, and J.S. Brown. Visual memory and the perception of a stable visual environment. *Perc. Psychophy.*, 47:35–46, 1990.

[6] R. Lal and M.J. Freedlander. Gating of retinal transmission by afferent eye position and movement signals. *Science*, 243:93–96, 1989.

[7] Y. LeCun, B. Boser, J.S. Denker, D. Henderson, R.E. Howard, and L.D. Jackel. Backpropagation applied to handwritten zip code recognition. *Neural Computation*, 1:540–566, 1990.

[8] J.E.W. Mayhew. After-effects of movement contingent on direction of gaze. *Vision Res.*, 13:877–880, 1973.

[9] J.T. Mc Ilwain. Saccadic eye movements evoked by electrical stimulation of the cat visual cortex. *Visual Neurosc.*, 1:135–143, 1988.

[10] J.K. O'Regan and A. Levy-Schoen. Integrating visual information from successive fixations : does trans-saccadic fusion exist? *Vision Res.*, 23:765–768, 1983.

[11] D.E. Rumelhart, G.E. Hinton, and R.J. Williams. Learning internal representations by error propagation. In D. E. Rumelhart, J. L. McClelland, and the PDP Research Group, editors, *Parallel Distributed Processing*, volume 1, chapter 8, pages 318–362. MIT Press, Cambridge, MA, 1986.

[12] Y. Trotter, S. Celebrini, S.J. Thorpe, and Imbert M. Modulation of stereoscopic processing in primate visual cortex v1 by the distance of fixation. In *Neurosc. Abs.*, New-Orleans, 1991.

[13] T.G. Weyand and J.G. Malpeli. Responses of neurons in primary visual cortex are influenced by eye position. In *Neurosc. Abs.*, page 419.7, St Louis, 1990.

[14] D. Zipser and R.A. Andersen. A back-propagation programmed network that stimulates reponse properties of a subset of posterior parietal neurons. *Nature*, 331:679–684, 1988.

VISIT: A Neural Model of Covert Visual Attention

Subutai Ahmad[*]
Siemens Research and Development,
ZFE ST SN6, Otto-Hahn Ring 6,
8000 Munich 83, Germany.
ahmad%bsun4@ztivax.siemens.com

Abstract

Visual attention is the ability to dynamically restrict processing to a subset
of the visual field. Researchers have long argued that such a mechanism is
necessary to efficiently perform many intermediate level visual tasks. This
paper describes *VISIT*, a novel neural network model of visual attention.
The current system models the search for target objects in scenes containing multiple distractors. This is a natural task for people, it is studied
extensively by psychologists, and it requires attention. The network's behavior closely matches the known psychophysical data on visual search
and visual attention. *VISIT* also matches much of the physiological data
on attention and provides a novel view of the functionality of a number of
visual areas. This paper concentrates on the biological plausibility of the
model and its relationship to the primary visual cortex, pulvinar, superior
colliculus and posterior parietal areas.

1 INTRODUCTION

Visual attention is perhaps best understood in the context of visual search, i.e.
the detection of a target object in images containing multiple distractor objects.
This task requires solving the binding problem and has been extensively studied in
psychology (see[16] for a review). The basic experimental finding is that a target
object containing a single distinguishing feature can be detected in constant time,
independent of the number of distractors. Detection based on a conjunction of
features, however, takes time linear in the number of objects, implying a sequential
search process (there are exceptions to this general rule). It is generally accepted

---

[*]Thanks to Steve Omohundro, Anne Treisman, Joe Malpeli, and Bill Baird for enlight-
ening discussions. Much of this research was conducted at the International Computer
Science Institute, Berkeley, CA.

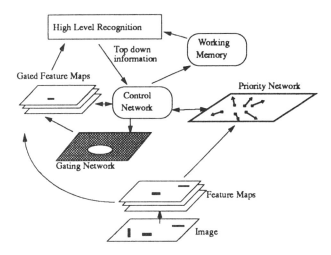

Figure 1: Overview of *VISIT*

that some form of covert attention[1] is necessary to accomplish this task. The following sections describe *VISIT*, a connectionist model of this process. The current paper concentrates on the relationships to the physiology of attention, although the psychological studies are briefly touched on. For further details on the psychological aspects see[1, 2].

2   OVERVIEW OF *VISIT*

We first outline the essential characteristics of *VISIT*. Figure 1 shows the basic architecture. A set of features are first computed from the image. These features are analogous to the topographic maps computed early in the visual system. There is one unit per location per feature, with each unit computing some local property of the image. Our current implementation uses four feature maps: red, blue, horizontal, and vertical. A parallel global sum of each feature map's activity is computed and is used to detect the presence of activity in individual maps.

The feature information is fed through two different systems: a gating network and a priority network. The gating network implements the focus - its function is to restrict higher level processing to a single circular region. Each gate unit receives the coordinates of a circle as input. If it is outside the circle, it turns on and inhibits corresponding locations in the gated feature maps. Thus the network can filter image properties based on an external control signal. The required computation is a simple second order weighted sum and takes two time steps[1].

---

[1] *Covert attention* refers to the ability to concentrate processing on a single image region without any overt actions such as eye movements.

The priority network ranks image locations in parallel and encodes the information in a manner suited to the updating of the focus of attention. There are three units per location in the priority map. The activity of the first unit represents the location's relevance to the current task. It receives activation from the feature maps in a local neighborhood of the image. The value of the i'th such unit is calculated as:

$$A_i = G(\sum_{x,y \in RF_i} \sum_{f \in F} P_f A_{fxy}) \tag{1}$$

where A_{fxy} is the activation of the unit computing feature f at location (x, y). RF_i denotes the receptive field of unit i, P_f is the priority given to feature map f, and G is a monotonically increasing function such as the sigmoid. P_f is represented as the real valued activation of individual units and can be dynamically adjusted according to the task. Thus by setting P_f for a particular feature to 1 and all others to 0, only objects containing that feature will influence the priority map. Section 2.1 describes a good strategy for setting P_f. The other two units at each location encode an "error vector", i.e. the vector difference between the units' location and center of the focus. These vectors are continually updated as the focus of attention moves around. To shift the focus to the most relevant location, the network simply adds the error vector corresponding to the highest priority unit to the activations of the units representing the focii's center. Once a location has been visited, the corresponding relevance unit is inhibited, preventing the network from continually attending to the highest priority location.

The control networks are responsible for mediating the information flow between the gating and priority networks, as well as incorporating top-down knowledge. The following section describes the part which sets the priority values for the feature maps. The rest of the networks are described in detail in [1]. Note that the control functions are fully implemented as networks of simple units and thus requires no "homunculus" to oversee the process.

2.1   *SWIFT*: A FAST SEARCH STRATEGY

The main function of *SWIFT* is to integrate top-down and bottom-up knowledge to efficiently guide the search process. Top down information about the target features are stored in a set of units. Let T be this set of features. Since the desired object must contain all the features of T, any of the corresponding feature maps may be searched. Using the ability to weight feature maps differently, the network removes the influence of all but one of the features in T. By setting this map's priority to 1, and all others to 0, the system will effectively prune objects which do not contain this feature.*SWIFT*[2] To minimize search time, it should choose the feature corresponding to the smallest number of objects. Since it is difficult to count the number of objects in parallel, the network chooses the map with the minimal total activity as the one likely to contain the minimal number of objects. (If the target features are not known in advance, *SWIFT* chooses the minimal feature map over all features. The net effect is to always pick the most distinctive feature.)

---

[2]Hence the name *SWIFT*: Search WIth Features Thrown out.

2.2   RELATIONSHIP TO PSYCHOPHYSICAL DATA

The run time behavior of the system closely matches the data on human visual search. Visual attention in people is known to be very quick, taking as little as 40-80 msecs to engage. Given that cortical neurons can fire about once every 10 msecs, this leaves time for at most 8 sequential steps. In *VISIT*, unlike other implementations of attention[10], the calculation of the next location is separated from the gating process. This allows the gating to be extremely fast, requiring only 2 time steps. Iterative models, which select the most active object through lateral inhibition, require time proportional to the distance in pixels between maximally separated objects. These models are not consistent with the 80msecs time requirement.

During visual search, *SWIFT* always searches the minimal feature map. The critical variable that determines search time is M, the number of objects in the minimal feature map. Search time will be linear in M. It can be shown that *VISIT* plus *SWIFT* is consistent with all of Treisman's original experiments including single feature search, conjunctive search, 2:1 slope ratios, search asymmetries, and illusory conjuncts[16], as well as the exceptions reported in[5, 14]. With an assumption about the features that are coded (consistent with current physiological knowledge), the results in[7, 11] can also be modeled. (This is described in more detail in [2]).

3   PHYSIOLOGY OF VISUAL ATTENTION

The above sections have described the general architecture of *VISIT*. There is a fairly strong correspondence between the modules in *VISIT* and the various visual areas involved in attention. The rest of the paper discusses these relationships.

3.1   TOPOGRAPHIC FEATURE MAPS

Each of the early visual areas, LGN, $V1$, and $V2$, form several topographic maps of retinal activity. In $V1$ alone there are a thousand times as many neurons as there are fibers in the optic nerve, enough to form several hundred feature maps. There is a diverse list of features thought to be computed in these areas, including orientations, colors, spatial frequencies, motion, etc.[6]. These areas are analogous to the set of early feature maps computed in *VISIT*.

In *VISIT* there are actually two separate sets of feature maps: early features computed directly from the image and gated feature maps. It might seem inefficient to have two copies of the same features. An alternate possibility is to directly inhibit the early feature maps themselves, and so eliminate the need for two sets. However, in a focused state, such a network would be unable to make global decisions based on the features. With the configuration described above, at some hardware cost, the network can efficiently access both local and global information simultaneously. *SWIFT* relies on this ability to efficiently carry out visual search.

There is evidence for a similar setup in the human visual system. Although people have actively searched, no local attentional effects have been found in the early feature maps. (Only *global* effects, such as an overall increase in firing rate, have been noticed.) The above reasoning provides a possible computational explanation of this phenomenon.

A natural question to ask is: what is the best set of features? For fast visual search, if *SWIFT* is used as a constraint, then we want the set of features that minimize M over all possible images and target objects, i.e. the features that best discriminate objects. It is easy to see that the optimal set of features should be maximally uncorrelated with a near uniform distribution of feature values. Extracting the principal components of the distribution of images gives us exactly those features. It is well known that a single Hebb neuron extracts the largest principal component; sets of such neurons can be connected to select successively smaller components. Moreover, as some researchers have demonstrated, simple Hebbian learning can lead to features that look very similar to the features in visual cortex (see [3] for a review). If the early features in visual cortex do in fact represent principal components, then *SWIFT* is a simple strategy that takes advantage of it.

3.2   THE PULVINAR

Contrary to the early visual system, local attentional effects have been discovered in the pulvinar. Recordings of cells in the lateral pulvinar of awake, behaving monkeys have demonstrated a spatially localized enhancement effect tied to selective attention[17]. Given this property it is tempting to pinpoint the pulvinar as the locus of the gated feature maps.

The general connectivity patterns provide some support for this hypothesis. The pulvinar is located in the dorsal part of the thalamus and is strongly connected to just about every visual area including LGN, $V1$, $V2$, superior colliculus, the frontal eye fields, and posterior parietal cortex. The projections are topography preserving and non-overlapping. As a result, the pulvinar contains several high-resolution maps of visual space, possibly one map for each one in primary visual cortex. In addition, there is a thin sheet of neurons around the pulvinar, the reticular complex, with exclusively inhibitory connections to the neurons within [4]. This is exactly the structure necessary to implement *VISIT*'s gating system.

There are other clues which also point to the thalamus as the gating system. Human patients with thalamic lesions have difficulty engaging attention and inhibiting crosstalk from other locations. Lesioned monkeys give slower responses when competing events are present in the visual field[12].

The hypothesis can be tested by further experiments. In particular, if a map in the pulvinar corresponding to a particular cortical area is damaged, then there should be a corresponding deficit in the ability to bind those specific features in the presence of distractors. In the absence of distractors, the performance should remain unchanged.

3.3   SUPERIOR COLLICULUS

The SC is involved in both the generation of eye saccades[15] and possibly with covert attention[12]. It is probably also involved in the integration of location information from various different modalities. Like the pulvinar, the superior colliculus (SC) is a structure with converging inputs from several different modalities including visual, auditory, and somatosensory[15]. The superior colliculus contains a representation similar to *VISIT*'s error maps for eye saccades[15]. At each location, groups of neurons represent the vector in motor coordinates required to shift the eye to that spot. In [13] the authors studied patients with a particular form of Parkinson's disease where the *SC* is damaged. These patients are able to make horizontal, but not vertical eye saccades. The experiments showed that although the patients were still able to move their covert attention in both the horizontal and vertical directions, the speed of orienting in the vertical direction was much slower. In addition [12] mentions that patients with this damage shift attention to previously attended locations as readily as new ones, suggesting a deficit in the mechanism that inhibits previously attended locations.

These findings are consistent with the priority map in *VISIT*. A first guess would identify the superior colliculus as the priority map, however this is probably inaccurate. More recent evidence suggests that the *SC* might be involved only in bottom-up shifts of attention (induced by exogenous stimuli as opposed to endogenous control signals) (Rafal, personal communication). There is also evidence that the frontal eye fields (*FEF*) are involved in saccade generation in a manner similar to the superior colliculus, particularly for saccades to complex stimuli[17]. The role of the *FEF* in covert attention is currently unknown.

3.4 POSTERIOR PARIETAL AREAS

The posterior paretal cortex *PP* may provide an answer. One hypothesis that is consistent with the data is that there are several different priority maps, for bottom-up and top-down stimuli. The top-down maps exist within *PP*, whereas the bottom-up maps exist in *SC* and possibly *FEF*. *PP* receives a significant projection from superior colliculus and may be involved in the production of voluntary eye saccades[17]. Experiments suggest that it is also involved in covert shifts of attention. There is evidence that neurons in *PP* increase their firing rate when in a state of attentive fixation[9]. Damage to *PP* leads to deficits in the ability to disengage covert attention away from a target[12]. In the context of eye saccades, there exist neurons in *PP* that fire about 55 msecs before an actual saccade. These results suggest that the control structure and the aspects of the network that integrate priority information from the various modules might also reside within *PP*.

4   DISCUSSION AND CONCLUSIONS

The above relationships between *VISIT* and the brain provides a coherent picture of the functionality of the visual areas. The literature is consistent with having the *LGN*, *V*1, and *V*2 as the early feature maps, the pulvinar as a gating system, the superior colliculus, and frontal eye fields, as a bottom-up priority map, and posterior parietal cortex as the locus of a higher level priority map as well as the the control networks. Figure 2 displays the various visual areas together with their proposed functional relationships.

In [12] the authors suggest that neurons in parietal lobe disengage attention from the present focus, those in superior colliculus shift attention to the target, and neurons in pulvinar engage attention on it. This hypothesis looks at the time course of an attentional shift (disengage, move, engage) and assigns three different areas to

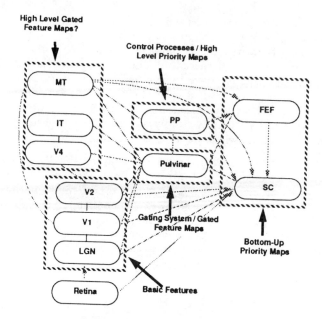

Figure 2: Proposed functionality of various visual areas. Lines denote major pathways. Those connections without arrows are known to be bi-directional.

the three different intervals within that temporal sequence. In *VISIT*, these three correspond to a single operation (add a new update vector to the current location) and a single module (the control network). Instead, the emphasis is on assigning different computational responsibilities to the various modules. Each module operates continuously but is involved in a different computation. While the gating network is being updated to a new location, the priority network and portions of the control network are continuously updating the priorities.

The model doesn't yet explain the findings in [8] where neurons in $V4$ exhibited a localized attentional response, but only if the stimuli were within the receptive fields. However, these neurons have relatively large receptive fields and are known to code for fairly high-level features. It is possible that this corresponds to a different form of attention working at a much higher level.

By no means is *VISIT* intended to be a detailed physiological model of attention. Precise modeling of even a single neuron can require significant computational resources. There are many physiological details that are not incorporated. However, at the macro level there are interesting relationships between the individual modules in *VISIT* and the known functionality of the different areas. The advantage of an implemented computational model such as *VISIT* is that it allows us to examine the underlying computations involved and hopefully better understand the underlying processes.

References

[1] S. Ahmad. *VISIT: An Efficient Computational Model of Human Visual Attention.* PhD thesis, University of Illinois at Urbana-Champaign, Champaign, IL, September 1991. Also TR-91-049, International Computer Science Institute, Berkeley, CA.

[2] S. Ahmad and S. Omohundro. Efficient visual search: A connectionist solution. In *13th Annual Conference of the Cognitive Science Society*, Chicago, IL, August 1991.

[3] S. Becker. Unsupervised learning procedures for neural networks. *International Journal of Neural Systems*, 12, 1991.

[4] F. Crick. Function of the thalamic reticular complex: the searchlight hypothesis. In *National Academy of Sciences*, volume 81, pages 4586–4590, 1984.

[5] H.E. Egeth, R.A. Virzi, and H. Garbart. Searching for conjunctively defined targets. *Journal of Experimental Psychology: Human Perception and Performance*, 10(1):32–39, 1984.

[6] D. Van Essen and C. H. Anderson. Information processing strategies and pathways in the primate retina and visual cortex. In S.F. Zornetzer, J.L. Davis, and C. Lau, editors, *An Introduction to Neural and Electronic Networks*. Academic Press, 1990.

[7] P. McLeod, J. Driver, and J. Crisp. Visual search for a conjunction of movement and form is parallel. *Nature*, 332:154–155, 1988.

[8] J. Moran and R. Desimone. Selective attention gates visual processing in the extrastriate cortex. *Science*, 229, March 1985.

[9] V.B. Mountcastle, R.A. Anderson, and B.C. Motter. The influence of attention fixation upon the excitability of the light-sensitive neurons of the posterior parietal cortex. *The Journal of Neuroscience*, 1(11):1218–1235, 1981.

[10] M. Mozer. *The Perception of Multiple Objects: A Connectionist Approach.* MIT Press, Cambridge, MA, 1991.

[11] K. Nakayama and G. Silverman. Serial and parallel processing of visual feature conjunctions. *Nature*, 320:264–265, 1986.

[12] M.I. Posner and S.E. Petersen. The attention system of the human brain. *Annual Review of Neuroscience*, 13:25–42, 1990.

[13] M.I. Posner, J.A. Walker, and R.D. Rafal. Effects of parietal injury on covert orienting of attention. *The Journal of Neuroscience*, 4(7):1863–1874, 1982.

[14] P.T. Quinlan and G.W. Humphreys. Visual search for targets defined by combinations of color, shape, and size: An examination of the task constraints of feature and conjunction searches. *Perception & Psychophysics*, 41:455–472, 1987.

[15] D. L. Sparks. Translation of sensory signals into commands for control of saccadic eye movements: Role of primate superior colliculus. *Physiological Reviews*, 66(1), 1986.

[16] A. Treisman. Features and objects: The Fourteenth Bartlett Memorial Lecture. *The Quarterly Journal of Experimental Psychology*, 40A(2), 1988.

[17] R.H. Wurtz and M.E. Goldberg, editors. *The Neurobiology of Saccadic Eye Movements.* Elsevier, New York, 1989.

Visual Grammars and their Neural Nets

Eric Mjolsness
Department of Computer Science
Yale University
New Haven, CT 06520-2158

Abstract

I exhibit a systematic way to derive neural nets for vision problems. It involves formulating a vision problem as Bayesian inference or decision on a comprehensive model of the visual domain given by a probabilistic *grammar*.

1 INTRODUCTION

I show how systematically to derive optimizing neural networks that represent quantitative visual models and match them to data. This involves a design methodology which starts from first principles, namely a probabilistic model of a visual domain, and proceeds via Bayesian inference to a neural network which performs a visual task. The key problem is to find probability distributions sufficiently intricate to model general visual tasks and yet tractable enough for theory. This is achieved by probabilistic and expressive *grammars* which model the image-formation process, including heterogeneous sources of noise each modelled with a grammar rule. In particular these grammars include a crucial "relabelling" rule that removes the undetectable internal labels (or indices) of detectable features and substitutes an uninformed labeling scheme used by the perceiver.

This paper is a brief summary of the contents of [Mjolsness, 1991].

428

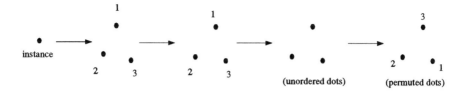

Figure 1: Operation of random dot grammar. The first arrow illustrates dot placement; the next shows dot jitter; the next arrow shows the pure, un-numbered feature locations; and the final arrow is the uninformed renumbering scheme of the
perceiver.

2   EXAMPLE: A RANDOM-DOT GRAMMAR

The first example grammar is a generative model of pictures consisting of a number
of dots (e.g. a sum of delta functions) whose relative locations are determined by
one out of M stored models. But the dots are subject to unknown independent jitter
and an unknown global translation, and the identities of the dots (their numerical
labels) are hidden from the perceiver by a random permutation operation. For
example each model might represent an imaginary asterism of equally bright stars
whose locations have been corrupted by instrument noise. One useful task would
be to recognize which model generated the image data. The random-dot grammar
is shown in (1).

model and location	Γ^0 :	root	$\rightarrow$	instance of model α at $\mathbf{x}$
		$E_0(\mathbf{x})$	$=$	$\frac{1}{2\sigma_r^2}|\mathbf{x}|^2$
dot locations	Γ^1 :	instance$(\alpha, \mathbf{x})$	$\rightarrow$	$\{\text{dotloc}(\alpha, m, \hat{\mathbf{x}}_m = \mathbf{x} + \mathbf{u}_m^\alpha)\}$
		$E_1(\{\hat{\mathbf{x}}_m\})$	$=$	$-\log \prod_m \delta(\hat{\mathbf{x}}_m - \mathbf{x} - \mathbf{u}_m^\alpha),$ where $< \mathbf{u}_m^\alpha >_m = 0$
			$\approx$	$\lim_{\sigma_\delta \to 0} \frac{1}{2\sigma_\delta^2} \sum_m |\mathbf{x}_m - \mathbf{x} - \mathbf{u}_m^\alpha|^2 + c(\sigma_\delta)$
dot jitter	Γ^2 :	dotloc$(\alpha, m, \hat{\mathbf{x}}_m)$	$\rightarrow$	dot$(m, \mathbf{x}_m)$
		$E_2(\mathbf{x}_m)$	$=$	$\frac{1}{2\sigma_{jt}^2}|\hat{\mathbf{x}}_m - \mathbf{x}_m|^2$
scramble all dots	Γ^3 :	$\{\text{dot}(m, \mathbf{x}_m)\}$	$\rightarrow$	$\{\text{imagedot}(\mathbf{x}_i = \sum_m P_{m,i}\mathbf{x}_m)\}$
		$E_3(\{\mathbf{x}_i\})$	$=$	$-\log \left[\Pr(P) \prod_i \delta(\mathbf{x}_i - \sum_m P_{m,i}\mathbf{x}_m) \right]$ where P is a permutation

$$(1)$$

The final joint probability distribution for this grammar allows recognition and other problems to be posed as Bayesian inference and solved by neural network optimization of

$$E_{\text{final}}(\alpha, P, \mathbf{x}) = \sum_{mi} P_{m,i} \left(\frac{1}{2N\sigma_r^2} |\mathbf{x}|^2 + \frac{1}{2\sigma_{jt}^2} |\mathbf{x}_i - \mathbf{x} - \mathbf{u}_m^\alpha|^2 \right). \tag{2}$$

A sum over all permutations has been approximated by the optimization over near-permutations, as usual for Mean Field Theory networks [Yuille, 1990], resulting in a neural network implementable as an analog circuit. The fact that P appears only linearly in E_{final} makes the optimization problems easier; it is a generalized "assignment" problem.

2.1   APPROXIMATE NEURAL NETWORK WITHOUT MATCH VARIABLES

Short of approximating a P configuration sum via Mean Field Theory neural nets, there is a simpler, cheaper, less accurate approximation that we have used on matching problems similar to the model recognition problem (find α and $\mathbf{x}$) for the dot-matching grammar. Under this approximation,

$$\text{argmax}_{\alpha,\mathbf{x}} \Pr(\alpha, \mathbf{x}|\{\mathbf{x}_i\}) \approx \text{argmax}_{\alpha,\mathbf{x}} \sum_{m,i} \exp -\frac{1}{T} \left(\frac{1}{2N\sigma_r^2} |\mathbf{x}|^2 + \frac{1}{2\sigma_{jt}^2} |\mathbf{x}_i - \mathbf{x} - \mathbf{u}_m^\alpha|^2 \right),$$
$$\tag{3}$$

for $T = 1$. This objective function has a simple interpretation when $\sigma_r \to \infty$: it minimizes the Euclidean distance between two Gaussian-blurred images containing the $\mathbf{x}_i$ dots and a shifted version of the $\mathbf{u}_m$ dots respectively:

$$
\begin{aligned}
& \text{argmin}_{\alpha,\mathbf{x}} \int d\mathbf{z} \, |G * I_1(\mathbf{z}) - G * I_2(\mathbf{z} - \mathbf{x})|^2 \\
= \ & \text{argmin}_{\alpha,\mathbf{x}} \int d\mathbf{z} \left| G_{\sigma/\sqrt{2}} * \sum_i \delta(\mathbf{z} - \mathbf{x}_i) - G_{\sigma/\sqrt{2}} * \sum_m \delta(\mathbf{z} - \mathbf{x} - \mathbf{u}_m^\alpha) \right|^2 \\
= \ & \text{argmin}_{\alpha,\mathbf{x}} \left[C_1 - 2\sum_{mi} \int d\mathbf{z} \exp -\frac{1}{\sigma^2} \left[|\mathbf{z} - \mathbf{x}_i|^2 + |\mathbf{z} - \mathbf{x} - \mathbf{u}_m^\alpha|^2 \right] \right] \\
= \ & \text{argmax}_{\alpha,\mathbf{x}} \sum_{mi} \exp -\frac{1}{2\sigma^2} |\mathbf{x}_i - \mathbf{x} - \mathbf{u}_m^\alpha|^2
\end{aligned}
\tag{4}
$$

Deterministic annealing from $T = \infty$ down to $T = 1$, which is a good strategy for finding global maxima in equation (3), corresponds to a coarse-to-fine correlation matching algorithm: the global shift $\mathbf{x}$ is computed by repeated local optimization while gradually decreasing the Gaussian blur parameter σ down to σ_{jt}.

The approximation (3) has the effect of eliminating the discrete P_{mi} variables, rather than replacing them with continuous versions V_{mi}. The same can be said for the "elastic net" method [Durbin and Willshaw, 1987]. Compared to the elastic net, the present objective function is simpler, more symmetric between rows and columns, has a nicer interpretation in terms of known algorithms (correlation matching in scale space), and is expected to be less accurate.

3   EXPERIMENTS IN IMAGE REGISTRATION

Equation (3) is an objective function for recovering the global two-dimensional (2D) translation of a model consisting of arbitrarily placed dots, to match up with similar dots with jittered positions. We use it instead to find the best 2D *rotation* and horizontal translation, for two images which actually differ by a horizontal *3D* translation with roughly constant camera orientation. The images consist of *line segments* rather than single dots, some of which are *missing or extra* data. In addition, there are strong *boundary effects* due to parts of the scene being translated outside the camera's field of view. The jitter is replaced by whatever positional inaccuracies come from an actual camera producing an 128 × 128 image [Williams and Hanson, 1988] which is then processed by a high quality line-segment finding algorithm [Burns, 1986]. Better results would be expected of objective functions derived from grammars which explicitly model more of these noise processes, such as the grammars described in Section 4.

We experimented with minimizing this objective function with respect to unknown global translations and (sometimes) rotations, using the continuation method and sets of line segments derived from real images. The results are shown in Figures 2, 3 and 4.

4   MORE GRAMMARS

Going beyond the random-dot grammar, we have studied several grammars of increasing complexity. One can add rotation and dot deletion as new sources of noise, or introduce a two-level hierarchy, in which models are sets of clusters of dots. In [Mjolsness et al., 1991] we present a grammar for multiple curves in a single image, each of which is represented in the image as a set of dots that may be hard to group into their original curves. This grammar illustrates how flexible objects can be handled in our formalism.

We approach a modest plateau of generality by augmenting the hierarchical version of the random-dot grammar with multiple objects in a single scene. This degree of complexity is sufficient to introduce many interesting features of knowledge representation in high-level vision, such as multiple instances of a model in a scene, as well as requiring segmentation and grouping as part of the recognition process. We have shown [Mjolsness, 1991] that such a grammar can yield neural networks nearly identical to the "Frameville" neural networks we have previously studied as a means of mixing simple Artificial Intelligence frame systems (or semantic networks) with optimization-based neural networks. What is more, the transformation leading to Frameville is very natural. It simply pushes the permutation matrix as far back into the grammar as possible.

Figure 2: A simple image registration problem. (a) Stair image. (b) Long line segments derived from stair image. (c) Two unregistered line segment images derived from two images taken from two horizontally translated viewpoints in three dimensions. The images are a pair of successive frames in an image sequence. (d) Registered viersions of same data: superposed long line segments extracted from two stair images (taken from viewpoints differing by a small horizontal translation in three dimensions) that have been optimally registered in two dimensions.

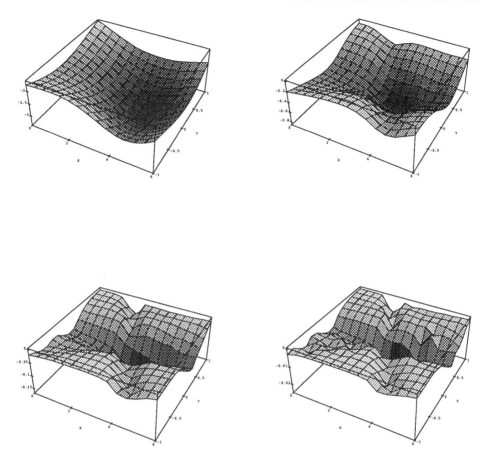

Figure 3: Continuation method (deterministic annealing). (a) Objective function at $\sigma = .0863$. (b) Objective function at $\sigma = .300$. (c) Objective function at $\sigma = .105$. (d) Objective function at $\sigma = .0364$.

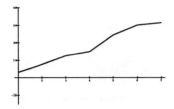
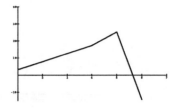

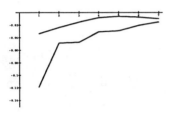
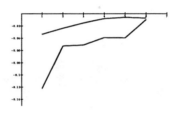

Figure 4: Image sequence displacement recovery. Frame 2 is matched to frames 3-8 in the stair image sequence. Horizontal displacements are recovered. Other starting frames yield similar results except for frame 1, which was much worse. (a) Horizontal displacement recovered, assuming no 2-d rotation. Recovered dispacement as a function of frame number is monotonic. (b) Horizontal displacement recovered, along with 2-d rotation which is found to be small except for the final frame. Displacements are in qualitative agreement with (a), more so for small displacements. (c) Objective function before and after displacement is recovered (upper and lower curves) without rotation. Note gradual decrease in ΔE with frame number (and hence with displacement). (d) Objective function before and after displacement is recovered (upper and lower curves) with rotation.

Acknowlegements

Charles Garrett performed the computer simulations and helped formulate the line-matching objective function used therein.

References

[Burns, 1986] Burns, J. B. (1986). Extracting straight lines. *IEEE Trans. PAMI*, 8(4):425–455.

[Durbin and Willshaw, 1987] Durbin, R. and Willshaw, D. (1987). An analog approach to the travelling salesman problem using an elastic net method. *Nature*, 326:689–691.

[Mjolsness, 1991] Mjolsness, E. (1991). Bayesian inference on visual grammars by neural nets that optimize. Technical Report YALEU/DCS/TR854, Yale University Department of Computer Science.

[Mjolsness et al., 1991] Mjolsness, E., Rangarajan, A., and Garrett, C. (1991). A neural net for reconstruction of multiple curves with a visual grammar. In *Seattle International Joint Conference on Neural Networks*.

[Williams and Hanson, 1988] Williams, L. R. and Hanson, A. R. (1988). Translating optical flow into token matches and depth from looming. In *Second International Conference on Computer Vision*, pages 441–448. Staircase test image sequence.

[Yuille, 1990] Yuille, A. L. (1990). Generalized deformable models, statistical physics, and matching problems. *Neural Computation*, 2(1):1–24.

Learning to Segment Images
Using Dynamic Feature Binding

Michael C. Mozer
Dept. of Comp. Science &
Inst. of Cognitive Science
University of Colorado
Boulder, CO 80309–0430

Richard S. Zemel
Dept. of Comp. Science
University of Toronto
Toronto, Ontario
Canada M5S 1A4

Marlene Behrmann
Dept. of Psychology &
Faculty of Medicine
University of Toronto
Toronto, Ontario
Canada M5S 1A1

Abstract

Despite the fact that complex visual scenes contain multiple, overlapping objects, people perform object recognition with ease and accuracy. One operation that facilitates recognition is an early segmentation process in which features of objects are grouped and labeled according to which object they belong. Current computational systems that perform this operation are based on predefined grouping heuristics. We describe a system called MAGIC that *learns* how to group features based on a set of pre-segmented examples. In many cases, MAGIC discovers grouping heuristics similar to those previously proposed, but it also has the capability of finding nonintuitive structural regularities in images. Grouping is performed by a relaxation network that attempts to dynamically bind related features. Features transmit a complex-valued signal (amplitude and phase) to one another; binding can thus be represented by phase locking related features. MAGIC's training procedure is a generalization of recurrent back propagation to complex-valued units.

When a visual image contains multiple, overlapping objects, recognition is difficult because features in the image are not grouped according to which object they belong. Without the capability to form such groupings, it would be necessary to undergo a massive search through all subsets of image features. For this reason, most machine vision recognition systems include a component that performs feature grouping or *image segmentation* (e.g., Guzman, 1968; Lowe, 1985; Marr, 1982).

436

A multitude of heuristics have been proposed for segmenting images. Gestalt psychologists have explored how people group elements of a display and have suggested a range of grouping principles that govern human perception (Rock & Palmer, 1990). Computer vision researchers have studied the problem from a more computational perspective. They have investigated methods of grouping elements of an image based on *nonaccidental regularities*—feature combinations that are unlikely to occur by chance when several objects are juxtaposed, and are thus indicative of a single object (Kanade, 1981; Lowe & Binford, 1982).

In these earlier approaches, the researchers have hypothesized a set of grouping heuristics and then tested their psychological validity or computational utility. In our work, we have taken an *adaptive* approach to the problem of image segmentation in which a system learns how to group features based on a set of examples. We call the system MAGIC, an acronym for multiple-object adaptive grouping of image components. In many cases MAGIC discovers grouping heuristics similar to those proposed in earlier work, but it also has the capability of finding nonintuitive structural regularities in images.

MAGIC is trained on a set of presegmented images containing multiple objects. By "presegmented," we mean that each image feature is labeled as to which object it belongs. MAGIC learns to detect configurations of the image features that have a consistent labeling in relation to one another across the training examples. Identifying these configurations allows MAGIC to then label features in novel, unsegmented images in a manner consistent with the training examples.

1   REPRESENTING FEATURE LABELINGS

Before describing MAGIC, we must first discuss a representation that allows for the labeling of features. Von der Malsburg (1981), von der Malsburg & Schneider (1986), Gray et al. (1989), and Eckhorn et al. (1988), among others, have suggested a biologically plausible mechanism of labeling through temporal correlations among neural signals, either the relative timing of neuronal spikes or the synchronization of oscillatory activities in the nervous system. The key idea here is that each processing unit conveys not just an activation value—average firing frequency in neural terms—but also a second, independent value which represents the relative *phase* of firing. The dynamic grouping or *binding* of a set of features is accomplished by aligning the phases of the features. Recent work (Goebel, 1991; Hummel & Biederman, in press) has used this notion of dynamic binding for grouping image features, but has been based on relatively simple, predetermined grouping heuristics.

2   THE DOMAIN

Our initial work has been conducted in the domain of two-dimensional geometric contours, including rectangles, diamonds, crosses, triangles, hexagons, and octagons. The contours are constructed from four primitive feature types—oriented line segments at 0°, 45°, 90°, and 135°—and are laid out on a 15 × 20 grid. At each location on the grid are units, called *feature units*, that detect each of the four primitive feature types. In our present experiments, images contain two contours. Contours are not permitted to overlap in their activation of the same feature unit.

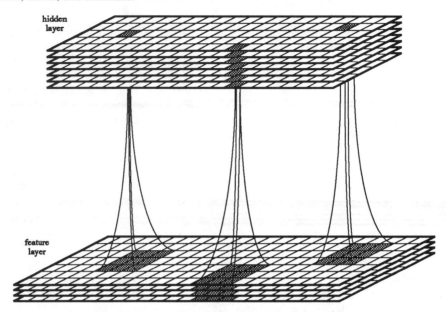

Figure 1: The architecture of MAGIC. The lower layer contains the feature units; the upper layer contains the hidden units. Each layer is arranged in a spatiotopic array with a number of different feature types at each position in the array. Each plane in the feature layer corresponds to a different feature type. The grayed hidden units are reciprocally connected to all features in the corresponding grayed region of the feature layer. The lines between layers represent projections in both directions.

3   THE ARCHITECTURE

The input to MAGIC is a pattern of activity over the feature units indicating which features are present in an image. The initial phases of the units are random. MAGIC's task is to assign appropriate phase values to the units. Thus, the network performs a type of pattern completion.

The network architecture consists of two layers of units, as shown in Figure 1. The lower (input) layer contains the feature units, arranged in spatiotopic arrays with one array per feature type. The upper layer contains hidden units that help to align the phases of the feature units; their response properties are determined by training. Each hidden unit is reciprocally connected to the units in a local spatial region of all feature arrays. We refer to this region as a *patch*; in our current simulations, the patch has dimensions 4 × 4. For each patch there is a corresponding fixed-size *pool* of hidden units. To achieve uniformity of response across the image, the pools are arranged in a spatiotopic array in which neighboring pools respond to neighboring patches and the weights of all pools are constrained to be the same.

The feature units activate the hidden units, which in turn feed back to the feature units. Through a relaxation process, the system settles on an assignment of phases to the features.

4 NETWORK DYNAMICS

Formally, the response of each feature unit i, x_i, is a complex value in polar form, (a_i, p_i), where a_i is the amplitude or activation and p_i is the phase. Similarly, the response of each hidden unit j, y_j, has components (b_j, q_j). The weight connecting unit i to unit j, w_{ji}, is also complex valued, having components (ρ_{ji}, θ_{ji}). The activation rule we propose is a generalization of the dot product to the complex domain:

$$
\begin{aligned}
net_j &= \mathbf{x} \cdot \mathbf{w}_j \\
&= \sum_i x_i \bar{w}_{ji} \\
&= \left(\left[\left(\sum_i a_i \rho_{ji} \cos(p_i - \theta_{ji}) \right)^2 + \left(\sum_i a_i \rho_{ji} \sin(p_i - \theta_{ji}) \right)^2 \right]^{\frac{1}{2}}, \right. \\
&\qquad \left. \tan^{-1} \left[\frac{\sum_i a_i \rho_{ji} \sin(p_i - \theta_{ji})}{\sum_i a_i \rho_{ji} \cos(p_i - \theta_{ji})} \right] \right)
\end{aligned}
$$

where net_j is the net input to hidden unit j. The net input is passed through a squashing nonlinearity that maps the amplitude of the response from the range $0 \to \infty$ to $0 \to 1$ but leaves the phase unaffected:

$$
y_j = \frac{net_j}{|net_j|} \left(1 - e^{-|net_j|^2} \right).
$$

The flow of activation from the hidden layer to the feature layer follows the same dynamics, although in the current implementation the amplitudes of the features are clamped, hence the top-down flow affects only the phases. One could imagine a more general architecture in which the relaxation process determined not only the phase values, but cleaned up noise in the feature amplitudes as well.

The intuition underlying the activation rule is as follows. The activity of a hidden unit, b_j, should be monotonically related to how well the feature response pattern matches the hidden unit weight vector, just as in the standard real-valued activation rule. Indeed, one can readily see that if the feature and weight phases are equal $(p_i = \theta_{ji})$, the rule for b_j reduces to the real-valued case. Even if the feature and weight phases differ by a constant $(p_i = \theta_{ji} + c)$, b_j is unaffected. This is a critical property of the activation rule: Because *absolute* phase values have no intrinsic meaning, the response of a unit should depend only on the *relative* phases. The activation rule achieves this by essentially ignoring the average difference in phase between the feature units and the weights. The hidden phase, q_j, reflects this average difference.

5 LEARNING ALGORITHM

During training, we would like the hidden units to learn to detect configurations of features that reliably indicate phase relationships among the features. We have experimented with a variety of training algorithms. The one with which we have had greatest success involves running the network for a fixed number of iterations and, after each iteration, attempting to adjust the weights so that the feature phase pattern will match a target phase pattern. Each training trial proceeds as follows:

1. A training example is generated at random. This involves selecting two contours and instantiating them in an image. The features of one contour have *target* phase $0°$ and the features of the other contour have target phase $180°$.

2. The training example is presented to MAGIC by clamping the amplitude of a feature unit to 1.0 if its corresponding image feature is present, or 0.0 otherwise. The phases of the feature units are set to random values in the range $0°$ to $360°$.

3. Activity is allowed to flow from the feature units to the hidden units and back to the feature units. Because the feature amplitudes are clamped, they are unaffected.

4. The new phase pattern over the feature units is compared to the target phase pattern (see step 1), and an error measure is computed:

$$E = -\left(\sum_i a_i \cos(\bar{p}_i - p_i)\right)^2 - \left(\sum_i a_i \sin(\bar{p}_i - p_i)\right)^2,$$

where $\bar{p}$ is the target phase pattern. This error ignores the absolute difference between the target and actual phases. That is, E is minimized when $\bar{p}_i - p_i$ is a constant for all i, regardless of the value of $\bar{p}_i - p_i$.

5. Using a generalization of back propagation to complex valued units, error gradients are computed for the feature-to-hidden and hidden-to-feature weights.

6. Steps 3–5 are repeated for a maximum of 30 iterations. The trial is terminated if the error increases on five consecutive iterations.

7. Weights are updated by an amount proportional to the average error gradient over iterations.

Learning is more robust when the feature-to-hidden weights are constrained to be symmetric with the hidden-to-feature weights. For complex weights, symmetry means that the weight from feature unit i to hidden unit j is the complex conjugate of the weight from hidden unit j to feature unit i. Weight symmetry ensures that MAGIC will converge to a fixed point. (The proof is based on discrete-time update and a two-layer architecture with sequential layer updates and no intralayer connections.)

Simulations reported below use a learning rate of .005 for the amplitudes and 0.02 for the phases. About 10,000 learning trials are required for stable performance, although MAGIC rapidly picks up on the most salient aspects of the domain.

6   SIMULATION RESULTS

We trained a network with 20 hidden units per pool on images containing either two rectangles, two diamonds, or a rectangle and a diamond. The shapes were of varying size and appeared in various locations. A subset of the resulting weights are shown in Figure 2. Each hidden unit attempts to detect and reinstantiate activity patterns that match its weights. One clear and prevalent pattern in the weights is the collinear arrangement of segments of a given orientation, all having the same phase value. When a hidden unit having weights of this form responds to a patch of the feature array, it tries align the phases of the patch with the phases of its weight vector. By synchronizing the phases of features, it acts to group the features. Thus, one can interpret the weight vectors as the rules by which features are grouped.

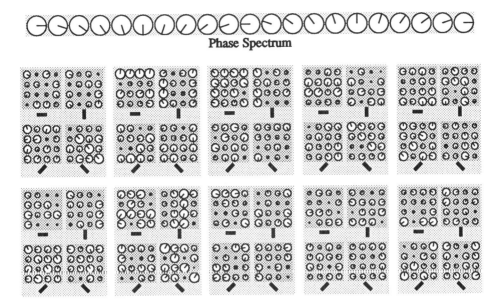

Phase Spectrum

Figure 2: Sample of feature-to-hidden weights learned by MAGIC. The area of a circle represents the amplitude of a weight, the orientation of the internal tick mark represents the phase angle. The weights are arranged such that the connections into each hidden unit are presented on a light gray background. Each hidden unit has a total of 64 incoming weights—4 × 4 locations in its receptive field and four feature types at each location. The weights are further grouped by feature type, and for each feature type they are arranged in a 4 × 4 pattern homologous to the image patch itself.

Whereas traditional grouping principles indicate the conditions under which features should be bound together as part of the same object, the grouping principles learned by MAGIC also indicate when features should be segregated into different objects. For example, the weights of the vertical and horizontal segments are generally 180° out of phase with the diagonal segments. This allows MAGIC to segregate the vertical and horizontal features of a rectangle from the diagonal features of a diamond. We had anticipated that the weights to each hidden unit would contain two phase values at most because each image patch contains at most two objects. However, some units make use of three or more phases, suggesting that the hidden unit is performing several distinct functions. As is the usual case with hidden unit weights, these patterns are difficult to interpret.

Figure 3 presents an example of the network segmenting an image. The image contains two diamonds. The top left panel shows the features of the diamonds and their initial random phases. The succeeding panels show the network's response during the relaxation process. The lower right panel shows the network response at equilibrium. Features of each object have been assigned a uniform phase, and the two objects are 180° out of phase. The task here may appear simple, but it is quite challenging due to the illusory diamond generated by the overlapping diamonds.

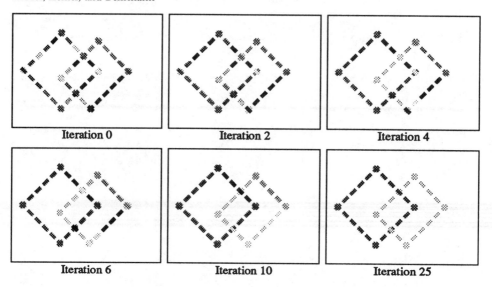

Figure 3: An example of MAGIC segmenting an image. The "iteration" refers to the number of times activity has flowed from the feature units to the hidden units and back. The phase value of a feature is represented by a gray level. The periodic phase continuum can only be approximated by the linear gray level continuum, but the basic information is conveyed nonetheless.

7   CURRENT DIRECTIONS

We are currently extending MAGIC in several directions, which we outline here.

- A natural principle for the hierarchical decomposition of objects emerges from the relative frequency of feature configurations during training. More frequent configurations result in a robust hidden representation, and hence the features forming these configurations will be tightly coupled. A coarse quantization of phases will lead to parses of the image in which only the highest frequency configurations are considered as "objects." Finer quantizations will lead to a further decomposition of the image. Thus, the continuous phase representation allows for the construction of hierarchical descriptions of objects.

- Spatially local grouping principles are unlikely to be sufficient for the image segmentation task. Indeed, we have encountered incorrect solutions produced by MAGIC that are locally consistent but globally inconsistent. To solve this problem, we are investigating an architecture in which the image is processed at several spatial scales simultaneously.

- Simulations are also underway to examine MAGIC's performance on real-world images—overlapping handwritten letters and digits—where it is somewhat less clear to which types of patterns the hidden units should respond.

- Zemel, Williams, and Mozer (to appear) have proposed a mathematical framework that—with slight modifications to the model—allow it to be interpreted as a mean-field approximation to a stochastic phase model.

- Behrmann, Zemel, and Mozer (to appear) are conducting psychological experiments to examine whether limitations of the model match human limitations.

Acknowledgements

This research was supported by NSF Presidential Young Investigator award IRI–9058450, grant 90–21 from the James S. McDonnell Foundation, and DEC external research grant 1250 to MM, and by a National Sciences and Engineering Research Council Postgraduate Scholarship to RZ. Our thanks to Paul Smolensky, Chris Williams, Geoffrey Hinton, and Jürgen Schmidhuber for helpful comments regarding this work.

References

Eckhorn, R., Bauer, R., Jordan, W., Brosch, M., Kruse, W., Munk, M., & Reitboek, H. J. (1988). Coherent oscillations: A mechanism of feature linking in the visual cortex? *Biological Cybernetics, 60*, 121–130.

Goebel, R. (1991). An oscillatory neural network model of visual attention, pattern recognition, and response generation. Manuscript in preparation.

Gray, C. M., Koenig, P., Engel, A. K., & Singer, W. (1989). Oscillatory responses in cat visual cortex exhibit intercolumnar synchronization which reflects global stimulus properties. *Nature (London), 338*, 334–337.

Guzman, A. (1968). Decomposition of a visual scene into three-dimensional bodies. *AFIPS Fall Joint Computer Conference, 33*, 291–304.

Hummel, J. E., & Biederman, I. (1992). Dynamic binding in a neural network for shape recognition. *Psychological Review*. In Press.

Kanade, T. (1981). Recovery of the three-dimensional shape of an object from a single view. *Artificial Intelligence, 17*, 409–460.

Lowe, D. G. (1985). *Perceptual Organization and Visual Recognition*. Boston: Kluwer Academic Publishers.

Lowe, D. G., & Binford, T. O. (1982). Segmentation and aggregation: An approach to figure-ground phenomena. In *Proceedings of the DARPA IU Workshop* (pp. 168–178). Palo Alto, CA: (null).

Marr, D. (1982). *Vision*. San Francisco: Freeman.

Rock, I., & Palmer, S. E. (1990). The legacy of Gestalt psychology. *Scientific American, 263*, 84–90.

von der Malsburg, C. (1981). *The correlation theory of brain function* (Internal Report 81-2). Goettingen: Department of Neurobiology, Max Planck Intitute for Biophysical Chemistry.

von der Malsburg, C., & Schneider, W. (1986). A neural cocktail-party processor. *Biological Cybernetics, 54*, 29–40.

Combined Neural Network and Rule-Based Framework for Probabilistic Pattern Recognition and Discovery

Hayit K. Greenspan and Rodney Goodman
Department of Electrical Engineering
California Institute of Technology, 116-81
Pasadena, CA 91125

Rama Chellappa
Department of Electrical Engineering
Institute for Advanced Computer Studies and Center for Automation Research
University of Maryland, College Park, MD 20742

Abstract

A combined neural network and rule-based approach is suggested as a general framework for pattern recognition. This approach enables unsupervised and supervised learning, respectively, while providing probability estimates for the output classes. The probability maps are utilized for higher level analysis such as a feedback for smoothing over the output label maps and the identification of unknown patterns (pattern "discovery"). The suggested approach is presented and demonstrated in the texture - analysis task. A correct classification rate in the 90 percentile is achieved for both unstructured and structured natural texture mosaics. The advantages of the probabilistic approach to pattern analysis are demonstrated.

1   INTRODUCTION

In this work we extend a recently suggested framework (Greenspan et al,1991) for a combined neural network and rule-based approach to pattern recognition. This approach enables unsupervised and supervised learning, respectively, as presented

444

in Fig. 1. In the unsupervised learning phase a neural network clustering scheme is used for the quantization of the input features. A supervised stage follows in which labeling of the quantized attributes is achieved using a rule based system. This information theoretic technique is utilized to find the most informative correlations between the attributes and the pattern class specification, while providing probability estimates for the output classes. Ultimately, a minimal representation for a library of patterns is learned in a training mode, following which the classification of new patterns is achieved.

The suggested approach is presented and demonstrated in the texture - analysis task. Recent results (Greenspan et al, 1991) have demonstrated a correct classification rate of 95 - 99% for synthetic (texton) textures and in the 90 percentile for 2 - 3 class natural texture mosaics. In this paper we utilize the output probability maps for high-level analysis in the pattern recognition process. A feedback based on the confidence measures associated with each class enables a smoothing operation over the output maps to achieve a high degree of classification in more difficult (natural texture) pattern mosaics. In addition, a generalization of the recognition process to identify unknown classes (pattern "discovery"), in itself a most challenging task, is demonstrated.

2   FEATURE EXTRACTION STAGE

The initial stage for a classification system is the feature extraction phase through which the attributes of the input domain are extracted and presented towards further processing. The chosen attributes are to form a representation of the input domain, which encompasses information for any desired future task.

In the texture-analysis task there is both biological and computational evidence supporting the use of Gabor filters for the feature - extraction phase (Malik and Perona, 1990; Bovik et al, 1990). Gabor functions are complex sinusoidal gratings modulated by 2-D Gaussian functions in the space domain, and shifted Gaussians in the frequency domain. The 2-D Gabor filters form a complete but non-orthogonal basis which can be used for image encoding into multiple spatial frequency and orientation channels. The Gabor filters are appropriate for textural analysis as they have tunable orientation and radial frequency bandwidths, tunable center frequencies, and optimally achieve joint resolution in space and spatial frequency.

In this work, we use the Log Gabor pyramid, or the Gabor wavelet decomposition to define an initial finite set of filters. We implement a pyramidal approach in the filtering stage reminiscent of the Laplacian Pyramid (Burt and Adelson, 1983). In our simulations a computationally efficient scheme involves a pyramidal representation of the image which is convolved with fixed spatial support oriented Gabor filters. Three scales are used with 4 orientations per scale (0,90,45,-45 degrees), together with a non-oriented component, to produce a 15-dimensional feature vector for every local window in the original image, as the output of the feature extraction stage.

The pyramidal approach allows for a hierarchical, multiscale framework for the image analysis. This is a desirable property as it enables the identification of features at various scales of the image and thus is attractive for scale-invariant pattern recognition.

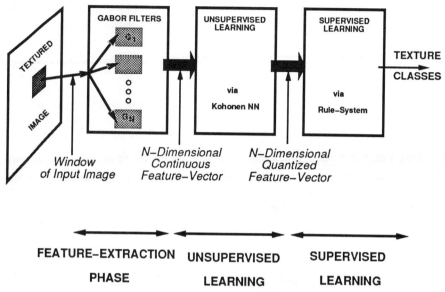

Figure 1: System Block Diagram

3 QUANTIZATION VIA UNSUPERVISED LEARNING

The unsupervised learning phase can be viewed as a preprocessing stage for achieving yet another, more compact representation, of the filtered input. The goal is to quantize the continuous valued features which are the result of the initial filtering stage. The need for discretization becomes evident when trying to learn associations between attributes in a statistically-based framework, such as a rule-based system. Moreover, in an extended framework, the network can reduce the dimension of the feature domain. This shift in representation is in accordance with biological based models.

The output of the filtering stage consists of N $(=15)$ continuous valued feature maps; each representing a filtered version of the original input. Thus, each local area of the input image is represented via an N-dimensional feature vector. An array of such N-dimensional vectors, viewed across the input image, is the input to the learning stage. We wish to detect characteristic behavior across the N-dimensional feature space for the family of textures to be learned. By projecting an input set of samples onto the N-dimensional space, we search for clusters to be related to corresponding code-vectors, and later on, recognized as possible texture classes. A neural-network quantization procedure, based on Kohonen's model (Kohonen, 1984) is utilized for this stage.

In this work each dimension, out of the N-dimensional attribute vector, is individually clustered. All samples are thus projected onto each axis of the space and one-dimensional clusters are found; this scalar quantization case closely resembles the K-means clustering algorithm. The output of the preprocessing stage is an N-dimensional quantized vector of attributes which is the result of concatenating the discrete valued codewords of the individual dimensions. Each dimension can be seen to contribute a probabilistic differentiation onto the different classes via the clusters found. As some of the dimensions are more representative than others, it is the goal of the supervised stage to find the most informative dimensions for the desired task (with the higher differentiation capability) and to label the combined clustered domain.

4   SUPERVISED LEARNING VIA A RULE-BASED SYSTEM

In the supervised stage we utilize the existing information in the feature maps for higher level analysis, such as input labeling and classification. In particular we need to learn a classifier which maps the output attributes of the unsupervised stage to the texture class labels. Any classification scheme could be used. However, we utilize a rule - based information theoretic approach which is an extension of a first order Bayesian classifier, because of its ability to output probability estimates for the output classes (Goodman et al, 1992). The classifier defines correlations between input features and output classes as probabilistic rules of the form: If $Y = y$ then $X = x$ with prob. p, where Y represents the attribute vector and X is the class variable. A data driven supervised learning approach utilizes an information theoretic measure to learn the most informative links or rules between the attributes and the class labels. Such a measure was introduced as the J measure (Smyth and Goodman, 1991) which represents the information content of a rule as the average bits of information that attribute values y give about the class X. The most informative set of rules via the J measure is learned in a training stage, following which the classifier uses them to provide an estimate of the probability of a given class being true. When presented with a new input evidence vector, Y, a set of rules can be considered to "fire". The classifier estimates the log posterior probability of each class given the rules that fire as:

$$\log p(x | rules \ that \ fire) = \log p(x) + \sum_j W_j$$

$$W_j = \log \left(\frac{p(x|y)}{p(x)} \right)$$

where $p(x)$ is the prior probability of the class x, and W_j represents the evidential support for the class as provided by rule j. Each class estimate can now be computed by accumulating the "weights of evidence" incident it from the rules that fire. The largest estimate is chosen as the initial class label decision. The probability estimates for the output classes can now be used for feedback purposes and further higher level processing.

The rule-based classification system can be mapped into a 3 layer feed forward architecture as shown in Fig. 2. The input layer contains a node for each attribute.

The hidden layer contains a node for each rule and the output layer contains a node for each class. Each rule (second layer node j) is connected to a class via the multiplicative weight of evidence W_j.

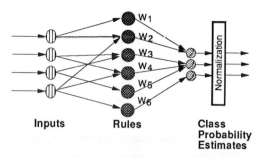

Figure 2: Rule-Based Network

5   RESULTS

In previous results (Greenspan et al, 1991) we have shown the capability of the proposed system to recognize successfully both artificial ("texton") and natural textures. A classification rate of 95-99% was obtained for 2 and 3 class artificial images. 90-98% was achieved for 2 and 3 class natural texture mosaics. In this work we wish to demonstrate the advantage of utilizing the output probability maps in the pattern recognition process. The probability maps are utilized for higher level analysis such as a feedback for smoothing and the identification of unknown patterns (pattern "discovery"). An example of a 5 - class natural texture classification is presented in Fig. 3. The mosaic is comprised of grass, raffia, herring, wood and wool (center square) textures. The input mosaic is presented (top left), followed by the labeled output map (top right) and the corresponding probability maps for a prelearned library of 6 textures (grass, raffia, wood, calf, herring and wool, left to right, top to bottom, respectively). The input poses a very difficult task which is challenging even to our own visual perception. Based on the probability maps (with white indicating strong probability) the very satisfying result of the labeled output map is achieved. The 5 different regions have been identified and labeled correctly (in different shades of gray) with the boundaries between the regions very strongly evident. A feedback based on the probability maps was used for smoothing over the label map, to achieve the result presented. It is worthwhile noting that the probabilistic framework enables the analysis of both structural textures (such as the wood, raffia and herring) and unstructural textures (such as the grass and wool).

Fig. 4. demonstrates the generalization capability of our system to the identification of an unknown class. In this task a presented pattern which is not part of the prelearned library, is to be recognized as such and labeled as an unknown area of interest. This task is termed "pattern discovery" and its application is wide spread from identifying unexpected events to the presentation of areas-of-interest in scene exploratory studies. Learning the unknown is a difficult problem in which the probability estimates prove to be valuable. In the presented example a 3 texture library was learned, consisting of wood, raffia and grass textures. The input consists of wood, raffia and sand (top left). The output label map (top right) which is the result of the analysis of the respective probability maps (bottom) exhibits the accurate detection of the known raffia and wood textures, with the sand area labeled in black as an unknown class. This conclusion was based on the corresponding probability estimations which are zeroed out in this area for all the known classes. We have thus successfuly analyzed the scene based on the existing source of knowledge.

Our most recent results pretain to the application of the system to natural scenery analysis. This is a most challanging task as it relates to real-world applications, an example of which are NASA space exploratory goals. Initial simulation results are presented in Fig. 5. which presents a sand-rock scenerio. The training examples are presented, followed by two input images and their corresponding output label maps, left to right, respectively. Here, white represents rock, gray represents sand and black regions are classified as unknown. The system copes successfully with this challange. We can see that a distinction between the regions has been made and for a possible mission such as rock avoidence (landing purposes, navigation etc.) reliable results were achieved. These initial results are very encouraging and indicate the robustness of the system to cope with difficult real-world cases.

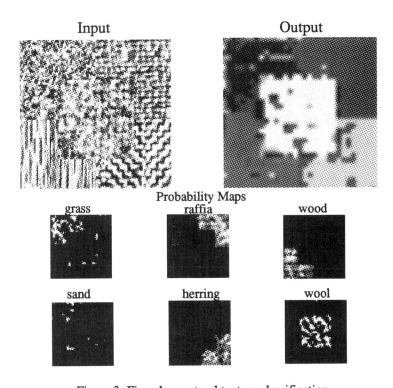

Figure 3: Five class natural texture classification

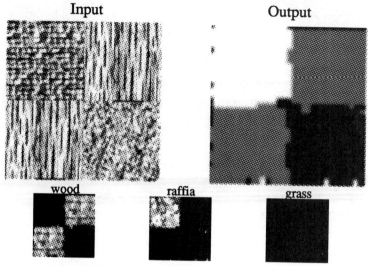

Figure 4: Identification of an unknown pattern

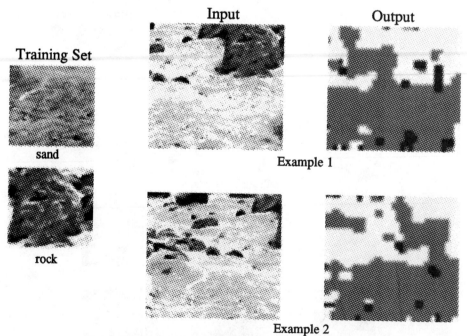

Figure 5: Natural scenery analysis

6 SUMMARY

The proposed learning scheme achieves a high percentage classification rate on both artificial and natural textures. The combined neural network and rule-based framework enables a probabilistic approach to pattern recognition. In this work we have demonstrated the advantage of utilizing the output probability maps in the pattern recognition process. Complicated patterns were analyzed accurately, with an extension to real-imagery applications. The generalization capability of the system to the discovery of unknown patterns was demonstrated. Future work includes research into scale and rotation invariance capabilities of the presented framework.

Acknowledgements

This work is funded in part by DARPA under the grant AFOSR-90-0199 and in part by the Army Research Office under the contract DAAL03-89-K-0126. Part of this work was done at Jet Propulsion Laboratory. The advice and software support of the image-analysis group there, especially that of Dr. Charlie Anderson, is greatly appreciated.

References

H. Greenspan, R. Goodman and R. Chellappa. (1991) Texture Analysis via Unsupervised and Supervised Learning. *Proceedings of the 1991 International Joint Conference on Neural Networks*, Vol. I:639-644.

R. M. Goodman, C. Higgins, J. Miller and P. Smyth. (1992) Rule-Based Networks for Classification and Probability Estimation. to appear in *Neural Computation*.

P. Smyth and R. M. Goodman. (1991) Rule Induction using Information Theory. In G. Piatetsky-Shapiro, W. Frawley (eds.), *Knowledge Discovery in Databases*, 159-176. AAAI Press.

J. Malik and P. Perona. (1990) Preattentive texture discrimination with early vision mechanisms. *Journal of Optical Society of America A*, Vol. 7[5]:923-932.

A. C. Bovik, M. Clark and W. S. Geisler. (1990) Multichannel Texture Analysis Using Localized Spatial Filters. *IEEE Transactions on Pattern Analysis and Machine Intelligence*, 12(1):55-73.

P.J. Burt and E. A. Adelson. (1983) The Laplacian Pyramid as a compact image code. *IEEE Trans. Commun.*,COM-31:532-540.

T. Kohonen. (1984) *Self Organisation and Associative Memory*. Springer-Verlag.

Linear Operator for Object Recognition

Ronen Basri   **Shimon Ullman***
M.I.T. Artificial Intelligence Laboratory
and Department of Brain and Cognitive Science
545 Technology Square
Cambridge, MA 02139

Abstract

Visual object recognition involves the identification of images of 3-D objects seen from arbitrary viewpoints. We suggest an approach to object recognition in which a view is represented as a collection of points given by their location in the image. An object is modeled by a set of 2-D views together with the correspondence between the views. We show that any novel view of the object can be expressed as a linear combination of the stored views. Consequently, we build a linear operator that distinguishes between views of a specific object and views of other objects. This operator can be implemented using neural network architectures with relatively simple structures.

1 Introduction

Visual object recognition involves the identification of images of 3-D objects seen from arbitrary viewpoints. In particular, objects often appear in images from previously unseen viewpoints. In this paper we suggest an approach to object recognition in which rigid objects are recognized from arbitrary viewpoint. The method can be implemented using neural network architectures with relatively simple structures.

In our approach a view is represented as a collection of points given by their location in the image, An object is modeled by a small set of views together with the correspondence between these views. We show that any novel view of the object

---

*Also, Weizmann Inst. of Science, Dept. of Applied Math., Rehovot 76100, Israel

can be expressed as a linear combination of the stored views. Consequently, we build a linear operator that distinguishes views of a specific object from views of other objects. This operator can be implemented by a neural network.

The method has several advantages. First, it handles correctly rigid objects, but is not restricted to such objects. Second, there is no need in this scheme to explicitly recover and represent the 3-D structure of objects. Third, the computations involved are often simpler than in previous schemes.

2   Previous Approaches

Object recognition involves a comparison of a viewed image against object models stored in memory. Many existing schemes to object recognition accomplish this task by performing a template comparison between the image and each of the models, often after compensating for certain variations due to the different positions and orientations in which the object is observed. Such an approach is called *alignment* (Ullman, 1989), and a similar approach is used in (Fischler & Bolles 1981, Lowe 1985, Faugeras & Hebert 1986, Chien & Aggarwal 1987, Huttenlocher & Ullman 1987, Thompson & Mundy 1987).

The majority of alignment schemes use object-centered representations to model the objects. In these models the 3-D structure of the objects is explicitly represented. The acquisition of models in these schemes therefore requires a separate process to recover the 3-D structure of the objects.

A number of recent studies use 2-D viewer-centered representations for object recognition. Abu-Mostafa & Pslatis (1987), for instance, developed a neural network that continuously collects and stores the observed views of objects. When a new view is observed it is recognized if it is sufficiently similar to one of the previously seen views. The system is very limited in its ability to recognize objects from novel views. It does not use information available from a collection of object views to extend the range of recognizable views beyond the range determined by each of the stored views separately.

In the scheme below we suggest a different kind of viewer-centered representations to model the objects. An object is modeled by a set of its observed images with the correspondence between points in the images. We show that only a small number of images is required to predict the appearance of the object from all possible viewpoints. These predictions are exact for rigid objects, but are not confined to such objects. We also suggest a neural network to implement the scheme.

A similar representation was recently used by Poggio & Edelman (1990) to develop a network that recognizes objects using radial basis functions (RBFs). The approach presented here has several advantages over this approach. First, by using the linear combinations of the stored views rather than applying radial basis functions to them we obtain exact predictions for the novel appearances of objects rather than an approximation. Moreover, a smaller number of views is required in our scheme to predict the appearance of objects from all possible views. For example, when a rigid object that does not introduce self occlusion (such as a wired object) is considered, predicting its appearance from all possible views requires only three views under the LC Scheme and about sixty views under the RBFs Scheme.

3   The Linear Combinations (LC) Scheme

In this section we introduce the Linear Combinations (LC) Scheme. Additional details about the scheme can be found in (Ullman & Basri, 1991). Our approach is based on the following observation. For many continuous transformations of interest in recognition, such as 3-D rotation, translation, and scaling, every possible view of a transforming object can be expressed as a linear combination of other views of the object. In other words, the set of possible images of an object undergoing rigid 3-D transformations and scaling is embedded in a linear space, spanned by a small number of 2-D images.

We start by showing that any image of an object undergoing rigid transformations followed by an orthographic projection can be expressed as a linear combination of a small number of views. The coefficients of this combination may differ for the x- and y-coordinates. That is, the intermediate view of the object may be given by two linear combinations, one for the x-coordinates and the other for the y-coordinates. In addition, certain functional restrictions may hold among the different coefficients.

We represent an image by two coordinate vectors, one contains the x-values of the object's points, and the other contains their y-values. In other words, an image P is described by $\mathbf{x} = (x_1, ..., x_n)$ and $\mathbf{y} = (y_1, ..., y_n)$ where every (x_i, y_i), $1 \leq i \leq n$, is an image point. The order of the points in these vectors is preserved in all the different views of the same object, namely, if P and P' are two views of the same object, then $(x_i, y_i) \in P$ and $(x_i', y_i') \in P'$ are in correspondence (or, in other words, they are the projections of the same object point).

Claim: The set of coordinate vectors of an object obtained from all different viewpoints is embedded in a 4-D linear space.
(A proof is given in Appendix A.)

Following this claim we can represent the entire space of views of an object by a basis that consists of any four linearly independent vectors taken from the space. In particular, we can construct a basis using familiar views of the object. Two images supply four such vectors and therefore are often sufficient to span the space. By considering the linear combinations of the model vectors we can reproduce any possible view of the object.

It is important to note that the set of views of a rigid object does not occupy the entire linear 4-D space. Rather, the coefficients of the linear combinations reproducing valid images follow in addition two quadratic constraints. (See Appendix A.) In order to verify that an object undergoes a rigid transformation (as opposed to a general 3-D affine transformation) the model must consist of at least three snapshots of the object.

Many 3-D rigid objects are bounded with smooth curved surfaces. The contours of such objects change their position on the object whenever the viewing position is changed. The linear combinations scheme can be extended to handle these objects as well. In this cases the scheme gives accurate approximations to the appearance of these objects (Ullman & Basri, 1991).

The linear combination scheme assumes that the same object points are visible in the different views. When the views are sufficiently different, this will no longer hold, due to self-occlusion. To represent an object from all possible viewing directions (e.g., both "front" and "back"), a number of different models of this type will be required. This notion is similar to the use of different object aspects suggested by Koenderink & Van Doorn (1979). (Other aspects of occlusion are discussed in the next section.)

4 Recognizing an Object Using the LC Scheme

In the previous section we have shown that the set of views of a rigid object is embedded in a linear space of a small dimension. In this section we define a linear operator that uses this property to recognize objects. We then show how this operator can be used in the recognition process.

Let $\mathbf{p}_1, ..., \mathbf{p}_k$ be the model views, and $\mathbf{p}$ be a novel view of the same object. According to the previous section there exist coefficients $a_1, ..., a_k$ such that: $\mathbf{p} = \sum_{i=1}^{k} a_i \mathbf{p}_i$. Suppose L is a linear operator such that $L\mathbf{p}_i = \mathbf{q}$ for every $1 \leq i \leq n$ and some constant vector $\mathbf{q}$, then L transforms $\mathbf{p}$ to $\mathbf{q}$ (up to a scale factor), $L\mathbf{p} = (\sum_{i=1}^{k} a_i)\mathbf{q}$. If in addition L transforms vectors outside the space spanned by the model to vectors other then $\mathbf{q}$ then L distinguishes views of the object from views of other objects. The vector $\mathbf{q}$ then serves as a "name" for the object. It can either be the zero vector, in which case L transforms every novel view of the object to zero, or it can be a familiar view of the object, in which case L has an associative property, namely, it takes a novel view of an object and transforms it to a familiar view. A constructive definition of L is given in appendix B.

The core of the recognition process we propose includes a neural network that implements the linear operator defined above. The input to this network is a coordinate vector created from the image, and the output is an indication whether the image is in fact an instance of the modeled object. The operator can be implemented by a simple, one layer, neural network with only feedforward connections, the type presented by Kohonen, Oja, & Lehtiö (1981). It is interesting to note that this operator can be modified to recognize several models in parallel.

To apply this network to the image the image should first be represented by its coordinate vectors. The construction of the coordinate vectors from the image can be implemented using cells with linear response properties, the type of cells encoding eye positions found by Zipser & Andersen (1988). The positions obtained should be ordered according to the correspondence of the image points with the model points. Establishing the correspondence is a difficult task and an obstacle to most existing recognition schemes. The phenomenon of apparent motion (Marr & Ullman 1981) suggests, however, that the human visual system is capable of handling this problem.

In many cases objects seen in the image are partially occluded. Sometimes also some of the points cannot be located reliably. To handle these cases the linear operator should be modified to exclude the missing points. The computation of the updated operator from the original one involves computing a pseudo-inverse. A method to compute the pseudo-inverse of a matrix in real time using neural networks has been suggested by Yeates (1991).

5   Summary

We have presented a method for recognizing 3-D objects from 2-D images. In this method, an object-model is represented by the linear combinations of several 2-D views of the object. It has been shown that for objects undergoing rigid transformations the set of possible images of a given object is embedded in a linear space spanned by a small number of views. Rigid transformations can be distinguished from more general linear transformations of the object by testing certain constraints placed upon the coefficients of the linear combinations. The method applies to objects with sharp as well as smooth boundaries.

We have proposed a linear operator to map the different views of the same object into a common representation, and we have presented a simple neural network that implements this operator. In addition, we have suggested a scheme to handle occlusions and unreliable measurements. One difficulty in this scheme is that it requires to find the correspondence between the image and the model views. This problem is left for future research.

The linear combination scheme described above was implemented and applied to a number of objects. Figures 1 and 2 show the application of the linear combinations method to artificially created and real life objects. The figures show a number of object models, their linear combinations, and the agreement between these linear combinations and actual images of the objects. Figure 3 shows the results of applying a linear operator with associative properties to artificial objects. It can be seen that whenever the operator is fed with a novel view of the object for which it was designed it returns a familiar view of the object.

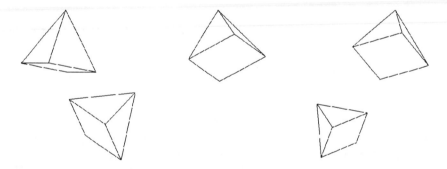

Figure 1: Top: three model pictures of a pyramid. Bottom: two of their linear combinations.

Appendix A

In this appendix we prove that the coordinate vectors of images of a rigid object lie in a 4-D linear space. We also show that the coefficients of the linear combinations that produce valid images of the object follow in addition two quadratic constraints.

Let O be a set of object points, and let $\mathbf{x} = (x_1, ..., x_n)$, $\mathbf{y} = (y_1, ..., y_n)$, and

Figure 2: Top: three model pictures of a VW car. Bottom: a linear combination of the three images (left), an actual edge image (middle), and the two images overlayed (right).

Figure 3: Top: applying an associative pyramidal operator to a pyramid (left) returns a model view of the pyramid (right, compare with Figure 1 top left). Bottom: applying the same operator to a cube (left) returns an unfamiliar image (right).

$\mathbf{z} = (z_1, ..., z_n)$ such that $(x_i, y_i, z_i) \in O$ for every $1 \leq i \leq n$. Let $\hat{P}$ be a view of the object, and let $\hat{\mathbf{x}} = (\hat{x}_1, ..., \hat{x}_n)$ and $\hat{\mathbf{y}} = (\hat{y}_1, ..., \hat{y}_n)$ such that $(\hat{x}_i, \hat{y}_i)$ is the position of (x_i, y_i, z_i) in $\hat{P}$. We call $\mathbf{x}$, $\mathbf{y}$, and $\mathbf{z}$ the coordinate vectors of O, and $\hat{\mathbf{x}}$ and $\hat{\mathbf{y}}$ the corresponding coordinate vectors in $\hat{P}$. Assume $\hat{P}$ is obtained from O by applying a rotation matrix R, a scale factor s, and a translation vector (t_x, t_y) followed by an orthographic projection.

Claim: There exist coefficients a_1, a_2, a_3, a_4 and b_1, b_2, b_3, b_4 such that:

$$\hat{\mathbf{x}} = a_1\mathbf{x} + a_2\mathbf{y} + a_3\mathbf{z} + a_4\mathbf{1}$$
$$\hat{\mathbf{y}} = b_1\mathbf{x} + b_2\mathbf{y} + b_3\mathbf{z} + b_4\mathbf{1}$$

where $\mathbf{1} = (1, ..., 1) \in \mathcal{R}^n$.

Proof: Simply by assigning:

$$
\begin{array}{llll}
a_1 & = & sr_{11} \qquad & b_1 = sr_{21} \\
a_2 & = & sr_{12} & b_2 = sr_{22} \\
a_3 & = & sr_{13} & b_3 = sr_{23} \\
a_4 & = & t_x & b_4 = t_y
\end{array}
$$

Therefore, $\hat{\mathbf{x}}, \hat{\mathbf{y}} \in span\{\mathbf{x}, \mathbf{y}, \mathbf{z}, \mathbf{1}\}$ regardless of the viewpoint from which $\hat{\mathbf{x}}$ and $\hat{\mathbf{y}}$ are taken. Notice that the set of views of a rigid object does not occupy the entire linear 4-D space. Rather, the coefficients follow in addition two quadratic constraints:

$$a_1^2 + a_2^2 + a_3^2 = b_1^2 + b_2^2 + b_3^2$$
$$a_1b_1 + a_2b_2 + a_3b_3 = 0$$

Appendix B

A "recognition matrix" is defined as follows. Let $\{\mathbf{p}_1, ..., \mathbf{p}_k\}$ be a set of k linearly independent vectors representing the model pictures. Let $\{\mathbf{p}_{k+1}, ..., \mathbf{p}_n\}$ be a set of vectors such that $\{\mathbf{p}_1, ..., \mathbf{p}_n\}$ are all linearly independent. We define the following matrices:

$$P = (\mathbf{p}_1, ..., \mathbf{p}_k, \mathbf{p}_{k+1}, ..., \mathbf{p}_n)$$
$$Q = (\mathbf{q}, ..., \mathbf{q}, \mathbf{p}_{k+1}, ..., \mathbf{p}_n)$$

We require that:

$$LP = Q$$

Therefore:

$$L = QP^{-1}$$

Note that since P is composed of n linearly independent vectors, the inverse matrix P^{-1} exists, therefore L can always be constructed.

Acknowledgments

We wish to thank Yael Moses for commenting on the final version of this paper. This report describes research done at the Massachusetts Institute of Technology within the Artificial Intelligence Laboratory. Support for the laboratory's artificial intelligence research is provided in part by the Advanced Research Projects Agency of the Department of Defense under Office of Naval Research contract N00014-85-K-0124. Ronen Basri is supported by the McDonnell-Pew and the Rothchild postdoctoral fellowships.

References

Abu-Mostafa, Y.S. & Pslatis, D. 1987. Optical neural computing. *Scientific American, 256*, 66-73.

Chien, C.H. & Aggarwal, J.K., 1987. Shape recognition from single silhouette. *Proc. of ICCV Conf. (London)* 481-490.

Faugeras, O.D. & Hebert, M., 1986. The representation, recognition and location of 3-D objects. *Int. J. Robotics Research*, 5(3), 27-52.

Fischler, M.A. & Bolles, R.C., 1981. Random sample consensus: a paradigm for model fitting with application to image analysis and automated cartography. *Communications of the ACM*, 24(6), 381-395.

Huttenlocher, D.P. & Ullman, S., 1987. Object recognition using alignment. *Proc. of ICCV Conf. (London)*, 102-111.

Koenderink, J.J. & Van Doorn, A.J., 1979. The internal representation of solid shape with respect to vision. *Biol. Cybernetics 32*, 211-216.

Kohonen, T., Oja, E., & Lehtiö, P., 1981. Storage and processing of information in distributed associative memory systems. *in Hinton, G.E. & Anderson, J.A., Parallel Models of Associative Memory. Hillsdale, NJ: Lawrence Erlbaum Associates*, 105-143.

Lowe, D.G., 1985. *Perceptual Organization and Visual Recognition.* Boston: Kluwer Academic Publishing.

Marr, D. & Ullman, S., 1981. Directional selectivity and its use in early visual processing. *Proc. R. Soc. Lond. B 211*, 151-180.

Poggio, T. & Edelman, S., 1990. A network that learns to recognize three dimensional objects. *Nature, Vol. 343*, 263-266.

Thompson, D.W. & Mundy J.L., 1987. Three dimensional model matching from an unconstrained viewpoint. *Proc. IEEE Int. Conf. on robotics and Automation*, Raleigh, N.C., 208-220.

S. Ullman and R. Basri, 1991. Recognition by Linear Combinations of Models. *IEEE Trans. on Pattern Analysis and Machine Intelligence, Vol. 13, No. 10*, pp. 992-1006

Ullman, S., 1989. Aligning pictorial descriptions: An approach to object recognition: *Cognition, 32(3)*, 193-254. Also: 1986, *A.I. Memo 931, The Artificial Intelligence Lab., M.I.T.*.

Yeates, M.C., 1991. A neural network for computing the pseudo-inverse of a matrix and application to Kalman filtering. *Tech. Report, California Institute of Technology.*

Zipser, D. & Andersen, R.A., 1988. A back-propagation programmed network that simulates response properties of a subset of posterior parietal neurons. *Nature, 331*, 679-684.

3D Object Recognition Using Unsupervised Feature Extraction

Nathan Intrator
Center for Neural Science,
Brown University
Providence, RI 02912, USA

Josh I. Gold
Center for Neural Science,
Brown University
Providence, RI 02912, USA

Heinrich H. Bülthoff
Dept. of Cognitive Science,
Brown University,
and Center for
Biological Information Processing,
MIT, Cambridge, MA 02139 USA

Shimon Edelman
Dept. of Applied Mathematics
and Computer Science,
Weizmann Institute of Science,
Rehovot 76100, Israel

Abstract

Intrator (1990) proposed a feature extraction method that is related to recent statistical theory (Huber, 1985; Friedman, 1987), and is based on a biologically motivated model of neuronal plasticity (Bienenstock et al., 1982). This method has been recently applied to feature extraction in the context of recognizing 3D objects from single 2D views (Intrator and Gold, 1991). Here we describe experiments designed to analyze the nature of the extracted features, and their relevance to the theory and psychophysics of object recognition.

1 Introduction

Results of recent computational studies of visual recognition (e.g., Poggio and Edelman, 1990) indicate that the problem of recognition of 3D objects can be effectively reformulated in terms of standard pattern classification theory. According to this approach, an object is represented by a few of its 2D views, encoded as clusters in multidimentional space. Recognition of a novel view is then carried out by interpolating among the stored views in the representation space. A major characteristic of the view interpolation scheme is its sensitivity to viewpoint: the farther the novel view is from the stored views, the lower the expected recognition rate.

This characteristic performance in the recognition of novel views of synthetic 3D stimuli was indeed found in human subjects by Bülthoff and Edelman (1991), who also replicated it in simulated psychophysical experiments that involved a computer implementation of the view interpolation model. Because of the high dimensionality of the raster images seen by the human subjects, it was impossible to use them directly for classification in the simulated experiments. Consequently, the simulations were simplified, in that the views presented to the model were encoded as lists of vertex locations of the objects (which resembled 3D wire frames).

This simplification amounts to what is referred to in the psychology of recognition as the feature extraction step (LaBerge, 1976). The discussion of the issue of features of recognition in recent psychological literature is relatively scarce, probably because of the abandonment of invariant feature theories (which postulate that objects are represented by clusters of points in multidimensional feature spaces (Duda and Hart, 1973)) in favor of structural models (see review in (Edelman, 1991)). Although some attempts have been made to generate and verify specific psychophysical predictions based on the feature space approach (see especially (Shepard, 1987)), current feature-based theories of perception seem to be more readily applicable to lower-level visual tasks than to the problem of object recognition.

In the present work, our aim was to explore a computationally tractable model of feature extraction conceived as dimensionality reduction, and to test its psychophysical validity. This work was guided by previous successful applications in pattern recognition of dimensionality reduction by a network model implementing Exploratory Projection Pursuit (Intrator, 1990; Intrator and Gold, 1991). We were also motivated by results of recent psychophysical experiments (Edelman and Bülthoff, 1990; Edelman et al., 1991) that found improvement in subjects' performance with increasing stimulus familiarity. These results are compatible with a feature-based recognition model which extracts problem-specific features in addition to universal ones. Specifically, the subjects' ability to discern key elements of the solution appears to increase as the problem becomes more familiar. This finding suggests that some of the features used by the visual system are based on the task-specific data, and therefore raises the question of how can such features be extracted. It was our conjecture that features found by the EPP model would turn out to be similar to the task-specific features in human vision.

1.1 Unsupervised Feature Extraction - The BCM Model

The feature extraction method briefly described below emphasizes dimensionality reduction, while seeking features of a set of objects that would best distinguish among the members of the set. This method does not rely on a general pre-defined set of features. This is not to imply, however, that the features are useful only in recognition of the original set of images from which they were extracted. In fact, the potential importance of these features is related to their invariance properties, or their ability to generalize. Invariance properties of features extracted by this method have been demonstrated previously in speech recognition (Intrator and Tajchman,

1991; Intrator, 1992).

From a mathematical viewpoint, extracting features from gray level images is related to dimensionality reduction in a high dimensional vector space, in which an $n \times k$ pixel image is considered to be a vector of length $n \times k$. The dimensionality reduction is achieved by replacing each image (or its high dimensional equivalent vector) by a low dimensional vector in which each element represents a projection of the image onto a vector of synaptic weights (constructed by a BCM neuron).

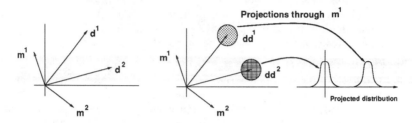

Figure 1: The stable solutions for a two dimensional two input problem are m_1 and m_2 (left) and similarly with a two-cluster data (right).

The feature extraction method we used (Intrator and Cooper, 1991) seeks multi-modality in the projected distribution of these high dimensional vectors. A simple example is illustrated in Figure 1. For a two-input problem in two dimensions, the stable solutions (projection directions) are m_1 and m_2, each has the property of being orthogonal to one of the inputs. In a higher dimensional space, for n linearly independent inputs, a stable solution is one that it is orthogonal to all but one of the inputs. In case of noisy but clustered inputs, a stable solution will be orthogonal to all but one of the cluster centers. As is seen in Figure 1 (right), this leads to a bimodal, or, in general, multi-modal, projected distribution. Further details are given in (Intrator and Cooper, 1991). In the present study, the features extracted by the above approach were used for classification as described in (Intrator and Gold, 1991; Intrator, 1992).

1.2   Experimental paradigm

We have studied the features extracted by the BCM model by replicating the experiments of Bülthoff and Edelman (1991), designed to test generalization from familiar to novel views of 3D objects. As in the psychophysical experiments, images of novel wire-like computer-generated objects (Bülthoff and Edelman, 1991; Edelman and Bülthoff, 1990) were used as stimuli. These objects proved to be easily manipulated, and yet complex enough to yield interesting results. Using wires also simplified the problem for the feature extractor, as they provided little or no occlusion of the key features from any viewpoint. The objects were generated by the Symbolics S-Geometry™ modeling package, and rendered with a visualization graphics tool (AVS, Stardent, Inc.). Each object consisted of seven connected equal-length segments, pointing in random directions and distributed equally around the origin (for further details, see Edelman and Bülthoff, 1990).

In the psychophysical experiments of Bülthoff and Edelman (1991), subjects were shown a target wire from two standard views, located 75° apart along the equator of the viewing sphere. The target oscillated around each of the two standard orientations with an amplitude of ±15° about a fixed vertical axis, with views spaced at 3° increments. Test views were located either along the equator – on the minor arc bounded by the two standard views (INTER condition) or on the corresponding major arc (EXTRA condition) – or on the meridian passing through one of the standard views (ORTHO condition). Testing was conducted according to a two-alternative forced choice (2AFC) paradigm, in which subjects were asked to indicate whether the displayed image constituted a view of the target object shown during the preceding training session. Test images were either unfamiliar views of the training object, or random views of a distractor (one of a distinct set of objects generated by the same procedure).

To apply the above paradigm to the BCM network, the objects were rendered in a 63 × 63 array, at 8 bits/pixel, under simulated illumination that combined ambient lighting of relative strength 0.3 with a point source of strength 1.0 at infinity. The study described below involved six-way classification, which is more difficult than the 2AFC task used in the psychophysical experiments. The six wires used

Figure 2: The six wires used in the computational experiments, as seen from a single view point.

in the experiments are depicted in Figure 2. Given the task of recognizing the six wires, the network extracted features that corresponded to small patches of the different images, namely areas that either remained relatively invariant under the rotation performed during training, or represented distinctive features of specific wires (Intrator and Gold, 1991). The classification results were in good agreement with the psychophysical data of Bülthoff and Edelman (1991): (1) the error rate was the lowest in the INTER condition, (2) recognition deteriorated to chance level with increased misorientation in the EXTRA and ORTHO conditions, and (3) horizontal training led to a better performance in the INTER condition than did vertical training.[1] The first two points were interpreted as resulting from the ability of the BCM network to extract rotation-invariant features. Indeed, features appearing in all the training views would be expected to correspond to the INTER condition. EXTRA and ORTHO views, on the other hand, are less familiar and therefore yield worse performance, and also may require features other than the rotation-invariant ones extracted by the model.

---

[1]The horizontal-vertical asymmetry might be related to an asymmetric structure of the visual field in humans (Hughes, 1977). This asymmetry was modeled by increasing the resolution along the horizontal axis.

2   Examining the Features of Recognition

To understand the meaning of the features extracted by the BCM network under the various conditions, and to establish a basis for further comparison between the psychophysical experiments and computational models, we developed a method for occluding key features from the images and examining the subsequent effects on the various recognition tasks.

2.1   The Occlusion Experiment

In this experiment, some of the features previously extracted by the network could be occluded during training and/or testing. Each input to a BCM neuron in our model corresponds to a particular point in the 2D input image, while "features" correspond to combinations of excitatory and inhibitory inputs. Assuming that inputs with strong positive weights constitute a significant proportion of the features, we occluded (set to 0) input pixels whose previously computed synaptic weight exceeded a preset threshold. Figure 3 shows a synaptic weight matrix defining a set of features, and the set of wires with the corresponding features occluded.

The main hypothesis we tested concerns the general utility of the extracted features for recognition. If the features extracted by the BCM network do capture rotation-invariant aspects of the object and can support recognition across a variety of rotations, then occluding those features during training should lead to a pronounced and general decline in recognition performance of the model. In particular, recognition should deteriorate most significantly in the INTER and EXTRA cases, since they lie in the plane of rotation during training and therefore can be expected to rely to a larger extent on rotation-invariant features. Little change should be seen in the ORTHO condition, on the other hand, because recognition of ORTHO views, situated outside the plane of rotation defined by the training phase, does not benefit from rotation-invariant features.

2.2   Results and Discussion

When there was no occlusion, the pattern of the model's performance replicated the results of the psychophysical experiments of (Bülthoff and Edelman, 1991). Specifically, the best performance was achieved for INTER views, with progressive deterioration under EXTRA and ORTHO conditions (Intrator and Gold, 1991; see Figure 4). The results of simulations involving occlusion of key features during training and no occlusion during testing are illustrated in Figure 5. Essentially the same results were obtained when occlusion was done during either training or testing.

Occlusion of the key features led to a number of interesting results. First, when features in the training image were occluded, occluding the same features during testing made little difference. This is not unexpected, since these features were not used to build the internal representation of the objects. Second, there was a general decline in performance within the plane of rotation used during training (especially in the INTER condition) when the extracted features were occluded. This is a strong indication that the features initially chosen by the network were in fact those features which best described the object across a range of rotations. Third, there

Figure 3: Wires occluded with a feature extracted by BCM network (left).

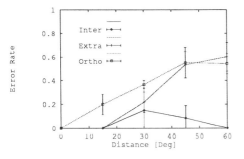

Figure 4: Misclassification performance, regular training.

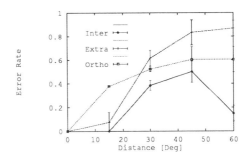

Figure 5: Misclassification performance, training on occluded images.

was little degradation of performance in the ORTHO condition when features were occluded during training. This result lends further support to the notion that the extracted features emphasized rotation-invariant characteristics of the objects, as abstracted in the training phase. Finally, we mention that the occlusion of the same features in a new psychophysical experiment caused the same selective deterioration found in the simulations to appear in the human subjects' performance. Specifically, the subjects' error rate was elevated in the INTER condition more than in the other conditions, and this effect was significantly stronger for occlusion masks obtained from the extracted features than for other, randomized, masks (Sklar et al., 1991).

To summarize, this work was undertaken to elucidate the nature of the *features of recognition* of 3D objects. We were especially interested in the features extracted by an unsupervised BCM network, and in their relation to computational and psychophysical findings concerning object recognition. We compared recognition performance of our model following training that involved features extracted by the BCM network with performance in the absence of these features. We found that the model's performance was affected by the occlusion of key features in a manner consistent with their predicted computational role. This method of testing the relative importance of features has also been applied in psychophysical experiments. Preliminary results of those experiments show that feature-derived masks have a stronger effect on human performance compared to other masks that occlude the same proportion of the image, but are not obtained via the BCM model. Taken together, these results demonstrate the strength of the dimensionality reduction approach to feature extraction, and provide a foundation for examining the link between computational and psychophysical studies of the features of recognition.

Acknowledgements

Research was supported by the National Science Foundation, the Army Research Office, and the Office of Naval Research.

References

Bienenstock, E. L., Cooper, L. N., and Munro, P. W. (1982). Theory for the development of neuron selectivity: orientation specificity and binocular interaction in visual cortex. *Journal Neuroscience*, 2:32–48.

Bülthoff, H. H. and Edelman, S. (1991). Psychophysical support for a 2D interpolation theory of object recognition. *Proceedings of the National Academy of Science.* to appear.

Duda, R. O. and Hart, P. E. (1973). *Pattern Classification and Scene Analysis.* John Wiley, New York.

Edelman, S. (1991). Features of recognition. CS-TR 10, Weizmann Institute of Science.

Edelman, S. and Bülthoff, H. H. (1990). Viewpoint-specific representations in three-dimensional object recognition. A.I. Memo No. 1239, Artificial Intelligence Laboratory, Massachusetts Institute of Technology.

Edelman, S., Bülthoff, H. H., and Sklar, E. (1991). Task and object learning in visual recognition. CBIP Memo No. 63, Center for Biological Information Processing, Massachusetts Institute of Technology.

Friedman, J. H. (1987). Exploratory projection pursuit. *Journal of the American Statistical Association*, 82:249–266.

Huber, P. J. (1985). Projection pursuit. (with discussion). *The Annals of Statistics*, 13:435–475.

Hughes, A. (1977). The topography of vision in mammals of contrasting live style: Comparative optics and retinal organisation. In Crescitelli, F., editor, *The Visual System in Vertebrates, Handbook of Sensory Physiology VII/5*, pages 613–756. Springer Verlag, Berlin.

Intrator, N. (1990). Feature extraction using an unsupervised neural network. In Touretzky, D. S., Ellman, J. L., Sejnowski, T. J., and Hinton, G. E., editors, *Proceedings of the 1990 Connectionist Models Summer School*, pages 310–318. Morgan Kaufmann, San Mateo, CA.

Intrator, N. (1992). Feature extraction using an unsupervised neural network. *Neural Computation*, 4:98–107.

Intrator, N. and Cooper, L. N. (1991). Objective function formulation of the BCM theory of visual cortical plasticity: Statistical connections, stability conditions. *Neural Networks.* To appear.

Intrator, N. and Gold, J. I. (1991). Three-dimensional object recognition of gray level images: The usefulness of distinguishing features. Submitted.

Intrator, N. and Tajchman, G. (1991). Supervised and unsupervised feature extraction from a cochlear model for speech recognition. In Juang, B. H., Kung, S. Y., and Kamm, C. A., editors, *Neural Networks for Signal Processing – Proceedings of the 1991 IEEE Workshop*, pages 460–469.

LaBerge, D. (1976). Perceptual learning and attention. In Estes, W. K., editor, *Handbook of learning and cognitive processes*, volume 4, pages 237–273. Lawrence Erlbaum, Hillsdale, New Jersey.

Poggio, T. and Edelman, S. (1990). A network that learns to recognize three-dimensional objects. *Nature*, 343:263–266.

Shepard, R. N. (1987). Toward a universal law of generalization for psychological science. *Science*, 237:1317–1323.

Sklar, E., Intrator, N., Gold, J. J., Edelman, S. Y., and Bülthoff, H. H. (1991). A hierarchical model for 3D object recognition based on 2D visual representation. In *Neurosci. Soc. Abs.*

PART VIII

OPTICAL CHARACTER RECOGNITION

Structural Risk Minimization
for Character Recognition

I. Guyon, V. Vapnik, B. Boser, L. Bottou, and S. A. Solla
AT&T Bell Laboratories
Holmdel, NJ 07733, USA

Abstract

The method of *Structural Risk Minimization* refers to tuning the capacity of the classifier to the available amount of training data. This capacity is influenced by several factors, including: (1) properties of the input space, (2) nature and structure of the classifier, and (3) learning algorithm. Actions based on these three factors are combined here to control the capacity of linear classifiers and improve generalization on the problem of handwritten digit recognition.

1 RISK MINIMIZATION AND CAPACITY

1.1 EMPIRICAL RISK MINIMIZATION

A common way of training a given classifier is to adjust the parameters $\mathbf{w}$ in the classification function $F(\mathbf{x}, \mathbf{w})$ to minimize the *training error* E_{train}, i.e. the frequency of errors on a set of p training examples. E_{train} estimates the expected risk based on the empirical data provided by the p available examples. The method is thus called *Empirical Risk Minimization*. But the classification function $F(\mathbf{x}, \mathbf{w}^*)$ which minimizes the empirical risk does not necessarily minimize the *generalization error*, i.e. the expected value of the risk over the full distribution of possible inputs and their corresponding outputs. Such generalization error E_{gene} cannot in general be computed, but it can be estimated on a separate test set (E_{test}). Other ways of estimating E_{gene} include the *leave-one-out* or *moving control* method [Vap82] (for a review, see [Moo92]).

1.2 CAPACITY AND GUARANTEED RISK

Any family of classification functions $\{F(\mathbf{x}, \mathbf{w})\}$ can be characterized by its capacity. The Vapnik-Chervonenkis dimension (or VC-dimension) [Vap82] is such a capacity, defined as the maximum number h of training examples which can be learnt without error, *for all possible binary labelings*. The VC-dimension is in some cases simply given by the number of free parameters of the classifier, but in most practical cases it is quite difficult to determine it analytically.

The VC-theory provides bounds. Let $\{F(\mathbf{x}, \mathbf{w})\}$ be a set of classification functions of capacity h. With probability $(1 - \eta)$, for a number of training examples $p > h$, simultaneously for all classification functions $F(\mathbf{x}, \mathbf{w})$, the generalization error E_{gene} is lower than a *guaranteed risk* defined by:

$$E_{guarant} = E_{train} + \epsilon(p, h, E_{train}, \eta) , \tag{1}$$

where $\epsilon(p, h, E_{train}, \eta)$ is proportional to $\epsilon_0 = [h(ln2p/h+1) - \eta]/p$ for small E_{train}, and to $\sqrt{\epsilon_0}$ for E_{train} close to one [Vap82,Vap92].

For a fixed number of training examples p, the training error decreases monotonically as the capacity h increases, while both guaranteed risk and generalization error go through a minimum. Before the minimum, the problem is *overdetermined*: the capacity is too small for the amount of training data. Beyond the minimum the problem is *underdetermined*. The key issue is therefore to match the capacity of the classifier to the amount of training data in order to get best generalization performance. The method of *Structural Risk Minimization* (SRM) [Vap82,Vap92] provides a way of achieving this goal.

1.3 STRUCTURAL RISK MINIMIZATION

Let us choose a family of classifiers $\{F(\mathbf{x}, \mathbf{w})\}$, and define a structure consisting of nested subsets of elements of the family: $S_1 \subset S_2 \subset ... \subset S_r \subset ....$ By defining such a structure, we ensure that the capacity h_r of the subset of classifiers S_r is less than h_{r+1} of subset S_{r+1}. The method of SRM amounts to finding the subset S^{opt} for which the classifier $F(\mathbf{x}, \mathbf{w}^*)$ which minimizes the empirical risk within such subset yields the best overall generalization performance.

Two problems arise in implementing SRM: (I) How to select S^{opt}? (II) How to find a good structure? Problem (I) arises because we have no direct access to E_{gene}. In our experiments, we will use the minimum of either E_{test} or $E_{guarant}$ to select S^{opt}, and show that these two minima are very close. A good structure reflects the *a priori* knowledge of the designer, and only few guidelines can be provided from the theory to solve problem (II). The designer must find the best compromise between two competing terms: E_{train} and ϵ. Reducing h causes ϵ to decrease, but E_{train} to increase. A good structure should be such that decreasing the VC-dimension happens at the expense of the smallest possible increase in training error. We now examine several ways in which such a structure can be built.

2   PRINCIPAL COMPONENT ANALYSIS, OPTIMAL BRAIN DAMAGE, AND WEIGHT DECAY

Consider three apparently different methods of improving generalization performance: Principal Component Analysis (a preprocessing transformation of input space) [The89], Optimal Brain Damage (an architectural modification through weight pruning) [LDS90], and a regularization method, Weight Decay (a modification of the learning algorithm) [Vap82]. For the case of a linear classifier, these three approaches are shown here to control the capacity of the learning system through the same underlying mechanism: a reduction of the *effective dimension* of weight space, based on the curvature properties of the Mean Squared Error (MSE) cost function used for training.

2.1   LINEAR CLASSIFIER AND MSE TRAINING

Consider a binary linear classifier $F(\mathbf{x}, \mathbf{w}) = \theta_0(\mathbf{w}^T \mathbf{x})$, where $\mathbf{w}^T$ is the transpose of $\mathbf{w}$ and the function θ_0 takes two values 0 and 1 indicating to which class $\mathbf{x}$ belongs. The VC-dimension of such classifier is equal to the dimension of input space [1] (or the number of weights): $h = dim(\mathbf{w}) = dim(\mathbf{x}) = n$.

The empirical risk is given by:

$$E_{train} = \frac{1}{p} \sum_{k=1}^{p} (y^k - \theta_0(\mathbf{w}^T \mathbf{x}^k))^2 \;, \qquad (2)$$

where $\mathbf{x}^k$ is the kth example, and y^k is the corresponding desired output. The problem of minimizing E_{train} as a function of $\mathbf{w}$ can be approached in different ways [DH73], but it is often replaced by the problem of minimizing a Mean Square Error (MSE) cost function, which differs from (2) in that the nonlinear function θ_0 has been removed.

2.2   CURVATURE PROPERTIES OF THE MSE COST FUNCTION

The three structures that we investigate rely on curvature properties of the MSE cost function. Consider the dependence of MSE on one of the parameters w_i. Training leads to the optimal value w_i^* for this parameter. One way of reducing the capacity is to set w_i to zero. For the linear classifier, this reduces the VC-dimension by one: $h' = dim(\mathbf{w}) - 1 = n - 1$. The MSE increase resulting from setting $w_i = 0$ is to lowest order proportional to the curvature of the MSE at w_i^*. Since the decrease in capacity should be achieved at the smallest possible expense in MSE increase, directions in weight space corresponding to small MSE curvature are good candidates for elimination.

The curvature of the MSE is specified by the Hessian matrix H of second derivatives of the MSE with respect to the weights. For a linear classifier, the Hessian matrix is given by twice the correlation matrix of the training inputs, $H = (2/p) \sum_{k=1}^{p} \mathbf{x}^k \mathbf{x}^{kT}$. The Hessian matrix is symmetric, and can be diagonalized to get rid of cross terms,

---

[1]We assume, for simplicity, that the first component of vector $\mathbf{x}$ is constant and set to 1, so that the corresponding weight introduces the bias value.

to facilitate decisions about the simultaneous elimination of several directions in weight space. The elements of the Hessian matrix after diagonalization are the eigenvalues λ_i; the corresponding eigenvectors give the principal directions w_i' of the MSE. In the rotated axis, the increase ΔMSE due to setting $w_i' = 0$ takes a simple form:

$$\Delta MSE \approx \frac{1}{2}\lambda_i(w_i'^*)^2 \qquad (3)$$

The quadratic approximation becomes an exact equality for the linear classifier. Principal directions w_i' corresponding to small eigenvalues λ_i of H are good candidates for elimination.

2.3 PRINCIPAL COMPONENT ANALYSIS

One common way of reducing the capacity of a classifier is to reduce the dimension of the input space and thereby reduce the number of necessary free parameters (or weights). *Principal Component Analysis* (PCA) is a feature extraction method based on eigenvalue analysis. Input vectors $\mathbf{x}$ of dimension n are approximated by a linear combination of $m \leq n$ vectors forming an ortho-normal basis. The coefficients of this linear combination form a vector $\mathbf{x}'$ of dimension m. The optimal basis in the least square sense is given by the m eigenvectors corresponding to the m largest eigenvalues of the correlation matrix of the training inputs (this matrix is $1/2$ of H). A structure is obtained by ranking the classifiers according to m. The VC-dimension of the classifier is reduced to: $h' = dim(\mathbf{x}') = m$.

2.4 OPTIMAL BRAIN DAMAGE

For a linear classifier, pruning can be implemented in two different but equivalent ways: (i) change input coordinates to a principal axis representation, prune the *components* corresponding to small eigenvalues according to PCA, and then train with the MSE cost function; (ii) change coordinates to a principal axis representation, train with MSE first, and then prune the *weights*, to get a weight vector $\mathbf{w}'$ of dimension $m \leq n$. Procedure (i) can be understood as a preprocessing, whereas procedure (ii) involves an *a posteriori* modification of the structure of the classifier (network architecture). The two procedures become identical if the weight elimination in (ii) is based on a 'smallest eigenvalue' criterion.

Procedure (ii) is very reminiscent of *Optimal Brain Damage* (OBD), a weight pruning procedure applied after training. In OBD, the best candidates for pruning are those weights which minimize the increase ΔMSE defined in equation (3). The m weights that are kept do not necessarily correspond to the largest m eigenvalues, due to the extra factor of $(w_i'^*)^2$ in equation (3). In either implementation, the VC-dimension is reduced to $h' = dim(\mathbf{w}') = dim(\mathbf{x}') = m$.

2.5 WEIGHT DECAY

Capacity can also be controlled through an additional term in the cost function, to be minimized simultaneously with MSE. Linear classifiers can be ranked according to the norm $\|\mathbf{w}\|^2 = \sum_{j=1}^{n} w_j^2$ of the weight vector. A structure is constructed by allowing within the subset S_r only those classifiers which satisfy $\|\mathbf{w}\|^2 \leq c_r$. The positive bounds c_r form an increasing sequence: $c_1 < c_2 < ... < c_r < ...$ This sequence can be matched with a monotonically decreasing sequence of positive Lagrange multipliers $\gamma_1 \geq \gamma_2 \geq ... \geq \gamma_r \geq ...$, such that our training problem stated as the minimization of MSE within a specific set S_r is implemented through the minimization of a new cost function: $MSE + \gamma_r \|\mathbf{w}\|^2$. This is equivalent to the Weight Decay procedure (WD). In a mechanical analogy, the term $\gamma_r \|\mathbf{w}\|^2$ is like the energy of a spring of tension γ_r which pulls the weights to zero. As it is easier to pull in the directions of small curvature of the MSE, WD pulls the weights to zero predominantly along the principal directions of the Hessian matrix H associated with small eigenvalues.

In the principal axis representation, the minimum $\mathbf{w}^\gamma$ of the cost function $MSE + \gamma\|\mathbf{w}\|^2$, is a simple function of the minimum $\mathbf{w}^0$ of the MSE in the $\gamma \rightarrow 0^+$ limit: $w_i^\gamma = w_i^0 \lambda_i / (\lambda_i + \gamma)$. The weight w_i^0 is attenuated by a factor $\lambda_i / (\lambda_i + \gamma)$. Weights become negligible for $\gamma \gg \lambda_i$, and remain unchanged for $\gamma \ll \lambda_i$. The effect of this attenuation can be compared to that of weight pruning. Pruning all weights such that $\lambda_i < \gamma$ reduces the capacity to:

$$h' = \sum_{i=1}^{n} \theta_\gamma(\lambda_i) , \qquad (4)$$

where $\theta_\gamma(u) = 1$ if $u > \gamma$ and $\theta_\gamma(u) = 0$ otherwise.

By analogy, we introduce the Weight Decay capacity:

$$h' = \sum_{i=1}^{n} \frac{\lambda_i}{\lambda_i + \gamma} . \qquad (5)$$

This expression arises in various theoretical frameworks [Moo92,McK92], and is valid only for broad spectra of eigenvalues.

3 SMOOTHING, HIGHER-ORDER UNITS, AND REGULARIZATION

Combining several different structures achieves further performance improvements. The combination of exponential smoothing (a preprocessing transformation of input space) and regularization (a modification of the learning algorithm) is shown here to improve character recognition. The generalization ability is dramatically improved by the further introduction of second-order units (an architectural modification).

3.1 SMOOTHING

Smoothing is a preprocessing which aims at reducing the effective dimension of input space by degrading the resolution: after smoothing, decimation of the inputs could be performed without further image degradation. Smoothing is achieved here through convolution with an exponential kernel:

$$BLURRED.PIXEL(i,j) = \frac{\sum_k \sum_l PIXEL(i+k,j+l)\, exp[-\frac{1}{\beta}\sqrt{k^2+l^2}]}{\sum_k \sum_l exp[-\frac{1}{\beta}\sqrt{k^2+l^2}]},$$

where β is the smoothing parameter which determines the structure.

Convolution with the chosen kernel is an invertible linear operation. Such preprocessing results in no capacity change for a MSE-trained linear classifier. Smoothing only modifies the spectrum of eigenvalues and must be combined with an eigenvalue-based regularization procedure such as OBD or WD, to obtain performance improvement through capacity decrease.

3.2   HIGHER-ORDER UNITS

Higher-order (or sigma-pi) units can be substituted for the linear units to get polynomial classifiers: $F(\mathbf{x}, \mathbf{w}) = \theta_0(\mathbf{w}^T \xi(\mathbf{x}))$, where $\xi(\mathbf{x})$ is an m-dimensional vector $(m \geq n)$ with components: $x_1, x_2, ..., x_n, (x_1 x_1), (x_1 x_2), ..., (x_n x_n), ..., (x_1 x_2 ... x_n)$. The structure is geared towards increasing the capacity, and is controlled by the order of the polynomial: S_1 contains all the linear terms, S_2 linear plus quadratic, etc. Computations are kept tractable with the method proposed in reference [Pog75].

4   EXPERIMENTAL RESULTS

Experiments were performed on the benchmark problem of handwritten digit recognition described in reference [GPP+89]. The database consists of 1200 (16 × 16) binary pixel images, divided into 600 training examples and 600 test examples.

In figure 1, we compare the results obtained by pruning inputs or weights with PCA and the results obtained with WD. The overall appearance of the curves is very similar. In both cases, the capacity (computed from (4) and (5)) decreases as a function of γ, whereas the training error increases. For the optimum value $\gamma*$, the capacity is only 1/3 of the nominal capacity, computed solely on the basis of the network architecture. At the price of some error on the training set, the error rate on the test set is only half the error rate obtained with $\gamma = 0^+$.

The competition between capacity and training error always results in a unique minimum of the guaranteed risk (1). It is remarkable that our experiments show the minimum of $E_{guarant}$ coinciding with the minimum of E_{test}. Any of these two quantities can therefore be used to determine $\gamma*$. In principle, another independent test set should be used to get a reliable estimate of E_{gene} (cross-validation). It seems therefore advantageous to determine $\gamma*$ using the minimum of $E_{guarant}$ and use the test set to predict the generalization performance.

Using $E_{guarant}$ to determine $\gamma*$ raises the problem of determining the capacity of the system. The capacity can be measured when analytic computation is not possible. Measurements performed with the method proposed by Vapnik, Levin, and Le Cun yield results in good agreement with those obtained using (5). The method yields an *effective VC-dimension* which accounts for the global capacity of the system, including the effects of input data, architecture, and learning algorithm [2].

---

[2]Schematically, measurements of the *effective VC-dimension* consist of splitting the training data into two subsets. The difference between E_{train} in these subsets is maximized. The value of h is extracted from the fit to a theoretical prediction for such maximal discrepancy.

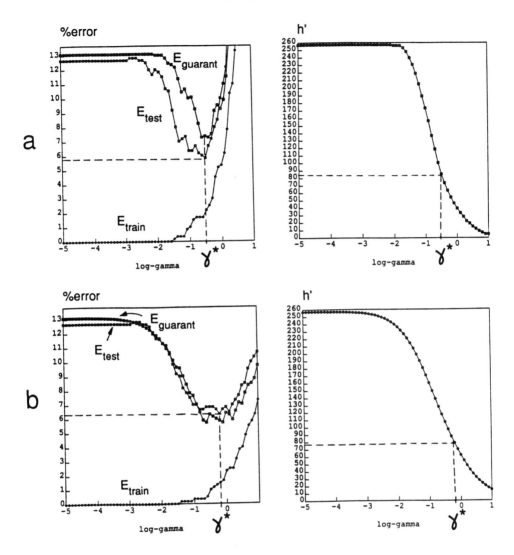

Figure 1: Percent error and capacity h' as a function of $\log \gamma$ (linear classifier, no smoothing): (a) weight/input pruning via PCA (γ is a threshold), (b) WD (γ is the decay parameter). The guaranteed risk has been rescaled to fit in the figure.

Table 1: E_{test} for Smoothing, WD, and Higher-Order Combined.

β	γ	1st order	2nd order
0	γ^*	6.3	1.5
1	γ^*	5.0	0.8
2	γ^*	4.5	1.2
10	γ^*	4.3	1.3
any	0^+	12.7	3.3

In table 1 we report results obtained when several structures are combined. Weight decay with $\gamma = \gamma^*$ reduces E_{test} by a factor of 2. Input space smoothing used in conjunction with WD results in an additional reduction by a factor of 1.5. The best performance is achieved for the highest level of smoothing, $\beta = 10$, for which the blurring is considerable. As expected, smoothing has no effect in the absence of WD.

The use of second-order units provides an additional factor of 5 reduction in E_{test}. For second order units, the number of weights scales like the square of the number of inputs $n^2 = 66049$. But the capacity (5) is found to be only 196, for the optimum values of γ and β.

5   CONCLUSIONS AND EPILOGUE

Our results indicate that the VC-dimension must measure the global capacity of the system. It is crucial to incorporate the effects of preprocessing of the input data and modifications of the learning algorithm. Capacities defined solely on the basis of the network architecture give overly pessimistic upper bounds.

The method of SRM provides a powerful tool for tuning the capacity. We have shown that structures acting at different levels (preprocessing, architecture, learning mechanism) can produce similar effects. We have then combined three different structures to improve generalization. These structures have interesting complementary properties. The introduction of higher-order units increases the capacity. Smoothing and weight decay act in conjunction to decrease it.

Elaborate neural networks for character recognition [LBD+90,GAL+91] also incorporate similar complementary structures. In multilayer sigmoid-unit networks, the capacity is increased through additional hidden units. Feature extracting neurons introduce smoothing, and regularization follows from prematurely stopping training before reaching the MSE minimum. When initial weights are chosen to be small, this stopping technique produces effects similar to those of weight decay.

Acknowledgments

We wish to thank L. Jackel's group at Bell Labs for useful discussions, and are particularly grateful to E. Levin and Y. Le Cun for communicating to us the unpublished method of computing the effective VC-dimension.

References

[DH73]   R.O. Duda and P.E. Hart. *Pattern Classification And Scene Analysis.* Wiley and Son, 1973.

[GAL+91]   I. Guyon, P. Albrecht, Y. Le Cun, J. Denker, and W. Hubbard. Design of a neural network character recognizer for a touch terminal. *Pattern Recognition*, 24(2), 1991.

[GPP+89]   I. Guyon, I. Poujaud, L. Personnaz, G. Dreyfus, J. Denker, and Y. Le Cun. Comparing different neural network architectures for classifying handwritten digits. In *Proceedings of the International Joint Conference on Neural Networks*, volume II, pages 127–132. IEEE, 1989.

[LBD+90]   Y. Le Cun, B. Boser, J. S. Denker, D. Henderson, R. E. Howard, W. Hubbard, and L. D. Jackel. Back-propagation applied to handwritten zipcode recognition. *Neural Computation*, 1(4), 1990.

[LDS90]   Y. Le Cun, J. S. Denker, and S. A. Solla. Optimal brain damage. In D. S. Touretzky, editor, *Advances in Neural Information Processing Systems 2 (NIPS 89)*, pages 598–605. Morgan Kaufmann, 1990.

[McK92]   D. McKay. A practical bayesian framework for backprop networks. In *this volume*, 1992.

[Moo92]   J. Moody. Generalization, weight decay and architecture selection for non-linear learning systems. In *this volume*, 1992.

[Pog75]   T. Poggio. On optimal nonlinear associative recall. *Biol. Cybern.*, (9)201, 1975.

[The89]   C. W. Therrien. *Decision, Estimation and Classification: An Introduction to Pattern Recognition and Related Topics.* Wiley, 1989.

[Vap82]   V. Vapnik. *Estimation of Dependences Based on Empirical Data.* Springer-Verlag, 1982.

[Vap92]   V Vapnik. Principles of risk minimization for learning theory. In *this volume*, 1992.

Image Segmentation with Networks of Variable Scales

Hans P. Graf   **Craig R. Nohl**   **Jan Ben**
AT&T Bell Laboratories
Crawfords Corner Road
Holmdel, NJ 07733, USA

ABSTRACT

We developed a neural net architecture for segmenting complex images, i.e., to localize two-dimensional geometrical shapes in a scene, without prior knowledge of the objects' positions and sizes. A scale variation is built into the network to deal with varying sizes. This algorithm has been applied to video images of railroad cars, to find their identification numbers. Over 95% of the characters were located correctly in a data base of 300 images, despite a large variation in lighting conditions and often a poor quality of the characters. A part of the network is executed on a processor board containing an analog neural net chip (Graf et al. 1991), while the rest is implemented as a software model on a workstation or a digital signal processor.

1 INTRODUCTION

Neural nets have been applied successfully to the classification of shapes, such as characters. However, typically, these networks do not tolerate large variations of an object's size. Rather, a normalization of the size has to be done before the network is able to perform a reliable classification. But in many machine vision applications an object's size is not known in advance and may vary over a wide range. If the objects are part of a complex image, finding their positions plus their sizes becomes a very difficult problem.

Traditional techniques to locate objects of variable scale include the generalized Hough transform (Ballard 1981) and constraint search techniques through a feature space (Grimson 1990), possibly with some relaxation mechanisms. These techniques start with a feature representation and then try to sort features into groups that may represent an object. Searches through feature maps tend to be very time consuming, since the number of comparisons that need to be made grows fast, typically exponentially, with the number of features. Therefore, practical techniques must focus on ways to minimize the time required for this search.

Our solution can be viewed as a large network, divided into two parts. The first layer of the network provides a feature representation of the image, while the second layer locates the objects. The key element for this network to be practical, is a neural net chip (Graf et al. 1991) which executes the first layer. The high compute power of this chip makes it possible to extract a large number of features. Hence features specific to the objects to be found can be extracted, reducing drastically the amount of computation required in the second layer.

The output of our network is not necessarily the final solution of a problem. Rather, its intended use is as part of a modular system, combined with other functional elements. Figure 1 shows an example of such a system that was used to read the identification numbers on railroad cars. In this system the network's outputs are the positions and sizes of characters. These are then classified in an additional network (LeCun et al. 1990), specialized for reading characters.

The net described here is not limited to finding characters. It can be combined with other classifiers and is applicable to a wide variety of object recognition tasks. Details of the network, for example the types of features that are extracted, are task specific and have to be optimized for the problem to be solved. But the overall architecture of the network and the data flow remains the same for many problems. Beside the application described here, we used this network for reading the license plates of cars, locating the address blocks on mail pieces, and for page layout analysis of printed documents.

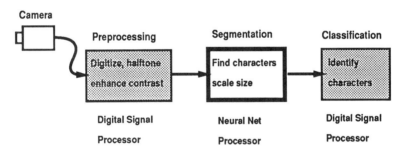

Figure 1: Schematic of the recognition system for reading the identification numbers on railroad cars. The network described here performs the part in the middle box, segmenting the image into characters and background.

2   THE NETWORK

2.1   THE ARCHITECTURE

The network consists of two parts, the input layer extracting features and the second layer, which locates the objects. The second layer is not rigidly coupled through connections to the first one. Before data move from the first layer to the second, the input fields of the neurons in the second layer are scaled to an appropriate size. This size depends on the data and is dynamically adjusted.

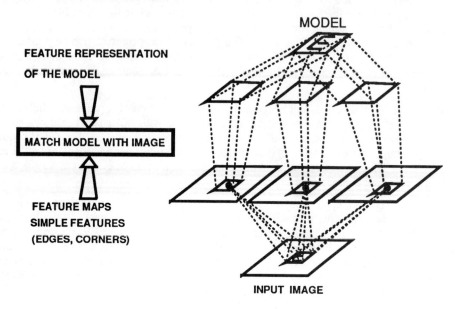

Figure 2: Schematic of the network.

Figure 2 shows a schematic of this whole network. The input data pass through the first layer of connections. From the other end of the net the model of the object is entered, and in the middle model and image are matched by scaling the input fields of the neurons in the second layer. In this way a network architecture is obtained that can handle a large variation of sizes. In the present paper we consider only scale variations, but other transformations, such as rotations can be integrated into this architecture as well.

And how can a model representation be scaled to the proper size before one knows an object's size? With a proper feature representation of the image, this can be done in a straight-forward and time-efficient way. Distances between pairs of features are measured and used to scale the input fields. In section 4 it is described in detail how the distances between corners provide a robust estimate of the sizes of characters. There is no need to determine an object's size with absolute certainty here. The goal is to limit the further search to just a few possible sizes, in order to reduce the amount of computation.

The time to evaluate the second layer of the network is reduced further by determining "areas-of-interest" and searching only these. Areas without any features, or without characteristic combinations of features, are excluded from the search. In this way, the neurons of the second layer have to analyze only a small part of the whole image. The key for the size estimates and the "area-of-interest" algorithm to work reliably, is a good feature representation. Thanks to the neural net chip, we can search an image for a large number of geometric features and have great freedom in choosing their shapes.

2.2 KERNELS FOR EXTRACTING FEATURES

The features extracted in the first layer have to be detectable regardless of an object's size. Many features, for example corners, are in principle independent of size. In practice however, one uses two-dimensional detectors of a finite extent. These detectors introduce a scale and tend to work best for a certain range of sizes. Hence, it may be necessary to use several detectors of different sizes for one feature. Simple features tend to be less sensitive to scale than complex ones. In the application described below, a variation of a factor of five in the characters' sizes is covered with just a single set of edge and corner detectors. Figure 3 shows a few of the convolution kernels used to extract these features.

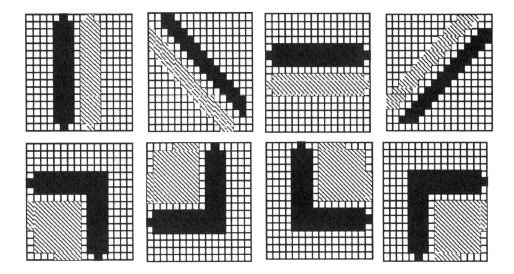

Figure 3: Examples of kernels for detecting edges and corners. Each of the kernels is stored as the connection weights of a neuron. These are ternary kernels with a size of 16 x 16 pixels. The values of the pixels are: black = -1, white = 0, hatched = +1. A total of 32 kernels of this size can be scanned simultaneously over an image with the neural net chip.

These kernels are scanned over an image with the neural net chip and wherever an edge or a corner of the proper orientation is located, the neuron tied to this kernel turns on. In this way, the neural net chip scans 32 kernels simultaneously over an image, creating 32 feature maps. The kernels containing the feature detectors have a size of 16 x 16 pixels. With kernels of such a large size, it is possible to create highly selective detectors. Moreover, a high noise immunity is obtained.

2.3   THE SECOND LAYER

The neurons of the second layer have a rectangular receptive field with 72 inputs, 3 x 3 inputs from eight feature maps. These neurons are trained with feature representations of shapes, normalized in size. The 3 x 3 input field of a neuron does not mean that only an area of 9 pixels in a feature map is used as input. Before a neuron is scanned over a part of a feature map, its input field is scaled to the size indicated by the size estimator. Therefore, each input corresponds to a rectangular area in a feature map. For finding objects in an image, the input fields, scaled to the proper size, are then scanned over the areas marked by the "area-of-interest" algorithm. If an output of a neuron is high, the area is marked as position of an object and is passed along to the classifier.

The second layer of the network does require only relatively few computations, typically a few hundred evaluations of neurons with 72 inputs. Therefore, this can be handled easily by a workstation or a digital signal processor. The same is true for the area-of-interest algorithm. The computationally expensive part is the feature extraction. On an image with 512 x 512 pixels this requires over 2 billion connection updates. In fact, on a workstation this takes typically about half an hour. Therefore, here a special purpose chip is crucial to provide a speed-up to make this approach useful for practical applications.

3   THE HARDWARE

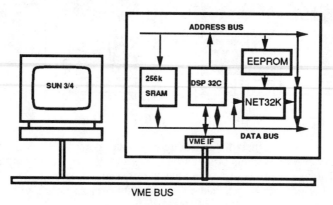

Figure 4: Schematic of the neural net board.

A schematic of the neural net board used for these applications is shown in Figure 4. The board contains an analog neural net chip, combined with a digital signal processor (DSP) and 256k of fast static memory. On the board, the DSP controls the data flow and the operation of the neural net chip. This board is connected over a VME bus to the host workstation. Signals, such as images, are sent from the host to the neural net board, where a local program operates on the data. The results are then sent back to the host for further processing and display. The time it takes to process an image of 512 x 512 pixels is one second, where the transfer of the data from the workstation to the board and back requires two thirds of this time.

The chip does a part of the computation in analog form. But analog signals are used only inside the chip, while all the input and the output data are digital. This chip works only with a low dynamic range of the signals. Therefore, the input signals are typically binarized before they are transferred to the chip. In the case of gray level images, the pictures are halftoned first and then the features are extracted form the binarized images. This is possible, since the large kernel sizes suppress the noise introduced by the halftoning process.

4 APPLICATION

This network was integrated into a system to read the identification numbers on railroad cars. Identifying a rail car by its number has to be done before a train enters the switching yard, where the cars are directed to different tracks. Today this is handled by human operators reading the numbers from video screens. The present investigation is a study to determine whether this process can be automated.

The pictures represent very difficult segmentation tasks, since the size of the characters varies by more than a factor of five and they are often of poor quality with parts rusted away or covered by dirt. Moreover, the positions of the characters can be almost anywhere in the picture, and they may be arranged in various ways, in single or in multiple lines. Also, they are written in many different fonts, and the contrast between characters and background varies substantially from one car to the next. Despite these difficulties, we were able to locate the characters correctly in over 95% of the cases, on a database of 300 video images of railroad cars.

As mentioned in section 2, in the first layer feature maps are created from which areas of interest are determined. Since the characters are arranged in horizontal lines, the first step is to determine where lines of characters might be present in the image. For that purpose the feature maps are projected onto a vertical line. Rows of characters produce strong responses of the corner detectors and are therefore detected as maxima in the projected densities. The orientation of a corner indicates whether it resulted from the lower end of a character or from the upper end. The simultaneous presence of maxima in the densities of lower and upper ends is therefore a strong indication for the presence of a row of characters. In this way, bands within the image are identified that may contain characters. A band not only indicates the presence of a row of characters, but also provides a good guess of their heights.

This simple heuristic proved to be very effective for the rail car images. It was made more robust by taking into account also the outputs of the vertical edge detectors. Characters produce strong responses of vertical edge detectors, while detractors, such as dirt create fewer and weaker responses.

At this stage we do not attempted to identify a character. All we need is a yes/no answer whether a part of the image should be analyzed by the classifier or not. The whole alphabet is grouped into five classes, and only one neuron to recognize any member within a class is created. A high output of one of these neurons therefore means that any character of its class may be present. Figures 5 and 6 show two examples produced by the segmentation network. The time required for the whole segmentation is less than three seconds, of which one second is spent for the feature extraction and the rest for the "focus-of-attention" algorithm and the second layer of the network.

Figure 5: Image of a tank car. The crosses mark where corner detectors gave a strong response. The inset shows an enlarged section around the identification number. The result of the segmentation network is indicated by the black lines.

5 CONCLUSION

The algorithm described combines neural net techniques with heuristics to obtain a practical solution for segmenting complex images reliably and fast. Clearly, a "conventional" neural net with a fixed architecture lacks the flexibility to handle the scale variations required in many machine vision applications. To extend the use of neural nets, transformations have to be built into the architecture.

We demonstrated the network's use for locating characters, but the same strategy works for a wide variety of other objects. Some details need to be adjusted to the objects to be found. In particular, the features extracted by the first layer are task specific. Their choice is critical, as they determine to a large extent the computational requirements for finding the objects in the second layer.

The use of a neural net chip is crucial to make this approach feasible, since it provides the computational power needed for the feature extraction. The extraction of geometrical features for pattern recognition applications has been studied extensively. However, its use is not wide spread, since it is computationally very demanding. The neural net chip opens the possibility for extracting large numbers of features in a short time. The large size of the convolution kernels, 16 x 16 pixels, provides a great flexibility in choosing the feature detectors' shapes. Their large size is also the main reason for a good noise suppression and a high robustness of the described network.

Figure 6: The result of the network on an image of high complexity. The white horizontal lines indicate the result of the "area-of-interest" algorithm. The final result is shown by the vertical white lines.

References

H.P. Graf, R. Janow, C.R. Nohl, and J. Ben, (1991), "A Neural-Net Board System for Machine Vision Applications", *Proc. Int. Joint Conf. Neural Networks*, Vol. 1, pp. 481 - 486.

D.H. Ballard, (1981), "Generalizing the Hough transform to detect arbitrary shapes", *Pattern Recognition*, Vol. 13, p. 111.

W.H. Grimson, (1990), "The Combinatorics of Object Recognition in Cluttered Environments Using Constraint Search", *Artificial Intelligence*, Vol. 44, p. 121.

Y. LeCun, B. Boser, J.S. Denker, D. Henderson, R.E. Howard, W. Hubbard, and L.D. Jackel, (1990), "Handwritten Digit Recognition with a Back-Propagation Network", in: Neural Information Processing Systems, Vol. 2, D. Touretzky (ed.), Morgan Kaufman, pp. 396 - 404.

Multi-Digit Recognition Using A Space Displacement Neural Network

Ofer Matan*, Christopher J.C. Burges,
Yann Le Cun and John S. Denker
AT&T Bell Laboratories, Holmdel, N. J. 07733

Abstract

We present a feed-forward network architecture for recognizing an unconstrained handwritten multi-digit string. This is an extension of previous work on recognizing isolated digits. In this architecture a single digit recognizer is replicated over the input. The output layer of the network is coupled to a Viterbi alignment module that chooses the best interpretation of the input. Training errors are propagated through the Viterbi module.

The novelty in this procedure is that segmentation is done on the feature maps developed in the Space Displacement Neural Network (SDNN) rather than the input (pixel) space.

1 Introduction

In previous work (Le Cun et al., 1990) we have demonstrated a feed-forward back-propagation network that recognizes isolated handwritten digits at state-of-the-art performance levels. The natural extension of this work is towards recognition of unconstrained *strings* of handwritten digits. The most straightforward solution is to divide the process into two: segmentation and recognition. The segmenter will divide the original image into pieces (each containing an isolated digit) and pass it to the recognizer for scoring. This approach assumes that segmentation and recognition can be decoupled. Except for very simple cases this is not true.

Speech-recognition research (Rabiner, 1989; Franzini, Lee and Waibel, 1990) has demonstrated the power of using the recognition engine to score each segment in

---

*Author's current address: Department of Computer Science, Stanford University, Stanford, CA 94305.

488

a candidate segmentation. The segmentation that gives the best combined score is chosen. "Recognition driven" segmentation is usually used in conjunction with dynamic programming, which can find the optimal solution very efficiently.

Though dynamic programming algorithms save us from exploring an exponential number of segment combinations, they are still linear in the number of possible segments – requiring one call to the recognition unit per candidate segment. In order to solve the problem in reasonable time it is necessary to: 1) limit the number of possible segments, or 2) have a rapid recognition unit.

We have built a ZIP code reading system that "prunes" the number of candidate segments (Matan et al., 1991). The candidate segments were generated by analyzing the image's pixel projection onto the horizontal axis. The strength of this system is that the number of calls to the recognizer is small (only slightly over twice the number of real digits). The weakness is that by generating only a small number of candidates one often misses the correct segmentation. In addition, generation of this small set is based on multi-parametric heuristics, making tuning the system difficult.

It would be attractive to discard heuristics and generate many more candidates, but then the time spent in the recognition unit would have to be reduced considerably. Reducing the computation of the recognizer usually gives rise to a reduction in recognition rates. However, it is possible to have our segments and eat them too. We propose an architecture which can explore many more candidates without compromising the richness of the recognition engine.

2   The Design

Let us describe a simplified and less efficient solution that will lead us to our final design. Consider a de-skewed image such as the one shown in Figure 1. The system will separate it into candidate segments using vertical cuts. A few examples of these are shown beneath the original image in Figure 1. In the process of finding the best overall segmentation each candidate segment will be passed to the recognizer described in (Le Cun et al., 1990). The scores will be converted to probabilities (Bridle, 1989) that are inserted into nodes of a direct acyclic graph. Each path on this graph represents a candidate segmentation where the length of each path is the product of the node values along it. The Viterbi algorithm is used to determine the longest path (which corresponds to the segmentation with the highest combined score).

It seems somewhat redundant to process the same pixels numerous times (as part of different, overlapping candidate segments). For this reason we propose to pass a whole size-normalized image to the recognition unit and to segment a feature map, after most of the neural network computation has been done. Since the first four layers in our recognizer are convolutional, we can easily extend the single-digit network by applying the convolution kernels to the multi-digit image.

Figure 2 shows the example image (Figure 1) processed by the extended network. We now proceed to segment the top layer. Since the network is convolutional, segmenting this feature-map layer is similar to segmenting the input layer. (Because of overlapping receptive fields and reduced resolution, it is not exactly equivalent.) This gives a speed-up of roughly an order of magnitude.

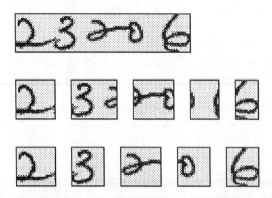

Figure 1: A sample ZIP code image and possible segmentations.

Figure 2: The example ZIP code processed by 4 layers of a convolutional feed-forward network.

In the single digit network, we can view the output layer as a 10-unit column vector that is connected to a zone of width 5 on the last feature layer. If we replicate the single digit network over the input in the horizontal direction, the output layer will be replicated. Each output vector will be connected to a different zone of width 5 on the feature layer. Since the width of a handwritten digit is highly variable, we construct alternate output vectors that are connected to feature segment zones of widths 4,3 and 2. The resulting output maps for the example ZIP code are shown in Figure 3.

The network we have constructed is a shared weight network reminiscent of a TDNN (Lang and Hinton, 1988). We have termed this architecture a Space Displacement Neural Network (SDNN). We rely on the fact that most digit strings lie on more or less one line; therefore, the network is replicated in the horizontal direction. For other applications it is conceivable to replicate in the vertical direction as well.

3   The Recognition Procedure

The output maps are processed by a Viterbi algorithm which chooses the set of output vectors corresponding to the segmentation giving the highest combined score. We currently assume that we know the number of digits in the image; however, this procedure can be generalized to an unknown number of digits. In Figure 3 the five output vectors that combined to give the best overall score are marked by thin lines beneath them.

4   The Training Procedure

During training we follow the above procedure and repeat it under the constraint that the winning combination corresponds to the ground truth. In Figure 4 the constrained-winning output vectors are marked by small circles. We perform back-propagation through both the ground truth vectors (reinforcement) and highest scoring vectors (negative reinforcement).

We have trained and tested this architecture on size normalized 5-digit ZIP codes taken from U.S Mail. 6000 images were used for training and 3000 where used for testing. The images were cleaned, deskewed and height normalized according to the assumed largest digit height. The data was not "cleaned" after the automatic preprocessing, leaving non centered images and non digits in both the training and test set.

Training was done using stochastic back propagation with some sweeps using Newton's method for adjusting the learning rates. We tried various methods of initializing the gradient on the last layer:

- Reinforce only units picked by the constrained Viterbi. (all other units have a gradient of zero).
- Same as above, but set negative feedback through units chosen by regular Viterbi that are different from those chosen by the constrained version. (Push down the incorrect segmentation if it is different from the correct answer). This speeds up the convergence.
- Reinforce units chosen by the constrained Viterbi. Set negative feed back

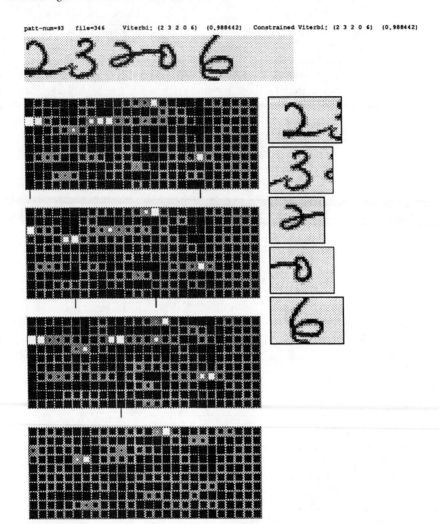

Figure 3: Recognition using the SDNN/Viterbi. The output maps of the SDNN are shown. White indicates a positive activation. The output vectors chosen by the Viterbi alignment are marked by a thin line beneath them. The input regions corresponding to these vectors are shown. One can see that the system centers on the individual digits. Each of the 4 output maps shown is connected to different size zone in the last feature layer (5,4,3 and 2, top to bottom). In order to implement weight sharing between output units connected to different zone sizes, the dangling connections to the output vectors of narrower zones are connected to feature units corresponding to background in the input.

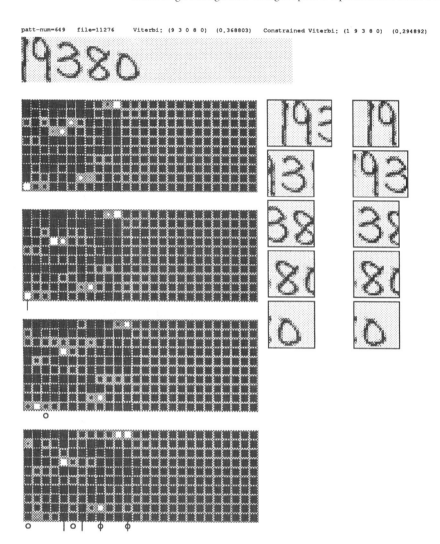

Figure 4: Training using the SDNN/Viterbi. The output vectors chosen by the Viterbi algorithm are marked by a thin line beneath them. The corresponding input regions are shown in the left column. The output vectors chosen by the constrained Viterbi algorithm are marked by small circles and their corresponding input regions are shown to the right. Given the ground truth the system can learn to center on the correct digit.

through all other units except those that are "similar" to ones in the correct set. ("similar" is defined by corresponding to a close center of frame in the input and responding with the correct class).

As one adds more units that have a non zero gradient, each training iteration is more similar to batch-training and is more prone to oscillations. In this case more Newton sweeps are required.

5   Results

The current raw recognition rates for the whole 5-digit string are 70% correct from the training set and 66% correct from the test set. Additional interesting statistics are the distribution of the number of correct digits across the whole ZIP code and the recognition rates for each digit's position within the ZIP code. These are presented in the tables shown below.

Table 1: Top: Distribution of test images according to the number of correct single digit classifications out of 5. Bottom: Rates of single digit classification according to position. Digits on the edges are classified more easily since one edge is predetermined.

Number of digits correct	Percent of cases
5	66.3
4	19.7
3	7.2
2	4.7
1	1.4
0	0.7

Digit position	Percent correct
1st	92
2nd	87
3rd	87
4th	86
5th	90

6   Conclusions and Future Work

The SDNN combined with the Viterbi algorithm learns to recognize strings of hand-written digits by "centering" on the individual digits in the string. This is similar in concept to other work in speech (Haffner, Franzini and Waibel, 1991) but differs from (Keeler, Rumelhart and Leow, 1991), where no alignment procedure is used.

The current recognition rates are still lower than our best system that uses pixel projection information to guide a recognition based segmenter. The SDNN is much faster and lends itself to parallel hardware. Possible improvements to the architecture may be:

- Modified constraints on the segmentation rules of the feature layer.
- Applying the Viterbi algorithm in the vertical direction as well might overcome problems due to height variance.
- It might be too hard to segment using local information only ; one might try using global information, such as pixel projection or recognizing doublets or triplets.

Though there is still considerable work to be done in order to reach state-of-the-art recognition levels, we believe that this type of approach is the correct direction for future image processing applications. Applying recognition based segmentation at the line, word and character level on high feature maps is necessary in order to achieve fast processing while exploring a large set of possible interpretations.

Acknowledgements

Support of this work by the Technology Resource Department of the U.S. Postal Service under Task Order 104230-90-C-2456 is gratefully acknowledged.

References

Bridle, J. S. (1989). Probabilistic Interpretation of Feedforward Classification Network Outputs with Relationships to Statistical Pattern Recognition. In Fogelman-Soulie, F. and Hérault, J., editors, *Neuro-computing: algorithms, architectures and applications*. Springer-Verlag.

Franzini, M., Lee, K. F., and Waibel, A. (1990). Connectionist Viterbi Training: A New Hybrid Method For Continuous Speech Recognition. In *Proceedings ICASSP 90*, pages 425–428. IEEE.

Haffner, P., Franzini, M., and Waibel, A. (1991). Integrating Time Alignment and Neural Networks for High Performance Continuous Speech Recognition. In *Proceedings ICASSP 91*. IEEE.

Keeler, J. D., Rumelhart, D. E., and Leow, W. (1991). Integrated Segmentation and Recognition of Handwritten-Printed Numerals. In Lippman, Moody, and Touretzky, editors, *Advances in Neural Information Processing Systems*, volume 3. Morgan Kaufman.

Lang, K. J. and Hinton, G. E. (1988). A Time Delay Neural Network Architecture for Speech Recognition. Technical Report CMU-cs-88-152, Carnegie-Mellon University, Pittsburgh PA.

Le Cun, Y., Matan, O., Boser, B., Denker, J. S., Henderson, D., Howard, R. E., Hubbard, W., Jackel, L. D., and Baird, H. S. (1990). Handwritten Zip Code Recognition with Multilayer Networks. In *Proceedings of the 10th International Conference on Pattern Recognition*. IEEE Computer Society Press.

Matan, O., Bromley, J., Burges, C. J. C., Denker, J. S., Jackel, L. D., Le Cun, Y., Pednault, E. P. D., Satterfield, W. D., Stenard, C. E., and Thompson, T. J. (1991). Reading Handwritten Digits: A ZIP code Recognition System (To appear in COMPUTER).

Rabiner, L. R. (1989). A Tutorial on Hidden Markov Models and Selected Applications in Speech Recognition. *Proceedings of the IEEE*, 77:257–286.

A Self-Organizing Integrated Segmentation And Recognition Neural Net

Jim Keeler *
MCC
3500 West Balcones Center Drive
Austin, TX 78729

David E. Rumelhart
Psychology Department
Stanford University
Stanford, CA 94305

Abstract

We present a neural network algorithm that simultaneously performs segmentation and recognition of input patterns that self-organizes to detect input pattern locations and pattern boundaries. We demonstrate this neural network architecture on character recognition using the NIST database and report on results herein. The resulting system simultaneously segments and recognizes touching or overlapping characters, broken characters, and noisy images with high accuracy.

1 INTRODUCTION

Standard pattern recognition systems usually involve a segmentation step prior to the recognition step. For example, it is very common in character recognition to segment characters in a pre-processing step then normalize the individual characters and pass them to a recognition engine such as a neural network, as in the work of LeCun et al. 1988, Martin and Pittman (1988).

This separation between segmentation and recognition becomes unreliable if the characters are touching each other, touching bounding boxes, broken, or noisy. Other applications such as scene analysis or continuous speech recognition pose similar and more severe segmentation problems. The difficulties encountered in these applications present an apparent dilemma: one cannot recognize the patterns

---

*keeler@mcc.com Reprint requests: coila@mcc.com or at the above address.

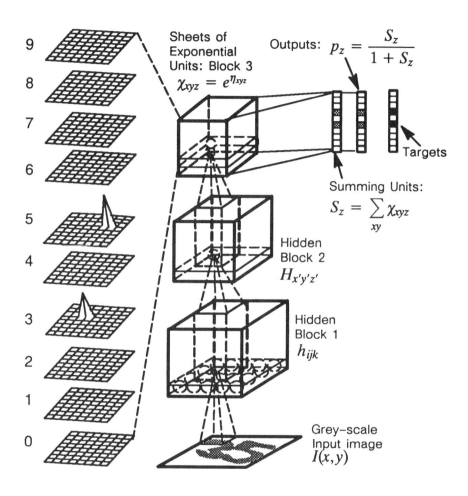

Figure 1: The ISR network architecture. The input image may contain several characters and is presented to the network in a two-dimensional grey-scale image. The units in the first block, h_{ijk}, have linked-local receptive field connections to the input image. Block 2, $H_{x'y'z'}$, has a three-dimensional linked-local receptive field to block 1, and the exponential unit block, block 3, has three-dimensional linked-local receptive field connections to block 2. These linked fields insure translational invariance (except for edge-effects at the boundary). The exponential unit block has one layer for each output category. These units are the output units in the test mode, but hidden units during training: the exponential unit activity is summed over (s_z) to project out the positional information, then converted to a probability p_z. Once trained, the exponential unit layers serve as "smart histograms" giving sharp peaks of activity directly above the corresponding characters in the input image, as shown to the left.

until they are segmented, yet in many cases one cannot segment the patterns until they are recognized.

A solution to this apparent dilemm is to simultaneously segment and recognize the patterns. Integration of the segmentation and recognition steps is essential for further progress in these difficult pattern recognition tasks, and much effort has been devoted to this topic in speech recognition. For example, Hidden Markov models integrate the task of segmentation and recognition as a part of the word-recognition module. Nevertheless, little neural network research in pattern recognition has focused on the integrated segmentation and recognition (ISR) problem.

There are several ways to achieve ISR in a neural network. The first use of back-propagation ISR neural networks for character recognition was reported by Keeler, Rumelhart and Leow (1991a). The ISR neural network architecture is similar to the time-delayed neural network architecture for speech recognition used by Lang, Hinton, and Waibel (1990).

The following section outlines the neural network algorithm and architecture. Details and rationale for the exact structure and assumptions of the network can be found in Keeler et al. (1991a,b).

2   NETWORK ARCHITECTURE AND ALGORITHM

The basic organization of the network is illustrated in Figure 2. The input consists of a two-dimensional grey-scale image representing the pattern to be processed. We designate this input pattern by the two-dimensional field $I(x, y)$. In general, we assume that any pattern can be presented at any location and that the characters may touch, overlap or be broken or noisy. The input then projects to a linked-local-receptive-field block of sigmoidal hidden units (to enforce translational invariance). We designate the activation of the sigmoidal units in this block by h_{ijk}.

The second block of hidden units, $H_{x'y'z'}$, is a linked-local receptive field block of sigmoidal units that receives input from a three-dimensional receptive field in the h_{ijk} block. In a standard neural network architecture we would normally connect block H to the output units. However we connect block H to a block of exponential units χ_{xyz}. The χ block serves as the outputs after the network has been trained; there is a sheet of exponential units for each output category. These units are connected to block H via a linked-local receptive field structure. $\chi_{xyz} = e^{\eta_{xyz}}$, where the net input to the unit is

$$\eta_{xyz} = \sum_{x'y'} W^{xyz}_{x'y'z'} H_{x'y'z'} + \beta_z, \tag{1}$$

and $W^{xyz}_{x'y'z'}$ is the weight from hidden unit $H_{x'y'z'}$ to the exponential unit χ_{xyz}. Since we use linked weights in each block, the entire structure is translationally invariant. We make use of this property in our training algorithm and project out the positional information by summing over the entire layer, $S_z = \sum_{xy} \chi_{xyz}$. This allows us to give non-specific target information in the form of "the input contains a 5 and a 3, but I will not say where." We do this by converting the summed information into an output probability, $p_z = \frac{S_z}{1+S_z}$.

2.1   The learning Rule

There are two objective functions that we have used to train ISR networks: cross entropy and total-sum-square-error. $l = \sum_z t_z ln p_z + (1 - t_z) ln(1 - p_z)$, where t_z equals 1 if pattern z is presented and 0 otherwise. Computing the gradient with respect to the net input to a particular exponential unit yields the following term in our learning rule:

$$\frac{\partial l}{\partial \eta_{xyz}} = (t_z - p_z)\frac{\chi_{xyz}}{\sum_{xy}\chi_{xyz}}. \tag{2}$$

It should be noted that this is a kind of *competitive* rule in which the learning is proportional to the relative strength of the activation at the unit at a particular location in the χ layer to the strength of activation in the entire layer. For example, suppose that $\chi_{2,3,5} = 1000$ and $\chi_{5,3,5} = 100$. Given the above rules, $\chi_{2,3,5}$ would receive about 10 times more of the output error than the unit $\chi_{5,3,5}$. Thus the units compete with each other for the credit or blame of the output, and the "rich get richer" until the proper target is achieved. This favors self-organization of highly localized spikes of activity in the exponential layers directly above the particular character that the exponential layer detects ("smart histograms" as shown in Figure 1). Note that we never give positional information in the network but that the network self-organizes the exponential unit activity to discern the positional information. The second function is the total-sum-square error, $E = \sum_z (t_z - p_z)^2$. For the total-sum-square error measure, the gradient term becomes

$$\frac{\partial E}{\partial \eta_{xyz}} = (t_z - p_z)\frac{\chi_{xyz}}{(1 + \sum_{xy}\chi_{xyz})^2}. \tag{3}$$

Again this has a competitive term, but the competition is only important for χ_{xyz} large, otherwise the denominator is dominated by 1 for small $\sum_{xy}\chi_{xyz}$. We used the quadratic error function for the networks reported in the next section.

3   NIST DATABASE RECOGNITION

3.1   Data

We tested this neural network algorithm on the problem of segmenting and recognizing handwritten numerals from the NIST database. This database contains approximately 273,000 samples of handwritten numerals collected from the Bureau of Census field staff. There were 50 different forms used in the study, each with 33 fields, 28 of which contain handwritten numerals ranging in length from 2 to 10 digits per field. We only used fields of length 2 to 6 (field numbers 6 to 30). We used two test sets: a small test set, Test Set A of approximately 4,000 digits, 1,000 fields, from forms labeled f1800 to f1840 and a larger test set, Test Set B, containing 20,000 numerals 5,000 fields and 200 forms from f1800 to f1899 and f2000 to f2199.

We used two different training sets: a hand-segmented training set containing approximately 33,000 digits from forms f0000 to f0636 (the Segmented Training Set) and another training set that was never hand-segmented from forms f0000 to f1800 (the Unsegmented Training Set. We pre-processed the fields with a simple box-removal and size-normalization program before they were input to the ISR net.

The hand segmentation was conventional in the sense that boxes were drawn around each of the characters, but we the boxes included any other portions of characters that may be nearby or touching in the natural context. Note that precise labeling of the characters is not essential at all. We have trained systems where only the center information the characters was used and found no degradation in performance. This is due to the fact that the system self-organizes the positional information, so it is only required that we know *whether* a character is in a field, not precisely *where*.

3.2   TRAINING

We trained several nets on the NIST database. The best training procedure was as follows: Step 1): train the network to an intermediate level of accuracy (96% or so on single characters, about 12 epochs of training set 1). Note that when we train on single characters, we do not need *isolated* characters – there are often portions of other nearby characters within the input field. Indeed, it helps the ISR performance to use this natural context. There are two reasons for this step: the first is speed – training goes much faster with single characters because we can use a small network. We also found a slight generalization accuracy benefit by including this training step. Step 2): copy the weights of this small network into a larger network and start training on 2 and 3 digit fields from the database without hand segmentation. These are fields numbered 6,7,11,15,19,20,23,24,27, and 28. The reason that we use these fields is that we do not have to hand-segment them – we present the fields to the net with the answer that the person was supposed to write in the field. (There were several cases where the person wrote the wrong numbers or didn't write anything. These cases were NOT screened from the training set.) Taking these fields from forms f0000 to f1800 gives us another 45,000 characters to train on without ever segmenting them.

There were several reasons that we use fields of length 2 and 3 and not fields of 4,5,or 6 for training (even though we used these in testing). First, 3 characters covers the most general case: a character either has no characters on either side, one to the left, one to the right or one on both sides (3 characters total). If we train on 3 characters and duplicate the weights, we have covered the most general case for any number of characters, and it is clearly faster to train on shorter fields. Second, training with more characters confuses the net. As pointed out in our previous work (keeler 1991a), the learning algorithm that we use is only valid for one or no characters of a given type presented in the input field. Thus, the field '39541' is ok to train on, but the field '288' violates one of the assumptions of the training rule. In this case the two 8's would be competing with each other for the answer and the rule favors only one winner. Even though this problem occurs 1/10th of the time for two digit fields, it is not serious enough to prevent the net from learning. (Clearly it would not learn fields of length 10 where all of the target units are turned on and there would be no chance for discrimination.) This problem could be avoided by incorporating order information into training and we have proposed several mechanisms for incorporating order information in training, but do not use them in the present system. Note that this biases the training toward the a-priori distribution of characters in the 2 and 3 digit fields, which is a different distribution from that of the testing set.

The two networks that we used had the following architectures: Net1: Input: 28x24 receptive fields 6x6 shift 2x2. hidden 1: 12x11x12 receptive fields 4x4x12 shift 2x2x12. hidden 2: 5x4x18 receptive fields 3x3x18 shift 1x1x18. exponentials (block 3): 3x2x10 10 summing, 10 outputs.

Net2: Input: 28x26 receptive fields 6x6 shift 2x4. hidden 1: 12x6x12 receptive fields 5x4x12 shift 1x2x12. hidden 2: 8x2x18 receptive fields 5x2x18 shift 1x1x18. exponentials (block 3): 4x1x10 10 summing, 10 outputs.

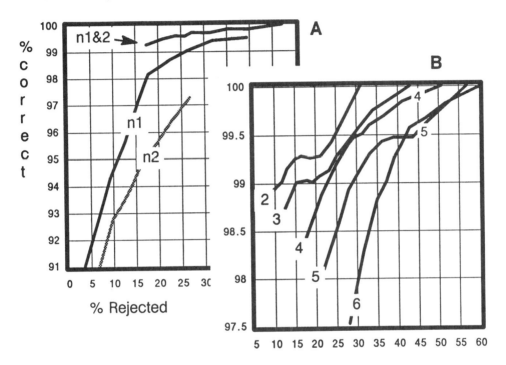

Figure 2: Average combined network performance on the NIST database. Figure 2A shows the generalization performance of two neural networks on the NIST Test Set A. The individual nets Net1 and Net2 (n1, n2 respectively) and the combined performance of nets 1 and 2 are shown where fields are rejected when the nets differ. The curves show results for fields ranging length 2 to 6 averaged over all fields for 1,000 total fields, 4,000 characters. Note that Net2 is not nearly as accurate as Net1 on fields, but that the combination of the two is significantly better than either. For this test set the rejection rate is 17% (83% acceptance) with an accuracy rate of 99.3% (error rate 0.7%) overall on fields of average length 4. Figure 2B shows the per-field performance for test-set B (5,000 fields, 20,000 digits) Again both nets are used for the rejection criterion. For comparison, 99% accuracy on fields of length 4 is achieved at 23% rejection.

Figure 2 shows the generalization performance on the NIST database for Net1, Net2 and their combination. For the combination, we accepted the answer only when the networks agreed and rejected further based on a simple confidence measure (the difference of the two highest activations) of each individual net.

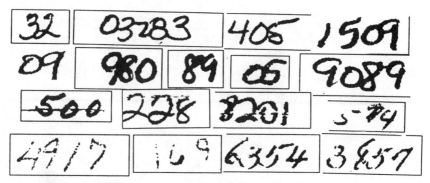

Figure 3: Examples of correctly recognized fields in the NIST database. This figure shows examples of fields that were correctly recognized by the ISR network. Note the cases of touching characters, multiple touching characters, characters touching in multiple places, fields with extrinsic noise, broken characters and touching, broken characters with noise. Because of the integrated nature of the segmentation and recognition, the same system is able to handle all of these cases.

4   DISCUSSION AND CONCLUSIONS

This investigation has demonstrated that the ISR algorithm can be used for integrated segmentation and recognition and achieve high-accuracy results on a large database of hand-printed numerals. The overall accuracy rates of 83% acceptance with 99.3% accuracy on fields of average length 4 is competitive with accuracy reported in commercial products. One should be careful making such comparisons. We found a variance of 7% or more in rejection performance on different test sets with more than 1,000 fields (a good statistical sample). Perhaps more important than the high accuracy, we have demonstrated that the ISR system is able to deal with touching, broken and noisy characters. In other investigations we have demonstrated the ISR system on alphabetic characters with good results, and on speech recognition (Keeler, Rumelhart, Zand-Biglari, 1991) where the results are slightly better than Hidden Markov Model results.

There are several attractive aspects about the ISR algorithm: 1) Labeling can be "sloppy" in the sense that the borders of the characters do not have to be defined. This reduces the labor burden of getting a system running. 2) The final weights can be duplicated so that the system can all run in parallel. Even with both networks running, the number of weights and activations needed to be stored in memory is quite small – about 30,000 floating point numbers, and the system is quite fast in the feed-forward mode: peak performance is about 2.5 characters/sec on a Dec 5000 (including everything: both networks running, input pre-processing, parsing the answers, printing results, etc.). This structure is ideal for VLSI implementation since it contains a very small number of weights (about 5,000). This is one possible way around the computational bottleneck facing encountered in processing complex scenes – the ISR net can do very-fast first-cut scene analysis with good discrimination of similar objects – an extremely difficult task. 3) The ISR algorithm and architecture presents a new and powerful approach of using forward models to convert position-independent training information into position-specific error signals. 4) There is no restriction to one-dimension; The same ISR structure has been used for two-dimensional parsing.

Nevertheless, there are several aspects of the ISR net that require improvement for future progress. First, the algorithmic assumption of having one pattern of a given type in the input field is too restrictive and can cause confusion in some training examples. Second, we are throwing some information away when we project out all of the positional information order information could be incorporated into the training information. This extra information should improve training performance due to the more-specific error signals. Finally, normalization is still a problem. We do a crude normalization, and the networks are able to segment and recognize characters as long as the difference in size is not too large. A factor of two in size difference is easily handled with the ISR system, but a factor of four decreases recognition accuracy by about 3-5% on the character recognition rates. This requires a tighter coupling between the segmentation/recognition and normalization. Just as one must segment and recognize simultaneously, in many cases one can't properly normalize until segmentation/recognition has occurred. Fortunately, in most document processing applications, crude normalization to within a factor of two is simple to achieve, allowing high accuracy networks.

Acknowledgements

We thank Wee-Kheng Leow, Steve O'Hara, John Canfield, for useful discussions and coding.

References

[1] J.D. Keeler, D.E. Rumelhart, and W.K. Leow (1991a) "Integrated Segmentation and Recognition of Hand-printed Numerals". In: Lippmann, Moody and Touretzky, Editors, *Neural Information Processing Systems* 3, 557-563.

[2] J.D. Keeler, D.E. Rumelhart, and S. Zand-Biglari (1991b) "A Neural Network For Integrated Segmentation and Recognition of Continuous Speech". MCC Technical Report ACT-NN-359-91.

[3] K. Lang, A. Waibel, G. Hinton. (1990) A time delay Neural Network Architecture for Isolated Word Recognition. *Neural Networks*, 3 23-44.

[4] Y. Le Cun, B. Boser, J.S. Denker, S. Solla, R. Howard, and L. Jackel. (1990) "Back-Propagation applied to Handwritten Zipcode Recognition." *Neural Computation* 1(4):541-551.

[5] G. Martin, J. Pittman (1990) "Recognizing hand-printed letters and digits." In D. Touretzky (Ed.). *Neural Information Processing Systems* 2, 405-414, Morgan Kauffman Publishers, San Mateo, CA.

[6] The NIST database can be obtained by writing to: Standard Reference Data National Institute of Standards and Technology 221/A323 Gaithersburg, MD 20899 USA and asking for NIST special database 1 (HWDB).

Recognizing Overlapping Hand–Printed Characters by Centered–Object Integrated Segmentation and Recognition

Gale L. Martin* & Mosfeq Rashid
MCC
Austin, Texas 78759 USA

Abstract

This paper describes an approach, called *centered object integrated segmentation and recognition* (COISR), for integrating object segmentation and recognition within a single neural network. The application is hand–printed character recognition. Two versions of the system are described. One uses a backpropagation network that scans exhaustively over a field of characters and is trained to recognize whether it is centered over a single character or between characters. When it is centered over a character, the net classifies the character. The approach is tested on a dataset of hand–printed digits. Very low error rates are reported. The second version, COISR–SACCADE, avoids the need for exhaustive scans. The net is trained as before, but also is trained to compute ballistic 'eye' movements that enable the input window to jump from one character to the next.

The common model of visual processing includes multiple, independent stages. First, filtering operations act on the raw image to segment or isolate and enhance to–be–recognized clumps. These clumps are normalized for factors such as size, and sometimes simplified further through feature extraction. The results are then fed to one or more classifiers. The operations prior to classification simplify the recognition task. Object segmentation restricts the number of features considered for classification to those associated with a single object, and enables normalization to be applied at the individual object level. Without such pre–processing, recognition may be an intractable problem. However, a weak point of this sequential stage model is that recognition and segmentation decisions are often inter–dependent. Not only does a correct recognition decision depend on first making a correct segmentation decision, but a correct segmentation decision often depends on first making a correct recognition decision.

This is a particularly serious problem in character recognition applications. OCR systems use intervening white space and related features to segment a field of characters into individual characters, so that classification can be accomplished one character at a time. This approach fails when characters touch each other or when an individual character is broken up by intervening white space. Some means of integrating the segmentation and recognition stages is needed.

This paper describes an approach, called *centered object integrated segmentation and recognition* (COISR), for integrating character segmentation and recognition within one

---

*Also with Eastman Kodak Company

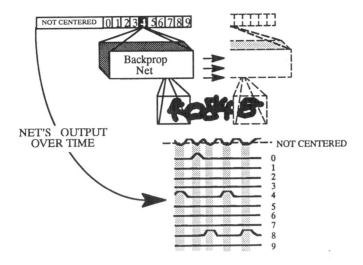

Figure 1: The COISR Exhaustive Scan Approach.

neural network. The general approach builds on previous work in pre-segmented character recognition (LeCun, Boser, Denker, Henderson, Howard, Hubbard, & Jackel, 1990; Martin & Pittman, 1990) and on the sliding window conception used in neural network speech applications, such as NETtalk (Sejnowski & Rosenberg(1986) and Time Delay Neural Networks (Waibel, Sawai, & Shikano, 1988). Two versions of the approach are described. In both cases, a net is trained to recognize what is centered in its input window as it slides along a character field. The window size is chosen to be large enough to include more than one character.

1   COISR VERSION 1: EXHAUSTIVE SCAN

As shown in Figure 1, the net is trained on an input window, and a target output vector representing what is in the center of the window. The top half of the figure shows the net's input window scanning successively across the field. Sometimes the middle of the window is centered on a character, and sometimes it is centered on a point between two characters. The target output vector consists of one node per category, and one node corresponding to a NOT–CENTERED condition. This latter node has a high target activation value when the input window is not centered over any character. A temporal stream of output vectors is created (shown at the bottom half of the figure) as the net scans the field. There is no need to explicitly segment characters, during training or testing, because recognition is defined as identifying what is in the center of the scanning window. The net learns to extract regularities in the shapes of individual characters even when those regularities occur in the context of overlapping and broken characters. The final stage of processing involves parsing the temporal stream generated as the net scans the field to yield an ascii string of recognized characters.

1.1 IMPLEMENTATION DETAILS

The COISR approach was tested using the National Institute of Standards and Technology (NIST) database of hand–printed digit fields, using fields 6–30 of the form, which correspond to five different fields of length 2, 3, 4, 5, or 6 digits each. The training data included roughly 80,000 digits (800 forms, 20,000 fields), and came from forms labeled f0000–f0499, and f1500–f1799 in the dataset. The test data consisted of roughly 20,000 digits (200 forms, 5,000 fields) and came from forms labeled f1800–f1899 and f2000–f2099 in the dataset. The large test set was used because considerable variations in test scores occurred with smaller test set sizes. The samples were scanned at a 300 pixel/inch resolution. Each field image was preprocessed to eliminate the white space and box surrounding the digit field. Each field was then size normalized with respect to the vertical height of the digit field to a vertical height of 20 pixels. Since the input is size normalized to the vertical height of the field of characters, the actual number of characters in the constant–width input window of 36 pixels varies depending on the height–to–width ratio for each character. The scan rate was a 3–pixel increment across the field.

A key design principle of the present approach is that highly accurate integrated seg-mentation and recognition requires training on both the shapes of characters and their positions within the input window. The field images used for training were labeled with the horizontal center positions of each character in the field. The human labeler simply pointed at the horizontal center of each digit in sequence with a mouse cursor and clicked on a mouse button. The horizontal position of each character was then paired with its category label (0–9) in a data file. The labeling process is not unlike a human reading teacher using a pointer to indicate the position of each character as he or she reads aloud the sequence of characters making up the word or sentence. During testing this position information is not used.

Position information about character centers is used to generate target output values for each possible position of the input window as it scans a field of characters. When the center position of a window is close to the center of a character, the target value of that character's output node is set at the maximum, with the target value of the NOT–CENTERED node set at the minimum. The activation values of all other char-acters' output nodes are set at the minimum. When the center position of a window is close to the half-way point between two character centers, the target value of all character output nodes are set to the minimum and the target value of the NOT-CENTERED node is set to a maximum. Between these two extremes, the target val-ues vary linearly with distance, creating a trapezoidal function (i.e., ⎯⎯⎯⎯⎯).

The neural network is a 2–hidden–layer backpropagation network, with local, shared connections in the first hidden layer, and local connections in the second hidden layer (see Figure 2). The first hidden layer consists of 2016 nodes, or more specifically 18 independent groups of 112 (16x7) nodes, with each group having local, shared connec-

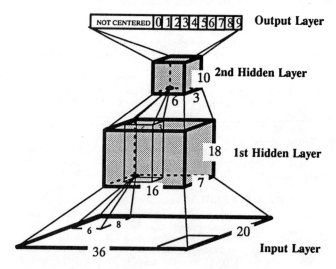

Figure 2: Architecture for the COISR–Exhaustive Scan Approach.

tions to the input layer. The local, overlapping receptive fields of size 6x8 are offset by 2 pixels, such that the region covered by each group of nodes spans the input layer. The second hidden layer consists of 180 nodes, having local, but NOT shared receptive fields of size 6x3. The output layer consists of 11 nodes, with each of these nodes connected to all of the nodes in the 2nd hidden layer. The net has a total of 2927 nodes (includes input and output nodes), and 157,068 connections. In a feedforward (non-learning) mode on a DEC 5000 workstation, in which the net is scanning a field of digits, the system processes about two digits per second, which includes image pre-processing and the necessary number of feedforward passes on the net.

As the net scans horizontally, the activation values of the 11 output nodes create a trace as shown in Figure 1. To convert this to an ascii string corresponding to the digits in the field, the state of the NOT-CENTERED node is monitored continuously. When it's activation value falls below a threshold, a summing process begins for each of the other nodes, and ends when the activation value of the NOT-CENTERED node exceeds the threshold. At this point the system decides that the input window has moved off of a character. The system then classifies the character on the basis of which output node has the highest summed activation for the position just passed over.

1.2 GENERALIZATION PERFORMANCE

As shown in Figure 3, the COISR technique achieves very low field-based error rates,

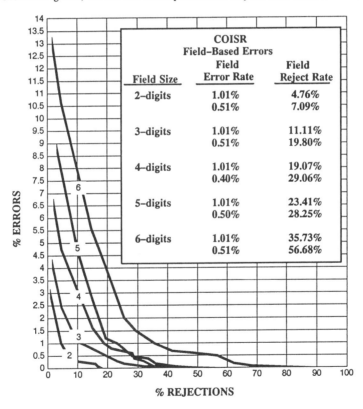

COISR Field-Based Errors		
Field Size	Field Error Rate	Field Reject Rate
2-digits	1.01%	4.76%
	0.51%	7.09%
3-digits	1.01%	11.11%
	0.51%	19.80%
4-digits	1.01%	19.07%
	0.40%	29.06%
5-digits	1.01%	23.41%
	0.50%	28.25%
6-digits	1.01%	35.73%
	0.51%	56.68%

Figure 3: Field-based Test Error and Reject Rates

particularly for a single classifier system. The error rates are field-based in the sense that if the network mis-classifies one character in the field, the entire field is considered as mis–classified. Error rates pertain to the fields remaining, after rejection. Rejections are based on placing a threshold for the acceptable distance between the highest and the next highest running activation total. In this way, by varying the threshold, the error rate can be traded off against the percentage of rejections. Since the reported data apply to fields, the threshold applies to the smallest distance value found across all of the characters in the field. Figure 4 provides examples, from the test set, of fields that the COISR network correctly classifies.

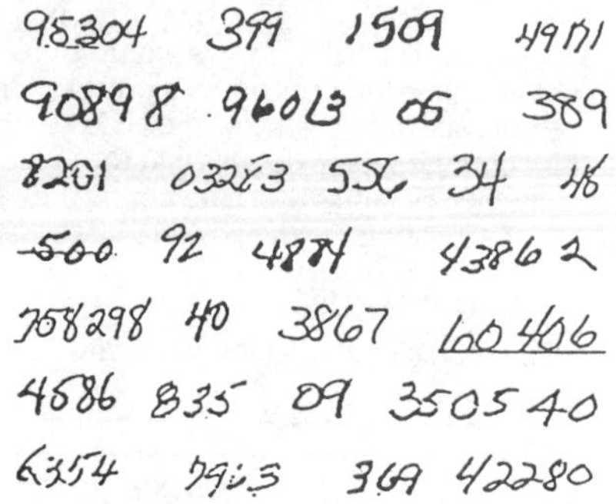

Figure 4: Test Set Examples of Touching and Broken Characters Correctly Recognized

The COISR technique is a success in the sense that it does something that conventional character recognition systems can not do. It robustly recognizes character fields containing touching, overlapping, and broken characters. One problem with the approach, however, lies with the exhaustive nature of the scan. The components needed to recognize a character in a given location are essentially replicated across the length of the to–be–classified input field, at the degree of resolution necessary to recognize the smallest and closest characters. While this has not presented any real difficulties for the present system, which processes 2 characters per second, it is likely to be troublesome when extensions are made to two–dimensional scans and larger vocabularies. A rough analogy with respect to human vision would be to require that all of the computational resources needed for recognizing objects at one point on the retina be replicated for each resolvable point on the retina. This design carries the notion of a compound eye to the ridiculous extreme.

2   COISR VERSION 2: SACCADIC SCAN

Taking a cue from natural vision systems, the second version of the COISR system uses a *saccadic scan*. The system is trained to make ballistic eye movements, so that it can effectively jump from character to character and over blank areas. This version is similar to the exhaustive scan version in the sense that a backprop net is trained to recognize when it's input window is centered on a character, and if so, to classify the character. In addition, the net is trained for navigation control (Pomerleau ,1991). At each point in a field of characters, the net is trained to estimate the distance to the next character on the right, and to estimate the degree to which the center–most character is off–center. The trained net accomodates for variations in character width, spacing between characters, writing styles, and other factors. At run–time, the system uses the computed character classification and distances to navigate along a character field. If the character classification judgment, for a given position, has a high degree of certainty, the system accesses the *next character* distance information computed by the net for the current position and executes the jump.   If the system gets off–track, so that a character can not be recognized with a high–degree of certainty, it makes a corrective saccade by accessing the *off-center character* distance computed by the net for the current position. This action corresponds to making a second attempt to center the character within the input window.

The primary advantage of this approach, over the exhaustive scan, is improved efficiency, as illustrated in Figure 5. The scanning input windows are shown at the top of the figure, for each approach, and each character–containing input window, shown below the scanned image for each approach, corresponds to a forward pass of the net. The exhaustive scan version requires about 4 times as many forward passes as the saccadic scan version. Greater improvements in efficiency can be achieved with wider input windows and images containing more blank areas. The system is still under development, but accuracy approaches that of the exhaustive scan system.

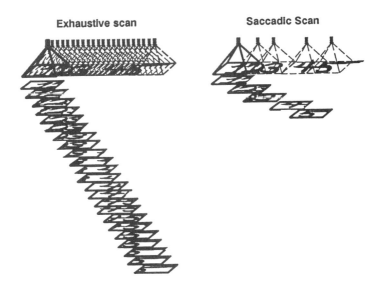

Figure 5: Number of Forward Passes for Saccadic & Exhaustive Scan Systems

3   COMPARISONS & CONCLUSIONS

In comparing accuracy rates between different OCR systems, one relevant factor that should be reported is the number of classifiers used. For a given system, increasing the number of classifiers typically reduces error rates but increases processing time. The low error rates reported here for the COISR–Exhaustive Scan approach come from a single classifier operating at 2 characters per second on a general purpose workstation. Most OCR systems employ multiple classifiers. For example, at the NIPS workshops this year, Jonathan Hull described the University of Buffalo zip code recognition system that contains five classifiers and requires about one minute to process a character. Keeler and Rumelhart, at this conference, also described a two–classifier neural net system for NIST digit recognition. The fact that the COISR approach achieved quite low error rates with a single classifier indicates that the approach is a promising one.

Clearly, another relevant factor in comparing systems is the ability to recognize touching and broken characters, since this is a dominant stumbling block for current OCR systems. Conventional systems can be altered to achieve integrated segmentation and recognition in limited cases, but this involves a lot of hand–crafting and a significant amount of time–consuming iterative processing (Fenrich. 1991). Essentially, multiple segmenters are used, and classification is performed for each such possible segmentation. The final segmentation and recognition decisions can thus be inter–dependent, but only at the cost of computing multiple segmentations and correspondingly, multiple classification decisions. The approach breaks down as the number of possible segmentations increases, as would occur for example if individual characters are broken or touching in multiple places or if multiple letters in a sequence are connected. The COISR system does not appear to have this problem.

The NIPS conference this year has included a number of other neural net approaches to integrated segmentation and recognition in OCR domains. Two approaches similar to the COISR–Exhaustive Scan system were those described by Faggin and by Keeler and Rumelhart. All three achieve integrated segmentation and recognition by convolving a neural network over a field of characters. Faggin described an analog hardware implementation of a neural–network–based OCR system that receives as input a window that slides along the machine–print digit field at the bottom of bank checks. Keeler and Rumelhart described a *self–organizing integrated segmentation and recognition* (SOISR) system. Initially, it is trained on characters that have been pre–segmented by a labeler effectively drawing a box around each. Then, in subsequent training, a net, with these pre–trained weights, is duplicated repetitively across the extent of a fixed–width input field, and is further trained on examples of entire fields that contain connecting or broken characters.

All three approaches have the weakness, described previously of performing essentially exhaustive scans or convolutions over the to–be–classified input field. This complaint is not necessarily directed at the specific applications dealt with at this year's NIPS conference, particularly if operating at the high levels of efficiency described by Faggin. Nor is the complaint directed at tasks that only require the visual system to focus on a few small clusters or fields in the larger, otherwise blank input field. In these cases, low–resolution filters may be sufficient to efficiently remove blank areas and enable efficient integrated segmentation and recognition. However, we use as an example, the saccadic scanning behavior of human vision in tasks, such as reading this paragraph. In such cases that require high–resolution sensitivity across a large, dense image and classification of a very large vocabulary of symbols, it seems clear that other, more flexible and efficient scanning mechanisms will be necessary. This high–density image domain is the focus of the COISR–Saccadic Scan approach, which integrates not only the segmentation and recognition of characters, but also control of the navigational aspects of vision.

Acknowledgements

We thank Lori Barski, John Canfield, David Chapman, Roger Gaborski, Jay Pittman, and Dave Rumelhart for helpful discussions and/or development of supporting image handling and network software. I also thank Jonathan Martin for help with the position labeling.

References

Fenrich, R. Segmentation of automatically located handwritten words. paper presented at the *International Workshop on frontiers in handwriting recognition*. Chateau de Bonas, France. 23–27 September 1991.

Keeler, J. D., Rumelhart, David E., Leow, Wee–Kheng. Integrated segmentation and recognition of hand–printed numerals, in R. P. Lippmann, John E. Moody, David S. Touretzky (Eds) *Advances in Neural Information Processing Systems 3*, p.557–563. San Mateo, CA: Morgan Kaufmann. 1991.

LeCun, Y., Boser, B., Denker, J., Henderson, D., Howard, R. E., Hubbard, W. & Jackel, L. D. Handwritten digit recognition with a backpropagation network, in D. S. Touretzky (Ed.) *Advances in Neural Information Processing Systems 2*. Morgan Kaufmann, 1990.

Martin, G. L. & Pittman, J. A. Recognizing hand–printed letters and digits. in D. S. Touretzky (Ed.) *Advances in Neural Information Processing Systems 2.* Morgan Kaufmann, 1990.

Pomerleau, D. A. Efficient training of artificial neural networks for autonomous navigation. *Neural Computation, 3,* 1991, 88–97.

Rumelhart, D. (1989) Learning and generalization in multi–layer networks. presentation given at the NATO Advanced Research Workshop on Neuro Computing Algorithms, Architectures and Applications. Les Arcs, France. February, 1989.

Sejnowski, T. J. & Rosenberg, C. R. (1986) NETtalk: a parallel network that learns to read aloud. Johns Hopkins University Electrical Engineering and Computer Science Technical Report JHU/EECS–86/01.

Waibel, A., Sawai, H., Shikano, K. (1988) Modularity and scaling in large phonemic neural networks. ATR Interpreting Telephony Research Laboratories Technical Report TR–I–0034.

Adaptive Elastic Models for Hand-Printed Character Recognition

Geoffrey E. Hinton, Christopher K. I. Williams and Michael D. Revow
Department of Computer Science, University of Toronto
Toronto, Ontario, Canada M5S 1A4

Abstract

Hand-printed digits can be modeled as splines that are governed by about 8 control points. For each known digit, the control points have preferred "home" locations, and deformations of the digit are generated by moving the control points away from their home locations. Images of digits can be produced by placing Gaussian ink generators uniformly along the spline. Real images can be recognized by finding the digit model most likely to have generated the data. For each digit model we use an elastic matching algorithm to minimize an energy function that includes both the deformation energy of the digit model and the log probability that the model would generate the inked pixels in the image. The model with the lowest total energy wins. If a uniform noise process is included in the model of image generation, some of the inked pixels can be rejected as noise as a digit model is fitting a poorly segmented image. The digit models learn by modifying the home locations of the control points.

1 Introduction

Given good bottom-up segmentation and normalization, feedforward neural networks are an efficient way to recognize digits in zip codes. (le Cun et al., 1990). However, in some cases, it is not possible to correctly segment and normalize the digits without using knowledge of their shapes, so to achieve close to human performance on images of whole zip codes it will be necessary to use models of shapes to influence the segmentation and normalization of the digits. One way of doing this is to use a large cooperative network that simultaneously segments, normalizes and recognizes all of the digits in a zip code. A first step in this direction is to take a poorly segmented image of a single digit and to explain the image properly in terms of an appropriately normalized, deformed digit model plus noise. The ability of the model to reject some parts of the image as noise is the first step towards model-driven segmentation.

512

2   Elastic models

One technique for recognizing a digit is to perform an elastic match with many different exemplars of each known digit-class and to pick the class of the nearest neighbor. Unfortunately this requires a large number of elastic matches, each of which is expensive. By using one elastic model to capture all the variations of a given digit we greatly reduce the number of elastic matches required. Burr (1981a, 1981b) has investigated several types of elastic model and elastic matching procedure. We describe a different kind of elastic model that is based on splines. Each elastic model contains parameters that define an ideal shape and also define a deformation energy for departures from this ideal. These parameters are initially set by hand but can be improved by learning. They are an efficient way to represent the many possible instances of a given digit.

Each digit is modelled by a deformable spline whose shape is determined by the positions of 8 control points. Every point on the spline is a weighted average of four control points, with the weighting coefficients changing smoothly as we move along the spline. [1] To generate an ideal example of a digit we put the 8 control points at their home locations for that model. To deform the digit we move the control points away from their home locations. Currently we assume that, for each model, the control points have independent, radial Gaussian distributions about their home locations. So the negative log probability of a deformation (its energy) is proportional to the sum of the squares of the departures of the control points from their home locations.

The deformation energy function only penalizes shape *deformations*. Translation, rotation, dilation, elongation, and shear do not change the shape of an object so we want the deformation energy to be invariant under these affine transformations. We achieve this by giving each model its own "object-based frame". Its deformation energy is computed relative to this frame, not in image coordinates. When we fit the model to data, we repeatedly recompute the best affine transformation between the object-based frame and the image (see section 4). The repeated recomputation of the affine transform during the model fit means that the shape of the digit is influencing the normalization.

Although we will use our digit models for recognizing images, it helps to start by considering how we would use them for generating images. The generative model is an elaboration of the probabilistic interpretation of the elastic net given by Durbin, Szeliski & Yuille (1989). Given a particular spline, we space a number of "beads" uniformly along the spline. Each bead defines the center of a Gaussian ink generator. The number of beads on the spline and the variance of the ink generators can easily be changed without changing the spline itself.

To generate a noisy image of a particular digit class, run the following procedure:

- Pick an affine transformation from the model's intrinsic reference frame to the image frame (i.e. pick a size, position, orientation, slant and elongation for the digit).

---

[1]In computing the weighting coefficients we use a cubic B-spline and we treat the first and last control points as if they were doubled.

- Pick a deformation of the model (i.e. move the control points away from their home locations). The probability of picking a deformation is $\frac{1}{Z}e^{-E_{deform}}$

- Repeat many times:
  Either (with probability π_{noise}) add a randomly positioned noise pixel
  Or pick a bead at random and generate a pixel from the Gaussian distribution defined by the bead.

3 Recognizing isolated digits

We recognize an image by finding which model is most likely to have generated it. Each possible model is fitted to the image and the one that has the lowest cost fit is the winner. The cost of a fit is the negative log probability of generating the image given the model.

$$E_{ideal} = -log \int_{\substack{I \in model \\ instances}} P(I)\ P(image \mid I)\ dI \qquad (1)$$

We can approximate this by just considering the best fitting model instance [2] and ignoring the fact that the model should not generate ink where there is no ink in the image:[3]

$$E = \lambda\ E_{deform} - \sum_{\substack{inked \\ pixels}} \log P(pixel \mid best\ model\ instance) \qquad (2)$$

The probability of an inked pixel is the sum of the probabilities of all the possible ways of generating it from the mixture of Gaussian beads or the uniform noise field.

$$P(i) = \frac{\pi_{noise}}{N} + \frac{\pi_{model}}{B} \sum_{beads} P_b(i) \qquad (3)$$

where N is the total number of pixels, B is the number of beads, π is a mixing proportion, and $P_b(i)$ is the probability density of pixel i under Gaussian bead b.

4 The search procedure for fitting a model to an image

Every Gaussian bead in a model has the same variance. When fitting data, we start with a big variance and gradually reduce it as in the elastic net algorithm of Durbin and Willshaw (1987) . Each iteration of the elastic matching algorithm involves three steps:

---

[2]In effect, we are assuming that the integral in equation 1 can be approximated by the height of the highest peak, and so we are ignoring variations between models in the width of the peak or the number of peaks.

[3]If the inked pixels are rare, poor models sin mainly by not inking those pixels that should be inked rather than by inking those pixels that should not be inked.

- Given the current locations of the Gaussians, compute the responsibility that each Gaussian has for each inked pixel. This is just the probability of generating the pixel from that Gaussian, normalized by the total probability of generating the pixel.

- Assuming that the responsibilities remain fixed, as in the EM algorithm of Dempster, Laird and Rubin (1977), we invert a 16×16 matrix to find the image locations for the 8 control points at which the forces pulling the control points towards their home locations are balanced by the forces exerted on the control points by the inked pixels. These forces come via the forces that the inked pixels exert on the Gaussian beads.

- Given the new image locations of the control points, we recompute the affine transformation from the object-based frame to the image frame. We choose the affine transformation that minimizes the sum of the squared distances, in object-based coordinates, between the control points and their home locations. The residual squared differences determine the deformation energy.

Some stages in the fitting of a model to data are shown in Fig. 1. This search technique avoids nearly all local minima when fitting models to isolated digits. But if we get a high deformation energy in the best fitting model, we can try alternative starting configurations for the models.

5 Learning the digit models

We can do discriminative learning by adjusting the home positions and variances of the control points to minimize the objective function

$$C = - \sum_{\substack{training \\ cases}} \log p(correct\ digit), \quad p(correct\ digit) = \frac{e^{-E_{correct}}}{\sum_{all\ digits} e^{-E_{digit}}} \quad (4)$$

For a model parameter such as the x coordinate of the home location of one of the control points we need $\partial C / \partial x$ in order to do gradient descent learning. Equation 4 allows us to express $\partial C / \partial x$ in terms of $\partial E / \partial x$ but there is a subtle problem: Changing a parameter of an elastic model causes a simple change in the energy of the configuration that the model previously settled to, but the model no longer settles to that configuration. So it appears that we need to consider how the energy is affected by the change in the configuration. Fortunately, derivatives are simple at an energy minimum because small changes in the configuration make no change in the energy (to first order). Thus the inner loop settling leads to simple derivatives for the outer loop learning, as in the Boltzmann machine (Hinton, 1989).

6 Results on the hand-filtered dataset

We are trying out the scheme out on a relatively simple task - we have a model of a two and a model of a three, and we want the two model to win on "two" images, and the three model to win on "three" images.

We have tried many variations of the character models, the preprocessing, the initial affine transformations of the models, the annealing schedule for the variances, the

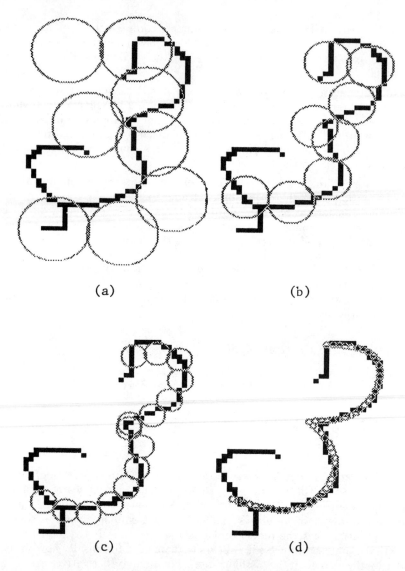

(a)   (b)

(c)   (d)

Figure 1: The sequence (a) to (d) shows some stages of fitting a model 3 to some data. The grey circles represent the beads on the spline, and the radius of the circle represents the standard deviation of the Gaussian. (a) shows the initial configuration, with eight beads equally spaced along the spline. In (b) and (c) the variance is progressively decreased and the number of beads is increased. The final fit using 60 beads is shown in (d). We use about three iterations at each of five variances on our "annealing schedule". In this example, we used $\pi_{noise} = 0.3$ which makes it cheaper to explain the extraneous noise pixels and the flourishes on the ends of the 3 as noise rather than deforming the model to bring Gaussian beads close to these pixels.

mixing proportion of the noise, and the relative importance of deformation energy versus data-fit energy.

Our current best performance is 10 errors (1.6%) on a test set of 304 two's and 304 three's. We reject cases if the best-fitting model is highly deformed, but on this test set the deformation energy never reached the rejection criterion. The training set has 418 cases, and we have a validation set of 200 cases to tell us when to stop learning. Figure 2 shows the effect of learning on the models. The initial affine transform is defined by the minimal vertical rectangle around the data.

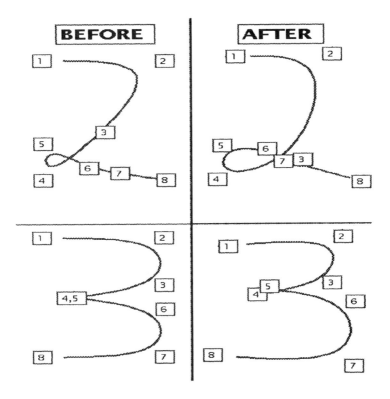

Figure 2: The two and three models before and after learning. The control points are labelled 1 through 8. We used maximum likelihood learning in which each digit model is trained only on instances of that digit. After each pass through all those instances, the home location of each control point (in the object-based frame) is redefined to be the average location of the control point in the final fits of the model of the digit to the instances of the digit. Most of the improvement in performance occurred after the fist pass, and after five updates of the home locations of the control points, performance on the validation set started to decrease. Similar results were obtained with discriminative training. We could also update the variance of each control point to be its variance in the final fits, though we did not adapt the variances in this simulation.

The images are preprocessed to eliminate variations due to stroke-width and paper and ink intensities. First, we use a standard local thresholding algorithm to make a binary decision for each pixel. Then we pick out the five largest connected components (hopefully digits). We put a box around each component, then thin all the data in the box. If we ourselves cannot recognize the resulting image we eliminate it from the data set. The training, validation and test data is all from the training portion of the United States Postal Service Handwritten ZIP Code Database (1987) which was made available by the USPS Office of Advanced Technology.

7   Discussion

Before we tried using splines to model digits, we used models that consisted of a fixed number of Gaussian beads with elastic energy constraints operating between neighboring beads. To constrain the curvature we used energy terms that involved triples of beads. With this type of energy function, we had great difficulty using a single model to capture topologically different instances of a digit. For example, when the central loop of a 3 changes to a cusp and then to an open bend, the sign of the curvature reverses. With a spline model it is easy to model these topological variants by small changes in the relative vertical locations of the central two control points (see figure 2). This advantage of spline models is pointed out by (Edelman, Ullman and Flash, 1990) who use a different kind of spline that they fit to character data by directly locating candidate knot points in the image.

Spline models also make it easy to increase the number of Gaussian beads as their variance is decreased. This coarse-to-fine strategy is much more efficient than using a large number of beads at all variances, but it is much harder to implement if the deformation energy explicitly depends on particular bead locations, since changing the number of beads then requires a new function for the deformation energy.

In determining where on the spline to place the Gaussian beads, we initially used a fixed set of blending coefficients for each bead. These coefficients are the weights used to specify the bead location as a weighted center of gravity of the locations of 4 control points. Unfortunately this yields too few beads in portions of a digit such as a long tail of a 2 which are governed by just a few control points. Performance was much improved by spacing the beads uniformly along the curve.

By using spline models, we build in a lot of prior knowledge about what characters look like, so we can describe the shape of a character using only a small number of parameters (16 coordinates and 8 variances). This means that the learning is exploring a much smaller space than a conventional feed-forward network. Also, because the parameters are easy to interpret, we can start with fairly good initial models of the characters. So learning only requires a few updates of the parameters.

Obvious extensions of the deformation energy function include using elliptical Gaussians for the distributions of the control points, or using full covariance matrices for neighboring pairs of control points. Another obvious modification is to use elliptical rather than circular Gaussians for the beads. If strokes curve gently relative to their thickness, the distribution of ink can be modelled much better using elliptical Gaussians. However, an ellipse takes about twice as many operations to fit and is not helpful in regions of sharp curvature. Our simulations suggest that, on average, two circular beads are more flexible than one elliptical bead.

Currently we do not impose any penalty on extremely sheared or elongated affine transformations, though this would probably improve performance. Having an explicit representation of the affine transformation of each digit should prove very helpful for recognizing multiple digits, since it will allow us to impose a penalty on differences in the affine transformations of neighboring digits.

Presegmented images of single digits contain many different kinds of noise that cannot be eliminated by simple bottom-up operations. These include descenders, underlines, and bits of other digits; corrections; dirt in recycled paper; smudges and misplaced postal franks. To really understand the image we probably need to model a wide variety of structured noise. We are currently experimenting with one simple way of incorporating noise models. After each digit model has been used to segment a noisy image into one digit instance plus noise, we try to fit more complicated noise models to the residual noise. A good fit greatly decreases the cost of that noise and hence improves this interpretation of the image. We intend to handle flourishes on the ends of characters in this way rather than using more elaborate digit models that include optional flourishes.

One of our main motivations in developing elastic models is the belief that a strong prior model should make learning easier, should reduce confident errors, and should allow top-down segmentation. Although we have shown that elastic spline models can be quite effective, we have not yet demonstrated that they are superior to feedforward nets and there is a serious weakness of our approach: Elastic matching is slow. Fitting the models to the data takes *much* more computation than a feedforward net. So in the same number of cycles, a feedforward net can try many alternative bottom-up segmentations and normalizations and select the overall segmentation that leads to the most recognizable digit string.

Acknowledgements

This research was funded by Apple and by the Ontario Information Technology Research Centre. We thank Allan Jepson and Richard Durbin for suggesting spline models.

References

Burr, D. J. (1981a). A dynamic model for image registration. *Comput. Graphics Image Process.*, 15:102–112.

Burr, D. J. (1981b). Elastic matching of line drawings. *IEEE Trans. Pattern Analysis and Machine Intelligence*, 3(6):708–713.

Dempster, A. P., Laird, N. M., and Rubin, D. B. (1977). Maximum likelihood from incomplete data via the EM algorithm. *Proc. Roy. Stat. Soc.*, B-39:1–38.

Durbin, R., Szeliski, R., and Yuille, A. L. (1989). An analysis of the elastic net approach to the travelling salesman problem. *Neural Computation*, 1:348–358.

Durbin, R. and Willshaw, D. (1987). An analogue approach to the travelling salesman problem. *Nature*, 326:689–691.

Edelman, S., Ullman, S., and Flash, T. (1990). Reading cursive handwriting by alignment of letter prototypes. *Internat. Journal of Comput. Vision*, 5(3):303–331.

Hinton, G. E. (1989). Deterministic Boltzmann learning performs steepest descent in weight-space. *Neural Computation*, 1:143–150.

le Cun, Y., Boser, B., Denker, J., Henderson, D., Howard, R., Hubbard, W., and Jackel, L. (1990). Handwritten digit recognition with a back-propagation network. In *Advances in Neural Information Processing Systems 2*, pages 396–404. Morgan Kaufmann.

PART IX

CONTROL AND PLANNING

Obstacle Avoidance through Reinforcement Learning

Tony J. Prescott and **John E. W. Mayhew**
Artificial Intelligence and Vision Research Unit,
University of Sheffield, S10 2TN, England.

Abstract

A method is described for generating plan-like, reflexive, obstacle avoidance behaviour in a mobile robot. The experiments reported here use a simulated vehicle with a primitive range sensor. Avoidance behaviour is encoded as a set of continuous functions of the perceptual input space. These functions are stored using CMACs and trained by a variant of Barto and Sutton's adaptive critic algorithm. As the vehicle explores its surroundings it adapts its responses to sensory stimuli so as to minimise the negative reinforcement arising from collisions. Strategies for local navigation are therefore acquired in an explicitly goal-driven fashion. The resulting trajectories form elegant collision-free paths through the environment

1 INTRODUCTION

Following Simon's (1969) observation that complex behaviour may simply be the reflection of a complex environment a number of researchers (eg. Braitenberg 1986, Anderson and Donath 1988, Chapman and Agre 1987) have taken the view that interesting, plan-like behaviour can emerge from the interplay of a set of pre-wired reflexes with regularities in the world. However, the temporal structure in an agent's interaction with its environment can act as more than just a trigger for fixed reactions. Given a suitable learning mechanism it can also be exploited to generate sequences of new responses more suited to the problem in hand. Hence, this paper attempts to show that obstacle avoidance, a basic level of navigation competence, can be developed through learning a set of *conditioned* responses to perceptual stimuli.

In the absence of a teacher a mobile robot can evaluate its performance only in terms of final outcomes. A negative reinforcement signal can be generated each time a collision occurs but this information tells the robot neither when nor how, in the train of actions preceding the crash, a mistake was made. In reinforcement learning this credit assignment problem is overcome by forming associations between sensory input patterns and predictions of future outcomes. This allows the generation of internal "secondary reinforcement" signals that can be used to select improved responses. Several authors have discussed the use of reinforcement learning for navigation, this research is inspired primarily by that of Barto, Sutton and co-workers (1981, 1982, 1983, 1989) and Werbos (1990). The principles underlying reinforcement learning have recently been given a firm mathematical basis by Watkins (1989) who has shown that these algorithms are implementing an on-line, incremental, approximation to the dynamic programming method for determining optimal control. Sutton (1990) has also made use of these ideas in formulating a novel theory of classical conditioning in animal learning.

We aim to develop a reinforcement learning system that will allow a simple mobile robot with minimal sensory apparatus to move at speed around an indoor environment avoiding collisions with stationary or slow moving obstacles. This paper reports preliminary results obtained using a simulation of such a robot.

2 THE ROBOT SIMULATION

Our simulation models a three-wheeled mobile vehicle, called the 'sprite', operating in a simple two-dimensional world (500x500 cm) consisting of walls and obstacles in which the sprite is represented by a square box (30x30 cm). Restrictions on the acceleration and the braking response of the vehicle model enforce a degree of realism in its ability to initiate fast avoidance behaviour. The perceptual system simulates a laser range-finder giving the logarithmically scaled distance to the nearest obstacle at set angles from its current orientation. An important feature of the research has been to explore the extent to which spatially sparse but frequent data can support complex behaviour. We show below results from simulations using only three rays emitted at angles -60°, 0°, and +60°. The controller operates directly on this unprocessed sensory input. The continuous trajectory of the vehicle is approximated by a sequence of discrete time steps. In each interval the sprite acquires new perceptual data then performs the associated response generating either a change in position or a feedback signal indicating that a collision has occured preventing the move. After a collision the sprite reverses slightly then attempts to rotate and move off at a random angle (90-180° from its original heading), if this is not possible it is relocated to a random starting position.

3 LEARNING ALGORITHM

The sprite learns a multi-parameter policy (Π) and an evaluation (V). These functions are stored using the CMAC coarse-coding architecture (Albus 1971), and updated by a reinforcement learning algorithm similar to that described by Watkins (1989). The action functions comprising the policy are acquired as gaussian probability distributions using the method proposed by Williams (1988). The following gives a brief summary of the algorithm used.

Let x_t be the perceptual input pattern at time t and r_t the external reward, then the reinforcement learning error (see Barto et al., 1989) is given by

$$\varepsilon_{t+1} = r_{t+1} + \gamma V_t(x_{t+1}) - V_t(x_t) \tag{1}$$

where γ is a constant ($0 < \gamma < 1$). This error is used to adjust V and Π by gradient descent ie.

$$V_{t+1}(x) = V_t(x) + \alpha \, \epsilon_{t+1} \, m_t(x) \quad \text{and} \tag{2}$$

$$\Pi_{t+1}(x) = \Pi_t(x) + \beta \, \epsilon_{t+1} \, n_t(x) \tag{3}$$

where α and β are learning rates and $m_t(x)$ and $n_t(x)$ are the evaluation and policy *eligibility traces* for pattern x. The eligibility traces can be thought of as activity in short-term memory that enables learning in the LTM store. The minimum STM requirement is to remember the last input pattern and the exploration gradient Δa_t of the last action taken (explained below), hence

$m_{t+1}(x) = 1$ and $n_{t+1}(x) = \Delta a_t$ iff x is the current pattern,

$m_{t+1}(x) = n_{t+1}(x) = 0$ otherwise. $\tag{4}$

Learning occurs faster, however, if the memory trace of each pattern is allowed to decay slowly over time with strength of activity being related to recency. Hence, if the rate of decay is given by λ ($0 <= \lambda <= 1$) then for patterns other than the current one

$m_{t+1}(x) = \lambda \, m_t(x)$ and $n_{t+1}(x) = \lambda \, n_t(x)$.

Using a decay rate of less than 1.0 the eligibility trace for any input becomes negligible within a short time, so in practice it is only necessary to store a list of the most recent patterns and actions (in our simulations only the last four values are stored).

The policy acquired by the learning system has two elements (f and ϑ) corresponding to the desired forward and angular velocities of the vehicle. Each element is specified by a gaussian pdf and is encoded by two adjustable parameters denoting its mean and standard deviation (hence the policy as a whole consists of four continuous functions of the input). In each time-step an action is chosen by selecting randomly from the two distributions associated with the current input pattern.

In order to update the policy the exploratory component of the action must be computed, this consists of a four-vector with two values for each gaussian element. Following Williams we define a standard gaussian density function g with parameters μ and σ and output y such that

$$g(y, \mu, \sigma) = \frac{1}{2\sqrt{\pi}\sigma} e^{-\frac{(y-\mu)^2}{2\sigma^2}}$$

the derivatives of the mean and standard deviation[1] are then given by

$$\Delta\mu = \frac{y-\mu}{\sigma^2} \quad \text{and} \quad \Delta\sigma = \frac{[(y-\mu)^2 - \sigma^2]}{\sigma^3} \tag{5}$$

The exploration gradient of the action as a whole is therefore the vector

$$\Delta a_t = [\Delta\mu_f, \Delta\sigma_f, \Delta\mu_\vartheta, \Delta\sigma_\vartheta]. \tag{6}$$

The four policy functions and the evaluation function are each stored using a CMAC table. This technique is a form of coarse-coding whereby the euclidean space in which a function lies is divided into a set of overlapping but offset tilings. Each tiling consists of regular regions of pre-defined size such that all points within each region are mapped to a single stored parameter. The value of the function at any point is given by the average of the parameters stored for the corresponding regions in all of the tilings. In our

---

[1] In practice we use (ln s) as the second adjustable parameter to ensure that the standard deviation of the gaussian never has a negative value (see Williams 1988 for details).

simulation each sensory dimension is quantised into five discrete bins resulting in a 5X5X5 tiling, five tilings are overlaid to form each CMAC. If the input space is enlarged (perhaps by adding further sensors) the storage requirements can be reduced by using a hashing function to map all the tiles onto a smaller number of parameters. This is a useful economy when there are large areas of the state space that are visited rarely or not at all.

4   EXPLORATION

In order for the sprite to learn useful obstacle avoidance behaviour it has to move around and explore its environment. If the sprite is rewarded simply for avoiding collisions an optimal strategy would be to remain still or to stay within a small, safe, circular orbit. Therefore to force the sprite to explore its world a second source of reinforcement is used which is a function of its current forward velocity and encourages it to maintain an optimal speed. To further promote adventurous behaviour the initial policy over the whole state-space is for the sprite to have a positive speed. A system which has a high initial expectation of future rewards will settle less rapidly for a locally optimal solution than a one with a low expectation.   Therefore the value function is set initially to the maximum reward attainable by the sprite.

Improved policies are found by deviating from the currently preferred set of actions. However, there is a trade-off to be made between exploiting the existing policy to maximise the short term reward and experimenting with untried actions that have potentially negative consequences but may eventually lead to a better policy.   This suggests that an annealing process should be applied to the degree of noise in the policy. In fact, the algorithm described above results in an automatic annealing process (Williams 88) since the variance of each gaussian element decreases as the mean behaviour converges to a local maximum. However, the width of each gaussian can also increase, if the mean is locally sub-optimal, allowing for more exploratory behaviour. The final width of the gaussian depends on whether the local peak in the action function is narrow or flat on top. The behaviour acquired by the system is therefore more than a set of simple reflexes. Rather, for each circumstance, there is a range of acceptable actions which is narrow if the robot is in a tight corner, where its behaviour is severely constrained, but wider in more open spaces.

5   RESULTS

To test the effectiveness of the learning algorithm the performance of the sprite was compared before and after fifty-thousand training steps on a number of simple environments. Over 10 independent runs[2] in the first environment shown in figure one the average distance travelled between collisions rose from approximately 0.9m (1b) before learning to 47.4m (1c) after training. At the same time the average velocity more than doubled to just below the optimal speed. The requirement of maintaining an optimum speed encourages the sprite to follow trajectories that avoid slowing down, stopping or reversing. However, if the sprite is placed too close to an obstacle to turn away safely, it can perform an n-point-turn manoeuvre requiring it to stop, back-off, turn and then move forward. It is thus capable of generating quite complex sequences of actions.

[2]Each measure was calculated over a sequence of five thousand simulation-steps with learning disabled.

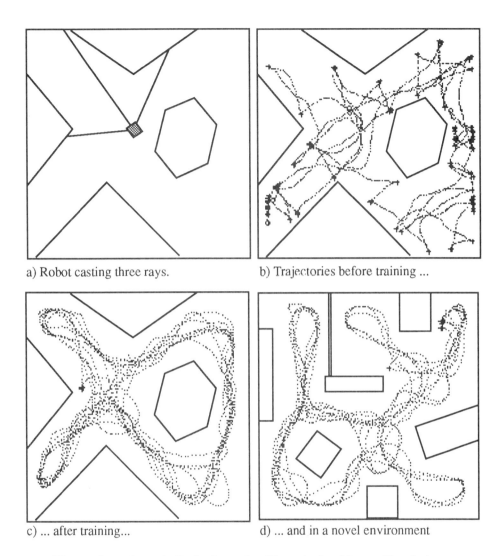

a) Robot casting three rays.

b) Trajectories before training ...

c) ... after training...

d) ... and in a novel environment

Figure One: Sample Paths from the Obstacle Avoidance Simulation.

The trajectories show the robot's movement over two thousand simulation steps before and after training.   After a collision the robot reverses slightly then rotates to move off at a random angle 90-180° from its original heading, if this is not possible it is relocated to a random position. Crosses indicate locations where collisions occured, circles show new starting positions.

Some differences have been found in the sprite's ability to negotiate different environments with the effectiveness of the avoidance learning system varying for different configurations of obstacles. However, only limited performance loss has been observed in transferring from a learned environment to an unseen one (eg. figure 1d), which is quickly made up if the sprite is allowed to adapt its strategies to suit the new circumstances. Hence we are encouraged to think that the learning system is capturing some fairly general strategies for obstacle avoidance.

The different kinds of tactical behaviour acquired by the sprite can be illustrated using three dimensional slices through the two policy functions (desired forward and angular velocities). Figure two shows samples of these functions recorded after fifty thousand training steps in an environment containing two slow moving rectangular obstacles. Each graph is a function of the three rays cast out by the sprite: the x and y axes show the depths of the left and right rays and the vertical slices correspond to different depths of the central ray (9, 35 and 74cm). The graphs show clearly several features that we might expect of effective avoidance behaviour. Most notably, there is a transition occuring over the three slices during which the policy changes from one of braking then reversing (graph a) to one of turning sharply (d) whilst maintaining speed or accelerating (e). This transition clearly corresponds to the threshold below which a collision cannot be avoided by swerving but requires backing-off instead. There is a considerable degree of left-right symmetry (reflection along the line left-ray=right-ray) in most of the graphs. This agrees with the observation that obstacle avoidance is by and large a symmetric problem. However some asymmetric behaviour is acquired in order to break the deadlock that arises when the sprite is faced with obstacles that are equidistant on both sides.

6   CONCLUSION

We have demonstrated that complex obstacle avoidance behaviour can arise from sequences of learned reactions to immediate perceptual stimuli. The trajectories generated often have the appearance of planned activity since individual actions are only appropriate as part of extended patterns of movement. However, planning only occurs as an implicit part of a learning process that allows experience of rewarding outcomes to be propagated backwards to influence future actions taken in similar contexts. This learning process is effective because it is able to exploit the underlying regularities in the robot's interaction with its world to find behaviours that consistently achieve its goals.

Acknowledgements

This work was supported by the Science and Engineering Research Council.

References

Albus, J.S., (1971) A theory of cerebellar function. *Math Biosci* 10:25-61.

Anderson, T.L., and Donath, M. (1988a) Synthesis of reflexive behaviour for a mobile robot based upon a stimulus-response paradigm. *SPIE Mobile Robots III*, 1007:198-210.

Anderson, T.L., and Donath, M. (1988b) A computational structure for enforcing reactive behaviour in a mobile robot. *SPIE Mobile Robots III* 1007:370-382.

Barto, A.G., Sutton, R.S., and Brouwer, P.S. (1981) Associative search network: A reinforcement learning associative memory". *Biological Cybernetics* 40:201-211.

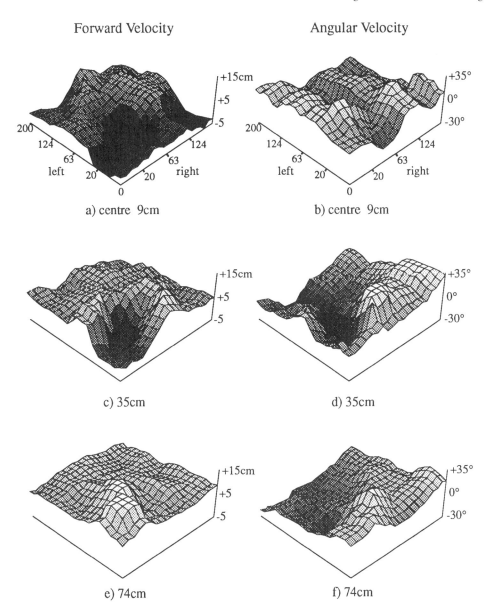

Figure Two: Surfaces showing action policies for depth measures
for the central ray of 9, 35 and 74 cm.

Barto, A.G., Anderson, C.W., and Sutton, R.S.(1982) Synthesis of nonlinear control surfaces by a layered associative search network. *Biological Cybernetics* 43:175-185.

Barto, A.G., Sutton, R.S., Anderson, C.W. (1983) Neuronlike adaptive elements that can solve difficult learning control problems. *IEEE Transactions on Systems, Man, and Cybernbetics* SMC-13:834-846.

Barto, A.G., Sutton, R.S., and Watkins, C.J.H.C (1989) Learning and sequential decision making. *COINS technical report.*

Braitenberg, V (1986) *Vehicles: experiments in synthetic psychology*, MIT Press, Cambridge, MA.

Chapman, D. and Agre, P.E. (1987) Pengi: An implementation of a theory of activity. AAAI-87.

Simon, H.A. (1969) *The sciences of the artificial.* MIT Press, Cambridge, Massachusetts.

Sutton, R.S. and Barto, A.G. (1990) Time-deriviative models of pavlovian reinforcement. in Moore, J.W., and Gabriel, M. (eds.) *Learning and Computational Neuroscience*, MIT Press, Cambridge, MA.

Watkins, C.J.H.C (1989) *Learning from delayed rewards.* Phd thesis, King's College, Cambridge University, UK.

Werbos, P.J. (1990) A menu of designs for reinforcement learning over time. in Millet, III, W.T., Sutton, R.S. and Werbos, P.J. *Neural networks for control*, MIT Press, Cambridge, MA.

Williams R.J., (1988) Towards a theory of reinforcement-learning connectionist systems. Technical Report NU-CCS-88-3, College of Computer Science, Northeastern University, Boston, MA.

Active Exploration in Dynamic Environments

Sebastian B. Thrun
School of Computer Science
Carnegie Mellon University
Pittsburgh, PA 15213
E-mail: thrun@cs.cmu.edu

Knut Möller
University of Bonn
Dept. of Computer Science
Römerstr. 164
D-5300 Bonn, Germany

Abstract

Whenever an agent learns to control an unknown environment, two opposing principles have to be combined, namely: *exploration* (long-term optimization) and *exploitation* (short-term optimization). Many real-valued connectionist approaches to learning control realize exploration by randomness in action selection. This might be disadvantageous when costs are assigned to "negative experiences". The basic idea presented in this paper is to make an agent explore unknown regions in a more directed manner. This is achieved by a so-called *competence map*, which is trained to predict the controller's accuracy, and is used for guiding exploration. Based on this, a bistable system enables smoothly switching attention between two behaviors – exploration and exploitation – depending on expected costs and knowledge gain.
The appropriateness of this method is demonstrated by a simple robot navigation task.

INTRODUCTION

The need for exploration in adaptive control has been recognized by various authors [MB89, Sut90, Moo90, Sch90, BBS91]. Many connectionist approaches (e.g. [Mel89, MB89]) distinguish a *random exploration phase*, at which a controller is constructed by generating actions randomly, and a subsequent *exploitation phase*. Random exploration usually suffers from three major disadvantages:

- Whenever *costs* are assigned to certain experiences – which is the case for various real-world tasks such as autonomous robot learning, chemical control, flight control etc. –, exploration may become unnecessarily expensive. Intuitively speaking, a child would burn itself again and again simply because it is

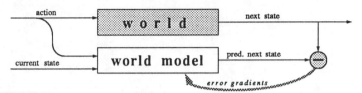

Figure 1: The training of the model network is a system identification task. Weights and biases of the network are estimated by gradient descent using the backpropagation algorithm.

in its random phase.

- Random exploration is often inefficient in terms of learning time, too [Whi91, Thr92]. Random actions usually make an agent waste plenty of time in already well-explored regions in state space, while other regions may still be poorly explored. Exploration happens by chance and is thus *undirected*.

- Once the exploitation phase begins, learning is finished and the system is unable to adapt to time-varying, dynamic environments.

However, more efficient exploration techniques rely on knowledge about the learning process itself, which is used for guiding exploration. Rather than selecting actions randomly, these exploration techniques select actions such that the expected knowledge gain is maximal. In discrete domains, this may be achieved by preferring states (or state-action pairs) that have been visited less frequently [BS90], or less recently [Sut90], or have previously shown a high prediction error [Moo90, Sch91][1]. For various discrete deterministic domains such exploration heuristics have been proved to prevent from exponential learning time [Thr92] (exponential in size of the state space). However, such techniques require a variable associated with each state-action pair, which is not feasible if states and actions are real-valued.

A novel real-valued generalization of these approaches is presented in this paper. A so-called *competence map* estimates the controller's accuracy. Using this estimation, the agent is driven into regions in state space with low accuracy, where the resulting learning effect is assumed to be maximal. This technique defines a *directed* exploration rule. In order to minimize costs during learning, exploration is combined with an exploitation mechanism using selective attention, which allows for switching between exploration and exploitation.

INDIRECT CONTROL USING FORWARD MODELS

In this paper we focus on an adaptive control scheme adopted from Jordan [Jor89]:

System identification (Fig. 1): Observing the input-output behavior of the unknown world (environment), a model is constructed by minimizing the difference of the observed outcome and its corresponding predictions. This is done with backpropagation.

Action search using the model network (Fig. 2): Let an actual state s and a goal state s^* be given. Optimal actions are searched using gradient descent in action space: starting with an initial action (e.g. randomly chosen), the next state

---

[1]Note that these two approaches [Moo90, Sch91] are real-valued.

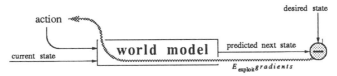

Figure 2: Using the model for optimizing actions (exploitation). Starting with some initial action, gradient descent through the model network progressively improves actions.

$\hat{s}$ is predicted with the world model. The *exploitation energy function*

$$E_{\text{exploit}} \;=\; (s^* - \hat{s})^T (s^* - \hat{s})$$

measures the LMS-deviation of the predicted and the desired state. Since the model network is differentiable, gradients of E_{exploit} can be propagated back through the model network. Using these gradients, actions are optimized progressively by gradient descent in action space, minimizing E_{exploit}. The resulting actions *exploit* the world.

THE COMPETENCE MAP

The general principle of many enhanced exploration schemes [BS90, Sut90, Moo90, TM91, Sch91, Thr92] is to select actions such that the resulting observations are expected to optimally improve the controller. In terms of the above control scheme, this may be realized by driving the agent into regions in state-action space where the accuracy of the model network is assumed to be low, and thus the knowledge gain by visiting these regions is assumed to be high. In order to estimate the accuracy of the model network, we introduce the notion of a *competence network* [Sch91, TM91]. Basically, this map estimates some upper bound of the LMS-error of the model network. This estimation is used for exploring the world by selecting actions which minimize the expected *competence* of the model, and thus maximize the resulting learning effect.

However, training the competence map is not as straightforward, since it is impossible to exactly predict the accuracy of the model network for regions in state space not visited for some time. The training procedure for the competence map is based on the assumption that the error increases (and thus competence decreases) slowly for such regions due to relearning and environmental dynamics:

1. At each time tick, backpropagation learning is applied using the last state-action pair as input, and the observed LMS-prediction error of the model as target value (c.f. Fig. 3), normalized to $(0, \varepsilon_{\max})$ ($0 \leq \varepsilon_{\max} \leq 1$, so far we used $\varepsilon_{\max} = 1$).

2. For some[2] randomly generated state-action pairs, the competence map is subsequently trained with target 1.0 ($\leq$ largest possible error $\varepsilon_{\max}$) [ACL+90]. This training step establishes a heuristic, realizing the loss of accuracy in unvisited regions: over time, the output values of the competence map increase for these regions.

Actions are now selected with respect to an energy function E which combines both

---

[2]in our simulations: five – with a small learning rate

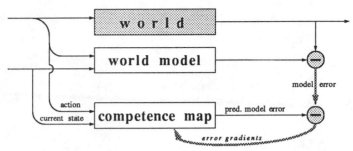

Figure 3: Training the competence map to predict the error of the model by gradient descent (see text).

exploration and exploitation:

$$E = (1-\Gamma) \cdot E_{\text{explore}} + \Gamma \cdot E_{\text{exploit}} \tag{1}$$

with gain parameter Γ ($0<\Gamma<1$). Here the *exploration energy*

$$E_{\text{explore}} = 1 - competence(action)$$

is evaluated using the competence map – minimizing E_{explore} is equivalent to maximizing the predicted model error. Since both the model net and the competence net are differentiable, gradient descent in action space may be used for minimizing Eq. (1). E combines exploration with exploitation: on the one hand minimizing E_{exploit} serves to avoid costs (short-term optimization), and on the other hand minimizing E_{explore} ensures exploration (long-term optimization). Γ determines the portion of both target functions – which can be viewed to represent behaviors – in the action selection process.

Note that ε_{max} determines the character of exploration: if ε_{max} is large, the agent is attracted by regions in state space which have previously shown *high prediction error*. The smaller ε_{max} is, the more the agent is attracted by *rarely-visited* regions.

EXPLORATION AND SELECTIVE ATTENTION

Clearly, exploration and exploitation are often conflicting and can hinder each other. E.g. if exploration and exploitation pull a mobile robot into opposite directions, the system will stay where it is. It therefore makes sense not to keep Γ constant during learning, but sometimes to focus more on exploration and sometimes more on exploitation, depending on expected costs and improvements. In our approach, this is achieved by determining the *focus of attention* Γ using the following bistable recursive function which allows for smoothly switching attention between both policies.

At each step of action search, let $e_{\text{exploit}} = \Delta E_{\text{exploit}}(a)$ and $e_{\text{explore}} = \Delta E_{\text{explore}}(a)$ denote the expected change of both energy functions by action a. With $f(\cdot)$ being a positive and monotonically increasing function[3],

$$\kappa \longleftarrow \Gamma \cdot f(e_{\text{exploit}}) - (1-\Gamma) \cdot f(e_{\text{explore}}) \tag{2}$$

compares the influence of action a on both energy functions *under the current focus of attention* Γ. The new Γ is then derived by squashing κ (with $c>0$):

$$\Gamma \longleftarrow \frac{1}{1 + e^{-c \cdot \kappa}} \tag{3}$$

---

[3] We chosed $f(x) = e^x$ in our simulations.

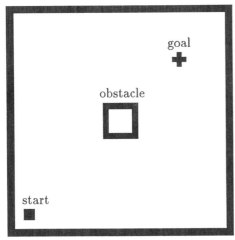
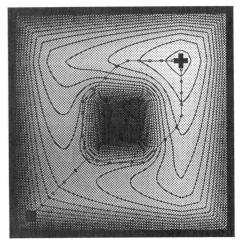

Figure 4: (a) Robot world – note that there are two equally good paths leading around the obstacle. (b) Potential field: In addition to the x-y-state vector, the environment returns for each state a *potential field value* (the darker the color, the larger the value). Gradient ascent in the potential field yields both optimal paths depicted. Learning this potential field function is part of the system identification task.

If $\kappa > 0$, the learning system is in exploitation mood and $\Gamma > 0.5$. Likewise, if $\kappa < 0$, the system is in exploration mood and $\Gamma < 0.5$. Since the actual attention Γ weighs both competing energy functions, in most cases Eqs. (2) and (3) establish two stable points (fixpoints), close to 0 and 1, respectively. Attention is switched only if κ changes its sign. The scalar c serves as *stability factor*: the larger c is, the closer is Γ to its extremal values and the larger the switching factors $\Gamma(1-\Gamma)^{-1}$ (taken from Eq. (2)).

A ROBOT NAVIGATION TASK

We now will demonstrate the benefits of active exploration using a competence map with selective attention by a simple robot navigation example. The environment is a 2-dimensional room with one obstacle and walls (see Fig. 4a), and x-y-states are evaluated by a potential field function (Fig. 4b). The goal is to navigate the robot from the start to the goal position without colliding with the obstacle or a wall.

Using a model network without hidden units for state prediction and a model with two hidden layers (10 units with gaussian activation functions in the first hidden layer, and 8 logistic units in the second) for potential field value prediction, we compared the following exploration techniques – Table 1 summarizes the results:

- **Pure random exploration.** In Fig. 5a the best result out of 20 runs is shown. The dark color in the middle indicates that the obstacle was touched extremely often. Moreover, the resulting controller (exploitation phase) did not find a path to the goal.
- **Pure exploitation** (see Fig. 5b). (With a bit of randomness in the beginning) this exploration technique found one of two paths but failed in both finding the other path and performing proper system identification. The number of crashes

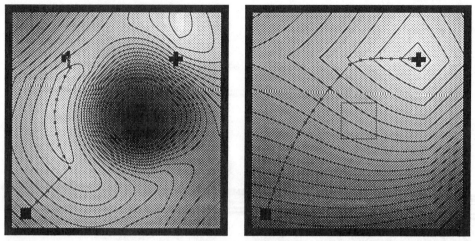

Figure 5: Resulting models of the potential field function. **(a) Random exploration**. The dark color in the middle indicates the high number of crashes against the obstacle. Note that the agent is restarted whenever it crashes against a wall or the obstacle – the probability for reaching the goal is 0.0007. **(b) Pure exploitation**: The resulting model is accurate along the path, but inaccurate elsewhere. Only one of two paths is identified.

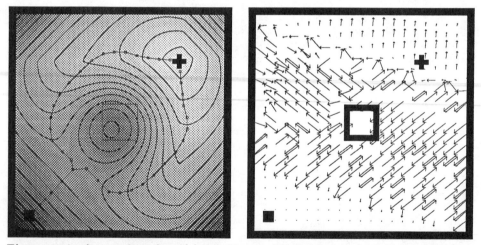

Figure 6: Active exploration. (a) Resulting model of the potential field function. This model is most accurate, and the number of crashes during training is the smallest. Both paths are found about equally often. (b) "Typical" competence map: The arrows indicate actions which maximize $E_{explore}$ (pure exploration).

	# runs	# crashes	# paths found	L_2-model error
random exploration	10 000	9 993	0	2.5 %
pure exploitation	15 000	11 000	1	0.7 %
active exploration	15 000	4 000	2	0.4 %

Table 1: Results (averaged over 20 runs). The L_2-model error is measured in relation to its initial value (= 100%).

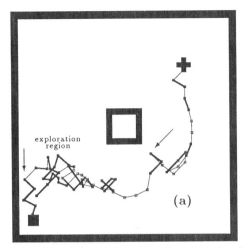
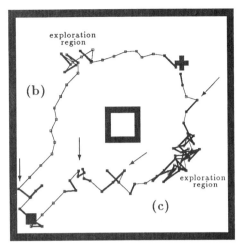

Figure 7: Three examples of trajectories during learning demonstrate the switching attention mechanism described in the paper. Thick lines indicate exploration mode ($\Gamma < 0.2$), and thin lines indicate exploitation ($\Gamma > 0.8$). The arrows mark some points where exploration is switched off due to a predicted collision.

during learning was significantly smaller than with random exploration.

- **Directed exploration with selective attention.** Using a competence network with two hidden layers (6 units each hidden layer), a proper model was found in all simulations we performed (Fig. 6a), and the number of collisions were the least. An intermediate state of the competence map is depicted in Fig. 6b, and three exploration runs are shown in Fig. 7.

DISCUSSION

We have presented an adaptive strategy for efficient exploration in non-discrete environments. A so-called competence map is trained to estimate the competence (error) of the world model, and is used for driving the agent to less familiar regions. In order to avoid unnecessary exploration costs, a selective attention mechanism switches between exploration and exploitation. The resulting learning system is dynamic in the sense that whenever one particular region in state space is preferred for several runs, sooner or later the exploration behavior forces the agent to leave this region. Benefits of this exploration technique have been demonstrated on a robot navigation task.

However, it should be noted that the exploration method presented seeks to explore more or less the *whole* state-action space. This may be reasonable for the above robot navigation task, but many state spaces, e.g. those typically found in traditional AI, are too large for getting exhaustively explored even once. In order to deal with such spaces, this method should be extended by some mechanism for cutting off exploration in "unrelevant" regions in state-action space, which may be determined by some notion of "relevance".

Note that the technique presented here does not depend on the particular control scheme at hand. E.g., some exploration techniques in the context of reinforcement learning may be found in [Sut90, BBS91], and are surveyed and compared in [Thr92].

Acknowledgements

The authors wish to thank Jonathan Bachrach, Andy Barto, Jörg Kindermann, Long-Ji Lin, Alexander Linden, Tom Mitchell, Andy Moore, Satinder Singh, Don Sofge, Alex Waibel, and the reinforcement learning group at CMU for interesting and fruitful discussions. S. Thrun gratefully acknowledges the support by German National Research Center for Computer Science (GMD) where part of the research was done, and also the financial support from Siemens Corp.

References

[ACL+90] L. Atlas, D. Cohn, R. Ladner, M.A. El-Sharkawi, R.J. Marks, M.E. Aggoune, and D.C. Park. Training connectionist networks with queries and selective sampling. In D. Touretzky (ed.) *Advances in Neural Information Processing Systems 2*, San Mateo, CA, 1990. IEEE, Morgan Kaufmann.

[BBS91] A.G. Barto, S.J. Bradtke, and S.P. Singh. Real-time learning and control using asynchronous dynamic programming. Technical Report COINS 91-57, Department of Computer Science, University of Massachusetts, MA, Aug. 1991.

[BS90] A.G. Barto and S.P. Singh. On the computational economics of reinforcement learning. In D.S. Touretzky et al. (eds.), *Connectionist Models, Proceedings of the 1990 Summer School*, San Mateo, CA, 1990. Morgan Kaufmann.

[Jor89] M.I. Jordan. Generic constraints on underspecified target trajectories. In *Proceedings of the First International Joint Conference on Neural Networks, Washington, DC*, IEEE TAB Neural Network Committee, San Diego, 1989.

[MB89] M.C. Mozer and J.R. Bachrach. Discovering the structure of a reactive environment by exploration. Technical Report CU-CS-451-89, Dept. of Computer Science, University of Colorado, Boulder, Nov. 1989.

[Mel89] B.W. Mel. Murphy: A neurally-inspired connectionist approach to learning and performance in vision-based robot motion planning. Technical Report CCSR-89-17A, Center for Complex Systems Research Beckman Institute, University of Illinois, 1989.

[Moo90] A.W. Moore. *Efficient Memory-based Learning for Robot Control*. PhD thesis, Trinity Hall, University of Cambridge, England, 1990.

[Sch90] J.H. Schmidhuber. Making the world differentiable: On using supervised learning fully recurrent neural networks for dynamic reinforcement learning and planning in non-stationary environments. Technical Report, Technische Universität München, Germany, 1990.

[Sch91] J.H. Schmidhuber. Adaptive confidence and adaptive curiosity. Technical Report FKI-149-91, Technische Universität München, Germany 1991.

[Sut90] R.S. Sutton. Integrated architectures for learning, planning, and reacting based on approximating dynamic programming. In *Proceedings of the Seventh International Conference on Machine Learning*, June 1990.

[TM91] S.B. Thrun and K. Möller. On planning and exploration in non-discrete environments. Technical Report 528, GMD, St.Augustin, FRG, 1991.

[Thr92] S.B. Thrun. Efficient exploration in reinforcement learning. Technical Report CMU-CS-92-102, Carnegie Mellon University, Pittsburgh, Jan. 1992.

[Whi91] S.D. Whitehead. A study of cooperative mechanisms for faster reinforcement learning. Technical Report 365, University of Rochester, Computer Science Department, Rochester, NY, March 1991.

Oscillatory Neural Fields for Globally Optimal Path Planning

Michael Lemmon
Dept. of Electrical Engineering
University of Notre Dame
Notre Dame, Indiana 46556

Abstract

A neural network solution is proposed for solving path planning problems faced by mobile robots. The proposed network is a two-dimensional sheet of neurons forming a distributed representation of the robot's workspace. Lateral interconnections between neurons are "cooperative", so that the network exhibits oscillatory behaviour. These oscillations are used to generate solutions of Bellman's dynamic programming equation in the context of path planning. Simulation experiments imply that these networks locate global optimal paths even in the presence of substantial levels of circuit noise.

1 Dynamic Programming and Path Planning

Consider a 2-DOF robot moving about in a 2-dimensional world. A robot's location is denoted by the real vector, $\mathbf{p}$. The collection of all locations forms a set called the workspace. An admissible point in the workspace is any location which the robot may occupy. The set of all admissible points is called the free workspace. The free workspace's complement represents a collection of obstacles. The robot moves through the workspace along a path which is denoted by the parameterized curve, $\mathbf{p}(t)$. An admissible path is one which lies wholly in the robot's free workspace. Assume that there is an initial robot position, $\mathbf{p}_0$, and a desired final position, $\mathbf{p}_f$. The robot path planning problem is to find an admissible path with $\mathbf{p}_0$ and $\mathbf{p}_f$ as endpoints such that some "optimality" criterion is satisfied.

The path planning problem may be stated more precisely from an optimal control

539

theorist's viewpoint. Treat the robot as a dynamic system which is characterized by a state vector, $\mathbf{p}$, and a control vector, $\mathbf{u}$. For the highest levels in a control hierarchy, it can be assumed that the robot's dynamics are modeled by the differential equation, $\dot{\mathbf{p}} = \mathbf{u}$. This equation says that the state velocity equals the applied control. To define what is meant by "optimal", a performance functional is introduced.

$$J(\mathbf{u}) = ||\mathbf{p}(t_f) - \mathbf{p}_f||^2 + \int_0^{t_f} c(\mathbf{p})\mathbf{u}^t\mathbf{u}\,dt \tag{1}$$

where $||\mathbf{x}||$ is the norm of vector $\mathbf{x}$ and where the functional $c(\mathbf{p})$ is unity if $\mathbf{p}$ lies in the free workspace and is infinite otherwise. This weighting functional is used to insure that the control does not take the robot into obstacles. Equation 1's optimality criterion minimizes the robot's control effort while penalizing controls which do not satisfy the terminal constraints.

With the preceding definitions, the optimal path planning problem states that for some final time, t_f, find the control $\mathbf{u}(t)$ which minimizes the performance functional $J(\mathbf{u})$. One very powerful method for tackling this minimization problem is to use dynamic programming (Bryson, 1975). According to dynamic programming, the optimal control, $\mathbf{u}_{opt}$, is obtained from the gradient of an "optimal return function", $J^o(\mathbf{p})$. In other words, $\mathbf{u}_{opt} = \nabla J^o$. The optimal return functional satisfies the Hamilton-Jacobi-Bellman (HJB) equation. For the dynamic optimization problem given above, the HJB equation is easily shown to be

$$\frac{\partial J^o}{\partial t} = \begin{cases} -\frac{1}{4}(\nabla J^o)^t(\nabla J^o) & c(\mathbf{p}) = 1 \\ 0 & c(\mathbf{p}) = \infty \end{cases} \tag{2}$$

This is a first order nonlinear partial differential equation (PDE) with terminal (boundary) condition, $J^o(t_f) = ||\mathbf{p}(t_f) - \mathbf{p}_f||^2$. Once equation 2 has been solved for the J^o, then the optimal "path" is determined by following the gradient of J^o.

Solutions to equation 2 must generally be obtained numerically. One solution approach numerically integrates a full discretization of equation 2 backwards in time using the terminal condition, $J^o(t_f)$, as the starting point. The proposed numerical solution is attempting to find characteristic trajectories of the nonlinear first-order PDE. The PDE nonlinearities, however, only insure that these characteristics exist locally (i.e., in an open neighborhood about the terminal condition). The resulting numerical solutions are, therefore, only valid in a "local" sense. This is reflected in the fact that truncation errors introduced by the discretization process will eventually result in numerical solutions violating the underlying principle of optimality embodied by the HJB equation.

In solving path planning problems, local solutions based on the numerical integration of equation 2 are not acceptable due to the "local" nature of the resulting solutions. Global solutions are required and these may be obtained by solving an associated variational problem (Benton, 1977). Assume that the optimal return function at time t_f is known on a closed set B. The variational solution for equation 2 states that the optimal return at time $t < t_f$ at a point $\mathbf{p}$ in the neighborhood of the boundary set B will be given by

$$J^o(\mathbf{p}, t) = \min_{\mathbf{y} \in B} \left\{ J^o(\mathbf{y}, t_f) + \frac{||\mathbf{p} - \mathbf{y}||^2}{(t_f - t)} \right\} \tag{3}$$

where $||\mathbf{p}||$ denotes the L_2 norm of vector $\mathbf{p}$. Equation 3 is easily generalized to other vector norms and only applies in regions where $c(\mathbf{p}) = 1$ (i.e. the robot's free workspace). For obstacles, $J^o(\mathbf{p}, t) = J^o(\mathbf{p}, t_f)$ for all $t < t_f$. In other words, the optimal return is unchanged in obstacles.

2   Oscillatory Neural Fields

The proposed neural network consists of MN neurons arranged as a 2-d sheet called a "neural field". The neurons are put in a one-to-one correspondence with the ordered pairs, (i, j) where $i = 1, \ldots, N$ and $j = 1, \ldots, M$. The ordered pair (i, j) will sometimes be called the (i, j)th neuron's "label". Associated with the (i, j)th neuron is a set of neuron labels denoted by $\mathbf{N}_{i,j}$. The neurons' whose labels lie in $\mathbf{N}_{i,j}$ are called the "neighbors" of the (i, j)th neuron.

The (i, j)th neuron is characterized by two states. The short term activity (STA) state, $x_{i,j}$, is a scalar representing the neuron's activity in response to the currently applied stimulus. The long term activity (LTA) state, $w_{i,j}$, is a scalar representing the neuron's "average" activity in response to recently applied stimuli. Each neuron produces an output, $f(x_{i,j})$, which is a unit step function of the STA state. (i.e., $f(x) = 1$ if $x > 0$ and $f(x) = 0$ if $x \leq 0$). A neuron will be called "active" or "inactive" if its output is unity or zero, respectively.

Each neuron is also characterized by a set of constants. These constants are either externally applied inputs or internal parameters. They are the disturbance $y_{i,j}$, the rate constant $\lambda_{i,j}$, and the position vector $\mathbf{p}_{i,j}$. The position vector is a 2-d vector mapping the neuron onto the robot's workspace. The rate constant models the STA state's underlying dynamic time constant. The rate constant is used to encode whether or not a neuron maps onto an obstacle in the robot's workspace. The external disturbance is used to initiate the network's search for the optimal path.

The evolution of the STA and LTA states is controlled by the state equations. These equations are assumed to change in a synchronous fashion. The STA state equation is

$$x_{i,j}^+ = G\left(x_{i,j}^- + \lambda_{i,j} y_{i,j} + \lambda_{i,j} \sum_{(k,l) \in \mathbf{N}_{i,j}} D_{kl} f(x_{k,l})\right) \tag{4}$$

where the summation is over all neurons contained within the neighborhood, $\mathbf{N}_{i,j}$, of the (i, j)th neuron. The function $G(x)$ is zero if $x < 0$ and is x if $x \geq 0$. This function is used to prevent the neuron's activity level from falling below zero. D_{kl} are network parameters controlling the strength of lateral interactions between neurons. The LTA state equation is

$$w_{i,j}^+ = w_{i,j}^- + |f'(x_{i,j})| \tag{5}$$

Equation 5 means that the LTA state is incremented by one every time the (i, j)th neuron's output changes.

Specific choices for the interconnection weights result in oscillatory behaviour. The specific network under consideration is a cooperative field where $D_{kl} = 1$ if $(k, l) \neq$

(i, j) and $D_{kl} = -A < 0$ if $(k, l) = (i, j)$. Without loss of generality it will also be assumed that the external disturbances are bounded between zero and one. It is also assumed that the rate constants, $\lambda_{i,j}$ are either zero or unity. In the path planning application, rate constants will be used to encode whether or not a given neuron represents an obstacle or a point in the free-workspace. Consequently, any neuron where $\lambda_{i,j} = 0$ will be called an "obstacle" neuron and any neuron where $\lambda_{i,j} = 1$ will be called a "free-space" neuron. Under these assumptions, it has been shown (Lemmon, 1991a) that once a free-space neuron turns active it will be oscillating with a period of 2 provided it has at least one free-space neuron as a neighbor.

3   Path Planning and Neural Fields

The oscillatory neural field introduced above can be used to generate solutions of the Bellman iteration (Eq. 3) with respect to the supremum norm. Assume that all neuron STA and LTA states are zero at time 0. Assume that the position vectors form a regular grid of points, $\mathbf{p}_{i,j} = (i\Delta, j\Delta)^t$ where Δ is a constant controlling the grid's size. Assume that all external disturbances but one are zero. In other words, for a specific neuron with label (i, j), $y_{k,l} = 1$ if $(k, l) = (i, j)$ and is zero otherwise. Also assume a neighborhood structure where $\mathbf{N}_{i,j}$ consist of the (i, j)th neuron and its eight nearest neighbors, $\mathbf{N}_{i,j} = \{(i + k, j + l); k = -1, 0, 1; l = -1, 0, 1\}$. WIth these assumptions it has been shown (Lemmon, 1991a) that the LTA state for the (i, j)th neuron at time n will be given by $G(n - \rho_{kl})$ where ρ_{kl} is the length of the shortest path from $\mathbf{p}_{k,l}$ and $\mathbf{p}_{i,j}$ with respect to the supremum norm.

This fact can be seen quite clearly by examining the LTA state's dynamics in a small closed neighborhood about the (k, l)th neuron. First note that the LTA state equation simply increments the LTA state by one every time the neuron's STA state toggles its output. Since a neuron oscillates after it has been initially activated, the LTA state, will represent the time at which the neuron was first activated. This time, in turn, will simply be the "length" of the shortest path from the site of the initial distrubance. In particular, consider the neighborhood set for the (k, l)th neuron and let's assume that the (k, l)th neuron has not yet been activated. If the neighbor has been activated, with an LTA state of a given value, then we see that the (k, l)th neuron will be activated on the next cycle and we have

$$w_{k,l} = \max_{(m,n) \in \mathbf{N}_{k,l}} \left(w_{m,n} - \frac{\|\mathbf{p}_{k,l} - \mathbf{p}_{m,n}\|_\infty}{\Delta} \right) \tag{6}$$

This is simply a dual form of the Bellman iteration shown in equation 3. In other words, over the free-space neurons, we can conclude that the network is solving the Bellman equation with respect to the supremum norm.

In light of the preceding discussion, the use of cooperative neural fields for path planning is straightforward. First apply a disturbance at the neuron mapping onto the desired terminal position, $\mathbf{p}_f$ and allow the field to generate STA oscillations. When the neuron mapping onto the robot's current position is activated, stop the oscillatory behaviour. The resulting LTA state distribution for the (i, j)th neuron equals the negative of the minimum distance (with respect to the sup norm) from that neuron to the initial disturbance. The optimal path is then generated by a sequence of controls which ascends the gradient of the LTA state distribution.

fig 1. STA activity waves   fig 2. LTA distribution

Several simulations of the cooperative neural path planner have been implemented. The most complex case studied by these simulations assumed an array of 100 by 100 neurons. Several obstacles of irregular shape and size were randomly distributed over the workspace. An initial disturbance was introduced at the desired terminal location and STA oscillations were observed. A snapshot of the neuronal outputs is shown in figure 1. This figure clearly shows wavefronts of neuronal activity propagating away from the initial disturbance (neuron (70,10) in the upper right hand corner of figure 1). The "activity" waves propagate around obstacles without any reflections. When the activity waves reach the neuron mapping onto the robot's current position, the STA oscillations were turned off. The LTA distribution resulting from this particular simulation run is shown in figure 2. In this figure, light regions denote areas of large LTA state and dark regions denote areas of small LTA state.

The generation of the optimal path can be computed as the robot is moving towards its goal. Let the robot's current position be the (i, j)th neuron's position vector. The robot will then generate a control which takes it to the position associated with one of the (i, j)th neuron's neighbors. In particular, the control is chosen so that the robot moves to the neuron whose LTA state is largest in the neighborhood set, $\mathbf{N}_{i,j}$. In other words, the next position vector to be chosen is $\mathbf{p}_{k,l}$ such that its LTA state is

$$w_{k,l} = \max_{(x,y) \in \mathbf{N}_{i,j}} w_{x,y} \tag{7}$$

Because of the LTA distribution's optimality property, this local control strategy is guaranteed to generate the optimal path (with respect to the sup norm) connecting the robot to its desired terminal position. It should be noted that the selection of the control can also be done with an analog neural network. In this case, the LTA states of neurons in the neighborhood set, $\mathbf{N}_{i,j}$ are used as inputs to a competitively inhibited neural net. The competitive interactions in this network will always select the direction with the largest LTA state.

Since neuronal dynamics are analog in nature, it is important to consider the impact of noise on the implementation. Analog systems will generally exhibit noise levels with effective dynamic ranges being at most 6 to 8 bits. Noise can enter the network in several ways. The LTA state equation can have a noise term (LTA noise), so that the LTA distribution may deviate from the optimal distribution. In our experiments, we assumed that LTA noise was additive and white. Noise may also enter in the selection of the robot's controls (selection noise). In this case, the robot's next position is the position vector, $\mathbf{p}_{k,l}$ such that $w_{k,l} = \max_{(x,y)\in\mathbf{N}_{i,j}}(w_{x,y} + v_{x,y})$ where $v_{x,y}$ is an i.i.d array of stochastic processes. Simulation results reported below assume that the noise processes, $v_{x,y}$, are positive and uniformly distributed i.i.d. processes. The introduction of noise places constraints on the "quality" of individual neurons, where quality is measured by the neuron's effective dynamic range. Two sets of simulation experiments have been conducted to assess the neural field's dynamic range requirements. In the following simulations, dynamic range is defined by the equation $-\log_2 |v_m|$, where $|v_m|$ is the maximum value the noise process can take. The unit for this measure of dynamic range is "bits".

The first set of simulation experiments selected robotic controls in a noisy fashion. Figure 3 shows the paths generated by a simulation run where the signal to noise ratio was 1 (0 bits). The results indicate that the impact of "selection" noise is to "confuse" the robot so it takes longer to find the desired terminal point. The path shown in figures 3 represents a random walk about the true optimal path. The important thing to note about this example is that the system is capable of tolerating extremely large amounts of "selection" noise.

The second set of simulation experiments introduced LTA noise. These noise experiments had a detrimental effect on the robot's path planning abilities in that several spurious extremals were generated in the LTA distribution. The result of the spurious extremals is to fool the robot into thinking it has reached its terminal destination when in fact it has not. As noise levels increase, the number of spurious states increase. Figure 4, shows how this increase varies with the neuron's effective dynamic range. The surprising thing about this result is that for neurons with as little as 3 bits of effective dynamic range the LTA distribution is free of spurious maxima. Even with less than 3 bits of dynamic range, the performance degradation is not catastrophic. LTA noise may cause the robot to stop early; but upon stopping the robot is closer to the desired terminal state. Therefore, the path planning module can be easily run again and because the robot is closer to its goal there will be a greater probability of success in the second trial.

4   Extensions and Conclusions

This paper reported on the use of oscillatory neural networks to solve path planning problems. It was shown that the proposed neural field can compute dynamic programming solutions to path planning problems with respect to the supremeum norm. Simulation experiments showed that this approach exhibited low sensitivity

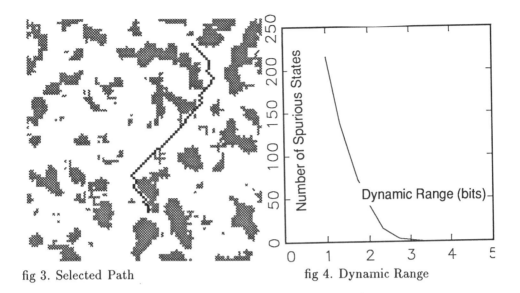

fig 3. Selected Path   fig 4. Dynamic Range

to noise, thereby supporting the feasibility of analog VLSI implementations.

The work reported here is related to resistive grid approaches for solving optimization problems (Chua, 1984). Resistive grid approaches may be viewed as "passive" relaxation methods, while the oscillatory neural field is an "active" approach. The primary virtue of the "active" approach lies in the network's potential to control the optimization criterion by selecting the interconnections and rate constants. In this paper and (Lemmon, 1991a), lateral interconnections were chosen to induce STA state oscillations and this choice yields a network which solves the Bellman equation with respect to the supremum norm. A slight modification of this model is currently under investigation in which the neuron's dynamics directly realize the iteration of equation 6 with respect to more general path metrics. This analog network is based on an SIMD approach originally proposed in (Lemmon, 1991). Results for this field are shown in figures 5 and 6. These figures show paths determined by networks utilizing different path metrics. In figure 5, the network penalizes movement in all directions equally. In figure 6, there is a strong penalty for horizontal or vertical movements. As a result of these penalties (which are implemented directly in the interconnection constants D_{kl}), the two networks' "optimal" paths are different. The path in figure 6 shows a clear preference for making diagonal rather than vertical or horizontal moves. These results clearly demonstrate the ability of an "active" neural field to solve path planning problems with respect to general path metrics. These different path metrics, of course, represent constraints on the system's path planning capabilities and as a result suggest that "active" networks may provide a systematic way of incorporating holonomic and nonholonomic constraints into the path planning process.

A final comment must be made on the apparent complexity of this approach.

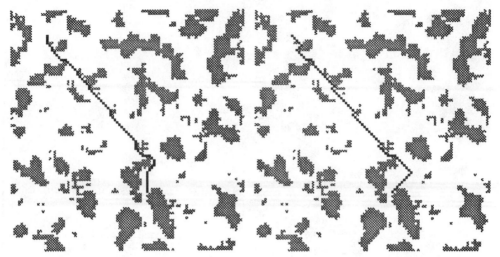

fig 5. No Direction Favored   fig 6. Diagonal Direction Favored

Clearly, if this method is to be of practical significance, it must be extended beyond the 2-DOF problem to arbitrary task domains. This extension, however, is nontrivial due to the "curse of dimensionality" experienced by straightforward applications of dynamic programming. An important area of future research therefore addresses the decomposition of real-world tasks into smaller subtasks which are amenable to the solution methodology proposed in this paper.

Acknowledgements

I would like to acknowledge the partial financial support of the National Science Foundation, grant number NSF-IRI-91-09298.

References

S.H. Benton Jr., (1977) *The Hamilton-Jacobi equation: A Global Approach.* Academic Press.

A.E. Bryson and Y.C. Ho, (1975) *Applied Optimal Control*, Hemisphere Publishing. Washington D.C.

L.O. Chua and G.N. Lin, (1984) Nonlinear programming without computation, *IEEE Trans. Circuits Syst.*, **CAS-31**:182-188

M.D. Lemmon, (1991) Real time optimal path planning using a distributed computing paradigm, *Proceedings of the Americal Control Conference*, Boston, MA, June 1991.

M.D. Lemmon, (1991a) 2-Degree-of-Freedom Robot Path Planning using Cooperative Neural Fields. *Neural Computation* 3(3):350-362.

Recognition of Manipulated Objects by Motor Learning

Hiroaki Gomi   **Mitsuo Kawato**
ATR Auditory and Visual Perception Research Laboratories,
Inui-dani, Sanpei-dani, Seika-cho, Soraku-gun, Kyoto 619-02, Japan

Abstract

We present two neural network controller learning schemes based on *feedback-error-learning* and modular architecture for recognition and control of multiple manipulated objects. In the first scheme, a Gating Network is trained to acquire object-specific representations for recognition of a number of objects (or sets of objects). In the second scheme, an Estimation Network is trained to acquire function-specific, rather than object-specific, representations which directly estimate physical parameters. Both recognition networks are trained to identify manipulated objects using somatic and/or visual information. After learning, appropriate motor commands for manipulation of each object are issued by the control networks.

1 INTRODUCTION

Conventional feedforward neural-network controllers (Barto et al., 1983; Psaltis et al., 1987; Kawato et al., 1987, 1990; Jordan, 1988; Katayama & Kawato, 1991) can not cope with multiple or changeable manipulated objects or disturbances because they cannot change immediately the control law corresponding to the object. In interaction with manipulated objects or, in more general terms, in interaction with an environment which contains unpredictable factor, feedback information is essential for control and object recognition. From these considerations, Gomi & Kawato (1990) have examined the adaptive feedback controller learning schemes using *feedback-error-learning*, from which *impedance control* (Hogan, 1985) can be obtained automatically. However, in that scheme, some higher system needs to supervise the setting of the appropriate mechanical impedance for each manipulated object or environment.

In this paper, we introduce semi-feedforward control schemes using neural networks which receive feedback and/or feedforward information for recognition of multiple manipulated objects based on *feedback-error-learning* and modular network architecture. These schemes have two advantages over previous ones as follows. (1) Learning is achieved without the

547

exact target motor command vector, which is unavailable during supervised motor learning. (2) Although somatic information alone was found to be sufficient to recognize objects, object identification is predictive and more reliable when both somatic and visual information are used.

2 RECOGNITION OF MANIPULATED OBJECTS

The most important issues in object manipulation are (1) how to recognize the manipulated object and (2) how to achieve uniform performance for different objects. There are several ways to acquire helpful information for recognizing manipulated objects. Visual information and somatic information (performance by motion) are most informative for object recognition for manipulation.

The physical characteristics useful for object manipulation such as mass, softness and slipperiness, can not be predicted without the experience of manipulating similar objects. In this respect, object recognition for manipulation should be learned through object manipulation.

3 MODULAR ARCHITECTURE USING GATING NETWORK

Jacobs et al. (1990, 1991) and Nowlan & Hinton (1990, 1991) have proposed a competitive modular network architecture which is applied to the task decomposition problem or classification problems. Jacobs (1991) applied this network architecture to the multi-payload robotics task in which each expert network controller is trained for each category of manipulated objects in terms of the object's mass. In his scheme, the payload's identity is fed to the gating network to select a suitable expert network which acts as a feedforward controller.

We examined modular network architecture using *feedback-error-learning* for simultaneous learning of object recognition and control task as shown in Fig.1.

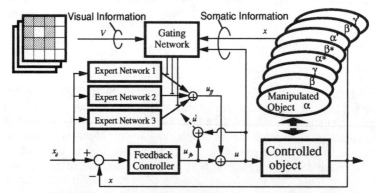

Fig.1 Configuration of the modular architecture using Gating Network for object manipulation based on feedback-error-learning

In this learning scheme, the quasi-target vector for combined output of expert networks is employed instead of the exact target vector. This is because it is unlikely that the exact target motor command vector can be provided in learning. The quasi-target vector of feedforward motor command, u' is produced by :

$$u' = u + u_{fb}. \tag{1}$$

Here, u denotes the previous final motor command and u_{fb} denotes the feedback motor command. Using this quasi-target vector, the gating and expert networks are trained to maximize the log-likelihood function, $\ln L$, by using backpropagation.

$$\ln L = \ln \sum_{i=1}^{n} g_i e^{-\|u'-u_i\|^2/2\sigma_i^2} \tag{2}$$

Here, u_i is the i th expert network output, σ_i is a variance scaling parameter of the i th expert network and g_i, the i th output of gating network, is calculated by

$$g_i = \frac{e^{s_i}}{\sum_{j=1}^{n} e^{s_j}}, \tag{3}$$

where s_i denotes the weighted input received by the i th output unit. The total output of the modular network is

$$u_{ff} = \sum_{i=1}^{n} g_i u_i . \tag{4}$$

By maximizing Eq.2 using steepest ascent method, the gating network learns to choose the expert network whose output is closest to the quasi-target command, and each expert network is tuned correctly when it is chosen by the gating network. The desired trajectory is fed to the expert networks so as to make them work as feedforward controllers.

4 SIMULATION OF OBJECT MANIPULATION BY MODULAR ARCHITECTURE WITH GATING NETWORK

We show the advantage of the learning schemes presented above by simulation results below. The configuration of the controlled object and manipulated object is shown in Fig.2 in which M, B, K respectively denote the mass, viscosity and stiffness of the coupled object (controlled- and manipulated-object). The manipulated object is changed every epoch (1 [sec]) while the coupled object is controlled to track the desired trajectory. Fig.3 shows the selected object, the feedforward and feedback motor commands, and the desired and actual trajectories before learning.

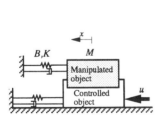

Fig.2 Configuration of the controlled object and the manipulated object

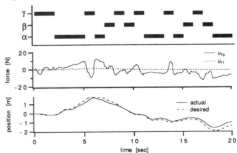

Fig.3 Temporal patterns of the selected object, the motor commands, the desired and actual trajectories before learning

The desired trajectory, x_d, was produced by Ornstein-Uhlenbeck random process. As shown in Fig.3, the error between the desired trajectory and the actual trajectory remained because the feedback controller in which the gains were fixed, was employed in this condition. (Physical characteristics of the objects used are listed in Fig.4a)

4.1 SOMATIC INFORMATION FOR GATING NETWORK

We call the actual trajectory vector, x, and the final motor command, u, "somatic information". Somatic information should be most useful for on-line (feedback) recognition of the dynamical characteristics of manipulated objects. The latest four times data of somatic information were used as the gating network inputs for identification of the coupled object in this simulation. s of Eq.3 is expressed as:

$$s(t) = \psi_1\big(x(t), x(t-1), x(t-2), x(t-3), u(t), u(t-1), u(t-2), u(t-3)\big). \quad (5)$$

The dynamical characteristics of coupled objects are shown in Fig.4a. The object was changed in every epoch (1 [sec]). The variance scaling parameter was $\sigma_i = 0.8$ and the learning rates were $\eta_{gate} = 1.0 \times 10^{-3}$ and $\eta_{expert\,i} = 1.0 \times 10^{-5}$. The three-layered feedforward neural network (input 16, hidden 30, output 3) was employed for the gating network and the two-layered linear networks (input 3, output 1) were used for the expert networks.

Comparing the expert's weights after learning and the coupled object characteristics in Fig.4a, we realize that expert networks No.1, No.2, No.3 obtained the inverse dynamics of coupled objects γ, β, α, respectively. The time variation of object, the gating network outputs, motor commands and trajectories after learning are shown in Fig.4b. The gating network outputs for the objects responded correctly in the most of the time and the feedback motor command, u_{fb}, was almost zero. As a consequence of adaptation, the actual trajectory almost perfectly corresponded with the desired trajectory.

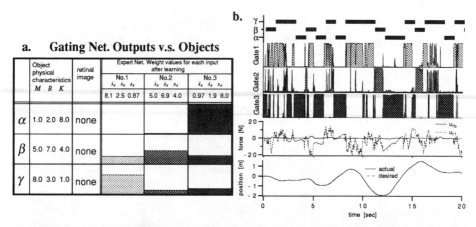

a.   Gating Net. Outputs v.s. Objects

Object physical characteristics $M\ B\ K$	retinal image	Expert Net. Weight values for each input after learning No.1 $\ddot{x}_t\ \dot{x}_t\ x_t$	No.2 $\ddot{x}_t\ \dot{x}_t\ x_t$	No.3 $\ddot{x}_t\ \dot{x}_t\ x_t$
		8.1 2.5 0.87	5.0 6.9 4.0	0.97 1.9 8.0
α 1.0 2.0 8.0	none			
β 5.0 7.0 4.0	none			
γ 8.0 3.0 1.0	none			

Fig.4 Somatic information for gating network, a. Statistical analysis of the correspondence of the expert networks with each object after learning (averaged gating outputs), **b.** Temporal patterns of objects, gating outputs, motor commands and trajectories after learning

4.2 VISUAL INFORMATION FOR GATING NETWORK

We usually assume the manipulated object's characteristics by using visual information. Visual information might be helpful for feedforward recognition. In this case, s of Eq.3 is expressed as:

$$s(t) = \psi_2\big(V(t)\big) \ . \quad (6)$$

We used three visual cues corresponding to each coupled object in this simulation as shown in Fig.5a. At each epoch in this simulation, one of three visual cues selected randomly is randomly placed at one of four possible locations on a 4×4 retinal matrix.

The visual cues of each object are different, but object α and $\alpha*$ have the same dynamical characteristics as shown in Fig.5a. The gating network should identify the object and select a suitable expert network for feedforward control by using this visual information. The learning coefficients were $\sigma_i = 0.7$, $\eta_{gate} = 1.0 \times 10^{-3}$, $\eta_{expert\ i} = 1.0 \times 10^{-5}$. The same networks used in above experiment were used in this simulation.

After learning, the expert network No.2 acquired the inverse dynamics of object α and $\alpha*$, and expert network No.3 accomplished this for object γ. It is recognized from Fig.5b that the gating network almost perfectly selected expert network No.2 for object α and $\alpha*$, and almost perfectly selected expert network No.3 for object γ. Expert network No.1 which did not acquire inverse dynamics corresponding to any of the three objects, was not selected in the test period after learning. The actual trajectory in the test period corresponded almost perfectly to the desired trajectory.

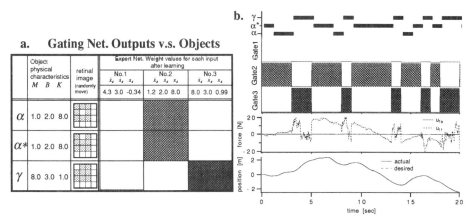

Fig. 5 Visual information for gating network, a. Statistical analysis of the correspondence of the expert networks with each object after learning (averaged gating outputs), **b.** Temporal patterns of objects, gating outputs, motor commands and trajectories after learning

4.3 SOMATIC & VISUAL INFORMATION FOR GATING NETWORK

We show here the simulation results by using both of somatic and visual information as the gating network inputs. In this case, s of Eq.3 is represented as:

$$s(t) = \psi_3\big(x(t),\cdots,x(t-3),u(t),\cdots,u(t-3),V(t)\big). \tag{7}$$

In this simulation, the object α and $\beta*$ had different dynamical characteristics, but shared same visual cue as listed in Fig.6a. Thus, to identify the coupled object one by one, it is necessary for the gating network to utilize not only visual information but also somatic information. The learning coefficients were $\sigma_i = 1.0$, $\eta_{gate} = 1.0 \times 10^{-3}$ and $\eta_{expert\ i} = 1.0 \times 10^{-5}$. The gating network had 32 input units, 50 hidden units, and 1 output unit, and the expert networks were the same as in the above experiment.

After learning, expert networks No.1, No.2, No.3 acquired the inverse dynamics of objects γ, $\beta*$, α respectively. As shown in Fig.6b, the gating network identified the object almost correctly.

a. Gating Net. Outputs v.s. Objects

Object physical characteristics M B K	retinal image (randomly move)	Expert Net. Weight values for each input after learning		
		No.1 $\ddot{x}_d$ $\dot{x}_d$ x_d	No.2 $\ddot{x}_d$ $\dot{x}_d$ x_d	No.3 $\ddot{x}_d$ $\dot{x}_d$ x_d
		8.1 2.4 0.8	5.1 6.9 4.0	1.0 1.9 8.0
α 1.0 2.0 8.0				
$\beta*$ 5.0 7.0 4.0				
γ 8.0 3.0 1.0				

b.

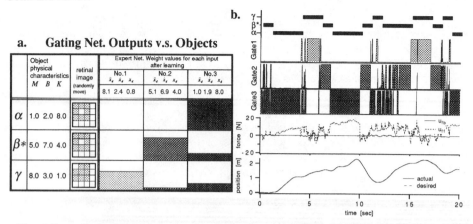

Fig. 6 Somatic & Visual information for gating network, a. Statistical analysis of the correspondence of the expert networks with each object after learning (averaged gating outputs), **b.** Temporal patterns of objects, gating outputs, motor commands and trajectories after learning

4.4 UNKNOWN OBJECT RECOGNITION BY USING SOMATIC INFORMATION

Fig.7b shows the responses for unknown objects whose physical characteristics were slightly different from known objects (see Fig.7a and Fig.4a) in the case using somatic information as the gating network inputs. Even if each tested object was not the same as any of the known (learned) objects, the closest expert network was selected. (compare Fig.4a and Fig.7a) During some period in the test phase, the feedback command increased because of an inappropriate feedforward command.

a. Gating Net. Outputs v.s. Objects

Object physical characteristics M B K	retinal image	Expert Net. Weight values for each input after learning		
		No.1 $\ddot{x}_d$ $\dot{x}_d$ x_d	No.2 $\ddot{x}_d$ $\dot{x}_d$ x_d	No.3 $\ddot{x}_d$ $\dot{x}_d$ x_d
		8.1 2.5 0.87	5.0 6.9 4.0	0.97 1.9 8.0
α' 2.0 3.0 7.0	none			
β' 4.0 6.0 5.0	none			
γ' 9.0 2.0 2.0	none			

b.

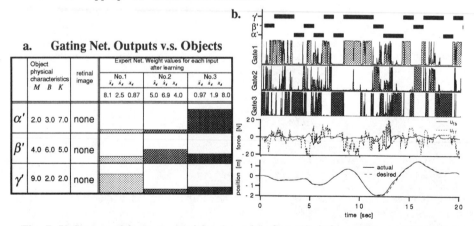

Fig. 7 Unknown objects recognition by using Somatic information, a. Statistical analysis of the correspondence of the expert networks with each object after learning (averaged gating outputs), **b.** Temporal patterns of objects, gating outputs, motor commands and trajectories after learning

5 MODULAR ARCHITECTURE
USING ESTIMATION NETWORK

The previous modular architecture is competitive in the sense that expert networks compete with each other to occupy its niche in the input space. We here propose a new cooperative modular architecture where expert networks specified for different functions cooperate to produce the required output. In this scheme, estimation networks are trained to recognize physical characteristics of manipulated objects by using feedback information. Using this method, an infinite number of manipulated objects in the limited domain can be treated by using a small number of estimation networks. We applied this method to recognizing the mass of the manipulated objects. (see Fig.8)

Fig.9a shows the output of the estimation network compared to actual masses. The realized trajectory almost coincided with the desired trajectory as shown in Fig.9b. This learning scheme can be applied not only to estimating mass but also to other physical characteristics such as softness or slipperiness.

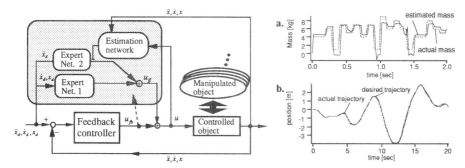

Fig. 8   Configuration of the modular architecture using mass estimation network for object manipulation by feedback-error-learning

Fig. 9 a. Comparison of actual & estimated mass, b. desired & actual trajectory

6 DISCUSSION

In the first scheme, the internal models for object manipulation (in this case, inverse dynamics) were represented not in terms of visual information but rather, of somatic information (see 4.2). Although the current simulation is primitive, it indicates the very important issue that functional internal-representations of objects (or environments), rather than declarative ones, were acquired by motor learning.

The quasi-target motor command in the first scheme and the motor command error in the second scheme are not always exactly correct in each time step because the proposed learning schemes are based on the *feedback-error-learning* method. Thus, the learning rates in the proposed schemes should be slower than those schemes in which exact target commands are employed. In our preliminary simulation, it was about five times slower. However, we emphasize that exact target motor commands are not available in supervised motor learning.

The limited number of controlled objects which can be dealt with by the modular network with a gating network is a considerable problem (Jacobs, 1991; Nowlan, 1990, 1991). This problem depends on choosing an appropriate number of expert networks and value of the variance scaling parameter, σ. Once this is done, the expert networks can interpolate the appropriate output for a number of unknown objects. Our second scheme provides a more satisfactory solution to this problem.

On the other hand, one possible drawback of the second scheme is that it may be difficult to estimate many physical parameters for complicated objects, even though the learning scheme which directly estimates the physical parameters can handle any number of objects.

We showed here basic examinations of two types of neural networks - a gating network and a direct estimation network. Both networks use feedback and/or feedforward information for recognition of multiple manipulated objects. In future, we will attempt to integrate these two architectures in order to model tasks involving skilled motor coordination and high level recognition.

Acknowledgment

We would like to thank Drs. E. Yodogawa and K. Nakane of ATR Auditory and Visual Perception Research Laboratories for their continuing encouragement. Supported by HFSP Grant to M.K.

References

Barto, A.G., Sutton, R.S., Anderson, C.W. (1983) Neuronlike adaptive elements that can solve difficult learning control problems; *IEEE Trans. on Sys. Man and Cybern.* SMC-13, pp.834-846

Gomi, H., Kawato, M. (1990) Learning control for a closed loop system using feedback-error-learning. *Proc. the 29th IEEE Conference on Decision and Control*, Hawaii, Dec., pp.3289-3294

Hogan, N. (1985) Impedance control: An approach to manipulation: Part I - Theory, Part II - Implementation, Part III - Applications, *ASME Journal of Dynamic Systems, Measurement*, and Control, Vol.107, pp.1-24

Jacobs, R.A., Jordan, M.I., Barto, A.G. (1990) Task decomposition through competition in a modular connectionist architecture: The what and where vision tasks, *COINS Technical Report 90-27*, pp.1-49

Jacobs, R.A., Jordan, M.I. (1991) A competitive modular connectionist architecture. In Lippmann, R.P. et al., (Eds.) *NIPS 3*, pp.767-773

Jordan, M.I. (1988) Supervised learning and systems with excess degrees of freedom, *COINS Technical Report 88-27*, pp.1-41

Kawato, M., Furukawa, K., Suzuki, R. (1987) A hierarchical neural-network model for control and learning of voluntary movement; *Biol. Cybern. 57*, pp.169-185

Kawato, M. (1990) Computational schemes and neural network models for formation and control of multijoint arm trajectory. In: Miller, T., Sutton, R.S., Werbos, P.J.(Eds.) *Neural Networks for Control*, The MIT Press, Cambridge, Massachusetts, pp.197-228

Katayama, M., Kawato, M. (1991) Learning trajectory and force control of an artificial muscle arm by parallel-hierarchical neural network model. In Lippmann, R.P. et al., (Eds.) *NIPS 3*, pp.436-442

Nowlan, S.J. (1990) Competing experts: An experimental investigation of associative mixture models, *Univ. Toronto Tech. Rep. CRG-TR-90-5*, pp.1-77

Nowlan, S.J., Hinton, G.E. (1991) Evaluation of adaptive mixtures of competing experts. In Lippmann, R.P. et al., (Eds.) *NIPS 3*, pp.774-780

Psaltis, D., Sideris, A., Yamamura, A. (1987) Neural controllers, *Proc. IEEE Int. Conf. Neural Networks*, Vol.4, pp.551-557

Refining PID Controllers using Neural Networks

Gary M. Scott
Department of Chemical Engineering
1415 Johnson Drive
University of Wisconsin
Madison, WI 53706

Jude W. Shavlik
Department of Computer Sciences
1210 W. Dayton Street
University of Wisconsin
Madison, WI 53706

W. Harmon Ray
Department of Chemical Engineering
1415 Johnson Drive
University of Wisconsin
Madison, WI 53706

Abstract

The KBANN approach uses neural networks to refine knowledge that can be written in the form of simple propositional rules. We extend this idea further by presenting the MANNCON algorithm by which the mathematical equations governing a PID controller determine the topology and initial weights of a network, which is further trained using backpropagation. We apply this method to the task of controlling the outflow and temperature of a water tank, producing statistically-significant gains in accuracy over both a standard neural network approach and a non-learning PID controller. Furthermore, using the PID knowledge to initialize the weights of the network produces statistically less variation in testset accuracy when compared to networks initialized with small random numbers.

1 INTRODUCTION

Research into the design of neural networks for process control has largely ignored existing knowledge about the task at hand. One form this knowledge (often called the "domain theory") can take is embodied in traditional controller paradigms. The

555

recently-developed KBANN (Knowledge-Based Artificial Neural Networks) approach (Towell et al., 1990) addresses this issue for tasks for which a domain theory (written using simple propositional rules) is available. The basis of this approach is to use the existing knowledge to determine an appropriate network topology and initial weights, such that the network begins its learning process at a "good" starting point.

This paper describes the MANNCON (Multivariable Artificial Neural Network Control) algorithm, a method of using a traditional controller paradigm to determine the topology and initial weights of a network. The used of a PID controller in this way eliminates network-design problems such as the choice of network topology (*i.e.*, the number of hidden units) and reduces the sensitivity of the network to the initial values of the weights. Furthermore, the initial configuration of the network is closer to its final state than it would normally be in a randomly-configured network. Thus, the MANNCON networks perform better and more consistently than the standard, randomly-initialized three-layer approach.

The task we examine here is learning to control a Multiple-Input, Multiple-Output (MIMO) system. There are a number of reasons to investigate this task using neural networks. One, it usually involves nonlinear input-output relationships, which matches the nonlinear nature of neural networks. Two, there have been a number of successful applications of neural networks to this task (Bhat & McAvoy, 1990; Jordan & Jacobs, 1990; Miller et al., 1990). Finally, there are a number of existing controller paradigms which can be used to determine the topology and the initial weights of the network.

2   CONTROLLER NETWORKS

The MANNCON algorithm uses a *Proportional–Integral–Derivative* (PID) controller (Stephanopoulos, 1984), one of the simplest of the traditional feedback controller schemes, as the basis for the construction and initialization of a neural network controller. The basic idea of PID control is that the control action $\mathbf{u}$ (a vector) should be proportional to the error, the integral of the error over time, and the temporal derivative of the error. Several tuning parameters determine the contribution of these various components. Figure 1 depicts the resulting network topology based on the PID controller paradigm. The first layer of the network, that from $\mathbf{y}_{sp}$ (desired process output or setpoint) and $\mathbf{y}_{(n-1)}$ (actual process output of the past time step), calculates the simple error (e). A simple vector difference,

$$\mathbf{e} = \mathbf{y}_{sp} - \mathbf{y}$$

accomplishes this. The second layer, that between $\mathbf{e}$, $\boldsymbol{\varepsilon}_{(n-1)}$, and $\boldsymbol{\varepsilon}$, calculates the actual error to be passed to the PID mechanism. In effect, this layer acts as a steady-state pre-compensator (Ray, 1981), where

$$\boldsymbol{\varepsilon} = \mathbf{G_I}\mathbf{e}$$

and produces the current error and the error signals at the past two time steps. This compensator is a constant matrix, $\mathbf{G_I}$, with values such that interactions at a steady state between the various control loops are eliminated. The final layer, that between $\boldsymbol{\varepsilon}$ and $\mathbf{u}_{(n)}$ (controller output/plant input), calculates the controller action

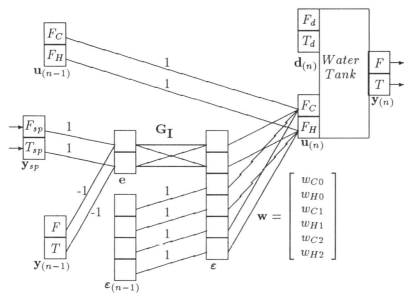

Figure 1: MANNCON network showing weights that are initialized using Ziegler-Nichols tuning parameters.

based on the velocity form of the discrete PID controller:

$$u_{C(n)} = u_{C(n-1)} + w_{C0}\varepsilon_{1(n)} + w_{C1}\varepsilon_{1(n-1)} + w_{C2}\varepsilon_{1(n-2)}$$

where w_{C0}, w_{C1}, and w_{C2} are constants determined by the tuning parameters of the controller for that loop. A similar set of equations and constants (w_{H0}, w_{H1}, w_{H2}) exist for the other controller loop.

Figure 2 shows a schematic of the water tank (Ray, 1981) that the network controls. This figure also shows the controller variables (F_C and F_H), the tank output variables ($F(h)$ and T), and the disturbance variables (F_d and T_d). The controller cannot measure the disturbances, which represent noise in the system.

MANNCON initializes the weights of Figure 1's network with values that mimic the behavior of a PID controller tuned with Ziegler-Nichols (Z-N) parameters (Stephanopoulos, 1984) at a particular operating condition. Using the KBANN approach (Towell et al., 1990), it adds weights to the network such that all units in a layer are connected to all units in all subsequent layers, and initializes these weights to small random numbers several orders of magnitude smaller than the weights determined by the PID parameters. We scaled the inputs and outputs of the network to be in the range [0, 1].

Initializing the weights of the network in the manner given above assumes that the activation functions of the units in the network are linear, that is,

$$o_{j,linear} = \sum w_{ji} o_i$$

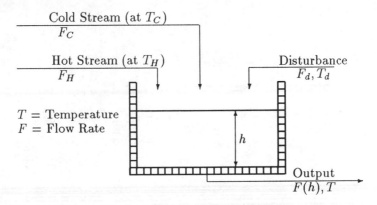

Figure 2: Stirred mixing tank requiring outflow and temperature control.

Table 1: Topology and initialization of networks.

Network	Topology	Weight Initialization
1. Standard neural network	3-layer (14 hidden units)	random
2. MANNCON network I	PID topology	random
3. MANNCON network II	PID topology	Z-N tuning

The strength of neural networks, however, lie in their having nonlinear (typically sigmoidal) activation functions. For this reason, the MANNCON system initially sets the weights (and the biases of the units) so that the linear response dictated by the PID initialization is *approximated* by a sigmoid over the output range of the unit. For units that have outputs in the range $[-1, 1]$, the activation function becomes

$$o_{j,sigmoid} = \frac{2}{1 + \exp(-2.31 \sum w_{ji} o_i)} - 1$$

where w_{ji} are the linear weights described above.

Once MANNCON configures and initializes the weights of the network, it uses a set of training examples and backpropagation to improve the accuracy of the network. The weights initialized with PID information, as well as those initialized with small random numbers, change during backpropagation training.

3   EXPERIMENTAL DETAILS

We compared the performance of three networks that differed in their topology and/or their method of initialization. Table 1 summarizes the network topology and weight initialization method for each network. In this table, "PID topology" is the network structure shown in Figure 1. "Random" weight initialization sets

Table 2: Range and average duration of setpoints for experiments.

Experiment	Training Set	Testing Set
1	$[0.1, 0.9]$	$[0.1, 0.9]$
	22 instances	22 instances
2	$[0.1, 0.9]$	$[0.1, 0.9]$
	22 instances	80 instances
3	$[0.4, 0.6]$	$[0.1, 0.9]$
	22 instances	80 instances

all weights to small random numbers centered around zero. We also compare these networks to a (non-learning) PID controller.

We trained the networks using backpropagation over a randomly-determined schedule of setpoint $\mathbf{y}_{sp}$ and disturbance $\mathbf{d}$ changes that did not repeat. The setpoints, which represent the desired output values that the controller is to maintain, are the temperature and outflow of the tank. The disturbances, which represent noise, are the inflow rate and temperature of a disturbance stream. The magnitudes of the setpoints and the disturbances formed a Gaussian distribution centered at 0.5. The number of training examples between changes in the setpoints and disturbances were exponentially distributed.

We performed three experiments in which the characteristics of the training and/or testing set differed. Table 2 summarizes the range of the setpoints as well as their average duration for each data set in the experiments. As can be seen, in Experiment 1, the training set and testing sets were qualitatively similar; in Experiment 2, the test set was of longer duration setpoints; and in Experiment 3, the training set was restricted to a subrange of the testing set. We periodically interrupted training and tested the network. Results are averaged over 10 runs (Scott, 1991).

We used the error at the output of the tank ($\mathbf{y}$ in Figure 1) to determine the network error (at $\mathbf{u}$) by propagating the error backward through the plant (Psaltis et al., 1988). In this method, the error signal at the input to the tank is given by

$$\delta_{ui} = f'(net_{ui}) \sum_j \delta_{yj} \frac{\partial y_i}{\partial u_i}$$

where δ_{yj} represents the simple error at the output of the water tank and δ_{ui} is the error signal at the input of the tank. Since we used a *model* of the process and not a real tank, we can calculate the partial derivatives from the process model equations.

4   RESULTS

Figure 3 compares the performance of the three networks for Experiment 1. As can be seen, the MANNCON networks show an increase in correctness over the standard neural network approach. Statistical analysis of the errors using a t-test show that they differ significantly at the 99.5% confidence level. Furthermore, while the difference in performance between MANNCON network I and MANNCON network II is

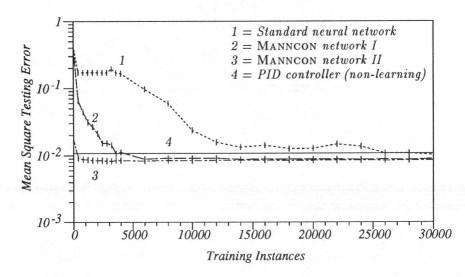

Figure 3: Mean square error of networks on the testset as a function of the number of training instances presented for Experiment 1.

not significant, the difference in the *variance* of the testing error over different runs is significant (99.5% confidence level). Finally, the MANNCON networks perform significantly better (99.95% confidence level) than the non-learning PID controller. The performance of the standard neural network represents the best of several trials with a varying number of hidden units ranging from 2 to 20.

A second observation from Figure 3 is that the MANNCON networks learned much more quickly than the standard neural-network approach. The MANNCON networks required significantly fewer training instances to reach a performance level within 5% of its final error rate. For each of the experiments, Table 3 summarizes the final mean error, as well as the number of training instances required to achieve a performance within 5% of this value.

In Experiments 2 and 3 we again see a significant gain in correctness of the MAN-NCON networks over both the standard neural network approach (99.95% confidence level) as well as the non-learning PID controller (99.95% confidence level). In these experiments, the MANNCON network initialized with Z-N tuning also learned significantly quicker (99.95% confidence level) than the standard neural network.

5   FUTURE WORK

One question is whether the introduction of extra hidden units into the network would improve the performance by giving the network "room" to learn concepts that are outside the given domain theory. The addition of extra hidden units as well as the removal of unneeded units is an area with much ongoing research.

Table 3: Comparison of network performance.

Method	Mean Square Error	Training Instances
Experiment 1		
1. Standard neural network	0.0103 ± 0.0004	$25,200 \pm 2,260$
2. MANNCON network I	0.0090 ± 0.0006	$5,000 \pm 3,340$
3. MANNCON network II	0.0086 ± 0.0001	640 ± 200
4. PID control (Z-N tuning)	0.0109	
5. Fixed control action	0.0190	
Experiment 2		
1. Standard neural network	0.0118 ± 0.00158	$14,400 \pm 3,150$
2. MANNCON network I	0.0040 ± 0.00014	$12,000 \pm 3,690$
3. MANNCON network II	0.0038 ± 0.00006	$2,080 \pm 300$
4. PID control (Z-N tuning)	0.0045	
5. Fixed control action	0.0181	
Experiment 3		
1. Standard neural network	0.0112 ± 0.00013	$25,200 \pm 2,360$
2. MANNCON network I	0.0039 ± 0.00008	$25,000 \pm 1,550$
3. MANNCON network II	0.0036 ± 0.00006	$9,400 \pm 1,180$
4. PID control (Z-N tuning)	0.0045	
5. Fixed control action	0.0181	

The "$\pm$" indicates that the true value lies within these bounds at a 95% confidence level. The values given for fixed control action (5) represent the errors resulting from fixing the control actions at a level that produces outputs of $[0.5, 0.5]$ at steady state.

"Ringing" (rapid changes in controller actions) occurred in some of the trained networks. A future enhancement of this approach would be to create a network architecture that prevented this ringing, perhaps by limiting the changes in the controller actions to some relatively small values.

Another important goal of this approach is the application of it to other real-world processes. The water tank in this project, while illustrative of the approach, was quite simple. Much more difficult problems (such as those containing significant time delays) exist and should be explored.

There are several other controller paradigms that could be used as a basis for network construction and initialization. There are several different digital controllers, such as Deadbeat or Dahlin's (Stephanopoulos, 1984), that could be used in place of the digital PID controller used in this project. Dynamic Matrix Control (DMC) (Pratt et al., 1980) and Internal Model Control (IMC) (Garcia & Morari, 1982) are also candidates for consideration for this approach.

Finally, neural networks are generally considered to be "black boxes," in that their inner workings are completely uninterpretable. Since the neural networks in this approach are initialized with information, it may be possible to interpret the weights of the network and extract useful information from the trained network.

6   CONCLUSIONS

We have described the MANNCON algorithm, which uses the information from a PID controller to determine a relevant network topology without resorting to trial-and-error methods. In addition, the algorithm, through initialization of the weights with prior knowledge, gives the backpropagtion algorithm an appropriate direction in which to continue learning. Finally, we have shown that using the MANNCON algorithm significantly improves the performance of the trained network in the following ways:

- Improved mean testset accuracy
- Less variability between runs
- Faster rate of learning
- Better generalization and extrapolation ability

Acknowledgements

This material based upon work partially supported under a National Science Foundation Graduate Fellowship (to Scott), Office of Naval Research Grant N00014-90-J-1941, and National Science Foundation Grants IRI-9002413 and CPT-8715051.

References

Bhat, N. & McAvoy, T. J. (1990). Use of neural nets for dynamic modeling and control of chemical process systems. *Computers and Chemical Engineering, 14,* 573–583.

Garcia, C. E. & Morari, M. (1982). Internal model control: 1. A unifying review and some new results. *I&EC Process Design & Development, 21,* 308–323.

Jordan, M. I. & Jacobs, R. A. (1990). Learning to control an unstable system with forward modeling. In *Advances in Neural Information Processing Systems* (Vol. 2, pp. 325–331). San Mateo, CA: Morgan Kaufmann.

Miller, W. T., Sutton, R. S., & Werbos, P. J. (Eds.)(1990). *Neural networks for control.* Cambridge, MA: MIT Press.

Pratt, D. M., Ramaker, B. L., & Cutler, C. R. (1980). Dynamic matrix control method. Patent 4,349,869, Shell Oil Company.

Psaltis, D., Sideris, A., & Yamamura, A. A. (1988). A multilayered neural network controller. *IEEE Control Systems Magazine, 8,* 17–21.

Ray, W. H. (1981). *Advanced process control.* New York: McGraw-Hill, Inc.

Scott, G. M. (1991). Refining PID controllers using neural networks. Master's project, University of Wisconsin, Department of Computer Sciences.

Stephanopoulos, G. (1984). *Chemical process control: An introduction to theory and practice.* Englewood Cliffs, NJ: Prentice Hall, Inc.

Towell, G., Shavlik, J., & Noordewier, M. (1990). Refinement of approximate domain theories by knowledge-base neural networks. In *Eighth National Conference on Aritificial Intelligence* (pp. 861–866). Menlo Park, CA: AAAI Press.

Fast Learning with Predictive Forward Models

Carlos Brody*
Dept. of Computer Science
IIMAS, UNAM
México D.F. 01000
México.
e-mail: carlos@hope.caltech.edu

Abstract

A method for transforming performance evaluation signals distal both in space and time into proximal signals usable by supervised learning algorithms, presented in [Jordan & Jacobs 90], is examined. A simple observation concerning differentiation through models trained with redundant inputs (as one of their networks is) explains a weakness in the original architecture and suggests a modification: an internal world model that encodes action-space exploration and, crucially, cancels input redundancy to the forward model is added. Learning time on an example task, cart-pole balancing, is thereby reduced about 50 to 100 times.

1 INTRODUCTION

In many learning control problems, the evaluation used to modify (and thus improve) control may not be available in terms of the controller's output: instead, it may be in terms of a spatial transformation of the controller's output variables (in which case we shall term it as being "distal in space"), or it may be available only several time steps into the future (termed as being "distal in time"). For example, control of a robot arm may be exerted in terms of joint angles, while evaluation may be in terms of the endpoint cartesian coordinates; furthermore, we may only wish to evaluate the endpoint coordinates reached after a certain period of time: the co-

---

*Current address: Computation and Neural Systems Program, California Institute of Technology, Pasadena CA.

ordinates reached <u>at the end</u> of some motion, for instance. In such cases, supervised learning methods are not directly applicable, and other techniques must be used. Here we study one such technique (proposed for cases where the evaluation is distal in both space and time by [Jordan & Jacobs 90]), analyse a source of its problems, and propose a simple solution for them which leads to fast, efficient learning.

We first describe two methods, and then combine them into the "predictive forward modeling" technique with which we are concerned.

1.1   FORWARD MODELING

"Forward Modeling" [Jordan & Rumelhart 90] is useful for dealing with evaluations which are distal in space; it involves the construction of a differentiable model to approximate the controller-action → evaluation transformation. Let our controller have internal parameters $\mathbf{w}$, output $\mathbf{c}$, and be evaluated in space $\mathbf{e}$, where $\mathbf{e} = \mathbf{e}(\mathbf{c})$ is an unknown but well-defined transformation. If there is a desired output in space $\mathbf{e}$, called $\mathbf{e}^*$, we can write an "error" function, that is, an evaluation we wish minimised, and differentiate it w.r.t. the controller's weights to obtain

$$E = (\mathbf{e}^* - \mathbf{e})^2 \qquad \frac{\partial E}{\partial \mathbf{w}} = \frac{\partial \mathbf{c}}{\partial \mathbf{w}} \cdot \frac{\partial \mathbf{e}}{\partial \mathbf{c}} \cdot \frac{\partial E}{\partial \mathbf{e}} \qquad (1)$$

Using a differentiable controller allows us to obtain the first factor in the second equation, and the third factor is also known; but the second factor is not. However, if we construct a differentiable model (called a "forward model") of $\mathbf{e}(\mathbf{c})$, then we can obtain an approximation to the second term by differentiating the model, and use this to obtain an estimate of the gradient $\partial E/\partial \mathbf{w}$ through equation (1); this can then be used for comparatively fast minimisation of E, and is what is known as "forward modeling".

1.2   PREDICTIVE CRITICS

To deal with evaluations which are distal in time, we may use a "critic" network, as in [Barto, Sutton & Anderson 83]. For a particular control policy implemented by the controller network, the critic is trained to predict the final evaluation that will be obtained given the current state – using, for example, Sutton's TD algorithm [Sutton 88]. The estimated final evaluation is then available as soon as we enter a state, and so may in turn be used to improve the control policy. This approach is closely related to dynamic programming [Barto, Sutton & Watkins 89].

1.3   PREDICTIVE FORWARD MODELS

While the estimated evaluation we obtain from the critic is no longer distal in time, it may still be distal in space. A natural proposal in such cases, where the evaluation signal is distal both in space and time, is to combine the two techniques described above: use a differentiable model as a predictive critic [Jordan & Jacobs 90]. If we know the desired final evaluation, we can then proceed as in equation (1) and obtain the gradient of the error w.r.t. the controller's weights. Schematically, this would look like figure 1. When using a backprop network for the predictive model,

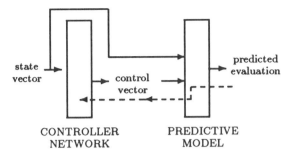

Figure 1: Jordan and Jacobs' predictive forward modeling architecture. Solid lines indicate data paths, the dashed line indicates backpropagation.

we would backpropagate through it, through it's control input, and then into the controller to modify the controller network. We should note that since predictions make no sense without a particular control policy, and the controller is only modified through the predictive model, both networks must be trained simultaneously.

[Jordan & Jacobs 90] applied this method to a well-known problem, that of learning to balance an inverted pendulum on a movable cart by exerting appropriate horizontal forces on the cart. The same task, without differentiating the critic, was studied in [Barto, Sutton & Anderson 83]. There, reinforcement learning methods were used instead to modify the controller's weights; these perform a search which in some cases may be shown to follow, *on average*, the gradient of the expected evaluation w.r.t. the network weights. Since differentiating the critic allows this gradient to be found directly, one would expect much faster learning when using the architecture of figure 1. However, Jordan and Jacobs' results show precisely the opposite: it is surprisingly slow.

2   THE REDUNDANCY PROBLEM

We can explain the above surprising result if we consider the fact that the predictive model network has redundant inputs: the control vector $\vec{c}$ is a function of the state vector $\vec{s}$ (call this $\vec{c} = \vec{\pi}(\vec{s})$). Let κ and σ be the number of components of the control and state vectors, respectively. Instead of drawing its inputs from the entire volume of $(\kappa + \sigma)$-dimensional input space, the predictor is trained **only** with inputs which lie on the σ-dimensional manifold defined by the relation $\vec{\pi}$. Away from the manifold the network is free to produce entirely arbitrary outputs. Differentiation of the model will then provide non-arbitrary gradients only for directions tangential to the manifold; this is a condition that the axes of the control dimensions will not, in general, satisfy.[1] This observation, which concerns any model trained with redundant inputs, is the very simple yet principal point of this paper.

One may argue that since the control policy is continually changing, the redundancy picture sketched out here is not in fact accurate: as the controller is modified, many

---

[1] Note that if $\vec{\pi}$ is single-valued, there is no way the manifold can "fold around" to cover all (or most) of the $\kappa + \sigma$ input space.

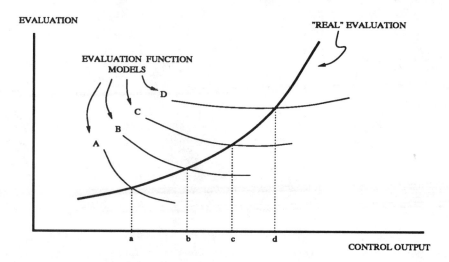

Figure 2: The evaluation as a function of control action. Curves A,B,C,D represent possible (wrong) estimates of the "real" curve made by the predictive model network.

possible control policies are "seen" by the predictor, so creating volume in input space and leading to correct gradients obtained from the predictor. However, the way in which this modification occurs is significant. An argument based on empirical observations will be made to sustain this.

Consider the example shown in figure 2. The graph shows what the "real" evaluation at some point in state space is, as a function of a component of the control action taken at that point; this function is what the predictive network should approximate. Suppose the function implemented by the predictive network initially looks like the curve which crosses the "real" evaluation function at point (a); suppose also that the current action taken also corresponds to point (a). Here we see a one-dimensional example of the redundancy problem: though the prediction at this point is entirely accurate, the gradient is not. If we wish to minimise the predicted evaluation, we would change the action in the direction of point (b). Examples of point (a) will no longer be presented to the predictive network, so it could quite plausibly modify itself simply so as to look like the estimated evaluation curve "B" which is shown crossing point (b) (a minimal change necessary to continue being correct). Again, the gradient is wrong and minimising the prediction will change the action in the same direction as before, perhaps to point (c); then to (d), and so on. Eventually, the prediction, though accurate, will have zero gradient, as in curve "D", and no modifications will occur. In practice, we have observed networks "getting stuck" in this fashion. Though the objective was to minimise the evaluation, the system stops "learning" at a point far from optimal.

The problem may be solved, as Jordan and Jacobs did, by introducing noise in the controller's output, thus breaking the redundancy. Unfortunately, this degrades

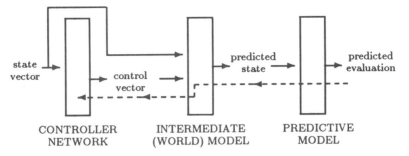

Figure 3: The proposed system architecture. Again, solid lines represent data paths while the dashed line represents backpropagation (or differentiation).

signal quality and means that since we are predicting future evaluations, we wish to predict the effects of future noise – a notoriously difficult objective. The predictive network eventually outputs the evaluation's expectation value, but this can take a long time.

3   USING AN INTERMEDIATE MODEL

3.1   AN EXTRA WORLD MODEL

Another way to solve the redundancy problem is through the use of what is here called an "intermediate model": a model of the world the controller is interacting with. That is, if $s(t)$ represents the state vector at time t, and $c(t)$ the controller output at time t, it is a model of the function I where $s(t+1) = I(s(t), c(t))$.

This model is used as represented schematically in figure 3. It helps in modularising the learning task faced by the predictive model [Chrisley 90], but more interestingly, it need not be trained simultaneously with the controller since its output does not depend on future control policy. Hence, it can be trained separately, with examples drawn from its *entire* (state x action) input space, providing gradient signals without arbitrary components when differentiated. Once trained, we freeze the intermediate model's weights and insert it into the system as in figure 3; we then proceed to train the controller and predictive model as before. The predictive model will no longer have redundant inputs when trained either, so it too will provide correct gradient signals. Since all arbitrary components have been eliminated, the speedup expected from using differentiable predictive models should now be obtainable.[2]

3.2   AN EXAMPLE TASK

The intermediate model architecture was tested on the same example task as used by Jordan and Jacobs, that of learning to balance a pole which is attached through a hinge on its lower end to a movable cart. The control action is a real valued-force

---

[2]This same architecture was independently proposed in [Werbos 90], but without the explanation as to why the intermediate model is necessary instead of merely desirable.

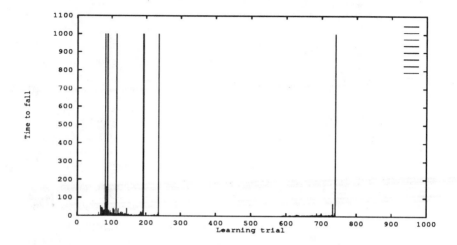

Figure 4: The evolution of eight different learning networks, using the intermediate model.

applied to the cart; the evaluation signal is a "0" while the pole has not fallen over, and the cart hasn't reached the edge of the finite-sized tracks it is allowed to move on, a "1" when either of these events happens. A trial is then said to have failed, and terminates.[3]

We count the number of learning trials needed before a controller is able to keep the pole balanced for a significant amount of a time (measured in simulated seconds). Figure 4 shows the evolution of eight networks; most reach balancing solutions within 100 to 300 faiulres. (These successful networks came from a batch of eleven: the other three never reached solutions.) This is 50 to 100 times faster than without the intermediate model, where 5000 to 30000 trials were needed to achieve similar balancing times [Jordan & Jacobs 90].

We must now take into account the overhead needed to train the intermediate model. This was done in 200 seconds of simulated time, while training the whole system typically required some 400 seconds– the overhead is small compared to the improvement achieved through the use of the intermediate model. However, off-line training of the intermediate model requires an additional agency to organise the selection and presentation of training examples. In the real world, we would either need some device which could initialise the system at any point in state space, or we would have to train through "flailing": applying random control actions, over many trials, so as to eventually cover all possible states and actions. As the dimensionality of the state representation rises for larger problems, intermediate model training will become more difficult.

---

[3]The differential equations which were used as a model of this system may be found in [Barto, Sutton & Anderson 83]. The parameters of the simulations were identical to those used in [Jordan & Jacobs 90].

3.3 REMARKS

We should note that the need for covering all state space is not merely due to the requirement of training an intermediate model: dynamic-programming based techniques such as the ones mentioned in this paper are guaranteed to lead us to an optimal control solution only if we explore the entire state space during learning. This is due to their generality, since no *a priori* structure of the state space is assumed. It might be possible to interleave the training of the intermediate model with the training of the controller and predictor networks, so as to achieve both concurrently. High-dimensional problems will still be problematic, but not just due to intermediate model training– the curse of dimensionality is not easily avoided!

4 CONCLUSIONS

If we differentiate through a model trained with redundant inputs, we eliminate possible arbitrary components (which are due to the arbitrary mixing of the inputs that the model may use) only if we differentiate tangentially along the manifold defined by the relationship between the inputs. For the architecture presented in [Jordan & Jacobs 90], this is problematic, since the axes of the control vector will typically not be tangential to the manifold. Once we take this into account, it is clear why the architecture was not as efficient as expected; and we can introduce an "intermediate" world model to avoid the problems that it had.

Using the intermediate model allows us to correctly obtain (through backpropagation, or differentiation) a real-valued vector evaluation on the controller's output. On the example task presented here, this led to a 50 to 100-fold increase in learning speed, and suggests a much better scaling-up performance and applicability to real-world problems than simple reinforcement learning, where real-valued outputs are not permitted, and vector control outputs would train very slowly.

Acknowledgements

Many thanks are due to Richard Rohwer, who supervised the beginning of this project, and to M. I. Jordan and R. Jacobs, who answered questions enlighteningly; thanks are also due to Dr F. Bracho at IIMAS, UNAM, who provided the environment for the project's conclusion. This work was supported by scholarships from CONACYT in Mexico and from Caltech in the U.S.

References

[Ackley 88] D. H. Ackley, "Associative Learning via Inhibitory Search", in D. S. Touretzky, ed., *Advances in Neural Information Processing Systems 1*, Morgan Kaufmann 1989

[Barto, Sutton & Anderson 83] A. G. Barto, R. S. Sutton, and C. W. Anderson, "Neuronlike Adaptive Elements that can Solve Difficult Control Problems", IEEE Transactions on Systems, Man, and Cybernetics, Vol. SMC-13, No. 5, Sept/Oct. 1983

[Barto, Sutton & Watkins 89] A. G. Barto, R. S. Sutton, and C. J. C. H. Watkins, "Learning and Sequential Decision Making", University of Massachusetts at Amherst COINS Technical Report 89-95, September 1989

[Chrisley 90] R. L. Chrisley, "Cognitive Map Construction and Use: A Parallel Distributed Approach", in Touretzky, Elman, Sejnowski, and Hinton, eds., *Connectionist Models: Proceedings of the 1990 Summer School*, Morgan Kaufmann 1991

[Jordan & Jacobs 90] M. I. Jordan and R. A. Jacobs, "Learning to Control an Unstable System with Forward Modeling", in D. S. Touretzky, ed., *Advances in Neural Information Processing Systems 2*, Morgan Kaufmann 1990

[Jordan & Rumelhart 90] M. I. Jordan and D. E. Rumelhart, "Supervised learning with a Distal Teacher", preprint.

[Nguyen & Widrow 90] D. Nguyen and B. Widrow, "The Truck Backer-Upper: An Example of Self-Learning in Neural Networks", in Miller, Sutton and Werbos, eds., *Neural Networks for Control*, MIT Press 1990

[Sutton 88] R. S. Sutton, "Learning to Predict by the Methods of Temporal Differences", Machine Learning **3**: 9–44, 1988

[Werbos 90] P. Werbos, "Architectures for Reinforcement Learning", in Miller, Sutton and Werbos, eds., *Neural Networks for Control*, MIT Press 1990

Fast, Robust Adaptive Control by Learning only Forward Models

Andrew W. Moore
MIT Artificial Intelligence Laboratory
545 Technology Square, Cambridge, MA 02139
awm@ai.mit.edu

Abstract

A large class of motor control tasks requires that on each cycle the controller is told its current state and must choose an action to achieve a specified, state-dependent, goal behaviour. This paper argues that the optimization of *learning rate*, the number of experimental control decisions before adequate performance is obtained, and *robustness* is of prime importance—if necessary at the expense of computation per control cycle and memory requirement. This is motivated by the observation that a robot which requires two thousand learning steps to achieve adequate performance, or a robot which occasionally gets stuck while learning, will always be undesirable, whereas moderate computational expense can be accommodated by increasingly powerful computer hardware. It is not unreasonable to assume the existence of inexpensive 100 Mflop controllers within a few years and so even processes with control cycles in the low tens of milliseconds will have millions of machine instructions in which to make their decisions. This paper outlines a learning control scheme which aims to make effective use of such computational power.

1 MEMORY BASED LEARNING

Memory-based learning is an approach applicable to both classification and function learning in which all experiences presented to the learning box are explicitly remembered. The memory, **Mem**, is a set of input-output pairs, **Mem** = $\{(x_1, y_1), (x_2, y_2), \ldots, (x_k, y_k)\}$. When a prediction is required of the output of a novel input x_{query}, the memory is searched to obtain experiences with inputs close to x_{query}. These local neighbours are used to determine a locally consistent output for the query. Three memory-based techniques, Nearest Neighbour, Kernel Regression, and Local Weighted Regression, are shown in the accompanying figure.

571

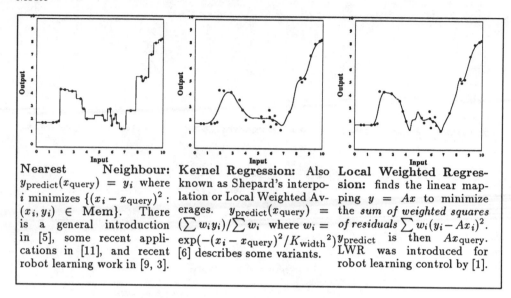

Nearest Neighbour: $y_{\text{predict}}(x_{\text{query}}) = y_i$ where i minimizes $\{(x_i - x_{\text{query}})^2 : (x_i, y_i) \in \text{Mem}\}$. There is a general introduction in [5], some recent applications in [11], and recent robot learning work in [9, 3].

Kernel Regression: Also known as Shepard's interpolation or Local Weighted Averages. $y_{\text{predict}}(x_{\text{query}}) = (\sum w_i y_i)/\sum w_i$ where $w_i = \exp(-(x_i - x_{\text{query}})^2/K_{\text{width}}^2)$ [6] describes some variants.

Local Weighted Regression: finds the linear mapping $y = Ax$ to minimize the *sum of weighted squares of residuals* $\sum w_i(y_i - Ax_i)^2$. y_{predict} is then Ax_{query}. LWR was introduced for robot learning control by [1].

2   A MEMORY-BASED INVERSE MODEL

An *inverse model* maps **State** × **Behaviour** → **Action** ($s \times b \rightarrow a$). Behaviour is the output of the system, typically the next state or time derivative of state. The learned inverse model provides a conceptually simple controller:

1. Observe s and b_{goal}.
2. $a := \text{inverse-model}(s, b_{\text{goal}})$
3. Perform action a and observe actual behaviour b_{actual}.
4. Update **MEM** with $(s, b_{\text{actual}} \rightarrow a)$: If we are ever again in state s and require behaviour b_{actual} we should apply action a.

Memory-based versions of this simple algorithm have used nearest neighbour [9] and LWR [3]. b_{goal} is the goal behaviour: depending on the task it may be fixed or it may vary between control cycles, perhaps as a function of state or time. The algorithm provides aggressive learning: during repeated attempts to achieve the same goal behaviour, the action which is applied is not an incrementally adjusted version of the previous action, but is instead the action which the memory and the memory-based learner predicts will directly achieve the required behaviour. If the function is locally linear then the sequence of actions which are chosen are closely related to the Secant method [4] for numerically finding the zero of a function by bisecting the line between the closest approximations that bracket the $y = 0$ axis. If learning begins with an initial error E_0 in the action choice, and we wish to reduce this error to E_0/K, the number of learning steps is $O(\log \log K)$: subject to benign conditions, the learner jumps to actions close to the ideal action very quickly.

A common objection to learning the inverse model is that it may be ill-defined. For a memory-based method the problems are particularly serious because of its update rule. It updates the inverse model near b_{actual} and therefore in those cases in which b_{goal} and b_{actual} differ greatly, the mapping near b_{goal} may not change. As a result, subsequent cycles will make identical mistakes. [10] discusses this further.

3   A MEMORY-BASED FORWARD MODEL

One fix for the problem of inverses becoming stuck is the addition of random noise to actions prior to their application. However, this can result in a large proportion of control cycles being wasted on experiments which the robot should have been able to predict as valueless, defeating the initial aim of learning as quickly as possible.

An alternative technique using multilayer neural nets has been to learn a forward model, which is necessarily well defined, to train a partial inverse. Updates to the forward model are obtained by standard supervised training, but updates to the inverse model are more sophisticated. The local Jacobian of the forward model is obtained and this value is used to drive an incremental change to the inverse model [8]. In conjunction with memory-based methods such an approach has the disadvantage that incremental changes to the inverse model loses the one-shot learning behaviour, and introduces the danger of becoming trapped in a local minimum.

Instead, this investigation only relies on learning the forward model. Then the inverse model is implicitly obtained from it by online numerical inversion instead of direct lookup. This is illustrated by the following algorithm:

1. Observe s and b_{goal}.
2. **Perform numerical inversion:**
   Search among a series of candidate actions $a_1, a_2 \ldots a_k$:
   $b_1^{predict} :=$ forward-model(s, a_1, MEM)
   $b_2^{predict} :=$ forward-model(s, a_2, MEM)
   $\vdots$
   $b_k^{predict} :=$ forward-model(s, a_k, MEM)

   Until TIME-OUT or $b_k^{predict} = b_{goal}$

3. If TIME-OUT then perform experimental action else perform a_k.
4. Update MEM with $(s, a_k \rightarrow b_{actual})$

A nice feature of this method is the absence of a preliminary training phase such as random flailing or feedback control. A variety of search techniques for numerical inversion can be applied. Global random search avoids local minima but is very slow for obtaining accurate actions, hill climbing is a robust local procedure and more aggressive procedures such as Newton's method can use partial derivative estimates from the forward model to make large second-order steps. The implementation used for subsequent results had a combination of global search and local hill climbing.

In very high speed applications in which there is only time to make a small number of forward model predictions, it is not difficult to regain much of the speed advantage of directly using an inverse model by commencing the action search with a_0 as the action predicted by a learned inverse model.

4   OTHER CONSIDERATIONS

Actions selected by a forward memory-based learner can be expected to converge very quickly to the correct action in benign cases, and will not become stuck in difficult cases, provided that the memory based representation can fit the true forward model. This proviso is weak compared with incremental learning control techniques which typically require stronger prior assumptions about the environment, such as near-linearity, or that an iterative function approximation procedure will avoid local minima. One-shot methods have an advantage in terms of number of control cycles before adequate performance whereas incremental methods have the advantage of only requiring trivial amounts of computation per cycle. However, the simple memory-based formalism described so far suffers from two major problems which some forms of adaptive and neural controllers may avoid.

- Brittle behaviour in the presence of outliers.
- Poor resistance to non-stationary environments.

Many incremental methods implicitly forget all experiences beyond a certain horizon. For example, in the delta rule $\Delta w_{ij} = \nu(y_i^{\text{actual}} - y_i^{\text{predict}})x_j$, the age beyond which experiences have a negligible effect is determined by the learning rate ν. As a result, the detrimental effect of misleading experiences is present for only a fixed amount of time and then fades away[1]. In contrast, memory-based methods remember everything for ever. Fortunately, two statistical techniques: *robust regression* and *cross-validation* allow extensions to the numerical inversion method in which we can have our cake and eat it too.

5   USING ROBUST REGRESSION

We can judge the quality of each experience $(x_i, y_i) \in \mathbf{Mem}$ by how well it is predicted by the rest of the experiences. A simple measure of the ith error is the *cross validation* error, in which the experience is first removed from the memory before prediction. $e_i^{\text{xve}} = | \mathbf{Predict}(x_i, \mathbf{Mem} - \{(x_i, y_i)\}) |$. With the memory-based formalism, in which all work takes place at prediction time, it is no more expensive to predict a value with one datapoint removed than with it included.

Once we have the measure e_i^{xve} of the quality of each experience, we can decide if it is worth keeping. Robust statistics [7] offers a wide range of methods: this implementation uses the *Median Absolute Deviation* (MAD) procedure.

6   FULL CROSS VALIDATION

The value $e_{\text{total}}^{\text{xve}} = \sum e_i^{\text{xve}}$, summed over all "good" experiences, provides a measure of how well the current representation fits the data. By optimizing this value with respect to internal learner parameters, such as the width of the local weighting function K_{width} used by kernel regression and LWR, the internal parameters can be found automatically. Another important set of parameters that can be optimized is the relative scaling of each input variable: an example of this procedure applied to a two-joint arm task may be found in Reference [2]. A useful feature of this procedure is its quick discovery (and subsequent ignoring) of irrelevant input variables.

Cross-validation can also be used to selectively forget old inaccurate experiences caused by a slowly drifting or suddenly changing environment. We have already seen that adaptive control algorithms such as the LMS rule can avoid such problems because the effects of experiences decay with time. Memory based methods can also forget things according to a forgetfulness parameter: all observations are weighted

---

[1] This also has disadvantages: persistence of excitation is required and multiple tasks can often require relearning if they have not been practised recently.

by not only the distance to the x_{query} but also by their age:

$$w_i = exp(-(x_i - x_{\text{query}})^2/K_{\text{width}}^2 - (n - i)/K_{\text{recall}}) \qquad (1)$$

where we assume the ordering of the experiences' indices i is temporal, with experience n the most recent.

We find the K_{recall} that minimizes the recent weighted average cross validation error $\sum_{i=0}^{n} e_i^{\text{xve}} exp(-(n - i)/\gamma)$, where γ is a human assigned 'meta-forgetfulness' constant, reflecting how many experiences the learner would need in order to benefit from observation of an environmental change. It should be noted that γ is a substantially less task dependent prescription of how far back to forget than would be a human specified K_{recall}. Some initial tests of this technique are included among the experiments of Section 8.

Architecture selection is another use of cross validation. Given a family of learners, the member with the least cross validation error is used for subsequent predictions.

7   COMPUTATIONAL CONSIDERATIONS

Unless the real time between control cycles is longer than a few seconds, cross validation is too expensive to perform after every cycle. Instead it can be performed as a separate parallel process, updating the best parameter values and removing outliers every few real control cycles. The usefulness of breaking a learning control task into an online realtime processes and offline mental simulation was noted by [12]. Initially, the small number of experiences means that cross validation optimizes the parameters very frequently, but the time between updates increases with the memory size. The decreasing frequency of cross validation updates is little cause for concern, because as time progresses, the estimated optimal parameter values are expected to become decreasingly variable.

If there is no time to make more than one memory based query per cycle, then memory based learning can nevertheless proceed by pushing even more of the computation into the offline component. If the offline process can identify meaningful states relevant to the task, then it can compute, for each of them, what the optimal action would be. The resulting state-action pairs are then used as a policy. The online process then need only look up the recommended action in the policy, apply it and then insert (s, a, b) into the memory.

8   COMPARATIVE TESTS

The ultimate goal of the investigation is to produce a learning control algorithm which can learn to control a fairly wide family of different tasks. Some basic, very different, tasks have been used for the initial tests.

The HARD task, graphed in Figure 1, is a one-dimensional direct relationship between action and behaviour which is both non-monotonic and discontinuous. The VARIER task (Figure 2) is a sinusoidal relation for which the phase continuously drifts, and occasionally alters catastrophically.

LINEAR is a noisy linear relation between 4-d states, 4-d actions and 4-d behaviours. For these first three tasks, the goal behaviour is selected randomly on each control cycle. ARM (Figure 3) is a simulated noisy dynamic two-joint arm acting under gravity in which state is perceived in cartesian coordinates and actions are produced in joint-torque coordinates. Its task is to follow the circular trajectory. BILLIARDS is a simulation of the real billiards robot described shortly in which 5% of experiences are entirely random outliers.

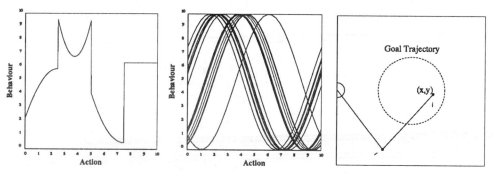

Figure 1: The HARD relation.   Figure 2: VARIER relation.   Figure 3: The ARM task.

The following learning methods were tested: nearest neighbour, kernel regression and LWR, all searching the forward model and using a form of uncertainty-based intelligent experimentation [10] when the forward search proved inadequate. Another method under test was sole use of the inverse, learned by LWR. Finally a "best-possible" value was obtained by numerically inverting the real simulated forward model instead of a learned model.

All tasks were run for only 200 control cycles. In each case the quality of the learner was measured by the number of successful actions in the final hundred cycles, where "successful" was defined as producing behaviour within a small tolerance of b_{goal}.

Results are displayed in Table 1. There is little space to discuss them in detail, but they generally support the arguments of the previous sections. The inverse model on its own was generally inferior to the forward method, even in those cases in which the inverse is well-defined. Outlier removal improved performance on the BILLIARDS task over non-robustified versions. Interestingly, outlier removal also greatly benefited the inverse only method. The selectively forgetful methods performed better than than their non-forgetful counterparts on the VARIER task, but in the stationary environments they did not pay a great penalty. Cross validation for K_{width} was useful: for the HARD task, LWR found a very small K_{width} but in the LINEAR task it unsurprisingly preferred an enormous K_{width}.

Some experiments were also performed with a real billiards robot shown in Figure 4. Sensing is visual: one camera looks along the cue stick and the other looks down at the table. The cue stick swivels around the cue ball, which starts each shot at the same position. At the start of each attempt the object ball is placed at a random position in the half of the table opposite the cue stick. The camera above the table obtains the (x, y) image coordinates of the object ball, which constitute the state. The action is the x-coordinate of the image of the object ball on the cue stick camera. A motor swivels the cue stick until the centroid of the actual image of the object ball coincides with the chosen x-coordinate value. The shot is then performed and observed by the overhead camera. The behaviour is defined as the cushion and position on the cushion with which the object ball first collides.

Controller type. (K = use MAD outlier removal, X = use cross-validation for K_{width}, R = use cross-validation for K_{recall}, IF = obtain initial candidate action from the inverse model then search the forward model.)	VARIER	HARD	LINEAR	ARM	BIL'DS
Best Possible: Obtained from numerically inverting simulated world	100 ± 0	100 ± 0	75 ± 3	94 ± 1	82 ± 4
Inverse only, learned with LWR	15 ± 9	24 ± 11	7 ± 6	76 ± 28	71 ± 5
Inverse only, learned with LWR, KRX	48 ± 16	72 ± 8	70 ± 4	89 ± 4	70 ± 10
LWR: IF	14 ± 10	11 ± 5	58 ± 4	83 ± 4	55 ± 12
LWR: IF X	19 ± 9	72 ± 4	70 ± 4	89 ± 3	61 ± 9
LWR: IF KX	22 ± 15	51 ± 27	73 ± 3	90 ± 3	75 ± 7
LWR: IF KRX	54 ± 8	65 ± 28	70 ± 5	89 ± 2	69 ± 7
LWR: Forward only, KRX	56 ± 9	53 ± 17	73 ± 1	89 ± 1	69 ± 7
Kernel Regression: IF	8 ± 2	6 ± 2	13 ± 3	3 ± 2	1 ± 1
Kernel Regression: IF KRX	15 ± 8	42 ± 21	14 ± 2	23 ± 10	30 ± 5
Nearest Neighbour: IF	22 ± 4	92 ± 2	0 ± 0	44 ± 6	10 ± 2
Nearest Neighbour: IF K	26 ± 10	69 ± 4	0 ± 0	40 ± 6	9 ± 3
Nearest Neighbour: IF KR	44 ± 8	68 ± 3	0 ± 0	40 ± 7	11 ± 3
Nearest Neighbour: Forward only, KR	43 ± 8	66 ± 5	0 ± 0	37 ± 3	8 ± 1
Global Linear Regression: IF	8 ± 3	7 ± 3	74 ± 5	60 ± 17	23 ± 6
Global Linear Regression: IF KR	20 ± 13	9 ± 2	73 ± 4	72 ± 3	21 ± 4
Global Quadratic Regression: IF	14 ± 7	5 ± 3	64 ± 2	70 ± 22	40 ± 11

Table 1: Relative performance of a family of learners on a family of tasks. Each combination of learner and task was run ten times to provide the mean number of successes and standard deviation shown in the table.

The controller uses the memory based learner to choose the action to maximize the probability that the ball will enter the nearer of the two pockets at the end of the table. A histogram of the number of successes against trial number is shown in Figure 5. In this experiment, the learner was LWR using outlier removal and cross validation for K_{width}. After 100 experiences, control choice running on a Sun-4 was taking 0.8 seconds[2]. Sinking the ball requires better than 1% accuracy in the choice of action, the world contains discontinuities and there are random outliers in the data and so it is encouraging that within less than 100 experiences the robot had reached a 70% success rate—substantially better than the author can achieve.

ACKNOWLEDGEMENTS

Some of the work discussed in this paper is being performed in collaboration with Chris Atkeson. The robot cue stick was designed and built by Wes Huang with help from Gerrit van Zyl. Dan Hill also helped considerably with the billiards robot. The author is supported by a Postdoctoral Fellowship from SERC/NATO. Support was provided under Air Force Office of Scientific Research grant AFOSR-89-0500 and a National Science Foundation Presidential Young Investigator Award to Christopher G. Atkeson.

[2]This could have been greatly improved with more appropriate hardware or better software techniques such as kd-trees for structuring data [11, 9].

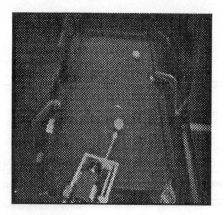

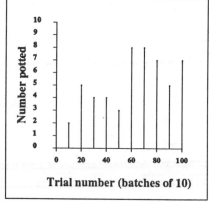

Trial number (batches of 10)

Figure 4: The billiards robot. In the foreground is the cue stick which attempts to sink balls in the far pockets.

Figure 5: Frequency of successes versus control cycle for the billiards task.

References

[1] C. G. Atkeson. Using Local Models to Control Movement. In *Proceedings of Neural Information Processing Systems Conference*, November 1989.

[2] C. G. Atkeson. Memory-Based Approaches to Approximating Continuous Functions. Technical report, M. I. T. Artificial Intelligence Laboratory, 1990.

[3] C. G. Atkeson and D. J. Reinkensmeyer. Using Associative Content-Addressable Memories to Control Robots. In Miller, Sutton, and Werbos, editors, *Neural Networks for Control.* MIT Press, 1989.

[4] S. D. Conte and C. De Boor. *Elementary Numerical Analysis.* McGraw Hill, 1980.

[5] R. O. Duda and P. E. Hart. *Pattern Classification and Scene Analysis.* John Wiley & Sons, 1973.

[6] R. Franke. Scattered Data Interpolation: Tests of Some Methods. *Mathematics of Computation*, 38(157), January 1982.

[7] F. Hampbell, P. Rousseeuw, E. Ronchetti, and W. Stahel. *Robust Statistics.* Wiley International, 1985.

[8] M. I. Jordan and D. E. Rumelhart. Forward Models: Supervised Learning with a Distal Teacher. Technical report, M. I. T., July 1990.

[9] A. W. Moore. Efficient Memory-based Learning for Robot Control. PhD. Thesis; Technical Report No. 209, Computer Laboratory, University of Cambridge, October 1990.

[10] A. W. Moore. Knowledge of Knowledge and Intelligent Experimentation for Learning Control. In *Proceedings of the 1991 Seattle International Joint Conference on Neural Networks*, July 1991.

[11] S. M. Omohundro. Efficient Algorithms with Neural Network Behaviour. *Journal of Complex Systems*, 1(2):273–347, 1987.

[12] R. S. Sutton. Integrated Architecture for Learning, Planning, and Reacting Based on Approximating Dynamic Programming. In *Proceedings of the 7th International Conference on Machine Learning.* Morgan Kaufman, June 1990.

Reverse TDNN: An Architecture for Trajectory Generation

Patrice Simard
AT&T Bell Laboratories
101 Crawford Corner Rd
Holmdel, NJ 07733

Yann Le Cun
AT&T Bell Laboratories
101 Crawford Corner Rd
Holmdel, NJ 07733

Abstract

The backpropagation algorithm can be used for both recognition and generation of time trajectories. When used as a recognizer, it has been shown that the performance of a network can be greatly improved by adding structure to the architecture. The same is true in trajectory generation. In particular a new architecture corresponding to a "reversed" TDNN is proposed. Results show dramatic improvement of performance in the generation of hand-written characters. A combination of TDNN and reversed TDNN for compact encoding is also suggested.

1 INTRODUCTION

Trajectory generation finds interesting applications in the field of robotics, automation, filtering, or time series prediction. Neural networks, with their ability to learn from examples, have been proposed very early on for solving non-linear control problems adaptively. Several neural net architectures have been proposed for trajectory generation, most notably recurrent networks, either with discrete time and external loops (Jordan, 1986), or with continuous time (Pearlmutter, 1988). Aside from being recurrent, these networks are not specifically tailored for trajectory generation. It has been shown that specific architectures, such as the Time Delay Neural Networks (Lang and Hinton, 1988), or convolutional networks in general, are better than fully connected networks at recognizing time sequences such as speech (Waibel et al., 1989), or pen trajectories (Guyon et al., 1991). We show that special architectures can also be devised for trajectory generation, with dramatic performance improvement.

Two main ideas are presented in this paper. The first one rests on the assumption that most trajectory generation problems deal with *continuous* trajectories. Following (Pearlmutter, 1988), we present the "differential units", in which the total input to the neuron controls the em rate of change (time derivative) of that unit state, instead of directly controlling its state. As will be shown the "differential units" can be implemented in terms of regular units.

The second idea comes from the fact that trajectories are usually come from a *plan*, resulting in the execution of a "motor program". Executing a complete motor program will typically involve executing a hierarchy of sub-programs, modified by the information coming from sensors. For example drawing characters on a piece of paper involves deciding which character to draw (and what size), then drawing each stroke of the character. Each stroke involves particular sub-programs which are likely to be common to several characters (straight lines of various orientations, curved lines, loops...). Each stroke is decomposed in precise motor patterns. In short, a plan can be described in a hierarchical fashion, starting from the most abstract level (which object to draw), which changes every half second or so, to the lower level (the precise muscle activation patterns) which changes every 5 or 10 milliseconds. It seems that this scheme can be particularly well embodied by an "Oversampled Reverse TDNN". a multilayer architecture in which the states of the units in the higher layers are updated at a faster rate than the states of units in lower layers. The ORTDNN resembles a Subsampled TDNN (Bottou et al., 1990)(Guyon et al., 1991), or a subsampled weight-sharing network (Le Cun et al., 1990a), in which all the connections have been reversed, and the input and output have been interchanged. The advantage of using the ORTDNN, as opposed to a table lookup, or a memory intensive scheme, is the ability to generalize the learned trajectories to unseen inputs (plans). With this new architecture it is shown that trajectory generation problems of large complexity can be solved with relatively small resources.

2   THE DIFFERENTIAL UNITS

In a time continuous network, the forward propagation can be written as:

$$T\frac{\partial x(t)}{\partial t} = -x(t) + g(wx(t)) + I(t) \tag{1}$$

where $x(t)$ is the activation vector for the units, T is a diagonal matrix such that T_{ii} is the time constant for unit i, I^t is the input vector at time t, w is a weight matrix such that w_{ij} is the connection from unit j to unit i, and g is a differentiable (multi-valued) function.

A reasonable discretization of this equation is:

$$\tilde{x}^{t+1} = \tilde{x}^t + \Delta t T^{-1}(-\tilde{x}^t + g(w\tilde{x}^t) + I^t) \tag{2}$$

where Δt is the time step used in the discretization, the superscript t means at time $t\Delta t$ (i.e. $\tilde{x}^t = \tilde{x}(t\Delta t)$). x_0 is the starting point and is a constant. t ranges from 0 to M, with $I^0 = 0$.

The cost function to be minimized is:

$$E = \frac{1}{2} \sum_{t=1}^{t=M} (S^t \tilde{x}^t - d^t)^{\top} (S^t \tilde{x}^t - d^t) \tag{3}$$

Where D^t is the desired output, and S^t is a rectangular matrix which has a 0 if the corresponding x_i^t is unconstrained and 1 otherwise. Each pattern is composed of pairs (I^t, D^t) for $t \in [1..M]$. To minimize equation 3 with the constraints given by equation 2 we express the Lagrage function (Le Cun, 1988):

$$L = \frac{1}{2} \sum_{t=1}^{t=M} (S^t \tilde{x}^t - D^t)(S^t \tilde{x}^t - D^t)^T + \sum_{t=0}^{t=M-1} (\tilde{b}^{t+1})^{\top} (-\tilde{x}^{t+1} + \tilde{x}^t + \Delta t T^{-1}(-\tilde{x}^t + g(w\tilde{x}^t) + I^t)) \tag{4}$$

Where $\tilde{b}^{t+1}$ are Lagrange multipliers (for $t \in [1..M]$). The superscript ^{T} means that the corresponding matrix is transposed. If we differentiate with respect to $\tilde{x}^t$ we get:

$$\left(\frac{\partial L}{\partial \tilde{x}^t}\right)^{\top} = \vec{0} = (S^t \tilde{x}^t - d^t) - \tilde{b}^t + \tilde{b}^{t+1} - \Delta t T^{-1} \tilde{b}^{t+1} - \Delta t T^{-1} w^T g'(w\tilde{x}^t)\tilde{b}^{t+1} \tag{5}$$

For $t \in [1..M-1]$ and $\frac{\partial L}{\partial \tilde{x}^M} = 0 = (S^t \tilde{x}^M - D^M) - \tilde{b}^M$ for the boundary condition. g' a diagonal matrix containing the derivatives of g ($g'(wx)w$ is the jacobian of g). From this an update rule for $\tilde{b}^t$ can be derived:

$$\begin{aligned} \tilde{b}^M &= (S^M \tilde{x}^M - d^M) \\ \tilde{b}^t &= (S^t \tilde{x}^t - d^t) + (1 - \Delta t T^{-1})\tilde{b}^{t+1} + \Delta t T^{-1} w^T \nabla g(w\tilde{x}^t)\tilde{b}^{t+1} \quad \text{for } t \in [1..M-1] \end{aligned} \tag{6}$$

This is the rule used to compute the gradient (backpropagation). If the Lagrangian is differentiated with respect to w_{ij}, the standard updating rule for the weight is obtained:

$$\frac{\partial L}{\partial w_{ij}} = \Delta t T^{-1} \sum_{t=1}^{t=M-1} \tilde{b}_i^{t+1} \tilde{x}_j^t g_i'(\sum_k w_{ik} \tilde{x}_k^t) \tag{7}$$

If the Lagrangian is differentiated with respect to T, we get:

$$\frac{\partial L}{\partial T} = -T^{-1} \sum_{t=0}^{t=M-1} (\tilde{x}^{t+1} - \tilde{x}^t)\tilde{b}^{t+1} \tag{8}$$

From the last two equations, we can derived a learning algorithm by gradient descent

$$\Delta w_{ij} = -\eta_w \frac{\partial L}{\partial w_{ij}} \tag{9}$$

$$\Delta \frac{1}{T_{ii}} = -\eta_T \frac{\partial L}{\partial \frac{1}{T_{ii}}} = -\eta_T \Delta t T_{ii} \sum_{t=0}^{t=M-1} (\tilde{x}^{t+1} - \tilde{x}^t)\tilde{b}^{t+1} \tag{10}$$

where η_w and η_T are respectively the learning rates for the weights and the time constants (in practice better results are obtained by having different learning rates $\eta_{w_{ij}}$ and $\eta_{T_{ii}}$ per connections). The constant η_T must be chosen with caution

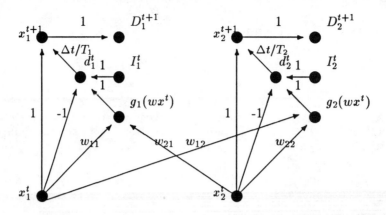

Figure 1: A backpropagation implementation of equation 2 for a two units network between time t and $t+1$. This figure repeats itself vertically for every time step from $t = 0$ to $t = M$. The quantities x_1^{t+1}, x_2^{t+1}, $d_1^t = -x_1^t + g_1(wx^t) + I_1^t$ and $d_2^t = -x_2^t + g_2(wx^t) + I_2^t$ are computed with linear units.

since if any time constants T_{ii} were to become less than one, the system would be unstable. Performing gradient descent in $\frac{1}{T_{ii}}$ instead of in T_{ii} is preferable for numerical stability reasons.

Equation 2 is implemented with a feed forward backpropagation network. It should first be noted that this equation can be written as a linear combination of x^t (the activation at the previous time), the input, and a non-linear function g of wx^t. Therefore, this can be implemented with two linear units and one nonlinear unit with activation function g. To keep the time constraint, the network is "unfolded" in time , with the weights shared from one time step to another. For instance a simple two fully connected units network with no threshold can be implemented as in Fig. 1 (only the layer between time t and $t+1$ is shown). The network repeats itself vertically for each time step with the weights shared between time steps. The main advantage of this implementation is that all equations 6, 7 and 8 are implemented implicitly by the back-propagation algorithm.

3   CHARACTER GENERATION: LEARNING TO GENERATE A SINGLE LETTER

In this section we describe a simple experiment designed to 1) illustrate how trajectory generation can be implemented with a recurrent network, 2) to show the advantages of using differential units instead of the traditional non linear units and 3) to show how the fully connected architecture (with differential units) severly limits the learning capacity of the network. The task is to draw the letter "A" with

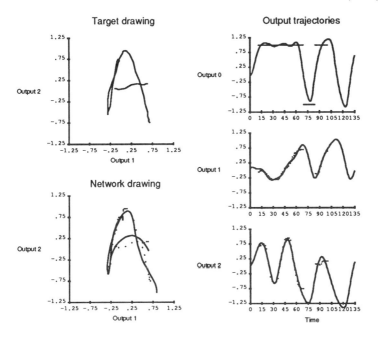

Figure 2: Top left: Trajectory representing the letter "A". Bottom left: Trajectory produced by the network after learning. The dots correspond to the target points of the original trajectory. The curve is produced by drawing output unit 2 as a function of output unit 1, using output unit 0 for deciding when the pen is up or down. Right: Trajectories of the three output units (pen-up/pen-down, X coordinate of the pen and Y coordinate of the pen) as a function of time. The dots corresponds to the target points of the original trajectory.

a pen. The network has 3 output units, two for the X and Y position of the pen, and one to code whether the pen is up or down. The network has a total 21 units, no input unit, 18 hidden units and 3 output units. The network is fully connected.

Character glyphs are obtained from a tablet which records points at successive instants of time. The data therefore is a sequence of triplets indicating the time, and the X and Y positions. When the pen is up, or if there are no constraint for some specific time steps (misreading of the tablet), the activation of the unit is left unconstrained. The letter to be learned is taken from a handwritten letter database and is displayed in figure 2 (top left).

The letter trajectory covers a maximum of 90 time stamps. The network is unfolded 135 steps (10 unconstrained steps are left at the begining to allow the network to settle and 35 additional steps are left at the end to monitor the network activity). The learning rate η_w is set to 1.0 (the actual learning rate is per connection and is obtained by dividing the global learning rate by the fanin to the destination unit, and by dividing by the number of connections sharing the same weight). The time constants are set to 10 to produce a smooth trajectory on the output. The learning rate η_T is equal to zero (no learning on the time constants). The initial values for the weights are picked from a uniform distribution between -1 and +1.

The trajectories fo units 0, 1 and 2 are shown in figure 2 (right). The top graphs represent the state of the pen as a function of time. The straight lines are the desired positions (1 means pen down, -1 means pen up). The middle and bottom graphs are the X and Y positions of the pen respectively. The network is unconstrained after time step 100. Even though the time constants are large, the output units reach the right values before time step 10. The top trajectory (pen-up/pen-down), however, is difficult to learn with time constants as large as 10 because it is not smooth.

The letter drawn by the network after learning is shown in figure 2 (left bottom). The network successfully learned to draw the letter on the fully connected network. Different fixed time constants were tried. For small time constant (like 1.0), the network was unable to learn the pattern for any learning rate η_w we tried. This is not surprising since the (vertical) weight sharing makes the trajectories very sensitive to any variation of the weights. This fact emphasizes the importance of using differential units. Larger time constants allow larger learning rate for the weights. Of course, if those are too large, fast trajectories can not be learned.

The error can be further improved by letting the time constant adapt as well. However the gain in doing so is minimal. If the learning rate η_T is small, the gain over $\eta_T = 0$ is negligible. If η_T is too big, learning becomes quickly unstable.

This simulation was done with no input, and the target trajectories were for the drawing of a single letter. In the next section, the problem is extended to that of learning to draw multiple letters, depending on an input vector.

4   LEARNING TO GENERATE MULTIPLE LETTERS: THE REVERSE TDNN ARCHITECTURE

In a first attempt, the fully connected network of the previous section was used to try to generate the eight first letters of the alphabet. Eight units were used for the input, 3 for the output, and various numbers of hidden units were tried. Every time, all the units, visible and hidden, were fully interconnected. Each input unit was associated to one letter, and the input patterns consisted of one +1 at the unit corresponding to the letter, and -1/7 for all other input units. No success was achieved for all the set of parameters which were tried. The error curves reached plateaus, and the letter glyphs were not recognizable. Even bringing the number of letter to two (one "A" and one "B") was unsuccessful. In all cases the network was acting like it was ignoring its input: the activation of the output units were almost identical for all input patterns. This was attributed to the network architecture.

A new kind of architecture was then used, which we call "Oversampled Reverse TDNN" because of its resemblance with a Subsampled TDNN with input and output interchanged. Subsampled TDNN have been used in speech recognition (Bottou et al., 1990), and on-line character recognition (Guyon et al., 1991). They can be seen one-dimensional versions of locally-connected, weight sharing networks (Le Cun, 1989)(Le Cun et al., 1990b). Time delay connections allow units to be connected to unit at an earlier time. Weight sharing in time implements a convolution of the input layer. In the Subsampled TDNN, the rate at which the units states are updated decreases gradually with the layer index. The subsampling provides

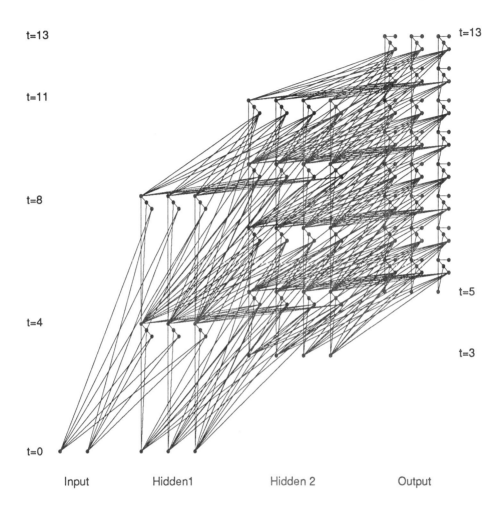

Figure 3: Architecture of a simple reverse TDNN. Time goes from bottom to top, data flows from left to right. The left module is the input and has 2 units. The next module (hidden1) has 3 units and is undersampled every 4 time steps. The following module (hidden2) has 4 units and is undersampled every 2 time steps. The right module is the output, has 3 units and is not undersampled. All modules have time delay connections from the preceding module. Thus the hidden1 is connected to hidden2 over a window of 5 time steps, and hidden2 to the output over a window of 3 time steps. For each pattern presented on the 2 input units, a trajectory of 8 time steps is produced by the network on each of the 3 units of the output.

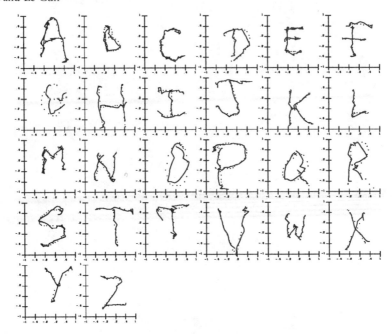

Figure 4: Letters drawn by the reverse TDNN network after 10000 iteration of learning.

a gradual reduction of the time resolution. In a reverse TDNN the subsampling starts from the units from the output (which have no subsampling) toward the input. Equivalently, each layer is oversampled when compared to the previous layer. This is illustrated in Figure 3 which shows a small reverse TDNN. The input is applied to the 2 units in the lower left. The next layer is unfolded in time two steps and has time delay connections toward step zero of the input. The next layer after this is unfolded in time 4 steps (with again time delay connections), and finally the output is completely unfolded in time. The advantage of such an architecture is its ability to generate trajectories progressively, starting with the lower frequency components at each layer. This parallels recognition TDNN's which extract features progressively. Since the weights are shared between time steps, the network on the figures has only 94 free weights.

With the reverse TDNN architecture, it was easy to learn the 26 letters of of the alphabet. We found that the learning is easier if all the weights are initialized to 0 except those with the shortest time delay. As a result, the network initially only sees its fastest connections. The influence of the remaining connections starts at zero and increase as the network learns. The glyphs drawn by the network after 10,000 training epochs are shown in figure 4. To avoid ambiguity, we give subsampling rates with respect to the output, although it would be more natural to mention oversampling rates with respect to the input. The network has 26 input units, 30 hidden units in the first layer subsampled at every 27 time steps, 25 units at the next layer subsampled at every 9 time steps, and 3 output units with no subsampling. Every layer has time delay connections from the previous layer, and is connected with 3 different updates of the previous layer. The time constants were not subject to learning and were initialized to 10 for the x and y output units, and to 1 for the remaining units. No effort was made to optimize these values.

Big initial time constants prevent the network from making fast variations on the output units and in general slow down the learning process. On the other hand, small time constants make learning more difficult. The correct strategy is to adapt the time constants to the intrinsic frequencies of the trajectory. With all the time constants equal to one, the network was not able to learn the alphabet (as it was the case in the experiment of the previous section). Good results are obtained with time constants of 10 for the two x-y output units and time constants of 1 for all other units.

5   VARIATIONS OF THE ORTDNN

Many variations of the Oversampled Reverse TDNN architecture can be imagined. For example, recurrent connections can be added: connections can go from right to left on figure 3, as long as they go up. Recurrent connections become necessary when information needs to be stored for an arbitrary long time. Another variation would be to add sensor inputs at various stages of the network, to allow adjustment of the trajectory based on sensor data, either on a global scale (first layers), or locally (last layers). Tasks requiring recurrent ORTDNN's and/or sensor input include dynamic robot control or speech synthesis.

Another interesting variation is an encoder network consisting of a Subsampled TDNN and an Oversmapled Reverse TDNN connected back to back. The Subsampled TDNN encodes the time sequence shown on its input, and the ORTDNN reconstructs an time sequence from the output of the TDNN. The main application of this network would be the compact encoding of time series. This network can be trained to reproduce its input on its output (auto-encoder), in which case the state of the middle layer can be used as a compact code of the input sequence.

6   CONCLUSION

We have presented a new architecture capable of learning to generate trajectories efficiently. The architecture is designed to favor hierarchical representations of trajectories in terms of subtasks.

The experiment shows how the ORTDNN can produce different letters as a function of the input. Although this application does not have practical consequences, it shows the learning capabilities of the model for generating trajectories. The task presented here was particularly difficult because there is no correlation between the patterns. The inputs for an A or a Z only differ on 2 of the 26 input units. Yet, the network produces totally different trajectories on the output units. This is promising since typical neural net application have very correlated patterns which are in general much easier to learn.

References

Bottou, L., Fogelman, F., Blanchet, P., and Liénard, J. S. (1990). Speaker independent isolated digit recognition: Multilayer perceptron vs Dynamic Time Warping. *Neural Networks*, 3:453–465.

Guyon, I., Albrecht, P., Le Cun, Y., Denker, J. S., and W., H. (1991). design of a neural network character recognizer for a touch terminal. *Pattern Recognition*, 24(2):105–119.

Jordan, M. I. (1986). Serial Order: A Parallel Distributed Processing Approach. Technical Report ICS-8604, Institute for Cognitive Science, University of California at San Diego, La Jolla, CA.

Lang, K. J. and Hinton, G. E. (1988). A Time Delay Neural Network Architecture for Speech Recognition. Technical Report CMU-cs-88-152, Carnegie-Mellon University, Pittsburgh PA.

Le Cun, Y. (1988). A theoretical framework for Back-Propagation. In Touretzky, D., Hinton, G., and Sejnowski, T., editors, *Proceedings of the 1988 Connectionist Models Summer School*, pages 21–28, CMU, Pittsburgh, Pa. Morgan Kaufmann.

Le Cun, Y. (1989). Generalization and Network Design Strategies. In Pfeifer, R., Schreter, Z., Fogelman, F., and Steels, L., editors, *Connectionism in Perspective*, Zurich, Switzerland. Elsevier. an extended version was published as a technical report of the University of Toronto.

Le Cun, Y., Boser, B., Denker, J. S., Henderson, D., Howard, R. E., Hubbard, W., and Jackel, L. D. (1990a). Handwritten digit recognition with a back-propagation network. In Touretzky, D., editor, *Advances in Neural Information Processing Systems 2 (NIPS*89)*, Denver, CO. Morgan Kaufman.

Le Cun, Y., Boser, B., Denker, J. S., Henderson, D., Howard, R. E., Hubbard, W., and Jackel, L. D. (1990b). Back-Propagation Applied to Handwritten Zipcode Recognition. *Neural Computation*.

Pearlmutter, B. (1988). Learning State Space Trajectories in Recurrent Neural Networks. *Neural Computation*, 1(2).

Waibel, A., Hanazawa, T., Hinton, G., Shikano, K., and Lang, K. (1989). Phoneme Recognition Using Time-Delay Neural Networks. *IEEE Transactions on Acoustics, Speech and Signal Processing*, 37:328–339.

Learning Global Direct Inverse Kinematics

David DeMers[*]
Computer Science & Eng.
UC San Diego
La Jolla, CA 92093-0114

Kenneth Kreutz-Delgado[†]
Electrical & Computer Eng.
UC San Diego
La Jolla, CA 92093-0407

Abstract

We introduce and demonstrate a bootstrap method for construction of an inverse function for the robot kinematic mapping using only sample configuration–space/workspace data. Unsupervised learning (clustering) techniques are used on pre–image neighborhoods in order to *learn* to partition the configuration space into subsets over which the kinematic mapping is invertible. Supervised learning is then used separately on each of the partitions to approximate the inverse function. The ill–posed inverse kinematics function is thereby regularized, and a global inverse kinematics solution for the wristless Puma manipulator is developed.

1 INTRODUCTION

The robot forward kinematics function is a continuous mapping

$$f : \mathcal{C} \subseteq \Theta^n \to \mathcal{W} \subseteq \mathcal{X}^m$$

which maps a set of n joint parameters from the *configuration space*, $\mathcal{C}$, to the m–dimensional *task space*, $\mathcal{W}$. If $m \leq n$, the robot has *redundant* degrees–of–freedom (dof's). In general, control objectives such as the positioning and orienting of the end–effector are specified with respect to task space co–ordinates; however, the manipulator is typically controlled only in the configuration space. Therefore, it is important to be able to find some $\vec{\theta} \in \mathcal{C}$ such that f($\vec{\theta}$) is a particular target value $\vec{x}_0 \in \mathcal{W}$. This is the *inverse kinematics problem*.

---

[*]e-mail: demers@cs.ucsd.edu
[†]e-mail: kreutz@ece.ucsd.edu

The inverse kinematics problem is ill–posed. If there are redundant dof's then the problem is *locally* ill–posed, because the solution is non–unique and consists of a non–trivial manifold[1] in C. With or without redundant dof's, the problem is generally *globally* ill–posed because of the existence of a finite set of solution branches — there will typically be multiple configurations which result in the same task space location. Thus computation of a *direct* inverse is problematic due to the many–to–one nature (and therefore non–invertibility) of the map f[2].

The inverse problem can be solved explicitly, that is, in closed form, for only certain kinds of manipulators. E.g. six dof elbow manipulators with separable wrist (where the first three joints are used for positioning and the last three have a common origin and are used for orientation), such as the Puma 560, are solvable, see (Craig, 86). The alternative to a closed form solution is a numerical solution, usually either using the inverse of the Jacobian , which is a Newton-style approach, or by using gradient descent (also a Jacobian–based method). These methods are iterative and require expensive Jacobian or gradient computation at each step, thus they are not well–suited for real–time control.

Neural networks can be used to find an inverse by implementing either direct inverse modeling (estimating the explicit function f^{-1}) or differential methods. Implementations of the direct inverse approach typically fail due to the non–linearity of the solution set[3], or resolve this problem by restriction to a single solution *a priori*. However, such a prior restriction of the solutions may not be possible or acceptable in all circumstances, and may drastically reduce the dexterity and manipulability of the arm.

The differential approaches either find only the nearest local solution, or resolve the multiplicity of solutions at training time, as with Jordan's forward modeling (Jordan & Rumelhart, 1990) or the approach of (Nguyen & Patel, 1990). We seek to regularize the mapping in such a way that all possible solutions are available at run–time, and can be computed efficiently as a direct constant–time inverse rather than approximated by slower iterative differential methods. To achieve the fast run–time solution, a significant cost in training time must be paid; however, it is not unreasonable to invest resources in off–line learning in order to attain on–line advantages. Thus we wish to gain the run–time computational efficiency of a direct inverse solution while also achieving the benefits of the differential approaches.

This paper introduces a method for performing *global* regularization; that is, identifying the complete, finite set of solutions to the inverse kinematics problem for a non–redundant manipulator. This will provide the ability to *choose* a particular solution at run time. Resolving redundancy is beyond the scope of this paper; however, preliminary work on a method which may be integrated with the work presented here is shown in (DeMers & Kreutz–Delgado, 1991). In the remainder of this paper it will be assumed that the manipulator does not have redundant dof's. It will also be assumed that all of the joints are revolute, thus the configuration space is a subset of the n-torus, T^n.

---

[1] Generically of dimensionality equal to $n - m$.

[2] The target values are assumed to be in the range of f, $\vec{x} \in \mathcal{W} = f(C)$, so the *existence* of a solution is not an issue in this paper.

[3] Training a network to minimize mean squared error with multiple target values for the same input value results in a "learned" response of the average of the targets. Since the targets lie on a number of non–linear manifolds (for the redundant case) or consist of a finite number of points (for the non–redundant case), the average of multiple targets will typically not be a correct target.

2   TOPOLOGY OF THE KINEMATICS FUNCTION

The kinematics mapping is continuous and smooth and, generically, neighborhoods in configuration space map to neighborhoods in the task space[4]. The configuration space, $\mathcal{C}$, is made up of a finite number of disjoint regions or partitions, separated by $n-1$ dimensional surfaces where the Jacobian loses rank (called *critical* surfaces), see (Burdick, 1988, Burdick, 1991).

Let $f : T^n \to \mathbf{R}^n$ be the kinematic mapping. Then

$$\mathcal{W} = f(\mathcal{C}) = \bigcup_{i=1}^{k} f_i(\mathcal{C}_i)$$

where f_i is the restriction of f to $\mathcal{C}_i$, $f_i : \mathcal{C}_i = \Theta^n/f \to \mathbf{R}^n$ and the factor space Θ^n/f is locally diffeomorphic to $\mathbf{R}^n$. The $\mathcal{C}_i$ are each a connected region such that

$$\forall \vec{\theta} \in \mathcal{C}_i, \quad \det\left(J(\vec{\theta})\right) \neq 0$$

where J is the Jacobian of f, $J = d_\theta f$. Define $\mathcal{W}_i$ as $f(\mathcal{C}_i)$. Generically, f_i is one–to–one and onto open neighborhoods of $\mathcal{W}_i$[5], thus by the inverse function theorem

$$\exists\, g_i(\vec{x}) = f_i^{-1} : \mathcal{W}_i \to \mathcal{C}_i, \text{ such that } f \circ g_i(\vec{x}) = \vec{x}, \quad \forall \vec{x} \in \mathcal{W}_i$$

In the general case, with redundant dof's, the kinematics over a single configuration–space region can be viewed as a fiber bundle, where the fibers are homeomorphic to T^{n-m}. The base space is the reachable workspace (the image of $\mathcal{C}_i$ under f). Solution branch resolution can be done by identifying distinct connected open coordinate neighborhoods of the configuration space which cover the workspace. Redundancy resolution can be done by a consistent parameterization of the fibers within each neighborhood. In the case at hand, without redundant dof's, the "fibers" are singleton sets and no resolution is needed.

In the remainder of this paper, we will use input/output data to identify the individual regions, $\mathcal{C}_i$, of a non–redundant manipulator, over which the mapping $f_i : \mathcal{C}_i \to \mathcal{W}_i$ is invertible. The input/output data will then be partitioned modulo the configuration regions $\mathcal{C}_i$, and each f_i^{-1} approximated individually.

3   SAMPLING APPROACH

If the manipulator can be measured and a large sample of $(\vec{\theta}, \vec{x})$ pairs taken, stored such that the $\vec{x}$ samples can be searched efficiently, a rough estimate of the inverse solutions at a particular target point $\vec{x}_0$ may be obtained by finding all of the $\vec{\theta}$ points whose image lies within some ϵ of $\vec{x}_0$. The pre–image of this ϵ–ball will generically consist of several distinct (distorted) balls in the configuration space. If the sampling is adequate then there will be one such ball for each of the inverse solution branches. If each of the the points in each ball is given a label for the solution branch, the labeled data may then be used for supervised

---

[4]This property fails when the manipulator is in a *singular* configuration, at which the Jacobian, $d_\theta f$, loses rank.

[5]Since it is generically true that J is non–singular.

learning of a classifier of solution branches in the configuration space. In this way we will have "bootstrapped" our way to the development of a solution branch classifier.

Taking advantage of the continuous nature of the forward mapping, note that if $\vec{x}_0$ is slightly perturbed by a "jump" to a neighboring target point then the pre–image balls will also be perturbed. We can assign labels to the new data consistent with labels already assigned to the previous data, by computing the distances between the new, unlabeled balls and the previously labeled balls. Continuing in this fashion, $\vec{x}_0$ traces a path through the entire workspace and solution branch labels may be given to all points in C which map to within ϵ of one of the selected $\vec{x}$ points along the sweep.

This procedure results in a significant and representative proportion of the data now being labeled as to solution branch. Thus we now have labeled data $(\vec{\theta}, \vec{x}, \mathcal{B}(\vec{\theta}))$, where $\mathcal{B}(\vec{\theta}) = \{1, \ldots, k\}$ indicates which of the k solution branches, C_i, the point $\vec{\theta}$ is in. We can now construct a classifier using supervised learning to compute the branches $\mathcal{B}(\vec{\theta})$ for a given $\vec{\theta}$. Once an estimate of $\mathcal{B}(\vec{\theta})$ is developed, we may use it to classify large amounts of $(\vec{\theta}, \vec{x})$ data, and partition the data into k sets, one for each of the solution branches, C_i.

4   RESOLUTION OF SOLUTION BRANCHES

We applied the above to the wristless Puma 560, a 3–R manipulator for end–effector positioning in $\mathbf{R}^3$. We took 40,000 samples of $(\vec{\theta}, \vec{x})$ points, and examined all points within 10 cm of selected target values $\vec{x}_i$. The $\vec{x}_i$ formed a grid of 90 locations in the workspace. 3,062 of the samples fell within 10 cm of one of the $\vec{x}_i$. The configuration space points for each target $\vec{x}_i$ were clustered into four groups, corresponding to the four possible solution branches of the wristless Puma 560. About 3% of the points were clustered into the wrong group, based on the labeling scheme used. These 3,062 points were then used as training patterns for a feedforward neural network classifier. A point was classified into the group associated with the output unit of the neural network with maximum activation. The output values were normalized to sum to 1.0. The network was tested on 50,000 new, previously unseen $(\vec{\theta}, \vec{x})$ pairs, and correctly classified more than 98% of them.

All of the erroneous classifications were for points near the critical surfaces. Therefore the activation levels of the output units can be used to estimate closeness to a critical surface. Examining the test data and assigning all $\vec{\theta}$ points for which no output unit has activation greater than or equal to 0.8 to the "near–a–singularity" class, the remaining points were 100% correctly classified.

Figure 1 shows the true critical manifold separating the regions of configuration space, and the estimated manifold consisting of points from the test set where the maximum activation of output units of the trained neural network is less than 0.8. The configuration space is a subset of the 3–torus, which is shown here "sliced" along three generators and represented as a cube. Because the Puma 560 has physical limits on the range of motion of its joints, the regions shown are in fact six distinct regions, and there is no wraparound in any direction.

This classifier network is our candidate for an estimate of $\mathcal{B}(\vec{\theta})$. With it, the samples can be separated into groups corresponding to the domains of each of the f_i, thus regularizing into $k = 6$ one–to–one invertible pieces[6].

---

[6]Although there are only four inverse solutions for any $\vec{x}$. If there were no joint limits, then the

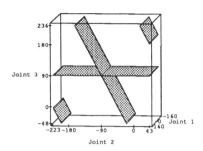
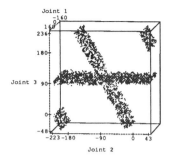

Figure 1: *The analytically derived critical surfaces, along with 1,000 points for which no unit of the neural network classifier has greater than 0.8 activation.*

5   DIRECT INVERSE SOLUTIONS

The classifier neural network can now be used to partition the data into four groups, one for each of the branches, C_i. For each of these data sets, we train a feedforward network to learn the mapping in the inverse direction. The target vectors were represented as vectors of the sine of the half–angle (a measure motivated by the quaternion representation of orientation). MSE under 0.001 were achieved for each of the four. This looks like a very small error, however, this error is somewhat misleading. The configuration space error is measured in units which are difficult to interpret. More important is the error in the workspace when the solution computed is used in the forward kinematics mapping to position the arm. Over a test set of 4,000 points, the average positioning error was 5.2 cm over the 92 cm radius workspace.

We have as yet made no attempts to optimize the network or training for the direct inverse; the thrust of our work is in achieving the regularization. It is clear that substantially better performance can be developed, for example, by following (Ritter, et al., 1989), and we expect end–effector positioning errors of less than 1% to be easily achievable.

6   DISCUSSION

We have shown that by exploiting the topological property of continuity of the kinematic mapping for a non–redundant 3–dof robot we can determine all of the solution regions of the inverse kinematic mapping. We have mapped out the configuration space critical surfaces and thus discovered an important topological property of the mapping, corresponding to an important physical property of the manipulator, by unsupervised learning. We can boostrap from the original input/output data, unlabeled as to solution branch, and construct an accurate classifier for the entire configuration space. The data can thereby be partitioned into sets which are individually one–to–one and invertible, and the inverse mapping can be directly approximated for each. Thus a large learning–time investment results in a fast run–time direct inverse kinematics solution.

cube shown would be a true 3–torus, with opposite faces identified. Thus the small pieces in the corners would be part of the larger regions by wraparound in the Joint 2 direction.

We need a thorough sampling of the configuration space in order to ensure that enough points will fall within each ϵ-ball, thus the data requirements are clearly exponential in the number of degrees of freedom of the manipulator. Even with efficient storage and retrieval in geometric data structures, such as a k–d tree, high dimensional systems may not be tractable by our methods.

Fortunately practical and useful robotic systems of six and seven degrees of freedom should be amenable to this method, especially if separable into positioning and orienting subsystems.

Acknowledgements

This work was supported in part by NSF Presidential Young Investigator award IRI–9057631 and a NASA/Netrologic grant. The first author would like to thank NIPS for providing student travel grants. We thank Gary Cottrell for his many helpful comments and enthusiastic discussions.

References

Joel Burdick (1991), "A Classification of 3R Regional Manipulator Singularities and Geometries", *Proc. 1991 IEEE Intl. Conf. Robotics & Automation*, Sacramento.

Joel Burdick (1988), "Kinematics and Design of Redundant Robot Manipulators", Stanford Ph.D. Thesis, Dept. of Mechanical Engineering.

John Craig (1986), *Introduction to Robotics*, Addison-Wesley.

David DeMers & Kenneth Kreutz–Delgado (1991), "Learning Global Topological Properties of Robot Kinematic Mappings for Neural Network-Based Configuration Control", in Bekey, ed. *Proc. USC Workshop on Neural Networks in Robotics*, (to appear).

Michael I. Jordan (1988), "Supervised Learning and Systems with Excess Degrees of Freedom", COINS Technical Report 88–27, University of Massachusetts at Amherst.

Michael I. Jordan & David E. Rumelhart (1990), "Forward Models: Supervised Learning with a Distal Teacher". Submitted to *Cognitive Science*.

L. Nguyen & R.V. Patel (1990), "A Neural Network Based Strategy for the Inverse Kinematics Problem in Robotics", in Jamshidi and Saif, eds., *Robotics and Manufacturing: recent Trends in Research, Education and Applications*, vol. 3, pp. 995–1000 (ASME Press).

Helge J. Ritter, Thomas M. Martinetz, & Klaus J. Schulten (1989), "Topology–Conserving Maps for Learning Visuo–Motor–Coordination", *Neural Networks*, Vol. 2, pp. 159–168.

A Neural Net Model for Adaptive Control of Saccadic Accuracy by Primate Cerebellum and Brainstem

Paul Dean[a], John E. W. Mayhew and Pat Langdon

Department of Psychology[a] and Artificial Intelligence
Vision Research Unit, University of Sheffield,
Sheffield S10 2TN, England.

Abstract

Accurate saccades require interaction between brainstem circuitry and the cerebellum. A model of this interaction is described, based on Kawato's principle of feedback-error-learning. In the model a part of the brainstem (the superior colliculus) acts as a simple feedback controller with no knowledge of initial eye position, and provides an error signal for the cerebellum to correct for eye-muscle nonlinearities. This teaches the cerebellum, modelled as a CMAC, to adjust appropriately the gain on the brainstem burst-generator's internal feedback loop and so alter the size of burst sent to the motoneurons. With direction-only errors the system rapidly learns to make accurate horizontal eye movements from any starting position, and adapts realistically to subsequent simulated eye-muscle weakening or displacement of the saccadic target.

1 INTRODUCTION

The use of artificial neural nets (ANNs) to control robot movement offers advantages in situations where the relevant analytic solutions are unknown, or where unforeseeable changes, perhaps as a result of damage or wear, are likely to occur. It is also a mode of control with considerable similarities to those used in biological systems. It may thus prove possible to use ideas derived from studies of ANNs in robots to help understand how the brain produces movements. This paper describes an attempt to do this for saccadic eye movements.

595

The structure of the human retina, with its small foveal area of high acuity, requires extensive use of eye-movements to inspect regions of interest. To minimise the time during which the retinal image is blurred, these saccadic refixation movements are very rapid - too rapid for visual feedback to be used in acquiring the target (Carpenter 1988). The saccadic control system must therefore know in advance the size of control signal to be sent to the eye muscles. This is a function of both target displacement from the fovea and initial eye-position. The latter is important because the eye-muscles and orbital tissues are elastic, so that more force is required to move the eye away from the straight-ahead position than towards it (Collins 1975).

Similar rapid movements may be required of robot cameras. Here too the desired control signal is usually a function of both target displacement and initial camera positions. Experiments with a simulated four degree-of-freedom stereo camera rig have shown that appropriate ANN architectures can learn this kind of function reasonably efficiently (Dean et al. 1991), provided the nets are given accurate error information. However, this information is only available if the relevant equations have been solved; how can ANNs be used in situations where this is not the case?

A possible solution to this kind of problem (derived in part from analysis of biological motor control systems) has been suggested by Kawato (1990), and was implemented for the simulated stereo camera rig (Fig 1). Two controllers are arranged in

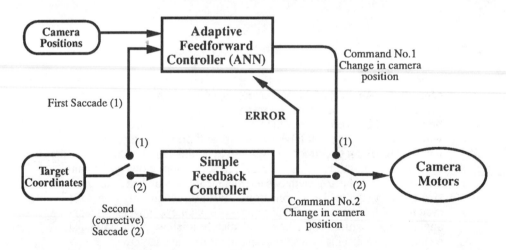

Fig 1: Control architecture for robot saccades

parallel. Target coordinates, together with information about camera positions, are passed to an adaptive feedforward controller in the form of an ANN, which then moves the cameras. If the movement is inaccurate, the new target coordinates are passed to the second controller. This knows nothing of initial camera position, but issues a corrective movement command that is simply proportional to target displacement. In the absence of the adaptive controller it can be used to home in on the target with a series of saccades:

though each individual saccade is ballistic, the sequence is generated by visual feedback, hence the term simple feedback controller. When the adaptive controller is present, however, the output of the simple feedback controller can be used not only to generate a corrective saccade but also as a motor error signal (Fig 1). Although this error signal is not accurate, its imperfections become less important as the ANN learns and so takes on more responsibility for the movement (for proof of convergence see Kawato 1990). The architecture is robust in that it learns on-line, does not require mathematical knowledge, and still functions to some extent when the adaptive controller is untrained or damaged.

These qualities are also important for control of saccades in biological systems, and it is therefore of interest that there are similarities between the architecture shown in Fig 1 and the structure of the primate saccadic system (Fig 2). The cerebellum is widely (though

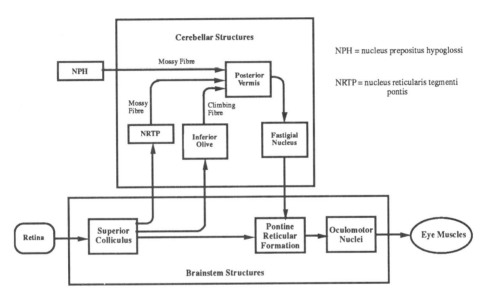

Fig 2: Schematic diagram of major components of primate saccadic control system

not universally) regarded as an adaptive controller, and when the relevant part of it is damaged the remaining brainstem structures function like the simple feedback controller of Fig 1. Saccades can still be made, but (i) they are not accurate; (ii) the degree of inaccuracy depends on initial eye position; (iii) multiple saccades are required to home in on the target; and (iv) the system never recovers (eg Ritchie 1976; Optican and Robinson 1980).

These similarities suggest that it is worth exploring the idea that the brainstem teaches the cerebellum to make accurate saccades (cf Grossberg and Kuperstein 1986), just as the simple feedback controller teaches the adaptive controller in the Kawato architecture. A model of the primate system was therefore constructed, using 'off-the-shelf' components wired together in accordance with known anatomy and physiology, and its performance assessed under a variety of conditions.

2 STRUCTURE OF MODEL

The overall structure of the model is shown in Fig 3. It has three main components: a simple feedback controller, a burst generator, and a CMAC. The simple feedback

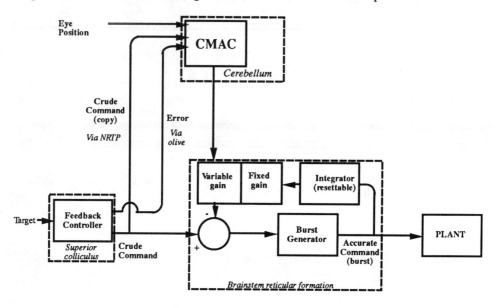

Figure 3: Main components of the model. The corresponding biological structures are shown in italics and dotted lines.

controller sends a signal proportional to target displacement from the fovea to the burst generator. The function of the burst generator is to translate this signal into an appropriate command for the eye muscles, and it is based here on the model of Robinson (Robinson 1975; van Gisbergen et al. 1981). Its output is a rapid burst of neural impulses, the frequency of which is esentially a velocity command. A crucial feature of Robinson's model is an internal feedback loop, in which the output of the generator is integrated and compared with the input command. The saccade terminates when the two are equal. This system ensures that the generator gives the output matching the input command in the face of disturbances that might alter burst frequency and hence saccade velocity.

The simple feedback controller sends to the CMAC (Albus 1981) a copy of its command to the burst generator. The CMAC (Cerebellar Model Arithmetic Computer) is a neural net model of the cerebellum incoporating theories of cerebellar function proposed independently by Marr (1969) and Albus (1971). Its function is to learn a mapping between a multidimensional input and a single-valued output, using a form of lookup table with local interpolation. The entries in the lookup table are modified using the delta rule, by an error signal which is either the difference between desired and actual output or some estimate of that difference. CMACs have been used successfully in a number of applications concerning prediction or control (eg Miller et al. 1987; Hormel 1990). In the present case the function to be learnt is that relating desired saccade amplitude and initial eye position (inputs) to gain adjustment in the internal feedback loop of the burst generator (output).

The correspondences between the model structure and the anatomy and physiology of the primate saccadic system are as follows.
(1) The simple feedback controller represents the superior colliculus.
(2) The burst generator corresponds to groups of neurons located in the brainstem.
(3) The CMAC models a particular region of cerebellar cortex, the posterior vermis.
(4) The pathway conveying a copy of the feedback controller's crude command corresponds to the projection from the superior colliculus to the nucleus reticularis tegmenti pontis, which in turn sendes a mossy fibre projection to the posterior vermis.
Space precludes detailed evaluation of the substantial evidence supporting the above correspondences (see eg Wurtz and Goldberg 1989). The remaining two connections have a less secure basis.
(5) The idea that the cerebellum adjusts saccadic accuracy by altering feedback gains in the burst generator is based on stimulation evidence (Keller 1989); details of the projection, including its anatomy, are not known.
(6) The error pathway from feedback controller to CMAC is represented by the anatomically identified projection from superior colliculus to inferior olive, and thence via climbing fibres to the posterior vermis. There is considerable debate concerning the functional role of climbing fibres, and in the case of the tecto-olivary projection the relevant physiological evidence appears to be lacking.

3 PERFORMANCE OF MODEL

The system shown in Fig 3 was trained to make horizontal movements only. The size of burst ΔI (arbitrary units) required to produce an accurate rightward saccade $\Delta\theta$ deg was calculated from Van Gisbergen and Van Opstal's (1989) analysis of the nonlinear relationship between eye position and muscle position as

$$\Delta I = a \ [\Delta\theta^2 + \ \Delta\theta \ (b \ + \ 2\theta)] \tag{1}$$

where θ is initial eye-position (measured in deg from extreme leftward eye-position) and a and b are constants. In the absence of the CMAC, the feedback controller and burst generator produce a burst of size

$$\Delta I \ = \ x. \ (c/d) \tag{2}$$

where x is the rightward horizontal displacement of the target, c is the gain constant of the feedback controller, and d a constant related to the fixed gain of the internal feedback loop of the burst generator. The kinematics of the eye are such that x (measured in deg of visual angle) is equal to $\Delta\theta$. The constants were chosen so that the performance of the system without the CMAC resembled that of the primate saccadic system after cerebellar damage (fig 4A), namely position-dependent overshoot (eg Ritchie 1976; Optican and

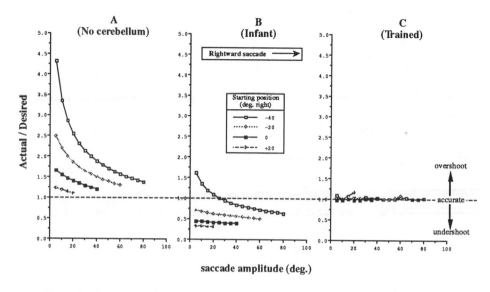

Fig 4. Performance of model under different conditions before and after training

Robinson 1980). When the CMAC is present, the size of burst changes to

$$\Delta I = x. [c/(g + d)] \qquad (3)$$

where g is the output of the CMAC. This was initialised to a value that produced a degree of saccadic undershoot (Fig 4b) characteristic of initial performance in human infants (eg Aslin 1987).

Training data were generated as 50,000 pairs of random numbers representing the initial position of the eye and the location of the target respectively. Each pair had to satisfy the constraints that (i) both lay within the oculomotor range (45 deg on either side of midline) and (ii) the target lay to the right of the starting position. For the test data the starting position varied from 40 deg left to 30 deg right in 10 degree steps. For each starting position there was a series of targets, starting at 5 deg to the right of the start and increasing in 5 degree steps up to 40 deg to the right of midline (a subset of the test data was used in Fig 4). The main measure of performance was the absolute gain error (ie the the difference between the actual gain and 1.0, always taken as positive) averaged over the test set.

The configuration of the CMAC was examined in pilot experiments. The CMAC coarse-codes its inputs, so that for a given resolution r, an input span of s can be represented as set of m measurement grids each dividing the input span into n compartments, where s/r = m.n. Combinations of m and n were examined, using perfect error feedback. A reasonable compromise between learning speed and asymptotic accuracy was achieved by using 10 coarse-coding grids each with 10x10 resolution (for the two input dimensions), giving a total of 1000 memory cells.

The main part of the study investigated first the effects of degrading the quality of the error feedback on learning. The main conclusion was that efficient learning could be obtained if the CMAC were told only the direction of the error, ie overshoot versus undershoot. This information was used to increase by a small fixed amount the weights in the activated cells (thereby producing increased gain in the internal feedback loop) when the saccade was too large, and to decreasing them similarly when it was too small. Appropriate choice of learning rate gave a realistic overall error of 5% (Fig 4c) after about 2000 trials. Direct comparison with learning rates of human infants, who take several months to achieve accuracy, is confounded by such factors as the maturation of the retina (Aslin 1987).

Learning parameters were then kept constant, and the model tested with simulations of two different conditions that produce saccadic plasticity in adult humans. One involved the effects of weakening the rightward pulling eye muscle in one eye. In people, the weakened eye can be trained by covering the normal eye with a patch, an effect which experiments with monkeys indicate depends on the cerebellum (Optican and Robinson 1980). For the model eye-weakening was simulated by increasing the constant a in equation (1) such that the trained system gave an average gain of about 0.5. Retraining required about 400-500 trials. Testing the previously normal eye (ie with the original value of a) showed that it now overshot, as is also the case in patients and experimental animals. Again normal performance was restored after 400-500 trials. These learning rates compare favourably with those observed in experimental animals.

Finally, the second simulation of adult saccadic plasticity concerned the effects of moving the target during a saccade. If the target is moved in the opposite direction to its original displacement the saccade will overshoot, but after a few trials adaptation occurs and the saccade becomes 'accurate' once more. Simulation of the procedure used by Deubel et al. (1986) gave system adaptation rates similar to those observed experimentally in people.

4 CONCLUSIONS

These results indicate that the model can account in general terms for the acquisition and maintenance of saccadic accuracy in primates (at least in one dimension). In addition to its general biologically attractive properties, the model's structure is consistent with current anatomical and physiological knowledge, and offers testable predictions about the functions of the hitherto mysterious projections from superior colliculus to posterior vermis. If these predictions are supported by experimental evidence, it would be appropriate to extend the model to incorporate greater physiological detail, for example concerning the precise location(s) of cerebellar plasticity.

Acknowledgements

This work was supported by the Joint Council Initiative in Cognitive Science.

References

Albus, J.A. (1971) A theory of cerebellar function. *Math. Biosci.* 10: 25-61.

Albus, J.A. (1981) *Brains, Behavior and Robotics.* BYTE books (McGraw-Hill), Peterborough New Hampshire.

Aslin, R.N. (1987) Motor aspects of visual development in infancy. In: *Handbook of Infant Perception*, eds. P. Salapatek and L. Cohen. Academic Press, New York, pp.43-113.

Collins, C.C. (1975) The human oculomotor control system. In: *Basic Mechanisms of Ocular Motility and their Clinical Implications*, eds. G. Lennerstrand and P. Bach-y-Rita. Pergamon Press, Oxford, pp. 145-180.

Dean, P., Mayhew, J.E.W., Thacker, T. and Langdon, P. (1991) Saccade control in a simulated robot camera-head system: neural net architectures for efficient learning of inverse kinematics. *Biol. Cybern.* 66: 27-36.

Deubel, H., Wolf, W. and Hauske, G. (1986) Adaptive gain control of saccadic eye movements. *Human Neurobiol.* 5: 245-253.

Grossberg, S. and Kuperstein, M. (1986) *Neural Dynamics of Adaptive Sensory-Motor Control: Ballistic Eye Movements.* Elsevier, Amsterdam.

Hormel, M. (1990) A self-organising associative memory system for control applications. In: *Advances in Neural Information Processing Systems 2*, ed. D.S. Touretzky. Morgan Kaufman, San Mateo, California, pp. 332-339.

Kawato, M. (1990) Feedback-error-learning neural network for supervised motor learning. In *Advanced Neural Computers*, ed. R. Eckmiller. Elsevier, Amsterdam, pp.365-372.

Keller, E.L. (1989) The cerebellum. In: *The Neurobiology of Saccadic Eye Movements*, eds. Wurtz, R.H. and Goldberg, M.E. Elsevier Science Publishers, North Holland, pp. 391-411.

Marr, D. (1969) A theory of cerebellar cortex. *J. Physiol.* 202: 437-470.

Miller, W.T. III, Glanz, F.H. and Gordon Kraft, L. III (1987) Application of a general learning algorithm to the control of robotic manipulators. *Int. J. Robotics Res.* 6: 84-98.

Optican, L.M. and Robinson, D.A. (1980) Cerebellar-dependent adaptive control of primate saccadic system. *J. Neurophysiol.* 44: 1058-1076.

Ritchie, L. (1976) Effects of cerebellar lesions on saccadic eye movements. *J. Neurophysiol.* 39: 1246-1256.

Robinson, D.A. (1975) Oculomotor control signals. In: *Basic Mechanisms of Ocular Motility and their Clinical Implications*, eds. Lennerstrand, G. and Bach-y-Rita, P. Pergamon Press, Oxford, pp. 337-374.

Van Gisbergen, J.A.M., Robinson, D.A. and Gielen, S. (1981) A quantitative analysis of generation of saccadic eye movements by burst neurons. *J. Neurophysiol.* 45: 417-442.

Van Gisbergen, J.A.M. and van Opstal, A.J. (1989) Models. In: *The Neurobiology of Saccadic Eye Movements*, eds. Wurtz, R.H. and Goldberg, M.E. Elsevier Science Publishers, North Holland, pp. 69-101.

Wurtz, R.H. and Goldberg, M.E. (1989) *The Neurobiology of Saccadic Eye Movements.* Elsevier Science Publishers, North Holland.

Learning in the Vestibular System: Simulations of Vestibular Compensation Using Recurrent Back-Propagation

Thomas J. Anastasio
University of Illinois
Beckman Institute
405 N. Mathews Ave.
Urbana, IL 61801

Abstract

Vestibular compensation is the process whereby normal functioning is regained following destruction of one member of the pair of peripheral vestibular receptors. Compensation was simulated by lesioning a dynamic neural network model of the vestibulo-ocular reflex (VOR) and retraining it using recurrent back-propagation. The model reproduced the pattern of VOR neuron activity experimentally observed in compensated animals, but only if connections heretofore considered uninvolved were allowed to be plastic. Because the model incorporated nonlinear units, it was able to reconcile previously conflicting, linear analyses of experimental results on the dynamic properties of VOR neurons in normal and compensated animals.

1 VESTIBULAR COMPENSATION

Vestibular compensation is one of the oldest and most well studied paradigms in motor learning. Although it is neurophysiologically well described, the adaptive mechanisms underlying vestibular compensation, and its effects on the dynamics of vestibular responses, are still poorly understood. The purpose of this study is to gain insight into the compensatory process by simulating it as learning in a recurrent neural network model of the vestibulo-ocular reflex (VOR).

The VOR stabilizes gaze by producing eye rotations that counterbalance head rotations. It is mediated by brainstem neurons in the vestibular nuclei (VN) that relay head velocity signals from vestibular sensory afferent neurons to the motoneurons of the eye muscles (Wilson and Melvill Jones 1979). The VOR circuitry also processes the canal signals, stretching out their time constants by four times before transmitting this signal to the motoneurons. This process of time constant lengthening is known as velocity storage (Raphan et al. 1979).

The VOR is a bilaterally symmetric structure that operates in push-pull. The VN are linked bilaterally by inhibitory commissural connections. Removal of the vestibular receptors from one side (hemilabyrinthectomy) unbalances the system, resulting in continuous eye movement that occurs in the absence of head movement, a condition known as spontaneous nystagmus. Such a lesion also reduces VOR sensitivity (gain) and eliminates velocity storage. Compensatory restoration of VOR occurs in stages (Fetter and Zee 1988). It begins by quickly eliminating spontaneous nystagmus, and continues by increasing VOR gain. Curiously, velocity storage never recovers.

2 NETWORK ARCHITECTURE

The horizontal VOR is modeled as a three-layered neural network (Figure 1). All of the units are nonlinear, passing their weighted input sums through the sigmoidal squashing function. This function bounds unit responses between zero and one. Input units represent afferents from the left (lhc) and right (rhc) horizontal semicircular canal receptors. Output units correspond to motoneurons of the lateral (lr) and medial (mr) rectus muscles of the left eye. Interneurons in the VN are represented by hidden units on the left ($lvn1$, $lvn2$) and right ($rvn1$, $rvn2$) sides of the model brainstem. Bias units stand for non-vestibular inputs, on the left (lb) and right (rb) sides.

Network connectivity reflects the known anatomy of mammalian VOR (Wilson and Melvill Jones 1979). Vestibular commissures are modeled as recurrent connections between hidden units on opposite sides. All connection weights to the hidden units are plastic, but those to the outputs are initially fixed, because it is generally believed that synaptic plasticity occurs only at the VN level in vestibular compensation (Galiana et al. 1984). Fixed hidden-to-output weights have a crossed, reciprocal pattern.

3 TRAINING THE NORMAL NETWORK

The simulations began by training the network shown in Figure 1, with both vestibular inputs intact (normal network), to produce the VOR with velocity storage (Anastasio 1991). The network was trained using recurrent back-propagation (Williams and Zipser 1989). The input and desired output sequences correspond to the canal afferent signals and motoneuron eye-velocity commands that would produce the VOR response to two impulse head rotational accelerations, one to the left and the other to the right. One input (rhc) and desired output (lr) sequence is shown in Figure 2A (dotted and dashed, respectivley). Those for lhc and mr (not shown) are identical but inverted. The desired output responses are equal in amplitude to the inputs,   producing VOR

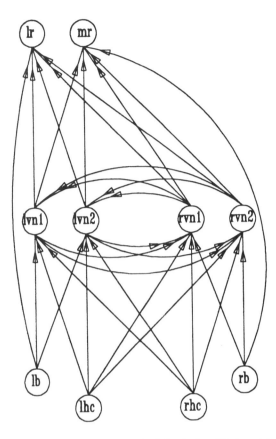

Figure 1.   Recurrent Neural Network Model of the Horizontal Vestibulo-Ocular Reflex (VOR). *lhc*, *rhc*: left and right horizontal semicircular canal afferents; *lvn1*, *lvn2*, *rvn1*, *rvn2*: vestibular nucleus neurons on left and right sides of model brainstem; *lr*, *mr*: lateral and medial rectus muscles of left eye; *lb*, *rb*: left and right non-vestibular inputs. This and subsequent figures redrawn from Anastasio (in press).

eye movements that would perfectly counterbalance head movements. The output responses decay more slowly than the input responses, reflecting velocity storage. Between head movements, both desired outputs have the same spontaneous firing rate of 0.50. With output spontaneous rates (SRs) balanced, no push-pull eye velocity command is given and, consequently, no VOR eye movement would be made.

The normal network learns the VOR transformation after about 4,000 training sequence presentations (passes). The network develops reciprocal connections from input to hidden units, as in the actual VOR (Wilson and Melvill Jones 1979). Inhibitory recurrent connections form an integrating (*lvn1*, *rvn1*) and a non-integrating (*lvn2*, *rvn2*) pair of hidden units (Anastasio 1991). The integrating pair subserve storage in the network. They have strong   mutual inhibition and exert net positive feedback on themselves. The non-integrating pair have almost no mutual inhibition.

4 SIMULATING VESTIBULAR COMPENSATION

After the normal network is constructed, with both inputs intact, vestibular compensation can be simulated by removing the input from one side and retraining with recurrent back-propagation. Left hemilabyrinthectomy produces deficits in the model that correspond to those observed experimentally. The responses of output unit *lr* acutely (i.e. immediately) following left input removal are shown in Figure 2A. The SR of *lr* (solid) is greatly increased above normal (dashed); that of *mr* (not shown) is decreased by the same amount. This output SR imbalance would result in eye movement to the left in the absence of head movement (spontaneous nystagmus). The gain of the outputs is greatly decreased. This is due to removal of one half the network input, and to the SR imbalance forcing the output units into the low gain extremes of the squashing function. Velocity storage is also eliminated by left input removal, due to events at the hidden unit level (see below).

During retraining, the time course of simulated compensation is similar to that

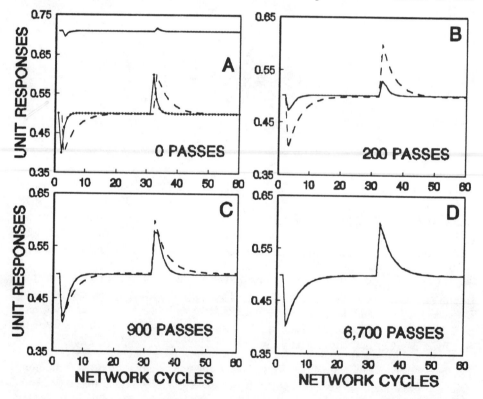

Figure 2. Simulated Compensation in the VOR Neural Network Model. Response of *lr* (solid) is shown at each stage of compensation: A, acutely (i.e. immediately) following the lesion; B, after spontaneous nystagmus has been eliminated; C, after VOR gain has been largely restored; D, after full recovery of VOR. Desired response of *lr* (dashed) shown in all plots. Intact input from *rhc* (dotted) shown in A only.

observed experimentally (Fetter and Zee 1988). Spontaneous nystagmus is eliminated after 200 passes, as the SRs of the output units are brought back to their normal level (Figure 2B). Output unit gain is largely restored by 900 passes, but time constant remains close to that of the inputs (Figure 2C). At this stage, VOR gain would have increased substantially, but its time constant would remain low, indicating loss of velocity storage. This stage approximates the extent of experimentally observed compensation (ibid.). Completely restoring the normal VOR, with full velocity storage, requires over seven times more retraining (Figure 2D).

The responses of the hidden units during each stage of simulated compensation are shown in Figure 3A and 3C. Average hidden unit SR and gain are shown as dotted lines in Figure 3A and 3C, respectively. Acutely following left input removal (AC stage), the SRs of left (dashed) and right (solid) hidden units decrease and increase, respectively (Figure 3A). One left hidden unit (*lvn1*) is actually silenced. Hidden unit gain at AC stage is greatly reduced bilaterally (Figure 3C), as for the outputs.

At the point where spontaneous nystagmus is eliminated (NE stage), hidden units SRs are balanced bilaterally, and none of the units are spontaneously silent (Figure 3A). When VOR gain is largely restored (GR stage, corresponding to experimentally observed compensation), the gains of the hidden units have substantially increased (Figure 3C). At GR stage, average hidden unit SR has also increased but the bilateral SR balance has been strictly maintained (Figure 3A). A comparison with experimental data (Yagi and Markham 1984; Newlands and Perachio 1990) reveals that the behavior of hidden units in the model does *not* correspond to that observed for real VN neurons in compensated animals. Rather than having bilateral SR balance, the average SR of VN neurons in compensated animals is lower on the lesion-side and higher on the intact-side. Moreover, many lesion-side VN neurons are permanently silenced. Also, rather than substantially recovering gain, the gains of VN neurons in compensated animals increase little from their low values acutely following the lesion.

The network model adopts its particular (and unphysiological) solution to vestibular compensation because, with fixed connection weights to the outputs, compensation can be brought about only by changes in hidden unit behavior. Thus, output SRs will be balanced only if hidden SRs are balanced, and output gain will increase only if hidden gain increases. The discrepancy between model and actual VN neuron data suggests that compensation cannot rely solely on synaptic plasticity at the VN level.

5 RELAXING CONSTRAINTS

A better match between model and experimental VN neuron data can be achieved by rerunning the compensation simulation with modifiable weights at all allowed network connections (Figure 1). Bias-to-output and hidden-to-output synaptic weights, which were previously fixed, are now made plastic. These extra degrees of freedom give the adapting network greater flexibility in achieving compensation, and release it from a strict dependency upon the behavior of the hidden units. The time course of compensation in the all-weights-modifiable example is similar to the previous case (Figure 2), but each stage is reached after fewer passes.

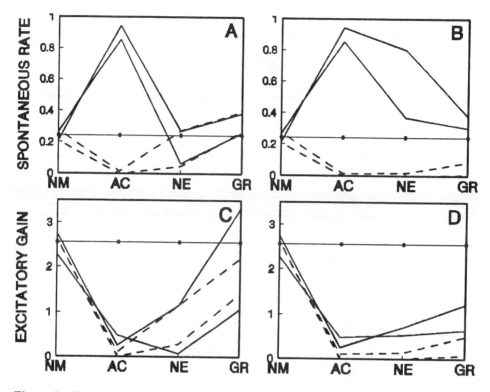

Figure 3. Behavior of Hidden Units at Various Stages of Compensation in the VOR Neural Network Model. Spontaneous rate (SR, A and B) and gain (C and D) are shown for networks with hidden layer weights only modifiable (A and C) or with all weights modifiable (B and D). Normal average SR (A and B) and gain (C and D) shown as dotted lines. NM, normal stage; AC, acutely following lesion; NE, after spontaneous nystagmus is eliminated; GR, after VOR gain is largely restored.

The behavior of the hidden units in the all-weights simulation more closely matches that of actual VN neurons in compensated animals (Figure 3B and 3D). At NE stage, even though spontaneous nystagmus is eliminated, there remains a large bilateral imbalance in hidden unit SR, and one lesion-side hidden unit (*lvn1*) is silenced (Figure 3B). At GR stage, hidden unit gain has increased only modestly from the low acute level (Figure 3D), and the bilateral SR imbalance persists, with *lvn1* still essentially spontaneously silent (Figure 3B). This modeling result constitutes a testable prediction that synaptic plasticity is occurring at the motoneuron as well as at the VN level in vestibular compensation.

6 NETWORK DYNAMICS

In the all-weights simulation at GR stage, as well as in compensated animals, some lesion-side VN neurons are silenced. Hidden unit *lvn1* is silenced by its inhibitory commissural interaction with *rvn1*, which in the normal network allowed the pair to form an integrating, recurrent loop. Silencing of *lvn1* breaks the commissural loop and consequently eliminates velocity storage in the network. VN neuron silencing could also account for the loss of velocity storage in the real, compensated VOR.

Loss of velocity storage in the model, in response to step head rotational acceleration stimuli, is shown in Figure 4. The output step response that would be expected given the longer VOR time constant is shown for *lr* in Figure 4A (dashed). The response of *mr* (not shown) is identical but inverted. Instead of expressing the longer VOR time constant, the actual step response of *lr* in the all-weights compensated network at GR stage (Figure 4A, dotted) has a rise time constant that is equal to the canal time constant, indicating complete loss of velocity storage. This is due to the behavior of the hidden units. The step responses of the integrating pair of hidden units in the compensated network at GR stage are shown in Figure 4B (*lvn1*, lower dotted; *rvn1*, upper dotted). Velocity storage is eliminated because *lvn1* is silenced, and this breaks the commissural loop that supports integration in the network.

Paradoxically, in the normal network with all hidden units spontaneously active, the output step response rise time constant is also equal to that of the canal afferents, again indicating a loss of velocity storage. This is shown for *lr* from the normal network in Figure 4A (solid). The step responses of the hidden units in the normal network are shown in Figure 4B (*lvn1*, dashed; *rvn1*, solid). Unit *lvn1*, which is spontaneously active in the normal network, is quickly driven into cut-off by the step stimulus. This breaks the commissural loop and eliminates velocity storage, accounting for the short rise time constants of hidden and output units network wide.

This result can explain some conflicting experimental findings concerning the

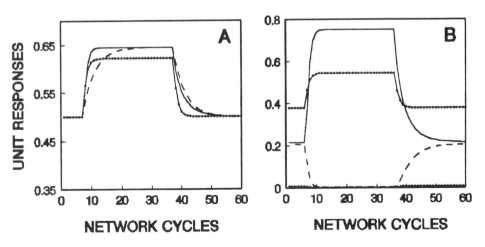

Figure 4. Responses of Units to Step Head Rotational Acceleration Stimuli in VOR Neural Network Model. A, expected response of *lr* with VOR time constant (dashed), and actual responses of *lr* in normal (solid) and all-weights compensated (dotted) networks. B, response of *lvn1* (dashed) and *rvn1* (solid) in normal network, and of *lvn1* (lower dotted) and *rvn1* (upper dotted) in all-weights compensated network.

dynamics of VN neurons in normal and compensated animals. Using sinusoidal stimuli, the time constants of VN neurons were found to be lower in compensated than in normal gerbils (Newlands and Perachio 1990). In contrast, using step stimuli, no difference in rise time constants were found for VN neurons in normal as compared to compensated cats (Yagi and Markham 1984).

Rather than being a species difference, the disagreement may involve the type of stimulus used. Step accelerations are intense stimuli that can drive VN neurons to extreme levels. In response to a step in their off-directions, many VN neurons in normal cats were observed to cut-off (ibid.). As shown in Figure 4, this would disrupt commissural interactions and reduce velocity storage and VN neuron rise time constants, just as if these neurons were silenced as they are in compensated animals. In fact, VN neuron rise time constants were observed to be low in both normal and compensated cats (ibid.). In contrast, sinusoidal stimuli at an intensity that does not cause widespread VN neuron cut-off would not be expected to disrupt velocity storage in normal animals.

Acknowledgements

This work was supported by a grant from the Whitaker Foundation.

References

Anastasio TJ (1991) Neural network models of velocity storage in the horizontal vestibulo-ocular reflex. Biol Cybern 64:187-196

Anastasio TJ (in press) Simulating vestibular compensation using recurrent back-propagation. Biol Cybern

Fetter M, Zee DS (1988) Recovery from unilateral labyrinthectomy in rhesus monkey. J Neurophysiol 59:370-393

Galiana HL, Flohr H, Melvill Jones G (1984) A reevauation of intervestibular nuclear coupling: its role in vestibular compensation. J Neurophysiol 51:242-259

Newlands SD, Perachio AA (1990) Compensation of horizontal canal related activity in the medial vestibular nucleus following unilateral labyrinth ablation in the decerebrate gerbil. I. type I neurons. Exp Brain Res 82:359-372

Raphan Th, Matsuo V, Cohen B (1979) Velocity storage in the vestibulo-ocular reflex arc (VOR). Exp Brain Res 35:229-248

Williams RJ, Zipser D (1989) A learning algorithm for continually running fully recurrent neural networks. Neural Comp 1:270-280

Wilson VJ, Melvill Jones G (1979) Mammalian vestibular physiology. Plenum Press, New York

Yagi T, Markham CH (1984) Neural correlates of compensation after hemilabyrinthectomy. Exp Neurol 84:98-108

A Cortico-Cerebellar Model that Learns to Generate Distributed Motor Commands to Control a Kinematic Arm

N.E. Berthier   S.P. Singh   A.G. Barto
Department of Computer Science
University of Massachusetts
Amherst, MA 01002

J.C. Houk
Department of Physiology
Northwestern University Medical School
Chicago, IL 60611

Abstract

A neurophysiologically-based model is presented that controls a simulated kinematic arm during goal-directed reaches. The network generates a quasi-feedforward motor command that is learned using training signals generated by corrective movements. For each target, the network selects and sets the output of a subset of pattern generators. During the movement, feedback from proprioceptors turns off the pattern generators. The task facing individual pattern generators is to recognize when the arm reaches the target and to turn off. A distributed representation of the motor command that resembles population vectors seen *in vivo* was produced naturally by these simulations.

1   INTRODUCTION

We have recently begun to explore the properties of sensorimotor networks with architectures inspired by the anatomy and physiology of the cerebellum and its interconnections with the red nucleus and the motor cortex (Houk 1989; Houk et al.,

1990). It is widely accepted that these brain regions are important in the control of limb movements (Kuypers, 1981; Ito, 1984), although relatively little attention has been devoted to probing how the different regions might function together in a cooperative manner. Starting from a foundation of known anatomical circuitry and the results of microelectrode recordings from neurons in these circuits, we proposed the concept of rubrocerebellar and corticocerebellar information processing modules that are arranged in parasagittal arrays and function as adjustable pattern generators (APGs) capable of the storage, recall and execution of motor programs.

The aim of the present paper is to extend the APG Model to a multiple degree-of-freedom task and to investigate how the motor representation developed by the model compares to the population vector representations seen by Georgopoulos and coworkers (e.g., Georopoulos, 1988). A complete description of the model and simulations reported here is contained in Berthier et al. (1991).

2   THE APG ARRAY MODEL

As shown in Figure 1 the model has three parts: a neural network that generates control signals, a muscle model that controls joint angle, and a planar, kinematic arm. The control network is an array of APGs that generate signals that are fed to the limb musculature. Because here we are interested in the basic issue of how a collection of APGs might cooperatively control multiple degree-of-freedom movements, we use a very simplified model of the limb that ignores dynamics. The muscles convert APG activity to changes in muscle length, which determine the changes in the joint angles. Activation of an APG causes movement of the arm in a direction in joint-angle space that is specific to that APG[1], and the magnitude of an APG's activity determines the velocity of that movement. The simultaneous activation of selected APGs determines the arm trajectory as the superposition of these movements. A learning rule, based on long-term depression (e.g., Ito, 1984), adjusts the subsets of APGs that are selected as well as characteristics of their activity in order to achieve desired movements.

Each APG consists of a positive feedback loop and a set of Purkinje cells (PCs). The positive feedback loop is a highly simplified model of a component of a complex cerebrocerebellar recurrent network. In the simplified model simulated here, each APG has its own feedback loop, and the loops associated with different APGs do not interact. When triggered by sufficiently strong activation, the neurons in these loops fire repetitively in a self-sustaining manner. An APG's motor command is generated through the action of its PCs which inhibit and modulate the buildup of activity in the feedback loop. The activity of loop cells is conveyed to spinal motor areas by rubrospinal fibers. PCs receive information that specifies and constrains the desired movements via parallel fibers.

We hypothesize that the response of PCs to particular parallel fiber inputs is adaptively adjusted through the influence of climbing fibers that respond to corrective movements (Houk & Barto, 1991). The APG array model assumes that climbing fibers and PCs are aligned in a way that climbing fibers provide specialized infor-

---

[1]To simplify these initial simulations we ignore changes in muscle moment arms with posture of the arm.

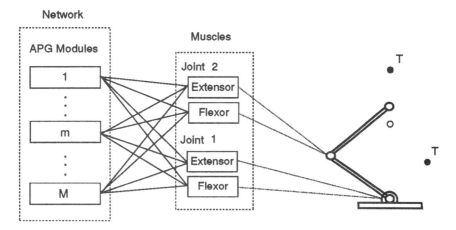

Figure 1: APG Control of Joint Angles. A collection of of APGs (adjustable pattern generators) is connected to a simulated two degree-of-freedom, kinematic, planar arm with antagonistic muscles at each joint. The task is to move the arm in the plane from a central starting location to one of eight symmetrically placed targets. Activation of an APG causes a movement of the arm that is specific to that APG, and the magnitude of an APG's activity determines the velocity of that movement. The simultaneous activation of selected APGs determines the arm trajectory as a superposition of these movements.

mation to PCs. Gellman et al. (1985) showed that proprioceptive climbing fibers are inhibited during planned movements, but the data of Gilbert and Thach (1977) suggest that they fire during corrective movements. In the present simulations, we assume that corrective movements are made when a movement fails to reach the target. These corrective movements stimulate proprioceptive climbing fibers which provides information to higher centers about the direction of the corrective movement. More detailed descriptions of APGs and relevant anatomy and physiology can be found in Houk (1989), Houk et al. (1990), and Berthier et al. (1991).

The generation of motor commands occurs in three phases. In the first phase, we assume that all positive feedback loops are off, and inputs provided by teleceptive and proprioceptive parallel fibers and basket cells determine the outputs of the PCs. We call this first phase selection. We assume that noise is present during the selection process so that individual PCs are turned off (i.e., selected) probabilistically. To begin the second phase, called the execution phase, loop activity is triggered by cortical activity. Once triggered, loop activity is self-sustaining because the loop cells have reciprocal positive connections. The triggering of loop activity causes the motor command to be "read out." The states of the PCs in the selection phase determine the speed and direction of the arm movement. As the movement is being performed, proprioceptive feedback and efference copy gradually depolarize the PCs. When a large proportion of the PCs are depolarized, PC inhibition reaches a critical value and terminates loop activity. In the third phase, the correction phase, corrective movements trigger climbing fiber activity that alters parallel fiber–PC connection weights.

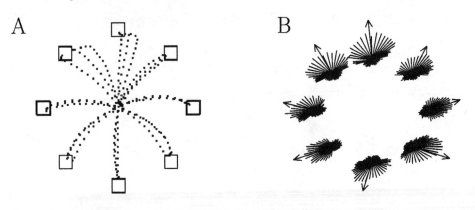

Figure 2: **A.** Movement Trajectories After Training. The starting point for each movement is the center of the workspace, and the target location is the center of the open square. The position of the arm at each time step is shown as a dot. Three movements are shown to each target. **B.** APG selection. APG selection for movements to a given target is illustrated by a vector plot at the position of the target. An individual APG is represented by a vector, the direction of which is equal to the direction of movement caused by that APG in Cartesian space. The vector length is proportional to output of the Purkinje cells during the selection phase. The arrow points in the direction of the vector sum.

3   SIMULATIONS

We trained the APG model to control a two degree-of-freedom, kinematic, planar arm. The task was similar to Georgopoulos (1988) and required APGs to move the arm from a central starting point to one of eight radially symmetric, equidistant targets. Each simulated trial started by placing the endpoint of the arm in the central starting location. The selection, execution, and correction phases of operation were then simulated. The task facing each of the selected APGs was to turn off at the proper time so that the movement stopped at the target.

Simulations showed that the model could learn to control movements to the eight targets. Training typically required about 700 trials per target until the arm endpoint was consistently moved to within 1 cm of the target. Figure 2 shows sample trajectories and population vectors of APG activity. Performance never resulted in precise movements due to the probabilistic nature of selection. Movement trajectories tended to follow straight lines in joint-angle space and were thus slightly curved lines in the workspace. About half of the APGs in the model were used to move to an individual target with population vectors similar to those seen by Georgopoulos (1988). The number of APGs used for each target was dependent on the sharpness of the climbing fiber receptive fields, with cardioid shaped receptive fields in joint-angle space giving population vectors that most resembled those experimentally observed.

4   ANALYSIS

In order to understand how the model worked we undertook a theoretical analysis of its simulated behavior. Analysis indicated that the expected trajectory of a movement was a straight line in joint-angle space from the starting position to the target. This is a special case of a mathematical result by Mussa-Ivaldi (1988). Because selection is probabilistic in the APG Array Model, trajectories in the workspace varied from the expected trajectory. In these cases, trajectories were piecewise linear because of the asynchronous termination of APG activity. Because of the Law of Large Numbers, the more PCs in each APG, the more closely the movement will resemble the expected movement.

The expected population of vectors of APG activity can be shown to be cosine-shaped in joint-angle space. That is, the length of the vector representing the activity of APG m is proportional to the cosine of the angle between the direction of action of APG m and the direction of the target in joint-angle space. The shape of the population vectors in Cartesian space is dependent on the Jacobian of the arm, which is a function of the arm posture.

The manner in which the outputs of PCs were set during selection leads to scaling of movement velocity with target distance. For any given movement direction, targets that are farther from the starting location lead to more rapid movements than closer targets.

Updating network weights based on the expected corrective movement will, in some cases, result in changing the weights in a way that they converge to the correct values. However, in other cases inappropriate changes are made. In the current simulations, we could largely avoid this problem by selecting parameter and initial weight values so that movements were initially small in amplitude. Random initialization of the weight values sometimes led to instances from which the learning rule could not recover.

5   DISCUSSION

In general, the present implementation of the model led to adequate control of the kinematic arm and mimicked the general output of nervous system seen in actual experiments. The network implemented a spatial to temporal transformation that transformed a target location into a time varying motor command. The model naturally generated population vectors that were similar to those seen *in vivo*. Further research is needed to improve the model's robustness and to extend it to more realistic control of a dynamical limb.

In the APG array model, APGs control arm movement in parallel so that the activity of all the modules taken together forms a distributed representation. The APG array executes a distributed motor program because it produces a spatiotemporal pattern of activity in the cerebrocerebellar recurrent network that is transmitted to the spinal cord to comprise a distributed motor command.

5.1   PARAMETRIZED MOTOR PROGRAMS

Certain features of the APG array model relate well to the ideas about parameterized motor programs discussed by Keele (1973), Schmidt (1988), and Adams (1971, 1977). The selection phase of the APG array model provides a feasible neuronal mechanism for preparing a parameterized motor program in advance of movement. The execution phase is also consistent with the open-loop ideas associated with motor programming concepts, except that, like Adams (1977), we explain the termination of the execution phase as being a consequence of proprioceptive feedback and efference copy.

In the APG array model, the counterpart of a generalized motor program is a set of parallel fiber weights for proprioceptive, efference copy, and target inputs. Given these weights, a particular constellation of parallel fiber inputs signifies that the desired endpoint of a movement is about to be reached, causing PCs to become depolarized. Once a set of parallel fiber weights corresponding to a desired endpoint is learned, the neuronal architecture and neurodynamics of the cerebellar network functions in a manner that parameterizes the motor program.

Movement velocity is parameterized in the selection phase of the model's operation. The velocity that is selected is automatically scaled so that velocity increases as the amplitude of the movement increases. While this type of scaling is often observed in motor performance studies, velocity can also be varied in an independent manner where velocity scaling can be applied simultaneously to all elements of a motor program to slow down or speed up the entire movement. Although we have not addressed this issue in the present report, simulation of velocity scaling under control of a neuromodulator can naturally be accomplished in the APG array model.

Movements terminate when the endpoint is recognized by PCs so that movement duration is dependent on the course of the movement instead of being determined by some internal clock because. Movement amplitude is parameterized by the weights of the target inputs, with smaller weights corresponding to larger amplitude movements.

5.2   CORRECTIVE MOVEMENTS

We assume that the training information conveyed to the APGs is the result of crude corrective movements stimulating proprioceptive receptors. This sensory information is conveyed to the cerebellum by climbing fibers. Learning in the APG array model therefore requires the existence of a low-level system capable of generating movements to spatial targets with at least a ballpark level of accuracy. Lesion (Yu et al., 1980) and developmental studies (von Hofsten, 1982) support the existence of a low-level system. Other evidence indicates that when limb movements are not proceeding accurately toward their intended targets, corrective components of the movements are generated by an unconscious, automatic control system (Goodale et al., 1986).

We assume that collaterals from the corticospinal and rubrospinal system that convey the motor commands to the spinal cord gate off sensory transmission through the proprioceptive climbing fiber pathway, thus preventing sensory responses to the initial limb movement. As the initial movement proceeds, the low-level system receives proprioceptive feedback from the limb and feedforward information about target location from the gaze control system. The latter information is updated as a consequence of corrective eye movements that typically occur after an initial gaze shift toward a visual target. Updated gaze information causes the spinal processor to generate a corrective component that is superimposed on the original motor command (Gielen & van Gisbergen, 1990; Flash & Henis, 1991). Since climbing fiber pathways would not be gated off by this low-level corrective process, climbing fibers should fire to indicate the direction of the corrective movement.

We assume that the network by which climbing fiber activity is generated is specifically wired to provide appropriate training information to the APGs (Houk & Barto, 1991). The training signal provided by a climbing fiber is specialized for the recipient APG in that it provides directional information in joint-angle space that is relative to the direction in which that APG moves the arm. The fact that training information is provided in terms of joint-angle space greatly simplifies the problem of providing errors in the correct system of reference. For example, if the network used visual error information, the error information would have to be transformed to joint errors.

The specialized training signals provided by the climbing fibers are determined by the structure of the ascending network conveying proprioceptive information. This ascending network has the same structure—but works in the opposite direction—as the network by which the APG array influences joint movement. This is reminiscent of the error backpropagation algorithm (e.g., Rumelhart et al., 1986, Parker, 1985) where the forward and backward passes through the network in the backpropagation algorithm are accomplished by the descending and ascending networks of the APG Array Model. This use of the ascending network to transform errors in the workspace to errors that are relative to a particular APG's direction of action is closely related to the use of error backpropagation for "learning with a distal teacher" as suggested by Jordan and Rumelhart (1991).

Houk and Barto (1991) suggested that the alignment of the ascending and descending networks might come about through trophic mechanisms stimulated by use-dependent alterations in synaptic efficacy. In the context of the present model, this hypothesis implies that the ascending network to the inferior olive, is established first, and that the descending network by which APGs influence motoneurons changes. We have not yet simulated this mechanism to see if it could actually generate the kind of alignment we assume in the present model.

Acknowledgements

This research was supported by ONR N00014-88-K-0339, NIMH Center Grant P50 MH48185, and a grant from the McDonnell-Pew Foundation for Cognitive Neuroscience supported by the James S. McDonnell Foundation and the Pew Charitable Trusts.

References

Adams JA (1971) A closed-loop theory of motor learning. *J Motor Beh* 3: 111-149
Adams JA (1977) Feedback theory of how joint receptors regulate the timing and positioning of a limb. *Psychol Rev* 84: 504-523

Berthier NE Singh SP Barto AG Houk JC (1991) Distributed representation of limb motor programs in arrays of adjustable pattern generators. NPB Technical Report 3, Institute for Neuroscience, Northwestern University, Chicago IL

Flash T Henis E (1991) Arm trajectory modifications during reaching towards visual targets. *J Cognitive Neurosci* 3:220-230

Gellman R Gibson AR Houk JC (1985) Inferior olivary neurons in the awake cat: Detection of contact and passive body displacement. J Neurophys 54:40-60.

Georgopoulos A (1988) Neural integration of movement: role of motor cortex in reaching. FASEB Journal 2:2849-2857.

Gielen CCAM Gisbergen van JAM (1990) The visual guidance of saccades and fast aiming movements. *News in Physiol Sci* 5: 58-63

Gilbert PFC Thach WT (1977) Purkinje cell activity during motor learning. *Brain Res* 128:309-328.

Goodale MA Pelisson D Prablanc C (1986) Large adjustments in visually guided reaching do not depend on vision of the hand or perception of target displacement. *Nature* 320: 748-750

Hofsten von C (1982) Eye-hand coordination in the newborn. *Dev Psychol* 18: 450-461

Houk JC (1989) Cooperative control of limb movements by the motor cortex, brainstem and cerebellum. In: Cotterill RMJ (ed) Models of Brain Function. Cambridge Univ Press Cambridge UK, 309-325

Houk JC Barto AG (1991) Distributed sensorimotor learning. NPB Technical Report 1, Institute for Neuroscience, Northwestern University, Chicago IL

Houk JC Singh SP Fisher C Barto AG (1990) An adaptive sensorimotor network inspired by the anatomy and physiology of the cerebellum. In: Miller WT Sutton RS Werbos PJ (eds) Neural Networks for Control. MIT Press Cambridge, MA 301-348

Ito M (1984) The Cerebellum and Neural Control. Raven Press New York

Ito M (1989) Long-term depression. *Annual review of Neuroscience* 12: 85-102

Jordan MI Rumelhart DE (1991) Forward models: Supervised learning with a distal teacher. Occasional Paper #40 MIT Center for Cognitive Science

Keele SW (1973) Attention and Human Performance. Goodyear Pacific Palisades, California

Kuypers HGJM (1981) Anatomy of the descending pathways. In: Brooks VB (ed) Handbook of Physiology Section I Volume II Part 1. American Physiological Society Bethesda MD 597-666

Mussa-Ivaldi FA (1988) Do neurons in the motor cortex encode movement direction? An alternative hypothesis. *Neurosci Lett* 91:106-111

Parker DB (1985) Learning-Logic. Technical Report TR-47, Massachusetts Institute of Technology Cambridge MA

Rumelhart DE Hinton GE Williams RJ (1986) Learning internal representations by error propagation. In: Rumelhart DE McClelland JL (eds) Parallel Distributed Processing. Explorations in the Microstructure of Cognition, Vol. 1: Foundations. Bradford Books/MIT Press Cambridge MA

Schmidt RA (1988) Motor Control and Motor Learning. Human Kinetics Champaign, Illinois

A Computational Mechanism To Account For Averaged Modified Hand Trajectories

Ealan A. Henis*and Tamar Flash
Department of Applied Mathematics and Computer Science
The Weizmann Institute of Science
Rehovot 76100, Israel

Abstract

Using the double-step target displacement paradigm the mechanisms underlying arm trajectory modification were investigated. Using short (10-110 msec) inter-stimulus intervals the resulting hand motions were initially directed in between the first and second target locations. The kinematic features of the modified motions were accounted for by the superposition scheme, which involves the vectorial addition of two independent point-to-point motion units: one for moving the hand toward an internally specified location and a second one for moving between that location and the final target location. The similarity between the inferred internally specified locations and previously reported measured end-points of the first saccades in double-step eye-movement studies may suggest similarities between perceived target locations in eye and hand motor control.

1   INTRODUCTION

The generation of reaching movements toward unexpectedly displaced targets involves more complicated planning and control problems than in reaching toward stationary ones, since the planning of the trajectory modification must be performed before the initial plan is entirely completed. One possible scheme to modify a trajectory plan is to abort the rest of the original motion plan, and replace it with a new one for moving toward the new target location. Another possible modifica-

---

*Current address IRCS/GRASP, University of Pennsylvania.

tion scheme is to superimpose a second plan with the initial one, without aborting it. Both schemes are discussed below.

Earlier studies of reaching movements toward static targets have shown that point-to-point reaching hand motions follow a roughly straight path, having a typical bell-shaped velocity profile. The kinematic features of these movements were successfully accounted for (Figure 1, left) by the minimum-jerk model (Flash & Hogan, 1985). In that model the X-components of hand motions (and analogously the Y-components) were represented by:

$$X(t) = X_A + (X_B - X_A)(10T^3 - 15T^4 + 6T^5), \quad T = \frac{t}{t_f} \tag{1}$$

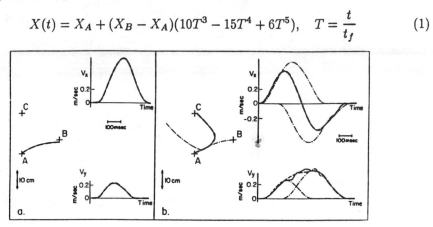

Figure 1: The Minimum-jerk Model and The Non-averaged Superposition Scheme

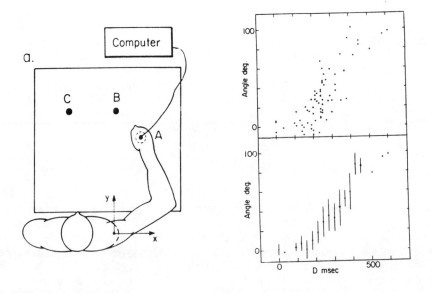

Figure 2: The Experimental Setup and The Initial Movement Direction Vs. D

where t_f is the movement duration, and $X_B - X_A$ is the X-component of movement amplitude. In a previous study (Henis & Flash, 1989; Flash & Henis, 1991) we have used the double-step target displacement paradigm (see below) with inter-stimulus intervals (ISIs) of 50-400 msec. Many of the resulting motions were found to be initially directed toward the first target location (*non-averaged*) (for larger ISIs a larger percentage of the motions were non-averaged). The kinematic features of these modified motions were successfully accounted for (Figure 1 right) by a superposition modification scheme that involves the vectorial addition of two time-shifted independent point-to-point motion units (Equation (1)) that have amplitudes that correspond to the two target displacements.

In the present study shorter ISIs of 10-110 msec were used, hence, all target displacements occurred before movement initiation. Most of the resulting hand motions were found to be initially directed in between the first and second target locations (*averaged* motions). For increasing values of D, where $D = RT_1 - ISI$ (RT_1 is the reaction time), the initial motion direction gradually shifted from the direction of the first toward the direction of the second stimulus (Figure 2 right). The averaging phenomenon has been previously reported for hand (Van Sonderen et al., 1988) and eye (Aslin & Shea, 1987; Van Gisbergen et al., 1987) motions. In this work we wished to account for the kinematic features of averaged trajectories as well as for the dependence of their initial direction on D.

It was observed (Van Sonderen et al., 1988) that when the first target displacement was toward the left and the second one was obliquely downwards and to the right most of the resulting motions were *averaged*. Averaged motions were also induced when the first target displacement was downwards and the second one was obliquely upwards and to the left. In this study we have used similar target displacements. Four naive subjects participated in the experiments. The motions were performed in the absence of visual feedback from the moving limb. In a typical trial, initially the hand was at rest at a starting position A (Figure 2 left). At $t = 0$ a visual target was presented at one of two equally probable positions B. It either remained lit (control condition, probability 0.4) or was shifted again, following an ISI, to one of two equally probable positions C (double-step condition, probability 0.3 each). In a block of trials one target configuration was used. Each block consisted of five groups of 56 trials, and within each group one ISI pair was used. The five ISI pairs were: 10 and 80, 20 and 110, 30 and 150, 40 and 200, and 50 and 300 msec. The target presentation sequence was randomized, and included appropriate control trials.

2 MODELING RATIONALE AND ANALYSIS

2.1 THE SUPERPOSITION SCHEME

The superposition scheme for *averaged* modified motions is based on the vectorial addition of two time-shifted independent elemental point-to-point hand motions that obey Equation (1). The first elemental trajectory plan is for moving between the initial hand location and an intermediate location B_i, internally specified. This plan continues unmodified until its intended completion. The second elemental trajectory plan is for moving between B_i and the final location of the target. The durations of the elemental motions may vary among trials, and are therefore a priori unknown. With short ISIs the elemental motion plans may be added (to give the modified plan) preceding movement initiation. Several possibilities for B_i were examined: a) the first location of the stimulus, b) an a priori unknown position, c) same as (b) with B_i constrained to lie on the line connecting the first and second locations of the stimulus, and d) same as (b) with B_i constrained to lie on the line of initial movement direction. Version (a) is equivalent to the superposition scheme that successfully accounted for *non-averaged* modified trajectories (Flash & Henis, 1991). In versions (b), (c) and (d) it was assumed that due to the quick displacement of the target, the specification of the end-point for the first motion plan may differ from the actual first location of the target. The first motion unit was represented by:

$$X_1(t) = X_A + (X_{B_i} - X_A)(10T^3 - 15T^4 + 6T^5), \quad \text{where} \quad T = \frac{t}{T_1}. \quad (2)$$

In (2), $(X_{B_i} - X_A)$ is the X-component of the first unit amplitude. The duration of this unit is denoted by T_1, a priori unknown. The expression for $Y_1(t)$ was analogous to Equation (2). The X-component of the second motion unit was taken to be:

$$X_2(t) = (X_C - X_{B_i})(10T^3 - 15T^4 + 6T^5), \quad \text{where} \quad T = \frac{t - t_s}{t_f - t_s} = \frac{t - t_s}{T_2}. \quad (3)$$

In (3), $(X_C - X_{B_i})$ is the X-component of the amplitude of the second trajectory unit. The start and end times of the second unit are denoted by t_s and t_f, respectively. The duration of the second motion unit $T_2 = t_f - t_s$ is a priori unknown. The X-component of the entire modified motion (and similarly for the Y-component) was represented by:

$$X(t) = X_1(t) + X_2(t). \quad (4)$$

The unknown parameters T_1, T_2, B_{iX} and B_{iY} that can best describe the entire measured trajectory were determined by using least-squares best-fit methods (Marquardt, 1963). This procedure minimized the sum of the position errors between the simulated and measured data points, taking into account (in versions (a), (c) and (d)) the assumed constraints on the location B_i.

2.2   THE ABORT-REPLAN SCHEME

In the abort-replan scheme it was assumed that initially a point-to-point trajectory plan is generated for moving toward an initial target (Equation (2)). The same four different possibilities for the end-point of the initial motion plan were examined. It was assumed that at some time-instant t_s the initial plan is aborted and replaced by a new plan for moving between the expected hand position at $t = t_s$ and the final target location. The new motion plan was assumed to be represented by:

$$X_{NEW}(t) = \sum_{i=0}^{5} a_i(t)^i. \quad (5)$$

The coefficients a_3, a_4 and a_5 were derived by using the the measured values of position, velocity and acceleration at $t = t_f$. For versions (b), (c) and (d) the analysis was performed simultaneously for the X and Y components of the trajectory. Choosing a trial B_i and T_1 the initial motion plan (Equation (2)) was calculated. Choosing a trial t_s, the remaining three unknown coefficients a_0, a_1 and a_2 of Equation (5) were calculated using the continuity conditions of the initial and new position, velocity and acceleration at $t = t_s$ (method I). Alternatively, these three coefficients were calculated using the corresponding *measured* values at $t = t_s$ (method II). To determine the best choice of the unknown parameters B_{iX}, B_{iY}, T_1 and t_s the same least squares methods (Marquardt, 1963) were used as described above. For version (a), for each cartesian component, a point-to-point minimum-jerk trajectory AB was speed-scaled to coincide with the initial part of the measured velocity profile. The time t_s of its deviation from the measured speed profile was extracted. From t_s on, the trajectory was represented by Equation (5). The values of a_0, a_1 and a_2 were derived by using the same least squares methods (method I). Alternatively, these values were determined by using the measured position, velocity and acceleration at $t = t_s$ (method II).

3   RESULTS

The motions recorded in the control trials were roughly straight with bell-shaped speed profiles. The mean reaction time in these control trials was 367.1 ± 94.6 msec ($N = 120$). The mean movement time was 574.1 ± 127.0 msec ($N = 120$). The change in target location elicited a graded movement toward an intermediate direction in between the two target locations, followed by a subsequent motion toward the final target (Figure 3, middle). Occasionally the hand went directly toward the final target location (Figure 3, right). For values of D less than 100 ms the movements were found to be initially directed toward the first target (Figure 3, left). As D increased, the initial direction of the motions gradually shifted (Figure 2, right) from the direction of the first (non-averaged) toward the direction of the second (direct) target locations (The initial direction depended on D rather than on ISI). The mean reaction time to the first stimulus (RT_1) was 350.4 ± 93.5 msec (N=192). The mean reaction time to the second stimulus (RT_2) (inferred from the superposition version (b)) was 382.8 ± 119.9 msec (N=192). This value is much smaller than that predicted by successive processing of information: $RT_2 = 2RT_1$-ISI (Poulton, 1981), and might be indicative of the presence of parallel planning. The mean durations T_1 and T_2 of the two trajectory units (of superposition version (b)) were: 373.0 ± 112.2 and 592.1 ± 98.1 msec ($N = 192$), respectively.

3.1   MODIFICATION SCHEMES

The most statistically successful model (Table-1) in accounting for the measured motions was the superposition version (b), which involves an internally specified location (a priori unknown) for the end-point of the first motion unit. In particular, the averaged initial direction of the measured motions was accounted for. Superposition version (d) was equivalent to version (b). The velocities simulated on the basis the other tested schemes substantially deviated from the measured ones (Table 1 and Figure 4). It should be noted that in both the superposition and abort-replan versions (b), (c) and (d) there were 4, 3 and 3 unknown parameters. In the abort-replan versions (aI) there were 3 unknown parameters, compared to 2 in the superposition version (a). Hence the relative success of the superposition version (b) in accounting for the data was not due to a larger number of free parameters.

Table 1: Normalized Velocity Deviations and The t-score With SP(b))

SP(a)	SP(b)	SP(c)	SP(d)	AB(aI)	AB(aII)	AB(bI)	AB(bII)	AB(cI)	AB(cII)	AB(dI)	AB(dII)
18.60	0.035	0.126	0.042	0.083	0.084	0.081	0.078	0.084	0.083	0.082	0.085
± 50.16	± 0.036	± 0.132	± 0.045	± 0.093	± 0.088	± 0.101	± 0.102	± 0.108	± 0.096	± 0.097	± 0.101
(4.711)	(0.000)	(8.465)	(1.546)	(6.126)	(6.559)	(5.460)	(5.050)	(5.478)	(5.959)	(5.782)	(5.935)

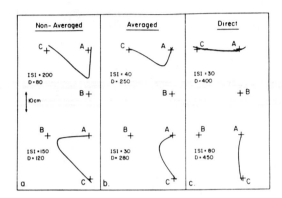

Figure 3: Types of Modified Trajectories

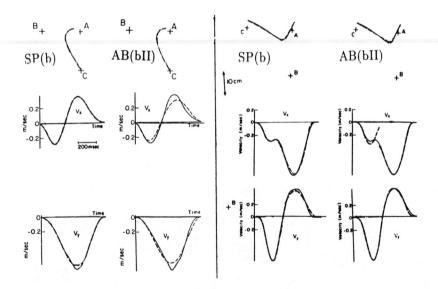

Figure 4: Representative Simulated Vs. Measured Trajectories

3.2   THE END-POINTS INFERRED FROM SUPERPOSITION (b)

The mean locations B_i resulting from different trials performed by the same subject were computed by pooling together B_i of movements with the same $D \pm 15$ msec (Figure 5 left). For $D \le 100$ msec, the measured motions were non-averaged and the inferred B_i were in the vicinity of the first target. For increasing values of D, B_i gradually shifted from the first toward the second target location, following a typical path that curved toward the initial hand position. For $D \ge 400$ msec, B_i were in the vicinity of the second target location. Since initially the motions are directed toward B_i, this gradual shift of B_i as a function of D may account for the observed dependence of the initial direction of motion on D. The locations B_i obtained on the basis of the other tested schemes did not show any regular behavior as functions of D.

4   DISCUSSION

This paper presents explicit possible mechanisms to account for the kinematic features of averaged modified trajectories. the most statistically successful scheme in accounting for the measured movements involves the vectorial addition of two independent point-to-point motion units: one for moving between the initial hand position and an internally specified location, and a second one for moving between that location and the final target location. Taken together with previous results for *non-averaged* modified trajectories (Flash & Henis, 1991), it was shown that the same superposition principle may account for both modified trajectory types. The differences between the observed types stem from differences in the time available to modify the end-point of the first unit. Our simulations have enabled us to infer the locations of the intermediate target locations, which were found to be similar to previously reported (Aslin & Shea, 1987) experimentally measured end-points of the first saccades, obtained by using the double-step paradigm (Figure 5 right[1]). This result may suggests underlying similarities between internally perceived target locations in eye and hand motor control and may suggest a common "where" command (Gielen et al., 1984; 1990) for both systems.

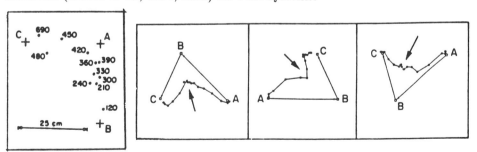

Figure 5: Inferred First Unit End-points and Measured Eye Positions

[1]Reprinted with permission from *Vision Res., Vol. 27, No. 11*, 1925-1942, Aslin, R.N. and Shea S.L.: The Amplitude And Angle of Saccades to Double-Step Target Displacements, Copyright [1987], Pergamon Press plc.

Why is the internally specified location dependent on D, which is a parameter associated with both sensory information and motor execution? One possible explanation is that following the target displacement the effect of the first stimulus on the motion planning decays, and that of the second stimulus becomes larger. These changes may occur in the transformations from the visual to the motor system. A purely sensory change in the perceived target location was also proposed (Van Sonderen et al., 1988; Becker & Jurgens 1979). Another possibility is that the direction of hand motion is internally coded in the motor system (Georgopoulos et al., 1986), and it gradually rotates (within the motor system) from the direction of the first to the direction of the second target. It is not clear which of these possibilities provides a better explanation for the observations.

In the superposition scheme there is no need to keep track of the actual or planned kinematic state of the hand. Hence, in contrast to the abort-replan scheme, an efference copy of the planned motion is not required. The successful use of motion plans expressed in extrapersonal coordinates provides support to the idea that arm movements are internally represented in terms of hand motion through external space. The construction of complex movements from simpler elementary building blocks is consistent with a hierarchical organization of the motor system. The independence of the elemental trajectories allows to plan them in parallel.

Acknowledgements

This research was supported by a grant no. 8800141 from the United-States Israel Binational Science Foundation (BSF), Jerusalem, Israel. Tamar Flash is incumbent of the Corinne S. Koshland career development chair.

References

Aslin, R.N. and Shea S.L. (1987). The Amplitude And Angle of Saccades to Double-Step Target Displacements. Vision Res., Vol. 27, No. 11, 1925-1942.

Becker W. and Jurgens R. (1979). An Analysis of The Saccadic System By Means of Double-Step Stimuli. Vision Res., 19, 967-983.

Flash T. and Henis E. (1991). Arm Trajectory Modification During Reaching Towards Visual Targets. Journal of Cognitive Neuroscience Vol. 3, no. 3, 220-230.

Flash, T. & Hogan, N. (1985). The coordination of arm movements: an experimentally confirmed mathematical model. J. Neurosci., 7, 1688-1703.

Georgopoulos A.P., Schwartz A.B. & Kettner R.E. (1986). Neuronal population coding of movement direction. Science 233, 1416-1419.

Gielen, C.C.A.M., Van den Heuvel, P.J.M. & Denier Van der Gon, J.J. (1984). Modification of muscle activation patterns during fast goal-directed arm movements. J. Motor Behavior, 16, 2-19.

Gielen C.C.A.M. & Van Gisbergen J.A.M. (1990). The visual guidance of saccades and fast aiming movements. News in Physiological Sciences Vol.5, 58-63.

Henis E. and Flash T. (1989). Mechanisms Subserving Arm Trajectory Modification. Perception 18(4):495.

Marquardt, D.W., (1963). An algorithm for least-squares estimation of non-linear parameters. J. SIAM, 11, 431-441.

Van Gisbergen, J.A.M., Van Opstal, A.J. & Roebroek, J.G.H. (1987). Stimulus-induced midflight modification of saccade trajectories. In J.K. O'Regan & A. Levy-Schoen (Eds.), Eye Movements: From Physiology to Cognition, Amsterdam: Elsevier, 27-36.

Van Sonderen, J.F., Denier Van Der Gon, J.J. & Gielen, C.C.A.M. (1988). Conditions determining early modification of motor programmes in response to change in target location. Exp. Brain Res., 71, 320-328.

Simulation of Optimal Movements Using the Minimum-Muscle-Tension-Change Model.

Menashe Dornay[*]   **Yoji Uno**[**]   **Mitsuo Kawato**[*]   **Ryoji Suzuki**[**]

[*]Cognitive Processes Department, ATR Auditory and Visual Perception Research Laboratories, Sanpeidani, Inuidani, Seika-Cho, Soraku-Gun, Kyoto 619-02 Japan.

[**]Department of Mathematical Engineering and Information Physics, Faculty of Engineering, University of Tokyo, Hongo, Bunkyo-ku, Tokyo, 113 Japan.

Abstract

This work discusses various optimization techniques which were proposed in models for controlling arm movements. In particular, the minimum-muscle-tension-change model is investigated. A dynamic simulator of the monkey's arm, including seventeen single and double joint muscles, is utilized to generate horizontal hand movements. The hand trajectories produced by this algorithm are discussed.

1   INTRODUCTION

To perform a voluntary hand movement, the primate nervous system must solve the following problems: (A) Which *trajectory* (hand path and velocity) should be used while moving the hand from the initial to the desired position. (B) What muscle forces should be generated. Those two problems are termed "ill-posed" because they can be solved in an infinite number of ways. The interesting question to us is: what strategy does the nervous system use while choosing a specific solution for these problems ? The chosen solutions must comply with the known experimental data: Human and monkey's free horizontal multi-joint hand movements have straight or gently curved paths. The hand velocity profiles are always roughly bell shaped (Bizzi & Abend 1986).

1.1   THE MINIMUM-JERK MODEL

Flash and Hogan (1985) proposed that a *global kinematic optimization* approach, the *minimum-jerk model*, defines a solution for the trajectory determination problem (problem A). Using this strategy, the nervous system is choosing the (unique) smoothest trajectory of the hand for any horizontal movement, without having to deal with the structure or dynamics of the arm. The minimum-jerk model produces reasonable approximations for hand trajectories in unconstrained point to point movements in the horizontal plane in front of the body (Flash & Hogan 1985; Morasso 1981; Uno et al. 1989a). It fails to describe, however, some important experimental findings for human arm movements (Uno et al. 1989a).

1.2   THE EQUILIBRIUM-TRAJECTORY HYPOTHESIS

According to the *equilibrium-trajectory hypothesis* (Feldman 1966), the nervous system generates movements by a gradual change in the equilibrium posture of the hand: at all times during the execution of a movement the muscle forces defines a stable posture which acts as a point of attraction in the configurational space of the limb. The actual hand movement is the *realized trajectory*. The realized hand trajectory is usually different from the attracting pre-planned *virtual trajectory* (Hogan 1984). Simulations by Flash (1987), have suggested that realistic multi-joint arm movements at moderate speed can be generated by moving the hand equilibrium position along a pre-planned *minimum-jerk* virtual trajectory. The interactions of the dynamic properties of the arm and the attracting virtual trajectory create together the actual realized trajectory. Flash did not suggest a solution to problem B.

A *static local optimization algorithm* related to the equilibrium-trajectory hypothesis and called *backdriving* was proposed by Mussa-Ivaldi et al. (1991). This algorithm can be used to solve problem B only after the virtual trajectory is known. The virtual trajectory is not necessarily a minimum-jerk trajectory. Driving the arm from a current equilibrium position to the next one on the virtual trajectory is performed by two steps: 1) simulate a passive displacement of the arm to the new position and 2) update the muscle forces so as to eliminate the induced hand force. A unique active change (step 2) is chosen by finding these muscle forces which minimize the change in the potential energy stored in the muscles. Using a static model of the monkey's arm, the first author has analyzed this **sequential computational approach**, including a solution for both the trajectory determination (A) and the muscle forces (B) problems (Dornay 1990, 1991a, 1991b).

The equilibrium-trajectory hypothesis which is using the minimum-jerk model was criticized by Katayama and Kawato (in preparation). According to their recent findings, the values of the dynamic stiffness used by Flash (1987) are too high to be realistic. They have found that a very complex virtual trajectory, completely different from the one predicted by the minimum-jerk model, is needed for coding realistic hand movements.

2   GLOBAL DYNAMIC OPTIMIZATIONS

A set of *global dynamic optimizations* have been proposed by Uno et al. (1989a, 1989b). Uno et al. suggested that the dynamic properties of the arm must be considered by any algorithm for controlling hand movements. They also proposed that the hand trajectory and the motor commands (joint torques, muscle tensions, etc.,) are computed **in parallel**.

2.1   THE MINIMUM-TORQUE-CHANGE MODEL

Uno et al. (1989a) have proposed the *minimum-torque-change model*. The model proposes that the hand trajectory and the joint torques are determined simultaneously, while the algorithm minimizes globally the rate of change of the joint torques. The minimum-torque-change model was criticized by Flash (1990), saying that the rotary inertia used was not realistic. If Flash's inertia values are used then the hand path predicted by the minimum-torque-change model is curved (Flash 1990).

2.2   THE MINIMUM-MUSCLE-TENSION-CHANGE MODEL

The *minimum-muscle-tension-change model* (Uno et al. 1989b, Dornay et al. 1991) is a parallel dynamic optimization approach in which the trajectory determination problem ($\mathbb{A}$) and the muscle force generation problem ($\mathbb{B}$) are solved simultaneously. No explicit trajectory is imposed on the hand, but that it must reach the final desired state (position, velocity, etc.) in a pre-specified time. The numerical solution used is a "penalty" method, in which the controller minimizes globally by iterations an energy function E :

$$E = \varepsilon \left(E_D + \lambda E_s \right) \tag{1}$$

E is the energy that must be minimized in iterations. E_D is a collection of hard constraints, like, for example that the hand must reach the desired position at the specified time. E_s is a smoothness constraint, like the minimum-muscle-tension-change model. λ is a regularization function, that needs to become smaller and smaller as the number of iterations increases. This is a key point because the hard constraints must be strictly satisfied at the end of the iterative process. ε is a small rate term. The smoothness constraint E_s , is the minimum-muscle-tension-change model, defined as:

$$E_S = 0.5 \int_{t_0}^{t_{fin}} \sum_{i=1}^{n} \left(df_i / dt \right)^2 dt \tag{2}$$

f_i is the tension of muscle i, n is the total number of muscles, t_0 is the initial time and t_{fin} is the final time of the movement.

Preliminary studies have shown (Uno et al. 1989b) that the minimum-muscle-tension-change model can simulate reasonable hand movements.

3   THE MONKEY'S ARM MODEL

The model used was recently described (Dornay 1991a; Dornay et al. 1991). It is based on anatomical study using the Rhesus monkey. Attachments of 17 shoulder, elbow and double joint muscles were marked on the skeleton. The skeleton was cleaned and reassembled to a natural configuration of a monkey during horizontal arm movements (Fig. 1). X-ray analysis was used to create a simplified horizontal model of the arm (Fig. 1). Effective origins and insertions of the muscles were estimated by computer simulations to ensure the postural stability of the hand at equilibrium (Dornay 1991a). The simplified dynamic model used in this study is described in Dornay et al. (1991).

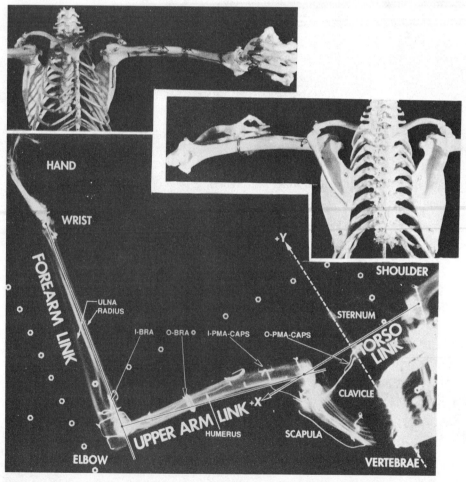

Figure 1: The Monkey's Arm Model. Top left is a ventral view of the skeleton. Middle right is a dorsal view. The bottom shows a top-down X-ray projection of the skeleton, with the axes marked on it. The photos were taken by Mr. H.S. Hall, MIT.

4   THE BEHAVIORAL TASK

We tried to simulate the horizontal arm movements reported by Uno et al. (1989a) for human subjects, using the monkey's model. Fig. 2 (left) shows a top view of the hand workspace of the monkey (light small dots). We used 7 hand positions defined by the following shoulder and elbow relative angles (in degrees): T_1 {14,122}; T_2 {67,100}; T_3 {75,64}; T_4 {63,45}; T_5 {35,54}; T_6 {-5,101} and T_7 {-25,45}. The joint angles used by Uno et al. (1989a) for T_4 and T_7, {77,22} and {0,0}, are out of the workspace of the monkey's hand (open circles in Fig 2, left). We approximated them by our T_4 and T_7 (filled circles). The behavioral task that we simulated using the minimum-muscle-tension-change model consisted of the 4 trajectories shown in Fig. 2 (right).

5   SIMULATION RESULTS

Figure 2 (right) shows the paths (T_2->T_6), (T_3->T_6), (T_4->T_1), and (T_7->T_5). The paths T_2->T_6, T_3->T_6 and T_7->T_5 are slightly convex. Slightly convex paths for T_2->T_6 were reported in human movements by Flash (1987), Uno et al. (1989a) and Morasso (1981). Human T_3->T_6 paths have a small tendency to be slightly convex (Uno et al. 1989a; Flash (1987). In our simulations, T_2->T_6 and T_3->T_6 have slightly larger curvatures than those reported in humans. Human large movements from the side of the body to the front of the body similar to our T_7->T_5 were reported by Uno et al. (1989a). The path of these movements is convex and similar to our simulation results. The simulated path of T_4->T_1 is slightly curved to the left and then to the right, but roughly straight. The human's T_4->T_1 paths look slightly straighter than in our simulations (Uno et al. 1989a; Flash 1987).

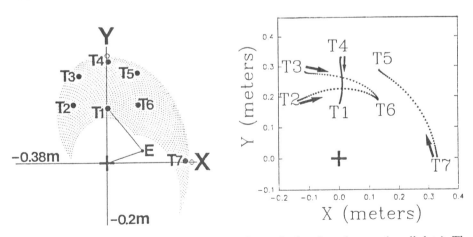

Figure 2. The Behavioral Task. The left side shows the hand workspace (small dots). The shoulder position and origin of coordinates (0,0) is marked by +. The elbow location when the hand is on position T_1 is marked by E. The right side shows 4 hand paths simulated by the minimum-muscle-tension-change model. Arrows indicate the directions of the movements.

Fig. 3 shows the corresponding simulated hand velocities. The velocity profiles have a single peak and are roughly bell shaped, like those reported for human subjects. The left side of the velocity profile of $T_4->T_1$ looks slightly irregular.

The hand trajectories simulated here are in general closer to human data than those reported by us in the past (Dornay et al. 1991). In the current study we used a much slower protocol for reducing λ than in the previous study, and we think that we are closer now to the optimal solution of the numerical calculation than in the previous study. Indeed, the hand velocity profiles and muscle tension profiles look smoother here than in the previous study. It is in general very difficult to guarantee that the optimal solution is achieved, unless an unpractical large number of iterations is used. Fig. 4 (top,left) shows the way E_D and E_S of equation 1 are changing as a function λ for the trajectory $T_7->T_5$. Ideally, both should reach a plato when the optimal solution is reached. The muscle tensions simulated for $T_7->T_5$ are shown in Fig. 4. They look quite smooth.

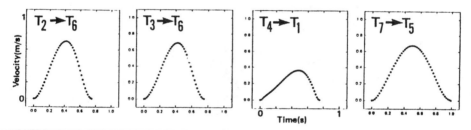

Figure 3. The Hand Tangential Velocity.

6   DISCUSSION

Various control strategies have been proposed to explain the roughly straight hand trajectory shown by primates in planar reaching movements. The minimum-jerk model (Flash & Hogan 1985) takes into account only the desired hand movement, and completely ignores the dynamic properties of the arm. This simplified approach is a good approximation for many movements, but cannot explain some experimental evidence (Uno et al. 1989a). A more demanding approach, the minimum-torque-change model (Uno et al. 1989a), takes into account the dynamics of the arm, but emphasizes only the torques at the joints, and completely ignores the properties of the muscles. This model was criticized to produce unrealistic hand trajectories when proper inertia values are used (Flash 1990). A third and more complicated model is the minimum-muscle-tension-change model (Uno et al. 1989b, Dornay et al. 1991). The minimum-muscle-tension-change model was shown here to produce gently curved hand movements, which although not identical, are quite close to the primate behavior. In the current study the initial and final tensions of the muscles were assumed to be zero. This is not a realistic assumption since even a static hand at an equilibrium is expected to have some stiffness. Using the minimum-muscle-tension-change model with non-zero initial and final muscle tensions is a logical

Muscle   Forces

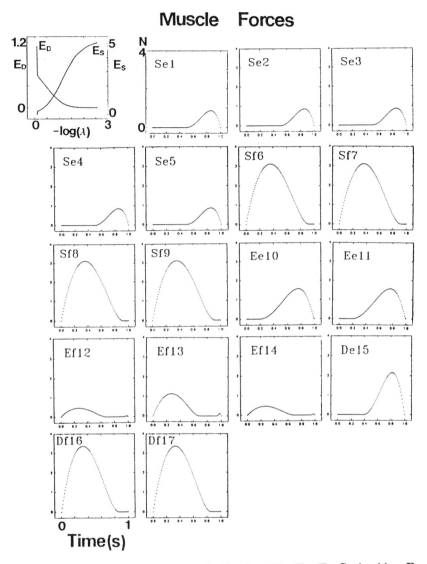

Figure 4. Numerical Analysis and Muscle Tensions For T_7->T_5. **S**=shoulder, **E**=elbow, **D**=double-joint muscle, **e**=extensor, **f**=flexor.

study which we intend to test in the near future. Still, the minimum-muscle-tension-change model considers only the muscle moment-arms (μ) and momvels ($\partial\mu/\partial\theta$) and ignores the muscle length-tension curves. A more complicated model which we are studying now is the minimum-motor-command-change model, which includes the length-tension curves.

Acknowledgements

M. Dornay and M. Kawato would like to thank Drs. K. Nakane and E. Yodogawa, ATR, for their valuable help and support. Preparation of the paper was supported by Human Frontier Science Program grant to M. Kawato.

References

1   E Bizzi & WK Abend (1986) Control of multijoint movements. In M.J. Cohen and F. Strumwasser (Eds.) *Comparative Neurobiology: Modes of Communication in the Nervous System*, John Wiley & Sons, pp. 255-277

2   M Dornay (1990) Control of movement and the postural stability of the monkey's arm. *Proc. 3rd International Symposium on Bioelectronic and Molecular Electronic Devices*, Kobe, Japan, December 18-20, pp. 101-102

3   M Dornay (1991a) Static analysis of posture and movement, using a 17-muscle model of the monkey's arm. *ATR Technical Report TR-A-0109*

4   M Dornay (1991b) Control of movement, postural stability, and muscle angular stiffness. *Proc. IEEE Systems, Man and Cybernetics*, Virginia, USA, pp. 1373-1379

5   M Dornay, Y Uno, M Kawato & R Suzuki (1991) Simulation of optimal movements using a 17-muscle model of the monkey's arm. *Proc. SICE 30th Annual Conference, ES-1-4*, July 17-19, Yonezawam Japan, pp. 919-922

6   AG Feldman (1966) Functional tuning of the nervous system with control of movement or maintenance of a steady posture. *Biophysics*, 11, pp. 766-775

7   T Flash & N Hogan (1985) The coordination of arm movements: an experimentally confirmed mathematical model. *J. Neurosci.*, 5, pp. 1688-1703

8   T Flash (1987) The control of hand equilibrium trajectories in multi-joint arm movements. *Biol. Cybern.*, 57, pp. 257-274

9   T Flash (1990) The organization of human arm trajectory control. In J. Winters and S. Woo (Eds.) *Multiple muscle systems: Biomechanics and movement organization*, Springer-Verlag, pp. 282-301

10   N Hogan (1984) An organizing principle for a class of voluntary movements. *J. Neurosci.*, 4, pp. 2745-2754

11   P Morasso (1981) Spatial control of arm movements. *Experimental Brain Research*, 42, pp. 223-227

12   FA Mussa-Ivaldi, P Morasso, N Hogan & E Bizzi (1991) Network models of motor systems with many degrees of freedom. In M.D. Fraser (Ed.) *Advances in control networks and large scale parallel distributed processing models*, Albex Publ. Corp.

13   Y Uno, M Kawato & R Suzuki (1989a) Formation and control of optimal trajectory in human multijoint arm movement - minimum-torque-change model. *Biol. Cybern.*, 61, pp. 89-101

14   Y Uno, R Suzuki & M Kawato (1989b) Minimum muscle-tension change model which reproduces human arm movement. *Proceedings of the 4th Symposium on Biological and Physiological Engineering*, pp. 299-302, (in Japanese)

PART X

APPLICATIONS

ANN Based Classification for Heart Defibrillators

M. Jabri, S. Pickard, P. Leong, Z. Chi, B. Flower, and Y. Xie

Sydney University Electrical Engineering

NSW 2006 Australia

Abstract

Current Intra-Cardia defibrillators make use of simple classification algorithms to determine patient conditions and subsequently to enable proper therapy. The simplicity is primarily due to the constraints on power dissipation and area available for implementation. Sub-threshold implementation of artificial neural networks offer potential classifiers with higher performance than commercially available defibrillators. In this paper we explore several classifier architectures and discuss micro-electronic implementation issues.

1.0 INTRODUCTION

Intra-Cardia Defibrillators (ICDs) represent an important therapy for people with heart disease. These devices are implanted and perform three types of actions:

> 1. monitor the heart
> 2. to pace the heart
> 3. to apply high energy/high voltage electric shock

They sense the electrical activity of the heart through leads attached to the heart tissue. Two types of sensing are commonly used:

Single Chamber: Lead attached to the Right Ventricular Apex (RVA)
Dual Chamber: An additional lead is attached to the High Right Atrium (HRA).

The actions performed by defibrillators are based on the outcome of a classification procedure based on the heart rhythms of different heart diseases (abnormal rhythms or "arrhythmias").

There are tens of different arrhythmias of interest to cardiologists. They are clustered into three groups according to the three therapies (actions) that ICDs perform.

Figure 1 shows an example of a Normal Sinus Rhythm. Note the regularity in the beats. Of interest to us is what is called the QRS complex which represents the electrical activity in the ventricle during a beat. The R point represents the peak, and the distance between two heart beats is usually referred to as the RR interval.

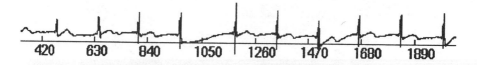

FIGURE 1. A Normal Sinus Rhythm (NSR) waveform

Figure 2 shows an example of a Ventricular Tachycardia (more precisely a Ventricular Tachycardia Slow or VTS). Note that the beats are faster in comparison with an NSR.

Ventricular Fibrillation (VF) is shown in Figure 3. Note the chaotic behavior and the absence of well defined heart beats.

FIGURE 2. A Ventricular Tachycardia (VT) waveform

The three waveforms discussed above are examples of Intra-Cardia Electro-Grams (ICEG). NSR, VT and VF are representative of the type of action a defibrillator has to takes. For an NSR, an action of "continue monitoring" is used. For a VT an action of "pacing" is performed, whereas for VF a high energy/high voltage shock is issued. Because they are near-field signals, ICEGs are different from external Eltro-Cardio-Grams (ECG). As a result, classification algorithms developed for ECG patterns may not be necessarily valuable for ICEG recognition.

The difficulties in ICEG classification lie in that many arrhythmias share similar features and fuzzy situations often need to be dealt with. For instance, many ICDs make use of the heart rate as a fundamental feature in the arrhythmia classification process. But several arrhythmias that require different type of therapeutic actions have similar heart rates. For example, a Sinus Tachycardia (ST) is an arrhythmia characterized with a heart rate that is higher than that of an NSR and in the vicinity of a VT. Many classifier would classify an ST as VT leading to a therapy of pacing, whereas an ST is supposed to be grouped under an NSR type of therapy. Another example is a fast VT which may be associated with heart rates that are indicative of

VF. In this case the defibrillator would apply a VF type of therapy when only a VT type therapy is required (pacing).

FIGURE 3. A Ventricular Fibrillation (VF) waveform.

The overlap of the classes when only heart rate is used as the main classification feature highlights the necessity of the consideration of further features with higher discrimination capabilities. Features that are commonly used in addition to the heart rate are:

1. average heart rate (over a period of time)
2. arrhythmia onset
3. arrhythmia probability density functions

Because of the limited power budget and area, arrhythmia classifiers in ICDs are kept extremely simple with respect to what could be achieved with more relaxed implementation constraints. As a result false positive (pacing or defibrillation when none is required) may be high and error rates may reach 13%.

Artificial neural network techniques offer the potential of higher classification performance. In order to maintain as lower power consumption as possible, VLSI micro-power implementation techniques need to be considered.

In this paper, we discuss several classifier architectures and sub-threshold implementation techniques. Both single and dual chamber based classifications are considered.

2.0 DATA

Data used in our experiments were collected from Electro-Physiological Studies (EPS) at hospitals in Australia and the UK. Altogether, and depending on whether single or dual chamber is considered, data from over 70 patients is available. Cardiologists from our commercial collaborator have labelled this data. All tests were performed on a testing set that was not used in classifier building. Arrhythmias recorded during EPS are produced by stimulation. As a result, no natural transitions are captured.

3.0 SINGLE CHAMBER CLASSIFICATION

We have evaluated several approaches for single chamber classification. It is important to note here that in the case of single chamber, not all arrhythmias could be correctly classified (not even by human experts). This is because data from the RVA lead represents mainly the ventricular electrical activity, and many atrial arrhythmias require atrial information for proper diagnosis.

3.1 MULTI-LAYER PERCEPTRONS

Table 1 shows the performance of multi-layer perceptrons (MLP) trained using vanilla back-propagation, conjugate gradient and a specialized limited precision training algorithm that we call Combined Search Algorithm (Xie and Jabri, 91). The input to the MLP are 21 features extracted from the time domain. There are three outputs representing three main groupings: NSR, VT and VF. We do not have the space here to elaborate on the choice of the input features. Interested readers are referenced to (Chi and Jabri, 91; Leong and Jabri, 91).

TABLE 1. Performance of Multi-layer Perceptron Based Classifiers

Network	Training Algorithm	Precision	Average Performance
21-5-3	backprop.	unlimited	96%
21-5-3	conj.-grad	unlimited	95.5%
21-5-3	CSA	6 bits	94.8%

The summary here indicates that a high performance single chamber based classification can be achieved for ventricular arrhythmias. It also indicates that limited precision training does not significantly degrade this performance. In the case of limited precision MLP, 6 bits plus a sign bit are used to represent network activities and weights.

3.2 INDUCTION OF DECISION TREES

The same training data used to train the MLP was used to create a decision tree using the C4.5 program developed by Ross Quinlan (a derivative of the ID3 algorithm). The resultant tree was then tested, and the performance was 95% correct classification. In order to achieve this high performance, the whole training data had to be used in the induction process (windowing disabled). This has a negative side effect in that the trees generated tend to be large.

The implementation of decision trees in VLSI is not a difficult procedure. The problem however is that because of the binary decision process, the branching thresholds are difficult to be implemented in digital (for large trees) and even more difficult to be implemented in micro-power analog. The latter implementation technique would be possible if the induction process can take advantage of the hardware characteristics in a similar way that "in-loop" training of sub-threshold VLSI MLP achieves the same objective.

4.0 DUAL CHAMBER BASED CLASSIFIERS

Two architectures for dual chamber based classifiers have been investigated: Multi-Module-Neural Networks and a hybrid Decision Tree/MLP. The difference between the classifier architectures is a function of which arrhythmia group is being targeted for classification.

4.1 MULTI-MODULE NEURAL NETWORK

The multi-module neural network architecture aims at improving the performance with respect to the classification of Supra-Ventricular Tachycardia (SVT). The architecture is shown in Figure 4 with the classifier being the right most block.

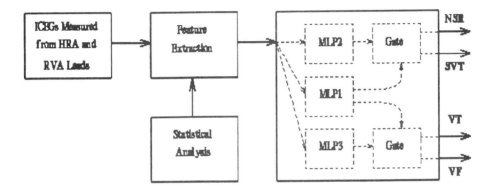

FIGURE 4. Multi-Module Neural Network Classifier

The idea behind this architecture is to divide the classification problem into that of discriminating between NSR and SVT on one hand and VF and VT on the other. The details of the operation and the training of this structured classifier can be found in (Chi and Jabri, 91).

In order to evaluate the performance of the MMNN classifier, a single large MLP was also developed. The single large MLP makes use of the same input features as the MMNN and targets the same classes. The performance comparison is shown in Table 2 which clearly shows that a higher performance is achieved using the MMNN.

4.2 HYBRID DECISION TREE/MLP

The hybrid decision tree/multi-layer perceptron "mimics" the classification process as performed by cardiologists. The architecture of the classifier is shown in Figure 5. The decision tree is used to produce a judgement on:

      1.The rate aspects of the ventricular and atrial channels,

      2.The relative timing between the atrial and ventricular beats.

In parallel with the decision tree, a morphology based classifier is used to perform template matching. The morphology classifier is a simple MLP with input that are signal samples (sampled at half the speed of the normal sampling rate of the signal).

The output of the timing and morphology classifiers are fed into an arbitrator which produces the class of the arrhythmia being observed. An "X out of Y" classifier is used to smooth out the

TABLE 2. Performance of Multi-Module Neural Network Classifier and comparison with that of a single large MLP.

Rhythms	MMNN Best %	MMNN Worst %	Single MLP %
NSR	95.3	93.8	93.4
ST	98.6	98.6	97.5
SVT	96.4	93.3	95.4
AT	95.9	93.2	71.2
AF	86.7	85.4	77.5
VT	99.4	99.4	100
VTF	100	100	80.3
VF	97	97	99.4
Average	96.2	95.1	89.3
SD	4.18	4.8	11.31

classification output by the arbitrator and to produce an "averaged" final output class. Further details on the implementation and the operation of the hybrid classifier can be found in (Leong and Jabri, 91).

This classifier achieves a high performance classification over several types of arrhythmia. Table 3 shows the performance on a multi-patient database and indicate a performance of over 99% correct classification.

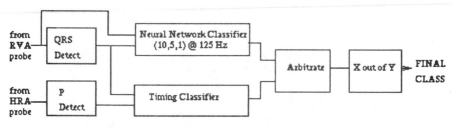

FIGURE 5. Architecture of the hybrid decision tree/neural network classifier.

5.0 MICROELECTRONIC IMPLEMENTATIONS

In all our classifier architecture investigations, micro-electronic implementation considerations were a constant constraint. Many other architectures that can achieve competitive performance were not discussed in this paper because of their unsuitability for low power/small area implementation. The main challenge in a low power/small area VLSI implementation of classifiers similar to those discussed above, is how to implement in very low power a MLP architecture that can reliably learn and achieve a performance comparable to that of the functional simulations. Several design strategies can achieve the low power and small area objectives.

TABLE 3. Performance of the hybrid decision tree/MLP classifier for dual chamber classification.

SubClass	Class	NSR	SVT	VT	VF
NSR	NSR	5247	4	2	0
ST	NSR	1535	24	2	1
SVT	SVT	0	1022	0	0
AT	SVT	0	52	0	0
AF	SVT	0	165	0	0
VT	VT	0	0	322	0
VT 1:1	VT	2	0	555	0
VF	VF	0	0	2	196
VTF	VF	0	2	0	116

Both digital and analog implementation techniques are being investigated and we report here on our analog implementation efforts only. Our analog implementations make use of the sub-threshold operation mode of MOS transistors in order to maintain a very low power dissipation.

5.1 MASTER PERTURBATOR CHIP

The architecture of this chip is shown in Figure 6(a). Weights are implemented using a differential capacitor scheme refreshed from digital RAM. Synapses are implemented as four quadrant Gilbert multipliers (Pickard et al, 92). The chip has been fabricated and is currently being tested. The building blocks have so far been successfully tested. Two networks are implemented a 7-5-3 (total of 50 synapses) and a small single layer network. The single layer network has been successfully trained to perform simple logic operations using the Weight Perturbation algorithm (Jabri and Flower, 91).

5.2 THE BOURKE CHIP

The BOURKE chip (Leong and Jabri, 92) makes use of Multiplying Digital to Analog Converters to implement the synapses. Weights are stored in digital registers. All neurons were implemented as external resistors for the sake of evaluation. Figure 6(b) shows the schematics of a synapse. The BOURKE chip has a small network 3-3-1 and has been successfully tested (it was successfully trained to perform an XOR). A larger version of this chip with a 10-6-4 network is being fabricated.

6.0 Conclusions

We have presented in this paper several architectures for single and dual chamber arrhythmia

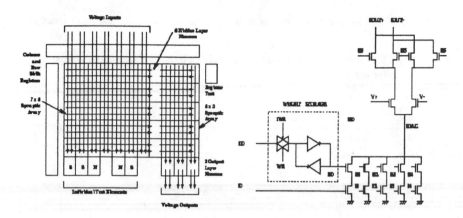

FIGURE 6. (a) Architecture of the Master Perturbator chip. (b) Schematics of the BOURKE chip synapse implementation.

classifiers. In both cases a good classification performance was achieved. In particular, for the case of dual chamber classification, the complexity of the problem calls on more structured classifier architectures. Two microelectronic low power implementation were briefly presented. Progress so far indicates that micro-power VLSI ANNs offer a technology that will enable the use of powerful classification strategies in implantable defibrillators.

Acknowledgment

Work presented in this paper was supported by the Australian Department of Industry Technology & Commerce, Telectronics Pacing Systems, and the Australian Research Council.

References

Z. Chi and M. Jabri (1991), "Identification of Supraventricular and Ventricular Arrhythmias Using a Combination of Three Neural Networks". Proceedings of the Computers in Cardiology Conference, Venice, Italy, September 1991.

M. Jabri and B. Flower (1991), ``Weight Perturbations: An optimal architecture and learning technique for analog VLSI feed-forward and recurrent multi-layer networks", Neural Computation, Vol. 3, No. 4, MIT Press.

P.H.W Leong and M. Jabri (1991), ``Arrhythmia Classification Using Two Intracardiac Leads", Proceedings of the Computers in Cardiology Conference, Venice, Italy.

P.H.W. Leong and M. Jabri (1992), ``An Analogue Low Power VLSI Neural Network", Proceedings of the Third Australian Conference on Neural Networks, pp. 147-150, Canberra, Australia.

S. Pickard, M. Jabri, P.H.W. Leong, B.G. Flower and P. Henderson (1992), ``Low Power Analogue VLSI Implementation of A Feed-Forward Neural Network", Proceedings of the Third Australian Conference on Neural Networks, pp. 88-91, Canberra, Australia.

Y. Xie and M. Jabri (1991), ``Training Algorithms for Limited Precision Feed-forward Neural Networks", submitted to IEEE Transactions on Neural Networks and Neural Computation.

Neural Network Diagnosis of Avascular Necrosis from Magnetic Resonance Images

Armando Manduca
Dept. of Physiology and Biophysics
Mayo Clinic
Rochester, MN 55905

Paul Christy
Dept. of Diagnostic Radiology
Mayo Clinic
Rochester, MN 55905

Richard Ehman
Dept. of Diagnostic Radiology
Mayo Clinic
Rochester, MN 55905

Abstract

Avascular necrosis (AVN) of the femoral head is a common yet potentially serious disorder which can be detected in its very early stages with magnetic resonance imaging. We have developed multi-layer perceptron networks, trained with conjugate gradient optimization, which diagnose AVN from single magnetic resonance images of the femoral head with 100% accuracy on training data and 97% accuracy on test data.

1 INTRODUCTION

Diagnostic radiology may be a very natural field of application for neural networks, since a simple answer is desired from a complex image, and the learning process that human experts undergo is to a large extent a supervised learning experience based on looking at large numbers of images with known interpretations. Although many workers have applied neural nets to various types of 1-dimensional medical data (e.g. ECG and EEG waveforms), little work has been done on applying neural nets to diagnosis directly from medical images.

We wanted to explore the use of neural networks in diagnostic radiology by (1) starting with a simple but real diagnostic problem, and (2) using only actual data. We chose the diagnosis of avascular necrosis from magnetic resonance images as an ideal initial problem, because: the area in question is small and well-defined, its size and shape do not vary greatly between individuals, the condition (if present) is usually visible even at low spatial and gray level resolution on a single image, and real data is readily available.

Avascular necrosis (AVN) is the deterioration of tissue due to a disruption in the blood supply. AVN of the femoral head (the ball at the upper end of the femur which fits into the socket formed by the hip bone) is an increasingly common clinical problem, with potentially crippling effects. Since the sole blood supply to the femoral head in adults traverses the femoral neck, AVN often occurs following hip fracture (e.g., Bo Jackson). It is now apparent that AVN can also occur as a side effect of treatment with corticosteroid drugs, which are commonly used for immunosuppression in transplant patients as well as for patients with asthma, rheumatoid arthritis and other autoimmune diseases. Although the pathogenesis of AVN secondary to corticosteroid use is not well understood, 6 - 10% of such patients appear to develop the disorder (Ternoven et al., 1990). AVN may be detected with magnetic resonance imaging (MRI) even in its very early stages, as a low signal region within the femoral head due to loss of water-containing bone marrow. MRI is expected to play an important future role in screening patients undergoing corticosteroid therapy for AVN.

2   METHODOLOGY

The data set selected for analysis consisted of 125 sagittal images of femoral heads from T1-weighted MRI scans of 40 adult patients, with 51% showing evidence of AVN, from early stages to quite severe (see Fig. 1). Often both femoral heads from the same patient were selected (typically only one has AVN if the cause is fracture-related while both sometimes have AVN if the cause is secondary to drug use), and often two or three different cross-sectional slices of the same femoral head were included (the appearance of AVN can change dramatically as one steps through different cross-sectional slices). The images were digitized and 128x128 regions centered on and just containing the femoral heads were manually selected. These 128x128 subimages with 256 gray levels were averaged down to 32x32 resolution and to 16 gray levels for most of the trials (see Fig. 2).

The neural networks used to analyze the data were standard feed-forward, fully-connected multilayer perceptrons with a single hidden layer of 4 to 30 nodes and 2 output nodes. The majority of the runs were with networks of 1024 input nodes, into which the 32x32 images were placed, with gray levels scaled so the input values ranged within +0.5. In other experiments with different input features the number of input nodes varied accordingly. Conjugate gradient optimization was used for training (Kramer and Sangiovanni-Vincentelli, 1989; Barnard and Cole 1989). Training was stopped at a maximum of 50 passes through the training set, though usually convergence was achieved before this point. Each training run took less than 1 minute on a SPARCstation 2.

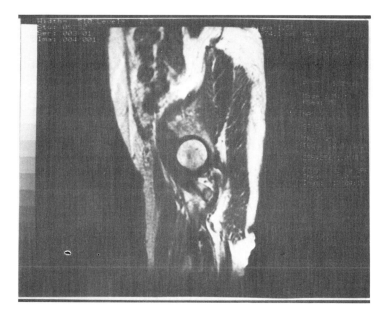

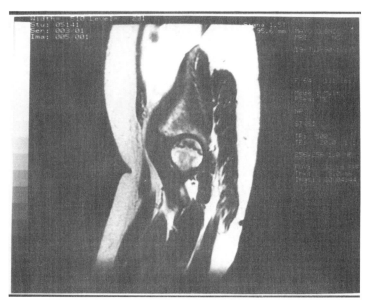

Figure 1: Representative sagittal hip T1 weighted MR images. The small circular area in the center of each picture is the femoral head (the ball joint at the upper end of the femur). The top image shows a normal femoral head; the bottom is a femoral head with severe avascular necrosis.

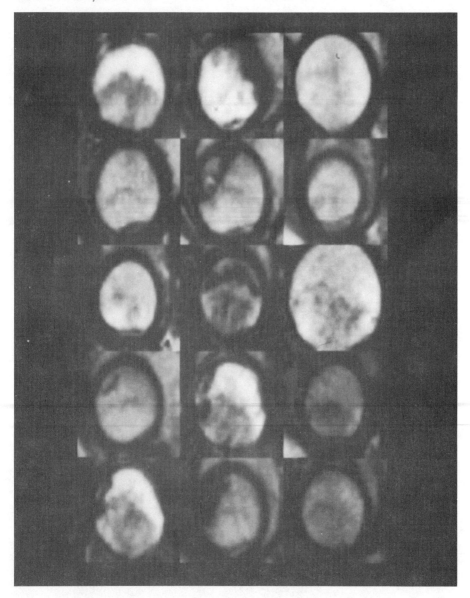

Figure 2: Sample images from our 32x32 pixel, 16 gray level data set. The five femoral heads in the right column are free of AVN, the five in the middle column have varying degrees of AVN, while the left column shows five images that were particularly difficult for both the networks and untrained humans to distinguish (only the last two have AVN).

Table 1: Diagnostic Accuracies on Test Data

(averages over 24 and 100 runs respectively)

hidden nodes	50% training	80% training
none	91.6%	92.6%
4	92.6%	95.5%
5	93.2%	96.4%
6	93.8%	96.4%
7	93.2%	97.0%
8	92.4%	96.8%
10	92.4%	96.1%
30	91.2%	94.1%

3   RESULTS

Two sets of runs with the image data were made, with the data randomly split 50%-50% and 80%-20% into training and test data sets respectively. In the first set, 4 different random splits of the data, with either half in turn serving as training or test data, and 3 different random weight initializations each were used for a total of 24 distinct runs for each network configuration. For the other set, since there was less test data, 10 different splits of the data with 10 different weight initializations each were used for a total of 100 distinct runs for each network configuration. The results are shown in Table 1. In all cases, the sensitivity and specificity were approximately equal. Standard deviations of the averages shown were typically 4.0% for the 24 run values and 3.0% for the 100 run values.

The overall data set is linearly separable, and networks with no hidden nodes readily achieved 100% on training data and better than 91% on test data. Networks with 2 or 3 hidden nodes were unable to converge on the training data much of the time, but with 4 hidden nodes convergence was restored and accuracy on test data was improved over the linear case. This accuracy increased up to 6 or 7 hidden nodes, and then began a gradual decrease as still more hidden nodes were added. This may be related to overfitting of the training data with the extra degrees of freedom, leading to poorer generalization. Adding a second hidden layer also decreased generalization accuracy.

Many other experiments were performed, using as inputs respectively: the 2-D FFT of the images, the power spectrum, features extracted with a ring-wedge detector in frequency space, the image data combined with each of the above, and multiple slight translations of the training and/or test data. None of these yielded an improvement in accuracy over the above, and no approach to date with significantly fewer than 1024 inputs maintained the high accuracies above. We are continuing experiments on other forms of reducing the dimensionality of the input data. A few experiments have been run with much larger networks, maintaining the full 128x128 resolution and 256 gray levels, but this also yields no improvement in the results.

4   DISCUSSION

The networks' performance at the 50% training level was comparable to that of humans with no training in radiology, who, supplied with the correct diagnosis for half of the images, averaged 92.5% accuracy on the remaining half. When the networks were trained on a larger set of data, their accuracy improved, to as high as 97.0% when 80% of the data was used for training. We expect this performance to continue to improve as larger data sets are collected.

It is difficult to compare the networks' performance to trained radiologists, who can diagnose AVN with essentially 100% accuracy, but who look at multiple cross-sectional images of far higher quality than our low-resolution, 16 gray-level data set. When presented with single images from our data set, they typically make no mistakes but set aside a few images as uncertain and strongly resist being forced to commit to an answer on those. We are currently experimenting with networks which can take inputs from multiple slices and which have an additional output representing uncertainty.

We consider the 97% accuracy achieved here to be very encouraging for further work on this problem and for the use of neural networks in more complex problems in diagnostic radiology. This is perhaps a very natural field of application for neural networks, since radiology resident training is essentially a four year experience with a very large training set, and the American College of Radiology teaching file is a classic example of a large collection of input/output training pairs (Boone et al., 1990). More complex diagnostic radiology problems may of course require fusing information from multiple images or imaging modalities, clinical data, and medical knowledge (perhaps as expert system rules). An especially intriguing possibility is that sophisticated network based systems could someday be presented with images which cannot currently be interpreted, supplied with the correct diagnosis as determined by other means, and learn to detect subtle distinctions in the images that are not apparent to human radiologists.

References

Barnard, E. and Cole, R. (1989) "A neural-net training program based on conjugate gradient optimization", Oregon Graduate Institute, Technical report CSE 89-014.

Boone, J. M., Sigillito, V. G. and Shaber, G. S. (1990), "Neural networks in radiology: An introduction and evaluation in a signal detection task", *Medical Physics*, **17**, 234-241.

Kramer, A. and Sangiovanni-Vincentelli, A. (1989), "Efficient Parallel Learning Algorithms for Neural Networks", in D. S. Touretzky (ed.) *Advances in Neural Information Processing Systems 1*, 40-48. Morgan-Kaufmann, San Mateo, CA.

Ternoven, O. et al. (1990), "Prevalence of Asymptomatic, Clinically Occult Avascular Necrosis of the Hip in a Population at Risk", *Radiology*, **177(P)**, 104.

Neural Network Analysis of Event Related Potentials and Electroencephalogram Predicts Vigilance

Rita Venturini   William W. Lytton

Terrence J. Sejnowski
Computational Neurobiology Laboratory
The Salk Institute
La Jolla, CA 92037

Abstract

Automated monitoring of vigilance in attention intensive tasks such as air traffic control or sonar operation is highly desirable. As the operator monitors the instrument, the instrument would monitor the operator, insuring against lapses. We have taken a first step toward this goal by using feedforward neural networks trained with backpropagation to interpret event related potentials (ERPs) and electroencephalogram (EEG) associated with periods of high and low vigilance. The accuracy of our system on an ERP data set averaged over 28 minutes was 96%, better than the 83% accuracy obtained using linear discriminant analysis. Practical vigilance monitoring will require prediction over shorter time periods. We were able to average the ERP over as little as 2 minutes and still get 90% correct prediction of a vigilance measure. Additionally, we achieved similarly good performance using segments of EEG power spectrum as short as 56 sec.

1 INTRODUCTION

Many tasks in society demand sustained attention to minimally varying stimuli over a long period of time. Detection of failure in vigilance during such tasks would be of enormous value. Different physiological variables like electroencephalogram

651

(EEG), electro-oculogram (EOG), heart rate, and pulse correlate to some extent with the level of attention (1, 2, 3). Profound changes in the appearance and spectrum of the EEG with sleep and drowsiness are well known. However, there is no agreement as to which EEG bands can best predict changes in vigilance. Recent studies (4) seem to indicate that there is a strong correlation between several EEG power spectra frequencies changes and attentional level in subjects performing a sustained task. Another measure that has been widely assessed in this context involves the use of event-related potentials (ERP)(5). These are voltage changes in the ongoing EEG that are time locked to sensory, motor, or cognitive events. They are usually too small to be recognized in the background electrical activity. The ERP's signal is typically extracted from the background noise of the EEG as a consequence of averaging over many trials. The ERP waveform remains constant for each repetition of the event, whereas the background EEG activity has random amplitude. Late cognitive event-related potentials, like the P300, are well known to be related to attentional allocation (6, 7, 8). Unfortunately, these ERPs are evoked only when the subject is attending to a stimulus. This condition is not present in a monitoring situation where monitoring is done precisely because the time of stimulus occurrence is unknown. Instead, shorter latency responses, evoked from unobtrusive task-irrelevant signals, need to be evaluated.

Data from a sonar simulation task was obtained from S.Makeig at al (9). They presented auditory targets only slightly louder than background noise to 13 male United States Navy personnel. Other tones, which the subjects were instructed to ignore, appeared randomly every 2-4 seconds (task irrelevant probes). Background EEG and ERP were both collected and analyzed. The ERPs evoked by the task irrelevant probes were classified into two groups depending on whether they appeared before a correctly identified target (pre-hit ERPs) or a missed target (pre-lapse ERPs). Pre-lapse ERPs showed a relative increase of P2 and N2 components and a decrease of the N1 deflection. N1, N2 and P2 designate the sign and time of peak of components in the ERP. Prior linear discriminant analysis (LDA) performed on the averages of each session, showed 83% correct classification using ERPs obtained from a single scalp site. Thus, the pre-hit and pre-lapse ERPs differed enough to permit classification by averaging over a large enough sample. In addition, EEG power spectra over 81 frequency bands were computed. EEG classification was made on the basis of a continuous measure of performance, the error rate, calculated as the mean of hits and lapses in a 32 sec moving window. Analysis of the EEG power spectrum (9) revealed that significant coherence is observed between various EEG frequencies and performance.

2   METHOD

2.1   THE DATA SET

Two different groups of input data were used (ERPs and EEG). For the former, a 600 msec sample of task irrelevant probe ERP was reduced to 40 points after low-pass filtering. We normalized the data on the basis of the maximum and minimum values of the entire set, maintaining amplitude variability. A single ERP was classified as being pre-hit or pre-lapse based on the subject's performance on the next target tone. EEG power spectrum, obtained every 1.6 seconds, was used as an input to predict a continuous estimate of vigilance (error rate), obtained by averaging the subject's performance during a 32 second window (normalized between -1 and 1). The five frequencies used (3, 10, 13, 19 and 39 Hz) had previously shown to be most strongly related to error rate changes (9). Each frequency was individually normalized to range between -1 and 1.

2.2   THE NETWORK

Feedforward networks were trained with backpropagation. We compared two-layer network to three-layer networks, varying the number of hidden units in different simulations between 2 and 8. Each architecture was trained ten times on the same task, resetting the weights every time with a different random seed. Initial simulations were performed to select network parameter values. We used a learning rate of 0.3 divided by the fan-in and weight initialization in a range between ±0.3. For the ERP data we used a jackknife procedure. For each simulation, a single pattern was excluded from the training set and considered to be the test pattern. Each pattern in turn was removed and used as the test pattern while the others are used for training. The EEG data set was not as limited as the ERP one and the simulations were performed using half of the data as training and the remaining part as testing set. Therefore, for subjects that had two runs each, the training and testing data came from separate sessions.

3   RESULTS

3.1   ERPs

The first simulation was done using a two-layer network to assess the adequacy of the neural network approach relative to the previous LDA results. The data set consisted of the grand averages of pre-hits and pre-lapses, from a single scalp site (Cz) of 9 subjects, three of them with a double session, giving a total of 24 patterns. The jackknife procedure was done in two different ways. First each ERP was considered individually, as had been done in the LDA study (pattern-jackknife). Second all the ERPs of a single subject were grouped together and removed together to form the test set (subject-jackknife). The network was trained for 10,000 epochs before testing. Figure 1 shows the weights for the 24 networks each trained with a set of ERPs obtained by removing a single ERP. The "waveform" of the weight values corresponds to features common to the pre-hit ERPs and to the negative of features common to the pre-lapse ERPs. Classification of patterns by the network was considerably more accurate than the 83% correct that had been obtained with the previous LDA analysis. 96% correct evaluation was seen in seven of the ten networks started with different random weight selections. The remaining three networks produced 92% correct responses (Fig. 2). The same two patterns were missed in all cases. Using hidden units did not improve generalization. The subject-jackknife results were very similar: 96% correct in two of ten networks and 92% in the remaining eight (Fig. 2). Thus, there was a somewhat increased difficulty in generalizing across individuals. The ability of the network to generalize over a shorter period of time was tested by progressively decreasing the number of trials used for testing using a network trained on the grand average ERPs. Subaverages

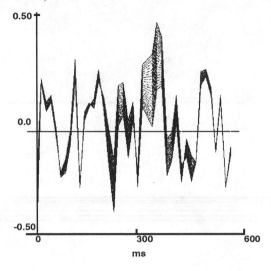

Figure 1: Weights from 24 two-layer networks trained from different initial weights: each value correspond to a sample point in time in the input data.

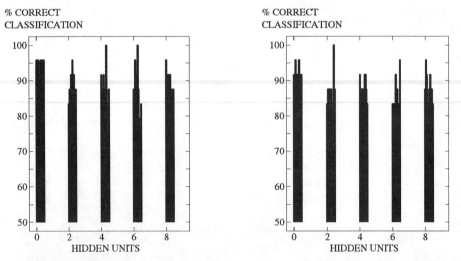

Figure 2: Generalization performance in Pattern (left) and Subject (right) Jack-knifes, using two-layer and three-layer networks with different number of hidden units. Each bar represents a different random start of the network.

**% CORRECT
CLASSIFICATION**

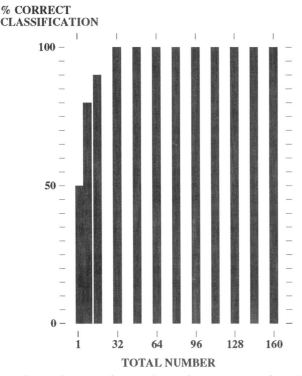

TOTAL NUMBER

Figure 3: Generalization for testing subaverages made using varying number of individual ERPs

were formed using from 1 to 160 individual ERPs (Figure 3). Performance with a single ERP is at chance. With 16 ERPs, corresponding to about 2 minutes, 90% accuracy was obtained.

3.2   EEG

We first report results using a two-layer network to compare with the previous LDA analysis. Five power spectrum frequency bands from a single scalp site (Cz) were used as input data. The error rate was averaged over 32 seconds at 1.6 second intervals. In the first set of runs both error rate and power spectra were filtered using a two minute time window. Good results could be obtained in cases where a subject made errors more than 40% of the time (Fig. 4). When the subject made few errors, training was more difficult and generalization was poor. These results were virtually identical to the LDA ones. The lack of improvement is probably due to the fact that the LDA performance was already close to 90% on this data set. Use of three-layer networks did not improve the generalization performance.

The use of a running average includes information in the EEG after the time at which the network is making a prediction. Causal prediction was attempted using multiple power spectra taken at 1.6 sec intervals over the past 56 sec, to predict the upcoming error rate. The results for one subject are shown in Figure 5. The predicted error rate differs from the target with a root mean square error of 0.3.

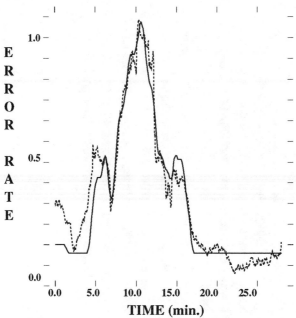

Figure 4: Generalization results predicting error rate from EEG. The dotted line is the network output, solid line the desired value.

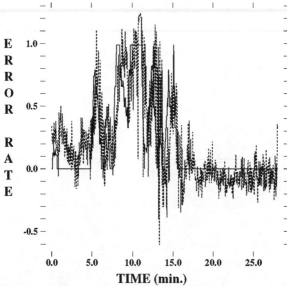

Figure 5: Causal prediction of error rate from EEG. The dotted line is the network output, solid line the desired value.

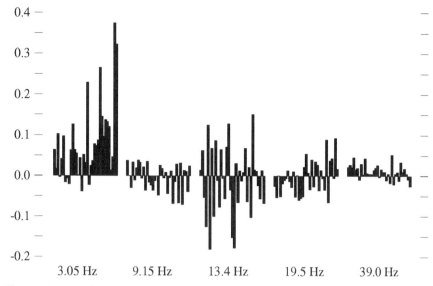

Figure 6: Weights from a two-layer causal prediction network. Each bar, within each frequency band, represents the influence on the output unit of power in that band at previous times ranging from 1 sec (right bar) to 56 sec (left bar).

Figure 6 shows the weights from a two-layer network trained to predict instantaneous error rate. The network mostly uses information from the 3.05 Hz and 13.4 Hz frequency bands in predicting the error rate changes. The values of the 3.05 Hz weights have a strong peak from the most recent time steps, indicating that power in this frequency band predicts the state of vigilance on a short time scale. The alternating positive and negative weights present in the 13.4 Hz set suggest that rapid changes in power in this band might be predictive of vigilance (i.e. the derivative of the power signal).

4 DISCUSSION

These results indicate that neural networks could be useful in analyzing electrophysiological measures. The EEG results suggest that the analysis can be applied to detect fluctuations of the attentional level of the subjects in real time. EEG analysis could also be a useful tool for understanding changes that occur in the electric activity of the brain during different states of attention.

In the ERP analysis, the lack of improvement with the introduction of hidden units might be due to the small size of the data set. If the data set is too small, adding hidden units and connections may reduce the ability to find a general solution to the problem. The ERP subject-jackknife results point out that inter-subject generalization is possible. This suggests the possibility of preparing a pre-programmed network that could be used with multiple subjects rather than training the network for each individual. The subaverages results suggest that the detection is possible in a relatively brief time interval. ERPs could be an useful completion to the EEG analysis in order to obtain an on line detector of attentional changes.

Future research will combination of these two measures along with EOG and heart rate. The idea is to let the model choose different network architectures and parameters, depending on the specific subtask.

ACKNOWLEDGEMENTS

We would like to thank Scott Makeig and Mark Inlow, Cognitive Performance and Psychophysiology Department, Naval Health Research Center, San Diego for providing the data and for invaluable discussions and Y. Le Cun and L.Y. Bottou from Neuristique who provided the SN2 simulator. RV was supported by Ministry of Public Instruction, Italy; WWL from a Physician Scientist Award, National Institute of Aging; TJS is an Investigator with the Howard Hughes Medical Institute. Research was supported by ONR Grant N00014-91-J-1674.

REFERENCES

1 Belyavin, A. and Wright, N.A.(1987). Changes in electrical activity of the brain with vigilance. *Electroencephalography and Clinical Neuroscience*, 66:137-144.

2 Torsvall, L. and Akerstedt, T.(1988). Extreme sleepiness: quantification of OG and spectral EEG parameters. *Int. J. Neuroscience*, 38:435-441.

3 Fruhstorfer, H., Langanke, P., Meinzer, K., Peter, J.H., and Pfaff, U.(1977). Neurophysiological vigilance indicators and operational analysis of a train vigilance monitoring device: a laboratory and field study. In R.R.Mackie(Ed.), *Vigilance Theory, Operational Performance, and Physiological Correlates*, 147-162, New York: Plenum Press.

4 Makeig, S. and Inlow M.(1991). Lapses in Alertness : Coherence of fluctuations in performance and EEG spectrum. Cognitive Performance and Psychophysiology Department, NHRC, San Diego. Technical Report.

5 Fruhstorfer, H. and Bergstrom, R.M.(1969). Human vigilance and auditory evoked responses. *Electroencephalography and Clinical Neurophysiology*, 27:346-355.

6 Polich, J.(1989). Habituation of P300 from auditory stimuli. *Psychobiology*, 17:19-28.

7 Polich, J.(1987). Task difficulty, probability, and inter-stimulus interval as determinants of P300 from auditory stimuli. *Electroencephalography and clinical Neurophysiology*, 68:311-320.

8 Polich, J.(1990). P300, Probability, and Interstimulus Interval. *Psychophysiology*, 27:396-403.

9 Makeig S., Elliot F.S., Inlow M. and Kobus D.A.(1991) Predicting Lapses in Vigilance Using Brain Evoked Responses to Irrelevant Auditory Probe. Cognitive Performance and Psychophysiology Department, NHRC, San Diego. Technical Report.

Neural Control for Rolling Mills: Incorporating Domain Theories to Overcome Data Deficiency

Martin Röscheisen
Computer Science Dept.
Munich Technical University
8 Munich 40, FRG

Reimar Hofmann
Computer Science Dept.
Edinburgh University
Edinburgh, EH89A, UK

Volker Tresp
Corporate R & D
Siemens AG
8 Munich 83, FRG

Abstract

In a Bayesian framework, we give a principled account of how domain-specific prior knowledge such as imperfect analytic domain theories can be optimally incorporated into networks of locally-tuned units: by choosing a specific architecture and by applying a specific training regimen. Our method proved successful in overcoming the data deficiency problem in a large-scale application to devise a neural control for a hot line rolling mill. It achieves in this application significantly higher accuracy than optimally-tuned standard algorithms such as sigmoidal backpropagation, and outperforms the state-of-the-art solution.

1 INTRODUCTION

Learning in connectionist networks typically requires many training examples and relies more or less explicitly on some kind of *syntactic* preference bias such as "minimal architecture" (Rumelhart, 1988; Le Cun *et al.*, 1990; Weigend, 1991; inter alia) or a smoothness constraint operator (Poggio *et al.*, 1990), but does not make use of explicit representations of domain-specific prior knowledge. If training data is deficient, learning a functional mapping inductively may no longer be feasible, whereas this may still be the case when guided by domain knowledge. Controlling a rolling mill is an example of a large-scale real-world application where training data is very scarce and noisy, yet there exist much refined, though still approximate, analytic models that have been applied for the past decades and embody many years of experience in this particular domain. Much in the spirit of Explanation-

659

Based Learning (see, for example, Mitchell *et al.*, 1986; Minton *et al.*, 1986), where domain knowledge is applied to get valid generalizations from only a few training examples, we consider an analytic model as an imperfect domain theory from which the training data is "explained" (see also Scott *et al.*, 1991; Bergadano *et al.*, 1990; Tecuci *et al.*, 1990). Using a Bayesian framework, we consider in Section 2 the optimal response of networks in the presence of noise on their input, and derive, in Section 2.1, a familiar localized network architecture (Moody *et al.*, 1989, 1990). In Section 2.2, we show how domain knowledge can be readily incorporated into this localized network by applying a specific training regimen. These results were applied as part of a project to devise a neural control for a hot line rolling mill, and, in Section 3, we describe experimental results which indicate that incorporating domain theories can be indispensable for connectionist networks to be successful in difficult engineering domains. (See also references for one of our more detailed papers.)

2 THEORETICAL FOUNDATION

2.1 NETWORK ARCHITECTURE

We apply a Bayesian framework to systems where the training data is assumed to be generated from the true model f, which itself is considered to be derived from a domain theory b that is represented as a function. Since the measurements in our application are very noisy and clustered, we took this as the paradigm case, and assume the actual input $X \in \mathbb{R}^d$ to be a noisy version of one of a small number (N) of prototypical input vectors $\vec{t}_1, \ldots, \vec{t}_N \in \mathbb{R}^d$ where the noise is additive with covariance matrix Σ. The corresponding true output values $f(\vec{t}_1), \ldots, f(\vec{t}_N) \in \mathbb{R}$ are assumed to be distributed around the values suggested by the domain theory, $b(\vec{t}_1), \ldots, b(\vec{t}_N)$ (variance σ^2_{prior}). Thus, each point in the training data $D := \{ (\vec{x}_i, y_i); \ i = 1, \ldots, M \}$ is considered to be generated as follows: $\vec{x}_i$ is obtained by selecting one of the $\vec{t}_k$ and adding zero-mean noise with covariance Σ, and y_i is generated by adding Gaussian zero-mean noise with variance σ^2_{data} to $f(\vec{t}_k)$.[1] We determine the system's response $O(\vec{x})$ to an input $\vec{x}$ to be optimal with respect to the expectation of the squared error (MMSE-estimate):

$$O(\vec{x}) := \underset{o(\vec{x})}{argmin} \ \mathcal{E}((f(T_{true}) - o(\vec{x}))^2).$$

The expectation is given by $\sum_{i=1}^{N} P(T_{true} = \vec{t}_i | X = \vec{x}) \cdot (f(\vec{t}_i) - o(\vec{x}))^2$. Bayes' Theorem states that $P(T_{true} = \vec{t}_i | X = \vec{x}) = p(X = \vec{x} | T_{true} = \vec{t}_i) \cdot P(T_{true} = \vec{t}_i) / p(X = \vec{x})$. Under the assumption that all $\vec{t}_i$ are equally likely, simplifying the derivative of the expectation yields

$$O(\vec{x}) = \frac{\sum_{i=1}^{N} p(X = \vec{x} | T_{true} = \vec{t}_i) \cdot C_i}{\sum_{i=1}^{N} p(X = \vec{x} | T_{true} = \vec{t}_i)}$$

---

[1] This approach is related to Nowlan (1990) and MacKay (1991), but we emphasize the influence of different priors over the hypothesis space by giving preference to hypotheses that are closer to the domain theory.

where C_i equals $\mathcal{E}(f(\vec{t_i})|D)$, *i.e.* the expected value of $f(\vec{t_i})$ given that the training data is exactly D. Assuming the input noise to be Gaussian and Σ, unless otherwise noted, to be diagonal, $\Sigma = (\delta_{ij}\sigma_i^2)_{1 \le i,j \le d}$, the probability density of X under the assumption that T_{true} equals $\vec{t_k}$ is given by

$$p(X = \vec{x}|T_{true} = \vec{t_k}) = \frac{1}{(2\pi)^{d/2} \cdot |\Sigma|^{1/2}} \exp\left[-\frac{1}{2}(\vec{x} - \vec{t_k})^t \, \Sigma^{-1} \, (\vec{x} - \vec{t_k})\right]$$

where $|.|$ is the determinant. The optimal response to an input $\vec{x}$ can now be written as

$$O(x) = \frac{\sum_{i=1}^{N} \exp[-\frac{1}{2}(\vec{x} - \vec{t_i})^t \, \Sigma^{-1} \, (\vec{x} - \vec{t_i})] \cdot C_i}{\sum_{i=1}^{N} \exp[-\frac{1}{2}(\vec{x} - \vec{t_i})^t \, \Sigma^{-1} \, (\vec{x} - \vec{t_i})]}. \tag{1}$$

Equation 1 corresponds to a network architecture with N Gaussian Basis Functions (GBFs) centered at $\vec{t_k}$, $k = 1, \dots, N$, each of which has a width σ_i, $i = 1, \dots, d$, along the i-th dimension, and an output weight C_k. This architecture is known to give smooth function approximations (Poggio *et al.*, 1990; see also Platt, 1990), and the normalized response function (partitioning to one) was noted earlier in studies by Moody *et al.* (1988, 1989, 1990) to be beneficial to network performance. Carving up an input space into hyperquadrics (typically hyperellipsoids or just hyperspheres) in this way suffers in practice from the severe drawback that as soon as the dimensionality of the input is higher, it becomes less feasible to cover the whole space with units of only local relevance ("curse of dimensionality"). The normalized response function has an essentially space-filling effect, and fewer units have to be allocated while, at the same time, most of the locality properties can be preserved such that efficient ball tree data structures (Omohundro, 1991) can still be used. If the distances between the centers are large with respect to their widths, the nearest-neighbor rule is recovered. With decreasing distances, the output of the network changes more smoothly between the centers.

2.2   TRAINING REGIMEN

The output weights C_i are given by

$$C_i = \mathcal{E}(f(\vec{t_i})|D) = \int_{-\infty}^{\infty} z \cdot p(f(\vec{t_i}) = z|D) \, dz \, .$$

Bayes' Theorem states that $p(f(\vec{t_i}) = z|D) = p(D|f(\vec{t_i}) = z) \cdot p(f(\vec{t_i}) = z) \, / \, p(D)$. Let $M(i)$ denote the set of indices j of the training data points (x_j, y_j) that were generated by adding noise to $(\vec{t_i}, f(\vec{t_i}))$, *i.e.* the points that "originated" from $\vec{t_i}$. Note that it is not known *a priori* which indices a set $M(i)$ contains; only posterior probabilities can be given. By applying Bayes' Theorem and by assuming the independence between different locations $\vec{t_i}$, the coefficients C_i can be written as[2]

$$C_i = \int_{-\infty}^{\infty} z \cdot \frac{\prod_{m \in M(i)} \exp\left[-\frac{1}{2}\frac{(z - y_m)^2}{\sigma_{data}^2}\right] \cdot \exp\left[-\frac{1}{2}\frac{(z - b(\vec{t_i}))^2}{\sigma_{prior}^2}\right]}{\int_{-\infty}^{\infty} \prod_{m \in M(i)} \exp\left[-\frac{1}{2}\frac{(v - y_m)^2}{\sigma_{data}^2}\right] \cdot \exp\left[-\frac{1}{2}\frac{(v - b(\vec{t_i}))^2}{\sigma_{prior}^2}\right] dv} \, dz \, .$$

---

[2]The normalization constants of the Gaussians in numerator and denominator cancel as well as the product for all $m \notin M(i)$ of the probabilities that $(\vec{x}_m, y_m)$ is in the data set.

It can be easily shown that this simplifies to

$$C_i = \frac{\sum_{m \in M(i)} y_m + k \cdot b(\vec{t}_i)}{|M(i)| + k} \qquad (2)$$

where $k = \sigma_{data}^2 / \sigma_{prior}^2$ and $|.|$ denotes the cardinality operator. In accordance with intuition, the coefficients C_i turn out to be a weighted mean between the value suggested by the domain theory b and the training data values which originated from $\vec{t}_i$. The weighting factor $k/(|M(i)| + k)$ reflects the relative reliability of the two sources of information, the empirical data and the prior knowledge.

Define S_i as $S_i = (C_i - b(\vec{t}_k)) \cdot k + \sum_{m \in M(i)} (C_i - y_m)$. Clearly, if $|S_i|$ is minimized to 0, then C_i reaches exactly the optimal value as it is given by equation 2. An adaptive solution to this is to update C_i according to $\dot{C}_i = -\gamma \cdot S_i$. Since the membership distribution for $M(i)$ is not known *a priori*, we approximate it using a posterior estimate of the probability $p(m \in M(i)|\vec{x}_m)$ that m is in $M(i)$ given that $\vec{x}_m$ was generated by some center $\vec{t}_k$, which is

$$p(m \in M(i)|\vec{x}_m) = \frac{p(X = \vec{x}_m | T_{true} = \vec{t}_i)}{\sum_{k=1}^{M} p(X = \vec{x}_m | T_{true} = \vec{t}_k)}.$$

$p(X = \vec{x}_m | T_{true} = \vec{t}_i)$ is the activation act_i of the i-th center, when the network is presented with input $\vec{x}_m$. Substituting the equation in the sum of S_i leads to the following training regimen: Using stochastic sample-by-sample learning, we present in each training step with probability $1 - \lambda$ a data point y_j, and with probability λ a point $b(\vec{t}_k)$ that is generated from the domain theory, where λ is given by

$$\lambda := \frac{k \cdot N}{k \cdot N + M}. \qquad (3)$$

(Recall that M is the total number of data points, and N is the number of centers.) λ varies from 0 (the data is far more reliable than the prior knowledge) to 1 (the data is unreliable in comparison with the prior knowledge). Thus, the change of C_i after each presentation is proportional to the error times the normalized activation of the i-th center, $act_i / \sum_{k=1}^{N} act_k$.

The optimal positions for the centers $\vec{t}_i$ are not known in advance, and we therefore perform standard LMS gradient descent on $\vec{t}_i$, and on the widths σ_i. The weight updates in a learning step are given by a discretization of the following dynamic equations (i=1,...,N; j=1,...,d):

$$\dot{t}_{ij} = 2\gamma \cdot \Delta \cdot act_i \cdot \frac{C_i - O(\vec{x})}{\sum_{k=1}^{N} act_k} \cdot \frac{1}{\sigma_{ij}^2} \cdot (x_j - t_{ij})$$

$$\left(\frac{1}{\sigma_{ij}^2} \right)^{\cdot} = -\gamma \cdot \Delta \cdot act_i \cdot \frac{C_i - O(\vec{x})}{\sum_{k=1}^{N} act_k} \cdot (x_j - t_{ij})^2$$

where Δ is the interpolation error, act_i is the (forward-computed) activity of the the i-th center, and t_{ij} and x_j are the j-th component of $\vec{t}_i$ and $\vec{x}$ respectively.

3 APPLICATION TO ROLLING MILL CONTROL

3.1 THE PROBLEM

In integrated steelworks, the finishing train of the hot line rolling mill transforms preprocessed steel from a casting successively into a homogeneously rolled steel-plate. Controlling this process is a notoriously hard problem: The underlying physical principles are only roughly known. The values of the control parameters depend on a large number of entities, and have to be determined from measurements that are very noisy, strongly clustered, "expensive," and scarce.[3] On the other hand, reliability and precision are at a premium. Unreasonable predictions have to be avoided under any circumstances, even in regions where no training data is available, and, by contract, an extremely high precision is required: the rolling tolerance has to be guaranteed to be less than typically 20μm, which is substantial, particularly in the light of the fact that the steel construction that holds the rolls itself expands for several millimeters under a rolling pressure of typically several thousands of tons. The considerable economic interest in improving adaptation methods in rolling mills derives from the fact that lower rolling tolerances are indispensable for the supplied industry, yet it has proven difficult to remain operational within the guaranteed bounds under these constraints.

The control problem consists of determining a reduction schedule that specifies for each pair of rolls their initial distance such that after the final roll pair the desired thickness of the steel-plate (the actual feedback) is achieved. This reinforcement problem can be reduced to a less complex approximation problem of predicting the rolling force that is created at each pair of rolls, since this force can directly and precisely be correlated to the reduction in thickness at a roll pair by conventional means. Our task was therefore to predict the rolling force on the basis of nine input variables like temperature and rolling speed, such that a subsequent conventional high-precision control can quickly reach the guaranteed rolling tolerance before much of a plate is lost.

The state-of-the-art solution to this problem is a parameterized analytic model that considers nine physical entities as input and makes use of a huge number of tabulated coefficients that are adapted separately for each material and each thickness class. The solution is known to give only approximate predictions about the actual force, and although the on-line corrections by the high-precision control are generally sufficient to reach the rolling tolerance, this process necessarily takes more time, the worse the prediction is—resulting in a waste of more of the beginning of a steel-plate. Furthermore, any improvement in the adaptation techniques will also shorten the initialization process for a rolling mill, which currently takes several months because of the poor generalization abilities of the applied method to other thickness classes or steel qualities.

The data for our simulations was drawn from a rolling mill that was being installed at the time of our experiments. It included measurements for around 200 different steel qualities; only a few qualities were represented more than 100 times.

---

[3]The costs for a single sheet of metal—giving three useful data points that have to be measured under difficult conditions—amount to a six-digit dollar sum. Only a limited number of plates of the same steel quality is processed every week, causing the data scarcity.

3.2   EXPERIMENTAL RESULTS

According to the results in Section 2, a network of the specified localized architecture was trained with data (artificially) generated from the domain theory and data derived from on-line measurements. The remaining design considerations for architecture selection were based on the extent to which a network had the capacity to represent an instantiation of the analytic model (our domain theory):

Table 1 shows the approximation error of partitioning-to-one architectures with different degrees of freedom on their centers' widths. The variances of the GBFs were either all equal and not adapted (GBFs with constant widths), or adapted individually for all centers (GBFs with spherical adaptation), or adapted individually for all centers and every input dimension—leading to axially oriented hyperellipsoids (GBFs with ellipsoidal adaptation). Networks with "full hyperquadric" GBFs, for

Method	Normalized Error Squares $[10^{-2}]$	Maximum Error $[10^{-2}]$
GBFs with partitioning		
constant widths	0.40	2.1
spherical adaptation	0.18	1.7
ellipsoidal "	0.096	0.41
GBFs no partitioning	0.85	5.3
MLP	0.38	3.4

Table 1: Approximation of an instantiation of the domain theory: localized architectures (GBFs) and a network with sigmoidal hidden units (MLP).

which the covariance matrix is no longer diagonal, were also tested, but performed clearly worse, apparently due to too many degrees of freedom. The table shows that the networks with "ellipsoidal" GBFs performed best. Convergence time of this type of network was also found to be superior. The table also gives the comparative numbers for two other architectures: GBFs without normalized response function achieved significantly lower accuracy—even if they had far more centers (performance is given for a net with 81 centers)—than those with partitioning and only 16 centers. Using up to 200 million sample presentations, sigmoidal networks trained with standard backpropagation (Rumelhart et al., 1986) achieved a yet lower level—despite the use of weight-elimination (Le Cun, 1990), and an analysis of the data's eigenvalue spectrum to optimize the learning rate (see also Le Cun, 1991). The indicated numbers are for networks with optimized numbers of hidden units.

The value for λ was determined according to equation 3 in Section 2.2 as $\lambda = 0.8$; the noise in our application could be easily estimated, since there are multiple measurements for each input point available and the reliability of the domain theory is known. Applying the described training regimen to the GBF-architecture with ellipsoidal adaptation led to promising results:

Figure 1 shows the points in a "slice" through a specific point in the input space: the measurements, the force as it is predicted by the analytic model and the network. It can be seen that the net exhibits fail-safe behavior: it sticks closely to the analytic model in regions where no data is available. If data points are available and suggest

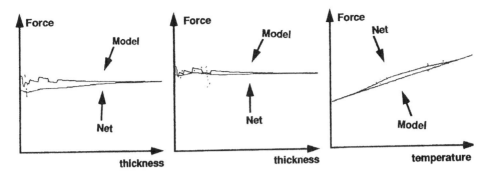

Figure 1: Prediction of the rolling force by the state-of-the-art model, by the neural network, and the measured data points as a function of the input 'sheet thickness,' and 'temperature.'

Method	Percent of Improvement on Trained Samples	Percent of Improvement at Generalization
Gaussian Units $\lambda = 0.8$	18	16
Gaussian Units $\lambda = 0.4$	41	14
MLP	3.9	3.1

Table 2: Relative improvement of the neural network solutions with respect to the state-of-the-art model: on the training data and on the cross-validation set.

a different force, then the network modifies its output in direction of the data.

Table 2 shows to what extent the neural network method performed superior to the currently applied state-of-the-art model (cross-validated mean). The numbers indicate the relative improvement of the mean squared error of the network solution with respect to an optimally-tuned analytic model. Although the data set was very sparse and noisy, it was nevertheless still possible to give a better prediction. The effect is also shown if a different value for λ were chosen: the higher value of λ, that is, more prior knowledge, keeps the net from memorizing the data, and improves generalization slightly. In case of the sigmoidal network, λ was simply optimized to give the smallest cross-validation error. When trained without prior knowledge, none of the architectures lead to an improvement.

4   CONCLUSION

In a large-scale applications to devise a neural control for a hot line rolling mill, training data turned out to be insufficient for learning to be feasible that is only based on syntactic preference biases. By using a Bayesian framework, an imperfect domain theory was incorporated as an inductive bias in a principled way. The method outperformed the state-of-the-art solution to an extent which steelworks automation experts consider highly convincing.

Acknowledgements

This paper describes the first two authors' joint university project, which was supported by grants from Siemens AG, Corporate R & D, and Studienstiftung des deutschen Volkes. H. Rein and F. Schmid of the Erlangen steelworks automation group helped identify the problem and sampled the data. W. Büttner and W. Finnoff made valuable suggestions.

References

Bergadano, F. and A. Giordana (1990). Guiding Induction with Domain Theories. In: Y. Kodratoff *et al.* (eds.), *Machine Learning*, Vol. 3, Morgan Kaufmann.

Cun, Y. Le, J. S. Denker, and S. A. Solla (1990). Optimal Brain Damage. In: D. S. Touretzky (ed.), *Advances in Neural Information Processing Systems 2*, Morgan Kaufmann.

Cun. Y. Le, I. Kanter and S. A. Solla (1991). Second Order Properties of Error Surfaces: Learning Time and Generalization. In: R. P. Lippman *et al.* (eds.), *Advances in Neural Information Processing 3*, Morgan Kaufmann.

Darken, Ch. and J. Moody (1990). Fast adaptive k-means clustering: some empirical results. In: *Proceedings of the IJCNN*, San Diego.

Duda, R. O. and P. E. Hart (1973). *Pattern Classification and Scene Analysis.* NY: Wiley.

MacKay, D. (1991). Bayesian Modeling. Ph.D. thesis, Caltech.

Minton, S. N., J. G. Carbonell *et al.* (1989). Explanation-based Learning: A problem-solving perspective. *Artificial Intelligence*, Vol. 40, pp. 63-118.

Mitchell, T. M., R. M. Keller and S. T. Kedar-Cabelli (1986). Explanation-based Learning: A unifying view. *Machine Learning*, Vol. 1, pp. 47-80.

Moody, J. (1990). Fast Learning in Multi-Resolution Hierarchies. In: D. S. Touretzky (ed.), *Advances in Neural Information Processing Systems 2*, Kaufmann, pp. 29-39.

Moody, J. and Ch. Darken (1989). Fast Learning in Networks of Locally-tuned Processing Units. *Neural Computation*, Vol. 1, pp. 281-294, MIT.

Moody, J. and Ch. Darken (1988). Learning with Localized Receptive Fields. In: D. Touretzky *et al.* (eds.), *Proc. of Connectionist Models Summer School*, Kaufmann.

Nowlan, St. J. (1990). Maximum Likelihood Competitive Learning. In: D. S. Touretzky (ed.,) *Advances in Neural Information Processing Systems 2*, Morgan Kaufmann.

Omohundro, S. M. (1991). Bump Trees for Efficient Function, Constraint, and Classification Learning. In: R. P. Lippman *et al.* (eds.), *Advances in Neural Information Processing 3*, Morgan Kaufmann.

Platt, J. (1990). A Resource-Allocating Network for Function Interpolation. In: D. S. Touretzky (ed.), *Advances in Neural Information Processing Systems 2*, Kaufmann.

Poggio, T. and F. Girosi (1990). A Theory of Networks for Approximation and Learning. A.I. Memo No. 1140 (extended in No. 1167 and No. 1253), MIT.

Röscheisen, M., R. Hofmann, and V. Tresp (1992). Incorporating Domain-Specific Prior Knowledge into Networks of Locally-Tuned Units. In: S. Hanson *et al.*(eds.), *Computational Learning Theory and Natural Learning Systems*, MIT Press.

Rumelhart, D. E., G. E. Hinton, and R. J. Williams (1986). Learning representations by back-propagating errors. *Nature*, 323(9):533-536, October.

Rumelhart, D. E. (1988). Plenary Address, IJCNN, San Diego.

Scott, G.M., J. W. Shavlik, and W. H. Ray (1991). Refining PID Controllers using Neural Networks. Technical Report, submitted to *Neural Computation*.

Tecuci, G. and Y. Kodratoff (1990). Apprenticeship Learning in Imperfect Domain Theories. In: Y. Kodratoff *et al.* (eds.), *Machine Learning*, Vol. 3, Morgan Kaufmann.

Weigend, A. (1991). Connectionist Architectures for Time-Series Prediction of Dynamical Systems. Ph.D. thesis, Stanford.

Fault Diagnosis of Antenna Pointing Systems using Hybrid Neural Network and Signal Processing Models

Padhraic Smyth, Jeff Mellstrom
Jet Propulsion Laboratory 238-420
California Institute of Technology
Pasadena, CA 91109

Abstract

We describe in this paper a novel application of neural networks to system health monitoring of a large antenna for deep space communications. The paper outlines our approach to building a monitoring system using hybrid signal processing and neural network techniques, including autoregressive modelling, pattern recognition, and Hidden Markov models. We discuss several problems which are somewhat generic in applications of this kind — in particular we address the problem of detecting classes which were not present in the training data. Experimental results indicate that the proposed system is sufficiently reliable for practical implementation.

1 Background: The Deep Space Network

The Deep Space Network (DSN) (designed and operated by the Jet Propulsion Laboratory (JPL) for the National Aeronautics and Space Administration (NASA)) is unique in terms of providing end-to-end telecommunication capabilities between earth and various interplanetary spacecraft throughout the solar system. The ground component of the DSN consists of three ground station complexes located in California, Spain and Australia, giving full 24-hour coverage for deep space communications. Since spacecraft are always severely limited in terms of available transmitter power (for example, each of the Voyager spacecraft only use 20 watts to transmit signals back to earth), all subsystems of the end-to-end communications link (radio telemetry, coding, receivers, amplifiers) tend to be pushed to the absolute limits of performance. The large steerable ground antennas (70m and 34m dishes) represent critical potential single points of failure in the network. In particular there is only a single 70m antenna at each complex because of the large cost and calibration effort involved in constructing and operating a steerable antenna of that size — the entire structure (including pedestal support) weighs over 8,000 tons.

The antenna pointing systems consist of azimuth and elevation axes drives which respond to computer-generated trajectory commands to steer the antenna in real-time. Pointing accuracy requirements for the antenna are such that there is little tolerance for component degradation. Achieving the necessary degree of positional accuracy is rendered difficult by various non-linearities in the gear and motor elements and environmental disturbances such as gusts of wind affecting the antenna dish structure. Off-beam pointing can result in rapid fall-off in signal-to-noise ratios and consequent potential loss of irrecoverable scientific data from the spacecraft.

The pointing systems are a complex mix of electro-mechanical and hydraulic components. A faulty component will manifest itself indirectly via a change in the characteristics of observed sensor readings in the pointing control loop. Because of the non-linearity and feedback present, direct causal relationships between fault conditions and observed symptoms can be difficult to establish — this makes manual fault diagnosis a slow and expensive process. In addition, if a pointing problem occurs while a spacecraft is being tracked, the antenna is often shut-down to prevent any potential damage to the structure, and the track is transferred to another antenna if possible. Hence, at present, diagnosis often occurs after the fact, where the original fault conditions may be difficult to replicate. An obvious strategy is to design an on-line automated monitoring system. Conventional control-theoretic models for fault detection are impractical due to the difficulties in constructing accurate models for such a non-linear system — an alternative is to learn the symptom-fault mapping directly from training data, the approach we follow here.

2   Fault Classification over Time

2.1   Data Collection and Feature Extraction

The observable data consists of various sensor readings (in the form of sampled time series) which can be monitored while the antenna is in tracking mode. The approach we take is to estimate the state of the system at discrete intervals in time. A feature vector $\underline{x}$ of dimension k is estimated from sets of successive windows of sensor data. A pattern recognition component then models the instantaneous estimate of the posterior class probability given the features, $p(\omega_i|\underline{x})$, $1 \leq i \leq m$. Finally, a hidden Markov model is used to take advantage of temporal context and estimate class probabilities conditioned on recent past history. This hierarchical pattern of information flow, where the time series data is transformed and mapped into a categorical representation (the fault classes) and integrated over time to enable robust decision-making, is quite generic to systems which must passively sense and monitor their environment in real-time.

Experimental data was gathered from a new antenna at a research ground-station at the Goldstone DSN complex in California. We introduced hardware faults in a controlled manner by switching faulty components in and out of the control loop. Obtaining data in this manner is an expensive and time-consuming procedure since the antenna is not currently instrumented for sensor data acquisition and is located in a remote location of the Mojave Desert in Southern California. Sensor variables monitored included wind speed, motor currents, tachometer voltages, estimated antenna position, and so forth, under three separate fault conditions (plus normal conditions).

The time series data was segmented into windows of 4 seconds duration (200 samples) to allow reasonably accurate estimates of the various features. The features consisted of order statistics (such as the range) and moments (such as the variance) of particular sensor channels. In addition we also applied an autoregressive-exogenous (ARX) modelling technique to the motor current data, where the ARX coefficients are estimated on each individual 4-second window of data. The autoregressive representation is particularly useful for discriminative purposes (Eggers and Khuon, 1990).

2.2   State Estimation with a Hidden Markov Model

If one applies a simple feed-forward network model to estimate the class probabilities at each discrete time instant t, the fact that faults are typically correlated over time is ignored. Rather than modelling the temporal dependence of features, $p(\underline{x}(t)|\underline{x}(t-1),\ldots,\underline{x}(0))$, a simpler approach is to model temporal dependence via the class variable using a Hidden Markov Model (HMM). The m classes comprise the Markov model states. Components of the Markov transition matrix $\mathbf{A}$ (of dimension $m \times m$) are specified *subjectively* rather than estimated from the data, since there is no reliable database of fault-transition information available at the component level from which to estimate these numbers. The *hidden* component of the HMM model arises from the fact that one cannot observe the states directly, but only indirectly via a stochastic mapping from states to symptoms (the features). For the results reported in this paper, the state probability estimates at time t are calculated using all the information available up to that point in time. The probability state vector is denoted by $p(\mathbf{s}(t))$. The probability estimate of state i at time t can be calculated recursively via the standard HMM equations:

$$\hat{\mathbf{u}}(t) = \mathbf{A}.p(\mathbf{s}(t-1)) \text{ and } p(s_i(t)) = \frac{\hat{u}_i(t)y_i(t)}{\sum_{j=1}^{m} \hat{u}_j(t)y_j(t)}$$

where the estimates are initialised by a prior probability vector $p(\mathbf{s}(0))$, the $u_i(t)$ are the components of $\mathbf{u}(t)$, $1 \leq i \leq m$, and the $y_i(t)$ are the likelihoods $p(\underline{x}|\omega_i)$ produced by the particular classifier being used (which can be estimated to within a normalising constant by $p(\omega_i|\underline{x})/p(\omega_i)$).

2.3   Classification Results

We compare a feedforward multi-layer perceptron model (single hidden layer with 12 sigmoidal units, trained using the squared error objective function and a conjugate-gradient version of backpropagation) and a simple maximum-likelihood Gaussian classifier (with an assumed diagonal covariance matrix, variances estimated from the data), both with and without the HMM component. Table 1 summarizes the

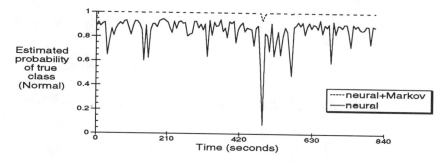

Figure 1: Stabilising effect of Markov component

overall classification accuracies obtained for each of the models — these results are for models trained on data collected in early 1991 (450 windows) which were then field-tested in real-time at the antenna site in November 1991 (596 windows). There were 12 features used in this particular experiment, including both ARX and time-domain features. Clearly, the neural-Markov model is the best model in the sense that no samples at all were misclassified — it is significantly better than the simple Gaussian classifier. Without the Markov component, the neural model still classified quite well (0.84% error rate). However all of its errors were false alarms (the classifier decision was a fault label, when in reality conditions were normal) which are highly undesirable from an operational viewpoint — in this context, the Markov model has significant practical benefit. Figure 1 demonstrates the stabilising effect of the Markov model over time. The vertical axis corresponds to the probability estimate of the model for the true class. Note the large fluctuations and general uncertainty in the neural output (due to the inherent noise in the feature data) compared to the stability when temporal context is modelled.

Table 1: Classification results for different models

Model	Percentage error rate in Field Test	
	Without HMM	With HMM
Gaussian model	16.94	14.42
Feedforward network	0.84	0.0

3   Detecting novel classes

While the neural model described above exhibits excellent performance in terms of discrimination, there is another aspect to classifier performance which we must consider for applications of this nature: how will the classifier respond if presented with data from a class which was not included in the training set ? Ideally, one would like the model to detect this situation. For fault diagnosis the chance that one will encounter such novel classes under operational conditions is quite high since there is little hope of having an exhaustive library of faults to train on.

In general, whether one uses a neural network, decision tree or other classification

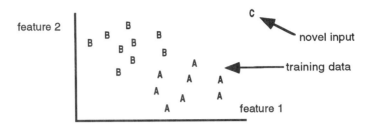

Figure 2: Data from a novel class C

method, there are few guarantees about the *extrapolation* behaviour of the trained classification model. Consider Figure 2, where point C is far away from the "A"s and "B"s on which the model is trained. The response of the trained model to point C may be somewhat arbitrary, since it may lie on either side of a decision boundary depending on a variety of factors such as initial conditions for the training algorithm, objective function used, particular training data, and so forth. One might hope that for a feedforward multi-layer perceptron, novel input vectors would lead to low response for all outputs. However, if units with non-local response functions are used in the model (such as the commonly used sigmoid function), the tendency of training algorithms such as backpropagation is to generate mappings which have a large response for at least one of the classes as the attributes take on values which extend well beyond the range of the training data values. Leonard and Kramer (1990) discuss this particular problem of poor extrapolation in the context of fault diagnosis of a chemical plant. The underlying problem lies in the basic nature of *discriminative* models which focus on estimating decision boundaries based on the differences between classes. In contrast, if one wants to detect data from novel classes, one must have a *generative* model for each known class, namely one which specifies how the data is generated for these classes. Hence, in a probabilistic framework, one seeks estimates of the probability density function of the data given a particular class, $f(\underline{x}|\omega_i)$, from which one can in turn use Bayes' rule for prediction:

$$p(\omega_i|\underline{x}) = \frac{f(\underline{x}|\omega_i)p(\omega_i)}{\sum_{j=1}^{m} f(\underline{x}|\omega_j)p(\omega_j)} \tag{1}$$

4   Kernel Density Estimation

Unless one assumes a particular parametric form for $f(\underline{x}|\omega_i)$, then it must be somehow estimated from the data. Let us ignore the multi-class nature of the problem temporarily and simply look at a single-class case. We focus here on the use of *kernel*-based methods (Silverman, 1986). Consider the 1-dimensional case of estimating the density $f(x)$ given samples $\{x_i\}$, $1 \leq i \leq N$. The idea is simple enough: we obtain an estimate $\hat{f}(x)$, where x is the point at which we wish to know the density, by summing the contributions of the kernel $K((x - x_i)/h)$ (where h is the *bandwidth* of the estimator, and $K(.)$ is the *kernel function*) over all the samples and normalizing such that the estimate is itself a density, i.e.,

$$\hat{f}(x) = \frac{1}{Nh} \sum_{i=1}^{N} K\left(\frac{x - x_i}{h}\right) \tag{2}$$

The estimate $\hat{f}(x)$ directly inherits the properties of $K(.)$, hence it is common to choose the kernel shape itself to be some well-known smooth function, such as a Gaussian. For the multi-dimensional case, the product kernel is commonly used:

$$\hat{f}(\underline{x}) = \frac{1}{Nh_1...h_d} \sum_{i=1}^{N} \left(\prod_{k=1}^{d} K\left(\frac{x^k - x_i^k}{h_k}\right) \right) \tag{3}$$

where x^k denotes the component in dimension k of vector $\underline{x}$, and the h_i represent different bandwidths in each dimension.

Various studies have shown that the quality of the estimate is typically much more sensitive to the choice of the bandwidth h than it is to the kernel shape $K(.)$ (Izenmann, 1991). Cross-validation techniques are usually the best method to estimate the bandwidths from the data, although this can be computationally intensive and the resulting estimates can have a high variance across particular data sets. A significant disadvantage of kernel models is the fact that all training data points must be stored and a distance measure between a new point and each of the stored points must be calculated for each class prediction. Another less obvious disadvantage is the lack of empirical results and experience with using these models for real-world applications — in particular there is a dearth of results for high-dimensional problems. In this context we now outline a *kernel approximation* model which is considerably simpler both to train and implement than the full kernel model.

5   Kernel Approximation using Mixture Densities

5.1   Generating a kernel approximation

An obvious simplification to the full kernel model is to replace clusters of data points by representative centroids, to be referred to as the *centroid kernel* model. Intuitively, the sum of the responses from a number of kernels is approximated by a single kernel of appropriate width. Omohundro (1992) has proposed algorithms for bottom-up merging of data points for problems of this nature. Here, however, we describe a top-down approach by observing that the kernel estimate is itself a special case of a *mixture* density. The underlying density is assumed to be a linear combination of L mixture components, i.e.,

$$f(x) = \sum_{i=1}^{L} \alpha_i f_i(x) \tag{4}$$

where the α_i are the mixing proportions. The full kernel estimate is itself a special case of a mixture model with $\alpha_i = 1/N$ and $f_i(x) = K(x)$. Hence, our centroid kernel model can also be treated as a mixture model but now the parameters of the mixture model (the mixing proportions or weights, and the widths and locations of the centroid kernels) must be estimated from the data. There is a well-known and

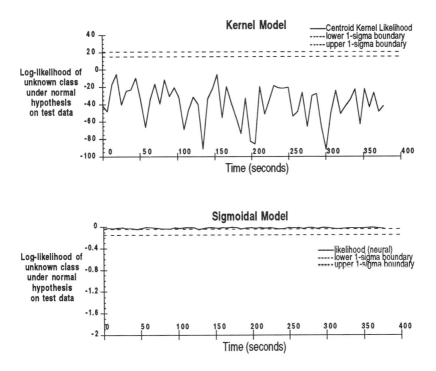

Figure 3: Likelihoods of kernel versus sigmoidal model on novel data

fast statistical procedure known as the EM (Expectation-Maximisation) algorithm for iteratively calculating these parameters, given some initial estimates (e.g., Redner and Walker, 1984). Hence, the procedure for generating a centroid kernel model is straightforward: divide the training data into homogeneous subsets according to class labels and then fit a mixture model with L components to each class using the EM procedure (initialisation can be based on randomly selected prototypes). Prediction of class labels then follows directly from Bayes' rule (Equation (1)). Note that there is a strong similarity between mixture/kernel models and Radial Basis Function (RBF) networks. However, unlike the RBF models, we do not train the output layer of our network in order to improve discriminative performance as this would potentially destroy the desired probability estimation properties of the model.

5.2   Experimental results on detecting novel classes

In Figure 3 we plot the log-likelihoods, $\log f(\underline{x}|\omega_i)$, as a function of time, for both a centroid kernel model (Gaussian kernel, $L = 5$) and the single-hidden layer sigmoidal network described in Section 2.2. Both of these models have been trained on only 3 of the original 4 classes (the discriminative performance of the models was roughly equivalent), excluding one of the known classes. The inputs $\{\underline{x}_i\}$ to the models are data from this fourth class. The dashed lines indicate the $\mu \pm \sigma$ boundaries on the log-likelihood for the normal class as calculated on the training data — this tells us the *typical* response of each model for class "normal" (note that the absolute values are irrelevant since the likelihoods have not been normalised via Bayes rule). For both models, the maximum response for the novel data came from the normal class. For the sigmoidal model, the novel response was actually greater than that on the training data — the network is very confident in its erroneous decision that the novel data belongs to class normal. Hence, in practice, the presence of a novel class would be completely masked. On the other hand, for the kernel model, the measured response on the novel data is significantly lower than that obtained on the training data. The classifier can directly calculate that it is highly unlikely that this new data belongs to any of the 3 classes on which the model was trained. In practice, for a centroid kernel model, the training data will almost certainly fit the model better than a new set of test data, even data from the same class. Hence, it is a matter of calibration to determine appropriate levels at which new data is deemed sufficiently unlikely to come from any of the known classes. Nonetheless, the main point is that a local kernel representation facilitates such detection, in contrast to models with global response functions (such as sigmoids).

In general, one does not expect a generative model which is not trained discriminatively to be fully competitive in terms of classification performance with discriminative models — on-going research involves developing hybrid discriminative-generative classifiers. In addition, on-line learning of novel classes once they have been detected is an interesting and important problem for applications of this nature. An initial version of the system we have described in this paper is currently undergoing test and evaluation for implementation at DSN antenna sites.

Acknowledgements

The research described in this paper was performed at the Jet Propulsion Laboratory, California Institute of Technology, under a contract with the National Aeronautics and Space Administration and was supported in part by DARPA under grant number AFOSR–90–0199.

References

M. Eggers and T. Khuon, 'Neural network data fusion concepts and application,' in *Proceedings of 1990 IJCNN*, San Diego, vol.II, 7–16, 1990.

M. A. Kramer and J. A. Leonard, 'Diagnosis using backpropagation neural networks — analysis and criticism,' *Computers in Chemical Engineering*, vol.14, no.12, pp.1323–1338, 1990.

B. Silverman, *Density Estimation for Statistics and Data Analysis*, New York: Chapman and Hall, 1986.

A. J. Izenmann, 'Recent developments in nonparametric density estimation,' *J. Amer. Stat. Assoc.*, vol.86, pp.205–224, March 1991.

S. Omohundro, 'Model-merging for improved generalization,' in this volume.

R. A. Redner and H. F. Walker, 'Mixture densities, maximum likelihood, and the EM algorithm,' *SIAM Review*, vol.26, no.2, pp.195–239, April 1984.

Multimodular Architecture for Remote Sensing Operations.

Sylvie Thiria[1,2]

Carlos Mejia[1]

Fouad Badran[1,2]

Michel Crépon[3]

[1] Laboratoire de Recherche en Informatique
Université de Paris Sud, B 490 - 91405 ORSAY Cedex France

[2] CEDRIC, Conservatoire National des Arts et Métiers
292 rue Saint Martin - 75 003 PARIS

[3] Laboratoire d'Océanographie et de Climatologie (LODYC)
T14 Université de PARIS 6 - 75005 PARIS (FRANCE)

Abstract

This paper deals with an application of Neural Networks to satellite remote sensing observations. Because of the complexity of the application and the large amount of data, the problem cannot be solved by using a single method. The solution we propose is to build multi-modules NN architectures where several NN cooperate together. Such system suffer from generic problem for whom we propose solutions. They allow to reach accurate performances for multi-valued function approximations and probability estimations. The results are compared with six other methods which have been used for this problem. We show that the methodology we have developed is general and can be used for a large variety of applications.

1   INTRODUCTION

Neural Networks have been used for many years to solve hard real world applications which involve large amounts of data. Most of the time, these problems cannot be solved with a unique technique and involve successive processing of the input data. Sophisticated NN architectures have thus been designed to provide good performances e.g. [Lecun et al. 90]. However this approach is limited for many reasons : the design of these architectures requires a lot of a priori knowledge about the task and is complicated. Such NN are difficult to train because of their large size and are dedicated to a specific problem. Moreover if the task is slightly modified, these NN have to be entirely redesigned and retrained. It is our feeling that complex problems cannot be solved efficiently with a single NN whatever sophisticated it is. A more fruitful approach is to use modular architectures where several simple NN modules cooperate together. This methodology is far more general and allows to easily build very sophisticated architectures which are able to handle the different processing steps which are necessary for example in speech or signal processing. These architectures can be easily modified to incorporate some additional knowledge about the problem or some changes in its specifications.

We have used these ideas to build a multi-module NN for a satellite remote sensing application. This is a hard problem which cannot be solved by a single NN. The different modules of our architecture are thus dedicated to specific tasks and allow to perform successive processing of the data. This approach allows to take into account in successive steps different informations about the problem. Furthermore, errors which may occur at the output of some modules may be corrected by others which allows to reach very good performances. Making these different modules cooperate raises several problems which appear to be generic for these architectures. It is thus interesting to study different solutions for their design, training, and the efficient information exchanges between modules. In the present paper, we first briefly describe the geophysical problem and its difficulties, we then present the different modules of our architecture and their cooperation, we compare our results to those of several other methods and discuss the advantages of our method.

2   THE GEOPHYSICAL PROBLEM

Scatterometers are active microwave radars which accurately measure the power of transmitted and backscatter signal radiations in order to compute the normalized radar cross section (σ_0) of the ocean surface. The σ_0 depends on the wind speed, the incidence angle θ (which is the angle between the radar beam and the vertical at the illuminated cell) and the azimuth angle (which is the horizontal angle χ between the wind and the antenna of the radar). The empirically based relationship between σ_0 and the local wind vector can be established which leads to the determination of a geophysical model function.

The model developed by A. Long gives a more precise form to this functional. It has been shown that for an angle of incidence θ, the general expression for σ_0 can be satisfactorily represented by a Fourrier series :

$$\sigma_0 = U.\left(\frac{1 + b_1.\cos\chi + b_2.\cos 2\chi}{1 + b_1 + b_2}\right),$$ (1)

with $U = A.v^\gamma$

Long's model specifies that A and γ only depend on the angle of incidence θ, and that b_1 and b_2 are a function of both the wind speed v and the angle of incidence θ (Figure 1).

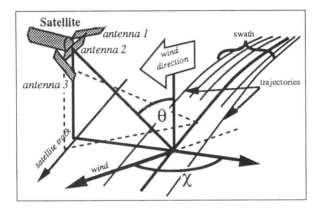

Figure 1 : Definition of the different geophysical scales.

For now, the different parameters b1, b2 A and γ used in this model are determined experimentally.

Conversely it becomes possible to compute the wind direction by using several antenna with different orientations with respect to the satellite track. The geophysical model function (1) can then be inverted using the three measurements of σ_0 given by the three antennas, it computes wind vector (direction and speed). Evidence shows that for a given trajectory within the swath (Figure 1) i.e. $(\theta_1,\theta_2,\theta_3)$ fixed, θ_i being the incidence angle of the beam linked to antenna i, the functional **F** is of the form presented in Fig.2 .

In the absence of noise, the determination of the wind direction would be unique in most cases. Noise-free ambiguities arise due to the bi-harmonic nature of the model function with respect to χ. The functional **F** presents singular points. At constant wind speed **F** yields a Lissajous curve ; in the singular points the direction is ambiguous with respect to the triplet measurements $(\sigma_1,\sigma_2,\sigma_3)$ as it is seen in Fig. 2. At these points **F** yields two directions differing by 160°. In practice, since the backscatter signal is noisy the number and the frequency of ambiguities is increased.

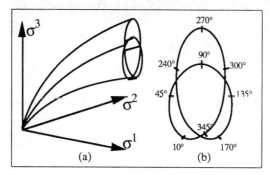

Figure 2 : (a) Representation of the Functional **F** for a given trajectory (b) Graphics obtained for a section of (a) at constant wind speed.

The problem is therefore how to set up an accurate (exact) wind map using the observed measurements $(\sigma_1, \sigma_2, \sigma_3)$.

3 THE METHOD

We propose to use multi-layered quasi-linear networks (MLP) to carry out this inversion phase. Indeed these nets are able of approximate complex non-linear functional relations; it becomes possible by using a set of measurements to determine **F** and to realize the inversion.

The determination of the wind's speed and direction lead to two problems of different complexity, each of them is solved using a dedicated multi-modular system. The two modules are then linked together to build a two level architecture. To take into account the strong dependence of the measurements with respect to the trajectory, each module (or level) consists of *n* distinct but similar systems, a specific system being dedicated to each satellite trajectory (*n* being the number of trajectories in a swath (Figure 1)).

The first level will allow the determination of the wind speed at every point of the swath. The results obtained will then be supplied to the second level as supplementary data which allow to compute the wind direction. Thus, we propose a two-level architecture which constitutes an automatic method for the computation of wind maps (Figure 3). The computation is performed sequentially between the different levels, each one supplying the next with the parameters needed.

Owing to the space variability of the wind, the measurements at a point are closely related to those performed in the neighbourhood. Taking into account this context must therefore bring important supplementary information to dealiase the ambiguities. At a point, the input data for a given system are therefore the measurements observed at that point and at it's eight closest neighbours.

All the networks used by the different systems are MLP trained with the back-propagation algorithm. The successive modifications were performed using a second order stochastic gradient : which is the approximation of the Levenberg-Marquardt rule.

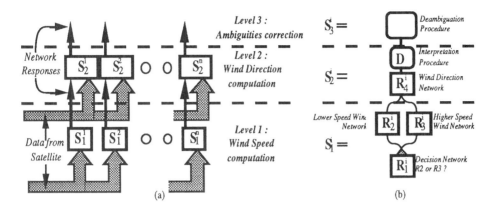

Figure 3 : The three systems S1, S2 and S3 for a given trajectory.

One system is dedicated to a proper trajectory. As a result the networks used on the same level of the global architecture are of the same type; only the learning set numerical values change from one system to another. Each network learning set will therefore consist of the data mesured on its trajectory. We present here the results for the central trajectory, performances for the others are similar.

3.1   THE NETWORK DECODING : FIRST LEVEL

A system (S1) in the first level allows to compute the wind speed (in ms^{-1}) along a trajectory. Because the function F_1 to be learned (signal $\rightarrow$ wind speed) is highly non-linear, each system is made of three networks (see Figure 3) : R1 allows to decide the range of the wind speed ($4 \leq v < 12$ or $12 \leq v < 20$); according to the R1 output an accurate value is computed using R2 for the first range and R3 for the other. The first level is built from 10 of these systems (one for each trajectory).

Each network (R1, R2, R3) consists of four fully connected layers. For a given point, we have introduced the knowledge of the radar measurements at the neighbouring points. The same experiments were performed without introducing this notion of vicinity, the learning and test performances were reduced by 17%, which proves the advantages of this approach. The input layer of each network consists of 27 automata : these 9x3 automata correspond to the σ_0 values relative to each antenna for the point to be considered and its eight neighbours.

R1 output layer has two cells : one for $4 \leq v < 12$ and the other for $12 \leq v < 20$; so its 4 layers are respectively built of 27, 25, 25, 2 automata.

R2 and R3 compute the exact wind speed. The output layer is represented by a unique output automaton and codes this wind speed v at the point considered between $[-1, +1]$. The four layers of each network are respectively formed of 27, 25, 25, 1 automata.

3.2   DECODING THE DIRECTION : SECOND LEVEL

Now the function F_2 (signal → wind direction) has to be learned. This level is located after the first one, so the wind speed has already been computed at all points. For each trajectory a system S2 allows to compute the wind direction, it is made of an MLP and a Decision Direction Process (we call it D). As for F1 we used for each point a contextual information. Thus, the input layer of the MLP consists of 30 automata : the first 9x3 correspond to the σ_0 values for each antenna, the last three represent three times the first level computed wind speed. However, because the original function has major ambiguities it is more convenient to compute, for a given input, several output values with their probabilities. For this reason we have discretized the desired output. It has been coded in degrees and 36 possible classes have been considered, each representing a 10° interval (between 0° and 360°). So, the MLP is four layered with respectively 30, 25, 25, 36 automata. It can be shown, according to the coding of the desired output, that the network approximates Bayes discriminant function or Bayes probability distribution related to the discretized transfer function F_2 [White, 89]. The interpretation of the MLP outputs using the D process allows to compute with accuracy the required function F_2. The network outputs represents the 36 classes corresponding to the 36 10° intervals. For a given input, a computed output is a $\mathcal{R}^{36}$ vector whose components can be interpreted to predict the wind direction in degrees. Each component, which is a Bayes discriminant function approximation, can be used as a coefficient of likelihood for each class. The Decision Direction Process D (see Fig. 3) computes real directions using this information. It performs the interpolation of the peaks' curve. D gives for each peak ist wind direction with its coefficients of likelihood.

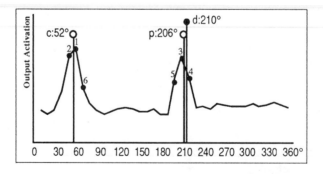

Figure 4 : network's output. The points in the x-axis correspond to the 36 outputs. Each represents an interval of 10° between 0 and 360°. The Y-axis points give the automata computed output. The point indicated by a $\underline{d}$ corresponds to the desired output angle, $\underline{c}$ is the most likely solution proposed by D and p is the second one.

The computed wind speed and the most likely wind direction computed by the first two levels allow to build a complete map which still includes errors in the directions. As we have seen in section 2, the physical problem has intrinsic ambiguities, they appear in the results (table 2). The removal of these errors is done by a third level of NN.

3.3   CORRECTING THE REMAINING ERRORS : THIRD LEVEL

This problem has been dealt with in [Badran & al 91] and is not discussed here. The method is related to image processing using MLP as optimal filter. The use of different filters taking into account the 5x5 vicinities of the point considered permits to detect the erroneous directions and to choose among the alternative proposed solutions. This method enables to correct up to 99.5% of the errors.

4   RESULTS

As actual data does not exist yet, we have tested the method on values computed from real meteorological models. The swaths of the scatterometer ERS1 were simulated by flying a satellite on wind fields given by the ECMWF forecasting model. The sea roughness values ($\sigma_1, \sigma_2, \sigma_3$) given by the three antennas were computed by inverting the Long model. Noise was then added to the simulated measurements in order to reproduce the errors made by the scatterometer. (A gaussian noise of zero average and of standard deviation 9.5% for both lateral antennas and 8.7% for the central antenna was added at each measurement).Twenty two maps obtained for the southern Atlantic Ocean were used to establish the learning sets. The 22 maps were selected randomly during the 30 days of September 1985 and nine remaining maps were used for the tests.

4.1   DECODING THE SPEED : FIRST LEVEL

In the results presented in Table 1, a predicted measurement is considered correct if it differs from the desired output by 1 m/s. It has to be noticed that the oceanographer's specification is 2 m/s; the present results illustrate the precision of the method.

Table 1 : performances on the wind speed

Performances		performances	bias
Accuracy 1 m/s	learning	99.3%	0.045m/s
	test	98.4 %	0.038m/s

4.2   DECODING THE DIRECTION : SECOND LEVEL

It is found that good performances are obtained after the interpretation of the best two peaks only. When it is compared to usual methods which propose up to six possible directions, this method appears to be very powerful. Table 2 shows the performances using one or two peaks. The function F and its singularities have been recovered with a good accuracy, the noise added during the simulations in order to reproduce the noise made by the measuring devices has been removed.

Table 2 : performances on the wind direction using the complete system

Performances		one peak	two peaks
Precision 20°	learning	68.0 %	99.1 %
	test	72.0 %	99.2 %

5   VALIDATION OF THE RESULTS

In order to prove the power of the NN approach, table 3 compare our results with six classical methods [Chi & Li 88].

Table 3 shows that the NN results are very good compared to other techniques, moreover all the classical methods are based on the assumption that a precise analytical function $((v,\chi) \to \sigma)$ exists, the NN method is more general and does not depend on such an assumption. Moreover the decoding of a point with NN requires approximately 23 ms on a SUN4 working station. This time is to be compared with the 0.25 second necessary for the decoding by present methods.

Table 3 : performances simulation results E_{rms} (in m/s) for different fixed wind speed

Speed	WLSL	ML	LS	WLS	AWLS	L1	LWSS	N.N
Low	0.92	0.66	0.67	0.74	0.69	0.63	1.02	0.49
Middle	0.89	0.85	1.10	1.31	0.89	0.98	0.87	0.53
Hight	3.71	3.44	4.11	5.52	3.52	4.06	3.49	1.18

The wind vector error e is defined as follows : $e = V1 - V2$ where $V1$ is the true wind vector and $V2$ is the estimated wind vector, $E_{rms} = E(\| e \|)$.

6   CONCLUSION

Performances reached when processing satellite remote sensing observations have proved that multi-modular architectures where simple NN modules cooperate can cope with real world applications. The methodology we have developed is general and can be used for a large variety of applications, it provides solutions to generic problems arising when dealing with NN cooperation.

References

Badran F, Thiria S, Crepon M (1991) : Wind ambiguity removal by the use of neural network techniques, *J.G.R Journal of Geophysical Research vol 96 n°C 11 p 20521-20529, November 15.*

Chong-Yung C, Fuk K Li (1969) : A Comparative Study of Several Wind Estimation Algorithms for Spacebornes scatterometers. *IEEE transactions on geoscience and remote sensing, vol 26, No 2.*

Le Cun Y., Boser B., & al., (1990) : Handwritten Digit Recognition with a Back-Propagation Network- in D.Touretzky (ed.) *Advances in Neural Information Processing Systems 2* , 396-404, Morgan Kaufmann

White H. (1989) : Learning in Artificial Neural Networks : A Statistical Perspective. *Neural Computation, 1, 425-464.*

Principled Architecture Selection for Neural Networks: Application to Corporate Bond Rating Prediction

John Moody
Department of Computer Science
Yale University
P. O. Box 2158 Yale Station
New Haven, CT 06520

Joachim Utans
Department of Electrical Engineering
Yale University
P. O. Box 2157 Yale Station
New Haven, CT 06520

Abstract

The notion of generalization ability can be defined precisely as the *prediction risk*, the expected performance of an estimator in predicting new observations. In this paper, we propose the prediction risk as a measure of the generalization ability of multi–layer perceptron networks and use it to select an optimal network architecture from a set of possible architectures. We also propose a heuristic search strategy to explore the space of possible architectures. The prediction risk is estimated from the available data; here we estimate the prediction risk by *v–fold cross–validation* and by asymptotic approximations of *generalized cross–validation* or Akaike's *final prediction error*. We apply the technique to the problem of predicting corporate bond ratings. This problem is very attractive as a case study, since it is characterized by the limited availability of the data and by the lack of a complete *a priori* model which could be used to impose a structure to the network architecture.

1 Generalization and Prediction Risk

The notion of generalization ability can be defined precisely as the *prediction risk*, the expected performance of an estimator is predicting new observations. Consider a set of observations $D = \{(\vec{x}_j, t_j); j = 1 \ldots N\}$ that are assumed to be generated

683

as

$$t_j = \mu(x_j) + \epsilon_j \qquad (1)$$

where $\mu(x)$ is an unknown function, the inputs x_j are drawn independently with an unknown stationary probability density function $p(x)$, the ϵ_j are independent random variables with zero mean ($\bar{\epsilon} = 0$) and variance σ_ϵ^2, and the t_j are the observed target values.

The learning or regression problem is to find an estimate $\hat{\mu}_\lambda(x; D)$ of $\mu(x)$ given the data set D from a class of predictors or models $\mu_\lambda(x)$ indexed by λ. In general, $\lambda \in \Lambda = (S, A, W)$, where $S \subset X$ denotes a chosen subset of the set of available input variables X, A is a selected architecture within a class of model architectures $\mathcal{A}$, and W are the adjustable parameters (weights) of architecture A.

The *prediction risk* $P(\lambda)$ is defined as the expected performance on future data and can be approximated by the expected performance on a finite test set:

$$P(\lambda) = \int dx\, p(x)[\mu(x) - \hat{\mu}(x)]^2 + \sigma_\epsilon^2 \approx E\{\frac{1}{N}\sum_{j=1}^{N}(t_j^* - \hat{\mu}_\lambda(x_j^*))^2\} \qquad (2)$$

where (x_j^*, t_j^*) are new observations that were not used in constructing $\hat{\mu}_\lambda(x)$. In what follows, we shall use $P(\lambda)$ as a measure of the generalization ability of a model. See [4] and [6] for more detailed presentations.

2   Estimates of Prediction Risk

Since we cannot directly calculate the prediction risk P_λ, we have to estimate it from the available data D. The standard method based on test–set validation is not advisable when the data set is small. In this paper we consider such a case; the prediction of corporate bond ratings from a database of only 196 firms. Cross-validation (CV) is a sample re–use method for estimating prediction risk; it makes maximally efficient use of the available data. Other methods are the generalized cross–validation (GCV) and the final prediction error (FPE) criteria, which combine the average training squared error ASE with a measure of the model complexity. These will be discussed in the next sections.

2.1   Cross Validation

Cross–Validation is a method that makes minimal assumptions on the statistics of the data. The idea of cross validation can be traced back to Mosteller and Tukey [7]. For reviews, see Stone [8, 9], Geisser [5] and Eubank [4].

Let $\hat{\mu}_{\lambda(j)}(x)$ be a predictor trained using all observations except (x_j, t_j) such that $\hat{\mu}_{\lambda(j)}(x)$ minimizes

$$ASE_j = \frac{1}{(N-1)}\sum_{k \neq j}\left(t_k - \hat{\mu}_{\lambda(j)}(x_k)\right)^2$$

Then, an estimator for the prediction risk $P(\lambda)$ is the *cross validation average squared error*

$$CV(\lambda) = \frac{1}{N} \sum_{j=1}^{N} \left(t_j - \hat{\mu}_{\lambda(j)}(x_j) \right)^2 \tag{3}$$

This form of $CV(\lambda)$ is known as *leave–one–out* cross–validation.

However, $CV(\lambda)$ in (3) is expensive to compute for neural network models; it involves constructing N networks, each trained with $N - 1$ patterns. For the work described in this paper we therefore use a variation of the method, *v-fold cross–validation*, that was introduced by Geisser [5] and Wahba *et al* [12]. Instead of leaving out only one observation for the computation of the sum in (3) we delete larger subsets of D.

Let the data D be divided into v randomly selected disjoint subsets P_j of roughly equal size: $\cup_{j=1}^{v} P_j = D$ and $\forall i \neq j$, $P_i \cap P_j = \emptyset$. Let N_j denote the number of observations in subset P_j. Let $\hat{\mu}_{\lambda(P_j)}(x)$ be an estimator trained on all data except for $(x,t) \subset P_j$. Then, the cross-validation average squared error for subset j is defined as

$$CV_{P_j}(\lambda) = \frac{1}{N_j} \sum_{(x_k, t_k) \in P_j} \left(t_k - \hat{\mu}_{\lambda(P_j)}(x_k) \right)^2,$$

and

$$CV_P(\lambda) = \frac{1}{v} \sum_j CV_{P_j}(\lambda). \tag{4}$$

Typical choices for v are 5 and 10. Note that leave–one–out CV is obtained in the limit $v = N$.

2.2   Generalized Cross-Validation and Final Prediction Error

For linear models, two useful criteria for selecting a model architecture are *generalized cross–validation (GCV)* (Wahba [11]) and Akaike's *final prediction error (FPE)* ([1]):

$$GCV(\lambda) = ASE(\lambda) \frac{1}{\left(1 - \frac{S(\lambda)}{N} \right)^2} \qquad FPE(\lambda) = ASE(\lambda) \left(\frac{1 + \frac{S(\lambda)}{N}}{1 - \frac{S(\lambda)}{N}} \right).$$

$S(\lambda)$ denotes the number of weights of model λ. See [4] for a tutorial treatment. Note that although they are slightly different for small sample sizes, they are asymptotically equivalent for large N:

$$\hat{P}(\lambda) \equiv ASE(\lambda) \left(1 + 2\frac{S(\lambda)}{N} \right) \approx GCV(\lambda) \approx FPE(\lambda) \tag{5}$$

We shall use this asymptotic estimate for the prediction risk in our analysis of the bond rating models.

It has been shown by Moody [6] that FPE and therefore $\hat{P}(\lambda)$ is an unbiased estimate of the prediction risk for the neural network models considered here provided that (1) the noise ϵ_j in the observed targets t_j is independent and identically distributed,

(2) weight decay is not used, and (3) the resulting model is unbiased. (In practice, however, essentially all neural network fits to data will be biased (see Moody [6]).) FPE is a special case of Barron's PSE [2] and Moody's GPE [6]. Although FPE and $\hat{P}(\lambda)$ are unbiased only under the above assumptions, they are much cheaper to compute than CV_P since no retraining is required.

3   A Case Study: Prediction of Corporate Bond Ratings

A bond is a debt security which constitutes a promise by the issuing firm to pay a given rate of interest on the original issue price and to redeem the bond at face value at maturity. Bonds are rated according to the default risk of the issuing firm by independent rating agencies such as Standard & Poors (S&P) and Moody's Investor Service. The firm is in default if it is not able make the promised interest payments.

Representation of S&P Bond Ratings												
CCC	B-	B	...	BBB+	A-	A	A+	AA-	AA	AA+	AAA-	AAA
2	3	4	...	11	12	13	14	15	16	17	18	19
high default risk					....					low default risk		

Table 1: Key to S&P bond ratings. We only used the range from 'AAA' or 'very low default risk' to 'CCC' meaning 'very high default risk'. (Note that AAA- is a not a standard category; its inclusion was suggested to us by a Wall Street analyst.) Bonds with rating BBB- or better are "investment grade" while "junk bonds" have ratings BB+ or below. For our output representation, we assigned an integer number to each rating as shown.

S&P and Moody's determine the rating from various financial variables and possibly other information, but the exact set of variables is unknown. It is commonly believed that the rating is at least to some degree judged on the basis of subjective factors and on variables not directly related to a particular firm. In addition, the method used for assigning the rating based on the input variables is unknown. The problem we are considering here is to predict the S&P rating of a bond based on fundamental financial information about the issuer which is publicly available. Since the rating agencies update their bond ratings infrequently, there is considerable value to being able to anticipate rating changes before they are announced. A predictive model which maps fundamental financial factors onto an estimated rating can accomplish this.

The input data for our model consists of 10 financial ratios reflecting the fundamental characteristics of the firms. The database was prepared for us by analysts at a major financial institution. Since we did not attempt to include all information in the input variables that could possibly be related to a firms bond rating (e.g. all fundamental or technical financial factors, or qualitative information such as quality of management), we can only attempt to approximate the S&P rating.

3.1   A Linear Bond Rating Predictor

For comparison with the neural network models, we computed a standard linear regression model. All input variables were used to predict the rating which is represented by a number in $[0, 1]$. The rating varies continuously from one category to the next higher or next lower one and this "smoothness" is captured in the single output representation and should make the task easier. To interpret the network

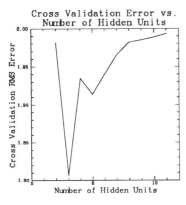
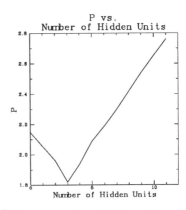

Figure 1: Cross validation error $CV_P(\lambda)$ and $\hat{P}(\lambda)$ versus number of hidden units.

response, the output was rescaled from $[0, 1]$ to $[2, 19]$ and rounded to the nearest integer; 19 corresponds to a rating of 'AAA' and 2 to 'CCC' and below (see Table 1). The input variables were normalized to the interval $[0, 1]$ since the original financial ratios differed widely in magnitude. The model predicted the rating of 21.4 % of the firms correctly, for 37.2 % the error was one notch and for 21.9 % two notches (thus predicting 80.5 % of the data within two notches from the correct target). The RMS training error was 1.93 and the estimate of the prediction risk $\hat{P} = 2.038$.

3.2   Beyond Linear Regression: Prediction by Two Layer Perceptrons

The class of models we are considering as predictors are two-layer perceptron networks with I_λ input variables, H_λ internal units and a single output unit having the form

$$\hat{\mu}_\lambda(x) = f\left(v_0 + \sum_{\alpha=1}^{H_\lambda} v_\alpha\, g(w_{\alpha 0} + \sum_{\beta=1}^{I_\lambda} w_{\alpha\beta}\, x_\beta)\right). \tag{6}$$

The hidden units have a sigmoidal transfer function while our single output unit uses a piecewise linear function.

3.3   Heuristic Search over the Space of Perceptron Architectures

Our proposed heuristic search algorithm over the space of perceptron architectures is as follows. First, we select the optimal number of internal units from a sequence of fully connected networks with increasing number of hidden units. Then, using the optimal fully connected network, we prune weights and input variables in parallel resulting in two separately pruned networks. Lastly, the methods were combined and the resulting networks is retrained to yield the final model

3.3.1   Selecting the Number of Hidden Units

We initially trained fully connected networks with all 10 available inputs variables but with the number of hidden units H_λ varying from 2 to 11. Five–fold cross–

Training Error 3 Hidden Units			
$|E_{notch}|$	firms	%	cum. %
0	67	34.2	34.2
1	84	42.9	77.1
2	34	17.3	94.4
> 2	11	5.6	100.0
number of weights			37
standard deviation			1.206
mean absolute deviation			0.898
training error			1.320

Cross Validation Error 3 Hidden Units			
$|E_{notch}|$	firms	%	cum. %
0	54	28.6	28.6
1	77	38.8	67.3
2	35	17.3	84.7
> 2	30	15.3	100.0
number of weights			37
standard deviation			1.630
mean absolute deviation			1.148
cross validation error			1.807

Table 2: Results for the network with 3 hidden units. The standard deviation and the mean absolute deviation are computed after rescaling the output of the network to [2,19] and rounding to the nearest integer (notches). The RMS training error is computed using the rescaled output of the network before rounding. The table also describes the predictive ability of the network by a histogram; the error column gives the number of rating categories the network was off from the correct target. The network with 3 hidden units significantly outperformed the linear regression model. On the right Cross Validation results for the network with 3 hidden units are shown. In order to predict the rating for a firm, we choose among the networks trained for the cross-validation procedure the one that was not trained using the subset the firm belongs to. Thus the results concerning the predictive ability of the model reflect the expected performance of the model trained on all the data with new data in the cross–validation–sense.

validation and $\hat{P}(\lambda)$ were used to select the number of hidden units. We compute $CV_P(\lambda)$ according to equation (4); the data set was partitioned into $v = 5$ subsets. We also computed $\hat{P}(\lambda)$ according to equation (5). The results of the two methods are consistent, having a common minimum for $H_\lambda = 3$ internal units (see figure 1).

Table 2(left) shows the results for the network with $H_\lambda = 3$ trained on the entire data set. A more accurate description of the performance of the model is shown in table 2(right) were the predictive ability is calculated from the hold–out sets of the cross–validation procedure.

3.3.2   Pruning of Input Variables via Sensitivity Analysis

Next, we attempted to further reduce the number of weights of the network by eliminating some of the input variables. To test which inputs are most significant for determining the network output, we perform a sensitivity analysis. We define the "Sensitivity" of the network model to variable β as:

$$S_\beta = \frac{1}{N} \sum_{j=1}^{N} ASE(\overline{x}_\beta) - ASE(x_\beta) \ \ \text{with} \ \ \overline{x}_\beta = \frac{1}{N} \sum_{j=1}^{N} x_{\beta_j} \ .$$

Here, x_{β_j} is the βth input variable of the jth exemplar. S_β measures the effect on the training ASE of replacing the βth input x_β by its average $\overline{x}_\beta$. Replacement of a variable by its average value removes its influence on the network output. Again we use 5-fold cross–validation and $\hat{P}$ to estimate the prediction risk P_λ. We constructed a sequence of models by deleting an increasing number of input variables in order of increasing S_β. For each model, CV_P and $\hat{P}$ was computed, figure 2 shows the results. A minimum was attained for the model with $I_\lambda = 8$ input variables (2 inputs were removed). This reduces the number of weights by $2H_\lambda = 6$.

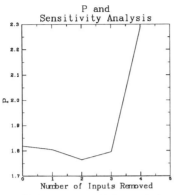
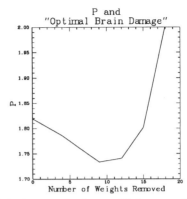

Figure 2: $\hat{P}(\lambda)$ for the sensitivity analysis and OBD. In both cases, the Cross validation error $CV_P(\lambda)$ has a minimum for the same λ.

3.3.3   Weight Pruning via "Optimal Brain Damage"

Optimal Brain Damage (OBD) was introduced by Le Cun *at al* [3] as a method to reduce the number of weights in a neural network to avoid overfitting. OBD is designed to select those weights in the network whose removal will have a small effect on the training *ASE*. Assuming that the original network was too large, removing these weights and retraining the now smaller network should improve the generalization performance. The method approximates *ASE* at a minimum in weight space by a diagonal quadratic expansion. The saliency

$$s_i = \frac{1}{2}\frac{\partial^2 ASE}{\partial w_i^2}w_i^2$$

computed after training has stopped is a measure (in the diagonal approximation) for the change of *ASE* when weight w_i is removed from the network.

CV_P and $\hat{P}$ were computed to select the optimal model. We find that CV_P and $\hat{P}$ are minimized when 9 weights are deleted from the network using all input variables. However, some overlap exists when compared to the sensitivity analysis described above: 5 of the deleted weights would also have been removed by the sensitivity method.

Table 3 show the overall performance of our model when the two techniques were combined to yield the final architecture. This architecture is obtained by deleting the union of the sets of weights that were deleted using weight and input pruning separately. Note the improvement in estimated prediction performance (CV error) in table 3 relative to 2.

4   Summary

Our example shows that (1) nonlinear network models can out–perform linear regression models, and (2) substantial benefits in performance can be obtained by the use of principled architecture selection methods. The resulting structured networks

Training Error, 3 Hidden Units 2 Inputs and 9 Connections Removed			
$|E_{notch}|$	firms	%	cum. %
0	69	35.2	35.2
1	81	41.3	76.5
2	32	16.3	92.8
> 2	14	7.2	100.0
number of weights		27	
standard deviation		1.208	
mean absolute deviation		0.882	
training error		1.356	

Cross Validation Error, 3 Hidden Units 2 Inputs and 9 Connections Removed			
$|E_{notch}|$	firms	%	cum. %
0	58	29.6	29.6
1	76	38.8	68.4
2	37	18.9	87.2
> 2	26	12.8	100.0
number of weights		27	
standard deviation		1.546	
mean absolute deviation		1.117	
cross validation error		1.697	

Table 3: Results for the network with 3 hidden units with both, sensitivity analysis and OBD applied. Note the improvement in CV error performance of relative to Table 2.

are optimized with respect to the task at hand, even though it may not be possible to design them based on *a priori* knowledge.

Estimates of the prediction risk offer a sound basis for assessing the performance of the model on new data and can be used as a tool for principled architecture selection. Cross–validation, GCV and FPE provide computationally feasible means of estimating the prediction risk. These estimates of prediction risk provide very effective criteria for selecting the number of internal units and performing sensitivity analysis and OBD.

References

[1] H. Akaike. Statistical predictor identification. *Ann. Inst. Statist. Math.*, 22:203–217, 1970.

[2] A. Barron. Predicted squared error: a criterion for automatic model selection. In S. Farlow, editor, *Self–Organizing Methods in Modeling*. Marcel Dekker, New York, 1984.

[3] Y. Le Cun, J. S. Denker, and S. A. Solla. Optimal brain damage. In D. S. Touretzky, editor, *Advances in Neural Information Processing Systems 2*. Morgan Kaufmann Publishers, 1990.

[4] Randall L. Eubank. *Spline Smoothing and Nonparametric Regression*. Marcel Dekker, Inc., 1988.

[5] Seymour Geisser. The predictive sample reuse method with applications. *Journal of The American Statistical Association*, 70(350), June 1975.

[6] John Moody. The effective number of parameters: an analysis of generalization and regularization in nonlinear learning systems. *short version in this volume, long version to appear*, 1992.

[7] F. Mosteller and J. W. Tukey. Data analysis, including statistics. In G. Lindzey and E. Aronson, editors, *Handbook of Social Psychology, Vol. 2*. Addison–Wesley, 1968 (first edition 1954).

[8] M. Stone. Cross–validatory choice and assessment of statistical predictions. *Roy. Stat. Soc.*, B36, 1974.

[9] M. Stone. Cross–validation: A review. *Math. Operationsforsch. Statist.*, Ser. Statistics, 9(1), 1978.

[10] Joachim Utans and John Moody. Selecting neural network architectures via the prediction risk: Application to corporate bond rating prediction. In *Proceedings of the First International Conference on Artifical Intelligence Applications on Wall Street*. IEEE Computer Society Press, Los Alamitos, CA, 1991.

[11] G. Wahba. *Spline Models for Observational Data*, volume 59 of *Regional Conference Series in Applied Mathematics*. SIAM Press, Philadelphia, 1990.

[12] G. Wahba and S. Wold. A completely automatic french curve: Fitting spline functions by cross–validation. *Communications in Statistics*, 4(1):1–17, 1975.

Adaptive Development of Connectionist Decoders for Complex Error-Correcting Codes

Sheri L. Gish   **Mario Blaum**
IBM Research Division
Almaden Research Center
650 Harry Road
San Jose, CA 95120

Abstract

We present an approach for development of a decoder for any complex binary error-correcting code (ECC) via training from examples of decoded received words. Our decoder is a connectionist architecture. We describe two separate solutions: A system-level solution (the Cascaded Networks Decoder); and the ECC-Enhanced Decoder, a solution which simplifies the mapping problem which must be solved for decoding. Although both solutions meet our basic approach constraint for simplicity and compactness, only the ECC-Enhanced Decoder meets our second basic constraint of being a generic solution.

1   INTRODUCTION

1.1   THE DECODING PROBLEM

An error-correcting code (ECC) is used to identify and correct errors in a received binary vector which is possibly corrupted due to transmission across a noisy channel. In order to use a selected error-correcting code, the *information bits*, or the bits containing the message, are *encoded* into a valid ECC codeword by the addition of a set of extra bits, the *redundancy*, determined by the properties of the selected ECC. To decode a received word, there is a pre-processing step first in which a *syndrome* is calculated from the word. The syndrome is a vector whose length is equal to the redundancy. If the syndrome is the all-zero vector, then the received

691

word is a valid codeword (no errors). The non-zero syndromes have a one-to-one relationship with the error vectors provided the number of errors does not exceed the error-correcting capability of the code. (An error vector is a binary vector equal in length to an ECC codeword with the error positions having a value of 1 while the rest of the positions have the value 0). The *decoding* process is defined as the mapping of a syndrome to its associated error vector. Once an error vector is found, the corrected codeword can be calculated by XORing the error vector with the received word. For more background in error-correcting codes, the reader is referred to any book in the field, such as [2, 9].

ECC's differ in the number of errors which they can correct and also in the distance (measured as a Hamming distance in codespace) which can be recognized between the received word and a true codeword. Codes which can correct more errors and cover greater distances are considered more powerful. However, in practice the difficulty of developing an efficient decoder which can correct many errors prevents the use of most ECC's in the solution of real world problems. Although decoding can be done for any ECC via lookup table, this method quickly becomes intractable as the length of codewords and the number of errors possibly corrected increase. Development of an efficient decoder for a particular ECC is not straightforward. Moreover, it was shown that decoding of a random code is an NP-hard problem [1, 4].

The purpose of our work is to develop an ECC decoder using the trainable machine paradigm; i.e. we develop a decoder via training using examples of decoded received words. To prove our concept, we have selected a binary block code, the (23,12,7) Golay Code, which has "real world" complexity. The Golay Code corrects up to 3 errors and has minimum distance 7. A Golay codeword is 23 bits long (12 information bits, 11 bit redundancy); the syndrome is 11 bits long. There exist many efficient decoding methods for the Golay code [2, 3, 9], but the code complexity represents quite a challenge for our proposed approach.

1.2   A CONNECTIONIST ECC DECODER

We use a connectionist architecture as our ECC decoder; the input is a syndrome (we assume that the straightforward step of syndrome calculation is pre-processing) and the output is the portion of the error vector corresponding to the information bits in the received word (we ignore the redundancy). The primary reason for our choice of a connectionist architecture is its inherent simplicity and compactness; a connectionist architecture solution is readily implemented in either hardware or software solutions to complex real world problems. The particular architecture we use is the multi-layer feedforward network with one hidden layer. There are full connections only between adjacent layers. The number of nodes in the input layer is the number of bits in the syndrome, and the number of nodes in the output layer is the number of information bits in the ECC codeword. The number of nodes in the hidden layer is a free parameter, but typically this number is no more than 1 or 2 nodes greater than the number of nodes in the input layer. Our activation function is the logistic function and our training algorithm is backpropagation (see [10] for a description of both). This architectural approach has been demonstrated to be both cost-effective and a superior performer compared to classical statistical alternative methods in the solution of complex mapping problems when it is used as a trainable pattern classifier [6, 7].

There are two basic constraints which we have placed on our trainable connectionist decoder. First, the final connectionist architecture must be simple and contain as few nodes as possible. Second, the method we use to develop our decoder must be able to be generalized to any binary ECC. To meet the second constraint, we insured that the training dataset contained only examples of decoded words (i.e. no a priori knowledge of code patterning or existing decoding algorithms was included), and also that the training dataset was as small a subset of the possible error vectors as was required to obtain generalization by trained networks.

2   RESULTS

2.1   THE CASCADED NETWORKS DECODER

Using our basic approach, we have developed two separate solutions. One, the Cascaded Networks Decoder (see Figure 1) a system-level solution which parses the decoding problem into a set of more tractable problems each addressed by a separate network. These smaller networks each solve either simple classification problems (binary decisions) or are specialized decoders. Performance of the Cascaded Networks Decoder is 95% correct for the Golay code (tested on all 2^{11} possible error vectors), and the whole system is small and compact. However, this solution does not meet our constraint that the solution method be generic since the parsing of the original problem does require some a priori knowledge about the ECC, and the training of each network is done on a separate, self-contained schedule.

2.2   THE ECC-ENHANCED DECODER

The approach taken by the Cascaded Networks Decoder simplifies the solution strategy of the decoding problem, while the ECC-Enhanced Decoder simplifies the mapping problem to be solved by the decoder. In the ECC-Enhanced Decoder, both the input syndrome and the output error vector are encoded as codewords of an ECC. Such encoding should serve to separate the inputs in input space and the outputs in output space, creating a "region-to-region" mapping which is much easier than the "point-to-point" mapping required without encoding [8]. In addition, the decoding of the network output compensates for some level of uncertainty in the network's performance; an output vector within a small distance of the target vector will be corrected to the actual target by the ECC. This enhances training procedures [5, 8].

We have found that the ECC-Enhanced Decoder method meets all of our constraints for a connectionist architecture. However, we also have found that choosing the best ECC for encoding the input and for encoding the output represents two critical and quite separate problems which must be solved in order for the method to succeed.

2.2.1   Choosing the Input ECC Encoding

The goal for the chosen ECC into which the input is encoded is to achieve maximum separation of input patterns in code space. The major constraint is the size of the codeword (number of bits which the length of the redundancy must be), because longer codewords increase the complexity of training and the size (in number of

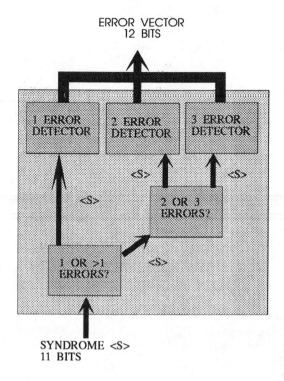

ERROR VECTOR
12 BITS

Figure 1: Cascaded Networks Decoder. A system-level solution incorporating 5 cascaded neural networks.

nodes) of the connectionist architecture. To determine the effect of different types of ECC's on the separation of input patterns in code space, we constructed a 325 pattern training dataset (mapping 11 bit syndrome to 12 bit error vector) and encoded only the inputs using 4 different ECC's. The candidate ECC's (with the size of redundancy required to encode the 11 bit syndrome) were

- Hamming (bit level, 4 bit redundancy)
- Extended Hamming (bit level, 5 bit redundancy)
- Reed Solomon (4 bit byte level, 2 byte redundancy)
- Fire (bit level, 11 bit redundancy)

We trained 5 networks (1 with no encoding of input, 1 each with a different ECC encoding) using this training dataset. Empirically, we had determined that this training dataset is slightly too small to achieve generalization for this task; we trained each network until its performance level on a 435 pattern test dataset (different patterns from the training dataset but encoded identically) degraded 20%. We then analyzed the effect of the input encoding on the patterning of error positions we observed for the output vectors.

The results of our analysis are illustrated in Figures 2 and 3. These bar graphs look only at output vectors found to have 2 or more errors, and show the proximity of error positions within an output vector. Each bar corresponds to the maximum distance of error positions within a vector (adjacent positions have a distance of 1). The bar height represents the total frequency of vectors with a given maximum distance; each bar is color-coded to break down the frequency by total number of errors per vector. This type of measurement shows the degree of burst (clustering of error positions) in the errors; knowing whether or not one has burst errors influences the likelihood of correction of those errors by an ECC (for instance, Fire codes are burst correcting codes).

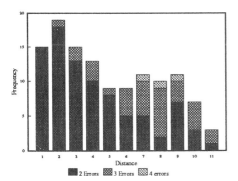 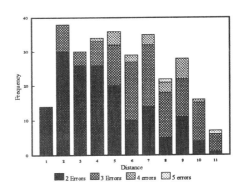

Figure 2: Bar Graphs of Output Errors Made by the Decoder. There was no encoding of the input in this instance. Training dataset results are on left, test dataset results are on right.

Our analysis shows that the Reed Solomon ECC is the only input encoding which separated the input patterns in a way which made use of an output pattern ECC encoding effective (resulted in more burst-type errors, decreased the total number of error positions in output vectors which had errors). The 11 bit redundancy required by the Fire code for input encoding increased complexity so that this solution was worse than the others in terms of performance. Thus, we have chosen the Reed Solomon ECC for input encoding in our ECC-Enhanced Decoder.

2.2.2   Choosing the Output ECC Encoding

The goal for the chosen ECC into which the output is encoded is correction of the maximum number of errors made by the decoder. Like the constraint imposed on the chosen ECC for input encoding, the ECC selected for encoding the output

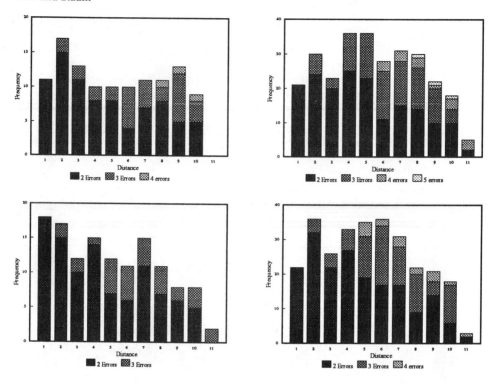

Figure 3: Bar Graphs of Effects of Different ECC Input Encodings on Output Errors Made by the Decoder. Training dataset results are on left, test dataset results are on right. Top row is Hamming code encoding, bottom row is Reed Solomon encoding.

should add as small a redundancy as possible. However, there is another even more important constraint on the choice of ECC for output encoding: decoding simplicity. The major advantage gained from encoding the output is the correction of slight uncertainty in the performance of the decoder, and this advantage is gained after the output is decoded. Thus, any ECC selected for output encoding should be one which can be decoded efficiently.

The error separation results we gained from our analysis of the effects of input encoding were used to guide our choices for an ECC into which the output would be encoded. We chose our ECC from the 4 candidates we considered for the input (these ECC's all can be decoded efficiently). The redundancy cost for encoding a 12 bit error vector was the same as in the 11 bit input case for the Reed Solomon and Fire codes, but was increased by 1 bit for the Hamming codes. Based on the result that a Reed Solomon encoding of the input both increased the amount of burst errors and decreased the total number of errors per output vector, we chose the Hamming code and the Fire code for our output encoding ECC. Both encodings yielded excellent performance on the Golay code decoding problem; the Fire code output encoding resulted in better generalization by the network and thus better performance (87% correct) than the Hamming code output encoding (84% correct).

References

[1] E. R. Berlekamp, R. J. McEliece and H. C. A. van Tilborg, "On the Inherent Intractability of Certain Coding Problems," *IEEE Trans. on Inf. Theory*, Vol. IT-8, pp. 384-386, May 1978.

[2] R. E. Blahut, *Theory and Practice of Error Control Codes*, Addison-Wesley, 1983.

[3] M. Blaum and J. Bruck, "Decoding the Golay Code with Venn Diagrams," *IEEE Trans. on Inf. Theory*, Vol. IT-36, pp. 906-910, July 1990.

[4] J. Bruck and M. Naor, "The Hardness of Decoding Linear Codes with Preprocessing," *IEEE Trans. on Inf. Theory*, Vol. IT-36, pp. 381-385, March 1990.

[5] T. G. Dietterich and G. Bakiri, "Error-Correcting Output Codes: A General Method for Improving Multiclass Inductive Learning Programs," Oregon State University Computer Science TR 91-30-2, 1991.

[6] S. L. Gish and W. E. Blanz, "Comparing a Connectionist Trainable Classifier with Classical Statistical Decision Analysis Methods," IBM Research Report RJ 6891 (65717), June 1989.

[7] S. L. Gish and W. E. Blanz, "Comparing the Performance of a Connectionist and Statistical Classifiers on an Image Segmentation Problem," in D. S. Touretzky (ed) *Neural Information Processing Systems 2*, pp. 614-621, Morgan Kaufmann Publishers, 1990.

[8] H. Li, T. Kronander and I. Ingemarsson, "A Pattern Classifier Integrating Multilayer Perceptron and Error-Correcting Code," in Proceedings of the IAPR Workshop on Machine Vision Applications, pp. 113-116, Tokyo, November 1990.

[9] F. J. MacWilliams and N. J. A. Sloane, *The Theory of Error-Correcting Codes*, Amsterdam, The Netherlands: North-Holland, 1977.

[10] D. E. Rumelhart, G. E. Hinton, and R. J. Williams, "Learning Internal Representations by Error Propagation," in D. E. Rumelhart, J. L. McClelland et. al. (eds) *Parallel Distributed Processing* Vol. 1, Chapter 8, MIT Press, 1986.

Application of Neural Network Methodology to the Modelling of the Yield Strength in a Steel Rolling Plate Mill

Ah Chung Tsoi
Department of Electrical Engineering
University of Queensland,
St Lucia, Queensland 4072,
Australia.

Abstract

In this paper, a tree based neural network viz. MARS (Friedman, 1991) for the modelling of the yield strength of a steel rolling plate mill is described. The inputs to the time series model are temperature, strain, strain rate, and interpass time and the output is the corresponding yield stress. It is found that the MARS-based model reveals which variable's functional dependence is nonlinear, and significant. The results are compared with those obtained by using a Kalman filter based online tuning method and other classification methods, e.g. CART, C4.5, Bayesian classification. It is found that the MARS-based method consistently outperforms the other methods.

1   Introduction

Hot rolling of steel slabs into flat plates is a common process in a steel mill. This technology has been in use for many years. The process of rolling hot slabs into plates is relatively well understood [see, e.g., Underwood, 1950]. But with the intense intrnational market competition, there is more and more demand on the quality of the finished plates. This demand for quality fuels the search for a better understanding of the underlying mechanisms of the transformation of hot slabs into plates, and a better control of the parameters involved. Hopefully, a better understanding of the controlling parameters will lead to a more optimal setting of the control on the process, which will lead ultimately to a better quality final product.

In this paper, we consider the problem of modelling the plate yield stress in a hot steel rolling plate mill. Rolling is a process of plastic deformation and its objective is achieved by subjecting the material to forces of such a magnitude that the resulting stresses produce permanent change of shape. Apart from the obvious dependence on the materials used, the characteristics of the material undergoing plastic deformation are described by stress, strain and temperature, if the rolling is performed on hot slabs. In addition, the interpass time, i.e., the time between passes of the slab through the rollers (an indirect measure of the rolling velocity), directly influences the metallurgical structure of the metal during rolling.

There is considerable evidence that the yield stress is also dependent on the strain rate. In fact, it is observed that as the strain rate increases, the initial yield point increases appreciably, but after an extension is achieved, the effect of strain rate on the yield stress is very much reduced [see, e.g., Underwood, 1950].

The effect of temperature on the yield stress is important. It is shown that the resistance to deformation increases with a decrease in temperature. The resistance to deformation versus temperature diagram shows a "hump" in the curve, which corresponds to the temperature at which the structure of material changes fundamentally [see, e.g., Underwood, 1950, Hodgson & Collinson, 1990].

Using, e.g., an energy method, it is possible to formulate a theoretical model of the dependence of deformation resistance on temperature, strain, strain rate, velocity (indirectly, the interpass time). One may then validate the theoretical model by performing a rolling experiment on a piece of material, perhaps under laboratory conditions [see .e.g., Horihata, Motomura, 1988, for consideration of a three roller system].

It is difficult to apply the derived theoretical model to a practical situation, due to the fact that in a practical process, the measurement of strain and strain rate are not accurate. Secondly, one cannot possibly perform a rolling experiment on each new piece of material to be rolled. Thus though the theoretical model may serve as a guide to our understanding of the process, it is not suitable for controller design purposes.

There are empirical models relating the resistance of deformation to temperature, strain and strain rate [see, e.g., Underwood, 1950, for an account of older models]. These models are often obtained by fitting the observed data to a general data model.

The following model has been found useful in fitting the observed practical data

$$k_m = a\epsilon^b \sinh^{-1}(c\dot{\epsilon}\exp(\frac{d}{T})^f) \tag{1}$$

where k_m is the yield stress, ϵ is the strain, $\dot{\epsilon}$ is the corresponding strain rate, and T is the temperature. a, b, c, d and f are unknown constants. It is claimed that this model will give a good prediction of the yield stress, especially at lower temperatures, and for thin plate passes [Hodgson & Collinson, 1990].

This model does not always give good predictions over all temperatures as mill conditions vary with time, and the model is only "tuned" on a limited set of data.

In order to overcome this problem, McFarlane, Telford, and Petersen [1991] have experimented with a recursive model based on the Kalman filter in control theory to update the parameters (see, e.g. Anderson, Moore, [1980]), a, b, c, d, f in the above model. To better describe the material behaviour at different temperatures, the model explicitly incorporates two separate sub-models with a temperature dependence:

1. Full crystallisation ($T < T_{upper}$)

$$k_m = a\epsilon^b \sinh^{-1}(c\dot{\epsilon}\exp(\frac{d}{T})^f) \qquad (2)$$

The constants a, b, c, d, f are model coefficients.

2. Partial recrystallisation ($T_{lower} \leq T \leq T_{upper}$).

$$k_m = a(\epsilon + \epsilon^*)^b \sinh^{-1}(c\dot{\epsilon}\exp(\frac{d}{T})^f) \qquad (3)$$

$$t_{0.5} = j(\lambda_{i-1}\epsilon_{i-1} + \epsilon_i)^g f_1((q(T_{i-1}, T_i)h)) \qquad (4)$$

$$\lambda_i = f_2(t, t_{0.5}) \qquad (5)$$

where λ is the fractional retained strain; ϵ^*, expressed as a Taylor series expansion of $\lambda_{i-1}\epsilon_{i-1}$, is the retained strain; t is the interpass time; $t_{0.5}$ is the 50 % recrystallisation time; $q(T_{i-1}, T_i)$ is a prescribed nonlinear function of T_{i-1} and T_i; $f_1(.)$ and $f_2(.)$ are pre-specified nonlinear functions; i, the roll pass number; j, h, g are the model coefficients; T_{upper} is an experimentally determined temperature at which the material undergoes a permanent change in structure; and T_{lower} is a temperature below which the material does not exhibit any plastic behaviour.

Model coefficients a, b, c, d, f, g, h, j are either estimated in a batch mode (i.e., all the past data are assumed to be available simultaneously) or adapted recursively on-line (i.e., only a limited number of the past data is available) using a Kalman filter algorithm in order to provide the best model predictions [McFarlane, Telford, Petersen, 1991].

It is noted that these models are motivated by the desire to fit a nonlinear model of a special type, i.e., one which has an inverse hyperbolic sine function. But, since the basic operation is data fitting, i.e., to fit a model to the set of given data, it is possible to consider more general nonlinear models. These models may not have any ready interpretation in metallurgical terms, but these models may be better in fitting a nonlinear model to the given data set in the sense that it may give a better prediction of the output.

It has been shown (see, e.g., Hornik et al, 1989) that a class of artificial neural networks, viz., a multilayer perceptron with a single hidden layer can approximate any arbitrary input output function to an arbitrary degree of accuracy. Thus it is reasonable to experiment with different classes of artificial neural network or induction tree structures for fitting the set of given data and to examine which structure gives the best performance.

The structure of the paper is as follows: in section 2, a brief review of a special class of neural networks is given. In section 3, results in applying the neural network model to the plate mill data are given.

2   A Tree Based Neural Network model

Friedman [1991] introduced a new class of neural network architecture which is called MARS (Multivariate Adaptive Regression Spline). This class of methods can be interpreted as a tree of neurons, in which each leaf of the tree consists of a neuron. The model of the neuron may be a piecewise linear polynomial, or a cubic polynomial, with the knot as a variable. In view of the lack of space, we will refer the interested readers to Friedman's paper [1991] for details on this method.

3   Results

MARS has been applied to the platemill data. We have used the data in the following manner.

We concatenate different runs of the plate mill into a single time series. This consists of 2877 points corresponding to 180 individual plates with approximately 16 passes on each plate. There are 4 independent variables, viz., interpass time, temperature, strain, and strain rate. The desired output variable is the yield stress.

A plot of the individual variables, viz temperature, strain, strain rate, interpass time and stress versus time reveal that the variables can vary rather considerably over the entire time series. In addition, a plot of stress versus temperature, stress versus strain, stress versus strain rate and stress versus interpass time reveals that the functional dependence could be highly nonlinear.

We have chosen to use an additive model (Friedman [1991]), instead of the more general multivariate model, as this will allow us to observe any possible nonlinear functional dependencies of the output as a function of the inputs.

$$k_m = k_1 f_1(T) + k_2 f_2(\epsilon) + k_3 f_3(\dot{\epsilon}) + k_4 f_4(t) \tag{6}$$

where $k_i, i = 1, 2, 3, 4$ are gains, and $f_i, i = 1, 2, 3, 4$ are piecewise nonlinear polynomial models found by MARS.

The results are as follows:

Both the piecewise linear polynomial and the piecewise cubic polynomial are used to study this set of data. It is found that the cubic polynomial gives a better fit than the linear polynomial fit. Figure 1(a) shows the error plot between the estimated output from a cubic spline fit, and the training data. It is observed that the error is very small. The maximum error is about -0.07. Figure 1(b) shows the plot of the predicted yield stress and the original yield stress over the set of training data.

These figures indicate that the cubic polynomial fit has captured most of the variation of the data. It is interesting to note that in this model, the interpass time

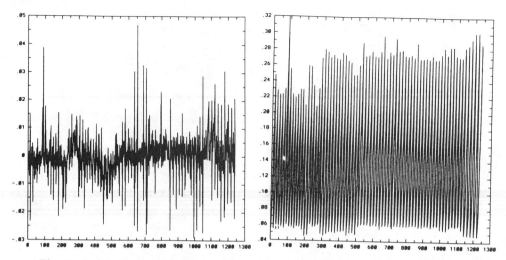

Figure 1: (a) The prediction error on the training data set (b) The prediction and the training data set superimposed

plays no significant part. This feature may be a peculiar aspect of this set of data points. It is not true in general.

It is found that the strain rate has the most influence on the data, followed by temperature, and followed by strain. The model, once obtained, can be used to predict the yield stress from a given set of temperature, strain, and strain rate.

Figure 2(a) shows the prediction error between the yield stress and the predicted yield stress on a set of testing data, i.e. the data which is not used to train the model and Figure 2(b) shows a plot of the predicted value of yield stress superimposed on the original yield stress.

It is observed that the prediction on the set of testing data is reasonable. This indicates that the MARS model has captured most of the dynamics underlying the original training data, and is capable of extending this captured knowledge onto a set of hitherto unseen data.

4   Comparison with the results obtained by conventional approaches

In order to compare the artificial neural network approach to more conventional methods for model tuning, the same data set was processed using:

1. A MARS model with cubic polynomials
2. An inverse hyperbolic sine law model using least square batch parameter tuning

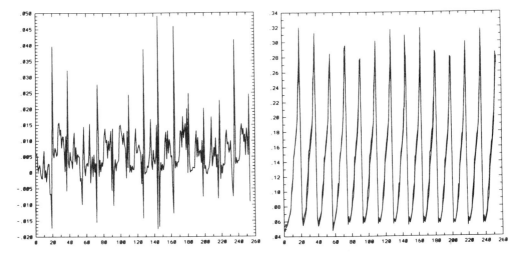

Figure 2: (a) The prediction error on the testing data set (b) The prediction and the testing data set superimposed

3. An inverse hyperbolic sine law model using a recursive least squares tuning

4. CART based classification [Briemen et. al., 1984]

5. C4.5 based method [Quinlan, 1986,1987]

6. Bayesian classification [Buntine, [1990]

In each case, we used a training data set of 78 plates (1242 passes) and a testing data set of 16 plates (252 passes). In the cases of CART, C4.5, and Bayesian classification methods, the yield stress variable is divided equally into 10 classes, and this is used as the desired output instead of the original real values.

The comparison of the results between MARS and the Kalman filter based approach are shown in the following table

	B_{11}	B_{12}	A_{11}	A_{12}	C_{11}	C_{12}
mean%	-.64	1.69	-.64	2.38	-0.2	4.5
mean abs%	4.61	4.22	4.61	5.3	3.5	5.3
std %	6.26	5.11	6.26	6.25	4.7	4.9

where
B_{11} = Batch Tuning: tuning model (forgetting factors =1 in adaption) on the training data
B_{12} = Batch Tuning: running tuned model on the testing data
A_{11} = Adaptation: on the training data
A_{12} = Adaptation: on the testing data

C_{11} = MARS on the training data
C_{12} = MARS on the testing data,

and $mean\% = mean((k_{meas} - k_{pred})/k_{meas})$,
$meanabs\% = mean(abs((k_{meas} - k_{pred})/k_{meas}))$,
$std\% = stdev((k_{meas} - k_{pred})/k_{meas})$; where mean and stdev stands for the mean and the standard deviations respectively, and k_{meas}, k_{pred} represents the measured and predicted values of the yield stress respectively.

It is found that the MARS based model performs extremely well compared with the other methods. The standard deviation of the prediction errors in a MARS model is considerably less than the corresponding standard deviation of prediction errors in a Kalman filter type batch or online tuning model on the testing data set.

We have also compared MARS with both the CART based method and the C4.5 based method. As both CART and C4.5 operate only on an output category, rather than a continuous output value, it is necessary to convert the yield stress into a category type of variable. We have chosen to divide equally the yield stress into 10 classes. With this modification, the CART and C4.5 methods are readily applicable.

The following table summarises the results of this comparison. The values given are the percentage of the prediction error on the testing data set for various methods. In the case of MARS, we have converted the prediction error from a continuous variable into the corresponding classes as used in the CART and C4.5 methods.

Bayes	CART	C4.5	MARS
65.4	12.99	16.14	6.2

It is found that the MARS model is more consistent in predicting the output classes than either the CART method, the C4.5 based method, or the Bayesian classifier. The fact that the MARS model performs better than the CART model can be seen as a confirmation that the MARS model is a generalisation of the CART model (see Friedman [1991]). But it is rather surprising to see that the MARS model outperforms a Bayesian classifier.

The results are similar over a number of other typical data sets, e.g., when the interpass time variable becomes significant.

5   Conclusion

It is found that MARS can be applied to model the platemill data with very good accuracy. In terms of predictive power on unseen data, it performs better than the more traditional methods, e.g., Kalman filter batch or online tuning methods, CART, C4.5 or Bayesian classifier.

It is almost impossible to convert the MARS model into one given in section 1. The Hodgson-Collinson model places a breakpoint at a temperature of $925 \deg C$, while in the MARS model, the temperature breakpoints are found to be at $1017 \deg C$ and $1129 \deg C$ respectively. Hence it is difficult to convert the MARS model into those given by the Hodgson-Collinson model, the Kalman filter type models or vice versa.

A possible improvement to the current MARS technique would be to restrict the breakpoints, so that they must exist within a temperature region where microstructural changes are known to occur.

6   Acknowledgement

The author acknowledges the assistance given by the staff at the BHP Melbourne Research Laboratory in providing the data, as well as in providing the background material in this paper. He specially thanks Dr D McFarlane in giving his generous time in assisting in the understanding of the more traditional approaches, and also for providing the results on the Kalman filtering approach. Also, he is indebted to Dr W Buntine, RIACS, NASA, Ames Research Center for providing an early version of the induction tree based programs.

7   References

Anderson, B.D.O., Moore, J.B., (1980). *Optimal Fitering*. Prentice Hall, Eaglewood, NJ.

Brieman, L., Friedman, J., Olshen, R.A., Stone, C.J., (1984). *Classification and Regression Trees*. Wadworth, Belmont, CA.

Buntine, W, (1990). *A Theory of Learning Classification Rules*. PhD Thesis submitted to the University of Technology, Sydney.

Friedman, J, (1991). "Multivariate Adaptive Regression Splines". *Ann Stat.* to appear. (Also, the implication of the paper on neural network models was presented orally in the 1990 NIPS Conference)

Hodgson, Collinson, (1990). Manuscript under preparation (authors are with BHP Research Lab., Melbourne, Australia).

Horihata, M, Motomura, M, (1988). "Theoretical analysis of 3-roll Rolling Process by the energy method". *Trans of the Iron and Steel Institute of Japan*, **28**:6, 434-439.

Hornik, K., Stinchcombe, M., White, H., (1989). "Multilayer Feedforward Networks are Universal Approximators". *Neural Networks*, **2**, 359-366.

McFarlane, D, Telford, A, Petersen, I, (1991). Manuscript under preparation

Quinlan, R. (1986). "Induction of Decision Trees". *Machine Learning.* **1**, 81-106.

Quinlan, R. (1987). "Simplifying Decision Trees". *International J Man-Machine Studies.* **27**, 221-234.

Underwood, L R, (1950). *The Rolling of Metals*. Chapman & Hall, London.

Computer Recognition of Wave Location in Graphical Data by a Neural Network

Donald T. Freeman
School of Medicine
University of Pittsburgh
Pittsburgh, PA 15261

Abstract

Five experiments were performed using several neural network architectures to identify the location of a wave in the time ordered graphical results from a medical test. Baseline results from the first experiment found correct identification of the target wave in 85% of cases (n=20). Other experiments investigated the effect of different architectures and preprocessing the raw data on the results. The methods used seem most appropriate for time oriented graphical data which has a clear starting point such as electrophoresis or spectrometry rather than continuous tests such as ECGs and EEGs.

1 INTRODUCTION

Complex wave form recognition is generally considered to be a difficult task for machines. Analytical approaches to this problem have been described and they work with reasonable accuracy (Gabriel et al. 1980, Valdes-Sosa et al. 1987) The use of these techniques, however, requires substantial mathematical training and the process is often time consuming and labor intensive (Boston 1987). Mathematical modeling also requires substantial knowledge of the particular details of the wave forms in order to determine how to apply the models and to determine detection criteria. Rule-based expert systems have also been used for the recognition of wave forms (Boston 1989). They require that a knowledge engineer work closely with a domain expert to extract the rules that the expert uses to perform the recognition. If the rules are *ad hoc* or if it is difficult for experts to articulate the rules they use, then rule-based expert systems are cumbersome to implement.

This paper describes the use of neural networks to recognize the location of peak V from the wave-form recording of brain stem auditory evoked potential tests. General discussions of connectionist networks can be found in (Rumelhart and McClelland 1986). The main features of neural networks that are relevant for our purposes revolve around their ease of use as compared to other modeling techniques. Neural networks provide several advantages over modeling with differential equations or rule-based systems. First, there is no knowledge engineering phase. The network is trained automatically using a series of examples along with the "right answer" to each example. Second, the resulting network typically has significant predictive power when novel examples are presented. So, neural network technology allows expert performance to be mimicked without requiring that expert knowledge be codified in a traditional fashion. In addition, neural networks, when used to perform signal analysis, require vastly less restrictive assumptions about the structure of the input signal than analytical techniques (Gorman and Sejnowski 1988). Still, neural nets have not yet been widely applied to problems of this sort (DeRoach 1989). Nevertheless, it seems that interest is growing in using computers, especially neural networks, to solve advanced problems in medical decision making (Stubbs 1988).

1.1 BRAIN STEM AUDITORY EVOKED POTENTIAL (BAEP)

Sensory evoked potentials are electric signals from the brain that occur in response to transient auditory, somatosensory, or visual stimuli such as a click, pinprick, or flash of light. The signals, recorded from electrodes placed on a subject's scalp, are a measure of the electrical activity in the subject's brain both from response to the stimulus and from the spontaneous electroencephalographic (EEG) activity of the brain. One way of discerning the response to the stimulus from the background EEG noise is to average the individual responses from many identical stimuli. When "cortical noise" has been removed in this way, evoked potentials can be an important noninvasive measure of central nervous system function. They are used in studies of physiology and psychology, for the diagnosis of neurologic disorders (Greenberg et al. 1981). Recently attention has focused on continuous automated monitoring of the BAEP intraoperatively as well as post-operatively for evaluation of central nervous system function (Moulton et al. 1991). Brain stem auditory evoked potentials (BAEP) are generated in the auditory pathways of the brain stem. They can be used to asses hearing and brain stem function even in unresponsive or uncooperative patients.

The BAEP test involves placing headphones on the patient, flooding one ear with white noise, and delivering clicks into the other ear. Electrodes on the scalp both on the same side (ipsilateral) and opposite side (contralateral) of the clicks record the electric potentials of brain activity for 10 msec. following each click. In the protocol used at the University of Pittsburgh Presbyterian University Hospital (PUH), a series of 2000 clicks is delivered and the results from each click - a graph of electrode activity over the 10 msec. - are averaged into a single graph. Results from the stimulation of one ear with the clicks is referred to as "one ear of data".

A graph of the wave form which results from the averaging of many stimuli appears as a series of peaks following the stimulus (Figure 1). The resulting graph typically has 7 important peaks but often includes other peaks resulting from the noise which remains after averaging. Each important peak represents the firing of a group of neurons in the auditory neural pathway[1]. The time of arrival of the peaks (the peak latencies) and the amplitudes of the peaks are used to characterize the response. The latencies of peaks I, III, and V are typically used to determine if there is evidence of slowed central nervous system conduction which is of value in the diagnosis of multiple sclerosis and other disease states[2]. Conduction delay may be seen in the left, right, or both BAEP pathways. It is of interest that the time of arrival of a wave on the ipsilateral and contralateral sides may be slightly different. This effect becomes more exagerated the more distant the correlated peaks are from the origin (Durrant, Boston, and Martin 1990).

Typically there are several issues in the interpretation of the graphs. First, it must be clear that some neural response to the auditory stimulus is represented in the wave form. If a response is present, the peaks which correspond to normal and abnormal responses must be distinguished from noise which remains in the signal even after averaging. Wave IV and wave V occasionally fuse, forming a wave IV/V complex, confounding this

---

[1]Putative generators are: I–Acoustic nerve; II–Cochlear nucleus; III–Superior olivary nucleus; IV–Lateral lemniscus; V–Inferior colliculus; VI–Medial geniculate nucleus; VII–Auditory radiations.

[2]Other disorders include brain edema, acoustic neuroma, gliomas, and central pontine myelinolysis.

process. In these cases we say that wave V is absent. Finally, the latencies and possibly the amplitudes of the identified peaks are be measured and a diagnostic explanation for them is developed.

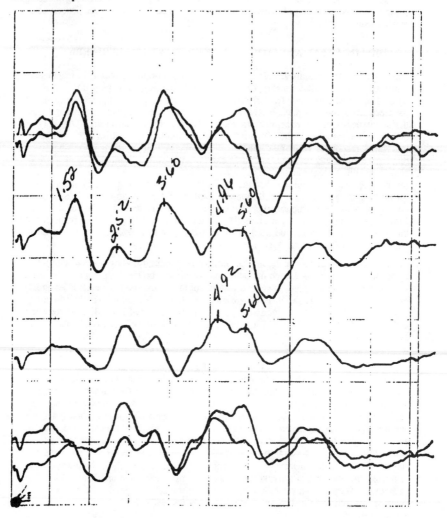

Figure 1. BAEP chart with the time of arrival for waves I to V identified.

2   METHODS AND PROCEDURES

2.1   DATA

Plots of BAEP tests were obtained from the evoked potential files from the last 4 years at PUH. A preliminary group of *training cases* consisting of 13 patients or 26 ears was selected by traversing the files alphabetically from the beginning of the alphabet. This group was subsequently extended to 25 patients or 50 ears, 39 normals and 11 abnormals. Most BAEP tests show no abnormalities; only 1 of the first 40 ears was abnormal. In order to create a training set with an adequate number of abnormal cases we included only patients with abnormal ears after these first 40 had been selected. Ten abnormal ears were obtained from a search of 60 patient files. *Test cases* were selected from files starting at the end of the alphabet, moving toward the beginning, the opposite of the process used for the training cases. Unlike the training set - where some cases were selected over others - all cases were included in the test set without bias. No cases were common to both sets. A total of 10 patients or 20 ears were selected. Table 1 summarizes the input data.

For one of the experiments, another data set was made using the ipsilateral data for 80 inputs and the derivative of the curve for the other 80 inputs. The derivative was computed by subtracting the amplitude of the point's successor from the amplitude of the point and dividing by 0.1.

The ipsilateral and contralateral wave recordings were transformed to machine readable format by manual tracing with a BitPad Plus® digitizer. A formal protocol was followed to ensure that a high fidelity transcription had been effected. The approximately 400 points which resulted from the digitization of each ear were graphed and compared to the original tracings. If the tracings did not match, then the transcription was performed again. In addition, the originally recorded latency values for peak V were corrected for any distortion in the digitizing process. The distortion was judged by a neurologist to be minimal.

Table 1: Composition of Input Data

Cases	Normal Ears	Abnormal Ears			Total Ears
		Prolonged V	Absent V	Total	
Training	39	8	3	11	50
Testing	18	0	2	2	20

A program was written to process the digital wave forms, creating an output file readable by the neural network simulator. The program discarded the first and last 1 msec. of the recordings. The remaining points were sampled at 0.1 msec. intervals using linear interpolation to estimate an amplitude if a point had not been recorded within 0.01 msec. of the desired time. These points were then normalized to the range <-1,1>. The resulting 80 points for the ipsilateral wave and 80 points for the contralateral wave (a total of 160 points) were used as the initial activations for the input layer of processing elements.

2.2   ARCHITECTURES

Each of the four network architectures had 160 input nodes. Each node represented the amplitude of the wave at each sample time (1.0 to 8.9 ms, every 0.1 ms). Each architecture also had 80 output nodes with a similar temporal interpretation (Figure 2). Architecture 1 (A1) had 30 hidden units connected only to the ipsilateral input units, 5 hidden units connected only to the contralateral input units and 5 hidden units connected to all the input units. The hidden units for all architectures were fully connected to the output units. Architecture 2 (A2) reversed these proportions. Architecture 3 (A3) was fully connected to the inputs. Architecture 4 (A4) preserved the proportions of A1 but had 16 ipsilateral hidden units, 3 contralateral, and 3 connected to both. All architectures used the sigmoid transfer function at both the hidden and output layers and all units were attached to a bias unit.

The distribution of the hidden units was chosen with the knowledge that human experts usually use information from the ipsilateral side but refer to the contralateral side only when features in the ipsilateral side are too obscure to resolve. The selection of the number of hidden units in neural network models remains an art. In order to determine whether the size of the hidden unit layer could be changed, we repeated the experiments using Architecture 2 where the number of hidden units was reduced to 16, with 10 connected to the ipsilateral inputs, 3 to the contralateral inputs, and 3 connected to all the inputs.

2.3   TRAINING

For training, target values for the output layer were all 0.0 except for the output nodes representing the time of arrival for wave V (reported on the BAEP chart) and one node on each side of it. The peak node target was 0.95 and the two adjacent nodes had targets of 0.90. For cases in which wave V was absent, the target for all the output nodes was 0.0.

A neural network simulator (NeuralWorks Professional II® version 3.5) was used to construct the networks and run the simulations. The back-propagation learning algorithm was used to train the networks. The random number generator was initialized with random number seeds taken from a random number table. Then network weights were initialized to random values between -0.2 and 0.2 and the training begun. Since our random number generator is deterministic – given the random number seed – these trials are replicable.

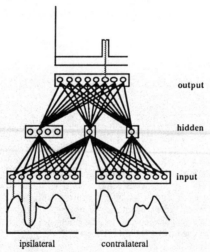

Figure 2. Diagram of Architecture 1 with representation of input and output data shown.

Each of the 50 ears of data in the training set was presented using a randomize, shuffle, and deal technique. Network weights were saved at various stages of learning, usually after every 1000 presentations (20 epochs) until the cumulative RMS error for an epoch fell below 0.01. The contribution of each training example to the total error was examined to determine whether a few examples were the source of most of the error. If so, training was continued until these examples had been learned to an error level comparable to the rest of the cases. After training, the 20 ears in the test set were presented to each of the saved networks and the output nodes of the net were examined for each test case.

2.4   ANALYSIS OF RESULTS

A threshold method was used to analyze the data. For each of the test cases the actual location of the maximum valued output unit was compared to the expected location of the maximum valued output unit. For a network result to be classified as a correct identification in the wave V present (true positive), we require that the maximum valued output unit have an activation which is over an activity-threshold (0.50) and that the unit be within a distance-threshold (0.2 msec.) of the expected location of wave V. For a true negative identification of wave V – a correct identification of wave V being absent – we require that all the output activities be below the activity threshold and that the case have no wave V to find. The network makes a false positive prediction of the location of wave V if some activity is above the activity threshold for a case which has no wave V. Finally, there are two ways for the network to make a false negative identification of wave V. In both instances, wave V must be present in the case. In one instance, some output node has activity above the activity threshold, but it is outside of the distance threshold. This corresponds to the identification of a wave V but in the wrong place. In the other instance, no node attains activity over the activity threshold, corresponding to a failure to find a wave V when there exists a wave V in the case to find.

2.5   EXPERIMENTS

Five experiments were performed. The first four used different architectures on the same data set and the last used architecture A1 on the derivatives data set. Each of the network architectures was trained from different random starting positions. For each trial, a network was randomized and trained as described above. The networks were sampled as learning progressed.

Experiment 1 determined how well archtecture A1 could identify wave V and provided baseline results for the remaining experiments. Experiments 2 and 3 tested whether our use of more hidden units attached to ipsilateral data made sense by reversing the proportion of hidden units alloted to ipsilateral data processing (experiment 2) and by tring a fully connected network (experiment 3). Experiment 4 determined whether fewer hidden units could be used. Experiment 5 investigated whether preprocessing of the input data to make derivative information available would facilitate network identification of peak location.

3   RESULTS

Results from the best network found for each of five experiments are shown in Table 2.

Table 2: Results from presentation of 20 test cases to various network architectures.

Experiment	Network	TP	TN	Total	FP	FN	Total
1	A1	16	1	1 7	1	2	3
2	A2	16	0	1 6	2	2	4
3	A3	16	0	1 6	2	2	4
4	A4	15	0	1 5	3	2	5
5	A1	15	1	1 6	1	3	4

4   DISCUSSION

In Experiment 1, the three cases which were incorrectly identified were examined closely. It is not evident from inspection why the net failed to identify the peaks or identified peaks where there were none to identify. Where peaks are present, they are not unusually located or surrounded by noise. The appearance of their shape seems similar to the cases which were identified correctly. We believe that more training examples which are "similar" to these 3 test cases, as well as examples with greater variety, will improve recognition of these cases. This improvement comes not from better generalization but rather from a reduced requirement for generalization. If the net is trained with cases which are increasingly similar to the cases which will be used to test it, then recognition of the test cases becomes easier at any given level of generalization.

The distribution of hidden units in A1 was chosen with the knowledge that human experts use information primarily from the ipsilateral side, referring to the contralateral side only when ipsilateral features are too obscure to resolve. Experiments 2 and 3 investigate whether this reliance on ipsilateral data suggests that there should be more hidden units for the ipsilateral side or for the contralateral side. The identical results from these experiments are similar to those of Experiment 1. One interpretation is that it is possible to make diagnoses of BAEPs using very few features from the ipsilateral side. Another interpretation is that it is possible to use the contralateral data as the chief information source, contrary to our expert's belief.

Experiment 4 investigates whether fewer features are needed by restricting the hidden layer to 20 hidden units. The slight degradation of performance indicates that it is possible to make BAEP diagnoses with fewer ipsilateral features. Experiment 5 utilized the ipsilateral waveform and its derivative to determine whether this pre-processing would improve the results. Surprisingly, the results did not improve, but it is possible that a better estimator of the derivative will prove this method useful.

Finally, when the weights from all the networks above were examined, we found that amplitudes from only the area where wave V falls were used. This suggests that it is not necessary to know the location of wave III before determining the location of wave V, in sharp contrast to expert's intuition. We believe the networks form a "local expert" for the identification of wave V which does not need to interact with data from other parts of the graph, and that other such local experts will be formed as we expand the project's scope.

5   CONCLUSIONS

Automated wave form recognition is considered to be a difficult task for machines and an especially difficult task for neural networks. Our results offer some encouragement that in some domains neural networks may be applied to perform wave form recognition and that the technique will be extensible as problem complexity increases.

Still, the accuracy of the networks we have discussed is not high enough for clinical use. Several extensions have been attempted and others considered including 1) increasing the sampling rate to decrease the granularity of the input data, 2) increasing the training set size, 3) using a different representation of the output for wave V absent cases, 4) using a different representation of the input, such as the derivative of the amplitudes, and 5) architectures which allow hybrids of these ideas.

Finally, since many other tests in medicine as well as other fields require the interpretation of graphical data, it is tempting to consider extending this method to other domains. Many other tests in medicine as well as other fields require the interpretation of graphical data.One distinguishing feature of the BAEP is that there is no difficulty with the time registration of the data; we always know where to start looking for the wave. This is in contrast to an EKG, for example, which may require substantial effort just to identify the beginning of a QRS complex. Our results indicate that the interpretation of graphs where the time registration of data is not an issue is possible using neural networks. Medical tests for which this technique would be appropriate include: other evoked potentials, spectrometry, and gel electrophoresis.

Acknowledgements

The author wishes to thank Dr. Scott Shoemaker of the Department of Neurology for his expertise, encouragement, constructive criticism, patience, and collaboration throughout the progress of this work. This research has been supported by NLM Training grant T15 LM-07059.

References

Boston, J.R. 1987. Detection criteria for sensory evoked potentials. Proceedings of 9th Ann. IEEE/EMBS Conf., Boston, MA.

Boston, J.R. 1989. Automated interpretation of brainstem auditory evoked potentials: a prototype system. IEEE Trans. Biomed. Eng. 36 (5) : 528-532.

DeRoach, J.N. 1989. Neural networks - an artificial intelligence approach to the analysis of clinical data. Austral. Phys. & Eng. Sci. in Med. 12 (2) : 100-106.

Durrant, J.D., J.R. Boston, and W.H. Martin. 1990. Correlation study of two-channel recordings of the brain stem auditory evoked potential. Ear and Hearing 11 (3) : 215-221.

Gabriel, S., J.D. Durrant, A.E. Dickter, and J.E. Kephart. 1980. Computer identification of waves in the auditory brain stem evoked potentials. EEG and Clin. Neurophys. 49 : 421-423.

Gorman, R. Paul, and Terrence J. Sejnowski. 1988. Analysis of hidden units in a layered network trained to classify sonar targets. Neural Networks 1 : 75-89.

Greenberg, R.P., P.G. Newlon, M.S. Hyatt, R.K. Narayan, and D.P. Becker. 1981. Prognostic implications of early multimodality evoked potentials in severely head-injured patients. J. Neurosurg 5 : 227-236.

Moùlton, Richard, Peter Kresta, Mario Ramirez, and William Tucker. 1991. Continuous automated monitoring of somatosensory evoked potentials in posttraumatic coma. Journal of Trauma 31 (5) : 676-685.

Rumelhart, David E., and James L. McClelland. 1986. Parallel distributed processing. Cambridge, Mass: MIT Press.

Stubbs, D F. 1988. Neurocomputers. MD Comput 5 (3) : 14-24.

Valdes-Sosa, M.J., M.A. Bobes, M.C. Perez-abalo, M. Perra, J.A. Carballo, and P. Valdes-Sosa. 1987. Comparison of auditory evoked potential detection methods using signal detection theory. Audiol 26 : 166-178.

A Neural Network for Motion Detection of Drift-Balanced Stimuli

Hilary Tunley*
School of Cognitive and Computer Sciences
Sussex University
Brighton, England.

Abstract

This paper briefly describes an artificial neural network for preattentive visual processing. The network is capable of determining image motion in a type of stimulus which defeats most popular methods of motion detection – a subset of second-order visual motion stimuli known as drift-balanced stimuli(DBS). The processing stages of the network described in this paper are integratable into a model capable of simultaneous motion extraction, edge detection, and the determination of occlusion.

1 INTRODUCTION

Previous methods of motion detection have generally been based on one of two underlying approaches: correlation; and gradient-filter. Probably the best known example of the correlation approach is the Reichardt movement detector [Reichardt 1961]. The gradient-filter (GF) approach underlies the work of Adelson and Bergen [Adelson 1985], and Heeger [Heeger 1988], amongst others.

These motion-detecting methods cannot track DBS, because DBS lack essential components of information needed by such methods. Both the correlation and GF approaches impose constraints on the input stimuli. Throughout the image sequence, correlation methods require information that is spatiotemporally correlatable; and GF motion detectors assume temporally constant spatial gradients.

---

*Current address: Experimental Psychology, School of Biological Sciences, Sussex University.

The network discussed here does not impose such constraints. Instead, it extracts motion *energy* and exploits the spatial coherence of movement (defined more formally in the Gestalt theory of *common fate* [Koffka 1935]) to achieve tracking.

The remainder of this paper discusses DBS image sequences, then correlation methods, then GF methods in more detail, followed by a qualitative description of this network which *can* process DBS.

2   SECOND-ORDER AND DRIFT-BALANCED STIMULI

There has been a lot of recent interest in second-order visual stimuli, and DBS in particular ([Chubb 1989, Landy 1991]). DBS are stimuli which give a clear percept of directional motion, yet Fourier analysis reveals a lack of coherent motion energy, or energy present in a direction opposing that of the displacement (hence the term 'drift-balanced'). Examples of DBS include image sequences in which the contrast polarity of edges present reverses between frames.

A subset of DBS, which are also processed by the network, are known as micro-balanced stimuli (MBS). MBS contain no correlatable features and are drift-balanced at all scales. The MBS image sequences used for this work were created from a random-dot image in which an area is successively shifted by a constant displacement between each frame and *simultaneously* re-randomised.

3   EXISTING METHODS OF MOTION DETECTION

3.1   CORRELATION METHODS

Correlation methods perform a local cross-correlation in image space: the matching of features in local neighbourhoods (depending upon displacement/speed) between image frames underlies the motion detection. Examples of this method include [Van Santen 1985]. Most correlation models suffer from noise degradation in that any noise features extracted by the edge detection are available for spurious correlation.

There has been much recent debate questioning the validity of correlation methods for modelling human motion detection abilities. In addition to DBS, there is also increasing psychophysical evidence ([Landy 1991, Mather 1991]) which correlation methods cannot account for.

These factors suggest that correlation techniques are not suitable for low-level motion processing where no information is available concerning *what* is moving (as with MBS). However, correlation is a more plausible method when working with higher level constructs such as tracking in model-based vision (e.g. [Bray 1990]).

3.2   GRADIENT-FILTER (GF) METHODS

GF methods use a combination of spatial filtering to determine edge positions and temporal filtering to determine whether such edges are moving. A common assumption used by GF methods is that *spatial gradients are constant*. A recent method by Verri [Verri 1990], for example, argues that flow detection is based upon the notion

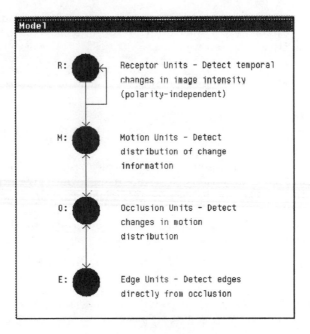

Figure 1: The Network (Schematic)

of tracking spatial gradient magnitude and/or direction, and that any variation in the spatial gradient is due to some form of motion deformation – i.e. rotation, expansion or shear. Whilst for scenes containing smooth surfaces this is a valid approximation, it is *not* the case for second-order stimuli such as DBS.

4   THE NETWORK

A simplified diagram illustrating the basic structure of the network (based upon earlier work ([Tunley 1990, Tunley 1991a, Tunley 1991b]) is shown in Figure 1 (the edge detection stage is discussed elsewhere ([Tunley 1990, Tunley 1991b, Tunley 1992]).

4.1   INPUT RECEPTOR UNITS

The units in the input layer respond to rectified local changes in image intensity over time. Each unit has a variable adaption rate, resulting in temporal sensitivity – a fast adaption rate gives a high temporal filtering rate. The main advantages for this temporal averaging processing are:

- Averaging removes the D.C. component of image intensity. This eliminates problematic gain for motion in high brightness areas of the image. [Heeger 1988].

- The random nature of DBS/MBS generation cannot guarantee that each pixel change is due to local image motion. Local temporal averaging smooths the moving regions, thus creating a more coherently structured input for the motion units.

The input units have a pointwise rectifying response governed by an autoregressive filter of the following form:

$$R_n = (1 - \alpha).R_{n-1} + \alpha.|I_n - I_{n-1}| \tag{1}$$

where $\alpha \in [0, 1]$ is a variable which controls the degree of temporal filtering of the change in input intensity, n and $n - 1$ are successive image frames, and R_n and I_n are the filter output and input, respectively.

The receptor unit responses for two different α values are shown in Figure 2. α can thus be used to alter the amount of motion blur produced for a particular frame rate, effectively producing a unit with differing velocity sensitivity.

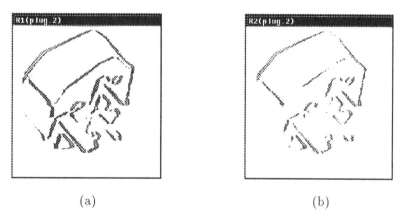

(a)   (b)

Figure 2: Receptor Unit Response: (a) $\alpha = 0.3$; (b) $\alpha = 0.7$.

4.2 MOTION UNITS

These units determine the *coherence* of image changes indicated by corresponding receptor units. First-order motion produces highly-tuned motion activity – i.e. a strong response in a particular direction – whilst second-order motion results in less coherent output.

The operation of a basic motion detector can be described by:

$$M_{ijkdn} = |R_{ijn} - R_{i'j'n-1}| \tag{2}$$

where M is the detector, (i', j') is a point in frame n at a distance d from (i, j), a point in frame $n - 1$, in the direction k. Therefore, for coherent motion (i.e. first-order), in direction k at a speed of d units/frame, as $n \to \infty$:

$$M_{ijkdn} \to 0 \tag{3}$$

The convergence of motion activity can be seen using an example. The stimulus sequence used consists of a bar of re-randomising texture moving to the right in front of a leftward moving background with the same texture (i.e. random dots). The bar motion is second-order as it contains no correlatable features, whilst the background consists of a simple first-order shifting of dots between frames. Figures 3, 4 and 5 show two-dimensional images of the leftward motion activity for the stimulus after 3, 4 and 6 frames respectively. The background, which has coherent leftward movement (at speed d units/frame) is gradually reducing to zero whilst the microbalanced rightwards-moving bar, remains active. The fact that a non-zero response is obtained for second-order motion suggests, according to the definition of Chubb and Sperling [Chubb 1989], that first-order detectors produce no response to MBS, that this detector is second-order with regard to motion detection.

Figure 3: Leftward Motion Response to Third Frame in Sequence.

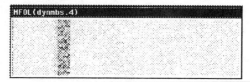

Figure 4: Leftward Motion Response to Fourth Frame.

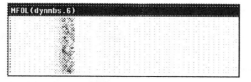

Figure 5: Leftward Motion Response to Sixth Frame.

The motion units in this model are arranged on a hexagonal grid. This grid is known as a flow web as it allows information to flow, both laterally between units of the same type, and between the different units in the model (motion, occlusion or edge). Each flow web unit is represented by three variables – a position (a, b) and a direction k, which is evenly spaced between 0 and 360 degrees. In this model each k is an integer between 1 and k_{max} – the value of k_{max} can be varied to vary the sensitivity of the units.

A way of using first-order techniques to discriminate between first and second-order motions is through the concept of coherence. At any point in the motion-processed images in Figures 3-5, a measure of the overall variation in motion activity can be used to distinguish between the motion of the micro-balanced bar and its background. The motion energy for a detector with displacement d, and orientation

k, at position (a, b), can be represented by E_{abkd}. For each motion unit, responding over distance d, in each cluster the energy present can be defined as:

$$E_{abkdn} = \frac{\min_k(M_{abkd})}{M_{abkd}} \tag{4}$$

where $\min_k(x_k)$ is the minimum value of x found searching over k values. If motion is coherent, and of approximately the correct speed for the detector M, then as $n \to \infty$:

$$E_{abk_m dn} \to 1 \tag{5}$$

where k_m is in the actual direction of the motion. In reality n need only approach around 5 for convergence to occur. Also, more importantly, under the same convergence conditions:

$$E_{abkdn} \to 0 \; \forall k \neq k_m \tag{6}$$

This is due to the fact that the minimum activation value in a group of first-order detectors at point (a, b) will be the same as the actual value in the direction, k_m. By similar reasoning, for non-coherent motion as $n \to \infty$:

$$E_{abkdn} \to 1 \; \forall k \tag{7}$$

in other words there is no peak of activity in a given direction. The motion energy is ambiguous at a large number of points in most images, except at discontinuities and on well-textured surfaces.

A measure of motion coherence used for the motion units can now be defined as:

$$M_c(abkd) = \frac{E_{abkd}}{\sum_{k=1}^{k_{max}} E_{abkd}} \tag{8}$$

For coherent motion in direction k_m as $n \to \infty$:

$$M_c(abk_m d) \to 1 \tag{9}$$

Whilst for second-order motion, also as $n \to \infty$:

$$M_c(abkd) \to 1/k_{max} \; \forall k \tag{10}$$

Using this approach the total M_c activity at each position – regardless of coherence, or lack of it – is unity. Motion energy is the same in all moving regions, the difference is in the distribution, or *tuning* of that energy.

Figures 6, 7 and 8 show how motion coherence allows the flow web structure to reveal the presence of motion in microbalanced areas whilst not affecting the easily detected background motion for the stimulus.

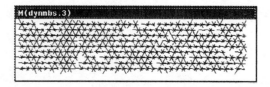

Figure 6: Motion Coherence Response to Third Frame

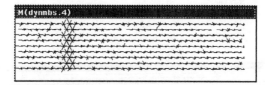

Figure 7: Motion Coherence Response to Fourth Frame

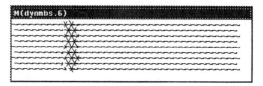

Figure 8: Motion Coherence Response to Sixth Frame

4.3   OCCLUSION UNITS

These units identify discontinuities in second-order motion which are vitally important when computing the direction of that motion. They determine spatial and temporal changes in motion coherence and can process single or multiple motions at each image point. Established and newly-activated occlusion units work, through a gating process, to enhance continuously-displacing surfaces, utilising the concept of visual inertia.

The implementation details of the occlusion stage of this model are discussed elsewhere [Tunley 1992], but some output from the occlusion units to the above second-order stimulus are shown in Figures 9 and 10. The figures show how the edges of the bar can be determined.

References

[Adelson 1985]   E.H. Adelson and J.R. Bergen. Spatiotemporal energy models for the perception of motion. *J. Opt. Soc. Am.* 2, 1985.

[Bray 1990]   A.J. Bray. Tracking objects using image disparities. *Image and Vision Computing*, 8, 1990.

[Chubb 1989]   C. Chubb and G. Sperling. Second-order motion perception: Space/time separable mechanisms. In *Proc. Workshop on Visual Motion, Irvine, CA, USA*, 1989.

Figure 9: Occluding Motion Information: Occlusion activity produced by an increase in motion coherence activity.

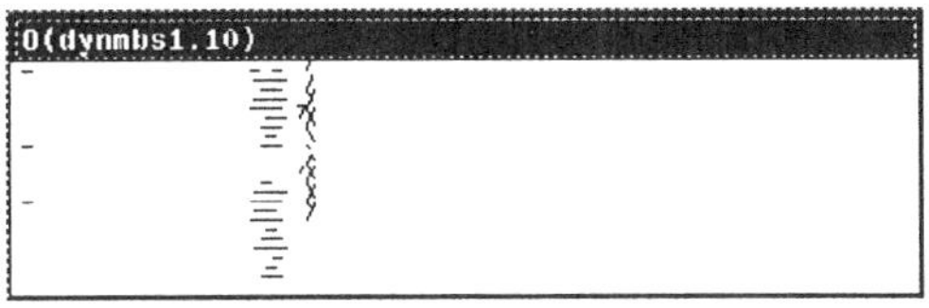

O(dynmbs1.10)

Figure 10: Occluding Motion Information: Occlusion activity produced by a decrease in motion activity at a point. Some spurious activity is produced due to the random nature of the second-order motion information.

[Heeger 1988]   D.J. Heeger. Optical Flow using spatiotemporal filters. *Int. J. Comp. Vision*, 1, 1988.

[Koffka 1935]   K. Koffka. *Principles of Gestalt Psychology*. Harcourt Brace, 1935.

[Landy 1991]   M.S. Landy, B.A. Dosher, G. Sperling and M.E. Perkins. The kinetic depth effect and optic flow II: First- and second-order motion. *Vis. Res.* 31, 1991.

[Mather 1991]   G. Mather. Personal Communication.

[Reichardt 1961] W. Reichardt. Autocorrelation, a principle for the evaluation of sensory information by the central nervous system. In W. Rosenblith, editor, *Sensory Communications*. Wiley NY, 1961.

[Van Santen 1985] J.P.H. Van Santen and G. Sperling. Elaborated Reichardt detectors. *J. Opt. Soc. Am.* 2, 1985.

[Tunley 1990]   H. Tunley. Segmenting Moving Images. In *Proc. Int. Neural Network Conf. (INNC90), Paris, France*, 1990.

[Tunley 1991a]   H. Tunley. Distributed dynamic processing for edge detection. In *Proc. British Machine Vision Conf. (BMVC91), Glasgow, Scotland*, 1991.

[Tunley 1991b]   H. Tunley. Dynamic segmentation and optic flow extraction. In. *Proc. Int. Joint. Conf. Neural Networks (IJCNN91), Seattle, USA*, 1991.

[Tunley 1992]   H. Tunley. Sceond-order motion processing: A distributed approach. CSRP 211, School of Cognitive and Computing Sciences, University of Sussex (forthcoming).

[Verri 1990]   A. Verri, F. Girosi and V. Torre. Differential techniques for optic flow. *J. Opt. Soc. Am.* 7, 1990.

Neural Network Routing for Random Multistage Interconnection Networks

Mark W. Goudreau
Princeton University
and
NEC Research Institute, Inc.
4 Independence Way
Princeton, NJ 08540

C. Lee Giles
NEC Research Institute, Inc.
4 Independence Way
Princeton, NJ 08540

Abstract

A routing scheme that uses a neural network has been developed that can aid in establishing point-to-point communication routes through multistage interconnection networks (MINs). The neural network is a network of the type that was examined by Hopfield (Hopfield, 1984 and 1985). In this work, the problem of establishing routes through random MINs (RMINs) in a shared-memory, distributed computing system is addressed. The performance of the neural network routing scheme is compared to two more traditional approaches - exhaustive search routing and greedy routing. The results suggest that a neural network router may be competitive for certain RMINs.

1 INTRODUCTION

A neural network has been developed that can aid in establishing point-to-point communication routes through multistage interconnection networks (MINs) (Goudreau and Giles, 1991). Such interconnection networks have been widely studied (Huang, 1984; Siegel, 1990). The routing problem is of great interest due to its broad applicability. Although the neural network routing scheme can accommodate many types of communication systems, this work concentrates on its use in a shared-memory, distributed computing system.

Neural networks have sometimes been used to solve certain interconnection network

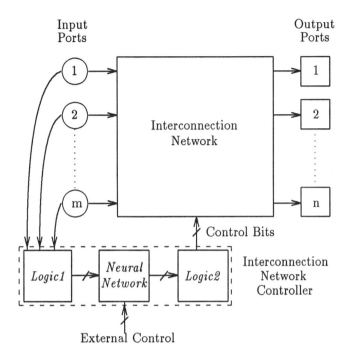

Figure 1: The communication system with a neural network router. The input ports (processors) are on the left, while the output ports (memory modules) are on the right.

problems, such as finding legal routes (Brown, 1989; Hakim and Meadows, 1990) and increasing the throughput of an interconnection network (Brown and Liu, 1990; Marrakchi and Troudet, 1989). The neural network router that is the subject of this work, however, differs significantly from these other routers and is specially designed to handle parallel processing systems that have MINs with random interstage connections. Such random MINs are called RMINs. RMINs tend to have greater fault-tolerance than regular MINs.

The problem is to allow a set of processors to access a set of memory modules through the RMIN. A picture of the communication system with the neural network router is shown in Figure 1. The are m processors and n memory modules. The system is assumed to be synchronous. At the beginning of a message cycle, some set of processors may desire to access some set of memory modules. It is the job of the router to establish as many of these desired connections as possible in a non-conflicting manner. Obtaining the optimal solution is not critical. Stymied processors may attempt communication again during the subsequent message cycle. It is the combination of speed and the quality of the solution that is important.

The object of this work was to discover if the neural network router could be competitive with other types of routers in terms of *quality of solution*, *speed*, and *resource*

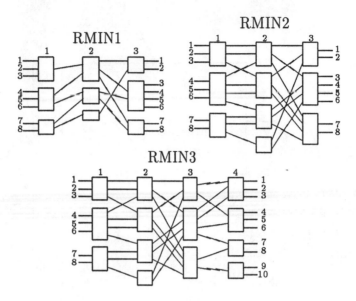

Figure 2: Three random multistage interconnection networks. The blocks that are shown are crossbar switches, for which each input may be connected to each output.

utilization. To this end, the neural network routing scheme was compared to two other schemes for routing in RMINs - namely, exhaustive search routing and greedy routing. So far, the results of this investigation suggest that the neural network router may indeed be a practicable alternative for routing in RMINs that are not too large.

2   EXHAUSTIVE SEARCH ROUTING

The exhaustive search routing method is optimal in terms of the ability of the router to find the best solution. There are many ways to implement such a router. One approach is described here.

For a given interconnection network, every route from each input to each output was stored in a database. (The RMINs that were used as test cases in this paper always had at least one route from each processor to each memory module.) When a new message cycle began and a new message set was presented to the router, the router would search through the database for a combination of routes for the message set that had no conflicts. A conflict was said to occur if more than one route in the set of routes used a single bus in the interconnection network. In the case where every combination of routes for the message set had a conflict, the router would find a combination of routes that could establish the largest possible number of desired connections.

If there are k possible routes for each message, this algorithm needs a memory of size $\Theta(mnk)$ and, in the worst case, takes exponential time with respect to the size of the message set. Consequently, it is an impractical approach for most RMINs, but it provides a convenient upper bound for the performance of other routers.

3 GREEDY ROUTING

When greedy routing is applied, message connections are established one at a time. Once a route is established in a given message cycle, it may not be removed. Greedy routing does not always provide the optimal routing solution.

The greedy routing algorithm that was used required the same route database as the exhaustive search router did. However, it selects a combination of routes in the following manner. When a new message set is present, the router chooses one desired message and looks at the first route on that message's list of routes. The router then establishes that route. Next, the router examines a second message (assuming a second desired message was requested) and sees if one of the routes in the second message's route list can be established without conflicting with the already established first message. If such a route does exist, the router establishes that route and moves on to the next desired message.

In the worst case, the speed of the greedy router is quadratic with respect to the size of the message set.

4 NEURAL NETWORK ROUTING

The focal point of the neural network router is a neural network of the type that was examined by Hopfield (Hopfield, 1984 and 1985). The problem of establishing a set of non-conflicting routes can be reduced to a constraint satisfaction problem. The structure of the neural network router is completely determined by the RMIN. When a new set of routes is desired, only certain bias currents in the network change. The neural network routing scheme also has certain fault-tolerant properties that will not be described here.

The neural network calculates the routes by converging to a legal *routing array*. A legal routing array is 3-dimensional. Therefore, each element of the routing array will have three indices. If element $a_{i,j,k}$ is equal to 1 then message i is routed through output port k of stage j. We say $a_{i,j,k}$ and $a_{l,m,n}$ are in the same *row* if $i = l$ and $k = n$. They are in the same *column* if $i = l$ and $j = m$. Finally, they are in the same *rod* if $j = m$ and $k = n$.

A legal routing array will satisfy the following three constraints:

1. one and only one element in each column is equal to 1.

2. the elements in successive columns that are equal to 1 represent output ports that can be connected in the interconnection network.

3. no more than one element in each rod is equal to 1.

The first restriction ensures that each message will be routed through one and only one output port at each stage of the interconnection network. The second restriction ensures that each message will be routed through a legal path in the interconnection network. The third restriction ensures that any resource contention in the interconnection network is resolved. In other words, only one message can use a certain output port at a certain stage in the interconnection network. When all three of these constraints are met, the routing array will provide a legal route for each message in the message set.

Like the routing array, the neural network router will naturally have a 3-dimensional structure. Each $a_{i,j,k}$ of a routing array is represented by the output voltage of a neuron, $V_{i,j,k}$. At the beginning of a message cycle, the neurons have a random output voltage. If the neural network settles in one of the global minima, the problem will have been solved.

A continuous time mode network was chosen. It was simulated digitally. The neural network has N neurons. The input to neuron i is u_i, its input bias current is I_i, and its output is V_i. The input u_i is converted to the output V_i by a sigmoid function, $g(x)$. Neuron i influences neuron j by a connection represented by T_{ji}. Similarly, neuron j affects neuron i through connection T_{ij}. In order for the Liapunov function (Equation 5) to be constructed, T_{ij} must equal T_{ji}. We further assume that $T_{ii} = 0$. For the synchronous updating model, there is also a time constant, denoted by τ.

The equations which describe the output of a neuron i are:

$$\frac{du_i}{dt} = -\frac{u_i}{\tau} + \sum_{j=1}^{N} T_{ij} V_j + I_i \tag{1}$$

$$\tau = RC \tag{2}$$

$$V_j = g(u_j) \tag{3}$$

$$g(x) = \frac{1}{1 + e^{-x}} \tag{4}$$

The equations above force the neural net into stable states that are the local minima of this approximate energy equation

$$E = -\frac{1}{2} \sum_{i=1}^{N} \sum_{j=1}^{N} T_{ij} V_i V_j - \sum_{i=1}^{N} V_i I_i \tag{5}$$

For the neural network, the weights (T_{ij}'s) are set, as are the bias currents (I_i's). It is the output voltages (V_i's) that vary to to minimize E.

Let M be the number of messages in a message set, let S be the number of stages in the RMIN, and let P be the number of ports per stage (P may be a function of the stage number). Below are the energy functions that implement the three constraints discussed above:

$$E_1 = \frac{A}{2} \sum_{m=1}^{M} \sum_{s=1}^{S-1} \sum_{p=1}^{P} V_{m,s,p} \left(-V_{m,s,p} + \sum_{i=1}^{P} V_{m,s,i} \right) \tag{6}$$

$$E_2 = \frac{B}{2} \sum_{s=1}^{S-1} \sum_{p=1}^{P} \sum_{m=1}^{M} V_{m,s,p} \left(-V_{m,s,p} + \sum_{i=1}^{M} V_{i,s,p} \right) \tag{7}$$

$$E_3 = \frac{C}{2} \sum_{m=1}^{M} \sum_{s=1}^{S-1} \sum_{p=1}^{P} (-2V_{m,s,p} + V_{m,s,p}(-V_{m,s,p} + \sum_{i=1}^{P} V_{m,s,i})) \qquad (8)$$

$$E_4 = D \sum_{m=1}^{M} \left[\sum_{s=2}^{S-1} \sum_{p=1}^{P} \sum_{i=1}^{P} d(s,p,i) V_{m,s-1,p} V_{m,s,i} \qquad (9) \right.$$

$$\left. + \sum_{j=1}^{P} (d(1,\alpha_m,j) V_{m,1,j} + d(S,j,\beta_m) V_{m,S-1,j}) \right]$$

A, B, C, and D are arbitrary positive constants.[1] E_1 and E_3 handle the first constraint in the routing array. E_4 deals with the second constraint. E_2 ensures the third. From the equation for E_4, the function $d(s1,p1,p2)$ represents the "distance" between output port $p1$ from stage $s1 - 1$ and output port $p2$ from stage $s1$. If $p1$ can connect to $p2$ through stage $s1$, then this distance may be set to zero. If $p1$ and $p2$ are not connected through stage $s1$, then the distance may be set to one. Also, α_m is the source address of message m, while β_m is the destination address of message m.

The entire energy function is:

$$E = E_1 + E_2 + E_3 + E_4 \qquad (10)$$

Solving for the connection and bias current values as shown in Equation 5 results in the following equations:

$$T_{(m1,s1,p1),(m2,s2,p2)} = -(A+C)\delta_{m1,m2}\delta_{s1,s2}(1 - \delta_{p1,p2}) \qquad (11)$$
$$-B\delta_{s1,s2}\delta_{p1,p2}(1 - \delta_{m1,m2})$$
$$-D\delta_{m1,m2}[\delta_{s1+1,s2}d(s2,p1,p2) + \delta_{s1,s2+1}d(s1,p2,p1)]$$

$$I_{m,s,p} = C - D[\delta_{s,1}d(1,\alpha_m,p) + \delta_{s,S-1}d(S,p,\beta_m)] \qquad (12)$$

$\delta_{i,j}$ is a Kronecker delta ($\delta_{i,j} = 1$ when $i = j$, and 0 otherwise).

Essentially, this approach is promising because the neural network is acting as a parallel computer. The hope is that the neural network will generate solutions much faster than conventional approaches for routing in RMINs.

The neural network that is used here has the standard problem - namely, a global minimum is not always reached. But this is not a serious difficulty. Typically, when the globally minimal energy is not reached by the neural network, some of the desired routes will have been calculated while others will not have. Even a locally minimal solution may partially solve the routing problem. Consequently, this would seem to be a particularly encouraging type of application for this type of neural network. For this application, the traditional problem of not reaching the global minimum may not hurt the system's performance very much, while the expected speed of the neural network in calculating the solution will be a great asset.

---

[1]For the simulations, $r = 1.0$, $A = C = D = 3.0$, and $B = 6.0$. These values for A, B, C, and D were chosen empirically.

Table 1: Routing results for the RMINs shown in Figure 2. The * entries were not calculated due to their computational complexity.

M	RMIN1			RMIN2			RMIN3		
	E_{es}	E_{gr}	E_{nn}	E_{es}	E_{gr}	E_{nn}	E_{es}	E_{gr}	E_{nn}
1	1.00	1.00	1.00	1.00	1.00	1.00	1.00	1.00	1.00
2	1.86	1.83	1.87	1.97	1.97	1.98	1.99	1.88	1.94
3	2.54	2.48	2.51	2.91	2.91	2.93	2.99	2.71	2.87
4	3.08	2.98	2.98	3.80	3.79	3.80	3.94	3.49	3.72
5	3.53	3.38	3.24	4.65	4.62	4.61	*	4.22	4.54
6	3.89	3.67	3.45	5.44	5.39	5.36	*	4.90	5.23
7	4.16	3.91	3.66	6.17	6.13	6.13	*	5.52	5.80
8	4.33	4.10	3.78	6.86	6.82	6.80	*	6.10	6.06

The neural network router uses a large number of neurons. If there are m input ports, and m output ports for each stage of the RMIN, an upper bound on the number of neurons needed is $m^2 S$. Often, however, the number of neurons actually required is much smaller than this upper bound.

It has been shown empirically that neural networks of the type used here can converge to a solution in essentially constant time. For example, this claim is made for the neural network described in (Takefuji and Lee, 1991), which is a slight variation of the model used here.

5   SIMULATION RESULTS

Figure 2 shows three RMINs that were examined. The routing results for the three routing schemes are shown in Table 1. E_{es} represents the expected number of messages to be routed using exhaustive search routing. E_{gr} is for greedy routing while E_{nn} is for neural network routing. These values are functions of the size of the message set, M. Only message sets that did not have obvious conflicts were examined. For example, no message set could have two processors trying to communicate to the same memory module. The table shows that, for at least these three RMINs, the three routing schemes produce solutions that are of similar virtue.

In some cases, the neural network router appears to outperform the supposedly optimal exhaustive search router. That is because the E_{es} and E_{gr} values were calculated by testing *every* message set of size M, while E_{nn} was calculated by testing *1,000 randomly generated message sets of size M*. For the neural network router to appear to perform best, it must have gotten message sets that were easier to route than average.

In general, the performance of the neural network router degenerates as the size of the RMIN increases. It is felt that the neural network router in its present form will not scale well for large RMINs. This is because other work has shown that large neural networks of the type used here have difficulty converging to a valid solution (Hopfield, 1985).

6   CONCLUSIONS

The results show that there is not much difference, in terms of quality of solution, for the three routing methodologies working on these relatively small sample RMINs. The exhaustive search approach is clearly not a practical approach since it is too time consuming. But when considering the asymptotic analyses for these three methodologies one should keep in mind the performance degradation of the greedy router and the neural network router as the size of the RMIN increases.

Greedy routing and neural network routing would appear to be valid approaches for RMINs of moderate size. But since asymptotic analysis has a very limited significance here, the best way to compare the speeds of these two routing schemes would be to build actual implementations.

Since the neural network router essentially calculates the routes *in parallel*, it can reasonably be hoped that a fast, analog implementation for the neural network router may find solutions faster than the exhaustive search router and even the greedy router. Thus, the neural network router may be a viable alternative for RMINs that are not too large.

References

Brown, T. X., (1989), "Neural networks for switching," *IEEE Commun. Mag.*, Vol. 27, pp. 72-81, Nov. 1989.

Brown, T. X. and Liu, K. H., (1990), "Neural network design of a banyan network controller," *IEEE J. on Selected Areas of Comm.*, pp. 1428-1438, Oct. 1990.

Goudreau, M. W. and Giles, C. L., (1991), "Neural network routing for multiple stage interconnection networks," *Proc. IJCNN 91*, Vol. II, p. A-885, July 1991.

Hakim, N. Z. and Meadows, H. E., (1990), "A neural network approach to the setup of the Benes switch," in *Infocom 90*, pp. 397-402.

Hopfield, J. J., (1984), "Neurons with graded response have collective computational properties like those of two-state neurons," *Proc. Natl. Acad. Sci. USA*, Vol. 81, pp. 3088-3092, May 1984.

Hopfield, J. J., (1985), "Neural computation on decisions in optimization problems," *Biol. Cybern.*, Vol. 52, pp. 141-152, 1985.

Huang, K. and Briggs, F. A., (1984), *Computer Architecture and Parallel Processing*, McGraw-Hill, New York, 1984.

Marrakchi, A. M. and Troudet, T., (1989), "A neural net arbitrator for large crossbar packet-switches," *IEEE Trans. on Circ. and Sys.*, Vol. 36, pp. 1039-1041, July 1989.

Siegel, H. J., (1990), *Interconnection Networks for Large Scale Parallel Processing*, McGraw-Hill, New York, 1990.

Takefuji, Y. and Lee, K. C., (1991), "An artificial hysteresis binary neuron: a model suppressing the oscillatory behaviors of neural dynamics", *Biological Cybernetics*, Vol. 64, pp. 353-356, 1991.

Networks for the Separation of Sources that are Superimposed and Delayed

John C. Platt   Federico Faggin
Synaptics, Inc.
2860 Zanker Road, Suite 206
San Jose, CA 95134

ABSTRACT

We have created new networks to unmix signals which have been mixed either with time delays or via filtering. We first show that a subset of the Hérault-Jutten learning rules fulfills a principle of minimum output power. We then apply this principle to extensions of the Hérault-Jutten network which have delays in the feedback path. Our networks perform well on real speech and music signals that have been mixed using time delays or filtering.

1   INTRODUCTION

Recently, there has been much interest in neural architectures to solve the "blind separation of signals" problem (Hérault & Jutten, 1986) (Vittoz & Arreguit, 1989). The separation is called "blind," because nothing is assumed known about the frequency or phase of the signals.

A concrete example of blind separation of sources is when the pure signals are sounds generated in a room and the mixed signals are the output of some microphones. The mixture process would model the delay of the sound to each microphone, and the mixing of the sounds at each microphone. The inputs to the neural network would be the microphone outputs, and the neural network would try to produce the pure signals.

The mixing process can take on different mathematical forms in different situations. To express these forms, we denote the pure signal i as P_i, the mixed signal i as I_i (which is the ith input to the network), and the output signal i as O_i.

The simplest form to unmix is linear superposition:

$$I_i(t) = P_i(t) + \sum_{j \neq i} M_{ij}(t) P_j(t). \tag{1}$$

730

A more realistic, but more difficult form to unmix is superposition with single delays:

$$I_i(t) = P_i(t) + \sum_{j \neq i} M_{ij}(t) P_j(t - D_{ij}(t)). \tag{2}$$

Finally, a rather general mixing process would be superposition with causal filtering:

$$I_i(t) = P_i(t) + \sum_{j \neq i} \sum_k M_{ijk}(t) P_j(t - \delta_k). \tag{3}$$

Blind separation is interesting for many different reasons. The network must adapt on-line and without a supervisor, which is a challenging type of learning. One could imagine using a blind separation network to clean up an input to a speech understanding system. (Jutten & Hérault, 1991) uses a blind separation network to deskew images. Finally, researchers have implemented blind separation networks using analog VLSI to yield systems which are capable of performing the separation of sources in real time (Vittoz & Arreguit, 1990) (Cohen, et. al., 1992).

1.1   Previous Work

Interest in adaptive systems which perform noise cancellation dates back to the 1960s and 1970s (Widrow, et. al., 1975). The first neural network to unmix on-line a linear superposition of sources was (Hérault & Jutten, 1986). Further work on off-line blind separation was performed by (Cardoso, 1989). Recently, a network to unmix filtered signals was proposed in (Jutten, et. al., 1991), independently of this paper.

2   PRINCIPLE OF MINIMUM OUTPUT POWER

In this section, we apply the mathematics of noise-cancelling networks (Widrow, et. al., 1975) to the network in (Hérault & Jutten, 1986) in order to generalize to new networks that can handle delays in the mixing process.

2.1   Noise-cancellation Networks

A noise-cancellation network tries to purify a signal which is corrupted by filtered noise (Widrow, et. al., 1975). The network has access to the isolated noise signal. The interference equation is

$$I(t) = P(t) + \sum_j M_j N(t - \delta_j). \tag{4}$$

The adaptive filter inverts the interference equation, to yield an output:

$$O(t) = I(t) - \sum_j C_j N(t - \delta_j). \tag{5}$$

The adaptation of a noise-cancellation network relies on an elegant notion: if a signal is impure, it will have a higher power than a pure signal, because the noise power adds to the signal power. The true pure signal has the lowest power. This minimum output power principle is used to determine adaptation laws for noise-cancellation networks. Specifically, at any time t, C_j is adjusted by taking a step that minimizes $O(t)^2$

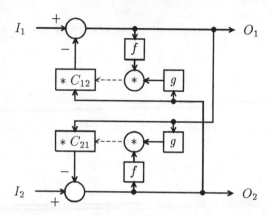

Figure 1: The network described in (Hérault & Jutten, 1986). The dashed arrows represent adaptation.

2.2 The Hérault-Jutten Network

The Hérault-Jutten network (see Figure 1) uses a purely additive model of interference. The interference is modeled by

$$I_i = P_i + \sum_{j \neq i} M_{ij} P_j. \tag{6}$$

Notice the Hérault-Jutten network solves a more general problem than previous noise-cancellation networks: the Hérault-Jutten network has no access to any pure signal.

In (Hérault & Jutten, 1986), the authors also propose inverting the interference model:

$$O_i = I_i - \sum_{j \neq i} C_{ij} O_j. \tag{7}$$

The Hérault-Jutten network can be understood intuitively by assuming that the network has already adapted so that the outputs are the pure signals ($O_j = P_j$). Each connection C_{ij} subtracts just the right amount of the pure signal P_j from the input I_i to yield the pure signal P_i. So, the Hérault-Jutten network will produce pure signals if the $C_{ij} = M_{ij}$.

In (Hérault & Jutten, 1986), the authors propose a very general adaptation rule for the C_{ij}:

$$\Delta C_{ij}(t) = \eta f(O_i(t)) g(O_j(t)). \tag{8}$$

for some non-linear functions f and g. (Sorouchyari, 1991) proves that the network converges for $f(x) = x^3$.

In this paper, we propose that the same elegant minimization principle that governs the noise-cancellation networks can be used to justify a subset of Hérault-Jutten learning algorithms. Let $g(x) = x$ and $f(x)$ be a derivative of some convex function $h(x)$, with a minimum at $x = 0$. In this case, each output of the Hérault-Jutten network *independently* minimizes a function $h(x)$.

A Hérault-Jutten network can be made by setting $h(x) = x^2$. Unfortunately, this network will not converge, because the update rules for two connections C_{ij} and C_{ji} are identical:

$$\Delta C_{ij}(t) = \Delta C_{ji}(t) = O_i(t)O_j(t). \tag{9}$$

Under this condition, the two parameters C_{ij} and C_{ji} will track one another and not converge to the correct answer. Therefore, a non-linear adaptation rule is needed to break the symmetry between the outputs.

The next two sections of the paper describe how the minimum output power principle can be applied to generalizations of the Hérault-Jutten architecture.

3   NETWORK FOR UNMIXING DELAYED SIGNALS

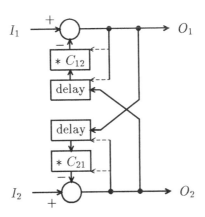

Figure 2:   Our network for unmixing signals mixed with single delays. The adjustable delay in the feedback path avoids the degeneracy in the learning rule. The dashed arrows represent adaptation: the source of the arrow is the source of the error used by gradient descent.

Our new network is an extension of the Hérault-Jutten network (see Figure 2). We assume that the interference is delayed by a certain amount:

$$I_i(t) = P_i(t) + \sum_{i \neq j} M_{ij} P_j(t - D_{ij}(t)). \tag{10}$$

Compare this to equation (6): our network can handle delayed interference, while the Hérault-Jutten network cannot. We introduce an adjustable delay in the feedback path in order to cancel the delay of the interference:

$$O_i(t) = I(t) - \sum_{i \neq j} C_{ij} O_j(t - d_{ij}(t)). \tag{11}$$

We apply the minimum output power principle to adapt the mixing coefficients C_{ij} and the delays d_{ij}:

$$\Delta C_{ij}(t) = \alpha O_i(t) O_j(t - d_{ij}(t)),$$
$$\Delta d_{ij}(t) = -\beta C_{ij}(t) O_i(t) \frac{dO_j}{dt}(t - d_{ij}(t)). \tag{12}$$

By introducing a delay in the feedback, we prevent degeneracy in the learning rule, hence we can use a quadratic power to adjust the coefficients.

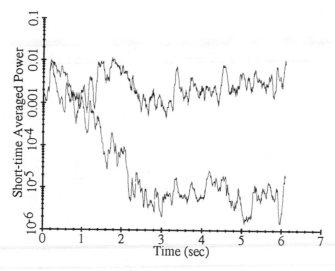

Figure 3: The results of the network applied to a speech/music superposition. These curves are short-time averages of the power of signals. The upper curve shows the power of the pure speech signal. The lower curve shows the power of the difference between the speech output of the network, and the pure speech signal. The gap between the curves is the amount that the network attenuates the interference between the music and speech: the adaptation of the network tries to drive the lower curve to zero. As you can see, the network quickly isolates the pure speech signal.

For a test of our network, we took two signals, one speech and one music, and mixed them together via software to form two new signals: the first being speech plus a delayed, attenuated music; the second being music plus delayed, attenuated speech. Figure 3 shows the results of our network applied to these two signals: the interference was attenuated by approximately 22 dB. One output of the network sounds like speech, with superimposed music which quickly fades away. The other output of the network sounds like music, with a superimposed speech signal which quickly fades away.

Our network can also be extended to more than two sources, like the Hérault-Jutten network. If the network tries to separate S sources, it requires S non-identical inputs. Each output connects to one input, and a delayed version of each of the other outputs, for a total of $2S(S-1)$ adaptive coefficients.

4   NETWORK FOR UNMIXING FILTERED SIGNALS

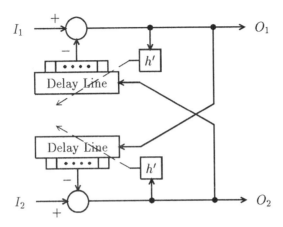

Figure 4:   A network to unmix signals that have been mixed via filtering. The filters in the feedback path are adjusted to independently minimize the power $h(O_i)$ of each output.

For the mixing process that involves filtering,

$$I_i(t) = P_i(t) + \sum_{j \neq i} \sum_k M_{ijk} P_j(t - \delta_k), \tag{13}$$

we put filters in the feedback path of each output:

$$O_i(t) = I_i(t) - \sum_{j \neq i} \sum_k C_{ijk} O_j(t - \delta_k). \tag{14}$$

(Jutten, et. al., 1991) also independently developed this architecture. We can use the principle of minimum output power to develop a learning rule for this architecture:

$$\Delta C_{ijk} = \eta h'(O_i(t)) O_j(t - \delta_k) \tag{15}$$

for some convex function h. (Jutten, et. al., 1991) suggests using an adaptation rule that is equivalent to choosing $h(x) = x^4$.

Interestingly, neither the choice of $h(x) = x^2$ nor $h(x) = x^4$ converges to the correct solution. For both $h(x) = x^2$ and $h(x) = x^4$, if the coefficients start at the correct solution, they stay there. However, if the coefficients start at zero, they converge to a solution that is only roughly correct (see Figure 5). These experiments show

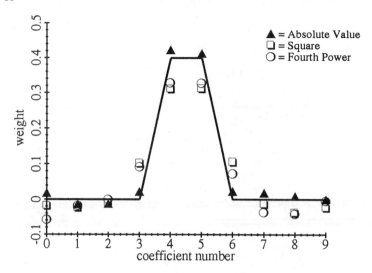

Figure 5: The coefficients for one filter in the feedback path of the network. The weights were initialized to zero. Two different speech/music mixtures were applied to the network. The solid line indicates the correct solution for the coefficients. When minimizing either $h(x) = x^2$ or $h(x) = x^4$, the network converges to an incorrect solution. Minimizing $h(x) = |x|$ seems to work well.

that the learning algorithm has multiple stable states. Experimentally, the spurious stable states seem to perform roughly as well as the true answer.

To account for these multiple stable states, we came up with a conjecture: that the different minimizations performed by each output fought against one another and created the multiple stable states. Optimization theory suggests using an exact penalty method to avoid fighting between multiple terms in a single optimization criteria (Gill, 1981). The exact penalty method minimizes a function $h(x)$ that has a non-zero derivative for x close to 0. We tried a simple exact penalty method of $h(x) = |x|$, and it empirically converged to the correct solution (see Figure 5). The adaptation rule is then

$$\Delta C_{ijk} = \eta \, \text{sgn}(O_i(t)) O_j(t - \delta_k) \qquad (16)$$

In this case, the non-linearity of the adaptation rule seems to be important for the network to converge to the true answer. For a speech/music mixture, we achieved a signal-to-noise ratio of 20 dB using the update rule (16).

5   FUTURE WORK

The networks described in the last two sections were found to converge empirically. In the future, proving conditions for convergence would be useful. There are some known pathological cases which cause these networks not to converge. For example, using white noise as the pure signals for the network in section 3 causes it to fail, because there is no sensible way for the network to change the delays.

More exploration of the choice of optimization function needs to be performed in the future. The work in section 4 is just a first step which illustrates the possible usefulness of the absolute value function.

Another avenue of future work is to try to express the blind separation problem as a global optimization problem, perhaps by trying to minimize the mutual information between the outputs. (Feinstein, Becker, personal communication)

6   CONCLUSIONS

We have found that the minimum output power principle can generate a subset of the Hérault-Jutten network learning rules. We use this principle to adapt extensions of the Hérault-Jutten network, which have delays in the feedback path. These new networks unmix signals which have been mixed with single delays or via filtering.

Acknowledgements

We would like to thank Kannan Parthasarathy for his assistance in some of the experiments. We would also like to thank David Feinstein, Sue Becker, and David Mackay for useful discussions.

References

Cardoso, J. F., (1989) "Blind Identification of Independent Components," *Proceedings of the Workshop on Higher-Order Spectral Analysis*, Vail, Colorado, pp. 157–160, (1989).

Cohen, M. H., Pouliquen, P. O., Andreou, A. G., (1992) "Analog VLSI Implementation of an Auto-Adaptive Network for Real-Time Separation of Independent Signals," *Advances in Neural Information Processing Systems 4*, Morgan-Kaufmann, San Mateo, CA.

Gill, P. E., Murray, W., Wright, M. H., (1981) *Practical Optimization*, Academic Press, London.

Herault, J., Jutten, C., (1986) "Space or Time Adaptive Signal Processing by Neural Network Models," *Neural Networks for Computing*, AIP Conference Proceedings 151, pp. 207–211, Snowbird, Utah.

Jutten, C., Thi, L. N., Dijkstra, E., Vittoz, E., Caelen, J., (1991) "Blind Separation of Sources: an Algorithm for Separation of Convolutive Mixtures," *Proc. Intl. Workshop on High Order Statistics*, Chamrousse France, July 1991.

Jutten, C., Herault, J., (1991) "Blind Separation of Sources, part I: An Adaptive Algorithm Based on Neuromimetic Architecture," *Signal Processing*, vol. 24, pp. 1–10.

Sorouchyari, E., (1991) "Blind Separation of Sources, Part III: Stability analysis," *Signal Processing*, vol. 24, pp. 21–29.

Vittoz, E. A., Arreguit, X., (1989) "CMOS Integration of Herault-Jutten Cells for Separation of Sources," *Proc. Workshop on Analog VLSI and Neural Systems*, Portland, Oregon, May 1989.

Widrow, B., Glover, J., McCool, J., Kaunitz, J., Williams, C., Hearn, R., Zeidler, J., Dong, E., Goodlin, R., (1975) "Adaptive Noise Cancelling: Principles and Applications," *Proc. IEEE*, vol. 63, no. 12, pp. 1692–1716.

PART XI

IMPLEMENTATION

CCD Neural Network Processors for Pattern Recognition

Alice M. Chiang   Michael L. Chuang   Jeffrey R. LaFranchise

MIT Lincoln Laboratory
244 Wood Street
Lexington, MA 02173

Abstract

A CCD-based processor that we call the NNC2 is presented. The NNC2 implements a fully connected 192-input, 32-output two-layer network and can be cascaded to form multilayer networks or used in parallel for additional input or output nodes. The device computes 1.92×10^9 connections/sec when clocked at 10 MHz. Network weights can be specified to six bits of accuracy and are stored on-chip in programmable digital memories. A neural network pattern recognition system using NNC2 and CCD image feature extractor (IFE) devices is described. Additionally, we report a CCD output circuit that exploits inherent nonlinearities in the charge injection process to realize an adjustable-threshold sigmoid in a chip area of $40 \times 80 \ \mu\text{m}^2$.

1 INTRODUCTION

A neural network chip based on charge-coupled device (CCD) technology, the NNC2, is presented. The NNC2 implements a fully connected two-layer net and can be cascaded to form multilayer networks. An image feature extractor (IFE) device (Chiang and Chuang, 1991) is briefly reviewed. The IFE is suited for neural networks with local connections and shared weights and can also be used for image preprocessing tasks. A neural network pattern recognition system based on feature extraction using IFEs and classification using NNC2s is proposed. The efficacy of neural networks with local connections and shared weights for feature extraction in character recognition and phoneme recognition tasks has been demonstrated by researchers such as (LeCun *et. al.* 1989) and (Waibel *et. al.*, 1989), respectively. More complex recognition tasks are likely to prove amenable to a system using locally connected networks as a front end with outputs generated by a highly-connected classifier. Both the IFE and the NNC2 are hybrids composed of analog and digital components. Network weights are stored digitally while neuron states and computation results are represented in analog form. Data enter and leave the devices in digital form for ease of integration into digital systems.

The sigmoid is used in many network models as the nonlinear neuron output function. We have designed, fabricated and tested a compact CCD sigmoidal output circuit that is described below. The paper concludes with a discussion of strategies for implementing networks with particularly high or low fan-in to fan-out ratios.

2   THE NNC2 AND IFE DEVICES

The NNC2 is a neural network processor that implements a fully connected two-layer net with 192 input nodes and 32 output nodes. The device is an expanded version of a previous neural network classifier (NNC) chip (Chiang, 1990) hence the appellation "NNC2." The NNC2 consists of a 192-stage CCD tapped delay line for holding and shifting input values, 192 four-quadrant multipliers, and 192 32-word local memories for weight storage. When clocked at 10 MHz, the NNC2 performs 1.92×10^9 connections/sec. The device was fabricated using a 2-μm minimum feature size double-metal, double-polysilicon CCD/CMOS process. The NNC2 measures 8.8×9.2 mm^2 and is depicted in Figure 1.

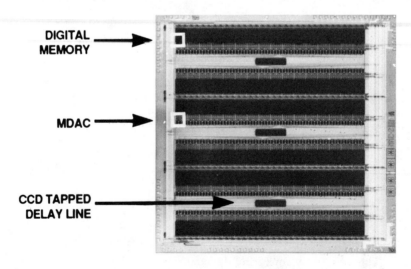

Figure 1: Photomicrograph of the NNC2

Tests indicate that the NNC2 has an output dynamic range exceeding 42 dB. Figure 2 shows the output of the NNC2 when the input consists of the cosine waveforms $f_n = 0.2cos(2\pi 2n/192) + 0.4cos(2\pi 3n/192)$ and the weights are set to

$cos(2\pi nk/192)$, $k = \pm1, \pm2, ..., \pm16$. Due to the orthogonality of sinusoids of different frequencies, the output correlations $g_k = \sum_{n=0}^{191} f_n cos(2\pi nk/192)$ should yield scaled impulses with amplitudes of ±0.2 and ±0.4 for $k = \pm2$ and ±3 only; this is indeed the case as the output (lower trace) in Figure 2 shows. This test demonstrates the linearity of the weighted sum (inner product) computed by the NNC2.

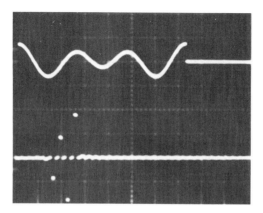

Figure 2: Response of the NNC2 to input cosine waveforms

Locally connected, shared weight networks can be implemented using the IFE which raster scans up to 20 sets of 7×7 weights over an input image. At every window position the inner product of the windowed pixels and each of the 20 sets of weights is computed. For additonal details, see (Chiang and Chuang, 1991). The IFE and the NNC2 share a number of common features that are described below.

2.1   MDACS

The multiplications of the inner product are performed in parallel by multiplying-D/A-converters (MDACs), of which there are 192 in the NNC2 and 49 in the IFE. Each MDAC produces a charge packet proportional to the product of an input and a digital weight. The partial products are summed on an output line common to all the MDACs, yielding a complete inner product every clock cycle. The design and operation of an MDAC are described in detail in (Chiang, 1990). Using a 2-μm design rule, a four-quadrant MDAC with 8-bit weights occupies an area of 200×200 μm^2.

2.2   WEIGHT STORAGE

The NNC2 and IFE feature on-chip digital storage of programmable network weights, specified to 6 and 8 bits, respectively. The NNC2 contains 192 local memories of 32 words each, while the IFE has forty-nine 20-word memories. Individual words can be addressed by means of a row pointer and a column pointer. Each bit of the CCD shift register memories is equipped with a feedback enable switch that obviates the need to refresh the volatile CCD storage medium explicitly; words are rewritten as they are read for use in computation, so that no cycles need be devoted to memory refresh.

2.3   INPUT BUFFER

Inputs to the NNC2 are held in a 192-stage CCD analog floating-gate tapped delay line. At each stage the floating gate is coupled to the input of the corresponding MDAC, permitting inputs to be sensed nondestructively for computation. The NNC2 delay line is composed of three 64-stage subsections (see Figure 1). This partionning allows the NNC2 to compute either the weighted sum of 192 inputs or three 64-point inner products. The latter capability is well-matched to Time-Delay Neural Networks (TDNNs) that implement a moving temporal window for phoneme recognition (Waibel *et. al.*, 1989). The IFE contains a similar 775-stage delay line that holds six lines of a 128-pixel input image plus an additional seven pixels. Taps are placed on the first seven of every 128 stages in the IFE delay line so that the 1-dimensional line emulates a 2-dimensional window.

3   CCD SIGMOIDAL OUTPUT CIRCUIT

A sigmoidal charge-domain nonlinear detection circuit is shown in Figure 3. The circuit has a programmable input-threshold controlled by the amplitude of the transfer gate voltage, V_{TG}. If the incoming signal charge is below the threshold set by V_{TG} no charge is transferred to the output port and the incoming signal is ignored. If the input is above threshold, the amount of charge transferred to the output port is the difference between the charge input and the threshold level. The circuit design is based on the ability to calculate the charge transfer efficiency from an n^+ diffusion region over a bias gate to a receiving well as a function of device parameters and exploits the fact that under certain operating conditions a nonlinear dependence exists between the input and output charge (Thornber, 1971). The maximum output produced can be bounded by the size and gate voltage of the receiving well. The predicted and measured responses of the circuit for two different threshold levels are shown in the bottom of Figure 3. The circuit has an area of $40 \times 80 \ \mu m^2$ and can be integrated with the NNC2 or IFE chips to perform both the weighted-sum and output-nonlinearity computations on a single device.

4   DESIGN STRATEGIES

The NNC2 uses a time-multiplexed output (TMO) structure (Figure 4a), where the number of multipliers and the number of local memories is equal to the number of inputs, N. The depth of each local memory is equal to the number of output nodes, M, and the outputs are computed serially as each set of weights is read in sequence from the memories. A 256-input, 256-output device with 64k 8-bit weights has been designed and can be realized in a chip area of $14 \times 14 \ mm^2$. This chip is reconfigurable so that a single such device can be used to implement multilayer networks. If a network with a large (>1000) number of input nodes is required, then a time-multiplexed input (TMI) architecture with M multipliers may be more suitable (Figure 4b). In contrast to a TMO system that computes the M inner products

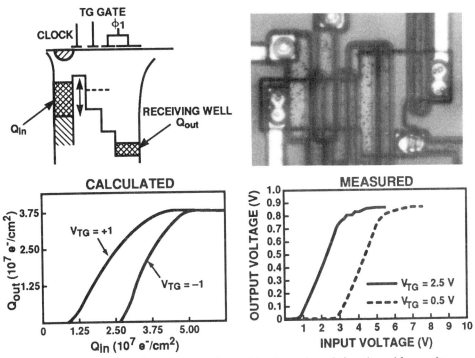

Figure 3: Schematic, micrograph, and test results of the sigmoid circuit

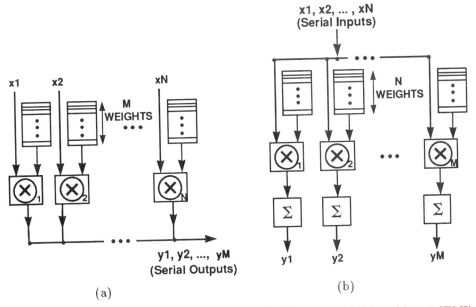

Figure 4: (a) Time-multiplexed output (TMO), (b) Time-multiplexed input (TMI)

sequentially (the multiplications of each inner product are performed in parallel), a TMI structure performs N sets of M multiplications each (all M inner products are serially computed in parallel). As each input element arrives it is broadcast to all M multipliers. Each multiplier multiplies the input by an appropriate weight from its N-word deep local memory and places the result in an accumulator. The M inner products appear in the accumulators one cycle after receipt of the final, N^{th} input.

5 SUMMARY

We have presented the NNC2, a CCD chip that implements a fully connected two-layer network at the rate of 1.92×10^9 connections/second. The NNC2 may be used in concert with IFE devices to form a CCD-based neural network pattern recogniton system or as a co-processor to speed up neural network simulations on conventional computers. A VME-bus board for the NNC2 is presently being constructed. A compact CCD circuit that generates a sigmoidal output function was described, and finally, the relative merits of time-multiplexing input or output nodes in neural network devices were enumerated. Table 1 below is a comparison of recent neural network chips.

	MIT LINCOLN LAB NNC2	CIT NN	INTEL ETANN	MITSUBISHI NN	AT&T NN	HITACHI WSINN	ADAPT. SOL. X1
No. OF OUTPUT NODES	32	256	TWO 64	168	16 (or 256)	576	64
No. OF INPUT NODES	192	256	TWO 64	168	256 (or 16)	64	4 k
SYNAPSE ACCURACY	6 b × ANALOG	1 b × ANALOG	ANALOG × ANALOG	ANALOG × ANALOG	3 b × 6 b	8 b × 9 b	9 b × 16 b
PROGRAMMABLE SYNAPSES	6 k	64 k	10 k	28 k	4 k	37 k	256 k
THROUGHPUT RATE (10^9 Connections/s)	1.92	0.5	2	?	5.1	1.2	1.6
CHIP AREA (mm²)	8.8 × 9.2	?	11.2 × 7.5	14.5 × 14.5	4.5 × 7	125 × 125	26.2 × 27.5
CLOCK RATE	10 MHz	1.5 MHz	400 kHz	?	20 MHz	2.1 MHz[a]	25 MHz
WEIGHT STORAGE	DIGITAL[b]	ANALOG	ANALOG	ANALOG	ANALOG	DIGITAL	DIGITAL
ON CHIP LEARNING	NO	NO	NO	YES[c]	NO	NO	YES
DESIGN RULE	2 µm CCD/CMOS	2 µm CCD	1 µm CMOS	1 µm CMOS	0.9 µm CMOS	0.8 µm CMOS	0.8 µm CMOS
REPORTED AT:	NIPS 91	IJCNN 90	IJCNN 89	ISSCC 91	ISSCC 91	IJCNN 90	ISSCC 91

NOTE:
a - CLOCK RATE FOR WSINN IS EXTRAPOLATED BASED ON 1/STEP TIME.
b - NO DEGRADATION OBSERVED ON DIGITALLY STORED AND REFRESHED WEIGHTS.
c - A SIMPLIFIED BOLTZMANN MACHINE LEARNING ALGORITHM IS USED.

Table 1: Selected neural network chips

Acknowledgements

This work was supported by DARPA, the Office of Naval Research, and the Department of the Air Force. The IFE and NNC2 were fabricated by Orbit Semiconductor.

References

A. J. Agranat, C. F. Neugebauer and A. Yariv, "A CCD Based Neural Network Integrated Circuit with 64k Analog Programmable Synapses," *IJCNN, 1990 Proceedings*, pp. II-551-II-555.

Y. Arima *et. al.*, "A 336-Neuron 28-k Synapse Self-Learning Neural Network Chip with branch-Neuron-Unit Architecture," in *ISSCC Dig. of Tech. Papers*, pp. 182-183, Feb. 1991.

B. E. Boser and E. Säckinger, "An Analog Neural Network Processor with Programmable Network Topology," in *ISSCC Dig. of Tech. Papers*, pp. 184-185, Feb. 1991.

A. M. Chiang, "A CCD Programmable Signal Processor," *IEEE Jour. Solid-State Circ.*, vol. 25, no. 6, pp. 1510-1517, Dec. 1990.

A. M. Chiang and M. L. Chuang, "A CCD Programmable Image Processor and its Neural Network Applications," *IEEE Jour. Solid-State Circ.*, vol. 26, no. 12, pp. 1894-1901, Dec. 1991.

D. Hammerstrom, "A VLSI Architecture for High-Performance, Low-Cost On-chip Learning," *IJCNN, 1990 Proceedings*, pp. II-537-II-543.

M. Holler *et. al.*, "An Electrically Trainable Artificial Neural Network (ETANN) with 10240 "Floating Gate" Synapses," *IJCNN, 1989 Proceedings*, pp. II-191-II-196.

Y. Le Cun *et. al.*, "Handwritten Digit Recognition with a Back-Propagation Network," in D. S. Touretzky (ed.), *Advances in Neural Information Processing Systems 2*, pp. 396-404, San Mateo, CA: Morgan Kaufmann, 1989.

K. K. Thornber, "Incomplete Charge Transfer in IGFET Bucket-Brigade Shift Registers," *IEEE Trans. Elect. Dev.*, vol. ED-18, no. 10, pp.941-950, 1971.

A. Waibel *et. al.*, "Phoneme Recognition Using Time-Delay Neural Networks," *IEEE Trans. on Acoust., Speech, Sig. Proc.*, vol. 37, no. 3, pp. 329-339, March 1989.

M. Yasunaga *et. al.*, "Design, Fabrication and Evaluation of a 5-Inch Wafer Scale Neural Network LSI Composed of 576 Digital Neurons," *IJCNN, 1990 Proceedings*, pp. II-527-II-535.

A Parallel Analog CCD/CMOS Signal Processor

Charles F. Neugebauer   **Amnon Yariv**
Department of Applied Physics
California Institute of Technology
Pasadena, CA 91125

Abstract

A CCD based signal processing IC that computes a fully parallel single
quadrant vector-matrix multiplication has been designed and fabricated with a
2µm CCD/CMOS process. The device incorporates an array of Charge
Coupled Devices (CCD) which hold an analog matrix of charge encoding the
matrix elements. Input vectors are digital with 1 - 8 bit accuracy.

1 INTRODUCTION

Vector-matrix multiplication (VMM) is often used in neural network theories to describe
the aggregation of signals by neurons. An input vector encoding the activation levels of
input neurons is multiplied by a matrix encoding the synaptic connection strengths to
create an output vector. The analog VLSI architecture presented here has been devised to
perform the vector-matrix multiplication using CCD technology. The architecture
calculates a VMM in one clock cycle, an improvement over previous semiparallel devices
(Agranat et al., 1988), (Chiang, 1990). This architecture is also useful for general signal
processing applications where moderate resolution is required, such as image processing.

As most neural models have robust behavior in the presence of noise and inaccuracies,
analog VLSI offers the potential for highly compact neural circuitry. Analog
multiplication circuitry can be made much smaller than its digital equivalent, offering
substantial savings in power and IC size at the expense of limited accuracy and
programmability. Digital I/O, however, is desirable as it allows the use of standard
memory and control circuits at the system level. The device presented here has digital
input and analog output and elucidates all relevant performance characteristics including

748

accuracy, speed, power dissipation and charge retention of the VMM. In practice, on-chip charge domain A/D converters are used for converting analog output signals to facilitate digital communication with off-chip devices.

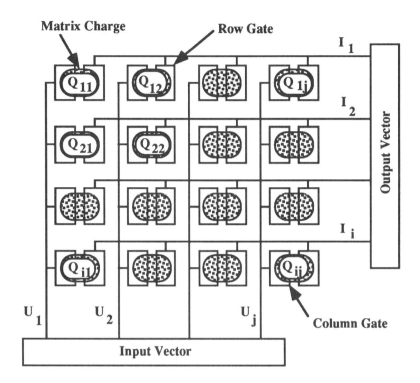

Figure 1: Simplified Schematic of CID Vector Matrix Multiplier

2 ARCHITECTURE DESCRIPTION

The vector-matrix multiplier consists of a matrix of CCD cells that resemble Charge Injection Device (CID) imager pixels in that one of the cell's gates is connected vertically from cell to cell forming a column electrode while another gate is connected horizontally forming a row electrode. The charge stored beneath the row and column gates encodes the matrix. A simplified schematic in Figure 1 shows the array organization.

2.1 BINARY VECTOR MATRIX MULTIPLICATION

In its most basic configuration, the VMM circuit computes the product of a binary input vector, U_j, and an analog matrix of charge. The computation done by each CID cell in the matrix is a multiply-accumulate in which the charge, Q_{ij}, is multiplied by a binary input vector element, U_j, encoded on the column line and this product is summed with other products in the same row to form the vector product, I_i, on the row lines. Multiplication by a binary number is equivalent to adding or not adding the charge at a particular matrix element to its associated row line.

The matrix element operation is shown in Figure 2 which displays a cross-section of one of the rows with the associated potential wells at different times in the computation.

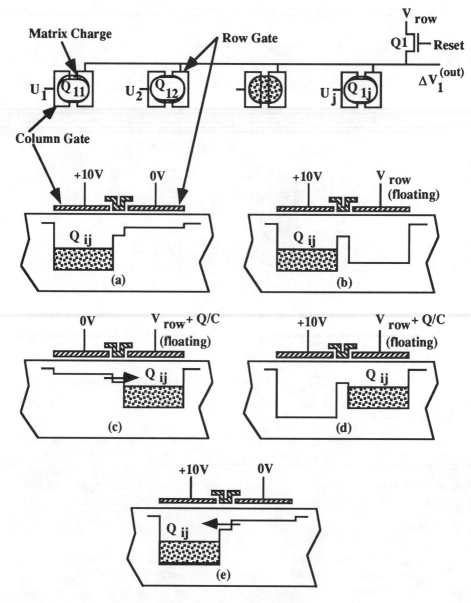

Figure 2: CID Cell Operation

In the initial state, prior to the VMM computation, the matrix of charges Q_{ij} is moved beneath the column electrodes by placing a positive voltage on all column lines, shown in Figure 2(a). A positive voltage creates a deep potential well for electrons. At this point, the row lines are reset to a reference voltage, V_{row}, by FETs Q1 and then disconnected from the voltage source, shown in Figure 2(b). The computation occurs when the column lines are pulsed to a negative voltage corresponding to the input vector U_j, shown in Figure 2(c). The binary U_j is represented by a negative pulse on the jth column line if the element U_j is a binary 1, otherwise the column line is kept at the positive voltage. This causes the charges in the columns that correspond to binary 1's in the input vector to be transferred to their respective row electrodes which thus experience a voltage change given by

$$\Delta V_i = \sum_{j=0}^{N-1} \frac{Q_{ij}U_j}{C_{row}}$$

where N is the number of elements in the input vector and C_{row} is the total capacitance of the row electrode. Once the charge has been transferred, the column lines are reset to their original positive voltages[1], resulting in the potential diagram in Figure 2(d). The voltage changes on the row lines are then sampled and the matrix of charges are returned to the column electrodes in preparation for the next VMM by pulsing the row electrodes negative as in Figure 2(e). In this manner, a complete binary vector is multiplied by an analog matrix of charge in one CCD clock cycle.

3 DESIGN AND OPERATION

The implementation of this architecture contains facilities for electronic loading of the matrix. Originally proposed as an optically loaded device (Agranat et al., 1988), the electronically loaded version has proven more reliable and consistent.

3.1 LOADING THE CCD ARRAY WITH MATRIX ELEMENTS

The CCD matrix elements described above can be modified to operate as standard four phase CCD shift registers by simply adding another gate. The matrix cell is shown in Figure 3. The fabricated single quadrant cell size is 24μm by 24μm using a 2μm minimum feature size CCD/CMOS process. More aggressive design rules in the same process can reduce this to 20μm by 20μm. These cells, when abutted with each other in a row, form a horizontal shift register which is used to load the matrix. Electronic loading of the matrix is accomplished in a fashion similar to CCD imagers. A fast CCD shift register running vertically is added along one side of the matrix which is loaded with one column of matrix charges from a single external analog data source. Once the fast shift register is loaded, it is transferred into the array by clocking the matrix electrodes to act as an array of horizontal shift registers, shown in Figure 3(a). This process is repeated until the entire matrix has been filled with charge.

---

[1]Returning the column lines to their original voltage levels has the effect of canceling the effect of stray capacitive coupling between the row and column lines, since the net column voltage change is zero.

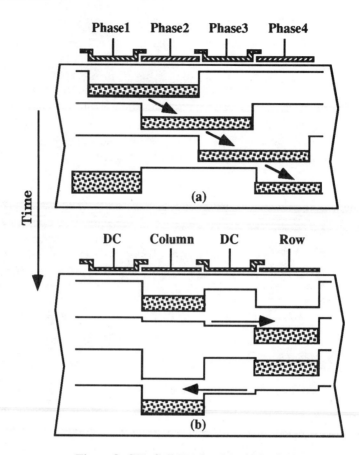

Figure 3: CID Cell Used to Load Matrix

When the matrix has been loaded, the charge can be used for computation with two of the four gates at each matrix cell kept at constant potentials, shown in Figure 3(b). The computation process moves the charge repeatedly between two electrodes. Incomplete charge transfer, a problem with our previous architecture (Agranat et al., 1990), does not degrade performance since any charge left behind under the column gates during computation is picked up on the next cycle, shown in Figure 2(e). Only dark current generation degrades the matrix charges during VMM, causing them to increase nonuniformly. In order to limit the effects of dark current generation on the matrix precision, the matrix charge must be refreshed periodically.

3.2 FLOATING GATE ROW AMPLIFIERS

In order to achieve better linearity when sensing charge, a floating gate amplifier is often used in CCD circuits. In the scheme described above, the induced voltage change of the row electrode significantly modifies its parasitic capacitance, resulting in a nonlinear voltage versus charge characteristic. To alleviate this problem, an operational amplifier with a capacitor in the feedback loop is added to each row line, shown in Figure 4. When charge is moved underneath the row line in the course of a VMM operation, the row voltage is kept constant by the action of the op-amp with an output voltage given by

$$\Delta V_i = \sum_{j=0}^{N-1} \frac{Q_{ij}U_j}{C_f}$$

where C_f is the feedback capacitance.

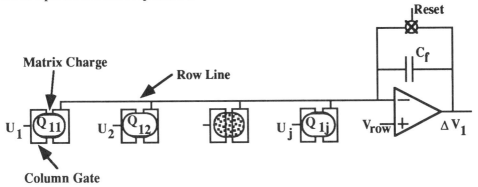

Figure 4: Linear Charge Sensing

The feedback capacitor is a poly-poly structure with vastly improved linearity compared to the row capacitance. This enhancement also has the effect of speeding the row line summation due to the well known benefits of current mode transmission. In addition, the possibility of digitally selecting a feedback capacitor value by switching power-of-two sized capacitors into the feedback loops creates a practical means of controlling the gain of the output amplifiers, with the potential for significantly extending the dynamic range of the device.

3.3 DIGITAL INPUT BUFFER AND DIVIDE-BY-TWO CIRCUITRY

Many applications such as image processing require multilevel input capability. This can easily be implemented by using the VMM circuitry in a bit-serial mode. The operation of the device is identical to the structure described above except that processing n-bit input precision requires n cycles of the device. Digital shift registers are added to each input column line that sequentially present the column lines with successively more significant bits of the input vector, shown in Figure 5. Using the notation $U_j^{(n-1)}$, which represents the binary vector formed by taking the nth bits of all the input elements, the first VMM done by the circuit is given by

$$\Delta V_i^{(0)} = \sum_{j=0}^{N-1} \frac{Q_{ij}U_j^{(0)}}{C_f}$$

where $\Delta V_i^{(0)}$ is the output vector represented as voltage changes on the row lines. The row voltages are stored on large capacitors, C1, which are allowed to share charge with another set of equally sized capacitors, C2, effectively dividing the output vector by two.

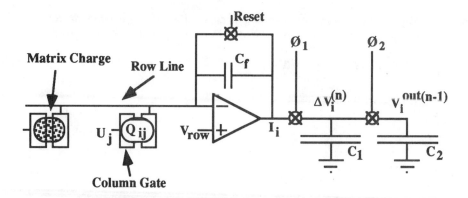

Figure 5: Switched Capacitor Divide-By-Two Circuit

The next most significant bit input vector, $U_j^{(1)}$, is then multiplied and creates another set of row voltage changes which are stored and shared to add another charge to the previously divided charge giving

$$V_i^{out\ (1)} = \sum_{j=0}^{N-1} \frac{Q_{ij}U_j^{(1)}}{C_f} + \frac{1}{2}\sum_{j=0}^{N-1} \frac{Q_{ij}U_j^{(0)}}{C_f}$$

where $V_i^{out(1)}$ is the voltage on C2 after two clock cycles. The process is repeated n times, effectively weighting each successive bit's data by the proper power of two factor giving a total output voltage of

$$V_i^{out\ (n-1)} = \frac{1}{C_f}\left(\sum_{j=0}^{N-1} Q_{ij}\left(\sum_{k=1}^{n} 2^{k-n}U_i^{(n-1)}\right)\right) = \frac{1}{C_f}\sum_{j=0}^{N-1} Q_{ij}D_j$$

after n clock cycles where D_j now represents the multivalued digital input vector. In this manner, multivalued input of n-bit precision can be processed where n is only limited by the analog accuracy of the components[2].

4 EXPERIMENTAL RESULTS

A number of VMM circuits have been fabricated implementing the architecture described above in a 2μm double-poly CCD/CMOS process. The largest circuit contains a 128x128 array of matrix elements. The matrix is loaded electronically through a single pin using the CCD shift register mode of the CID cell, shown in Figure 3. Matrix element mismatches due to threshold variations are avoided since all matrix elements are created by the same set of electrodes.

A list of relevant system characteristics is given in Table 1. The matrix of charge is

---

[2] If 4-bit input is required the device is simply clocked four times. Since the power of two scaling is divisive, the most significant bit is always given the same weighting regardless of the input word length.

loaded in 4ms and needs to be refreshed every 20ms to retain acceptable weight accuracy at room temperature, giving a refresh overhead of 20%. A simple linear filter bank was loaded with a sinusoidal matrix and multiplied with a slowly chirped input signal to determine the linearity and noise limits.

Table1: Experimental Results

Charge Transfer Efficiency	0.99995
Cell Size	24μm x 24μm
Bit Rate	4 MHz
Refresh Time	4ms
Noise Limits	7 bits
Linearity	5 bits
Power Consumption	
(excluding output drivers)	<100mW
Connections Per Second	
(binary input vectors)	6.4×10^{10}

5 SUMMARY

A CCD based vector matrix multiplication scheme has been developed that offers high speed and low power in addition to provisions for digital I/O. Intended for neural network and image processing applications, the architecture is intended to integrate well into digital environments.

Acknowledgements

This work was supported by a grant from the U.S. Army Center for Signals Warfare.

References

A. Agranat, C. F. Neugebauer and A. Yariv. (1988) Parallel Optoelectronic Realization of Neural Network Models Using CID Technology. *Applied Optics 27* :4354-4355.

A. Agranat, C. F. Neugebauer, R.D. Nelson and A. Yariv. (1990) The CCD Neural Processor: A Neural Integrated Circuit with 65,536 Programmable Analog Synapses. *IEEE Trans. on Circuits and Systems 37* :1073-1075.

A. M. Chiang. (1990) A CCD Programmable Signal Processor. *IEEE Journal of Solid State Circuits 25* :1510-1517.

Direction Selective Silicon Retina that uses Null Inhibition

Ronald G. Benson and Tobi Delbrück
Computation and Neural Systems Program, 139-74
California Institute of Technology
Pasadena CA 91125
email: benson@cns.caltech.edu and tdelbruck@caltech.edu

Abstract

Biological retinas extract spatial and temporal features in an attempt to reduce the complexity of performing visual tasks. We have built and tested a silicon retina which encodes several useful temporal features found in vertebrate retinas. The cells in our silicon retina are selective to direction, highly sensitive to positive contrast changes around an ambient light level, and tuned to a particular velocity. Inhibitory connections in the null direction perform the direction selectivity we desire. This silicon retina is on a $4.6 \times 6.8mm$ die and consists of a 47×41 array of photoreceptors.

1 INTRODUCTION

The ability to sense motion in the visual world is essential to survival in animals. Visual motion processing is indispensable; it tells us about predators and prey, our own motion and image stablization on the retina. Many algorithms for performing early visual motion processing have been proposed [HK87] [Nak85]. A key salient feature of motion is direction selectivity, *ie* the ability to detect the direction of moving features. We have implemented Barlow and Levick's model, [BHL64], which hypothesizes inhibition in the null direction to accomplish direction selectivity.

In contrast to our work, Boahen, [BA91], in these proceedings, describes a silicon retina that is specialized to do spatial filtering of the image. Mahowald, [Mah91], describes a silicon retina that has surround interactions and adapts over mulitple time scales. Her silicon retina is designed to act as an analog preprocessor and

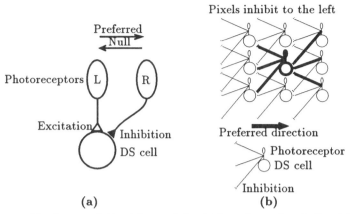

Figure 1: Barlow and Levick model of direction selectivity (DS). (a) Shows how two cells are connected in an inhibitory fashion and (b) a mosaic of such cells.

so the gain of the output stage is rather low. In addition there is no rectification into on- and off-pathways. This and earlier work on silicon early vision systems have stressed spatial processing performed by biological retinas at the expense of temporal processing.

The work we describe here and the work described by Delbrück, [DM91], emphasizes temporal processing. Temporal differentiation and separation of intensity changes into on- and off-pathways are important computations performed by vertebrate retinas. Additionally, specialized vertebrate retinas, [BHL64], have cells which are sensitive to moving stimuli and respond maximally to a preferred direction; they have almost zero response in the opposite or null direction. We have designed and tested a silicon retina that models these direction selective velocity tuned cells. These receptors excite cells which respond to positive contrast changes only and are selective for a particular direction of stimuli. Our silicon retina may be useful as a preprocessor for later visual processing and certainly as an enhancement for the already existing spatial retinas. It is a striking demonstration of the perceptual saliency of contrast changes and directed motion in the visual world.

2   INHIBITION IN THE NULL DIRECTION

Barlow and Levick, [BHL64], described a mechanism for direction selectivity found in the rabbit retina which postulates inhibitory connections to achieve the desired direction selectivity. Their model is shown in Figure 1(a) . As a moving edge passes over the photoreceptors from left to right, the left photoreceptor is excited first, causing its direction selective (DS) cell to fire. The right photoreceptor fires when the edge reaches it and since it has an inhibitory connection to the left DS cell, the right photoreceptor retards further output from the left DS cell. If an edge is moving in the opposite or null direction (right to left), the activity evoked in the right photoreceptor completely inhibits the left DS cell from firing, thus creating a direction selective cell.

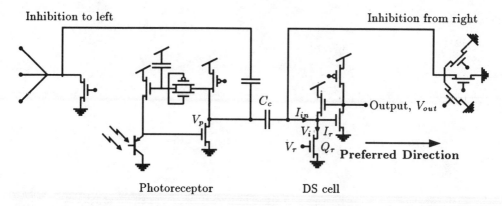

Inhibition to left   Inhibition from right

Photoreceptor   DS cell

Figure 2: Photoreceptor and direction selective (DS) cell. The output of the high-gain, adaptive photoreceptor is fed capacitively to the input of the DS cell. The output of the photoreceptor sends inhibition to the left. Inhibition from the right photoreceptors connect to the input of the DS cell.

In the above explanation with the edge moving in the preferred direction (left to right), as the edge moves faster, the inhibition from leading photoreceptors truncates the output of the DS cell ever sooner. In fact, it is this inhibitory connection which leads to velocity tuning in the preferred direction.

By tiling these cells as shown in Figure 1(b), it is possible to obtain an array of directionally tuned cells. This is the architecture we used in our chip. Direction selectivity is inherent in the connections of the mosaic, *ie* the hardwiring of the inhibitory connections leads to directionally tuned cells.

3   PIXEL OPERATION

A pixel consists of a photoreceptor, a direction selective (DS) cell and inhibition to and from other pixels as shown in Figure 2. The photoreceptor has high-gain and is adaptive [Mah91, DM91]. The output from this receptor, V_p, is coupled into the DS cell which acts as a rectifying gain element, [MS91], that is only sensitive to positive-going transitions due to increases in light intensity at the receptor input. Additionally, the output from the photoreceptor is capacitively coupled to the inhibitory synapses which send their inhibition to the left and are coupled into the DS cell of the neighboring cells.

A more detailed analysis of the DS cell yields several insights into this cell's functionality. A step increase of ΔV at V_p, caused by a step increase in light intensity incident upon the phototransistor, results in a charge injection of $C_c\Delta V$ at V_i. This charge is leaked away by Q_τ at a rate I_τ, set by voltage V_τ. Hence, to first order, the output pulse width T is simply

$$T = \frac{C_c\Delta V}{I_\tau}.$$

There is also a threshold minimum step input size that will result in enough change

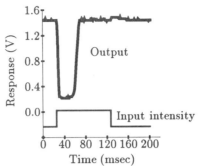

Figure 3: Pixel response to intensity step. Bottom trace is intensity; top trace is pixel output.

in V_i to pull V_{out} all the way to ground. This threshold is set by C_c and the gain of the photoreceptor.

When the input to the rectifying gain element is not a step, but instead a steady increase in voltage, the current I_{in} flowing into node V_i is

$$I_{\text{in}} = C_c \dot{V}_p.$$

When this current exceeds I_τ there is a net increase in the voltage V_i, and the output V_{out} will quickly go low. The condition $I_{\text{in}} = I_\tau$ defines the threshold limit for stimuli detection, *i.e.* input stimuli resulting in an $I_{\text{in}} < I_\tau$ are not perceptible to the pixel. For a changing intensity $\dot{I}$, the adaptive photoreceptor stage outputs a voltage V_p proportional to $\dot{I}/I$, where I is the input light intensity. This photoreceptor behavior means that the pixel threshold will occur at whatever $\dot{I}/I$ causes $C_c\dot{V}_p$ to exceed the constant current I_τ.

The inhibitory synapses (shown as Inhibition from right in Figure 2) provide additional leakage from V_i resulting in a shortened response width from the DS cell.

This analysis suggests that a characterization of the pixel should investigate both the response amplitude, measured as pulse width versus input intensity step size, and the response threshold, measured with temporal intensity contrast. In the next section we show such measurements.

4   CHARACTERIZATION OF THE PIXEL

We have tested both an isolated pixel and a complete 2-dimensional retina of 47×41 pixels. Both circuits were fabricated in a 2μm p-well CMOS double poly process available through the MOSIS facility. The retina is scanned out onto a monitor using a completely integrated on-chip scanner[MD91]. The only external components are a video amplifier and a crystal.

We show a typical response of the isolated pixel to an input step of intensity in Figure 3. In response to the input step increase of intensity, the pixel output goes low and saturates for a time set by the bias V_τ in Figure 2. Eventually the pixel recovers and the output returns to its quiescent level. In response to the step decrease of intensity there is almost no response as seen in Figure 3.

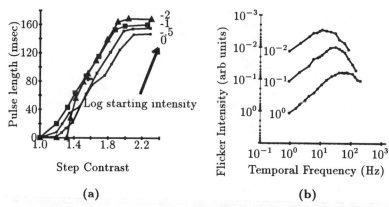

Figure 4: (a) Pulse width of response as function of input contrast step size. The abscissa is measured in units of ratio-intensity, i.e., a value of 1 means no intensity step, a value of 1.1 means a step from a normalized intensity of 1 to a normalized intensity of 1.1, and so forth. The different curves show the response at different absolute light levels; the number in the figure legend is the log of the absolute intensity. **(b) Receptor threshold measurements.** At each temporal frequency, we determined the minimum necessary amplitude of triangular intensity variations to make the pixel respond. The different curves were taken at different background intensity levels, shown to the left of each curve. For example, the bottom curve was taken at a background level of 1 unit of intensity; at 8 Hz, the threshold occurred at a variation of 0.2 units of intensity.

The output from the pixel is essentially quantized in amplitude, but the resulting pulse has a finite duration related to the input intensity step. The analysis in Section 3 showed that the output pulse width, T, should be linear in the input intensity contrast step. In Figure 4(a), we show the measured pulse-width as a function of input contrast step. To show the adaptive nature of the receptor, we did this same measurement at several different absolute intensity levels.

Our silicon retina sees some features of a moving image and not others. Detection of a moving feature depends on its contrast and velocity. To characterize this behavior, we measured a receptor's thresholds for intensity variations, as a function of temporal frequency.

These measurements are shown in Figure 4(b); the curves define "zones of visibility"; if stimuli lie below a curve, they are visible, if they fall above a curve they are not. (The different curves are for different absolute intensity levels.) For low temporal frequencies stimuli are visible only if they are high contrast; at higher temporal frequencies, but still below the photoreceptor cutoff frequency, lower contrast stimuli are visible. Simply put, if the input image has low contrast and is slowly moving, it is not seen. Only high contrast or quickly moving features are salient stimuli. More precisely, for temporal frequencies below the photoreceptor cutoff frequency, the threshold occurs at a constant value of the temporal intensity contrast $\dot{I}/I$.

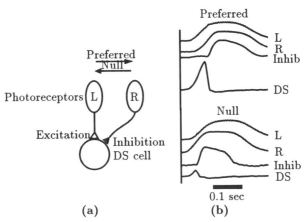

Figure 5: (a) shows the basic connectivity of the tested cell. (b) top trace is the response due to an edge moving in the preferred direction (left to right). (b) bottom trace is the response due to an edged moving in the null direction (right to left).

5   NULL DIRECTION INHIBITION PROPERTIES

We performed a series of tests to characterize the inhibition for various orientations and velocities. The data in Figure 5(b) shows the outputs of two photoreceptors, the inhibitory signal and the output of a DS cell. The top panel in Figure 5(b) shows the outputs in the preferred direction and the bottom panel shows them in the null direction. Notice that the output of the left photoreceptor (L in Figure 5(b) top panel) precedes the right (R). The output of the DS cell is quite pronounced, but is truncated by the inhibition from the right photoreceptor. On the other hand, the bottom panel shows that the output of the DS cell is almost completely truncated by the inhibitory input.

A DS cell receives most inhibition when the stimulus is travelling exactly in the null direction. As seen in Figure 6(a) as the angle of stimulus is rotated, the maximum response from the DS cell is obtained when the stimulus is moving in the preferred direction (directly opposite to the null direction). As the bar is rotated toward the null direction, the response of the cell is reduced due to the increasing amount of inhibition received from the neighboring photoreceptors.

If a bar is moving in the preferred direction with varying velocity, there is a velocity, V_{max}, for which the DS cell responds maximally as shown in Figure 6(b). As the bar is moved faster than V_{max}, inhibition arrives at the cell sooner, thus truncating the response. As the cell is moved slower than V_{max}, less input is provided to the DS cell as described in Section 3. In the null direction (negative in Figure 6(b)) the cell does not respond, as expected, until the bar is travelling fast enough to beat the inhibition's onset (recall delay from Figure 5).

In Figure 7 we show the response of the entire silicon retina to a rotating fan. When the fan blades are moving to the left the retina does not respond, but when moving to the right, note the large response. Note the largest response when the blades are moving exactly in the preferred direction.

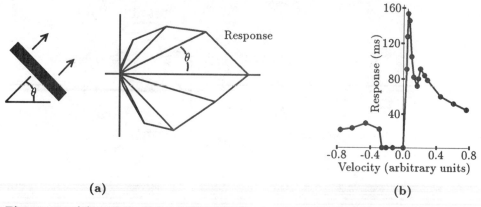

(a)   (b)

Figure 6: (a) polar plot which shows the pixels are directionally tuned. (b) shows velocity tuning of the DS cell (positive velocities are in the preferred direction).

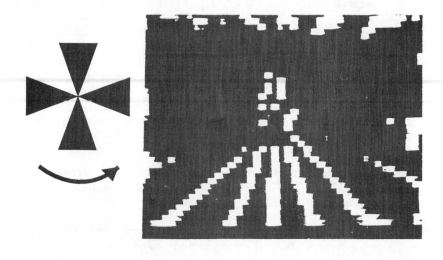

(a)   (b)

Figure 7: (a) Rotating fan used as stimulus to the retina. (b) Output of the retina.

6 CONCLUSION

We have designed and tested a silicon retina that detects temporal changes in an image. The salient image features are sufficiently high contrast stimuli, relatively fast increase in intensity (measured with respect to the recent past history of the intensity), direction and velocity of moving stimuli. These saliency measures result in a large compression of information, which will be useful in later processing stages.

Acknowledgments

Our thanks to Carver Mead and John Hopfield for their guidance and encouragement, to the Office of Naval Research for their support under grant NAV N00014-89-J-1675, and, of course, to the MOSIS fabrication service.

References

[BA91] K. Boahen and A. Andreou. A contrast sensitive silicon retina with reciprocal synapses. In S. Hanson J. Moody and R. Lippmann, editors, *Advances in Neural Information Processing Systems, Volume 4*. Morgan Kaufmann, Palo Alto, CA, 1991.

[BHL64] H.B. Barlow, M.R. Hill, and W.R. Levick. Retinal ganglion cells responding selectively to direction and speed of image motion in the rabbit. *J. Physiol.*, 173:377–407, 1964.

[DM91] T. Delbrück and Carver Mead. Silicon adaptive photoreceptor array that computes temporal intensity derivatives. In *Proc. SPIE 1541*, volume 1541-12, pages 92–99, San Diego, CA, July 1991. Infrared Sensors: Detectors, Electronics, and Signal Processing.

[HK87] E. Hildreth and C. Koch. The analysis of visual motion: From computational theory to neuronal mechanisms. *Annual Review in Neuroscience*, 10:477–533, 1987.

[Mah91] M.A. Mahowald. Silicon retina with adaptive photoreceptor. In *SPIE Technical Symposia on Optical Engineering and Photonics in Aerospace Sensing*, Orlando, FL, April 1991. Visual Information Processing: From Neurons to Chips.

[MD91] C.A. Mead and T. Delbrück. Scanners for use in visualizing analog VLSI circuitry. *Analog Integrated Circuits and Signal Processing*, 1:93–106, 1991.

[MS91] C.A. Mead and R. Sarpeshkar. An axon circuit. Internal Memo, Physics of Computation Laboratory, Caltech, 1991.

[Nak85] K. Nakayama. Biological image motion processing: A review. *Vision Research*, 25(5):625–660, 1985.

A Contrast Sensitive Silicon Retina with Reciprocal Synapses

Kwabena A. Boahen
Computation and Neural Systems
California Institute of Technology
Pasadena, CA 91125

Andreas G. Andreou
Electrical and Computer Engineering
Johns Hopkins University
Baltimore, MD 21218

Abstract

The goal of perception is to extract invariant properties of the underlying world. By computing contrast at edges, the retina reduces incident light intensities spanning twelve decades to a twentyfold variation. In one stroke, it solves the dynamic range problem and extracts relative reflec tivity, bringing us a step closer to the goal. We have built a contrast-sensitive silicon retina that models all major synaptic interactions in the outer–plexiform layer of the vertebrate retina using current–mode CMOS circuits: namely, reciprocal synapses between cones and horizontal cells, which produce the antagonistic center/surround receptive field, and cone and horizontal cell gap junctions, which determine its size. The chip has 90×92 pixels on a 6.8×6.9mm die in 2μm n–well technology and is fully functional.

1 INTRODUCTION

Retinal cones use both intracellular and extracellular mechanisms to adapt their gain to the input intensity level and hence remain sensitive over a large dynamic range. For example, photochemical processes within the cone modulate the pho tocurrents while shunting inhibitory feedback from the network adjusts its membrane conductance. Adaptation makes the light sensitivity inversely proportional to the recent input level and the membrane conductance proportional to the background intensity. As a result, the cone's membrane potential is proportional to the ratio between the input and its spatial or temporal average, i.e. contrast. We have

764

developed a contrast–sensitive silicon retina using shunting inhibition.

This silicon retina is the first to include variable inter–receptor coupling, allowing one to trade–off resolution for enhanced signal–to–noise ratio, thereby revealing low–contrast stimuli in the presence of large transistor mismatch. In the vertebrate retina, gap junctions between photoreceptors perform this function [5]. At these specialized synapses, pores in the cell membranes are juxtaposed, allowing ions to diffuse directly from one cell to another [6]. Thus, each receptor's response is a weighted average over a local region. The signal–to–noise ratio increases for features larger than this region—in direct proportion to the space constant [5].

Our chip achieves a four–fold improvement in density over previous designs [2]. We use innovative current–mode circuits [7] that provide very high functionality while faithfully modeling the neurocircuitry. A bipolar phototransistor models the photocurrents supplied by the outer–segment of the cone. We use a novel single–transistor implementation of gap junctions that exploits the physics of MOS transistors. Chemical synapses are also modeled very efficiently with a single device.

Mahowald and Mead's pioneering silicon retina [2] coded the logarithm of contrast. However, a logarithmic encoding degrades the signal–to–noise ratio because large signals are compressed more than smaller ones. Mead et. al. have subsequently improved this design by including network–level adaptation [4] and adaptive photoreceptors [3, 4] but do not implement shunting inhibition. Our silicon retina was designed to encode contrast directly using shunting inhibition.

The remainder of this paper is organized as follows. The neurocircuitry of the distal retina is described in Section 2. Diffusors and the contrast–sensitive silicon retina circuit are featured in Section 3. We show that a linearized version of this circuit computes the regularized solution for edge detection. Responses from a one–dimensional retina showing receptive field organization and contrast sensitivity, and images from the two–dimensional chip showing spatial averaging and edge enhancement are presented in Section 4. Section 5 concludes the paper.

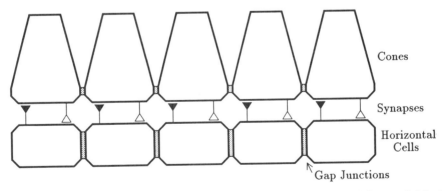

Figure 1: Neurocircuitry of the outer–plexiform layer. The white and black triangles are excitatory and inhibitory chemical synapses, respectively. The grey regions between adjacent cells are electrical gap junctions.

2   THE RETINA

The outer plexiform layer of the retina produces the well–known antagonistic center/surround receptive field organization first described in detail by Kuffler in the cat [11]. The functional neurocircuitry, based on the red cone system in the turtle [10, 8, 6], is shown in Figure 1. Cones and horizontal cells are coupled by gap junctions, forming two syncytia within which signals diffuse freely. The gap junctions between horizontal cells are larger in area (larger number of elementary pores), so signals diffuse relatively far in the horizontal cell syncytium. On the other hand, signals diffuse poorly in the cone syncytium and therefore remain relatively strong locally. When light falls on a cone, its activity increases and it excites adjacent horizontal cells which reciprocate with inhibition. Due to the way signals spread, the excitation received by nearby cones is stronger than the inhibition from horizontal cells, producing net excitation in the center. Beyond a certain distance, however, the reverse is true and so there is net inhibition in the surround.

The inhibition from horizontal cells is of the shunting kind and this gives rise to to contrast sensitivity. Horizontal cells depolarize the cones by closing chloride channels while light hyperpolarizes them by closing sodium channels [9, 1]. The cone's membrane potential is given by

$$V = \frac{g_{Na}E_{Na} + g_D V_{net}}{g_{Na} + g_{Cl} + g_D} \tag{1}$$

where the conductances are proportional to the number of channels that are open and voltages are referred to the reversal potential for chloride. g_D and V_{net} describe the effect of gap junctions to neighboring cones. Since the horizontal cells pool signals over a relatively large area, g_{Cl} will depend on the background intensity. Therefore, the membrane voltage will be proportional to the ratio between the input, which determines g_{Na}, and the background.

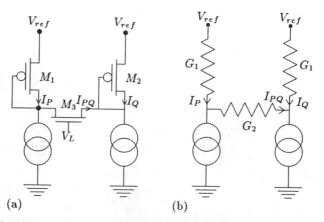

Figure 2: (a) Diffusor circuit. (b) Resistor circuit. The diffusor circuit simulates the currents in this linear resistive network.

3   SILICON MODELS

In the subthreshold region of operation, a MOS transistor mimics the behavior of a gap junction. Current flows by *diffusion:* the current through the channel is linearly proportional to the difference in carrier concentrations across it [2]. Therefore, the channel is directly analogous to a porous membrane and carrier concentration is the analog of ionic species concentration. In conformity with the underlying physics, we call transistors in this novel mode of operation *diffusors.* The gate modulates the carrier concentrations at the drain and the source multiplicatively and therefore sets the *diffusivity.* In addition to offering a compact gap junction with electronically adjustable 'area,' the diffusor has a large dynamic range—at least five decades.

A current–mode diffusor circuit is shown in Figure 2a. The currents through the diode–connected well devices M_1 and M_2 are proportional to the carrier concentrations at either end of the diffusor M_3. Consequently, the diffusor current is proportional to the current difference between M_1 and M_2. Starting with the equation describing subthreshold conduction [2, p. 36], we obtain an expression for the current I_{PQ} in terms of the currents I_P and I_Q, the reference voltage V_{ref} and the bias voltage V_L :

$$I_{PQ} = e^{\kappa V_L - V_{ref}}(I_Q^{1/\kappa} - I_P^{1/\kappa}) \tag{2}$$

For simplicity, voltages and currents are in units of $V_T = kT/q$, and I_0, the zero bias current, respectively; all devices are assumed to have the same κ and I_0. The ineffectiveness of the gate in controlling the channel potential, measured by $\kappa \approx 0.75$, introduces a small nonideality. There is a direct analogy between this circuit and the resistive circuit shown in Figure 2b for which $I_{PQ} = (G_2/G_1)(I_Q - I_P)$. The currents in these circuits are identical if $G_2/G_1 = \exp(\kappa V_L - V_{ref})$ and $\kappa = 1$. Increasing V_L or reducing V_{ref} has the same effect as increasing G_2 or reducing G_1.

Chemical synapses are also modeled using a single MOS transistor. Synaptic inputs to the turtle cone have a much higher resistance, typically 0.6GΩ or more [1], than the input conductance of a cone in the network which is 50MΩ or less [8]. Thus the synaptic inputs are essentially current sources. This also holds true for horizontal cells which are even more tightly coupled. Accordingly, chemical synapses are modeled by a MOS transistor in *saturation.* In this regime, it behaves like a current source driving the postsynapse controlled by a voltage in the presynapse. The same applies to the light–sensitive input supplied by the cone outer–segment; its peak conductance is about 0.4GΩ in the tiger salamander [9]. Therefore, the cone outer–segment is modeled by a bipolar phototransistor, also in saturation, which produces a current proportional to incident light intensity.

Shunting inhibition is not readily realized in silicon because the 'synapses' are current sources. However, to first order, we achieve the same effect by modulating the gap junction diffusivity g_D (see Equation 1). In the silicon retina circuit, we set V_L globally for a given diffusivity and control V_{ref} locally to implement shunting inhibition.

A one–dimensional version of the current–mode silicon retina circuit is shown in Figure 3. This is a direct mapping of the neurocircuitry of the outer–plexiform layer (shown in Figure 1) onto silicon using one transistor per chemical synapse/gap junction. Devices M_1 and M_2 model the reciprocal synapses. M_4 and M_5 model

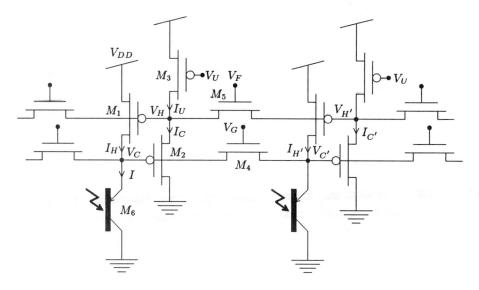

Figure 3: Current–mode Outer–Plexiform Circuit.

the gap junctions; their diffusitivities are set globally by the bias voltages V_G and V_F. The phototransistor M_6 models the light–sensitive input from the cone outer segment. The transistor M_3, with a fixed gate bias V_U, is analogous to a leak in the horizontal cell membrane that counterbalances synaptic input from the cone.

The circuit operation is as follows. The currents I_C and I_H represent the responses of the cone and the horizontal cell, respectively. These signals are actually in the post–synaptic circuit—the nodes with voltage V_C and V_H correspond to the presynaptic signals but they encode the logarithm of the response. Increasing the photocurrent will cause V_C to drop, turning on M_2 and increasing its current I_C; this is excitation. I_C pulls V_H down, turning on M_1 and increasing its current I_H; another excitatory effect. I_H, in turn, pulls V_C up, turning off M_2 and reducing its current I_C; this is inhibition.

The diffusors in this circuit behave just like those in Figure 2 although the well devices are not diode–connected. The relationship between the currents given by Equation 2 still holds because the voltages across the diffusor are determined by the currents through the well devices. However, the reference voltage for the diffusors between 'cones' (M_4) is not fixed but depends on the 'horizontal cell' response. Since $I_H = \exp(V_{DD} - \kappa V_H)$, the diffusivity in the cone network will be proportional to the horizontal cell response. This produces shunting inhibition.

3.1   RELATION TO LINEAR MODELS

Assuming the horizontal cell activities are locally very similar due to strong coupling, we can replace the cone network diffusivity by $\hat{g} = \langle I_H \rangle g$, where $\langle I_H \rangle$ is the local average. Now we treat the diffusors between the 'cones' as if they had a fixed diffusitivity $\hat{g}$; the diffusivity in the 'horizontal cell' network is denoted by h. Then the equations describing the full two–dimensional circuit on a square grid are:

$$I_H(x_m, y_n) = I(x_m, y_n) + \hat{g} \sum_{\substack{i = m \pm 1 \\ j = n \pm 1}} \{I_C(x_i, y_j) - I_C(x_m, y_n)\} \tag{3}$$

$$I_C(x_m, y_n) = I_U + h \sum_{\substack{i = m \pm 1 \\ j = n \pm 1}} \{I_H(x_m, y_n) - I_H(x_i, y_j)\} \tag{4}$$

This system is a special case of the dual layer outer plexiform model proposed by Yagi [12]—we have the membrane admittances set to zero and the synaptic strengths set to unity. Using the second–difference approximation for the laplacian, we obtain the continuous versions of these equations

$$I_H(x, y) = I(x, y) + \hat{g}\nabla^2 I_C(x, y) \tag{5}$$

$$I_C(x, y) = I_U - h\nabla^2 I_H(x, y) \tag{6}$$

with the internode distance normalized to unity. Solving for $I_H(x, y)$, we find

$$\lambda \nabla^2 \nabla^2 I_H(x, y) + I_H(x, y) = I(x, y) \tag{7}$$

This is the *biharmonic* equation used in computer vision to find an optimally smooth interpolating function '$I_H(x, y)$' for the noisy, discrete data '$I(x, y)$' [13]. The co-efficient $\lambda = \hat{g}h$ is called the regularizing parameter; it determines the trade–off between smoothing and fitting the data. In this context, the function of the horizontal cells is to compute a smoothed version of the image while the cones perform edge detection by taking the laplacian of the smoothed image as given by Equation 6. The space constant of the solutions is $\lambda^{1/4}$ [13]. This predicts that the receptive field size of our retina circuit will be weakly dependent on the input intensity since $\hat{g}$ is proportional to the horizontal cell activity.

4 CHIP PERFORMANCE

Data from the one–dimensional chip showing receptive field organization is in Figure 4. As the 'cone' coupling increases, the gain decreases and the excitatory and inhibitory subregions of the receptive field become larger. Increasing the 'horizontal cell' coupling also enlarges the receptive field but in this case the gain increases. This is because stronger diffusion results in weaker signals locally and so the inhibition decreases. Figure 5(a) shows the variation of receptive field size with intensity— roughly doubling in size for each decade. This indicates a one–third power dependence which is close to the theoretical prediction of one–fourth for the linear model. The discrepancy is due to the body effect on transistor M_2 (see Figure 3) which makes the diffusor strength increase with a power of $1/\kappa^2$.

Contrast sensitivity measurements are shown in Figure 5(b). The S–shaped curves are plots of the Michaelis–Menten equation used by physiologists to fit responses of cones [6]:

$$V = V_{max} \frac{I^n}{I^n + \sigma^n} \tag{8}$$

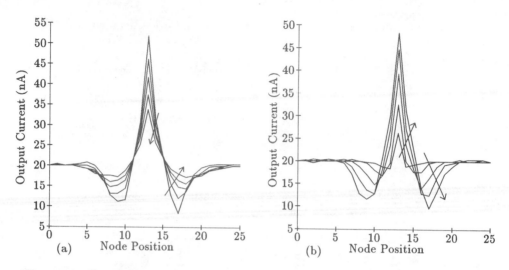

Figure 4: Receptive fields measured for 25×1 pixel chip; arrows indicate increasing diffusor gate voltages. The inputs were 50nA at the center and 10nA elsewhere, and the output current I_U was set to 20nA. (a) Increasing inter–receptor diffusor voltages in 15mV steps. (b) Increasing inter–horizontal cell diffusor voltages in 50mV steps.

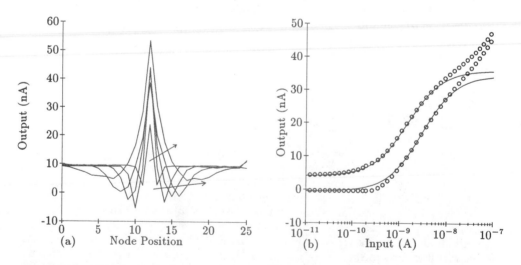

Figure 5: (a) Dependence of receptive field on intensity; arrows indicate increasing intensity. Center inputs were 500pA, 5nA, 15nA, 50nA, and 500nA. The background input was always one–fifth of the center input. (b) Contrast sensitivity measurements at two background intensity levels. Lines are fits of the Michaelis–Menten equation.

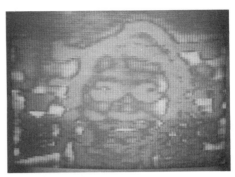

Figure 6: Video images from 90×92 pixel chip with and without cone coupling. The vertical lines between pixels are artifacts of the scanning circuitry.

where σ is the background intensity and the exponent n determines the slope of the S–curve. A vertical offset is included to account for the dependence of transistor mismatch on the intensity level. The circuit deviates at high intensities due to increasing inter–receptor coupling strength. For these fits, n is 1.2 in both cases, compared to the physiologically observed value of 1.0 for cones [6], and σ is 1.5nA and 3.0nA; the actual background intensities were 0.56nA and 1.8nA. Thus the responses are centered at a higher intensity and did not shift horizontally as much as expected with intensity. This is due to the difference in gain for inputs above and below the background level. As the inputs decrease the cone coupling reduces and so the gain increases. Hence there is a smaller range of operation below the background level.

Figure 6 shows video images of a face produced by the two–dimensional silicon retina chip. The chip includes scanning circuitry which rasterizes the image and generates all the signals required to drive a multiscan monitor [14]. The image on the left shows a considerable amount of spatial noise due to transistor mismatch. The face is hardly recognizable. In the other image the inter–cone diffusors have been turned on and greatly enhance the signal–to–noise. The center–surround processing highlights edges, producing the 'halo' around her head, and regions with high curvature, like the cheeks.

5   CONCLUSIONS

Using a current–mode approach, we have built a dense, robust, contrast–sensitive silicon retina modeled closely after the vertebrate retina. Our single–transistor gap junctions and chemical synapses yield very efficient implementations of neural networks. Unfortunately, the implementation of shunting inhibition used here makes the receptive fields enlarge with increasing intensity. We are presently developing new circuits that address this problem.

Acknowledgements

We are very grateful to Carver Mead for his support and encouragement. KB is supported by a graduate fellowship from Caltech. AA is supported by a Research Initiation Award from NSF (MIP-9010364). KB thanks Tobi Delbrück, Andy Moore, Lloyd Watts, Misha Mahowald, and Xavier Arreguit for their help. Chip fabrication was provided by MOSIS and computing facilities in the Mead Lab by Hewlett–Packard.

References

[1] A. Kaneko, T. Ohtsuka et.al., "GABA Sensitivity in Solitary Turtle Cones," in *Neurocircuitry of the Retina: A Cajal Memorial*, pp. 89-97, A. Gallego and P. Gouras, Eds, Elsevier, New York NY, 1985.

[2] C. A. Mead, *Analog VLSI and Neural Systems*, Addison–Wesley, Reading MA, 1989.

[3] T. Delbrück and C. A. Mead, "An electronic Photoreceptor sensitive to small changes in Intensity," in *Advances in Neural Information Processing Systems I*, D. S. Touretsky ed. Morgan Kauffman , San Mateo CA, 1989.

[4] M. A. Mahowald, "Silicon Retina with Adaptive Photoreceptors," in *SPIE/SPSE Symposium on Electronic Science and Technology: From Neurons to Chips*. Orlando, FL, April 1991.

[5] T. D. Lamb and E. J. Simon, "The Relation between Intercellular Coupling and Electrical Noise in Turtle Photoreceptors," *J. Physiol.*, 263, pp. 257-286, 1976.

[6] J. E. Dowling, *The Retina: An Approachable part of the Brain*, Harvard University Press, Cambridge MA, 1987.

[7] A. G. Andreou et.al., "Current–Mode Subthreshold MOS Circuits for Analog VLSI Neural Systems," *IEEE Trans. on Neural Networks*, vol. 2, no. 2., pp. 205-213, March 1991.

[8] P. B. Detwiler and A. L. Hodgkin, "Electrical Coupling between Cones in the Turtle Retina," *J. Physiol.*, 291, pp. 75-100, 1979.

[9] D. Attwell, F. S. Werblin et. al., "The Properties of Single Cones isolated from the Tiger Salamander Retina," *J. Physiol.*, 328, pp. 259-283, 1982.

[10] D. A. Baylor, M. G. F. Fourtes et. al., "Receptive Fields of Cones in the Retina of the Turtle," *J. Physiol.*, 214, pp. 265-294, 1971.

[11] S. W. Kuffler, "Discharge Patterns and Functional Organization of Mammalian Retina," *J. Neurophysiol.*, 16, pp. 37-68, 1953.

[12] T. Yagi, Y. Funahashi, and F. Ariki, "Dynamic Model of Dual Layer Neural Network for Vertebrate Retina," *Proceedings of IJCNN-89,* Washington DC, June 1989.

[13] T. Poggio, H. Voorhees, and A. Yuille, "A Regularized Solution to Edge Detection," Massachusetts Institute of Technology, AI Lab Memo 833, May 1985.

[14] C. A. Mead and T. Delbück, "Scanners for use in visualizing analog VLSI circuitry," *in press*, 1992.

A Neurocomputer Board Based on the ANNA Neural Network Chip

Eduard Säckinger, Bernhard E. Boser, and Lawrence D. Jackel
AT&T Bell Laboratories
Crawfords Corner Road, Holmdel, NJ 07733

Abstract

A board is described that contains the ANNA neural-network chip, and a DSP32C digital signal processor. The ANNA (Analog Neural Network Arithmetic unit) chip performs mixed analog/digital processing. The combination of ANNA with the DSP allows high-speed, end-to-end execution of numerous signal-processing applications, including the preprocessing, the neural-net calculations, and the postprocessing steps. The ANNA board evaluates neural networks 10 to 100 times faster than the DSP alone. The board is suitable for implementing large (million connections) networks with sparse weight matrices. Three applications have been implemented on the board: a convolver network for slant detection of text blocks, a handwritten digit recognizer, and a neural network for recognition-based segmentation.

1 INTRODUCTION

Many researchers have built neural-network chips, but few chips have been installed in board-level systems, even though this next level of integration provides insights and advantages that can't be attained on a chip testing station. Building a board demonstrates whether or not the chip can be effectively integrated into the larger systems required for real applications. A board also exposes bottlenecks in the system data paths. Most importantly, a working board moves the neural-network chip from the realm of a research exercise, to that of a practical system, readily available to users whose primary interest is actual applications. An additional bonus of carrying the integration to the board level is that the chip designer can gain the user feedback that will assist in designing new chips with greater utility.

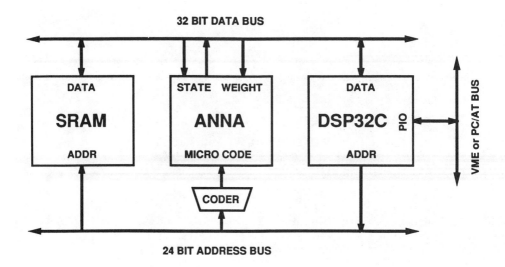

Figure 1: Block Diagram of the ANNA Board

2   ARCHITECTURE

The neurocomputer board contains a special purpose chip called ANNA (Boser et al., 1991), for the parallel evaluation of neuron functions (a squashing function applied to a weighted sum) and a general purpose digital signal processor, DSP32C. The board also contains interface and clock synchronization logic as well as 1 MByte of static memory, SRAM (see Fig. 1). Two version of this board with two different bus interfaces have been built: a double height VME board (see Fig. 2) and a PC/AT board (see Fig. 3).

The ANNA neural network chip is an ALU (Arithmetic and Logic Unit) specialized for neural network functions. It contains a 12-bit wide state-data input, a 12-bit wide state-data output, a 12-bit wide weight-data input, and a 37-bit micro-instruction input. The instructions that can be executed by the chip are the following (parameters are not shown):

RFSH Write weight values from the weight-data input into the dynamic on-chip weight storage.

SHIFT Shift on-chip barrel shifter to the left and load up to four new state values from state-data input into the right end of the shifter.

STORE Transfer state vector from the shifter into the on-chip state storage and/or into the state-data latches of the arithmetic unit.

CALC Calculate eight dot-products between on-chip weight vectors and the contents of the above mentioned data latches; subsequently evaluate the squashing function.

OUT Transfer the results of the calculation to the state-data output.

Figure 2: ANNA Board with VME Bus Interface

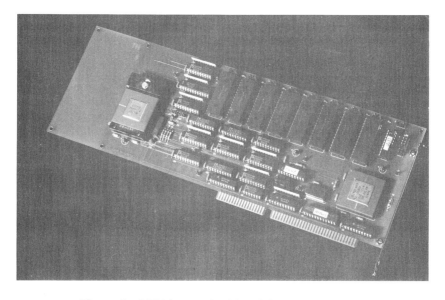

Figure 3: ANNA Board with PC/AT Bus Interface

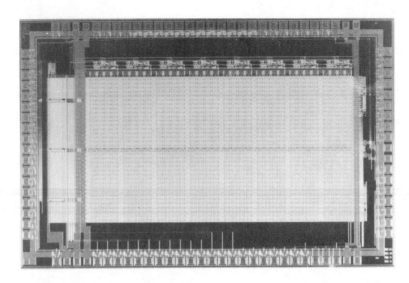

Figure 4: Photo Micrograph of the ANNA Chip

Some of the instructions (like **SHIFT** and **CALC**) can be executed in parallel. The barrel shifter at the input as well as the on-chip state storage make the ANNA chip very effective for evaluating locally-connected, weight-sharing networks such as feature extraction and time-delay neural networks (TDNN).

The ANNA neural network chip, implemented in a $0.9\,\mu m$ CMOS technology, contains 180,000 transistors on a $4.5 \times 7\,mm^2$ die (see Fig. 4). The chip implements 4,096 *physical* synapses which can be time multiplexed in order to realize networks with many more than 4,096 connections. The resolution of the synaptic weights is 6 bits and that of the states (input/output of the neurons) is 3 bits. Additionally, a 4-bit scaling factor can be programmed for each neuron to extend the dynamic range of the weights. The weight values are stored as charge packets on capacitors and are periodically refreshed by two on chip 6-bit D/A converter. The synapses are realized by multiplying 3-bit D/A converters (analog weight times digital state). The analog results of this multiplication are added by means of current summing and then converted back to digital by a saturating 3-bit A/D converter. Although the chip uses analog computing internally, all input/output is digital. This combines the advantages of the high synaptic density, the high speed, and the low power of analog with the ease of interfacing to a digital system like a digital signal processor (DSP).

The 32-bit floating-point digital signal processor (DSP32C) on the same board runs at 40 MHz without wait states (100 ns per instruction) and is connected to 1 MByte of static RAM. The DSP has several functions: (1) It generates the micro instructions for the ANNA chip. (2) It is responsible for accessing the pixel, feature, and weight data from the memory and then storing the results of the chip in the memory. (3) If the precision of the ANNA chip is not sufficient the DSP can do the calculations with 32-bit floating-point precision. (4) Learning algorithms can be run on the DSP. (5) The DSP is useful as a pre- and post-processor for neural networks. In this way a whole task can be carried out on the board without exchanging intermediate results with the host.

As shown by Fig. 1 ANNA instructions are supplied over the DSP address bus, while state and weight data is transferred over the data bus. This arrangement makes it possible to supply or store ANNA data *and* execute a micro instruction simultaneously, i.e., using only one DSP instruction. The ANNA clock is automatically generated whenever the DSP issues a micro instruction to the ANNA chip.

3   PERFORMANCE

Using a DSP for supplying micro instructions as well as accessing the data from the memory makes the board very flexible and fairly simple. Both data and instruction flow to and from the ANNA chip are under software control and can be programmed using the C or DSP32C assembly language.

Because of DSP32C features such as one-instruction 32-bit memory-to-memory transfer with auto increment and overhead free looping, ANNA instruction sequences can be generated at a rate of approximately 5 MIPS. A similar rate of 5 MByte/s is achieved for reading and writing ANNA data from and to the memory.

The speed of the board depends on the application and how well it makes use of the chip's parallelism and ranges between 30 MC/s and 400 MC/s. For concrete examples see the section on Applications. Compared to the DSP32C which performs at about 3 MC/s (for sparsely connected networks) the board with the ANNA chip is 10 to 100 times faster.

The speed of the board is not limited by the ANNA chip but by the above mentioned data rates. The use of a dedicated hardware sequencer will improve the speed by up to ten times. The board can thus be used for prototyping an application, before building more specialized hardware.

4   SOFTWARE

To make the board easily usable we implemented a LISP interpreter on the host computer (a SUN workstation) which allows us to make remote procedure calls (RPC) to the ANNA board. After starting the LISP interpreter on the host it will download the DSP object code to the board and start the main program on the DSP. Then, the DSP will transfer the addresses of all procedures that are available to the user to the LISP interpreter. From then on, all these procedures can be called as LISP functions of the form (==> anna *procedure parameter(s)*) from the host. Parameters and return value are handled automatically by the LISP interpreter.

Three ways of using the ANNA board are described. The first two methods do not require DSP programming; everything is controlled from the LISP interpreter. The third method requires DSP programming and results in maximum speed for any application.

1. The simplest way to use the board together with this LISP interpreter is to call existing library functions on the board. For example a neural network for recognizing handwritten digits can be called as follows:

(==> anna down-weight *weight-matrix*)
(setq *class* (==> anna down-rec-up *digit-pattern*))

The first LISP function activates the **down-weight** function on the ANNA board that transfers the LISP matrix, *weight-matrix*, to the board. This function defines all the weights of the network and has to be called only once. The second LISP function calls the **down-rec-up** function which takes the *digit-pattern* (pixel image) as an input, downloads this pattern, runs the recognizer, and uploads the *class* number (0 ... 9).

This method requires no knowledge of the ANNA or DSP instruction set. The library functions are fast since they have been optimized by the implementer. At the moment library functions for nonlinear convolution, character recognition, and testing are available.

2. If a function which is not part of the library has to be implemented, an ANNA program must be written. A collection of LISP functions (ANNANAS), support the translation of symbolic ANNA program into micro code. The micro code is then run on the ANNA chip by means of a software sequencer implemented on the DSP. Assembling and running a simple ANNA program using ANNANAS looks like this:

```
(anna-repeat 16)        ; REPEAT 16           start of loop
(anna-shift 4 0)        ;  SHIFT 4,R0;        ANNA shift instruction
(anna-store 0 'a 2)     ;  STORE R0,A.L2;     ANNA store instruction
(anna-endrep)           ; ENDREP              end of loop
(anna-stop)             ; STOP                end of program

(anna-run 0)            ;                     start sequencer
```

In this way, all the features of the ANNA chip and board can be used without DSP programming. This mode is also helpful for testing and debugging ANNA programs. Beside the assembler, ANNANAS also provides several monitoring and debugging tools.

3. If maximum speed is imperative, an application specific sequencer has to be written (as opposed to the slower generic sequencer described above). To do this a DSP assembler and C compiler are required. A toolbox of assembly macros and C functions help implementing this sequencer. Besides the sequencer, pre- and post-processing software can also be implemented on the fast DSP hardware. After successfully testing the program it can be added to the library as a new function.

5   APPLICATIONS

5.1   CONVOLVER NETWORK

In this application the ANNA chip is configured for 16 neurons with 256 synapses each. First, each of these neurons connect to the upper left 16 × 16 field of a

Table 1: Performance of the Recognizer.

IMPLEMENTATION	ERROR RATE	REJECT RATE FOR 1 % ERROR
Full Precision	4.9 %	9.1 %
ANNA/DSP	5.3 ± 0.2 %	13.5 ± 0.8 %
ANNA/DSP/Retraining	4.9 ± 0.2 %	11.5 ± 0.8 %

large image. The 16 neurons are then scanned horizontally and vertically over the whole image. The network constructed by the above procedure carries out a nonlinear convolution with 16 kernels (corresponding to the number of neurons) of size 16 × 16. This network is well suited for the chip and runs at 385 MC/s on the board. This is about 100 times faster than evaluating the same network on a DSP.

Such a network can be used to determine the slant angle of a text block for subsequent deslanting. In this case the sixteen kernels consist of line detectors at various angles. The threshold of the neurons is set to a high value, such that the output activates only if there is a strong response from the detector. The feature map at the output of the network containing the highest number of active neurons corresponds to the slant angle.

5.2   HANDWRITTEN DIGIT RECOGNIZER

A five-layer feed-forward network for handwritten character recognition, similar to the one described in (LeCun et al., 1990), containing 136,000 connections has been implemented on the board as a practical application example. A detailed description of this implementation can be found in (Säckinger et al., 1992).

The first three layers of this network contain 97 % of the connections and are evaluated with the ANNA chip. The last two layers require higher precision and therefore run on the DSP. Processing of the first three layers with a total of 132,000 connections takes 4.9 ms corresponding to 27 MC/s. The last two layers, which contain only 4,200 connections, are evaluated by the DSP in 1.7 ms (2.5 MC/s). The lower speed performance of the ANNA part compared to the convolver network is due to the smaller neurons (less synapses per neuron). Therefore, some of the chips parallelism cannot be used by this application. Still, the speed-up is approximately 10 over a DSP implementation.

The recognition performance drops slightly when porting the network onto the board. However, retraining the last layer with the chip in the loop restores the performance almost to its original value. The performance figures are summarized in Table 1. Besides the error rate, the number of patterns that have to be rejected in order to make less than 1 % error are also given. Note that the recognizer on the ANNA board does not give exactly the same performance every time it is tested because the first three layers are evaluated by *analog* hardware subject to noise. Therefore, the performance is measured with 100 runs through the test set and the mean and standard deviation is given in the table.

5.3 RECOGNITION BASED SEGMENTATION

Before individual digits can be passed to a recognizer as described in the previous section, they typically have to be isolated (segmented) from a string of characters (e.g. a ZIP code). When characters overlap, segmentation is a difficult problem and simple algorithms which look for connected components or histograms fail.

A promising solution to this problem is to combine recognition and segmentation (Keeler et al., 1992, Matan et al., 1992). For instance recognizers like the one described above can be replicated horizontally and vertically over the region of interest. This will guarantee, that there is a recognizer centered over each character. It is crucial, however, to train the recognizer such that it rejects partial characters. Such a replicated version of the recognizer (at 31 times 6 locations) with approximately 2 million connections has been implemented on the ANNA board and was used to segment ZIP codes.

6 CONCLUSION

A board with a neural-network chip and a digital signal processor (DSP) has been built. Large pattern recognition applications have been implemented on the board giving a speed advantage of 10 to 100 over the DSP alone.

Acknowledgements

The authors would like to thank Steve Deiss for his excellent job in building the boards and Yann LeCun and Jane Bromley for their help with the digit recognizer.

References

Bernhard Boser, Eduard Säckinger, Jane Bromley, Yann LeCun, and Lawrence D. Jackel. An analog neural network processor with programmable network topology. *IEEE J. Solid-State Circuits*, 26(12):2017–2025, December 1991.

Yann Le Cun, Bernhard Boser, John S. Denker, Donnie Henderson, Richard E. Howard, Wayne Hubbard, and Lawrence D. Jackel. Handwritten digit recognition with a back-propagation network. In David S. Touretzky, editor, *Neural Information Processing Systems*, volume 2, pages 396–404. Morgan Kaufmann Publishers, San Mateo, CA, 1990.

Eduard Säckinger, Bernhard Boser, Jane Bromley, Yann LeCun, and Lawrence D. Jackel. Application of the ANNA neural network chip to high-speed character recognition. *IEEE Trans. Neural Networks*, 3(2), March 1992.

J. D. Keeler and D. E. Rumelhart. Self-organizing segmentation and recognition neural network. In J. M. Moody, S. J. Hanson, and R. P. Lippman, editors, *Neural Information Processing Systems*, volume 4. Morgan Kaufmann Publishers, San Mateo, CA, 1992.

Ofer Matan, Christopher J. C. Burges, Yann LeCun, and John S. Denker. Multi-digit recognition using a space delay neural network. In J. M. Moody, S. J. Hanson, and R. P. Lippman, editors, *Neural Information Processing Systems*, volume 4. Morgan Kaufmann Publishers, San Mateo, CA, 1992.

Software for ANN training on a Ring Array Processor

Phil Kohn, Jeff Bilmes, Nelson Morgan, James Beck
International Computer Science Institute,
1947 Center St., Berkeley CA 94704, USA

Abstract

Experimental research on Artificial Neural Network (ANN) algorithms requires either writing variations on the same program or making one monolithic program with many parameters and options. By using an object-oriented library, the size of these experimental programs is reduced while making them easier to read, write and modify. An efficient and flexible realization of this idea is Connectionist Layered Object-oriented Network Simulator (CLONES). CLONES runs on UNIX[1] workstations and on the 100-1000 MFLOP Ring Array Processor (RAP) that we built with ANN algorithms in mind. In this report we describe CLONES and show how it is implemented on the RAP.

1 Overview

As we continue to experiment with Artificial Neural Networks (ANNs) to generate phoneme probabilities for speech recognition (Bourlard & Morgan, 1991), two things have become increasingly clear:

1. Because of the diversity and continuing evolution of ANN algorithms, the programming environment must be both powerful and flexible.

2. These algorithms are very computationally intensive when applied to large databases of training patterns.

Ideally we would like to implement and test ideas at about the same rate that we come up with them. We have approached this goal both by developing application specific parallel

---

[1]UNIX is a trademark of AT&T

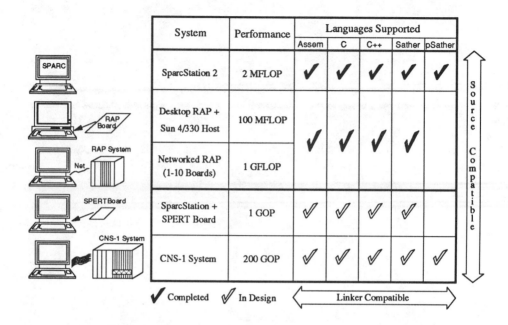

System	Performance	Languages Supported					
		Assem	C	C++	Sather	pSather	
SparcStation 2	2 MFLOP	✔	✔	✔	✔	✔	Source Compatible
Desktop RAP + Sun 4/330 Host	100 MFLOP	✔	✔	✔	✔		
Networked RAP (1-10 Boards)	1 GFLOP						
SparcStation + SPERT Board	1 GOP	✔ (in design)	✔ (in design)	✔ (in design)	✔ (in design)		
CNS-1 System	200 GOP	✔ (in design)	✔ (in design)	✔ (in design)	✔ (in design)	✔ (in design)	

✔ Completed   ✔ In Design   ⟨ Linker Compatible ⟩

Figure 1: Hardware and software configurations

hardware, the Ring Array Processor (RAP) (Morgan et al., 1990; Beck, 1990; Morgan et al., 1992), and by building an object-oriented software environment, the Connectionist Layered Object-oriented Network Simulator (CLONES) (Kohn, 1991). By using an object-oriented library, the size of experimental ANN programs can be greatly reduced while making them easier to read, write and modify. CLONES is written in C++ and utilizes libraries previously written in C and assembler.

Our ANN research currently encompasses two hardware platforms and several languages, shown in Figure 1. Two new hardware platforms, the SPERT board (Asanović et al., 1991) and the CNS-1 system are in design (unfilled check marks), and will support source code compatibility with the existing machines. The SPERT design is a custom VLSI parallel processor installed on an SBUS card plugged into a SPARC workstation. Using variable precision fixed point arithmetic, a single SPERT board will have performance comparable to a 10 board RAP system with 40 processors. The CNS-1 system is based on multiple VLSI parallel processors interconnected by high speed communication rings.

Because the investment in software is generally large, we insist on source level compatibility across hardware platforms at the level of the system libraries. These libraries include matrix and vector classes that free the user from concern about the hardware configuration. It is also considered important to allow routines in different languages to be linked together. This includes support for Sather, an object-oriented language that has been developed at ICSI for workstations. The parallel version of Sather, called pSather, will be supported on the CNS-1.

CLONES is seen as the ANN researcher's interface to this multiplatform, multilanguage environment. Although CLONES is an application written specifically for ANN algorithms, it's object-orientation gives it the ability to easily include previously developed libraries. CLONES currently runs on UNIX workstations and the RAP; this paper focuses on the RAP implementation.

2   RAP hardware

The RAP consists of cards that are added to a UNIX host machine (currently a VME based Sun SPARC). A RAP card has four 32 MFlop Digital Signal Processor (DSP) chips (TI TMS320C30), each with its own local 256KB or 1MB of fast static RAM and 16MB of DRAM.

Instead of sharing memory, the processors communicate on a high speed ring that shifts data in a single machine cycle. For each board, the peak transfer rate between 4 nodes is 64 million words/sec (256 Mbytes/second). This is a good balance to the 64 million multiply-accumulates per second (128 MFLOPS) peak performance of the computational elements.

Up to 16 of these boards can be interconnected and used as one Single Program operating on Multiple Data stream (SPMD) machine. In this style of parallel computation, all the processors run the same program and are doing the same operations to different pieces of the same matrix or vector [2]. The RAP can run other styles of parallel computation, including pipelines where each processor is doing a different operation on different data streams. However, for fully connected back-propagation networks, SPMD parallelism works well and is also much easier to program since there is only one flow of control to worry about.

A reasonable design for networks in which all processors need all unit outputs is a single broadcast bus. However, this design is not appropriate for other related algorithms such as the backward phase of the back-propagation learning algorithm. By using a ring, back-propagation can be efficiently parallelized without the need to have the complete weight matrix on all processors. The number of ring operations required for each complete matrix update cycle is of the same order as the number of units, **not** the square of the number of units. It should also be noted that we are using a stochastic or on-line learning algorithm. The training examples are **not** dividing among the processors then the weights batch updated after a complete pass. All weights are updated for each training example. This procedure greatly decreases the training time for large redundant training sets since more steps are being taken in the weight-space per training example.

We have empirically derived formulae that predict the performance improvement on back-propagation training as a function of the number of boards. Theoretical peak performance is 128 MFlops/board, with sustained performance of 30-90% for back-propagation problems of interest to us. Systems with up to 40 nodes have been tested, for which throughputs

---

[2]The hardware does not automatically keep the processors in lock step; for example, they may become out of sync because of branches conditioned on the processor's node number or on the data. However, when the processors must communicate with each other through the ring, hardware synchronization automatically occurs. A node that attempts to read before data is ready, or to write when there is already data waiting, will stop executing until the data can be moved.

of up to 574 Million Connections Per Second (MCPS) have been measured, as well as learning rates of up to 106 Million Connection Updates Per Second (MCUPS) for training. Practical considerations such as workstation address space and clock skew restrict current implementations to 64 nodes, but in principle the architecture scales to about 16,000 nodes for back-propagation.

We now have considerable experience with the RAP as a day-to-day computational tool for our research. With the aid of the RAP hardware and software, we have done network training studies that would have over a century on a UNIX workstation such as the SPARCstation-2. We have also used the RAP to simulate variable precision arithmetic to guide us in the design of higher performance hardware such as SPERT.

The RAP hardware remains very flexible because of the extensive use of programmable logic arrays. These parts are automatically downloaded when the host machine boots up. By changing the download files, the functionality of the communications ring and the host interface can be modified or extended without any physical changes to the board.

3   RAP software

The RAP DSP software is built in three levels (Kohn & Bilmes, 1990; Bilmes & Kohn, 1990). At the lowest level are hand coded assembler routines for matrix, vector and ring operations. Many standard matrix and vector operations are currently supported as well as some operations specialized for efficient back-propagation. These matrix and vector routines do not use the communications ring or split up data among processing nodes. There is also a UNIX compatible library including most standard C functions for file, math and string operations. All UNIX kernel calls (such as file input or output) cause requests to be made to the host SPARC over the VMEbus. A RAP dæmon process running under UNIX has all of the RAP memory mapped into its virtual address space. It responds to the RAP system call interrupts (from the RAP device driver) and can access RAP memory with a direct memory copy function or assignment statement.

An intermediate level consists of matrix and vector object classes coded in C++. A programmer writing at this level or above can program the RAP as if it were a conventional serial machine. These object classes divide the data and processing among the available processing nodes, using the communication ring to redistribute data as needed. For example, to multiply a matrix by a vector, each processor would have its own subset of the matrix rows that must be multiplied. This is equivalent to partitioning the output vector elements among the processors. If the complete output vector is needed by all processors, a ring broadcast routine is called to redistribute the part of the output vector from each processor to all the other processors.

The top level of RAP software is the CLONES environment. CLONES is an object-oriented library for constructing, training and utilizing connectionist networks. It is designed to run efficiently on data parallel computers as well as uniprocessor workstations. While efficiency and portability to parallel computers are the primary goals, there are several secondary design goals:

1. minimize the learning curve for using CLONES;
2. minimize the additional code required for new experiments;
3. maximize the variety of artificial neural network algorithms supported;

4. allow heterogeneous algorithms and training procedures to be interconnected and trained together;

5. allow the trained network to be easily embedded into other programs.

The size of experimental ANN programs is greatly reduced by using an object-oriented library; at the same time these programs are easier to read, write and evolve.

Researchers often generate either a proliferation of versions of the same basic program, or one giant program with a large number of options and many potential interactions and side-effects. Some simulator programs include (or worse, evolve) their own language for describing networks. We feel that a modern object-oriented language (such as C++) has all the functionality needed to build and train ANNs. By using an object-oriented design, we attempt to make the most frequently changed parts of the program very small and well localized. The parts that rarely change are in a centralized library. One of the many advantages of an object-oriented library for experimental work is that any part can be specialized by making a new class of object that inherits the desired operations from a library class.

4   CLONES overview

To make CLONES easier to learn, we restrict ourselves to a subset of the many features of C++. Excluded features include multiple inheritance, operator overloading (however, function overloading is used) and references. Since the multiple inheritance feature of C++ is not used, CLONES classes can be viewed as a collection of simple inheritance trees. This means that all classes of objects in CLONES either have no parent class (top of a class tree) or inherit the functions and variables of a single parent class.

CLONES consists of a library of C++ classes that represent networks (**Net**), their components (**Net_part**) and training procedures. There are also utility classes used during training such as: databases of training data (**Database**), tables of parameters and arguments (**Param**), and performance statistics (**Stats**). **Database** and **Param** do not inherit from any other class. Their class trees are independent of the rest of CLONES and each other. The **Stats** class inherits from **Net_behavior**.

The top level of the CLONES class tree is a class called **Net_behavior**. It defines function interfaces for many general functions including file save or restore and debugging. It also contains behavior functions that are called during different phases of running or training a network. For example, there are functions that are called before or after a complete training run (**pre_training**, **post_training**), before or after a pass over the database (**pre_epoch**, **post_epoch**) and before or after a forward or backward run of the network (**pre_forw_pass**, **post_forw_pass**, **pre_back_pass**, **post_back_pass**). The **Net**, **Net_part** and **Stats** classes inherit from this class.

All network components used to construct ANNs are derived from the two classes **Layer** and **Connect**. Both of these inherit from class **Net_part**. A CLONES network can be viewed as a graph where the nodes are **Layer** objects and the arcs are **Connect** objects. Each **Connect** connects a single input **Layer** with a single output **Layer**. A **Layer** holds the data for a set of units (such as an activation vector), while a **Connect** transforms the data as it passes between **Layers**. Data flows along **Connects** between the pair of **Layers** by calling **forw_propagate** (input to output) or **back_propagate** (output to input) behavior functions in the **Connect** object.

CLONES does not have objects that represent single units (or artificial neurons). Instead, **Layer** objects are used to represent a set of units. Because arrays of units are passed down to the lowest level routines, most of the computation time is focused into a few small assembly coded loops that easily fit into the processor instruction cache. Time spent in all of the levels of control code that call these loops becomes less significant as the size of the **Layer** is increased.

The **Layer** class does not place any restrictions on the representation of its internal information. For example, the representation for activations may be a floating point number for each unit (**Analog_layer**), or it may be a set of unit indices, indicating which units are active (**Binary_layer**). **Analog_layer** and **Binary_layer** are built into the CLONES library as subclasses of the class **Layer**. The **Analog_layer** class specifies the representation of activations, but it still leaves open the procedures that use and update the activation array. **BP_analog_layer** is a subclass of **Analog_layer** that specify these procedures for the back-propagation algorithm. Subclasses of **Analog_layer** may also add new data structures to hold extra internal state such as the error vector in the case of **BP_analog_layer**. The **BP_Analog_layer** class has subclasses for various transfer functions such as **BP_sigmoid_layer** and **BP_linear_layer**.

Layer classes also have behavior functions that are called in the course of running the network. For example, one of these functions (**pre_forw_propagate**) initializes the **Layer** for a forward pass, perhaps by clearing its activation vector. After all of the connections coming into it are run, another **Layer** behavior function (**post_forw_propagate**) is called that computes the activation vector from the partial results left by these connections. For example, this function may apply a transfer function such as the sigmoid to the accumulated sum of all the input activations.

These behavior functions can be changed by making a subclass. **BP_analog_layer** leaves open the activation transfer function (or squashing function) and its derivative. Subclasses define new transfer functions to be applied to the activations. A new class of back-propagation layer with a customized transfer function (instead of the default sigmoid) can be created with the following C++ code:

```
class My_new_BP_layer_class : public BP_analog_layer {

  My_new_BP_layer_class(int number_of_units)
    : BP_analog_layer(number_of_units);    // constructor

  void transfer(Fvec *activation) {
    /* apply forward transfer function to my activation vector */
  }

  void d_transfer(Fvec *activation, Fvec *err)  {
    /* apply backward error transfer to err (given activation) */
  }
};
```

A **Connect** class includes two behavior functions: one that transforms activations from the incoming **Layer** into partial results in the outgoing **Layer** (**forw_propagate**) and one that takes outgoing errors and generates partial results in the incoming **Layer** (**back_propagate**).

The structure of a partial result is part of the **Layer** class. The subclasses of **Connect** include: **Bus_connect** (one to one), **Full_connect** (all to all) and **Sparse_connect** (some to some).

Each subclass of **Connect** may contain a set of internal parameters such as the weight matrix in a **BP_full_connect**. Subclasses of **Connect** also specify which pairs of **Layer** subclasses can be connected. When a pair of **Layer** objects are connected, type checking by the C++ compiler insures that the input and output **Layer** subclasses are supported by the **Connect** object.

In order to do its job efficiently, a **Connect** must know something about the internal representation of the layers that are connected. By using C++ overloading, the **Connect** function selected depends not only on the class of **Connect**, but also on the classes of the two layers that are connected. Not all **Connect** classes are defined for all pairs of **Layer** classes. However, **Connects** that convert between **Layer** classes can be utilized to compensate for missing functions.

CLONES allows the user to view layers and connections much like tinker-toy wheels and rods. ANNs are built up by creating **Layer** objects and passing them to the create functions of the desired **Connect** classes. Changing the interconnection pattern does not require any changes to the **Layer** classes or objects and vice-versa.

At the highest level, a **Net** object delineates a subset of a network and controls its training. Operations can be performed on these subsets by calling functions on their **Net** objects. The **Layers** of a **Net** are specified by calling one of **new_input_layer**, **new_hidden_layer**, or **new_output_layer** on the **Net** object for each **Layer**. Given the **Layers**, the **Connects** that belong to the **Net** are deduced by the **Net_order** objects (see below). **Layer** and **Connect** objects can belong to any number of **Nets**.

The **Net** labels all of its **Layers** as one of input, output or hidden. These labels are used by the **Net_order** objects to determine the order in which the behavior functions of the **Net_parts** are called. For example, a **Net** object contains **Net_order** objects called **forward_pass_order** and **backward_pass_order** that control the execution sequence for a forward or backward pass. The **Net** object also has functions that call a function by the same name on all of its component parts (for example **set_learning_rate**).

When a **Net_order** object is built it scans the connectivity of the **Net**. The rules that relate topology to order of execution are centralized and encapsulated in subclasses of **Net_order**. Changes to the structure of the **Net** are localized to just the code that creates the **Layers** and **Connects**; one does not need to update separate code that contains explicit knowledge about the order of evaluation for running a forward or backward pass.

The training procedure is divided into a series of steps, each of which is a call to a function in the **Net** object. At the top level, calling **run_training** on a **Net** performs a complete training run. In addition to calling **pre_training, post_training** behavior functions, it calls **run_epoch** in a loop until the the **next_learning_rate** function returns zero. The **run_epoch** function calls **run_forward** and **run_backward**.

At a lower level there are functions that interface the database(s) of the **Net** object to the **Layers** of the **Net**. For example, **set_input** sets the activations of the input **Layers** for a given pattern number of the database. Another of these sets the error vector of the output layer (**set_error**). Some of these functions, such as **is_correct** evaluate the performance of the **Net** on the current pattern.

In addition to database related functions, the **Net** object also contains useful global variables for all of its components. A pointer to the **Net** object is always passed to all behavior functions of its **Layers** and **Connects** when they are called. One of these variables is a **Param** object that contains a table of parameter names, each with a list of values. These parameters usually come from the command line and/or parameter files. Other variables include: the current pattern, the correct target output, the epoch number, etc.

5   Conclusions

CLONES is a useful tool for training ANNs especially when working with large training databases and networks. It runs efficiently on a variety of parallel hardware as well as on UNIX workstations.

Acknowledgements

Special thanks to Steve Renals for daring to be the first CLONES user and making significant contributions to the design and implementation. Others who provided valuable input to this work were: Krste Asanović, Steve Omohundro, Jerry Feldman, Heinz Schmidt and Chuck Wooters. Support from the International Computer Science Institute is gratefully acknowledged.

References

Asanović, K., Beck, J., Kingsbury, B., Kohn, P., Morgan, N., & Wawrzynek, J. (1991). SPERT: A VLIW/SIMD Microprocessor for Artificial Neural Network Computations. Tech. rep. TR-91-072, International Computer Science Institute.

Beck, J. (1990). The Ring Array Processor (RAP): Hardware. Tech. rep. TR-90-048, International Computer Science Institute.

Bilmes, J. & Kohn, P. (1990). The Ring Array Processor (RAP): Software Architecture. Tech. rep. TR-90-050, International Computer Science Institute.

Bourlard, H. & Morgan, N. (1991). Connectionist approaches to the use of Markov models for continuous speech recognition. In Touretzky, D. S. (Ed.), *Advances in Neural Information Processing Systems*, Vol. 3. Morgan Kaufmann, San Mateo CA.

Kohn, P. & Bilmes, J. (1990). The Ring Array Processor (RAP): Software Users Manual Version 1.0. Tech. rep. TR-90-049, International Computer Science Institute.

Kohn, P. (1991). CLONES: Connectionist Layered Object-oriented NEtwork Simulator. Tech. rep. TR-91-073, International Computer Science Institute.

Morgan, N., Beck, J., Kohn, P., Bilmes, J., Allman, E., & Beer, J. (1990). The RAP: a ring array processor for layered network calculations. In *Proceedings IEEE International Conference on Application Specific Array Processors*, pp. 296–308 Princeton NJ.

Morgan, N., Beck, J., Kohn, P., & Bilmes, J. (1992). Neurocomputing on the RAP. In Przytula, K. W. & Prasanna, V. K. (Eds.), *Digital Parallel Implementations of Neural Networks*. Prentice-Hall, Englewood Cliffs NJ.

Constrained Optimization Applied to the Parameter Setting Problem for Analog Circuits

David Kirk, Kurt Fleischer, Lloyd Watts,* Alan Barr
Computer Graphics 350-74
California Institute of Technology
Pasadena, CA 91125

Abstract

We use constrained optimization to select operating parameters for two circuits: a simple 3-transistor square root circuit, and an analog VLSI artificial cochlea. This automated method uses computer controlled measurement and test equipment to choose chip parameters which minimize the difference between the actual circuit's behavior and a specified goal behavior. Choosing the proper circuit parameters is important to compensate for manufacturing deviations or adjust circuit performance within a certain range. As biologically-motivated analog VLSI circuits become increasingly complex, implying more parameters, setting these parameters by hand will become more cumbersome. Thus an automated parameter setting method can be of great value [Fleischer 90]. Automated parameter setting is an integral part of a *goal-based engineering design methodology* in which circuits are constructed with parameters enabling a wide range of behaviors, and are then "tuned" to the desired behaviors automatically.

1   Introduction

Constrained optimization methods are useful for setting the parameters of analog circuits. We present two experiments in which an automated method successfully finds parameter settings which cause our circuit's behavior to closely approximate the desired behavior. These parameter-setting experiments are described in Section 3. The difficult subproblems encountered were (1) building the electronic setup

---

*Dept of Electrical Engineering 116-81

to acquire the data and control the circuit, and (2) specifying the computation of deviation from desired behavior in a mathematical form suitable for the optimization tools. We describe the necessary components of the electronic setup in Section 2, and we discuss the selection of optimization technique toward the end of Section 3.

Automated parameter setting can be an important component of a system to build accurate analog circuits. The power of this method is enhanced by including appropriate parameters in the initial design of a circuit: we can build circuits with a wide range of behaviors and then "tune" them to the desired behavior. In Section 6, we describe a comprehensive design methodology which embodies this strategy.

2   Implementation

We have assembled a system which allows us to test these ideas. The system can be conceptually decomposed into four distinct parts:

circuit: an analog VLSI chip intended to compute a particular function.

target function: a computational model quantitatively describing the desired behavior of the circuit. This model may have the same parameters as the circuit, or may be expressed in terms of biological data that the circuit is to mimic.

error metric: compares the target to the actual circuit function, and computes a difference measure.

constrained optimization tool: a numerical analysis tool, chosen based on the characteristics of the particular problem posed by this circuit.

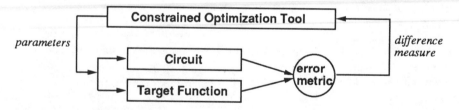

The constrained optimization tool uses the error metric to compute the difference between the performance of the circuit and the target function. It then adjusts the parameters to minimize the error metric, causing the actual circuit behavior to approach the target function as closely as possible.

2.1   A Generic Physical Setup for Optimization

A typical physical setup for choosing chip parameters under computer control has the following elements: an analog VLSI circuit, a digital computer to control the optimization process, computer programmable voltage/current sources to drive the chip, and computer programmable measurement devices, such as electrometers and oscilloscopes, to measure the chip's response.

The combination of all of these elements provides a self-contained environment for testing chips. The setting of parameters can then be performed at whatever level of automation is desirable. In this way, *all* inputs to the chip and all measurements of the outputs can be controlled by the computer.

3   The Experiments

We perform two experiments to set parameters of analog VLSI circuits using constrained optimization. The first experiment is a simple one-parameter system, a 3-transistor "square root" circuit. The second experiment uses a more complex time-varying multi-parameter system, an analog VLSI electronic cochlea. The artificial cochlea is composed of cascaded 2nd order section filters.

3.1   Square Root Experiment

In the first experiment we examine a "square-root" circuit [Mead 89], which actually computes $ax^\alpha + b$, where α is typically near 0.4. We introduce a parameter (V) into this circuit which varies α indirectly. By adjusting the voltage V in the square root circuit, as shown in Figure 1(a), we can alter the shape of the response curve.

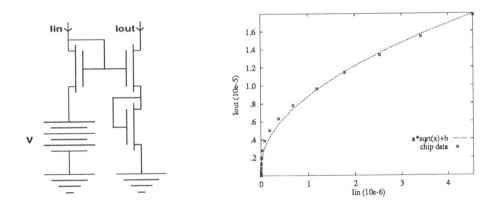

Figure 1: (a) Square root circuit. (b) Resulting fit.

We have little control over the values of a and b in this circuit, so we choose an error metric which optimizes α, targeting a curve which has a slope of 0.5 in log-log I_{in} vs. I_{out} space. Since $b << a\sqrt{x}$, we can safely ignore b for the purposes of this parameter-setting experiment. The entire optimization process takes only a few minutes for this simple one-parameter system. Figure 1(b) shows the final results of the square root computation, with the circuit output normalized by a and b.

3.2   Analog VLSI Cochlea

As an example of a more complex system on which to test the constrained optimization technique, we chose a silicon cochlea, as described by [Lyon 88]. The silicon cochlea is a cascade of lowpass second-order filter sections arranged such that the natural frequency τ of the stages decreases exponentially with distance into the cascade, while the quality factor Q of the filters is the same for each section (tap). The value of Q determines the peak gain at each tap.

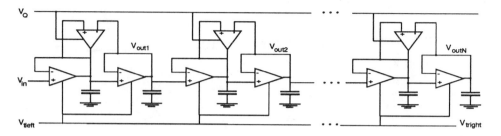

Figure 2: Cochlea circuit

To specify the performance of such a cochlea, we need to specify the natural frequencies of the first and last taps, and the peak gain at each tap. These performance parameters are controlled by bias voltages V_{τ_L} V_{τ_R}, and V_Q, respectively. The parameter-setting problem for this circuit is to find the bias voltages that give the desired performance. This optimization task is more lengthy than the square root optimization. Each measurement of the frequency response takes a few minutes, since it is composed of many individual instrument readings.

3.2.1   Cochlea Results

The results of our attempts to set parameters for the analog VLSI cochlea are quite encouraging.

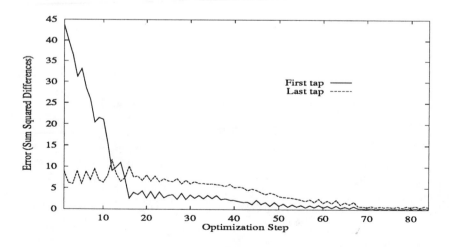

Figure 3: Error metric trajectories for gradient descent on cochlea

Figure 3 shows the trajectories of the error metrics for the first and last tap of the cochlea. Most of the progress is made in the early steps, after which the optimization is proceeding along the valley of the error surface, shown in Figure 5.

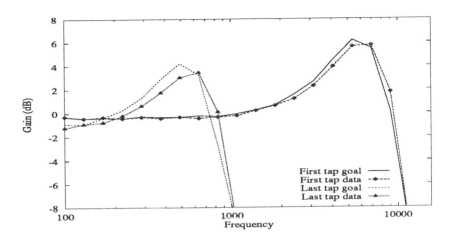

Figure 4: Target frequency response and gradient descent optimized data for cochlea

Figure 4 shows both the target frequency response data and the frequency responses which result from our chosen parameter settings. The curves are quite similar, and the differences are at the scale of measurement noise and instrument resolution in our system.

3.2.2   Cochlea Optimization Strategies

We explored several optimization strategies for finding the best parameters for the electronic cochlea. Of these, two are of particular interest:

special knowledge: use a priori knowledge of the effect of each knob to guide the optimization

gradient descent: assume that we know nothing except the input/output relation of the chip. Then we can estimate the gradient for gradient descent by varying the inputs. Robust numerical techniques such as conjugate gradient can also be helpful when the energy landscape is steep.

We found the gradient descent technique to be reliable, although it did not converge nearly as quickly as the "special knowledge" optimization. This corresponds with our intuition that any special knowledge we have about the circuit's operation will aid us in setting the parameters.

4   Choosing An Appropriate Optimization Method

One element of our system which has worked without much difficulty is the optimization. However, more complex circuits may require more sophisticated optimization methods. A wide variety of constrained optimization algorithms exist which are

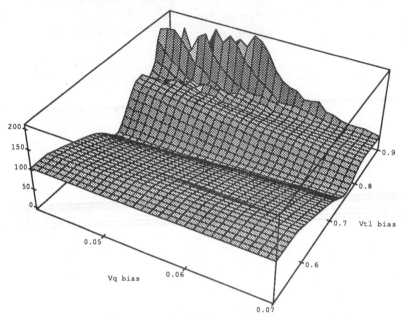

Figure 5: The error surface for the error metric for the frequency response of the first tap of the cochlea. Note the narrow valley in the error surface. Our target (the minimum) lies near the far left, at the deepest part of the valley.

effective on particular classes of problems (gradient descent, quasi-newton, simulated annealing, etc) [Platt 89, Gill 81, Press 86, Fleischer 90], and we can choose a method appropriate to the problem at hand. Techniques such as simulated annealing can find optimal parameter combinations for multi-parameter systems with complex behavior, which gives us confidence that our methods will work for more complex circuits.

The choice of error metric may also need to be reconsidered for more complex circuits. For systems with time-varying signals, we can use an error metric which captures the time course of the signal. We can deal with hysteresis by beginning at a known state and following the same path for each optimization step. Noisy and non-smooth functions can be improved by averaging data and using robust numeric techniques which are less sensitive to noise.

5   Conclusions

The constrained optimization technique works well when a well-defined goal for chip operation can be specified. We can compare automated parameter setting with adjustment by hand: consider that humans often fail in the same situations where optimization fails (eg. multiple local minima). In contrast, for larger dimensional spaces, hand adjustment is very difficult, while an optimization technique may succeed. We expect to integrate the technique into our chip development process, and future developments will move the optimization and learning process gradually into the chip. It is interesting to note that our gradient descent method "learns" the parameters of the chip in a manner similar to backpropagation. Seen from this perspective, this work is a step on the path toward robust on-chip learning.

In order to use this technique, there are two moderately difficult problems to address. First, one must assemble and interface the equipment to set parameters and record results from the circuit under computer control (eg. voltage and current sources, electrometer, digital oscilloscope, etc). This is a one-time cost since a similar setup can be used for many different circuits. A more difficult issue is how to specify the target function of a circuit, and how to compute the error metric. For example, in the simple square-root circuit, one might be more concerned about behavior in a particular region, or perhaps along the entire range of operation. Care must be taken to ensure that the combination of the target model and the error metric accurately describes the desired behavior of the circuit.

The existence of an automated parameter setting mechanism opens up a new avenue for producing accurate analog circuits. The goal of *accurately* computing a function differs from the approach of providing a cheap (simple) circuit which loosely *approximates* the function [Gilbert 68] [Mead 89]. By providing appropriate parameters in the design of a circuit, we can ensure that the desired function is in the domain of possible circuit behaviors (given expected manufacturing tolerances). Thus we define the domain of the circuit in anticipation of the parameter setting apparatus. The optimization methods will then be able to find the best solution in the domain, which could potentially be accurate to a high degree of precision.

6   The Goal-based Engineering Design Technique

The results of our optimization experiments suggest the adoption of a comprehensive *Goal-based Engineering Design Technique* that directly affects how we design and test chips.

Our results change the types of circuits we will try to build. The optimization techniques allow us to aggresively design and build ambitious circuits and more frequently have them work as expected, meeting our design goals. As a corollary, we can confidently attack larger and more interesting problems.

The technique is composed of the following four steps:

1) **goal-setting:** identify the target function, or behavioral goals, of the design

2) **circuit design:** design the circuit with "knobs" (adjustable parameters) in it, attempting to make sure desired (target) circuit behavior is in gamut of the actual circuit, given expected manufacturing variation and device characteristics.

3) **optimization plan:** devise optimization strategy to explore parameter settings. This includes capabilities such as a digital computer to control the optimization, and computer-driven instruments which can apply voltages/currents to the chip and measure voltage/current outputs.

4) **optimization:** use optimization procedure to select parameters to minimize deviation of actual circuit performance from the target function the optimization may make use of *special knowledge* about the circuit, such as "I know that this knob has effect x," or interaction, such as "I know that this is a good region, so explore here."

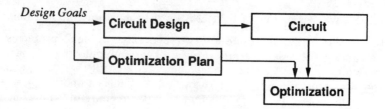

The goal-setting process produces design goals that influence both the circuit design and the form of the optimization plan. It is important to produce a match between the design of the circuit and the plan for optimizing its parameters.

Acknowledgements

Many thanks to Carver Mead for ideas, encouragement, and support for this project. Thanks also to John Lemoncheck for help getting our physical setup together. Thanks to Hewlett-Packard for equipment donation. This work was supported in part by an AT&T Bell Laboratories Ph.D. Fellowship. Additional support was provided by NSF (ASC-89-20219). All opinions, findings, conclusions, or recommendations expressed in this document are those of the author and do not necessarily reflect the views of the sponsoring agencies.

References

[Fleischer 90] Fleischer, K., J. Platt, and A. Barr, "An Approach to Solving the Parameter Setting Problem," IEEE/ACM 23rd Intl Conf on System Sciences, January 1990.

[Gilbert 68] Gilbert, B., "A Precise Four-Quadrant Multiplier with Sub-nanosecond Response," *IEEE Journal of Solid-State Circuits*, SC-3:365, 1968.

[Gill 81] Gill, P. E., W. Murray, and M. H. Wright, "Practical Optimization," Academic Press, 1981.

[Lyon 88] Lyon, R. A., and C. A. Mead, "An Analog Electronic Cochlea," IEEE Trans. Acous. Speech, and Signal Proc., Volume 36, Number 7, July, 1988, pp. 1119-1134.

[Mead 89] Mead, C. A., "Analog VLSI and Neural Systems," Addison-Wesley, 1989.

[Platt 89] Platt, J. C., "Constrained Optimization for Neural Networks and Computer Graphics," Ph.D. Thesis, California Institute of Technology, Caltech-CS-TR-89-07, June, 1989.

[Press 86] Press, W., Flannery, B., Teukolsky, S., Vetterling, W., "Numerical Recipes: the Art of Scientific Computing," Cambridge University Press, Cambridge, 1986.

Segmentation Circuits Using Constrained Optimization

John G. Harris*
MIT AI Lab
545 Technology Sq., Rm 767
Cambridge, MA 02139

Abstract

A novel segmentation algorithm has been developed utilizing an absolute-value smoothness penalty instead of the more common quadratic regularizer. This functional imposes a piece-wise constant constraint on the segmented data. Since the minimized energy is guaranteed to be convex, there are no problems with local minima and no complex continuation methods are necessary to find the unique global minimum. By interpreting the minimized energy as the generalized power of a nonlinear resistive network, a continuous-time analog segmentation circuit was constructed.

1 INTRODUCTION

Analog hardware has obvious advantages in terms of its size, speed, cost, and power consumption. Analog chip designers, however, should not feel constrained to mapping existing digital algorithms to silicon. Many times, new algorithms must be adapted or invented to ensure efficient implementation in analog hardware. Novel analog algorithms embedded in the hardware must be simple and obey the natural constraints of physics. Much algorithm intuition can be gained from experimenting with these continuous-time nonlinear systems. For example, the algorithm described in this paper arose from experimentation with existing analog segmentation hardware. Surprisingly, many of these "analog" algorithms may prove useful even if a computer vision researcher is limited to simulating the analog hardware on a digital computer [7].

---

*A portion of this work is part of a Ph.D dissertation at Caltech [7].

2   ABSOLUTE-VALUE SMOOTHNESS TERM

Rather than deal with systems that have many possible stable states, a network
that has a unique stable state will be studied. Consider a network that minimizes:

$$E(u) = \frac{1}{2} \sum_i (d_i - u_i)^2 + \lambda \sum_i |u_{i+1} - u_i| \qquad (2)$$

The absolute-value function is used for the smoothness penalty instead of the more
familiar quadratic term. There are two intuitive reasons why the absolute-value
penalty is an improvement over the quadratic penalty for piece-wise constant seg-
mentation. First, for large values of $|u_i - u_{i+1}|$, the penalty is not as severe, which
means that edges will be smoothed less. Second, small values of $|u_i - u_{i+1}|$ are
penalized more than they are in the quadratic case, resulting in a flatter surface
between edges. Since no complex continuation or annealing methods are necessary
to avoid local minima, this computational model is of interest to vision researchers
independent of any hardware implications.

This method is very similar to constrained optimization methods discussed by Platt
[14] and Gill [4]. Under this interpretation, the problem is to minimize $\sum (d_i - u_i)^2$
with the constraint that $u_i = u_{i+1}$ for all i. Equation 1 is an instance of the penalty
method, as $\lambda \to \infty$, the constraint $u_i = u_{i+1}$ is fulfilled exactly. The absolute-value
value penalty function given in Equation 2 is an example of a nondifferential penalty.
The constraint $u_i = u_{i+1}$ is fulfilled exactly for a finite value of λ. However, unlike
typical constrained optimization methods, this application requires some of these
"exact" constraints to fail (at discontinuities) and others to be fulfilled.

This algorithm also resembles techniques in robust statistics, a field pioneered and
formalized by Huber [9]. The need for robust estimation techniques in visual processing is clear since, a single outlier may cause wild variations in standard regularization networks which rely on quadratic data constraints [17]. Rather than use the
quadratic data constraints, robust regression techniques tend to limit the influence
of outlier data points.[2] The absolute-value function is one method commonly used
to reduce outlier susceptability. In fact, the absolute-value network developed in
this paper is a robust method if discontinuities in the data are interpreted as outliers. The line process or resistive fuse networks can also be interpreted as robust
methods using a more complex influence functions.

3   ANALOG MODELS

As pointed out by Poggio and Koch [15], the notion of minimizing power in linear
networks implementing quadratic "regularized" algorithms must be replaced by the
more general notion of minimizing the total resistor co-content [13] for nonlinear
networks. For a voltage-controlled resistor characterized by $I = f(V)$, the co-
content is defined as

$$J(V) = \int_0^V f(V')dV' \qquad (3)$$

---

[2]Outlier detection techniques have been mapped to analog hardware [8].

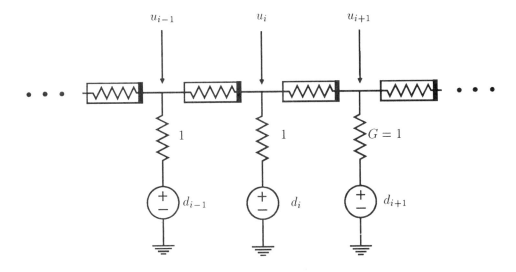

Figure 1: Nonlinear resistive network for piece-wise constant segmentation.

One-dimensional surface interpolation from dense data will be used as the model problem in this paper, but these techniques generalize to sparse data in multiple dimensions. A standard technique for smoothing or interpolating noisy inputs d_i is to minimize an energy[1] of the form:

$$E(u) = \sum_i (d_i - u_i)^2 + \lambda \sum_i (u_{i+1} - u_i)^2 \tag{1}$$

The first term ensures that the solution u_i will be close to the data while the second term implements a smoothness constraint. The parameter λ controls the tradeoff between the degree of smoothness and the fidelity to the data. Equation 1 can be interpreted as a regularization method [1] or as the power dissipated the linear version of the resistive network shown in Figure 1 [16].

Since the energy given by Equation 1 oversmoothes discontinuities, numerous researchers (starting with Geman and Geman [3]) have modified Equation 1 with line processes and successfully demonstrated piece-wise smooth segmentation. In these methods, the resultant energy is nonconvex and complex annealing or continuation methods are required to converge to a good local minima of the energy space. This problem is solved using probabilistic [11] or deterministic annealing techniques [2, 10]. Line-process discontinuities have been successfully demonstrated in analog hardware using resistive fuse networks [5], but continuation methods are still required to find a good solution [6].

---

[1]The term *energy* is used throughout this paper as a cost functional to be minimized. It does not necessarily relate to any true energy dissipated in the real world.

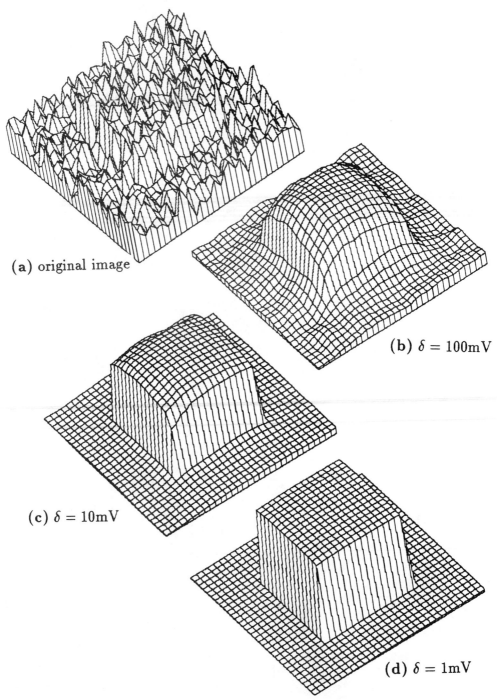

Figure 2: Various examples of tiny-tanh network simulation for varying δ. The I-V characteristic of the saturating resistors is $I = \lambda \tanh(V/\delta)$. (a) shows a synthetic 1.0V tower image with additive Gaussian noise of $\sigma = 0.3$V which is input to the network. The network outputs are shown in Figures (b) $\delta = 100$mV, (c) $\delta = 10$mV and (d) $\delta = 1$mV. For all simulations $\lambda = 1$.

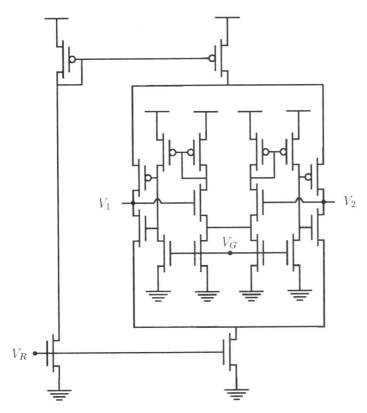

Figure 3: Tiny tanh circuit. The saturating tanh characteristic is measured between nodes V_1 and V_2. Controls V_R and V_G set the conductance and saturation voltage for the device.

For a linear resistor, $I = GV$, the co-content is given by $\frac{1}{2}GV^2$, which is half the dissipated power $P = GV^2$.

The absolute-value functional in Equation 2 is not strictly convex. Also, since the absolute-value function is nondifferentiable at the origin, hardware and software methods of solution will be plagued with instabilities and oscillations. We approximate Equation 2 with the following well-behaved convex co-content:

$$\frac{1}{2}\sum_i (u_i - d_i)^2 + \sum_i \int_0^{u_{i+1} - u_i} \lambda \tanh(v/\delta)dv \tag{4}$$

The co-content becomes the absolute-value cost function in Equation 2 in the limiting case as $\delta \to 0$. The derivative of Equation 2 yields Kirchoff's current equation at each node of the resistive network in Figure 1:

$$(u_i - d_i) + \lambda \tanh(\frac{u_i - u_{i+1}}{\delta}) + \lambda \tanh(\frac{u_i - u_{i-1}}{\delta}) = 0 \tag{5}$$

Therefore, construction of this network requires a nonlinear resistor with a hyperbolic tangent I-V characteristic with an extremely narrow linear region. For this reason, this element is called the *tiny-tanh* resistor. This saturating resistor is used as the nonlinear element in the resistive network shown in Figure 1. Its I-V characteristic is $I = \lambda \tanh(V/\delta)$. It is well-known that any circuit made of independent voltage sources and two-terminal resistors with strictly increasing I-V characteristics has a unique stable state.

4   COMPUTER SIMULATIONS

Figure 2a shows a synthetic 1.0V tower image with additive Gaussian noise of $\sigma = 0.3$V. Figure 2b shows the simulated result for $\delta = 100$mV and $\lambda = 1$. As Mead has observed, a network of saturating resistors has a limited segmentation effect [12]. Unfortunately, as seen in the figure, noise is still evident in the output, and the curves on either side of the step have started to slope toward one another. As λ is increased to further smooth the noise, the two sides of the step will blend together into one homogeneous region. However, as the width of the linear region of the saturating resistor is reduced, network segmentation properties are greatly enhanced. Segmentation performance improves for $\delta = 10$mV shown in Figure 2c and further improves for $\delta = 1mV$ in Figure 2d. The best segmentation occurs when the I-V curve resembles a step function, and co-content, therefore, approximates an absolute-value. Decreasing δ less than 1mV shows no discernible change in the output.[3]

One drawback of this network is that it does not recover the exact heights of input steps. Rather it subtracts a constant from the height of each input. It is straightforward to show that the amount each uniform region is pulled towards the background is given by λ(perimeter/area) [7]. Significant features with large area/perimeter ratios will retain their original height. Noise points have small area/perimeter ratios and therefore will be pulled towards the background. Typically, the exact values of the heights are less important than the location of the discontinuities. Furthermore, it would not be difficult to construct a two-stage network to recover the exact values of the step heights if desired. In this scheme a tiny-tanh network would control the switches on a second fuse network.

5   ANALOG IMPLEMENTATION

Mead has constructed a CMOS saturating resistor with an I-V characteristic of the form $I = \lambda \tanh(V/\delta)$, where delta must be larger than 50mV because of fundamental physical limitations [12]. Simulation results from section 4 suggest that for a tower of height h to be segmented, h/δ must be at least on the order of 1000. Therefore a network using Mead's saturating resistor ($\delta = 50$mV) could segment a tower on the order of 50V, which is much too large a voltage to input to these chips. Furthermore, since we are typically interested in segmenting images into more than two levels even higher voltages would be required. The tiny-tanh circuit (shown in Figure 3) builds upon an older version of Mead's saturating resistor [18] using a gain stage to decrease the linear region of the device. This device can be made to saturate at voltages as low as 5mV.

---

[3]These simulations were also used to smooth and segment noisy depth data from a correlation-based stereo algorithm run on real images [7].

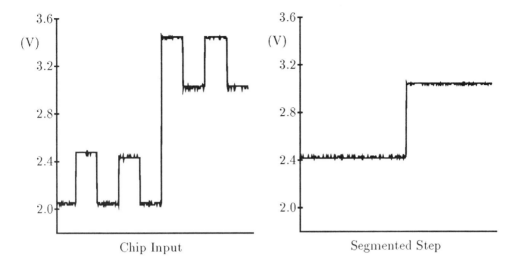

Figure 4: Measured segmentation performance of the tiny-tanh network for a step. The input shown on the left is about a 1V step. The output shown on the right is a segmented step about 0.5V in height.

By implementing the nonlinear resistors in Figure 1 with the tiny-tanh circuit, a 1D segmentation network was successfully fabricated and tested. Figure 4 shows the segmentation which resulted when a step (about 1V) was scanned into the chip. The segmented step has been reduced to about 0.5V. No special annealing methods were necessary because a convex energy is being minimized.

6   CONCLUSION

A novel energy functional was developed for piece-wise constant segmentation.[4] This computational model is of interest to vision researchers independent of any hardware implications, because a convex energy is minimized. In sharp contrast to previous solutions of this problem, no complex continuation or annealing methods are necessary to avoid local minima. By interpreting this Lyapunov energy as the co-content of a nonlinear circuit, we have built and demonstrated the tiny-tanh network, a continuous-time segmentation network in analog VLSI.

Acknowledgements

Much of this work was perform at Caltech with the support of Christof Koch and Carver Mead. A Hughes Aircraft graduate student fellowship and an NSF postdoctoral fellowship are gratefully acknowledged.

---

[4]This work has also been extended to segment piece-wise linear regions, instead of the purely piece-wise constant processing discussed in this paper [7].

References

[1] M. Bertero, T. Poggio, and V. Torre. Ill-posed problems in early vision. *Proc. IEEE*, 76:869–889, 1988.

[2] A. Blake and A. Zisserman. *Visual Reconstruction*. MIT Press, Cambridge, MA, 1987.

[3] S. Geman and D. Geman. Stochastic relaxation, gibbs distribution and the bayesian restoration of images. *IEEE Trans. Pattern Anal. Mach. Intell.*, 6:721–741, 1984.

[4] P. E. Gill, W. Murray, and M. H. Wright. *Practical Optimization*. Academic Press, 1981.

[5] J. G. Harris, C. Koch, and J. Luo. A two-dimensional analog VLSI circuit for detecting discontinuities in early vision. *Science*, 248:1209–1211, 1990.

[6] J. G. Harris, C. Koch, J. Luo, and J. Wyatt. Resistive fuses: analog hardware for detecting discontinuities in early vision. In M. Mead, C.and Ismail, editor, *Analog VLSI Implementations of Neural Systems*. Kluwer, Norwell, MA, 1989.

[7] J.G. Harris. *Analog models for early vision*. PhD thesis, California Institute of Technology, Pasadena, CA, 1991. Dept. of Computation and Neural Systems.

[8] J.G. Harris, S.C. Liu, and B. Mathur. Discarding outliers in a nonlinear resistive network. In *International Joint Conference on Neural Networks*, pages 501–506, Seattle, WA., July 1991.

[9] P.J. Huber. *Robust Statistics*. J. Wiley & Sons, 1981.

[10] C. Koch, J. Marroquin, and A. Yuille. Analog "neuronal" networks in early vision. *Proc Natl. Acad. Sci. B. USA*, 83:4263–4267, 1987.

[11] J. Marroquin, S. Mitter, and T. Poggio. Probabilistic solution of ill-posed problems in computational vision. *J. Am. Statistic Assoc*, 82:76–89, 1987.

[12] C. Mead. *Analog VLSI and Neural Systems*. Addison-Wesley, 1989.

[13] W. Millar. Some general theorems for non-linear systems possessing resistance. *Phil. Mag.*, 42:1150–1160, 1951.

[14] J. Platt. Constraint methods for neural networks and computer graphics. Dept. of Computer Science Technical Report Caltech-CS-TR-89-07, California Institute of Technology, Pasadena, CA, 1990.

[15] T. Poggio and C. Koch. An analog model of computation for the ill-posed problems of early vision. Technical report, MIT Artificial Intelligence Laboratory, Cambridge, MA, 1984. AI Memo No. 783.

[16] T. Poggio and C. Koch. Ill-posed problems in early vision: from computational theory to analogue networks. *Proc. R. Soc. Lond. B*, 226:303–323, 1985.

[17] B.G. Schunck. Robust computational vision. In *Robust methods in computer vision workshop.*, 1989.

[18] M. A. Sivilotti, M. A. Mahowald, and C. A. Mead. Real-time visual computation using analog CMOS processing arrays. In *1987 Stanford Conference on Very Large Scale Integration*, Cambridge, MA, 1987. MIT Press.

Analog LSI Implementation of an Auto-Adaptive Network for Real-Time Separation of Independent Signals

Marc H. Cohen, Philippe O. Pouliquen and Andreas G. Andreou*
Electrical and Computer Engineering
The Johns Hopkins University, Baltimore, MD 21218, USA

Abstract

We present experimental data from an analog CMOS LSI chip that implements the Herault-Jutten adaptive neural network. Testing procedures and results in time and frequency-domain are described. These include weight convergence trajectories, extraction of a signal in noise, and separation of statistically complex signals such as speech.

1 Introduction

In its most general form, the N x N independent component analyzer (In.C.A.) network (Herault 1986, Jutten 1987, 1991) can be used to solve the following classical signal processing problem; given N physically distinct measurements of *a priori* unknown linear combinations of N independent signal sources, the network auto-adaptively extracts N equivalent independent signals.

The network consists of a set of N simple processing units interconnected by inhibitory synapses (see figure 1). A processing unit i calculates its output $S_i(t)$ based on its input $E_i(t)$ and the weighted sum of the outputs from the remaining $N-1$ units. The weights are updated using a modified Hebbian learning rule (Hebb 1949, Herault 1986, Jutten 1987, 1991).

This architecture has led to various CMOS implementations (Vittoz 1989, Cohen 1991a). We have implemented three different CMOS designs using different learn-

---

*Please address correspondence to Andreas G. Andreou.

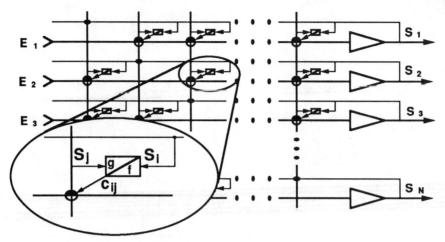

Figure 1: The $N \times N$ network architecture

ing rules, circuits and design methodologies. Two of them employ both above- and below-threshold CMOS circuits, the third (Cohen 1991a, 1992) employs only subthreshold MOS technology. The particulars of the circuits and learning rules employed in our implementations have been described in detail elsewhere (Cohen 1991a, 1991b, 1991c, 1992); this paper concentrates on the test procedures and results using different type of input signals.

In section 2 we describe the test procedure used to observe the evolution of the weights in time from reset to convergence of the network. In section 3 we describe tests designed to observe the frequency domain characteristics of the network. In section 4 we describe more ambitious tests involving speech signals and other audio-band signals.

All results presented here were obtained from the first design: a chip that used the learning rules and design techniques of Vittoz and Arreguit (Vittoz 1989). Our improvements on their original implementation were mostly in the details of the circuits and resulted in a system that had less systematic offsets in the individual components (Cohen 1991a). However, similar tests where performed on the other two designs with similar results.

2   Time domain results

This test was chosen to match conditions used for digital simulations of the network, and to compare the evolution of the weights in their weight-space. Two sine waves of approximately 1kHz were mixed in two different ratios, and the mixed signals (E_1 and E_2) were presented to the chip. The chip output signals (S_1 and S_2) and the weights (C_{12} and C_{21}) were digitized and plotted.

The results are shown in figure 2. Figure 2(a) is a phase plot of the network's input signals, and figure 2(b) is a phase plot of the network's output signals after

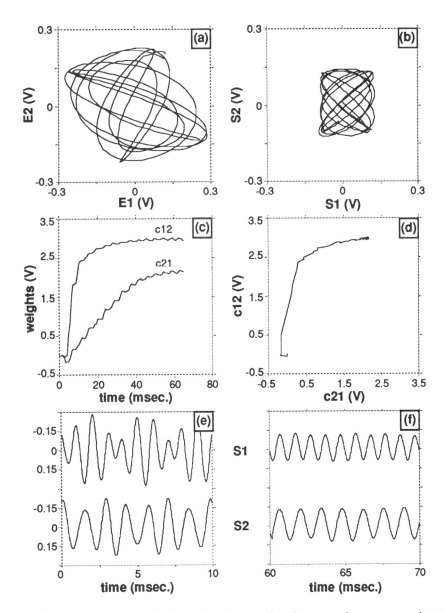

Figure 2: Test results for a 2 × 2 network using two sine waves as input.

convergence of the weights: note how the plot has been transformed from a parallel-ogram into a rectangle. Figure 2(c) is a plot of the network's weights as a function of time, beginning from the reset state where the weight capacitors are grounded. Figure 2(d) is a phase plot of the network's weights: in this instance, the initial rapid change in the phase space of the weights is due to offsets in the circuits used. That is, once the system was turned on it assumed an operating point for weights other than the (0,0). Figures 2(e) and 2(f) plot the output signals of the network immediately after reset and after convergence of the weights respectively. Other implementations exhibited similar behaviors except that initial offsets in the weight space (although certainly not catastrophic here) were eliminated by using improved circuit techniques.

This test is not applied to larger networks due to the large number of signals required to observe the weights. By comparing the convergence results of the 2×2 networks for which the weights were externally observable with other networks for which the weights were not observable, it was determined that the addition of the observation circuitry slowed convergence by a factor of 5.

3   Frequency domain results

This procedure is designed to test an implementation's ability to extract a signal which is "buried" in background noise.

The signal (X_1, a sinusoid) is to be extracted from bandpass filtered white noise (X_2), which has peak amplitude 10dB greater than the signal and "center" frequency around the frequency of the signal.

Test results are plotted in figure 3: the magnitude spectrum of the original signals, the input signals to the network, and the output signals of the network after convergence are shown. The chip is able to reduce the background noise by 30dB, and extract the sinusoid.

Larger networks (6×6) were tested with a mixture of six sinusoidal signals around 1kHz spaced at not regular intervals approximately 20Hz apart. The networks successfully separated each pure sinusoid into a separate output channel and suppressed all adjacent sinusoids by approximately 20dB. No convergence problems were encountered with this larger network.

4   Audio-band results

These In.C.A. networks were not necessarily intended for filtering the type of signals that are usually synthesized in a laboratory. Therefore the networks were also tested using music and speech, signals that have more complex statistical properties.

For instance, a recording of a segment of text read in English and a segment of text read in greek by the same speaker were mixed in two slightly different ratios to produce unintelligible input signals for the 2×2 networks. The spectrogram of a typical segment of the mixed signals is shown in figure 4. The networks easily recovered the two original recordings: the spectrograms of the outputs are shown

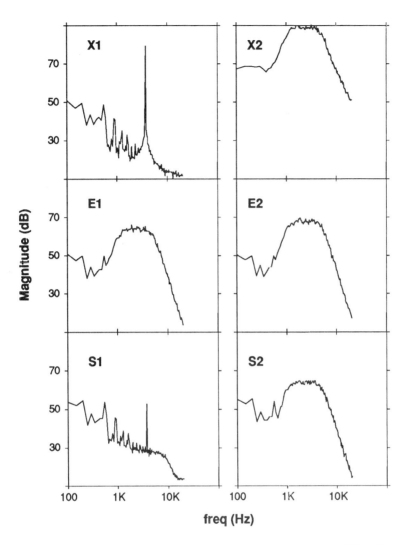

Figure 3: Test results for a 2 × 2 network using a sine wave and bandpass filtered white noise as input.

in figure 5. Similar results were obtained with mixed recordings of music, or combinations of music and speech.

5   Conclusion

We have described the results of a network which performs auto-adaptive filtering. By using analog VLSI technology we have achieved a real-time, scalable and low

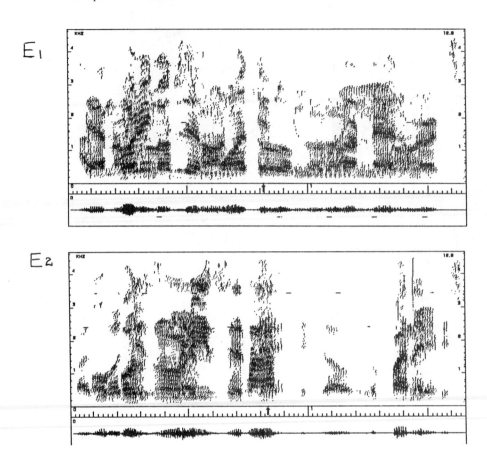

Figure 4: Spectrograms of segments of mixed speech used as input to the 2 × 2 networks.

power realization of the network. We believe it will have many applications, to name but a few;

- three dimensional object reconstruction from stereoscopic vision,
- removing crosstalk in telephone/digital communication lines, and
- separation of evoked potential signals from background EEG and EMG noise.

Using MOS technology and micropower techniques real-time separation of signals in the audio spectrum and up to about 1MHz is possible. Current-mode techniques (Cohen 1992) using bipolar devices, and higher current levels should enable real-time processing of signals of a few hundred MHz.

Future work will involve developing the capability to handle signal delays introduced by the medium through which the signals propagate before reaching the sensors (as

S_1

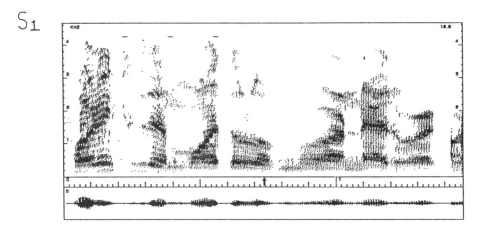

S_2

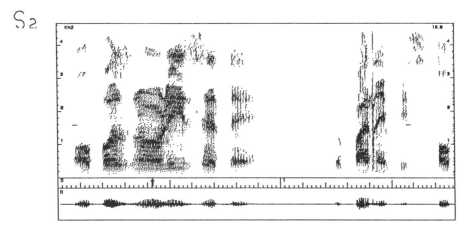

Figure 5: Spectrogram of segments of the output of a 2 × 2 network showing separation of the speech signals.

in the "cocktail party" problem). Such modifications to the algorithm have been proposed by Jutten (Jutten 1987) and recently by Platt and Faggin (Platt 1991).

References

Cohen M. H. (1991a) "Analog VLSI Implementation of an Auto-Adaptive Synthetic Neural Network for Real-Time Separation of Independent Signal Sources." M.S.E. Thesis, Biomedical Engineering, The Johns Hopkins University.

Cohen M. H., Pouliquen P. O. and Andreou A. G. (1991b) "Silicon Implementation of an Auto-Adaptive Network for Real-Time Separation of Independent Signals." *Proceedings of the 1991 International Symposium on Circuits and Systems,* Singapore, 2971–2974.

Cohen M. H., Pouliquen P. O. and Andreou A. G. (1991c) "Silicon VLSI Implementation of an Auto-Adaptive Network for the Real-Time Separation of Independent Signal Sources." *Proceedings of the 25th Annual Conference on Information Sciences and Systems,* The Johns Hopkins University, Baltimore, Maryland, 856–861.

Cohen M. H., Pouliquen P. O. and Andreou A. G. (1991d) "An Auto-Adaptive Synthetic Neural Network for Real-Time Separation of Independent Signal Sources." *Proceedings of the 1991 International Joint Conference on Neural Networks,* Seattle, WA, I-211–214.

Cohen M. H. and Andreou A. G. (1992) "Current-Mode Subthreshold MOS Implementation of the Herault-Jutten Auto-Adaptive Network." *IEEE Journal of Solid-State Circuits* 27(5), May 1992.

Hebb D. O. (1949) "*The Organisation of Behavior*" Wiley, New York.

Herault J. and Jutten C. (1986) "Space or Time Adaptive Signal Processing by Neural Network Models." *Neural Networks for Computing,* AIP Conference Proceedings 151, Snowbird, UT. Edited by John S. Denker.

Jutten C. (1987) "Calcul Neuromimétique et Traitement du Signal, Analyse en Composantes Indépendantes." Ph.D. Thesis, Université Scientifique et Médicale¡ - Institut National Polytechnique, Grenoble, France.

Jutten C. and Herault J. (1991) "Blind Separation of Sources, Part I: An Adaptive Algorithm based on Neuromimetic Architecture." *Signal Processing* 24:1–10, Elsevier Science Publishers.

Platt J. and Faggin F. "A Network for the Separation of Sources that are Superimposed and Delayed." *Advances in Neural Information Processing Systems 4* Morgan Kaufmann Publishers, San Mateo, 1992.

Vittoz E. A. and Arreguit X. (1989) "CMOS Integration of Herault-Jutten Cells for Separation of Sources." *Workshop on Analog VLSI and Neural Systems* Portland, Oregon. Kluwer Academic Press, Norwell, MA.

Temporal Adaptation
in a
Silicon Auditory Nerve

John Lazzaro

CS Division
UC Berkeley
571 Evans Hall
Berkeley, CA 94720

Abstract

Many auditory theorists consider the temporal adaptation of the auditory nerve a key aspect of speech coding in the auditory periphery. Experiments with models of auditory localization and pitch perception also suggest temporal adaptation is an important element of practical auditory processing. I have designed, fabricated, and successfully tested an analog integrated circuit that models many aspects of auditory nerve response, including temporal adaptation.

1. INTRODUCTION

We are modeling known and proposed auditory structures in the brain using analog VLSI circuits, with the goal of making contributions both to engineering practice and biological understanding. Computational neuroscience involves modeling biology at many levels of abstraction. The first silicon auditory models were constructed at a fairly high level of abstraction (Lyon and Mead, 1988; Lazzaro and Mead, 1989ab; Mead et al., 1991; Lyon, 1991). The functional limitations of these silicon systems have prompted a new generation of auditory neural circuits designed at a lower level of abstraction (Watts et al., 1991; Liu et al., 1991). 813

The silicon model of auditory nerve response models sensory transduction and spike generation in the auditory periphery at a high level of abstraction (Lazzaro and Mead, 1989c); this circuit is a component in silicon models of auditory localization, pitch perception, and spectral shape enhancement (Lazzaro and Mead, 1989ab; Lazzaro, 1991a). Among other limitations, this circuit does not model the short-term temporal adaptation of the auditory nerve. Many auditory theorists consider the temporal adaptation of the auditory nerve a key aspect of speech coding in the auditory periphery (Delgutte and Kiang, 1984). From the engineering perspective, the pitch perception and auditory localization chips perform well with sustained sounds as input; temporal adaptation in the silicon auditory nerve should improve performance for transient sounds.

I have designed, fabricated, and tested an integrated circuit that models the temporal adaptation of spiral ganglion neurons in the auditory periphery. The circuit receives an analog voltage input, corresponding to the signal at an output tap of a silicon cochlea, and produces fixed-width, fixed-height pulses that are correlates to the action potentials of an auditory nerve fiber. I have also fabricated and tested an integrated circuit that combines an array of these neurons with a silicon cochlea (Lyon and Mead, 1988); this design is a silicon model of auditory nerve response. Both circuits were fabricated using the Orbit double polysilicon n-well $2\mu m$ process.

2. TEMPORAL ADAPTATION

Figure 1 shows data from the temporal adaptation circuit; the data in this figure was taken by connecting signals directly to the inner hair cell circuit input, bypassing silicon cochlea processing. In (a), we apply a 1 kHz pure tone burst of 20ms in duration to the input of the hair cell circuit (top trace), and see an adapting sequence of spikes as the output (middle trace). If this tone burst in repeated at 80ms intervals, each response in unique; by averaging the responses to 64 consecutive tone bursts (bottom trace), we see the envelope of the temporal adaptation superimposed on the cycle-by-cycle phase-locking of the spike train. These behaviors qualitatively match biological experiments (Kiang et al., 1965).

In biological auditory nerve fibers, cycle-by-cycle phase locking ceases for auditory fibers tuned to sufficiently high frequencies, but the temporal adaptation property remains. In the silicon spiral ganglion neuron, a 10kHz pure tone burst fails to elicit phase-locking (Figure 1(b), trace identities as in (a)). Temporal adaptation remains, however, qualitatively matching biological experiments (Kiang et al., 1965).

To compare this data with the previous generation of silicon auditory nerve circuits, we set the control parameters of the new spiral ganglion model to eliminate temporal adaptation. Figure 1(c) shows the 1 kHz tone burst response (trace identities as in (a)). Phase locking occurs without temporal adaptation. The uneven response of the averaged spike outputs is due to beat frequencies between the input tone frequency and the output spike rate; in practice, the circuit noise of the silicon cochleas adds random variation to the auditory input and smooths this response (Lazzaro and Mead, 1989c).

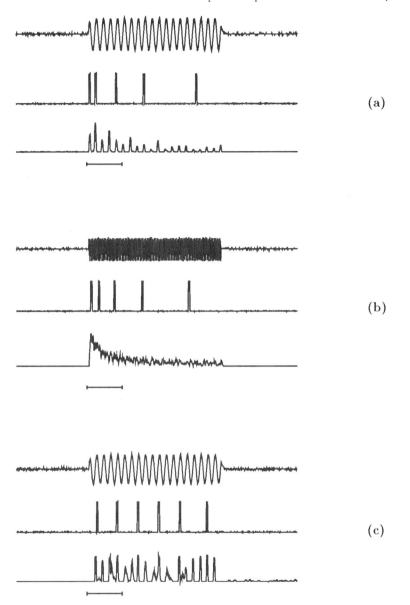

Figure 1. Responses of test chip to pure tone bursts. Horizontal axis is time for all plots, all horizontal rules measure 5 ms. **(a)** Chip response to a 1 kHz, 20 ms tone burst. Top trace shows tone burst input, middle trace shows a sample response from the chip, bottom trace shows averaged output of 64 responses to tone bursts. Averaged response shows both temporal adaptation and phase locking. **(b)** Chip response to a 10 kHz, 20 ms tone burst. Trace identifications identical to (a). Response shows temporal adaptation without phase locking. **(c)** Chip response to a 1 kHz, 20 ms tone burst, with adaptation circuitry disabled. Trace identifications identical to (a). Response shows phase locking without temporal adaptation.

3. CIRCUIT DESIGN

Figure 2 shows a block diagram of the model. The circuits modeling inner hair cell transduction remain unchanged from the original model (Lazzaro and Mead, 1989c), and are shown as a single box. This box performs time differentiation, nonlinear compression and half-wave rectification on the input waveform V_i, producing a unidirectional current waveform as output. The dependent current source represents this processed signal.

The axon hillock circuit (Mead, 1989), drawn as a box marked with a pulse, converts this current signal into a series of fixed-width, fixed height spikes; V_o is the output of the model. The current signal is connected to the pulse generator using a novel current mirror circuit, that serves as the control element to regulate temporal adaptation. This current mirror circuit has an additional high impedance input, V_a, that exponentially scales the current entering the axon hillock circuit (the current mirror operates in the subthreshold region). The adaptation capacitor C_a is associated with the control voltage V_a.

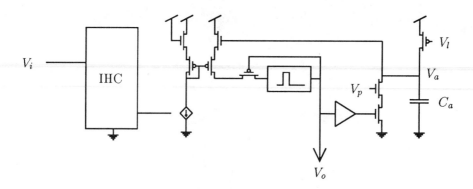

Figure 2. Circuit schematic of the enhanced silicon model of auditory nerve response. The circuit converts the analog voltage input V_i into the pulse train V_o; control voltages V_l and V_p control the temporal adaptation of state variable V_a on capacitor C_a. See text for details.

C_a is constantly charged by the PFET transistor associated with control voltage V_l, and is discharged during every pulse output of the axon hillock circuit, by an amount set by the control voltage V_p. During periods with no input signal, V_a is charged to V_{dd}, and the current mirror is set to deliver maximum current with the onset of an input signal. If an input signal occurs and neuron activity begins, the capacitor V_a is discharged with every spike, degrading the output of the current mirror. In this way, temporal adaptation occurs, with characteristics determined by V_p and V_l.

The nonlinear differential equations for this adaptation circuit are similar to the equations governing the adaptive baroreceptor circuit (Lazzaro et al., 1991); the publication describing this circuit includes an analysis deriving a recurrence relation that describes the pulse output of the circuit given a step input.

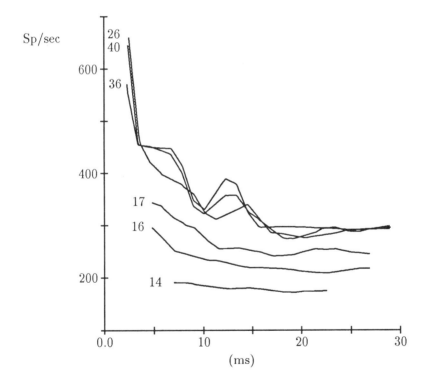

Figure 3. Instantaneous firing rate of the adaptive neuron, as a function of time; tone burst begins at 0 ms. Each curve is marked with the amplitude of presented tone burst, in dB. Tone burst frequency is 1Khz.

4. DATA ANALYSIS

The experiment shown in Figure 1(a) was repeated for tone bursts of different amplitudes; this data set was used to produce several standard measures of adaptive response (Hewitt and Meddis, 1991). The integrated auditory nerve circuit was used for this set of experiments. Data was taken from an adaptive auditory nerve output that had a best frequency of 1 Khz.; the frequency of all tone bursts was also 1 Khz.

Figure 3 shows the instantaneous firing rate of the auditory nerve output as a function of time, for tone bursts of different amplitudes. Adaptation was more pronounced for more intense sounds. This difference is also seen in Figure 4. In this figure, instantaneous firing rate is plotted as a function of amplitude, both at response onset and after full adaptation.

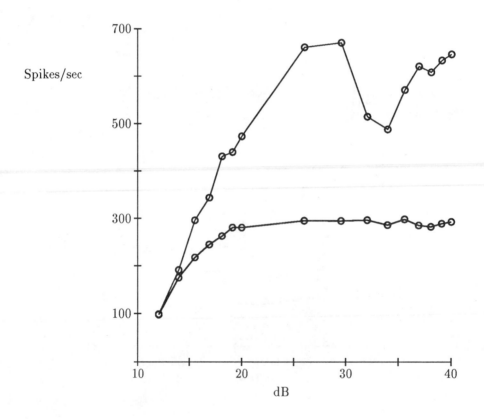

Figure 4. Instantaneous firing rate of the adaptive neuron, as a function of amplitude (in dB). Top curve is firing rate at onset of response, bottom curve is firing rate after adaptation. Tone burst frequency is 1Khz.

Figure 4 shows that the instantaneous spike rate saturates at moderate intensity after full adaptation; at these moderate intensities, however, the onset instantaneous spike rate continues to encode intensity. Figure 4 shows a non-monotonicity at high intensities in the onset response; this undesired non-monotonicity is a result of the undesired saturation of the silicon cochlea circuit (Lazzaro, 1991b).

5. CONCLUSION

This circuit improves the silicon model of auditory response, by adding temporal adaptation. We expect this improvement to enhance existing architectures for auditory localization and pitch perception, and aid the creation of new circuits for speech processing.

Acknowledgements

Thanks to K. Johnson of CU Boulder and J. Wawrzynek of UC Berkeley for hosting this research in their laboratories. I also thank the Caltech auditory research community, specifically C. Mead, D. Lyon, M. Konishi, L. Watts, M. Godfrey, and X. Arreguit. This work was funded by the National Science Foundation.

References

Delgutte, B., and Kiang, Y. S. (1984). Speech coding in the auditory nerve I-V. *J. Acoust. Soc. Am* **75**:3, 866–918.

Hewitt, M. J. and Meddis, R. (1991). An evaluation of eight computer models of mammalian inner hair-cell function. *J. Acoust. Soc. Am* **90**:2, 904.

Kiang, N. Y.-s, Watenabe, T., Thomas, E.C., and Clark, L.F. (1965). *Discharge Patterns of Single Fibers in the Cat's Auditory Nerve.* Cambridge, MA: M.I.T Press.

Lazzaro, J. and Mead, C. (1989a). A silicon model of auditory localization. *Neural Computation* **1**: 41–70.

Lazzaro, J. and Mead, C. (1989b). Silicon modeling of pitch perception. *Proceedings National Academy of Sciences* **86**: 9597–9601.

Lazzaro, J. and Mead, C. (1989c). Circuit models of sensory transduction in the cochlea. In Mead, C. and Ismail, M. (eds), *Analog VLSI Implementations of Neural Networks.* Norwell, MA: Kluwer Academic Publishers, pp. 85-101.

Lazzaro, J. P. (1991a). A silicon model of an auditory neural representation of spectral shape. *IEEE Journal Solid State Circuits* **26**: 772–777.

Lazzaro, J. P. (1991b). Biologically-based auditory signal processing in analog VLSI. *IEEE Asilomar Conference on Signals, Systems, and Computers.*

Lazzaro, J. P., Schwaber, J., and Rogers, W. (1991). Silicon baroreceptors: modeling cardiovascular pressure transduction in analog VLSI. In Sequin, C. (ed), *Ad-*

vanced Research in VLSI, Proceedings of the 1991 Santa Cruz Conference, Cambridge, MA: MIT Press, pp. 163–177.

Liu, W., Andreou, A., and Goldstein, M. (1991). Analog VLSI implementation of an auditory periphery model. *25 Annual Conference on Information Sciences and Systems,* Baltimore, MD, 1991.

Lyon, R. and Mead, C. (1988). An analog electronic cochlea. *IEEE Trans. Acoust., Speech, Signal Processing* **36**: 1119–1134.

Lyon, R. (1991). CCD correlators for auditory models. *IEEE Asilomar Conference on Signals, Systems, and Computers.*

Mead, C. A., Arreguit, X., Lazzaro, J. P. (1991) Analog VLSI models of binaural hearing. *IEEE Journal of Neural Networks,* **2**: 230–236.

Mead, C. A. (1989). *Analog VLSI and Neural Systems.* Reading, MA: Addison-Wesley.

Watts, L., Lyon, R., and Mead, C. (1991). A bidirectional analog VLSI cochlear model. In Sequin, C. (ed), *Advanced Research in VLSI, Proceedings of the 1991 Santa Cruz Conference,* Cambridge, MA: MIT Press, pp. 153–163.

Optical Implementation of a Self-Organizing Feature Extractor

Dana Z. Anderson*, Claus Benkert, Verena Hebler, Ju-Seog Jang, Don Montgomery, and Mark Saffman.

Joint Institute for Laboratory Astrophysics, University of Colorado and the Department of Physics, University of Colorado, Boulder Colorado 80309-0440

Abstract

We demonstrate a self-organizing system based on photorefractive ring oscillators. We employ the system in two ways that can both be thought of as feature extractors; one acts on a set of images exposed repeatedly to the system strictly as a linear feature extractor, and the other serves as a signal demultiplexer for fiber optic communications. Both systems implement unsupervised competitive learning embedded within the mode interaction dynamics between the modes of a set of ring oscillators. After a training period, the modes of the rings become associated with the different image features or carrier frequencies within the incoming data stream.

1 Introduction

Self-organizing networks (Kohonen, Hertz, Domany) discover features or qualities about their input environment on their own; they learn without a teacher making explicit what is to be learned. This property reminds us of several ubiquitous behaviors we see in the physical and natural sciences such as pattern formation, morphogenesis and phase transitions (Domany). While in the natural case one is usually satisfied simply to *analyze* and understand the behavior of a self-organizing system, we usually have a specific function in mind that we wish a neural network to perform. That is, in the network case we wish to *synthesize* a system that will perform the desired function. Self-organizing principles are particularly valuable when one does not know ahead of time exactly what to expect from the input to be processed and when it is some property of the input itself that is of interest. For example, one may wish to determine some quality about the input statistics - this one can often do by applying self-organization principles. However, when one wishes to attribute some meaning to the data, self-organization principles are probably poor candidates for this task.

821

It is the behavioral similarity between self-organizing network models and physical systems that has lead us to investigate the possibility of implementing a self-organizing network function by designing the dynamics for a set of optical oscillators. Modes of sets of oscillators undergo competition (Anderson, Benkert) much like that employed in competitive learning network models. Using photorefractive elements, we have tailored the dynamics of the mode interaction to perform a learning task. A physical optical implementation of self-organized learning serves two functions. Unlike a computer simulation, the physical system *must* obey certain physical laws just like a biological system does. We have in mind the consequences of energy conservation, finite gain and the effects of noise. Therefore, we might expect to learn something about general principles applicable to biological systems from our physical versions. Second, there are some applications where an optical system serves as an ideal "front end" to signal processing.

Here we take a commonly used supervised approach for extracting features from a stream of images and demonstrate how this task can be done in a self-organizing manner. The conventional approach employs a holographic correlator (Vander Lugt). In this technique, various patterns are chosen for recognition by the optical system and then recorded in holographic media using angle-encoded reference beams. When a specific pattern is presented to the holographic correlator, the output is determined by the correlation between the presented pattern and the patterns that have been recorded as holograms during the 'learning phase'. The angles and intensities of the reconstructed reference beams identify the features present in the pattern. Because the processing time-scale in holographic systems is determined by the time necessary for light to scatter off of the holographic grating, the optical correlation takes place virtually instantaneously. It is the speed of this correlation that makes the holographic approach so interesting.

While its speed is an asset, the holographic correlator approach to feature extraction from images is a supervised approach to the problem: an external supervisor must choose the relevant image features to store in the correlator holograms. Moreover the supervisor must provide an angle-encoded reference beam for each stored feature. For many applications, it is desirable to have an adaptive system that has the innate capacity to discover, in an unsupervised fashion, the underlying structure within the input data.

A photorefractive ring resonator circuit that learns to extract spatially orthogonal features from images is illustrated schematically in figure 1. The resonator rings in figure 1 are constructed physically from optical fibers cables. The resonator is self-starting and is pumped by images containing the input data (White). The resonator learns to associate each feature in the input data set with one and only one of the available resonator rings. In other words, when the proper feature is present in the input data, the resonator ring with which it has become associated will light up. When this feature is absent from the input data, the corresponding resonator ring will be dark.

The self-organizing capabilities of this system arise from the nonlinear dynam-

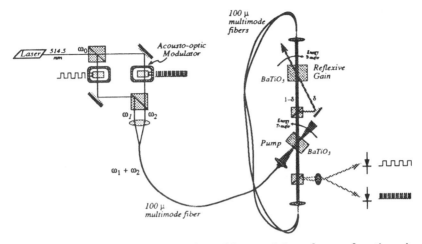

Figure 1: Schematic diagram of the self-organizing photorefractive ring resonator. The two signal frequencies, ω_1 amd ω_2, are identical when the circuit is used as a feature extractor and are separated by 280 MHz when the system is used as a frequency demultiplexer.

ics of competition between resonator modes for optical energy within the common photorefractive pump crystal (Benkert). We have used this system to accomplish two optical signal processing tasks. In the first case, the resonator can learn to distinguish between two spatially orthogonal input images that are impressed on the common pump beam in a piece-wise constant fashion. In the second case, frequency demultiplexing of a composite input image constructed from two spatially orthogonal image components of different optical frequencies can be accomplished (Saffman, 1991b). In both cases, the optical system has no *a priori* knowledge of the input data and self-discovers the important structural elements.

2 A Self-Organizing Photorefractive Ring Resonator

The experimental design that realizes an optical self-organizing feature extractor is shown in figure 1. The optical system consists of a two ring, multimode, unidirectional photorefractive ring resonator in which the rings are spatially distinct. The resonator rings are defined by loops of 100 μ core multimode optical fiber. The gain for both modes is provided by a common $BaTiO_3$ crystal that is pumped by optical images presented as speckle patterns from a single 100 μ multimode optical fiber. The light source is a single frequency argon-ion laser operating at 514.5 nm. The second $BaTiO_3$ crystal provides reflexive coupling within the resonator, which ensures that each resonator ring becomes associated with only one input feature.

The input images are generated by splitting the source beam and passing it through two acousto-optic modulator cells. The optical signals generated by the acousto-optic modulators are then focused into a single 1.5 meter long stepindex, 100 μ core, multimode optical fiber. The difference in the angle of incidence for the two signal beams at the fiber end face is sufficient to ensure that the corresponding speckle pattern images are spatially orthogonal (Saffman,

1991a). The acousto-optic cells are used in a conventional fashion to shift the optical frequency of the carrier signal, and are also used as shutters to impress time modulated information on the input signals. When the resonator is operating as a feature extractor, both input signals are carried on the same optical frequency, but are presented to the resonator sequentially. The presentation cycle time of 500 Hz was chosen to be much smaller than the characteristic time constant of the BaTiO$_3$ pump crystal. When operating as a frequency demultiplexer, the acousto-optic modulators shift the optical carrier frequencies of the input signals such that they are separated by 280 MHz. The two input carrier signals are time modulated and mixed into the optical fiber to form a composite image composed of two spatially orthogonal speckle patterns having different optical frequencies. This composite image is used as the pump beam for the resonator.

3 Unsupervised Competitive Learning

Correlations between the optical electric fields in images establish the criterion for a measure of similarity between different image features. The best measure of these correlations is the inner product between the complex-valued spatial electric field distribution across the input images,

$$S_{12} = \left| \iint d^2 x E_1^*(x) E_2(x) \right|$$

When $S_{12} = 0$ the images are uncorrelated and we define such images as spatially orthogonal. When the resonator begins to oscillate, neither resonator ring has any preference for a particular input feature or frequency. The system modes have no internal bias (*i.e.*, no *a priori* knowledge) for the input data. As the gain for photorefractive two-beam coupling in the common BaTiO$_3$ pump crystal saturates, the two resonator rings begin to compete with each other for the available pump energy. This competitive coupling leads to 'winner-takes-all' dynamics in the resonator in which each resonator ring becomes associated with one or the other spatially orthogonal input images. In other words, the rings become labels for each spatially orthogonal feature present in the input image set.

Phenomenologically, the dynamics of this mode competition can be described by Lotka-Volterra equations (Benkert, Lotka, Volterra),

$$\frac{dI_{i,p}}{dt} = I_{i,p} \left(\alpha_{i,p} - \beta_{i,p} I_{i,p} - \sum_{j,l} \theta_{i,p;j,l} I_{j,l} \right)$$

Where $I_{i,p}$ is the intensity of the oscillating energy in ring i due to energy transferred from the input feature p, $\alpha_{i,p}$ is the gain for two-beam coupling between ring i and feature p, $\beta_{i,p}$ is the self-saturation coefficient, and $\theta_{i,p;j,l}$ are the cross-saturation coefficients. The self-organizing dynamics are determined by the values of the cross coupling coefficients. Thus the competitive learning algorithm that drives the self-organization in this optical system is embedded

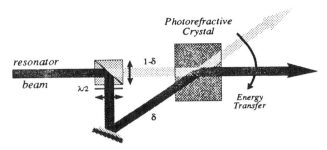

Figure 2: Reflexive gain interaction. A fraction, δ, of the incident intensity is removed from the resonator beam, and then coupled back into itself by photorefractive two beam coupling. This ensures 'Winner-takes-all' competitive dynamics between the resonator rings.

within the nonlinear dynamics of mode competition in the pump crystal.

Once the system has learned, the spatially orthogonal features in the training set are represented as holograms in the $BaTiO_3$ pump crystal. These holograms act as linear projection operators, and any new image constructed from features in the training set will be projected in a linear fashion onto the learned feature basis set. The relative intensity of light oscillating in each ring corresponds to the fraction of each learned feature in the new image. Thus, the resonator functions as a feature extractor (Kohonen).

4 Reflexive Gain

If each resonator ring was single mode, then competitive dynamics in the common pump crystal would be sufficient for feature extraction. However, a multimode ring system allows stability for certain pathological feature extracting states. The multimode character of each resonator ring can permit simultaneous oscillation of two spatially orthogonal modes within a single ring. Ostensibly, the system is performing feature extraction, but this form of output is not useful for further processing. These pathological states are excluded by introducing reflexive gain into the cavity.

Any system that twists back upon itself and closes a loop is referred to as *reflexive* (Hofstadter, pg. 3). A reflexive gain interaction is achieved by removing a portion of the oscillating energy from each ring and then coupling it back into the same ring by photorefractive two-beam coupling, as illustrated in figure 2. The standard equations for photorefractive two-beam coupling (Kukhtarev, Hall) can be used to derive an expression for the steady-state transmission, T, through the reflexive gain element in terms of the number of spatially orthogonal modes, N, that are oscillating simultaneously within a single ring,

$$T = \left[1 + \frac{\delta}{1-\delta}\exp\left(\frac{-G_0}{N}\right)\right]^{-1}$$

Here, $\exp(G_0)$ is the small signal gain and δ is the fraction of light removed

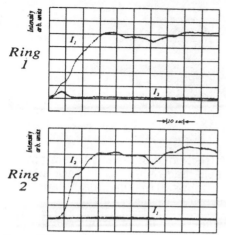

Figure 3: Time evolution of the intensities within each resonator ring due to ω_1 (I_1) and ω_2(I_2). After about 30 seconds, the system has learned to demultiplex the two input frequencies. Ring 1 has become associated with ω_1 and Ring 2 has become associated with ω_2. The contrast ratio between I_1 and I_2 in each ring is about 40:1.

from the resonator. The transmission decreases for $N > 1$ causing larger cavity losses for the case of simultaneous oscillation of spatially orthogonal modes within a single ring. Therefore, the system favors 'winner-takes-all' dynamics over other pathological feature extracting states.

5 Experimental Results

The self-organizing dynamics within the optical circuit require several seconds to reach steady state. In the case of frequency demultiplexing, the dynamical evolution of the system was observed by detecting the envelopes of the carrier modulation, as shown in figure 3. In the case of the feature extractor, transient system dynamics were observed by synchronizing the observation with the modulation of one feature or the other, as shown in figure 4. The frequency demultiplexing (figure 3) and feature extracting (figure 4) states develop a high contrast ratio and are stable for as long as the pump beam is present. Measurements with a spectrum analyzer show an output contrast ratio of better than 40:1 in the frequency demultiplexing case.

The circuit described here extracts spatially orthogonal features while contin-

Figure 4: Time evolution of the intensities in each resonator ring due to the two input pictures. The system requires about 30 seconds to learn to extract features from the input images. Picture 1 is associated with Ring 1 and picture 2 is associated with Ring2.

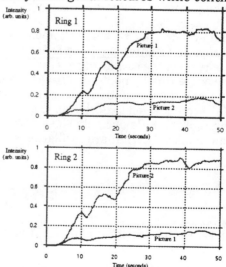

uously adapting to slow variations in the spatial mode superposition due to drifts in the carrier frequency or perturbations to the fibers. Thus, the system is adaptive as well as unsupervised.

6 Summary

An optical implementation of a self-organizing feature extractor that is adaptive has been demonstrated. The circuit exhibits the desirable dynamical property that is often referred to in the parlance of the neural networks as 'unsupervised learning'. The essential properties of this system arise from the nonlinear dynamics of mode competition within the optical ring resonator. The learning algorithm is embedded in these dynamics and they contribute to its capacity to adapt to slow changes in the input signal. The circuit learns to associate different spatially orthogonal images with different rings in an optical resonator. The learned feature set can represent orthogonal basis vectors in an image or different frequencies in a multiplexed optical signal. Because a wide variety of information can be encoded onto the input images presented to the feature extractor described here, it has the potential to find general application for tasks where the speed and adaptability of self-organizing and all-optical processing is desirable.

Acknowledgements

We are grateful for the support of both the Office of Naval Research, contract #N00014-91-J-1212 and the Air Force Office of Scientific Research, contract #AFOSR-90-0198. Mark Saffman would like to acknowledge support provided by a U.S. Air Force Office of Scientific Research laboratory graduate fellowship.

References

D.Z. Anderson and R. Saxena, *Theory of Multimode Operation of a Unidirectional Ring Oscillator having Photorefractive Gain: Weak Field Limit*, J. Opt. Soc. Am. B, **4**, 164 (1987).

C. Benkert and D.Z. Anderson, *Controlled competitive dynamics in a photorefractive ring oscillator: "Winner-takes-all" and the "voting-paradox" dynamics*, Phys. Rev. A, **44**, 4633 (1991).

E. Domany, J.L. van Hemmen and K. Schulten, eds., *Models of Neural Networks*; Springer-Verlag (1991).

T.J. Hall, R. Jaura, L.M. Connors and P.D. Foote, *The Photorefractive Effect - A Review*; Prog. Quant. Electr., **10**, 77 (1985).

J. Hertz, A. Krogh and R.G. Palmer, *Introduction to the Theory of Neural Computation*; Addison-Wesley (1991).

D. R. Hofstadter, *Metamagical Themas: Questing for the Essence of Mind and Pattern*; Bantam Books (1985).

T. Kohonen, *Self-Organization and Associative Memory*, 3rd Edition; Springer-Verlag (1989).

N. V. Kukhtarev, V.B. Markov, S.G. Odulov, M.S. Soskin and V.L. Vinetskii, *Holographic Storage in Electrooptic Crystals. I. Steady State*; Ferroelectrics, **22**, 949 (1979).

N. V. Kukhtarev, V.B. Markov, S.G. Odulov, M.S. Soskin and V.L. Vinetskii, *Holographic Storage in Electrooptic Crystals. II. Beam Coupling - Light Amplification;* Ferroelectrics, **22**, 961 (1979).

A.J. Lotka, *Elements of Physical Biology*; Baltimore (1925).

M. Saffman and D.Z. Anderson, *Mode multiplexing and holographic demultiplexing communications channels on a multimode fiber*, Opt. Lett., **16**, 300 (1991a).

M. Saffman, C. Benkert and D.Z. Anderson, *Self-organizing photorefractive frequency demultiplexer*, Opt. Lett., **16**, 1993 (1991b).

A. Vander Lugt, *Signal Detection by Complex Spatial Filtering*; IEEE Trans. Inform. Theor., **IT-10**, 139 (1964).

V. Volterra, *Leçons sur la Théorie Mathematiques de la Lutte pour la Vie*; Gauthier-Villars (1931).

J.O. White, M. Cronin-Golomb, B. Fischer, and A. Yariv, *Coherent Oscillation by Self-Induced Gratings in the Photorefractive Crystal BaTiO3*; Appl. Phys. Lett., **40**, 450 (1982).

PART XII

LEARNING AND GENERALIZATION

Principles of Risk Minimization
for Learning Theory

V. Vapnik
AT&T Bell Laboratories
Holmdel, NJ 07733, USA

Abstract

Learning is posed as a problem of function estimation, for which two principles of solution are considered: empirical risk minimization and structural risk minimization. These two principles are applied to two different statements of the function estimation problem: global and local. Systematic improvements in prediction power are illustrated in application to zip-code recognition.

1   INTRODUCTION

The structure of the theory of learning differs from that of most other theories for applied problems. The search for a solution to an applied problem usually requires the three following steps:

1. State the problem in mathematical terms.
2. Formulate a general principle to look for a solution to the problem.
3. Develop an algorithm based on such general principle.

The first two steps of this procedure offer in general no major difficulties; the third step requires most efforts, in developing computational algorithms to solve the problem at hand.

In the case of learning theory, however, many algorithms have been developed, but we still lack a clear understanding of the mathematical statement needed to describe the learning procedure, and of the general principle on which the search for solutions should be based. This paper is devoted to these first two steps, the statement of the problem and the general principle of solution.

The paper is organized as follows. First, the problem of function estimation is stated, and two principles of solution are discussed: the principle of empirical risk minimization and the principle of structural risk minimization. A new statement is then given: that of local estimation of function, to which the same principles are applied. An application to zip-code recognition is used to illustrate these ideas.

2   FUNCTION ESTIMATION MODEL

The learning process is described through three components:

1. A generator of random vectors x, drawn independently from a fixed but unknown distribution $P(x)$.
2. A supervisor which returns an output vector y to every input vector x, according to a conditional distribution function $P(y|x)$, also fixed but unknown.
3. A learning machine capable of implementing a set of functions $f(x, w)$, $w \in W$.

The problem of learning is that of choosing from the given set of functions the one which approximates best the supervisor's response. The selection is based on a training set of ℓ independent observations:

$$(x_1, y_1), ..., (x_\ell, y_\ell). \tag{1}$$

The formulation given above implies that learning corresponds to the problem of function approximation.

3   PROBLEM OF RISK MINIMIZATION

In order to choose the best available approximation to the supervisor's response, we measure the loss or discrepancy $L(y, f(x, w))$ between the response y of the supervisor to a given input x and the response $f(x, w)$ provided by the learning machine. Consider the expected value of the loss, given by the risk functional

$$R(w) = \int L(y, f(x, w)) dP(x, y). \tag{2}$$

The goal is to minimize the risk functional $R(w)$ over the class of functions $f(x, w)$, $w \in W$. But the joint probability distribution $P(x, y) = P(y|x)P(x)$ is unknown and the only available information is contained in the training set (1).

4   EMPIRICAL RISK MINIMIZATION

In order to solve this problem, the following induction principle is proposed: the risk functional $R(w)$ is replaced by the empirical risk functional

$$E(w) = \frac{1}{\ell} \sum_{i=1}^{\ell} L(y_i, f(x_i, w)) \tag{3}$$

constructed on the basis of the training set (1). The induction principle of empirical risk minimization (ERM) assumes that the function $f(x, w_\ell^*)$,which minimizes $E(w)$ over the set $w \in W$, results in a risk $R(w_\ell^*)$ which is close to its minimum.

This induction principle is quite general; many classical methods such as least square or maximum likelihood are realizations of the ERM principle.

The evaluation of the soundness of the ERM principle requires answers to the following two questions:

1. Is the principle consistent? (Does $R(w_\ell^*)$ converge to its minimum value on the set $w \in W$ when $\ell \to \infty$?)

2. How fast is the convergence as ℓ increases?

The answers to these two questions have been shown (Vapnik et al., 1989) to be equivalent to the answers to the following two questions:

1. Does the empirical risk $E(w)$ converge uniformly to the actual risk $R(w)$ over the full set $f(x, w)$, $w \in W$? Uniform convergence is defined as

$$\text{Prob}\{ \sup_{w \in W} |R(w) - E(w)| > \varepsilon \} \longrightarrow 0 \quad \text{as} \quad \ell \to \infty. \tag{4}$$

2. What is the rate of convergence?

It is important to stress that uniform convergence (4) for the full set of functions is a *necessary* and *sufficient* condition for the consistency of the ERM principle.

5   VC-DIMENSION OF THE SET OF FUNCTIONS

The theory of uniform convergence of empirical risk to actual risk developed in the 70's and 80's, includes a description of necessary and sufficient conditions as well as bounds for the rate of convergence (Vapnik, 1982). These bounds, which are independent of the distribution function $P(x, y)$, are based on a quantitative measure of the capacity of the set of functions implemented by the learning machine: the VC-dimension of the set.

For simplicity, these bounds will be discussed here only for the case of binary pattern recognition, for which $y \in \{0, 1\}$ and $f(x, w)$, $w \in W$ is the class of indicator functions. The loss function takes only two values $L(y, f(x, w)) = 0$ if $y = f(x, w)$ and $L(y, f(x, w)) = 1$ otherwise. In this case , the risk functional (2) is the probability of error, denoted by $P(w)$. The empirical risk functional (3), denoted by $\nu(w)$, is the frequency of error in the training set.

The VC-dimension of a set of indicator functions is the maximum number h of vectors which can be shattered in all possible 2^h ways using functions in the set. For instance, $h = n + 1$ for linear decision rules in n-dimensional space, since they can shatter at most $n + 1$ points.

6   RATES OF UNIFORM CONVERGENCE

The notion of VC-dimension provides a bound to the rate of uniform convergence. For a set of indicator functions with VC-dimension h, the following inequality holds:

$$\text{Prob}\{ \sup_{w \in W} |P(w) - \nu(w)| > \varepsilon \} < (\frac{2\ell e}{h})^h \exp\{-\varepsilon^2 \ell\}. \tag{5}$$

It then follows that with probability $1 - \eta$, simultaneously for all $w \in W$,

$$P(w) < \nu(w) + C_0(\ell/h, \eta), \tag{6}$$

with confidence interval

$$C_0(\ell/h, \eta) = \sqrt{\frac{h(\ln 2\ell/h + 1) - \ln \eta}{\ell}}. \tag{7}$$

This important result provides a bound to the actual risk $P(w)$ for all $w \in W$, including the w^* which minimizes the empirical risk $\nu(w)$.

The deviation $|P(w) - \nu(w)|$ in (5) is expected to be maximum for $P(w)$ close to $1/2$, since it is this value of $P(w)$ which maximizes the error variance $\sigma(w) = \sqrt{P(w)(1 - P(w))}$. The worst case bound for the confidence interval (7) is thus likely be controlled by the worst decision rule. The bound (6) is achieved for the worst case $P(w) = 1/2$, but not for small $P(w)$, which is the case of interest. A uniformly good approximation to $P(w)$ follows from considering

$$\text{Prob}\{ \sup_{w \in W} \frac{P(w) - \nu(w)}{\sigma(w)} > \varepsilon \}. \tag{8}$$

The variance of the relative deviation $(P(w) - \nu(w))/\sigma(w)$ is now independent of w. A bound for the probability (8), if available, would yield a uniformly good bound for actual risks for all $P(w)$.

Such a bound has not yet been established. But for $P(w) << 1$, the approximation $\sigma(w) \simeq \sqrt{P(w)}$ is true, and the following inequality holds:

$$\text{Prob}\{ \sup_{w \in W} \frac{P(w) - \nu(w)}{\sqrt{P(w)}} > \varepsilon \} < (\frac{2\ell e}{h})^h \exp\{-\frac{\varepsilon^2 \ell}{4}\}. \tag{9}$$

It then follows that with probability $1 - \eta$, simultaneously for all $w \in W$,

$$P(w) < \nu(w) + C_1(\ell/h, \nu(w), \eta), \tag{10}$$

with confidence interval

$$C_1(\ell/h, \nu(w), \eta) = 2 \left(\frac{h(\ln 2\ell/h + 1) - \ln \eta}{\ell} \right) \left(1 + \sqrt{1 + \frac{\nu(w)\ell}{h(\ln 2\ell/h + 1) - \ln \eta}} \right). \tag{11}$$

Note that the confidence interval now depends on $\nu(w)$, and that for $\nu(w) = 0$ it reduces to

$$C_1(\ell/h, 0, \eta) = 2C_0^2(\ell/h, \eta),$$

which provides a more precise bound for real case learning.

7   STRUCTURAL RISK MINIMIZATION

The method of ERM can be theoretically justified by considering the inequalities (6) or (10). When ℓ/h is large, the confidence intervals C_0 or C_1 become small, and can be neglected. The actual risk is then bound by only the empirical risk, and the probability of error on the test set can be expected to be small when the frequency of error in the training set is small.

However, if ℓ/h is small, the confidence interval cannot be neglected, and even $\nu(w) = 0$ does not guarantee a small probability of error. In this case the minimization of $P(w)$ requires a new principle, based on the simultaneous minimization of $\nu(w)$ and the confidence interval. It is then necessary to control the VC-dimension of the learning machine.

To do this, we introduce a nested structure of subsets $S_p = \{f(x, w), w \in W_p\}$, such that

$$S_1 \subset S_2 \subset ... \subset S_n.$$

The corresponding VC-dimensions of the subsets satisfy

$$h_1 < h_2 < ... < h_n.$$

The principle of structure risk minimization (SRM) requires a two-step process: the empirical risk has to be minimized for each element of the structure. The optimal element S^* is then selected to minimize the guaranteed risk, defined as the sum of the empirical risk and the confidence interval. This process involves a trade-off: as h increases the minimum empirical risk decreases, but the confidence interval increases.

8   EXAMPLES OF STRUCTURES FOR NEURAL NETS

The general principle of SRM can be implemented in many different ways. Here we consider three different examples of structures built for the set of functions implemented by a neural network.

1. Structure given by the architecture of the neural network. Consider an ensemble of fully connected neural networks in which the number of units in one of the hidden layers is monotonically increased. The set of implementable functions makes a structure as the number of hidden units is increased.

2. Structure given by the learning procedure. Consider the set of functions $S = \{f(x, w), \; w \in W\}$ implementable by a neural net of fixed architecture. The parameters $\{w\}$ are the weights of the neural network. A structure is introduced through $S_p = \{f(x, w), \; \|w\| \leq C_p\}$ and $C_1 < C_2 < ... < C_n$. For a convex loss function, the minimization of the empirical risk within the element S_p of the structure is achieved through the minimization of

$$E(w, \gamma_p) = \frac{1}{\ell} \sum_{i=1}^{\ell} L(y_i, f(x_i, w)) + \gamma_p \|w\|^2$$

with appropriately chosen Lagrange multipliers $\gamma_1 > \gamma_2 > ... > \gamma_n$. The well-known "weight decay" procedure refers to the minimization of this functional.

3. Structure given by preprocessing. Consider a neural net with fixed architecture. The input representation is modified by a transformation $z = K(x, \beta)$, where the parameter β controls the degree of the degeneracy introduced by this transformation (for instance β could be the width of a smoothing kernel).

A structure is introduced in the set of functions $S = \{f(K(x, \beta), w),\ w \in W\}$ through $\beta \geq C_p$, and $C_1 > C_2 > ... > C_n$.

9   PROBLEM OF LOCAL FUNCTION ESTIMATION

The problem of learning has been formulated as the problem of selecting from the class of functions $f(x, w)$, $w \in W$ that which provides the best available approximation to the response of the supervisor. Such a statement of the learning problem implies that a unique function $f(x, w^*)$ will be used for prediction over the full input space X. This is not necessarily a good strategy: the set $f(x, w)$, $w \in W$ might not contain a good predictor for the full input space, but might contain functions capable of good prediction on specified regions of input space.

In order to formulate the learning problem as a problem of local function approximation, consider a kernel $K(x - x_0, b) \geq 0$ which selects a region of input space of width b, centered at x_0. For example, consider the rectangular kernel,

$$K_r(x - x_0, b) = \left\{ \begin{array}{ll} 1 & \text{if } |x - x_0| \leq b \\ 0 & \text{otherwise} \end{array} \right.$$

and a more general general continuous kernel, such as the gaussian

$$K_g(x - x_0, b) = \exp -\{\frac{(x - x_0)^2}{b^2}\}.$$

The goal is to minimize the local risk functional

$$R(w, b, x_0) = \int L(y, f(x, w))\frac{K(x - x_0, b)}{K(x_0, b)}\,dP(x, y). \tag{12}$$

The normalization is defined by

$$K(x_0, b) = \int K(x - x_0, b)\,dP(x). \tag{13}$$

The local risk functional (12) is to be minimized over the class of functions $f(x, w)$, $w \in W$ and over all possible neighborhoods $b \in (0, \infty)$ centered at x_0. As before, the joint probability distribution $P(x, y)$ is unknown, and the only available information is contained in the training set (1).

10   EMPIRICAL RISK MINIMIZATION FOR LOCAL ESTIMATION

In order to solve this problem, the following induction principle is proposed: for fixed b, the local risk functional (12) is replaced by the empirical risk functional

$$E(w, b, x_0) = \frac{1}{\ell} \sum_{i=1}^{\ell} L(y_i, f(x_i, w))\frac{K(x_i - x_0, b)}{K(x_0, b)}, \tag{14}$$

constructed on the basis of the training set. The empirical risk functional (14) is to be minimized over $w \in W$. In the simplest case, the class of functions is that of constant functions, $f(x,w) = C(w)$. Consider the following examples:

1. **K-Nearest Neighbors Method:** For the case of binary pattern recognition, the class of constant indicator functions contains only two functions: either $f(x,w) = 0$ for all x, or $f(x,w) = 1$ for all x. The minimization of the empirical risk functional (14) with the rectangular kernel $K_r(x - x_0, b)$ leads to the K-nearest neighbors algorithm.

2. **Watson-Nadaraya Method:** For the case $y \in R$, the class of constant functions contains an infinite number of elements, $f(x,w) = C(w)$, $C(w) \in R$. The minimization of the empirical risk functional (14) for general kernel and a quadratic loss function $L(y, f(x,w)) = (y - f(x,w))^2$ leads to the estimator

$$f(x_0) = \sum_{i=1}^{\ell} y_i \frac{K(x_i - x_0, b)}{\sum_{j=1}^{\ell} K(x_j - x_0, b)},$$

which defines the Watson-Nadaraya algorithm.

These classical methods minimize (14) with a fixed b over the class of constant functions. The supervisor's response in the vicinity of x_0 is thus approximated by a constant, and the characteristic size b of the neighborhood is kept fixed, independent of x_0.

A truly local algorithm would adjust the parameter b to the characteristics of the region in input space centered at x_0. Further improvement is possible by allowing for a richer class of predictor functions $f(x,w)$ within the selected neighborhood. The SRM principle for local estimation provides a tool for incorporating these two features.

11 STRUCTURAL RISK MINIMIZATION FOR LOCAL ESTIMATION

The arguments that lead to the inequality (6) for the risk functional (2) can be extended to the local risk functional (12), to obtain the following result: with probability $1 - \eta$, and simultaneously for all $w \in W$ and all $b \in (0, \infty)$

$$R(w, b, x_0) < E(w, b, x_0) + C_2(\ell/h, b, \eta). \tag{15}$$

The confidence interval $C_2(\ell/h, b, \eta)$ reduces to $C_0(\ell/h, \eta)$ in the $b \to \infty$ limit.

As before, a nested structure is introduced in the class of functions, and the empirical risk (14) is minimized with respect to both $w \in W$ and $b \in (0, \infty)$ for each element of the structure. The optimal element is then selected to minimize the guaranteed risk, defined as the sum of the empirical risk and the confidence interval. For fixed b this process involves an already discussed trade-off: as h increases, the empirical risk decreases but the confidence interval increases. A new trade-off appears by varying b at fixed h: as b increases the empirical risk increases, but the confidence interval decreases. The use of b as an additional free parameter allows us to find deeper minima of the guaranteed risk.

12   APPLICATION TO ZIP-CODE RECOGNITION

We now discuss results for the recognition of the hand written and printed digits in the US Postal database, containing 9709 training examples and 2007 testing examples. Human recognition of this task results in an approximately 2.5% prediction error (Säckinger et al., 1991).

The learning machine considered here is a five-layer neural network with shared weights and limited receptive fields. When trained with a back-propagation algorithm for the minimization of the empirical risk, the network achieves 5.1% prediction error (Le Cun et al., 1990).

Further performance improvement with the same network architecture has required the introduction a new induction principle. Methods based on SRM have achieved prediction errors of 4.1% (training based on a double-back-propagation algorithm which incorporates a special form of weight decay (Drucker, 1991)) and 3.95% (using a smoothing transformation in input space (Simard, 1991)).

The best result achieved so far, of 3.3% prediction error, is based on the use of the SRM for local estimation of the predictor function (Bottou, 1991).

It is obvious from these results that dramatic gains cannot be achieved through minor algorithmic modifications, but require the introduction of new principles.

Acknowledgements

I thank the members of the Neural Networks research group at Bell Labs, Holmdel, for supportive and useful discussions. Sara Solla, Leon Bottou, and Larry Jackel provided invaluable help to render my presentation more clear and accessible to the neural networks community.

References

V. N. Vapnik (1982), *Estimation of Dependencies Based on Empirical Data*, Springer-Verlag (New York).

V. N. Vapnik and A. Ja. Chervonenkis (1989) 'Necessary and sufficient conditions for consistency of the method of empirical risk minimization' [in Russian], *Yearbook of the Academy of Sciences of the USSR* on *Recognition, Classification, and Forecasting*, **2**, 217-249, Nauka (Moscow) (English translation in preparation).

E. Säckinger and J. Bromley (1991), private communication.

Y. Le Cun, B. Boser, J. S. Denker, D. Henderson, R. E. Howard, W. Hubbard and L. D. Jackel (1990) 'Handwritten digit recognition with a back-propagation network', *Neural Information Processing Systems 2*, 396-404, ed. by D. S. Touretzky, Morgan Kaufmann (California).

H. Drucker (1991), private communication.

P. Simard (1991), private communication.

L. Bottou (1991), private communication.

Bayesian Model Comparison and Backprop Nets

David J.C. MacKay*
Computation and Neural Systems
California Institute of Technology 139–74
Pasadena CA 91125
mackay@ras.phy.cam.ac.uk

Abstract

The Bayesian model comparison framework is reviewed, and the Bayesian Occam's razor is explained. This framework can be applied to feedforward networks, making possible (1) objective comparisons between solutions using alternative network architectures; (2) objective choice of magnitude and type of weight decay terms; (3) quantified estimates of the error bars on network parameters and on network output. The framework also generates a measure of the effective number of parameters determined by the data.

The relationship of Bayesian model comparison to recent work on prediction of generalisation ability (Guyon *et al.*, 1992, Moody, 1992) is discussed.

1 BAYESIAN INFERENCE AND OCCAM'S RAZOR

In science, a central task is to develop and compare models to account for the data that are gathered. Typically, two levels of **inference** are involved in the task of data modelling. At the first level of inference, we assume that one of the models that we invented is true, and we fit that model to the data. Typically a model includes some free parameters; fitting the model to the data involves inferring what values those parameters should probably take, given the data. This is repeated for each model. The second level of inference is the task of model comparison. Here,

---

*Current address: Darwin College, Cambridge CB3 9EU, U.K.

we wish to compare the models in the light of the data, and assign some sort of preference or ranking to the alternatives.[1]

For example, consider the task of interpolating a noisy data set. The data set could be interpolated using a splines model, polynomials, or feedforward neural networks. At the first level of inference, we find for each individual model the best fit interpolant (a process sometimes known as 'learning'). At the second level of inference we want to rank the alternative models and state for our particular data set that, for example, 'splines are probably the best interpolation model', or 'if the interpolant is modelled as a polynomial, it should probably be a cubic', or 'the best neural network for this data set has eight hidden units'.

Model comparison is a difficult task because it is not possible simply to choose the model that fits the data best: more complex models can always fit the data better, so the maximum likelihood model choice leads us inevitably to implausible over–parameterised models which generalise poorly. 'Occam's razor' is the principle that states that unnecessarily complex models should not be preferred to simpler ones. Bayesian methods automatically and quantitatively embody Occam's razor (Gull, 1988, Jeffreys, 1939), without the introduction of ad hoc penalty terms. Complex models are automatically self–penalising under Bayes' rule.

Let us write down Bayes' rule for the two levels of inference described above. Assume each model $\mathcal{H}_i$ has a vector of parameters $\mathbf{w}$. A model is defined by its functional form and two probability distributions: a 'prior' distribution $P(\mathbf{w}|\mathcal{H}_i)$ which states what values the model's parameters might plausibly take; and the predictions $P(D|\mathbf{w}, \mathcal{H}_i)$ that the model makes about the data D when its parameters have a particular value $\mathbf{w}$. Note that models with the same parameterisation but different priors over the parameters are therefore defined to be different models.

1. Model fitting. At the first level of inference, we assume that one model $\mathcal{H}_i$ is true, and we infer what the model's parameters $\mathbf{w}$ might be given the data D. Using Bayes' rule, the **posterior probability** of the parameters $\mathbf{w}$ is:

$$P(\mathbf{w}|D, \mathcal{H}_i) = \frac{P(D|\mathbf{w}, \mathcal{H}_i)P(\mathbf{w}|\mathcal{H}_i)}{P(D|\mathcal{H}_i)} \tag{1}$$

In words:

$$\text{Posterior} = \frac{\text{Likelihood} \times \text{Prior}}{\text{Evidence}}$$

It is common to use gradient–based methods to find the maximum of the posterior, which defines the most probable value for the parameters, $\mathbf{w}_{\mathrm{MP}}$; it is then common to summarise the posterior distribution by the value of $\mathbf{w}_{\mathrm{MP}}$, and error bars on these best fit parameters. The error bars are obtained from the curvature of the posterior; writing the Hessian $\mathbf{A} = -\nabla\nabla \log P(\mathbf{w}|D, \mathcal{H}_i)$ and Taylor–expanding the log posterior with $\Delta\mathbf{w} = \mathbf{w} - \mathbf{w}_{\mathrm{MP}}$,

$$P(\mathbf{w}|D, \mathcal{H}_i) \simeq P(\mathbf{w}_{\mathrm{MP}}|D, \mathcal{H}_i) \exp\left(-\tfrac{1}{2}\Delta\mathbf{w}^{\mathrm{T}}\mathbf{A}\Delta\mathbf{w}\right) \tag{2}$$

---

[1] Note that both levels of inference are distinct from *decision theory*. The goal of inference is, given a defined hypothesis space and a particular data set, to assign probabilities to hypotheses. Decision theory chooses between alternative actions on the basis of these probabilities so as to minimise the expectation of a 'loss function'.

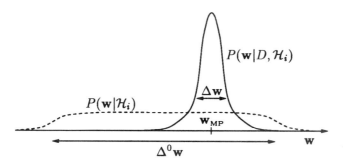

Figure 1: **The Occam factor**
This figure shows the quantities that determine the Occam factor for a hypothesis $\mathcal{H}_i$ having a single parameter $\mathbf{w}$. The prior distribution (dotted line) for the parameter has width $\Delta^0\mathbf{w}$. The posterior distribution (solid line) has a single peak at $\mathbf{w}_{\mathrm{MP}}$ with characteristic width $\Delta\mathbf{w}$. The Occam factor is $\frac{\Delta\mathbf{w}}{\Delta^0\mathbf{w}}$.

we see that the posterior can be locally approximated as a gaussian with covariance matrix (error bars) $\mathbf{A}^{-1}$.

2. Model comparison. At the second level of inference, we wish to infer which model is most plausible given the data. The posterior probability of each model is:

$$P(\mathcal{H}_i|D) \propto P(D|\mathcal{H}_i)P(\mathcal{H}_i) \tag{3}$$

Notice that the objective data–dependent term $P(D|\mathcal{H}_i)$ is the evidence for $\mathcal{H}_i$, which appeared as the normalising constant in (1). The second term, $P(\mathcal{H}_i)$, is a 'subjective' prior over our hypothesis space. Assuming that we have no reason to assign strongly differing priors $P(\mathcal{H}_i)$ to the alternative models, **models $\mathcal{H}_i$ are ranked by evaluating the evidence.**

This concept is very general: the evidence can be evaluated for parametric and 'non–parametric' models alike; whether our data modelling task is a regression problem, a classification problem, or a density estimation problem, the evidence is the Bayesian's transportable quantity for comparing alternative models. In all these cases the evidence naturally embodies Occam's razor, as we will now see. The evidence is the normalising constant for equation (1):

$$P(D|\mathcal{H}_i) = \int P(D|\mathbf{w},\mathcal{H}_i)P(\mathbf{w}|\mathcal{H}_i)\,d\mathbf{w} \tag{4}$$

For many problems, including interpolation, it is common for the posterior $P(\mathbf{w}|D,\mathcal{H}_i) \propto P(D|\mathbf{w},\mathcal{H}_i)P(\mathbf{w}|\mathcal{H}_i)$ to have a strong peak at the most probable parameters $\mathbf{w}_{\mathrm{MP}}$ (figure 1). Then the evidence can be approximated by the height of the peak of the integrand $P(D|\mathbf{w},\mathcal{H}_i)P(\mathbf{w}|\mathcal{H}_i)$ times its width, $\Delta\mathbf{w}$:

$$P(D|\mathcal{H}_i) \simeq \underbrace{P(D|\mathbf{w}_{\mathrm{MP}},\mathcal{H}_i)}_{} \underbrace{P(\mathbf{w}_{\mathrm{MP}}|\mathcal{H}_i)\,\Delta\mathbf{w}}_{} \tag{5}$$

$$\text{Evidence} \simeq \text{Best fit likelihood} \quad \text{Occam factor}$$

Thus the evidence is found by taking the best fit likelihood that the model can achieve and multiplying it by an 'Occam factor' (Gull, 1988), which is a term with magnitude less than one that penalises $\mathcal{H}_i$ for having the parameter $\mathbf{w}$.

Interpretation of the Occam factor

The quantity $\Delta \mathbf{w}$ is the posterior uncertainty in $\mathbf{w}$. Imagine for simplicity that the prior $P(\mathbf{w}|\mathcal{H}_i)$ is uniform on some large interval $\Delta^0 \mathbf{w}$ (figure 1), so that $P(\mathbf{w}_{\text{MP}}|\mathcal{H}_i) = \frac{1}{\Delta^0 \mathbf{w}}$; then

$$\text{Occam factor} = \frac{\Delta \mathbf{w}}{\Delta^0 \mathbf{w}},$$

i.e. **the ratio of the posterior accessible volume of $\mathcal{H}_i$'s parameter space to the prior accessible volume** (Gull, 1988, Jeffreys, 1939). The log of the Occam factor can be interpreted as the amount of information we gain about the model $\mathcal{H}_i$ when the data arrive.

Typically, a complex or flexible model with many parameters, each of which is free to vary over a large range $\Delta^0 \mathbf{w}$, will be penalised with a larger Occam factor than a simpler model. The Occam factor also penalises models which have to be finely tuned to fit the data. Which model achieves the greatest evidence is determined by a trade–off between minimising this natural complexity measure and minimising the data misfit.

Occam factor for several parameters

If $\mathbf{w}$ is k-dimensional, and if the posterior is well approximated by a gaussian, the Occam factor is given by the determinant of the gaussian's covariance matrix:

$$P(D|\mathcal{H}_i) \simeq \underbrace{P(D|\mathbf{w}_{\text{MP}}, H_i)}_{\text{Evidence} \simeq \text{Best fit likelihood}} \underbrace{P(\mathbf{w}_{\text{MP}}|\mathcal{H}_i)(2\pi)^{k/2}\det^{-\frac{1}{2}}\mathbf{A}}_{\text{Occam factor}} \qquad (6)$$

where $\mathbf{A} = -\nabla\nabla \log P(\mathbf{w}|D, \mathcal{H}_i)$, the Hessian which we already evaluated when we calculated the error bars on $\mathbf{w}_{\text{MP}}$. As the amount of data collected, N, increases, this gaussian approximation is expected to become increasingly accurate on account of the central limit theorem.

Thus Bayesian model selection is a simple extension of maximum likelihood model selection: **the evidence is obtained by multiplying the best fit likelihood by the Occam factor.** To evaluate the Occam factor all we need is the Hessian $\mathbf{A}$, if the gaussian approximation is good. Thus the Bayesian method of model comparison by evaluating the evidence is computationally no more demanding than the task of finding for each model the best fit parameters and their error bars.

2   THE EVIDENCE FOR NEURAL NETWORKS

Neural network learning procedures include a host of control parameters such as the number of hidden units and weight decay rates. These parameters are difficult to set because there is an Occam's razor problem: if we just set the parameters so as to minimise the error on the training set, we would be led to over–complex and under–regularised models which over-fit the data. Figure 2a illustrates this problem by showing the test error versus the training error of a hundred networks of varying complexity all trained on the same interpolation problem.

Of course if we had unlimited resources, we could compare these networks by measuring the error on an unseen test set or by similar cross–validation techniques. However these techniques may require us to devote a large amount of data to the test set, and may be computationally demanding. If there are several parameters like weight decay rates, it is preferable if they can be optimised on line.

Using the Bayesian framework, it is possible for all our data to have a say in both the model fitting and the model comparison levels of inference. We can rank alternative neural network solutions by evaluating the 'evidence'. Weight decay rates can also be optimised by finding the 'most probable' weight decay rate. Alternative weight decay schemes can be compared using the evidence. The evidence also makes it possible to compare neural network solutions with other interpolation models, for example, splines or radial basis functions, and to choose control parameters such as spline order or RBF kernel. The framework can be applied to classification networks as well as the interpolation networks discussed here. For details of the theoretical framework (which is due to Gull and Skilling (1989)) and for more complete discussion and bibliography, MacKay (1991) should be consulted.

2.1   THE PROBABILISTIC INTERPRETATION

Fitting a backprop network to a data set $D = \{\mathbf{x}, \mathbf{t}\}$ often involves minimising an objective function $M(\mathbf{w}) = \beta E_D(\mathbf{w}; D) + \alpha E_W(\mathbf{w})$. The first term is the data error, for example $E_D = \sum \frac{1}{2}(\mathbf{y} - \mathbf{t})^2$, and the second term is a regulariser (weight decay term), for example $E_W = \sum \frac{1}{2} w_h^2$. (There may be several regularisers with independent constants $\{\alpha_c\}$. The Bayesian framework also covers that case.) A model $\mathcal{H}$ has three components $\{\mathcal{A}, \mathcal{N}, \mathcal{R}\}$: The architecture $\mathcal{A}$ specifies the functional dependence of the input–output mapping on the network's parameters $\mathbf{w}$. The noise model $\mathcal{N}$ specifies the functional form of the data error. Within the probabilistic interpretation (Tishby *et al.*, 1989), the data error is viewed as relating to a likelihood, $P(D|\mathbf{w}, \beta, \mathcal{A}, \mathcal{N}) = \exp(-\beta E_D)/Z_D$. For example, a quadratic E_D corresponds to the assumption that the distribution of errors between the data and the true interpolant is Gaussian, with variance $\sigma_\nu^2 = 1/\beta$. Lastly, the regulariser $\mathcal{R}$, with associated regularisation constant α, is interpreted as specifying a prior on the parameters $\mathbf{w}$, $P(\mathbf{w}|\alpha, \mathcal{A}, \mathcal{R}) = \exp(-\alpha E_W)$. For example, the use of a plain quadratic regulariser corresponds to a Gaussian prior distribution for the parameters.

Given this probabilistic interpretation, interpolation with neural networks can then be decomposed into three levels of inference:

1	Fitting a regularised model	$P(\mathbf{w}\|D, \alpha, \beta, \mathcal{H}_i) = \dfrac{P(D\|\mathbf{w}, \beta, \mathcal{H}_i) P(\mathbf{w}\|\alpha, \mathcal{H}_i)}{P(D\|\alpha, \beta, \mathcal{H}_i)}$
2a	Setting regularisation constants and estimating noise level	$P(\alpha, \beta\|D, \mathcal{H}_i) = \dfrac{P(D\|\alpha, \beta, \mathcal{H}_i) P(\alpha, \beta\|\mathcal{H}_i)}{P(D\|\mathcal{H}_i)}$
2	Model comparison	$P(\mathcal{H}_i\|D) \propto P(D\|\mathcal{H}_i) P(\mathcal{H}_i)$

Both levels 2a and 2 require Occam's razor. For both levels the key step is to evaluate the evidence $P(D|\alpha, \beta, \mathcal{H})$, which, within the quadratic approximation

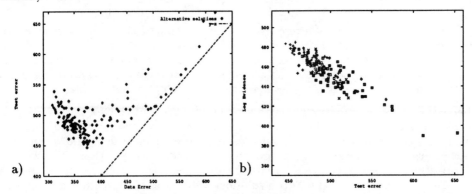

Figure 2: **The evidence solves the neural networks' Occam problem**
a) Test error vs. data error. Each point represents the performance of a single trained
neural network on the training set and on the test set. This graph illustrates the fact that
the best generalisation is not achieved by the models which fit the training data best.
b) Log Evidence vs. test error.

around $\mathbf{w}_{\mathrm{MP}}$, is given by:

$$\log P(D|\alpha,\beta,\mathcal{H}) = -\alpha E_W^{\mathrm{MP}} - \beta E_D^{\mathrm{MP}} - \frac{1}{2}\log\det\mathbf{A} - \log Z_W(\alpha) - \log Z_D(\beta) + \frac{k}{2}\log 2\pi. \tag{7}$$

At level 2a we can find the most probable value for the regularisation constant α
and noise level $1/\beta$ by differentiating (7) with respect to α and β. The result is

$$\chi_W^2 \equiv 2\alpha E_W = \gamma \qquad \text{and} \qquad \chi_D^2 \equiv 2\beta E_D = N - \gamma, \tag{8}$$

where γ is 'the effective number of parameters determined by the data' (Gull, 1989),

$$\gamma = k - \alpha\mathrm{Trace}\mathbf{A}^{-1} = \sum_{a=1}^{k}\frac{\lambda_a}{\lambda_a + \alpha}, \tag{9}$$

where λ_a are the eigenvalues of $\nabla\nabla\beta E_D$ in the natural basis of E_W. Each term
in the sum is a number between 0 and 1 which measures how well one parame-
ter is determined by the data rather than by the prior. The expressions (8), or
approximations to them, can be used to re–estimate weight decay rates on line.

The central quantity in the evidence and in γ is the inverse hessian $\mathbf{A}^{-1}$, which
describes the error bars on the parameters $\mathbf{w}$. From this we can also obtain error
bars on the outputs of a network (Denker and Le Cun, 1991, MacKay, 1991). These
error bars are closely related to the predicted generalisation error calculated by
Levin *et al.*(1989). In (MacKay, 1991) the practical utility of these error bars is
demonstrated for both regression and classification networks.

Figure 2b shows the Bayesian 'evidence' for each of the solutions in figure 2a against
the test error. It can be seen that the correlation between the evidence and the
test error is extremely good. This good correlation depends on the model being
well–matched to the problem; when an inconsistent weight decay scheme was used
(forcing all weights to decay at the same rate), it was found that the correlation between the evidence and the test error was much poorer. Such comparisons between
Bayesian and traditional methods are powerful tools for human learning.

3   RELATION TO THEORIES OF GENERALISATION

The Bayesian 'evidence' framework assesses within a well–defined hypothesis space *how probable* a set of alternative models are. However, what we really want to know is how well each model is expected to generalise. Empirically, the correlation between the evidence and generalisation error is surprisingly good. But a theoretical connection linking the two is not yet established. Here, a brief discussion is given of similarities and differences between the evidence and quantities arising in recent work on prediction of generalisation error.

3.1   RELATION TO MOODY'S 'G.P.E.'

Moody's (1992) 'Generalised Prediction Error' is a generalisation of Akaike's 'F.P.E.' to non–linear regularised models. The F.P.E. is an estimator of generalisation error which can be derived without making assumptions about the distribution of errors between the data and true interpolant, and without assuming a known class to which the true interpolant belongs. The difference between F.P.E. and G.P.E. is that the total number of parameters k in F.P.E. is replaced by an effective number of parameters, which is in fact identical to the quantity γ arising in the Bayesian analysis (9). If E_D is as defined earlier,

$$\text{G.P.E.} = \left(E_D + \sigma_\nu^2 \gamma\right)/N. \tag{10}$$

Like the log evidence, the G.P.E. has the form of the data error plus a term that penalises complexity. However, although the same quantity γ arises in the Bayesian analysis, the Bayesian Occam factor does *not* have the same scaling behaviour as the G.P.E. term (see discussion below). And empirically, the G.P.E. is not always a good predictor of generalisation. The reason for this is that in the derivation of the G.P.E., it is assumed that the distribution over $\mathbf{x}$ values is well approximated by a sum of delta functions at the samples in the training set. This is equivalent to assuming test samples will be drawn only at the $\mathbf{x}$ locations at which we have already received data. This assumption breaks down for over–parameterised and over–flexible models. An additional distinction that between the G.P.E. and the evidence framework is that the G.P.E. is defined for regression problems only; the evidence can be evaluated for regression, classification and density estimation models.

3.2   RELATION TO THE EFFECTIVE V–C DIMENSION

Recent work on 'structural risk minimisation' (Guyon *et al.*, 1992) utilises empirical expressions of the form:

$$E_{\text{gen}} \simeq E_D/N + c_1 \frac{\log(N/\gamma) + c_2}{N/\gamma} \tag{11}$$

where γ is the 'effective V–C dimension' of the model, and is identical to the quantity arising in (9). The constants c_1 and c_2 are determined by experiment. The structural risk theory is currently intended to be applied only to nested families of classification models (hence the absence of β: E_D is dimensionless) with monotonic effective V–C dimension, whereas the evidence can be evaluated for any models. However, it is very interesting that the scaling behaviour of this expression (11) is identical to the scaling behaviour of the log evidence (7), subject to the following assumptions. Assume that the value of the regularisation constant satisfies (8). Assume furthermore that the significant eigenvalues ($\lambda_a > \alpha$) scale as $\lambda_a \sim N\alpha/\gamma$ (It can be confirmed that this scaling is obtained for example in the interpolation models consisting of a sequence of steps of independent heights, as we vary the number of steps.) Then it can be shown that the scaling of the log evidence is:

$$- \log P(D|\alpha, \beta, \mathcal{H}) \sim \beta E_D^{\text{MP}} + \frac{1}{2} \left(\gamma \log(N/\gamma) + \gamma \right) \tag{12}$$

(Readers familiar with MDL will recognise the dominant $\frac{\gamma}{2} \log N$ term; MDL and Bayes are identical.) Thus the scaling behaviour of the log evidence is identical to the structural risk minimisation expression (11), if $c_1 = \frac{1}{2}$ and $c_2 = 1$. I. Guyon (personal communication) has confirmed that the empirically determined values for c_1 and c_2 are indeed close to these Bayesian values. It will be interesting to try and understand and develop this relationship.

Acknowledgements

This work was supported by studentships from Caltech and SERC, UK.

References

J.S. Denker and Y. Le Cun (1991). 'Transforming neural-net output levels to probability distributions', in *Advances in neural information processing systems 3*, ed. R.P. Lippmann *et al.*, 853–859, Morgan Kaufmann.

S.F. Gull (1988). 'Bayesian inductive inference and maximum entropy', in *Maximum Entropy and Bayesian Methods in science and engineering, vol. 1: Foundations*, G.J. Erickson and C.R. Smith, eds., Kluwer.

S.F. Gull (1989). 'Developments in Maximum entropy data analysis', in J. Skilling, ed., 53–71.

I. Guyon, V.N. Vapnik, B.E. Boser, L.Y. Bottou and S.A. Solla (1992). 'Structural risk minimization for character recognition', this volume.

H. Jeffreys (1939). *Theory of Probability*, Oxford Univ. Press.

E. Levin, N. Tishby and S. Solla (1989). 'A statistical approach to learning and generalization in layered neural networks', in *COLT '89: 2nd workshop on computational learning theory*, 245–260.

D.J.C. MacKay (1991) 'Bayesian Methods for Adaptive Models', Ph.D. Thesis, Caltech. Also 'Bayesian interpolation', 'A practical Bayesian framework for backprop networks', 'Information–based objective functions for active data selection', to appear in *Neural computation*. And 'The evidence framework applied to classification networks', submitted to *Neural computation*.

J.E. Moody (1992). 'Generalization, regularization and architecture selection in nonlinear learning systems', this volume.

N. Tishby, E. Levin and S.A. Solla (1989). 'Consistent inference of probabilities in layered networks: predictions and generalization', in *Proc. IJCNN*, Washington.

The *Effective* Number of Parameters:
An Analysis of Generalization and Regularization
in Nonlinear Learning Systems

John E. Moody
Department of Computer Science, Yale University
P.O. Box 2158 Yale Station, New Haven, CT 06520-2158
Internet: moody@cs.yale.edu, Phone: (203)432-1200

Abstract

We present an analysis of how the generalization performance (expected test set error) relates to the expected training set error for nonlinear learning systems, such as multilayer perceptrons and radial basis functions. The principal result is the following relationship (computed to second order) between the expected test set and training set errors:

$$\langle \mathcal{E}_{test}(\lambda) \rangle_{\xi\xi'} \approx \langle \mathcal{E}_{train}(\lambda) \rangle_{\xi} + 2\sigma_{eff}^2 \frac{p_{eff}(\lambda)}{n} \ . \tag{1}$$

Here, n is the size of the training sample ξ, σ_{eff}^2 is the effective noise variance in the response variable(s), λ is a regularization or weight decay parameter, and $p_{eff}(\lambda)$ is the *effective number of parameters* in the nonlinear model. The expectations $\langle \ \rangle$ of training set and test set errors are taken over possible training sets ξ and training and test sets ξ' respectively. The effective number of parameters $p_{eff}(\lambda)$ usually differs from the true number of model parameters p for nonlinear or regularized models; this theoretical conclusion is supported by Monte Carlo experiments. In addition to the surprising result that $p_{eff}(\lambda) \neq p$, we propose an estimate of (1) called the *generalized prediction error* (GPE) which generalizes well established estimates of prediction risk such as Akaike's FPE and AIC, Mallows C_P, and Barron's PSE to the nonlinear setting.[1]

---

[1]GPE and $p_{eff}(\lambda)$ were previously introduced in Moody (1991).

1 Background and Motivation

Many of the nonlinear learning systems of current interest for adaptive control, adaptive signal processing, and time series prediction, are supervised learning systems of the regression type. Understanding the relationship between generalization performance and training error and being able to estimate the generalization performance of such systems is of crucial importance. We will take the *prediction risk* (expected test set error) as our measure of generalization performance.

2 Learning from Examples

Consider a set of n real-valued input/output data pairs $\xi(n) = \{\xi^i = (x^i, y^i); i = 1, \ldots, n\}$ drawn from a stationary density $\Xi(\xi)$. The observations can be viewed as being generated according to the *signal plus noise* model[2]

$$y^i = \mu(x^i) + \epsilon^i \tag{2}$$

where y^i is the observed response (dependent variable), x^i are the independent variables sampled with input probability density $\Omega(x)$, ϵ^i is independent, identically-distributed (iid) noise sampled with density $\Phi(\epsilon)$ having mean 0 and variance σ^2,[3] and $\mu(x)$ is the *conditional mean*, an unknown function. From the signal plus noise perspective, the density $\Xi(\xi) = \Xi(x, y)$ can be represented as the product of two components, the conditional density $\Psi(y|x)$ and the input density $\Omega(x)$:

$$
\begin{aligned}
\Xi(x, y) &= \Psi(y|x)\,\Omega(x) \\
&\equiv \Phi(y - \mu(x))\,\Omega(x) \ .
\end{aligned}
\tag{3}
$$

The learning problem is then to find an estimate $\widehat{\mu}(x)$ of the conditional mean $\mu(x)$ on the basis of the training set $\xi(n)$.

In many real world problems, few *a priori* assumptions can be made about the functional form of $\mu(x)$. Since a parametric function class is usually not known, one must resort to a *nonparametric regression* approach, whereby one constructs an estimate $\widehat{\mu}(x) = f(x)$ for $\mu(x)$ from a large class of functions $\mathcal{F}$ known to have good approximation properties (for example, $\mathcal{F}$ could be all possible radial basis function networks and multilayer perceptrons). The class of approximation functions is usually the union of a countable set of subclasses (specific network architectures)[4] $\mathcal{A} \subset \mathcal{F}$ for which the elements of each subclass $f(w, x) \in \mathcal{A}$ are continuously parametrized by a set of $p = p(\mathcal{A})$ weights $w = \{w^\alpha; \alpha = 1, \ldots, p\}$. The task of finding the estimate $f(x)$ thus consists of two problems: choosing the best architecture $\widehat{\mathcal{A}}$ and choosing the best set of weights $\widehat{w}$ given the architecture. Note that in

---

[2]The assumption of additive noise ϵ which is independent of x is a standard assumption and is not overly restrictive. Many other conceivable signal/noise models can be transformed into this form. For example, the multiplicative model $y = \mu(x)(1 + \epsilon)$ becomes $y' = \mu'(x) + \epsilon'$ for the transformed variable $y' = \log(y)$.

[3]Note that we have made only a minimal assumption about the noise ϵ, that it is has finite variance σ^2 independent of x. Specifically, we do not need to make the assumption that the noise density $\Phi(\epsilon)$ is of known form (*e.g.* gaussian) for the following development.

[4]For example, a "fully connected two layer perceptron with five internal units".

the nonparametric setting, there does not typically exist a function $f(w^*, x) \in \mathcal{F}$ with a finite number of parameters such that $f(w^*, x) = \mu(x)$ for arbitrary $\mu(x)$. For this reason, the estimators $\widehat{\mu}(x) = f(\widehat{w}, x)$ will be *biased* estimators of $\mu(x)$.[5]

The first problem (finding the architecture $\mathcal{A}$) requires a search over possible architectures (*e.g.* network sizes and topologies), usually starting with small architectures and then considering larger ones. By necessity, the search is not usually exhaustive and must use heuristics to reduce search complexity. (A heuristic search procedure for two layer networks is presented in Moody and Utans (1992).)

The second problem (finding a good set of weights for $f(w, x)$) is accomplished by minimizing an objective function:

$$\widehat{w}_\lambda = \operatorname{argmin}_w U(\lambda, w, \xi(n)) \ . \tag{4}$$

The objective function U consists of an error function plus a regularizer:

$$U(\lambda, w, \xi(n)) = n\, \mathcal{E}_{train}(w, \xi(n)) + \lambda\, S(w) \tag{5}$$

Here, the error $\mathcal{E}_{train}(w, \xi(n))$ measures the "distance" between the target response values y^i and the fitted values $f(w, x^i)$:

$$\mathcal{E}_{train}(w, \xi(n)) = \frac{1}{n} \sum_{i=1}^{n} \mathcal{E}[y^i, f(w, x^i)] \ , \tag{6}$$

and $S(w)$ is a regularization or weight-decay function which biases the solution toward functions with *a priori* "desirable" characteristics, such as smoothness. The parameter $\lambda \geq 0$ is the regularization or weight decay parameter and must itself be optimized.[6]

The most familiar example of an objective function uses the squared error[7] $\mathcal{E}[y^i, f(w, x^i)] = [y^i - f(w, x^i)]^2$ and a weight decay term:

$$U(\lambda, w, \xi(n)) = \sum_{i=1}^{n}(y^i - f(w, x^i))^2 + \lambda \sum_{\alpha=1}^{p} g(w^\alpha) \ . \tag{7}$$

The first term is the sum of squared errors (SSE) of the model $f(w, x)$ with respect to the training data, while the second term penalizes either small, medium, or large weights, depending on the form of $g(w^\alpha)$. Two common examples of weight decay functions are the ridge regression form $g(w^\alpha) = (w^\alpha)^2$ (which penalizes large weights) and the Rumelhart form $g(w^\alpha) = (w^\alpha)^2 / [(w^0)^2 + (w^\alpha)^2]$ (which penalizes weights of intermediate values near w^0).

---

[5] By *biased*, we mean that the mean squared bias is nonzero: $MSB = \int \rho(x)(\langle\widehat{\mu}(x)\rangle_\xi - \mu(x))^2 dx \ > \ 0$. Here, $\rho(x)$ is some positive weighting function on the input space and $\langle \rangle_\xi$ denotes an expected valued taken over possible training sets $\xi(n)$. For unbiasedness ($MSB = 0$) to occur, there must exist a set of weights w^* such that $f(w^*, x) = \mu(x)$, and the learned weights $\widehat{w}$ must be "close to" w^*. For "near unbiasedness", we must have $w^* \equiv \operatorname{argmin}_w MSB(w)$ such that $(MSB(w^*) \approx 0)$ and $\widehat{w}$ "close to" w^*.

[6] The optimization of λ will be discussed in Moody (1992).

[7] Other error functions, such as those used in generalized linear models (see for example McCullagh and Nelder 1983) or robust statistics (see for example Huber 1981) are more appropriate than the squared error if the noise is known to be non-gaussian or the data contains many outliers.

An example of a regularizer which is not explicitly a weight decay term is:

$$S(w) = \int_x dx \Omega(x) \|\partial_{xx} f(w, x)\|^2 \ . \tag{8}$$

This is a smoothing term which penalizes functional fits with high curvature.

3 Prediction Risk

With $\widehat{\mu}(x) = f(\widehat{w}[\xi(n)], x)$ denoting an estimate of the true regression function $\mu(x)$ trained on a data set $\xi(n)$, we wish to estimate the prediction risk P, which is the expected error of $\widehat{\mu}(x)$ in predicting future data. In principle, we can either define P for models $\widehat{\mu}(x)$ trained on arbitrary training sets of size n sampled from the unknown density $\Psi(y|x)\Omega(x)$ or for training sets of size n with input density equal to the empirical density defined by the single training set available:

$$\Omega'(x) = \frac{1}{n} \sum_{i=1}^{n} \delta(x - x^i) \ . \tag{9}$$

For such training sets, the n inputs x^i are held fixed, but the response variables y^i are sampled with the conditional densities $\Psi(y|x^i)$. Since $\Omega'(x)$ is known, but $\Omega(x)$ is generally not known *a priori*, we adopt the latter approach.

For a large ensemble of such training sets, the *expected training set error* is[8]

$$
\begin{aligned}
\langle \mathcal{E}_{train}(\lambda) \rangle_\xi &= \left\langle \frac{1}{n} \sum_{i=1}^{n} \mathcal{E}[y^i, f(\widehat{w}[\xi(n)], x^i)] \right\rangle_\xi \\
&= \int \frac{1}{n} \sum_{i=1}^{n} \mathcal{E}[y^i, f(\widehat{w}[\xi(n)], x^i)] \left\{ \prod_{i=1}^{n} \Psi(y^i|x^i) dy^i \right\} \tag{10}
\end{aligned}
$$

For a future exemplar (x,z) sampled with density $\Psi(z|x)\Omega(x)$, the prediction risk P is defined as:

$$P = \int \mathcal{E}[z, f(\widehat{w}[\xi(n)], x)] \Psi(z|x)\Omega(x) \left\{ \prod_{i=1}^{n} \Psi(y^i|x^i) dy^i \right\} dz dx \tag{11}$$

Again, however, we don't assume that $\Omega(x)$ is known, so computing (11) is not possible.

Following Akaike (1970), Barron (1984), and numerous other authors (see Eubank 1988), we can define the prediction risk P as the *expected test set error* for test sets of size n $\xi'(n) = \{\xi^{i\prime} = (x^i, z^i);\ i = 1, \ldots, n\}$ having the empirical input density $\Omega'(x)$. This expected test set error has form:

$$
\begin{aligned}
\langle \mathcal{E}_{test}(\lambda) \rangle_{\xi\xi'} &= \left\langle \frac{1}{n} \sum_{i=1}^{n} \mathcal{E}[z^i, f(\widehat{w}[\xi(n)], x^i)] \right\rangle_{\xi\xi'} \tag{12} \\
&= \int \frac{1}{n} \sum_{i=1}^{n} \mathcal{E}[z^i, f(\widehat{w}[\xi(n)], x^i)] \left\{ \prod_{i=1}^{n} \Psi(y^i|x^i)\Psi(z^i|x^i) dy^i dz^i \right\}
\end{aligned}
$$

---

[8] Following the physics convention, we use angled brackets $\langle\ \rangle$ to denote expected values. The subscripts denote the random variables being integrated over.

We take (12) as a proxy for the true prediction risk P.

In order to compute (12), it will not be necessary to know the precise functional form of the noise density $\Phi(\epsilon)$. Knowing just the noise variance σ^2 will enable an exact calculation for linear models trained with the SSE error and an approximate calculation correct to second order for general nonlinear models. The results of these calculations are presented in the next two sections.

4   The Expected Test Set Error for Linear Models

The relationship between expected training set and expected test set errors for *linear models* trained using the SSE error function with no regularizer is well known in statistics (Akaike 1970, Barron 1984, Eubank 1988). The exact relation for test and training sets with density (9):

$$\langle \mathcal{E}_{test} \rangle_{\xi\xi'} = \langle \mathcal{E}_{train} \rangle_\xi + 2\sigma^2 \frac{p}{n} \ . \tag{13}$$

As pointed out by Barron (1984), (13) can also apply approximately to the case of a nonlinear model $f(w, x)$ trained by minimizing the sum of squared errors SSE. This approximation can be arrived at in two ways. First, the model $f(\widehat{w}, x)$ can be treated as *locally linear* in a neighborhood of $\widehat{w}$. This approximation ignores the hessian and higher order shape of $f(w, x)$ in parameter space. Alternatively, the model $f(w, x)$ can be assumed to be *locally quadratic* in parameter space w and *unbiased*.

However, the extension of (13) as an approximate relation for nonlinear models breaks down if any of the following situations hold:

The SSE error function is not used. (For example, one may use a robust error measure (Huber 1981) or log likelihood error measure instead.)

A regularization term is included in the objective function. (This introduces bias.)

The *locally linear* approximation for $f(w, x)$ is not good.

The *unbiasedness* assumption for $f(w, x)$ is incorrect.

5   The Expected Test Set Error for Nonlinear Models

For neural network models, which are typically nonparametric (thus biased) and highly nonlinear, a new relationship is needed to replace (13). We have derived such a result correct to second order for nonlinear models:

$$\langle \mathcal{E}_{test}(\lambda) \rangle_{\xi\xi'} \approx \langle \mathcal{E}_{train}(\lambda) \rangle_\xi + 2\sigma^2_{eff} \frac{p_{eff}(\lambda)}{n} \ . \tag{14}$$

This result differs from the classical result (13) by the appearance of $p_{eff}(\lambda)$ (the *effective number of parameters*), σ^2_{eff} (the effective noise variance in the response variable(s)), and a dependence on λ (the regularization or weight decay parameter).

A full derivation of (14) will be presented in a longer paper (Moody 1992). The result is obtained by considering the noise terms ϵ^i for both the training and test sets as perturbations to an idealized model fit to noise free data. The perturbative expansion is computed out to second order in the ϵ^i's subject to the constraint that the estimated weights $\hat{w}$ minimize the perturbed objective function. Computing expectation values and comparing the expansions for expected test and training errors yields (14). It is important to re-emphasize that deriving (14) does not require knowing the precise form of the noise density $\Phi(\epsilon)$. Only a knowledge of σ^2 is assumed.

The effective number of parameters $p_{eff}(\lambda)$ usually differs from the true number of model parameters p and depends upon the amount of model bias, model non-linearity, and on our prior model preferences (eg. smoothness) as determined by the regularization parameter λ and the form of our regularizer. The precise form of $p_{eff}(\lambda)$ is

$$p_{eff}(\lambda) \equiv \operatorname{tr} G \equiv \frac{1}{2} \sum_{i\alpha\beta} T_{i\alpha} U_{\alpha\beta}^{-1} T_{\beta i} \;, \tag{15}$$

where G is the *generalized influence matrix* which generalizes the standard *influence* or *hat* matrix of linear regression, $T_{i\alpha}$ is the $n \times p$ matrix of derivatives of the training error function

$$T_{i\alpha} \equiv \frac{\partial}{\partial y^i} \frac{\partial}{\partial w^\alpha} n\mathcal{E}(w, \xi(n)) \;, \tag{16}$$

and $U_{\alpha\beta}^{-1}$ is the inverse of the hessian of the total objective function

$$U_{\alpha\beta} \equiv \frac{\partial}{\partial w^\alpha} \frac{\partial}{\partial w^\beta} \mathcal{U}(\lambda, w, \xi(n)) \;. \tag{17}$$

In the general case that $\sigma^2(x)$ varies with location in the input space x, the effective noise variance σ^2_{eff} is a weighted average of the noise variances $\sigma^2(x^i)$. For the uniform signal plus noise model model we have described above, $\sigma^2_{eff} = \sigma^2$.

6   The Effects of Regularization

In the neural network community, the most commonly used regularizers are weight decay functions. The use of weight decay is motivated by the intuitive notion that it removes unnecessary weights from the model. An analysis of $p_{eff}(\lambda)$ with weight decay ($\lambda > 0$) confirms this intuitive notion. Furthermore, whenever $\sigma^2 > 0$ and $n < \infty$, there exists some $\lambda_{optimal} > 0$ such that the expected test set error (12) is minimized. This is because weight decay methods yield models with lower model variance, even though they are biased. These effects will be discussed further in Moody (1992).

For models trained with squared error (SSE) and quadratic weight decay $g(w^\alpha) = (w^\alpha)^2$, the assumptions of unbiasedness[9] or local linearizability lead to the following expression for $p_{eff}(\lambda)$ which we call the *linearized effective* number of parameters $p_{lin}(\lambda)$:

$$p_{lin}(\lambda) = \sum_{\alpha=1}^{p} \frac{\kappa^\alpha}{\kappa^\alpha + \lambda} \;. \tag{18}$$

---

[9]Strictly speaking, a model with quadratic weight decay is unbiased only if the "true" weights are 0.

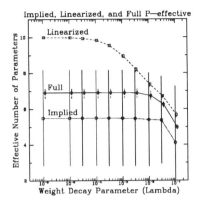

Figure 1: The full $p_{eff}(\lambda)$ (15) agrees with the implied $p_{imp}(\lambda)$ (19) to within experimental error, whereas the linearized $p_{lin}(\lambda)$ (18) does not (except for very large λ). These results verify the significance of (14) and (15) for nonlinear models.

Here, κ^α is the αth eigenvalue of the $p \times p$ matrix $K = T^\dagger T$, with T as defined in (16).

The form of $p_{eff}(\lambda)$ can be computed easily for other weight decay functions, such as the Rumelhart form $g(w^\alpha) = (w^\alpha)^2/[(w^0)^2 + (w^\alpha)^2]$. The basic result for all weight decay or regularization functions, however, is that $p_{eff}(\lambda)$ is a decreasing function of λ with $p_{eff}(0) = p$ and $p_{eff}(\infty) = 0$, as is evident in the special case (18). If the model is nonlinear and biased, then $p_{eff}(0)$ generally differs from p.

7   Testing the Theory

To test the result (14) in a nonlinear context, we computed the full $p_{eff}(\lambda)$ (15), the linearized $p_{lin}(\lambda)$ (18), and the *implied number of parameters* $p_{imp}(\lambda)$ (19) for a nonlinear test problem. The value of $p_{imp}(\lambda)$ is obtained by computing the expected training and test errors for an ensemble of training sets of size n with known noise variance σ^2 and solving for $p_{eff}(\lambda)$ in equation (14):

$$\widehat{p}_{imp}(\lambda) = \frac{n}{2\sigma^2}\left[\langle\widehat{\mathcal{E}_{test}(\lambda)}\rangle_{\xi\xi'} - \langle\widehat{\mathcal{E}_{train}(\lambda)}\rangle_\xi\right] \qquad (19)$$

The ^s indicate Monte Carlo estimates based on computations using a finite ensemble (10 in our experiments) of training sets. The test problem was to fit training sets of size 50 generated as a sum of three sigmoids plus noise, with the noise sampled from the uniform density. The model architecture $f(w, x)$ was also a sum of three sigmoids and the weights $\widehat{w}$ were estimated by minimizing (7) with quadratic weight decay. See figure 1.

8   GPE: An Estimate of Prediction Risk for Nonlinear Systems

A number of well established, closely related criteria for estimating the prediction risk for linear or linearizable models are available. These include Akaike's FPE (1970), Akaike's AIC (1973) Mallow's C_P (1973), and Barron's PSE (1984). (See also Akaike (1974) and Eubank (1988).) These estimates are all based on equation (13).

The generalized prediction error (GPE) generalizes the classical estimators FPE, AIC, C_P, and PSE to the nonlinear setting by estimating (14) as follows:

$$GPE(\lambda) = \widehat{P}_{GPE} = \mathcal{E}_{train}(n) + 2\widehat{\sigma}_{eff}^2 \frac{\widehat{p}_{eff}(\lambda)}{n} \ . \tag{20}$$

The estimation process and the quality of the resulting GPE estimates will be described in greater detail elsewhere.

Acknowledgements

The author wishes to thank Andrew Barron and Joseph Chang for helpful conversations. This research was supported by AFOSR grant 89-0478 and ONR grant N00014-89-J-1228.

References

H. Akaike. (1970). Statistical predictor identification. *Ann. Inst. Stat. Math.*, **22**:203.

H. Akaike. (1973). Information theory and an extension of the maximum likelihood principle. In *2nd Intl. Symp. on Information Theory*, Akademia Kiado, Budapest, 267.

H. Akaike. (1974). A new look at the statistical model identification. *IEEE Trans. Auto. Control*, **19**:716-723.

A. Barron. (1984). Predicted squared error: a criterion for automatic model selection. In *Self-Organizing Methods in Modeling*, S. Farlow, ed., Marcel Dekker, New York.

R. Eubank. (1988). *Spline Smoothing and Nonparametric Regression.* Marcel Dekker, New York.

P. J. Huber. (1981). *Robust Statistics.* Wiley, New York.

C. L. Mallows. (1973). Some comments on C_P. *Technometrics* **15**:661-675.

P. McCullagh and J.A. Nelder. (1983). *Generalized Linear Models.* Chapman and Hall, New York.

J. Moody. (1991). Note on Generalization, Regularization, and Architecture Selection in Nonlinear Learning Systems. In B.H. Juang, S.Y. Kung, and C.A. Kamm, editors, *Neural Networks for Signal Processing*, IEEE Press, Piscataway, NJ.

J. Moody. (1992). Long version of this paper, in preparation.

J. Moody and J. Utans. (1992). Principled architecture selection for neural networks: application to corporate bond rating prediction. In this volume.

Estimating Average-Case Learning Curves Using Bayesian, Statistical Physics and VC Dimension Methods

David Haussler
University of California
Santa Cruz, California

Michael Kearns*
AT&T Bell Laboratories
Murray Hill, New Jersey

Manfred Opper
Institut für Theoretische Physik
Universität Giessen, Germany

Robert Schapire
AT&T Bell Laboratories
Murray Hill, New Jersey

Abstract

In this paper we investigate an average-case model of concept learning, and give results that place the popular statistical physics and VC dimension theories of learning curve behavior in a common framework.

1 INTRODUCTION

In this paper we study a simple concept learning model in which the learner attempts to infer an unknown *target concept* f, chosen from a known *concept class* $\mathcal{F}$ of $\{0, 1\}$-valued functions over an input space X. At each trial i, the learner is given a point $x_i \in X$ and asked to predict the value of $f(x_i)$. If the learner predicts $f(x_i)$ incorrectly, we say the learner makes a *mistake*. After making its prediction, the learner is told the correct value.

This simple theoretical paradigm applies to many areas of machine learning, including much of the research in neural networks. The quantity of fundamental interest in this setting is the *learning curve*, which is the function of m defined as the prob-

---

*Contact author. Address: AT&T Bell Laboratories, 600 Mountain Avenue, Room 2A-423, Murray Hill, New Jersey 07974. Electronic mail: mkearns@research.att.com.

ability the learning algorithm makes a mistake predicting $f(x_{m+1})$, having already
seen the examples $(x_1, f(x_1)), \ldots, (x_m, f(x_m))$.

In this paper we study learning curves in an average-case setting that admits a prior
distribution over the concepts in $\mathcal{F}$. We examine learning curve behavior for the
optimal *Bayes* algorithm and for the related *Gibbs* algorithm that has been studied
in statistical physics analyses of learning curve behavior. For both algorithms we
give new upper and lower bounds on the learning curve in terms of the Shannon
information gain.

The main contribution of this research is in showing that the average-case or
Bayesian model provides a unifying framework for the popular statistical physics
and VC dimension theories of learning curves. By beginning in an average-case setting and deriving bounds in information-theoretic terms, we can gradually recover
a worst-case theory by removing the averaging in favor of combinatorial parameters
that upper bound certain expectations.

Due to space limitations, the paper is technically dense and almost all derivations
and proofs have been omitted. We strongly encourage the reader to refer to our
longer and more complete versions [4, 6] for additional motivation and technical
detail.

2   NOTATIONAL CONVENTIONS

Let X be a set called the *instance space*. A *concept class* $\mathcal{F}$ over X is a (possibly
infinite) collection of subsets of X. We will find it convenient to view a concept
$f \in \mathcal{F}$ as a function $f : X \to \{0, 1\}$, where we interpret $f(x) = 1$ to mean that
$x \in X$ is a *positive example* of f, and $f(x) = 0$ to mean x is a *negative example*.

The symbols $\mathcal{P}$ and $\mathcal{D}$ are used to denote probability distributions. The distribution
$\mathcal{P}$ is over $\mathcal{F}$, and $\mathcal{D}$ is over X. When $\mathcal{F}$ and X are countable we assume that these
distributions are defined as probability mass functions. For uncountable $\mathcal{F}$ and X
they are assumed to be probability measures over some appropriate σ-algebra. All
of our results hold for both countable and uncountable $\mathcal{F}$ and X.

We use the notation $\mathbf{E}_{f \in \mathcal{P}}[\chi(f)]$ for the expectation of the random variable χ with
respect to the distribution $\mathcal{P}$, and $\mathbf{Pr}_{f \in \mathcal{P}}[cond(f)]$ for the probability with respect
to the distribution $\mathcal{P}$ of the set of all f satisfying the predicate $cond(f)$. Everything
that needs to be measurable is assumed to be measurable.

3   INFORMATION GAIN AND LEARNING

Let $\mathcal{F}$ be a concept class over the instance space X. Fix a *target concept* $f \in \mathcal{F}$ and
an infinite sequence of instances $\mathbf{x} = x_1, \ldots, x_m, x_{m+1}, \ldots$ with $x_m \in X$ for all m.
For now we assume that the fixed instance sequence $\mathbf{x}$ is known in advance to the
learner, but that the target concept f is not. Let $\mathcal{P}$ be a probability distribution
over the concept class $\mathcal{F}$. We think of $\mathcal{P}$ in the Bayesian sense as representing the
prior beliefs of the learner about which target concept it will be learning.

In our setting, the learner receives information about f incrementally via the label sequence $f(x_1), \ldots, f(x_m), f(x_{m+1}), \ldots$. At time m, the learner receives the label $f(x_m)$. For any $m \geq 1$ we define (with respect to $\mathbf{x}, f$) the mth *version space*

$$\mathcal{F}_m(\mathbf{x}, f) = \{\hat{f} \in \mathcal{F} : \hat{f}(x_1) = f(x_1), \ldots, \hat{f}(x_m) = f(x_m)\}$$

and the mth *volume* $V_m^{\mathcal{P}}(\mathbf{x}, f) = \mathcal{P}[\mathcal{F}_m(\mathbf{x}, f)]$. We define $\mathcal{F}_0(\mathbf{x}, f) = \mathcal{F}$ for all $\mathbf{x}$ and f, so $V_0^{\mathcal{P}}(\mathbf{x}, f) = 1$. The version space at time m is simply the class of all concepts in $\mathcal{F}$ consistent with the first m labels of f (with respect to $\mathbf{x}$), and the mth volume is the measure of this class under $\mathcal{P}$. For the first part of the paper, the infinite instance sequence $\mathbf{x}$ and the prior $\mathcal{P}$ are fixed; thus we simply write $\mathcal{F}_m(f)$ and $V_m(f)$. Later, when the sequence $\mathbf{x}$ is chosen randomly, we will reintroduce this dependence explicitly. We adopt this notational practice of omitting any dependence on a fixed $\mathbf{x}$ in many other places as well.

For each $m \geq 0$ let us define the mth *posterior distribution* $\mathcal{P}_m(\mathbf{x}, f) = \mathcal{P}_m$ by restricting $\mathcal{P}$ to the mth version space $\mathcal{F}_m(f)$; that is, for all (measurable) $S \subset \mathcal{F}$, $\mathcal{P}_m[S] = \mathcal{P}[S \cap \mathcal{F}_m(f)]/\mathcal{P}[\mathcal{F}_m(f)] = \mathcal{P}[S \cap \mathcal{F}_m(f)]/V_m(f)$.

Having already seen $f(x_1), \ldots, f(x_m)$, how much information (assuming the prior $\mathcal{P}$) does the learner expect to gain by seeing $f(x_{m+1})$? If we let $\mathcal{I}_{m+1}(\mathbf{x}, f)$ (abbreviated $\mathcal{I}_{m+1}(f)$ since $\mathbf{x}$ is fixed for now) be a random variable whose value is the (Shannon) information gained from $f(x_{m+1})$, then it can be shown that the expected information is

$$\mathbf{E}_{f \in \mathcal{P}}[\mathcal{I}_{m+1}(f)] = \mathbf{E}_{f \in \mathcal{P}}\left[-\log \frac{V_{m+1}(f)}{V_m(f)}\right] = \mathbf{E}_{f \in \mathcal{P}}[-\log \chi_{m+1}(f)] \qquad (1)$$

where we define the $(m+1)$st *volume ratio* by $\chi_{m+1}^{\mathcal{P}}(\mathbf{x}, f) = \chi_{m+1}(f) = V_{m+1}(f)/V_m(f)$.

We now return to our learning problem, which we define to be that of predicting the label $f(x_{m+1})$ given only the previous labels $f(x_1), \ldots, f(x_m)$. The first learning algorithm we consider is called the *Bayes optimal classification algorithm*, or the *Bayes* algorithm for short. For any m and $b \in \{0, 1\}$, define $\mathcal{F}_m^b(\mathbf{x}, f) = \mathcal{F}_m^b(f) = \{\hat{f} \in \mathcal{F}_m(\mathbf{x}, f) : \hat{f}(x_{m+1}) = b\}$. Then the Bayes algorithm is:

If $\mathcal{P}_m[\mathcal{F}_m^1(f)] > \mathcal{P}_m[\mathcal{F}_m^0(f)]$, predict $f(x_{m+1}) = 1$.

If $\mathcal{P}_m[\mathcal{F}_m^1(f)] < \mathcal{P}_m[\mathcal{F}_m^0(f)]$, predict $f(x_{m+1}) = 0$.

If $\mathcal{P}_m[\mathcal{F}_m^1(f)] = \mathcal{P}_m[\mathcal{F}_m^0(f)]$, flip a fair coin to predict $f(x_{m+1})$.

It is well known that if the target concept f is drawn at random according to the prior distribution $\mathcal{P}$, then the Bayes algorithm is optimal in the sense that it minimizes the probability that $f(x_{m+1})$ is predicted incorrectly. Furthermore, if we let $Bayes_{m+1}^{\mathcal{P}}(\mathbf{x}, f)$ (abbreviated $Bayes_{m+1}^{\mathcal{P}}(f)$ since $\mathbf{x}$ is fixed for now) be a random variable whose value is 1 if the Bayes algorithm predicts $f(x_{m+1})$ correctly and 0 otherwise, then it can be shown that the probability of a mistake for a random f is

$$\mathbf{E}_{f \in \mathcal{P}}[Bayes_{m+1}^{\mathcal{P}}(f)] = \mathbf{E}_{f \in \mathcal{P}}\left[\Theta\left(\frac{1}{2} - \chi_{m+1}(f)\right)\right]. \qquad (2)$$

Despite the optimality of the Bayes algorithm, it suffers the drawback that its *hypothesis* at any time m may not be a member of the target class $\mathcal{F}$. (Here we define the hypothesis of an algorithm at time m to be the (possibly probabilistic) mapping $\hat{f} : X \to \{0, 1\}$ obtained by letting $\hat{f}(x)$ be the prediction of the algorithm when $x_{m+1} = x$.) This drawback is absent in our second learning algorithm, which we call the *Gibbs* algorithm [6]:

Given $f(x_1), \ldots, f(x_m)$, choose a hypothesis concept $\hat{f}$ randomly from $\mathcal{P}_m$.

Given x_{m+1}, predict $f(x_{m+1}) = \hat{f}(x_{m+1})$.

The Gibbs algorithm is the "zero-temperature" limit of the learning algorithm studied in several recent papers [2, 3, 8, 9]. If we let $Gibbs_{m+1}^{\mathcal{P}}(\mathbf{x}, f)$ (abbreviated $Gibbs_{m+1}^{\mathcal{P}}(f)$ since $\mathbf{x}$ is fixed for now) be a random variable whose value is 1 if the Gibbs algorithm predicts $f(x_{m+1})$ correctly and 0 otherwise, then it can be shown that the probability of a mistake for a random f is

$$\mathbf{E}_{f \in \mathcal{P}}[Gibbs_{m+1}^{\mathcal{P}}(f)] = \mathbf{E}_{f \in \mathcal{P}}[1 - \chi_{m+1}(f)]. \tag{3}$$

Note that by the definition of the Gibbs algorithm, Equation (3) is exactly the average probability of mistake of a consistent hypothesis, using the distribution on $\mathcal{F}$ defined by the prior. Thus bounds on this expectation provide an interesting contrast to those obtained via VC dimension analysis, which always gives bounds on the probability of mistake of the *worst* consistent hypothesis.

4   THE MAIN INEQUALITY

In this section we state one of our main results: a chain of inequalities that upper and lower bounds the expected error for both the Bayes and Gibbs algorithms by simple functions of the expected information gain. More precisely, using the characterizations of the expectations in terms of the volume ratio $\chi_{m+1}(f)$ given by Equations (1), (2) and (3), we can prove the following, which we refer to as the main inequality:

$$\begin{aligned}
\mathcal{H}^{-1}(\mathbf{E}_{f \in \mathcal{P}}[\mathcal{I}_{m+1}(f)]) &\leq \mathbf{E}_{f \in \mathcal{P}}[Bayes_{m+1}(f)] \\
&\leq \mathbf{E}_{f \in \mathcal{P}}[Gibbs_{m+1}(f)] \leq \frac{1}{2}\mathbf{E}_{f \in \mathcal{P}}[\mathcal{I}_{m+1}(f)].
\end{aligned} \tag{4}$$

Here we have defined an inverse to the binary entropy function $\mathcal{H}(p) = -p \log p - (1 - p) \log(1 - p)$ by letting $\mathcal{H}^{-1}(q)$, for $q \in [0, 1]$, be the unique $p \in [0, 1/2]$ such that $\mathcal{H}(p) = q$. Note that the bounds given depend on properties of the particular prior $\mathcal{P}$, and on properties of the particular fixed sequence $\mathbf{x}$. These upper and lower bounds are equal (and therefore tight) at both extremes $\mathbf{E}_{f \in \mathcal{P}}[\mathcal{I}_{m+1}(f)] = 1$ (maximal information gain) and $\mathbf{E}_{f \in \mathcal{P}}[\mathcal{I}_{m+1}(f)] = 0$ (minimal information gain). To obtain a weaker but perhaps more convenient lower bound, it can also be shown that there is a constant $c_0 > 0$ such that for all $p > 0$, $\mathcal{H}^{-1}(p) \geq c_0 p / \log(2/p)$.

Finally, if all that is wanted is a direct comparison of the performances of the Gibbs and Bayes algorithms, we can also show:

$$\mathbf{E}_{f \in \mathcal{P}}[Bayes_{m+1}(f)] \leq \mathbf{E}_{f \in \mathcal{P}}[Gibbs_{m+1}(f)] \leq 2\mathbf{E}_{f \in \mathcal{P}}[Bayes_{m+1}(f)]. \tag{5}$$

5   THE MAIN INEQUALITY: CUMULATIVE VERSION

In this section we state a cumulative version of the main inequality: namely, bounds on the expected *cumulative* number of mistakes made in the first m trials (rather than just the instantaneous expectations).

First, for the cumulative information gain, it can be shown that $\mathbf{E}_{f \in \mathcal{P}}[\sum_{i=1}^{m} \mathcal{I}_i(f)] = \mathbf{E}_{f \in \mathcal{P}}[-\log V_m(f)]$. This expression has a natural interpretation. The first m instances $x_1, \ldots, x_m$ of $\mathbf{x}$ induce a partition $\Pi_m^{\mathcal{F}}(\mathbf{x})$ of the concept class $\mathcal{F}$ defined by $\Pi_m^{\mathcal{F}}(\mathbf{x}) = \Pi_m^{\mathcal{F}} = \{\mathcal{F}_m(\mathbf{x}, f) : f \in \mathcal{F}\}$. Note that $|\Pi_m^{\mathcal{F}}|$ is always at most 2^m, but may be considerably smaller, depending on the interaction between $\mathcal{F}$ and $x_1, \ldots, x_m$. It is clear that $\mathbf{E}_{f \in \mathcal{P}}[-\log V_m(f)] = -\sum_{\pi \in \Pi_m^{\mathcal{F}}} \mathcal{P}[\pi] \log \mathcal{P}[\pi]$. Thus the expected cumulative information gained from the labels of $x_1, \ldots, x_m$ is simply the entropy of the partition $\Pi_m^{\mathcal{F}}$ under the distribution $\mathcal{P}$. We shall denote this entropy by $\mathcal{H}^{\mathcal{P}}(\Pi_m^{\mathcal{F}}(\mathbf{x})) = \mathcal{H}_m^{\mathcal{P}}(\mathbf{x}) = \mathcal{H}_m^{\mathcal{P}}$. Now analogous to the main inequality for the instantaneous case (Inequality (4)), we can show:

$$
\begin{aligned}
\frac{c_0 \mathcal{H}_m^{\mathcal{P}}}{\log(2m/\mathcal{H}_m^{\mathcal{P}})} &\leq m \mathcal{H}^{-1}\left(\frac{1}{m}\mathcal{H}_m^{\mathcal{P}}\right) \leq \mathbf{E}_{f \in \mathcal{P}}\left[\sum_{i=1}^{m} Bayes_i(f)\right] \\
&\leq \mathbf{E}_{f \in \mathcal{P}}\left[\sum_{i=1}^{m} Gibbs_i(f)\right] \leq \frac{1}{2}\mathcal{H}_m^{\mathcal{P}}.
\end{aligned}
\tag{6}
$$

Here we have applied the inequality $\mathcal{H}^{-1}(p) \geq c_0 p/\log(2/p)$ in order to give the lower bound in more convenient form. As in the instantaneous case, the upper and lower bounds here depend on properties of the particular $\mathcal{P}$ and $\mathbf{x}$. When the cumulative information gain is maximum ($\mathcal{H}_m^{\mathcal{P}} = m$), the upper and lower bounds are tight.

These bounds on learning performance in terms of a partition entropy are of special importance to us, since they will form the crucial link between the Bayesian setting and the Vapnik-Chervonenkis dimension theory.

6   MOVING TO A WORST-CASE THEORY: BOUNDING THE INFORMATION GAIN BY THE VC DIMENSION

Although we have given upper bounds on the expected cumulative number of mistakes for the Bayes and Gibbs algorithms in terms of $\mathcal{H}_m^{\mathcal{P}}(\mathbf{x})$, we are still left with the problem of evaluating this entropy, or at least obtaining reasonable upper bounds on it. We can intuitively see that the "worst case" for learning occurs when the partition entropy $\mathcal{H}_m^{\mathcal{P}}(\mathbf{x})$ is as large as possible. In our context, the entropy is qualitatively maximized when two conditions hold: (1) the instance sequence $\mathbf{x}$ induces a partition of $\mathcal{F}$ that is the largest possible, and (2) the prior $\mathcal{P}$ gives equal weight to each element of this partition.

In this section, we move away from our Bayesian average-case setting to obtain worst-case bounds by formalizing these two conditions in terms of combinatorial parameters depending only on the concept class $\mathcal{F}$. In doing so, we form the link between the theory developed so far and the VC dimension theory.

The second of the two conditions above is easily quantified. Since the entropy of a partition is at most the logarithm of the number of classes in it, a trivial upper bound on the entropy which holds for all priors $\mathcal{P}$ is $\mathcal{H}_m^{\mathcal{P}}(\mathbf{x}) \leq \log |\Pi_m^{\mathcal{F}}(\mathbf{x})|$. VC dimension theory provides an upper bound on $\log |\Pi_m^{\mathcal{F}}(\mathbf{x})|$ as follows.

For any sequence $\mathbf{x} = x_1, x_2, \ldots$ of instances and for $m \geq 1$, let $\dim_m(\mathcal{F}, \mathbf{x})$ denote the largest $d > 0$ such that there exists a subsequence $x_{i_1}, \ldots, x_{i_d}$ of $x_1, \ldots, x_m$ with $|\Pi_m^{\mathcal{F}}(\langle x_{i_1}, \ldots, x_{i_d} \rangle)| = 2^d$; that is, for every possible labeling of $x_{i_1}, \ldots, x_{i_d}$ there is some target concept in $\mathcal{F}$ that gives this labeling. The *Vapnik-Chervonenkis (VC) dimension* of $\mathcal{F}$ is defined by $\dim(\mathcal{F}) = \max\{\dim_m(\mathcal{F}, \mathbf{x}) : m \geq 1$ and $x_1, x_2, \ldots \in X\}$. It can be shown [7, 10] that for all $\mathbf{x}$ and $m \geq d \geq 1$,

$$\log |\Pi_m^{\mathcal{F}}(\mathbf{x})| \leq (1 + o(1)) \dim_m(\mathcal{F}, \mathbf{x}) \log \frac{m}{\dim_m(\mathcal{F}, \mathbf{x})} \tag{7}$$

where $o(1)$ is a quantity that goes to zero as $\alpha = m/\dim_m(\mathcal{F}, \mathbf{x})$ goes to infinity.

In all of our discussions so far, we have assumed that the instance sequence $\mathbf{x}$ is fixed in advance, but that the target concept f is drawn randomly according to $\mathcal{P}$. We now move to the completely probabilistic model, in which f is drawn according to $\mathcal{P}$, and each instance x_m in the sequence $\mathbf{x}$ is drawn randomly and independently according to a distribution $\mathcal{D}$ over the instance space X (this infinite sequence of draws from $\mathcal{D}$ will be denoted $\mathbf{x} \in \mathcal{D}^*$). Under these assumptions, it follows from Inequalities (6) and (7), and the observation above that $\mathcal{H}_m^{\mathcal{P}}(\mathbf{x}) \leq \log |\Pi_m^{\mathcal{F}}(\mathbf{x})|$ that for any $\mathcal{P}$ and any $\mathcal{D}$,

$$\mathbf{E}_{f \in \mathcal{P}, \mathbf{x} \in \mathcal{D}^*} \left[\sum_{i=1}^m Bayes_i(\mathbf{x}, f) \right] \leq \mathbf{E}_{f \in \mathcal{P}, \mathbf{x} \in \mathcal{D}^*} \left[\sum_{i=1}^m Gibbs_i(\mathbf{x}, f) \right]$$

$$\leq \frac{1}{2} \mathbf{E}_{\mathbf{x} \in \mathcal{D}^*} [\log |\Pi_m^{\mathcal{F}}(\mathbf{x})|]$$

$$\leq (1 + o(1)) \mathbf{E}_{\mathbf{x} \in \mathcal{D}^*} \left[\frac{\dim_m(\mathcal{F}, \mathbf{x})}{2} \log \frac{m}{\dim_m(\mathcal{F}, \mathbf{x})} \right]$$

$$\leq (1 + o(1)) \frac{\dim(\mathcal{F})}{2} \log \frac{m}{\dim(\mathcal{F})}. \tag{8}$$

The expectation $\mathbf{E}_{\mathbf{x} \in \mathcal{D}^*} [\log |\Pi_m^{\mathcal{F}}(\mathbf{x})|]$ is the *VC entropy* defined by Vapnik and Chervonenkis in their seminal paper on uniform convergence [11].

In terms of instantaneous mistake bounds, using more sophisticated techniques [4], we can show that for any $\mathcal{P}$ and any $\mathcal{D}$,

$$\mathbf{E}_{f \in \mathcal{P}, \mathbf{x} \in \mathcal{D}^*} [Bayes_m(\mathbf{x}, f)] \leq \mathbf{E}_{\mathbf{x} \in \mathcal{D}^*} \left[\frac{\dim_m(\mathcal{F}, \mathbf{x})}{m} \right] \leq \frac{\dim(\mathcal{F})}{m} \tag{9}$$

$$\mathbf{E}_{f \in \mathcal{P}, \mathbf{x} \in \mathcal{D}^*} [Gibbs_m(\mathbf{x}, f)] \leq \mathbf{E}_{\mathbf{x} \in \mathcal{D}^*} \left[\frac{2 \dim_m(\mathcal{F}, \mathbf{x})}{m} \right] \leq \frac{2 \dim(\mathcal{F})}{m} \tag{10}$$

Haussler, Littlestone and Warmuth [5] construct specific $\mathcal{D}$, $\mathcal{P}$ and $\mathcal{F}$ for which the last bound given by Inequality (8) is tight to within a factor of $1/\ln(2) \approx 1.44$; thus this bound cannot be improved by more than this factor in general.[1] Similarly, the

---

[1] It follows that the expected total number of mistakes of the Bayes and the Gibbs algorithms differ by a factor of at most about 1.44 in each of these cases; this was not previously known.

bound given by Inequality (9) cannot be improved by more than a factor of 2 in general.

For specific $\mathcal{D}$, $\mathcal{P}$ and $\mathcal{F}$, however, it is possible to improve the general bounds given in Inequalities (8), (9) and (10) by more than the factors indicated above. We calculate the instantaneous mistake bounds for the Bayes and Gibbs algorithms in the natural case that $\mathcal{F}$ is the set of homogeneous linear threshold functions on $\mathbf{R}^d$ and both the distribution $\mathcal{D}$ and the prior $\mathcal{P}$ on possible target concepts (represented also by vectors in $\mathbf{R}^d$) are uniform on the unit sphere in $\mathbf{R}^d$. This class has VC dimension d. In this case, under certain reasonable assumptions used in statistical mechanics, it can be shown that for $m \gg d \gg 1$,

$$\mathbf{E}_{f \in \mathcal{P}, \mathbf{x} \in \mathcal{D}^*}[Bayes_m(\mathbf{x}, f)] \quad \approx \quad \frac{0.44d}{m}$$

(compared with the upper bound of d/m given by Inequality (9) for any class of VC dimension d) and

$$\mathbf{E}_{f \in \mathcal{P}, \mathbf{x} \in \mathcal{D}^*}[Gibbs_m(\mathbf{x}, f)] \quad \approx \quad \frac{0.62d}{m}$$

(compared with the upper bound of $2d/m$ in Inequality (10)). The ratio of these asymptotic bounds is $\sqrt{2}$. We can also show that this performance advantage of Bayes over Gibbs is quite robust even when $\mathcal{P}$ and $\mathcal{D}$ vary, and there is noise in the examples [6].

7 OTHER RESULTS AND CONCLUSIONS

We have a number of other results, and briefly describe here one that may be of particular interest to neural network researchers. In the case that the class $\mathcal{F}$ has infinite VC dimension (for instance, if $\mathcal{F}$ is the class of all multi-layer perceptrons of finite size), we can still obtain bounds on the number of cumulative mistakes by decomposing $\mathcal{F}$ into $\mathcal{F}_1, \mathcal{F}_2, \ldots, \mathcal{F}_i, \ldots$, where each $\mathcal{F}_i$ has finite VC dimension, and by decomposing the prior $\mathcal{P}$ over $\mathcal{F}$ as a linear sum $\mathcal{P} = \sum_{i=1}^{\infty} \alpha_i \mathcal{P}_i$, where each $\mathcal{P}_i$ is an arbitrary prior over $\mathcal{F}_i$, and $\sum_{i=1}^{\infty} \alpha_i = 1$. A typical decomposition might let $\mathcal{F}_i$ be all multi-layer perceptrons of a given architecture with at most i weights, in which case $d_i = O(i \log i)$ [1]. Here we can show an upper bound on the cumulative mistakes during the first m examples of roughly $\mathcal{H}\{\alpha_i\} + [\sum_{i=1}^{\infty} \alpha_i d_i] \log m$ for both the Bayes and Gibbs algorithms, where $\mathcal{H}\{\alpha_i\} = -\sum_{i=1}^{\infty} \alpha_i \log \alpha_i$. The quantity $\sum_{i=1}^{\infty} \alpha_i d_i$ plays the role of an "effective VC dimension" relative to the prior weights $\{\alpha_i\}$. In the case that $\mathbf{x}$ is also chosen randomly, we can bound the probability of mistake on the mth trial by roughly $\frac{1}{m}(\mathcal{H}\{\alpha_i\} + [\sum_{i=1}^{\infty} \alpha_i d_i] \log m)$.

In our current research we are working on extending the basic theory presented here to the problems of learning with noise (see Opper and Haussler [6]), learning multi-valued functions, and learning with other loss functions.

Perhaps the most important general conclusion to be drawn from the work presented here is that the various theories of learning curves based on diverse ideas from information theory, statistical physics and the VC dimension are all in fact closely related, and can be naturally and beneficially placed in a common Bayesian framework.

Acknowledgements

We are greatly indebted to Ron Rivest for his valuable suggestions and guidance, and to Sara Solla and Naftali Tishby for insightful ideas in the early stages of this investigation. We also thank Andrew Barron, Andy Kahn, Nick Littlestone, Phil Long, Terry Sejnowski and Haim Sompolinsky for stimulating discussions on these topics. This research was supported by ONR grant N00014-91-J-1162, AFOSR grant AFOSR-89-0506, ARO grant DAAL03-86-K-0171, DARPA contract N00014-89-J-1988, and a grant from the Siemens Corporation. This research was conducted in part while M. Kearns was at the M.I.T. Laboratory for Computer Science and the International Computer Science Institute, and while R. Schapire was at the M.I.T. Laboratory for Computer Science and Harvard University.

References

[1] E. Baum and D. Haussler. What size net gives valid generalization? *Neural Computation*, 1(1):151–160, 1989.

[2] J. Denker, D. Schwartz, B. Wittner, S. Solla, R. Howard, L. Jackel, and J. Hopfield. Automatic learning, rule extraction and generalization. *Complex Systems*, 1:877–922, 1987.

[3] G. Györgi and N. Tishby. Statistical theory of learning a rule. In *Neural Networks and Spin Glasses*. World Scientific, 1990.

[4] D. Haussler, M. Kearns, and R. Schapire. Bounds on the sample complexity of Bayesian learning using information theory and the VC dimension. In *Computational Learning Theory: Proceedings of the Fourth Annual Workshop*. Morgan Kaufmann, 1991.

[5] D. Haussler, N. Littlestone, and M. Warmuth. Predicting {0, 1}-functions on randomly drawn points. Technical Report UCSC-CRL-90-54, University of California Santa Cruz, Computer Research Laboratory, Dec. 1990.

[6] M. Opper and D. Haussler. Calculation of the learning curve of Bayes optimal classification algorithm for learning a perceptron with noise. In *Computational Learning Theory: Proceedings of the Fourth Annual Workshop*. Morgan Kaufmann, 1991.

[7] N. Sauer. On the density of families of sets. *Journal of Combinatorial Theory (Series A)*, 13:145–147, 1972.

[8] H. Sompolinsky, N. Tishby, and H. Seung. Learning from examples in large neural networks. *Physics Review Letters*, 65:1683–1686, 1990.

[9] N. Tishby, E. Levin, and S. Solla. Consistent inference of probabilities in layered networks: predictions and generalizations. In *IJCNN International Joint Conference on Neural Networks*, volume II, pages 403–409. IEEE, 1989.

[10] V. N. Vapnik. *Estimation of Dependences Based on Empirical Data*. Springer-Verlag, New York, 1982.

[11] V. N. Vapnik and A. Y. Chervonenkis. On the uniform convergence of relative frequencies of events to their probabilities. *Theory of Probability and its Applications*, 16(2):264–80, 1971.

Constant-Time Loading of Shallow 1-Dimensional Networks

Stephen Judd
Siemens Corporate Research,
755 College Rd. E.,
Princeton, NJ 08540
judd@learning.siemens.com

Abstract

The complexity of learning in shallow 1-Dimensional neural networks has been shown elsewhere to be linear in the size of the network. However, when the network has a huge number of units (as cortex has) even linear time might be unacceptable. Furthermore, the algorithm that was given to achieve this time was based on a single serial processor and was biologically implausible.

In this work we consider the more natural parallel model of processing and demonstrate an expected-time complexity that is *constant* (i.e. independent of the size of the network). This holds even when inter-node communication channels are short and local, thus adhering to more biological and VLSI constraints.

1 Introduction

Shallow neural networks are defined in [Jud90]; the definition effectively limits the depth of networks while allowing the width to grow arbitrarily, and it is used as a model of neurological tissue like cortex where neurons are arranged in arrays tens of millions of neurons wide but only tens of neurons deep. Figure 1 exemplifies a family of networks which are not only shallow but "1-dimensional" as well—we allow the network to be extended as far as one liked in width (i.e. to the right) by repeating the design segments shown. The question we address is how learning time scales with the width. In [Jud88], it was proved that the worst case time complexity

863

of training this family is linear in the width. But the proof involved an algorithm that was biologically very implausible and it is this objection that will be somewhat redressed in this paper.

The problem with the given algorithm is that it operates only a monolithic serial computer; the single-CPU model of computing has no overt constraints on communication capacities and therefore is too liberal a model to be relevant to our neural machinery. Furthermore, the algorithm reveals very little about how to do the processing in a parallel and distributed fashion. In this paper we alter the model of computing to attain a degree of biological plausibility. We allow a linear number processors and put explicit constraints on the time required to communicate between processors. Both of these changes make the model much more biological (and also closer to the connectionist style of processing).

This change alone, however, does not alter the time complexity—the worst case training time is still linear. But when we change the complexity question being asked, a different answer is obtained. We define a class of tasks (viz. training data) that are drawn at random and then ask for the *expected* time to load these tasks, rather than the worst-case time. This alteration makes the question much more environmentally relevant. It also leads us into a different domain of algorithms and yields fast loading times.

2   Shallow 1-D Loading

2.1   Loading

A *family* of the example shallow 1-dimensional architectures that we shall examine is characterized solely by an integer, d, which defines the depth of each architecture in the family. An example is shown in figure 1 for $d = 3$. The example also happens to have a fixed fan-in of 2 and a very regular structure, but this is not essential. A *member* of the family is specified by giving the width n, which we will take to be the number of output nodes.

A *task* is a set of pairs of binary vectors, each specifying a stimulus to a net and its desired response. A random task of size t is a set of t pairs of independently drawn random strings; there is no guarantee it is a function.

Our primary question has to do with the following problem, which is parameterized by some fixed depth d, and by a *node function set* (which is the collection of different transfer functions that a node can be tuned to perform):

Shallow 1-D Loading :
    Instance: An integer n, and a task.
    Objective: Find a function (from the node function set) for each node in the network in the shallow 1-D architecture defined by d and n such that the resulting circuit maps all the stimuli in the task to their associated responses.

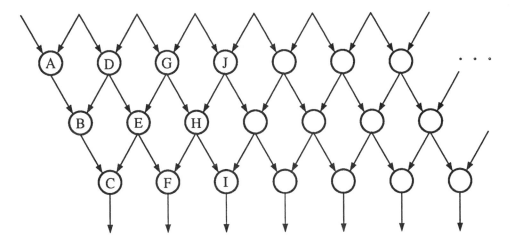

Figure 1: A Example Shallow 1-D Architecture

2.2   Model of Computation

Our machine model for solving this question is the following: For an instance of shallow 1-D loading of width n, we allow n processors. Each one has access to a piece of the task, namely processor i has access to bits i through $i + d$ of each stimulus, and to bit i of each response. Each processor i has a communication link only to its two neighbours, namely processors $i - 1$ and $i + 1$. (The first and n^{th} processors have only one neighbour.) It takes one time step to communicate a fixed amount of data between neighbours. There is no charge for computation, but this is not an unreasonable cheat because we can show that a matrix multiply is sufficient for this problem, and the size of the matrix is a function only of d (which is fixed).

This definition accepts the usual connectionist ideal of having the processor closely identified with the network nodes for which it is "finding the weights", and data available at the processor is restricted to the same "local" data that connectionist machines have.

This sort of computation sets the stage for a complexity question,

2.3   Question and Approach

We wish to demonstrate that

Claim 1 *This parallel machine solves shallow 1-D loading where each processor is finished in constant expected time The constant is dependent on the depth of the architecture and on the size of the task, but not on the width. The expectation is over the tasks.*

For simplicity we shall focus on one particular processor—the one at the leftmost end—and we shall further restrict our attention to finding a node function for one particular node.

To operate in parallel, it is necessary and sufficient for each processor to make its local decisions in a "safe" manner—that is, it must make choices for its nodes in such a way as to facilitate a global solution. Constant-time loading precludes being able to see all the data; and if only local data is accessible to a processor, then its plight is essentially to find an assignment that is compatible with *all* nonlocal satisfying assignments.

Theorem 2 *The expected communication complexity of finding a "safe" node function assignment for a particular node in a shallow 1-D architecture is a constant dependent on d and t, but not on n.*

If decisions about assignments to single nodes can be made easily and essentially without having to communicate with most of the network, then the induced partitioning of the problem admits of fast parallel computation. There are some complications to the details because all these decisions must be made in a coordinated fashion, but we omit these details here and claim they are secondary issues that do not affect the gross complexity measurements.

The proof of the theorem comes in two pieces. First, we define a computational problem called path finding and the graph-theoretic notion of domination which is its fundamental core. Then we argue that the loading problem can be reduced to path finding in constant parallel time and give an upper bound for determining domination.

3   Path Finding

The following problem is parameterized by an integer K, which is fixed.

Path finding :
Instance: An integer n defining the number of parts in a partite graph, and a series of $K \times K$ adjacency matrices, $M_1, M_2, \ldots M_{n-1}$. M_i indicates connections between the K nodes of part i and the K nodes of part $i + 1$.
Objective: Find a path of n nodes, one from each part of the n-partite graph.

Define X_h to be the binary matrix representing connectivity between the first part of the graph and the ith part: $X_1 = M_1$ and $X_h(j, k) = 1$ iff $\exists m$ such that $X_h(j, m) = 1$ and $M_h(m, k) = 1$. We say "*i includes j at h*" if every bit in the ith row of X_h is 1 whenever the corresponding bit in the jth row of X_h is 1. We say "*i dominates at h*" or "*i is a dominator*" if for all rows j, i includes j at h.

Lemma 3 *Before an algorithm can select a node i from the first part of the graph to be on the path, it is necessary and sufficient for i to have been proven to be a dominator at some h.*   □

The minimum h required to prove domination stands as our measure of "communication complexity".

Lemma 4 *Shallow 1-D Loading can be reduced to path finding in constant parallel time.*

Proof: Each output node in a shallow architecture has a set of nodes leading into it called a support cone (or "receptive field"), and the collection of functions assigned to those nodes will determine whether or not the output bit is correct in each response. Nodes A,B,C,D,E,G in Figure 1 are the support cone for the first output node (node C), and D,E,F,G,H,J are the cone for the second. Construct each part of the graph as a set of points each corresponding to an assignment over the whole support cone that makes its output bit always correct. This can be done for each cone in parallel, and since the depth (and the fan-in) is fixed, the set of all possible assignments for the support cone can be enumerated in constant time. Now insert edges between adjacent parts wherever two points correspond to assignments that are mutually compatible. (Note that since the support cones overlap one another, we need to ensure that assignments are consistent with each other.) This also can be done in constant parallel time. We call this construction a *compatibility graph*.

A solution to the loading problem corresponds exactly to a path in the compatibility graph. □

A dominator in this path-finding graph is exactly what was meant above by a "safe" assignment in the loading problem.

4   Proof of Theorem

Since it is possible that there is no assignments to certain cones that correctly map the stimuli it is trivial to prove the theorem, but as a practical matter we are interested in the case where the architecture is actually capable of performing the task. We will prove the theorem using a somewhat more satisfying event.

Proof of theorem 2: For each support cone there is 1 output bit per response and there are t such responses. Given the way they are generated, these responses could all be the same with probability $.5^{t-1}$. The probability of two adjacent cones both having to perform such a constant mapping is $.5^{2(t-1)}$.

Imagine the labelling in Figure 1 to be such that there were many support cones to the left (and right) of the piece shown. Any path through the left side of the compatibility graph that arrived at some point in the part for the cone to the left of C would imply an assignment for nodes A, B, and D. Any path through the right side of the compatibility graph that arrived at some point in the part for the cone of I would imply an assignment for nodes G, H, and J. If cones C and F were both required to merely perform constant mappings, then any and all assignments to A, B, and D would be compatible with any and all assignments to G, H, and J (because nodes C and F could be assigned constant functions themselves, thereby making the others irrelevant). This insures that any point on a path to the left will dominate at the part for I.

Thus $2^{2(t-1)}$ (the inverse of the probability of this happening) is an upper bound on the domination distance, i.e. the communication complexity, i.e. the loading time.   □

More accurately, the complexity is $\min(c(d,t), f(t), n)$, where c and f are some unknown functions. But the operative term here is usually c because d is unlikely to get so large as to bring f into play (and of course n is unbounded).

The analysis in the proof is sufficient, but it is a far cry from complete. The actual Markovian process in the sequence of X's is much richer; there are so many events in the compatibility graph that cause domination to occur that is takes a lot of careful effort to construct a task that will *avoid* it!

5   Measuring the Constants

Unfortunately, the very complications that give rise to the pleasant robustness of the domination event also make it fiendishly difficult to analyze quantitatively. So to get estimates for the actual constants involved we ran Monte Carlo experiments.

We ran experiments for 4 different cases. The first experiment was to measure the distance one would have to explore before finding a dominating assignment for the node labeled A in figure 1. The node function set used was the set of linearly separable functions. In all experiments, if domination occurred for the degenerate reason that there were no solutions (paths) at all, then that datum was thrown out and the run was restarted with a different seed.

Figure 2 reports the constants for the four cases. There is one curve for each experiment. The abscissa represents t, the size of the task. The ordinate is the number of support cones that must be consulted before domination can be expected to occur. All points given are the average of at least 500 trials. Since t is an integer the data should not have been interpolated between points, but they are easier to see as connected lines. The solid line (labeled LSA) is for the case just described. It has a bell shape, reflecting three facts:

- when the task is very small almost every choice of node function for one node is compatible with choices for the neighbouring nodes.
- when the task is very large, there so many constraints on what a node must compute that it is easy to resolve what that should be without going far afield.
- when the task is intermediate-sized, the problem is harder.

Note the very low distances involved—even the peak of the curve is well below 2, so nowhere would you expect to have to pass data more than 2 support cones away. Although this worst-expected-case would surely be larger for deeper nets, current work is attempting to see how badly this would scale with depth (larger d).

The curve labeled LUA is for the case where all Boolean functions are used as the node function set. Note that it is significantly higher in the region $6 \leq t \leq 12$. The implication is that although the node function set being used here is a superset of the linearly separable functions, it takes *more* computation at loading time to be able to exploit that extra power.

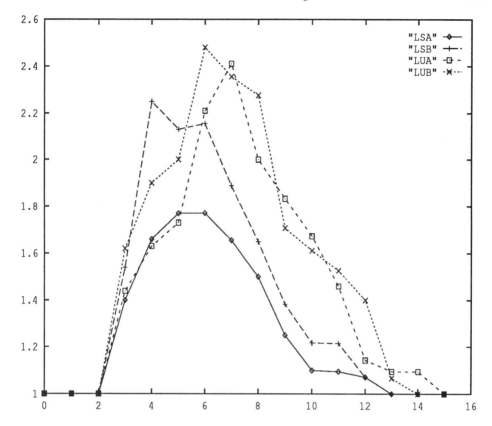

Figure 2: Measured Domination Distances.

The curve labeled LSB shows the expected distance one has to explore before finding a dominating assignment for the node labelled B in figure 1. The node function set used was the set of linearly separable functions. Note that it is everywhere higher that the LSA curve, indicating that the difficulty of settling on a correct node function for a second-layer node is somewhat higher than finding one for a first-layer node.

Finally, there is a curve for node B when all Boolean functions are used (LUB). It is generally higher than when just linearly separable functions are used, but not so markedly so as in the case of node A.

6 Conclusions

The model of computation used here is much more biologically relevant than the ones previously used for complexity results, but the algorithm used here runs in an off-line "batch mode" (i.e. it has all the data before it starts processing). This has an unbiological nature, but no more so than the customary connectionist habit of repeating the data many times.

A weakness of our analysis is that (as formulated here) it is only for discrete node functions, exact answers, and noise-free data. Extensions for any of these additional difficulties may be possible, and the bell shape of the curves should survive.

The peculiarities of the regular 3-layer network examined here may appear restrictive, but it was taken as an example only; what is really implied by the term "1-D" is only that the bandwidth of the SCI graph for the architecture be bounded (see [Jud90] for definitions). This constraint allows several degrees of freedom in choosing the architecture, but domination is such a robust combinatoric event that the essential observation about bell-shaped curves made in this paper will persist even in the face of large changes from these examples.

We suggest that whatever architectures and node function sets a designer cares to use, the notion of domination distance will help reveal important computational characteristics of the design.

Acknowledgements

Thanks go to Siemens and CalTech for wads of computer time.

References

[Jud88] J. S. Judd. On the complexity of loading shallow neural networks. *Journal of Complexity*, September 1988. Special issue on Neural Computation, in press.

[Jud90] J. Stephen Judd. *Neural Network Design and the Complexity of Learning.* MIT Press, Cambridge, Massachusetts, 1990.

Experimental Evaluation of Learning in a Neural Microsystem

Joshua Alspector Anthony Jayakumar Stephan Luna†
Bellcore
Morristown, NJ 07962-1910

Abstract

We report learning measurements from a system composed of a cascadable learning chip, data generators and analyzers for training pattern presentation, and an X-windows based software interface. The 32 neuron learning chip has 496 adaptive synapses and can perform Boltzmann and mean-field learning using separate noise and gain controls. We have used this system to do learning experiments on the parity and replication problem. The system settling time limits the learning speed to about 100,000 patterns per second roughly independent of system size.

1. INTRODUCTION

We have implemented a model of learning in neural networks using feedback connections and a local learning rule. Even though back-propagation[1] (Rumelhart,1986) networks are feedforward in processing, they have separate, implicit feedback paths during learning for error propagation. Networks with explicit, full-time feedback paths can perform pattern completion[2] (Hopfield,1982), can learn many-to-one mappings, can learn probability distributions, and can have interesting temporal and dynamical properties in contrast to the single forward pass processing of multilayer perceptrons trained with back-propagation or other means. Because of the potential for complex dynamics, feedback networks require a reliable method of relaxation for learning and retrieval of static patterns. The Boltzmann machine[3] (Ackley,1985) uses stochastic settling while the mean-field theory version[4] (Peterson,1987) uses a more computationally efficient deterministic technique.

We have previously shown that Boltzmann learning can be implemented in VLSI[5] (Alspector,1989). We have also shown, by simulation,[6] (Alspector,1991a) that Boltzmann and mean-field networks can have powerful learning and representation properties just like the more thoroughly studied back-propagation methods. In this paper, we demonstrate these properties using new, expandable parallel hardware for on-chip learning.

---

† Permanent address: University of California, Berkeley; EECS Dep't, Cory Hall; Berkeley, CA 94720

2. VLSI IMPLEMENTATION

2.1 Electronic Model

We have implemented these feedback networks in VLSI which speeds up learning by many orders of magnitude due to the parallel nature of weight adjustment and neuron state update. Our choice of learning technique for implementation is due mainly to the local learning rule which makes it much easier to cast these networks into electronics than back-propagation.

Individual neurons in the Boltzmann machine have a probabilistic decision rule such that neuron i is in state $s_i = 1$ with probability

$$\Pr(s_i = 1) = \frac{1}{1+e^{-u_i/T}} \tag{1}$$

where $u_i = \sum_j w_{ij} s_j$ is the net input to each neuron calculated by current summing and T is a parameter that acts like temperature in a physical system and is represented by the noise and gain terms in Eq. (2), which follows. In the electronic model we use, each neuron performs the activation computation

$$s_i = f\left(\beta * (u_i + v_i)\right) \tag{2}$$

where f is a monotonic non-linear function such as *tanh*. The noise, v, is chosen from a zero mean gaussian distribution whose width is proportional to the temperature. This closely approximates the distribution in Eq. (1) and comes from our hardware implementation, which supplies uncorrelated noise in the form of a binomial distribution[7] (Alspector,1991b) to each neuron. The noise is slowly reduced as annealing proceeds. For mean-field learning, the noise is zero but the gain, β, has a finite value proportional to $1/T$ taken from the annealing schedule. Thus the non-linearity sharpens as 'annealing' proceeds.

The network is annealed in two phases, + and −, corresponding to clamping the outputs in the desired state (teacher phase) and allowing them to run free (student phase) at each pattern presentation. The learning rule which adjusts the weights w_{ij} from neuron j to neuron i is

$$\Delta w_{ij} = sgn\left[(s_i s_j)^+ - (s_i s_j)^- \right]. \tag{3}$$

Note that this measures the instantaneous correlations after annealing. For both phases each synapse memorizes the correlations measured at the end of the annealing cycle and weight adjustment is then made, (i.e., online). The *sgn* matches our hardware implementation which changes weights by one each time.

2.2 Learning Microchip

Fig. 1 shows the learning microchip which has been fabricated. It contains 32 neurons and 992 connections (496 bidirectional synapses). On the extreme right is a noise generator which supplies 32 uncorrelated pseudo-random noise sources[7] (Alspector,1991b) to the neurons to their left. These noise sources are summed in the form of current along with the weighted post-synaptic signals from other neurons at the input to each neuron in order to implement the simulated annealing process of the stochastic Boltzmann machine. The neuron amplifiers implement a non-linear activation

Figure 1. Photo of 32-Neuron Cascadable Learning Chip

function which has variable gain to provide for the gain sharpening function of the mean-field technique. The range of neuron gain can also be adjusted to allow for scaling in summing currents due to adjustable network size.

Most of the area is occupied by the synapse array. Each synapse digitally stores a weight ranging from -15 to +15 as 4 bits plus a sign. It multiples the voltage input from the presynaptic neuron by this weight to output a current. One conductance direction can be disconnected so that we can experiment with asymmetric networks[8] (Allen,1990). Although the synapses can have their weights set externally, they are designed to be adaptive. They store correlations, in parallel, using the local learning rule of Eq. (3) and adjust their weights accordingly. A neuron state range of -1 to 1 is assumed by the digital learning processor in each synapse on the chip.

Fig. 2a shows a family of transfer functions of a neuron, showing how the gain is continually adjustable by varying a control voltage. Fig. 2b shows the transfer function of a synapse as different weights are loaded. The input linear range is about 2 volts.

Fig. 3 shows waveforms during exclusive-OR learning using the noise annealing of the Boltzmann machine. The top three traces are hidden neurons while the bottom trace is the output neuron which is clamped during the + phase. There are two input patterns presented during the time interval displayed, (-1,+1) and (+1,-1), both of which should output a +1 (note the state clamped to high voltage on the output neuron). Note the sequence of steps involved in each pattern presentation. 1) Outputs from the previous pattern are unclamped. 2) The new pattern is presented to the input neurons. 3) Noise is presented to the network and annealed. 4) The student phase latch captures the

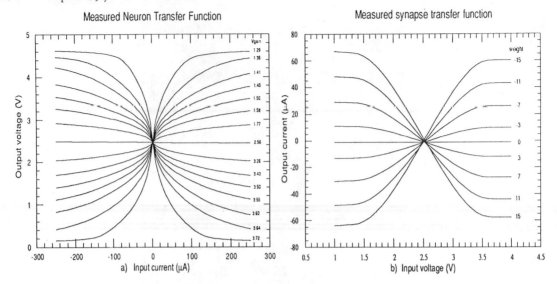

Figure 2. Transfer Functions of Electronic Neuron (2a) and Synapse (2b)

correlations. 5) Data from the neuron states is read into the data analyzer. 6) The output neurons are clamped (no annealing is necessary for a three layer network). 7) The teacher phase latch captures the correlations. 8) Weights are adjusted (go to step 1).

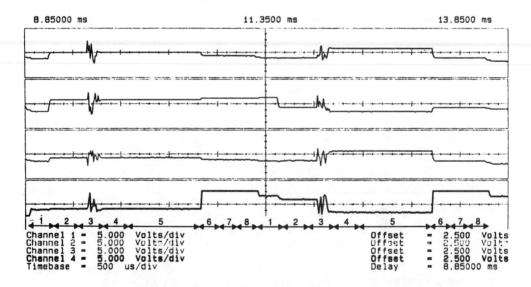

Figure 3. Neuron Signals during Learning (see text for steps involved)

Fig. 4a shows an expanded view of 4 neuron waveforms during the noise annealing portion of the chip operation during Boltzmann learning. Fig. 4b shows a similar portion during gain annealing. Note that, at low gain, the neuron states start at 2.5 *volts* and settle to an analog value between 0 and 5 *volts*. For the purposes of classification for the

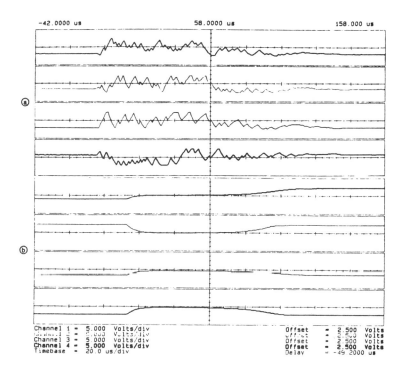

Figure 4. Neuron Signals during Annealing with Noise (4a) and Gain (4b)

digital problems we investigated, neurons are either +1 or -1 depending on whether their voltage is above or below 2.5 *volts*. This isn't clear until after settling. There are several instances in Figs. 3 and 4 where the neuron state changes after noise or gain annealing.

The speed of pattern presentations is limited by the length of the annealing signal for system settling (100 μsec in Fig. 3). The rest of the operations can be made negligibly short in comparison. The annealing time could be reduced to 10 μsec or so, leading to a rate of about 100,000 patterns/sec. In comparison, a 10-10-10 replication problem, which fits on a single chip, takes about a second per pattern on a SPARCstation 2. This time scales roughly with the number of weights on a sequential machine, but is almost constant on the learning chip due to its parallel nature.

We can do even larger problems in a multiple chip system because the chip is designed to be cascaded with other similar chips in a board-level system which can be accessed by a computer. The nodes which sum current from synapses for net input into a neuron are available externally for connection to other chips and for external clamping of neurons or other external input. We are currently building such a system with a VME bus interface for tighter coupling to our software than is allowed by the GPIB instrument bus we are using at the time of this writing.

2.3 Learning Experiments

To study learning as a function of problem size, we chose the parity and replication (identity) problems. This facilitates comparisons with our previous simulations[6]

(Alspector,1991a). The parity problem is the generalization of exclusive-OR for arbitrary input size. It is difficult because the classification regions are disjoint with every change of input bit, but it has only one output. The goal of the replication problem is for the output to duplicate the bit pattern found on the input after being encoded by the hidden layer. Note that the output bits can be shifted or scrambled in any order without affecting the difficulty of the problem. There are as many output neurons as input. For the replication problem, we chose the hidden layer to have the same number of neurons as the input layer, while for parity we chose the hidden layer to have twice the number as the input layer.

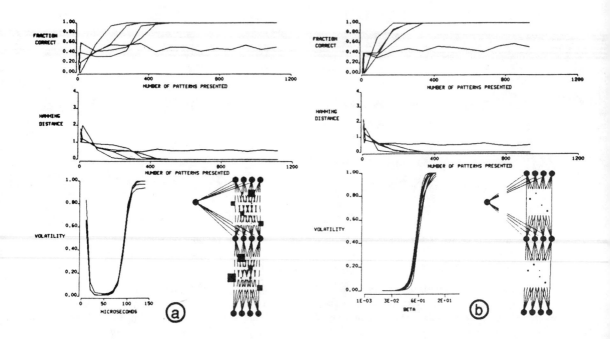

Figure 5. X-window Display for Learning on Chip (5a) and in Software (5b)

Fig. 5 shows the X-window display for 5 mean-field runs for learning the 4 input, 4 hidden, 4 output (4-4-4) replication on the chip (5a) and in the simulator (5b). The user specification is the same for both. Only the learning calculation module is different. Both have displays of the network topology, the neuron states (color and pie-shaped arc of circles) and the network weights (color and size of squares). There are also graphs of percent correct and error (Hamming distance for replication) and one of volatility of neuron states[9] (Alspector,1992) as a measure of the system temperature. The learning curves look quite similar. In both cases, one of the 5 runs failed to learn to 100 %. The boxes representing weights are signed currents (about 4 μamp per unit weight) in 5a and integers from -15 to +15 in 5b. Volatility is plotted as a function of time (μsec) in 5a and shows that, in hardware (see Fig. 4), time is needed for a gain decrease at the start of the annealing as well as for the gain increase of the annealing proper. The volatility in 5b is plotted as a function of gain (BETA) which increases logarithmically in the simulator at each anneal step.

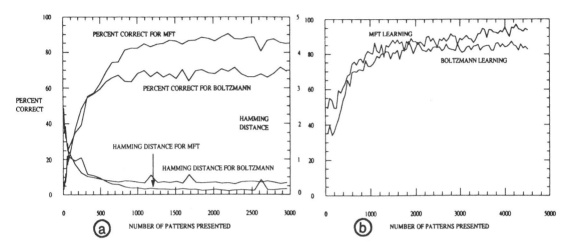

Figure 6. On-chip Learning for 6 Input Replication (6a) and Parity (6b)

Fig. 6a displays data from the average of 10 runs of 6-6-6 replication for both Boltzmann (BZ) and mean-field (MFT) learning. While the percent correct saturates at 90 % (70 % for Boltzmann), the output error as measured by the Hamming distance between input and output is less than 1 bit out of 6. Boltzmann learning is somewhat poorer in this experiment probably because circuit parameters have not yet been optimized. We expect that a combination of noise and gain annealing will yield the best results but have not tested this possibility at this writing. Fig. 6b is a similar plot for 6-12-1 parity.

We have done on-chip learning experiments using noise and gain annealing for parity and replication up to 8 input bits, nearly utilizing all the neurons on a single chip. To judge scaling behavior in these early experiments, we note the number of patterns required until no further improvement in percent correct is visible by eye. Fig. 7a plots, for an average of 10 runs of the parity problem, the number of patterns required to learn up to the saturation value for percent correct for both Boltzmann and mean-field learning. This scales roughly as an exponential in number of inputs for learning on chip just as it did in simulation[6] (Alspector,1991a) since the training set size is exponential. The final percent correct is indicated on the plot. Fig. 7b plots the equivalent data for the replication problem. Outliers are due to low saturation values. Overall, the training time per pattern on-chip is quite similar to our simulations. However, in real-time, it can be about 100,000 times as fast for a single chip and will be even faster for multiple chip systems. The speed for either learning or evaluation is roughly 10^8 connections per second per chip.

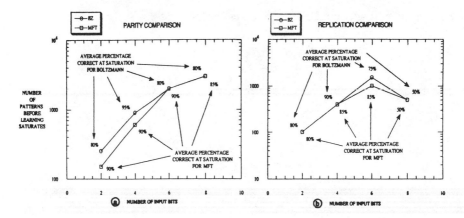

Figure 7. Scaling of Parity (7a) and Replication (7b) Problem with Input Size

3. CONCLUSION

We have shown that Boltzmann and mean-field learning networks can be implemented in a parallel, analog VLSI system. While we report early experiments on a single-chip digital system, a multiple-chip VME-based electronic system with analog I/O is being constructed for use on larger problems.

ACKNOWLEDGMENT:

This work has been partially supported by AFOSR contract F49620-90-C-0042, DEF.

REFERENCES

1. D.E. Rumelhart, G.E. Hinton, & R.J. Williams, "Learning Internal Representations by Error Propagation", in *Parallel Distributed Processing: Explorations in the Microstructure of Cognition. Vol. 1: Foundations*, D.E. Rumelhart & J.L. McClelland (eds.), MIT Press, Cambridge, MA (1986), p. 318.

2. J.J. Hopfield, "Neural Networks and Physical Systems with Emergent Collective Computational Abilities", *Proc. Natl. Acad. Sci. USA*, **79**, 2554-2558 (1982).

3. D.H. Ackley, G.E. Hinton, & T.J. Sejnowski, "A Learning Algorithm for Boltzmann Machines", *Cognitive Science* **9** (1985) pp. 147-169.

4. C. Peterson & J.R. Anderson, "A Mean Field Learning Algorithm for Neural Networks", *Complex Systems*, **1:5**, 995-1019, (1987).

5. J. Alspector, B. Gupta, & R.B. Allen, "Performance of a Stochastic Learning Microchip" in *Advances in Neural Information Processing Systems 1*, D. Touretzky (ed.), Morgan-Kaufmann, Palo Alto, (1989), pp. 748-760.

6. J. Alspector, R.B. Allen, A. Jayakumar, T. Zeppenfeld, & R. Meir "Relaxation Networks for Large Supervised Learning Problems" in *Advances in Neural Information Processing Systems 3*, R.P Lippmann, J.E. Moody, & D.S. Touretzky (eds.), Morgan-Kaufmann, Palo Alto, (1991), pp. 1015-1021.

7. J. Alspector, J.W. Gannett, S. Haber, M.B. Parker, & R. Chu, "A VLSI-Efficient Technique for Generating Multiple Uncorrelated Noise Sources and Its Application to Stochastic Neural Networks", *IEEE Trans. Circuits & Systems*, **38**, 109, (Jan., 1991).

8. R.B. Allen & J. Alspector, "Learning of Stable States in Stochastic Asymmetric Networks", *IEEE Trans. Neural Networks*, **1**, 233-238, (1990).

9. J. Alspector, T. Zeppenfeld & S. Luna, "A Volatility Measure for Annealing in Feedback Neural Networks", to appear in *Neural Computation*, (1992).

Threshold Network Learning in the Presence of Equivalences

John Shawe-Taylor
Department of Computer Science
Royal Holloway and Bedford New College
University of London
Egham, Surrey TW20 0EX, UK

Abstract

This paper applies the theory of Probably Approximately Correct (PAC) learning to multiple output feedforward threshold networks in which the weights conform to certain equivalences. It is shown that the sample size for reliable learning can be bounded above by a formula similar to that required for single output networks with no equivalences. The best previously obtained bounds are improved for all cases.

1 INTRODUCTION

This paper develops the results of Baum and Haussler [3] bounding the sample sizes required for reliable generalisation of a single output feedforward threshold network. They prove their result using the theory of Probably Approximately Correct (PAC) learning introduced by Valiant [11]. They show that for $0 < \epsilon \leq 1/2$, if a sample of size

$$m \geq m_0 = \frac{64W}{\epsilon} \log \frac{64N}{\epsilon}$$

is loaded into a feedforward network of linear threshold units with N nodes and W weights, so that a fraction $1 - \epsilon/2$ of the examples are correctly classified, then with confidence approaching certainty the network will correctly classify a fraction $1 - \epsilon$ of future examples drawn according to the same distribution. A similar bound was obtained for the case when the network correctly classified the whole sample. The results below will imply a significant improvement to both of these bounds.

In many cases training can be simplified if known properties of a problem can be incorporated into the structure of a network before training begins. One such technique is described by Shawe-Taylor [9], though many similar techniques have been applied as for example in TDNN's [6]. The effect of these restrictions is to constrain groups of weights to take the same value and learning algorithms are adapted to respect this constraint.

In this paper we consider the effect of this restriction on the generalisation performance of the networks and in particular the sample sizes required to obtain a given level of generalisation. This extends the work described above by Baum and Haussler [3] by improving their bounds and also improving the results of Shawe-Taylor and Anthony [10], who consider generalisation of multiple-output threshold networks. The remarkable fact is that in all cases the formula obtained is the same, where we now understand the number of weights W to be the number of weight classes, but N is still the number of computational nodes.

2   DEFINITIONS AND MAIN RESULTS

2.1   SYMMETRY AND EQUIVALENCE NETWORKS

We begin with a definition of threshold networks. To simplify the exposition it is convenient to incorporate the threshold value into the set of weights. This is done by creating a distinguished input that always has value 1 and is called the threshold input. The following is a formal notation for these systems.

A network $\mathcal{N} = (C, I, O, n_0, E)$ is specified by a set C of computational nodes, a set I of input nodes, a subset $O \subseteq C$ of output nodes and a node $n_0 \in I$, called the threshold node. The connectivity is given by a set $E \subseteq (C \cup I) \times C$ of connections, with $\{n_0\} \times C \subseteq E$.

With network $\mathcal{N}$ we associate a weight function w from the set of connections to the real numbers. We say that the network $\mathcal{N}$ is in state w. For input vector $\mathbf{i}$ with values in some subset of the set $\mathcal{R}$ of real numbers, the network computes a function $F_{\mathcal{N}}(w, \mathbf{i})$.

An automorphism γ of a network $\mathcal{N} = (C, I, O, n_0, E)$ is a bijection of the nodes of $\mathcal{N}$ which fixes I setwise and $\{n_0\} \cup O$ pointwise, such that the induced action fixes E setwise. We say that an automorphism γ preserves the weight assignment w if $w_{ji} = w_{(\gamma j)(\gamma i)}$ for all $i \in I \cup C$, $j \in C$. Let γ be an automorphism of a network $\mathcal{N} = (C, I, O, n_0, E)$ and let $\mathbf{i}$ be an input to $\mathcal{N}$. We denote by $\mathbf{i}^\gamma$ the input whose value on input k is that of $\mathbf{i}$ on input $\gamma^{-1}k$.

The following theorem is a natural generalisation of part of the Group Invariance Theorem of Minsky and Pappert [8] to multi-layer perceptrons.

Theorem 2.1 *[9] Let γ be a weight preserving automorphism of the network $\mathcal{N} = (C, I, O, n_0, E)$ in state w. Then for every input vector $\mathbf{i}$*

$$F_{\mathcal{N}}(w, \mathbf{i}) = F_{\mathcal{N}}(w, \mathbf{i}^\gamma).$$

Following this theorem it is natural to consider the concept of a *symmetry network* [9]. This is a pair $(\mathcal{N}, \Gamma)$, where $\mathcal{N}$ is a network and Γ a group of weight preserving automorphims of $\mathcal{N}$. We will also refer to the automorphisms as symmetries. For a symmetry network $(\mathcal{N}, \Gamma)$, we term the orbits of the connections E under the action of Γ the weight classes.

Finally we introduce the concept of an *equivalence network*. This definition abstracts from the symmetry networks precisely those properties we require to obtain our results. The class of equivalence networks is, however, far larger than that of symmetry networks and includes many classes of networks studied by other researchers [6, 7].

Definition 2.2 *An equivalence network is a threshold network in which an equivalence relation is defined on both weights and nodes. The two relations are required to be compatible in that weights in the same class are connected to nodes in the same class, while nodes in the same class have the same set of input weight connection types. The weights in an equivalence class are at all times required to remain equal.*

Note that every threshold network can be viewed as an equivalence network by taking the trivial equivalence relations. We now show that symmetry networks are indeed equivalence networks with the same weight classes and give a further technical lemma. For both lemmas proofs are omitted.

Lemma 2.3 *A symmetry network $(\mathcal{N}, \Gamma)$ is an equivalence network, where the equivalence classes are the orbits of connections and nodes respectively.*

Lemma 2.4 *Let $\mathcal{N}$ be an equivalence network and C be the set of classes of nodes. Then there is an indexing of the classes, C_i, $i = 1, \ldots, n$, such that nodes in C_i do not have connections from nodes in C_j for $j \geq i$.*

2.2   MAIN RESULTS

We are now in a position to state our main results. Note that throughout this paper log means natural logarithm, while an explicit subscript is used for other bases.

Theorem 2.5 *Let $\mathcal{N}$ be an equivalence network with W weight classes and N computational nodes. If the network correctly computes a function on a set of m inputs drawn independently according to a fixed probability distribution, where*

$$m \geq m_0(\epsilon, \delta) = \frac{1}{\epsilon(1 - \sqrt{\epsilon})} \left[\log \left(\frac{1.3}{\delta} \right) + 2W \log \left(\frac{6\sqrt{N}}{\epsilon} \right) \right]$$

then with probability at least $1 - \delta$ the error rate of the network will be less than ϵ on inputs drawn according to the same distribution.

Theorem 2.6 *Let $\mathcal{N}$ be an equivalence network with W weight classes and N computational nodes. If the network correctly computes a function on a fraction $1 - (1 - \gamma)\epsilon$ of m inputs drawn independently according to a fixed probability distribution, where*

$$m \geq m_0(\epsilon, \delta, \gamma) = \frac{1}{\gamma^2 \epsilon(1 - \sqrt{\epsilon/N})} \left[4 \log \left(\frac{4}{\delta} \right) + 6W \log \left(\frac{4N}{\gamma^{2/3}\epsilon} \right) \right]$$

then with probability at least $1 - \delta$ the error rate of the network will be less than ϵ on inputs drawn according to the same distribution.

3   THEORETICAL BACKGROUND

3.1   DEFINITIONS AND PREVIOUS RESULTS

In order to present results for binary outputs ($\{0, 1\}$ functions) and larger ranges in a unified way we will consider throughout the task of learning the graph of a function. All the definitions reduce to the standard ones when the outputs are binary.

We consider learning from examples as selecting a suitable function from a set H of hypotheses, being functions from a space X to set Y, which has at most countable size. At all times we consider an (unknown) target function

$$c : X \longrightarrow Y$$

which we are attempting to learn. To this end the space X is required to be a probability space (X, Σ, μ), with appropriate regularity conditions so that the sets considered are measurable [4]. In particular the hypotheses should be measurable when Y is given the discrete topology as should the error sets defined below. The space $S = X \times Y$ is equipped with a σ-algebra $\Sigma \times 2^Y$ and measure $\nu = \nu(\mu, c)$, defined by its value on sets of the form $U \times \{y\}$:

$$\nu(U \times \{y\}) = \mu\left(U \cap c^{-1}(y)\right).$$

Using this measure the error of a hypothesis is defined to be

$$\mathrm{er}_\nu(h) = \nu\{(x, y) \in S | h(x) \neq y\}.$$

The introduction of ν allows us to consider samples being drawn from S, as they will automatically reflect the output value of the target. This approach freely generalises to stochastic concepts though we will restrict ourselves to target functions for the purposes of this paper. The error of a hypothesis h on a sample $\mathbf{x} = ((x_1, y_1), \ldots, (x_m, y_m)) \in S^m$ is defined to be

$$\mathrm{er}_{\mathbf{x}}(h) = \frac{1}{m} \left|\{i | h(x_i) \neq y_i\}\right|.$$

We also define the VC dimension of a set of hypotheses by reference to the product space S. Consider a sample $\mathbf{x} = ((x_1, y_1), \ldots, (x_m, y_m)) \in S^m$ and the function

$$\mathbf{x}^\star : H \longrightarrow \{0, 1\}^m,$$

given by $\mathbf{x}^\star(h)_i = 1$ if and only if $h(x_i) = y_i$, for $i = 1, \ldots, m$. We can now define the growth function $B_H(m)$ as

$$B_H(m) = \max_{\mathbf{x} \in S^m} |\{\mathbf{x}^\star(h) | h \in H\}| \leq 2^m.$$

The Vapnik-Chervonenkis dimension of a hypothesis space H is defined as

$$\mathrm{VCdim}(H) = \begin{cases} \infty; & \text{if } B_H(m) = 2^m, \text{ for all } m; \\ \max\{m | B_H(m) = 2^m\}; & \text{otherwise.} \end{cases}$$

In the case of a threshold network $\mathcal{N}$, the set of functions obtainable using all possible weight assignments is termed the hypothesis space of $\mathcal{N}$ and we will refer to it as $\mathcal{N}$. For a threshold network $\mathcal{N}$, we also introduce the state growth function $S_{\mathcal{N}}(m)$. This is defined by first considering all computational nodes to be output nodes, and then counting different output sequences.

$$S_{\mathcal{N}}(m) = \max_{\mathbf{x}=(\mathbf{i}_1,\ldots,\mathbf{i}_m)\in X^m} |\{(F_{\mathcal{N}'}(w,\mathbf{i}_1), F_{\mathcal{N}'}(w,\mathbf{i}_2),\ldots, F_{\mathcal{N}'}(w,\mathbf{i}_m))|w : E \to \mathcal{R}\}|$$

where $X = [0,1]^{|I|}$ and $\mathcal{N}'$ is obtained from $\mathcal{N}$ by setting $O = C$. We clearly have that for all $\mathcal{N}$ and m, $B_{\mathcal{N}}(m) \leq S_{\mathcal{N}}(m)$.

Theorem 3.1 *[2] If a hypothesis space H has growth function $B_H(m)$ then for any $\epsilon > 0$ and $k > m$ and*

$$0 < r < 1 - \frac{1}{\sqrt{\epsilon k}}$$

the probability that there is a function in H which agrees with a randomly chosen m sample and has error greater than ϵ is less than

$$\frac{\epsilon k(1-r)^2}{\epsilon k(1-r)^2 - 1} B_H(m+k) \exp\left\{-r\epsilon \frac{km}{m+k}\right\}.$$

This result can be used to obtain the following bound on sample size required for PAC learnability of a hypothesis space with VC dimension d. The theorem improves the bounds reported by Blumer et al. [4].

Theorem 3.2 *[2] If a hypothesis space H has finite VC dimension $d > 1$, then there is $m_0 = m_0(\epsilon, \delta)$ such that if $m > m_0$ then the probability that a hypothesis consistent with a randomly chosen sample of size m has error greater than ϵ is less than δ. A suitable value of m_0 is*

$$m_0 = \frac{1}{\epsilon(1-\sqrt{\epsilon})}\left[\log\left(\frac{d/(d-1)}{\delta}\right) + 2d\log\left(\frac{6}{\epsilon}\right)\right].$$

$\square$

For the case when we allow our hypothesis to incorrectly compute the function on a small fraction of the training sample, we have the following result. Note that we are still considering the discrete metric and so in the case where we are considering multiple output feedforward networks a single output in error would count as an overall error.

Theorem 3.3 *[10] Let $0 < \epsilon < 1$ and $0 < \gamma \leq 1$. Suppose H is a hypothesis space of functions from an input space X to a possibly countable set Y, and let ν be any probability measure on $S = X \times Y$. Then the probability (with respect to ν^m) that, for $\mathbf{x} \in S^m$, there is some $h \in H$ such that*

$$\mathrm{er}_\nu(h) > \epsilon \quad \text{and} \quad \mathrm{er}_{\mathbf{x}}(h) \leq (1-\gamma)\mathrm{er}_\nu(h)$$

is at most

$$4\, B_H(2m) \exp\left(-\frac{\gamma^2 \epsilon m}{4}\right).$$

Furthermore, if H has finite VC dimension d, this quantity is less than δ for

$$m > m_0(\epsilon, \delta, \gamma) = \frac{1}{\gamma^2 \epsilon(1-\sqrt{\epsilon})}\left[4\log\left(\frac{4}{\delta}\right) + 6d\log\left(\frac{4}{\gamma^{2/3}\epsilon}\right)\right].$$

$\square$

4   THE GROWTH FUNCTION FOR EQUIVALENCE NETWORKS

We will bound the number of output sequences $B_{\mathcal{N}}(m)$ for a number m of inputs by the number of distinct state sequences $S_{\mathcal{N}}(m)$ that can be generated from the m inputs by different weight assignments. This follows the approach taken in [10].

Theorem 4.1 *Let $\mathcal{N}$ be an equivalence network with W weight equivalence classes and a total of N computational nodes. Then we can bound $S_{\mathcal{N}}(m)$ by*

$$S_{\mathcal{N}}(m) \leq \left(\frac{Nem}{W}\right)^W.$$

Idea of Proof: Let C_i, $i = 1,\ldots,n$, be the equivalence classes of nodes indexed as guaranteed by Lemma 2.4 with $|C_i| = c_i$ and the number of inputs for nodes in C_i being n_i (including the threshold input). Denote by $\mathcal{N}_j$ the network obtained by taking only the first j node equivalence classes. We omit a proof by induction that

$$S_{\mathcal{N}_j}(m) \leq \prod_{i=1}^{j} B_i(mc_i),$$

where B_i is the growth function for nodes in the class C_i.

Using the well known bound on the growth function of a threshold node with n_i inputs we obtain

$$S_{\mathcal{N}}(m) \leq \prod_{i=1}^{n} \left(\frac{emc_i}{n_i}\right)^{n_i}.$$

Consider the function $f(x) = x \log x$. This is a convex function and so for a set of values $x_1,\ldots,x_M$, we have that the average of $f(x_i)$ is greater than or equal to f applied to the average of x_i. Consider taking the x's to be c_i copies of n_i/c_i for each $i = 1,\ldots n$. We obtain

$$\frac{1}{N}\sum_{i=1}^{n} n_i \log \frac{n_i}{c_i} \geq \frac{W}{N} \log \frac{W}{N} \quad \text{or} \quad \prod_{i=1}^{n} \left(\frac{c_i}{n_i}\right)^{n_i} \leq \left(\frac{N}{W}\right)^W,$$

and so

$$S_{\mathcal{N}}(m) \leq \left(\frac{emN}{W}\right)^W,$$

as required. ∎

The bounds we have obtained make it possible to bound the Vapnik-Chervonenkis dimension of equivalence networks. Though we we will not need these results, we give them here for completeness.

Proposition 4.2 *The Vapnik-Chervonenkis dimension of an equivalence network with W weight classes and N computational nodes is bounded by*

$$2W \log_2 eN.$$

5   PROOF OF MAIN RESULTS

Using the results of the last section we are now in a position to prove Theorems 2.5 and 2.6.

Proof of Theorem 2.5 : (Outline) We use Theorem 3.1 which bounds the probability that a hypothesis with error greater than ϵ can match an m-sample. Substituting our bound on the growth function of an equivalence network and choosing

$$k = \left\lceil m \left(\frac{r\epsilon m}{W} - 1 \right) \right\rceil,$$

and r as in [1], we obtain the following bound on the probability

$$\left(\frac{d}{d-1} \right) \left(\frac{e^4 \epsilon m^2}{W^2} \right)^W N^W \exp(-\epsilon m).$$

By choosing $m > m_0$ where m_0 is given by

$$m_0 = m_0(\epsilon, \delta) = \frac{1}{\epsilon(1 - \sqrt{\epsilon})} \left[\log \left(\frac{1.3}{\delta} \right) + 2W \log \left(\frac{6\sqrt{N}}{\epsilon} \right) \right]$$

we guarantee that the above probability is less than δ as required. ∎

Our second main result can be obtained more directly.

Proof of Theorem 2.6 : (Outline) We use Theorem 3.3 which bounds the probability that a hypothesis with error greater than ϵ can match all but a fraction $(1 - \gamma)$ of an m-sample. The bound on the sample size is obtained from the probability bound by using the inequality for $B_H(2m)$. By adjusting the parameters we will convert the probability expression to that obtained by substituting our growth function. We can then read off a sample size by the corresponding substitution in the sample size formula. Consider setting $d = W$, $\epsilon = \epsilon'/N$ and $m = Nm'$. With these substitutions the sample size formula is

$$m' = \frac{1}{\gamma^2 \epsilon'(1 - \sqrt{\epsilon'/N})} \left[4 \log \left(\frac{4}{\delta} \right) + 6W \log \left(\frac{4N}{\gamma^{2/3} \epsilon'} \right) \right]$$

as required. ∎

6   CONCLUSION

The problem of training feedforward neural networks remains a major hurdle to the application of this approach to large scale systems. A very promising technique for simplifying the training problem is to include equivalences in the network structure which can be justified by a priori knowledge of the application domain. This paper has extended previous results concerning sample sizes for feedforward networks to cover so called equivalence networks in which weights are constrained in this way. At the same time we have improved the sample size bounds previously obtained for standard threshold networks [3] and multiple output networks [10].

The results are of the same order as previous results and imply similar bounds on the Vapnik-Chervonenkis namely $2W \log_2 eN$. They perhaps give circumstancial evidence for the conjecture that the $\log_2 eN$ factor in this expression is real, in that the same expression obtains even if the number of computational nodes is increased by expanding the equivalence classes of weights. Equivalence networks may be a useful area to search for high growth functions and perhaps show that for certain classes the VC dimension is $\Omega(W \log N)$.

References

[1] Martin Anthony, Norman Biggs and John Shawe-Taylor, Learnability and Formal Concept Analysis, RHBNC Department of Computer Science, Technical Report, CSD-TR-624, 1990.

[2] Martin Anthony, Norman Biggs and John Shawe-Taylor, The learnability of formal concepts, Proc. COLT '90, Rochester, NY. (eds Mark Fulk and John Case) (1990) 246–257.

[3] Eric Baum and David Haussler, What size net gives valid generalization, Neural Computation, 1 (1) (1989) 151–160.

[4] Anselm Blumer, Andrzej Ehrenfeucht, David Haussler and Manfred K. Warmuth, Learnability and the Vapnik-Chervonenkis dimension, JACM, 36 (4) (1989) 929–965.

[5] David Haussler, preliminary extended abstract, COLT '89.

[6] K. Lang and G.E. Hinton, The development of TDNN architecture for speech recognition, Technical Report CMU-CS-88-152, Carnegie-Mellon University, 1988.

[7] Y. le Cun, A theoretical framework for back propagation, in D. Touretzsky, editor, *Connectionist Models: A Summer School*, Morgan-Kaufmann, 1988.

[8] M. Minsky and S. Papert, Perceptrons, expanded edition, MIT Press, Cambridge, USA, 1988.

[9] John Shawe-Taylor, Building Symmetries into Feedforward Network Architectures, Proceedings of First IEE Conference on Artificial Neural Networks, London, 1989, 158–162.

[10] John Shawe-Taylor and Martin Anthony, Sample Sizes for Multiple Output Feedforward Networks, Network, 2 (1991) 107–117.

[11] Leslie G. Valiant, A theory of the learnable, Communications of the ACM, 27 (1984) 1134–1142.

Gradient Descent: Second-Order Momentum and Saturating Error

Barak Pearlmutter
Department of Psychology
P.O. Box 11A Yale Station
New Haven, CT 06520-7447
pearlmutter-barak@yale.edu

Abstract

Batch gradient descent, $\Delta w(t) = -\eta dE/dw(t)$, converges to a minimum of quadratic form with a time constant no better than $\frac{1}{4}\lambda_{\max}/\lambda_{\min}$ where $\lambda_{\min}$ and $\lambda_{\max}$ are the minimum and maximum eigenvalues of the Hessian matrix of E with respect to w. It was recently shown that adding a momentum term $\Delta w(t) = -\eta dE/dw(t) + \alpha\Delta w(t-1)$ improves this to $\frac{1}{4}\sqrt{\lambda_{\max}/\lambda_{\min}}$, although only in the batch case. Here we show that second-order momentum, $\Delta w(t) = -\eta dE/dw(t) + \alpha\Delta w(t-1) + \beta\Delta w(t-2)$, can lower this no further. We then regard gradient descent with momentum as a dynamic system and explore a nonquadratic error surface, showing that saturation of the error accounts for a variety of effects observed in simulations and justifies some popular heuristics.

1 INTRODUCTION

Gradient descent is the bread-and-butter optimization technique in neural networks. Some people build special purpose hardware to accelerate gradient descent optimization of backpropagation networks. Understanding the dynamics of gradient descent on such surfaces is therefore of great practical value.

Here we briefly review the known results in the convergence of batch gradient descent; show that second-order momentum does not give any speedup; simulate a real network and observe some effect not predicted by theory; and account for these effects by analyzing gradient descent with momentum on a saturating error surface.

887

1.1   SIMPLE GRADIENT DESCENT

First, let us review the bounds on the convergence rate of simple gradient descent without momentum to a minimum of quadratic form [11, 1]. Let w^* be the minimum of E, the error, $H = d^2E/d\mathbf{w}^2(\mathbf{w}^*)$, and λ_i, $\mathbf{v}_i$ be the eigenvalues and eigenvectors of H. The weight change equation

$$\Delta\mathbf{w} = -\eta\frac{dE}{d\mathbf{w}} \tag{1}$$

(where $\Delta f(t) \equiv f(t+1) - f(t)$) is limited by

$$0 < \eta < 2/\lambda_{\max} \tag{2}$$

We can substitute $\eta = 2/\lambda_{\max}$ into the weight change equation to obtain convergence that tightly bounds any achievable in practice, getting a time constant of convergence of $-1/\log(1-2s) = (2s)^{-1} + O(1)$, or

$$E - E^* \;\succ\; \exp(-4st) \tag{3}$$

where we use $s = \lambda_{\min}/\lambda_{\max}$ for the inverse eigenvalues spread of H and $\succ$ is read "asymptotically converges to zero more slowly than."

1.2   FIRST-ORDER MOMENTUM

Sometimes a momentum term is used, the weight update (1) being modified to incorporate a momentum term $\alpha < 1$ [5, equation 16],

$$\Delta\mathbf{w}(t) = -\eta\frac{dE}{d\mathbf{w}}(t) + \alpha\Delta\mathbf{w}(t-1). \tag{4}$$

The Momentum LMS algorithm, MLMS, has been analyzed by Shynk and Roy [6], who have shown that the momentum term can not speed convergence in the online, or stochastic gradient, case. In the batch case, which we consider here, Tuğay and Tanik [9] have shown that momentum is stable when

$$\alpha < 1 \quad\text{and}\quad 0 < \eta < 2(\alpha+1)/\lambda_{\max} \tag{5}$$

which speeds convergence to

$$E - E^* \succ \exp(-(4\sqrt{s} + O(s))\,t) \tag{6}$$

by

$$\alpha^* = \frac{2 - 4\sqrt{s(1-s)}}{(1-2s)^2} - 1 = 1 - 4\sqrt{s} + O(s), \qquad \eta^* = 2(\alpha^*+1)/\lambda_{\max}. \tag{7}$$

2   SECOND-ORDER MOMENTUM

The time constant of asymptotic convergence can be changed from $O(\lambda_{\max}/\lambda_{\min})$ to $O(\sqrt{\lambda_{\max}/\lambda_{\min}})$ by going from a first-order system, (1), to a second-order system, (4). Making a physical analogy, the first-order system corresponds to a circuit with

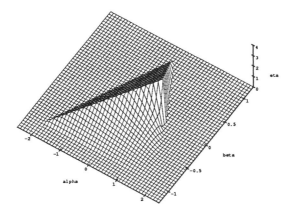

Figure 1: Second-order momentum converges if $\eta\lambda_{\max}$ is less than the value plotted as "eta," as a function of α and β. The region of convergence is bounded by four smooth surfaces: three planes and one hyperbola. One of the planes is parallel to the η axis, even though the sampling of the plotting program makes it appear slightly sloped. Another is at $\eta = 0$ and thus hidden. The peak is at 4.

a resistor, and the second-order system adds a capacitor to make an RC oscillator. One might ask whether further gains can be had by going to a third-order system,

$$\Delta\mathbf{w}(t) = -\eta\frac{dE}{d\mathbf{w}} + \alpha\Delta\mathbf{w}(t-1) + \beta\Delta\mathbf{w}(t-2). \tag{8}$$

For convergence, all the eigenvalues of the matrix

$$M_i = \begin{pmatrix} 0 & 1 & 0 \\ 0 & 0 & 1 \\ -\beta & -\alpha+\beta & 1-\eta\lambda_i+\alpha \end{pmatrix}$$

in $(c_i(t-1)\ c_i(t)\ c_i(t+1))^T \approx M_i(c_i(t-2)\ c_i(t-1)\ c_i(t))^T$ must have absolute value less than or equal to 1, which occurs precisely when

$$\begin{aligned} -1 \ \le\ &\beta\ \le\ 1 \\ 0 \ \le\ &\eta\ \le\ 4(\beta+1)/\lambda_i \\ \eta\lambda_i/2 - (1-\beta)\ \le\ &\alpha\ \le\ \beta\eta\lambda_i/2 + (1-\beta). \end{aligned}$$

For $\beta \le 0$ this is most restrictive for $\lambda_{\max}$, but for $\beta > 0$ $\lambda_{\min}$ also comes into play. Taking the limit as $\lambda_{\min} \to 0$, this gives convergence conditions for gradient descent with second-order momentum of

$$\begin{aligned} -1 \le\ &\beta \\ \beta - 1 \le\ &\alpha\ \le 1-\beta \\ \text{when } \alpha \le 3\beta+1: \hspace{3cm} &\tag{9} \\ 0 \le\ &\eta\ \le \frac{2}{\lambda_{\max}}(1+\alpha-\beta) \\ \text{when } \alpha \ge 3\beta+1: & \\ 0 <\ &\eta\ < \frac{\beta+1}{\lambda_{\max}\beta}(\alpha+\beta-1) \end{aligned}$$

a region shown in figure 1.

Fastest convergence for $\lambda_{\min}$ within this region lies along the ridge $\alpha = 3\beta + 1$, $\eta = 2(1 + \alpha - \beta)/\lambda_{\max}$. Unfortunately, although convergence is slightly faster than with first-order momentum, the relative advantage tends to zero as $s \to 0$, giving negligible speedup when $\lambda_{\max} \gg \lambda_{\min}$. For small s, the optimal settings of the parameters are

$$
\begin{aligned}
\alpha^{**} &= 1 - \frac{9}{4}\sqrt{s} + O(s) \\
\beta^{**} &= -\frac{3}{4}\sqrt{s} + O(s) \\
\eta^{**} &= 4(1 - \sqrt{s}) + O(s)
\end{aligned}
\tag{10}
$$

where α^* is as in (7).

3   SIMULATIONS

We constructed a standard three layer backpropagation network with 10 input units, 3 sigmoidal hidden units, and 10 sigmoidal output units. 15 associations between random 10 bit binary input and output vectors were constructed, and the weights were initialized to uniformly chosen random values between -1 and $+1$. Training was performed with a square error measure, batch weight updates, targets of 0 and 1, and a weight decay coefficient of 0.01.

To get past the initial transients, the network was run at $\eta = 0.45, \alpha = 0$ for 150 epochs, and at $\eta = 0.3, \alpha = 0.9$ for another 200 epochs. The weights were then saved, and the network run for 200 epochs for η ranging from 0 to 0.5 and α ranging from 0 to 1 from that starting point.

Figure 3 shows that the region of convergence has the shape predicted by theory. Calculation of the eigenvalues of $d^2E/d\mathbf{w}^2$ confirms that the location of the boundary is correctly predicted. Figure 2 shows that momentum speeded convergence by the amount predicted by theory. Figure 3 shows that the parameter setting that give the most rapid convergence in practice are the settings predicted by theory.

However, within the region that does not converge to the minimum, there appear to be two regimes: one that is characterized by apparently chaotic fluctuations of the error, and one which slopes up gradually from the global minimum. Since this phenomenon is so atypical of a quadratic minimum in a linear system, which either converges or diverges, and this phenomenon seems important in practice, we decided to investigate a simple system to see if this behavior could be replicated and understood, which is the subject of the next section.

4   GRADIENT DESCENT WITH SATURATING ERROR

The analysis of the sections above may be objected to on the grounds that it assumes the minimum to have quadratic form and then performs an analysis in the neighborhood of that minimum, which is equivalent to analyzing a linear unit. Surely our nonlinear backpropagation networks are richer than that.

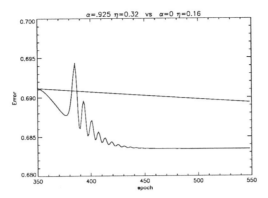

Figure 2: Error plotted as a function of time for two settings of the learning parameters, both determined empirically: the one that minimized the error the most, and the one with $\alpha = 0$ that minimized the error the most. There exists a less aggressive setting of the parameters that converges nearly as fast as the quickly converging curve but does not oscillate.

A clue that this might be the case was shown in figure 3. The region where the system converges to the minimum is of the expected shape, but rather than simply diverging outside of this region, as would a linear system, more complex phenomena are observed, in particular a sloping region.

Acting on the hypothesis that this region is caused by λ_{max} being maximal at the minimum, and gradually decreasing away from it (it must decrease to zero in the limit, since the hidden units saturate and the squared error is thus bounded) we decided to perform a dynamic systems analysis of the convergence of gradient descent on a one dimensional nonquadratic error surface. We chose

$$E = 1 - \frac{1}{1 + w^2} \tag{11}$$

which is shown in figure 4, as this results in a bounded E.

Letting

$$f(w) = w - \eta E'(w) = \frac{w(1 - 2\eta + 2w^2 + w^4)}{(1 + w^2)^2} \tag{12}$$

be our transfer function, a local analysis at the minimum gives $\lambda_{max} = E''(0) = 2$ which limits convergence to $\eta < 1$. Since the gradient towards the minimum is always less than predicted by a second-order series at the minimum, such η are in fact globally convergent. As η passes 1 the fixedpoint bifurcates into the limit cycle

$$w = \pm\sqrt{\sqrt{\eta} - 1}, \tag{13}$$

which remains stable until $\eta \to 16/9 = 1.77777\ldots$, at which point the single symmetric binary limit cycle splits into two asymmetric limit cycles, each still of period two. These in turn remain stable until $\eta \to 2.0732261475-$, at which point repeated period doubling to chaos occurs. This progression is shown in figure 7.

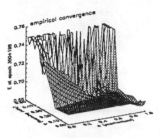 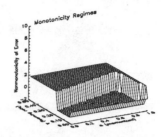 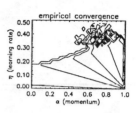

Figure 3: (Left) the error at epoch 550 as a function of the learning regime. Shading is based on the height, but most of the vertical scale is devoted to nonconvergent networks in order to show the mysterious nonconvergent sloping region. The minimum, corresponding to the most darkly shaded point, is on the plateau of convergence at the location predicted by the theory. (Center) the region in which the network is convergent, as measured by a strictly monotonically decreasing error. Learning parameter settings for which the error was strictly decreasing have a low value while those for which it was not have a high one. The lip at $\eta = 0$ has a value of 0, given where the error did not change. The rim at $\alpha = 1$ corresponds to damped oscillation caused by $\eta > 4\alpha\lambda/(1 - \alpha)^2$. (Right) contour plot of the convergent plateau shows that the regions of equal error have linear boundaries in the nonoscillatory region in the center, as predicted by theory.

As usual in a bifurcation, w rises sharply as η passes 1. But recall that figure 3, with the smooth sloping region, plotted the error E rather than the weights. The analogous graph here is shown in figure 6 where we see the same qualitative feature of a smooth gradual rise, which first begins to jitter as the limit cycle becomes asymmetric, and then becomes more and more jagged as the period doubles its way to chaos. From figure 7 it is clear that for higher η the peak error of the attractor will continue to rise gently until it saturates.

Next, we add momentum to the system. This simple one dimensional system duplicates the phenomena we found earlier, as can be seen by comparing figure 3 with figure 5. We see that momentum delays the bifurcation of the fixed point attractor at the minimum by the amount predicted by (5), namely until η approaches $1 + \alpha$. At this point the fixedpoint bifurcates into a symmetric limit cycle of period 2 at

$$w = \pm\sqrt{\sqrt{\frac{\eta}{1 + \alpha}} - 1}, \qquad (14)$$

a formula of which (13) is a special case. This limit cycle is stable for

$$\eta < \frac{16}{9}(1 + \alpha), \qquad (15)$$

but as η reaches this limit, which happens at the same time that w reaches $\pm 1/\sqrt{3}$ (the inflection point of E where $E = 1/4$) the limit cycle becomes unstable. However, for α near 1 the cycle breaks down more quickly in practice, as it becomes haloed by more complex attractors which make it progressively less likely that a sequence of iterations will actually converge to the limit cycle in question. Both boundaries of this strip, $\eta = 1 + \alpha$ and $\eta = \frac{16}{9}(1 + \alpha)$, are visible in figure 5,

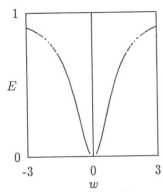

Figure 4: A one dimensional tulip-shaped nonlinear error surface $E = 1 - (1 + w^2)^{-1}$.

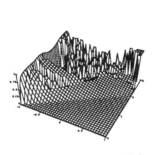

Figure 5: E after 50 iterations from a starting point of 0.05, as a function of η and α.

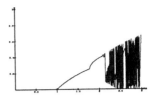

Figure 6: E as a function of η with $\alpha = 0$. When convergent, the final value is shown; otherwise E after 100 iterations from a starting point of $w = 1.0$. This a more detailed graph of a slice of figure 5 at $\alpha = 0$.

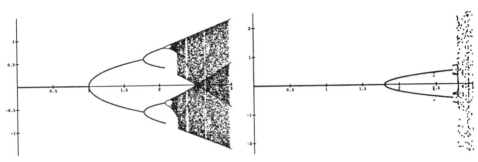

Figure 7: The attractor in w as a function of η is shown, with the progression from a single attractor at the minimum of E to a limit cycle of period two, which bifurcates and then doubles to chaos. $\alpha = 0$ (left) and $\alpha = 0.8$ (right). For the numerical simulations portions of the graphs, iterations 100 through 150 from a starting point of $w = 1$ or $w = 0.05$ are shown.

particularly since in the region between them E obeys

$$E = 1 - \sqrt{\frac{1 + \alpha}{\eta}} \tag{16}$$

The bifurcation and subsequent transition to chaos with momentum is shown for $\alpha = 0.8$ in figure 7. This α is high enough that the limit cycle fails to be reached by the iteration procedure long before it actually becomes unstable. Note that this diagram was made with w started near the minimum. If it had been started far from it, the system would usually not reach the attractor at $w = 0$ but instead enter a halo attractor. This accounts for the policy of backpropagation experts, who gradually raise momentum as the optimization proceeds.

5   CONCLUSIONS

The convergence bounds derived assume that the learning parameters are set optimally. Finding these optimal values in practice is beyond the scope of this paper, but some techniques for achieving nearly optimal learning rates are available [4, 10, 8, 7, 3]. Adjusting the momentum feels easier to practitioners than adjusting the learning rate, as too high a value leads to small oscillations rather than divergence, and techniques from control theory can be applied to the problem [2].

However, because error surfaces in practice saturate, techniques for adjusting the learning parameters automatically as learning proceeds can not be derived under the quadratic minimum assumption, but must take into account the bifurcation and limit cycle and the sloping region of the error, or they may mistake this regime of stable error for convergence, leading to premature termination.

References

[1] S. Thomas Alexander. *Adaptive Signal Processing*. Springer-Verlag, 1986.

[2] H. S. Dabis and T. J. Moir. Least mean squares as a control system. *International Journal of Control*, 54(2):321–335, 1991.

[3] Yan Fang and Terrence J. Sejnowski. Faster learning for dynamic recurrent backpropagation. *Neural Computation*, 2(3):270–273, 1990.

[4] Robert A. Jacobs. Increased rates of convergence through learning rate adaptation. *Neural Networks*, 1(4):295–307, 1988.

[5] David E. Rumelhart, Geoffrey E. Hinton, and R. J. Williams. Learning internal representations by error propagation. In D. E. Rumelhart, J. L. McClelland, and the PDP research group., editors, *Parallel distributed processing: Explorations in the microstructure of cognition, Volume 1: Foundations*. MIT Press, 1986.

[6] J. J. Shynk and S. Roy. The LMS algorithm with momentum updating. In *Proceedings of the IEEE International Symposium on Circuits and Systems*, pages 2651–2654, June 6–9 1988.

[7] F. M. Silva and L. B. Almeida. Acceleration techniques for the backpropagation algorithm. In L. B. Almeida and C. J. Wellekens, editors, *Proceedings of the 1990 EURASIP Workshop on Neural Networks*. Springer-Verlag, February 1990. (Lecture Notes in Computer Science series).

[8] Tom Tollenaere. SuperSAB: Fast adaptive back propagation with good scaling properties. *Neural Networks*, 3(5):561–573, 1990.

[9] Mehmet Ali Tuğay and Yalçin Tanik. Properties of the momentum LMS algorithm. *Signal Processing*, 18(2):117–127, October 1989.

[10] T. P. Vogl, J. K. Mangis, A. K. Zigler, W. T. Zink, and D. L. Alkon. Accelerating the convergence of the back-propagation method. *Biological Cybernetics*, 59:257–263, September 1988.

[11] B. Widrow, J. M. McCool, M. G. Larimore, and C. R. Johnson Jr. Stational and nonstationary learning characteristics of the LMS adaptive filter. *Proceedings of the IEEE*, 64:1151–1162, 1979.

Tangent Prop – A formalism for specifying selected invariances in an adaptive network

Patrice Simard
AT&T Bell Laboratories
101 Crawford Corner Rd
Holmdel, NJ 07733

Bernard Victorri
Université de Caen
Caen 14032 Cedex
France

Yann Le Cun
AT&T Bell Laboratories
101 Crawford Corner Rd
Holmdel, NJ 07733

John Denker
AT&T Bell Laboratories
101 Crawford Corner Rd
Holmdel, NJ 07733

Abstract

In many machine learning applications, one has access, not only to training data, but also to some high-level *a priori* knowledge about the desired behavior of the system. For example, it is known in advance that the output of a character recognizer should be invariant with respect to small spatial distortions of the input images (translations, rotations, scale changes, etcetera).

We have implemented a scheme that allows a network to learn the derivative of its outputs with respect to distortion operators of our choosing. This not only reduces the learning time and the amount of training data, but also provides a powerful *language* for specifying what generalizations we wish the network to perform.

1 INTRODUCTION

In machine learning, one very often knows more about the function to be learned than just the training data. An interesting case is when certain *directional derivatives* of the desired function are known at certain points. For example, an image

895

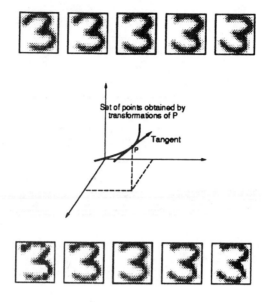

Figure 1: Top: Small rotations of an original digital image of the digit "3" (center). Middle: Representation of the effect of the rotation in the input vector space space (assuming there are only 3 pixels). Bottom: Images obtained by moving along the tangent to the transformation curve for the same original digital image (middle).

recognition system might need to be invariant with respect to small distortions of the input image such as translations, rotations, scalings, etc.; a speech recognition system might need to be invariant to time distortions or pitch shifts. In other words, the derivative of the system's output should be equal to zero when the input is transformed in certain ways.

Given a large amount of training data and unlimited training time, the system could learn these invariances from the data alone, but this is often infeasible. The limitation on data can be overcome by training the system with additional data obtained by distorting (translating, rotating, etc.) the original patterns (Baird, 1990). The top of Fig. 1 shows artificial data generated by rotating a digital image of the digit "3" (with the original in the center). This procedure, called the "distortion model", has two drawbacks. First, the user must choose the magnitude of distortion and how many instances should be generated. Second, and more importantly, the distorted data is highly correlated with the original data. This makes traditional learning algorithms such as backpropagation very inefficient. The distorted data carries only a very small incremental amount of information, since the distorted patterns are not very different from the original ones. It may not be possible to adjust the learning system so that learning the invariances proceeds at a reasonable rate while learning the original points is non-divergent.

The key idea in this paper is that it is possible to directly learn the effect on the output of distorting the input, *independently* from learning the undistorted

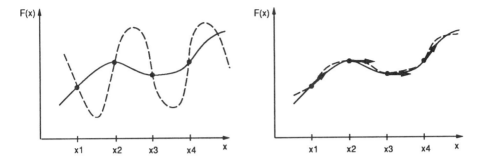

Figure 2: Learning a given function (solid line) from a limited set of example (x_1 to x_4). The fitted curves are shown in dotted line. Top: The only constraint is that the fitted curve goes through the examples. Bottom: The fitted curves not only goes through each examples but also its derivatives evaluated at the examples agree with the derivatives of the given function.

patterns. When a pattern P is transformed (e.g. rotated) with a transformation s that depends on one parameter α (e.g. the angle of the rotation), the set of all the transformed patterns $S(P) = \{s(\alpha, P) \ \forall \alpha\}$ is a one dimensional curve in the vector space of the inputs (see Fig. 1). In certain cases, such as rotations of digital images, this curve must be made continuous using smoothing techniques, as will be shown below. When the set of transformations is parameterized by n parameters α_i (rotation, translation, scaling, etc.), $S(P)$ is a manifold of at most n dimensions. The patterns in $S(P)$ that are obtained through *small* transformations of P, i.e. the part of $S(P)$ that is close to P, can be approximated by a plane tangent to the manifold $S(P)$ at point P. Small transformations of P can be obtained by adding to P a linear combination of vectors that span the tangent plane (tangent vectors). The images at the bottom of Fig. 1 were obtained by that procedure. More importantly, the tangent vectors can be used to specify high order constraints on the function to be learned, as explained below.

To illustrate the method, consider the problem of learning a single-valued function F from a limited set of examples. Fig. 2 (left) represents a simple case where the desired function F (solid line) is to be approximated by a function G (dotted line) from four examples $\{(x_i, F(x_i))\}_{i=1,2,3,4}$. As exemplified in the picture, the fitted function G largely disagrees with the desired function F between the examples. If the functions F and G are assumed to be differentiable (which is generally the case), the approximation G can be greatly improved by requiring that G's derivatives evaluated at the points $\{x_i\}$ are equal to the derivatives of F at the same points (Fig. 2 right). This result can be extended to multidimensional inputs. In this case, we can impose the equality of the derivatives of F and G in *certain directions*, not necessarily in all directions of the input space.

Such constraints find immediate use in traditional learning problems. It is often the case that *a priori* knowledge is available on how the desired function varies with

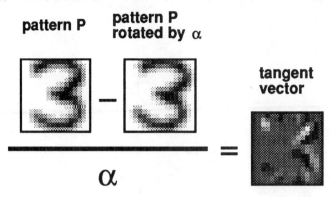

Figure 3: How to compute a tangent vector for a given transformation (in this case a rotation).

respect to some transformations of the input. It is straightforward to derive the corresponding constraint on the directional derivatives of the fitted function G in the directions of the transformations (previously named tangent vectors). Typical examples can be found in pattern recognition where the desired classification function is known to be invariant with respect to some transformation of the input such as translation, rotation, scaling, etc., in other words, the directional derivatives of the classification function in the directions of these transformations is zero.

2   IMPLEMENTATION

The implementation can be divided into two parts. The first part consists in computing the tangent vectors. This part is independent from the learning algorithm used subsequently. The second part consists in modifying the learning algorithm (for instance backprop) to incorporate the information about the tangent vectors.

Part I: Let x be an input pattern and s be a transformation operator acting on the input space and depending on a parameter α. If s is a rotation operator for instance, then $s(\alpha, x)$ denotes the input x rotated by the angle α. We will require that the transformation operator s be differentiable with respect to α and x, and that $s(0, x) = x$. The tangent vector is by definition $\partial s(\alpha, x)/\partial \alpha$. It can be approximated by a finite difference, as shown in Fig. 3. In the figure, the input space is a 16 by 16 pixel image and the patterns are images of handwritten digits. The transformations considered are rotations of the digit images. The tangent vector is obtained in two steps. First the image is rotated by an infinitesimal amount α. This is done by computing the rotated coordinates of each pixel and interpolating the gray level values at the new coordinates. This operation can be advantageously combined with some smoothing using a convolution. A convolution with a Gaussian provides an efficient interpolation scheme in $O(nm)$ multiply-adds, where n and m are the (gaussian) kernel and image sizes respectively. The next step is to subtract (pixel by pixel) the rotated image from the original image and to divide the result by the scalar α (see Fig. 3). If k types of transformations are considered, there will be k different tangent vectors per pattern. For most algorithms, these do not require any storage space since they can be generated as needed from the original pattern at negligible cost.

Part II: Tangent prop is an extension of the backpropagation algorithm, allowing it to learn directional derivatives. Other algorithms such as radial basis functions can be extended in a similar fashion.

To implement our idea, we will modify the usual weight-update rule:

$$\Delta w = -\eta \frac{\partial E}{\partial w} \quad \text{is replaced with} \quad \Delta w = -\eta \frac{\partial}{\partial w}(E + \mu E_r) \tag{1}$$

where η is the learning rate, E the usual objective function, E_r an additional objective function (a *regularizer*) that measures the discrepancy between the actual and desired directional derivatives in the directions of some selected transformations, and μ is a weighting coefficient.

Let x be an input pattern, $y = G(x)$ be the input-output function of the network. The regularizer E_r is of the form

$$E_r = \sum_{x \in \text{training set}} E_r(x)$$

where $E_r(x)$ is

$$E_r(x) = \sum_i \left\| K_i(x) - \left(\frac{\partial G(s_i(\alpha, x))}{\partial \alpha} \right)_{\alpha=0} \right\|^2 \tag{2}$$

Here, $K_i(x)$ is the desired directional derivative of G in the direction induced by transformation s_i applied to pattern x. The second term in the norm symbol is the actual directional derivative, which can be rewritten as

$$\left. \frac{\partial G(s_i(\alpha, x))}{\partial \alpha} \right|_{\alpha=0} = G'(x) \cdot \left. \frac{\partial s_i(\alpha, x)}{\partial \alpha} \right|_{\alpha=0}$$

where $G'(x)$ is the Jacobian of G for pattern x, and $\partial s_i(\alpha, x)/\partial \alpha$ is the *tangent vector* associated to transformation s_i as described in Part I. Multiplying the tangent vector by the Jacobian involves one forward propagation through a "linearized" version of the network. In the special case where *local invariance* with respect to the s_i's is desired, $K_i(x)$ is simply set to 0.

Composition of transformations: The theory of Lie groups (Gilmore, 1974) ensures that compositions of local (small) transformations s_i correspond to linear combinations of the corresponding tangent vectors (the local transformations s_i have a structure of Lie algebra). Consequently, if $E_r(x) = 0$ is verified, the network derivative in the direction of a linear combination of the tangent vectors is equal to the same linear combination of the desired derivatives. In other words if the network is successfully trained to be locally invariant with respect to, say, horizontal translation and vertical translations, it will be invariant with respect to compositions thereof.

We have derived and implemented an efficient algorithm, "tangent prop", for performing the weight update (Eq. 1). It is analogous to ordinary backpropagation,

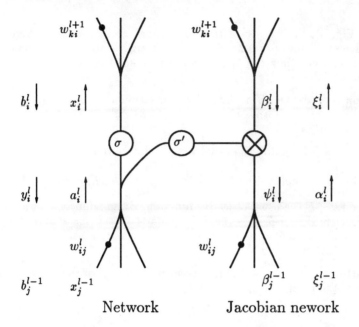

Network   Jacobian nework

Figure 4: forward propagated variables (a, x, α, ξ), and backward propagated variables (b, y, β, ψ) in the regular network (roman symbols) and the Jacobian (linearized) network (greek symbols)

but in addition to propagating neuron activations, it also propagates the tangent vectors. The equations can be easily derived from Fig. 4.

Forward propagation:

$$a_i^l = \sum_j w_{ij}^l x_j^{l-1} \qquad x_i^l = \sigma(a_i^l) \tag{3}$$

Tangent forward propagation:

$$\alpha_i^l = \sum_j w_{ij}^l \xi_j^{l-1} \qquad \xi_i^l = \sigma'(a_i^l)\alpha_i^l \tag{4}$$

Tangent gradient backpropagation:

$$\beta_i^l = \sum_k w_{ki}^{l+1} \psi_k^{l+1} \qquad \psi_i^l = \sigma'(a_i^l)\beta_i^l \tag{5}$$

Gradient backpropagation:

$$b_i^l = \sum_k w_{ki}^{l+1} y_k^{l+1} \qquad y_i^l = \sigma'(a_i^l)b_i^l + \sigma''(a_i^l)\alpha_i^l\beta_i \tag{6}$$

Weight update:

$$\frac{\partial[E(W, U_p) + \mu E_r(W, U_p, T_p)]}{\partial w_{ij}^l} = x_j^{l-1} y_i^l + \mu \xi_j^{l-1} \psi_i^l \tag{7}$$

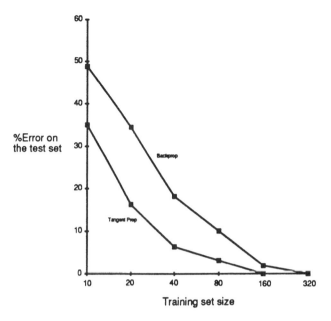

Figure 5: Generalization performance curve as a function of the training set size for the tangent prop and the backprop algorithms

The regularization parameter μ is tremendously important, because it determines the tradeoff between minimizing the usual objective function and minimizing the directional derivative error.

3   RESULTS

Two experiments illustrate the advantages of tangent prop. The first experiment is a classification task, using a small (linearly separable) set of 480 binarized hand-written digit. The training sets consist of 10, 20, 40, 80, 160 or 320 patterns, and the training set contains the remaining 160 patterns. The patterns are smoothed using a gaussian kernel with standard deviation of one half pixel. For each of the training set patterns, the tangent vectors for horizontal and vertical translation are computed. The network has two hidden layers with locally connected shared weights, and one output layer with 10 units (5194 connections, 1060 free parameters) (Le Cun, 1989). The generalization performance as a function of the training set size for traditional backprop and tangent prop are compared in Fig. 5. We have conducted additional experiments in which we implemented not only translations but also rotations, expansions and hyperbolic deformations. This set of 6 generators is a basis for all linear transformations of coordinates for two dimensional images. It is straightforward to implement other generators including gray-level-shifting, "smooth" segmentation, local continuous coordinate transformations and independent image segment transformations.

The next experiment is designed to show that in applications where data is highly

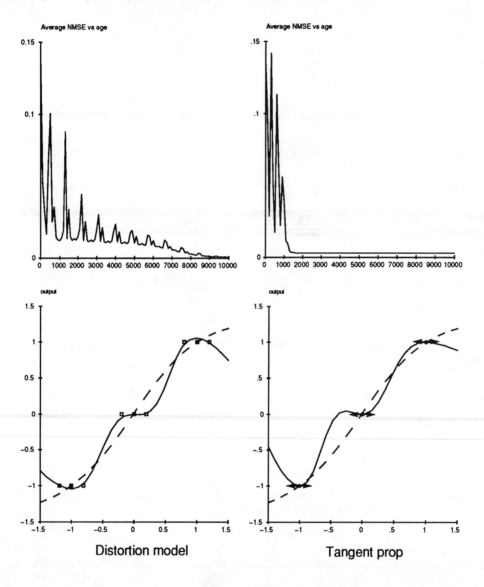

Figure 6: Comparison of the distortion model (left column) and tangent prop (right column). The top row gives the learning curves (error versus number of sweeps through the training set). The bottom row gives the final input-output function of the network; the dashed line is the result for unadorned back prop.

correlated, tangent prop yields a large speed advantage. Since the distortion model implies adding lots of highly correlated data, the advantage of tangent prop over the distortion model becomes clear.

The task is to approximate a function that has plateaus at three locations. We want to enforce local invariance near each of the training points (Fig. 6, bottom). The network has one input unit, 20 hidden units and one output unit. Two strategies are possible: either generate a small set of training point covering each of the plateaus (open squares on Fig. 6 bottom), or generate one training point for each plateau (closed squares), and enforce local invariance around them (by setting the desired derivative to 0). The training set of the former method is used as a measure the performance for both methods. All parameters were adjusted for approximately optimal performance in all cases. The learning curves for both models are shown in Fig. 6 (top). Each sweep through the training set for tangent prop is a little faster since it requires only 6 forward propagations, while it requires 9 in the distortion model. As can be seen, stable performance is achieved after 1300 sweeps for the tangent prop, versus 8000 for the distortion model. The overall speedup is therefore about 10.

Tangent prop in this example can take advantage of a very large regularization term. The distortion model is at a disadvantage because the only parameter that effectively controls the amount of regularization is the magnitude of the distortions, and this cannot be increased to large values because the right answer is only invariant under *small* distortions.

4   CONCLUSIONS

When *a priori* information about invariances exists, this information must be made available to the adaptive system. There are several ways of doing this, including the distortion model and tangent prop. The latter may be much more efficient in some applications, and it permits separate control of the emphasis and learning rate for the invariances, relative to the original training data points. Training a system to have zero derivatives in some directions is a powerful tool to express invariances to transformations of our choosing. Tests of this procedure on large-scale applications (handwritten zipcode recognition) are in progress.

References

Baird, H. S. (1990). Document Image Defect Models. In *IAPR 1990 Workshop on Sytactic and Structural Pattern Recognition*, pages 38–46, Murray Hill, NJ.

Gilmore, R. (1974). *Lie Groups, Lie Algebras and some of their Applications*. Wiley, New York.

Le Cun, Y. (1989). Generalization and Network Design Strategies. In Pfeifer, R., Schreter, Z., Fogelman, F., and Steels, L., editors, *Connectionism in Perspective*, Zurich, Switzerland. Elsevier. an extended version was published as a technical report of the University of Toronto.

Polynomial Uniform Convergence of Relative Frequencies to Probabilities

Alberto Bertoni, Paola Campadelli* Anna Morpurgo, Sandra Panizza
Dipartimento di Scienze dell'Informazione
Università degli Studi di Milano
via Comelico, 39 - 20135 Milano - Italy

Abstract

We define the concept of *polynomial uniform convergence* of relative frequencies to probabilities in the *distribution–dependent* context. Let $X_n = \{0,1\}^n$, let P_n be a probability distribution on X_n and let $F_n \subset 2^{X_n}$ be a family of events. The family $\{\langle X_n, P_n, F_n \rangle\}_{n \geq 1}$ has the property of polynomial uniform convergence if the probability that the maximum difference (over F_n) between the relative frequency and the probability of an event exceed a given positive ε be at most δ $(0 < \delta < 1)$, when the sample on which the frequency is evaluated has size polynomial in $n, 1/\varepsilon, 1/\delta$. Given a t-sample $(x_1, \ldots, x_t)$, let $\mathcal{C}_n^{(t)}(x_1, \ldots, x_t)$ be the Vapnik–Chervonenkis dimension of the family $\{\{x_1, \ldots, x_t\} \cap f \mid f \in F_n\}$ and $M(n,t)$ the expectation $\mathrm{E}(\mathcal{C}_n^{(t)}/t)$. We show that $\{\langle X_n, P_n, F_n \rangle\}_{n \geq 1}$ has the property of polynomial uniform convergence iff there exists $\beta > 0$ such that $M(n,t) = O(n/t^\beta)$. Applications to distribution–dependent PAC learning are discussed.

1 INTRODUCTION

The probably approximately correct (PAC) learning model proposed by Valiant [Valiant, 1984] provides a complexity theoretical basis for learning from examples produced by an arbitrary distribution. As shown in [Blumer et al., 1989], a cen-

---

*Also at CNR, Istituto di Fisiologia dei Centri Nervosi, via Mario Bianco 9, 20131 Milano, Italy.

tral notion for distribution–free learnability is the Vapnik–Chervonenkis dimension, which allows obtaining estimations of the sample size adequate to learn at a given level of approximation and confidence. This combinatorial notion has been defined in [Vapnik & Chervonenkis, 1971] to study the problem of uniform convergence of relative frequencies of events to their corresponding probabilities in a distribution–free framework.

In this work we define the concept of *polynomial uniform convergence* of relative frequencies of events to probabilities in the *distribution-dependent* setting. More precisely, consider, for any n, a probability distribution on $\{0,1\}^n$ and a family of events $F_n \subseteq 2^{\{0,1\}^n}$: our request is that the probability that the maximum difference (over F_n) between the relative frequency and the probability of an event exceed a given arbitrarily small positive constant ε be at most δ ($0 < \delta < 1$) when the sample on which we evaluate the relative frequencies has size polynomial in $n, 1/\varepsilon, 1/\delta$.

The main result we present here is a necessary and sufficient condition for polynomial uniform convergence in terms of "average information per example".

In section 2 we give preliminary notations and results; in section 3 we introduce the concept of polynomial uniform convergence in the distribution–dependent context and we state our main result, which we prove in section 4. Some applications to distribution–dependent PAC learning are discussed in section 5.

2   PRELIMINARY DEFINITIONS AND RESULTS

Let X be a set of elementary events on which a probability measure P is defined and let F be a collection of boolean functions on X, i.e. functions $f : X \to \{0,1\}$. For $f \in F$ the set $f^{-1}(1)$ is said event, and $\mathcal{P}_f$ denotes its probability. A *t-sample* (or sample of size t) on X is a sequence $\underline{x} = (x_1, \ldots, x_t)$, where $x_k \in X$ ($1 \leq k \leq t$). Let $X^{(t)}$ denote the space of t-samples and $P^{(t)}$ the probability distribution induced by P on $X^{(t)}$, such that $P^{(t)}(x_1, \ldots, x_t) = P(x_1)P(x_2) \cdots P(x_t)$.

Given a t-sample $\underline{x}$ and a set $f \in F$, let $\nu_f^{(t)}(\underline{x})$ be the relative frequency of f in the t-sample $\underline{x}$, i.e.

$$\nu_f^{(t)}(\underline{x}) = \frac{\sum_{i=1}^{t} f(x_i)}{t}.$$

Consider now the random variable $\Pi_F^{(t)} : X^{(t)} \to [0\,1]$, defined over $\langle X^{(t)}, P^{(t)} \rangle$, where

$$\Pi_F^{(t)}(x_1, \ldots, x_t) = \sup_{f \in F} |\, \nu_f^{(t)}(x_1, \ldots, x_t) - \mathcal{P}_f \,|.$$

The relative frequencies of the events are said to converge to the probabilities uniformly over F if, for every $\varepsilon > 0$, $\lim_{t \to \infty} P^{(t)}\{\underline{x} \mid \Pi_F^{(t)}(\underline{x}) > \varepsilon\} = 0$.

In order to study the problem of uniform convergence of the relative frequencies to the probabilities, the notion of index $\Delta_F(\underline{x})$ of a family F with respect to a t-sample $\underline{x}$ has been introduced [Vapnik & Chervonenkis, 1971]. Fixed a t-sample $\underline{x} = (x_1, \ldots, x_t)$,

$$\Delta_F(\underline{x}) = \#\{f^{-1}(1) \cap \{x_1, \ldots, x_t\} | f \in F\}.$$

Obviously $\Delta_F(x_1, \ldots, x_t) \leq 2^t$; a set $\{x_1, \ldots, x_t\}$ is said *shattered* by F iff $\Delta_F(x_1, \ldots, x_t) = 2^t$; the maximum t such that there is a set $\{x_1, \ldots, x_t\}$ shattered by F is said the *Vapnik–Chervonenkis dimension* d_F of F. The following result holds [Vapnik & Chervonenkis, 1971].

Theorem 2.1 *For all distribution probabilities on X, the relative frequencies of the events converge (in probability) to their corresponding probabilities uniformly over F iff $d_F < \infty$.*

We recall that the Vapnik–Chervonenkis dimension is a very useful notion in the distribution–independent PAC learning model [Blumer et al., 1989]. In the distribution–dependent framework, where the probability measure P is fixed and known, let us consider the expectation $E[\log_2 \Delta_F(\underline{x})]$, called entropy $H_F(t)$ of the family F in samples of size t; obviously $H_F(t)$ depends on the probability distribution P. The relevance of this notion is showed by the following result [Vapnik & Chervonenkis, 1971].

Theorem 2.2 *A necessary and sufficient condition for the relative frequencies of the events in F to converge uniformly over F (in probability) to their corresponding probabilities is that*

$$\lim_{t \to \infty} \frac{H_F(t)}{t} = 0.$$

3   POLYNOMIAL UNIFORM CONVERGENCE

Consider the family $\{\langle X_n, P_n, F_n \rangle\}_{n \geq 1}$, where $X_n = \{0,1\}^n$, P_n is a probability distribution on X_n and F_n is a family of boolean functions on X_n.

Since X_n is finite, the frequencies trivially converge uniformly to the probabilities; therefore we are interested in studying the problem of convergence with constraints on the sample size. To be more precise, we introduce the following definition.

Definition 3.1 *Given the family $\{\langle X_n, P_n, F_n \rangle\}_{n \geq 1}$, the relative frequencies of the events in F_n converge polynomially to their corresponding probabilities uniformly over F_n iff there exists a polynomial $p(n, 1/\varepsilon, 1/\delta)$ such that*

$$\forall \varepsilon, \delta > 0 \; \forall n \; \left(t \geq p(n, 1/\varepsilon, 1/\delta) \Rightarrow P^{(t)}\{\underline{x} \mid \Pi_{F_n}^{(t)}(\underline{x}) > \varepsilon\} < \delta \right).$$

In this context ε and δ are the approximation and confidence parameters, respectively.

The problem we consider now is to characterize the family $\{\langle X_n, P_n, F_n \rangle\}_{n \geq 1}$ such that the relative frequencies of events in F_n converge polynomially to the probabilities. Let us introduce the random variable $C_n^{(t)} : X_n^{(t)} \to N$, defined as

$$C_n^{(t)}(x_1, \ldots, x_t) = \max\{\#A \mid A \subseteq \{x_1, \ldots, x_t\} \wedge A \text{ is shattered by } F_n\}.$$

In this notation it is understood that $C_n^{(t)}$ refers to F_n. The random variable $C_n^{(t)}$ and the index function Δ_{F_n} are related to one another; in fact, the following result can be easily proved.

Lemma 3.1 $C_n^{(t)}(\underline{x}) \leq \log \Delta_{F_n}(\underline{x}) \leq C_n^{(t)}(\underline{x}) \log t$.

Let $M(n,t) = \mathrm{E}(\dfrac{C_n^{(t)}}{t})$ be the expectation of the random variable $\dfrac{C_n^{(t)}}{t}$. From Lemma 3.1 readily follows that

$$M(n,t) \leq \frac{H_{F_n}(t)}{t} \leq M(n,t) \log t;$$

therefore $M(n,t)$ is very close to $H_{F_n}(t)/t$, which can be interpreted as "average information for example" for samples of size t.

Our main result shows that $M(n,t)$ is a useful measure to verify whether $\{\langle X_n, P_n, F_n \rangle\}_{n \geq 1}$ satisfies the property of polynomial convergence, as shown by the following theorem.

Theorem 3.1 *Given* $\{\langle X_n, P_n, F_n \rangle\}_{n \geq 1}$, *the following conditions are equivalent:*

C1. *The relative frequencies of events in F_n converge polynomially to their corresponding probabilities.*

C2. *There exists $\beta > 0$ such that $M(n,t) = O(n/t^\beta)$.*

C3. *There exists a polynomial $\psi(n, 1/\varepsilon)$ such that*

$$\forall \varepsilon \, \forall n \, \left(t \geq \psi(n, 1/\varepsilon) \Rightarrow M(n,t) \leq \varepsilon \right).$$

Proof.

- **C2 $\Rightarrow$ C3** is readily verified. In fact, condition C2 says there exist $\alpha, \beta > 0$ such that $M(n,t) \leq \alpha n/t^\beta$; now, observing that $t \geq (\alpha n/\varepsilon)^{\frac{1}{\beta}}$ implies $\alpha n/t^\beta \leq \varepsilon$, condition C3 immediately follows.

- **C3 $\Rightarrow$ C2.** As stated by condition C3, there exist $a, b, c > 0$ such that if $t \geq an^b/\varepsilon^c$ then $M(n,t) \leq \varepsilon$. Solving the first inequality with respect to ε gives, in the worst case, $\varepsilon = (an^b/t)^{\frac{1}{c}}$, and substituting for ε in the second inequality yields $M(n,t) \leq (an^b/t)^{\frac{1}{c}} = a^{\frac{1}{c}}n^{\frac{b}{c}}/t^{\frac{1}{c}}$. If $\frac{b}{c} \leq 1$ we immediately obtain $M(n,t) \leq a^{\frac{1}{c}}n^{\frac{b}{c}}/t^{\frac{1}{c}} \leq a^{\frac{1}{c}}n/t^{\frac{1}{c}}$. Otherwise, if $\frac{b}{c} > 1$, since $M(n,t) \leq 1$, we have $M(n,t) \leq \min\{1, a^{\frac{1}{c}}n^{\frac{b}{c}}/t^{\frac{1}{c}}\} \leq \min\{1, (a^{\frac{1}{c}}n^{\frac{b}{c}}/t^{\frac{1}{c}})^{\frac{c}{b}}\} \leq a^{\frac{1}{b}}n/t^{\frac{1}{b}}$. $\square$

The proof of the equivalence between propositions C1 and C3 will be given in the next section.

4 PROOF OF THE MAIN THEOREM

First of all, we prove that condition C3 implies condition C1. The proof is based on the following lemma, which is obtained by minor modifications of [Vapnik & Chervonenkis, 1971 (Lemma 2, Theorem 4, and Lemma 4)].

Lemma 4.1 *Given the family* $\{\langle X_n, P_n, F_n\rangle\}_{n\geq 1}$, *if* $\lim_{t\to\infty} \dfrac{H_{F_n}(t)}{t} = 0$ *then*

$$\forall\varepsilon\,\forall\delta\,\forall n\,\left(t \geq \frac{132t_0}{\varepsilon^2\delta} \Rightarrow P_n^{(t)}\{\underline{x} \mid \Pi_{F_n}^{(t)}(\underline{x}) > \varepsilon\} < \delta\right),$$

where t_0 *is such that* $H_{F_n}(t_0)/t_0 \leq \varepsilon^2/64$.

As a consequence, we can prove the following.

Theorem 4.1 *Given* $\{\langle X_n, P_n, F_n\rangle\}_{n\geq 1}$, *if there exists a polynomial* $\psi(n, 1/\varepsilon)$ *such that*

$$\forall\varepsilon\,\forall n\,\left(t \geq \psi(n, 1/\varepsilon) \Rightarrow \frac{H_{F_n}(t)}{t} \leq \varepsilon\right),$$

then the relative frequencies of events in F_n *converge polynomially to their probabilities.*

Proof (outline). It is sufficient to observe that if we choose $t_0 = \psi(n, 64/\varepsilon^2)$, by hypothesis it holds that $H_{F_n}(t_0)/t_0 \leq \varepsilon^2/64$; therefore, from Lemma 4.1, if

$$t \geq \frac{132t_0}{\varepsilon^2\delta} = \frac{132}{\varepsilon^2\delta}\,\psi(n, \frac{64}{\varepsilon^2}),$$

then $P_n^{(t)}\{\underline{x} \mid \Pi_{F_n}^{(t)}(\underline{x}) > \varepsilon\} < \delta$.   □

An immediate consequence of Theorem 4.1 and of the relation $M(n,t) \leq H_{F_n}(t)/t \leq M(n,t)\log t$ is that condition C3 implies condition C1.

We now prove that condition C1 implies condition C3. For the sake of simplicity it is convenient to introduce the following notations:

$$a_n^{(t)} = \frac{C_n^{(t)}}{t} \qquad P_a(n, \varepsilon, t) = P_n^{(t)}\{\underline{x} \mid a_n^{(t)}(\underline{x}) \leq \varepsilon\}.$$

The following lemma, which relates the problem of polynomial uniform convergence of a family of events to the parameter $P_a(n, \varepsilon, t)$, will only be stated since it can be proved by minor modifications of Theorem 4 in [Vapnik & Chervonenkis, 1971].

Lemma 4.2 *If* $t \geq 16/\varepsilon^2$ *then* $P_n^{(t)}\{\underline{x} \mid \Pi_{F_n}^{(t)}(\underline{x}) > \varepsilon\} \geq \frac{1}{4}(1 - P_a(n, 8\varepsilon, 2t))$.

A relevant property of $P_a(n, \varepsilon, t)$ is given by the following lemma.

Lemma 4.3 $\forall\alpha \geq 1\ P_a(n, \varepsilon/\alpha, \alpha t) \leq P_a^\alpha(n, \varepsilon, t)$.

Proof. Let $(\underline{x}_1, \ldots, \underline{x}_\alpha)$ be an αt-sample obtained by the concatenation of α elements $\underline{x}_1, \ldots, \underline{x}_\alpha \in X^{(t)}$. It is easy to verify that $C_n^{(\alpha t)}(\underline{x}_1, \ldots, \underline{x}_\alpha) \geq \max_{i=1,\ldots,\alpha} C_n^{(t)}(\underline{x}_i)$. Therefore

$$P_n^{(\alpha t)}\{C_n^{(\alpha t)}(\underline{x}_1, \ldots, \underline{x}_\alpha) \leq k\} \leq P_n^{(\alpha t)}\{C_n^{(t)}(\underline{x}_1) \leq k \wedge \cdots \wedge C_n^{(t)}(\underline{x}_\alpha) \leq k\}.$$

By the independency of the events $C_n^{(t)}(\underline{x}_i) \leq k$ we obtain

$$P_n^{(\alpha t)}\{C_n^{(\alpha t)}(\underline{x}_1, \ldots, \underline{x}_\alpha) \leq k\} \leq \prod_{i=1}^{\alpha} P_n^{(t)}\{C_n^{(t)}(\underline{x}_i) \leq k\}.$$

Recalling that $a_n^{(t)} = C_n^{(t)}/t$ and substituting $k = \varepsilon t$, the thesis follows. $\quad\square$

A relation between $P_a(n, \varepsilon, t)$ and the parameter $M(n, t)$, which we have introduced to characterize the polynomial uniform convergence of $\{\langle X_n, P_n, F_n\rangle\}_{n\geq 1}$, is shown in the following lemma.

Lemma 4.4 *For every ε $(0 < \varepsilon < 1/4)$, if $M(n,t) > 2\sqrt{\varepsilon}$ then $P_a(n, \varepsilon, t) < 1/2$.*

Proof. For the sake of simplicity, let $m = M(n, l)$. If $m > \delta > 0$, we have

$$\delta < m = \int_0^1 x\, dP_a = \int_0^{\delta/2} x\, dP_a + \int_{\delta/2}^1 x\, dP_a$$

$$\leq \frac{\delta}{2} P_a(n, \frac{\delta}{2}, l) + 1 - P_a(n, \frac{\delta}{2}, l).$$

Since $0 < \delta < 1$, we obtain

$$P_a(n, \frac{\delta}{2}, l) < \frac{1 - \delta}{1 - \delta/2} \leq 1 - \frac{\delta}{2}.$$

By applying Lemma 4.3 it is proved that, for every $\alpha \geq 1$,

$$P_a(n, \frac{\delta}{2\alpha}, \alpha l) \leq \left(1 - \frac{\delta}{2}\right)^\alpha.$$

For $\alpha = \dfrac{2}{\delta}$ we obtain

$$P_a(n, \frac{\delta^2}{4}, \frac{2l}{\delta}) < e^{-1} < \frac{1}{2}.$$

For $\varepsilon = \delta^2/4$ and $t = 2l/\delta$, the previous result implies that, if $M(n, t\sqrt{\varepsilon}) > 2\sqrt{\varepsilon}$, then $P_a(n, \varepsilon, t) < 1/2$.

It is easy to verify that $C_n^{(\alpha t)}(\underline{x}_1, \ldots, \underline{x}_\alpha) \leq \sum_{i=1}^\alpha C_n^{(t)}(\underline{x}_i)$ for every $\alpha \geq 1$. This implies $M(n, \alpha t) \leq M(n, t)$ for $\alpha \geq 1$, hence $M(n, t\sqrt{\varepsilon}) \geq M(n, t)$, from which the thesis follows. $\quad\square$

Theorem 4.2 *If for the family $\{\langle X_n, P_n, \mathcal{F}_n\rangle\}_{n\geq 1}$ the relative frequencies of events in F_n converge polynomially to their probabilities, then there exists a polynomial $\psi(n, 1/\varepsilon)$ such that*

$$\forall \varepsilon\, \forall n\, (t \geq \psi(n, 1/\varepsilon) \Rightarrow M(n, t) \leq \varepsilon).$$

Proof. By contradiction. Let us suppose that $\{\langle X_n, P_n, F_n\rangle\}_{n\geq 1}$ polynomially converges and that for all polynomial functions $\psi(n, 1/\varepsilon)$ there exist ε, n, t such that $t \geq \psi(n, 1/\varepsilon)$ and $M(n, t) > \varepsilon$.

Since $M(n, t)$ is a monotone, non–increasing function with respect to t it follows that for every ψ there exist ε, n such that $M(n, \psi(n, 1/\varepsilon)) > \varepsilon$. Considering the one-to-one corrispondence T between polynomial functions defined by $T\psi(n, 1/\varepsilon) = \varphi(n, 4/\varepsilon^2)$, we can conclude that for any φ there exist ε, n such that $M(n, \varphi(n, 1/\varepsilon)) > 2\sqrt{\varepsilon}$. From Lemma 4.4 it follows that

$$\forall \varphi\, \exists n\, \exists \varepsilon\, \left(P_a(n, \varepsilon, \varphi(n, \frac{1}{\varepsilon})) \leq \frac{1}{2}\right). \tag{1}$$

Since, by hypothesis, $\{\langle X_n, P_n, F_n \rangle\}_{n \geq 1}$ polynomially converges, fixed $\delta = 1/20$, there exists a polynomial ϕ such that

$$\forall \varepsilon \; \forall n \; \forall \phi \left(t \geq \phi(n, \frac{1}{\varepsilon}) \Rightarrow P_n^{(t)}\{\underline{x} \mid \Pi_{F_n}^{(t)}(\underline{x}) > \varepsilon\} < \frac{1}{20} \right)$$

From Lemma 4.2 we know that if $t \geq 16/\varepsilon^2$ then

$$P_n^{(t)}\{\underline{x} \mid \Pi_{F_n}^{(t)}(\underline{x}) > \varepsilon\} \geq \frac{1}{4}(1 - P_a(n, 8\varepsilon, 2t))$$

If $t \geq \max\{16/\varepsilon^2, \phi(n, 1/\varepsilon)\}$, then $\frac{1}{4}(1 - P_a(n, 8\varepsilon, 2t)) < \frac{1}{20}$, hence $P_a(n, 8\varepsilon, 2t) > \frac{4}{5}$.

Fixed a polynomial $\overline{p}(n, 1/\varepsilon)$ such that $2\overline{p}(n, 8/\varepsilon) \geq \max\{16/\varepsilon^2, \phi(n, 1/\varepsilon)\}$, we can conclude that

$$\forall \varepsilon \; \forall n \; \left(P_a(n, \varepsilon, \overline{p}(n, \frac{1}{\varepsilon})) > \frac{4}{5} \right). \tag{2}$$

From assertions (1) and (2) the contradiction $\frac{1}{2} < \frac{4}{5}$ can easily be derived.   □

An immediate consequence of Theorem 4.2 is that, in Theorem 3.1, condition C1 implies condition C3. Theorem 3.1 is thus proved.

5   DISTRIBUTION–DEPENDENT PAC LEARNING

In this section we briefly recall the notion of learnability in the distribution–dependent PAC model and we discuss some applications of the previous results. Given $\{\langle X_n, P_n, F_n \rangle\}_{n \geq 1}$, a labelled t-sample S_f for $f \in F_n$ is a sequence $(\langle x_1, f(x_1) \rangle, \ldots, \langle x_t, f(x_t) \rangle)$, where $(x_1, \ldots, x_t)$ is a t-sample on X_n. We say that $f_1, f_2 \in F_n$ are ε-close with respect to P_n iff $P_n\{x \mid f_1(x) \neq f_2(x)\} \leq \varepsilon$.

A learning algorithm A for $\{\langle X_n, P_n, F_n \rangle\}_{n \geq 1}$ is an algorithm that, given in input $\varepsilon, \delta > 0$, a labelled t-sample S_f with $f \in F_n$, outputs the representation of a function g which, with probability $1 - \delta$, is ε-close to f. The family $\{\langle X_n, P_n, F_n \rangle\}_{n \geq 1}$ is said *polynomially learnable* iff there exists a learning algorithm A working in time bounded by a polynomial $p(n, 1/\varepsilon, 1/\delta)$.

Bounds on the sample size necessary to learn at approximation ε and confidence $1 - \delta$ have been given in terms of ε-covers [Benedek & Itai, 1988]; classes which are not learnable in the distribution–free model, but are learnable for some specific distribution, have been shown (e.g. l-terms DNF [Kucera et al., 1988]).

The following notion is expressed in terms of relative frequencies.

Definition 5.1 *A quasi–consistent algorithm for the family* $\{\langle X_n, P_n, F_n \rangle\}_{n \geq 1}$ *is an algorithm that, given in input* $\delta, \varepsilon > 0$ *and a labelled t-sample* S_f *with* $f \in F_n$, *outputs in time bounded by a polynomial* $p(n, 1/\varepsilon, 1/\delta)$ *the representation of a function* $g \in F_n$ *such that*

$$P_n^{(t)}\{\underline{x} \mid \nu_{f \oplus g}^{(t)}(\underline{x}) > \varepsilon\} < \delta$$

By Theorem 3.1 the following result can easily be derived.

Theorem 5.1 *Given* $\{\langle X_n, P_n, F_n\rangle\}_{n\geq1}$, *if there exists* $\beta > 0$ *such that* $M(n,t) = O(n/t^\beta)$ *and there exists a quasi-consistent algorithm for* $\{\langle X_n, P_n, F_n\rangle\}_{n\geq1}$ *then* $\{\langle X_n, P_n, F_n\rangle\}_{n\geq1}$ *is polynomially learnable.*

6 CONCLUSIONS AND OPEN PROBLEMS

We have characterized the property of polynomial uniform convergence of $\{\langle X_n, P_n, F_n\rangle\}_{n\geq1}$ by means of the parameter $M(n,t)$. In particular we proved that $\{\langle X_n, P_n, F_n\rangle\}_{n\geq1}$ has the property of polynomial convergence iff there exists $\beta > 0$ such that $M(n,t) = O(n/t^\beta)$, but no attempt has been made to obtain better upper and lower bounds on the sample size in terms of $M(n,t)$.

With respect to the relation between polynomial uniform convergence and PAC learning in the distribution–dependent context, we have shown that if a family $\{\langle X_n, P_n, F_n\rangle\}_{n\geq1}$ satisfies the property of polynomial uniform convergence then it can be PAC learned with a sample of size bounded by a polynomial function in n, $1/\varepsilon$, $1/\delta$.

It is an open problem whether the converse implication also holds.

Acknowledgements

This research was supported by CNR, project Sistemi Informatici e Calcolo Parallelo.

References

G. Benedek, A. Itai. (1988) "Learnability by Fixed Distributions". *Proc. COLT'88*, 80-90.

A. Blumer, A. Ehrenfeucht, D. Haussler, K. Warmuth. (1989) "Learnability and the Vapnik–Chervonenkis Dimension". *J. ACM* **36**, 929-965.

L. Kucera, A. Marchetti–Spaccamela, M. Protasi. (1988) "On the Learnability of DNF Formulae". *Proc. XV Coll. on Automata, Languages, and Programming*, L.N.C.S. **317**, Springer Verlag.

L.G. Valiant. (1984) "A Theory of the Learnable". *Communications of the ACM* **27** (11), 1134-1142.

V.N. Vapnik, A.Ya. Chervonenkis. (1971) "On the uniform convergence of relative frequencies of events to their probabilities". *Theory of Prob. and its Appl.* **16** (2), 265-280.

Unsupervised learning
of distributions on binary vectors
using two layer networks

Yoav Freund *
Computer and Information Sciences
University of California Santa Cruz
Santa Cruz, CA 95064

David Haussler
Computer and Information Sciences
University of California Santa Cruz
Santa Cruz, CA 95064

Abstract

We study a particular type of Boltzmann machine with a bipartite graph structure called a harmonium. Our interest is in using such a machine to model a probability distribution on binary input vectors. We analyze the class of probability distributions that can be modeled by such machines, showing that for each $n \geq 1$ this class includes arbitrarily good approximations to any distribution on the set of all n-vectors of binary inputs. We then present two learning algorithms for these machines. The first learning algorithm is the standard gradient ascent heuristic for computing maximum likelihood estimates for the parameters (i.e. weights and thresholds) of the model. Here we give a closed form for this gradient that is significantly easier to compute than the corresponding gradient for the general Boltzmann machine. The second learning algorithm is a greedy method that creates the hidden units and computes their weights one at a time. This method is a variant of the standard method for projection pursuit density estimation. We give experimental results for these learning methods on synthetic data and natural data from the domain of handwritten digits.

1 Introduction

Let us suppose that each example in our input data is a binary vector $\vec{x} = \{x_1, \ldots, x_n\} \in \{\pm 1\}^n$, and that each such example is generated independently at random according some unknown distribution on $\{\pm 1\}^n$. This situation arises, for instance, when each example consists of (possibly noisy) measurements of n different binary attributes of a randomly selected object. In such a situation, unsupervised learning can be usefully defined as using the input data to find a good model of the unknown distribution on $\{\pm 1\}^n$ and thereby learning the structure in the data.

The process of learning an unknown distribution from examples is usually called *density estimation* or *parameter estimation* in statistics, depending on the nature of the class of distributions used as models. Connectionist models of this type include Bayes networks [14], mixture models [3,13], and Markov random fields [14,8]. Network models based on the notion of energy minimization such as Hopfield nets [9] and Boltzmann machines [1] can also be used as models of probability distributions.

---

*yoav@cis.ucsc.edu

The models defined by Hopfield networks are a special case of the more general Markov random field models in which the local interactions are restricted to symmetric pairwise interactions between components of the input. Boltzmann machines also use only pairwise interactions, but in addition they include *hidden units*, which correspond to unobserved variables. These unobserved variables interact with the observed variables represented by components of the input vector. The overall distribution on the set of possible input vectors is defined as the marginal distribution induced on the components of the input vector by the Markov random field over all variables, both observed and hidden. While the Hopfield network is relatively well understood, it is limited in the types of distributions that it can model. On the other hand, Boltzmann machines are universal in the sense that they are powerful enough to model any distribution (to any degree of approximation), but the mathematical analysis of their capabilities is often intractable. Moreover, the standard learning algorithm for the Boltzmann machine, a gradient ascent heuristic to compute the maximum likelihood estimates for the weights and thresholds, requires repeated stochastic approximation, which results in unacceptably slow learning. [1] In this work we attempt to narrow the gap between Hopfield networks and Boltzmann machines by finding a model that will be powerful enough to be universal, [2] yet simple enough to be analyzable and computationally efficient. [3] We have found such a model in a minor variant of the special type of Boltzmann machine defined by Smolensky in his *harmony theory* [16][Ch.6]. This special type of Boltzmann machine is defined by a network with a simple bipartite graph structure, which he called a *harmonium*.

The harmonium consists of two types of units: input units, each of which holds one component of the input vector, and hidden units, representing hidden variables. There is a weighted connection between each input unit and each hidden unit, and no connections between input units or between hidden units (see Figure (1)). The presence of the hidden units induces dependencies, or correlations, between the variables modeled by input units. To illustrate the kind of model that results, consider the distribution of people that visit a specific coffee shop on Sunday. Let each of the n input variables represent the presence $(+1)$ or absence (-1) of a particular person that Sunday. These random variables are clearly not independent, e.g. if Fred's wife and daughter are there, it is more likely that Fred is there, if you see three members of the golf club, you expect to see other members of the golf club, if Bill is there you are unlikely to see Brenda there, etc. This situation can be modeled by a harmonium model in which each hidden variable represents the presence or absence of a social group. The weights connecting a hidden unit and an input unit measure the tendency of the corresponding person to be associated with the corresponding group. In this coffee shop situation, several social groups may be present at one time, exerting a combined influence on the distribution of customers. This can be modeled easily with the harmonium, but is difficult to model using Bayes networks or mixture models. [4]

2   The Model

Let us begin by formalizing the harmonium model. To model a distribution on $\{\pm 1\}^n$ we will use n input units and some number $m \geq 0$ of hidden units. These units are connected in a bipartite graph as illustrated in Figure (1).

The random variables represented by the input units each take values in $\{+1, -1\}$, while the hidden variables, represented by the hidden units, take values in $\{0, 1\}$. The state of the machine is defined by the values of these random variables. Define $\vec{x} = (x_1, \ldots, x_n) \in \{\pm 1\}^n$ to be the state of the input units, and $\vec{h} = (h_1, \ldots, h_m) \in \{0, 1\}^m$ to be the state of the hidden units.

The connection weights between the input units and the ith hidden unit are denoted [5] by $\vec{\omega}^{(i)} \in R^n$ and the bias of the ith hidden unit is denoted by $\theta^{(i)} \in R$. The parameter vector $\phi = \{(\vec{\omega}^{(1)}, \theta^{(1)}), \ldots, (\vec{\omega}^{(m)}, \theta^{(m)})\}$

---

[1] One possible solution to this is the mean-field approximation [15], discussed further in section 2 below.

[2] In [4] we show that any distribution over $\{\pm 1\}^n$ can be approximated to within any desired accuracy by a harmonium model using 2^n hidden units.

[3] See also other work relating Bayes nets and Boltzmann machines [12,7].

[4] Noisy-OR gates have been introduced in the framework of Bayes Networks to allow for such combinations. However, using this in networks with hidden units has not been studied, to the best of our knowledge.

[5] In [16][Ch.6], binary connection weights are used. Here we use real-valued weights.

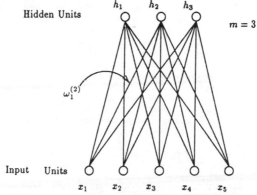

Figure 1: The bipartite graph of the harmonium

defines the entire network, and thus also the probability model induced by the network. For a given ϕ, the energy of a state configuration of hidden and input units is defined to be

$$E(\vec{x}, \vec{h}|\phi) = -\sum_{i=1}^{m}(\vec{\omega}^{(i)} \cdot \vec{x} + \theta^{(i)})h_i \tag{1}$$

and the probability of a configuration is

$$Pr(\vec{x}, \vec{h}|\phi) = \frac{1}{Z}e^{-E(\vec{x}, \vec{h}|\phi)} \quad \text{where} \quad Z = \sum_{\vec{x}, \vec{h}} e^{-E(\vec{x}, \vec{h}|\phi)}.$$

Summing over $\vec{h}$, it is easy to show that in the general case the probability distribution over possible state vectors on the input units is given by

$$Pr(\vec{x}|\phi) = \sum_{\vec{h} \in \{0,1\}^m} Pr(\vec{x}, \vec{h}|\phi) = \frac{1}{Z}\sum_{\vec{h} \in \{0,1\}^m} \exp\left(\sum_{i=1}^{m}(\vec{\omega}^{(i)} \cdot \vec{x} + \theta^{(i)})h_i\right) = \frac{1}{Z}\prod_{i=1}^{m}\left(1 + e^{\vec{\omega}^{(i)} \cdot \vec{x} + \theta^{(i)}}\right), \tag{2}$$

This product form is particular to the harmonium structure, and does not hold for general Boltzmann machines. Product form distribution models have been used for density estimation in Projection Pursuit [10,6,5]. We shall look further into this relationship in section 5.

3   Discussion of the model

The right hand side of Equation (2) has a simple intuitive interpretation. The ith factor in the product corresponds to the hidden variable h_i and is an increasing function of the dot product between $\vec{x}$ and the weight vector of the ith hidden unit. Hence an input vector $\vec{x}$ will tend to have large probability when it is in the direction of one of the weight vectors $\vec{\omega}^{(i)}$ (i.e. when $\vec{\omega}^{(i)} \cdot \vec{x}$ is large), and small probability otherwise. This is the way that the hidden variables can be seen to exert their "influence"; each corresponds to a preferred or "prototypical" direction in space.

The next to the last formula in Equation (2) shows that the harmonium model can be written as a mixture of 2^m distributions of the form

$$\frac{1}{Z(\vec{h})} \exp\left(\sum_{i=1}^{m}(\vec{\omega}^{(i)} \cdot \vec{x} + \theta^{(i)})h_i\right),$$

where $\vec{h} \in \{0,1\}^m$ and $Z(\vec{h})$ is the appropriate normalization factor. It is easily verified that each of these distributions is in fact a product of n Bernoulli distributions on $\{+1, -1\}$, one for each input variable x_j. Hence the harmonium model can be interpreted as a kind of mixture model. However, the number of components in the mixture represented by a harmonium is exponential in the number of hidden units.

It is interesting to compare the class of harmonium models to the standard class of models defined by a mixture of products of Bernoulli distributions. The same bipartite graph described in Figure (1) can be used to define a standard mixture model. Assign each of the m hidden units a weight vector $\vec{w}^{(i)}$ and a probability p_i such that $\sum_{i=1}^{m} p_i = 1$. To generate an example, choose *one* of the hidden units according to the distribution defined by the p_i's, and then choose the vector $\vec{x}$ according to $P_i(\vec{x}) = \frac{1}{Z_i} e^{\vec{w}^{(i)} \cdot \vec{x}}$, where Z_i is the appropriate normalization factor so that $\sum_{\vec{x} \in \{\pm 1\}^n} P_i(\vec{x}) = 1$. We thus get the distribution

$$P(\vec{x}) = \sum_{i=1}^{m} \frac{p_i}{Z_i} e^{\vec{w}^{(i)} \cdot \vec{x}} \tag{3}$$

This form for presenting the standard mixture model emphasizes the similarity between this model and the harmonium model. A vector $\vec{x}$ will have large probability if the dot product $\vec{w}^{(i)} \cdot \vec{x}$ is large for some $1 \leq i \leq m$ (so long as p_i is not too small). However, unlike the standard mixture model, the harmonium model allows more than one hidden variable to be $+1$ for any generated example. This means that several hidden influences can combine in the generation of a single example, because several hidden variables can be $+1$ at the same time. To see why this is useful, consider the coffee shop example given in the introduction. At any moment of time it is reasonable to find *several* social groups of people sitting in the shop. The harmonium model will have a natural representation for this situation, while in order for the standard mixture model to describe it accurately, a hidden variable has to be assigned to each combination of social groups that is likely to be found in the shop at the same time. In such cases the harmonium model is exponentially more succinct than the standard mixture model.

4   Learning by gradient ascent on the log-likelihood

We now suppose that we are given a sample consisting of a set S of vectors in $\{\pm 1\}^n$ drawn independently at random from some unknown distribution. Our goal is use the sample S to find a good model for this unknown distribution using a harmonium with m hidden units, if possible. The method we investigate here is the method of maximum likelihood estimation using gradient ascent. The goal of learning is thus reduced to finding the set of parameters for the harmonium that maximize the (log of the) probability of the set of examples S. In fact, this gives the standard learning algorithm for general Boltzmann machines. For a general Boltzmann machine this would require stochastic estimation of the parameters. As stochastic estimation is very time-consuming, the result is that learning is very slow. In this section we show that stochastic estimation need not be used for the harmonium model.

From (2), the log likelihood of a sample of input vectors $S = \{\vec{x}^{(1)}, \vec{x}^{(2)}, \ldots, \vec{x}^{(N)}\}$, given a particular setting $\phi = \{(\vec{w}^{(1)}, \theta^{(1)}), \ldots, (\vec{w}^{(m)}, \theta^{(m)})\}$ of the parameters of the model is:

$$\text{log-likelihood}(\phi) = \sum_{\vec{x} \in S} \ln Pr(\vec{x}|\phi) = \sum_{i=1}^{m} \left(\sum_{\vec{x} \in S} \ln(1 + e^{\vec{w}^{(i)} \cdot \vec{x} + \theta^{(i)}}) \right) - N \ln Z . \tag{4}$$

Taking the gradient of the log-likelihood results in the following formula for the jth component of $\vec{w}^{(i)}$

$$\frac{\partial}{\partial w_j^{(i)}} \text{log-likelihood}(\phi) = \sum_{\vec{x} \in S} x_j \frac{1}{1 + e^{-(\vec{w}^{(i)} \cdot \vec{x} + \theta^{(i)})}} - N \sum_{\vec{x} \in \{\pm 1\}^n} Pr(\vec{x}|\phi) x_j \frac{1}{1 + e^{-(\vec{w}^{(i)} \cdot \vec{x} + \theta^{(i)})}} \tag{5}$$

A similar formula holds for the derivative of the bias term.

The purpose of the clamped and unclamped phases in the Boltzmann machine learning algorithm is to approximate these two terms. In general, this requires stochastic methods. However, here the clamped term is easy to calculate, it requires summing a logistic type function over all training examples. The same term is obtained by making the mean field approximation for the clamped phase in the general algorithm [15], which is exact in this case. It is more difficult to compute the sleep phase term, as it is an explicit sum over the entire input space, and within each term of this sum there is an implicit sum over the entire space of configurations of hidden units in the factor $Pr(\vec{x}|\phi)$. However, again taking advantage of the special structure of the harmonium, we can reduce this sleep phase gradient term to a sum only over the configurations of the hidden units, yielding for each component of $\vec{\omega}^{(i)}$

$$\frac{\partial}{\partial \omega_j^{(i)}}\text{log-likelihood}(\phi) = \sum_{\vec{x} \in S} x_j \frac{1}{1 + e^{-(\vec{\omega}^{(i)} \cdot \vec{x} + \theta^{(i)})}} - N \sum_{\vec{h} \in \{0,1\}^m} Pr(\vec{h}|\phi) h_i \tanh(\sum_{k=1}^m h_k \omega_j^{(k)}) \qquad (6)$$

where

$$Pr(\vec{h}|\phi) = \frac{\exp(\sum_{i=1}^m h_i \theta^{(i)}) \prod_{j=1}^n \cosh(\sum_{i=1}^m h_i \omega_j^{(i)})}{\sum_{\vec{h}' \in \{0,1\}^m} \left[\exp(\sum_{i=1}^m h_i' \theta^{(i)}) \prod_{j=1}^n \cosh(\sum_{i=1}^m h_i' \omega_j^{(i)}) \right]}$$

Direct computation of (6) is fast for small m in contrast to the case for general Boltzmann machines (we have performed experiments with $m \leq 10$). However, for large m it is not possible to compute all 2^m terms. There is a way to avoid this exponential explosion if we can assume that a small number of terms dominate the sums. If, for instance, we assume that the probability that more than k hidden units are active ($+1$) at the same time is negligibly small we can get a good approximation by computing only $O(m^k)$ terms. Alternately, if we are not sure which states of the hidden units have non-negligible probability, we can dynamically search, as part of the learning process, for the significant terms in the sum. This way we get an algorithm that is always accurate, and is efficient when the number of significant terms is small. In the extreme case where we assume that only one hidden unit is active at a time (i.e. $k = 1$), the harmonium model essentially reduces to the standard mixture model as discussed is section 3. For larger k, this type of assumption provides a middle ground between the generality of the harmonium model and the simplicity of the mixture model.

5   Projection Pursuit methods

A statistical method that has a close relationship with the harmonium model is the Projection Pursuit (PP) technique [10,6;5]. The use of projection pursuit in the context of neural networks has been studied by several researchers (e.g. [11]). Most of the work is in *exploratory* projection pursuit and projection pursuit *regression*. In this paper we are interested in projection pursuit *density estimation*. Here PP avoids the exponential blowup of the standard gradient ascent technique, and also has that advantage that the number m of hidden units is estimated from the sample as well, rather than being specified in advance.

Projection pursuit density estimation [6] is based on several types of analysis, using the central limit theorem, that lead to the following general conclusion. *If $\vec{x} \in R^n$ is a random vector for which the different coordinates are independent, and $\vec{\omega} \in R^n$ is a vector from the n dimensional unit sphere, then the distribution of the projection $\vec{\omega} \cdot \vec{x}$ is close to gaussian for most $\vec{\omega}$.* Thus searching for those directions $\vec{\omega}$ for which the projection of a sample is most non-gaussian is a way for detecting dependencies between the coordinates in high dimensional distributions. Several "projection-indices" have been studied in the literature for measuring the "non-gaussianity" of projection, each enhancing different properties of the projected distribution. In order to find more than one projection direction, several methods of "structure elimination" have been devised. These methods transform the sample in such a way that the the direction in which non-gaussianity has been detected appears to be gaussian, thus enabling the algorithm to detect non-gaussian projections that would otherwise be obscured. The search for a description of the distribution of a sample in terms of its projections can be formalized in the context of maximal likelihood density estimation [6]. In order to create a formal relation between the harmonium model and projection pursuit, we define a variant of the model that defines a density over R^n instead of a distribution over $\{\pm 1\}^n$. Based on this form we devise a projection index and a structure removal method that are the basis of the following learning algorithm (described fully in [4])

- **Initialization**
  Set S_0 to be the input sample.
  Set p_0 to be the initial distribution (Gaussian).

- **Iteration**
  Repeat the following steps for $i = 1, 2 \ldots$ until no single-variable harmonium model has a significantly higher likelihood than the Gaussian distribution with respect to S_i.

  1. Perform an estimate-maximize (EM) [2] search on the log-likelihood of a single hidden variable model on the sample S_{i-1}. Denote by θ_i and $\vec{w}^{(i)}$ the parameters found by the search, and create a new hidden unit with associated binary r.v. h_i with these weights and bias.

  2. Transform S_{i-1} into S_i using the following structure removal procedure. For each example $\vec{x} \in S_{i-1}$ compute the probability that the hidden variable h_i found in the last step is 1 on this input:

  $$P(h_i = 1) = \left(1 + e^{-(\theta_i + \vec{w}^{(i)} \cdot \vec{x})}\right)^{-1}$$

  Flip a coin that has probability of "head" equal to $P(h_i = 1)$. If the coin turns out "head" then add $\vec{x} - \vec{w}^{(i)}$ to S_i else add $\vec{x}$ to S_i.

  3. Set $p_i(\vec{x})$ to be $p_{i-1}(\vec{x}) Z_i^{-1} \left(1 + e^{\theta_i + \vec{w}^{(i)} \cdot \vec{x}}\right)$.

6   Experimental work

We have carried out several experiments to test the performance of unsupervised learning using the harmonium model. These are not, at this stage, extensive experimental comparisons, but they do provide initial insights into the issues regarding our learning algorithms and the use of the harmonium model for learning real world tasks.

The first set of experiments studies two methods for learning the harmonium model. The first is the gradient ascent method, and the second is the projection pursuit method. The experiments in this set were performed on synthetically generated data. The input consisted of binary vectors of 64 bits that represent 8 x 8 binary images. The images are synthesized using a harmonium model with 10 hidden units whose weights were set as in Figure (2,a). The ultimate goal of the learning algorithms was to retrieve the model that generated the data. To measure the quality of the models generated by the algorithms we use three different measures. The likelihood of the model, [6] the fraction of correct predictions the model makes when used to predict the value of a single input bit given all the other bits, and the performance of the model when used to reconstruct the input from the most probable state of the hidden units. [7] All experiments use a test set and a train set, each containing 1000 examples. The gradient ascent method used a standard momentum term, and typically needed about 1000 epochs to stabilize. In the projection pursuit algorithm, 4 iterations of EM per hidden unit proved sufficient to find a stable solution. The results are summarized in the following table and in Figure (2).

	likelihood		single bit prediction		input reconstruction	
	train	test	train	test	train	test
gradient ascent for 1000 epochs	0.399	0.425	0.098	0.100	0.311	0.338
projection pursuit	0.799	0.802	0.119	0.114	0.475	0.480
Projection pursuit followed by gradient ascent for 100 epochs	0.411	0.430	0.091	0.089	0.315	0.334
Projection pursuit followed by gradient ascent for 1000 epochs	0.377	0.405	0.071	0.082	0.261	0.287
true model	0.372	0.404	0.062	0.071	0.252	0.283

Looking at the table and Figure (2), and taking into account execution times, it appears that gradient ascent is slow but eventually finds much of the underlying structure in the distribution, although several of the hidden units (see units 1,2,6,7, counting from the left, in Figure (2,a)) have no obvious relation to the true model, In contrast, PP is fast and finds all of the features of the true model albeit sometimes

---

[6] We present the negation of the log-likelihood, scaled so that the uniform distribution will have likelihood 1.0

[7] More precisely, for each input unit i we compute the probability p_i that it has value +1. Then for example $(x_1, \ldots, x_n)$, we measure $-\sum_{i=1}^{n} \log_2(1/2 + x_i(p_i - 1/2))$.

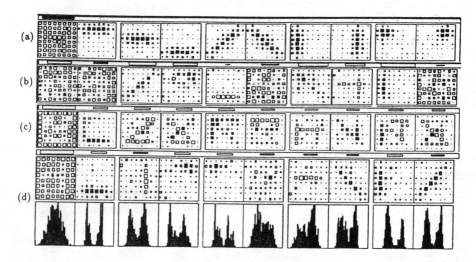

Figure 2: The weight vectors of the models in the synthetic data experiments. Each matrix represents the 64 weights of one hidden unit. The square above the matrix represents the units bias. positive weights are displayed as full squares and negative weights as empty squares, the area of the square is proportional to the absolute value of the weight. (a) The weights in the model found by gradient ascent alone. (b) The weights in the model found by projection pursuit alone. (c) The weights in the model used for generating the data. (d) The weights in the model found by projection pursuit followed by gradient ascent. For this last model we also show the histograms of the projection of the examples on the directions defined by those weight vectors; the bimodality expected from projection pursuit analysis is evident.

in combinations, However, the error measurements show that something is still missing from the models found by our implementation of PP. Following PP by a gradient ascent phase seems to give the best of both algorithms, finding a good approximation after only 140 epochs (40 PP + 100 gradient) and recovering the true model almost exactly after 1040 epochs.

In the second set of experiments we compare the performance of the harmonium model to that of the mixture model. The comparison uses real world data extracted from the NIST handwritten data base [8], Examples are 16×16 binary images (see Figure (3)). We use 60 hidden units to model the distribution in both of the models. Because of the large number of hidden units we cannot use gradient ascent learning and instead use projection pursuit. For the same reason it was not possible to compute the likelihood of the harmonium model and only the other two measures of error were used. Each test was run several times to get accuracy bounds on the measurements. The results are summarized in the following table

	single bit prediction		input reconstruction	
	train	test	train	test
Mixture model	0.185 ± 0.005	0.258 ± 0.005	0.518 ± 0.002	0.715 ± 0.002
Harmonium model	0.20 ± 0.01	0.21 ± 0.01	0.63 ± 0.05	0.66 ± 0.03

In Figure (4) we show some typical weight vectors found for the mixture model and for the harmonium model, it is clear that while the mixture model finds weights that are some kind of average prototypes of complete digits, the harmonium model finds weights that correspond to local features such as lines and contrasts. There is a small but definite improvement in the errors of the harmonium model with respect to the errors of the mixture model. As the experiments on synthetic data have shown that PP does not reach

[8] NIST Special Database 1, HWDB Rel1-1.1, May 1990.

Figure 3: A few examples from the handwritten digits sample.

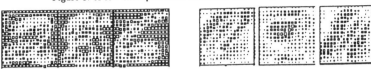

Figure 4: Typical weight vectors found by the mixture model (left) and the harmonium model (right)

optimal solutions by itself we expect the advantage of the harmonium model over the mixture model will increase further by using improved learning methods. Of course, the harmonium model is a very general distribution model and is not specifically tuned to the domain of handwritten digit images, thus it cannot be compared to models specifically developed to capture structures in this domain. However, the experimental results supports our claim that the harmonium model is a simple and tractable mathematical model for describing distributions in which several correlation patterns combine to generate each individual example.

References

[1] D. H. Ackley, G. E. Hinton, and T. J. Sejnowski. A learning algorithm for Boltzmann machines. *Cognitive Science*, 9:147–169, 1985.

[2] A. Dempster, N. Laird, and D. Rubin. Maximum likelihood from incomplete data via the EM algorithm. *J. Roy. Statist. Soc. B*, 39:1–38, 1977.

[3] B. Everitt and D. Hand. *Finite mixture distributions*. Chapman and Hall, 1981.

[4] Y. Freund and D. Haussler. Unsupervised learning of distributions on binary vectors using two layer networks. Technical Report UCSC-CRL-91-20, Univ. of Calif. Computer Research Lab, Santa Cruz, CA, 1992 (To appear).

[5] J. H. Friedman. Exploratory projection pursuit. *J. Amer. Stat.Assoc.*, 82(397):599–608, Mar. 1987.

[6] J. H. Friedman, W.Stuetzle, and A. Schroeder. Projection pursuit density estimation. *J. Amer. Stat.Assoc.*, 79:599–608, 1984.

[7] H. Gefner and J. Pearl. On the probabilistic semantics of connectionist networks. Technical Report CSD-870033, UCLA Computer Science Department, July 1987.

[8] S. Geman and D. Geman. Stochastic relaxations, Gibbs distributions and the Bayesian restoration of images. *IEEE Trans. on Pattern Analysis and Machine Intelligence*, 6:721–742, 1984.

[9] J. Hopfield. Neural networks and physical systems with emergent collective computational abilities. *Proc. Natl. Acad Sci. USA*, 79:2554–2558, Apr. 1982.

[10] P. Huber. Projection pursuit (with discussion). *Ann. Stat.*, 13:435–525, 1985.

[11] N. Intrator. Feature extraction using an unsupervised neural network. In D. Touretzky, J. Ellman, T. Sejnowski, and G. Hinton, editors, *Proceedings of the 1990 Connectionist Models Summer School*, pages 310–318. Morgan Kaufmann, San Mateo, CA., 1990.

[12] R. M. Neal. Learning stochastic feedforward networks. Technical report, Department of Computer Science, University of Toronto, Nov. 1990.

[13] S. Nowlan. Maximum likelihood competitive learning. In D. Touretsky, editor, *Advances in Neural Information Processing Systems*, volume 2, pages 574–582. Morgan Kaufmann, 1990.

[14] J. Pearl. *Probabilistic Reasoning in Intelligent Systems*. Morgan Kaufmann, 1988.

[15] C. Peterson and J. R. Anderson. A mean field theory learning algorithm for neural networks. *Complex Systems*, 1:995–1019, 1987.

[16] D. E. Rumelhart and J. L. McClelland. *Parallel Distributed Processing: Explorations in the Microstructure of Cognition. Volume 1: Foundations*. MIT Press, Cambridge, Mass., 1986.

Incrementally Learning Time-varying Half-planes

Anthony Kuh[*]
Dept. of Electrical Engineering
University of Hawaii at Manoa
Honolulu, HI 96822

Thomas Petsche[†]
Siemens Corporate Research
755 College Road East
Princeton, NJ 08540

Ronald L. Rivest[‡]
Laboratory for Computer Science
MIT
Cambridge, MA 02139

Abstract

We present a distribution-free model for incremental learning when concepts vary with time. Concepts are caused to change by an adversary while an incremental learning algorithm attempts to track the changing concepts by minimizing the error between the current target concept and the hypothesis. For a single half-plane and the intersection of two half-planes, we show that the average mistake rate depends on the maximum rate at which an adversary can modify the concept. These theoretical predictions are verified with simulations of several learning algorithms including back propagation.

1 INTRODUCTION

The goal of our research is to better understand the problem of learning when concepts are allowed to change over time. For a dichotomy, concept drift means that the classification function changes over time. We want to extend the theoretical analyses of learning to include time-varying concepts; to explore the behavior of current learning algorithms in the face of concept drift; and to devise tracking algorithms to better handle concept drift. In this paper, we briefly describe our theoretical model and then present the results of simulations

---
[*]kuh@wiliki.eng.hawaii.edu   [†]petsche@learning.siemens.com   [‡]rivest@theory.lcs.mit.edu

in which several tracking algorithms, including an on-line version of back-propagation, are applied to time-varying half-spaces.

For many interesting real world applications, the concept to be learned or estimated is not static, i.e., it can change over time. For example, a speaker's voice may change due to fatigue, illness, stress or background noise (Galletti and Abbott, 1989), as can handwriting. The output of a sensor may drift as the components age or as the temperature changes. In control applications, the behavior of a plant may change over time and require incremental modifications to the model.

Haussler, *et al.* (1987) and Littlestone (1989) have derived bounds on the number of mistakes an on-line learning algorithm will make while learning any concept in a given concept class. However, in that and most other learning theory research, the concept is assumed to be fixed. Helmbold and Long (1991) consider the problem of concept drift, but their results apply to memory-based tracking algorithms while ours apply to incremental algorithms. In addition, we consider different types of adversaries and use different methods of analysis.

2 DEFINITIONS

We use much the same notation as most learning theory, but we augment many symbols with a subscript to denote time. As usual, X is the instance space and x_t is an instance drawn at time t according to a *fixed*, arbitrary distribution P_X. The function $c_t : X \rightarrow \{0, 1\}$ is the active concept at time t, that is, at time t any instance is labeled according to c_t. The label of the instance is $a_t = c_t(x_t)$. Each active concept c_i is a member of the concept class C. A sequence of active concepts is denoted **c**. At any time t, the tracker uses an algorithm $\mathcal{L}$ to generate a hypothesis $\hat{c}_t$ of the active concept.

We use a symmetric distance function to measure the difference between two concepts: $d(c, c') = P_X[x : c(x) \neq c'(x)]$.

As we alluded to in the introduction, we distinguish between two types of tracking algorithms. A *memory-based* tracker stores the most recent m examples and chooses a hypothesis based on those stored examples. Helmbold and Long (1991), for example, use an algorithm that chooses as the hypothesis the concept that minimizes the number of disagreements between $\hat{c}_t(x_t)$ and $c_t(x_t)$. An *incremental* tracker uses only the previous hypothesis and the most recent examples to form the new hypothesis. In what follows, we focus on incremental trackers.

The task for a tracking algorithm is, at each iteration t, to form a "good" estimate $\hat{c}_t$ of the active concept c_t using the sequence of previous examples. Here "good" means that the probability of a disagreement between the label predicted by the tracker and the actual label is small. In the time-invariant case, this would mean that the tracker would incrementally improve its hypothesis as it collects more examples. In the time-varying case, however, we introduce an adversary whose task is to change the active concept at each iteration.

Given the existence of a tracker and an adversary, each iteration of the tracking problem consists of five steps: (1) the adversary chooses the active concept c_t; (2) the tracker is given an unlabeled instance, x_t, chosen randomly according to P_X; (3) the tracker predicts a label using the current hypothesis: $\hat{a}_t = \hat{c}_{t-1}(x_t)$; (4) the tracker is given the correct label $a_t = c_t(x_t)$; (5) the tracker forms a new hypothesis: $\hat{c}_t = \mathcal{L}(\hat{c}_{t-1}, \langle x_t, a_t \rangle)$.

It is clear that an unrestricted adversary can always choose a concept sequence (a sequence of active concepts) that the tracker can not track. Therefore, it is necessary to restrict the changes that the adversary can induce. In this paper, we require that two subsequent concepts differ by no more than γ, that is, $d(c_t, c_{t-1}) \leq \gamma$ for all t. We define the restricted concept sequence space $C_\gamma = \{\mathbf{c} : c_t \in C, \ d(c_t, c_{t+1}) \leq \gamma\}$. In the following, we are concerned with two types of adversaries: a *benign* adversary which causes changes that are independent of the hypothesis; and a *greedy* adversary which always chooses a change that will maximize $d(c_t, c_{t-1})$ constrained by the upper-bound.

Since we have restricted the adversary, it seems only fair to restrict the tracker too. We require that a tracking algorithm be: *deterministic*, i.e., that the process generating the hypotheses be deterministic; *prudent*, i.e., that the label predicted for an instance be a deterministic function of the current hypothesis: $\hat{a}_t = \hat{c}_{t-1}(x_t)$; and *conservative*, i.e., that the hypothesis is modified only when an example is mislabeled. The restriction that a tracker be conservative rules out algorithms which attempt to predict the adversary's movements and is the most restrictive of the three. On the other hand, when the tracker does update its hypothesis, there are no restrictions on $d(\hat{c}_t, \hat{c}_{t-1})$.

To measure performance, we focus on the mistake rate of the tracker. A *mistake* occurs when the tracker mislabels an instance, i.e., whenever $\hat{c}_{t-1}(x_t) \neq c_t(x_t)$. For convenience, we define a mistake indicator function, $M(x_t, c_t, \hat{c}_{t-1})$ which is 1 if $\hat{c}_{t-1}(x_t) \neq c_t(x_t)$ and 0 otherwise. Note that if a mistake occurs, it occurs before the hypothesis is updated — a conservative tracker is always a step behind the adversary. We are interested in the *asymptotic mistake rate*, $\mu = \liminf_{t \to \infty} \frac{1}{t} \sum_{i=0}^{t} M(x_t, c_t, \hat{c}_{t-1})$.

Following Helmbold and Long (1991), we say that an algorithm (μ, γ)-tracks a sequence space C if, for all $\mathbf{c} \in C_\gamma$ and all drift rates γ' not greater than γ, the mistake rate μ' is at most μ.

We are interested in bounding the asymptotic mistake rate of a tracking algorithm based on the concept class and the adversary. To derive a lower bound on the mistake rate, we hypothesize the existence of a perfect conservative tracker, i.e., one that is always able to guess the correct concept each time it makes a mistake. We say that such a tracker has *complete side information* (CSI). No conservative tracker can do better than one with CSI. Thus, the mistake rate for a tracker with CSI is a lower bound on the mistake rate achievable by any conservative tracker.

To upper bound the mistake rate, it is necessary that we hypothesize a particular tracking algorithm when *no side information* (NSI) is available, that is, when the tracker only knows it mislabeled an instance and nothing else. In our analysis, we study a simple tracking algorithm which modifies the previous hypothesis just enough to correct the mistake.

3 ANALYSIS

We consider two concept classes in this paper, half-planes and the intersection of two half-planes which can be defined by lines in the plane that pass through the origin. We call these classes HS_2 and IHS_2. In this section, we present our analysis for HS_2.

Without loss of generality, since the lines pass through the origin, we take the instance space to be the circumference of the unit circle. A half-plane in HS_2 is defined by a vector $\mathbf{w}$ such that for an instance x, $c(x) = 1$ if $\mathbf{w}x \geq 0$ and $c(x) = 0$ otherwise. Without loss of

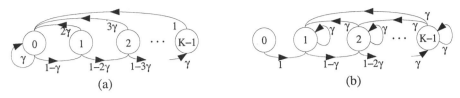

Figure 1: Markov chain for the greedy adversary and (a) CSI and (b) COVER trackers.

generality, as we will show later, we assume that the instances are chosen uniformly.

To begin, we assume a greedy adversary as follows: Every time the tracker guesses the correct target concept (that is, $\hat{c}_{t-1} = c_{t-1}$), the greedy adversary randomly chooses a vector $\mathbf{r}$ orthogonal to $\mathbf{w}$ and at every iteration, the adversary rotates $\mathbf{w}$ by $\pi\gamma$ radians in the direction defined by $\mathbf{r}$. We have shown that a greedy adversary maximizes the asymptotic mistake rate for a conservative tracker but do not present the proof here.

To lower bound the achievable error rate, we assume a conservative tracker with complete side information so that the hypothesis is unchanged if no mistake occurs and is updated to the correct concept otherwise. The state of this system is fully described by $d(c_t, \hat{c}_t)$ and, for $\gamma = 1/K$ for some integer K, is modeled by the Markov chain shown in figure 1a. In each state s_i (labeled i in the figure), $d(c_t, \hat{c}_t) = i\gamma$. The asymptotic mistake rate is equal to the probability of state 0 which is lower bounded by

$$l(\gamma) = \sqrt{2\gamma/\pi} - 2\gamma/\pi$$

Since $l(\gamma)$ depends only on γ which, in turn, is defined in terms of the probability measure, the results holds for all distributions. Therefore, since this result applies to the best of all possible conservative trackers, we can say that

Theorem 1. *For* HS_2, *if* $d(c_t, c_{t-1}) \leq \gamma$, *then there exists a concept sequence* $\mathbf{c} \in \mathcal{C}_\gamma$ *such that the mistake rate* $\mu > l(\gamma)$. *Equivalently,* $\mathcal{C}_\gamma$ *is not* (γ, μ)-*trackable whenever* $\mu < l(\gamma)$.

To upper bound the achievable mistake rate, we must choose a realizable tracking algorithm. We have analyzed the behavior of a simple algorithm we call COVER which rotates the hypothesize line just far enough to cover the incorrectly labeled instance. Mathematically, if $\hat{\mathbf{w}}_t$ is the hypothesized normal vector at time t and x_t is the mislabeled instance:

$$\hat{\mathbf{w}}_t = \hat{\mathbf{w}}_{t-1} - (x_t \cdot \hat{\mathbf{w}}_{t-1})x_t. \tag{1}$$

In this case, a mistake in state s_i can lead to a transition to any state s_j for $j \leq i$ as shown in Figure 1b. The asymptotic probability of a mistake is the sum of the equilibrium transition probabilities $P(s_j|s_i)$ for all $j \leq i$. Solving for these probabilities leads to an upper bound $u(\gamma)$ on the mistake rate:

$$u(\gamma) = \sqrt{\pi\gamma/2} + \gamma(2 + \sqrt{1/e})$$

Again this depends only on γ and so is distribution independent and we can say that:

Theorem 2. *For* HS_2, *for all concept sequences* $\mathbf{c} \in \mathcal{C}_\gamma$ *the mistake rate for* COVER $\mu \leq u(\gamma)$. *Equivalently,* $\mathcal{C}_\gamma$ *is* (γ, μ)-*trackable whenever* $\mu < u(\gamma)$.

If the adversary is benign, it is as likely to decrease as to increase the probability of a mistake. Unfortunately, although this makes the task of the tracker easier, it also makes the analysis more difficult. So far, we can show that:

Theorem 3. *For* HS_2 *and a benign adversary, there exists a concept sequence* $\mathbf{c} \in C_\gamma$ *such that the mistake rate* μ *is* $O(\gamma^{2/3})$.

4   SIMULATIONS

To test the predictions of the theory and explore some areas for which we currently have no theory, we have run simulations for a variety of concept classes, adversaries, and tracking algorithms. Here we will present the results for single half-planes and the intersection of two half-planes; both greedy and benign adversaries; an ideal tracker; and two types of trackers that use no side information.

4.1   HALF-PLANES

The simplest concept class we have simulated is the set of all half-planes defined by lines passing through the origin. This is equivalent to the set classifications realizable with 2-dimensional perceptrons with zero threshold. In other words, if $\mathbf{w}$ is the normal vector and x is a point in space, $c(x) = 1$ if $\mathbf{w} \cdot x \geq 0$ and $c(x) = 0$ otherwise. The mistake rate reported for each data point is the average of 1,000,000 iterations. The instances were chosen uniformly from the circumference of the unit circle.

We also simulated the ideal tracker using an algorithm called CSI and tested a tracking algorithm called COVER, which is a simple implementation of the tracking algorithm analyzed in the theory. If a tracker using COVER mislabels an instance, it rotates the normal vector in the plane defined by it and the instance so that the instance lies exactly on the new hypothesis line, as described by equation 1.

4.1.1   Greedy adversary

Whenever CSI or COVER makes a mistake and then guesses the concept exactly, the greedy adversary uniformly at random chooses a direction orthogonal to the normal vector of the hyperplane. Whenever COVER makes a mistake and $\hat{\mathbf{w}}_t \neq \mathbf{w}_t$, the greedy adversary choose the rotation direction to be in the plane defined by $\mathbf{w}_t$ and $\hat{\mathbf{w}}_t$ and orthogonal to $\mathbf{w}_t$. At every iteration, the adversary rotates the normal vector of the hyperplane in the most recently chosen direction so that $d(c_t, c_{t+1}) = \gamma$, or equivalently, $\mathbf{w}_t \cdot \mathbf{w}_{t-1} = \cos(\pi\gamma)$.

Figure 2 shows that the theoretical lower bound very closely matches the simulation results for CSI when γ is small. For small γ, the simulation results for COVER lie very close to the theoretical predictions for the NSI case. In other words, the bounds predicted in theorems 1 and 2 are tight and the mistake rates for CSI and COVER differ by only a factor of $\pi/2$.

4.1.2   Benign adversary

At every iteration, the benign adversary uniformly at random chooses a direction orthogonal to the normal vector of the hyperplane and rotates the hyperplane in that direction so that $d(c_t, c_{t+1}) = \gamma$. Figure 3 shows that CSI behaves as predicted by Theorem 3 when $\mu = 0.6\gamma^{2/3}$. The figure also shows that COVER performs very well compared to CSI.

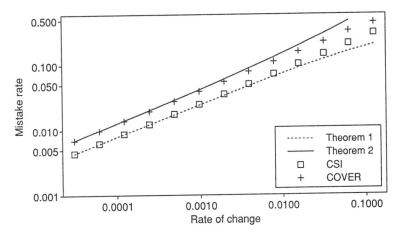

Figure 2: The mistake rate, μ, as a function of the rate of change, γ, for HS$_2$ when the adversary is greedy.

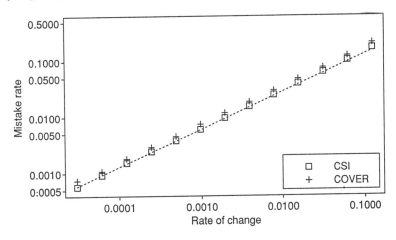

Figure 3: The mistake rate, μ, as a function of the rate of change, γ, for HS$_2$ when the adversary is benign. The line is $\mu = 0.6\gamma^{2/3}$.

4.2   INTERSECTION OF TWO HALF-PLANES

The other concept class we consider here is the intersection of two half-spaces defined by lines through the origin. That is, $c(x) = 1$ if $\mathbf{w}_1 x \geq 0$ and $\mathbf{w}_2 x \geq 0$ and $c(x) = 0$ otherwise. We tested two tracking algorithms using no side information for this concept class.

The first is a variation on the previous COVER algorithm. For each mislabeled instance: if both half-spaces label x_t differently than $c_t(x_t)$, then the line that is closest in euclidean distance to x_t is updated according to COVER; otherwise, the half-space labeling x_t differently than $c_t(x_t)$ is updated.

The second is a feed-forward network with 2 input, 2 hidden and 1 output nodes. The

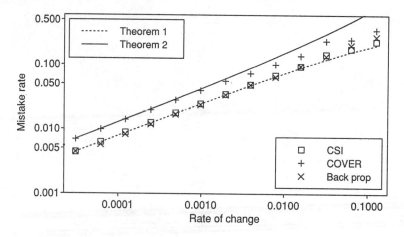

Figure 4: The mistake rate, μ, as a function of the rate of change, γ, for IHS_2 when the adversary is greedy.

thresholds of all the neurons and the weights from the hidden to output layers are fixed, i.e., only the input weights can be modified. The output of each neuron is $f(\mathbf{u}) = (1 + e^{-10\mathbf{wu}})^{-1}$. For classification, the instance was labeled one if the output of the network was greater than 0.5 and zero otherwise. If the difference between the actual and desired outputs was greater than 0.1, back-propagation was run using only the most recent example until the difference was below 0.1. The learning rate was fixed at 0.01 and no momentum was used. Since the model may be updated without making a mistake, this algorithm is not conservative.

4.2.1 Greedy Adversary

At each iteration, the greedy adversary rotates each hyperplane in a direction orthogonal to its normal vector. Each rotation direction is based on an initial direction chosen uniformly at random from the set of vectors orthogonal to the normal vector. At each iteration, both the normal vector and the rotation vector are rotated $\pi\gamma/2$ radians in the plane they define so that $d(c_t, c_{t-1}) = \gamma$ for every iteration. Figure 4 shows that the simulations match the predictions well for small γ. Non-conservative back-propagation performs about as well as conservative CSI and slightly better than conservative COVER.

4.2.2 Benign Adversary

At each iteration, the benign adversary uniformly at random chooses a direction orthogonal to $\mathbf{w}_i$ and rotates the hyperplane in that direction such that $d(c_t, c_{t-1}) = \gamma$. The theory for the benign adversary in this case is not yet fully developed, but figure 5 shows that the simulations approximate the optimal performance for HS_2 against a benign adversary with $\mathbf{c} \in C_{\gamma/2}$. Non-conservative back-propagation does not perform as well for very small γ, but catches up for $\gamma > .001$. This is likely due to the particular choice of learning rate.

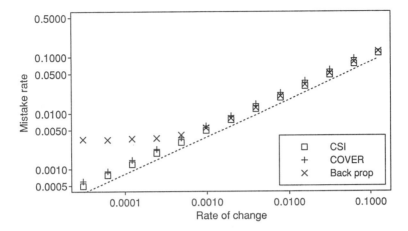

Figure 5: The mistake rate, μ, as a function of the rate of change, γ, for IHS_2 when the adversary is benign. The dashed line is $\mu = 0.6(\gamma/2)^{2/3}$.

5   CONCLUSIONS

We have presented the results of some of our research applied to the problem of tracking time-varying half-spaces. For HS_2 and IHS_2 presented here, simulation results match the theory quite well. For IHS_2, non-conservative back-propagation performs quite well.

We have extended the theorems presented in this paper to higher-dimensional input vectors and more general geometric concept classes. In Theorem 3, $\mu \geq c\gamma^{2/3}$ for some constant c and we are working to find a good value for that constant. We are also working to develop an analysis of non-conservative trackers and to better understand the difference between conservative and non-conservative algorithms.

Acknowledgments

Anthony Kuh gratefully acknowledges the support of the National Science Foundation through grant EET-8857711 and Siemens Corporate Research. Ronald L. Rivest gratefully acknowledges support from NSF grant CCR-8914428, ARO grant N00014-89-J-1988 and a grant from the Siemens Corporation.

References

Galletti, I. and Abbott, M. (1989). Development of an advanced airborne speech recognizer for direct voice input. *Speech Technology*, pages 60–63.

Haussler, D., Littlestone, N., and Warmuth, M. K. (1987). Expected mistake bounds for on-line learning algorithms. (Unpublished).

Helmbold, D. P. and Long, P. M. (1991). Tracking drifting concepts using random examples. In Valiant, L. G. and Warmuth, M. K., editors, *Proceedings of the Fourth Annual Workshop on Computational Learning Theory*, pages 13–23. Morgan Kaufmann.

Littlestone, N. (1989). Mistake bounds and logarithmic linear-threshold learning algorithms. Technical Report UCSC-CRL-89-11, Univ. of California at Santa Cruz.

The VC-Dimension versus the Statistical Capacity of Multilayer Networks

Chuanyi Ji *and Demetri Psaltis
Department of Electrical Engineering
California Institute of Technology
Pasadena, CA 91125

Abstract

A general relationship is developed between the VC-dimension and the statistical lower epsilon-capacity which shows that the VC-dimension can be lower bounded (in order) by the statistical lower epsilon-capacity of a network trained with random samples. This relationship explains quantitatively how generalization takes place after memorization, and relates the concept of generalization (consistency) with the capacity of the optimal classifier over a class of classifiers with the same structure and the capacity of the Bayesian classifier. Furthermore, it provides a general methodology to evaluate a lower bound for the VC-dimension of feedforward multilayer neural networks.

This general methodology is applied to two types of networks which are important for hardware implementations: two layer $(N - 2L - 1)$ networks with binary weights, integer thresholds for the hidden units and zero threshold for the output unit, and a single neuron $((N - 1)$ networks) with binary weigths and a zero threshold. Specifically, we obtain $O(\frac{W}{lnL}) \leq d_2 \leq O(W)$, and $d_1 \sim O(N)$. Here W is the total number of weights of the $(N - 2L - 1)$ networks. d_1 and d_2 represent the VC-dimensions for the $(N - 1)$ and $(N - 2L - 1)$ networks respectively.

1 Introduction

The information capacity and the VC-dimension are two important quantities that characterize multilayer feedforward neural networks. The former characterizes their

---

*Present Address: Department of Electrical Computer and System Engineering, Rensselaer Polytech Institute, Troy, NY 12180.

memorization capability, while the latter represents the sample complexity needed for generalization. Discovering their relationships is of importance for obtaining a better understanding of the fundamental properties of multilayer networks in learning and generalization.

In this work we show that the VC-dimension of feedforward multilayer neural networks, which is a distribution-and network-parameter-indenpent quantity, can be lower bounded (in order) by the statistical lower epsilon-capacity C_ϵ^- (McEliece et.al, (1987)), which is a distribution-and network-dependent quantity, when the samples are drawn from two classes: $\Omega_1(+1)$ and $\Omega_2(-1)$. The only requirement on the distribution from which samples are drawn is that the optimal classification error achievable, the Bayes error P_{be}, is greater than zero. Then we will show that the VC-dimension d and the statistical lower epsilon-capacity C_ϵ^- are related by

$$C_\epsilon^- \leq Ad, \qquad (1)$$

where $\epsilon = P_{eo} - \epsilon'$ for $0 < \epsilon' \leq P_{eo}$; or $\epsilon = P_{be} - \epsilon'$ for $0 < \epsilon' \leq P_{be}$. Here ϵ is the error tolerance, and P_{eo} represents the optimal error rate achievable on the class of classifiers considered. It is obvious that $P_{eo} \geq P_{be}$. The relation given in Equation (1) is non-trivial if $P_{be} > 0$, $P_{eo} \leq \epsilon'$ or $P_{be} \leq \epsilon'$ so that ϵ is a non-negative quantity. Ad is called the universal sample bound for generalization, where $A < \frac{128 ln \frac{1}{\epsilon}}{\epsilon'^2}$ is a positive constant. When the sample complexity exceeds Ad, all the networks of the same architechture for all distributions of the samples can generalize with almost probability 1 for d large. A special case of interest, in which $P_{be} = \frac{1}{2}$, corresponds to random assignments of samples. Then C_ϵ^- represents the random storage capacity which characterizes the memorizing capability of networks.

Although the VC-dimension is a key parameter in generalization, there exists no systematic way of finding it. The relationship we have obtained, however, brings concomitantly a constructive method of finding a lower bound for the VC-dimension of multilayer networks. That is, if the weights of a network are properly constructed using random samples drawn from a chosen distribution, the statistical lower epsilon-capacity can be evaluated and then utilized as bounds for the VC-dimension. In this paper we will show how this constructive approach contributes to finding lower bounds of the VC-dimension of multilayer networks with binary weights.

2   A Relationship Between the VC-Dimension and the Statistical Capacity

2.1   Definition of the Statistical Capacity

Consider a network s whose weights are constructed from M random samples belonging to two classes. Let $\hat{r}(s) = \frac{Z}{M}$, where Z is the total number of samples classified incorrectly by the network s. Then the random variable $\hat{r}(s)$ is the training error rate. Let

$$P_c(M) = \Pr(\hat{r}(s) \leq \epsilon), \qquad (2)$$

where $0 \leq \epsilon \leq 1$. Then the statistical lower epsilon-capacity (statistical capacity in short) C_ϵ^- is the maximum M such that $P_\epsilon(M) \geq 1 - \eta$, where η can be arbitrarily small for sufficiently large N.

Roughly speaking, the statistical lower epsilon-capacity defined here can be regarded as a sharp transition point on the curve $P_\epsilon(M)$ shown in Fig.1. When the number of samples used is below this sharp transition, the network can memorize them perfectly.

2.2   The Universal Sample Bound for Generalization

Let $P_e(x|s)$ be the true probability of error for the network s. Then the generalization error $\Delta E(s)$ satisfies $\Delta E(s) = | \hat{r}(s) - P_e(x|s) |$. We can show that the probability for the generalization error to exceed a given small quantity ϵ satisfies the following relation.

Theorem 1

$$\Pr(\max_{s \in S} \Delta E(s) > \epsilon') \leq h(2M; d, \epsilon'), \tag{3}$$

where

$$h(2M; d, \epsilon') = \begin{cases} 1; & either\ 2M \leq d,\ or\ 6\frac{(2M)^d}{d!}e^{-\frac{\epsilon'^2 M}{8}} \geq 1 \& 2M > d, \\ 6\frac{(2M)^d}{d!}e^{-\frac{\epsilon'^2 M}{8}}; & otherwise. \end{cases}$$

Here S is a class of networks with the same architecture. The function $h(2M; d, \epsilon')$ has one sharp transition occurring at Ad shown in Fig.1, where A is a constant satisfying the equation $A = ln(2A) + 1 - \frac{\epsilon'^2}{8}A = 0$.

This theorem says that when the number M of samples used exceeds Ad, generalization happens with probability 1. Since Ad is a distribution-and network-parameter-independent quantity, we call it the universal sample bound for generalization.

2.3   A Relationship between The VC-Dimension and C_ϵ^-

Roughly speaking, since both the statistical capacity and the VC-dimension represent sharp transition points, it is natural to ask whether they are related. The relationship can actually be given through the theorem below.

Theorem 2 *Let samples belonging to two classes $\Omega_1(+1)$ and $\Omega_2(-1)$ be drawn independently from some distribution. The only requirement on the distributions considered is that the Bayes error P_{be} satisfies $0 < P_{be} \leq \frac{1}{2}$. Let S be a class of feedforward multilayer networks with a fixed structure consisting of threshold elements and s_1 be one network in S, where the weights of s_1 are constructed from M (training) samples drawn from one distribution as specified above. For a given distribution, let P_{eo} be the optimal error rate achievable on S and P_{be} be the Bayes error rate. Then*

$$\Pr(\hat{r}(s_1) < P_{eo} - \epsilon') \leq h(2M; d, \epsilon'), \tag{4}$$

and

$$\Pr(\hat{r}(s_1) < P_{be} - \epsilon') \leq h(2M; d, \epsilon'), \tag{5}$$

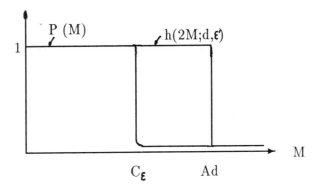

Figure 1: Two sharp transition points for the capacity and the universal sample bound for generalization.

where $\hat{r}(s_1)$ is equal to the training error rate of s_1. (It is also called the resubstitution error estimator in the pattern recognition literature.) These relations are nontrivial if $P_{eo} > \epsilon'$, $P_{be} > \epsilon'$ and $\epsilon' > 0$ small.

The key idea of this result is illustrated in Fig.1. That is, the sharp transition which stands for the lower epsilon-capacity is below the sharp transition for the universal sample bound for generalization.

To interpret this relation, let us compare Equation (2) and Equation (5) and examine the range of ϵ and ϵ' respectively. Since ϵ', which is initially given in Inequality (3), represents a bound on the generalization error, it is usually quite small. For most of practical problems, P_{be} is small also. If the structure of the class of networks is properly chosen so that $P_{eo} \approx P_{be}$, then $\epsilon = P_{eo} - \epsilon'$ will be a small quantity. Although the epsilon-capacity is a valid quantity depending on M for any network in the class, for M sufficiently large, the meaningful networks to be considered through this relation is only a small subset in the class whose true probability of error is close to P_{eo}. That is, this small subset contains only those networks which can approximate the best classifier contained in this class.

For a special case in which samples are assigned randomly to two classes with equal probability, we have a result stated in Corollary 1.

Corollary 1 *Let samples be drawn independently from some distribution and then assigned randomly to two classes $\Omega_1(+1)$ and $\Omega_2(-1)$ with equal probability. This is equivalent to the case that the two class conditional distributions have complete overlap with one another. That is, $\Pr(x \mid \Omega_1) = \Pr(x \mid \Omega_2)$. Then the Bayes error is $\frac{1}{2}$. Using the same notation as in the above theorem, we have*

$$C_{\frac{1}{2}-\epsilon'}^{-} \leq Ad. \tag{6}$$

Although the distributions specified here give an uninteresting case for classification purposes, we will see later that the random statistical epsilon-capacity in Inequality (6) can be used to characterize the memorizing capability of networks, and to formulate a constructive approach to find a lower bound for the VC-dimension.

3 Bounds for the VC-Dimension of Two Networks with Binary Weights

3.1 A Constructive Methodology

One of the applications of this relation is that it provides a general constructive approach to find a lower bound for the VC-dimension for a class of networks. Specifically, using the relationship given in Inequality (6), the procedures can be described as follows.

1) Select a distribution.

2) Draw samples independently from the chosen distribution, and then assign them randomly to two classes.

3) Evaluate the lower epsilon-capacity and then use it as a lower bound for the VC-dimension.

Two example are given below to demonstrate how this general approach can be applied to find lower bounds for the VC-dimension.

3.2 Bounds for Two-Layer Networks with Binary Weigths

Two-layer $(N - 2L - 1)$ networks with binary weights and integer thresholds are considered in this section.

3.2.1 A lower Bound

The construction of the network we consider is motivated by the one used by Baum (Baum, 1988) in finding the capacity for two layer networks with *real* weights. Although this particular network will fail if the accuracy of the weights and the thresholds is reduced, the idea of using the grandmother-cell type of network will be adopted to construct our network.

We consider a two layer binary network with $2L$ hidden threshold units and one output threshold unit shown in Fig.2 a).

The weights at the second layer are fixed and equal to $+1$ and -1 alternately. The hidden units are allowed to have integer thresholds in $[-N, N]$, and the threshold for the output unit is zero.

Let $\vec{X}_l^{(m)} = (x_{l1}^{(m)}, ..., x_{lN}^{(m)})$ be a N dimensional random vector, where $x_{li}^{(m)}$'s are independent random variables taking $(+1)$ and (-1) with equal probability $\frac{1}{2}$, $0 \leq l \leq L$, and $0 \leq m \leq M$. Consider the lth pair of hidden units. The weights at the first layer for this pair of hidden units are equal. Let w_{li} denote the weight from the ith input to these two hidden units, then we have

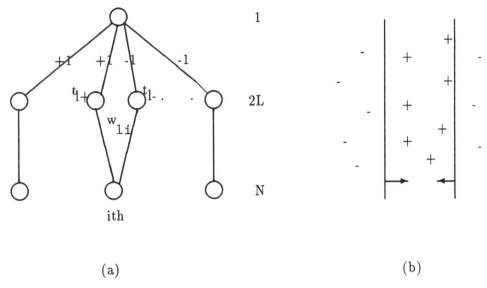

(a)   (b)

Figure 2: a) The two-layer network with binary weights. b) Illustration on how a pair of hidden units separates samples.

$$w_{li} = sgn(\alpha_l \sum_{m=1}^{M} x_{li}^{(m)}), \tag{7}$$

where $sgn(x) = 1$ if $x > 0$, and -1 otherwise. α_l's , $1 \leq l \leq L$, which are independent random variables which take on two values $+1$ or -1 with equal probability, represent the random assignments of the LM samples into two classes $\Omega_1(+1)$ and $\Omega_2(-1)$.

The thresholds for these two units are different and are given as

$$t_{l\pm} = \alpha_l \lfloor (1 \mp k) \sqrt{\frac{2}{\pi}} \frac{N}{\sqrt{M}} \rfloor, \tag{8}$$

where $0 < k < 1$, and $t_{l\pm}$ correspond to the thresholds for the units with weight $+1$ and -1 at the second layer respectively.

Fig.2 b) illustrates how this network works. Each pair of hidden units forms two parallel hyperplanes separated by the two thresholds, which will generates a presynaptic input either $+2$ or (-2) to the output unit only for the samples stored in this pair which fall in between the planes when α_l equals either $+1$ or -1, and a presynaptic input 0 for the samples falling outside. When the samples as well as the parallel hyperplanes are random, with a certain probability they will fall either between a pair of parallel hyperplanes or outside. Therefore, statistical analysis is needed to obtain the lower epsilon-capacity.

Theorem 3 *A lower bound $C_{\frac{1}{2}-\epsilon'}^{-'}$ for the lower epsilon-capacity $C_{\frac{1}{2}-\epsilon'}^{-}$ for this network is:*

$$C_{\frac{1}{2}-\epsilon'}^{-'} = \frac{(1-k)^2 NL}{\pi (ln \frac{4\sqrt{\pi}\epsilon'^2}{9}L - \frac{1}{2}lnlnL)}$$

$$\sim O(\frac{W}{lnL}). \tag{9}$$

3.2.2   An Upper Bound

Since the total number of possible mappings of two layer $(N-2L-1)$ networks with binary weights and integer thresholds ranging in $[-N, N]$ is bounded by $2^{W+L\log 2N}$, the VC-dimension d_2 is upper bounded by $W + L\log 2N$, which is in the order of W. Then $d_2 \leq O(W)$. By combining both the upper and lower bounds, we have

$$O(\frac{W}{lnL}) \leq d_2 \leq O(W). \tag{10}$$

3.3   Bounds for One-Layer Networks with Binary Weigths

The one-layer network we consider here is equivalent to one hidden unit in the above $(N-2L-1)$ network. Specifically, the weight from the i-th input unit to the neuron is

$$w_i = sgn(\sum_{m=1}^{M} \alpha_m x_i^{(m)}), \tag{11}$$

where $(1 \leq i \leq N)$, $x_i^{(m)}$'s and α_m's are independent and equally probable binary(± 1) random variables, which represent elements of N-dimensional sample vectors and their random assignments to two classes respectively.

Theorem 4 *The lower epsilon-capacity $C_{\frac{1}{2}-\epsilon'}^{-}$ of this network satisfies*

$$C_{\frac{1}{2}-\epsilon'}^{-} \approx \frac{N}{\pi^2\epsilon^2}. \tag{12}$$

Then by Corollary 1 we have $O(N) \leq O(d_1)$, where d_1 is the VC-dimension of one-layer $(N-1)$ networks.

Using the similar counting arguement, an upper bound can be obtained as $d_1 \leq N$. Then combining the lower and upper bounds, we have $d_1 \sim O(N)$

4   Discussions

The general relationship we have drawn between the VC-dimension and the statistical lower epsilon-capacity provides a new view on the sample complexity for generalization. Specifically, it has two implications to learning and generalziation.

1) For random assignments of the samples ($P_{be} = \frac{1}{2}$), the relationship confirms that generalization occurs after memorization, since the statistical lower epsilon-capacity

for this case is the random storage capacity which charaterizes the memorizing capability of networks and it is upper bounded by the universal sample bound for generalization.

2) For cases where the Bayes error is smaller than $\frac{1}{2}$, the relationship indicates that an appropriate choice of a network structure is very important. If a network structure is properly chosen so that the optimal achievable error rate P_{eo} is close to the Bayes error P_{eb}, than the optimal network in this class is the one which has the largest lower epsilon-capacity. Since a suitable structure can hardly be chosen a priori due to the lack of knowledge about the underlying distribution, searching for network structures as well as weight values becomes necessary. Similar idea has been addressed by Devroye (Devroye, 1988) and by Vapnik (Vapnik, 1982) for structural minimization.

We have applied this relation as a general constructive approach to obtain lower bounds for the VC-dimension of two-layer and one-layer networks with binary interconnections. For the one-layer networks, the lower bound is tight and matches the upper bound. For the two-layer networks, the lower bound is smaller than the upper bound (in order) by a ln factor. In an independent work by Littlestone (Littlestone, 1988), the VC-dimension of so-called DNF expressions were obtained. Since any DNF expression can be implemented by a two layer network of threshold units with binary weights and integer thresholds, this result is equivalent to showing that the VC-dimension of such networks is $O(W)$. We believe that the ln factor in our lower bound is due to the limitations of the grandmother-cell type of networks used in our construction.

Acknowledgement

The authors would like to thank Yaser Abu-Mostafa and David Haussler for helpful discussions. The support of AFOSR and DARPA is gratefully acknowledged.

References

E. Baum. (1988) On the Capacity of Multilayer Perceptron. *J. of Complexity*, 4:193-215.

L. Devroye. (1988) Automatic Pattern Recognition: A Study of Probability of Error. *IEEE Trans. on Pattern Recognition and Machine Intelligence*, Vol. 10, No.4: 530-543.

N. Littlestone. (1988) Learning Quickly When Irrelevant Attributes Abound: A New Linear-Threshold Algorithm. *Machine Learning 2:* 285-318.

R.J . McEliece, E.C . Posner, E.R . Rodemich, S.S . Venkatesh. (1987) The Capacity of the Hopfield Associative Memory. *IEEE Trans. Inform. Theory*, Vol. IT-33, No. 4, 461-482.

V.N . Vapnik (1982) *Estimation of Dependences Based on Empirical Data*, New York: Springer-Verlag.

Some Approximation Properties of Projection Pursuit Learning Networks

Ying Zhao   Christopher G. Atkeson
The Artificial Intelligence Laboratory
Massachusetts Institute of Technology
Cambridge, MA 02139

Abstract

This paper will address an important question in machine learning: What kind of network architectures work better on what kind of problems? A projection pursuit learning network has a very similar structure to a one hidden layer sigmoidal neural network. A general method based on a continuous version of projection pursuit regression is developed to show that projection pursuit regression works better on angular smooth functions than on Laplacian smooth functions. There exists a ridge function approximation scheme to avoid the curse of dimensionality for approximating functions in $L^2(\phi_d)$.

1   INTRODUCTION

Projection pursuit is a nonparametric statistical technique to find "interesting" low dimensional projections of high dimensional data sets. It has been used for nonparametric fitting and other data-analytic purposes (Friedman and Stuetzle, 1981, Huber, 1985). Approximation properties have been studied by Diaconis & Shahshahani (1984) and Donoho & Johnstone (1989). It was first introduced into the context of learning networks by Barron & Barron (1988). A one hidden layer sigmoidal feedforward neural network approximates $f(\mathbf{x})$ using the structure (Figure 1(a)):

$$g(\mathbf{x}) = \sum_{j=1}^{n} \alpha_j \sigma(p_j \theta_j^T \mathbf{x} + \delta_j) \tag{1}$$

936

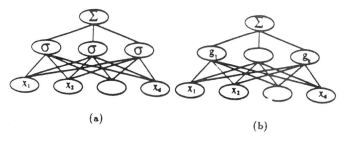

Figure 1: (a) A One Hidden Layer Feedforward Neural Network. (b) A Projection Pursuit Learning Network.

where σ is a sigmoidal function. θ_j are direction parameters with $\|\theta_j\| = 1$, and α_j, p_j, δ_j are function parameters. A projection pursuit learning network based on projection pursuit regression (PPR) (Friedman and Stuetzle, 1981) or a ridge function approximation scheme (RA) has a very similar structure (Figure 1(b)).

$$g(\mathbf{x}) = \sum_{j=1}^{n} g_j(\theta_j^T \mathbf{x}) \tag{2}$$

where θ_j are also direction parameters with $\|\theta_j\| = 1$. The corresponding function parameters are ridge functions g_j which are any smooth function to be learned from the data. Since σ is replaced by a more general smooth function g_j, projection pursuit learning networks can be viewed as a generalization of one hidden layer sigmoidal feedforward neural networks. This paper will discuss some approximation properties of PPR:

1. Projection pursuit learning networks work better on angular smooth functions than on Laplacian smooth functions. Here "work better" means that for fixed complexities of hidden unit functions and a certain accuracy, fewer hidden units are required. For the two dimensional case ($d = 2$), Donoho and Johnstone (1989) show this result using equispaced directions. The equispaced directions may not be available when $d > 2$. We use a set of directions generated from zeros of orthogonal polynomials and uniformly distributed directions on an unit sphere instead. The analysis method in D & J's paper is limited to two dimensions. We apply the theory of spherical harmonics (Muller, 1966) to develop a continuous ridge function representation of any arbitray smooth functions and then employ different numerical integration schemes to discretize it for cases when $d > 2$.

2. The curse of dimensionality can be avoided when a proper ridge function approximation is applied. Once a continuous ridge function representation is established for any function in $L^2(\phi_d)$, a Monte Carlo type of integration scheme can be applied which has a RMS error convergence rate $O(N^{-\frac{1}{2}})$ where N is the number of ridge functions in the linear combinations. This is a similar result to Barron's result (Barron, 1991) except that we have less restrictions on the underlying function class.

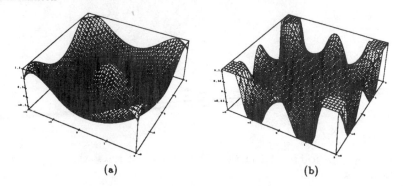

(a) (b)

Figure 2: (a) A radial basis element J_{014}. (b) a harmonic basis element J_{810}.

2   SMOOTHNESS CLASSES AND A $L^2(\phi_d)$ BASIS

We use $L^2(\phi_d)$ as our underlying function space with Gaussian measure $\phi_d = (\frac{1}{2\pi})^{\frac{d}{2}} e^{-\frac{|\mathbf{x}|^2}{2}}$. $\|f\|^2 = \int_{R^d} f^2 \phi_d d\mathbf{x}$. The smoothness classes characterize the rates of convergence. Let Δ_d be the Laplacian operator and Δ_d^* be the Laplacian-Beltrami operator (Muller, 1966). The smoothness classes can be defined as:

Definition 1 *The function $f \in L^2(\phi_d)$ will be said to have Cartesian smoothness of order p if it has p derivatives and these derivatives are all in $L^2(\phi_d)$. It will be said to have angular smoothness of order q if $\Delta_d^{*q} f \in L^2(\phi_d)$. It will be said to have Laplacian smoothness of order r if $\Delta_d^r f \in L^2(\phi_d)$. Let $\mathcal{F}_p$ be the class of functions with Cartesian smoothness p, A_{pq} be the class of functions with Cartesian smoothness p and angular smoothness q and $\mathcal{L}_{pr}$ be the class of functions with Cartesian smoothness p and Laplacian smoothness r.*

We derive an orthogonal basis in $L^2(\phi_d)$ from the eigenfunctions of a self-adjoint operator. The basis element is defined as:

$$J_{njm}(\mathbf{x}) = \gamma_m \underbrace{r^n S_{nj}(\xi)}_{harmonic} \underbrace{L_m^\alpha(\frac{r^2}{2})}_{radial} \tag{3}$$

where $\mathbf{x} = r\xi$, $n = 0, ..., \infty$, $m = 0, ..., \infty$, $j = 1, ..., N(d,n)$, $\gamma_m = (-2)^m m!$, $\alpha = n + \frac{d-2}{2}$. $S_{nj}(\xi)$ are linearly independent spherical harmonics of degree n in d dimensions (Muller, 1966). $L_m^\alpha(\frac{r^2}{2})$ is a Laguerre polynomial. The advantage of the basis comes from its representation as a product of a spherical harmonic and a radial polynomial. Specifically J_{0jm} is a radial polynomial for $n = 0$ and J_{nj0} is a harmonic polynomial for $m = 0$. Figure 2(a),(b) show a radial basis element and a harmonic basis element when $n + 2m = 8$. The basis element J_{njm} has an orthogonality:

$$E(J_{njm}(r,\xi) J_{kil}(r,\xi)) = \delta_n^k \delta_j^i \delta_m^l \frac{2^{n+2m-1}}{\pi^{\frac{d}{2}}} \Gamma(m + n + \frac{d}{2}) \Gamma(m+1) \tag{4}$$

where E denotes expectation with respect to ϕ_d. Since it is a basis in $L^2(\phi_d)$, any function $f \in L^2(\phi_d)$ has an expansion in terms of basis elements J_{njm}

$$f = \sum_{n,j,m} c_{njm} J_{njm} \tag{5}$$

The circular harmonic $e^{in\theta}$ is a special case of the spherical harmonic $S_{nj}(\xi)$. In two dimensions, $d = 2$, $N(d, n) = 2$ and $\mathbf{x} = (r\cos\theta, r\sin\theta)$. The spherical harmonic $S_{nj}(\xi)$ can be reduced to the following: $S_{n1}(\xi) = \frac{1}{\sqrt{\pi}}\cos n\theta$, $S_{n2}(\xi) = \frac{1}{\sqrt{\pi}}\sin n\theta$, which is the circular harmonic.

Smoothness classes can also be defined qualitatively from expansions of functions in terms of basis elements J_{njm}. Since $\|f\|^2 = \sum c_{njm}^2 J_{njm}^2$, one can think of $p_{njm}(f) = \frac{c_{njm}^2 J_{njm}^2}{\sum c_{njm}^2 J_{njm}^2}$ as representing the distribution of energy in f among the different modes of oscillation J_{njm}. If f is cartesian smooth, $p_{njm}(f)$ peaks around small $n + 2m$. If f is angular smooth, $p_{njm}(f)$ peaks around small n. If f is Laplacian smooth, $p_{njm}(f)$ peaks around small m. To explain why PPR works better on angular smooth functions than on Laplacian smooth functions, we first examine how to represent these $L^2(\phi_d)$ basis elements systematically in terms of ridge functions and then use the expansion (5) to derive a error bound of RA for general smooth functions.

3   CONTINUOUS RIDGE FUNCTION SCHEMES

There exists a continuous ridge function representation for any function $f(\mathbf{x}) \in L^2(\phi_d)$ which is an integral of ridge functions through all possible directions.

$$f(\mathbf{x}) = \int_{\Omega_d} g(\mathbf{x}^T\eta, \eta)d\omega_d(\eta). \tag{6}$$

This works intuitively because any object is determined by any infinite set of radiographs. More precisely, any function $f(\mathbf{x}) \in L^2(\phi_d)$ can be approximated arbitrarily well by a linear combination of ridge functions $\sum_k g(\mathbf{x}^T\eta_k, \eta_k)$ provided infinitely many combination units (Jones, 1987). As $k \to \infty$, we have (6). The natural discrete approximation to (6) has the form: $f_n(\mathbf{x}) = \sum_{j=1}^n w_j g(\mathbf{x}^T\eta_j, \eta_j)$, which becomes the usual PPR (2). We proved a continuous ridge function representation of basis elements J_{njm} which is shown in Lemma 1.

Lemma 1 *The continuous ridge function representation of J_{njm} is:*

$$J_{njm}(\mathbf{x}) = \lambda_{nmd} \int_{\Omega_d} H_{n+2m}(\eta^T\mathbf{x})S_{nj}(\eta)d\omega_d(\eta) \tag{7}$$

where λ_{nmd} is a constant and $H_{n+2m}(x)$ is a Hermite polynomial.

Therefore any function $f \in L^2(\phi_d)$ has a continuous ridge function representation (6) with

$$g(\mathbf{x}^T\eta, \eta) = \sum c_{njm}\lambda_{nmd}H_{n+2m}(\mathbf{x}^T\eta)S_{nj}(\eta) \tag{8}$$

Gaussian quadrature and Monte Carlo integration schemes can be used to discretize (6).

4   GAUSSIAN QUADRATURE

Since $\int_{\Omega_d} g(\mathbf{x}^T\eta, \eta)d\omega_d(\eta) = \int_{\Omega_{d-1}} \int_{-1}^1 g(\mathbf{x}^T\eta, \eta)(1 - t_{d-1}^2)^{\frac{d-3}{2}} dt_{d-1}d\omega_{d-1}(\eta_{d-1})$, simple product rules using Gaussian quadrature formulae can be used here. $t_{ij}, i =$

(a)

(b)

Figure 3: Directions (a) for a radial polynomial (b) for a harmonic polynomial

$d - 1, ..., 1, j = 1, ..., n$ are zeros of orthogonal polynomials with weights $(1 - t^2)^{\frac{i-2}{2}}$. $N = n^{d-1}$ points on the unit sphere Ω_d can be formed using t_{ij} through

$$\eta = \begin{bmatrix} \sqrt{1 - t_{d-1}^2} \cdots \sqrt{1 - t_1^2} \\ \sqrt{1 - t_{d-1}^2} \cdots t_1 \\ \cdots \\ t_{d-1} \end{bmatrix} \tag{9}$$

If $g(x^T \eta, \eta)$ is a polynomial of degree at most $2n - 1$ (in terms of $t_1, ..., t_{d-1}$), then $N = n^{d-1}$ points (directions) are sufficient to represent the integral exactly. This can be demonstrated with two examples by taking $d = 3$.

Example 1: a radial function

$$x^4 + y^4 + z^4 + 2x^2 y^2 + 2x^2 z^2 + 2y^2 z^2 = c_1 \int_{\Omega_3} (x^T \eta)^4 d\omega_3(\eta) \tag{10}$$

$d = 3, n = 3$. $n^2 = 9$ directions from (9) are sufficient to represent this polynomial with $t_2 = 0, \sqrt{\frac{3}{5}}, -\sqrt{\frac{3}{5}}$ (zeros of a degree 3 Legendre polynomial) and $t_1 = 0, \frac{\sqrt{3}}{2}, -\frac{\sqrt{3}}{2}$ (zeros of a degree 3 Tschebyscheff polynomial). More directions are needed to represent a harmonic function with exactly the same number of terms of monomials but with different coefficients.

Example 2: a harmonic function

$$\frac{1}{8}(8z^4 + 3y^4 + 3z^4 - 24z^2 y^2 - 24z^2 z^2 + 6y^2 z^2) = c_2 \int_{\Omega_3} (x^T \eta)^4 S_{4j}(\eta) d\omega_3(\eta) \tag{11}$$

where $S_{4j}(\eta) = \frac{1}{8}(35t^4 - 30t^2 + 3), \eta = t\epsilon_3 + \sqrt{1 - t^2}\eta_2$. $n = 5, n^2 = 25$ directions from (9) are sufficient to represent the polynomial with $t_2 = 0, 0.90618, -0.90618, 0.53847, -0.53847$ and $t_1 = \cos\frac{2j-1}{10}\pi, j = 1, ..., 5$. The distribution of these directions on a unit sphere are shown in Figure 3(a) and (b). In general, $N = (n + m + 1)^{d-1}$ directions are sufficient to represent J_{njm} exactly by using zeros of orthogonal polynomials. If $p = n + 2m$ (the degree of the basis) is fixed, $N = (p - m + 1)^{d-1} = (\frac{p+n}{2} + 1)^{d-1}$ is minimised when $n = 0$ which corresponds to the radial basis element. N is maximised when $m = 0$ which is the harmonic element. Using definitions of smoothness classes in Section 2. we can show that ridge function approximation works better on angular smooth functions. The basic result is as follows:

Theorem 1 $f \in \mathcal{A}_{pq}$, let $R_N f$ denote a sum of ridge functions which best approximate f by using a set of directions generated by zeros of orthogonal polynomials. Then

$$E_N = \|R_N f - f\|_{\mathcal{A}_{pq}}^2 \leq B_p N^{-\frac{p}{d-1}} + B_q N^{-\frac{4q}{d-1}} \tag{12}$$

This error bound says that ridge function approximation does take advantage of angular smoothness. Radial functions are the most angular smooth functions with $q = +\infty$ and harmonic functions are the least angular smooth functions when the Cartesian smoothness p is fixed. Therefore ridge function approximation works better on angular smooth functions than on Laplacian smooth functions. Radial and harmonic functions are the two extreme cases.

5 UNIFORMLY DISTRIBUTED DIRECTIONS ON Ω_d

Instead of using directions from zeros of orthogonal polynomials, N uniformly distributed directions on Ω_d is an alternative to generalizing equispaced directions. This is a Monte Carlo type of integration scheme on Ω_d.

To approximate the integral (7), N uniformly distributed directions η_1, η_2, ..., η_N on Ω_d drawn from the density $f(\eta) = 1/\omega_d$ on Ω_d are used:

$$\hat{J}_{njm}(\mathbf{x}) = \frac{\omega_d}{N} \lambda_{nmd} \sum_{k=1}^{N} H_{n+2m}(\mathbf{x}^T \eta_k) S_{nj}(\eta_k) \tag{13}$$

The mean value for $\hat{J}_{njm}(\mathbf{x})$ is

$$m_N(\mathbf{x}) = \frac{\omega_d}{N} \lambda_{nmd} \sum_{k=1}^{N} \int_{\Omega_d} H_{n+2m}(\mathbf{x}^T \eta_k) S_{nj}(\eta_k) \frac{1}{\omega_d} d\omega_d(\eta_k) = J_{njm}(\mathbf{x}) \tag{14}$$

The variance is

$$\sigma_N^2(\mathbf{x}) = \frac{\sigma^2(\mathbf{x})}{N} \tag{15}$$

where $\sigma^2(\mathbf{x}) = \int_{\Omega_d} \left[\lambda_{nmd}\omega_d H_{n+2m}(\mathbf{x}^T \eta) S_{nj}(\eta) - J_{njm}(\mathbf{x}) \right]^2 \frac{1}{\omega_d} d\omega_d(\eta)$. Therefore $\hat{J}_{njm}(\mathbf{x})$ approximates $J_{njm}(\mathbf{x})$ with a rate $\sigma(\mathbf{x})/\sqrt{N}$. The difference between a radial basis and a harmonic basis is $\sigma(\mathbf{x})$. Let us average $\sigma(\mathbf{x})$ with respect to ϕ_d:

$$\|\sigma(\mathbf{x})\|^2 = \|J_{njm}\|^2 \left[\frac{\|J_{njm}\|^2 \omega_d}{\Gamma(n+2m+1)} - 1 \right] = \|J_{njm}\|^2 \alpha_{njm} \tag{16}$$

For a fixed $n + 2m = p$, $\|\sigma(\mathbf{x})\|^2$ is minimized at $n = 0$ (a radial element) and maximized at $m = 0$ (a harmonic element).

The same justification can be done for a general function $f \in L^2(\phi_d)$ with (6) and (8). A RA scheme is:

$$\hat{f}(\mathbf{x}) = \frac{\omega_d}{N} \sum_{k=1}^{N} g(\mathbf{x}^T \eta_k, \eta_k)$$

$m_N(\mathbf{x}) = f(\mathbf{x})$, $\sigma_N^2(\mathbf{x}) = \frac{\sigma^2(\mathbf{x})}{N}$, $\sigma^2(\mathbf{x}) = \int_{\Omega_d} \omega_d g^2(\mathbf{x}^T \eta, \eta) d\omega_d(\eta) - f^2(\mathbf{x})$ and $\|\sigma(\mathbf{x})\|^2 = \sum c_{njm}^2 \|J_{njm}\|^2 \alpha_{njm}$. Since α_{njm} is small when n is small, large when m is small and recall the distribution $p_{njm}(f)$ in Section 3, $\|\sigma\|^2 / \|f\|^2$ is small when f is smooth. Among these smooth functions, if f is angular smooth, $\|\sigma\|^2 / \|f\|^2$ is smaller than that if f is Laplacian smooth. The RMS error convergence rate $\frac{\|\sigma_N\|}{\|f\|} = \frac{\|\sigma\|}{\|f\|\sqrt{N}}$ is consequently smaller for f being angular smooth than for f being Laplacian smooth. But both rates are $O(N^{-\frac{1}{2}})$ no matter what class the underlying function belongs to. The difference is the constant which is related to the distribution of energy in f among the different modes of oscillations (angular or Laplacian). The radial and harmonic functions are two extremes.

6   THE CURSE OF DIMENSIONALITY IN RA

Generally, if N directions η_1, η_2, ..., η_N, on Ω_d drawn from any distribution $p(\eta)$ on the sphere Ω_d to approximate (6)

$$\hat{f}(\mathbf{x}) = \frac{1}{N} \sum_{k=1}^{N} \frac{g(\mathbf{x}^T \eta_k, \eta_k)}{p(\eta_k)}) \qquad (17)$$

$m_N = f(\mathbf{x})$ $\sigma_N^2 = \frac{\sigma^2}{N}$ where $\sigma^2(\mathbf{x}) = \int_{\Omega_d} \frac{1}{p(\eta)} g^2(\mathbf{x}^T \eta, \eta) d\omega_d(\eta) - f^2(\mathbf{x})$. And

$$\|\sigma(\mathbf{x})\|^2 = \int_{\Omega_d} \frac{1}{p(\eta)} \|g_\eta\|^2 d\omega_d(\eta) - \|f\|^2 = c_f \qquad (18)$$

Then

$$\|\hat{f}(\mathbf{x}) - f(\mathbf{x})\|^2 \leq \frac{\|\sigma(\mathbf{x})\|^2}{N} = \frac{c_f}{N} \qquad (19)$$

That is, $\hat{f}(\mathbf{x}) \to f(\mathbf{x})$ with a rate $O(N^{-\frac{1}{2}})$. Equation (19) shows that there is no curse of dimensionality if a ridge function approximation scheme (17) is used for $f(\mathbf{x})$. The same conclusion can be drawn when sigmoidal hidden unit function neural networks are applied to Barron's class of underlying function (Barron, 1991). But our function class here is the function class that can be represented by a continuous ridge function (6), which is a much larger function class than Barron's. Any function $f \in L^2(\phi_d)$ has a representation (6)(Section 4). Therefore, for any function $f \in L^2(\phi_d)$, there exists a node function $g(\mathbf{x}^T \eta, \eta)$ and related ridge function approximation scheme (17) to approximate $f(\mathbf{x})$ with a rate $O(N^{-\frac{1}{2}})$, which has no curse of dimensionality. In other words, if we are allowed to choose a node function $g(\mathbf{x}^T \eta, \eta)$ according to the property of data, which is the characteristic of PPR, then ridge function approximation scheme can avoid the curse of dimensionality. That is a generalization of Barron's result that the curse of dimensionality goes away if certain types of node function (e.g., cos and σ) are considered.

The smoothness of a underlying function determines the size of the constant c_f. As shown in the previous section, if $p(\eta) = 1/\omega_d$ (i.e., uniformly distributed directions), then angular smooth functions have smaller c_f than Laplacian smooth functions do. Choosing different $p(\eta)$ does not change this conclusion. But a properly chosen $p(\eta)$ reduces c_f in general. If $f(\mathbf{x})$ is smooth enough, the node function $g(\mathbf{x}^T \eta, \eta)$ can be computed from the Radon transform $R_\eta f$ of f in the direction η which is defined as

$$R_\eta f(\mathbf{x}^T \eta = s) = \int_{R^{d-1}} f(\mathbf{x}^T \eta \eta + \mathbf{x}_{d-1} \eta_{d-1}) d\mathbf{x}_{d-1} \tag{20}$$

and we proved: $g(\mathbf{x}^T \eta, \eta) = \mathcal{F}^{-1}(F_\eta(t)|t|^{d-1})\,|_{t=\mathbf{x}^T \eta}$, where $F_\eta(t)$ is the Fourier transform of $R_\eta f(s)$ and $\mathcal{F}^{-1}$ denotes the inverse Fourier transform. In practice, learning $g(\mathbf{x}^T \eta, \eta)$ is usually replaced by a smoothing step which seeks a one dimensional function to fit $\mathbf{x}^T \eta$ best to the residual in this direction (Friedman and Stuetzle, 1981, Zhao and Atkeson, 1991).

7   CONCLUSION

As we showed, PPR works better on angular smooth function than on Laplacian smooth functions by discretizing a continuous ridge function representation. PPR can avoid the curse of dimensionality by learning node functions from data.

Acknowledgments

Support was provided under Air Force Office of Scientific Research grant AFOSR-89-0500. Support for CGA was provided by a National Science Foundation Presidential Young Investigator Award, an Alfred P. Sloan Research Fellowship, and the W. M. Keck Foundation Associate Professorship in Biomedical Engineering. Special thanks goes to Prof. Zhengfang Zhou and Prof. Peter Huber at Math Dept. in MIT, who provided useful discussions.

References

Barron, A. R. and Barron, R. L. (1988) "Statistical Learning Networks: A Unifying View." *Computing Science and Statistics: Proceedings of 20th Symposium on the Interface.* Ed Wegman, editor, Amer. Statist. Assoc., Washington, D. C., 192-203.

Barron, A. R. (1991) "Universal Approximation Bounds for Superpositions of A Sigmoidal Function". TR. 58. Dept. of Stat., Univ. of Illinois at Urbana-Champaign.

Donoho, D. L. and Johnstone, I. (1989). "Projection-based Approximation, and Duality with Kernel Methods". *Ann. Statist., 17, 58-106.*

Diaconis, P. and Shahshahani, M. (1984) "On Non-linear Functions of Linear Combinations", *SIAM J. Sci. Stat. Compt. 5, 175-191.*

Friedman, J. H. and Stuetzle, W. (1981) "Projection Pursuit Regression". *J. Amer. Stat. Assoc.*, 76, 817-823.

Huber, P. J. (1985) "Projection Pursuit (with discussion)", *Ann. Statist., 13, 435-475.*

Jones, L. (1987) "On A Conjecture of Huber Concerning the Convergence of Projection Pursuit Regression". *Ann. Statist., 15, 880-882.*

Muller, C. (1966), *Spherical Harmonics.* Lecture Notes in Mathematics, no.17.

Zhao, Y. and C. G. Atkeson (1991) "Projection Pursuit Learning", Proc. IJCNN-91-SEATTLE.

Neural Computing with Small Weights

Kai-Yeung Siu
Dept. of Electrical & Computer Engineering
University of California, Irvine
Irvine, CA 92717

Jehoshua Bruck
IBM Research Division
Almaden Research Center
San Jose, CA 95120-6099

Abstract

An important issue in neural computation is the dynamic range of weights in the neural networks. Many experimental results on learning indicate that the weights in the networks can grow prohibitively large with the size of the inputs. Here we address this issue by studying the tradeoffs between the depth and the size of weights in polynomial-size networks of linear threshold elements (LTEs). We show that there is an efficient way of simulating a network of LTEs with large weights by a network of LTEs with small weights. In particular, we prove that every depth-d, polynomial-size network of LTEs with *exponentially large* integer weights can be simulated by a depth-$(2d + 1)$, polynomial-size network of LTEs with *polynomially bounded* integer weights. To prove these results, we use tools from harmonic analysis of Boolean functions. Our technique is quite general, it provides insights to some other problems. For example, we are able to improve the best known results on the depth of a network of linear threshold elements that computes the $COMPARISON$, SUM and $PRODUCT$ of two n-bits numbers, and the $MAXIMUM$ and the $SORTING$ of n n-bit numbers.

1 Introduction

The motivation for this work comes from the area of neural networks, where a linear threshold element is the basic processing element. Many experimental results on learning have indicated that the magnitudes of the coefficients in the threshold elements grow very fast with the size of the inputs and therefore limit the practical use of the network. One natural question to ask is the following: How limited is the computational power of the network if we restrict ourselves to threshold elements with only "small" growth in the coefficients? We answer this question by showing that we can trade-off an exponential growth with a polynomial growth in the magnitudes of coefficients by increasing the depth of the network by a factor of almost two and a polynomial growth in the size.

Linear Threshold Functions: A linear threshold function $f(X)$ is a Boolean function such that

$$f(X) = sgn(F(X)) = \left\{ \begin{array}{rl} 1 & \text{if } F(X) > 0 \\ -1 & \text{if } F(X) < 0 \end{array} \right.$$

where

$$F(X) = \sum_{i=1}^{n} w_i \cdot x_i + w_0$$

Throughout this paper, a *Boolean function* will be defined as $f : \{1, -1\}^n \rightarrow \{1, -1\}$; namely, 0 and 1 are represented by 1 and -1, respectively. Without loss of generality, we can assume $F(X) \neq 0$ for all $X \in \{1, -1\}^n$. The coefficients w_i are commonly referred to as the *weights* of the threshold function. We denote the class of all linear threshold functions by LT_1.

$\widehat{LT}_1$ **functions:** In this paper, we shall study a subclass of LT_1 which we denote by $\widehat{LT}_1$. Each function $f(X) = sgn(\sum_{i=1}^{n} w_i \cdot x_i + w_0)$ in $\widehat{LT}_1$ is characterized by the property that the weights w_i are integers and bounded by a polynomial in n, i.e. $|w_i| \leq n^c$ for some constant $c > 0$.

Threshold Circuits: A *threshold circuit* [5, 10] is a Boolean network in which every gate computes an $\widehat{LT}_1$ function. The *size* of a threshold circuit is the number of $\widehat{LT}_1$ elements in the circuit. Let $\widehat{LT}_k$ denote the class of threshold circuits of *depth k* with the *size bounded by a polynomial* in the number of inputs. We define LT_k similarly except that we allow each gate in LT_k to compute an LT_1 function.

Although the definition of (LT_1) linear threshold function allows the weights to be real numbers, it is known [12] that we can replace each of the real weights by integers of $O(n \log n)$ bits, where n is the number of input Boolean variables. So in the rest of the paper, we shall assume without loss of generality that all weights are integers. However, this still allows the magnitudes of the weights to increase exponentially fast with the size of the inputs. It is natural to ask if this is necessary. In other words, is there a linear threshold function that must require exponentially large weights? Since there are $2^{\Omega(n^2)}$ linear threshold functions in n variables [8, 14, 15], there exists at least one which requires $\Omega(n^2)$ bits to specify the weights. By the pigeonhole principle, at least one weight of such a function must need $\Omega(n)$ bits, and thus is exponentially large in magnitude. i.e.

$$\widehat{LT}_1 \subsetneq LT_1$$

The above result was proved in [9] using a different method by explicitly constructing an LT_1 function and proving that it is not in $\widehat{LT}_1$. In the following section, we shall show that the $COMPARISON$ function (to be defined later) also requires exponentially large weights. We will refer to this function later on in the proof of our main results. **Main Results:** The fact that we can simulate a linear threshold function with exponentially large weights in a 'constant' number of layers of elements with 'small' weights follows from the results in [3] and [11]. Their results showed that the sum of n n-bit numbers is computable in a constant number of layers of 'counting' gates, which in turn can be simulated by a constant number of layers of threshold elements with 'small' weights. However, it was not explicitly stated how many layers are needed in each step of their construction and direct application of their results would yield a constant such as 13. In this paper, we shall reduce the constant to 3 by giving a more 'depth'-efficient algorithm and by using harmonic analysis of Boolean functions [1, 2, 6]. We then generalize this result to higher depth circuits and show how to simulate a threshold circuit of depth-d and exponentially large weights in a depth-$(2d + 1)$ threshold circuit of 'small' weights, $i.e.$ $LT_d \subseteq \widehat{LT}_{2d+1}$.

As another application of harmonic analysis, we also show that the $COMPARISON$ and $ADDITION$ of two n-bit numbers is computable with only two layers of elements with 'small' weights, while it was only known to be computable in 3 layers [5]. We also indicate how our 'depth'-efficient algorithm can be applied to show that the product of two n-bit numbers can be computed in $\widehat{LT}_4$. In addition, we show that the $MAXIMUM$ and $SORTING$ of n n-bit numbers can be computed in $\widehat{LT}_3$ and $\widehat{LT}_4$, respectively.

2   Main Results

Definition: Let $X = (x_1, \ldots, x_n)$, $Y = (y_1, \ldots, y_n) \in \{1, -1\}^n$. We consider X and Y as two n-bit numbers representing $\sum_{i=1}^{n} x_i \cdot 2^i$ and $\sum_{i=1}^{n} y_i \cdot 2^i$, respectively.

The COMPARISON function is defined as

$$C(X, Y) = 1 \text{ iff } X \geq Y$$

In other words,

$$C(X, Y) = sgn\{\sum_{i=1}^{n} 2^i(x_i - y_i) + 1\}$$

Lemma 1

$$COMPARISON \notin \widehat{LT}_1$$

On the other hand, using harmonic analysis [2], we can show the following:

Lemma 2

$$COMPARISON \in \widehat{LT}_2$$

Spectral representation of Boolean functions: Recently, harmonic analysis has been found to be a powerful tool in studying the *computational complexity* of Boolean functions [1, 2, 7]. The idea is that every Boolean function $f : \{1, -1\}^n \to \{1, -1\}$ can be represented as a polynomial over the field of rational numbers as follows:

$$f(X) = \sum_{\alpha \in \{0,1\}^n} a_\alpha X^\alpha$$

where $X^\alpha = x_1^{\alpha_1} x_2^{\alpha_2} \dots x_n^{\alpha_n}$.

Such representation is unique and the coefficients of the polynomial, $\{a_\alpha | \alpha \in \{0,1\}^n\}$, are called the *spectral coefficients* of f.

We shall define the L_1 *spectral norm* of f to be

$$\|f\| = \sum_{\alpha \in \{0,1\}^n} |a_\alpha|.$$

The proof of Lemma 2 is based on the spectral techniques developed in [2]. Using probabilistic arguments, it was proved in [2] that if a Boolean function has L_1 spectral norm which is polynomially bounded, then the function is computable in $\widehat{LT}_2$. We observe (together with Noga Alon) that the techniques in [2] can be generalized to show that any Boolean function with polynomially bounded L_1 spectral norm can even be closely *approximated by a sparse polynomial*. This observation is crucial when we extend our result from a single element to networks of elements with large weights.

Lemma 3 *Let $f(X) : \{1,-1\}^n \to \{1,-1\}$ such that $\|f\| \leq n^c$ for some c. Then for any $k > 0$, there exists a sparse polynomial*

$$F(X) = \frac{1}{N} \sum_{\alpha \in S} w_\alpha X^\alpha \text{ such that}$$

$$|F(X) - f(X)| \leq n^{-k},$$

where w_α and N are integers, $S \subset \{0,1\}^n$, the size of S, w_α and N are all bounded by a polynomial in n. Hence, $f(X) \in \widehat{LT}_2$.

As a consequence of this result, Lemma 2 follows since it can be shown that $COMPARISON$ has a polynomially bounded L_1 spectral norm.

Now we are ready to state our main results. Although most linear threshold functions require exponentially large weights, we can always simulate them by 3 layers of $\widehat{LT}_1$ elements.

Theorem 1

$$LT_1 \subsetneq \widehat{LT}_3$$

The result stated in Theorem 1 implies that a depth-d threshold circuit with exponentially large weights can be simulated by a depth-$3d$ threshold circuit with polynomially large weights. Using the result of Lemma 3, we can actually obtain a more depth-efficient simulation .

Theorem 2

$$LT_d \subseteq \widehat{LT}_{2d+1}$$

As another consequence of Lemma 3, we have the following :

Corollary 1 *Let $f_1(X), ..., f_m(X)$ be functions with polynomially bounded L_1 spectral norms, and $g(f_1(X), ..., f_m(X))$ be an $\widehat{LT}_1$ function with $f_i(X)$'s as inputs, i.e.*

$$g(f_1(X), ..., f_m(X)) = sgn(\sum_{i=1}^{m} w_i f_i(X) + w_0)$$

Then g can be expressed as a sign of a sparse polynomial in X with polynomially many number of monomial terms X^α's and polynomially bounded integer coefficients. Hence $g \in \widehat{LT}_2$.

If all LT_1 functions have polynomially bounded L_1 spectral norms, then it would follow that $LT_1 \subset \widehat{LT}_2$. However, even the simple MAJORITY function does not have a polynomially bounded L_1 spectral norm. We shall prove this fact via the following theorem. (As in Lemma 3, by a sparse polynomial we mean a polynomial with only polynomially many monomial terms X^α's).

Theorem 3 *The $\widehat{LT}_1$ function MAJORITY:*

$$sgn(\sum_{i=1}^{n} x_i)$$

cannot be approximated by a sparse polynomial with an error $o(n^{-1})$.

Other applications of the harmonic analysis techniques and the results of Lemma 3 yields the following theorems:

Theorem 4

Let x, y be two n-bit numbers. Then

$$ADDITION(x, y) \in \widehat{LT}_2$$

Theorem 5 *The product of two n-bit integers can be computed in $\widehat{LT}_4$.*

Theorem 6 *The MAXIMUM of n n-bit numbers can be computed in $\widehat{LT}_3$.*

Theorem 7 *The SORTING of n n-bit numbers can be computed in $\widehat{LT}_4$.*

3   Concluding Remarks

Our main result indicates that for networks of linear threshold elements, we can trade-off arbitrary real weights with polynomially bounded integer weights, at the expense of a polynomial increase in the size and a factor of almost two in the depth of the network. The proofs of the results in this paper can be found in [13]. We would like to mention that our results have recently been improved by Goldmann, Hastad and Razborov [4]. They showed that any polynomial-size depth-d network of linear threshold elements with arbitrary weights can be simulated by a polynomial-size depth-$(d+1)$ network with "small" (polynomially bounded integer) weights. While our construction can be made explicit, only the existence of the simulation result is proved in [4]; it is left as an open problem in [4] if there is an explicit construction of their results.

Acknowledgements

This work was done while Kai-Yeung Siu was a research student associate at IBM Almaden Research Center and was supported in part by the Joint Services Program at Stanford University (US Army, US Navy, US Air Force) under Contract DAAL03-88-C-0011, and the Department of the Navy (NAVELEX), NASA Headquarters, Center for Aeronautics and Space Information Sciences under Grant NAGW-419-S6.

References

[1] J. Bruck. Harmonic Analysis of Polynomial Threshold Functions. *SIAM Journal on Discrete Mathematics*, May 1990.

[2] J. Bruck and R. Smolensky. Polynomial Threshold Functions, AC^0 Functions and Spectral Norms. Technical Report RJ 7140, IBM Research, November 1989. Appeared in IEEE Symp. on Found. of Comp. Sci. October, 1990.

[3] A. K. Chandra, L. Stockmeyer, and U. Vishkin. Constant depth reducibility. *Siam J. Comput.*, 13:423–439, 1984.

[4] M. Goldmann, J. Hastad, and A. Razborov Majority Gates vs. General Weighted Threshold Gates. Unpublished Manuscript.

[5] A. Hajnal, W. Maass, P. Pudlak, M. Szegedy, and G. Turan. Threshold circuits of bounded depth. *IEEE Symp. Found. Comp. Sci.*, 28:99–110, 1987.

[6] R. J. Lechner. Harmonic analysis of switching functions. In A. Mukhopadhyay, editor, *Recent Development in Switching Theory*. Academic Press, 1971.

[7] N. Linial, Y. Mansour, and N. Nisan. Constant Depth Circuits, Fourier Transforms, and Learnability. *Proc. 30th IEEE Symp. Found. Comp. Sci.*, 1989.

[8] S. Muroga and I. Toda. Lower Bound of the Number of Threshold Functions. *IEEE Trans. on Electronic Computers*, EC 15, 1966.

[9] J. Myhill and W. H. Kautz. On the Size of Weights Required for Linear-Input Switching Functions. *IRE Trans. on Electronic Computers*, EC 10, 1961.

[10] I. Parberry and G. Schnitger. Parallel Computation with Threshold Functions . *Journal of Computer and System Sciences*, 36(3):278–302, 1988.

[11] N. Pippenger. The complexity of computations by networks. *IBM J. Res. Develop.*, 31(2), March 1987.

[12] P. Raghavan. Learning in Threshold Networks: A Computation Model and Applications. Technical Report RC 13859, IBM Research, July 1988.

[13] K.-Y. Siu and J. Bruck. On the Power of Threshold Circuits with Small Weights . *SIAM J. Discrete Math.*, 4(3):423–435, August 1991.

[14] D. R. Smith. Bounds on the Number of Threshold Functions. *IEEE Trans. on Electronic Computers*, EC 15, 1966.

[15] S. Yajima and T. Ibaraki. A Lower Bound on the Number of Threshold Functions. *IEEE Trans. on Electronic Computers*, EC 14, 1965.

A Simple Weight Decay Can Improve Generalization

Anders Krogh*
CONNECT, The Niels Bohr Institute
Blegdamsvej 17
DK-2100 Copenhagen, Denmark
krogh@cse.ucsc.edu

John A. Hertz
Nordita
Blegdamsvej 17
DK-2100 Copenhagen, Denmark
hertz@nordita.dk

Abstract

It has been observed in numerical simulations that a weight decay can improve generalization in a feed-forward neural network. This paper explains why. It is proven that a weight decay has two effects in a linear network. First, it suppresses any irrelevant components of the weight vector by choosing the smallest vector that solves the learning problem. Second, if the size is chosen right, a weight decay can suppress some of the effects of static noise on the targets, which improves generalization quite a lot. It is then shown how to extend these results to networks with hidden layers and non-linear units. Finally the theory is confirmed by some numerical simulations using the data from NetTalk.

1 INTRODUCTION

Many recent studies have shown that the generalization ability of a neural network (or any other 'learning machine') depends on a balance between the information in the training examples and the complexity of the network, see for instance [1,2,3]. Bad generalization occurs if the information does not match the complexity, *e.g.* if the network is very complex and there is little information in the training set. In this last instance the network will be over-fitting the data, and the opposite situation corresponds to under-fitting.

---

*Present address: Computer and Information Sciences, Univ. of California Santa Cruz, Santa Cruz, CA 95064.

Often the number of free parameters, *i.e.* the number of weights and thresholds, is used as a measure of the network complexity, and algorithms have been developed, which minimizes the number of weights while still keeping the error on the training examples small [4,5,6]. This minimization of the number of free parameters is not always what is needed.

A different way to constrain a network, and thus decrease its complexity, is to limit the growth of the weights through some kind of weight decay. It should prevent the weights from growing too large unless it is really necessary. It can be realized by adding a term to the cost function that penalizes large weights,

$$E(\boldsymbol{w}) = E_0(\boldsymbol{w}) + \frac{1}{2}\lambda \sum_i w_i^2, \tag{1}$$

where E_0 is one's favorite error measure (usually the sum of squared errors), and λ is a parameter governing how strongly large weights are penalized. $\boldsymbol{w}$ is a vector containing all parameters of the network, it will be called the weight vector. If gradient descend is used for learning, the last term in the cost function leads to a new term $-\lambda w_i$ in the weight update:

$$\dot{w}_i \propto -\frac{\partial E_0}{\partial w_i} - \lambda w_i. \tag{2}$$

Here it is formulated in continuous time. If the gradient of E_0 (the 'force term') were not present this equation would lead to an exponential decay of the weights.

Obviously there are infinitely many possibilities for choosing other forms of the additional term in (1), but here we will concentrate on this simple form.

It has been known for a long time that a weight decay of this form can improve generalization [7], but until now not very widely recognized. The aim of this paper is to analyze this effect both theoretically and experimentally. Weight decay as a special kind of regularization is also discussed in [8,9].

2 FEED-FORWARD NETWORKS

A feed-forward neural network implements a function of the inputs that depends on the weight vector $\boldsymbol{w}$, it is called f_w. For simplicity it is assumed that there is only one output unit. When the input is $\boldsymbol{\xi}$ the output is $f_w(\boldsymbol{\xi})$. Note that the input vector is a vector in the N-dimensional input space, whereas the weight vector is a vector in the weight space which has a different dimension W.

The aim of the learning is not only to learn the examples, but to learn the underlying function that produces the targets for the learning process. First, we assume that this *target function* can actually be implemented by the network. This means there exists a weight vector $\boldsymbol{u}$ such that the target function is equal to f_u. The network with parameters $\boldsymbol{u}$ is often called the *teacher*, because from input vectors it can produce the right targets. The sum of squared errors is

$$E_0(\boldsymbol{w}) = \frac{1}{2}\sum_{\mu=1}^{p}[f_u(\boldsymbol{\xi}^\mu) - f_w(\boldsymbol{\xi}^\mu)]^2, \tag{3}$$

where p is the number of training patterns. The learning equation (2) can then be written

$$\dot{w}_i \propto \sum_\mu [f_u(\boldsymbol{\xi}^\mu) - f_w(\boldsymbol{\xi}^\mu)] \frac{\partial f_w(\boldsymbol{\xi})}{\partial w_i} - \lambda w_i. \tag{4}$$

Now the idea is to expand this around the solution $\boldsymbol{u}$, but first the linear case will be analyzed in some detail.

3   THE LINEAR PERCEPTRON

The simplest kind of 'network' is the linear perceptron characterized by

$$f_w(\boldsymbol{\xi}) = N^{-1/2} \sum_i w_i \xi_i \tag{5}$$

where the $N^{-1/2}$ is just a convenient normalization factor. Here the dimension of the weight space (W) is the same as the dimension of the input space (N).

The learning equation then takes the simple form

$$\dot{w}_i \propto \sum_\mu N^{-1} \sum_j [u_j - w_j] \xi_j^\mu \xi_i^\mu - \lambda w_i. \tag{6}$$

Defining

$$v_i \equiv u_i - w_i \tag{7}$$

and

$$A_{ij} = N^{-1} \sum_\mu \xi_i^\mu \xi_j^\mu \tag{8}$$

it becomes

$$\dot{v}_i \propto -\sum_j A_{ij} v_j + \lambda(u_i - v_i). \tag{9}$$

Transforming this equation to the basis where $\mathbf{A}$ is diagonal yields

$$\dot{v}_r \propto -(A_r + \lambda)v_r + \lambda u_r, \tag{10}$$

where A_r are the eigenvalues of $\mathbf{A}$, and a subscript r indicates transformation to this basis. The generalization error is defined as the error averaged over the distribution of input vectors

$$F = \langle [f_u(\boldsymbol{\xi}) - f_w(\boldsymbol{\xi})]^2 \rangle_\xi = \langle N^{-1}(\sum_i v_i \xi_i)^2 \rangle_\xi = N^{-1} \sum_{ij} v_i v_j \langle \xi_i \xi_j \rangle_\xi$$

$$= N^{-1} \sum_i v_i^2. \tag{11}$$

Here it is assumed that $\langle \xi_i \xi_j \rangle_\xi = \delta_{ij}$. The generalization error F is thus proportional to $|\boldsymbol{v}|^2$, which is also quite natural.

The eigenvalues of the covariance matrix $\mathbf{A}$ are non-negative, and its rank can easily be shown to be less than or equal to p. It is also easily seen that all eigenvectors belonging to eigenvalues larger than 0 lies in the subspace of weight space spanned by the input patterns $\boldsymbol{\xi}^1, \ldots, \boldsymbol{\xi}^p$. This subspace, called the pattern subspace, will be denoted V_p, and the orthogonal subspace is denoted by $V_p^\perp$. When there are sufficiently many examples they span the whole space, and there will be no zero eigenvalues. This can only happen for $p \geq N$.

When $\lambda = 0$ the solution to (10) inside V_p is just a simple exponential decay to $v_r = 0$. Outside the pattern subspace $A_r = 0$, and the corresponding part of v_r will be constant. Any weight vector which has the same projection onto the pattern subspace as $\boldsymbol{u}$ gives a learning error 0. One can think of this as a 'valley' in the error surface given by $\boldsymbol{u} + V_p^\perp$.

The training set contains no information that can help us choose between all these solutions to the learning problem. When learning with a weight decay $\lambda > 0$, the constant part in $V_p^\perp$ will decay to zero asymptotically (as $e^{-\lambda t}$, where t is the time). An infinitesimal weight decay will therefore choose the solution with the smallest norm out of all the solutions in the valley described above. This solution can be shown to be the optimal one on average.

4   LEARNING WITH AN UNRELIABLE TEACHER

Random errors made by the teacher can be modeled by adding a random term η to the targets:

$$f_u(\boldsymbol{\xi}^\mu) \longrightarrow f_u(\boldsymbol{\xi}^\mu) + \eta^\mu. \tag{12}$$

The variance of η is called σ^2, and it is assumed to have zero mean. Note that these targets are not exactly realizable by the network (for $\alpha > 0$), and therefore this is a simple model for studying learning of an unrealizable function.

With this noise the learning equation (2) becomes

$$\dot{w}_i \propto \sum_\mu (N^{-1} \sum_j v_j \xi_j^\mu + N^{-1/2} \eta^\mu) \xi_i^\mu - \lambda w_i. \tag{13}$$

Transforming it to the basis where $\mathbf{A}$ is diagonal as before,

$$\dot{v}_r \propto -(A_r + \lambda) v_r + \lambda u_r - N^{-1/2} \sum_\mu \eta^\mu \xi_r^\mu. \tag{14}$$

The asymptotic solution to this equation is

$$v_r = \frac{\lambda u_r - N^{-1/2} \sum_\mu \eta^\mu \xi_r^\mu}{\lambda + A_r}. \tag{15}$$

The contribution to the generalization error is the square of this summed over all r. If averaged over the noise (shown by the bar) it becomes for each r

$$F_r = \overline{v_r^2} = \frac{\lambda^2 u_r^2 + N^{-1} \sum_\mu (\xi_r^\mu)^2 \overline{(\eta^\mu)^2}}{(\lambda + A_r)^2} = \frac{\lambda^2 u_r^2 + A_r \sigma^2}{(\lambda + A_r)^2}. \tag{16}$$

The last expression has a minimum in λ, which can be found by putting the derivative with respect to λ equal to zero, $\lambda_{\text{optimal}}^r = \sigma^2 / u_r^2$. Remarkably it depends only

Figure 1: Generalization error as a function of $\alpha = p/N$. The full line is for $\lambda = \sigma^2 = 0.2$, and the dashed line for $\lambda = 0$. The dotted line is the generalization error with no noise and $\lambda = 0$.

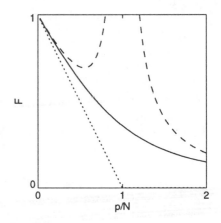

on $\boldsymbol{u}$ and the variance of the noise, and *not* on $\mathbf{A}$. If it is assumed that $\boldsymbol{u}$ is random (16) can be averaged over $\boldsymbol{u}$. This yields an optimal λ independent of r,

$$\lambda_{\text{optimal}} = \frac{\sigma^2}{u^2}, \qquad (17)$$

where u^2 is the average of $N^{-1}|\boldsymbol{u}|^2$.

In this case the weight decay to some extent prevents the network from fitting the noise.

From equation (14) one can see that the noise is projected onto the pattern subspace. Therefore the contribution to the generalization error from $V_p^{\perp}$ is the same as before, and this contribution is on average minimized by a weight decay of any size.

Equation (17) was derived in [10] in the context of a particular eigenvalue spectrum. Figure fig. 1 shows the dramatic improvement in generalization error when the optimal weight decay is used in this case. The present treatment shows that (17) is independent of the spectrum of $\mathbf{A}$.

We conclude that a weight decay has two positive effects on generalization in a linear network: 1) It suppresses any irrelevant components of the weight vector by choosing the smallest vector that solves the learning problem. 2) If the size is chosen right, it can suppress some of the effect of static noise on the targets.

5   NON-LINEAR NETWORKS

It is not possible to analyze a general non-linear network exactly, as done above for the linear case. By a local linearization, it is however, possible to draw some interesting conclusions from the results in the previous section.

Assume the function is realizable, $f = f_u$. Then learning corresponds to solving the p equations

$$f_w(\boldsymbol{\xi}^{\mu}) = f_u(\boldsymbol{\xi}^{\mu}) \qquad (18)$$

in W variables, where W is the number of weights. For $p < W$ these equations define a manifold in weight space of dimension at least $W - p$. Any point $\tilde{w}$ on this manifold gives a learning error of zero, and therefore (4) can be expanded around $\tilde{w}$. Putting $v = \tilde{w} - w$, expanding f_w in v, and using it in (4) yields

$$\dot{v}_i \;\; \propto \;\; -\sum_{\mu,j} \left(\frac{\partial f_w(\boldsymbol{\xi}^\mu)}{\partial w_j} \right) v_j \frac{\partial f_w(\boldsymbol{\xi}^\mu)}{\partial w_i} + \lambda(\tilde{w}_i - v_i)$$

$$= \;\; -\sum_j \mathcal{A}_{ij}(\tilde{w})v_j - \lambda v_i + \lambda \tilde{w}_i \qquad (19)$$

(The derivatives in this equation should be taken at $\tilde{w}$.)

The analogue of **A** is defined as

$$\mathcal{A}_{ij}(\tilde{w}) \equiv \sum_\mu \frac{\partial f_w(\boldsymbol{\xi}^\mu)}{\partial w_i} \frac{\partial f_w(\boldsymbol{\xi}^\mu)}{\partial w_j}. \qquad (20)$$

Since it is of outer product form (like **A**) its rank $R(\tilde{w}) \leq \min\{p, W\}$. Thus when $p < W$, $\mathcal{A}$ is *never* of full rank. The rank of $\mathcal{A}$ is of course equal to W minus the dimension of the manifold mentioned above.

From these simple observations one can argue that good generalization should *not* be expected for $p < W$. This is in accordance with other results (cf. [3]), and with current 'folk-lore'. The difference from the linear case is that the 'rain gutter' need not be (and most probably is not) linear, but curved in this case. There may in fact be other valleys or rain gutters disconnected from the one containing u. One can also see that if $\mathcal{A}$ has full rank, all points in the immediate neighborhood of $\tilde{w} = u$ give a learning error larger than 0, *i.e.* there is a simple minimum at u.

Assume that the learning finds one of these valleys. A small weight decay will pick out the point in the valley with the smallest norm among all the points in the valley. In general it can not be proven that picking that solution is the best strategy. But, at least from a philosophical point of view, it seems sensible, because it is (in a loose sense) the solution with the smallest complexity—the one that Ockham would probably have chosen.

The value of a weight decay is more evident if there are small errors in the targets. In that case one can go through exactly the same line of arguments as for the linear case to show that a weight decay can improve generalization, and even with the same optimal choice (17) of λ. This is strictly true only for small errors (where the linear approximation is valid).

6 NUMERICAL EXPERIMENTS

A weight decay has been tested on the NetTalk problem [11]. In the simulations back-propagation derived from the 'entropic error measure' [12] with a momentum term fixed at 0.8 was used. The network had 7×26 input units, 40 hidden units and 26 output units. In all about 8400 weights. It was trained on 400 to 5000 random words from the data base of around 20.000 words, and tested on a different set of 1000 random words. The training set and test set were independent from run to run.

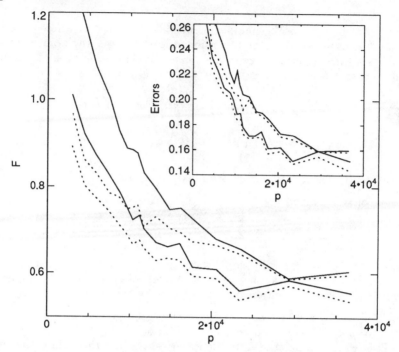

Figure 2: The top full line corresponds to the generalization error after 300 epochs (300 cycles through the training set) without a weight decay. The lower full line is with a weight decay. The top dotted line is the lowest error seen during learning without a weight decay, and the lower dotted with a weight decay. The size of the weight decay was $\lambda = 0.00008$.

Insert: Same figure except that the error rate is shown instead of the squared error. The error rate is the fraction of wrong phonemes when the phoneme vector with the smallest angle to the actual output is chosen, see [11].

Results are shown in fig. 2. There is a clear improvement in generalization error when weight decay is used. There is also an improvement in error rate (insert of fig. 2), but it is less pronounced in terms of relative improvement. Results shown here are for a weight decay of $\lambda = 0.00008$. The values 0.00005 and 0.0001 was also tried and gave basically the same curves.

7   CONCLUSION

It was shown how a weight decay can improve generalization in two ways: 1) It suppresses any irrelevant components of the weight vector by choosing the smallest vector that solves the learning problem. 2) If the size is chosen right, a weight decay can suppress some of the effect of static noise on the targets. Static noise on the targets can be viewed as a model of learning an unrealizable function. The analysis assumed that the network could be expanded around an optimal weight vector, and therefore it is strictly only valid in a little neighborhood around that vector.

The improvement from a weight decay was also tested by simulations. For the NetTalk data it was shown that a weight decay can decrease the generalization error (squared error) and also, although less significantly, the actual mistake rate of the network when the phoneme closest to the output is chosen.

Acknowledgements

AK acknowledges support from the Danish Natural Science Council and the Danish Technical Research Council through the Computational Neural Network Center (CONNECT).

References

[1] D.B. Schwartz, V.K. Samalam, S.A. Solla, and J.S. Denker. Exhaustive learning. *Neural Computation*, 2:371–382, 1990.

[2] N. Tishby, E. Levin, and S.A. Solla. Consistent inference of probabilities in layered networks: predictions and generalization. In *International Joint Conference on Neural Networks*, pages 403–410, (Washington 1989), IEEE, New York, 1989.

[3] E.B. Baum and D. Haussler. What size net gives valid generalization? *Neural Computation*, 1:151–160, 1989.

[4] Y. Le Cun, J.S. Denker, and S.A. Solla. Optimal brain damage. In D.S. Touretzky, editor, *Advances in Neural Information Processing Systems*, pages 598–605, (Denver 1989), Morgan Kaufmann, San Mateo, 1990.

[5] H.H. Thodberg. Improving generalization of neural networks through pruning. *International Journal of Neural Systems*, 1:317–326, 1990.

[6] D.H. Weigend, D.E. Rumelhart, and B.A. Huberman. Generalization by weight-elimination with application to forecasting. In R.P. Lippmann et al, editors, *Advances in Neural Information Processing Systems*, page 875–882, (Denver 1989), Morgan Kaufmann, San Mateo, 1991.

[7] G.E. Hinton. Learning translation invariant recognition in a massively parallel network. In G. Goos and J. Hartmanis, editors, *PARLE: Parallel Architectures and Languages Europe. Lecture Notes in Computer Science*, pages 1–13, Springer-Verlag, Berlin, 1987.

[8] J .Moody. Generalization, weight decay, and architecture selection for nonlinear learning systems. These proceedings.

[9] D. MacKay. A practical bayesian framework for backprop networks. These proceedings.

[10] A. Krogh and J.A. Hertz. Generalization in a Linear Perceptron in the Presence of Noise. To appear in *Journal of Physics A* 1992.

[11] T.J. Sejnowski and C.R. Rosenberg. Parallel networks that learn to pronounce english text. *Complex Systems*, 1:145–168, 1987.

[12] J.A. Hertz, A. Krogh, and R.G. Palmer. *Introduction to the Theory of Neural Computation*. Addison-Wesley, Redwood City, 1991.

Best-First Model Merging for
Dynamic Learning and Recognition

Stephen M. Omohundro
International Computer Science Institute
1947 Center Street, Suite 600
Berkeley, California 94704

Abstract

"Best-first model merging" is a general technique for dynamically choosing the structure of a neural or related architecture while avoiding overfitting. It is applicable to both learning and recognition tasks and often generalizes significantly better than fixed structures. We demonstrate the approach applied to the tasks of choosing radial basis functions for function learning, choosing local affine models for curve and constraint surface modelling, and choosing the structure of a balltree or bumptree to maximize efficiency of access.

1 TOWARD MORE COGNITIVE LEARNING

Standard backpropagation neural networks learn in a way which appears to be quite different from human learning. Viewed as a cognitive system, a standard network always maintains a complete model of its domain. This model is mostly wrong initially, but gets gradually better and better as data appears. The net deals with all data in much the same way and has no representation for the strength of evidence behind a certain conclusion. The network architecture is usually chosen before any data is seen and the processing is much the same in the early phases of learning as in the late phases.

Human and animal learning appears to proceed in quite a different manner. When an organism has not had many experiences in a domain of importance to it, each individual experience is critical. Rather than use such an experience to slightly modify the parameters of a global model, a better strategy is to remember the experience in detail. Early in learning, an organism doesn't know which features of an experience are important unless it has a strong prior knowledge of the domain. Without such prior knowledge,its best strategy is to generalize on the basis of a similarity measure to individual stored experiences. (Shepard, 1987) shows that there is a universal exponentially decaying form for this kind of similarity based generalization over a wide variety of sensory domains in several studied species. As experiences accumulate, the organism eventually gets enough data to reliably validate models from complex classes. At this point the animal need no longer remember individual experiences, but rather only the discovered generalities (eg. as rules). With such a strategy, it is possible for a system to maintain a measure of confidence in it its predictions while building ever more complex models of its environment.

Systems based on these two types of learning have also appeared in the neural network, statistics and machine learning communities. In the learning literature one finds both "table-lookup" or "memory-based" methods and "parameter-fitting" methods. In statistics the distinction is made between "non-parametric" and "parametric" methods. Table-lookup methods work by storing examples and generalize to new situations on the basis of similarity to the old ones. Such methods are capable of one-shot learning and have a measure of the applicability of their knowledge to new situations but are limited in their generalization capability. Parameter fitting models choose the parameters of a predetermined model to best fit a set of examples. They usually take longer to train and are susceptible to computational difficulties such as local maxima but can potentially generalize better by extending the influence of examples over the whole space. Aside from computational difficulties, their fundamental problem is overfitting, ie. having insufficient data to validate a particular parameter setting as useful for generalization.

2 OVERFITTING IN LEARNING AND RECOGNITION

There have been many recent results (eg. based on the Vapnik-Chervonenkis dimension) which identify the number of examples needed to validate choices made from specific parametric model families. We would like a learning system to be able to induce extremely complex models of the world but we don't want to have to present it with the enormous amount of data needed to validate such a model unless it is really needed. (Vapnik, 1982) proposes a technique for avoiding overfitting while allowing models of arbitrary complexity. The idea is to start with a nested familty of model spaces, whose members contain ever more complex models. When the system has only a small amount of data it can only validate models in in the smaller model classes. As more data arrives, however, the more complex classes may be considered. If at any point a fit is found to within desired tolerances, however, only the amount of data needed by the smallest class containing the chosen model is needed. Thus there is the potential for choosing complex models without penalizing situations in which the model is simple. The model merging approach may be viewed in these terms except that instead of a single nested family, there is a widely branching tree of model spaces.

Like learning, recognition processes (visual, auditory, etc.) aim at constructing models from data. As such they are subject to the same considerations regarding overfitting. Figure 1 shows a perceptual example where a simpler model (a single segment) is perceptually chosen to explain the data (4 almost collinear dots) than a more complex model (two segments) which fits the data better. An intuitive explanations is that if the dots were generated by two segments, it would be an amazing coincidence that they are almost collinear, if it were generated by one, that fact is easily explained. Many of the Gestalt phenomena can be considered in the same terms. Many of the processes used in recognition (eg. segmentation, grouping) have direct analogs in learning and vice versa.

Figure 1: An example of Occam's razor in recognition.

There has been much recent interest in the network community in Bayesian methods for model selection while avoiding overfitting (eg. Buntine and Weigend, 1992 and MacKay 1992). Learning and recognition fit naturally together in a Bayesian framework. The Bayesian approach makes explicit the need for a prior distribution. The posterior distribution generated by learning becomes the prior distribution for recognition. The model merging process described in this paper is applicable to both phases and the knowledge representation it suggests may be used for both processes as well.

There are at least three properties of the world that may be encoded in a prior distribution and have a dramatic effect on learning and recognition and are essential to the model merging approach. The *continuity prior* is that the world is geometric and unless there is contrary data a system should prefer continuous models over discontinuous ones. This prior leads to a wide variety of what may be called "geometric learning algorithms" (Omohundro, 1990). The *sparseness prior* is that the world is sparsely interacting. This says that probable models naturally decompose into components which only directly affect one another in a sparse manner. The primary origin of this prior is that physical objects usually only directly affect nearby objects in space and time. This prior is responsible for the success of representations such as Markov random fields and Bayesian networks which encode conditional independence relations. Even if the individual models consist of sparsely interacting components, it still might be that the data we receive for learning or recognition depends in an intricate way on all components. The *locality prior* prefers models in which the data decomposes into components which are directly affected by only a small number of model components. For example, in the learning setting only a small portion of the knowledge base will be relevant to any specific situation. In the recognition setting, an individual pixel is determined by only a small number of objects in the scene. In geometric settings, a localized representation allows only a small number of model parameters to affect any individual prediction.

3 MODEL MERGING

Based on the above considerations, an ideal learning or recognition system should model the world using a collection of sparsely connected, smoothly parameterized, localized models. This is an apt description of many of the neural network models currently in use. Bayesian methods provide an optimal means for induction with such a choice of prior over models but are computationally intractable in complex situations. We would therefore like to develop heuristic approaches which approximate the Bayesian solution and avoid overfitting. Based on the idealization of animal learning in the first section, we would like is a system which smoothly moves between a memory-based regime in which the models are the data into ever more complex parameterized models. Because of the locality prior, model components only affect a subset of the data. We can therefore choose the complexity of components which are relevant to different portions of the data space according to the data which has been received there. This allows for reliably validated models of extremely high complexity in some regions of the space while other portions are modeled with low complexity. If only a small number of examples have been seen in some region, these are simply remembered and generalization is based on similarity. As more data arrives, if regularities are found and there is enough data present to justify them, more complex parameterized models are incorporated.

There are many possible approaches to implementing such a strategy. We have investigated a particular heuristic which can be made computationally efficient and appears to work well in a variety of areas. The *best-first model merging* approach is applicable in a variety of situations in which complex models are constructed by combining simple ones. The idea is to improve a complex model by replacing two of its component models by a single model. This "merged" model may be in the same family as the original components. More interestingly, because the combined data from the merged components is used in determining the parameters of the merged model, it may come from a larger parameterized class. The critical idea is to never allow the system to hypothesize a model which is more complex than can be justified by the data it is based on. The "best-first" aspect is to always choose to merge the pair of models which decrease the likelihood of the data the least. The merging may be stopped according to a variety of criteria which are now applied to individual model components rather than the entire model. Examples of such criteria are those based on cross-validation, Bayesian Occam factors, VC bounds, etc. In experiments in a variety of domains, this approach does an excellent job of discovering regularities and allocating modelling resources efficiently.

3 MODEL MERGING VS. K-MEANS FOR RBF'S

Our first example is the problem of choosing centers in radial basis function networks for approximating functions. In the simplest approach, a radial basis function (eg. a Gaussian) is located at each training input location. The induced function is a linear combination of these basis functions which minimizes the mean square error of the training examples. Better models may be obtained by using fewer basis functions than data points. Most work on choosing the centers of these functions uses a clustering technique such as k-means (eg. Moody and Darken, 1989). This is reasonable because it puts the representational power of the model in the regions of highest density where errors are more critical. It ignores the structure of the modelled function, however. The model merging approach starts with a basis function at each training point and successively merges pairs which increase the training error the least. We compared this approach with the k-means approach in a variety of circumstances.

Figure 2 shows an example where the function on the plane to be learned is a sigmoid in x centered at 0 and is constant in y. Thus the function varies most along the y axis. The data is drawn from a Gaussian distribution which is centered at (-.5,0). 21 training samples were drawn from this distribution and from these a radial basis function network with 6 Gaussian basis functions was learned. The X's in the figure show the centers chosen by k-means. As expected, they are clustered near the center fo the Gaussian source distribution. The triangles show the centers chosen by best-first model merging. While there is some tendency to focus on the source center, there is also a tendency to represent the region where the modelled function varies the most. The training error is over 10 times less with model merging and the test error on an independent test set is about 3 times lower. These results were typical in variety of test runs. This simple example shows one way in which underlying structure is naturally discovered by the merging technique.

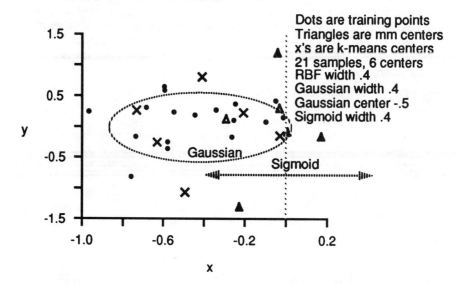

Figure 2: Radial basis function centers in two dimensions chosen by model merging and by k-means. The dots show the 21 training samples. The x's are the centers chosen by k-means, the triangles by model merging. The training error was .008098 for k-means and .000604 for model merging. The test error was .012463 for k-means and .004638 for model merging.

4   APPROXIMATING CURVES AND SURFACES

As a second intuitive example, consider the problem of modelling a curve in the plane by a combination of straight line segments. The error function may be taken as the mean square error over each curve point to the nearest segment point. A merging step in this case consists of replacing two segments by a single segment. We always choose that pair such that the merged segment increases the error the least. Figure 3 shows the approximations generated by this strategy. It does an excellent job at identifying the essentially linear portions of the curve and puts the boundaries between component models at the "corners". The corresponding "top-down" approach would start with a single segment and repeatedly split it. This approach sometimes has to make decisions too early and often misses the corners in the curve. While not shown in the figure, as repeated mergings take place, more data is available for each segment. This would allow us to use more complex models than linear segments such as Bezier curves. It is possible to reliably induce a representation which is linear in some portions and higher order in others. Such models potentially have many parameters and would be subject to overfitting if they were learned directly rather than by going through merge steps.

Exactly the same strategy may be applied to modelling higher-dimensional constraint surfaces by hyperplanes or functions by piecewise linear portions. The model merging approach naturally complements the efficient mapping and constraint surface representations described in (Omohundro, 1991) based on bumptrees.

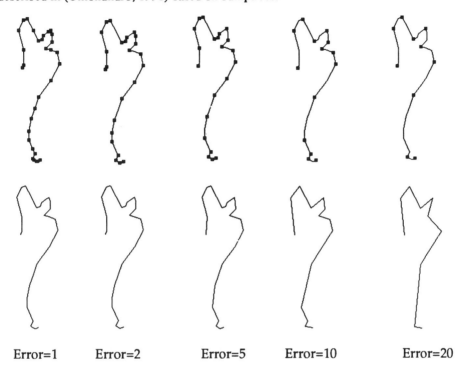

| Error=1 | Error=2 | Error=5 | Error=10 | Error=20 |

Figure 3: Approximation of a curve by best-first merging of segment models. The top row shows the endpoints chosen by the algorithm at various levels of allowed error. The bottom row shows the corresponding approximation to the curve.

Notice, in this example, that we need only consider merging neighboring segments as the increased error in merging non-adjoining segments would be too great. This imposes a locality on the problem which allows for extremely efficient computation. The idea is to maintain a priority queue with all potential merges on it ordered by the increase in error caused by the merge. This consists of only the neighboring pairs (of which there are n-1 if there are n segments). The top pair on the queue is removed and the merge operation it represents is performed if it doesn't violate the stopping critera. The other potential merge pairs which incorporated the merged segments must be removed from the queue and the new possible mergings with the generated segment must be inserted (alternatively, nothing need be removed and each pair is checked for viability when it reaches the top of the queue). The neighborhood structure allows each of the operations to be performed quickly with the appropriate data structures and the entire merging process takes a time which is linear (or linear times logarithmic) in the number of component models. Complex time-varying curves may easily be processed in real time on typical workstations. In higher dimensions, hierarchical geometric data structures (as in Omohundro, 1987, 1990) allow a similar reduction in computation based on locality.

5 BALLTREE CONSTRUCTION

The model merging approach is applicable to a wide variety of adaptive structures. The "balltree" structure described in (Omohundro, 1989) provides efficient access to regions in geometric spaces. It consists of a nested hierarchy of hyper-balls surrounding given leaf balls and efficiently supports querries which test for intersection, inclusion, or nearness to a leaf ball. The balltree construction algorithm itself provides an example of a best-first merge approach in a higher dimensional space. To determine the best hierarchy we can merge the leaf balls pairwise in such a way that the total volume of all the merged regions is as small as possible. The figure compares the quality of balltrees constructed using best-first merging to those constructed using top-down and incremental algorithms. As in other domains, the top-down approach has to make major decisions too early and often makes suboptimal choices. The merging approach only makes global decisions after many local decisions which adapt well to the structure.

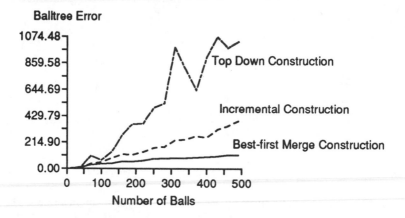

Figure 4: Balltree error as a function of number of balls for the top-down, incremental, and best-first merging construction methods. Leaf balls have uniformly distributed centers in 5 dimensions with radii uniformly distributed less than .1.

6 CONCLUSION

We have described a simple but powerful heuristic for dynamically building models for both learning and recognition which constructs complex models that adapt well to the underlying structure. We presented three different examples which only begin to touch on the possibilities. To hint at the broad applicability, we will briefly describe several other applications we are currently examining.

In (Omohundro, 1991) we presented an efficient structure for modelling mappings based on a collection of local mapping models which were combined according to a partition of unity formed by "influence functions" associated with each model. This representation is very flexible and can be made computationally efficient. While in the experiments of that paper, the local models were affine functions (constant plus linear), they may be chosen from any desired class. The model merging approach builds such a mapping representation by successively merging models and replacing them with a new model whose influence function extends over the range of the two original influence functions. Because it is based on more data, the new model can be chosen from a larger complexity class of functions than the originals.

One of the most fundamental inductive tasks is density estimation, ie. estimating a probablity distribution from samples drawn from it. A powerful standard technique is adaptvie kernel estimation in which a normalized Gaussian (or other kernel) is placed at each sample point with a width determined by the local sample density (Devroye and Gyorfi, 1985). Model merging can be applied to improve the generalization performance of this approach by choosing successively more complex component densities once enough data has accumulated by merging. For example, consider a density supported on a curve in a high dimensional space. Initially the estimate will consist of radially-symmetric Gaussians at each sample point. After successive mergings, however, the one-dimensional linear structure can be discovered (and the Gaussian components be chosen from the larger class of extended Gaussians) and the generalization dramatically improved.

Other natural areas of application include inducing the structure of hidden Markov models, stochastic context-free grammars, Markov random fields, and Bayesian networks.

References

D. H. Ballard and C. M. Brown. *(1982) Computer Vision.* Englewood Cliffs, N. J: Prentice-Hall.

W. L. Buntine and A. S. Weigend. (1992) Bayesian Back-Propagation. To appear in: *Complex Systems.*

L. Devroye and L. Gyorfi. (1985) *Nonparametric Density Estimation: The L1 View*, New York: Wiley.

D. J. MacKay. (1992) A Practical Bayesian Framework for Backprop Networks. Caltech preprint.

J. Moody and C. Darken. (1989) Fast learning in networks of locally-tuned processing units. *Neural Computation*, 1, 281-294.

S. M. Omohundro. (1987) Efficient algorithms with neural network behavior. *Complex Systems* 1:273-347.

S. M. Omohundro. (1989) Five balltree construction algorithms. *International Computer Science Institute Technical Report* TR-89-063.

S. M. Omohundro. (1990) Geometric learning algorithms. *Physica D* 42:307-321.

S. M. Omohundro. (1991) Bumptrees for Efficient Function, Constraint, and Classification Learning. In Lippmann, Moody, and Touretzky, (eds.) *Advances in Neural Information Processing Systems 3*. San Mateo, CA: Morgan Kaufmann Publishers.

R. N. Shepard. (1987) Toward a universal law of generalization for psychological science. *Science.*

V. Vapnik. (1982) *Estimation of Dependences Based on Empirical Data*, New York: Springer-Verlag.

PART XIII

ARCHITECTURES AND ALGORITHMS

Rule Induction through Integrated Symbolic and Subsymbolic Processing

Clayton McMillan, Michael C. Mozer, Paul Smolensky
Department of Computer Science and
Institute of Cognitive Science
University of Colorado
Boulder, CO 80309–0430

Abstract

We describe a neural network, called *RuleNet*, that learns explicit, symbolic condition-action rules in a formal string manipulation domain. RuleNet discovers functional categories over elements of the domain, and, at various points during learning, extracts rules that operate on these categories. The rules are then injected back into RuleNet and training continues, in a process called *iterative projection*. By incorporating rules in this way, RuleNet exhibits enhanced learning and generalization performance over alternative neural net approaches. By integrating symbolic rule learning and subsymbolic category learning, RuleNet has capabilities that go beyond a purely symbolic system. We show how this architecture can be applied to the problem of case-role assignment in natural language processing, yielding a novel rule-based solution.

1 INTRODUCTION

We believe that neural networks are capable of more than pattern recognition; they can also perform higher cognitive tasks which are fundamentally rule-governed. Further we believe that they can perform higher cognitive tasks *better* if they incorporate rules rather than eliminate them. A number of well known cognitive models, particularly of language, have been criticized for going too far in eliminating rules in fundamentally rule-governed domains. We argue that with a suitable choice of high-level, rule-governed task, representation, processing architecture, and learning algorithm, neural networks can represent and learn rules involving higher-level categories while simultaneously learning those categories. The resulting networks can exhibit better learning and task performance than neural networks that do not incorporate rules, have capabilities that go beyond that of a purely symbolic rule-learning algorithm.

We describe an architecture, called *RuleNet*, which induces symbolic condition-action rules in a string mapping domain. In the following sections we describe this domain, the task and network architecture, simulations that demonstrate the potential for this approach, and finally, future directions of the research leading toward more general and complex domains.

2 DOMAIN

We are interested in domains that map input strings to output strings. A string consists of *n* *slots*, each containing a symbol. For example, the string **abcd** contains the symbol **c** in slot 3. The domains we have studied are intrinsically rule-based, meaning that the mapping function from input to output strings can be completely characterized by explicit, mutually exclusive condition-action rules. These rules are of the general form "*if certain symbols are present in the input then perform a certain mapping from the input slots to the output slots.*" The conditions do not operate directly on the input symbols, but rather on *categories* defined over the input symbols. Input symbols can belong to multiple categories. For example, the words **boy** and `girl` are instances of the higher level category **HUMAN**. We denote instances with lowercase bold font, and categories with uppercase bold font. It should be apparent from context whether a letter string refers to a single instance, such as **boy**, or a string of instances, such as **abcd**.

Three types of conditions are allowed: 1) a *simple* condition, which states that an instance of some category must be present in a particular slot of the input string, 2) a *conjunction* of two simple conditions, and 3) a *disjunction* of two simple conditions. A typical condition might be that an instance of the category **W** must be present in slot 1 of the input string and an instance of category **Y** must be present in slot 3.

The action performed by a rule produces an output string in which the content of each slot is either a fixed symbol or a function of a particular input slot, with the additional constraint that each input slot maps to at most one output slot. In the present work, this function of the input slots is the identity function. A typical action might be to switch the symbols in slots 1 and 2 of the input, replace slot 3 with the symbol **a**, and copy slot 4 of the input to the output string unchanged, e.g., **abcd** → **baad**.

We call rules of this general form *second-order categorical permutation (SCP) rules*. The number of rules grows exponentially with the length of the strings and the number of input symbols. An example of an SCP rule for strings of length four is:

if (*input$_1$* is an instance of **W** and *input$_3$* is an instance of **Y**) **then**
  (*output$_1$* = *input$_2$*, *output$_2$* = *input$_1$*, *output$_3$* = **a**, *output$_4$*=*input$_4$*)

where *input$_\alpha$* and *output$_\beta$* denote input slot α and output slot β, respectively. As a shorthand for this rule, we write [∧ **W_Y_** → **21a4**], where the square brackets indicate this is a rule, the "∧" denotes a conjunctive condition, and the "_" denotes a *wildcard* symbol. A disjunction is denoted by "∨".

This formal string manipulation task can be viewed as an abstraction of several interesting cognitive models in the connectionist literature, including case-role assignment (McClelland & Kawamoto, 1986), grapheme-phoneme mapping (Sejnowski & Rosenberg, 1987), and mapping verb stems to the past tense (Rumelhart & McClelland, 1986).

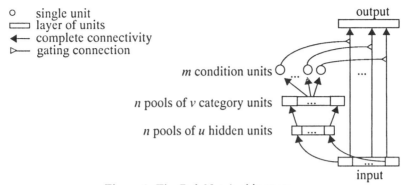

Figure 1: The RuleNet Architecture

3 TASK

RuleNet's task is to induce a compact set of rules that accurately characterizes a set of training examples. We generate training examples using a predefined rule base. The rules are over strings of length four and alphabets which are subsets of {**a**, **b**, **c**, **d**, **e**, **f**, **g**, **h**, **i**, **j**, **k**, **l**}. For example, the rule [v **Y_W_** →**4h21**] may be used to generate the exemplars:

$$\texttt{hedk} \rightarrow \texttt{kheh}, \texttt{cldk} \rightarrow \texttt{khlc}, \texttt{gbdj} \rightarrow \texttt{jhbg}, \texttt{gdbk} \rightarrow \texttt{khdg}$$

where category **W** consists of **a**, **b**, **c**, **d**, **i**, and category **Y** consists of **f**, **g**, **h**. Such exemplars form the corpus used to train RuleNet. Exemplars whose input strings meet the conditions of several rules are excluded. RuleNet's task is twofold: It must discover the categories solely based upon the usage of their instances, and it must induce rules based upon those categories.

The rule bases used to generate examples are minimal in the sense that no smaller set of rules could have produced the examples. Therefore, in our simulations the target number of rules to be induced is the same as the number used to generate the training corpus.

There are several traditional, symbolic systems, e.g., COBWEB (Fisher, 1987), that induce rules for classifying inputs based upon training examples. It seems likely that, given the correct representation, a system such as COBWEB could learn rules that would *classify* patterns in our domain. However, it is not clear whether such a system could also learn the action associated with each class. Classifier systems (Booker, et al., 1989) learn both conditions and actions, but there is no obvious way to map a symbol in slot α of the input to slot β of the output. We have also devised a greedy combinatoric algorithm for inducing this type of rule, which has a number of shortcomings in comparison to RuleNet. See McMillan (1992) for comparisons of RuleNet and alternative symbolic approaches.

4 ARCHITECTURE

RuleNet can implement SCP rules of the type outlined above. As shown in Figure 1, RuleNet has five layers of units: an *input* layer, an *output* layer, a layer of *category* units, a layer of *condition* units, and a layer of *hidden* units. The operation of RuleNet can be divided into three functional components: categorization is performed in the mapping from the input layer to the category layer via the hidden units, the conditions are evaluated in the mapping from the category layer to the condition layer, and actions are performed in the mapping from the input layer to the output layer, gated by the condition units.

The input layer is divided into n pools of units, one for each slot, and activates the category layer, which is also divided into n pools. Input pool α maps to category pool α. Units in category pool α represent possible categorizations of the symbol in input slot α. One or more category units will respond to each input symbol. The activation of the hidden and category units is computed with a logistic squashing function. There are m units in the condition layer, one per rule. The activation of condition unit i, p_i, is computed as follows:

$$p_i = \frac{\text{logistic}(net_i)}{\sum_j \text{logistic}(net_j)}$$

The activation p_i represents the probability that rule i applies to the current input. The normalization enforces a soft winner-take-all competition among condition units. To the degree that a condition unit wins, it enables a set of weights from the input layer to the output layer. These weights correspond to the action for a particular rule. There is one set of weights, A_i, for each of the m rules. The activation of the output layer, y, is calculated from the input layer, x, as follows:

$$y = \sum_i^m p_i A_i x$$

Essentially, the transformation A_i for rule each rule i is applied to the input, and it contributes to the output to the degree that condition i is satisfied. Ideally, just one condition unit will be fully activated by a given input, and the rest will remain inactive.

This architecture is based on the local expert architecture of Jacobs, Jordan, Nowlan, and Hinton (1991), but is independently motivated in our work by the demands of the task domain. RuleNet has essentially the same structure as the Jacobs network, where the action substructure of RuleNet corresponds to their *local experts* and the condition substructure corresponds to their *gating network*. However, their goal—to minimize crosstalk between logically independent subtasks—is quite different than ours.

4.1 Weight Templates

In order to interpret the weights in RuleNet as symbolic SCP rules, it is necessary to establish a correspondence between regions of weight space and SCP rules.

A *weight template* is a parameterized set of constraints on some weights—a manifold in weight space—that has a direct correspondence to an SCP rule. The strategy behind iterative projection is twofold: constrain gradient descent so that weights stay close to templates in weight space, and periodically project the learned weights to the nearest template, which can then readily be interpreted as a set of SCP rules.

For SCP rules, there are three types of weight templates: one dealing with categorization, one with rule conditions, and one with rule actions. Each type of template is defined over a subset of the weights in RuleNet. The categorization templates are defined over the weights from input to category units, the condition templates are defined over the weights from category to condition units for each rule i, c_i, and the action templates are defined over the weights from input to output units for each rule i, A_i.

Category templates. The category templates specify that the mapping from each input slot α to category pool α, for $1 \leq \alpha \leq n$, is uniform. This imposes category invariance across the input string.

Condition templates. The weight vector c_i, which maps category activities to the activity of condition unit i, has vn elements—v being the number of category units per slot and n being the number of slots. The fact that the condition unit should respond to at most one category in each slot implies that at most one weight in each v-element subvector of c_i should be nonzero. For example, assuming there are three categories, **W**, **X**, and **Y**, the vector c_i that detects the simple condition *"$input_2$ is an instance of **X**"* is: (000 0φ0 000 000), where φ is an arbitrary parameter. Additionally, a bias is required to ensure that the net input will be negative unless the condition is satisfied. Here, a bias value, b, of -0.5φ will suffice. For disjunctive and conjunctive conditions, weights in *two* slots should be equal to φ, the rest zero, and the appropriate bias is $-.5\varphi$ or -1.5φ, respectively. There is a weight template for each condition type and each combination of slots that takes part in a condition. We generalize these templates further in a variety of ways. For instance, in the case where each input symbol falls into exactly one category, if a constant ε_α is added to all weights of c_i corresponding to slot α and ε_α is also subtracted from b, the net input to condition unit i will be unaffected. Thus, the weight template must include the $\{\varepsilon_\alpha\}$.

Action templates. If we wish the actions carried out by the network to correspond to the string manipulations allowed by our rule domain, it is necessary to impose some restrictions on the values assigned to the action weights for rule i, A_i. A_i has an $n \times n$ block form, where n is the length of input/output strings. Each block is a $k \times k$ submatrix, where k is the number of elements in the representation of each input symbol. The block at block-row β, block-column α of A_i copies $input_\alpha$ to $output_\beta$ if it is the identity matrix. Thus, the weight templates restrict each block to being either the identity matrix or the zero matrix. If $output_\beta$ is to be a fixed symbol, then block-row β must be all zero except for the output bias weights in block-row β.

The weight templates are defined over a submatrix $A_{i\beta}$, the set of weights mapping the input to an output slot β. There are $n+1$ templates, one for the mapping of each input slot to the output, and one for the writing of a fixed symbol to the output. An additional constraint that only one block may be nonzero in block-column α of A_i ensures that $input_\alpha$ maps to at most one output slot.

4.2 Constraints on Weight Changes

Recall that the strategy in iterative projection is to constrain weights to be close to the templates described above, in order that they may be readily interpreted as symbolic rules. We use a combination of hard and soft constraints, some of which we briefly describe here.

To ensure that during learning every block in A_i approaches the identity or zero matrix, we constrain the off-diagonal terms to be zero and constrain weights along the diagonal of each block to be the same, thus limiting the degrees of freedom to one parameter within each block. All weights in c_i except the bias are constrained to positive or zero values. Two soft constraints are imposed upon the network to encourage all-or-none categorization of input instances: A decay term is used on all weights in c_i except the maximum in each slot, and a second cost term encourages binary activation of the category units.

4.3 Projection

The constraints described above do not guarantee that learning will produce weights that correspond exactly to SCP rules. However, using projection, it is possible to transform the condition and action weights such that the resulting network can be interpreted as rules. The essential idea of projection is to take a set of learned weights, such as c_i, and compute values for the parameters in each of the corresponding weight templates such that the resulting weights match the learned weights. The weight template parameters are estimated using a least squares procedure, and the closest template, based upon a Euclidean distance metric, is taken to be the projected weights.

5 SIMULATIONS

We ran simulations on 14 different training sets, averaging the performance of the network over at least five runs with different initial weights for each set. The training data were generated from SCP rule bases containing 2–8 rules and strings of length four. Between four and eight categories were used. Alphabets ranged from eight to 12 symbols. Symbols were represented by either local or distributed activity vectors. Training set sizes ranged from 3–15% of possible examples.

Iterative projection involved the following steps: (1) start with one rule (one set of c_i-A_i weights), (2) perform gradient descent for 500-5,000 epochs, (3) project to the nearest set of SCP rules and add a new rule. Steps (2) and (3) were repeated until the training set was fully covered.

In virtually every run on each data set in which RuleNet converged to a set of rules that completely covered the training set, the rules extracted were exactly the original rules used to generate the training set. In the few remaining runs, RuleNet discovered an equivalent set of rules.

It is instructive to examine the evolution of a rule set. The rightmost column of Figure 2 shows a set of five rules over four categories, used to generate 200 exemplars, and the left portion of the Figure shows the evolution of the hypothesis set of rules learned by RuleNet over 20,000 training epochs, projecting every 4000 epochs. At epoch 8000, RuleNet has discovered two rules over two categories, covering 24.5% of the training set. At epoch 12,000, RuleNet has discovered three rules over three categories, covering 52% of the training set. At epoch 20,000, RuleNet has induced five rules over four categories that

epoch 8000	epoch 12,000	epoch 20,000	original rules/categ.
[∨ B_C_ → 4h21] [∧ _B_C → 341f]	[∨ B_C_ → 4h21] [∧ __EC → 2413] [∧ _B_B → 321f]	[∨ B_C_ → 4h21] [B__ → 4213] [∨ _E_D → 342f] [∧ _D_B → 3214] [∨ __EC → 2413]	[∨ Y_W_ → 4h21] [_Y__ → 4213] [∨ _Z_X → 342f] [∧ _X_Y → 3214] [∨ __ZW → 2413]
Categ. Instance B f g h C a b c i	Categ. Instance B f g h C a b c d i E a i j k	Categ. Instance C a b c d i D e g l B f g h E a c i j k	Categ. Instance W a b c d i X e g l Y f g h Z a c i j k

Figure 2: Evolution of a Rule Set

Table 1: Generalization performance of RuleNet (average of five runs)

% of patterns correctly mapped

Architecture	Data Set 1 (8 Rules)		Data Set 2 (3 Rules)		Data Set 3 (3 Rules)		Data Set 4 (5 Rules)	
	train	test	train	test	train	test	train	test
RuleNet	100	100	100	100	100	100	100	100
Jacobs architecture	100	22	100	7	100	14	100	27
3-layer backprop	100	27	100	7	100	14	100	35
# of patterns in set	120	1635	45	1380	45	1380	75	1995

cover 100% of the training examples. A close comparison of these rules with the original rules shows that they only differ in the arbitrary labels RuleNet has attached to the categories.

Learning rules can greatly enhance generalization. In cases where RuleNet learns the original rules, it can be expected to generalize perfectly to any pattern created by those rules. We compared the performance of RuleNet to that of a standard three-layer backprop network (with 15 hidden units per rule) and a version of the Jacobs architecture, which in principle has the capacity to perform the task. Four rule bases were tested, and roughly 5% of the possible examples were used for training and the remainder were used for generalization testing. Outputs were thresholded to 0 or 1. The *cleaned up* outputs were compared to the targets to determine which were mapped correctly. All three learn the training set perfectly. However, on the test set, RuleNet's ability to generalize is 300% to 2000% better than the other systems (Table1).

Finally, we applied RuleNet to case-role assignment, as considered by McClelland and Kawamoto (1986). Case-role assignment is the problem of mapping syntactic constituents of a sentence to underlying semantic, or thematic, roles. For example, in the sentence, "The boy broke the window", *boy* is the subject at the syntactic level and the *agent*, or acting entity, at the semantic level. *Window* is the *object* at the syntactic level and the *patient*, or entity being acted upon, at the semantic level. The words of a sentence can be represented as a string of *n* slots, where each slot is labeled with a constituent, such as *subject*, and that slot is filled with the corresponding word, such as *boy*. The output is handled analogously. We used McClelland and Kawamoto's 152 sentences over 34 nouns and verbs as RuleNet's training set. The five categories and six rules induced by RuleNet are shown in Table 2, where S = subject, O = object, and wNP = noun in the *with* noun-phrase. We conjecture that RuleNet has induced such a small set of rules in part because it employs

Table 2: SCP Rules Induced by RuleNet in Case-Role Assignment

Rule	Sample of Sentences Handled Correctly
if O = **VICTIM then** wNP→modifier	*The boy ate the pasta with cheese.*
if O = **THING** ∧ wNP = **UTENSIL** **then** wNP→instrument	*The boy ate the pasta with the fork.*
if S = **BREAKER then** S→instrument	*The rock broke the window.*
if S = **THING then** S→patient	*The window broke. The fork moved.*
if V = **moved then** **self**→patient	*The man moved.*
if S = **ANIMATE then** **food**→patient	*The lion ate.*

implicit conflict resolution, automatically assigning strengths to categories and conditions. These rules cover 97% of the training set and perform the correct case-role assignments on 84% of the 1307 sentences in the test set.

6 DISCUSSION

RuleNet is but one example of a general methodology for rule induction in neural networks. This methodology involves five steps: 1) identify a fundamentally rule-governed domain, 2) identify a class of rules that characterizes that domain, 3) design a general architecture, 4) establish a correspondence between components of symbolic rules and manifolds of weight space—weight templates, and 5) devise a weight-template-based learning procedure.

Using this methodology, we have shown that RuleNet is able to perform both category and rule learning. Category learning strikes us as an intrinsically *subsymbolic* process. Functional categories are often fairly arbitrary (consider the classification of words as nouns or verbs) or have complex statistical structure (consider the classes "liberals" and "conservatives"). Consequently, real-world categories can seldom be described in terms of boolean (symbolic) expressions; subsymbolic representations are more appropriate.

While category learning is intrinsically subsymbolic, rule learning is intrinsically a symbolic process. The integration of the two is what makes RuleNet a unique and powerful system. Traditional symbolic machine learning approaches aren't well equipped to deal with subsymbolic learning, and connectionist approaches aren't well equipped to deal with the symbolic. RuleNet combines the strengths of each approach.

Acknowledgments

This research was supported by NSF Presidential Young Investigator award IRI-9058450, grant 90-21 from the James S. McDonnell Foundation, and DEC external research grant 1250 to MM; NSF grants IRI-8609599 and ECE-8617947 to PS; by a grant from the Sloan Foundation's computational neuroscience program to PS; and by the Optical Connectionist Machine Program of the NSF Engineering Research Center for Optoelectronic Computing Systems at the University of Colorado at Boulder.

References

Booker, L.B., Goldberg, D.E., and Holland, J.H. (1989). Classifier systems and genetic algorithms, *Artificial Intelligence* 40:235-282.

Fisher, D.H. (1987). Knowledge acquisition via incremental concept clustering. *Machine Learning* 2:139-172.

Jacobs, R., Jordan, M., Nowlan, S., Hinton, G. (1991). Adaptive mixtures of local experts. *Neural Computation*, 3:79-87.

McClelland, J. & Kawamoto, A. (1986). Mechanisms of sentence processing: assigning roles to constituents. In J.L. McClelland, D.E. Rumelhart, & the PDP Research Group, *Parallel Distributed Processing: Explorations in the microstructure of cognition, Vol. 2*. Cambridge, MA: MIT Press/Bradford Books.

McMillan, C. (1992). Rule induction in a neural network through integrated symbolic and subsymbolic processing. Unpublished Ph.D. Thesis. Boulder, CO: Department of Computer Science, University of Colorado.

Rumelhart, D., & McClelland, J. (1986). On learning the past tense of English verbs. In J.L. McClelland, D.E. Rumelhart, & the PDP Research Group, *Parallel Distributed Processing: Explorations in the microstructure of cognition. Vol. 2*. Cambridge, MA: MIT Press/Bradford Books.

Sejnowski, T. J. & Rosenberg, C. R. (1987). Parallel networks that learn to pronounce English text, *Complex Systems*, 1: 145-168.

Interpretation of Artificial Neural Networks: Mapping Knowledge-Based Neural Networks into Rules

Geoffrey Towell   Jude W. Shavlik
Computer Sciences Department
University of Wisconsin
Madison, WI 53706

Abstract

We propose and empirically evaluate a method for the extraction of expert-comprehensible rules from trained neural networks. Our method operates in the context of a three-step process for learning that uses rule-based domain knowledge in combination with neural networks. Empirical tests using real-worlds problems from molecular biology show that the rules our method extracts from trained neural networks: closely reproduce the accuracy of the network from which they came, are superior to the rules derived by a learning system that directly refines symbolic rules, and are expert-comprehensible.

1 Introduction

Artificial neural networks (ANNs) have proven to be a powerful and general technique for machine learning [1, 11]. However, ANNs have several well-known shortcomings. Perhaps the most significant of these shortcomings is that determining why a trained ANN makes a particular decision is all but impossible. Without the ability to explain their decisions, it is hard to be confident in the reliability of a network that addresses a real-world problem. Moreover, this shortcoming makes it difficult to transfer the information learned by a network to the solution of related problems. Therefore, methods for the extraction of comprehensible, symbolic rules from trained networks are desirable.

Our approach to understanding trained networks uses the three-link chain illustrated by Figure 1. The first link inserts domain knowledge, which need be neither complete nor correct, into a neural network using KBANN [13] — see Section 2. (Networks created using KBANN are called KNNs.) The second link trains the KNN using a set of classified

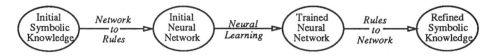

Figure 1: Rule refinement using neural networks.

training examples and standard neural learning methods [9]. The final link extracts rules from trained KNNs. Rule extraction is an extremely difficult task for arbitrarily-configured networks, but is somewhat less daunting for KNNs due to their initial comprehensibility. Our method (described in Section 3) takes advantage of this property to efficiently extract rules from trained KNNs.

Significantly, when evaluated in terms of the ability to correctly classify examples not seen during training, our method produces rules that are equal or superior to the networks from which they came (see Section 4). Moreover, the extracted rules are superior to the rules resulting from methods that act *directly* on the rules (rather than their re-representation as a neural network). Also, our method is superior to the most widely-published algorithm for the extraction of rules from general neural networks.

2   The KBANN Algorithm

The KBANN algorithm translates symbolic domain knowledge into neural networks; defining the topology and connection weights of the networks it creates. It uses a knowledge base of domain-specific inference rules to define what is initially known about a topic. A detailed explanation of this rule-translation appears in [13].

As an example of the KBANN method, consider the sample domain knowledge in Figure 2a that defines membership in category A. Figure 2b represents the hierarchical structure of these rules: solid and dotted lines represent necessary and prohibitory dependencies, respectively. Figure 2c represents the KNN that results from the translation into a neural network of this domain knowledge. Units X and Y in Figure 2c are introduced into the KNN to handle the disjunction in the rule set. Otherwise, each unit in the KNN corresponds to a consequent or an antecedent in the domain knowledge. The thick lines in Figure 2c represent heavily-weighted links in the KNN that correspond to dependencies in the domain knowledge. The thin lines represent the links added to the network to allow refinement of the domain knowledge. Weights and biases in the network are set so that, prior to learning, the network's response to inputs is exactly the same as the domain knowledge.

This example illustrates the two principal benefits of using KBANN to initialize KNNs. First, the algorithm indicates the features that are believed to be important to an example's classification. Second, it specifies important derived features, thereby guiding the choice of the number and connectivity of *hidden units*.

3   Rule Extraction

Almost every method of rule extraction makes two assumptions about networks. First, that training does not significantly shift the meaning of units. By making this assumption, the methods are able to attach labels to rules that correspond to terms in the domain knowledge

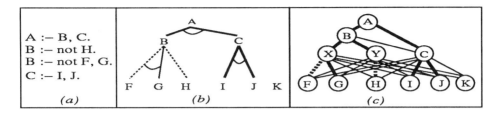

Figure 2: Translation of domain knowledge into a KNN.

upon which the network is based. These labels enhance the comprehensibility of the rules. The second assumption is that the units in a trained KNN are always either active (≈ 1) or inactive (≈ 0). Under this assumption each non-input unit in a trained KNN can be treated as a Boolean rule. Therefore, the problem for rule extraction is to determine the situations in which the "rule" is true. Examination of trained KNNs validates both of these assumptions.

Given these assumptions, the simplest method for extracting rules we call the SUBSET method. This method operates by exhaustively searching for subsets of the links into a unit such that the sum of the weights of the links in the subset guarantees that the total input to the unit exceeds its bias. In the limit, SUBSET extracts a set of rules that reproduces the behavior of the network. However, the combinatorics of this method render it impossible to implement. Heuristics can be added to reduce the complexity of the search at some cost in the accuracy of the resulting rules. Using heuristic search, SUBSET tends to produce repetitive rules whose preconditions are difficult to interpret. (See [10] or [2] for more detailed explanations of SUBSET.)

Our algorithm, called NOFM, addresses both the combinatorial and presentation problems inherent to the SUBSET algorithm. It differs from SUBSET in that it explicitly searches for rules of the form: ``If (N of these M antecedents are true) ...'' This method arose because we noticed that rule sets discovered by the SUBSET method often contain N-of-M style concepts. Further support for this method comes from experiments that indicate neural networks are good at learning N-of-M concepts [1] as well as experiments that show a bias towards N-of-M style concepts is useful [5]. Finally, note that purely conjunctive rules result if $N = M$, while a set of disjunctive rules results when $N = 1$; hence, using N-of-M rules does not restrict generality.

The idea underlying NOFM (summarized in Table 1) is that individual antecedents (links) do not have unique importance. Rather, groups of antecedents form equivalence classes in which each antecedent has the same importance as, and is interchangeable with, other members of the class. This equivalence-class idea allows NOFM to consider groups of links without worrying about particular links within the group. Unfortunately, training using backpropagation does not naturally bunch links into equivalence classes. Hence, the first step of NOFM groups links into equivalence classes.

This grouping can be done using standard clustering methods [3] in which clustering is stopped when no clusters are closer than a user-set distance (we use 0.25). After clustering, the links to the unit in the upper-right corner of Figure 3 form two groups, one of four links with weight near one and one of three links with weight near six. (The effect of this grouping is very similar to the training method suggested by Nowlan and Hinton [7].)

Table 1: The NOFM algorithm for rule extraction.

(1)   With each hidden and output unit, form groups of similarly-weighted links.

(2)   Set link weights of all group members to the average of the group.

(3)   Eliminate any groups that do not affect whether the unit will be active or inactive.

(4)   Holding all links weights constant, optimize biases of hidden and output units.

(5)   Form a single rule for each hidden and output unit. The rule consists of a threshold given by the bias and weighted antecedents specified by remaining links.

(6)   Where possible, simplify rules to eliminate spperfluous weights and thresholds.

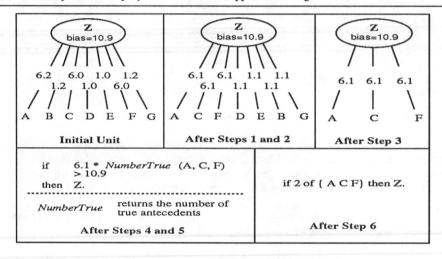

Figure 3: Rule extraction using NOFM.

Once the groups are formed, the procedure next attempts to identify and eliminate groups that do not contribute to the calculation of the consequent. In the extreme case, this analysis is trivial; clusters can be eliminated solely on the basis of their weight. In Figure 3 no combination of the cluster of links with weight 1.1 can cause the summed weights to exceed the bias on unit Z. Hence, links with weight 1.1 are eliminated from Figure 3 after step 3.

More often, the assessment of a cluster's utility uses heuristics. The heuristic we use is to scan each training example and determine which groups can be eliminated while leaving the example correctly categorized. Groups not required by any example are eliminated.

With unimportant groups eliminated, the next step of the procedure is to optimize the bias on each unit. Optimization is required to adjust the network so that it accurately reflects the assumption that units are boolean. This can be done by freezing link weights (so that the groups stay intact) and retraining the bias terms in the network.

After optimization, rules are formed that simply re-express the network. Note that these rules are considerable simpler than the trained network; they have fewer antecedents and those antecedents tend to be in a few weight classes.

Finally, rules are simplified whenever possible to eliminate the weights and thresholds. Simplification is accomplished by a scan of each restated rule to determine combinations of clusters that exceed the threshold. In Figure 3 the result of this scan is a single N-of-M style rule. When a rule has more than one cluster, this scan may return multiple combinations each of which has several N-of-M predicates. In such cases, rules are left in their original form of weights and a threshold.

4   Experiments in Rule Extraction

This section presents a set of experiments designed to determine the relative strengths and weaknesses of the two rule-extraction methods described above. Rule-extraction techniques are compared using two measures: *quality*, which is measured both by the accuracy of the rules; and *comprehensibility* which is approximated by analysis of extracted rule sets.

4.1   Testing Methodology

Following Weiss and Kulikowski [14], we use repeated 10-fold cross-validation[1] for testing learning on two tasks from molecular biology: promoter recognition [13] and splice-junction determination [6]. Networks are trained using the *cross-entropy*. Following Hinton's [4] suggestion for improved network interpretability, all weights "decay" gently during training.

4.2   Accuracy of Extracted Rules

Figure 4 addresses the issue of the accuracy of extracted rules. It plots percentage of errors on the testing and training sets, averaged over eleven repetitions of 10-fold cross-validation, for both the promoter and splice-junction tasks. For comparison, Figure 4 includes the accuracy of the trained KNNs prior to rule extraction (the bars labeled "Network"). Also included in Figure 4 is the accuracy of the EITHER system, an "all symbolic" method for the empirical adaptation of rules [8]. (EITHER has not been applied to the splice-junction problem.)

The initial rule sets for promoter recognition and splice-junction determination correctly categorized 50% and 61%, respectively, of the examples. Hence, each of the systems plotted in Figure 4 improved upon the initial rules. Comparing only the systems that result in refined rules, the NOFM method is the clear winner. On training examples, the error rate for rules extracted by NOFM is slightly worse than EITHER but superior to the rules extracted using SUBSET. On the testing examples the NOFM rules are more accurate than both EITHER and SUBSET. (One-tailed, paired-sample *t*-tests indicate that for both domains the NOFM rules are superior to the SUBSET rules with 99.5% confidence.)

Perhaps the most significant result in this paper is that, on the testing set, the error rate of the NOFM rules is equal or superior to that of the networks from which the rules were extracted. Conversely, the error rate of the SUBSET rules on testing examples is statistically worse than the networks in both problem domains. The discussion at the end of this paper

---

[1]In N-fold cross-validation, the set of examples is partitioned into N sets of equal size. Networks are trained using $N - 1$ of the sets and tested using the remaining set. This procedure is repeated N times so that each set is used as the testing set once. We actually used only $N - 2$ of the sets for training. One set was used for testing and the other to stop training to prevent overfitting of the training set.

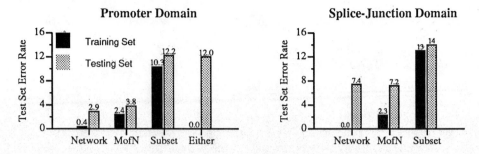

Figure 4: Error rates of extracted rules.

analyses the reasons why NOFM's rules can be superior to the networks from which they came.

4.3 Comprehensibility

To be useful, the extracted rules must not only be accurate, they also must be understandable. To assess rule comprehensibility, we looked at rule sets extracted by the NOFM method. Table 3 presents the rules extracted by NOFM for promoter recognition. The rules extracted by NOFM for splice-junction determination are not shown because they have much the same character as those of the promoter domain.

While Table 3 is somewhat murky, it is vastly more comprehensible than the network of 3000 links from which it was extracted. Moreover, the rules in this table can be rewritten in a form very similar to one used in the biological community [12], namely weight matrices.

One major pattern in the extracted rules is that the network learns to disregard a major portion of the initial rules. These same rules are dropped by other rule-refinement systems (e.g., EITHER). This suggests that the deletion of these rules is not merely an artifact of NOFM, but instead reflects an underlying property of the data. Hence, we demonstrate that machine learning methods can provide valuable evidence about biological theories.

Looking beyond the dropped rules, the rules NOFM extracts confirm the importance of the bases identified in the initial rules (Table 2). However, whereas the initial rules required matching every base, the extracted rules allow a less than perfect match. In addition, the extracted rules point to places in which changes to the sequence are important. For instance, in the first *minus10* rule, a 'T' in position 11 is a strong indicator that the rule is true. However, replacing the 'T' with either a 'G' or an 'A' prevents the rule from being satisfied.

5   Discussion and Conclusions

Our results indicate that the NOFM method not only can extract meaningful, symbolic rules from trained KNNs, the extracted rules can be superior at classifying examples not seen during training to the networks from which they came. Additionally, the NOFM method produces rules whose accuracy is substantially better than EITHER, an approach that directly modifies the initial set of rules [8]. While the rule set produced by the NOFM algorithm is

Table 2: Partial set of original rules for promoter-recognition.

```
promoter        :- contact, conformation.
contact         :- minus-35, minus-10.
minus-35        :- @-37 'CTTGAC'.    --- three additional rules
minus-10        :- @-14 'TATAAT'.    --- three additional rules
conformation    :- @-45 'AA--A'.     --- three additional rules
```

Examples are 57 base-pair long strands of DNA. Rules refer to bases by stating a sequence location followed by a subsequnce. So, @-37 'CT' indicates a 'C' in position -37 and a 'T' in position -36.

Table 3: Promoter rules NoFM extracts.

```
Promoter :- Minus35, Minus10.

Minus-35                              Minus-10 :- 2 of @-14 '---CA---T' and
 :-10 < 4.0 * nt(@-37 '--TTGAT-') +            not 1 of @-14 '---RB---S'.
        1.5 * nt(@-37 '----TCC-') +   Minus-10
        0.5 * nt(@-37 '---MC---') -    :-10 < 3.0 * nt(@-14 '--TAT--T-') +
        1.5 * nt(@-37 '--GGAGG-').            1.8 * nt(@-14 '-----GA--') +
Minus-35                                      0.7 * nt(@-14 '----GAT--') -
 :-10 < 5.0 * nt(@-37 '--T-G--A') +           0.7 * nt(@-14 '--GKCCCS ').
        3.1 * nt(@-37 '---GT---') +   Minus-10
        1.9 * nt(@-37 '----C-CT') +    :-10 < 3.8 * nt(@-14 '--TA-A-T-') +
        1.5 * nt(@-37 '---C--A-') -           3.0 * nt(@-14 '--G--C---') +
        1.5 * nt(@-37 '------GC') -           1.0 * nt(@-14 '---T---A-') -
        1.9 * nt(@-37 '--CAW---') -           1.0 * nt(@-14 '--CS-G-S-') -
        3.1 * nt(@-37 '--A----C').            3.0 * nt(@-14 '--A--T---').
Minus-35 :- @-37 '-C-TGAC-'.         Minus-10 :- @-14 '-TAWA-T--'.
Minus-35 :- @-37 '--TTD-CA'.
```

"nt()" returns the number of enclosed in the parentheses antecedents that match the given sequence. So, nt(@-14 '- - - C - - G - -') would return 1 when matched against the sequence @-14 'AAACAAAAA'.

Table 4: Standard nucleotide ambiguity codes.

Code	Meaning	Code	Meaning	Code	Meaning	Code	Meaning
M	A or C	R	A or G	W	A or T	S	C or G
K	G or T	D	A or G or T	B	C or G or T		

slightly larger than that produced by EITHER, the sets of rules produced by both of these algorithms is small enough to be easily understood. Hence, although weighing the tradeoff between accuracy and understandability is problem and user-specific, the NOFM approach combined with KBANN offers an appealing mixture.

The superiority of the NOFM rules over the networks from which they are extracted may occur because the rule-extraction process reduces overfitting of the training examples. The principle evidence in support of this hypothesis is that the difference in ability to correctly categorize testing and training examples is smaller for NOFM rules than for trained KNNs. Thus, the rules extracted by NOFM sacrifice some training set accuracy to achieve higher testing set accuracy.

Additionally, in earlier tests this effect was more pronounced; the NOFM rules were superior to the networks from which they came on both datasets (with 99according to a one-tailed t-test). Modifications to training to reduce overfitting improved generalization by networks without significantly affecting NOFM's rules. The result of the change in training method is that the differences between the network and NOFM arc not statistically significant in either dataset. However, the result is significant in that it supports the overfitting hypothesis.

In summary, the NOFM method extracts accurate, comprehensible rules from trained KNNs. The method is currently limited to KNNs; randomly-configured networks violate its assumptions. New training methods [7] may broaden the applicability of the method. Even without different methods for training, our results show that NOFM provides a mechanism through which networks can make expert comprehensible explanations of their behavior. In addition, the extracted rules allow for the transfer of learning to the solution of related problems.

Acknowledgments

This work is partially supported by Office of Naval Research Grant N00014-90-J-1941, National Science Foundation Grant IRI-9002413, and Department of Energy Grant DE-FG02-91ER61129.

References

[1] D. H. Fisher and K. B. McKusick. An empirical comparison of ID3 and back-propagation. In *Proceedings of the Eleventh International Joint Conference on Artificial Intelligence*, pages 788–793, Detroit, MI, August 1989.

[2] L. M. Fu. Rule learning by searching on adapted nets. In *Proceedings of the Ninth National Conference on Artificial Intelligence*, pages 590–595, Anaheim, CA, 1991.

[3] J. A. Hartigan. *Clustering Algorithms*. Wiley, New York, 1975.

[4] G. E. Hinton. Connectionist learning procedures. *Artificial Intelligence*, 40:185–234, 1989.

[5] P. M. Murphy and M. J. Pazzani. ID2-of-3: Constructive induction of N-of-M concepts for discriminators in decision trees. In *Proceedings of the Eighth International Machine Learning Workshop*, pages 183–187, Evanston, IL, 1991.

[6] M. O. Noordewier, G. G. Towell, and J. W. Shavlik. Training knowledge-based neural networks to recognize genes in DNA sequences. In *Advances in Neural Information Processing Systems*, 3, Denver, CO, 1991. Morgan Kaufmann.

[7] S. J. Nowlan and G. E. Hinton. Simplifying neural networks by soft weight-sharing. In *Advances in Neural Information Processing Systems*, 4, Denver, CO, 1991. Morgan Kaufmann.

[8] D. Ourston and R. J. Mooney. Changing the rules: A comprehensive approach to theory refinement. In *Proceedings of the Eighth National Conference on Artificial Intelligence*, pages 815–820, Boston, MA, Aug 1990.

[9] D. E. Rumelhart, G. E. Hinton, and R. J. Williams. Learning internal representations by error propagation. In D. E. Rumelhart and J. L. McClelland, editors, *Parallel Distributed Processing: Explorations in the microstructure of cognition. Volume 1: Foundations*, pages 318–363. MIT Press, Cambridge, MA, 1986.

[10] K. Saito and R. Nakano. Medical diagnostic expert system based on PDP model. In *Proceedings of IEEE International Conference on Neural Networks*, volume 1, pages 255–262, 1988.

[11] J. W. Shavlik, R. J. Mooney, and G. G. Towell. Symbolic and neural net learning algorithms: An empirical comparison. *Machine Learning*, 6:111–143, 1991.

[12] G. D. Stormo. Consensus patterns in DNA. In *Methods in Enzymology*, volume 183, pages 211–221. Academic Press, Orlando, FL, 1990.

[13] G. G. Towell, J. W. Shavlik, and M. O. Noordewier. Refinement of approximately correct domain theories by knowledge-based neural networks. In *Proceedings of the Eighth National Conference on Artificial Intelligence*, pages 861–866, Boston, MA, 1990.

[14] S. M. Weiss and C. A. Kulikowski. *Computer Systems that Learn*. Morgan Kaufmann, San Mateo, CA, 1990.

Hierarchies of adaptive experts

Michael I. Jordan   Robert A. Jacobs
Department of Brain and Cognitive Sciences
Massachusetts Institute of Technology
Cambridge, MA 02139

Abstract

In this paper we present a neural network architecture that discovers a recursive decomposition of its input space. Based on a generalization of the modular architecture of Jacobs, Jordan, Nowlan, and Hinton (1991), the architecture uses competition among networks to recursively split the input space into nested regions and to learn separate associative mappings within each region. The learning algorithm is shown to perform gradient ascent in a log likelihood function that captures the architecture's hierarchical structure.

1   INTRODUCTION

Neural network learning architectures such as the multilayer perceptron and adaptive radial basis function (RBF) networks are a natural nonlinear generalization of classical statistical techniques such as linear regression, logistic regression and additive modeling. Another class of nonlinear algorithms, exemplified by CART (Breiman, Friedman, Olshen, & Stone, 1984) and MARS (Friedman, 1990), generalizes classical techniques by partitioning the training data into non-overlapping regions and fitting separate models in each of the regions. These two classes of algorithms extend linear techniques in essentially independent directions, thus it seems worthwhile to investigate algorithms that incorporate aspects of both approaches to model estimation. Such algorithms would be related to CART and MARS as multilayer neural networks are related to linear statistical techniques. In this paper we present a candidate for such an algorithm. The algorithm that we present partitions its training data in the manner of CART or MARS, but it does so in a parallel, on-line manner that can be described as the stochastic optimization of an appropriate cost functional.

985

Why is it sensible to partition the training data and to fit separate models within each of the partitions? Essentially this approach enhances the flexibility of the learner and allows the data to influence the choice between local and global representations. For example, if the data suggest a discontinuity in the function being approximated, then it may be more sensible to fit separate models on both sides of the discontinuity than to adapt a global model across the discontinuity. Similarly, if the data suggest a simple functional form in some region, then it may be more sensible to fit a global model in that region than to approximate the function locally with a large number of local models. Although global algorithms such as backpropagation and local algorithms such as adaptive RBF networks have some degree of flexibility in the tradeoff that they realize between global and local representation, they do not have the flexibility of adaptive partitioning schemes such as CART and MARS.

In a previous paper we presented a modular neural network architecture in which a number of "expert networks" compete to learn a set of training data (Jacobs, Jordan, Nowlan & Hinton, 1991). As a result of the competition, the architecture adaptively splits the input space into regions, and learns separate associative mappings within each region. The architecture that we discuss here is a generalization of the earlier work and arises from considering what would be an appropriate internal structure for the expert networks in the competing experts architecture. In our earlier work, the expert networks were multilayer perceptrons or radial basis function networks. If the arguments in support of data partitioning are valid, however, then they apply equally well to a region in the input space as they do to the entire input space, and therefore each expert should itself be composed of competing sub-experts. Thus we are led to consider recursively-defined hierarchies of adaptive experts.

2   THE ARCHITECTURE

Figure 1 shows two hierarchical levels of the architecture. (We restrict ourselves to two levels throughout the paper to simplify the exposition; the algorithm that we develop, however, generalizes readily to trees of arbitrary depth). The architecture has a number of *expert networks* that map from the input vector $\mathbf{x}$ to output vectors $\mathbf{y}_{ij}$. There are also a number of *gating networks* that define the hierarchical structure of the architecture. There is a gating network for each cluster of expert networks and a gating network that serves to combine the outputs of the clusters. The output of the ith cluster is given by

$$\mathbf{y}_i = \sum_j g_{j|i}\mathbf{y}_{ij} \tag{1}$$

where $g_{j|i}$ is the activation of the jth output unit of the gating network in the ith cluster. The output of the architecture as a whole is given by

$$\mathbf{y} = \sum_i g_i\mathbf{y}_i \tag{2}$$

where g_i is the activation of the ith output unit of the top-level gating network.

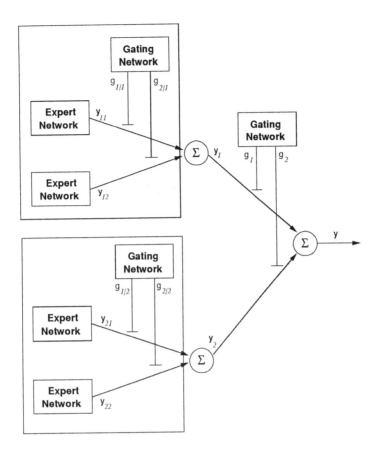

Figure 1: Two hierarchical levels of adaptive experts. All of the expert networks and all of the gating networks have the same input vector.

We assume that the outputs of the gating networks are given by the normalizing *softmax* function (Bridle, 1989):

$$g_i = \frac{e^{s_i}}{\sum_j e^{s_j}} \qquad (3)$$

and

$$g_{j|i} = \frac{e^{s_{j|i}}}{\sum_k e^{s_{k|i}}} \qquad (4)$$

where s_i and $s_{j|i}$ are the weighted sums arriving at the output units of the corresponding gating networks.

The gating networks in the architecture are essentially classifiers that are responsible for partitioning the input space. Their choice of partition is based on the ability of the expert networks to model the input-output functions within their respective regions (as quantified by their posterior probabilities; see below). The nested arrangement of gating networks in the architecture (cf. Figure 1) yields a nested partitioning much like that found in CART or MARS. The architecture is a more general mathematical object than a CART or MARS tree, however, given that the gating networks have non-binary outputs and given that they may form nonlinear decision surfaces.

3   THE LEARNING ALGORITHM

We derive a learning algorithm for our architecture by developing a probabilistic model of a tree-structured estimation problem. The environment is assumed to be characterized by a finite number of stochastic processes that map input vectors $\mathbf{x}$ into output vectors $\mathbf{y}^*$. These processes are partitioned into nested collections of processes that have commonalities in their input-output parameterizations. Data are assumed to be generated by the model in the following way. For any given $\mathbf{x}$, collection i is chosen with probability g_i, and a particular process j is then chosen with conditional probability $g_{j|i}$. The selected process produces an output vector $\mathbf{y}^*$ according to the probability density $f(\mathbf{y}^* \mid \mathbf{x}; \mathbf{y}_{ij})$, where $\mathbf{y}_{ij}$ is a vector of parameters. The total probability of generating $\mathbf{y}^*$ is:

$$P(\mathbf{y}^* \mid \mathbf{x}) = \sum_i g_i \sum_j g_{j|i} f(\mathbf{y}^* \mid \mathbf{x}; \mathbf{y}_{ij}), \tag{5}$$

where g_i, $g_{j|i}$, and $\mathbf{y}_{ij}$ are unknown nonlinear functions of $\mathbf{x}$.

Treating the probability $P(\mathbf{y}^* \mid \mathbf{x})$ as a likelihood function in the unknown parameters g_i, $g_{j|i}$, and $\mathbf{y}_{ij}$, we obtain a learning algorithm by using gradient ascent to maximize the log likelihood. Let us assume that the probability density associated with the residual vector $(\mathbf{y}^* - \mathbf{y}_{ij})$ is the multivariate normal density, where $\mathbf{y}_{ij}$ is the mean of the jth process of the ith cluster (or the $(i,j)^{\text{th}}$ expert network) and Σ_{ij} is its covariance matrix. Ignoring the constant terms in the normal density, the log likelihood is:

$$\ln L = \ln \sum_i g_i \sum_j g_{j|i} |\Sigma_{ij}|^{-\frac{1}{2}} e^{-\frac{1}{2}(\mathbf{y}^* - \mathbf{y}_{ij})^T \Sigma_{ij}^{-1} (\mathbf{y}^* - \mathbf{y}_{ij})}. \tag{6}$$

We define the following posterior probability:

$$h_i = \frac{g_i \sum_j g_{j|i} |\Sigma_{ij}|^{-\frac{1}{2}} e^{-\frac{1}{2}(\mathbf{y}^* - \mathbf{y}_{ij})^T \Sigma_{ij}^{-1} (\mathbf{y}^* - \mathbf{y}_{ij})}}{\sum_i g_i \sum_j g_{j|i} |\Sigma_{ij}|^{-\frac{1}{2}} e^{-\frac{1}{2}(\mathbf{y}^* - \mathbf{y}_{ij})^T \Sigma_{ij}^{-1} (\mathbf{y}^* - \mathbf{y}_{ij})}}, \tag{7}$$

which is the posterior probability that a process in the ith cluster generates a particular target vector $\mathbf{y}^*$. We also define the conditional posterior probability:

$$h_{j|i} = \frac{g_{j|i} |\Sigma_{ij}|^{-\frac{1}{2}} e^{-\frac{1}{2}(\mathbf{y}^* - \mathbf{y}_{ij})^T \Sigma_{ij}^{-1} (\mathbf{y}^* - \mathbf{y}_{ij})}}{\sum_j g_{j|i} |\Sigma_{ij}|^{-\frac{1}{2}} e^{-\frac{1}{2}(\mathbf{y}^* - \mathbf{y}_{ij})^T \Sigma_{ij}^{-1} (\mathbf{y}^* - \mathbf{y}_{ij})}}, \tag{8}$$

which is the conditional posterior probability that the jth expert in the ith cluster generates a particular target vector $\mathbf{y}^*$. Differentiating 6, and using Equations 3, 4,

7, and 8, we obtain the partial derivative of the log likelihood with respect to the output of the $(i, j)^{\text{th}}$ expert network:

$$\frac{\partial \ln L}{\partial \mathbf{y}_{ij}} = h_i \, h_{j|i} \, (\mathbf{y}^* - \mathbf{y}_{ij}). \tag{9}$$

This partial derivative is a supervised error term modulated by the appropriate posterior probabilities. Similarly, the partial derivatives of the log likelihood with respect to the weighted sums at the output units of the gating networks are given by:

$$\frac{\partial \ln L}{\partial s_i} = h_i - g_i \tag{10}$$

and

$$\frac{\partial \ln L}{\partial s_{j|i}} = h_i \, (h_{j|i} - g_{j|i}). \tag{11}$$

These derivatives move the prior probabilities associated with the gating networks toward the corresponding posterior probabilities.

It is interesting to note that the posterior probability h_i appears in the gradient for the experts in the ith cluster (Equation 9) and in the gradient for the gating network in the ith cluster (Equation 11). This ties experts within a cluster to each other and implies that experts within a cluster tend to learn similar mappings early in the training process. They differentiate later in training as the probabilities associated with the cluster to which they belong become larger. Thus the architecture tends to acquire coarse structure before acquiring fine structure. This feature of the architecture is significant because it implies a natural robustness to problems with overfitting in deep hierarchies.

We have also found it useful in practice to obtain an additional degree of control over the coarse-to-fine development of the algorithm. This is achieved with a heuristic that adjusts the learning rate at a given level of the tree as a function of the time-average entropy of the gating network at the next higher level of the tree:

$$\mu_{\cdot|i}(t+1) = \alpha\mu_{\cdot|i}(t) + \beta(M_i + \sum_j g_{j|i} \ln g_{j|i})$$

where M_i is the maximum possible entropy at level i of the tree. This equation has the effect that the networks at level $i + 1$ are less inclined to diversify if the superordinate cluster at level i has yet to diversify (where diversification is quantified by the entropy of the gating network).

4   SIMULATIONS

We present simulation results from an unsupervised learning task and two supervised learning tasks.

In the unsupervised learning task, the problem was to extract regularities from a set of measurements of leaf morphology. Two hundred examples of maple, poplar, oak, and birch leaves were generated from the data shown in Table 1. The architecture that we used had two hierarchical levels, two clusters of experts, and two experts

	Maple	Poplar	Oak	Birch
Length	3,4,5,6	1,2,3	5,6,7,8,9	2,3,4,5
Width	3,4,5	1,2	2,3,4,5	1,2,3
Flare	0	0,1	0	1
Lobes	5	1	7,9	1
Margin	Entire	Crenate, Serrate	Entire	Doubly-Serrate
Apex	Acute	Acute	Rounded	Acute
Base	Truncate	Rounded	Cumeate	Rounded
Color	Light	Yellow	Light	Dark

Table 1: Data used to generate examples of leaves from four types of trees. The columns correspond to the type of tree; the rows correspond to the features of a tree's leaf. The table's entries give the possible values for each feature for each type of leaf. See Preston (1976).

within each cluster. Each expert network was an auto-associator that maps forty-eight input units into forty-eight output units through a bottleneck of two hidden units. Within the experts, backpropagation was used to convert the derivatives in Equation 9 into changes to the weights. The gating networks at both levels were affine. We found that the hierarchical architecture consistently discovers the decomposition of the data that preserves the natural classes of tree species (cf. Preston, 1976). That is, within one cluster of expert networks, one expert learns the maple training patterns and the other expert learns the oak patterns. Within the other cluster, one expert learns the poplar patterns and the other expert learns the birch patterns. Moreover, due to the use of the autoassociator experts, the hidden unit representations within each expert are principal component decompositions that are specific to a particular species of leaf.

We have also studied a supervised learning problem in which the learner must predict the grayscale pixel values in noisy images of human faces based on values of the pixels in surrounding $5x5$ masks. There were 5000 masks in the training set. We used a four-level binary tree, with affine experts (each expert mapped from twenty-five input units to a single output unit) and affine gating networks. We compared the performance of the hierarchical architecture to CART and to backpropagation.[1] In the case of backpropagation and the hierarchical architecture, we utilized cross-validation (using a test set of 5000 masks) to stop the iterative training procedure. As shown in Figure 2, the performance of the hierarchical architecture is comparable to backpropagation and better than CART.

Finally we also studied a system identification problem involving learning the simulated forward dynamics of a four-joint, three-dimensional robot arm. The task was to predict the joint accelerations from the joint positions, sines and cosines of joint positions, joint velocities, and torques. There were 6000 data items in the training set. We used a four-level tree with trinary splits at the top two levels, and binary splits at lower levels. The tree had affine experts (each expert mapped

---

[1]Fifty hidden units were used in the backpropagation network, making the number of parameters in the backpropagation network and the hierarchical network roughly comparable.

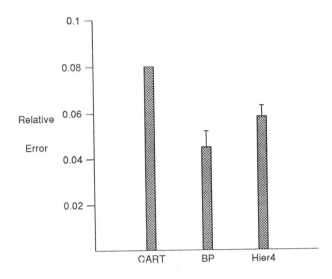

Figure 2: The results on the image restoration task. The dependent measure is relative error on the test set (cf. Breiman, et al., 1984).

from twenty input units to four output units) and affine gating networks. We once again compared the performance of the hierarchical architecture to CART and to backpropagation. In the case of backpropagation and the hierarchical architecture, we utilized a conjugate gradient technique, and halted the training process after 1000 iterations. In the case of CART, we ran the algorithm four separate times on the four output variables. Two of these runs produced 100 percent relative error, a third produced 75 percent relative error, and the fourth (the most proximal joint acceleration) yielded 46 percent relative error, which is the value we report in Figure 3. As shown in the figure, the hierarchical architecture and backpropagation achieve comparable levels of performance.

5   DISCUSSION

In this paper we have presented a neural network learning algorithm that captures aspects of the recursive approach to function approximation exemplified by algorithms such as CART and MARS. The results obtained thus far suggest that the algorithm is computationally viable, comparing favorably to backpropagation in terms of generalization performance on a set of small and medium-sized tasks. The algorithm also has a number of appealing theoretical properties when compared to backpropagation: In the affine case, it is possible to show that (1) no backward propagation of error terms is required to adjust parameters in multi-level trees (cf. the activation-dependence of the multiplicative terms in Equations 9 and 11), (2) all of the parameters in the tree are maximum likelihood estimators. The latter property suggests that the affine architecture may be a particularly suitable architecture in which to explore the effects of priors on the parameter space (cf. Nowlan

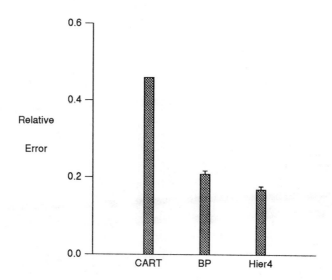

Figure 3: The results on the system identification task.

& Hinton, this volume).

Acknowledgements

This project was supported by grant IRI-9013991 awarded by the National Science Foundation, by a grant from Siemens Corporation, by a grant from ATR Auditory and Visual Perception Research Laboratories, by a grant from the Human Frontier Science Program, and by an NSF Presidential Young Investigator Award to the first author.

References

Breiman, L., Friedman, J.H., Olshen, R.A., & Stone, C.J. (1984) *Classification and Regression Trees.* Belmont, CA: Wadsworth International Group.

Bridle, J. (1989) Probabilistic interpretation of feedforward classification network outputs, with relationships to statistical pattern recognition. In F. Fogelman–Soulie & J. Hérault (Eds.), *Neuro–computing: Algorithms, Architectures, and Applications.* New York: Springer–Verlag.

Friedman, J.H. (1990) Multivariate adaptive regression splines. *The Annals of Statistics, 19,* 1–141.

Jacobs, R.A, Jordan, M.I., Nowlan, S.J., & Hinton, G.E. (1991) Adaptive mixtures of local experts. *Neural Computation, 3,* 79–87.

Preston, R.J. (1976) *North American Trees (Third Edition).* Ames, IA: Iowa State University Press.

Adaptive Soft Weight Tying
using Gaussian Mixtures

Steven J. Nowlan
Computational Neuroscience Laboratory
The Salk Institute, P.O. Box 5800
San Diego, CA 92186-5800

Geoffrey E. Hinton
Department of Computer Science
University of Toronto
Toronto, Canada M5S 1A4

Abstract

One way of simplifying neural networks so they generalize better is to add
an extra term to the error function that will penalize complexity. We
propose a new penalty term in which the distribution of weight values
is modelled as a mixture of multiple gaussians. Under this model, a set
of weights is simple if the weights can be clustered into subsets so that
the weights in each cluster have similar values. We allow the parameters
of the mixture model to adapt at the same time as the network learns.
Simulations demonstrate that this complexity term is more effective than
previous complexity terms.

1 Introduction

A major problem in training artificial neural networks is to ensure that they will
generalize well to cases that they have not been trained on. Some recent theoretical
results (Baum and Haussler, 1989) have suggested that in order to guarantee good
generalization the amount of information required to directly specify the output
vectors of all the training cases must be considerably larger than the number of
independent weights in the network. In many practical problems there is only
a small amount of labelled data available for training and this creates problems
for any approach that uses a large, homogeneous network with many independent
weights. As a result, there has been much recent interest in techniques that can
train large networks with relatively small amounts of labelled data and still provide
good generalization performance.

In order to improve generalization, the number of free parameters in the network
must be reduced. One of the oldest and simplest approaches to removing excess
degrees of freedom from a network is to add an extra term to the error function

993

that penalizes complexity:

$$\text{cost} = \text{data-misfit} + \lambda \, \text{complexity} \tag{1}$$

During learning, the network is trying to find a locally optimal trade-off between the data-misfit (the usual error term) and the complexity of the net. The relative importance of these two terms can be estimated by finding the value of λ that optimizes generalization to a validation set. Probably the simplest approximation to complexity is the sum of the squares of the weights, $\sum_i w_i^2$. Differentiating this complexity measure leads to simple *weight decay* (Plaut, Nowlan and Hinton, 1986) in which each weight decays towards zero at a rate that is proportional to its magnitude. This decay is countered by the gradient of the error term, so weights which are not critical to network performance, and hence always have small error gradients, decay away leaving only the weights necessary to solve the problem.

The use of a $\sum_i w_i^2$ penalty term can also be interpreted from a Bayesian perspective.[1] The "complexity" of a set of weights, $\lambda \sum_i w_i^2$, may be described as its negative log probability density under a radially symmetric gaussian prior distribution on the weights. The distribution is centered at the origin and has variance $1/\lambda$. For multilayer networks, it is hard to find a good theoretical justification for this prior, but Hinton (1987) justifies it empirically by showing that it greatly improves generalization on a very difficult task. More recently, Mackay (1991) has shown that even better generalization can be achieved by using different values of λ for the weights in different layers.

2   A more complex measure of network complexity

If we wish to eliminate small weights without forcing large weights away from the values they need to model the data, we can use a prior which is a mixture of a narrow (n) and a broad (b) gaussian, both centered at zero.

$$p(w) = \pi_n \frac{1}{\sqrt{2\pi}\sigma_n} e^{-\frac{w^2}{2\sigma_n^2}} + \pi_b \frac{1}{\sqrt{2\pi}\sigma_b} e^{-\frac{w^2}{2\sigma_b^2}} \tag{2}$$

where π_n and π_b are the mixing proportions of the two gaussians and are therefore constrained to sum to 1.

Assuming that the weight values were generated from a gaussian mixture, the conditional probability that a particular weight, w_i, was generated by a particular gaussian, j, is called the *responsibility* of that gaussian for the weight and is:

$$r_j(w_i) = \frac{\pi_j p_j(w_i)}{\sum_k \pi_k p_k(w_i)} \tag{3}$$

where $p_j(w_i)$ is the probability density of w_i under gaussian j.

When the mixing proportions of the two gaussians are comparable, the narrow gaussian gets most of the responsibility for a small weight. Adopting the Bayesian perspective, the cost of a weight under the narrow gaussian is proportional to $w^2/2\sigma_n^2$. As long as σ_n is quite small there will be strong pressure to reduce the magnitude

---

[1]R. Szeliski, personal communication, 1985.

of small weights even further. Conversely, the broad gaussian takes most of the responsibility for large weight values, so there is much less pressure to reduce them. In the limiting case when the broad gaussian becomes a uniform distribution, there is almost no pressure to reduce very large weights because they are almost certainly generated by the uniform distribution. A complexity term very similar to this limiting case is used in the "weight elimination" technique of (Weigend, Huberman and Rumelhart, 1990) to improve generalization for a time series prediction task. [2]

3   Adaptive Gaussian Mixtures and Soft Weight-Sharing

A mixture of a narrow, zero-mean gaussian with a broad gaussian or a uniform allows us to favor networks with many near-zero weights, and this improves generalization on many tasks. But practical experience with hand-coded weight constraints has also shown that great improvements can be achieved by constraining particular subsets of the weights to share the same value (Lang, Waibel and Hinton, 1990; Le Cun, 1989). Mixtures of zero-mean gaussians and uniforms cannot implement this type of symmetry constraint. If however, we use multiple gaussians and allow their means and variances to adapt as the network learns, we can implement a "soft" version of weight-sharing in which the learning algorithm decides for itself which weights should be tied together. (We may also allow the mixing proportions to adapt so that we are not assuming all sets of tied weights are the same size.)

The basic idea is that a gaussian which takes responsibility for a subset of the weights will squeeze those weights together since it can then have a lower variance and assign a higher probability density to each weight. If the gaussians all start with high variance, the initial division of weights into subsets will be very soft. As the variances shrink and the network learns, the decisions about how to group the weights into subsets are influenced by the task the network is learning to perform.

To make these intuitive ideas a bit more concrete, we may define a cost function of the general form given in (1):

$$C = \frac{K}{\sigma_y^2} \sum_c \frac{1}{2}(y_c - d_c)^2 - \sum_i \log\left(\sum_j \pi_j p_j(w_i)\right) \tag{4}$$

where σ_y^2 is the variance of the squared error and each $p_j(w_i)$ is a gaussian density with mean μ_j and standard deviation σ_j. We optimize this function by adjusting the w_i and the mixture parameters π_j, μ_j, and σ_j, and σ_y.[3]

The partial derivative of C with respect to each weight is the sum of the usual squared error derivative and a term due to the complexity cost for the weight:

$$\frac{\partial C}{\partial w_i} = \frac{K}{\sigma_y^2} \sum_c (y_c - d_c)\frac{\partial y_c}{\partial w_i} - \sum_j r_j(w_i)\frac{(\mu_j - w_i)}{\sigma_j^2} \tag{5}$$

---

[2] See (Nowlan, 1991) for a precise description of the relationship between mixture models and the model used by (Weigend, Huberman and Rumelhart, 1990).

[3] $1/\sigma_y^2$ may be thought of as playing the same role as λ in equation 1 in determining a trade-off between the misfit and complexity costs. K is a normalizing factor based on a gaussian error model.

Method	Train % Correct	Test % Correct
Vanilla Back Prop.	100.0 ± 0.0	67.3 ± 5.7
Cross Valid.	98.8 ± 1.1	83.5 ± 5.1
Weight Elimination	100.0 ± 0.0	89.8 ± 3.0
Soft-share - 5 Comp.	100.0 ± 0.0	95.6 ± 2.7
Soft-share - 10 Comp.	100.0 ± 0.0	97.1 ± 2.1

Table 1: Summary of generalization performance of 5 different training techniques on the shift detection problem.

The derivative of the complexity cost term is simply a weighted sum of the difference between the weight value and the center of each of the gaussians. The weighting factors are the *responsibility* measures defined in equation 3 and if over time a single gaussian claims most of the responsibility for a particular weight the effect of the complexity cost term is simply to pull the weight towards the center of the responsible gaussian. The strength of this force is inversely proportional to the variance of the gaussian.

In the simulations described below, all of the parameters $(w_i, \mu_j, \sigma_j, \pi_j)$ are updated *simultaneously* using a conjugate gradient descent procedure. To prevent variances shrinking too fast or going negative we optimize $\log \sigma_j$ rather than σ_j. To ensure that the mixing proportions sum to 1 and are positive, we optimize x_j where $\pi_j = exp(x_j)/\sum exp(x_k)$. For further details see (Nowlan and Hinton, 1992).

4   Simulation Results

We compared the generalization performance of soft weight-tying to other techniques on two different problems. The first problem, a 20 input, one output shift detection network, was chosen because it was binary problem for which solutions which generalize well exhibit a lot of repeated weight structure. The generalization performance of networks trained using the cost criterion given in equation 4 was compared to networks trained in three other ways: No cost term to penalize complexity; No explicit complexity cost term, but use of a validation set to terminate learning; Weight elimination (Weigend, Huberman and Rumelhart, 1990)[4]. The simulation results are summarized in Table 1.

The network had 20 input units, 10 hidden units, and a single output unit and contained 101 weights. The first 10 input units in this network were given a random binary pattern, and the second group of 10 input units were given the same pattern circularly shifted by 1 bit left or right. The desired output of the network was $+1$ for a left shift and -1 for a right shift. A data set of 2400 patterns was created by randomly generating a 10 bit string, and choosing with equal probability to shift the string left or right. The data set was divided into 100 training cases, 1000 validation cases, and 1300 test cases. The training set was deliberately chosen to be very small ($< 5\%$ of possible patterns) to explore the region in which complexity penalties should have the largest impact. Ten simulations were performed with each

---

[4]With a fixed value of λ chosen by cross-validation.

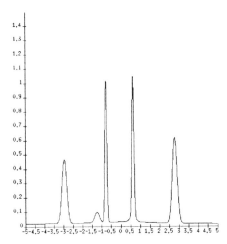

Figure 1: Final mixture probability density for a typical solution to the shift detection problem. Five of the components in the mixture can be seen as distinct bumps in the probability density. Of the remaining five components, two have been eliminated by having their mixing proportions go to zero and the other three are very broad and form the baseline offset of the density function.

method, starting from ten different initial weight sets (*i.e.* each method used the same ten initial weight configurations).

The final weight distributions discovered by the soft weight-tying technique are shown in Figure 1. There is no significant component with mean 0. The classical assumption that the network contains a large number of inessential weights which can be eliminated to improve generalization is not appropriate for this problem and network architecture. This may explain why the weight elimination model used by Weigend *et al* (Weigend, Huberman and Rumelhart, 1990) performs relatively poorly in this situation.

The second task chosen to evaluate the effectiveness of our complexity penalty was the prediction of the yearly sunspot average from the averages of previous years. This task has been well studied as a time-series prediction benchmark in the statistics literature (Priestley, 1991b; Priestley, 1991a) and has also been investigated by (Weigend, Huberman and Rumelhart, 1990) using a complexity penalty similar to the one discussed in section 2.

The network architecture used was identical to the one used in the study by Weigend *et al*. The network had 12 input units which represented the yearly average from the preceding 12 years, 8 hidden units, and a single linear output unit which represented the prediction for the average number of sunspots in the current year. Yearly sunspot data from 1700 to 1920 was used to train the network to perform this one-step prediction task, and the evaluation of the network was based on data from

Method	Test arv
TAR	0.097
RBF	0.092
WRH	0.086
Soft-share - 3 Comp.	0.077 ± 0.0029
Soft-share - 8 Comp.	0.072 ± 0.0022

Table 2: Summary of average relative variance of 5 different models on the one-step sunspot prediction problem.

1921 to 1955.[5] The evaluation of prediction performance used the *average relative variance* (*arv*) measure discussed in (Weigend, Huberman and Rumelhart, 1990).

Simulations were performed using the same conjugate gradient method used for the first problem. Complexity measures based on gaussian mixtures with 3 and 8 components were used and ten simulations were performed with each (using the same training data but different initial weight configurations). The results of these simulations are summarized in Table 2 along with the best result obtained by Weigend *et al* (Weigend, Huberman and Rumelhart, 1990) (*WRH*), the bilinear auto-regression model of Tong and Lim (Tong and Lim, 1980) (*TAR*)[6], and the multi-layer RBF network of He and Lapedes (He and Lapedes, 1991) (*RBF*). All figures represent the *arv* on the test set. For the mixture complexity models, this is the *average* over the ten simulations, plus or minus one standard deviation.

Since the results for the models other than the mixture complexity trained networks are based on a single simulation it is difficult to assign statistical signifigance to the differences shown in Table 2. We may note however, that the difference between the 3 and 8 component mixture complexity models is significant ($p > 0.95$) and the differences between the 8 component model and the other models are much larger.

Figure 2 shows an 8 component mixture model of the final weight distribution. It is quite unlike the distribution in Figure 1 and is actually quite close to a mixture of two zero-mean gaussians, one broad and one narrow. This may explain why weight elimination works quite well for this task.

Weigend *et al* point out that for time series prediction tasks such as the sunspot task a much more interesting measure of performance is the ability of the model to predict more than one time step into the future. One way to approach the multi-step prediction problem is to use *iterated single-step prediction*. In this method, the predicted output is fed back as input for the next prediction and all other input units have their values shifted back one unit. Thus the input typically consists of a combination of actual and predicted values. When predicting more than one step into the future, the prediction error depends both on how many steps into the future one is predicting (I) and on what point in the time series the prediction began. An appropriate error measure for iterated prediction is the *average relative I-times iterated prediction variance* (Weigend, Huberman and Rumelhart, 1990)

---

[5]The authors thank Andreas Weigend for providing his version of this data.

[6]This was the model favored by Priestly (Priestley, 1991a) in a recent evaluation of classical statistical approaches to this task.

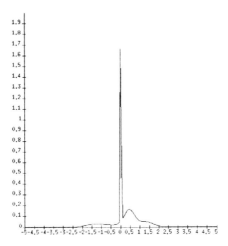

Figure 2: Typical final mixture probability density for the sunspot prediction problem with a model containing 8 mixture components.

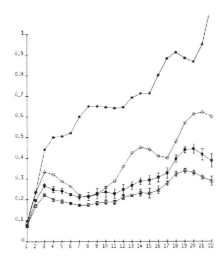

Figure 3: Average relative I-times iterated prediction variance versus number of prediction iterations for the sunspot time series from 1921 to 1955. Closed circles represent the TAR model, open circles the WRH model, closed squares the 3 component complexity model, and open squares the 8 component complexity model. Ten different sets of initial weights were used for the 3 and 8 component complexity models and one standard deviation error bars are shown.

which averages predictions I steps into the future over all possible starting points. Using this measure, the performance of various models is shown in Figure 3.

5   Summary

The simulations we have described provide evidence that the use of a more flexible model for the distribution of weights in a network can lead to better generalization performance than weight decay, weight elimination, or techniques that control the learning time. The flexibility of our model is clearly demonstrated in the very different final weight distributions discovered for the two different problems investigated in this paper. The ability to automatically adapt to individual problems suggests that the method should have broad applicability.

Acknowledgements

This research was funded by the Ontario ITRC, the Canadian NSERC and the Howard Hughes Medical Institute. Hinton is the Noranda fellow of the Canadian Institute for Advanced Research.

References

Baum, E. B. and Haussler, D. (1989). What size net gives valid generalization? *Neural Computation*, 1:151–160.

He, X. and Lapedes, A. (1991). Nonlinear modelling and prediction by successive approximation using Radial Basis Functions. Technical Report LA-UR-91-1375, Los Alamos National Laboratory.

Hinton, G. E. (1987). Learning translation invariant recognition in a massively parallel network. In *Proc. Conf. Parallel Architectures and Languages Europe*, Eindhoven.

Lang, K. J., Waibel, A. H., and Hinton, G. E. (1990). A time-delay neural network architecture for isolated word recognition. *Neural Networks*, 3:23–43.

Le Cun, Y. (1989). Generalization and network design strategies. Technical Report CRG-TR-89-4, University of Toronto.

MacKay, D. J. C. (1991). *Bayesian Modelling and Neural Networks*. PhD thesis, Computation and Neural Systems, California Institute of Technology, Pasadena, CA.

Nowlan, S. J. (1991). *Soft Competitive Adaptation: Neural Network Learning Algorithms based on Fitting Statistical Mixtures*. PhD thesis, School of Computer Science, Carnegie Mellon University, Pittsburgh, PA.

Nowlan, S. J. and Hinton, G. E. (1992). Simplifying neural networks by soft weight-sharing. *Neural Computation*. In press.

Plaut, D. C., Nowlan, S. J., and Hinton, G. E. (1986). Experiments on learning by back-propagation. Technical Report CMU-CS-86-126, Carnegie-Mellon University, Pittsburgh PA 15213.

Priestley, M. B. (1991a). *Non-linear and Non-stationary Time Series Analysis*. Academic Press.

Priestley, M. B. (1991b). *Spectral Analysis and Time Series*. Academic Press.

Tong, H. and Lim, K. S. (1980). Threshold autoregression, limit cycles, and cyclical data. *Journal Royal Statistical Society B*, 42.

Weigend, A. S., Huberman, B. A., and Rumelhart, D. E. (1990). Predicting the future: A connectionist approach. *International Journal of Neural Systems*, 1.

Repeat Until Bored: A Pattern Selection Strategy

Paul W. Munro
Department of Information Science
University of Pittsburgh
Pittsburgh, PA   15260

ABSTRACT

An alternative to the typical technique of selecting training examples independently from a fixed distribution is formulated and analyzed, in which the current example is presented repeatedly until the error for that item is reduced to some criterion value, β; then, another item is randomly selected. The convergence time can be dramatically increased or decreased by this heuristic, depending on the task, and is very sensitive to the value of β.

1   INTRODUCTION

In order to implement the back propagation learning procedure (Werbos, 1974; Parker, 1985; Rumelhart, Hinton and Williams, 1986), several issues must be addressed. In addition to designing an appropriate network architecture and determining appropriate values for the learning parameters, the batch size and a scheme for selecting training examples must be chosen. The batch size is the number of patterns presented for which the corresponding weight changes are computed before they are actually implemented; immediate update is equivalent to a batch size of one. The principal pattern selection schemes are independent selections from a stationary distribution (independent identically distributed, or i.i.d.) and epochal, in which the training set is presented cyclically (here, each cycle through the training set is called an epoch). Under i.i.d. pattern selection, the learning performance is sensitive to the sequence of training examples. This observation suggests that there may exist selection strategies that facilitate learning. Several studies have shown the benefit of strategic pattern selection (e.g., Mozer and Bachrach, 1990; Atlas, Cohn, and Ladner, 1990; Baum and Lang, 1991).

Typically, online learning is implemented by independent identically distributed pattern selection, which cannot (by definition) take advantage of useful sequencing strategy. It seems likely, or certainly plausible, that the success of learning depends to some extent on the order in which stimuli are presented. An extreme, though negative, example would be to restrict learning to a portion of the available training sct; i.e. to reduce the effective training set. Let sampling functions that depend on the state of the learner in a constructive way be termed *pedagogical*.

Determination of a particular input may require information exogenous to the learner; that is, just as training algorithms have been classified as supervised and unsupervised, so can pedagogical pattern selection techniques. For example, selection may depend on the network's performance relative to a desired schedule. The intent of this study is to explore an unsupervised selection procedure (even though a supervised learning rule, backpropagation, is used). The initial selection heuristic investigated was to evaluate the errors across the entire pattern set for each iteration and to present the pattern with the highest error; of course, this technique has a large computational overhead, but the question was whether it would reduce the number of learning trials. The results were quite to the contrary; preliminary trials on small tasks (two and three bit parity), show that this scheme performs very poorly with all patterns maintaining high error.

A new unsupervised selection technique is introduced here. The "Repeat-Until-Bored" heuristic is easily implemented and simply stated: if the current training example generates a high error (i.e. greater than a fixed criterion value), it is repeated; otherwise, another one is randomly selected. This approach was motivated by casual observations of behavior in small children; they seem to repeat seemingly arbitrary tasks several times, and then abruptly stop and move to some seemingly arbitrary alternative (Piaget, 1952). For the following discussion, IID and RUB will denote the two selection procedures to be compared.

2 METHODOLOGY

RUB can be implemented by adding a condition to the IID statement; in C, this is simply

```
old(IID):  patno = random() % numpats;
new(RUB):  if (paterror<beta) patno = random() % numpats;
```

where *patno* identifies the selected pattern, *numpats* is the number of patterns in the training set, and *paterror* is the sum squared error on a particular pattern. Thus, an example is presented and repeated until it has been learned by the network to some criterion level, the squared error summed across the output units is less than a "boredom" criterion β; then, another pattern is randomly selected.

The action of RUB in weight space is illustrated in Figure 1, for a two dimensional environment consisting of just two patterns. Corresponding to each pattern, there is an isocline (or equilibrium surface) , defined by the locus of weight vectors that yield the desired response to that pattern (here, **a** or **b**). Since the delta rule drives the weight parallel to the presented pattern, trajectories in weight space are perpendicular to the pattern's isocline. Here, RUB is compared with alternate pattern selection.

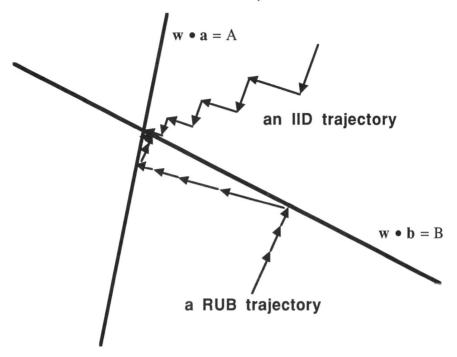

Figure 1. *Effect of pattern selection on weight state trajectory.* A linear unit can be trained to give arbitrary responses (A and B) to given stimuli (**a** and **b**). The isoclines (bold lines) are defined to be the set of weights that satisfy each stimulus-response pair. Thus, the intersection is the weight state that satisfies both constraints. The delta rule drives the weights toward the isocline that corresponds to the presented pattern. The RUB procedure repeats a pattern until the state approaches the isocline.

The RUB procedure was tested for a broad range of β across several tasks. Two performance measures were used; in both cases, performance was averaged across several (20-100) trials with different initial random weights. For the parity tasks, performance was measured as the fraction of trials for which the squared error summed over the training set reached a sufficiently low value (usually 0.1) within a specified number of training examples. Since the parity task always converged for sufficiently large β, performance was measured as the number of trials that converged within a prespecified number of iterations required to reduce the total squared error summed across the pattern set to a low value (typically, 0.1). Note that each iteration of weight modification during a set of repeated examples was explicitly counted in the performance measure, so the comparison between IID and RUB is fair. Also, for each task, the learning rate and momentum were fixed (ususally 0.1 and 0.9, respectively).

Consideration of RUB (see the above C implementation, for example) indicates that, for very small values of β, the first example will be repeated indefinitely, and the task can therefore not be learned. At the other extreme, for β greater than or equal to the maximum possible squared error (2.0, in this case), performance should match IID.

3 RESULTS

3.1. PARITY

While the expected behavior for RUB on the two and three bit parity tasks (Figure 2) is observed for low and high values of β, there are some surprises in the intermediate range. Rather than proceeding monotonically from zero to its IID value, the performance curve exhibits an "up-down-up" behavior; it reaches a maximum in the range 0.2<β<0.25, then plummets to zero at β=0.25, remains there for an interval, then partially recovers at its final (IID) level. This "dead zone" phenomenon is not as pronounced when the momentum parameter is set to zero (Figure 3).

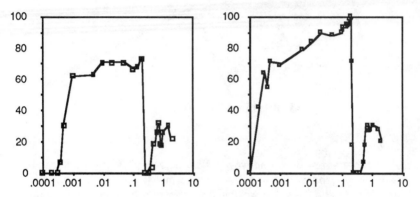

Figure 2. *Performance profiles for the parity task.* Each point is the average number of successful simulations out of 100 trials. A log scale is used so that the behavior for very low values of the error criterion is evident. Note the critical falloff at β≈0.25 for both the XOR task (left) and three-bit parity (right).

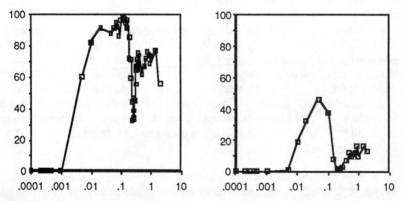

Figure 3. *Performance profiles with zero momemtum.* For these two tasks, the up-down-up phenomenon is still evident, but there is no "dead zone".
Left: XOR Right: Three bit parity

3.2 ENCODERS

The 4-2-4 encoder shows no significant improvement over the IID for any value of RUB. Here, performance was measured both in terms of success rate and average number of iterations to success. Even though all simulations converge for $\beta > .001$ (i.e., there is no dead zone), the effect of β is reflected in another performance measure: average number of iterations to convergence (Figure 4). However, experiments with the 5-2-5 encoder task show an effect. While backprop converges for all values of β (except very small values), the performance, as measured by number of pattern presentations, does show a pronounced decrement. The 8-3-8 encoder shows a significant, but less dramatic, effect.

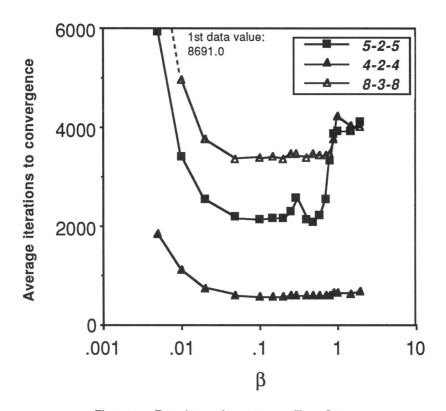

Figure 4. *Encoder performance profiles.* See text.

3.3 THE MESH

The mesh (Figure 5, left) is a 2-D classification task that can be solved by a strictly layered net with five hidden units. Like the encoder and unlike parity, IID is found to converge on 100% of trials; however, there is a critical value of β and a well-defined dead zone (Figure 5, right). Note that the curve depicting average number of iterations to convergence decreases monotonically, interrupted at the dead zone but continuing its apparent trend for higher values of β.

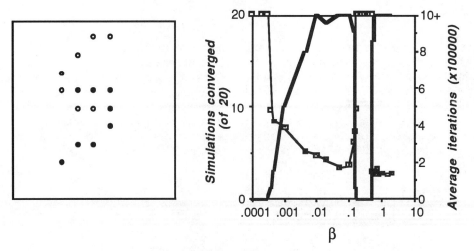

Figure 5. *The mesh task.* **Left:** the task. **Right:** Performance profile. Number of simulations that converge is plotted along the bold line (left vertical) axis. Average number of iterations are plotted as squares (right vertical axis).

3.4 NONCONVERGENCE

Nonconvergence was examined in detail for three values of β, corresponding to high performance, poor performance (the dead zone), and IID, for the three bit parity task. The error for each of the eight patterns is plotted over time. For trials that do not converge (Figure 6), the patterns interact differently, depending on the value of β. At $\beta=0.05$ (a "good" value of β for this task), the error traces for the four odd-parity patterns are strongly correlated in an irregular oscillatory mode, as are the four even-parity traces, but the two groups are strongly anticorrelated. In the odd parity group, the error remains low for three of the patterns (001, 010, and 100), but ranges from less than 0.1 to values greater than 0.95 for the fourth (111). Traces for the even parity patterns correspond almost identically; i.e. not only are they correlated, but all four maintain virtually the same value.

At this point, the dead zone phenomenon has only been observed in tasks with a single output unit. This property hints at the following explanation. Note first that each input/output pair in the training set divides the weight space into two halves, characterized by the sign of the linear activation into the output unit; that is, whether the output is above or below 0.5, and hence whether the magnitude of the difference between the actual and desired responses is above or below 0.5. Since β is the value of the *squared* error, learning is repeated for $\beta=0.25$ only for examples for which the state is on the wrong *half* of weight space. Just when it is about to cross the category boundary, which would bring the absolute value of the error below .5, RUB switches to another example, and the state is not pushed to the other side of the boundary. This conjecture suggests that for tasks with multiple output units, this effect might be reduced or eliminated, as has been demonstrated in the encoder examples.

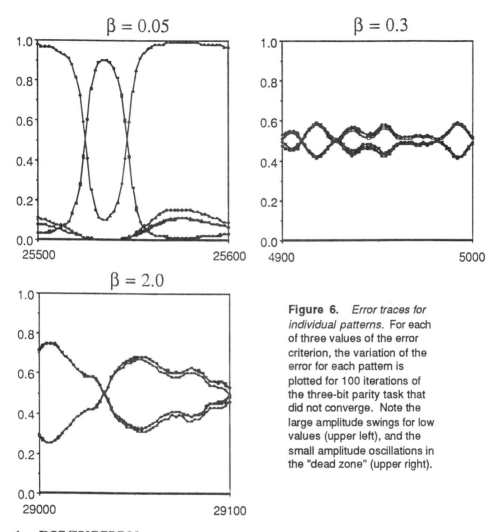

Figure 6. *Error traces for individual patterns.* For each of three values of the error criterion, the variation of the error for each pattern is plotted for 100 iterations of the three-bit parity task that did not converge. Note the large amplitude swings for low values (upper left), and the small amplitude oscillations in the "dead zone" (upper right).

4   DISCUSSION

Active learning and boredom. The sequence of training examples has an undeniable effect on learning, both in the real world and in simulated learning systems. While the RUB procedure influences this sequence such that the learning performance is either positively or negatively affected, it is just a minimal instance of active learning; more elaborate learning systems have explored similar notions of "boredom" (eg., Scott and Markovitch, 1989).

Nonconvergence. From Figure 6 it can be seen, for both RUB and IID, that nonconvergence does not correspond to a local minimum in weight space. In situations where the overall error is "stuck" at a non-zero value, the error on the individual patterns continues to change. The weight trajectory is thus "trapped" in a nonoptimal *orbit,* rather than a nonoptimal equilibrium *point.*

Acknowledgements

This research was supported in part by NSF grant IRI-8910368 and by Siemens Corporate Research, which kindly provided the author with financial support and a stimulating research environment during the summer of 1990. David Cohn and Rik Belew were helpful in bringing relevant work to my attention.

References

Baum, E. and Lang, K. (1991) Constructing multi-layer neural networks by searching input space rather than weight space. In: *Advances in Neural Information Processing Systems 3*. D. S. Touretsky, ed. Morgan Kaufmann.

Cohn, D., Atlas, L., and Ladner, R. (1990) Training connectionist networks with queries and selective sampling. In: *Advances in Neural Information Processing Systems 2*. D. S. Touretsky, ed. Morgan Kaufmann.

Mozer, M. and Bachrach, J. (1990) Discovering the structure of a reactive environment by exploration. In: *Advances in Neural Information Processing Systems 2*. D. S. Touretsky, ed. Morgan Kaufmann.

Parker, D. (1985) Learning logic. TR-47. MIT Center for Computational Economics and Statistics. Cambridge MA.

Piaget, J. (1952) *The Origins of Intelligence in Children*. Norton.

Rumelhart D., Hinton G., and Williams R. (1986) Learning representations by back-propagating errors. *Nature* 3 2 3:533-536.

Scott, P. D. and Markovitch, S. (1989) Uncertainty based selection of learning experiences. *Sixth International Workshop on Machine Learning*. pp.358-361

Werbos, P. (1974) Beyond regression: new tools for prediction and analysis in the behavioral sciences. Unpublished doctoral dissertation, Harvard University.

Towards Faster Stochastic Gradient Search

Christian Darken and John Moody
Yale Computer Science, P.O. Box 2158, New Haven, CT 06520
Email: darken@cs.yale.edu

Abstract

Stochastic gradient descent is a general algorithm which includes LMS, on-line backpropagation, and adaptive k-means clustering as special cases. The standard choices of the learning rate η (both adaptive and fixed functions of time) often perform quite poorly. In contrast, our recently proposed class of "search then converge" learning rate schedules (Darken and Moody, 1990) display the *theoretically optimal* asymptotic convergence rate and a superior ability to escape from poor local minima. However, the user is responsible for setting a key parameter. We propose here a new methodology for creating the first completely automatic adaptive learning rates which achieve the *optimal rate of convergence*.

Introduction

The stochastic gradient descent algorithm is

$$\Delta W(t) = -\eta \nabla_W E(W(t), X(t)).$$

where η is the learning rate, t is the "time", and $X(t)$ is the independent random exemplar chosen at time t. The purpose of the algorithm is to find a parameter vector W which minimizes a function $G(W)$ which for learning algorithms has the form $\mathcal{E}_X E(W, X)$, i.e. G is the average of an objective function over the exemplars, labeled E and X respectively. We can rewrite $\Delta W(t)$ in terms of G as

$$\Delta W(t) = -\eta [\nabla_W G(W(t)) + \xi(t, W(t))],$$

where the ξ are independent zero-mean noises. Stochastic gradient descent may be preferable to deterministic gradient descent when the exemplar set is increasing in size over time or large, making the average over exemplars expensive to compute.

1009

Additionally, the noise in the gradient can help the system escape from local minima. The fundamental algorithmic issue is **how to best adjust η as a function of time and the exemplars?**

State of the Art Schedules

The usual non-adaptive choices of η (i.e. η depends on the time only) often yield poor performance. The simple expedient of taking η to be constant results in persistent residual fluctuations whose magnitude and the resulting degradation of system performance are difficult to anticipate (see fig. 3). Taking a smaller constant η reduces the magnitude of the fluctuations, but seriously slows convergence and causes problems with metastable local minima. Taking $\eta(t) = c/t$, the common choice in the stochastic approximation literature of the last forty years, typically results in slow convergence to bad solutions for small c, and parameter blow-up for small t if c is large (Darken and Moody, 1990).

The available adaptive schedules (i.e. η depends on the time *and* on previous exemplars) have problems as well. Classical methods which involve estimating the hessian of G are often unusable because they require $O(N^2)$ storage and computation for each update, which is too expensive for large N (many parameter systems— e.g. large neural nets). Methods such as those of Fabian (1960) and Kesten (1958) require the user to specify an entire function and thus are not practical methods as they stand. The delta-bar-delta learning rule, which was developed in the context of deterministic gradient descent (Jacobs, 1988), is often useful in locating the general vicinity of a solution in the stochastic setting. However it hovers about the solution without converging (see fig. 4). A schedule developed by Urasiev is proven to converge in principle, but in practice it converges slowly if at all (see fig. 5). The literature is widely scattered over time and disciplines, however to our knowledge no published $O(N)$ technique attains the optimal convergence speed.

Search-Then-Converge Schedules

Our recently proposed solution is the "search then converge" learning rate schedule. η is chosen to be a fixed function of time such as the following:

$$\eta(t) = \eta_0 \frac{1 + \frac{c}{\eta_0}\frac{t}{\tau}}{1 + \frac{c}{\eta_0}\frac{t}{\tau} + \tau\frac{t^2}{\tau^2}}$$

This function is approximately constant with value η_0 at times small compared to τ (the "search phase"). At times large compared with τ (the "converge phase"), the function decreases as c/t. See for example the eta vs. time curves for figs. 6 and 7. This schedule has demonstrated a dramatic improvement in convergence speed and quality of solution as compared to the traditional fixed learning rate schedule for k-means clustering (Darken and Moody, 1990). However, these benefits apply to supervised learning as well. Compare the error curve of fig. 3 with those of figs. 6 and 7.

This schedule yields optimally fast asymptotic convergence if $c > c^*$, $c^* \equiv 1/2\alpha$, where α is the smallest eigenvalue of the hessian of the function G (defined above)

Little Drift   **Much Drift**

Figure 1: Two contrasting parameter vector trajectories illustrating the notion of drift

at the pertinent minimum (Fabian, 1968) (Major and Revesz, 1973) (Goldstein, 1987). The penalty for choosing $c < c^*$ is that the ratio of the excess error given c too small to the excess error with c large enough gets arbitrarily large as training time grows, i.e.

$$\lim_{t \to \infty} \frac{E_{c<c^*}}{E_{c>c^*}} = \infty,$$

where E is the excess error above that at the minimum. The same holds for the ratio of the two distances to the location of the minimum in parameter space.

While the above schedule works well, its asymptotic performance depends upon the user's choice of c. Since neither η_0 nor τ affects the asymptotic behavior of the system, we will discuss their selection elsewhere. Setting $c > c^*$, however, is vital. Can such a c be determined automatically? Directly estimating α with conventional methods (by calculating the smallest eigenvalue of the hessian at our current estimate of the minimum) is too computationally demanding. This would take at least $O(N^2)$ storage and computation time for each estimate, and would have to be done repeatedly (N is the number of parameters). We are investigating the possibility of a low complexity direct estimation of α by performing a second optimization. However here we take a more unusual approach: we shall determine whether c is large enough by observing the trajectory of the parameter (or "weight") vector.

On-line Determination of Whether $c < c^*$

We propose that excessive correlation in the parameter change vectors (i.e. "drift") indicates that c is too small (see fig. 1). We define the drift as

$$D(t) \equiv \sum_k d_k^2(t)$$

$$d_k(t) \equiv \sqrt{T} \frac{\langle \delta_k(t) \rangle_T}{[\langle (\delta_k(t) - \langle \delta_k(t) \rangle_T)^2 \rangle_T]^{1/2}}$$

where $\delta_k(t)$ is the change in the kth component of the parameter vector at time t and the angled brackets denote an average over T parameter changes. We take $T = at$, where $a << 1$. Notice that the numerator is the average parameter step while the

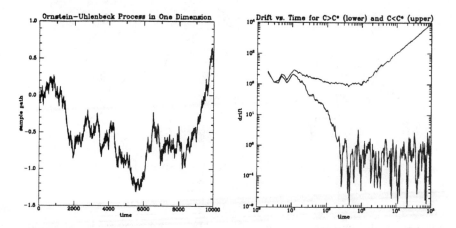

Figure 2: (Left) An Ornstein–Uhlenbeck process. This process is zero-mean, gaussian, and stationary (in fact strongly ergodic). It may be thought of as a random walk with a restoring force towards zero. (Right) Measurement of the drift for the runs $c = .1c^*$ and $c = 10c^*$ which are discussed in figs. 7 and 8 below.

denominator is the standard deviation of the steps. As a point of reference, if the δ_k were independent normal random variables, then the d_k would be "T-distributed" with Γ degrees of freedom, i.e. approximately unit-variance normals for moderate to large T. We find that δ_k may also be taken to be the kth component of the noisy gradient to the same effect.

Asymptotically, we will take the learning rate to go as c/t. Choosing c too small results in a slow drift of the parameter vector towards the solution in a relatively linear trajectory. When $c > c^*$ however, the trajectory is much more jagged. Compare figs. 7 and 8. More precisely, we find that $D(t)$ **blows up like a power of t when c is too small, but remains finite otherwise.** Our experiments confirm this (for an example, see fig. 2). This provides us with a signal to use in future adaptive learning rate schemes for ensuring that c is large enough.

The bold-printed statement above implies that an arbitrarily small change in c which moves it to the opposite side of c^* has dramatic consequences for the behavior of the drift. The following rough argument outlines how one might prove this statement, focusing on the source of this interesting discontinuity in behavior. We simplify the argument by taking the δ_k's to be gradient measurements as mentioned above. We consider a one-dimensional problem, and modify d_1 to be $\sqrt{T}\langle \delta_1 \rangle_T$ (i.e. we ignore the denominator). Then since $T = at$ as stated above, we approximate

$$d_1 \equiv \sqrt{T}\langle \delta_1(t) \rangle_T \approx \langle \sqrt{t}\delta_1(t) \rangle_T = \langle \sqrt{t}[\nabla G(t) + \xi(t)] \rangle_T$$

Recall the definitions of G and ξ from the introduction above. As $t \to \infty$, $\nabla G(t) \to K[W(t) - W_0]$ for the appropriate K by the Taylor's expansion for G around W_0, the location of the local minimum. Thus

$$\lim_{t \to \infty} d_1 \approx \langle K\sqrt{t}[W(t) - W_0] \rangle_T + \langle \sqrt{t}\xi(t) \rangle_T$$

Define $X(t) \equiv \sqrt{t}[W(t) - W_0]$. Now according to (Kushner, 1978), $X(e^t)$ converges

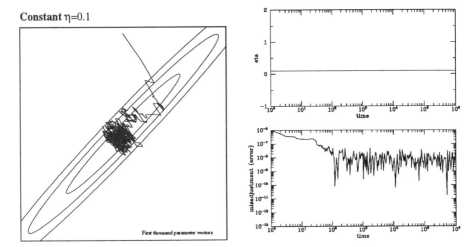

Constant η=0.1

Figure 3: The constant η schedule, commonly used in training backpropagation networks, does not converge in the stochastic setting.

in distribution to the well-known Ornstein-Uhlenbeck process (fig. 2) when $c > c^*$. By extending this work, one can show that $X(t)$ converges in distribution to a *deterministic* power law, t^p with $p > 0$ when $c < c^*$. Since the ξ's are independent and have uniformly bounded variances for smooth objective functions, the second term converges in distribution to a finite-variance random variable. The first term converges to a finite-variance random variable if $c > c^*$, but to a power of t if $c < c^*$.

Qualitative Behavior of Schedules

We compare several fixed and adaptive learning rate schedules on a toy stochastic problem. Notice the difficulties that are encountered by some schedules even on a fairly easy problem due to noise in the gradient. The problem is learning a two parameter adaline in the presence of independent uniformly distributed $[-0.5, 0.5]$ noise on the exemplar labels. Exemplars were independently uniformly distributed on $[-1, 1]$. The objective function has a condition number of 10, indicating the presence of the narrow ravine indicated by the elliptical isopleths in the figures. All runs start from the same parameter (weight) vector and receive the same sequence of exemplars. The misadjustment is defined as the Euclidean distance in parameter space to the minimum. Multiples of this quantity bound the usual sum of squares error measure above and below, i.e. sum of squares error is roughly proportional to the misadjustment. Results are presented in figs. 3–8.

Conclusions

Our empirical tests agree with our theoretical expectations that drift can be used to determine whether the crucial parameter c is large enough. Using this statistic, it will be possible to produce the first fully automatic learning rates which converge at optimal speed. We are currently investigating candidate schedules which we expect to be useful for large-scale LMS, backpropagation, and clustering applications.

Stochastic Delta-Bar-Delta

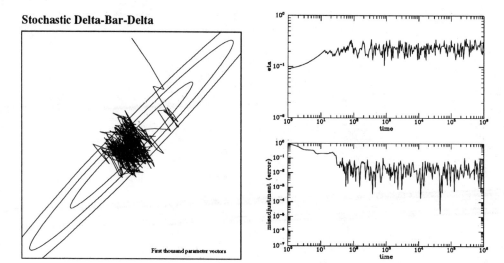

Figure 4: Delta-bar-delta (Jacobs, 1988) was apparently developed for use with deterministic gradient descent. It is also useful for stochastic problems with little noise, which is however not the case for this test problem. In this example η *increases* from its initial value, and then stabilizes. We use the algorithm exactly as it appears in Jacobs' paper with noisy gradients substituted for the true gradient (which is unavailable in the stochastic setting). Parameters used were $\eta_0 = 0.1$, $\theta = 0.3$, $\kappa = 0.01$, and $\phi = 0.1$.

Urasiev

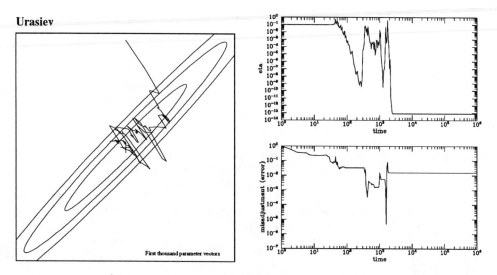

Figure 5: Urasiev's technique (Urasiev, 1988) varies η erratically over several orders of magnitude. The large fluctuations apparently cause η to completely stop changing after a while due to finite precision effects. Parameters used were $D = 0.2$, $R = 2$, and $U = 1$.

Fixed Search-Then-Converge, c=c*

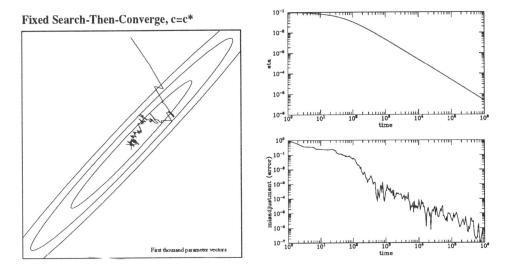

Figure 6: The fixed search-then-converge schedule with $c = c^*$ gives excellent performance. However if c^* is not known, you may get performance as in the next two examples. An adaptive technique is called for.

Fixed Search-Then-Converge, c=10c*

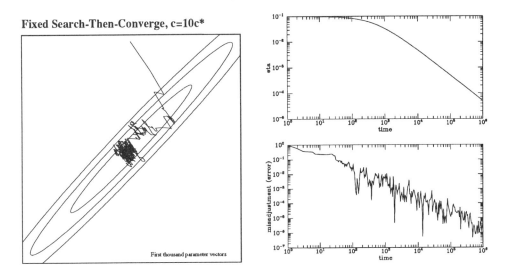

Figure 7: Note that taking $c > c^*$ slows convergence a bit as compared to the $c = c^*$ example in fig. 6, though it could aid escape from bad local minima in a nonlinear problem.

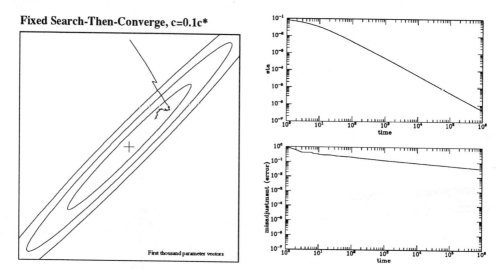

Fixed Search-Then-Converge, c=0.1c*

First thousand parameter vectors

Figure 8: This run illustrates the penalty to be paid if $c < c^*$.

References

C. Darken and J. Moody. (1990) Note on learning rate schedules for stochastic optimization. *Advances in Neural Information Processing Systems 3.* 832-838.

V.Fabian. (1960) Stochastic approximation methods. *Czechoslovak Math J.* **10** (85) : 123-159.

V. Fabian. (1968) On asymptotic normality in stochastic approximation. *Ann. Math. Stat.* **39**(4):1327-1332.

L. Goldstein. (1987) Mean square optimality in the continuous time Robbins Monro procedure. Technical Report DRB-306. Department of Mathematics, University of Southern California.

R. Jacobs. (1988) Increased rates of convergence through learning rate adaptation. *Neural Networks.* **1**:295-307.

H. Kesten. (1958) Accelerated stochastic approximation. *Annals of Mathematical Statistics.* **29**:41-59.

H. Kushner. (1978) Rates of convergence for sequential Monte Carlo optimization methods. *SIAM J. Control and Optimization.* **16**:150-168.

P. Major and P.Revesz. (1973) A limit theorem for the Robbins-Monro approximation. *Z. Wahrscheinlichkeitstheorie verw. Geb.* **27**:79-86.

S. Urasiev. (1988) Adaptive stochastic quasigradient procedures. In *Numerical Techniques for Stochastic Optimization.* Y. Ermoliev and R. Wets Eds. Springer-Verlag.

Competitive Anti-Hebbian Learning of Invariants

Nicol N. Schraudolph
Computer Science & Engr. Dept.
University of California, San Diego
La Jolla, CA 92093–0114
nici@cs.ucsd.edu

Terrence J. Sejnowski
Computational Neurobiology Laboratory
The Salk Institute for Biological Studies
La Jolla, CA 92186-5800
tsejnowski@ucsd.edu

Abstract

Although the detection of *invariant* structure in a given set of input patterns is vital to many recognition tasks, connectionist learning rules tend to focus on directions of high variance *(principal components)*. The *prediction paradigm* is often used to reconcile this dichotomy; here we suggest a more direct approach to invariant learning based on an *anti-Hebbian* learning rule. An unsupervised two-layer network implementing this method in a competitive setting learns to extract coherent depth information from random-dot stereograms.

1 INTRODUCTION: LEARNING INVARIANT STRUCTURE

Many connectionist learning algorithms share with principal component analysis (Jolliffe, 1986) the strategy of extracting the directions of highest variance from the input. A single Hebbian neuron, for instance, will come to encode the input's first principal component (Oja and Karhunen, 1985); various forms of lateral interaction can be used to force a layer of such nodes to differentiate and span the principal component subspace — cf. (Sanger, 1989; Kung, 1990; Leen, 1991), and others. The same type of representation also develops in the hidden layer of backpropagation autoassociator networks (Baldi and Hornik, 1989).

However, the directions of highest variance need not always be those that yield the most information, or — as the case may be — the information we are interested in (Intrator, 1991). In fact, it is sometimes desirable to extract the *invariant structure* of a stimulus instead, learning to encode those aspects that vary the least. The problem, then, is how to achieve this within a connectionist framework that is so closely tied to the maximization of variance.

In (Földiák, 1991), spatial invariance is turned into a temporal feature by presenting *transformation sequences* within invariance classes as a stimulus. A built-in temporal smoothness constraint enables Hebbian neurons to learn these transformations, and hence the invariance classes. Although this is an efficient and neurobiologically attractive strategy it is limited by its strong assumptions about the nature of the stimulus.

A more general approach is to make information about invariant structure available in the error signal of a supervised network. The most popular way of doing this is to require the network to predict the next patch of some structured input from the preceding context, as in (Elman, 1990); the same prediction technique can be used across space as well as time. It is also possible to explicitly derive an error signal from the mutual information between two patches of structured input (Becker and Hinton, 1992), a technique which has been applied to viewpoint-invariant object recognition (Zemel and Hinton, 1991).

2   METHODS

2.1   ANTI-HEBBIAN FEEDFORWARD LEARNING

In most formulations of the covariance learning rule it is quietly assumed that the learning rate be positive. By reversing the sign of this constant in a recurrent autoassociator, Kohonen constructed a "novelty filter" that learned to be insensitive to familiar features in its input (Kohonen, 1989). More recently, such anti-Hebbian synapses have been used for lateral decorrelation of feature detectors (Barlow and Földiák, 1989; Leen, 1991) as well as — in differential form — removal of temporal variations from the input (Mitchison, 1991).

We suggest that in certain cases the use of anti-Hebbian feedforward connections to learn invariant structure may eliminate the need to bring in the heavy machinery of supervised learning algorithms required by the prediction paradigm, with its associated lack of neurobiological plausibility. Specifically, this holds for linear problems, where the stimuli lie near a hyperplane in the input space: the weight vector of an anti-Hebbian neuron will move into a direction normal to that hyperplane, thus characterizing the invariant structure.

Of course a set of Hebbian feature detectors whose weight vectors span the hyperplane would characterize the associated class of stimuli just as well. The anti-Hebbian learning algorithm, however, provides a more efficient representation when the dimensionality of the hyperplane is more than half that of the input space, since less normal vectors than spanning vectors are required for unique characterization in this case. Since they remove rather than extract the variance within a stimulus class, anti-Hebbian neurons also present a very different output representation to subsequent layers.

Unfortunately it is not sufficient to simply negate the learning rate of a layer of Hebbian feature detectors in order to turn them into working anti-Hebbian invariance detectors: although such a change of sign does superficially achieve the intended effect, many of the subtleties that make Hebb's rule work in practice do not survive the transformation. In what follows we address some of the problems thus introduced.

Like the Hebb rule, anti-Hebbian learning requires weight normalization, in this case to prevent weight vectors from collapsing to zero. Oja's active decay rule (Oja, 1982) is a popular local approximation to explicit weight normalization:

$$\Delta \vec{w} = \eta(\vec{x}y - \vec{w}y^2), \text{ where } y = \vec{w}^T \vec{x} \tag{1}$$

Here the first term in parentheses represents the standard Hebb rule, while the second is the active decay. Unfortunately, Oja's rule can not be used for weight growth in anti-Hebbian neurons since it is unstable for negative learning rates ($\eta < 0$), as is evident from the observation that the growth/decay term is proportional to $\vec{w}$. In our experiments, explicit L_2-normalization of weight vectors was therefore used instead.

Hebbian feature detectors attain maximal activation for the class of stimuli they represent. Since the weight vectors of anti-Hebbian invariance detectors are *normal* to the invariance class they represent, membership in that class is signalled by a zero activation. In other words, linear anti-Hebbian nodes signal *violations* of the constraints they encode rather than compliance. While such an output representation can be highly desirable for some applications[1], it is unsuitable for others, such as the classification of mixtures of invariants described below.

We therefore use a symmetric activation function that responds maximally for a zero net input, and decays towards zero for large net inputs. More specifically, we use Gaussian activation functions, since these allow us to interpret the nodes' outputs as class membership probabilities. Soft competition between nodes in a layer can then be implemented simply by normalizing these probabilities (i.e. dividing each output by the sum of outputs in a layer), then using them to scale weight changes (Nowlan, 1990).

2.2   AN ANTI-HEBBIAN OBJECTIVE FUNCTION

The magnitude of weight change in a Hebbian neuron is proportional to the cosine of the angle between input and weight vectors. This means that nodes that best represent the current input learn faster than those which are further away, thus encouraging differentiation among weight vectors. Since anti-Hebbian weight vectors are normal to the hyperplanes they represent, those that best encode a given stimulus will experience the *least* change in weights. As a result, weight vectors will tend to clump together unless weight changes are rescaled to counteract this deficiency. In our experiments, this is done by the soft competition mechanism; here we present a more general framework towards this end.

A simple Hebbian neuron maximizes the variance of its output y through stochastic approximation by performing gradient ascent in $\frac{1}{2}y^2$ (Oja and Karhunen, 1985):

$$\Delta w_i \propto \frac{\partial}{\partial w_i} \frac{1}{2} y^2 = y \frac{\partial}{\partial w_i} y = x_i y \tag{2}$$

As seen above, it is not sufficient for an anti-Hebbian neuron to simply perform gradient descent in the same function. Instead, an objective function whose derivative has inverse magnitude to the above at every point is needed, as given by

$$\Delta w_i \propto \frac{\partial}{\partial w_i} \frac{1}{2} \log(y^2) = \frac{1}{y} \frac{\partial}{\partial w_i} y = \frac{x_i}{y} \tag{3}$$

---

[1]Consider the *subsumption architecture* of a hierarchical network in which higher layers only receive information that is not accounted for by earlier layers.

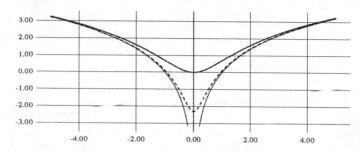

Figure 1: Possible objective functions for anti-Hebbian learning (see text).

Unfortunately, the pole at $y = 0$ presents a severe problem for simple gradient descent methods: the near-infinite derivatives in its vicinity lead to catastrophically large step sizes. More sophisticated optimization methods deal with this problem by explicitly controlling the step size; for plain gradient descent we suggest reshaping the objective function at the pole such that its partials never exceed the input in magnitude:

$$\Delta w_i \propto \frac{\partial}{\partial w_i} \varepsilon \log(y^2 + \varepsilon^2) = \frac{2\varepsilon x_i y}{y^2 + \varepsilon^2}, \tag{4}$$

where $\varepsilon > 0$ is a free parameter determining at which point the logarithmic slope is abandoned in favor of a quadratic function which forms an optimal trapping region for simple gradient descent (Figure 1).

3   RESULTS ON RANDOM-DOT STEREOGRAMS

In random-dot stereograms, stimuli of a given stereo disparity lie on a hyperplane whose dimensionality is half that of the input space plus the disparity in pixels. This is easily appreciated by considering that given, say, the left half-image and the disparity, one can predict the right half-image except for the pixels shifted in at the edge. Thus stereo disparities that are small compared to the receptive field width can be learned equally well by Hebbian and anti-Hebbian algorithms; when the disparity approaches receptive field width, however, anti-Hebbian neurons have a distinct advantage.

3.1   SINGLE LAYER NETWORK: LOCAL DISPARITY TUNING

Our training set consisted of stereo images of 5,000 frontoparallel strips at uniformly random depth covered densely with Gaussian features of random location, width, polarity and power. The images were discretized by integrating over pixel bins in order to allow for sub-pixel disparity acuity. Figure 2 shows that a single cluster of five anti-Hebbian nodes with soft competition develops near-perfect tuning curves for local stereo disparity after 10 sweeps through this training set. This disparity tuning is achieved by learning to have corresponding weights (at the given disparity) be of equal magnitude but opposite sign, so that any stimulus pattern at that disparity yields a zero net input and thus maximal response.

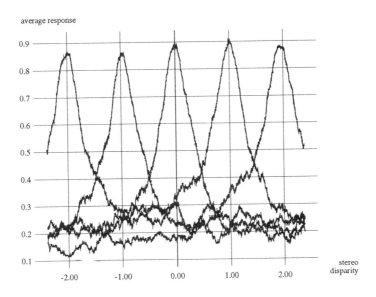

Figure 2: Sliding window average response of first-layer nodes after presentation of 50,000 stereograms as a function of stimulus disparity: strong disparity tuning is evident.

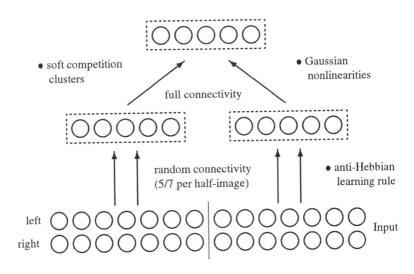

Figure 3: Architecture of the network (see text).

Note, however, that this type of detector suffers from false positives: input patterns that happen to yield near-zero net input even though they have a different stereo disparity. Although the individual response of a tuned node to an input pattern of the wrong disparity is therefore highly idiosyncratic, the sliding window average of each response with its 250 closest neighbors (with respect to disparity) shown in Figure 2 is far more well-behaved. This indicates that the average activity over a number of patterns (in a "moving stereogram" paradigm) — or, alternatively, over a population of nodes tuned to the same disparity — allows discrimination of disparities with sub-pixel accuracy.

3.2   TWO-LAYER NETWORK: COHERENT DISPARITY TUNING

In order to investigate the potential for hierarchical application of this architecture, it was extended to two layers as shown in Figure 3. The two first-layer clusters with non-overlapping receptive fields extract local stereo disparity as before; their output is monitored by a second-layer cluster. Note that there is no backpropagation of derivatives: all three clusters use the same unsupervised learning algorithm.

This network was trained on coherent input, i.e. stimuli for which the stereo disparity was identical across the receptive field boundary of first-layer clusters. As shown in Figure 4, the second layer learns to preserve the first layer's disparity tuning for coherent patterns, albeit in in somewhat degraded form. Each node in the second layer learns to pick out exactly the two corresponding nodes in the first-layer clusters, again by giving them weights of equal magnitude but opposite sign.

However, the second layer represents more than just a noisy copy of the first layer: it meaningfully integrates coherence information from the two receptive fields. This can be demonstrated by testing the trained network on non-coherent stimuli which exhibit a depth discontinuity between the receptive fields of first-layer clusters. The overall response of the second layer is tuned to the coherent stimuli it was trained on (Figure 5).

4   DISCUSSION

Although a negation of the learning rate introduces various problems to the Hebb rule, feedforward anti-Hebbian networks can pick up invariant structure from the input. We have demonstrated this in a competitive classification setting; other applications of this framework are possible. We find the *subsumption* aspect of anti-Hebbian learning particularly intriguing: the real world is so rich in redundant data that a learning rule which can adaptively *ignore* much of it must surely be an advantage. From this point of view, the promising first experiments we have reported here use quite impoverished inputs; one of our goals is therefore to extend this work towards real-world stimuli.

Acknowledgements

We would like to thank Geoffrey Hinton, Sue Becker, Tony Bell and Steve Nowlan for the stimulating and helpful discussions we had. Special thanks to Sue Becker for permission to use her random-dot stereogram generator early in our investigation. This work was supported by a fellowship stipend from the McDonnell-Pew Center for Cognitive Neuro-science at San Diego to the first author, who also received a NIPS travel grant enabling him to attend the conference.

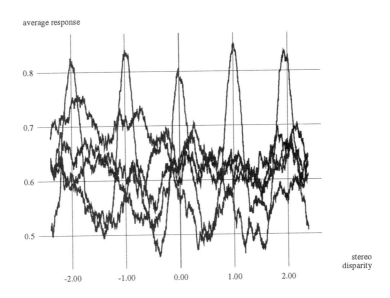

Figure 4: Sliding window average response of second-layer nodes after presentation of 250,000 coherent stereograms as a function of stimulus disparity: disparity tuning is preserved in degraded form.

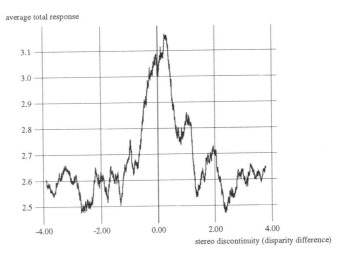

Figure 5: Sliding window average of total second-layer response to non-coherent input as a function of stimulus discontinuity: second layer is tuned to coherent patterns.

References

Baldi, P. and Hornik, K. (1989). Neural networks and principal component analysis: Learning from examples without local minima. *Neural Networks*, 2:53–58.

Barlow, H. B. and Földiák, P. (1989). Adaptation and decorrelation in the cortex. In Durbin, R. M., Miall, C., and Mitchison, G. J., editors, *The Computing Neuron*, chapter 4, pages 54–72. Addison-Wesley, Wokingham.

Becker, S. and Hinton, G. E. (1992). A self-organizing neural network that discovers surfaces in random-dot stereograms. *Nature*, to appear.

Elman, J. (1990). Finding structure in time. *Cognitive Science*, 14:179–211.

Földiák, P. (1991). Learning invariance from transformation sequences. *Neural Computation*, 3:194–200.

Intrator, N. (1991). Exploratory feature extraction in speech signals. In (Lippmann et al., 1991), pages 241–247.

Jolliffe, I. (1986). *Principal Component Analysis*. Springer-Verlag, New York.

Kohonen, T. (1989). *Self-Organization and Associative Memory*. Springer-Verlag, Berlin, 3 edition.

Kung, S. Y. (1990). Neural networks for extracting constrained principal components. submitted to *IEEE Trans. Neural Networks*.

Leen, T. K. (1991). Dynamics of learning in linear feature-discovery networks. *Network*, 2:85–105.

Lippmann, R. P., Moody, J. E., and Touretzky, D. S., editors (1991). *Advances in Neural Information Processing Systems*, volume 3, Denver 1990. Morgan Kaufmann, San Mateo.

Mitchison, G. (1991). Removing time variation with the anti-hebbian differential synapse. *Neural Computation*, 3:312–320.

Nowlan, S. J. (1990). Maximum likelihood competitive learning. In Touretzky, D. S., editor, *Advances in Neural Information Processing Systems*, volume 2, pages 574–582, Denver 1989. Morgan Kaufmann, San Mateo.

Oja, E. (1982). A simplified neuron model as a principal component analyzer. *Journal of Mathematical Biology*, 15:267–273.

Oja, E. and Karhunen, J. (1985). On stochastic approximation of the eigenvectors and eigenvalues of the expectation of a random matrix. *Journal of Mathematical Analysis and Applications*, 106:69–84.

Sanger, T. D. (1989). Optimal unsupervised learning in a single-layer linear feedforward neural network. *Neural Networks*, 2:459–473.

Zemel, R. S. and Hinton, G. E. (1991). Discovering viewpoint-invariant relationships that characterize objects. In (Lippmann et al., 1991), pages 299–305.

Merging Constrained Optimisation with Deterministic Annealing to "Solve" Combinatorially Hard Problems

Paul Stolorz*
Santa Fe Institute
1660 Old Pecos Trail, Suite A
Santa Fe, NM 87501

ABSTRACT

Several parallel analogue algorithms, based upon mean field theory (MFT) approximations to an underlying statistical mechanics formulation, and requiring an externally prescribed annealing schedule, now exist for finding approximate solutions to difficult combinatorial optimisation problems. They have been applied to the Travelling Salesman Problem (TSP), as well as to various issues in computational vision and cluster analysis. I show here that any given MFT algorithm can be combined in a natural way with notions from the areas of constrained optimisation and adaptive simulated annealing to yield a single homogenous and efficient parallel relaxation technique, for which an externally prescribed annealing schedule is no longer required. The results of numerical simulations on 50-city and 100-city TSP problems are presented, which show that the ensuing algorithms are typically an order of magnitude faster than the MFT algorithms alone, and which also show, on occasion, superior solutions as well.

1   INTRODUCTION

Several promising parallel analogue algorithms, which can be loosely described by the term "deterministic annealing", or "mean field theory (MFT) annealing", have

---

*also at Theoretical Division and Center for Nonlinear Studies, MSB213, Los Alamos National Laboratory, Los Alamos, NM 87545.

recently been proposed as heuristics for tackling difficult combinatorial optimisation problems [1, 2, 3, 4, 5, 6, 7]. However, the annealing schedules must be imposed externally in a somewhat *ad hoc* manner in these procedures (although they can be made adaptive to a limited degree [8]). As a result, a number of authors [9, 10, 11] have considered the alternative analogue approach of Lagrangian relaxation, a form of constrained optimisation due originally to Arrow [12], as a different means of tackling these problems. The various alternatives require the introduction of a new set of variables, the Lagrange multipliers. Unfortunately, these usually lead in turn to either the inclusion of expensive penalty terms, or the consideration of restricted classes of problem constraints. The penalty terms also tend to introduce unwanted local minima in the objective function, and they must be included even when the algorithms are exact [13, 10]. These drawbacks prevent their easy application to large-scale combinatorial problems, containing 100 or more variables.

In this paper I show that the technical features of analogue mean field approximations can be merged with both Lagrangian relaxation methods, and with the broad philosophy of adaptive annealing without, importantly, requiring the large computational resources that typically accompany the Lagrangian methods. The result is a systematic procedure for crafting from any given MFT algorithm a single parallel homogeneous relaxation technique which needs no externally prescribed annealing schedule. In this way the computational power of the analogue heuristics is greatly enhanced. In particular, the Lagrangian framework can be used to construct an efficient adaptation of the elastic net algorithm [2], which is perhaps the most promising of the analogue heuristics. The results of numerical experiments are presented which display both increased computational efficiency, and on occasion, better solutions (avoidance of some local minima) over deterministic annealing. Also, the qualitative mechanism at the root of this behaviour is described. Finally, I note that the apparatus can be generalised to a procedure that uses several multipliers, in a manner that roughly parallels the notion of different temperatures at different physical locations in the simulated annealing heuristic.

2   DETERMINISTIC ANNEALING

The deterministic annealing procedures consist of tracking the local minimum of an objective function of the form

$$F(\underline{x}) = U(\underline{x}) - TS(\underline{x}) \tag{1}$$

where $\underline{x}$ represents the analogue variables used to describe the particular problem at hand, and $T \geq 0$ (initially chosen large) is an adjustable annealing, or temperature, parameter. As T is lowered, the objective function undergoes a qualitative change from a convex to a distinctly non-convex function. Provided the annealing shedule is slow enough, however, it is hoped that the local minimum near $T = 0$ is a close approximation to the global solution of the problem.

The function $S(\underline{x})$ represents an analogue approximation [5, 4, 7] to the entropy of an underlying discrete statistical physics system, while $F(\underline{x})$ approximates its free energy. The underlying discrete system forms the basis of the simulated annealing heuristic [14]. Although a general and powerful technique, this heuristic is an inherently stochastic procedure which must consider many individual discrete tours at each and every temperature T. The deterministic annealing approximations have the advantage of being deterministic, so that an approximate solution at a given temperature can be found with much less computational effort. In both cases, however, the complexity of the problem under consideration shows up in the need to determine with great care an annealing schedule for lowering the temperature parameter.

The primary contribution of this paper consists in pursuing the relationship between deterministic annealing and statistical physics one step further, by making explicit use of the fact that due to the statistical physics embedding of the deterministic annealing procedures,

$$S(\underline{x}_{min}) \to 0 \text{ as } T \to 0 \tag{2}$$

where $\underline{x}_{min}$ is the local minimum obtained for the parameter value T. This deceptively simple observation allows the consideration of the somewhat different approach of Lagrange multiplier methods to automatically determine a dynamics for T in the analogue heuristics, using as a constraint the vanishing of the entropy function at zero temperature. This particular fact has not been explicitly used in any previous optimisation procedures based upon Lagrange multipliers, although it is implicit in the work of [9]. Most authors have focussed instead on the syntactic constraints contained in the function $U(\underline{x})$ when incorporating Lagrange multipliers. As a result the issue of eliminating an external annealing schedule has not been directly confronted.

3   LAGRANGE MULTIPLIERS

Multiplier methods seek the critical points of a "Lagrangian" function

$$F(\underline{x}, \lambda) = U(\underline{x}) - \lambda S(\underline{x}) \tag{3}$$

where the notation of (1) has been retained, in accordance with the philosophy discussed above. The only difference is that the parameter T has been replaced by a variable λ (the Lagrange multiplier), which is to be treated on the same basis as the variables $\underline{x}$. By definition, the critical points of $F(\underline{x}, \lambda)$ obey the so-called Kuhn-Tucker conditions

$$\begin{aligned} \nabla_{\underline{x}} F(\underline{x}, \lambda) &= 0 = \nabla_{\underline{x}} U(\underline{x}) - \lambda \nabla_{\underline{x}} S(\underline{x}) \\ \nabla_{\lambda} F(\underline{x}, \lambda) &= 0 = -S(\underline{x}) \end{aligned} \tag{4}$$

Thus, at any critical point of this function, the constraint $S(\underline{x}) = 0$ is satisfied. This corresponds to a vanishing entropy estimate in (1). Hopefully, in addition, $U(\underline{x})$ is minimised, subject to the constraint.

The difficulty with this approach when used in isolation is that finding the critical points of $F(\underline{x}, \lambda)$ entails, in general, the minimisation of a transformed "unconstrained" function, whose set of local minima contains the critical points of F as a subset. This transformed function is required in order to ensure an algorithm which is convergent, because the critical points of $F(\underline{x}, \lambda)$ are saddle points, not local minima. One well-known way to do this is to add a term $S^2(\underline{x})$ to (3), giving an augmented Lagrangian with the same fixed points as (3), but hopefully with better convergence properties. Unfortunately, the transformed function is invariably more complicated than $F(\underline{x}, \lambda)$, typically containing extra quadratic penalty terms (as in the above case), which tend to convert harmless saddle points into unwanted local minima. It also leads to greater computational overhead, usually in the form of either second derivatives of the functions $U(\underline{x})$ and $S(\underline{x})$, or of matrix inversions [13, 10] (although see [11] for an approach which minimises this overhead). For large-scale combinatorial problems such as the TSP these disadvantages become prohibitive. In addition, the entropic constraint functions occurring in deterministic annealing tend to be quite complicated nonlinear functions of the variables involved, often with peculiar behaviour near the constraint condition. In these cases (the Hopfield /Tank method is an example) a term quadratic in the entropy cannot simply be added to (3) in a straightforward way to produce a suitable augmented Lagrangian (of course, such a procedure *is* possible with several of the terms in the internal energy $U(\underline{x})$).

4   COMBINING BOTH METHODS

The best features of each of the two approaches outlined above may be retained by using the following modification of the original first-order Arrow technique:

$$
\dot{x}_i \;\; = -\nabla_{x_i}\hat{F}(\underline{x},\lambda) \;\; = -\nabla_{x_i}U(\underline{x})+\lambda\nabla_{x_i}S(\underline{x}) \tag{5}
$$
$$
\dot{\lambda} \;\; = +\nabla_\lambda\hat{F}(\underline{x},\lambda) \;\; = -S(\underline{x})+c/\lambda
$$

where $\hat{F}(\underline{x},\lambda)$ is a slightly modified "free energy" function given by

$$
\hat{F}(\underline{x},\lambda) = U(\underline{x}) - \lambda S(\underline{x}) + c\ln\lambda \tag{6}
$$

In these expressions, $c > 0$ is a constant, chosen small on the scale of the other parameters, and characterises the sole, inexpensive, penalty requirement. It is needed purely in order to ensure that λ remain positive. In fact, in the numerical experiment that I will present, this penalty term for λ was not even used - the algorithm was simply terminated at a suitably small value of λ.

The reason for insisting upon $\lambda > 0$, in contrast to most first-order relaxation methods, is that it ensures that the free energy objective function is bounded below with respect to the $\underline{x}$ variables. This in turn allows (5) to be proven locally convergent [15] using techniques discussed in [13]. Furthermore, the methods described by (5) are found empirically to be globally convergent as well. This feature is in fact the key to their computational efficiency, as it means that they need not be grafted onto more sophisticated and inefficient methods in order to ensure convergence. This behaviour can be traced to the fact that the "free energy" functions, while non-convex overall with respect to $\underline{x}$, are nevertheless convex over large volumes of the solution space. The point can be illustrated by the construction of an energy function similar to that used by Platt and Barr [9], which also displays the mechanism by which some of the unwanted local minima in deterministic annealing may be avoided. These issues are discussed further in Section 6.

The algorithms described above have several features which distinguish them from previous work. Firstly, the entropy estimate $S(\underline{x})$ has been chosen explicitly as the appropriate constraint function, a fact which has previously been unexploited in the optimisation context (although a related piecewise linear function has been used by [9]). Further, since this estimate is usually positive for the mean field theory heuristics, λ (the only new variable) decreases monotonically in a manner roughly similar to the temperature decrease schedule used in simulated and deterministic annealing, but with the *ad hoc* drawback now removed. Moreover, there is no requirement that the system be at or near a fixed point each time λ is altered - there is simply one homogeneous dynamical system which must approach a fixed point only once at the very end of the simulation, and furthermore λ appears linearly except near the end of the procedure (a major reason for its efficiency). Finally, the algorithms do not require computationally cumbersome extra structure in the form of quadratic penalty terms, second derivatives or inverses, in contrast to the usual Lagrangian relaxation techniques. All of these features can be seen to be due to the statistical physics setting of the annealing "Lagrangian", and the use of an entropic constraint instead of the more usual syntactic constraints.

The apparatus outlined above can immediately be used to adapt the Hopfield/Tank heuristic for the Travelling Salesman Problem (TSP) [1], which can easily be written in the form (1). However, the elastic net method [2] is known to be a somewhat superior method, and is therefore a better candidate for modification. There is an impediment to the procedure here: the objective function for the elastic net is actually of the form

$$F(\underline{x}, \lambda) = U(\underline{x}) - \lambda S(\underline{x}, \lambda) \tag{7}$$

which precludes the use of a true Lagrange muliplier, since λ now appears non-trivially in the constraint function itself! However, I find surprisingly that the algorithm obtained by applying the Lagrangian relaxation apparatus in a straight-forward way as before still leads to a coherent algorithm. The equations are

$$
\begin{aligned}
\dot{x}_i &= -\nabla_{x_i} F(\underline{x}, \lambda) &= -\nabla_{x_i} U(\underline{x}) + \lambda \nabla_{x_i} S(\underline{x}) \\
\dot{\lambda} &= +\epsilon \nabla_\lambda F(\underline{x}, \lambda) &= -\epsilon [S(\underline{x}, \lambda) + \lambda \nabla_\lambda S(\underline{x}, \lambda)]
\end{aligned}
\tag{8}
$$

The parameter $\epsilon > 0$ is chosen so that an explicit barrier term for λ can be avoided. It is the only remaining externally prescribed part of the former annealing schedule, and is fixed just once at the begining of the algorithm.

It can be shown that the global convergence of (8) is highly plausible in general (and seems to always occur in practice), as in the simpler case described by (5). Secondly, and most importantly, it can be shown that the constraints that are obeyed at the new fixed points satisfy the syntax of the original discrete problem [15]. The procedure is not limited to the elastic net method for the TSP. The mean field approximations discussed in [3, 4, 5] all behave in a similar way, and can therefore be adapted successfully to Lagrangian relaxation methods. The form of the elastic net entropy function suggests a further natural generalisation of the procedure. A different "multiplier" λ_a can be assigned to each city a, each variable being responsible for satisfying a different additive component of the entropy constraint. The idea has an obvious parallel to the notion in simulated annealing of lowering the temperature in different geographical regions at different rates in response to the behaviour of the system. The number of extra variables required is a modest computational investment, since there are typically many more tour points than city points for a given implementation.

5   RESULTS FOR THE TSP

Numerical simulations were performed on various TSP instances using the elastic net method, the Lagrangian adaptation with a single global Lagrange multiplier, and the modification discussed above involving one Lagrange multiplier for each city. The results are shown in Table 1. The tours for the Lagrangian relaxation methods are about 0.5% shorter than those for the elastic net, although these differences are not yet at a statistically significant level. The differences in the computational requirements are, however, much more dramatic. No attempt has been made to optimise any of the techniques by using sophisticated descent procedures, although the size of the update step has been chosen to seperately optimise each method.

Table 1: Performance of heuristics described in the text on a set of 40 randomly distibuted 50-city instances of the TSP in the unit square. CPU times quoted are for a SUN SPARC Station 1+. α and β are the standard tuning parameters [4].

METHOD	α	β	TOUR LENGTH	CPU(SEC)
Elastic net	0.2	2.5	5.95 ± 0.10	260 ± 33
Global multiplier	0.4	2.5	5.92 ± 0.09	49 ± 5
Local multipliers	0.4	2.5	5.92 ± 0.08	82 ± 12

I have also been able to obtain a superior solution to the 100-city problem analysed by Durbin and Willshaw [2], namely a solution of length 7.746 [15] (c.f. length 7.783 for the elastic net) in a fraction of the time taken by elastic net annealing. This represents an improvement of roughly 0.5%. Although still about 0.5% longer than the best tour found by simulated annealing, this result is quite encouraging, because it was obtained with far less CPU time than simulated annealing, and in substantially less time than the elastic net: improvements upon solutions within about 1% of optimality typically require a substantial increase in CPU investment.

6   HOW IT WORKS - VALLEY ASCENT

Inspection of the solutions obtained by the various methods indicates that the multiplier schemes can sometimes exchange enough "inertial" energy to overcome the energy barriers which trap the annealing methods, thus offering better solutions as well as much-improved computational efficiency. This point is illustrated in Figure 1(a), which displays the evolution of the following function during the algorithm for a typical set of parameters:

$$E = \frac{1}{2} \sum_i \dot{x_i}^2 + \frac{1}{2} \dot{\lambda}^2 \tag{9}$$

The two terms can be thought of as different components of an overall kinetic energy E. During the procedure, energy can be exchanged between these two components, so the function $E(t)$ does not decrease monotonically with time. This allows the system to occasionally escape from local minima. Nevertheless, after a long enough

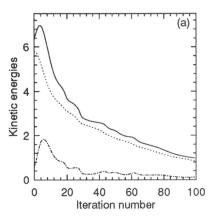
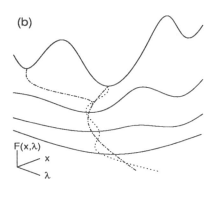

Figure 1: (a) Evolution of variables for a typical 50-city TSP. The solid curve shows the total kinetic energy E given by (9). The dotted curve shows the λ component of this energy, and the dash-dotted curve shows the $\underline{x}$ component. (b) Trajectories taken by various algorithms on a schematic free energy surface. The two dash-dotted curves show possible paths for elastic net annealing, each ascending a valley floor. The dotted curve shows a Lagrangian relaxation, which displays oscillations about the valley floor leading to the superior solution.

time the function does decrease smoothly, ensuring convergence to a valid solution to the problem.

The basic mechanism can also be understood by plotting schematically the free energy "surface" $F(\underline{x}, \lambda)$, as shown in Figure 1(b). This surface has a single valley in the foreground, where λ is large. Bifurcations occur as λ becomes smaller, with a series of saddles, each a valid problem solution, being reached in the background at $\lambda = 0$. Deterministic annealing can be viewed as the ascent of just one of these valleys along the valley floor. It is hoped that the broadest and deepest minimum is chosen at each valley bifurcation, leading eventually to the lowest background saddle point as the optimal solution. A typical trajectory for one of the Lagrangian modifications also consists roughly of the ascent of one of these valleys. However, oscillations about the valley floor now occur on the way to the final saddle point, due to the interplay between the different kinetic components displayed in Figure 1(a). It is hoped that the extra degrees of freedom allow valleys to be explored more fully near bifurcation points, thus biasing the larger valleys more than deterministic annealing. Notice that in order to generate the λ dynamics, computational significance is now assigned to the actual *value* of the free energy in the new schemes, in contrast to the situation in regular annealing.

7   CONCLUSION

In summary, a simple yet effective framework has been developed for systematically generalising any algorithm described by a mean field theory approximation procedure to a Lagrangian method which replaces annealing by the relaxation of a single dynamical system. Even in the case of the elastic net, which has a slightly awkward form, the resulting method can be shown to be sensible, and I find in fact that it substantially improves the speed (and accuracy) of that method. The adaptations depend crucially upon the vanishing of the analogue entropy at zero temperature. This allows the entropy to be used as a powerful constraint function, even though it is a highly nonlinear function and might be expected at first sight to be unsuitable for the task. In fact, this observation can also be applied in a wider context to design objective functions and architectures for neural networks which seek to improve generalisation ability by limiting the number of network parameters [16].

References

[1] J.J. Hopfield and D.W. Tank. Neural computation of decisions in optimization problems. *Biol. Cybern.*, 52:141–152, 1985.

[2] R. Durbin and D. Willshaw. An analogue approach to the travelling salesman problem using an elsatic net method. *Nature*, 326:689–691, 1987.

[3] D. Geiger and F. Girosi. Coupled markov random fields and mean field theory. In D. Touretzky, editor, *Advances in Neural Information Processing Systems 2*, pages 660–667. Morgan Kaufmann, 1990.

[4] A.L. Yuille. Generalised deformable models, statistical physics, and matching problems. *Neural Comp.*, 2:1–24, 1990.

[5] P.D. Simic. Statistical mechanics as the underlying theory of "elastic" and "neural" optimisations. *NETWORK: Comp. Neural Syst.*, 1:89–103, 1990.

[6] A. Blake and A. Zisserman. *Visual Reconstruction*. MIT Press, 1987.

[7] C. Peterson and B. Soderberg. A new method for mapping optimization problems onto neural networks. *Int. J. Neural Syst.*, 1:3–22, 1989.

[8] D.J. Burr. An improved elastic net method for the travelling salesman problem. In *IEEE 2nd International Conf. on Neural Networks*, pages I–69–76, 1988.

[9] J.C. Platt and A.H. Barr. Constrained differential optimization. In D.Z. Anderson, editor, *Neural Information Proc. Systems*, pages 612–621. AIP, 1988.

[10] A.G. Tsirukis, G.V. Reklaitis, and M.F. Tenorio. Nonlinear optimization using generalised hopfield networks. *Neural Comp.*, 1:511–521, 1989.

[11] E. Mjolsness and C. Garrett. Algebraic transformations of objective functions. *Neural Networks*, 3:651–669, 1990.

[12] K.J. Arrow, L. Hurwicz, and H. Uzawa. *Studies in Linear and Nonlinear Programming*. Stanford University Press, 1958.

[13] D.P. Bertsekas. *Constrained Optimization and Lagrange Multiplier Methods*. Academic Press, 1982. See especially Chapter 4.

[14] S. Kirkpatrick, C.D. Gelatt Jr., and M.P. Vecchi. Optimization by simulated annealing. *Science*, 220:671–680, 1983.

[15] P. Stolorz. Merging constrained optimisation with deterministic annealing to "solve" combinatorially hard problems. Technical report, LA-UR-91-3593, Los Alamos National Laboratory, 1991.

[16] P.Stolorz. Analogue entropy as a constraint in adaptive learning and optimisation. Technical report, in preparation, Santa Fe Institute, 1992.

Kernel Regression and Backpropagation Training with Noise

Petri Koistinen and Lasse Holmström
Rolf Nevanlinna Institute, University of Helsinki
Teollisuuskatu 23, SF-00510 Helsinki, Finland

Abstract

One method proposed for improving the generalization capability of a feed-forward network trained with the backpropagation algorithm is to use artificial training vectors which are obtained by adding noise to the original training vectors. We discuss the connection of such backpropagation training with noise to kernel density and kernel regression estimation. We compare by simulated examples (1) backpropagation, (2) backpropagation with noise, and (3) kernel regression in mapping estimation and pattern classification contexts.

1 INTRODUCTION

Let X and Y be random vectors taking values in $\mathbf{R}^d$ and $\mathbf{R}^p$, respectively. Suppose that we want to estimate Y in terms of X using a feedforward network whose input-output mapping we denote by $y = g(x, w)$. Here the vector w includes all the weights and biases of the network. Backpropagation training using the quadratic loss (or error) function can be interpreted as an attempt to minimize the expected loss

$$\lambda(w) = E\|g(X, w) - Y\|^2. \tag{1}$$

Suppose that $E\|Y\|^2 < \infty$. Then the regression function

$$m(x) = E[Y|X = x]. \tag{2}$$

minimizes the loss $E\|b(X) - Y\|^2$ over all Borel measurable mappings b. Therefore, backpropagation training can also be viewed as an attempt to estimate m with the network g.

In practice, one cannot minimize λ directly because one does not know enough about the distribution of (X, Y). Instead one minimizes a sample estimate

$$\hat{\lambda}_n(w) = \frac{1}{n} \sum_{i=1}^{n} \|g(X_i, w) - Y_i\|^2 \tag{3}$$

in the hope that weight vectors w that are near optimal for $\hat{\lambda}_n$ are also near optimal for λ. In fact, under rather mild conditions the minimizer of $\hat{\lambda}_n$ actually converges towards the minimizing set of weights for λ as $n \to \infty$, with probability one (White, 1989). However, if n is small compared to the dimension of w, minimization of $\hat{\lambda}_n$ can easily lead to overfitting and poor generalization, *i.e.*, weights that render $\hat{\lambda}_n$ small may produce a large expected error λ.

Many cures for overfitting have been suggested. One can divide the available samples into a training set and a validation set, perform iterative minimization using the training set and stop minimization when network performance over the validation set begins to deteriorate (Holmström et al., 1990, Weigend et al., 1990). In another approach, the minimization objective function is modified to include a term which tries to discourage the network from becoming too complex (Weigend et al., 1990). Network pruning (see, *e.g.*, Sietsma and Dow, 1991) has similar motivation. Here we consider the approach of generating artificial training vectors by adding noise to the original samples. We have recently analyzed such an approach and proved its asymptotic consistency under certain technical conditions (Holmström and Koistinen, 1990).

2   ADDITIVE NOISE AND KERNEL REGRESSION

Suppose that we have n original training vectors (x_i, y_i) and want to generate artificial training vectors using additive noise. If the distributions of both X and Y are continuous it is natural to add noise to both x and y components of the sample. However, if the distribution of X is continuous and that of Y is discrete (*e.g.*, in pattern classification), it feels more natural to add noise to the x components only. In Figure 1 we present sampling procedures for both cases. In the x-only case the additive noise is generated from a random vector S_X with density K_X whereas in the x-and-y case the noise is generated from a random vector S_{XY} with density K_{XY}. Notice that we control the magnitude of noise with a scalar smoothing parameter $h > 0$.

In both cases the sampling procedures can be thought of as generating random samples from new random vectors $X_h^{(n)}$ and $Y_h^{(n)}$. Using the same argument as in the Introduction we see that a network trained with the artificial samples tends to approximate the regression function $E[Y_h^{(n)}|X_h^{(n)}]$. Generate I uniformly on $\{1, \ldots, n\}$ and denote by f and $f(\cdot|I = i)$ the density and conditional density of $X_h^{(n)}$. Then in the x-only case we get

$$m_h^{(n)}(X_h^{(n)}) := E[Y_h^{(n)}|X_h^{(n)}] = \sum_{i=1}^{n} y_i P(I = i|X_h^{(n)})$$

Procedure 1.	Procedure 2.
(Add noise to x only)	(Add noise to both x and y)
1. Select $i \in \{1, \ldots, n\}$ with equal probability for each index.	1. Select $i \in \{1, \ldots, n\}$ with equal probability for each index.
2. Draw a sample s_X from density K_X on $\mathbf{R}^d$.	2. Draw a sample (s_X, s_Y) from density K_{XY} on $\mathbf{R}^{d+p}$.
3. Set $\begin{aligned} x_h^{(n)} &= x_i + h s_X \\ y_h^{(n)} &= y_i. \end{aligned}$	3. Set $\begin{aligned} x_h^{(n)} &= x_i + h s_X \\ y_h^{(n)} &= y_i + h s_Y. \end{aligned}$

Figure 1: Two Procedures for Generating Artificial Training Vectors.

$$= \sum_{i=1}^{n} y_i \frac{f(X_h^{(n)}|I = i)P(I = i)}{f(X_h^{(n)})} = \sum_{i=1}^{n} y_i \frac{h^{-d}K_X((X_h^{(n)} - x_i)/h) \cdot n^{-1}}{\sum_{j=1}^{n} n^{-1}h^{-d}K_X((X_h^{(n)} - x_i)/h)}.$$

Denoting K_X by k we obtain

$$m_h^{(n)}(x) = \frac{\sum_{i=1}^{n} k((x - x_i)/h)y_i}{\sum_{i=1}^{n} k((x - x_i)/h)}. \qquad (4)$$

We result in the same expression also in the x-and-y case provided that $\int y K_{XY}(x, y) \, dy = 0$ and that we take $k(x) = \int K_{XY}(x, y) \, dy$ (Watson, 1964). The expression (4) is known as the (Nadaraya-Watson) kernel regression estimator (Nadaraya, 1964, Watson, 1964, Devroye and Wagner, 1980).

A common way to train a p-class neural network classifier is to train the network to associate a vector x from class j with the j'th unit vector $(0, \ldots, 0, 1, 0, \ldots, 0)$. It is easy to see that then the kernel regression estimator components estimate the class *a posteriori* probabilities using (Parzen-Rosenblatt) kernel density estimators for the class conditional densities. Specht (1990) argues that such a classifier can be considered a neural network. Analogously, a kernel regression estimator can be considered a neural network though such a network would need units proportional to the number of training samples. Recently Specht (1991) has advocated using kernel regression and has also presented a clustering variant requiring only a fixed amount of units. Notice also the resemblance of kernel regression to certain radial basis function schemes (Moody and Darken, 1989, Stokbro et al., 1990).

An often used method for choosing h is to minimize the cross-validated error (Härdle and Marron, 1985, Friedman and Silverman, 1989)

$$M(h) = \frac{1}{n} \sum_{i=1}^{n} \|m_{h,i}^{(n)}(x_i) - y_i\|^2, \qquad m_{h,i}^{(n)}(x) = \frac{\sum_{j \neq i} k((x - x_j)/h)y_j}{\sum_{j \neq i} k((x - x_j)/h)}. \qquad (5)$$

Another possibility is to use a method suggested by kernel density estimation theory (Duin, 1976, Habbema et al., 1974) whereby one chooses that h maximizing a cross-validated (pseudo) likelihood function

$$L_{XY}(h) = \prod_{i=1}^{n} f_{n,h,i}^{XY}(x_i, y_i), \qquad L_X(h) = \prod_{i=1}^{n} f_{n,h,i}^{X}(x_i), \qquad (6)$$

where $f_{n,h,i}^{XY}$ ($f_{n,h,i}^{X}$) is a kernel density estimate with kernel K_{XY} (K_X) and smoothing parameter h but with the i'th sample point left out.

3   EXPERIMENTS

In the first experiment we try to estimate a mapping g_0 from noisy data (x, y),

$$Y = g_0(X) + N_y = a \sin X + b + N_y, \qquad a = 0.4, b = 0.5$$
$$X \sim \text{UNI}(-\pi, \pi), \qquad N_y \sim N(0, \sigma^2), \qquad \sigma = 0.1.$$

Here UNI and N denote the uniform and the normal distribution. We experimented with backpropagation, backpropagation with noise and kernel regression. Backpropagation loss function was minimized using Marquardt's method. The network architecture was FN-1-13-1 with 40 adaptable weights (a feedforward network with one input, 13 hidden nodes, one output, and logistic activation functions in the hidden and output layers). We started the local optimizations from 3 different random initial weights and kept the weights giving the least value for $\hat{\lambda}_n$. Backpropagation training with noise was similar except that instead of the original n vectors we used $10n$ artificial vectors generated with Procedure 2 using $S_{XY} \sim N(0, I_2)$. Magnitude of noise was chosen with the criterion L_{XY} (which, for backpropagation, gave better results than M). In the kernel regression experiments S_{XY} was kept the same. Table 1 characterizes the distribution of J, the expected squared distance of the estimator g ($g(\cdot, w)$ or $m_h^{(n)}$) from g_0,

$$J = E[g(X) - g_0(X)]^2.$$

Table 2 characterizes the distribution of h chosen according to the criteria L_{XY} and M and Figure 2 shows the estimators in one instance. Notice that, on the average, kernel regression is better than backpropagation with noise which is better than plain backpropagation. The success of backpropagation with noise is partly due to the fact that σ and n have here been picked favorably. Notice too that in kernel regression the results with the two cross-validation methods are similar although the h values they suggest are clearly different.

In the second experiment we trained classifiers for a four-dimensional two-class problem with equal *a priori* probabilities and class-conditional densities $N(\mu_1, C_1)$ and $N(\mu_2, C_2)$,

$$\mu_1 = 2.32[1\ 0\ 0\ 0]^T, C_1 = I_4; \qquad \mu_2 = 0, C_2 = 4I_4.$$

An FN-4-6-2 with 44 adaptable weights was trained to associate vectors from class 1 with $[0.9\ 0.1]^T$ and vectors from class 2 with $[0.1\ 0.9]^T$. We generated $n/2$ original vectors from each class and a total of $10n$ artificial vectors using Procedure 1 with $S_X \sim N(0, I_4)$. We chose the smoothing parameters, h_1 and h_2, separately for the two classes using the criterion L_X: h_i was chosen by evaluating L_X on class i samples only. We formed separate kernel regression estimators for each class; the i'th estimator was trained to output 1 for class i vectors and 0 for the other sample vectors. The M criterion then produces equal values for h_1 and h_2. The classification rule was to classify x to class i if the output corresponding to the i'th class was the maximum output. The error rates are given in Table 3. (The error rate of the Bayesian classifier is 0.116 in this task.) Table 4 summarizes the distribution of h_1 and h_2 as selected by L_X and M.

Table 1: Results for Mapping Estimation. Mean value (left) and standard deviation (right) of J based on 100 repetitions are given for each method.

n	BP		BP+noise, L_{XY}		Kernel regression			
					L_{XY}		M	
40	.0218	.016	.0104	.0079	.00446	.0022	.00365	.0019
80	.00764	.0048	.00526	.0018	.00250	.00078	.00191	.00077

Table 2: Values of h Suggested by the Two Cross-validation Methods in the Mapping Estimation Experiment. Mean value and standard deviation based on 100 repetitions are given.

n	L_{XY}		M	
40	0.149	0.020	0.276	0.086
80	0.114	0.011	0.241	0.062

Table 3: Error Rates for the Different Classifiers. Mean value and standard deviation based on 25 repetitions are given for each method.

n	BP		BP+noise, L_X		Kernel regression			
					L_X		M	
44	.281	.054	.189	.018	.201	.022	.207	.027
88	.264	.028	.163	.011	.182	.010	.184	.013
176	.210	.023	.145	.010	.164	.0089	.164	.011

Table 4: Values of h_1 and h_2 Suggested by the Two Cross-validation Methods in the Classification Experiment. Mean value and standard deviation based on 25 repetitions are given.

n	L_X				M	
	h_1		h_2		$h_1 = h_2$	
44	.818	.078	1.61	.14	1.14	.27
88	.738	.056	1.48	.11	1.01	.19
176	.668	.048	1.35	.090	.868	.10

4 CONCLUSIONS

Additive noise can improve the generalization capability of a feedforward network trained with the backpropagation approach. The magnitude of the noise cannot be selected blindly, though. Cross-validation-type procedures seem to suit well for the selection of noise magnitude. Kernel regression, however, seems to perform well whenever backpropagation with noise performs well. If the kernel is fixed in kernel regression, we only have to choose the smoothing parameter h, and the method is not overly sensitive to its selection.

References

[Devroye and Wagner, 1980] Devroye, L. and Wagner, T. (1980). Distribution-free consistency results in nonparametric discrimination and regression function estimation. *The Annals of Statistics*, 8(2):231–239.

[Duin, 1976] Duin, R. P. W. (1976). On the choice of smoothing parameters for Parzen estimators of probability density functions. *IEEE Transactions on Computers*, C-25:1175–1179.

[Friedman and Silverman, 1989] Friedman, J. and Silverman, B. (1989). Flexible parsimonious smoothing and additive modeling. *Technometrics*, 31(1):3–21.

[Habbema et al., 1974] Habbema, J. D. F., Hermans, J., and van den Broek, K. (1974). A stepwise discriminant analysis program using density estimation. In Bruckmann, G., editor, *COMPSTAT 1974*, pages 101–110, Wien. Physica Verlag.

[Härdle and Marron, 1985] Härdle, W. and Marron, J. (1985). Optimal bandwidth selection in nonparametric regression function estimation. *The Annals of Statistics*, 13(4):1465–1481.

[Holmström and Koistinen, 1990] Holmström, L. and Koistinen, P. (1990). Using additive noise in back-propagation training. Research Reports A3, Rolf Nevanlinna Institute. To appear in *IEEE Trans. Neural Networks*.

[Holmström et al., 1990] Holmström, L., Koistinen, P., and Ilmoniemi, R. J. (1990). Classification of unaveraged evoked cortical magnetic fields. In *Proc. IJCNN-90-WASH DC*, pages II: 359–362. Lawrence Erlbaum Associates.

[Moody and Darken, 1989] Moody, J. and Darken, C. (1989). Fast learning in networks of locally-tuned processing units. *Neural Computation*, 1:281–294.

[Nadaraya, 1964] Nadaraya, E. (1964). On estimating regression. *Theor. Probability Appl.*, 9:141–142.

[Sietsma and Dow, 1991] Sietsma, J. and Dow, R. J. F. (1991). Creating artificial neural networks that generalize. *Neural Networks*, 4:67–79.

[Specht, 1991] Specht, D. (1991). A general regression neural network. *IEEE Transactions on Neural Networks*, 2(6):568–576.

[Specht, 1990] Specht, D. F. (1990). Probabilistic neural networks. *Neural Networks*, 3(1):109–118.

[Stokbro et al., 1990] Stokbro, K., Umberger, D., and Hertz, J. (1990). Exploiting neurons with localized receptive fields to learn chaos. NORDITA preprint.

[Watson, 1964] Watson, G. (1964). Smooth regression analysis. *Sankhyā Ser. A*, 26:359–372.

[Weigend et al., 1990] Weigend, A., Huberman, B., and Rumelhart, D. (1990). Predicting the future: A connectionist approach. *International Journal of Neural Systems*, 1(3):193–209.

[White, 1989] White, H. (1989). Learning in artificial neural networks: A statistical perspective. *Neural Computation*, 1:425–464.

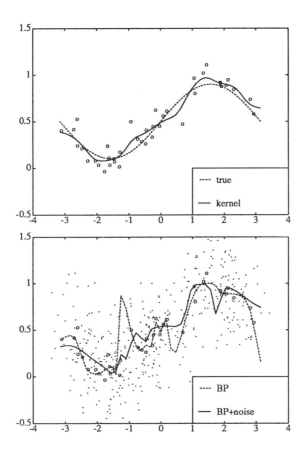

Figure 2: Results From a Mapping Estimation Experiment. Shown are the $n = 40$ original vectors (o's), the artificial vectors (dots), the true function $a \sin x + b$ and the fitting results using kernel regression, backpropagation and backpropagation with noise. Here $h = 0.16$ was chosen with L_{XY}. Values of J are 0.0075 (kernel regression), 0.014 (backpropagation with noise) and 0.038 (backpropagation).

Splines, Rational Functions and Neural Networks

Robert C. Williamson
Department of Systems Engineering
Australian National University
Canberra, 2601
Australia

Peter L. Bartlett
Department of Electrical Engineering
University of Queensland
Queensland, 4072
Australia

Abstract

Connections between spline approximation, approximation with rational functions, and feedforward neural networks are studied. The potential improvement in the degree of approximation in going from single to two hidden layer networks is examined. Some results of Birman and Solomjak regarding the degree of approximation achievable when knot positions are chosen on the basis of the probability distribution of examples rather than the function values are extended.

1 INTRODUCTION

Feedforward neural networks have been proposed as parametrized representations suitable for nonlinear regression. Their approximation theoretic properties are still not well understood. This paper shows some connections with the more widely known methods of spline and rational approximation. A result due to Vitushkin is applied to determine the relative improvement in degree of approximation possible by having more than one hidden layer. Furthermore, an approximation result relevant to statistical regression originally due to Birman and Solomjak for Sobolev space approximation is extended to more general Besov spaces. The two main results are theorems 3.1 and 4.2.

1040

2 SPLINES AND RATIONAL FUNCTIONS

The two most widely studied nonlinear approximation methods are splines with free knots and rational functions. It is natural to ask what connection, if any, these have with neural networks. It is already known that splines with free knots and rational functions are closely related, as Petrushev and Popov's remarkable result shows:

Theorem 2.1 ([10, chapter 8]) *Let*

$$R_n(f)_p := \inf\{\|f - r\|_p : r \text{ a rational function of degree } n\}$$

$$S_n^k(f)_p := \inf\{\|f - s\|_p : s \text{ a spline of degree } k - 1 \text{ with } n - 1 \text{ free knots}\}.$$

If $f \in L_p[a, b], \infty < a < b < \infty$, $1 < p < \infty$, $k \geq 1$, $0 < \alpha < k$, then

$$R_n(f)_p = O(n^{-\alpha}) \quad \text{if and only if} \quad S_n^k(f)_p = O(n^{-\alpha}).$$

In both cases the efficacy of the methods can be understood in terms of their flexibility in partitioning the domain of definition: the partitioning amounts to a "balancing" of the error of local linear approximation [4].

There is an obvious connection between single hidden layer neural networks and splines. For example, replacing the sigmoid $(1 + e^{-x})^{-1}$ by the piecewise linear function $(|x + 1| - |x - 1|)/2$ results in networks that are in one dimension splines, and in d dimensions can be written in "Canonical Piecewise Linear" form [3]:

$$f(x) := a + b^T x + \sum_{i=1}^{\kappa} c_i |\alpha_i^T x - \beta_i|$$

defines $f: \mathbb{R}^d \to \mathbb{R}$, where $a, c_i, \beta_i \in \mathbb{R}$ and $b, \alpha_i \in \mathbb{R}^d$. Note that canonical piecewise linear representations are unique on a compact domain if we use the form $f(x) := \sum_{i=1}^{\kappa+1} c_i |\alpha_i^T x - 1|$. Multilayer piecewise linear nets are not generally canonical piecewise linear: Let $g(x) := |x+y-1| - |x+y+1| - |x-y+1| - |x-y-1| + x + y$. Then $g(\cdot)$ is canonical piecewise linear, but $|g(x)|$ (a simple two-hidden layer network) is not.

The connection between certain single hidden layer networks and rational functions has been exploited in [13].

3 COMPOSITIONS OF RATIONAL FUNCTIONS

There has been little effort in the nonlinear approximation literature in understanding nonlinearly parametrized approximation classes "more complex" than splines or rational functions. Multiple hidden layer neural networks are in this more complex class. As a first step to understanding the utility of these representations we now consider the degree of approximation of certain smooth function classes via rational functions or compositions of rational functions in the sup-metric. A function $\phi: \mathbb{R} \to \mathbb{R}$ is rational of degree π if ϕ can be expressed as a ratio of polynomials in $x \in \mathbb{R}$ of degree at most π. Thus

$$(3.1) \qquad \phi_\theta := \phi_\theta(x) := \frac{\sum_{i=1}^{\pi} \alpha_i x^i}{\sum_{i=1}^{\pi} \beta_i x^i} \qquad x \in \mathbb{R}, \; \theta := [\alpha, \beta]$$

Let $\sigma_\pi(f, \phi) := \inf\{\|f - \phi_\theta\| : \deg \phi \leq \pi\}$ denote the degree of approximation of f by a rational function of degree π or less. Let $\psi := \phi \circ \rho$, where ϕ and ρ are rational functions: $\rho \colon \mathbb{R} \times \Theta_\rho \to \mathbb{R}$, $\phi \colon \mathbb{R} \times \Theta_\phi \to \mathbb{R}$, both of degree π. Let $\mathbb{F}$ be some function space (metrized by $\|\cdot\|_\infty$) and let $\sigma_\pi(\mathbb{F}, \cdot) := \sup\{\sigma_\pi(f, \cdot) : f \in \mathbb{F}\}$ denote the degree of approximation of the function class $\mathbb{F}$.

Theorem 3.1 *Let $\mathbb{F}_\alpha := W_\infty^\alpha(\Omega)$ denote the Sobolev space of functions from a compact subset $\Omega \subset \mathbb{R}$ to $\mathbb{R}$ with $s := \lfloor \alpha \rfloor$ continuous derivatives and the sth derivative satisfying a Lipschitz condition with order $\alpha - s$. Then there exist positive constants c_1 and c_2 not depending on π such that for sufficiently large π*

$$(3.2) \qquad \sigma_\pi(\mathbb{F}_\alpha, \rho) \geq c_1 \left(\frac{1}{2\pi}\right)^\alpha$$

and

$$(3.3) \qquad \sigma_\pi(\mathbb{F}_\alpha, \psi) \geq c_2 \left(\frac{1}{4\pi \log(\pi + 1)}\right)^\alpha$$

Note that (3.2) is tight: it is achievable. Whether (3.3) is achievable is unknown. The proof is a consequence of theorem 3.4. The above result, although only for rational functions of a single variable, suggests that no great benefit in terms of degree of approximation is to be obtained by using multiple hidden layer networks.

3.1   PROOF OF THEOREM

Definition 3.2 *Let $\Gamma^d \subset \mathbb{R}^d$. A map $r \colon \Gamma^d \to \mathbb{R}$ is called a piecewise rational function of degree k with barrier b_d^q of order q if there is a polynomial b_d^q of degree q in $x \in \Gamma^d$ such that on any connected component of $\gamma_i \subset \Gamma^d \setminus \{x : b_d^q(x) = 0\}$, r is a rational function on γ_i of degree k:*

$$r := r(x) := \frac{P_{d,i}^k(x)}{Q_{d,i}^k(x)} \qquad P_{d,i}^k, Q_{d,i}^k \in \mathbb{R}^d[x].$$

Note that at any point $x \in \overline{\gamma_i} \cap \overline{\gamma_j}$, $(i \neq j)$, r is not necessarily single valued.

Definition 3.3 *Let $\mathbb{F}$ be some function class defined on a set G metrized with $\|\cdot\|_\infty$ and let $\Theta = \mathbb{R}^\nu$. Then $F_{\varepsilon,\nu}^{k,q} \colon G \times \Theta \to \mathbb{R}$, $F_{\varepsilon,\nu}^{k,q} \colon (x, \theta) \mapsto F(x, \theta)$ where*

1. *$F(x, \theta)$ is a piecewise rational function of θ of degree k or less with barrier $b_\nu^{q,x}$ (possibly depending on x) of order q;*

2. *For all $f \in \mathbb{F}$ there is a $\theta \in \Theta$ such that $\|f - F(\cdot, \theta)\| \leq \varepsilon$;*

is called an ε-representation of $\mathbb{F}$ of degree k and order q.

Theorem 3.4 ([12, page 191, theorem 1]) *If $F_{\varepsilon,\nu}^{k,q}$ is an ε-representation of $\mathbb{F}_\alpha$ of degree k and order q with barrier b not depending on x, then for sufficiently small ε*

$$(3.4) \qquad \nu \log[(q+1)(k+1)] \geq c \left(\frac{1}{\varepsilon}\right)^{1/\alpha}$$

where c is a constant not dependent on ε, ν, k or q.

Theorem 3.4 holds for any ε-representation F and therefore (by rearrangement of (3.4) and setting $\nu = 2\pi$)

$$(3.5) \qquad \sigma_\pi(\mathbb{F}, F) \geq c \frac{1}{(2\pi \log[(q+1)(k+1)])^\alpha}$$

Now ϕ_θ given by (3.1) is, for any given and fixed $x \in \mathbb{R}$, a piecewise rational function of θ of degree 1 with barrier of degree 0 (no barrier is actually required). Thus (3.5) immediately gives (3.2).

Now consider $\psi_\theta = \phi \circ \rho$, where

$$\phi = \frac{\sum_{i=1}^{\pi_\phi} \alpha_i y^i}{\sum_{i=1}^{\pi_\phi} \beta_i y^i} \ (y \in \mathbb{R}) \quad \text{and} \quad \rho = \frac{\sum_{j=1}^{\pi_\rho} \gamma_j x^j}{\sum_{j=1}^{\pi_\rho} \delta_j x^j} \ (x \in \mathbb{R}).$$

Direct substitution and rearrangement gives

$$\psi_\theta = \frac{\sum_{i=1}^{\pi_\phi} \alpha_i \left[\sum_{j=1}^{\pi_\rho} \gamma_j x^j\right]^i \left[\sum_{j=1}^{\pi_\rho} \delta_j x^j\right]^{\pi_\phi - i}}{\sum_{i=1}^{\pi_\phi} \beta_i \left[\sum_{j=1}^{\pi_\rho} \gamma_j x^j\right]^i \left[\sum_{j=1}^{\pi_\rho} \delta_j x^j\right]^{\pi_\phi - i}}$$

where we write $\theta = [\alpha, \beta, \gamma, \delta]$ and for simplicity set $\pi_\phi = \pi_\rho = \pi$. Thus $\dim \theta = 4\pi =: \nu$. For arbitrary but fixed x, ψ is a rational function of degree $k = \pi$. No barrier is needed so $q = 0$ and hence by (3.4),

$$\sigma_\pi(\mathbb{F}_\alpha, \psi) \geq c_2 \left(\frac{1}{4\pi \log(\pi + 1)}\right)^\alpha.$$

3.2   OPEN PROBLEMS

An obvious further question is whether results as in the previous section hold for multivariable approximation, perhaps for multivariable rational approximation.

A popular method of d-dimensional nonlinear spline approximation uses dyadic splines [2,5,8]. They are piecewise polynomial representations where the partition used is a dyadic decomposition. Given that such a partition Ξ is a subset of a partition generated by the zero level set of a barrier polynomial of degree $\leq |\Xi|$, can Vitushkin's results be applied to this situation? Note that in Vitushkin's theory it is the *parametrization* that is piecewise rational (PR), not the *representation*. What connections are there in general (if any) between PR representations and PR parametrizations?

4   DEGREE OF APPROXIMATION AND LEARNING

Determining the degree of approximation for given parametrized function classes is not only of curiosity value. It is now well understood that the statistical sample complexity of learning depends on the size of the approximating class. Ideally the approximat*ing* class is small whilst well approximating as large as possible an approximat*ed* class. Furthermore, in order to make statements such as in [1] regarding the overall degree of approximation achieved by statistical learning, the classical degree of approximation is required.

For regression purposes the metric used is $L_{p,\mu}$, where

$$\|f - g\|_{L_{p,\mu}} := \left[\int (f(x) - g(x))^p \, d\mu(x)\right]^{1/p}$$

where μ is a probability measure. Ideally one would like to avoid calculating the degree of approximation for an endless series of different function spaces. Fortunately, for the case of spline approximation (with free knots) this not necessary because (thanks to Petrushev and others) there now exist both direct and converse theorems characterizing such approximation classes. Let $S_n(f)_p$ denote the error of n knot spline approximation in $L_p[0,1]$. Let I denote the identity operator and $T(h)$ the translation operator $(T(h)(f, x) := f(x + h))$ and let $\Delta_h^k := (T(h) - I)^k$, $k = 1, 2, \ldots$, be the difference operators. The modulus of smoothness of order k for $f \in L_p(\Omega)$ is

$$\omega_k(f, t)_p := \sum_{|h| \le t} \|\Delta_h^k f(\cdot)\|_{L_p(\Omega)}.$$

Petrushev [9] has obtained

Theorem 4.1 *Let* $\tau = (\alpha/d + 1/p)^{-1}$. *Then*

$$(4.1) \qquad \sum_{n=1}^{\infty} [n^\alpha S_n(f)_p]^k \frac{1}{n} < \infty$$

if and only if

$$(4.2) \qquad \int_0^\infty [t^{-\alpha} \omega_k(f, t)_\tau]^\tau \frac{dt}{t}.$$

The somewhat strange quantity in (4.2) is the norm of f in a Besov space $B_{\tau,\tau;k}^\alpha$. Note that for α large enough, $\tau < 1$. That is, the smoothness is measured in an L_p ($p < 1$) space. More generally [11], we have (on domain $[0, 1]$)

$$\|f\|_{B_{p,q;k}^\alpha} := \left(\int_0^1 (t^{-\alpha} \omega_k(f, t)_p)^q \frac{dt}{t}\right)^{1/q}$$

Besov spaces are generalizations of classical smoothness spaces such as Sobolev spaces (see [11]).

We are interested in approximation in $L_{p,\mu}$ and following Birman and Solomjak [2] ask what degree of approximation in $L_{p,\mu}$ can be obtained when the knot positions are chosen according to μ rather than f. This is of interest because it makes the problem of determining the parameter values on the basis of observations linear.

Theorem 4.2 *Let* $f \in L_{p,\mu}$ *where* $\mu \in L_\lambda$ *for some* $\lambda > 1$ *and is absolutely continuous. Choose the* n *knot positions of a spline approximant* v *to* f *on the basis of* μ *only. Then for all such* f *there is a constant* c *not dependent on* n *such that*

$$(4.3) \qquad \|f - v\|_{L_{p,\mu}} \le cn^{-\alpha} \|f\|_{B_{\sigma,\sigma;k}^\alpha}$$

where $\sigma = (\alpha + (1 - \lambda^{-1})p^{-1})^{-1}$ *and* $p < \sigma$. *The constant* c *depends on* μ *and* λ.

If $p \geq 1$ and $\sigma \leq p$, for any $\alpha < \sigma^{-1}$ for all f under the conditions above, there is a v such that

(4.4)
$$||f - v||_{L_{p,\mu}} \leq cn^{-\alpha + \frac{1}{\sigma} - \frac{1}{p}} ||f||_{B^{\alpha}_{\sigma;k}}$$

and again c depends on μ and λ but does not depend on n.

Proof First we prove (4.3). Let $[0,1]$ be partitioned by Ξ. Thus if v is the approximant to f on $[0,1]$ we have

$$||f - v||^p_{L_{p,\mu}} = \sum_{\Delta \in \Xi} ||f - v||^p_{L_{p,\mu}(\Delta)} = \sum_{\Delta \in \Xi} \int_{\Delta} |f(x) - v(x)|^p d\mu(x).$$

For any $\lambda \geq 1$,

$$\int_{\Delta} |f(x) - v(x)|^p d\mu(x) = \int_{\Delta} |f - v|^p \left(\frac{d\mu}{dx}\right) dx$$

$$\leq \left[\int_{\Delta} |f - v|^{p(1-\lambda^{-1})^{-1}} dx\right]^{1-\lambda^{-1}} \left[\int_{\Delta} \left(\frac{d\mu}{dx}\right)^{\lambda} dx\right]^{\lambda^{-1}}$$

$$= ||f - v||^p_{L_{\psi}(\Delta)} ||d\mu/dx||_{L_{\lambda}(\Delta)}$$

where $\psi = p(1 - \lambda^{-1})^{-1}$. Now Petrushev and Popov [10, p.216] have shown that there exists a polynomial of degree k on $\Delta = [r, s]$ such that

$$||f - v||^p_{L_{\psi}(\Delta)} \leq c||f||^p_{B(\Delta)}$$

where

$$||f||_{B(\Delta)} := \left(\int_0^{(s-r)/k} (t^{-\alpha} ||\Delta_t^k f(\cdot)||_{L_{\sigma}(r,s-kt)})^{\sigma} \frac{dt}{t}\right)^{1/\sigma}$$

and $\sigma := (\alpha + \psi^{-1})^{-1}$, $0 < \psi < \infty$ and $k \geq 1$. Let $|\Xi| =: n$ and choose $\Xi = \cup_i \Delta_i$ $(\Delta_i = [r_i, s_i])$ such that

$$\int_{\Delta_i} \left(\frac{d\mu}{dx}\right)^{\lambda} dx = \frac{1}{n}||d\mu/dx||^{\lambda}_{L_{\lambda}(0,1)}.$$

Thus $||d\mu/dx||_{L_{\lambda}(\Delta)} = n^{-1/\lambda}||d\mu/dx||_{L_{\lambda}(0,1)}$. Hence

(4.5)
$$||f - v||^p_{L_{p,\mu}} \leq c||d\mu/dx||_{L_{\lambda}} \sum_{\Delta \in \Xi} n^{-1/\lambda} ||f||^p_{B(\Delta)}.$$

Since (by hypothesis) $p < \sigma$, Holder's inequality gives

$$||f - v||^p_{L_{p,\mu}} \leq c||d\mu/dx||_{L_{\lambda}} \left[\sum_{\Delta \in \Xi} \left(\frac{1}{n}\right)^{\frac{1}{\lambda}\frac{1}{1-p/\sigma}}\right]^{1 - \frac{p}{\sigma}} \left[\sum_{\Delta \in \Xi} ||f||^{\sigma}_{B(\Delta)}\right]^{\frac{p}{\sigma}}$$

Now for arbitrary partitions Ξ of $[0,1]$ Petrushev and Popov [10, page 216] have shown

$$\sum_{\Delta \in \Xi} ||f||^{\sigma}_{B(\Delta)} \leq ||f||^{\sigma}_{B^{\alpha}_{\sigma;k}}$$

where $B^\alpha_{\sigma;k} = B^\alpha_{\sigma,\sigma;k} = B([0,1])$. Hence

$$\|f - v\|^p_{L_{p,\mu}} \le c\|d\mu/dx\|_{L_\lambda}\, n^{\frac{p}{\sigma}+1-\frac{1}{\lambda}}\, \|f\|^p_{B^\alpha_{\sigma;k}}$$

and so

(4.6) $$\|f - v\|_{L_{p,\mu}} \le c\|d\mu/dx\|^{1/p}_{L_\lambda}\, n^{-\alpha}\, \|f\|_{B^\alpha_{\sigma;k}}$$

with $\sigma = (\alpha + \psi^{-1})^{-1}$, $\psi = p(1 - \lambda^{-1})^{-1}$. Hence $\sigma = (\alpha + \frac{1-\lambda^{-1}}{p})^{-1}$. Thus given α and p, choosing different λ adjusts the σ used to measure f on the right-hand side of (4.6). This proves (4.3).

Note that because of the restriction that $p < \sigma$, $\alpha > 1$ is only achievable for $p < 1$ (which is rarely used in statistical regression [6]). Note also the effect of the term $\|d\mu/dx\|^{1/p}_{L_\lambda}$. When $\lambda = 1$ this is identically 1 (since μ is a probability measure). When $\lambda > 1$ it measures the departure from uniform distribution, suggesting the degree of approximation achievable under non-uniform distributions is worse than under uniform distributions.

Equation (4.4) is proved similarly. When $\sigma \le p$ with $p \ge 1$, for any $\alpha \le 1/\sigma$, we can set $\lambda := (1 - \frac{p}{\sigma} + p\alpha)^{-1} \ge 1$. From (4.5) we have

$$\|f - v\|^p_{L_{p,\mu}} \le c\|d\mu/dx\|_{L_\lambda} \sum_{\Delta \in \Xi} \left(\frac{1}{n}\right)^{1/\lambda} \|f\|^p_{B(\Delta)}$$

$$\le c\|d\mu/dx\|_{L_\lambda} \left(\frac{1}{n}\right)^{1/\lambda} \left[\sum_{\Delta \in \Xi} \|f\|^\sigma_{B(\Delta)}\right]^{p/\sigma}$$

$$\le c\|d\mu/dx\|_{L_\lambda} n^{-1+\frac{p}{\sigma}-p\alpha} \|f\|^p_{B^\alpha_{\sigma;k}}$$

and therefore

$$\|f - v\|_{L_{p,\mu}} \le c\|d\mu/dx\|^{1/p}_{L_\lambda} n^{-\alpha+\frac{1}{\sigma}-\frac{1}{p}} \|f\|_{B^\alpha_{\sigma;k}}.$$

■

5   CONCLUSIONS AND FURTHER WORK

In this paper a result of Vitushkin has been applied to "multi-layer" rational approximation. Furthermore, the degree of approximation achievable by spline approximation with free knots when the knots are chosen according to a probability distribution has been examined.

The degree of approximation of neural networks, particularly multiple layer networks, is an interesting open problem. Ideally one would like both direct and converse theorems, completely characterizing the degree of approximation. If it turns out that from an approximation point of view neural networks are no better than dyadic splines (say), then there is a strong incentive to study the PAC-like learning theory (of the style of [7]) for such spline representations. We are currently working on this topic.

Acknowledgements

This work was supported in part by the Australian Telecommunications and Electronics Research Board and OTC. The first author thanks Federico Girosi for providing him with a copy of [4]. The second author was supported by an Australian Postgraduate Research Award.

References

[1]   A. R. Barron, Approximation and Estimation Bounds for Artificial Neural Networks, To appear in Machine Learning, 1992.

[2]   M. S. Birman and M. Z. Solomjak, Piecewise-Polynomial Approximations of Functions of the Classes W_p^α, *Mathematics of the USSR — Sbornik*, **2** (1967), pp. 295–317.

[3]   L. Chua and A. -C. Deng, Canonical Piecewise-Linear Representation, *IEEE Transactions on Circuits and Systems*, **35** (1988), pp. 101–111.

[4]   R. A. DeVore. Degree of Nonlinear Approximation, in *Approximation Theory VI, Volume 1*, C. K. Chui, L. L. Schumaker and J. D. Ward, eds., Academic Press, Boston, 1991, pp. 175–201.

[5]   R. A. DeVore, B. Jawerth and V. Popov, Compression of Wavelet Decompositions, To appear in American Journal of Mathematics, 1992.

[6]   H. Ekblom, L_p-methods for Robust Regression, *BIT*, **14** (1974), pp. 22–32.

[7]   D. Haussler, Decision Theoretic Generalizations of the PAC Model for Neural Net and Other Learning Applications, Report UCSC-CRL-90-52, Baskin Center for Computer Engineering and Information Sciences, University of California, Santa Cruz, 1990.

[8]   P. Oswald, On the Degree of Nonlinear Spline Approximation in Besov-Sobolev Spaces, *Journal of Approximation Theory*, **61** (1990), pp. 131–157.

[9]   P. P. Petrushev, Direct and Converse Theorems for Spline and Rational Approximation and Besov Spaces, in *Function Spaces and Applications (Lecture Notes in Mathematics 1302)*, M. Cwikel, J. Peetre, Y. Sagher and H. Wallin, eds., Springer-Verlag, Berlin, 1988, pp. 363–377.

[10] P. P. Petrushev and V. A. Popov, *Rational Approximation of Real Functions*, Cambridge University Press, Cambridge, 1987.

[11] H. Triebel, *Theory of Function Spaces*, Birkhäuser Verlag, Basel, 1983.

[12] A. G. Vitushkin, *Theory of the Transmission and Processing of Information*, Pergamon Press, Oxford, 1961, Originally published as *Otsenka slozhnosti zadachi tabulirovaniya* (Estimation of the Complexity of the Tabulation Problem), Fizmatgiz, Moscow, 1959.

[13] R. C. Williamson and U. Helmke, Existence and Uniqueness Results for Neural Network Approximations, Submitted, 1992.

Networks with Learned Unit Response Functions

John Moody and Norman Yarvin
Yale Computer Science, 51 Prospect St.
P.O. Box 2158 Yale Station, New Haven, CT 06520-2158

Abstract

Feedforward networks composed of units which compute a sigmoidal function of a weighted sum of their inputs have been much investigated. We tested the approximation and estimation capabilities of networks using functions more complex than sigmoids. Three classes of functions were tested: polynomials, rational functions, and flexible Fourier series. Unlike sigmoids, these classes can fit non-monotonic functions. They were compared on three problems: prediction of Boston housing prices, the sunspot count, and robot arm inverse dynamics. The complex units attained clearly superior performance on the robot arm problem, which is a highly non-monotonic, pure approximation problem. On the noisy and only mildly nonlinear Boston housing and sunspot problems, differences among the complex units were revealed; polynomials did poorly, whereas rationals and flexible Fourier series were comparable to sigmoids.

1 Introduction

A commonly studied neural architecture is the feedforward network in which each unit of the network computes a nonlinear function $g(x)$ of a weighted sum of its inputs $x = w^t u$. Generally this function is a sigmoid, such as $g(x) = \tanh x$ or $g(x) = 1/(1 + e^{(x-\theta)})$. To these we compared units of a substantially different type: they also compute a nonlinear function of a weighted sum of their inputs, but the unit response function is able to fit a much higher degree of nonlinearity than can a sigmoid. The nonlinearities we considered were polynomials, rational functions (ratios of polynomials), and flexible Fourier series (sums of cosines.) Our comparisons were done in the context of two-layer networks consisting of one hidden layer of complex units and an output layer of a single linear unit.

1048

This network architecture is similar to that built by projection pursuit regression (PPR) [1, 2], another technique for function approximation. The one difference is that in PPR the nonlinear function of the units of the hidden layer is a nonparametric smooth. This nonparametric smooth has two disadvantages for neural modeling: it has many parameters, and, as a smooth, it is easily trained only if desired output values are available for that particular unit. The latter property makes the use of smooths in multilayer networks inconvenient. If a parametrized function of a type suitable for one-dimensional function approximation is used instead of the nonparametric smooth, then these disadvantages do not apply. The functions we used are all suitable for one-dimensional function approximation.

2   Representation

A few details of the representation of the unit response functions are worth noting.

Polynomials: Each polynomial unit computed the function

$$g(x) = a_1 x + a_2 x^2 + \ldots + a_n x^n$$

with $x = w^T u$ being the weighted sum of the input. A zero'th order term was not included in the above formula, since it would have been redundant among all the units. The zero'th order term was dealt with separately and only stored in one location.

Rationals: A rational function representation was adopted which could not have zeros in the denominator. This representation used a sum of squares of polynomials, as follows:

$$g(x) = \frac{a_0 + a_1 x + \ldots + a_n x^n}{1 + (b_0 + b_1 x)^2 + (b_2 x + b_3 x^2)^2 + (b_4 x + b_5 x^2 + b_6 x^3 + b_7 x^4)^2 + \ldots}$$

This representation has the qualities that the denominator is never less than 1, and that n parameters are used to produce a denominator of degree n. If the above formula were continued the next terms in the denominator would be of degrees eight, sixteen, and thirty-two. This powers-of-two sequence was used for the following reason: of the $2(n - m)$ terms in the square of a polynomial $p = a_m x^m + \ldots + a_n x^n$, it is possible by manipulating $a_m \ldots a_n$ to determine the $n - m$ highest coefficients, with the exception that the very highest coefficient must be non-negative. Thus if we consider the coefficients of the polynomial that results from squaring and adding together the terms of the denominator of the above formula, the highest degree squared polynomial may be regarded as determining the highest half of the coefficients, the second highest degree polynomial may be regarded as determining the highest half of the rest of the coefficients, and so forth. This process cannot set all the coefficients arbitrarily; some must be non-negative.

Flexible Fourier series: The flexible Fourier series units computed

$$g(x) = \sum_{i=0}^{n} a_i \cos(b_i x + c_i)$$

where the amplitudes a_i, frequencies b_i and phases c_i were unconstrained and could assume any value.

Sigmoids: We used the standard logistic function:

$$g(x) = 1/(1 + e^{(x-\theta)})$$

3   Training Method

All the results presented here were trained with the Levenberg-Marquardt modification of the Gauss-Newton nonlinear least squares algorithm. Stochastic gradient descent was also tried at first, but on the problems where the two were compared, Levenberg-Marquardt was much superior both in convergence time and in quality of result. Levenberg-Marquardt required substantially fewer iterations than stochastic gradient descent to converge. However, it needs $O(p^2)$ space and $O(p^2n)$ time per iteration in a network with p parameters and n input examples, as compared to $O(p)$ space and O(pn) time per epoch for stochastic gradient descent. Further details of the training method will be discussed in a longer paper.

With some data sets, a weight decay term was added to the energy function to be optimized. The added term was of the form $\lambda \sum_{i=1}^{n} w_i^2$. When weight decay was used, a range of values of λ was tried for every network trained.

Before training, all the data was normalized: each input variable was scaled so that its range was (-1,1), then scaled so that the maximum sum of squares of input variables for any example was 1. The output variable was scaled to have mean zero and mean absolute value 1. This helped the training algorithm, especially in the case of stochastic gradient descent.

4   Results

We present results of training our networks on three data sets: robot arm inverse dynamics, Boston housing data, and sunspot count prediction. The Boston and sunspot data sets are noisy, but have only mild nonlinearity. The robot arm inverse dynamics data has no noise, but a high degree of nonlinearity. Noise-free problems have low estimation error. Models for linear or mildly nonlinear problems typically have low approximation error. The robot arm inverse dynamics problem is thus a pure approximation problem, while performance on the noisy Boston and sunspots problems is limited more by estimation error than by approximation error.

Figure 1a is a graph, as those used in PPR, of the unit response function of a one-unit network trained on the Boston housing data. The x axis is a projection (a weighted sum of inputs $w^T u$) of the 13-dimensional input space onto 1 dimension, using those weights chosen by the unit in training. The y axis is the fit to data. The response function of the unit is a sum of three cosines. Figure 1b is the superposition of five graphs of the five unit response functions used in a five-unit rational function solution (RMS error less than 2%) of the robot arm inverse dynamics problem. The domain for each curve lies along a different direction in the six-dimensional input space. Four of the five fits along the projection directions are non-monotonic, and thus can be fit only poorly by a sigmoid.

Two different error measures are used in the following. The first is the RMS error, normalized so that error of 1 corresponds to no training. The second measure is the

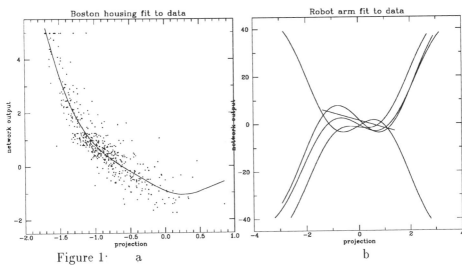

Figure 1·   a   b

square of the normalized RMS error, otherwise known as the fraction of explained variance. We used whichever error measure was used in earlier work on that data set.

4.1   Robot arm inverse dynamics

This problem is the determination of the torque necessary at the joints of a two-joint robot arm required to achieve a given acceleration of each segment of the arm, given each segment's velocity and position. There are six input variables to the network, and two output variables. This problem was treated as two separate estimation problems, one for the shoulder torque and one for the elbow torque. The shoulder torque was a slightly more difficult problem, for almost all networks. The 1000 points in the training set covered the input space relatively thoroughly. This, together with the fact that the problem had no noise, meant that there was little difference between training set error and test set error.

Polynomial networks of limited degree are not universal approximators, and that is quite evident on this data set; polynomial networks of low degree reached their minimum error after a few units. Figure 2a shows this. If polynomial, cosine, rational, and sigmoid networks are compared as in Figure 2b, leaving out low degree polynomials, the sigmoids have relatively high approximation error even for networks with 20 units. As shown in the following table, the complex units have more parameters each, but still get better performance with fewer parameters total.

Type	Units	Parameters	Error
degree 7 polynomial	5	65	.024
degree 6 rational	5	95	.027
2 term cosine	6	73	.020
sigmoid	10	81	.139
sigmoid	20	161	.119

Since the training set is noise-free, these errors represent pure approximation error.

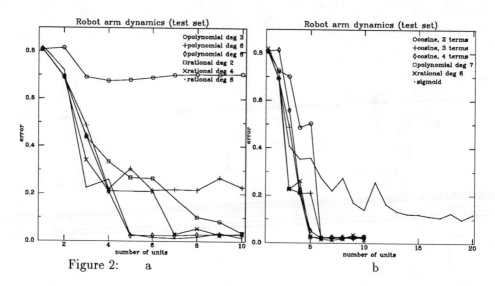

Figure 2:   a   b

The superior performance of the complex units on this problem is probably due to their ability to approximate non-monotonic functions.

4.2   Boston housing

The second data set is a benchmark for statistical algorithms: the prediction of Boston housing prices from 13 factors [3]. This data set contains 506 exemplars and is relatively simple; it can be approximated well with only a single unit. Networks of between one and six units were trained on this problem. Figure 3a is a graph of training set performance from networks trained on the entire data set; the error measure used was the fraction of explained variance. From this graph it is apparent

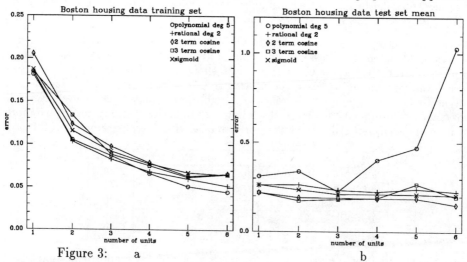

Figure 3:   a   b

that training set performance does not vary greatly between different types of units, though networks with more units do better.

On the test set there is a large difference. This is shown in Figure 3b. Each point on the graph is the average performance of ten networks of that type. Each network was trained using a different permutation of the data into test and training sets, the test set being 1/3 of the examples and the training set 2/3. It can be seen that the cosine nets perform the best, the sigmoid nets a close second, the rationals third, and the polynomials worst (with the error increasing quite a bit with increasing polynomial degree.)

It should be noted that the distribution of errors is far from a normal distribution, and that the training set error gives little clue as to the test set error. The following table of errors, for nine networks of four units using a degree 5 polynomial, is somewhat typical:

Set	Error								
training	0.095	0.062	0.060	0.090	0.076	0.065	0.068	0.066	0.091
test	0.085	1.677	0.171	0.197	0.143	0.546	0.250	0.158	0.395

Our speculation on the cause of these extremely high errors is that polynomial approximations do not extrapolate well; if the prediction of some data point results in a polynomial being evaluated slightly outside the region on which the polynomial was trained, the error may be extremely high. Rational functions where the numerator and denominator have equal degree have less of a problem with this, since asymptotically they are constant. However, over small intervals they can have the extrapolation characteristics of polynomials. Cosines are bounded, and so, though they may not extrapolate well if the function is not somewhat periodic, at least do not reach large values like polynomials.

4.3   Sunspots

The third problem was the prediction of the average monthly sunspot count in a given year from the values of the previous twelve years. We followed previous work in using as our error measure the fraction of variance explained, and in using as the training set the years 1700 through 1920 and as the test set the years 1921 through 1955. This was a relatively easy test set – every network of one unit which we trained (whether sigmoid, polynomial, rational, or cosine) had, in each of ten runs, a training set error between .147 and .153 and a test set error between .105 and .111. For comparison, the best test set error achieved by us or previous testers was about .085. A similar set of runs was done as those for the Boston housing data, but using at most four units; similar results were obtained. Figure 4a shows training set error and Figure 4b shows test set error on this problem.

4.4   Weight Decay

The performance of almost all networks was improved by some amount of weight decay. Figure 5 contains graphs of test set error for sigmoidal and polynomial units,

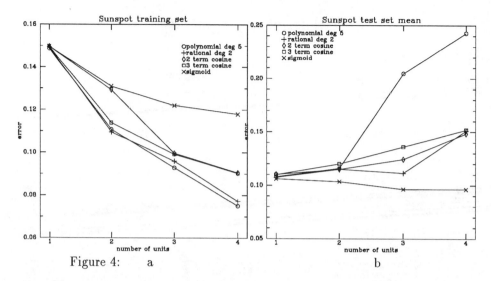

Figure 4:   a   b

using various values of the weight decay parameter λ. For the sigmoids, very little weight decay seems to be needed to give good results, and there is an order of magnitude range (between .001 and .01) which produces close to optimal results. For polynomials of degree 5, more weight decay seems to be necessary for good results; in fact, the highest value of weight decay is the best. Since very high values of weight decay are needed, and at those values there is little improvement over using a single unit, it may be supposed that using those values of weight decay restricts the multiple units to producing a very similar solution to the one-unit solution. Figure 6 contains the corresponding graphs for sunspots. Weight decay seems to help less here for the sigmoids, but for the polynomials, moderate amounts of weight decay produce an improvement over the one-unit solution.

Acknowledgements

The authors would like to acknowledge support from ONR grant N00014-89-J-1228, AFOSR grant 89-0478, and a fellowship from the John and Fannie Hertz Foundation. The robot arm data set was provided by Chris Atkeson.

References

[1] J. H. Friedman, W. Stuetzle, "Projection Pursuit Regression", *Journal of the American Statistical Association*, December 1981, Volume 76, Number 376, 817-823

[2] P. J. Huber, "Projection Pursuit", *The Annals of Statistics*, 1985 Vol. 13 No. 2, 435-475

[3] L. Breiman et al, *Classification and Regression Trees*, Wadsworth and Brooks, 1984, pp217-220

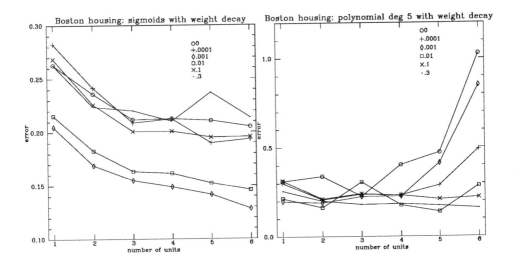

Figure 5: Boston housing test error with various amounts of weight decay

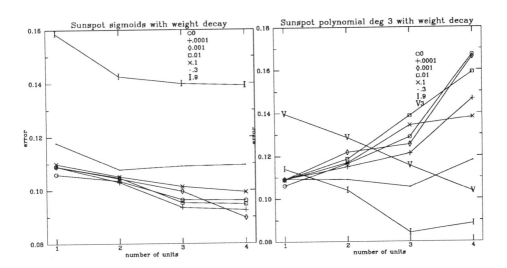

Figure 6: Sunspot test error with various amounts of weight decay

Learning in Feedforward Networks with Nonsmooth Functions

Nicholas J. Redding*
Information Technology Division
Defence Science and Tech. Org.
P.O. Box 1600 Salisbury
Adelaide SA 5108 Australia

T. Downs
Intelligent Machines Laboratory
Dept of Electrical Engineering
University of Queensland
Brisbane Q 4072 Australia

Abstract

This paper is concerned with the problem of learning in networks where some or all of the functions involved are not smooth. Examples of such networks are those whose neural transfer functions are piecewise-linear and those whose error function is defined in terms of the ℓ_∞ norm.

Up to now, networks whose neural transfer functions are piecewise-linear have received very little consideration in the literature, but the possibility of using an error function defined in terms of the ℓ_∞ norm has received some attention. In this latter work, however, the problems that can occur when gradient methods are used for nonsmooth error functions have not been addressed.

In this paper we draw upon some recent results from the field of nonsmooth optimization (NSO) to present an algorithm for the nonsmooth case. Our motivation for this work arose out of the fact that we have been able to show that, in backpropagation, an error function based upon the ℓ_∞ norm overcomes the difficulties which can occur when using the ℓ_2 norm.

1 INTRODUCTION

This paper is concerned with the problem of learning in networks where some or all of the functions involved are not smooth. Examples of such networks are those whose neural transfer functions are piecewise-linear and those whose error function is defined in terms of the ℓ_∞ norm.

---

*The author can be contacted via email at internet address redding@itd.dsto.oz.au.

Up to now, networks whose neural transfer functions are piecewise-linear have received very little consideration in the literature, but the possibility of using an error function defined in terms of the ℓ_∞ norm has received some attention [1]. In the work described in [1], however, the problems that can occur when gradient methods are used for nonsmooth error functions have not been addressed.

In this paper we draw upon some recent results from the field of nonsmooth optimization (NSO) to present an algorithm for the nonsmooth case. Our motivation for this work arose out of the fact that we have been able to show [2][1] that an error function based upon the ℓ_∞ norm overcomes the difficulties which can occur when using backpropagation's ℓ_2 norm [4].

The framework for NSO is the class of locally Lipschitzian functions [5]. Locally Lipschitzian functions are a broad class of functions that include, but are not limited to, "smooth" (completely differentiable) functions. (Note, however, that this framework does not include step-functions.) We here present a method for training feedforward networks (FFNs) whose behaviour can be described by a locally Lipschitzian function $\mathbf{y} = \mathbf{f}_{net}(\mathbf{w}, \mathbf{x})$, where the input vector $\mathbf{x} = (x_1, \ldots, x_n)$ is an element of the set of patterns $\mathcal{X} \subset \mathbf{R}^n$, $\mathbf{w} \in \mathbf{R}^b$ is the weight vector, and $\mathbf{y} \in \mathbf{R}^m$ is the m-dimensional output.

The possible networks that fit within the locally Lipschitzian framework include any network that has a continuous, piecewise differentiable description, *i.e.*, continuous functions with nondifferentiable points ("nonsmooth functions").

Training a network involves the selection of a weight vector $\mathbf{w}^*$ which minimizes an *error function* $E(\mathbf{w})$. As long as the error function E is locally Lipschitzian, then it can be trained by the procedure that we will outline, which is based upon a new technique for NSO [6].

In Section 2, a description of the difficulties that can occur when gradient methods are applied to nonsmooth problems is presented. In Section 3, a short overview of the Bundle-Trust algorithm [6] for NSO is presented. And in Section 4 details of applying a NSO procedure to training networks with an ℓ_∞ based error function are presented, along with simulation results that demonstrate the viability of the technique.

2   FAILURE OF GRADIENT METHODS

Two difficulties which arise when gradient methods are applied to nonsmooth problems will be discussed here. The first is that gradient descent sometimes fails to converge to a local minimum, and the second relates to the lack of a stopping criterion for gradient methods.

2.1   THE "JAMMING" EFFECT

We will now show that gradient methods can fail to converge to a local minimum (the "jamming" effect [7,8]). The particular example used here is taken from [9].

Consider the following function, that has a minimum at the point $\mathbf{w}^* = (0,0)$:

$$f_1(\mathbf{w}) = 3(w_1^2 + 2w_2^2). \tag{1}$$

If we start at the point $\mathbf{w}_0 = (2, 1)$, it is easily shown that a steepest descent algorithm[2] would generate the sequence $\mathbf{w}_1 = (2, -1)/3$, $\mathbf{w}_2 = (2, 1)/9$, $\ldots$, so that the sequence

---

[1]This is quite simple, using a theorem due to Krishnan [3].

[2]This is achieved by repeatedly performing a line search along the steepest descent direction.

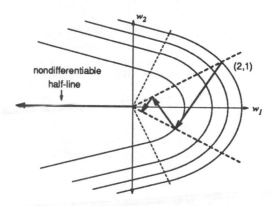

Figure 1: A contour plot of the function f_3.

$\{\mathbf{w}_k\}$ oscillates between points on the two half-lines $w_1 = 2w_2$ and $w_1 = -2w_2$ for $w_1 \geqslant 0$, converging to the optimal point $\mathbf{w}^* = (0,0)$. Next, from the function f_1, create a new function f_2 in the following manner:

$$f_2(\mathbf{w}) = \sqrt{f_1} = \sqrt{3(w_1^2 + 2w_2^2)}. \tag{2}$$

The gradient at any point of f_2 is proportional to the gradient at the same point on f_1, so the sequence of points generated by a gradient descent algorithm starting from $(2,1)$ on f_2 will be the same as the case for f_1, and will again converge[3] to the optimal point, again $\mathbf{w}^* = (0,0)$.

Lastly, we shift the optimal point away from $(0,0)$, but keep a region including the sequence $\{\mathbf{w}_k\}$ unchanged to create a new function $f_3(\mathbf{w})$:

$$f_3(\mathbf{w}) = \begin{cases} \sqrt{3(w_1^2 + 2w_2^2)} & \text{if } 0 \leqslant |w_2| \leqslant 2w_1 \\ \frac{1}{\sqrt{3}}(w_1 + 4|w_2|) & \text{elsewhere.} \end{cases} \tag{3}$$

The new function f_3, depicted in fig. 1, is continuous, has a discontinuous derivative only on the half-line $w_1 \leqslant 0$, $w_2 = 0$, and is convex with a "minimum" as $w_1 \to -\infty$. In spite of this, the steepest descent algorithm still converges to the now nonoptimal "jamming" point $(0,0)$. A multitude of possible variations to f_1 exist that will achieve a similar result, but the point is clear: gradient methods can lead to trouble when applied to nonsmooth problems.

This lesson is important, because the backpropagation learning algorithm is a smooth gradient descent technique, and as such will have the difficulties described when it, or an extension (*eg.*, [1]), are applied to a nonsmooth problem.

2.2 STOPPING CRITERION

The second significant problem associated with smooth descent techniques in a nonsmooth context occurs with the stopping criterion. In normal smooth circumstances, a stopping

---

[3]Note that for this new sequence of points, the gradient no longer converges to 0 at $(0,0)$, but oscillates between the values $\sqrt{2}(1, \pm 1)$.

criterion is determined using

$$\|\nabla f\| \leqslant \epsilon, \tag{4}$$

where ϵ is a small positive quantity determined by the required accuracy. However, it is frequently the case that the minimum of a nonsmooth function occurs at a nondifferentiable point or "kink", and the gradient is of little value around these points. For example, the gradient of $f(w) = |w|$ has a magnitude of 1 no matter how close w is to the optimum at $w = 0$.

3   NONSMOOTH OPTIMIZATION

For any locally Lipschitzian function f, the *generalized directional derivative* always exists, and can be used to define a *generalized gradient* or *subdifferential*, denoted by ∂f, which is a compact convex set[4] [5]. A particular element $\mathbf{g} \in \partial f(\mathbf{w})$ is termed a *subgradient* of f at $\mathbf{w}$ [5,10]. In situations where f is strictly differentiable at $\mathbf{w}$, the generalized gradient of f at $\mathbf{w}$ is equal to the gradient, *i.e.*, $\partial f(\mathbf{w}) = \nabla f(\mathbf{w})$.

We will now discuss the basic aspects of NSO and in particular the Bundle-Trust (BT) algorithm [6].

Quite naturally, subgradients in NSO provide a substitute for the gradients in standard smooth optimization using gradient descent. Accordingly, in an NSO procedure, we require the following to be satisfied:

$$\text{At every } \mathbf{w}, \text{ we can compute } f(\mathbf{w}) \text{ and any } \mathbf{g} \in \partial f(\mathbf{w}). \tag{5}$$

To overcome the jamming effect, however, it is not sufficient replace the gradient with a subgradient in a gradient descent algorithm — the strictly local information that this provides about the function's behaviour can be misleading. For example, an approach like this will not change the descent path taken from the starting point $(2, 1)$ on the function f_3 (see fig. 1).

The solution to this problem is to provide some "smearing" of the gradient information by enriching the information at $\mathbf{w}$ with knowledge of its surroundings. This can be achieved by replacing the strictly local subgradients $\mathbf{g} \in \partial f(\mathbf{w})$ by $\bigcup_{\mathbf{v} \in B} \mathbf{g} \in \partial f(\mathbf{v})$ where B is a suitable neighbourhood of $\mathbf{w}$, and then define the ϵ-*generalized gradient* $\partial_\epsilon f(\mathbf{w})$ as

$$\partial_\epsilon f(\mathbf{w}) \triangleq \text{co} \left\{ \bigcup_{\mathbf{v} \in B(\mathbf{w}, \epsilon)} \partial f(\mathbf{v}) \right\} \tag{6}$$

where $\epsilon > 0$ and small, and co denotes a convex hull. These ideas were first used by [7] to overcome the lack of continuity in minimax problems, and have become the basis for extensive work in NSO.

In an optimization procedure, points in a sequence $\{\mathbf{w}_k, k = 0, 1, \ldots\}$ are visited until a point is reached at which a stopping criterion is satisfied. In a NSO procedure, this occurs when a point $\mathbf{w}_k$ is reached that satisfies the condition $0 \in \partial_\epsilon f(\mathbf{w}_k)$, and the point is said to be ϵ-*optimal*. That is, in the case of convex f, the point $\mathbf{w}_k$ is ϵ-*optimal* if

$$f(\mathbf{w}_k) \leqslant f(\mathbf{w}) + \epsilon \|\mathbf{w} - \mathbf{w}_k\| + \epsilon \text{ for all } \mathbf{w} \in \Re^n \tag{7}$$

---

[4]In other words, a set of vectors will define the generalized gradient of a nonsmooth function at a single point, rather than a single vector in the case of smooth functions.

and in the case of nonconvex f,

$$f(\mathbf{w}_k) \leqslant f(\mathbf{w}) + \epsilon \|\mathbf{w} - \mathbf{w}_k\| + \epsilon \text{ for all } \mathbf{w} \in B \tag{8}$$

where B is some neighbourhood of $\mathbf{w}_k$ of nonzero dimension. Obviously, as $\epsilon \to 0$, then $\mathbf{w}_k \to \mathbf{w}^*$ at which $0 \in \partial f(\mathbf{w}^*)$, *i.e.*, $\mathbf{w}_k$ is "within ϵ" of the local minimum $\mathbf{w}^*$.

Usually the ϵ-generalized gradient is not available, and this is why the *bundle concept* is introduced. The basic idea of a bundle concept in NSO is to replace the ϵ-generalized gradient by some inner approximating polytope P which will then be used to compute a descent direction. If the polytope P is a sufficiently good approximation to f, then we will find a direction along which to descend (a so-called *serious step*). In the case where P is not a sufficiently good approximation to f to yield a descent direction, then we perform a *null step*, staying at our current position $\mathbf{w}$, and try to improve P by adding another subgradient $\partial f(\mathbf{v})$ at some nearby point $\mathbf{v}$ to our current position $\mathbf{w}$.

A natural way of approximating f is by using a *cutting plane* (CP) *approximation*. The CP approximation of $f(\mathbf{w})$ at the point $\mathbf{w}_k$ is given by the expression [6]

$$\max_{1 \leqslant i \leqslant k} \{g_i^{t}(\mathbf{w} - \mathbf{w}_i) + f(\mathbf{w}_i)\}, \tag{9}$$

where g_i is a subgradient of f at the point $\mathbf{w}_i$. We see then that (9) provides a piecewise linear approximation of convex[5] f from below, which will coincide with f at all points $\mathbf{w}_i$. For convenience, we redefine the CP approximation in terms of $\mathbf{d} = \mathbf{w} - \mathbf{w}_k$, $\mathbf{d} \in \mathbf{R}^b$, the vector difference of the point of approximation, $\mathbf{w}$, and the current point in the optimization sequence, $\mathbf{w}_k$, giving the CP approximation f_{CP} of f:

$$f_{CP}(\mathbf{w}_k, \mathbf{d}) = \max_{1 \leqslant i \leqslant k} \{g_i^{t}\mathbf{d} + g_i^{t}(\mathbf{w}_k - \mathbf{w}_i) + f(\mathbf{w}_i)\}. \tag{10}$$

Now, when the CP approximation is minimized to find a descent direction, there is no reason to trust the approximation far away from $\mathbf{w}_k$. So, to discourage a large step size, a stabilizing term $\frac{1}{2t_k}\mathbf{d}^{t}\mathbf{d}$, where t_k is positive, is added to the CP approximation.

If the CP approximation at $\mathbf{w}_k$ of f is good enough, then the $\mathbf{d}_k$ given by

$$\mathbf{d}_k = \arg \min_{\mathbf{d}} f_{CP}(\mathbf{w}_k, \mathbf{d}) + \frac{1}{2t_k}\mathbf{d}^{t}\mathbf{d} \tag{11}$$

will produce a descent direction such that a line search along $\mathbf{w}_k + \lambda \mathbf{d}_k$ will find a new point $\mathbf{w}_{k+1}$ at which $f(\mathbf{w}_{k+1}) < f(\mathbf{w}_k)$ (a *serious step*). It may happen that f_{CP} is such a poor approximation of f that a line search along $\mathbf{d}_k$ is not a descent direction, or yields only a marginal improvement in f. If this occurs, a *null step* is taken and one enriches the *bundle* of subgradients from which the CP approximation is computed by adding a subgradient from $\partial f(\mathbf{w}_k + \lambda \mathbf{d}_k)$ for small $\lambda > 0$. Each *serious step* guarantees a decrease in f, and a stopping criterion is provided by terminating the algorithm as soon as $\mathbf{d}_k$ in (11) satisfies the ϵ-optimality criterion, at which point $\mathbf{w}_k$ is ϵ-optimal. These details are the basis of bundle methods in NSO [9,10].

The bundle method described suffers from a weak point: its success depends on the delicate selection of the parameter t_k in (11) [6]. This weakness has led to the incorporation of a "trust region" concept [11] into the bundle method to obtain the BT (bundle-trust) algorithm [6].

---

[5]In the nonconvex f case, (9) is not an approximation to f from below, and additional tolerance parameters must be considered to accommodate this situation [6].

To incorporate a trust region, we define a "radius" that defines a ball in which we can "trust" that f_{CP} is a good approximation of f. In the BT algorithm, by following trust region concepts, the choice of t_k is not made *a priori* and is determined during the algorithm by varying t_k in a systematic way (*trust* part) and improving the CP approximation by *null steps* (*bundle* part) until a satisfactory CP approximation f_{CP} is obtained along with a ball (in terms of t_k) on which we can *trust* the approximation. Then the $\mathbf{d}_k$ in (11) will lead to a substantial decrease in f.

The full details of the BT algorithm can be found in [6], along with convergence proofs.

4   EXAMPLES

4.1   A SMOOTH NETWORK WITH NONSMOOTH ERROR FUNCTION

The particular network example we consider here is a two-layer FFN (*i.e.*, one with a single layer of hidden units) where each output unit's value y_i is computed from its discriminant function $Q_{o_i} = w_{i0} + \sum_{j=1}^{h} w_{ij} z_j$, by the transfer function $y_i = \tanh(Q_{o_i})$, where z_j is the output of the j-th hidden unit. The j-th hidden unit's output z_j is given by $z_j = \tanh(Q_{h_j})$, where $Q_{h_j} = v_{j0} + \sum_{k=1}^{n} v_{jk} x_k$ is its discriminant function. The ℓ_∞ error function (which is locally Lipschitzian) is defined to be

$$E(\mathbf{w}) = \max_{\mathbf{x} \in \mathcal{X}} \max_{1 \leqslant i \leqslant m} |Q_{o_i}(\mathbf{x}) - t_i(\mathbf{x})|, \tag{12}$$

where $t_i(\mathbf{x})$ is the desired output of output unit i for the input pattern $\mathbf{x} \in \mathcal{X}$.

To make use of the BT algorithm described in the previous section, it is necessary to obtain an expression from which a subgradient at $\mathbf{w}$ for $E(\mathbf{w})$ in (12) can be computed. Using the generalized gradient calculus in [5, Proposition 2.3.12], a subgradient $\mathbf{g} \in \partial E(\mathbf{w})$ is given by the expression[6]

$$\mathbf{g} = \operatorname{sgn}\left(Q_{o_{i'}}(\mathbf{x}') - t_{i'}(\mathbf{x}')\right) \nabla_{\mathbf{w}} Q_{o_{i'}}(\mathbf{x}') \quad \text{for some } i', \mathbf{x}' \in \mathcal{J} \tag{14}$$

where $\mathcal{J}$ is the set of patterns and output indices for which $E(\mathbf{w})$ in (12) obtains it maximum value, and the gradient $\nabla_{\mathbf{w}} Q_{o_{i'}}(\mathbf{x}')$ is given by

$$\nabla_{\mathbf{w}} Q_{o_{i'}}(\mathbf{x}') = \begin{cases} 1 & \text{w.r.t. } w_{i'0} \\ z_j & \text{w.r.t. } w_{i'j} \\ (1 - z_j^2) w_{i'j} & \text{w.r.t. } v_{j0} \\ x_k'(1 - z_j^2) w_{i'j} & \text{w.r.t. } v_{jk} \\ 0 & \text{elsewhere.} \end{cases} \tag{15}$$

(Note that here $j = 1, 2, \ldots, h$ and $k = 1, \ldots, n$).

The BT technique outlined in the previous section was applied to the standard XOR and 838 encoder problems using the ℓ_∞ error function in (12) and subgradients from (14,15).

---

[6]Note that for a function $f(w) = |w| = \max\{w, -w\}$, the generalized gradient is given by the expression

$$\partial f(w) = \begin{cases} 1 & w > 0 \\ \operatorname{co}\{1, -1\} & x = 0 \\ -1 & x < 0 \end{cases} \tag{13}$$

and a suitable subgradient $\mathbf{g} \in \partial f(w)$ can be obtained by choosing $\mathbf{g} = \operatorname{sgn}(w)$.

In all test runs, the BT algorithm was run until convergence to a local minimum of the ℓ_∞ error function occurred with ϵ set at 10^{-4}. On the XOR problem, over 20 test runs using a randomly initialized 2-2-1 network, an average of 52 function and subgradient evaluations were required. The minimum number of function and subgradient evaluations required in the test runs was 23 and the maximum was 126. On the 838 encoder problem, over 20 test runs using a randomly initialized 8-3-8 network, an average of 334 function and subgradient evaluations were required. For this problem, the minimum number of function and subgradient evaluations required in the test runs was 221 and the maximum was 512.

4.2   A NONSMOOTH NETWORK AND NONSMOOTH ERROR FUNCTION

In this section we will consider a particular example that employs a network function that is nonsmooth as well as a nonsmooth error function (the ℓ_∞ error function of the previous example).

Based on the piecewise-linear network employed by [12], let the i-th output of the network be given by the expression

$$y_i = \sum_{k=1}^{n} u_{ik} x_k + \sum_{j=1}^{h} w_{ij} \left| \sum_{k=1}^{n} v_{jk} x_k + v_{j0} \right| + w_{i0} \tag{16}$$

with an ℓ_∞-based error function

$$E(\mathbf{w}) = \max_{\mathbf{x} \in \mathcal{X}} \max_{1 \leqslant i \leqslant m} |y_i(\mathbf{x}) - t_i(\mathbf{x})|. \tag{17}$$

Once again using the generalized gradient calculus from [5, Proposition 2.3.12], a single subgradient $\mathbf{g} \in \partial E(\mathbf{w})$ is given by the expression

$$\mathbf{g} = \text{sgn}(y_{i'}(\mathbf{x}') - t_{i'}(\mathbf{x}')) \begin{cases} x_k & \text{w.r.t. } u_{i'k} \\ 1 & \text{w.r.t. } w_{i'0} \\ \left| \sum_{k=1}^{n} v_{jk} x_k + v_{j0} \right| & \text{w.r.t. } w_{i'j} \\ w_{i'j} \, \text{sgn}(\sum_{k=1}^{n} v_{jk} x_k + v_{j0}) & \text{w.r.t. } v_{j0} \\ w_{i'j} \, \text{sgn}(\sum_{k=1}^{n} v_{jk} x_k + v_{j0}) x'_k & \text{w.r.t. } v_{jk} \\ 0 & \text{elsewhere.} \end{cases} \tag{18}$$

(Note that $j = 1, 2, \ldots, h$, $k = 1, 2, \ldots, n$).

In all cases the ϵ-stopping criterion is set at 10^{-4}. On the XOR problem, over 20 test runs using a randomly initialized 2-2-1 network, an average of 43 function and subgradient evaluations were required. The minimum number of function and subgradient evaluations required in the test runs was 30 and the maximum was 60. On the 838 encoder problem, over 20 test runs using a randomly initialized 8-3-8 network, an average of 445 function and subgradient evaluations were required. For this problem, the minimum number of function and subgradient evaluations required in the test runs was 386 and the maximum was 502.

5   CONCLUSIONS

We have demonstrated the viability of employing NSO for training networks in the case where standard procedures, with their implicit smoothness assumption, would have difficulties or find impossible. The particular nonsmooth examples we considered involved an error function based on the ℓ_∞ norm, for the case of a network with sigmoidal characteristics and a network with a piecewise-linear characteristic.

Nonsmooth optimization problems can be dealt with in many different ways. A possible alternative approach to the one presented here (that works for most NSO problems) is to express the problem as a composite function and then solve it using the exact penalty method (termed *composite NSO*) [11]. Fletcher [11, p. 358] states that in practice this can require a great deal of storage or be too complicated to formulate. In contrast, the BT algorithm solves the more general *basic NSO* problem and so can be more widely applied than techniques based on composite functions. The BT algorithm is simpler to set up, but this can be at the cost of algorithm complexity and a computational overhead. The BT algorithm, however, does retain the gradient descent flavour of backpropagation because it uses the generalized gradient concept along with a chain rule for computing these (generalized) gradients. Nongradient-based and stochastic methods for NSO do exist, but they were not considered here because they do not retain the gradient-based deterministic flavour. It would be useful to see if these other techniques are faster for practical problems.

The message should be clear however — smooth gradient techniques should be treated with suspicion when a nonsmooth problem is encountered, and in general the more complicated nonsmooth methods should be employed.

References

[1] P. Burrascano, "A norm selection criterion for the generalized delta rule," *IEEE Transactions on Neural Networks* 2 (1991), 125–130.

[2] N. J. Redding, "Some Aspects of Representation and Learning in Artificial Neural Networks," University of Queensland, PhD Thesis, June, 1991.

[3] T. Krishnan, "On the threshold order of a Boolean function," *IEEE Transactions on Electronic Computers* EC-15 (1966), 369–372.

[4] M. L. Brady, R. Raghavan & J. Slawny, "Backpropagation fails to separate where perceptrons succeed," *IEEE Transactions on Circuits and Systems* 36 (1989).

[5] F. H. Clarke, *Optimization and Nonsmooth Analysis*, Canadian Mathematical Society Series of Monographs and Advanced Texts, John Wiley & Sons, New York, NY, 1983.

[6] H. Schramm & J. Zowe, "A version of the bundle idea for minimizing a nonsmooth function: conceptual ideas, convergence analysis, numerical results," *SIAM Journal on Optimization* (1991), to appear.

[7] V. F. Dem'yanov & V. N. Malozemov, *Introduction to Minimax*, John Wiley & Sons, New York, NY, 1974.

[8] P. Wolfe, "A method of conjugate subgradients for minimizing nondifferentiable functions," in *Nondifferentiable Optimization*, M. L. Balinski & P. Wolfe, eds., Mathematical Programming Study #3, North-Holland, Amsterdam, 1975, 145–173.

[9] C. Lemaréchal, "Nondifferentiable Optimization," in *Optimization*, G. L. Nemhauser, A. H. G. Rinnooy Kan & M. J. Todd, eds., Handbooks in Operations Research and Management Science #1, North-Holland, Amsterdam, 1989, 529–572.

[10] K. C. Kiwiel, *Methods of Descent for Nondifferentiable Optimization*, Lect. Notes in Math. #1133, Springer-Verlag, New York–Heidelberg–Berlin, 1985.

[11] R. Fletcher, *Practical Methods of Optimization* second edition, John Wiley & Sons, New York, NY, 1987.

[12] R. Batruni, "A multilayer neural network with piecewise-linear structure and backpropagation learning," *IEEE Transactions on Neural Networks* 2 (1991), 395–403.

Iterative Construction of
Sparse Polynomial Approximations

Terence D. Sanger
Massachusetts Institute
of Technology
Room E25-534
Cambridge, MA 02139
tds@ai.mit.edu

Richard S. Sutton
GTE Laboratories
Incorporated
40 Sylvan Road
Waltham, MA 02254
sutton@gte.com

Christopher J. Matheus
GTE Laboratories
Incorporated
40 Sylvan Road
Waltham, MA 02254
matheus@gte.com

Abstract

We present an iterative algorithm for nonlinear regression based on construction of sparse polynomials. Polynomials are built sequentially from lower to higher order. Selection of new terms is accomplished using a novel look-ahead approach that predicts whether a variable contributes to the remaining error. The algorithm is based on the tree-growing heuristic in LMS Trees which we have extended to approximation of arbitrary polynomials of the input features. In addition, we provide a new theoretical justification for this heuristic approach. The algorithm is shown to discover a known polynomial from samples, and to make accurate estimates of pixel values in an image-processing task.

1 INTRODUCTION

Linear regression attempts to approximate a target function by a model that is a linear combination of the input features. Its approximation ability is thus limited by the available features. We describe a method for adding new features that are products or powers of existing features. Repeated addition of new features leads to the construction of a polynomial in the original inputs, as in (Gabor 1961). Because there is an infinite number of possible product terms, we have developed a new method for predicting the usefulness of entire classes of features before they are included. The resulting nonlinear regression will be useful for approximating functions that can be described by sparse polynomials.

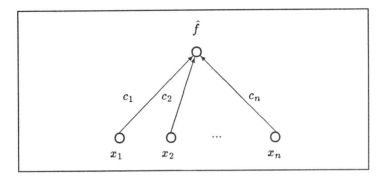

Figure 1: Network depiction of linear regression on a set of features x_i.

2   THEORY

Let $\{x_i\}_{i=1}^n$ be the set of features already included in a model that attempts to predict the function f. The output of the model is a linear combination

$$\hat{f} = \sum_{i=1}^n c_i x_i$$

where the c_i's are coefficients determined using linear regression. The model can also be depicted as a single-layer network as in figure 1. The approximation error is $e = f - \hat{f}$, and we will attempt to minimize $E[e^2]$ where E is the expectation operator.

The algorithm incrementally creates new features that are products of existing features. At each step, the goal is to select two features x_p and x_q already in the model and create a new feature $x_p x_q$ (see figure 2). Even if $x_p x_q$ does not decrease the approximation error, it is still possible that $x_p x_q x_r$ will decrease it for some x_r. So in order to decide whether to create a new feature that is a product with x_p, the algorithm must "look-ahead" to determine if there exists any polynomial a in the x_i's such that inclusion of $a x_p$ would significantly decrease the error. If no such polynomial exists, then we do not need to consider adding any features that are products with x_p.

Define the inner product between two polynomials a and b as $\langle a|b \rangle = E[ab]$ where the expected value is taken with respect to a probability measure μ over the (zero-mean) input values. The induced norm is $\|a\|^2 = E[a^2]$, and let P be the set of polynomials with finite norm. $\{P, \langle \cdot|\cdot \rangle\}$ is then an infinite-dimensional linear vector space. The Weierstrass approximation theorem proves that P is dense in the set of all square-integrable functions over μ, and thus justifies the assumption that any function of interest can be approximated by a member of P.

Assume that the error e is a polynomial in P. In order to test whether $a x_p$ participates in e for any polynomial $a \in P$, we write

$$e = a_p x_p + b_p$$

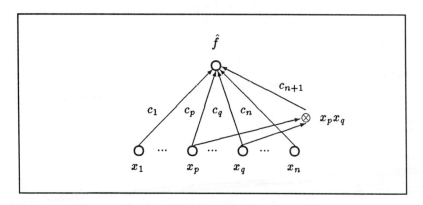

Figure 2: Incorporation of a new product term into the model.

where a_p and b_p are polynomials, and a_p is chosen to minimize $\|a_p x_p - e\|^2 = E[(a_p x_p - e)^2]$. The orthogonality principle then shows that $a_p x_p$ is the projection of the polynomial e onto the linear subspace of polynomials $x_p P$. Therefore, b_p is orthogonal to $x_p P$, so that $E[b_p g] = 0$ for all g in $x_p P$.

We now write

$$E[e^2] = E[a_p^2 x_p^2] + 2E[a_p x_p b_p] + E[b_p^2] = E[a_p^2 x_p^2] + E[b_p^2]$$

since $E[a_p x_p b_p] = 0$ by orthogonality. If $a_p x_p$ were included in the model, it would thus reduce $E[e^2]$ by $E[a_p^2 x_p^2]$, so we wish to choose x_p to maximize $E[a_p^2 x_p^2]$. Unfortunately, we have no direct measurement of a_p.

3   METHODS

Although $E[a_p^2 x_p^2]$ cannot be measured directly, Sanger (1991) suggests choosing x_p to maximize $E[e^2 x_p^2]$ instead, which is directly measurable. Moreover, note that

$$\begin{aligned}
E[e^2 x_p^2] &= E[a_p^2 x_p^4] + 2E[a_p x_p^3 b_p] + E[x_p^2 b_p^2] \\
&= E[a_p^2 x_p^4]
\end{aligned}$$

and thus $E[e^2 x_p^2]$ is related to the desired but unknown value $E[a_p^2 x_p^2]$. Perhaps better would be to use

$$\frac{E[e^2 x_p^2]}{E[x_p^2]} = \frac{E[a_p^2 x_p^4]}{E[x_p^2]}$$

which can be thought of as the regression of $(a_p^2 x_p^2) x_p$ against x_p.

More recently, (Sutton and Matheus 1991) suggest using the regression coefficients of e^2 against x_i^2 for all i as the basis for comparison. The regression coefficients w_i are called "potentials", and lead to a linear approximation of the squared error:

$$\widehat{e^2} = \sum_{i=1}^{n} w_i x_i^2 \tag{1}$$

If a new term $a_p x_p$ were included in the model of f, then the squared error would be b_p^2 which is orthogonal to any polynomial in $x_p P$ and in particular to x_p^2. Thus the coefficient of x_p^2 in (1) would be zero after inclusion of $a_p x_p$, and $w_p E[x_p^2]$ is an approximation to the decrease in mean-squared error $E[e^2] - E[b_p^2]$ which we can expect from inclusion of $a_p x_p$. We thus choose x_p by maximizing $w_p E[x_p^2]$.

This procedure is a form of look-ahead which allows us to predict the utility of a high-order term $a_p x_p$ without actually including it in the regression. This is perhaps most useful when the term is predicted to make only a small contribution for the optimal a_p, because in this case we can drop from consideration any new features that include x_p.

We can choose a different variable x_q similarly, and test the usefulness of incorporating the product $x_p x_q$ by computing a "joint potential" w_{pq} which is the regression of the squared error against the model including a new term $x_p^2 x_q^2$. The joint potential attempts to predict the magnitude of the term $E[a_{pq}^2 x_p^2 x_q^2]$.

We now use this method to choose a single new feature $x_p x_q$ to include in the model. For all pairs $x_i x_j$ such that x_i and x_j individually have high potentials, we perform a third regression to determine the joint potentials of the product terms $x_i x_j$. Any term with a high joint potential is likely to participate in f. We choose to include the new term $x_p x_q$ with the largest joint potential. In the network model, this results in the construction of a new unit that computes the product of x_p and x_q, as in figure 2. The new unit is incorporated into the regression, and the resulting error e will be orthogonal to this unit and all previous units. Iteration of this technique leads to the successive addition of new regression terms and the successive decrease in mean-squared error $E[e^2]$. The process stops when the residual mean-squared error drops below a chosen threshold, and the final model consists of a sparse polynomial in the original inputs.

We have implemented this algorithm both in a non-iterative version that computes coefficients and potentials based on a fixed data set, and in an iterative version that uses the LMS algorithm (Widrow and Hoff 1960) to compute both coefficients and potentials incrementally in response to continually arriving data. In the iterative version, new terms are added at fixed intervals and are chosen by maximizing over the potentials approximated by the LMS algorithm. The growing polynomial is efficiently represented as a tree-structure, as in (Sanger 1991a).

Although the algorithm involves three separate regressions, each is over only $O(n)$ terms, and thus the iterative version of the algorithm is only of $O(n)$ complexity per input pattern processed.

4   RELATION TO OTHER ALGORITHMS

Approximation of functions over a fixed monomial basis is not a new technique (Gabor 1961, for example). However, it performs very poorly for high-dimensional input spaces, since the set of all monomials (even of very low order) can be prohibitively large. This has led to a search for methods which allow the generation of sparse polynomials. A recent example and bibliography are provided in (Grigoriev et al. 1990), which describes an algorithm applicable to finite fields (but not to

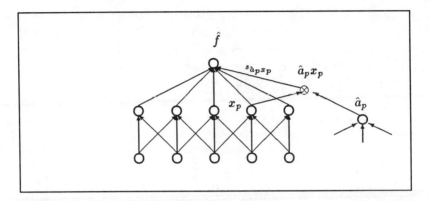

Figure 3: Products of hidden units in a sigmoidal feedforward network lead to a polynomial in the hidden units themselves.

real-valued random variables).

The GMDH algorithm (Ivakhnenko 1971, Ikeda *et al.* 1976, Barron *et al.* 1984) incrementally adds new terms to a polynomial by forming a second (or higher) order polynomial in 2 (or more) of the current terms, and including this polynomial as a new term if it correlates with the error. Since GMDH does not use look-ahead, it risks avoiding terms which would be useful at future steps. For example, if the polynomial to be approximated is xyz where all three variables are independent, then no polynomial in x and y alone will correlate with the error, and thus the term xy may never be included. However, x^2y^2 does correlate with $x^2y^2z^2$, so the look-ahead algorithm presented here would include this term, even though the error did not decrease until a later step. Although GMDH can be extended to test polynomials of more than 2 variables, it will always be testing a finite-order polynomial in a finite number of variables, so there will always exist target functions which it will not be able to approximate.

Although look-ahead avoids this problem, it is not always useful. For practical purposes, we may be interested in the best Nth-order approximation to a function, so it may not be helpful to include terms which participate in monomials of order greater than N, even if these monomials would cause a large decrease in error. For example, the best 2nd-order approximation to $x^2 + y^{1000} + z^{1000}$ may be x^2, even though the other two terms contribute more to the error. In practice, some combination of both infinite look-ahead and GMDH-type heuristics may be useful.

5   APPLICATION TO OTHER STRUCTURES

These methods have a natural application to other network structures. The inputs to the polynomial network can be sinusoids (leading to high-dimensional Fourier representations), Gaussians (leading to high-dimensional Radial Basis Functions) or other appropriate functions (Sanger 1991a, Sanger 1991b). Polynomials can even be applied with sigmoidal networks as input, so that

$$x_i = \sigma \left(\sum s_{ij} z_j \right)$$

where the z_j's are the original inputs, and the s_{ij}'s are the weights to a sigmoidal hidden unit whose value is the polynomial term x_i. The last layer of hidden units in a multilayer network is considered to be the set of input features x_i to a linear output unit, and we can compute the potentials of these features to determine the hidden unit x_p that would most decrease the error if $a_p x_p$ were included in the model (for the optimal polynomial a_p). But a_p can now be approximated using a subnetwork of any desired type. This subnetwork is used to add a new hidden unit $\hat{a}_p x_p$ that is the product of x_p with the subnetwork output $\hat{a}_p$, as in figure 3.

In order to train the $\hat{a}_p$ subnetwork iteratively using gradient descent, we need to compute the effect of changes in $\hat{a}_p$ on the network error $\mathcal{E} = E[(f - \hat{f})^2]$. We have

$$\frac{\partial \mathcal{E}}{\partial \hat{a}_p} = -2E[(f - \hat{f})s_{\hat{a}_p x_p} x_p]$$

where $s_{\hat{a}_p x_p}$ is the weight from the new hidden unit to the output. Without loss of generality we can set $s_{\hat{a}_p x_p} = 1$ by including this factor within $\hat{a}_p$. Thus the error term for iteratively training the subnetwork $\hat{a}_p$ is

$$(f - \hat{f})x_p$$

which can be used to drive a standard backpropagation-type gradient descent algorithm. This gives a method for constructing new hidden nodes and a learning algorithm for training these nodes. The same technique can be applied to deeper layers in a multilayer network.

6   EXAMPLES

We have applied the algorithm to approximation of known polynomials in the presence of irrelevant noise variables, and to a simple image-processing task.

Figure 4 shows the results of applying the algorithm to 200 samples of the polynomial $2 + 3x_1 x_2 + 4x_3 x_4 x_5$ with 4 irrelevant noise variables. The algorithm correctly finds the true polynomial in 4 steps, requiring about 5 minutes on a Symbolics Lisp Machine. Note that although the error did not decrease after cycle 1, the term $x_4 x_5$ was incorporated since it would be useful in a later step to reduce the error as part of $x_3 x_4 x_5$ in cycle 2.

The image processing task is to predict a pixel value on the succeeding scan line from a 2x5 block of pixels on the preceding 2 scan lines. If successful, the resulting polynomial can be used as part of a DPCM image coding strategy. The network was trained on random blocks from a single face image, and tested on a different image. Figure 5 shows the original training and test images, the pixel predictions, and remaining error . Figure 6 shows the resulting 55-term polynomial. Learning this polynomial required less than 10 minutes on a Sun Sparcstation 1.

200 samples of $y = 2 + 3x_1 x_2 + 4x_3 x_4 x_5$
with 4 additional irrelevant inputs, $x_6 - x_9$

Original MSE: 1.0

Cycle 1:

MSE:	0.967								
Terms:	X_1	X_2	X_3	X_4	X_5	X_6	X_7	X_8	X_9
Coeffs:	-0.19	0.14	0.24	0.31	0.17	0.48	0.03	0.05	0.58
Potentials:	0.22	0.24	0.25	0.32	0.33	0.01	0.08	0.01	0.05
Top Pairs:	(5 4) (5 3) (4 3) (4 4)								
New Term:	$X_{10} = X_4 X_5$								

Cycle 2:

MSE:	0.966									
Terms:	X_1	X_2	X_3	X_4	X_5	X_6	X_7	X_8	X_9	X_{10}
Coeffs:	-0.19	0.14	0.24	0.30	0.18	0.48	0.03	0.05	0.57	0.05
Potentials:	0.25	0.22	0.25	0.05	0.02	0.03	0.08	0.02	0.03	0.47
Top Pairs:	(10 3) (10 1) (10 2) (10 10)									
New Term:	$X_{11} = X_{10} X_3 = X_3 X_4 X_5$									

Cycle 3:

MSE:	0.349										
Terms:	X_1	X_2	X_3	X_4	X_5	X_6	X_7	X_8	X_9	X_{10}	X_{11}
Coeffs:	0.04	-0.26	0.09	0.37	-0.04	0.27	0.10	0.22	0.42	-0.26	4.07
Potentials:	0.52	0.59	0.03	0.02	-0.08	0.03	-0.05	-0.06	0.05	-0.05	0.05
Top Pairs:	(2 1) (2 9) (2 2) (1 9)										
New Term:	$X_{12} = X_1 X_2$										

Cycle 4:

MSE:	0.000											
Terms:	X_1	X_2	X_3	X_4	X_5	X_6	X_7	X_8	X_9	X_{10}	X_{11}	X_{12}
Coeffs:	-0.00	-0.00	-0.00	0.00	-0.00	0.00	0.00	0.00	0.00	-0.00	4.00	3.00

Solution: $2 + 3X_1 X_2 + 4X_3 X_4 X_5$

Figure 4: A simple example of polynomial learning.

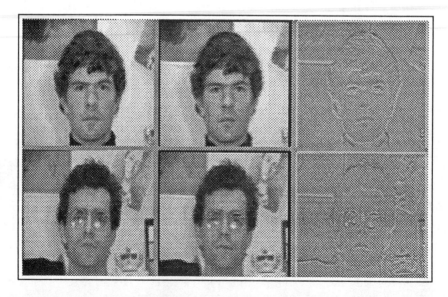

Figure 5: Original, predicted, and error images. The top row is the training image
(RMS error 8.4), and the bottom row is the test image (RMS error 9.4).

$-40.1x_0 + -23.9x_1 + -5.4x_2 + -17.1x_3 +$
$(1.1x_5 + 2.4x_8 + -1.1x_2 + -1.5x_0 + -2.0x_1 + 1.3x_4 + 2.3x_6 + 3.1x_7 + -25.6)x_4 +$
$($
$\quad (-2.9x_9 + 3.0x_8 + -2.9x_4 + -2.8x_3 + -2.9x_2 + -1.9x_5 + -6.3x_0 + -5.2x_1 + 2.5x_6 + 6.7x_7 + 1.1)x_9 +$
$\quad (3.9x_8 + x_5 + 3.3x_4 + 1.6x_3 + 1.1x_2 + 2.9x_6 + 5.0x_7 + 16.1)x_8 +$
$\quad -2.3x_3 + -2.1x_2 + -1.6x_1 + 1.1x_4 + 2.1x_6 + 3.5x_7 + 28.6)x_5 +$
$87.1x_6 + 128.1x_7 + 80.5x_8 +$
$($
$\quad (-2.6x_9 + -2.4x_5 + -4.5x_0 + -3.9x_1 + 3.4x_6 + 7.3x_7 + -2.5)x_9 +$
$\quad 21.7x_8 + -16.0x_4 + -12.1x_3 + -8.8x_2 + 31.4)x_9 +$
2.6

Figure 6: 55-term polynomial used to generate figure 5.

Acknowledgments

We would like to thank Richard Brandau for his helpful comments and suggestions on an earlier draft of this paper. This report describes research done both at GTE Laboratories Incorporated, in Waltham MA, and at the laboratory of Dr. Emilio Bizzi in the department of Brain and Cognitive Sciences at MIT. T. Sanger was supported during this work by a National Defense Science and Engineering Graduate Fellowship, and by NIH grants 5R37AR26710 and 5R01NS09343 to Dr. Bizzi.

References

Barron R. L., Mucciardi A. N., Cook F. J., Craig J. N., Barron A. R., 1984, Adaptive learning networks: Development and application in the United States of algorithms related to GMDH, In Farlow S. J., ed., *Self-Organizing Methods in Modeling*, pages 25–65, Marcel Dekker, New York.

Gabor D., 1961, A universal nonlinear filter, predictor, and simulator which optimizes itself by a learning process, *Proc. IEE*, 108B:422–438.

Grigoriev D. Y., Karpinski M., Singer M. F., 1990, Fast parallel algorithms for sparse polynomial interpolation over finite fields, *SIAM J. Computing*, 19(6):1059–1063.

Ikeda S., Ochiai M., Sawaragi Y., 1976, Sequential GMDH algorithm and its application to river flow prediction, *IEEE Trans. Systems, Man, and Cybernetics*, SMC-6(7):473–479.

Ivakhnenko A. G., 1971, Polynomial theory of complex systems, *IEEE Trans. Systems, Man, and Cybernetics*, SMC-1(4):364–378.

Sanger T. D., 1991a, Basis-function trees as a generalization of local variable selection methods for function approximation, In Lippmann R. P., Moody J. E., Touretzky D. S., ed.s, *Advances in Neural Information Processing Systems 3*, pages 700–706, Morgan Kaufmann, Proc. NIPS'90, Denver CO.

Sanger T. D., 1991b, A tree-structured adaptive network for function approximation in high dimensional spaces, *IEEE Trans. Neural Networks*, 2(2):285–293.

Sutton R. S., Matheus C. J., 1991, Learning polynomial functions by feature construction, In *Proc. Eighth Intl. Workshop on Machine Learning*, Chicago.

Widrow B., Hoff M. E., 1960, Adaptive switching circuits, In *IRE WESCON Conv. Record, Part 4*, pages 96–104.

Node Splitting: A Constructive Algorithm for Feed-Forward Neural Networks

Mike Wynne-Jones
Research Initiative in Pattern Recognition
St. Andrews Road, Great Malvern
WR14 3PS, UK
mikewj@hermes.mod.uk

Abstract

A constructive algorithm is proposed for feed-forward neural networks, which uses node-splitting in the hidden layers to build large networks from smaller ones. The small network forms an approximate model of a set of training data, and the split creates a larger more powerful network which is initialised with the approximate solution already found. The insufficiency of the smaller network in modelling the system which generated the data leads to oscillation in those hidden nodes whose weight vectors cover regions in the input space where more detail is required in the model. These nodes are identified and split in two using principal component analysis, allowing the new nodes to cover the two main modes of each oscillating vector. Nodes are selected for splitting using principal component analysis on the oscillating weight vectors, or by examining the Hessian matrix of second derivatives of the network error with respect to the weights. The second derivative method can also be applied to the input layer, where it provides a useful indication of the relative importances of parameters for the classification task. Node splitting in a standard Multi Layer Perceptron is equivalent to introducing a hinge in the decision boundary to allow more detail to be learned. Initial results were promising, but further evaluation indicates that the long range effects of decision boundaries cause the new nodes to slip back to the old node position, and nothing is gained. This problem does not occur in networks of localised receptive fields such as radial basis functions or gaussian mixtures, where the technique appears to work well.

1   Introduction

To achieve good generalisation in neural networks and other techniques for inferring a model from data, we aim to match the number of degrees of freedom of the model to that of the system generating the data. With too small a model we learn an incomplete solution, while too many free parameters capture individual training samples and noise.

Since the optimum size of network is seldom known in advance, there are two alternative ways of finding it. The *constructive algorithm* aims to build an approximate model, and then add new nodes to learn more detail, thereby approaching the optimum network size from below. *Pruning* algorithms, on the other hand, start with a network which is known to be too big, and then cut out nodes or weights which do not contribute to the model. A review of recent techniques [WJ91a] has led the author to favour the constructive approach, since pruning still requires an estimate of the optimum size, and the initial large networks can take a long time to train. Constructive algorithms offer fast training of the initial small networks, with the network size and training slowness reflecting the amount of information already learned. The best approach of all would be a constructive algorithm which also allowed the pruning of unnecessary nodes or weights from the network.

The constructive algorithm trains a network until no further detail of the training data can be learned, and then adds new nodes to the network. New nodes can be added with random weights, or with pre-determined weights. Random weights are likely to disrupt the approximate solution already found, and are unlikely to be initially placed in parts of the weight space where they can learn something useful, although encouraging results have been reported in this area.[Ash89] This problem is likely to be accentuated in higher dimensional spaces. Alternatively, weights can be pre-determined by measurements on the performance of the seed network, and this is the approach adopted here. One node is turned into two, each with half the output weight. A divergence is introduced in the weights into the nodes which is sufficient for them behave independently in future training without disrupting the approximate solution already found.

2   Node-Splitting

A network is trained using standard techniques until no further improvement on training set performance is achieved. Since we begin with a small network, we have an approximate model of the data, which captures the dominant properties of the generating system but lacks detail. We now freeze the weights in the network, and calculate the updates which would be made them, using simple gradient descent, by each separate training pattern. Figure 1 shows the frozen vector of weights into a single hidden node, and the scatter of proposed updates around the equilibrium position.

The picture shows the case of a hidden node where there is one clear direction of oscillation. This might be caused by two clusters of data within a class, each trying to use the node in its own area of the input space, or by a decision boundary pulled clockwise by some patterns and anticlockwise by others. If the oscillation is strong, either in its exhibition of a clear direction or in comparison with other

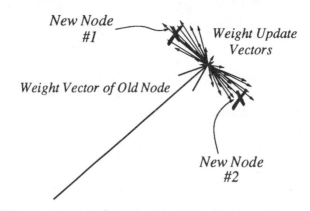

Figure 1: A hidden node weight vector and updates proposed by individual training patterns

nodes in the same layer, then the node is split in two. The new nodes are placed one standard deviation either side of the old position. While this divergence gives the nodes a push in the right direction, allowing them to continue to diverge in later training, the overall effect on the network is small. In most cases there is very little degradation in performance as a result of the split.

The direction and size of oscillation are calculated by principal component analysis of the weight updates. By a traditional method, we are required to make a covariance matrix of the weight updates for the weight vector into each node:

$$\mathbf{C} = \sum_p \delta\mathbf{w}\delta\mathbf{w}^T \tag{1}$$

where p is the number of patterns. The matrix is then decomposed to a set of eigenvalues and eigenvectors; the largest eigenvalue is the variance of oscillation and the corresponding eigenvector is its direction. Suitable techniques for performing this decomposition include Singular Value Decomposition and Householder Reduction. [Vet86] A much more suitable way of calculating the principal components of a stream of continuous measurements such as weight updates is iterative estimation. An estimate is stored for each required principal component vector, and the estimates are updated using each sample. [Oja83, San89] By Oja's method, the scalar product of the current sample vector with each current estimate of the eigenvectors is used as a matching coefficient, M. The matching coefficient is used to re-estimate the eigenvalues and eigenvectors, in conjunction with a gain term λ which decays as the number of patterns seen increases. The eigenvectors are updated by a proportion λM of the current sample, and the eigenvalues by λM^2. The trace (sum of eigenvalues) can also be estimated simply as the mean of the traces (sum of diagonal elements) of the individual sample covariance matrices. The principal component vectors are renormalised and orthogonalised after every few updates. This algorithm is of order n, the number of eigenvalues required, for the re-estimation, and $O(n^2)$ for the orthogonalisation; the matrix decomposition method can take exponential time, and is always much slower in practice.

In a recent paper on *Meiosis Networks*, Hanson introduced stochastic weights in the multi layer perceptron, with the aim of avoiding local minima in training.[Han90] A sample was taken from a gaussian distribution each time a weight was used; the mean was updated by gradient descent, and the variance reflected the network convergence. The variance was allowed to decay with time, so that the network would approach a deterministic state, but was increased in proportion to the updates made to the mean. While the network was far from convergence these updates were large, and the variance remained large. Node splitting was implemented in this system, in nodes where the variances on the weights were large compared with the means. In such cases, two new nodes were created with the weights one standard deviation either side of the old mean: one SD is added to all weights to one node, and subtracted for all weights to the other. Preliminary results were promising, but there appear to be two problems with this approach for node-splitting. First, the splitting criterion is not good: a useless node with all weights close to zero could have comparatively large variances on the weights owing to noise. This node would be split indefinitely. Secondly and more interestingly, the split is made without regard to the correlations in sign between the weight updates, shown as dots in the scatter plots of figure 2. In figure 2a, Meiosis would correctly place new nodes in the positions marked with crosses, while in figure 2b, the new nodes would be placed in completely the wrong places. This problem does not occur in the node splitting scheme based on principal component analysis.

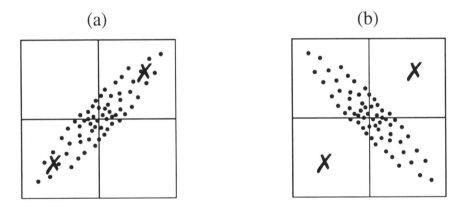

Figure 2: Meiosis networks split correctly if the weight updates are correlated in sign (a), but fail when they are not (b).

3   Selecting nodes for splitting

Node splitting is carried out in the direction of maximum variance of the scatter plot of weight updates proposed by individual training samples. The hidden layer nodes most likely to benefit from splitting are those for which the non-spherical nature of the scatter plot is most pronounced. In later implementations this criterion was measured by comparing the largest eigenvalue with the sum of the eigenvalues, both these quantities being calculated by the iterative method. This is less simple in cases where there are a number of dominant directions of variance; the scatter plot might, for example be a four dimensional disk in a ten dimensional space, and hence present the possibility of splitting one node into eight. It is hoped that these more complicated splits will be the subject of further research.

An alternative approach in determining the need of nodes to be split, in comparison with other nodes in the same layer, is to use the second derivatives of the network error with respect to a parameter of the nodes which is normalised across all nodes in a given layer of the network. Such a parameter was proposed by Mozer and Smolensky in [Smo89]: a multiplicative gating function is applied to the outputs of the nodes, with its gating parameter set to one. Small increments in this parameter can be used to characterise the error surface around the unity value, with the result that derivatives are normalised across all nodes in a given layer of the network. Mozer and Smolensky replaced the sum squared error criterion with a modulus error criterion to preserve non-zero gradients close to the local minimum reached in training; we prefer to characterise the true error surface by means of second derivatives, which can be calculated by repeated use of the chain rule (backpropagation). Backpropagation of second derivatives has previously been reported in [Sol90] and [Hea90].

Since a high curvature error minimum in the space of the gating parameter for a particular node indicates steep gradients surrounding the minimum, it is these nodes which exhibit the greatest instability in their weight-space position. In the weight space, if the curvature is high only in certain directions, we have the situation in figure 1, where the node is oscillating, and is in need of splitting. If the curvature is high in all directions in comparison with other nodes, the network is highly sensitive to changes in the node or its weights, and again it will benefit from splitting.

At the other end of the scale of curvature sensitivity, a node or weight with very low curvature is one to which the network error is quite insensitive, and the parameter is a suitable candidate for pruning. This scheme has previously been used for weight pruning by Le Cun, Denker et al. [Sol90], and offers the potential for an integrated system of splitting and pruning - a truly adaptive network architecture.

3.1   Applying the sensitivity measure to input nodes

In addition to using the gating parameter sensitivity to select nodes for pruning, Mozer and Smolensky mention the possibility of using it on the input nodes to indicate those inputs to which the classification is most sensitive. This has been implemented in our system with the second derivative sensitivity measure, and applied to a large financial classification problem supplied by THORN EMI Research. The analysis was carried out on the 78-dimensional data, and the input sensitivities varied over several orders of magnitude. The inputs were grouped into four sets according to sensitivity, and MLPs of 10 hidden nodes were trained on each subset of the data. While the low sensitivity groups failed to learn anything at all, the higher sensitivity groups quickly attained a reasonable classification rate. Identification of useless inputs leads to greatly increased training speed in future analysis, and can yield valuable economies in future data collection. This work is reported in more detail in [WJ91b].

4   Evaluation in Multi Layer Perceptron networks

Despite the promising results from initial evaluations, further testing showed that the splitter technique was often unable to improve on the performance of the network used as a seed for the first split. These test were carried out on a number of different classification problems, where large numbers of hidden nodes were already known to be required, and with a number of different splitting criteria. Prolonged experimentation and consideration of this failure lead to the hypothesis that a split might be made to correct some misclassified patterns in one region of the input space but, owing to the long range effects of MLP decision boundaries, the changed positions of the planes might cause a much greater number of misclassifications elsewhere. These would tend to cause the newly created nodes to slip back to the position of the node from which they were created, with no overall benefit. This possibility was tested by re-implementing the splitter technique in a gaussian mixture modeling system, which uses a network of localised receptive fields, and hence does not have the long range effects which occurred in the multi layer perceptron.

5   Implementation of the splitter in a Gaussian Mixture Model, and the results

The Gaussian Mixtures Model [Cox91] is a clustering algorithm, which attempts to model the distribution of a points in a data set. It consists of a number of multivariate gaussian distributions in different positions in the input space, and with different variances in different directions. The responses of these receptive fields (bumps) are weighted and summed together; the weights are calculated to satisfy the PDF constraint that the responses should sum to one over the data set. For the experiments on node splitting, the variance was the same in all directions for a particular bump, leading to a model which is a sum of weighted spherical gaussian distributions of different sizes and in different positions. The model is trained by gradient ascent in the likelihood of the model fitting the data, which leads to a set of learning rules for re-estimating the weights, then the centre positions of the receptive fields, then their variances.

For the splitter, a small model is trained until nothing more can be learned, and the parameters are frozen. The training set is run through once more, and the updates are calculated which each pattern attempts to make to the centre position of each receptive field. The first principal component and trace of these updates are calculated by the iterative method, and any nodes for which the principal component variance is a large proportion of the trace is split in two.

The algorithm is quick to converge, and is slowed down only a little by the overhead of computing the principal component and trace. Figure 3 shows the application of the gaussian mixture splitter to modelling a circle and an enclosing annulus; in the circle (a) there is no dominant principal component direction in the data covered by the receptive field of each node (shown at one standard deviation by a circle), while in (b) three nodes are clearly insufficient to model the annulus, and one has just undergone a split. (c) shows the same data set and model a little later in training after a number of splits have taken place. The technique has been evaluated on a number of other simple problems, with no negative results to date.

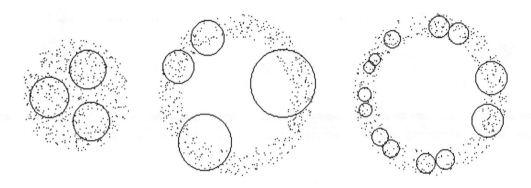

Figure 3: Gaussian mixture model with node-splitting applied to a circle and surrounding annulus

6   Conclusions

The splitter technique based on taking the principal component of the influences on hidden nodes in a network, has been shown to be useful in the multi layer perceptron in only a very limited number of cases. The split in this kind of network corresponds to a hinge in the decision boundary, which corrects the errors for which it was calculated, but usually caused for more errors in other parts of the input space. This problem does not occur in networks of localised receptive fields such as radial basis functions of gaussian mixture distributions, where it appears to work very well. Further studies will include splitting nodes into more than two, in cases where there is more than one dominant principal component, and applying node-splitting to different modelling algorithms, and to gaussian mixtures in hidden markov models for speech recognition.

The analysis of the sensitivity of the network error to individual nodes gives an ordered list which can be used for both splitting and pruning in the same network, although splitting does not generally work in the MLP. This measure has been demonstrated in the input layer, to identify which network inputs are more or less useful in the classification task.

Acknowledgements

The author is greatly indebted to John Bridle and Steve Luttrell of RSRE, Neil Thacker of Sheffield University, and colleagues in the Research Initiative in Pattern

Recognition and its member companies for helpful comments and advice; also to David Bounds of Aston University and RIPR for advice and encouragement.

References

[Ash89]   Timur Ash. Dynamic node creation in backpropagation networks. Technical Report 8901, Institute for Cognitive Science, UCSD, La Jolla, California 92093, February 1989.

[Cox91]   John S Bridle & Stephen J Cox. Recnorm: Simultaneous normalisation and classification applied to speech recognition. In Richard P Lippmann & John E Moody & David S Touretzky, editor, *Advances in Neural Information Processing Systems 3*, pages 234–240, San Mateo, CA, September 1991. Morgan Kaufmann Publishers.

[Han90]   Stephen José Hanson. Meiosis networks. In David S Touretzky, editor, *Advances in Neural Information Processing Systems 2*, pages 533–541, San Mateo, CA, April 1990. Morgan Kaufmann Publishers.

[Hea90]   Anthony JR Heading. An analysis of noise tolerance in multi-layer perceptrons. Research Note SP4 122, Royal Signals and Radar Establishment, St Andrews Road, Malvern, Worcestershire, WR14 3PS, UK, July 1990.

[Oja83]   E Oja. *Subspace Methods of Pattern Recognition*. Research Studies Press Ltd, Letchworth, UK, 1983.

[San89]   TD Sanger. Optimal unsupervised learning in a single-layer linear feedforward neural network. *Neural Networks*, 2:459–473, 1989.

[Smo89]   MC Mozer & P Smolensky. Skeletonization: A technique for trimming the fat from a neural network. In DS Touretzky, editor, *Advances in Neural Information Processing Systems 1*, pages 107–115, San Mateo, CA, April 1989. Morgan Kaufmann Publishers.

[Sol90]   Yann Le Cun & John S Denker & Sara A Solla. Optimal brain damage. In David S Touretzky, editor, *Advances in Neural Information Processing Systems 2*, pages 598–605, San Mateo, CA, April 1990. Morgan Kaufmann Publishers.

[Vet86]   WH Press & BP Flannery & SA Teukolsky & WT Vetterling. *Numerical Recipes in C: The Art of Scientific Computing*. Cambrigde University Press, 1986.

[WJ91a]   Mike Wynne-Jones. Constructive algorithms and pruning: Improving the multi layer perceptron. In R Vichnevetsky & JJH Miller, editor, *Proceedings of the 13th IMACS World Congress on Computation and Applied Mathematics*, pages 747–750, Dublin, July 1991. IMACS '91, IMACS.

[WJ91b]   Mike Wynne-Jones. Self-configuring neural networks, a new constructive algorithm, and assessing the importance of individual inputs. Technical Report X2345/1, Thorn EMI Central Research Laboratories, Dawley Road, Hayes, Middlesex, UB3 1HH, UK, March 1991.

Information Measure Based Skeletonisation

Sowmya Ramachandran
Department of Computer Science
University of Texas at Austin
Austin, TX 78712-1188

Lorien Y. Pratt *
Department of Computer Science
Rutgers University
New Brunswick, NJ 08903

Abstract

Automatic determination of proper neural network topology by trimming over-sized networks is an important area of study, which has previously been addressed using a variety of techniques. In this paper, we present Information Measure Based Skeletonisation (IMBS), a new approach to this problem where *superfluous* hidden units are removed based on their *information measure* (IM). This measure, borrowed from decision tree induction techniques, reflects the degree to which the hyperplane formed by a hidden unit discriminates between training data classes. We show the results of applying IMBS to three classification tasks and demonstrate that it removes a substantial number of hidden units without significantly affecting network performance.

1 INTRODUCTION

Neural networks can be evaluated based on their learning speed, the space and time complexity of the learned network, and generalisation performance. Pruning over-sized networks (skeletonisation) has the potential to improve networks along these dimensions as follows:

- Learning Speed: Empirical observation indicates that networks which have been constrained to have fewer parameters lack flexibility during search, and so tend to learn slower. Training a network that is larger than necessary and

*This work was partially supported by DOE #DE-FG02-91ER61129, through subcontract #097P753 from the University of Wisconsin.

trimming it back to a reduced architecture could lead to improved learning speed.

- Network Complexity: Skeletonisation improves both space and time complexity by reducing the number of weights and hidden units.

- Generalisation: Skeletonisation could constrain networks to generalise better by reducing the number of parameters used to fit the data.

Various techniques have been proposed for skeletonisation. One approach [Hanson and Pratt, 1989, Chauvin, 1989, Weigend *et al.*, 1991] is to add a cost term or bias to the objective function. This causes weights to decay to zero unless they are reinforced. Another technique is to measure the increase in error caused by removing a parameter or a unit, as in [Mozer and Smolensky, 1989, Le Cun *et al.*, 1990]. Parameters that have the least effect on the error may be pruned from the network.

In this paper, we present Information Measure Based Skeletonisation (IMBS), an alternate approach to this problem, in which *superfluous* hidden units in a single hidden-layer network are removed based on their *information measure* (IM). This idea is somewhat related to that presented in [Siestma and Dow, 1991], though we use a different algorithm for detecting superfluous hidden units.

We also demonstrate that when IMBS is applied to a vowel recognition task, to a subset of the Peterson-Barney 10-vowel classification problem, and to a heart disease diagnosis problem, it removes a substantial number of hidden units without significantly affecting network performance.

2   IM AND THE HIDDEN LAYER

Several decision tree induction schemes use a particular information-theoretic measure, called IM, of the degree to which an attribute separates (discriminates between the classes of) a given set of training data [Quinlan, 1986]. IM is a measure of the information gained by knowing the value of an attribute for the purpose of classification. The higher the IM of an attribute, the greater the uniformity of class data in the subsets of feature space it creates.

A useful simplification of the sigmoidal activation function used in back-propagation networks [Rumelhart *et al.*, 1986] is to reduce this function to a threshold by mapping activations greater than 0.5 to 1 and less than 0.5 to 0. In this simplified model, the hidden units form hyperplanes in the feature space which separate data. Thus, they can be considered analogous to binary-valued attributes, and the IM of each hidden unit can be calculated as in decision tree induction [Quinlan, 1986].

Figure 1 shows the training data for a fabricated two-feature, two-class problem and a possible configuration of the hyperplanes formed by each hidden unit at the end of training. Hyperplane $h1$'s higher IM corresponds to the fact that it separates the two classes better than $h2$.

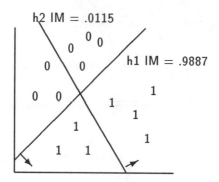

Figure 1: Hyperplanes and their IM. Arrows indicate regions where hidden units have activations > 0.5.

3   IM TO DETECT SUPERFLUOUS HIDDEN UNITS

One of the important goals of training is to adjust the set of hyperplanes formed by the hidden layer so that they separate the training data.[1] We define *superfluous* units as those whose corresponding hyperplanes are not necessary for the proper separation of training data. For example, in Figure 1, hyperplane $h2$ is superfluous because:

1. $h1$ separates the data better than $h2$ and
2. $h2$ does not separate the data in either of the two regions created by $h1$.

The IMBS algorithm to identify superfluous hidden units, shown in Figure 2, recursively finds hidden units that are necessary to separate the data and classifies the rest as superfluous. It is similar to the decision tree induction algorithm in [Quinlan, 1986].

The hidden layer is skeletonised by removing the superfluous hidden units. Since the removal of these units perturbs the inputs to the output layer, the network will have to be trained further after skeletonisation to recover lost performance.

4   RESULTS

We have tested IMBS on three classification problems, as follows:

1. Train a network to an acceptable level of performance.
2. Identify and remove superfluous hidden units.
3. Train the skeletonised network further to an acceptable level of performance.

We will refer to the stopping point of training at step 1 as the *skeletonisation point (SP)*; further training will be referred to in terms of SP + number of training epochs.

---

[1]This again is not strictly true for hidden units with sigmoidal activation, but holds for the approximate model.

Input:
   Training data
   Hidden unit activations for each training data pattern.
Output:
   List of superfluous hidden units.
Method:
   main ident-superfluous-hu
   begin
      data-set← training data
      useful-hu-list← nil
      pick-best-hu(data-set,useful-hu-list)
      output hidden units that are not in useful-hu-list
   end
   procedure pick-best-hu(data-set, useful-hu-list)
   begin
      if all the data in data-set belong to the same class then return
      Calculate IM of each hidden unit.
      h1← hidden unit with best IM.
      add h1 to the useful-hu list
      ds1← all the data in data-set for which h1 has an activation of > .5
      ds2← all the data in data-set for which h1 has an activation of <= .5
      pick-best-hu(ds1, useful-hu-list)
      pick-best-hu(ds2, useful-hu-list)
   end

Figure 2: IMBS: An Algorithm for Identifying Superfluous Hidden Units

For each problem, data was divided into a training set and a test set. Several networks were run for a few epochs with different back-propagation parameters η (learning rate) and α (momentum) to determine their locally optimal values.

For each problem, we chose an initial architecture and trained 10 networks with different random initial weights for the same number of epochs. The performances of the original (i.e. the network before skeletonisation) and the skeletonised networks, measured as number of correct classifications of the training and test sets, was measured both at SP and after further training. The retrained skeletonised network was compared with the original network at SP as well as the original network that had been trained further for the same number of weight updates.[2] All training was via the standard back-propagation algorithm with a sigmoidal activation function and updates after every pattern presentation [Rumelhart et al., 1986]. A paired T-test [Siegel, 1988] was used to measure the significance of the difference in performance between the skeletonised and original networks. Our experimental results are summarised in Figure 3, and Tables 1 and 2; detailed experimental conditions are given below.

---

[2]This was ensured by adjusting the number of epochs a network was trained after skeletonisation according to the number of hidden units in the network. Thus, a network with 10 hidden units was trained on twice as many epochs as one with 20 hidden units.

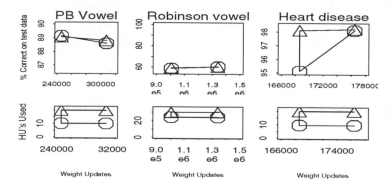

Figure 3: Summary of experimental results. Circles represent skeletonised networks; triangles represent unskeletonised networks for comparison. Note that when performance drops upon skeletonisation, the original performance level is recovered within a few weight updates. In all cases, hidden unit count is reduced.

4.1 PETERSON-BARNEY DATA

IMBS was first evaluated on a 3-class subset of the Peterson-Barney 10-vowel classification data set, originally described in [Peterson and Barney, 1952], and recreated by [Watrous, 1991]. This data consists of the formant values F1 and F2 for each of two repetitions of each of ten vowels by 76 speaker (1520 utterances). The vowels were pronounced in isolated words consisting of the consonant "h", followed by a vowel, followed by "d". This set was randomly divided into a $\frac{2}{3}, \frac{1}{3}$ training/test split, with 298 and 150 patterns, respectively.

Our initial architecture was a fully connected network with 2 input units, one hidden layer with 20 units, and 3 output units. We trained the networks with $\eta = 1.0$ and $\alpha = 0.001$ until the TSS (total sum of squared error) scores seemed to reach a plateau. The networks were trained for 2000 epochs and then skeletonised.

The skeletonisation procedure removed an average of 10.1 (50.5%) hidden units. Though the average performance of the skeletonised networks was worse than that of the original, this difference was not statistically significant ($p = 0.001$).

4.2 ROBINSON VOWEL RECOGNITION

Using data from [Robinson, 1989], we trained networks to perform speaker independent recognition of the 11 steady-state vowels of British English using a training set of LPC-derived log area ratios. Training and test sets were as used by [Robinson, 1989], with 528 and 462 patterns, respectively.

The initial network architecture was fully connected, with 10 input units, 11 output units, and 30 hidden units. Networks were trained with $\eta = 1.0$ and $\alpha = 0.01$, until the performance on the training set exceeded 95%. The networks were trained for 1500 epochs and then skeletonised. The skeletonisation procedure removed an average of 5.8 (19.3%) hidden units. The difference in performance was not statistically significant ($p = 0.001$).

Table 1: Performance of unskeletonised networks

	correct classifications	
	Training set	Test set
Peterson-Barney		
SP	262.90 (88.22%)	133.61 (89.07%)
SP + 500	263.28 (88.35%)	133.20 (88.80%)
Vowel Recognition		
SP	501.60 (95.00%)	273.69 (59.24%)
SP + 500	506.99 (96.02%)	277.80 (60.13%)
Heart Disease		
SP	805.8 (98.27%)	402.20 (98.10%)
SP + 14	806.40 (98.34%)	402.60 (98.20%)

Table 2: Mean difference in the number of correct classifications between the original and skeletonised networks. Positive differences indicate that the original network did better after further training. The numbers in parentheses indicate the 99.9% confidence intervals for the mean.

comparison points		mean difference	
Original	Skeletonised	Training set	Test set
Peterson-Barney			
SP	SP	3.10 [-0.83, 7.03]	-0.10 [-2.05, 1.84]
SP	SP+1010	-0.1 [-1.76, 1.56]	0.7 [-0.73, 2.13]
SP+500	SP+1010	0.20 [-1.52, 1.91]	0.30 [-1.30, 1.90]
Robinson Vowel			
SP	SP	1.70 [-2.40, 5.80]	2.40 [-2.39, 7.19]
SP	SP+620	-8.2 [-20.33, 3.93]	-4.4 [-18.26, 9.46]
SP+500	SP+620	-0.30 [-3.15, 2.55]	-0.30 [-8.36, 7.76]
Heart Disease			
SP	SP	20.80 [-5.66, 47.26]	12.20 [-1.65, 26.05]
SP	SP+33	0 [-4.28, +4.28]	0 [-2.85, 2.85]
SP+14	SP+33	0.60 [-4.55, 5.75]	0.40 [-3.03, 3.83]

4.3   HEART DISEASE DATA

Using a 14-attribute set of diagnosis information, we trained networks on a heart disease diagnosis problem [Detrano *et al.*, 1989]. Training and test data were chosen randomly in a $\frac{2}{3}$, $\frac{1}{3}$ split of 820 and 410 patterns, respectively. The initial networks were fully connected, with 25 input units, one hidden layer with 20 units, and 2 output units. The networks were trained with $\alpha = 1.25$ and $\eta = 0.005$. Training was stopped when the TSS scores seemed to reach a plateau. The networks were trained for 300 epochs and then skeletonised.

The skeletonisation procedure removed an average of 9.6 (48%) hidden units. Here, removing superfluous units degraded the performance by an average of 2.5% on the training set and 3.0% on the test set. However, after being trained further for only 30 epochs, the skeletonised networks recovered to do as well as the original networks.

5   CONCLUSION AND EXTENSIONS

We have introduced an algorithm, called IMBS, which uses an information measure borrowed from decision tree induction schemes to skeletonise over-sized back-propagation networks. Empirical tests showed that IMBS removed a substantial percentage of hidden units without significantly affecting the network performance.

Potential extensions to this work include:

- Using decision tree reduction schemes to allow for trimming not only superfluous hyperplanes, but also those responsible for overfitting the training data, in an effort to improve generalisation.

- Extending IMBS to better identify superfluous hidden units under conditions of less than 100% performance on the training data.

- Extending IMBS to work for networks with more than one hidden layer.

- Performing more rigorous empirical evaluation.

- Making IMBS less sensitive to the hyperplane-as-threshold assumption. In particular, a model with variable-width hyperplanes (depending on the sigmoidal gain) may be effective.

Acknowledgements

Our thanks to Haym Hirsh and Tom Lee for insightful comments on earlier drafts of this paper, to Christian Roehr for an update to the IMBS algorithm, and to Vince Sgro, David Lubinsky, David Loewenstern and Jack Mostow for feedback on later drafts. Matthias Pfister, M.D., of University Hospital in Zurich, Switzerland was responsible for collection of the heart disease data. We used software distributed with [McClelland and Rumelhart, 1988] for many of our simulations.

References

[Chauvin, 1989] Chauvin, Y. 1989. A back-propagation algorithm with optimal use of hidden units. In Touretzky, D. S., editor 1989, *Advances in Neural Information Processing Systems 1*. Morgan Kaufmann, San Mateo, CA. 519–526.

[Detrano *et al.*, 1989] Detrano, R.; Janosi, A.; Steinbrunn, W.; Pfisterer, M.; Schmid, J.; Sandhu, S.; Guppy, K.; Lee, S.; and Froelicher, V. 1989. International application of a new probability algorithm for the diagnosis of coronary artery disease. *American Journal of Cardiology* 64:304–310.

[Hanson and Pratt, 1989] Hanson, Stephen José and Pratt, Lorien Y. 1989. Comparing biases for minimal network construction with back-propagation. In Touretzky, D. S., editor 1989, *Advances in Neural Information Processing Systems 1*. Morgan Kaufmann, San Mateo, CA. 177–185.

[Le Cun *et al.*, 1990] Le Cun, Yann; Denker, John; Solla, Sara A.; Howard, Richard E.; and Jackel, Lawrence D. 1990. Optimal brain damage. In Touretzky, D. S., editor 1990, *Advances in Neural Information Processing Systems 2*. Morgan Kaufmann, San Mateo, CA.

[McClelland and Rumelhart, 1988] McClelland, James L. and Rumelhart, David E. 1988. *Explorations in Parallel Distributed Processing: A Handbook of Models, Programs, and Exercises*. Cambridge, MA, The MIT Press.

[Mozer and Smolensky, 1989] Mozer, Michael C. and Smolensky, Paul 1989. Skeletonization: A technique for trimming the fat from a network via relevance assessment. In Touretzky, D. S., editor 1989, *Advances in Neural Information Processing Systems 1*. Morgan Kaufmann, San Mateo, CA. 107–115.

[Peterson and Barney, 1952] Peterson, and Barney, 1952. Control methods used in a study of the vowels. *J. Acoust. Soc. Am.* 24(2):175–184.

[Quinlan, 1986] Quinlan, J. R. 1986. Induction of decision trees. *Machine Learning* 1(1):81–106.

[Robinson, 1989] Robinson, Anthony John 1989. *Dynamic Error Propagation Networks*. Ph.D. Dissertation, Cambridge University, Engineering Department.

[Rumelhart *et al.*, 1986] Rumelhart, D.; Hinton, G.; and Williams, R. 1986. Learning representations by back-propagating errors. *Nature* 323:533–536.

[Siegel, 1988] Siegel, Andrew F. 1988. *Statistics and data analysis: An Introduction.* John Wiley and Sons. chapter 15, 336–339.

[Siestma and Dow, 1991] Siestma, Jocelyn and Dow, Robert J. F. 1991. Creating artificial neural networks that generalize. *Neural Networks* 4:67–79.

[Watrous, 1991] Watrous, Raymond L. 1991. Current status of peterson-barney vowel formant data. *Journal of the Acoustical Society of America* 89(3):2459–60.

[Weigend *et al.*, 1991] Weigend, Andreas S.; Rumelhart, David E.; and Huberman, Bernardo A. 1991. Generalization by weight-elimination with application to forecasting. In Lippmann, R. P.; Moody, J. E.; and Touretzky, D. S., editors 1991, *Advances in Neural Information Processing Systems 3*. Morgan Kaufmann, San Mateo, CA. 875–882.

Data Analysis using G/SPLINES

David Rogers[*]
Research Institute for Advanced Computer Science
MS T041-5, NASA/Ames Research Center
Moffett Field, CA 94035
INTERNET: drogers@riacs.edu

Abstract

G/SPLINES is an algorithm for building functional models of data. It uses genetic search to discover combinations of basis functions which are then used to build a least-squares regression model. Because it produces a population of models which evolve over time rather than a single model, it allows analysis not possible with other regression-based approaches.

1 INTRODUCTION

G/SPLINES is a hybrid of Friedman's Multivariable Adaptive Regression Splines (MARS) algorithm (Friedman, 1990) with Holland's Genetic Algorithm (Holland, 1975).

G/SPLINES has advantages over MARS in that it requires fewer least-squares computations, is easily extendable to non-spline basis functions, may discover models inaccessible to local-variable selection algorithms, and allows significantly larger problems to be considered. These issues are discussed in (Rogers, 1991).

This paper begins with a discussion of linear regression models, followed by a description of the G/SPLINES algorithm, and finishes with a series of experiments illustrating its performance, robustness, and analysis capabilities.

---

* Currently at Polygen/Molecular Simulations, Inc., 796 N. Pastoria Ave., Sunnyvale, CA 94086, INTERNET: drogers@msi.com.

2 LINEAR MODELS

A common assumption used in data modeling is that the data samples are derived from an underlying function:

$$y_i = f(X_i) + \text{error}$$
$$"" = f(x_{i1}, ..., x_{in}) + \text{error}$$

The goal of analysis is to develop a model F(X) which minimizes the least-squares error:

$$\text{LSE}(F) = \frac{1}{N} \sum_{i=1}^{N} (y_i - F(X_i))^2$$

The function F(X) can then be used to estimate the underlying function f at previously-seen data samples (*recall*) or at new data samples (*prediction*). Samples used to construct the function F(X) are in the *training set*; samples used to test prediction are in the *test set*.

In constructing F(X), if we assume the model F can be written as a linear combination of basis function$\{\phi_k\}$:

$$F(X) = a_0 + \sum_{k=1}^{M} a_k \phi_k(X)$$

then standard least-squares regression can find the optimal coefficients $\{a_k\}$. However, selecting an appropriate set of basis functions for high-dimensional models can be difficult. G/SPLINES is a primarily a method for selecting this set.

3 G/SPLINES

Many techniques develop a regression model by incremental addition or deletion of basis functions to a single model. The primary idea of G/SPLINES is to keep a *collection* of models, and use the genetic algorithm to recombine among these models.

G/SPLINES begins with a collection of models containing randomly-generated basis functions.

$$F_1: \{\phi_1 \; \phi_2 \; \phi_3 \; \phi_4 \; \phi_5 \; \phi_6 \; \phi_7 \; \phi_8 \; \phi_9 \; \phi_{10} \; \phi_{11} \; \phi_{12} \; \phi_{13} \; \phi_{14}\}$$
$$F_2: \{\delta_1 \; \delta_2 \; \delta_3 \; \delta_4 \; \delta_5 \; \delta_6 \; \delta_7 \; \delta_8 \; \delta_9 \; \delta_{10} \; \delta_{11}\}$$
$$\vdots \qquad \vdots$$
$$F_K: \{\sigma_1 \; \sigma_2 \; \sigma_3 \; \sigma_4 \; \sigma_5 \; \sigma_6 \; \sigma_7 \; \sigma_8 \; \sigma_9 \; \sigma_{10} \; \sigma_{11} \; \sigma_{12}\}$$

The basis functions are functions which use a small number of the variables in the data set, such as $SIN(x_2 - 1)$ or $(x_4 - .4)(x_5 - .1)$. The model coefficients $\{a_k\}$ are determined using least-squares regression.

Each model is scored using Friedman's "lack of fit" (LOF) measure, which is a penalized least-squares measure for goodness of fit; this measure takes into account factors such as the number of data samples, the least-squares error, and the number of model parameters.

At this point, we repeatedly perform the *genetic crossover* operation:

- Two good models are probabilistically selected as "parents". The likelihood of being chosen is inversely proportional to a model's LOF score.

- Each parent is randomly "cut" into two sections, and a new model is created using a piece from each parent:

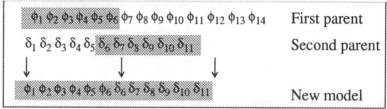

- Optional mutation operators may alter the newly-created model.

- The model with the worst LOF score is replaced by this new model.

This process ends when the average fitness of the population stops improving.

Some features of the G/SPLINES algorithm are significantly different from MARS:

Unlike incremental search, full-sized models are tested at every step.
The algorithm automatically determines the proper size for models.
Many fewer models are tested than with MARS.
A population of models offers information not available from single-model methods.

4 MUTATION OPERATORS

Additional mutation operators were added to the system to counteract some negative tendencies of a purely crossover-based algorithm.

Problem: genetic diversity is reduced as process proceeds (fewer basis functions in population)

<u>NEW</u>: creates a new basis function by randomly choosing a basis function type and then randomly filling in the parameters.

Problem: need process for constructing useful multidimensional basis functions

<u>MERGE</u>: takes a random basis function from each parent, and creates a new basis function by multiplying them together.

Problem: models contain "hitchhiking" basis functions which contribute little

<u>DELETION</u>: ranks the basis functions in order of minimum maximum contribution to the approximation. It removes one or more of the least-contributing basis functions.

5 EXPERIMENTAL

Experiments were conducted on data derived from a function used by Friedman (1988):

$$f(X) = SIN(\pi X_1 X_2) + 20(X_3 - \frac{1}{2})^2 + 10X_4 + 5X_5$$

Standard experimental conditions are as follows. Experiments used a training set containing 200 samples, and a test set containing 200 samples. Each sample contained 10 predictor variables (5 informative, 5 noninformative) and a response. Sample points were randomly selected from within the unit hypercube. The signal/noise ratio was 4.8/1.0

The G/SPLINE population consisted of 100 models. Linear truncated-power splines were used as basis functions. After each crossover, a model had a 50% chance of getting a new basis function created by operator NEW or MERGE and the least-contributing 10% of its basis functions deleted using operator DELETE.

The standard training phase involved 10,000 crossover operations. After training, the models were tested against a set of 200 previously-unseen test samples.

5.1 G/SPLINES VS. MARS

Question: is G/SPLINE competitive with MARS?

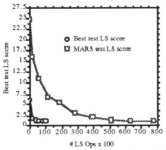

Figure 1. Test least-squares scores versus number of least-squares regressions for G/SPLINES and MARS.

The MARS algorithm was close to convergence after 50,000 least-squares regressions, and showed no further improvement after 80,000. The G/SPLINES algorithm was close to convergence after 4,000 least-squared regressions, and showed no further improvement after 10,000. [Note: the number of least-squares regressions is not a direct measure of the computational efficiency of the algorithms, as MARS uses a technique (applicable only to linear truncated-power splines) to greatly reduce cost of doing least-squares-regression.]

To complete the comparison, we need results on the quality of the discovered models:

Final average least-squared error of the best 4 G/SPLINES models was: ~1.17
Final least-squared error of the MARS model was: ~1.12
The "best" model has a least-squared error (from the added noise) of: ~1.08

Using only linear truncated-power splines, G/SPLINES builds models comparable (though slightly inferior) to MARS. However, by using basis functions other than linear truncated power splines, G/SPLINES can build improved models. If we repeat the experiment with additional basis function types of step functions, linear splines, and quadratic splines, we get improved results:

With additional basis functions, the final average least-squared error was: ~1.095.

I suggest that by including basis functions which reflect the underlying structure of f, the quality of the discovered models is improved.

5.2 VARIABLE ELIMINATION

Question: does variable usage in the population reflect the underlying function? (Recall that the data samples contained 10 variables; only the first 5 were used to calculate f.)

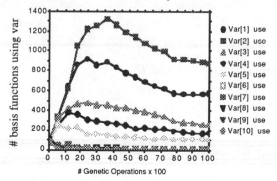

Figure 2. # of basis functions using a variable vs. # of crossover operations.

G/SPLINES correctly focuses on basis functions which use the first five variables The relative usage of these five variables reflects the complexity of the relationship between an input variable and the response in a given dimension.

Question: is the rate of elimination of variables affected by sample size?

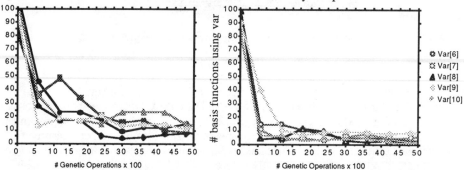

Figure 3. Close-up of Figure 2, showing the five variables not affecting the response. The left graph is the standard experiment; the right from a training with 50 samples.

The left graph plots the number of basis functions containing a variable versus the number of genetic operations for the five noninformative variables in the standard experiment. The variables are slowly eliminated from consideration. The right graph plots the same information, using a training set size of 50 samples. The variables are rapidly eliminated. Smaller training sets force the algorithm to work with most predictive variables, causing a faster elimination of less predictive variables.

Question: Is variable elimination effective with increased numbers of noninformative variables?

This experiment used the standard conditions but increased the number of predictor variables in the training and test sets to 100 (5 informative, <u>95</u> noninformative).

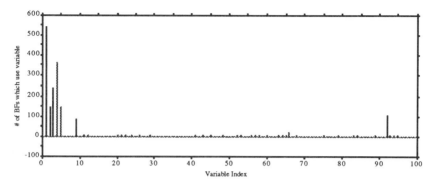

Figure 4. Number of basis functions which used a variable vs. variable index, after 10,000 genetic operations.

Figure 4 shows that elimination behavior was still apparent in this high-dimensional data set. The five informative variables were the first five in order of use.

5.3 MODEL SIZE

Question: What is the effect of the genetic algorithm on model size?

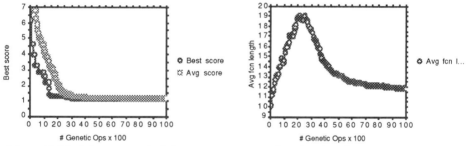

Figure 5. Model scores on training set and average function length.

The left graph plots the best and average LOF score for the training set versus the number of genetic operations. The right graph plots the average number of basis functions in a model versus the number of genetic operations.

Even after the LOF error is minimized, the average model length continues to decrease. This is likely due to pressure from the genetic algorithm; a compact representation is more likely to survive the crossover operation without loss. (In fact, due to the nature of the LOF function, the least-squared errors of the best models is slightly increased by this procedure. The system considers the increase a fair trade-off for smaller model size.)

5.4 RESISTANCE TO OVERFITTING

Question: Does Friedman's LOF function resist overfitting with small training sets?

Training was conducted with data sets of two sizes: 200 and 50. The left graph in Figure 6 plots the population average least-squared error for the training set and the test set versus the number of genetic operations, using a training set size of 200 samples. The right graph

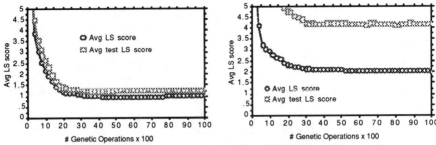

Figure 6. LS error vs. # of operations for training with 200 and 50 samples.

plots the same information, but for a system using a training set size of 50 samples.

In both cases, little overfitting is seen, even when the algorithm is allowed to run long after the point where improvement ceases. Training with a small number of samples still leads to models which resist overfitting.

Question: What is the effect of additive noise on overfitting?

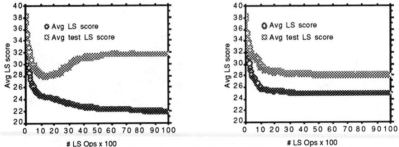

Figure 7. LS error vs. # of operations for low and high noise data sets.

Training was conducted with training sets having a signal/noise ratio of 1.0/1.0. The left graph plots the least-squared error for the training and test set versus the number of genetic operations. The right graph plots the same information, but with a higher setting of Friedman's smoothing parameter.

Noisy data results in a higher risk of overfitting. However, this can be accommodated if we set a higher value for Friedman's smoothing parameter.

5.5 ADDITIONAL BASIS FUNCTION TYPES AND TRAINING SET SIZES

Question: What is the effect of changes in training set size on the type of basis functions selected?

The experiment in Figure 8 used the standard conditions, but using many additional basis function types. The left graph plots the use of different types of basis functions using a training set of size 50.The right graph plots the same information using a training set size of 200. Simply put, different training set sizes lead to significant changes in preferences among function types. A detailed analysis of these graphs can give insight into the nature of the data and the best components for model construction.

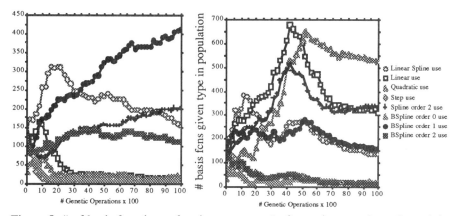

Figure 8. # of basis functions of a given type vs. # of genetic operations, for training sets of 50 and 200 samples.

6 CONCLUSIONS

G/SPLINES is a new algorithm related to state-of-the-art statistical modeling techniques such as MARS. The strengths of this algorithm are that G/SPLINES builds models that are comparable in quality to MARS, with a greatly reduced number of intermediate model constructions; is capable of building models from data sets that are too large for the MARS algorithm; and is easily extendable to basis functions that are not spline-based.

Weaknesses of this algorithm include the ad-hoc nature of the mutation operators; the lack of studies of the real-time performance of G/SPLINES vs. other model builders such as MARS; the need for theoretical analysis of the algorithm's convergence behavior; the LOF function needs to be changed to reflect additional basis function types.

The WOLF program source code, which implements G/SPLINES, is available free to other researchers in either Macintosh or UNIX/C formats. Contact the author (drogers@riacs.edu) for information.

Acknowledgments

This work was supported in part by Cooperative Agreements NCC 2-387 and NCC 2-408 between the National Aeronautics and Space Administration (NASA) and the Universities Space Research Association (USRA). Special thanks to my domestic partner Doug Brockman, who shared my enthusiasm even though he didn't know what the hell I was up to; and my father, Philip, who made me want to become a scientist.

References

Friedman, J., "Multivariate Adaptive Regression Splines," Technical Report No. 102, Laboratory for Computational Statistics, Department of Statistics, Stanford University, November 1988 (revised August 1990).

Holland, J., *Adaptation in Artificial and Natural Systems*, University of Michigan Press, Ann Arbor, MI, 1975.

Rogers, David, "G/SPLINES: A Hybrid of Friedman's Multivariate Adaptive Splines (MARS) Algorithm with Holland's Genetic Algorithm," in *Proceedings of the Fourth International Conference on Genetic Algorithms*, San Diego, July, 1991.

Unsupervised Classifiers, Mutual Information and 'Phantom Targets'

John S. Bridle
Anthony J.R. Heading
Defence Research Agency
St. Andrew's Road, Malvern
Worcs. WR14 3PS, U.K.

David J.C. MacKay
California Institute of Technology 139–74
Pasadena CA 91125 U.S.A

Abstract

We derive criteria for training adaptive classifier networks to perform unsupervised data analysis. The first criterion turns a simple Gaussian classifier into a simple Gaussian mixture analyser. The second criterion, which is much more generally applicable, is based on mutual information. It simplifies to an intuitively reasonable difference between two entropy functions, one encouraging 'decisiveness,' the other 'fairness' to the alternative interpretations of the input. This 'firm but fair' criterion can be applied to any network that produces probability-type outputs, but it does not necessarily lead to useful behavior.

1   Unsupervised Classification

One of the main distinctions made in discussing neural network architectures, and pattern analysis algorithms generally, is between supervised and unsupervised data analysis. We should therefore be interested in any method of building bridges between techniques in these two categories. For instance, it is possible to use an unsupervised system such as a Boltzmann machine to learn the joint distribution of inputs and a teacher's classification labels. The particular type of bridge we seek is a method of taking a supervised pattern classifier and turning it into an unsupervised data analyser. That is, we are interested in methods of "bootstrapping" classifiers.

Consider a classifier system. Its input is a vector $\mathbf{x}$, and the output is a probability vector $\mathbf{y}(\mathbf{x})$. (That is, the elements of $\mathbf{y}$ are positive and sum to 1.) The elements of $\mathbf{y}$, $(y_i(\mathbf{x}), i = 1 \ldots N_c)$ are to be taken as the probabilities that $\mathbf{x}$ should be assigned to each of N_c classes. (Note that our definition of classifier does not include a decision process.)

To enforce the conditions we require for the output values, we recommend using a generalised logistic (normalised exponential, or SoftMax) output stage. We call the unnormalised log probabilities of the classes a_i, and the softmax performs:

$$y_i = e^{a_i}/Z \quad \text{with} \quad Z = \sum_i e^{a_i} \tag{1}$$

Normally the parameters of such a system would be adjusted using a training set comprising examples of inputs and corresponding classes, $\{(\mathbf{x}_i, c_i)\}$. We assume that the system includes means to convert derivatives of a training criterion with respect to the outputs into a form suitable for adjusting the values of the parameters, for instance by "backpropagation".

Imagine however that we have *un*labelled data, $\mathbf{x}_m, m = 1 \ldots N_{ts}$, and wish to use it to 'improve' the classifier. We could think of this as self–supervised learning, to hone an already good system on lots of easily–obtained unlabelled real–world data, or to adapt to a slowly changing environment, or as a way of turning a classifier into some sort of cluster analyser. (Just what kind depends on details of the classifier itself.) The ideal method would be theoretically well-founded, general-purpose (independent of the details of the classifier), and computationally tractable.

One well known approach to unsupervised data analysis is to minimise a reconstruction error: for linear projections and squared euclidean distance this leads to principal components analysis, while reference-point based classifiers lead to vector quantizer design methods, such as the LBG algorithm . Variants on VQ, such as Kohonen's feature maps, can be motivated by requiring robustness to distortions in the code space . Reconstruction error is only available as a training criterion if reconstruction is defined: in general we are only given class label probabilities.

2   A Data Likelihood Criterion

For the special case of a Gaussian clustering of an unlabelled data set, it was demonstrated in [1] that gradient ascent on the likelihood of the data has an appealing interpretation in terms of backpropagation in an equivalent unit-Gaussian classifier network: for each input $\mathbf{x}$ presented to the network, the output $\mathbf{y}$ is doubled to give 'phantom targets' $\mathbf{t} = 2\mathbf{y}$; when the derivatives of the log likelihood criterion $J = -\Sigma_i t_i \log y_i$ relative to these targets are propagated back through the network, it turns out that the resulting gradient is identical to the gradient of the likelihood of the data given a Gaussian mixture model.

For the unit-Gaussian classifier, the activations a_i in (1) are

$$a_i = -|\mathbf{x} - \mathbf{w}_i|^2, \tag{2}$$

so the outputs of the network are

$$y_i = P(\text{class} = i \mid \mathbf{x}, \mathbf{w}) \tag{3}$$

where we assume the inputs are drawn from equi-probable unit-Gaussian distributions with the mean of the distribution of the ith class equal to $\mathbf{w}_i$.

This result was only derived in a limited context, and it was speculated that it might be generalisable to arbitrary classification models. The above phantom target rule has been re-derived for a larger class of networks [4], but the conditions for strict applicability are quite severe. Briefly, there should be exponential density functions for each class, and the normalizing factors for these densities should be independent of the parameters. Thus Gaussians with fixed covariance matrices are acceptable, but variable covariances are not, and neither are linear transformations preceeding the Gaussians.

The next section introduces a new objective function which is independent of details of the classifier.

3   Mutual Information Criterion

Intuitively, an unsupervised adaptive classifier is doing a plausible job if its outputs usually give a fairly clear indication of the class of an input vector, and if there is also an even distribution of input patterns between the classes. We could label these desiderata 'decisive' and 'fair' respectively. Note that it is trivial to achieve either of them alone. For a poorly regularised model it may also be trivial to achieve both.

There are several ways to proceed. We could devise *ad–hoc* measures corresponding to our notions of decisiveness and fairness, or we could consider particular types of classifier and their unsupervised equivalents, seeking a general way of turning one into the other. Our approach is to return to the general idea that the class predictions should retain as much information about the input values as possible. We use a measure of the information about $\mathbf{x}$ which is conveyed by the output distribution, *i.e.* the mutual information between the inputs and the outputs. We interpret the outputs $\mathbf{y}$ as a probability distribution over a discrete random variable c (the class label), thus $\mathbf{y} = p(c|\mathbf{x})$. The mutual information between $\mathbf{x}$ and c is

$$
\begin{aligned}
\mathcal{I}(c\,;\mathbf{x}) &= \iint dc\,d\mathbf{x}\,p(c,\mathbf{x})\log\frac{p(c,\mathbf{x})}{p(c)p(\mathbf{x})} \tag{4} \\
&= \int d\mathbf{x}\,p(\mathbf{x})\int dc\,p(c|\mathbf{x})\log\frac{p(c|\mathbf{x})}{p(c)} \tag{5} \\
&= \int d\mathbf{x}\,p(\mathbf{x})\int dc\,p(c|\mathbf{x})\log\frac{p(c|\mathbf{x})}{\int d\mathbf{x}\,p(\mathbf{x})p(c|\mathbf{x})} \tag{6}
\end{aligned}
$$

The elements of this expression are separately recognizable:

$\int d\mathbf{x}\,p(\mathbf{x})(\cdot)$ is equivalent to an average over a training set $\frac{1}{N_{ts}}\sum_{ts}(\cdot)$;

$p(c|\mathbf{x})$ is simply the network output y_c;

$\int dc\,(\cdot)$ is a sum over the class labels and corresponding network outputs.

Hence:

$$
\mathcal{I}(c\,;\mathbf{x}) = \frac{1}{N_{ts}}\sum_{ts}\sum_{i=1}^{N_c} y_i\log\frac{y_i}{\bar{y}_i} \tag{7}
$$

$$= -\sum_{i=1}^{N_c} \overline{y}_i \log \overline{y}_i + \frac{1}{N_{ts}} \sum_{ts} \sum_{i=1}^{N_c} y_i \log y_i \qquad (8)$$

$$= \mathcal{H}(\overline{\mathbf{y}}) - \overline{\mathcal{H}(\mathbf{y})} \qquad (9)$$

The objective function I is the difference between the entropy of the average of the outputs, and the average of the entropy of the outputs, where both averages are over the training set. $\mathcal{H}(\overline{\mathbf{y}})$ has its maximum value when the average activities of the separate outputs are equal – this is 'fairness'. $\overline{\mathcal{H}(\mathbf{y})}$ has its minimum value when one output is full on and the rest are off for every training case – this is 'firmness'.

We now evaluate $\mathcal{I}$ for the training set, and take the gradient of $\mathcal{I}$.

4   Gradient descent

To use this criterion with back–propagation network training, we need its derivatives with respect to the network outputs.

$$\frac{\partial \mathcal{I}(c\,;\mathbf{x})}{\partial y_i} = \frac{\partial}{\partial y_i} \frac{1}{N_{ts}} \sum_{ts} \sum_{i=1}^{N_c} y_i \log \frac{y_i}{\overline{y}_i} \qquad (10)$$

$$= \frac{1}{N_{ts}} \sum_{ts} [1 + \log y_i - 1 - \log \overline{y}_i] \qquad (11)$$

$$= \frac{1}{N_{ts}} \sum_{ts} \log \frac{y_i}{\overline{y}_i} \qquad (12)$$

The resulting expression is quite simple, but note that the presence of a $\overline{y}_i$ term means that two passes through the training set are required: the first to calculate the average output node activations, and the second to back–propagate the derivatives.

5   Illustrations

Figures 1 shows $\mathcal{I}$ (divided by its maximum possible value, $\log N_c$) for a run of a particular unit-Gaussian classifier network. The 30 data points are drawn from a 2-d isotropic Gaussian. Figure 2 shows the fairness and firmness criteria separately. (The upper curve is 'fairness' $\mathcal{H}(\overline{\mathbf{y}})/\log N_c$, and the lower curve is 'firmness' $(1 - \overline{\mathcal{H}(\mathbf{y})}/\log N_c)$.)

The ten reference points had starting values drawn from the same distribution as the data. Figure 3 shows their movement during training. From initial positions within the data cluster, they move outwards into a circle around the data. The resulting classification regions are shown in Figure 4. (The grey level is proportional to the value of the maximum response at each point, and since the outputs are positive normalised this value drops to 0.5 or less at the decision boundaries.) We observe that the space is being partitioned into regions with roughly equal numbers of points. It might be surprising at first that the reference points do not end up near

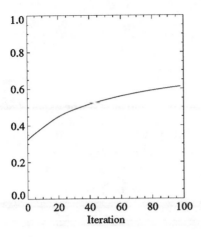

1. The M.I. criterion

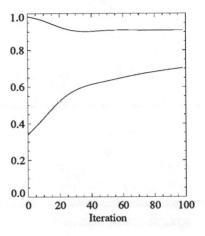

2. Firm and Fair separately

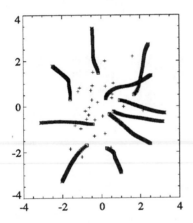

3. Tracks of reference points

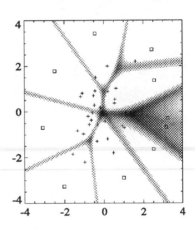

4. Decision Regions

the data. However, it is only the transformation from data **x** to outputs **y** that is being trained, and the reference points are just parameters of that transformation. As the reference points move further away from one another the decision boundaries grow firmer. In this example the fairness criterion happens to decrease in favour of the firmness, and this usually happens. We could consider different weightings of the two components of the criterion.

6 Comments

The usefulness of this objective function will prove will depend very much on the form of classifier that it is applied to. For a poorly regularised classifier, maximisation of the criterion alone will not necessarily lead to good solutions to unsupervised classification; it could be maximised by any implausible classification of the input that is completely hard (*i.e.* the output vector always has one 1 and all the other outputs 0), and that chops the training set into regions containing similar numbers of training points; such a solution would be one of many global maxima, regardless of whether it chopped the data into natural classes.

The meaning of a 'natural' partition in this context is, of course, rather ill-defined. Simple models often do not have the capacity to break a pattern space into highly contorted regions – the decision boundaries shown in the figure below is an example of model producing a reasonable result as a consequence of its inherent simplicity. When we use more complex models, however, we must ensure that we find simpler solutions in preference to more complex ones. Thus this criterion encourages us to pursue objective techniques for regularising classification networks [2, 3]; such techniques are probably long overdue.

Copyright © Controller HMSO London 1992

References

[1] J.S. Bridle (1988). The phantom target cluster network: a peculiar relative of (unsupervised) maximum likelihood stochastic modelling and (supervised) error backpropagation, RSRE Research Note SP4: 66, DRA Malvern UK.

[2] D.J.C. MacKay (1991). Bayesian interpolation, submitted to *Neural computation*.

[3] D.J.C. MacKay (1991). A practical Bayesian framework for backprop networks, submitted to *Neural computation*.

[4] J S Bridle and S J Cox. Recnorm: Simultaneous normalisation and classification applied to speech recognition. In *Advances in Neural Information Processing Systems 3*. Morgan Kaufmann, 1991.

[5] J S Bridle. Training stochastic model recognition algorithms as networks can lead to maximum mutual information estimation of parameters. In *Advances in Neural Information Processing Systems 2*. Morgan Kaufmann, 1990.

A Network of Localized Linear Discriminants

Martin S. Glassman
Siemens Corporate Research
755 College Road East
Princeton, NJ 08540
msg@siemens.siemens.com

Abstract

The localized linear discriminant network (LLDN) has been designed to address classification problems containing relatively closely spaced data from different classes (*encounter zones* [1], the accuracy problem [2]). Locally trained hyperplane segments are an effective way to define the decision boundaries for these regions [3]. The LLD uses a modified perceptron training algorithm for effective discovery of separating hyperplane/sigmoid units within narrow boundaries. The basic unit of the network is the *discriminant receptive field* (DRF) which combines the LLD function with Gaussians representing the dispersion of the local training data with respect to the hyperplane. The DRF implements a local distance measure [4], and obtains the benefits of networks of localized units [5]. A constructive algorithm for the two-class case is described which incorporates DRF's into the hidden layer to solve local discrimination problems. The output unit produces a smoothed, piecewise linear decision boundary. Preliminary results indicate the ability of the LLDN to efficiently achieve separation when boundaries are narrow and complex, in cases where both the "standard" multilayer perceptron (MLP) and k-nearest neighbor (KNN) yield high error rates on training data.

1 The LLD Training Algorithm and DRF Generation

The LLD is defined by the hyperplane normal vector V and its "midpoint" M (a translated origin [1] near the center of gravity of the training data in feature space). Incremental corrections to V and M accrue for each training token feature vector Y_j in the training set, as illustrated in figure 1 (exaggerated magnitudes). The surface of the hyperplane is appropriately moved either towards or away from Y_j by rotating V, and shifting M along the axis defined by V. M is always shifted towards Y_j in the "radial" direction R_j (which is the component of D_j orthogonal to V, where $D_j = Y_j - M$):

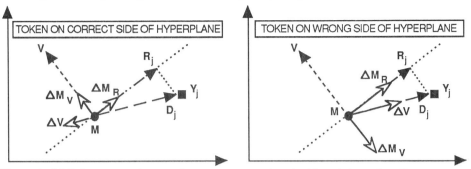

Figure 1: LLD incremental correction vectors associated with training token Y_j are shown above, and the corresponding LLD update rules below:

$$\Delta \vec{V} = \mu(n) \sum_j \Delta \vec{V}_j = \mu(n) \sum_j (\frac{-s_c w_c \varepsilon_j}{\|\vec{D}_j\|}) \vec{D}_j$$

$$\Delta \vec{M}_{\vec{V}} = \gamma(n) \sum_j \Delta \vec{M}_{\vec{V}_j} = \gamma(n) \sum_j (-s_c w_c \varepsilon_j) \vec{V}$$

$$\Delta \vec{M}_{\vec{R}} = \beta(n) \sum_j \Delta \vec{M}_{\vec{R}_j} = \beta(n) \sum_j (w_c \varepsilon_j) \vec{R}_j$$

The batch mode summation is over tokens in the local training set, and n is the iteration index. The polarity of ΔV_j and ΔM_{R_j} is set by s_c (c = the class of Y_j), where $s_c = 1$ if Y_j is classified correctly, and $s_c = -1$ if not. Corrections for each token are scaled by a sigmoidal error term: $\varepsilon_j = 1/(1 + \exp((s_c \eta/\lambda) \mid \vec{V}^T \vec{D}_j \mid))$, a function of the distance of the token to the plane, the sign of s_c, and a data-dependent scaling parameter: $\lambda = \mid \vec{V}^T [\vec{B}_0 - \vec{B}_1] \mid$, where η is a fixed (experimental) scaling parameter. The scaling of the sigmoid is proportional to an estimate of the boundary region width along the axis of V. B_c is a weighted average of the class c token vectors: $\vec{B}_c(n + 1) = (1 - \alpha)\vec{B}_c(n) + \alpha w_c \sum_{j \in c} \epsilon_{j,c}(n)\vec{Y}_j(n)$, where $\epsilon_{j,c}$ is a sigmoid with the same scaling as ε_j, except that it is centered on B_c instead of M, emphasizing tokens of class c nearest the hyperplane surface. For small η's, B_c will settle near the cluster center of gravity, and for large η's, B_c will approach the tokens closest to the hyperplane surface. (The rate of the movement of B_c is limited by the value of α, which is not critical.) The inverse of the number of tokens in class c, w_c, balances the weight of the corrections from each class. If a more Bayesian-like solution is required, the slope of ε can be made class dependent (for example, replacing η with $\eta_c \propto w_c$). Since the slope of the sigmoid error term is limited and distribution dependent, the use of w_c, along with the nonlinear weighting of tokens near the hyperplane surface, is important for the development of separating planes in relatively narrow boundaries (the assumption is that the distributions near these boundaries are non-Gaussian). The setting of η simultaneously (for convenience) controls the focus on the "inner edges" of the class clusters and the slope of the sigmoid relative to the distance between the inner edges, with some resultant control over generalization performance. This local scaling of the error also aids the convergence rate. The range of good values for η has been found to be reasonably wide, and identical values have been used successfully with speech, ecg, and synthetic data; it could also be set/optimized using cross-validation. Separate adaptive learning rates ($\mu(n)$, $\gamma(n)$, and $\beta(n)$) are used in order to take advantage of the distinct nature of the geometric function of each component. Convergence is also improved by maintaining M within the local region; this controls the rate at which the hyperplane can sweep through the boundary region, making the effect of ΔV more predictable. The LLD normal vector update is simply: $\vec{V}(n+1) = (\vec{V}(n) + \Delta\vec{V})/\|\vec{V}(n) + \Delta\vec{V}\|$, so that V is always normalized to unit magnitude. The midpoint is just shifted: $\vec{M}(n+1) = \vec{M}(n) + \Delta\vec{M}_{\vec{R}} + \Delta\vec{M}_{\vec{V}}$.

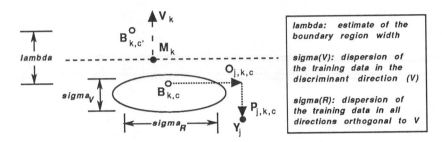

Figure 2: Vectors and parameters associated with the DRF for class c, for LLD k

DRF's are used to localize the response of the LLD to the region of feature space in which it was trained, and are constructed after completion of LLD training. Each DRF represents one class, and the localizing component of the DRF is a Gaussian function based on simple statistics of the training data for that class. Two measures of the dispersion of the data are used: σ_V ("normal" dispersion), obtained using the mean average deviation of the lengths of $P_{j,k,c}$, and σ_R ("radial" dispersion), obtained correspondingly using the $O_{j,k,c}$'s. (As shown, $P_{j,k,c}$ is the normal component, and $O_{j,k,c}$ the radial component of $Y_j - B_{k,c}$.) The output in response to an input vector Y_j from the class c DRF associated with the LLD k is $\phi_{j,k,c}$:

$$\phi_{j,k,c} = \Theta_{k,c}(\varepsilon_{j,k} - 0.5)/\exp(\sqrt{d_{\vec{V}j,k,c}^2 + d_{\vec{R}j,k,c}^2}); \quad \varepsilon_{j,k} = 1/(1 + \exp((\eta/\lambda_k) \mid \vec{V}_k^T [\vec{Y}_j - \vec{M}_k] \mid))$$

Two components of the DRF incorporate the LLD discriminant; one is the sigmoid error function used in training the LLD but shifted down to a value of zero at the hyperplane surface. The other is $\Theta_{k,c}$, which is 1 if Y_j is on the class c side of LLD k, and zero if not. (In retrospect, for generalization performance, it may not be desirable to introduce this discontinuity to the discriminant component.) The contribution of the Gaussian is based on the normal and radial dispersion weighted distances of the input vector to $B_{k,c}$:

$$d_{\vec{V}j,k,c} = \|\vec{P}_{j,k,c}\|/\sigma_{\vec{V},k,c}, \quad and. \quad d_{\vec{R}j,k,c} = \|\vec{O}_{j,k,c}\|/\sigma_{\vec{R},k,c}.$$

2   Network Construction

Segmentation of the boundary between classes is accomplished by "growing" LLD's within the boundary region. An LLD is initialized using a closely spaced pair of tokens from each class. The LLD is grown by adding nearby tokens to the training set, using the k-nearest neighbors to the LLD midpoint at each growth stage as candidates for permanent inclusion. Candidate DRF's are generated after incremental training of the LLD to accommodate each new candidate token. Two error measures are used to assess the effect of each candidate, the peak value of ε_j over the local training set, and ϖ, which is a measure of misclassification error due to the receptive fields of the candidate DRF's extending over the *entire* training set. The candidate token with the lowest average ϖ is permanently added, as long as both its ε_j and ϖ are below fixed thresholds. Growth the the LLD is halted if no candidate has both error measures below threshold. The ε_j and ϖ thresholds directly affect the granularity of the DRF representation of the data; they need to be set to minimize the number of DRF's generated, while allowing sufficient resolution of local discrimination problems. They should perhaps be adaptive so as to encourage coarse grained solutions to develop before fine grain structure.

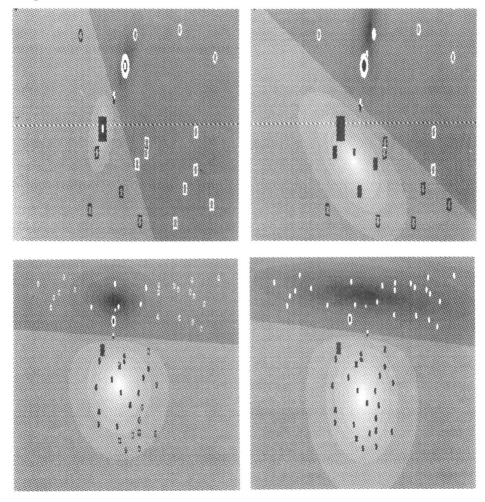

Figure 3: Four "snapshots" in the growth of an LLD/DRF pair. The upper two are "close-ups." The initial LLD/DRF pair is shown in the upper left, along with the seed pair. Filled rectangles and ellipses represent the tokens from each class in the permanent local training set at each stage. The large markers are the B points, and the cross is the LLD midpoint. The amplitude of the DRF outputs are coded in greyscale.

At this point the DRF's are fixed and added to the network; this represents the addition of two new localized features available for use by the network's output layer in solving the global discrimination problem. In this implementation, the output "layer" is a single LLD used to generate a two-class decision. The architecture is shown below:

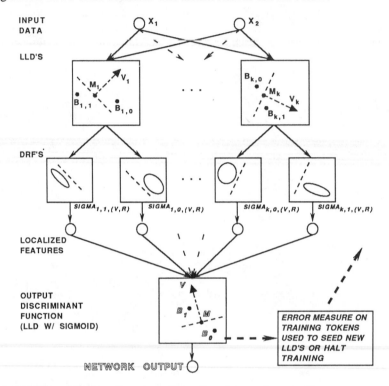

Figure 4: LLDN architecture for a two-dimensional, two-class problem

The ouput unit is completely retrained after addition of a new DRF pair, using the *entire* training set. The output of the network to the input Y_j is: $\varphi_j = 1/(1+\exp((\eta/\lambda_{\mathcal{O}})\vec{\mathcal{V}}^T[\vec{\Phi}_j - \mathcal{M}]))$, where $\lambda_{\mathcal{O}} = |\vec{\mathcal{V}}^T[\vec{\mathcal{B}}_0 - \vec{\mathcal{B}}_1]|$, and $\vec{\Phi}_j = [\phi_{j,1}, \ldots, \phi_{j,p}]$ is the p dimensional vector of DRF outputs presented to the output unit. $\mathcal{V}$ is the output LLD normal vector, $\mathcal{M}$ the midpoint, and $\mathcal{B}_c$'s the cluster edge points in the internal feature space. The output error for each token is then used to select a new seed pair for development of the next LLD/DRF pair. If all tokens are classified with sufficient confidence, of course, construction of the LLDN is complete. There are three possibilities for insufficient confidence: a token is covered by a DRF of the wrong class, it is not yet covered sufficiently by any DRF's, or it is in a region of "conflict" between DRF's of different classes. A heuristic is used to prevent the repeated selection of the same seed pair tokens, since there is no guarantee that a given DRF will significantly reduce the error for the data it covers after output unit retraining. This heuristic alternates between the types of error and the class for selection of the primary seed token. Redundancy in DRF shapes is also minimized by error-weighting the dispersion computations so that the resultant Gaussian focuses more on the higher error regions of the local training data. A simple but reasonably effective pruning algorithm was incorporated to further eliminate unnecessary DRF's.

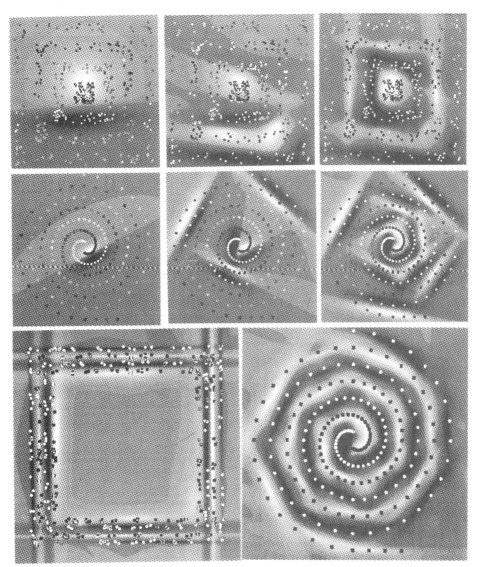

Figure 5: Network response plots illustrating network development. The upper two sequences, beginning with the first LLD/DRF pair, and the bottom two plots show final network responses for these two problems. A solution to a harder version of the nested squares problem is on the lower left.

3   Experimental Results

The first experiment demonstrates comparative convergence properties of the LLD and a single hyperplane trained by the standard generalized delta rule (GDR) method (no hidden units, single output unit "network" is used) on 14 linearly separable, minimal consonant pair data sets. The data is 256 dimensional (time/frequency matrix, described in [6]), with 80 exemplars per consonant. The results compare the best performance obtainable from each technique. The LLD converges roughly 12 times faster in iteration counts. The GDR often fails to .completely separate f/th, f/v, and s/sh; in the results in figure 6 it fails on the f/th data set at a plateau of 25% error. In both experiments described in this paper, networks were run for relatively long times to insure confidence in declaring failure to

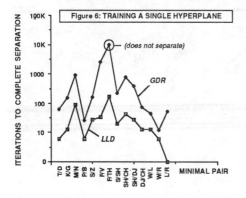

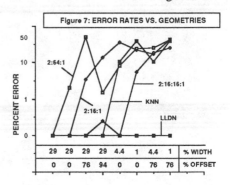

solve the problem. The second experiment involves complete networks on synthetic two-dimensional problems. Two examples of the nested squares problem (random distributions of tokens near the surface of squares of alternating class, 400 tokens total) are shown in figure 5. Two parameters controlling data set generation are explored: the relative boundary region width, and the relative offset from the origin of the data set center of gravity (while keeping the upper right corner of the outside square near the (1,1) coordinate); all data is kept within the unit square (except for geometry number 2). Relative boundary widths of 29%, 4.4%, and 1% are used with offsets of 0%, 76%, and 94%. The best results over parameter settings are reported for each network for each geometry. Four MLP architectures were used: 2:16:1, 2:32:1, 2:64:1, and 2:16:16:1; all of these converge to a solution for the easiest problem (wide boundaries, no offset), but all eventually fail as the boundaries narrow and/or the offset increases. The worst performing net (2:64:1) fails for 7/8 problems (maximum error rate of 49%); the best net (2:16:16:1) fails in 3/8 (maximum of 24% error). The LLDN is 1 to 3 orders of magnitude faster in cpu time when the MLP does converge, even though it does not use adaptive learning rates in this experiment. (The average running time for the LLDN was 34 minutes; for the MLP's it was 3481 minutes [Stardent 3040, single cpu], but which includes non-converging runs. The 2:16:16:1 net did, however, take 4740 minutes to solve problem 6, which was solved in 7 minutes by the LLDN.) The best LLDN's converge to zero errors over the problem set (fig. 6), and are not too sensitive to parameter variation, which primarily affect convergence time and number of DRF's generated. In contrast, finding good values for learning rate and momentum for the MLP's for each problem was a time-consuming process. The effect of random weight initialization in the MLP is not known because of the long running times required. The KNN error rate was estimated using the leave-one-out method, and yields error rates of 0%, 10.5%, and 38.75% (for the best k's) respectively for the three values of boundary width. The LLDN is insensitive to offset and scale (like the KNN) because of the use of the local origin (M) and error scaling (λ). While global offset and scaling problems for the MLP can be ameliorated through normalization and origin translation, this method cannot guarantee elimination of local offset and scaling problems. The LLDN's utilization of DRF's was reasonably efficient, with the smallest networks (after pruning) using 20, 32, and 54 DRF's for the three boundary widths. A simple pruning algorithm, which starts up after convergence, iteratively removes the DRF's with the lowest connection weights to the output unit (which is retrained after each link is removed). A range of roughly 20% to 40% of the DRF's were removed before developing misclassification errors on the training sets. The LLDN was also tested on the "two-spirals" problem, which is know to be difficult for the standard MLP methods. Because of the boundary segmentation process, solution of the two-spirals problem was straightforward for the LLDN, and could be tuned to converge in as fast as 2.5 minutes on an Apollo DN10000. The solution shown in fig. 5 uses 50 DRF's (not pruned). The generalization pattern is relatively "nice" (for training on the sparse version of the data set), and perhaps demonstrates the practical nature of the smoothed piecewise linear boundary for nonlinear problems.

4   Discussion

The effect of LLDN parameters on generalization performance needs to be studied. In the nested squares problem it is clear that the MLP's will have better generalization *when they converge*; this illustrates the potential utility of a multi-scale approach to developing localized discriminants. A number of extensions are possible: Localized feature selection can be implemented by simply zeroing components of V. The DRF Gaussians could model the radial dispersion of the data more effectively (in greater than two dimensions) by generating principal component axes which are orthogonal to V. Extension to the multiclass case can be based on DRF sets developed for discrimination between each class and all other classes, using the DRF's as features for a multi-output classifier. The use of multiple hidden layers offers the prospect of more complex localized receptive fields. Improvement in generalization might be gained by including a procedure for merging neighboring DRF's. While it is felt that the LLD parameters should remain fixed, it may be advantageous to allow adjustment of the DRF Gaussian dispersions as part of the output layer training. A stopping rule for LLD training needs to be developed so that adaptive learning rates can be utilized effectively. This rule may also be useful in identifying poor token candidates early in the incremental LLD training.

References

[1] J. Sklansky and G.N. Wassel. *Pattern Classifiers and Trainable Machines.* Springer Verlag, New York, 1981

[2] S. Makram-Ebeid, J.A. Sirat, and J.R. Viala. A rationalized error backpropagation learning algorithm. *Proc. IJCNN*, 373-380, 1988

[3] J. Sklansky, and Y. Park. Automated design of multiple-class piecewise linear classifiers. *Journal of Classification*, 6:195-222, 1989

[4] R.D. Short, and K. Fukanaga. A new nearest neighbor distance measure. *Proc. Fifth Intl. Conf. on Pattern Rec.*, 81-88

[5] R. Lippmann. A critical overview of neural network pattern classifiers. *Neural Networks for Signal Processing (IEEE)*, 267-275, 1991

[6] M.S. Glassman and M.B. Starkey. Minimal consonant pair discrimination for speech therapy. *Proc. European Conf. on Speech Comm. and Tech.*, 273-276, 1989

A Weighted Probabilistic Neural Network

David Montana
Bolt Beranek and Newman Inc.
10 Moulton Street
Cambridge, MA 02138

Abstract

The Probabilistic Neural Network (PNN) algorithm represents the likelihood function of a given class as the sum of identical, isotropic Gaussians. In practice, PNN is often an excellent pattern classifier, outperforming other classifiers including backpropagation. However, it is not robust with respect to affine transformations of feature space, and this can lead to poor performance on certain data. We have derived an extension of PNN called Weighted PNN (WPNN) which compensates for this flaw by allowing anisotropic Gaussians, i.e. Gaussians whose covariance is not a multiple of the identity matrix. The covariance is optimized using a genetic algorithm, some interesting features of which are its redundant, logarithmic encoding and large population size. Experimental results validate our claims.

1 INTRODUCTION

1.1 PROBABILISTIC NEURAL NETWORKS (PNN)

PNN (Specht 1990) is a pattern classification algorithm which falls into the broad class of "nearest-neighbor-like" algorithms. It is called a "neural network" because of its natural mapping onto a two-layer feedforward network. It works as follows. Let the exemplars from class i be the k-vectors $\vec{x}_j^i$ for $j = 1, ..., N_i$. Then, the likelihood function for class i is

$$L_i(\vec{x}) = \frac{1}{N_i(2\pi\sigma)^{k/2}} \sum_{j=1}^{N_i} e^{-(\vec{x}-\vec{x}_j^i)^2/\sigma} \tag{1}$$

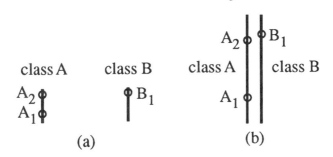

Figure 1: PNN is not robust with respect to affine transformations of feature space. Originally (a), A_2 is closer to its classmate A_1 than to B_1; however, after a simple affine transformation (b), A_2 is closer to B_1.

and the conditional probability for class i is

$$P_i(\vec{x}) = L_i(\vec{x}) / \sum_{j=1}^{M} L_j(\vec{x}) \tag{2}$$

Note that the class likelihood functions are sums of identical isotropic Gaussians centered at the exemplars.

The single free parameter of this algorithm is σ, the variance of the Gaussians (the rest of the terms in the likelihood functions are determined directly from the training data). Hence, training a PNN consists of optimizing σ relative to some evaluation criterion, typically the number of classification errors during cross-validation (see Sections 2.1 and 3). Since the search space is one-dimensional, the search procedure is trivial and is often performed by hand.

1.2   THE PROBLEM WITH PNN

The main drawback of PNN and other "nearest-neighbor-like" algorithms is that they are not robust with respect to affine transformations (i.e., transformations of the form $\vec{x} \mapsto A\vec{x} + \vec{b}$) of feature space. (Note that in theory affine transformations should not affect the performance of backpropagation, but the results of Section 3 show that this is not true in practice.) Figures 1 and 2 depict examples of how affine transformations of feature space affect classification performance. In Figures 1a and 2a, the point A_2 is closer (using Euclidean distance) to point A_1, which is also from class A, than to point B_1, which is from class B. Hence, with a training set consisting of the exemplars A_1 and B_1, PNN would classify A_2 correctly. Figures 1b and 2b depict the feature space after affine transformations. In both cases, A_2 is closer to B_1 than to A_1 and would hence be classified incorrectly. For the example of Figure 2, the transformation matrix A is not diagonal (i.e., the principle axes of the transformation are not the coordinate axes), and the adverse effects of this transformation cannot be undone by any affine transformation with diagonal A.

This problem has motivated us to generalize the PNN algorithm in such a way that it is robust with respect to affine transformations of the feature space.

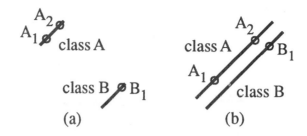

Figure 2: The principle axes of the affine transformation do not necessarily correspond with the coordinate axes.

1.3   A SOLUTION: WEIGHTED PNN (WPNN)

This flaw of nearest-neighbor-like algorithms has been recognized before, and there have been a few proposed solutions. They all use what Dasarathy (1991) calls "modified metrics", which are non-Euclidean distance measures in feature space. All the approaches to modified metrics define criteria which the chosen metric should optimize. Some criteria allow explicit derivation of the new metrics (Short and Fukunuga 1981; Fukunuga and Flick 1984). However, the validity of these derivations relies on there being a very large number of exemplars in the training set. A more recent set of approaches (Atkeson 1991; Kelly and Davis 1991) (i) use criteria which measure the performance on the training set using leaving-one-out cross-validation (see (Stone 1974) and Section 2.1), (ii) restrict the number of parameters of the metric to increase statistical significance, and (iii) optimize the parameters of the metric using non-linear search techniques. For his technique of "locally weighted regression", Atkeson (1991) uses an evaluation criterion which is the sum of the squares of the error using leaving-one-out. His metric has the form $d^2 = w_1(x_1 - y_1)^2 + ... + w_k(x_k - y_k)^2$, and hence has k free parameters $w_1, ..., w_k$. He uses Levenberg-Marquardt to optimize these parameters with respect to the evaluation criterion. For their Weighted K-Nearest Neighbors (WKNN) algorithm, Kelly and Davis (1991) use an evaluation criterion which is the total number of incorrect classifications under leaving-one-out. Their metric is the same as Atkeson's, and their optmization is done with a genetic algorithm.

We use an approach similar to that of Atkeson (1991) and Kelly and Davis (1991) to make PNN more robust with respect to affine transformations. Our approach, called Weighted PNN (WPNN), works by using anisotropic Gaussians rather than the isotropic Gaussians used by PNN. An anisotropic Gaussian has the form $\frac{1}{(2\pi)^{k/2}(\det \Sigma)^{1/2}} e^{-(\vec{x} - \vec{x}_0)^T \Sigma^{-1}(\vec{x} - \vec{x}_0)}$. The covariance Σ is a nonnegative-definite kxk symmetric matrix. Note that Σ enters into the exponent of the Gaussian so as to define a new distance metric, and hence the use of anisotropic Gaussians to extend PNN is analogous to the use of modified metrics to extend other nearest-neighbor-like algorithms.

The likelihood function for class i is

$$L_i(\vec{x}) = \frac{1}{N_i(2\pi)^{k/2}(\det \Sigma)^{1/2}} \sum_{j=1}^{N_i} e^{-(\vec{x} - \vec{x}_j^i)^T \Sigma^{-1}(\vec{x} - \vec{x}_j^i)} \qquad (3)$$

and the conditional probability is still as given in Equation 2. Note that when Σ is a multiple of the identity, i.e. $\Sigma = \sigma I$, Equation 3 reduces to Equation 1. Section 2 describes how we select the value of Σ.

To ensure good generalization, we have so far restricted ourselves to diagonal co-variances (and thus metrics of the form used by Atkeson (1991) and Kelly and Davis (1991). This reduces the number of degrees of freedom of the covariance from $k(k+1)/2$ to k. However, this restricted set of covariances is not sufficiently general to solve all the problems of PNN (as demonstrated in Section 3), and we therefore in Section 2 hint at some modifications which would allow us to use arbitrary co-variances.

2   OPTIMIZING THE COVARIANCE

We have used a genetic algorithm (Goldberg 1988) to optimize the covariance of the Gaussians. The code we used was a non-object-oriented C translation of the OOGA (Object-Oriented Genetic Algorithm) code (Davis 1991). This code preserves the features of OOGA including arbitrary encodings, exponential fitness, steady-state replacement, and adaptive operator probabilities. We now describe the distinguishing features of our genetic algorithm: (1) the evaluation function (Section 2.1), (2) the genetic encoding (Section 2.2), and (3) the population size (Section 2.3).

2.1   THE EVALUATION FUNCTION

To evaluate the performance of a particular covariance matrix on the training set, we use a technique called "leaving-one-out", which is a special form of cross-validation (Stone 1974). One exemplar at a time is withheld from the training set, and we then determine how well WPNN with that covariance matrix classifies the with-held exemplar. The full evaluation is the sum of the evaluations on the individual exemplars.

For the exemplar $\vec{x}_j^i$, let $\tilde{L}_q(\vec{x}_j^i)$ for $q = 1, ..., M$ denote the class likelihoods obtained upon withholding this exemplar and applying Equation 3, and let $\tilde{P}_q(\vec{x}_j^i)$ be the probabilities obtained from these likelihoods via Equation 2. Then, we define the performance as

$$E = \sum_{i=1}^{M} \sum_{j=1}^{N_i} ((1 - \tilde{P}_i(\vec{x}_j^i))^2 + \sum_{q \neq i} (\tilde{P}_q(\vec{x}_j^i))^2) \tag{4}$$

We have incorporated two heuristics to quickly identify covariances which are clearly bad and give them a value of ∞, the worst possible score. This greatly speeds up the optimization process because many of the generated covariances can be eliminated this way (see Section 2.3). The first heuristic identifies covariances which are too "small" based on the condition that, for some exemplar $\vec{x}_j^i$ and all $q = 1, ...M$, $\tilde{L}_q(\vec{x}_j^i) = 0$ to within the precision of IEEE double-precision floating-point format. In this case, the probabilities $\tilde{P}_q(\vec{x}_j^i)$ are not well-defined. (When Σ is this "small", WPNN is approximately equivalent to WKNN with $k = 1$, and if such a small Σ is indeed required, then the WKNN algorithm should be used instead.)

The second heuristic identifies covariances which are too "big" in the sense that too many exemplars contribute significantly to the likelihood functions. Empirical observations and theoretical arguments show that PNN (and WPNN) work best when only a small fraction of the exemplars contribute significantly. Hence, we reject a particular Σ if, for any exemplar $\vec{x}_j^i$,

$$\sum_{\vec{x} \neq \vec{x}_j^i} e^{-(\vec{x}-\vec{x}_j^i)^T \Sigma^{-1}(\vec{x}-\vec{x}_j^i)} > (\sum_{i=1}^M N_i)/P \tag{5}$$

Here, P is a parameter which we chose for our experiments to equal four.

Note: If we wish to improve the generalization by discarding some of the degrees of freedom of the covariance (which we will need to do when we allow non-diagonal covariances), we should modify the evaluation function by subtracting off a term which is montonically increasing with the number of degrees of freedom discarded.

2.2   THE GENETIC ENCODING

Recall from Section 1.3 that we have presently restricted the covariance to be diagonal. Hence, the set of all possible covariances is k-dimensional, where k is the dimension of the feature space. We encode the covariances as $k+1$ integers $(a_0, ..., a_k)$, where the a_i's are in the ranges $(a_0)_{min} \leq a_0 \leq (a_0)_{max}$ and $0 \leq a_i \leq a_{max}$ for $i = 1, ..., k$. The decoding map is

$$(a_0, ..., a_k) \mapsto \Sigma = \text{diag}(2^{-(C_1 a_0 + C_2 a_1)}, ..., 2^{-(C_1 a_0 + C_2 a_k)}) \tag{6}$$

We observe the following about this encoding. First, it is a "logarithmic encoding", i.e. the encoded parameters are related logarithmically to the original parameters. This provides a large dynamic range without the sacrifice of sufficient resolution at any scale and without making the search space unmanageably large. The constants C_1 and C_2 determine the resolution, while the constants $(a_0)_{min}$, $(a_0)_{max}$, and a_{max} determine the range. Second, it is possibly a "redundant" encoding, i.e. there may be multiple encodings of a single covariance. We use this redundant encoding, despite the seeming paradox, to reduce the size of the search space. The a_0 term encodes the size of the Gaussian, roughly equivalent to σ in PNN. The other a_i's encode the relative weighting of the various dimensions. If we dropped the a_0 term, the other a_i terms would have to have larger ranges to compensate, thus making the search space larger.

Note: If we wish to improve the generalization by discarding some of the degrees of freedom of the covariance, we need to allow all the entries besides a_0 to take on the value of ∞ in addition to the range of values defined above. When $a_i = \infty$, its corresponding entry in the covariance matrix is zero and is hence discarded.

2.3   POPULATION SIZE

For their success, genetic algorithms rely on having multiple individuals with partial information in the population. The problem we have encountered is that the ratio of the the area of the search space with partial information to the entire search space is small. In fact, with our very loose heuristics, on Dataset 1 (see Section 3) about

90% of the randomly generated individuals of the initial population evaluated to ∞. In fact, we estimate very roughly that only 1 in 50 or 1 in 100 randomly generated individuals contain partial information. To ensure that the initial population has multiple individuals with partial information requires a population size of many hundreds, and we conservatively used a population size of 1600. Note that with such a large population it is essential to use a steady-state genetic algorithm (Davis 1991) rather than generational replacement.

3   EXPERIMENTAL RESULTS

We have performed a series of experiments to verify our claims about WPNN. To do so, we have constructed a sequence of four datasets designed to illustrate the shortcomings of PNN and how WPNN in its present form can fix some of these shortcomings but not others. Dataset 1 is a training set we generated during an effort to classify simulated sonar signals. It has ten features, five classes, and 516 total exemplars. Dataset 2 is the same as Dataset 1 except that we supplemented the ten features of Dataset 1 with five additional features, which were random numbers uniformly distributed between zero and one (and hence contained no information relevant to classification), thus giving a total of 15 features. Dataset 3 is the same as Dataset 2 except with ten (rather than five) irrelevant features added and hence a total of 20 features. Like Dataset 3, Dataset 4 has 20 features. It is obtained from Dataset 3 as follows. Pair each of the true features with one of the irrelevant features. Call the feature values of the ith pair f_i and g_i. Then, replace these feature values with the values $0.5(f_i + g_i)$ and $0.5(f_i - g_i + 1)$, thus mixing up the relevant features with the irrelevant features via linear combinations.

To evaluate the performance of different pattern classification algorithms on these four datasets, we have used 10-fold cross-validation (Stone 1974). This involves splitting each dataset into ten disjoint subsets of similar size and similar distribution of exemplars by class. To evaluate a particular algorithm on a dataset requires ten training and test runs, where each subset is used as the test set for the algorithm trained on a training set consisting of the other nine subsets.

The pattern classification algorithms we have evaluated are backpropagation (with four hidden nodes), PNN (with $\sigma = 0.05$), WPNN and CART. The results of the experiments are shown in Figure 3. Note that the parenthesized quantities denote errors on the training data and are not compensated for the fact that each exemplar of the original dataset is in nine of the ten training sets used for cross-validation.

We can draw a number of conclusions from these results. First, the performance of PNN on Datasets 2-4 clearly demonstrates the problems which arise from its lack of robustness with respect to affine transformations of feature space. In each case, there exists an affine transformation which makes the problem essentially equivalent to Dataset 1 from the viewpoint of Euclidean distance, but the performance is clearly very different. Second, WPNN clearly eliminates this problem with PNN for Datasets 2 and 3 but not for Dataset 4. This points out both the progress we have made so far in using WPNN to make PNN more robust and the importance of extending the WPNN algorithm to allow non-diagonal covariances. Third, although backpropagation is in theory transparent to affine transformations of feature space (because the first layer of weights and biases implements an arbitrary affine

Dataset / Algorithm	1	2	3	4
Backprop	11 (69)	16 (51)	20 (27)	13 (64)
PNN	9	94	109	29
WPNN	10	11	11	25
CART	14	17	18	53

Figure 3: Performance on the four datasets of backprop, CART, PNN and WPNN (parenthesized quantities are training set errors).

transformation), in practice affine transformations effect its performance. Indeed, Dataset 4 is obtained from Dataset 3 by an affine transformation, yet backprop-agation performs very differently on them. Backpropagation does better on the training sets for Dataset 3 than on the training sets for Dataset 4 but does better on the test sets of Dataset 4 than the test sets of Dataset 3. This implies that for Dataset 4 during the training procedure backpropagation is not finding the globally optimum set of weights and biases but is missing in such a way that improves its generalization.

4   CONCLUSIONS AND FUTURE WORK

We have demonstrated through both theoretical arguments and experiments an inherent flaw of PNN, its lack or robustness with respect to affine transformations of feature space. To correct this flaw, we have proposed an extension of PNN, called WPNN, which uses anisotropic Gaussians rather than the isotropic Gaussians used by PNN. Under the assumption that the covariance of the Gaussians is diagonal, we have described how to use a genetic algorithm to optimize the covariance for optimal performance on the training set. Experiments have shown that WPNN can partially remedy the flaw with PNN.

What remains to be done is to modify the optimization procedure to allow arbitrary (i.e., non-diagonal) covariances. The main difficulty here is that the covariance matrix has a large number of degrees of freedom ($k(k+1)/2$, where k is the dimension of feature space), and we therefore need to ensure that the choice of covariance is not overfit to the data. We have presented some general ideas on how to approach this problem, but a true solution still needs to be developed.

Acknowledgements

This work was partially supported by DARPA via ONR under Contract N00014-89-C-0264 as part of the Artifical Neural Networks Initiative.

Thanks to Ken Theriault for his useful comments.

References

C.G. Atkeson. (1991) Using locally weighted regression for robot learning. *Proceedings of the 1991 IEEE Conference on Robotics and Automation*, pp. 958–963. Los Alamitos, CA: IEEE Computer Society Press.

B.V. Dasarathy. (1991) *Nearest Neighbor (NN) Norms: NN Pattern Classification Techniques*. Los Alamitos, CA: IEEE Computer Society Press.

L. Davis. (1991) *Handbook of Genetic Algorithms*. New York: Van Nostrand Reinhold.

K. Fukunaga and T.T. Flick. (1984) An optimal global nearest neighbor metric. *IEEE Transactions on Pattern Analysis and Machine Intelligence*, Vol. PAMI-6, No. 3, pp. 314–318.

D. Goldberg. (1988) *Genetic Algorithms in Machine Learning, Optimization and Search*. Redwood City, CA: Addison-Wesley.

J.D. Kelly, Jr. and L. Davis. (1991) Hybridizing the genetic algorithm and the k nearest neighbors classification algorithm. *Proceedings of the Fourth Internation Conference on Genetic Algorithms*, pp. 377–383. San Mateo, CA: Morgan Kaufmann.

R.D. Short and K. Fukunaga. (1981) The optimal distance measure for nearest neighbor classification. *IEEE Transactions on Information Theory*, Vol. IT-27, No. 5, pp. 622–627.

D.F. Specht. (1990) Probabilistic neural networks. *Neural Networks*, vol. 3, no. 1, pp. 109–118.

M. Stone. (1974) Cross-validatory choice and assessment of statistical predictions. *Journal of the Royal Statistical Society*, vol. 36, pp. 111–147.

Network generalization for production:
Learning and producing styled letterforms

Igor Grebert
541 Cutwater Ln.
Foster City, CA
94404

David G. Stork
Ricoh Calif. Research Cen.
2882 Sand Hill Rd.# 115
Menlo Park, CA 94025

Ron Keesing
Dept. Physiology
U. C. S. F.
San Francisco, CA
94143

Steve Mims
Electrical Engin.
Stanford U.
Stanford, CA
94305

Abstract

We designed and trained a connectionist network to generate
letterforms in a new font given just a *few* exemplars from
that font. During learning, our network constructed a
distributed internal representation of fonts as well as letters,
despite the fact that each training instance exemplified *both* a
font and a letter. It was necessary to have separate but
interconnected hidden units for "letter" and "font"
representations — several alternative architectures were not
successful.

1. INTRODUCTION

Generalization from examples is central to the notion of cognition and
intelligent behavior (Margolis, 1987). Much research centers on
generalization in *recognition*, as in optical character recognition, speech
recognition, and so forth. In all such cases, during the recognition event the
information content of the representation is reduced; sometimes
categorization is binary, representing just one bit of information. Thus the
information reduction in answering "Is this symphony by Mozart?" is very
large.

A different class of problems requires generalization for *production*, e.g.,
paint a portrait of Madonna in the style of Matisse. Here during the
production event a very low informational input ("Madonna," and
"Matisse") is used to create a very *high* informational output, including
color, form, etc. on the canvas. Such problems are a type of analogy, and
typically require the generalization system to abstract out invariants in both
the instance being presented (e.g., Madonna) *and* the style (e.g., Matisse),
and to integrate these representations in a meaningful way. This must be

done despite the fact that the system is never taught explicitly the features that correspond to Matisse's style alone, nor to Madonna's face alone, and is never presented an example of both simultaneously.

To explore this class of analogy and production issues, we addressed the following problem, derived from Hofstadter (1985):

Given just a few letters in a new font, draw the remaining letters.

Connectionist networks have recently been applied to production problems such as music composition (Todd, 1989), but our task is somewhat different. Whereas in music composition, memory and context (in the form of recurrent connections in a network) are used for pattern generation (melody or harmony), we have no such temporal or other explicit context information during the production of letterforms.

2. DATA, NETWORK AND TRAINING

Figure 1 illustrates schematically our class of problems, and shows a subset of the data used to train our network. The general problem is to draw all the remaining letterforms in a given font, such that those forms are recognizable as letters in the style of that font.

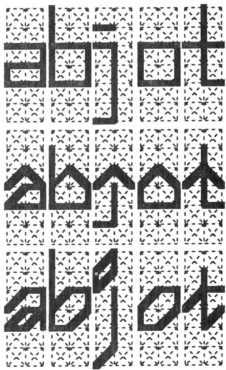

Figure 1: Several letters from three fonts (**Standard, House** and **Benzene right**) in Hofstadter's GridFont system. There are 56 fundamental horizontal, vertical and diagonal strokes, or "pixels," in the grid.

Each letterform in Figure 1 has a recognizable letter identity and "style" (or font). Each letter (columns) shares some invariant features as does each font (rows), though it would be quite difficult to describe what is the "same" in each of the **a**'s for instance, or for all letters in **Benzene right** font.

We trained our network with 26 letters in each of five fonts (**Standard, House, Slant, Benzene right** and **Benzene left**), and just 14 letters in the "test" font (**Hunt four** font). The task of the network was to reconstruct the missing 12 letters in **Hunt four** font. We used a structured three-level network (Figure 2) in which letter identity was represented in a 1-of-26 code (e.g., 010000... → b), and the font identity was represented in a similar 1-of-6 code. The letterforms were represented as 56-element binary vectors, with **1**'s for each stroke comprising the character, and were provided to the output units by a teacher. (Note that this network is "upside-down" from the typical use of connectionist networks for *categorization*.) The two sections of the input layer were each fully connected to the hidden layer, but the hidden layer-to-output layer connections were restricted (Figures 3 and 4). Such restricted hidden-to-output projections helped to prevent the learning of spurious and meaningless correlations between strokes in widely separate grid regions. There are unidirectional one-to-many intra-hidden layer connections from the letter section to the font section within the hidden layer (Figure 3).

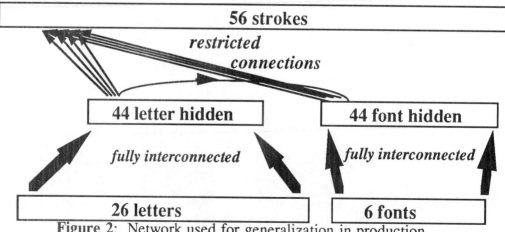

Figure 2: Network used for generalization in production. Note that the high-dimensional representation of strokes is at the *output* of the network, while the low-dimensional representation (a one-of-26 coding for letters and a one-of-six for fonts) is the *input*. The net has one-to-many connections from letter hidden units to font hidden units (cf. Figure 3)

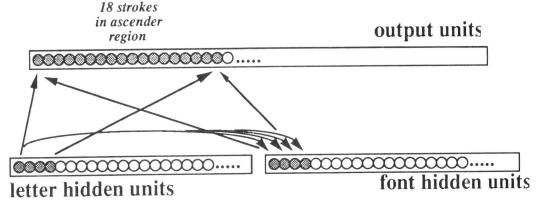

Figure 3: Expanded view of the hidden and output layers of the network of Figure 2. Four letter hidden units and four font hidden units (dark) project fully to the eighteen stroke (output) units representing the ascender region of the GridFont grid; these hidden units project to no other output units. Each of the four letter hidden units also projects to all four of the corresponding font hidden units. This basic structure is repeated across the network (see text).

All connection weights, including intra-hidden layer weights, were adjusted using backpropagation (Rumelhart, Hinton and Williams, 1986), with a learning rate of $\eta = 0.005$ and momentum $\alpha = 0.9$. The training error stopped decreasing after roughly 10,000 training epochs, where each epoch consisted of one presentation of each of the 144 patterns (26 letters x 5 fonts + 14 letters) in random order.

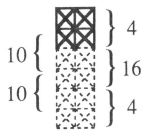

Figure 4: The number of hidden units projecting to each region of the output. Four font hidden units and four letter hidden units project to the 18 top strokes (ascender region) of the output layer, as indicated. Ten font hidden units and ten letter hidden units project to the next lower square region (20 strokes), etc. This restriction prevents the learning of meaningless correlations between particular strokes in the ascender and descender regions (for instance). Such spurious correlations disrupt learning and generalization only with a small training set such as ours.

3. RESULTS AND CONCLUSIONS

In order to produce any letterform, we presented as input to the trained network a (very sparse) 1-of-26 and 1-of-6 signal representing the target letter and font; the letterforms emerged at the output layer. Our network reproduced nearly perfectly all the patterns in the training set.

Figure 5 shows *untrained* letterforms generated by the network. Note that despite irregularities, all the letters except **z** can be easily recognized by humans. Moreover, the letterforms typically share the common style of **Hunt four** font — **b, c, g,** and **p** have the diamond-shaped "loop" of **o, q,** and other letters in the font; the **g** and **y** generated have the same right descender, similar to that in several letters of the original font, and so on; the **l** exactly matches the form designed by Hofstadter. Incidentally, we found that some of the letterforms produced by the network could be considered superior to those designed by Hofstadter. For instance, the generated **w** had the characteristic **Hunt four** diamond shape while the **w** designed by Hostadter did not. We must stress, though, that there is no "right" answer here; the letterforms provided by Hofstadter are merely one possible solution. Just as there is no single "correct" portrait of Madonna in the style of Matisse, so our system must be judged successful if the letterforms produced are both legible and have the style implied by the other letterforms in the test font.

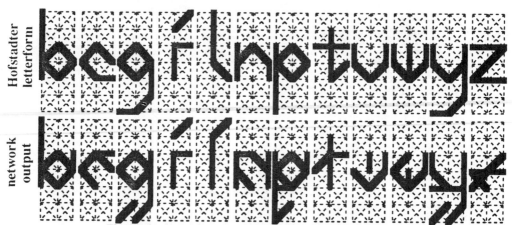

Figure 5: Hofstadter's letterforms from **Hunt four** font (above), and the output of our network (below) for the twelve letterforms that had never been presented during training. Hofstadter's letterforms serve merely as a guide; it is not necessary that the network reproduce these exactly to be judged successful.

Analysis of learned connection strengths (Grebert et al., 1992) reveals that different internal representations were formed for letter and for font characteristics, and that these are appropriate to the task at hand. The particular letter hidden unit shown in Figure 6 effectively "shuts down" any activity in the ascender region. Such a hidden unit would be useful when generating **a**, **c**, **e**, etc. Indeed this hidden unit receives strong input from all letters that have no ascenders. The particular font hidden unit shown in Figure 6 leads to excitation of the "loop" in **Slant** font, and is used in the generation of **o**, **b**, **d**, **g**, etc. in that font. We note further that our network integrated style information (e.g., the diamond shape of the "loop" for the **b**, **g**, the "dot" for the **l**, etc.) with the form information appropriate to the particular letter being generated.

exc   inh   exc   inh

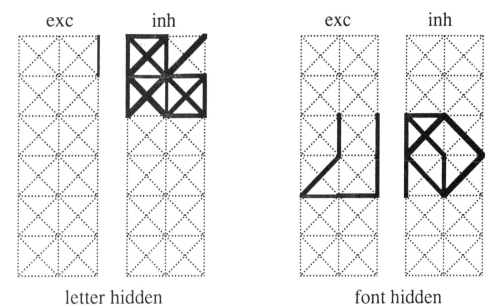

letter hidden   font hidden

Figure 6: Hidden unit representation for a single letter hidden unit (left) and font hidden unit (right).

In general, the network does quite well. The only letterform quite poorly represented is **z**. Evidently, the **z** letterform cannot be inferred from other information, presumably because **z** does not consist of any of the simplest fundamental features that make up a wide variety of other letters (left or right ascenders, loops, crosses for **t** and **f**, dots, right or left descenders).

The average adult has seen perhaps as many as 10^6 distinct examples of each letter in perhaps 10^{10} presentations; in contrast, our network experienced just five or six distinct examples of each letter in 10^4 presentations. Out of this tremendous number of letterforms, the human virtually never experiences a **g** that has a disconnected descender (to take one example), and would not have made the errors our network does. We suspect that the errors our network makes are similar to those a typical westerner would exhibit in generating novel characters in a completely foreign alphabet, such as Thai. Although our network similarly has experienced only **g**'s with connected descenders, it has a very small database over which to generalize; it is to be expected, then, that the network has not yet "deduced" the connectivity constraint for **g**. Indeed, it is somewhat surprising that our network performs as well as it does, and this gives us confidence that the architecture of Figure 2 is appropriate for the production task.

This conclusion is supported by the fact that alternative architectures gave very poor results. For instance a standard three-level backpropagation network produced illegible letterforms. Likewise, if the direct connections between letter hidden units and the output units in Figure 2 were removed, generalization performance was severely compromised.

Our network parameters could have been "fine tuned" for improved performance but such fine tuning would be appropriate for our problem alone, and not the *general* class of production problems. Even without such fine tuning, though, it is clear that the architecture of Figure 2 can successfully learn invariant features of both letter and font information, and integrate them for meaningful production of unseen letterforms. We believe this architecture can be applied to related problems, such as speech production, graphic image generation, etc.

ACKNOWLEDGEMENTS

Thanks to David Rumelhart and Douglas Hofstadter for useful discussions. Reprint requests should be addressed to Dr. Stork at the above address, or stork@crc.ricoh.com.

REFERENCES

Grebert, Igor, David G. Stork, Ron Keesing and Steve Mims, "Connectionist generalization for production: An example from GridFont," *Neural Networks* (1992, in press).

Hofstadter, Douglas, "Analogies and Roles in Human and Machine Thinking," Chapter 24, 547-603 in *Metamagical Themas: Questing for the Essence of Mind and Pattern* Basic Books (1985).

Margolis, Howard, *Patterns, Thinking, and Cognition: A Theory of Judgment* U. Chicago Press (1987).

Rumelhart, David E., Geoffrey E. Hinton and Ron J. Williams, "Learning Internal Representations by Error Propagation," Chapter 8, pp. 318-362 in *Parallel Distributed Processing: Explorations in the Microstructure of Cognition. Vol 1: Foundations* D. E. Rumelhart, and J. L. McClelland (eds.) MIT Press (1986).

Todd, Peter M., "A Connectionist approach to algorithmic composition," *Computer Music Journal*, **13**(4), 27-43, Winter 1989.

Shooting Craps in Search of an Optimal Strategy for Training Connectionist Pattern Classifiers

J. B. Hampshire II   and   **B. V. K. Vijaya Kumar**
Department of Electrical & Computer Engineering
Carnegie Mellon University
Pittsburgh, PA 15213-3890
hamps@speech1.cs.cmu.edu   and   kumar@gauss.ece.cmu.edu

Abstract

We compare two strategies for training connectionist (as well as non-connectionist) models for statistical pattern recognition. The *probabilistic strategy* is based on the notion that Bayesian discrimination (i.e., optimal classification) is achieved when the classifier learns the *a posteriori* class distributions of the random feature vector. The *differential strategy* is based on the notion that the identity of the largest class *a posteriori* probability of the feature vector is all that is needed to achieve Bayesian discrimination. Each strategy is directly linked to a family of objective functions that can be used in the supervised training procedure. We prove that the probabilistic strategy — linked with error measure objective functions such as mean-squared-error and cross-entropy — typically used to train classifiers necessarily requires larger training sets and more complex classifier architectures than those needed to approximate the Bayesian discriminant function. In contrast, we prove that the differential strategy — linked with *classification figure-of-merit* objective functions (CFM_{mono}) [3] — requires the minimum classifier functional complexity and the fewest training examples necessary to approximate the Bayesian discriminant function with specified precision (measured in probability of error). We present our proofs in the context of a game of chance in which an unfair C-sided die is tossed repeatedly. We show that this rigged game of dice is a paradigm at the root of all statistical pattern recognition tasks, and demonstrate how a simple extension of the concept leads us to a general information-theoretic model of sample complexity for statistical pattern recognition.

1 Introduction

Creating a connectionist pattern classifier that generalizes well to novel test data has recently focussed on the process of finding the network architecture with the minimum functional complexity necessary to model the training data accurately (see, for example, the works of Baum, Cover, Haussler, and Vapnik). Meanwhile, relatively little attention has been paid to the effect on generalization of the objective function used to train the classifier. In fact, the choice of objective function used to train the classifier is tantamount to a choice of training strategy, as described in the abstract [2, 3].

We formulate the proofs outlined in the abstract in the context of a rigged game of dice in which an unfair C-sided die is tossed repeatedly. Each face of the die has some probability of turning up. We assume that one face is always more likely than all the others. As a result, all the probabilities may be different, but at most $C - 1$ of them can be identical. The objective of the game is to identify the most likely die face with specified high confidence. The relationship between this rigged dice paradigm and statistical pattern recognition becomes clear if one realizes that *a single unfair die is analogous to a specific point on the domain of the random feature vector being classified.* Just as there are specific class probabilities associated with each *point* in feature vector space, each *die* has specific probabilities associated with each of its faces. The number of faces on the die equals the number of classes associated with the analogous point in feature vector space. Identifying the most likely die face is equivalent to identifying the maximum class *a posteriori* probability for the analogous point in feature vector space — the requirement for Bayesian discrimination. We formulate our proofs for the case of a single die, and conclude by showing how a simple extension of the mathematics leads to general expressions for pattern recognition involving both discrete and continuous random feature vectors.

Authors' Note: In the interest of brevity, our proofs are posed as answers to questions that pertain to the rigged game of dice. It is hoped that the reader will find the relevance of each question/answer to statistical pattern recognition clear. Owing to page limitations, we cannot provide our proofs in full detail; the reader seeking such detail should refer to [1]. Definitions of symbols used in the following proofs are given in table 1.

1.1 A Fixed-Point Representation

The M_q-bit approximation $q_M[x]$ to the real number $x \in (-1, 1]$ is of the form

$$MSB \quad \text{(most significant bit)} \quad = \quad \text{sign}[x]$$

$$MSB - 1 \quad = \quad 2^{-1} \tag{1}$$
$$\downarrow$$
$$LSB \quad \text{(least significant bit)} \quad = \quad 2^{-(M_q-1)}$$

with the specific value defined as the mid-point of the $2^{-(M_q-1)}$-wide interval in which x is located:

$$q_M[x] \triangleq \begin{cases} \text{sign}[x] \cdot \left(\lfloor |x| \cdot 2^{(M_q-1)} \rfloor \cdot 2^{-(M_q-1)} + 2^{-M_q} \right), & |x| < 1 \\ \\ \text{sign}[x] \cdot \left(1 - 2^{-M_q} \right), & |x| = 1 \end{cases} \tag{2}$$

The lower and upper bounds on the quantization interval are

$$L_{M_q}[x] < x \leq U_{M_q}[x] \tag{3}$$

Table 1: Definitions of symbols used to describe die faces, probabilities, probabilistic differences, and associated estimates.

Symbol	Definition
ω_{rj}	The true jth most likely die face ($\widehat{\omega_{rj}}$ is the estimated jth most likely face).
$P(\omega_{rj})$	The probability of the true jth most likely die face.
k_{rj}	The number of occurrences of the true jth most likely die face.
$\hat{P}(\omega_{rj})$	An empirical estimate of the probability of the true jth most likely die face: $$\hat{P}(\omega_{rj}) = \frac{k_{rj}}{n} \quad \text{(note } n \text{ denotes the sample size)}$$
Δ_{ri}	The probabilistic difference involving the true rankings and probabilities of the C die faces: $$\Delta_{ri} = P(\omega_{ri}) - \sup_{j \neq i} P(\omega_{rj})$$
$\hat{\Delta}_{ri}$	The probabilistic difference involving the true rankings but *empirically estimated* probabilities of the C die faces: $$\hat{\Delta}_{ri} = \hat{P}(\omega_{ri}) - \sup_{j \neq i} \hat{P}(\omega_{rj}) = \frac{k_{ri} - \sup_{j \neq i} k_{rj}}{n}$$

where

$$L_{M_q}[x] = q_M[x] - 2^{-M_q} \tag{4}$$

and

$$U_{M_q}[x] = q_M[x] + 2^{-M_q} \tag{5}$$

The fixed-point representation described by (1) – (5) differs from standard fixed-point representations in its choice of quantization interval. The choice of (2) – (5) represents zero as a negative — more precisely, a *non-positive* — finite precision number. See [1] for the motivation of this format choice.

1.2 A Mathematical Comparison of the Probabilistic and Differential Strategies

The probabilistic strategy for identifying the most likely face on a die with C faces involves estimating the C face probabilities. In order for us to distinguish $\hat{P}(\omega_{r1})$ from $\hat{P}(\omega_{r2})$, we must choose M_q (i.e. the number of bits in our fixed-point representation of the estimated probabilities) such that

$$q_M[\hat{P}(\omega_{r1})] > q_M[\hat{P}(\omega_{r2})] \tag{6}$$

The distinction between the differential and probabilistic strategies is made more clear if one considers the way in which the M_q-bit approximation $\hat{\Delta}_{r1}$ is computed from a random sample containing k_{r1} occurrences of die face $\hat{\omega}_{r1}$ and k_{r2} occurrences of die face $\hat{\omega}_{r2}$. For the differential strategy

$$\hat{\Delta}_{r1 \text{ differential}} \equiv q_M \left[\frac{k_{r1} - k_{r2}}{n} \right] \tag{7}$$

and for the probabilistic strategy

$$\hat{\Delta}_{r1 \text{ probabilistic}} \equiv q_M \left[\frac{k_{r1}}{n} \right] - q_M \left[\frac{k_{r2}}{n} \right] \tag{8}$$

where

$$\Delta_i \overset{\triangle}{=} P(\omega_i) - \sup_{j \neq i} P(\omega_j) \quad i = 1, 2, \ldots C \tag{9}$$

Note that when $i = r1$

$$\Delta_{i=r1} = P(\omega_{r1}) - P(\omega_{r2}) \tag{10}$$

and when $i \neq r1$

$$\Delta_{i \neq r1} = P(\omega_i) - P(\omega_{r1}) \tag{11}$$

Note also

$$\Delta_{r1} = -\Delta_{r2} \tag{12}$$

Since

$$\sum_{i=1}^{C} \Delta_i = \sum_{i=r3}^{rC} P(\omega_i) - (C - 2) P(\omega_{r1}) \tag{13}$$

we can show that the C differences of (9) yield the C probabilities by

$$P(\omega_{r1}) = \frac{1}{C} \left[1 - \sum_{i=r2}^{rC} \Delta_i \right] \tag{14}$$

$$P(\omega_{rj}) = \Delta_{rj} + P(\omega_{r1}) \quad \forall j > 1$$

Thus, estimating the C differences of (9) is equivalent to estimating the C probabilities $P(\omega_1), P(\omega_2), \ldots, P(\omega_C)$.

Clearly, the sign of $\hat{\Delta}_{r1}$ in (7) is modeled correctly (i.e., $\hat{\Delta}_{r1 \, differential}$ can correctly identify the most likely face) when $M_q = 1$, while this is typically not the case for $\hat{\Delta}_{r1 \, probabilistic}$ in (8). In the latter case, $\hat{\Delta}_{r1 \, probabilistic}$ is zero when $M_q = 1$ because $q_m[\hat{P}(\omega_{r1})]$ and $q_M[\hat{P}(\omega_{r2})]$ are indistinguishable for M_q below some minimal value implied by (6). That minimal value of M_q can be found by recognizing that the number of bits necessary for (6) to hold for asymptotically large n (i.e., for the quantized difference in (8) to exceed one LSB) is

$$M_{q \, min} = \begin{cases} \underbrace{1}_{\text{sign bit}} + \underbrace{\lceil -\log_2 \lceil \Delta_{r1} \rceil \rceil}_{\text{magnitude bits}}, & -\log_2 \left[P(\omega_{rj}) \right] \ni \mathcal{Z}^+ \quad j \in \{1, 2\} \\ \\ \underbrace{1}_{\text{sign bit}} + \underbrace{\lceil -\log_2 \lceil \Delta_{r1} \rceil \rceil + 1}_{\text{magnitude bits}}, & \text{otherwise} \end{cases}$$

$$\tag{15}$$

where $\mathcal{Z}^+$ represents the set of all positive integers. Note that the conditional nature of $M_{q \, min}$ in (15) prevents the case in which $\lim_{\varepsilon \to 0} P(\omega_{r1}) - \varepsilon = L_{M_q}[P(\omega_{r1})]$ or $P(\omega_{r2}) = U_{M_q}[P(\omega_{r2})]$; either case would require an infinitely large sample size before the variance of the corresponding estimated probability became small enough to distinguish $q_M[\hat{P}(\omega_{r1})]$ from $q_M[\hat{P}(\omega_{r2})]$. The sign bit in (15) is not required to estimate the probabilities themselves in (8), but it is necessary to compute the difference between the two probabilities in that equation — this difference being the ultimate computation by which we choose the most likely die face.

1.3   The Sample Complexity Product

We introduce the *sample complexity product* (SCP) as a measure of both the number of samples and the functional complexity (measured in bits) required to identify the most likely face of an unfair die with specified probability.

$$\text{SCP} \triangleq n \cdot M_q \quad s.t. \quad \text{P (most likely face correctly ID'd)} \geq \alpha \tag{16}$$

2   A Comparison of the Sample Complexity Requirements for the Probabilistic and Differential Strategies

Axiom 1 *We view the number of bits M_q in the finite-precision approximation $q_M[x]$ to the real number $x \in (-1, 1]$ as a measure of the approximation's functional complexity. That is, the functional complexity of an approximation is the number of bits with which it represents a real number on $(-1, 1]$.*

Assumption 1 *If $\hat{P}(\omega_{r1}) > \hat{P}(\omega_{r2})$, then $\hat{P}(\omega_{r1})$ will be greater than $\hat{P}(\omega_{rj})$ $\forall j > 2$ (see [1] for an analysis of cases in which this assumption is invalid).*

Question: What is the probability that the most likely face of an unfair die will be empirically identifiable after n tosses?

Answer for the probabilistic strategy:

$$P\left(q_M[\hat{P}(\omega_{r1})] > q_M[\hat{P}(\omega_{rj})], \ \forall j > 1 \right)$$

$$\cong \ n! \sum_{k_{r1}=\lambda_1}^{v_1} \frac{P(\omega_{r1})^{k_{r1}}}{k_{r1}!} \left[\sum_{k_{r2}=\lambda_2}^{v_2} \frac{P(\omega_{r2})^{k_{r2}} (1 - P(\omega_{r1}) - P(\omega_{r2}))^{(n-k_{r1}-k_{r2})}}{k_{r2}! \ (n - k_{r1} - k_{r2})!} \right] \tag{17}$$

where

$$
\begin{aligned}
\lambda_1 &= \max\left(\mathcal{B} + 1, \ \frac{n - k_{r2}}{\mathcal{C} - 1} + 1 \right) \qquad \forall \mathcal{C} > 2 \\
v_1 &= n \\
\lambda_2 &= 0 \\
v_2 &= \min(\mathcal{B}, \ n - k_{r1}) \\
\mathcal{B} &= \{\mathcal{B}_{M_q}\} = k_{U_{M_q}}[P(\omega_{r2})] = k_{L_{M_q}}[P(\omega_{r1})] - 1
\end{aligned}
\tag{18}
$$

There is a simple recursion in [1] by which every possible boundary for M_q-bit quantization leads to itself and two additional boundaries in the set $\{\mathcal{B}_{M_q}\}$ for $(M_q + 1)$-bit quantization.

Answer for the differential strategy:

$$P\left(L_{M_q}[\Delta_{r1}] < \hat{\Delta}_{r1} \leq U_{M_q}[\Delta_{r1}], \ \hat{\Delta}_{rj} < 0 \ \forall j > 1 \right)$$

$$\cong \quad n! \sum_{k_{r1}=\lambda_1}^{\upsilon_1} \frac{P(\omega_{r1})^{k_{r1}}}{k_{r1}!} \left[\sum_{k_{r2}=\lambda_2}^{\upsilon_2} \frac{P(\omega_{r2})^{k_{r2}} (1 - P(\omega_{r1}) - P(\omega_{r2}))^{(n-k_{r1}-k_{r2})}}{k_{r2}! \, (n - k_{r1} - k_{r2})!} \right] \quad (19)$$

where

$$\lambda_1 \;=\; \max\left(k_{L_{M_q}}[\Delta_{r1}], \; \frac{n - k_{r2}}{C - 1} + 1 \right) \qquad \forall C > 2$$

$$\upsilon_1 \;=\; n \qquad\qquad\qquad\qquad\qquad\qquad\qquad\quad (20)$$

$$\lambda_2 \;=\; \max\left(0, \; k_{r1} - k_{U_{M_q}}[\Delta_{r1}] \right)$$

$$\upsilon_2 \;=\; \min\left(k_{r1} - k_{L_{M_q}}[\Delta_{r1}], \; n - k_{r1} \right)$$

Since the multinomial distribution is positive semi-definite, it should be clear from a comparison of (17) – (18) and (19) – (20) that $P\left(L_{M_q}[\Delta_{r1}] < \hat{\Delta}_{r1} \leq U_{M_q}[\Delta_{r1}] \right)$ is largest (and larger than any possible $P\left(q_M[\hat{P}(\omega_{r1})] > q_M[\hat{P}(\omega_{rj})], \; \forall j > 1 \right)$) for a given sample size n when the differential strategy is employed with $M_q = 1$ such that $L_{M_q}[\Delta_{r1}] = 0$ and $U_{M_q}[\Delta_{r1}] = 1$ (i.e., $k_{L_{M_q}}[\Delta_{r1}] = 1$ and $k_{U_{M_q}}[\Delta_{r1}] = n$). The converse is also true, to wit:

Theorem 1 *For a fixed value of n in (19), the 1-bit approximation to Δ_{r1} yields the highest probability of identifying the most likely die face ω_{r1}.*

It can be shown that theorem 1 does not depend on the validity of assumption 1 [1]. Given Axiom 1, the following corollary to theorem 1 holds:

Corollary 1 *The differential strategy's minimum-complexity 1-bit approximation of Δ_{r1} yields the highest probability of identifying the most likely die face ω_{r1} for a given number of tosses n.*

Corollary 2 *The differential strategy's minimum-complexity 1-bit approximation of Δ_{r1} requires the smallest sample size necessary (n_{min}) to identify $P(\omega_{r1})$ — and thereby the most likely die face ω_{r1} — correctly with specified confidence. Thus, the differential strategy requires the minimum SCP necessary to identify the most likely die face with specified confidence.*

2.1 Theoretical Predictions versus Empirical Results

Figures 1 and 2 compare theoretical predictions of the number of samples n and the number of bits M_q necessary to identify the most likely face of a particular die versus the actual requirements obtained from 1000 games (3000 tosses of the die in each game). The die has five faces with probabilities $P(\omega_{r1}) = 0.37$, $P(\omega_{r2}) = 0.28$, $P(\omega_{r3}) = 0.2$, $P(\omega_{r4}) = 0.1$, and $P(\omega_{r1}) = 0.05$. The theoretical predictions for M_q and n (arrows with boxed labels based on iterative searches employing equations (17) and (19)) that would with 0.95 confidence correctly identify the most likely die face ω_{r1} are shown to correspond with the empirical results: in figure 1 the empirical 0.95 confidence interval is marked by the lower bound of the dark gray and the upper bound of the light gray; in figure 2 the empirical 0.95 confidence interval is marked by the lower bound of the $\hat{P}(\omega_{r1})$ distribution and the upper bound of the

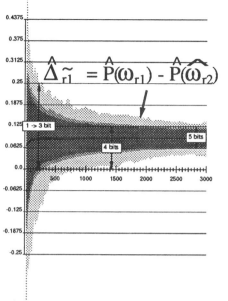

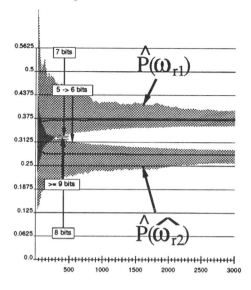

Figure 1: Theoretical predictions of the number of tosses needed to identify the most likely face ω_{r1} with 95% confidence (Die 1): Differential strategy prediction superimposed on empirical results of 1000 games (3000 tosses each).

Figure 2: Theoretical predictions of the number of tosses needed to identify the most likely face ω_{r1} with 95% confidence (Die 1): Probabilistic strategy prediction superimposed on empirical results of 1000 games (3000 tosses each).

$\hat{P}(\omega_{r2})$ distribution. These figures illustrate that the differential strategy's minimum SCP is 227 ($n = 227$, $M_q = 1$) while the minimum SCP for the probabilistic strategy is 2720 ($n = 544$, $M_q = 5$). A complete tabulation of SCP as a function of $P(\omega_{r1})$, $P(\omega_{r2})$, and the worst-case choice for $\mathcal{C}$ (the number of classes/die faces) is given in [1].

3   Conclusion

The sample complexity product (SCP) notion of functional complexity set forth herein is closely aligned with the complexity measures of Kolmogorov and Rissanen [4, 6]. We have used it to prove that the differential strategy for learning the Bayesian discriminant function is optimal in terms of its minimum requirements for classifier functional complexity and number of training examples when the classification task is identifying the most likely face of an unfair die. It is relatively straightforward to extend theorem 1 and its corollaries to the general pattern recognition case in order to show that the expected SCP for the 1-bit differential strategy

$$E\,[SCP]_{differential} \cong \int_{\mathbf{X}} n_{min}\left[P\left(\omega_{r1} \mid \mathbf{x}\right), P\left(\omega_{r2} \mid \mathbf{x}\right)\right] \cdot \underbrace{M_{q\,min}\left[P\left(\omega_{r1} \mid \mathbf{x}\right), P\left(\omega_{r2} \mid \mathbf{x}\right)\right]}_{=1} \rho(\mathbf{x})d\mathbf{x}$$

(21)

(or the discrete random vector analog of this equation) is minimal [1]. This is because n_{min} is by corollary 2 the smallest sample size necessary to distinguish any and all $P(\omega_{r1})$ from lesser $P(\omega_{r2})$. The resulting analysis confirms that the classifier trained with the differential strategy for statistical pattern recognition (i.e., using a CFM_{mono} objective function) has the highest probability of learning the Bayesian discriminant function when the functional capacity of the classifier and the available training data are both limited.

The relevance of this work to the process of designing and training robust connectionist pattern classifiers is evident if one considers the practical meaning of the terms $n_{min}\left[P\left(\omega_{r1}\mid x\right),P\left(\omega_{r2}\mid x\right)\right]$ and $M_{q\,min}\left[P\left(\omega_{r1}\mid x\right),P\left(\omega_{r2}\mid x\right)\right]$ in the sample complexity product of (21). Given one's choice of connectionist model to employ as a classifier, the $M_{q\,min}$ term dictates the minimum necessary connectivity of that model. For example, (21) can be used to prove that a partially connected radial basis function (RBF) with trainable variance parameters and three hidden layer "nodes" has the minimum M_q necessary for Bayesian discrimination in the 3-class task described by [5]. However, because *both* SCP terms are functions of the probabilistic nature of the random feature vector being classified *and the learning strategy employed*, that minimal RBF architecture *will only yield Bayesian discrimination if trained using the differential strategy*. The probabilistic strategy requires significantly more functional complexity in the RBF in order to meet the requirements of the probabilistic strategy's SCP [1]. Philosophical arguments regarding the use of the differential strategy in lieu of the more traditional probabilistic strategy are discussed at length in [1].

Acknowledgement

This research was funded by the Air Force Office of Scientific Research under grant AFOSR-89-0551. We gratefully acknowledge their support.

References

[1] J. B. Hampshire II. *A Differential Theory of Statistical Pattern Recognition*. PhD thesis, Carnegie Mellon University, Department of Electrical & Computer Engineering, Hammerschlag Hall, Pittsburgh, PA 15213-3890, 1992. manuscript in progress.

[2] J. B. Hampshire II and B. A. Pearlmutter. Equivalence Proofs for Multi-Layer Perceptron Classifiers and the Bayesian Discriminant Function. In Touretzky, Elman, Sejnowski, and Hinton, editors, *Proceedings of the 1990 Connectionist Models Summer School*, pages 159–172, San Mateo, CA, 1991. Morgan-Kaufmann.

[3] J. B. Hampshire II and A. H. Waibel. A Novel Objective Function for Improved Phoneme Recognition Using Time-Delay Neural Networks. *IEEE Transactions on Neural Networks*, 1(2):216–228, June 1990. A revised and extended version of work first presented at the 1989 International Joint Conference on Neural Networks, vol. I, pp. 235-241.

[4] A. N. Kolmogorov. Three Approaches to the Quantitative Definition of Information. *Problems of Information Transmission*, 1(1):1–7, Jan. - Mar. 1965. Faraday Press translation of Problemy Peredachi Informatsii.

[5] M. D. Richard and R. P. Lippmann. Neural Network Classifiers Estimate Bayesian *a posteriori* Probabilities. *Neural Computation*, 3(4):461–483, 1991.

[6] J. Rissanen. Modeling by shortest data description. *Automatica*, 14:465–471, 1978.

Improving the Performance of Radial Basis Function Networks by Learning Center Locations

Dietrich Wettschereck
Department of Computer Science
Oregon State University
Corvallis, OR 97331-3202

Thomas Dietterich
Department of Computer Science
Oregon State University
Corvallis, OR 97331-3202

Abstract

Three methods for improving the performance of (gaussian) radial basis function (RBF) networks were tested on the NETtalk task. In RBF, a new example is classified by computing its Euclidean distance to a set of *centers* chosen by unsupervised methods. The application of supervised learning to learn a non-Euclidean distance metric was found to reduce the error rate of RBF networks, while supervised learning of each center's variance resulted in inferior performance. The best improvement in accuracy was achieved by networks called generalized radial basis function (GRBF) networks. In GRBF, the center locations are determined by supervised learning. After training on 1000 words, RBF classifies 56.5% of letters correct, while GRBF scores 73.4% letters correct (on a separate test set). From these and other experiments, we conclude that supervised learning of center locations can be very important for radial basis function learning.

1 Introduction

Radial basis function (RBF) networks are 3-layer feed-forward networks in which each hidden unit α computes the function

$$f_\alpha(\mathbf{x}) = e^{-\frac{||\mathbf{X}-\mathbf{X}_\alpha||^2}{\sigma^2}},$$

and the output units compute a weighted sum of these hidden-unit activations:

$$f^*(\mathbf{x}) = \sum_{\alpha=1}^{N} c_\alpha f_\alpha(\mathbf{x}).$$

In other words, the value of $f^*(\mathbf{x})$ is determined by computing the Euclidean distance between $\mathbf{x}$ and a set of N **centers**, $\mathbf{x}_\alpha$. These distances are then passed through Gaussians (with variance σ^2 and zero mean), weighted by c_α, and summed.

Radial basis function networks (RBF networks) provide an attractive alternative to sigmoid networks for learning real-valued mappings: (a) they provide excellent approximations to smooth functions (Poggio & Girosi, 1989), (b) their "centers" are interpretable as "prototypes", and (c) they can be learned very quickly, because the center locations $(\mathbf{x}_\alpha)$ can be determined by unsupervised learning algorithms and the weights (c_α) can be computed by pseudo-inverse methods (Moody and Darken, 1989).

Although the application of unsupervised methods to learn the center locations does yield very efficient training, there is some evidence that the generalization performance of RBF networks is inferior to sigmoid networks. Moody and Darken (1989), for example, report that their RBF network must receive 10 times more training data than a standard sigmoidal network in order to attain comparable generalization performance on the Mackey-Glass time-series task.

There are several plausible explanations for this performance gap. First, in sigmoid networks, all parameters are determined by supervised learning, whereas in RBF networks, typically only the learning of the output weights has been supervised. Second, the use of Euclidean distance to compute $\|\mathbf{x} - \mathbf{x}_\alpha\|$ assumes that all input features are equally important. In many applications, this assumption is known to be false, so this could yield poor results.

The purpose of this paper is twofold. First, we carefully tested the performance of RBF networks on the well-known NETtalk task (Sejnowski & Rosenberg, 1987) and compared it to the performance of a wide variety of algorithms that we have previously tested on this task (Dietterich, Hild, & Bakiri, 1990). The results confirm that there is a substantial gap between RBF generalization and other methods.

Second, we evaluated the benefits of employing supervised learning to learn (a) the center locations $\mathbf{x}_\alpha$, (b) weights w_i for a weighted distance metric, and (c) variances σ_α^2 for each center. The results show that supervised learning of the center locations and weights improves performance, while supervised learning of the variances or of combinations of center locations, variances, and weights did not. The best performance was obtained by supervised learning of only the center locations (and the output weights, of course).

In the remainder of the paper we first describe our testing methodology and review the NETtalk domain. Then, we present results of our comparison of RBF with other methods. Finally, we describe the performance obtained from supervised learning of weights, variances, and center locations.

2   Methodology

All of the learning algorithms described in this paper have several parameters (such as the number of centers and the criterion for stopping training) that must be specified by the user. To set these parameters in a principled fashion, we employed the cross-validation methodology described by Lang, Hinton & Waibel (1990). First, as usual, we randomly partitioned our dataset into a training set and a test set. Then, we further divided the training set into a subtraining set and a cross-validation set. Alternative values for the user-specified parameters were then tried while training on the subtraining set and testing on the cross-validation set. The best-performing parameter values were then employed to train a network on the full training set. The generalization performance of the resulting network is then measured on the test set. Using this methodology, no information from the test set is used to determine any parameters during training.

We explored the following parameters: (a) the number of hidden units (centers) N, (b) the method for choosing the initial locations of the centers, (c) the variance σ^2 (when it was not subject to supervised learning), and (d) (whenever supervised training was involved) the stopping squared error per example. We tried $N = 50, 100, 150, 200$, and 250; $\sigma^2 = 1, 2, 4, 5, 10, 20$, and 50; and three different initialization procedures:

(a) Use a subset of the training examples,

(b) Use an unsupervised version of the IB2 algorithm of Aha, Kibler & Albert (1991), and

(c) Apply k-means clustering, starting with the centers from (a).

For all methods, we applied the pseudo-inverse technique of Penrose (1955) followed by Gaussian elimination to set the output weights.

To perform supervised learning of center locations, feature weights, and variances, we applied conjugate-gradient optimization. We modified the conjugate-gradient implementation of backpropagation supplied by Barnard & Cole (1989).

3   The NETtalk Domain

We tested all networks on the NETtalk task (Sejnowski & Rosenberg, 1987), in which the goal is to learn to pronounce English words by studying a dictionary of correct pronunciations. We replicated the formulation of Sejnowski & Rosenberg in which the task is to learn to map each individual letter in a word to a phoneme and a stress.

Two disjoint sets of 1000 words were drawn at random from the NETtalk dictionary of 20,002 words (made available by Sejnowski and Rosenberg): one for training and one for testing. The training set was further subdivided into an 800-word subtraining set and a 200-word cross-validation set.

To encode the words in the dictionary, we replicated the encoding of Sejnowski & Rosenberg (1987): Each input vector encodes a 7-letter window centered on the letter to be pronounced. Letters beyond the ends of the word are encoded as blanks. Each letter is locally encoded as a 29-bit string (26 bits for each letter, 1 bit for comma, space, and period) with exactly one bit on. This gives 203 input bits, seven of which are 1 while all others are 0.

Each phoneme and stress pair was encoded using the 26-bit distributed code developed by Sejnowski & Rosenberg in which the bit positions correspond to distinctive features of the phonemes and stresses (e.g., voiced/unvoiced, stop, etc.).

4   RBF Performance on the NETtalk Task

We began by testing RBF on the NETtalk task. Cross-validation training determined that peak RBF generalization was obtained with $N = 250$ (the number of centers), $\sigma^2 = 5$ (constant for all centers), and the locations of the centers computed by k-means clustering. Table 1 shows the performance of RBF on the 1000-word test set in comparison with several other algorithms: nearest neighbor, the decision tree algorithm ID3 (Quinlan, 1986), sigmoid networks trained via backpropagation (160 hidden units, cross-validation training, learning rate 0.25, momentum 0.9), Wolpert's (1990) HERBIE algorithm (with weights set via mutual information), and ID3 with error-correcting output codes (ECC, Dietterich & Bakiri, 1991).

Table 1: Generalization performance on the NETtalk task.

	% correct (1000-word test set)			
Algorithm	Word	Letter	Phoneme	Stress
Nearest neighbor	3.3	53.1	61.1	74.0
RBF	3.7	57.0*****	65.6*****	80.3*****
ID3	9.6*****	65.6*****	78.7*****	77.2*****
Back propagation	13.6**	70.6*****	80.8****	81.3*****
Wolpert	15.0	72.2*	82.6*****	80.2
ID3 + 127-bit ECC	20.0***	73.7*	85.6*****	81.1

Prior row different, $p < .05^*$ $.01^{**}$ $.005^{***}$ $.002^{****}$ $.001^{*****}$

Performance is shown at several levels of aggregation. The "stress" column indicates the percentage of stress assignments correctly classified. The "phoneme" column shows the percentage of phonemes correctly assigned. A "letter" is correct if the phoneme and stress are correctly assigned, and a "word" is correct if all letters in the word are correctly classified. Also shown are the results of a two-tailed test for the difference of two proportions, which was conducted for each row and the row preceding it in the table.

From this table, it is clear that RBF is performing substantially below virtually all of the algorithms except nearest neighbor. There is certainly room for supervised learning of RBF parameters to improve on this.

5   Supervised Learning of Additional RBF Parameters

In this section, we present our supervised learning experiments. In each case, we report only the cross-validation performance. Finally, we take the best supervised learning configuration, as determined by these cross-validation scores, train it on the entire training set and evaluate it on the test set.

5.1   Weighted Feature Norm and Centers With Adjustable Widths

The first form of supervised learning that we tested was the learning of a weighted norm. In the NETtalk domain, it is obvious that the various input features are not equally important. In particular, the features describing the letter at the center of the 7-letter window—the letter to be pronounced—are much more important than the features describing the other letters, which are only present to provide context. One way to capture the importance of different features is through a weighted norm:

$$||x - x_\alpha||^2_w = \sum_i w_i(x_i - x_{\alpha i})^2.$$

We employed supervised training to obtain the weights w_i. We call this configuration RBF_{FW}. On the cross-validation set, RBF_{FW} correctly classified 62.4% of the letters (N=200, $\sigma^2 = 5$, center locations determined by k-means clustering). This is a 4.7 percentage point improvement over standard RBF, which on the cross-validation set classifies only 57.7% of the letters correctly (N=250, $\sigma^2 = 5$, center locations determined by k-means clustering).

Moody & Darken (1989) suggested heuristics to set the variance of each center. They employed the inverse of the mean Euclidean distance from each center to its P-nearest neighbors to determine the variance. However, they found that in most cases a global value for all variances worked best. We replicated this experiment for P = 1 and P = 4, and we compared this to just setting the variances to a global value ($\sigma^2 = 5$) optimized by cross-validation. The performance on the cross-validation set was 53.6% (for P=1), 53.8% (for P=4), and 57.7% (for the global value).

In addition to these heuristic methods, we also tried supervised learning of the variances alone (which we call RBF_σ). On the cross-validation set, it classifies 57.4% of the letters correctly, as compared with 57.7% for standard RBF.

Hence, in all of our experiments, a single global value for σ^2 gives better results than any of the techniques for setting separate values for each center. Other researchers have obtained experimental results in other domains showing the usefulness of nonuniform variances. Hence, we must conclude that, while RBF_σ did not perform well in the NETtalk domain, it may be valuable in other domains.

5.2   Learning Center Locations (Generalized Radial Basis Functions)

Poggio and Girosi (1989) suggest using gradient descent methods to implement supervised learning of the center locations, a method that they call generalized radial basis functions (GRBF). We implemented and tested this approach. On the cross-validation set, GRBF correctly classifies 72.2% of the letters ($N = 200, \sigma^2 = 4$, centers initialized to a subset of training data) as compared to 57.7% for standard RBF. This is a remarkable 14.5 percentage-point improvement.

We also tested GRBF with previously learned feature weights ($GRBF_{FW}$) and in combination with learning variances ($GRBF_\sigma$). The performance of both of these methods was inferior to GRBF. For $GRBF_{FW}$, gradient search on the center locations failed to significantly improved performance of RBF_{FW} networks (RBF_{FW} 62.4% vs. $GRBF_{FW}$ 62.8%, RBF_{FW} 54.5% vs. $GRBF_{FW}$ 57.9%). This shows that through the use of a non-Euclidian, fixed metric found by RBF_{FW} the gradient search of $GRBF_{FW}$ is getting caught in a local minimum. One explanation for this is that feature weights and adjustable centers are two alternative ways of achieving the same effect—namely, of making some features more important than others. Redundancy can easily create local minima. To understand this explanation, consider the plots in Figure 1. Figure 1(A) shows the weights of the input features as they

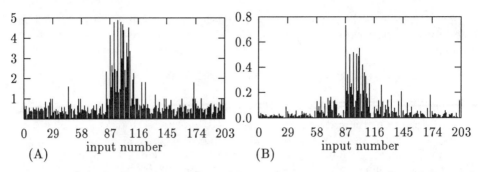

Figure 1: (A) displays the weights of input features as learned by RBF_{FW}. In (B) the mean square-distance between centers (separate for each dimension) from a $GRBF$ network ($N = 100$, $\sigma^2 = 4$) is shown.

were learned by RBF_{FW}. Features with weights near zero have no influence in the distance calculation when a new test example is classified. Figure 1(B) shows the mean squared distance between every center and every other center (computed separately for each input feature). Low values for the mean squared distance on feature i indicate that most centers have very similar values on feature i. Hence, this feature can play no role in determining which centers are activated by a new test example. In both plots, the features at the center of the window are clearly the most important. Therefore, it appears that GRBF is able to capture the information about the relative importance of features without the need for feature weights.

To explore the effect of learning the variances and center locations simultaneously, we introduced a scale factor to allow us to adjust the relative magnitudes of the gradients. We then varied this scale factor under cross validation. Generally, the larger we set the scale factor (to increase the gradient of the variance terms) the worse the performance became. As with $GRBF_{FW}$, we see that difficulties in gradient descent training are preventing us from finding a global minimum (or even re-discovering known local minima).

5.3   Summary

Based on the results of this section as summarized in Table 2, we chose GRBF as the best supervised learning configuration and applied it to the entire 1000-word training set (with testing on the 1000-word test set). We also combined it with a 63-bit error-correcting output code to see if this would improve its performance, since error-correcting output codes have been shown to boost the performance of backpropagation and ID3. The final comparison results are shown in Table 3. The results show that GRBF is superior to RBF at all levels of aggregation. Furthermore, GRBF is statistically indistinguishable from the best method that we have tested to date (ID3 with 127-bit error-correcting output code), except on phonemes where it is detectably inferior and on stresses where it is detectably superior. GRBF with error-correcting output codes is statistically indistinguishable from ID3 with error-correcting output codes.

Table 2: Percent of letters correctly classified on the 200-word cross-validation data set.

Method	% Letters Correct
RBF	57.7
RBF$_{FW}$	62.4
RBF$_\sigma$	57.4
GRBF	72.2
GRBF$_{FW}$	62.8
GRBF$_\sigma$	67.5

Table 3: Generalization performance on the NETtalk task.

Algorithm	% correct (1000-word test set)			
	Word	Letter	Phoneme	Stress
RBF	3.7	57.0	65.6	80.3
GRBF	19.8***	73.8***	84.1***	82.4**
ID3 + 127-bit ECC	20.0	73.7	85.6*	81.1*
GRBF + 63-bit ECC	19.2	74.6	85.3	82.2

Prior row different, $p < .05^*$ $.002^{**}$ $.001^{***}$

The near-identical performance of GRBF and the error-correcting code method and the fact that the use of error correcting output codes does not improve GRBF's performance significantly, suggests that the "bias" of GRBF (i.e., its implicit assumptions about the unknown function being learned) is particularly appropriate for the NETtalk task. This conjecture follows from the observation that error-correcting output codes provide a way of recovering from improper bias (such as the bias of ID3 in this task). This is somewhat surprising, since the mathematical justification for GRBF is based on the smoothness of the unknown function, which is certainly violated in classification tasks.

6   Conclusions

Radial basis function networks have many properties that make them attractive in comparison to networks of sigmoid units. However, our tests of RBF learning (unsupervised learning of center locations, supervised learning of output-layer weights) in the NETtalk domain found that RBF networks did not generalize nearly as well as sigmoid networks. This is consistent with results reported in other domains.

However, by employing supervised learning of the center locations as well as the output weights, the GRBF method is able to substantially exceed the generalization performance of sigmoid networks. Indeed, GRBF matches the performance of the best known method for the NETtalk task: ID3 with error-correcting output codes, which, however, is approximately 50 times faster to train.

We found that supervised learning of feature weights (alone) could also improve the performance of RBF networks, although not nearly as much as learning the center locations. Surprisingly, we found that supervised learning of the variances of the Gaussians located at each center hurt generalization performance. Also, combined supervised learning of center locations and feature weights did not perform as well as supervised learning of center locations alone. The training process is becoming stuck in local minima. For GRBF$_{FW}$, we presented data suggesting that feature weights are redundant and that they could be introducing local minima as a result.

Our implementation of GRBF, while efficient, still gives training times comparable to those required for backpropagation training of sigmoid networks. Hence, an important open problem is to develop more efficient methods for supervised learning of center locations.

While the results in this paper apply only to the NETtalk domain, the markedly superior performance of GRBF over RBF suggests that in new applications of RBF networks, it is important to consider supervised learning of center locations in order to obtain the best generalization performance.

Acknowledgments

This research was supported by a grant from the National Science Foundation Grant Number IRI-86-57316.

References

D. W. Aha, D. Kibler & M. K. Albert. (1991) Instance-based learning algorithms. *Machine Learning* 6(1):37-66.

E. Barnard & R. A. Cole. (1989) A neural-net training program based on conjugate-gradient optimization. Rep. No. CSE 89-014. Oregon Graduate Institute, Beaverton, OR.

T. G. Dietterich & G. Bakiri. (1991) Error-correcting output codes: A general method for improving multiclass inductive learning programs. *Proceedings of the Ninth National Conference on Artificial Intelligence (AAAI-91)*, Anaheim, CA: AAAI Press.

T. G. Dietterich, H. Hild, & G. Bakiri. (1990) A comparative study of ID3 and back-propagation for English text-to-speech mapping. *Proceedings of the 1990 Machine Learning Conference*, Austin, TX. 24–31.

K. J. Lang, A. H. Waibel & G. E. Hinton. (1990) A time-delay neural network architecture for isolated word recognition. *Neural Networks* 3:33-43.

J. MacQueen. (1967) Some methods of classification and analysis of multivariate observations. In LeCam, L. M. & Neyman, J. (Eds.), *Proceedings of the 5th Berkeley Symposium on Mathematics, Statistics, and Probability* (p. 281). Berkeley, CA: University of California Press.

J. Moody & C. J. Darken. (1989) Fast learning in networks of locally-tuned processing units. *Neural Computation* 1(2):281-294.

R. Penrose. (1955) A generalized inverse for matrices. *Proceedings of Cambridge Philosophical Society* 51:406-413.

T. Poggio & F. Girosi. (1989) A theory of networks for approximation and learning. Report Number AI-1140. MIT Artificial Intelligence Laboratory, Cambridge, MA.

J. R. Quinlan. (1986) Induction of decision trees. *Machine Learning* 1(1):81-106.

T. J. Sejnowski & C. R. Rosenberg. (1987) Parallel networks that learn to pronounce English text. *Complex Systems* 1:145-168.

D. Wolpert. (1990) Constructing a generalizer superior to NETtalk via a mathematical theory of generalization. *Neural Networks* 3:445-452.

A Topographic Product for the Optimization of Self-Organizing Feature Maps

Hans-Ulrich Bauer, Klaus Pawelzik, Theo Geisel
Institut für theoretische Physik and SFB Nichtlineare Dynamik
Universität Frankfurt
Robert-Mayer-Str. 8-10
W-6000 Frankfurt 11
Fed. Rep. of Germany
email: bauer@asgard.physik.uni-frankfurt.dbp

Abstract

Optimizing the performance of self-organizing feature maps like the Kohonen map involves the choice of the output space topology. We present a topographic product which measures the preservation of neighborhood relations as a criterion to optimize the output space topology of the map with regard to the global dimensionality D^A as well as to the dimensions in the individual directions. We test the topographic product method not only on synthetic mapping examples, but also on speech data. In the latter application our method suggests an output space dimensionality of $D^A = 3$, in coincidence with recent recognition results on the same data set.

1 INTRODUCTION

Self-organizing feature maps like the Kohonen map (Kohonen, 1989, Ritter et al., 1990) not only provide a plausible explanation for the formation of maps in brains, e.g. in the visual system (Obermayer et al., 1990), but have also been applied to problems like vector quantization, or robot arm control (Martinetz et al., 1990). The underlying organizing principle is the preservation of neighborhood relations. For this principle to lead to a most useful map, the topological structure of the output space must roughly fit the structure of the input data. However, in technical applications this structure is often not a priory known. For this reason several attempts have been made to modify the Kohonen-algorithm such, that not only the weights, but also the output space topology itself is adapted during learning (Kangas et al., 1990, Martinetz et al., 1991).

Our contribution is also concerned with optimal output space topologies, but we follow a different approach, which avoids a possibly complicated structure of the output space. First we describe a quantitative measure for the preservation of neighborhood relations in maps, the topographic product P. The topographic product had been invented under the name of "wavering product" in nonlinear dynamics in order to optimize the embeddings of chaotic attractors (Liebert et al., 1991). $P = 0$ indicates perfect match of the topologies. $P < 0$ ($P > 0$) indicates a folding of the output space into the input space (or vice versa), which can be caused by a too small (resp. too large) output space dimensionality. The topographic product can be computed for any self-organizing feature map, without regard to its specific learning rule. Since judging the degree of twisting and folding by visually inspecting a plot of the map is the only other way of "measuring" the preservation of neighborhoods, the topographic product is particularly helpful, if the input space dimensionality of the map exceeds $D^A = 3$ and the map can no more be visualized. Therefore the derivation of the topographic product is already of value by itself.

In the second part of the paper we demonstrate the use of the topographic product by two examples. The first example deals with maps from a 2D input space with nonflat stimulus distribution onto rectangles of different aspect ratios, the second example with the map of 19D speech data onto output spaces of different dimensionality. In both cases we show, how the output space topology can be optimized using our method.

2   DERIVATION OF THE TOPOGRAPHIC PRODUCT

2.1   KOHONEN-ALGORITHM

In order to introduce the notation necessary to derive the topographic product, we very briefly recall the Kohonen algorithm. It describes a map from an input space $\mathbf{V}$ into an output space A. Each node j in A has a weight vector $\mathbf{w}_j$ associated with it, which points into $\mathbf{V}$. A stimulus $\mathbf{v}$ is mapped onto that node i in the output space, which minimizes the input space distance $d^{\mathbf{V}}(\mathbf{w}_i, \mathbf{v})$:

$$i: \quad d^V(\mathbf{w}_i, \mathbf{v}) = \min_{j \in A} d^V(\mathbf{w}_j, \mathbf{v}). \tag{1}$$

During a learning step, a random stimulus is chosen in the input space and mapped onto an output node i according to Eq. 1. Then all weights $\mathbf{w}_j$ are shifted towards $\mathbf{v}$, with the amount of shift for each weight vector being determined by a neighborhood function $h^0_{i,j}$:

$$\delta \mathbf{w}_j = \epsilon h^0_{j,i}(d^A(j,i))(\mathbf{v} - \mathbf{w}_j) \quad \forall j \in A. \tag{2}$$

($d^A(j,i)$ measures distances in the output space.) $h^0_{j,i}$ effectively restricts the nodes participating in the learning step to nodes in the vicinity of i. A typical choice for the neighborhood function is

$$h^0_{j,i} = \exp\left(-\frac{(d^A)^2(j,i)}{2\sigma^2}\right). \tag{3}$$

In this way the neighborhood relations in the output space are enforced in the input space, and the output space topology becomes of crucial importance. Finally it should be mentioned that the learning step size ϵ as well as the width of the neighborhood function σ are decreased during the learning for the algorithm to converge to an equilibrium state. A typical choice is an exponential decrease. For a detailed discussion of the convergence properties of the algorithm, see (Ritter et al., 1988).

2.2 TOPOGRAPHIC PRODUCT

After the learning phase, the topographic product is computed as follows. For each output space node j, the nearest neighbor ordering in input space and output space is computed ($n^A_k(j)$ denotes the k-th nearest neighbor of j in A, $n^{\mathbf{V}}_k(j)$ in $\mathbf{V}$). Using these quantities, we define the ratios

$$Q_1(j,k) = \frac{d^{\mathbf{V}}(\mathbf{w}_j, \mathbf{w}_{n^A_k(j)})}{d^{\mathbf{V}}(\mathbf{w}_j, \mathbf{w}_{n^{\mathbf{V}}_k(j)})}, \tag{4}$$

$$Q_2(j,k) = \frac{d^A(j, n^A_k(j))}{d^A(j, n^{\mathbf{V}}_k(j))}. \tag{5}$$

One has $Q_1(j,k) = Q_2(j,k) = 1$ only, if the k-th nearest neighbors in $\mathbf{V}$ and A coincide. Any deviations of the nearest neighbor ordering will result in values for $Q_{1,2}$ deviating from 1. However, not all differences in the nearest neighbor orderings in $\mathbf{V}$ and A are necessarily induced by neighborhood violations. Some can be due to locally varying magnification factors of the map, which in turn are induced by spatially varying stimulus densities in $\mathbf{V}$. To cancel out the latter effects, we define the products

$$P_1(j,k) = \left(\Pi^k_{l=1} Q_1(j,l)\right)^{\frac{1}{k}}, \tag{6}$$

$$P_2(j,k) = \left(\Pi^k_{l=1} Q_2(j,l)\right)^{\frac{1}{k}}. \tag{7}$$

For these the relations

$$P_1(j,k) \geq 1,$$
$$P_2(j,k) \leq 1$$

hold. Large deviations of P_1 (resp. P_2) from the value 1 indicate neighborhood violations, when looking from the output space into the input space (resp. from the input space into the output space). In order to get a symmetric overall measure, we further multiply P_1 and P_2 and find

$$P_3(j,k) = \left(\Pi^k_{l=1} Q_1(j,k) Q_2(j,k)\right)^{\frac{1}{2k}}. \tag{8}$$

Further averaging over all nodes and neighborhood orders finally yields the topographic product

$$P = \frac{1}{N(N-1)} \sum_{j=1}^{N} \sum_{k=1}^{N-1} \log(P_3(j,k)). \tag{9}$$

The possible values for P are to be interpreted as follows:

$$P \leq 0 : \quad \text{output space dimension } D^A \text{ too low,}$$
$$P = 0 : \quad \text{output space dimension } D^A \text{ o.k.,}$$
$$P \geq 0 : \quad \text{output space dimension } D^A \text{ too high.}$$

These formulas suffice to understand how the product is to be computed. A more detailed explanation for the rational behind each individual step of the derivation can be found in a forthcoming publication (Bauer et al., 1991).

3   EXAMPLES

We conclude the paper with two examples which exemplify how the method works.

3.1   ILLUSTRATIVE EXAMPLE

The first example deals with the mapping from a 2D input space onto rectangles of different aspect ratios. The stimulus distribution is flat in one direction, Gaussian shaped in the other (Fig 1a). The example demonstrates two aspects of our method at once. First it shows that the method works fine with maps resulting from nonflat stimulus distributions. These induce spatially varying areal magnification factors of the map, which in turn lead to twists in the neighborhood ordering between input space and output space. Compensation for such twists was the purpose of the multiplication in Eqs (6) and (7).

Table 1: Topographic product P for the map from a square input space with a Gaussian stimulus distribution in one direction, onto rectangles with different aspect ratios. The values for P are averaged over 8 networks each. The 43×6-output space matches the input data best, since its topographic product is smallest.

N	aspect ratio	P
256×1	256	-0.04400
128×2	64	-0.03099
64×4	16	-0.00721
43×6	7.17	0.00127
32×8	4	0.00224
21×12	1.75	0.01335
16×16	1	0.02666

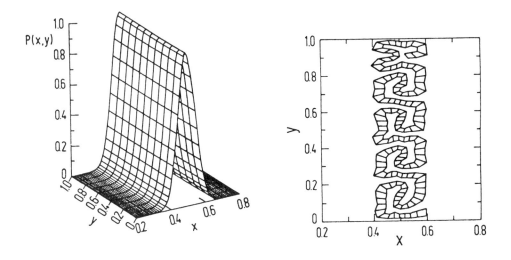

Fig. 1a   Fig. 1b

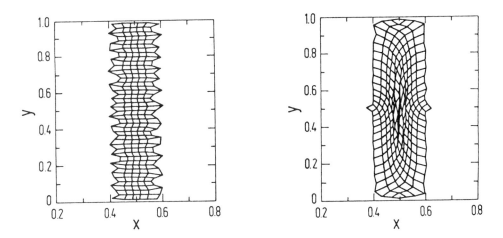

Fig. 1c   Fig. 1d

Figure 1: Self-organizing feature maps of a Gaussian shaped (a) 2-dimensional stimulus distribution onto output spaces with 128 × 2 (b), 43 × 6 (c) and 16 × 16 (d) output nodes. The 43 × 6-output space preserves neighborhood relations best.

Secondly the method cannot only be used to optimize the overall output space dimensionality, but also the individual dimensions in the different directions (i.e. the different aspect ratios). If the rectangles are too long, the resulting map is folded like a Peano curve (Fig. 1b), and neighborhood relations are severely violated perpendicular to the long side of the rectangle. If the aspect ratio fits, the map has a regular look (Fig. 1c), neighborhoods are preserved. The zig-zag-form at the outer boundary of the rectangle does not correspond to neighborhood violations. If the rectangle approaches a square, the output space is somewhat squashed into the input space, again violating neighborhood relations (Fig. 1d). The topographic product P coincides with this intuitive evaluation (Tab. 1) and picks the 43×6-net as the most neighborhood preserving one.

3.2   APPLICATION EXAMPLE

In our second example speech data is mapped onto output spaces of various dimensionality. The data represent utterances of the ten german digits, given as 19-dimensional acoustical feature vectors (Gramß et al., 1990). The P-values for the different maps are given in Tab. 2. For both the speaker-dependent as well as the speaker-independent case the method distinguishes the maps with $D^A = 3$ as most neighborhood preserving. Several points are interesting about these results. First of all, the suggested output space dimensionality exceeds the widely used $D^A = 2$. Secondly, the method does not generally judge larger output space dimensions as more neighborhood preserving, but puts an upper bound on D^A. The data seems to occupy a submanifold of the input space which is distinctly lower than four dimensional. Furthermore we see that the transition from one to several speakers does not change the value of D^A which is optimal under neighborhood considerations. This contradicts the expectation that the additional interspeaker variance in the data occupies a full additional dimension.

Table 2: Topographic product P for maps from speech feature vectors in a 19D input space onto output spaces of different dimensionality $D^{\mathbf{V}}$.

$D^{\mathbf{V}}$	N	P speaker-dependent	P speaker-independent
1	256	-0.156	-0.229
2	16×16	-0.028	-0.036
3	$7 \times 6 \times 6$	0.019	0.007
4	$4 \times 4 \times 4 \times 4$	0.037	0.034

What do these results mean for speech recognition? Let us suppose that several utterances of the same word lead to closeby feature vector sequences in the input space. If the mapping was not neighborhood preserving, one should expect the trajectories in the output space to be separated considerably. If a speech recognition system compares these output space trajectories with reference trajectories corresponding to reference utterances of the words, the probability of misclassification rises. So one should expect that a word recognition system with a Kohonen-map preprocessor and a subsequent trajectory classifier should perform better if the neighborhoods in the map are preserved.

The results of a recent speech recognition experiment coincide with these heuristic expectations (Brandt et al., 1991). The experiment was based on the same data set, made use of a Kohonen feature map as a preprocessor, and of a dynamic time-warping algorithm as a sequence classifier. The recognition performance of this hybrid system turned out to be better by about 7% for a 3D map, compared to a 2D map with a comparable number of nodes (0.795 vs. 0.725 recognition rate).

Acknowledgements

This work was supported by the Deutsche Forschungsgemeinschaft through SFB 185 "Nichtlineare Dynamik", TP A10.

References

H.-U. Bauer, K. Pawelzik, Quantifying the Neighborhood Preservation of Self-Organizing Feature Maps, submitted to IEEE TNN (1991).

W.D. Brandt, H. Behme, H.W. Strube, Bildung von Merkmalen zur Spracherkennung mittels Phonotopischer Karten, Fortschritte der Akustik - Proc. of DAGA 91 (DPG GmbH, Bad Honnef), 1057 (1991).

T. Gramß, H.W. Strube, Recognition of Isolated Words Based on Psychoacoustics and Neurobiology, Speech Comm. **9**, 35 (1990).

J.A. Kangas, T.K. Kohonen, J.T. Laaksonen, Variants of Self-Organizing Maps, IEEE Trans. Neur. Net. **1**, 93 (1990).

T. Kohonen, Self-Organization and Associative Memory, 3rd Ed., Springer (1989).

W. Liebert, K. Pawelzik, H.G. Schuster, Optimal Embeddings of Chaotic Attractors from Topological Considerations, Europhysics Lett. **14**, 521 (1991).

T. Martinetz, H. Ritter, K. Schulten, Three-Dimensional Neural Net for Learning Visuomotor Coordination of a Robot Arm, IEEE Trans. Neur. Net. **1**, 131 (1990).

T. Martinetz, K. Schulten, A "Neural-Gas" Network Learns Topologies, Proc. ICANN 91 Helsinki, ed. Kohonen et al., North-Holland, I-397 (1991).

K. Obermaier, H. Ritter, K. Schulten, A Principle for the Formation of the Spatial Structure of Cortical Feature Maps, Proc. Nat. Acad. Sci. USA **87**, 8345 (1990).

H. Ritter, K. Schulten, Convergence Properties of Kohonen's Topology Conserving Maps: Fluctuations, Stability and Dimension Selection, Biol. Cyb. **60**, 59-71 (1988).

H. Ritter, T. Martinetz, K. Schulten, Neuronale Netze, Addison Wesley (1990).

PART XIV

PERFORMANCE COMPARISONS

Human and Machine 'Quick Modeling'

Jakob Bernasconi
Asea Brown Boveri Ltd
Corporate Research
CH-5405 Baden,
SWITZERLAND

Karl Gustafson
University of Colorado
Department of Mathematics and
Optoelectronic Computing Center
Boulder, CO 80309

ABSTRACT

We present here an interesting experiment in 'quick modeling' by humans, performed independently on small samples, in several languages and two continents, over the last three years. Comparisons to decision tree procedures and neural net processing are given. From these, we conjecture that human reasoning is better represented by the latter, but substantially different from both. Implications for the 'strong convergence hypothesis' between neural networks and machine learning are discussed, now expanded to include human reasoning comparisons.

1   INTRODUCTION

Until recently the fields of symbolic and connectionist learning evolved separately. Suddenly in the last two years a significant number of papers comparing the two methodologies have appeared. A beginning synthesis of these two fields was forged at the NIPS '90 Workshop #5 last year (Pratt and Norton, 1990), where one may find a good bibliography of the recent work of Atlas, Dietterich, Omohundro, Sanger, Shavlik, Tsoi, Utgoff and others.

It was at that NIPS '90 Workshop that we learned of these studies, most of which concentrate on performance comparisons of decision tree algorithms (such as ID3, CART) and neural net algorithms (such as Perceptrons, Backpropagation). Independently three years ago we had looked at Quinlan's ID3 scheme (Quinlan, 1984) and intuitively and rather instantly not agreeing with the generalization he obtains by ID3 from a sample of 8 items generalized to 12 items, we subjected this example to a variety of human experiments. We report our findings, as compared to the performance of ID3 and also to various neural net computations.

1151

Because our focus on humans was substantially different from most of the other mentioned studies, we also briefly discuss some important related issues for further investigation. More details are given elsewhere (Bernasconi and Gustafson, to appear).

2   THE EXPERIMENT

To illustrate his ID3 induction algorithm, Quinlan (1984) considers a set C consisting of 8 objects, with attributes height, hair, and eyes. The objects are described in terms of their attribute values and classified into two classes, "+" and "−", respectively (see Table 1). The problem is to find a rule which correctly classifies all objects in C, and which is in some sense minimal.

Table 1: The set C of objects in Quinlan's classification example.

Object	Height	Hair	Eyes	Class
1	(s) short	(b) blond	(bl) blue	+
2	(t) tall	(b) blond	(br) brown	−
3	(t) tall	(r) red	(bl) blue	+
4	(s) short	(d) dark	(bl) blue	−
5	(t) tall	(d) dark	(bl) blue	−
6	(t) tall	(b) blond	(bl) blue	+
7	(t) tall	(d) dark	(br) brown	−
8	(s) short	(b) blond	(br) brown	−

The ID3 algorithm uses an information-theoretic approach to construct a "minimal" classification rule, in the form of a decision tree, which correctly classifies all objects in the learning set C. In Figure 1, we show two possible decision trees which correctly classify all 8 objects of the set C. Decision tree 1 is the one selected by the ID3 algorithm. As can be seen, "Hair" as root of the tree classifies four of the eight objects immediately. Decision tree 2 requires the same number of tests and has the same number of branches, but "Eyes" as root classifies only three objects at the first level of the tree.

Consider now how the decision trees of Figure 1 classify the remaining four possible objects in the set complement C'. Table 2 shows that the two decision trees lead to a different classification of the four objects of sample C'. We observe that the ID3-preferred decision tree 1 places a large importance on the "red" attribute (which occurs only in one object of sample C), while decision tree 2 puts much less emphasis on this particular attribute.

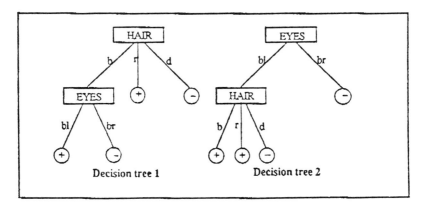

Figure 1: Two possible decision trees for the classification of sample C (Table 1)

Table 2: The set C' of the remaining four objects, and their classification by the decision trees of Figure 1.

Object	Attribute Values			Classification Tree 1	Tree 2
9	s	d	br	−	−
10	s	r	bl	+	+
11	s	r	br	+	−
12	t	r	br	+	−

3   GENERALIZATIONS BY HUMANS AND NEURAL NETS

Curious about these differences in the generalization behavior, we have asked some humans (colleagues, graduate students, undergraduate students, some nonscientists also) to "look" at the original sample C of 8 items, presented to them without warning, and to "use" this information to classify the remaining 4 objects. Over some time, we have accumulated a "human sample" of total size 73 from 3 continents representing 14 languages. The results of this human generalization experiment are summarized in Table 3. We observe that about 2/3 of the test persons generalized in the same manner as decision tree 2, and that less than 10 percent arrived at the generalization corresponding to the ID3-preferred decision tree 1.

Table 3: Classification of objects 9 through 12 by Humans and by a Neural Net. Based on a total sample of 73 humans. Each of the 4 contributing subsamples from different languages and locations gave consistent percentages.

Object	Attribute Values			Classification A	B	C	D	E	Other
9	s	d	br	−	−	−	−	−	⋮
10	s	r	bl	+	+	−	+	+	⋮
11	s	r	br	−	+	−	−	+	⋮
12	t	r	br	−	+	−	+	−	⋮
Humans:				65.8%	8.2%	4.1%	9.6%	—	12.3%
Neural Net:				71.4%	12.1%	9.4%	4.2%	2.9%	—

We also subjected this generalization problem to a variety of neural net computations. In particular, we analyzed a simple perceptron architecture with seven input units representing a unary coding of the attribute values (i.e., a separate input unit for each attribute value). The eight objects of sample C (Table 1) were used as training examples, and we employed the perceptron learning procedure (Rumelhart and McClelland, 1986) for a threshold output unit. In our initial experiment, the starting weights were chosen randomly in $(-1, 1)$ and the learning parameter h (the magnitude of the weight changes) was varied between 0.1 and 1. After training, the net was asked to classify the unseen objects 9 to 12 of Table 2. Out of the 16 possible classifications of this four object test set, only 5 were realized by the neural net (labelled A through E in Table 3). The percentage values given in Table 3 refer to a total of 9000 runs (3000 each for $h = 0.1, 0.5$, and 1.0, respectively). As can be seen, there is a remarkable correspondence between the solution profile of the neural net computations and that of the human experiment.

4   BACKWARD PREDICTION

There exist many different rules which all correctly classify the given set C of 8 objects (Table 1), but which lead to a different generalization behavior, i.e., to a different classification of the remaining objects 9 to 12 (see Tables 2 and 3). From a formal point of view, all of the 16 possible classifications of objects 9 to 12 are equally probable, so that no a priori criterion seems to exist to prefer one generalization over the other. We have nevertheless attempted to quantify the obviously ill-defined notion of "meaningful generalization". To estimate the relative "quality" of different classification rules, we propose to analyze the "backward prediction ability" of the respective generalizations. This is evaluated as follows. An appropriate learning method (e.g., neural nets) is used to construct rules which explain a given classification of objects 9 to 12, and these rules are applied to classify the initial set C of 8 objects. The 16 possible generalizations can then be rated according to their "backward prediction accuracy" with respect to the original classification of the sample C. We have performed a number of such calculations and consistently found that the 5 generalizations chosen by the neural nets in the forward prediction mode (cf. Table 3) have by far the highest backward prediction accuracy (on the average between 5 and 6 correct classifications). Their negations ("+" exchanged with "−"), on the other hand, predict only about 2 to 3 of the 8 original classifications correctly, while the remaining 6 possible generalizations all have a backward prediction accuracy close to 50% (4 out of 8 correct). These results, representing averages over 1000 runs, are given in Table 4.

Table 4: Neural Net backward prediction accuracy for the different classifications of objects 9 to 12.

Classification of objects				Backward prediction accuracy (%)
9	10	11	12	
−	+	−	−	76.0
−	+	+	−	71.2
−	+	+	+	71.1
−	+	−	+	67.9
−	−	−	−	61.9
−	−	+	−	52.6
−	−	−	+	52.5
+	+	−	−	52.5
+	+	+	−	47.4
+	+	−	+	47.3
−	−	+	+	47.0
+	+	+	+	37.2
+	−	+	−	31.7
+	−	−	−	30.1
+	−	−	+	28.3
+	−	+	+	23.6

In addition to Neural Nets, we have also used the ID3 method to evaluate the backward predictive power of different generalizations. This method generates fewer rules than the Neural Nets (often only a single one), but the resulting tables of backward prediction accuracies all exhibit the same qualitative features. As examples, we show in Figure 2 the ID3 backward prediction trees for two different generalizations, the ID3-preferred generalization which classifies the objects 9 to 12 as $(- + ++)$, and the Human and Neural Net generalization $(- + --)$. Both trees have a backward prediction accuracy of 75% (provided that "blond hair" in tree (a) is classified randomly).

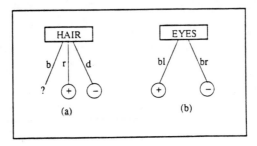

Figure 2: ID3 backward prediction trees, (a) for the ID3-preferred generalization
(− + ++), and (b) for the generalization preferred by Humans and Neural Nets,
(− + −−)

The overall backward prediction accuracy is not the only quantity of interest in these
calculations. We can, for example, examine how well the original classification of an
individual object in the set C is reproduced by predicting backwards from a given
generalization.

Some examples of such backward prediction profiles are shown in Figure 3. From
both the ID3 and the Neural Net calculations, it is evident that the backward
prediction behavior of the Human and Neural Net generalization is much more
informative than that of the ID3-solution, even though the two solutions have almost
the same average backward prediction accuracy.

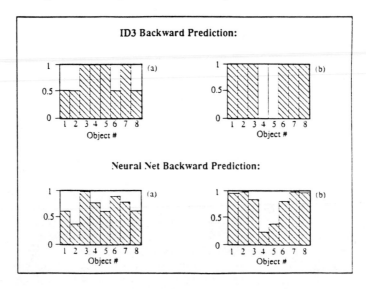

Figure 3: Individual backward prediction probabilities for the ID3-preferred generalization [graphs (a)], and for the Human and Neural Net generalization [graphs
(b)].

Finally, we have recently performed a Human backward prediction experiment. These results are given in Table 5. Details will be given elsewhere (Bernasconi and Gustafson, to appear). Note that the Backward Prediction results are commensurate with the Forward Prediction in both cases.

Table 5: Human backward predictions and accuracy from the two principal forward generalizations A (Neural Nets, Humans) and B (ID3).

Object	Class	Backward from A		Backward from B	
1	+	+	+	+	−
2	−	−	−	+	−
3	+	+	+	+	+
4	−	+	−	−	−
5	−	+	−	−	−
6	+	+	+	+	−
7	−	−	−	−	−
8	−	−	−	+	−
Humans:		59%	12%	33%	17%
Accuracy:		75%	100%	75%	75%

5   DISCUSSION AND CONCLUSIONS

Our basic conclusion from this experiment is that the "Strong Convergence Hypothesis" that Machine Learning and Neural Network algorithms are "close" can be sharpened, with the two fields then better distinguished, by comparison to Human Modelling. From the experiment described here, we conjecture a "Stronger Convergence Hypothesis" that Humans and Neural Nets are "closer."

Further conclusions related to minimal network size (re Pavel, Gluck, Henkle, 1989), crossvalidation (see Weiss and Kulikowski, 1991), sharing over nodes (as in Dietterich, Hild, Bakiri, to appear, and Atlas et al., 1990), and rule extracting (Shavlik et al., to appear), will appear elsewhere (Bernasconi and Gustafson, to appear). Although we have other experiments on other test sets underway, it should be stressed that our investigations especially toward Human comparisons are only preliminary and should be viewed as a stimulus to further investigations.

ACKNOWLEDGEMENT

This work was partially supported by the NFP 23 program of the Swiss National Science Foundation and by the US–NSF grant CDR8622236.

REFERENCES

L. Y. Pratt and S. W. Norton, "Neural Networks and Decision Tree Induction: Exploring the Relationship Between Two Research Areas," NIPS '90 Workshop #5 Summary (1990), 7 pp.

J. Ross Quinlan, "Learning Efficient Classification Procedures and Their Application to Chess End Games," in *Machine Learning: An Artificial Intelligence Approach*, edited by R. S. Michalski, J. G. Carbonell, and T. M. Mitchell, Springer-Verlag, Berlin (1984), 463–482.

D. E. Rumelhart and J. L. McClelland (Eds.), *Parallel Distributed Processing*, Vol. 1 MIT Press, Cambridge, MA (1986).

J. Bernasconi and K. Gustafson, "Inductive Inference and Neural Nets," to appear.

J. Bernasconi and K. Gustafson, "Generalization by Humans, Neural Nets, and ID3," IJCNN–91–Seattle.

Y. H. Pao, *Adaptive Pattern Recognition and Neural Networks*, Addison Wesley (1989), Chapter 4.

M. Pavel, M. A. Gluck and V. Henkle, "Constraints on Adaptive Networks for Modelling Human Generalization," in *Advances in Neural Information Processing Systems* 1, edited by D. Touretzky, Morgan Kaufmann, San Mateo, CA (1989), 2–10.

S. Weiss and C. Kulikowski, *Computer Systems that Learn*, Morgan Kaufmann (1991).

T. G. Dietterich, H. Hild, and G. Bakiri, "A Comparison of ID3 and Backpropagation for English Text-to-Speech Mapping," *Machine Learning*, to appear.

L. Atlas, R. Cole, J. Connor, M. El-Sharkawi, R. Marks, Y. Muthusamy, E. Barnard, "Performance Comparisons Between Backpropagation Networks and Classification Trees on Three Real-World Applications," in *Advances in Neural Information Processing Systems* 2, edited by D. Touretzky, Morgan Kaufmann (1990), 622–629.

J. Shavlik, R. Mooney, G. Towell, "Symbolic and Neural Learning Algorithms: An Experimental Comparison (revised)," *Machine Learning*, (1991, to appear).

A Comparison of Projection Pursuit and Neural Network Regression Modeling

Jenq-Neng Hwang, Hang Li,
Information Processing Laboratory
Dept. of Elect. Engr., FT-10
University of Washington
Seattle WA 98195

Martin Maechler, R. Douglas Martin, Jim Schimert
Department of Statistics
Mail Stop: GN-22
University of Washington
Seattle, WA 98195

Abstract

Two projection based feedforward network learning methods for model-free regression problems are studied and compared in this paper: one is the popular *back-propagation* learning (BPL); the other is the *projection pursuit* learning (PPL). Unlike the totally parametric BPL method, the PPL non-parametrically estimates unknown nonlinear functions sequentially (neuron-by-neuron and layer-by-layer) at each iteration while jointly estimating the interconnection weights. In terms of learning efficiency, both methods have comparable training speed when based on a Gauss-Newton optimization algorithm while the PPL is more parsimonious. In terms of learning robustness toward noise outliers, the BPL is more sensitive to the outliers.

1   INTRODUCTION

The back-propagation learning (BPL) networks have been used extensively for essentially two distinct problem types, namely model-free *regression* and *classification*,

1159

which have no *a priori* assumption about the unknown functions to be identified other than imposes a certain degree of smoothness. The projection pursuit learning (PPL) networks have also been proposed for both types of problems (Friedman85 [3]), but to date there appears to have been much less actual use of PPLs for both regression and classification than of BPLs. In this paper, we shall concentrate on regression modeling applications of BPLs and PPLs since the regression setting is one in which some fairly deep theory is available for PPLs in the case of low-dimensional regression (Donoho89 [2], Jones87 [6]).

A multivariate model-free regression problem can be stated as follows: given n pairs of vector observations, $(\mathbf{y}_l , \mathbf{x}_l) = (y_{l1}, \cdots, y_{lq}; x_{l1}, \cdots, x_{lp})$, which have been generated from unknown models

$$y_{li} = g_i(\mathbf{x}_l) + \epsilon_{li}, \quad l = 1, 2, \cdots, n; \quad i = 1, 2, \cdots, q \qquad (1)$$

where $\{\mathbf{y}_l\}$ are called the multivariable "response" vector and $\{\mathbf{x}_l\}$ are called the "independent variables" or the "carriers". The $\{g_i\}$ are unknown smooth non-parametric (model-free) functions from p-dimensional Euclidean space to the real line, i.e., $g_i : R^p \longrightarrow R, \forall i$. The $\{\epsilon_{li}\}$ are random variables with zero mean, $E[\epsilon_{li}] = 0$, and independent of $\{\mathbf{x}_l\}$. Often the $\{\epsilon_{li}\}$ are assumed to be independent and identically distributed (*iid*) as well.

The goal of regression is to generate the estimators, $\hat{g}_1, \hat{g}_2, \cdots, \hat{g}_q$, to best approximate the unknown functions, $g_1, g_2, \cdots, g_q$, so that they can be used for prediction of a new $\mathbf{y}$ given a new $\mathbf{x}$: $\hat{y}_i = \hat{g}_i(\mathbf{x}), \forall i$.

2   A TWO-LAYER PERCEPTRON AND BACK-PROPAGATION LEARNING

Several recent results have shown that a two-layer (one hidden layer) perceptron with sigmoidal nodes can in principle represent any Borel-measurable function to any desired accuracy, assuming "enough" hidden neurons are used. This, along with the fact that theoretical results are known for the PPL in the analogous two-layer case, justifies focusing on the two-layer perceptron for our studies here.

2.1   MATHEMATICAL FORMULATION

A two-layer perceptron can be mathematically formulated as follows:

$$u_k = \sum_{j=1}^{p} w_{kj} x_j - \theta_k = \mathbf{w}_k^T \mathbf{x} - \theta_k, \quad k = 1, 2, \cdots, m$$

$$y_i = \sum_{k=1}^{m} \beta_{ik} f_k(u_k) = \sum_{k=1}^{m} \beta_{ik} \sigma(u_k), \quad i = 1, 2, \cdots, q \qquad (2)$$

where u_k denotes the weighted sum input of the kth neuron in the hidden layer; θ_k denotes the bias of the kth neuron in the hidden layer; w_{kj} denotes the input-layer weight linked between the kth hidden neuron and the jth neuron of the input layer (or j^{th} element of the input vector $\mathbf{x}$); β_{ik} denotes the output-layer weight linked between the ith output neuron and the kth hidden neuron; f_k is the nonlinear activation function, which is usually assumed to be a fixed monotonically increasing (logistic) sigmoidal function, $\sigma(u) = 1/(1 + e^{-u})$.

The above formulation defines quite explicitly the parametric representation of functions which are being used to approximate $\{g_i(\mathbf{x}), \ i = 1, 2, \cdots, q\}$. A simple reparametrization allows us to write $\hat{g}_i(\mathbf{x})$ in the form:

$$\hat{g}_i(\mathbf{x}) = \sum_{k=1}^{m} \beta_{ik} \sigma(\frac{\alpha_k^T \mathbf{x} - \mu_k}{s_k}) \tag{3}$$

where α_k is a unit length version of weight vector $\mathbf{w}_k$. This formulation reveals how $\{\hat{g}_i\}$ are built up as a linear combination of sigmoids evaluated at translates (by μ_k) and scaled (by s_k) projection of $\mathbf{x}$ onto the unit length vector α_k.

2.2 BACK-PROPAGATION LEARNING AND ITS VARIATIONS

Historically, the training of a multilayer perceptron uses back-propagation learning (BPL). There are two common types of BPL: the *batch* one and the *sequential* one. The batch BPL updates the weights after the presentation of the complete set of training data. Hence, a training iteration incorporates one sweep through all the training patterns. On the other hand, the sequential BPL adjusts the network parameters as training patterns are presented, rather than after a complete pass through the training set. The sequential approach is a form of Robbins-Monro *Stochastic Approximation*.

While the two-layer perceptron provides a very powerful nonparametric modeling capability, the BPL training can be slow and inefficient since only the first derivative (or gradient) information about the training error is utilized. To speed up the training process, several *second-order* optimization algorithms, which take advantage of second derivative (or Hessian matrix) information, have been proposed for training perceptrons (Hwang90 [4]). For example, the Gauss-Newton method is also used in the PPL (Friedman85 [3]).

The fixed nonlinear nodal (sigmoidal) function is a monotone nondecreasing differentiable function with very simple first derivative form, and possesses nice properties for numerical computation. However, it does not interpolate/extrapolate efficiently in a wide variety of regression applications. Several attempts have been proposed to improve the choice of nonlinear nodal functions; e.g., the Gaussian or bell-shaped function, the locally tuned radial basis functions, and semi-parametric (non-fixed nodal function) nonlinear functions used in PPLs and hidden Markov models.

2.3 RELATIONSHIP TO KERNEL APPROXIMATION AND DATA SMOOTHING

It is instructive to compare the two-layer perceptron approximation in Eq. (3) with the well-known kernel method for regression. A *kernel* $K(\cdot)$ is a non-negative symmetric function which integrates to unity. Most kernels are also unimodal, with mode at the origin, $K(t_1) \geq K(t_2)$, $0 \leq t_1 < t_2$. A kernel estimate of $g_i(\mathbf{x})$ has the form

$$\hat{g}_{K,i}(\mathbf{x}) = \sum_{l=1}^{n} y_{li} \frac{1}{h^q} K(\frac{\|\mathbf{x} - \mathbf{x}_l\|}{h^q}), \tag{4}$$

where h is a bandwidth parameter and q is the dimension of $\mathbf{y}_l$ vector. Typically a good value of h will be chosen by a data-based cross-validation method. Consider for a moment the special case of the kernel approximator and the two-layer perceptron in Eq. (3) respectively, with *scalar* y_l and x_l, i.e., with $p = q = 1$ (hence unit length interconnection weight $\alpha = 1$ by definition):

$$\hat{g}_K(x) = \sum_{l=1}^{n} y_l \frac{1}{h} K(\frac{\|x - x_l\|}{h}) = \sum_{l=1}^{n} y_l \frac{1}{h} K(\frac{x - x_l}{h}), \tag{5}$$

$$\hat{g}(x) = \sum_{k=1}^{m} \beta_k \sigma(\frac{x - \mu_k}{s_k}) \tag{6}$$

This reveals some important connections between the two approaches.

Suppose that for $\hat{g}(x)$, we set $\sigma = K$, i.e., σ is a kernel and in fact identical to the kernel K, and that $\beta_k, \mu_k, s_k \equiv s$ have been chosen (trained), say by BPL. That is, all $\{s_k\}$ are constrained to a single unknown parameter value s. In general, $m \leq n$, or even m is a modest fraction of n when the unknown function $g(x)$ is reasonably smooth. Furthermore, suppose that h has been chosen by cross validation. Then one can expect $\hat{g}_K(x) \approx \hat{g}_\sigma(x)$, particularly in the event that the $\{\mu_k\}$ are close to the observed values $\{x_l\}$ and x is close to a specific μ_k value (relative to h). However, in this case where we force $s_k \equiv s$, one might expect $\hat{g}_K(x)$ to be a somewhat better estimate overall than $\hat{g}_\sigma(x)$, since the former is more local in character.

On the other hand, when one removes the restriction $s_k \equiv s$, then BPL leads to a local bandwidth selection, and in this case one may expect $\hat{g}_\sigma(x)$ to provide better approximation than $\hat{g}_K(x)$ when the function $g(x)$ has considerably varying curvature, $g''(x)$, and/or considerably varying error variance for the noise ϵ_{li} in Eq. (1). The reason is that a fixed bandwidth kernel estimate can not cope as well with changing curvature and/or noise variance as can a good smoothing method which uses a good local bandwidth selection method. A small caveat is in order: if m is fairly large, the estimation of a separate bandwidth for each kernel location, μ_k, may cause some increased variability in $\hat{g}_\sigma(x)$ by virtue of using many more parameters than are needed to adequately represent a nearly optimal local bandwidth selection method. Typically a nearly optimal local bandwidth function will have some degree of smoothness, which reflects smoothly varying curvature and/or noise variance, and a good local bandwidth selection method should reflect the smoothness constraints. This is the case in the high-quality "supersmoother", designed for applications like the PPL (to be discussed), which uses cross-validation to select bandwidth locally (Friedman85 [3]), and combines this feature with considerable speed.

The above arguments are probably equally valid without the restriction $\sigma = K$, because two sigmoids of opposite signs (via choice of two $\{\beta_k\}$) that are appropriately shifted, will approximate a kernel up to a scaling to enforce unity area. However, there is a novel aspect: one can have a separate local bandwidth for each half of the kernel, thereby using an asymmetric kernel, which might improve the approximation capabilities relative to symmetric kernels with a single local bandwidth in some situations.

In the multivariate case, the curse of dimensionality will often render useless the kernel approximator $\hat{g}_{K,i}(\mathbf{x})$ given by Eq. (4). Instead one might consider using a projection pursuit kernel (PPK) approximator:

$$\hat{g}_{PPK,i}(\mathbf{x}) = \sum_{l=1}^{n} \sum_{k=1}^{m} y_{li} \frac{1}{h_k} K(\frac{\alpha_k^T \mathbf{x} - \alpha_k^T \mathbf{x}_l}{h_k}) \tag{7}$$

where a different bandwidth h_k is used for each direction α_k. In this case, the similarities and differences between the PPK estimate and the BPL estimate $\hat{g}_{\sigma,i}(\mathbf{x})$ become evident.

The main difference between the two methods is that PPK performs explicit smoothing in each direction α_k using a kernel smoother, whereas BPL does implicit smoothing with both β_k (replacing y_{li}/h_k) and μ_k (replacing $\alpha_k^T \mathbf{x}_l$) being determined by nonlinear least squares optimization. In both PPK and BPL, the α_k and h_k are determined by nonlinear optimization (cross-validation choices of bandwidth parameters are inherently nonlinear optimization problems) (Friedman85 [3]).

3   PROJECTION PURSUIT LEARNING NETWORKS

The projection pursuit learning (PPL) is a statistical procedure proposed for multivariate data analysis using a two-layer network given in Eq. (2). This procedure derives its name from the fact that it interprets high dimensional data through well-chosen lower-dimensional projections. The "pursuit" part of the name refers to optimization with respect to the projection directions.

3.1   COMPARATIVE STRUCTURES OF PPL AND BPL

Similar to a BPL perceptron, a PPL network forms projections of the data in directions determined from the interconnection weights. However, unlike a BPL perceptron, which employs a fixed set of nonlinear (sigmoidal) functions, a PPL non-parametrically estimates the nonlinear nodal functions based on nonlinear optimization approach which involves use of a one-dimensional data-smoother (e.g., a least squares estimator followed by a variable window span data averaging mechanism) (Friedman85 [3]). Therefore, it is important to note that a PPL network is a semi-parametric learning network, which consists of both parametrically and non-parametrically estimated elements. This is in contrast to a BPL perceptron, which is a completely parametric model.

3.2   LEARNING STRATEGIES OF PPL

In comparison with a batch BPL, which employs either 1st-order gradient descent or 2nd-order Newton-like methods to estimate the weights of all layers *simultaneously* after all the training patterns are presented, a PPL learns neuron-by-neuron and layer-by-layer *cyclically* after all the training patterns are presented. Specifically, it applies linear least squares to estimate the output-layer weights, a one-dimensional data smoother to estimate the nonlinear nodal functions of each hidden neuron, and the Gauss-Newton nonlinear least squares method to estimate the input-layer weights.

The PPL procedure uses the batch learning technique to iteratively minimize the mean squared error, E, over all the training data. All the parameters to be estimated are hierarchically divided into m groups (each associated with one hidden neuron), and each group, say the kth group, is further divided into three subgroups: the output-layer weights, $\{\beta_{ik}, i = 1, \cdots, q\}$, connected to the kth hidden neuron; the nonlinear function, $f_k(u)$, of the kth hidden neuron; and the input-layer weights, $\{w_{kj}, j = 1, \cdots, p\}$, connected to the kth hidden neuron. The PPL starts from updating the parameters associated with the first hidden neuron (group) by updating each subgroup, $\{\beta_{i1}\}$, $f_1(u)$, and $\{w_{1j}\}$ consecutively (layer-by-layer) to minimize the mean squared error E. It then updates the parameters associated with the second hidden neuron by consecutively updating $\{\beta_{i2}\}$, $f_2(u)$, and $\{w_{2j}\}$. A complete updating pass ends at the updating of the parameters associated with the mth (the last) hidden neuron by consecutively updating $\{\beta_{im}\}$, $f_m(u)$, and $\{w_{mj}\}$. Repeated updating passes are made over all the groups until convergence (i.e., in our studies of Section 4, we use the stopping criterion that $\frac{|E^{(new)} - E^{(old)}|}{E^{(old)}}$ be smaller than a prespecified small constant, $\xi = 0.005$).

4   LEARNING EFFICIENCY IN BPL AND PPL

Having discussed the "parametric" BPL and the "semi-parametric" PPL from structural, computational, and theoretical viewpoints, we have also made a more practical comparison of learning efficiency via a simulation study. For simplicity of comparison, we confine the simulations to the two-dimensional univariate case, i.e., $p = 2$, $q = 1$. This is an important situation in practice, because the models can be visualized graphically as functions $y = g(x_1, x_2)$.

4.1   PROTOCOLS OF THE SIMULATIONS

Nonlinear Functions: There are five nonlinear functions $g^{(j)} : [0,1]^2 \rightarrow \mathbb{R}$ investigated (Maechler90 [7]), which are *scaled* such that the standard deviation is 1 (for a large regular grid of 2500 points on $[0,1]^2$), and *translated* to make the range nonnegative.

Training and Test Data: Two independent variables (carriers) (x_{l1}, x_{l2}) were generated from the uniform distribution $U([0,1]^2)$, i.e., the abscissa values $\{(x_{l1}, x_{l2})\}$ were generated as uniform random variates on $[0,1]$ and independent from each other. We generated 225 pairs $\{(x_{l1}, x_{l2})\}$ of abscissa values, and used this same set for experiments of all five different functions, thus eliminating an unnecessary extra random component of the simulation. In addition to one set of noiseless training data, another set of noisy training data was also generated by adding *iid* Gaussian noises.

Algorithm Used: The PPL simulations were conducted using the *S-Plus* package (S-Plus90 [1]) implementation of PPL, where 3 and 5 hidden neurons were tried (with 5 and 7 maximum working hidden neurons used separately to avoid the overfitting). The *S-Plus* implementation is based on the Friedman code (Friedman85 [3]), which uses a Gauss-Newton method for updating the lower layer weights. To obtain a fair comparison, the BPL was implemented using a batch Gauss-Newton method (rather than the usual gradient descent, which is slower) on two-layer perceptrons with linear output neurons and nonlinear sigmoidal hidden neurons (Hwang90 [4], Hwang91 [5]), where 5 and 10 hidden neurons were tried.

Independent Test Data Set: The assessment of performance was done by comparing the fitted models with the "true" function counterparts on a large independent test set. Throughout all the simulations, we used the same set of test data for performance assessment, i.e., $\{g^{(j)}(x_{l1}, x_{l2})\}$, of size $N = 10000$, namely a regularly spaced grid on $[0, 1]^2$, defined by its marginals.

4.2   SIMULATION RESULTS IN LEARNING EFFICIENCY

To summarize the simulation results in learning efficiency, we focused on the chosen three aspects: *accuracy*, *parsimony*, and *speed*.

Learning Accuracy: The accuracy determined by the absolute L_2 error measure of the independent test data in both learning methods are quite comparable either trained by noiseless or noisy data (Hwang91 [5]). Note that our comparisons are based on 5 & 10 hidden neurons of BPLs and 3 & 5 hidden neurons of PPLs. The reason of choosing different number of hidden neurons will be explained in the learning parsimony section.

Learning Parsimony: In comparison with BPL, the PPL is more parsimonious in training all types of nonlinear functions, i.e., in order to achieve comparable accuracy to the BPLs for a two-layer perceptrons, the PPLs require fewer hidden neurons (more parsimonious) to approximate the desired true function (Hwang91 [5]). Several factors may contribute to this favorable performance. First and foremost, the data-smoothing technique creates more pertinent nonlinear nodal functions, so the network adapts more efficiently to the observation data without using too many terms (hidden neurons) of interpolative projections. Secondly, the batch Gauss-Newton BPL updates all the weights in the network simultaneously while the PPL updates cyclically (neuron-by-neuron and layer-by-layer), which allows the most recent updating information to be used in the subsequent updating. That is, more important projection directions can be determined first so that the less important projections can have a easier search (the same argument used in favoring the Gauss-Seidel method over the Jacobi method in an iterative linear equation solver).

Learning Speed: As we reported earlier (Maechler90 [7]), the PPL took much less time (1-2 order of magnitude speedup) in achieving accuracy comparable with that of the sequential gradient descent BPL. Interestingly, when compared with the batch Gauss-Newton BPL, the PPL took quite similar amount of time over all the simulations (under the same number of hidden neurons and the same convergence threshold $\xi = 0.005$). In all simulations, both the BPLs and PPLs can converge under 100 iterations most of the time.

5   SENSITIVITY TO OUTLIERS

Both BPL's and PPL's are types of nonlinear least squares estimators. Hence like all least squares procedures, they are all sensitive to outliers. The outliers may come from large errors in measurements, generated by heavy tailed deviations from a Gaussian distribution for the noise ϵ_{li} in Eq. (1).

When in presence of additive Gaussian noises without outliers, most functions can be well approximated by 5-10 hidden neurons using BPL or with 3-5 hidden neurons using PPL. When the Gaussian noise is altered by adding one outlier, the BPL with 5-10 hidden neurons can still approximate the desired function reasonably well in general at the sacrifice of the magnified error around the vicinity of the outlier. If the number of outliers increases to 3 in the same corner, the BPL can only get a "distorted" approximation of the desired function. On the other hand, the PPL with 5 hidden neurons can successfully approximate the desired function and remove the single outlier. In case of three outliers, the PPL using simple data smoothing techniques can no longer keep its robustness in accuracy of approximation.

Acknowledgements

This research was partially supported through grants from the National Science Foundation under Grant No. ECS-9014243.

References

[1] *S-Plus* Users Manual (Version 3.0). Statistical Science Inc., Seattle, WA, 1990.

[2] D.L. Donoho and I.M. Johnstone. Projection–based approximation and a duality with kernel methods. The Annals of Statistics, Vol. 17, No. 1, pp. 58–106, 1989.

[3] J.H. Friedman. Classification and multiple regression through projection pursuit. Technical Report No. 12, Department of Statistics, Stanford University, January 1985.

[4] J. N. Hwang and P. S. Lewis. From nonlinear optimization to neural network learning. In Proc. *24th Asilomar Conf. on Signals, Systems, & Computers*, pp. 985-989, Pacific Grove, CA, November 1990.

[5] J. N. Hwang, H. Li, D. Martin, J. Schimert. The learning parsimony of projection pursuit and back-propagation networks. In *25th Asilomar Conf. on Signals, Systems, & Computers*, Pacific Grove, CA, November 1991.

[6] L.K. Jones. On a conjecture of Huber concerning the convergence of projection pursuit regression. The Annals of Statistics, Vol. 15, No. 2,880–882, 1987.

[7] M. Maechler, D. Martin, J. Schimert, M. Csoppenszky and J. N. Hwang. Projection pursuit learning networks for regression. in Proc. *2nd Int'l Conf. Tools for AI*, pp. 350-358, Washington D.C., November 1990.

Benchmarking Feed-Forward Neural Networks: Models and Measures

Leonard G. C. Hamey
Computing Discipline
Macquarie University
NSW 2109
AUSTRALIA

Abstract

Existing metrics for the learning performance of feed-forward neural networks do not provide a satisfactory basis for comparison because the choice of the training epoch limit can determine the results of the comparison. I propose new metrics which have the desirable property of being independent of the training epoch limit. The *efficiency* measures the yield of correct networks in proportion to the training effort expended. The *optimal* epoch limit provides the greatest efficiency. The learning performance is modelled statistically, and asymptotic performance is estimated. Implementation details may be found in (Hamey, 1992).

1 Introduction

The empirical comparison of neural network training algorithms is of great value in the development of improved techniques and in algorithm selection for problem solving. In view of the great sensitivity of learning times to the random starting weights (Kolen and Pollack, 1990), individual trial times such as reported in (Rumelhart, *et al.*, 1986) are almost useless as measures of learning performance.

Benchmarking experiments normally involve many training trials (typically $N = 25$ or 100, although Tesauro and Janssens (1988) use $N = 10000$). For each trial i, the training time to obtain a correct network t_i is recorded. Trials which are not successful within a limit of T epochs are considered failures; they are recorded as $t_i = T$. The mean successful training time $\bar{t}_T$ is defined as follows.

1167

$$\bar{t}_T = \frac{\sum_{t_i < T} t_i}{S}$$

where S is the number of successful trials. The median successful time $\tilde{t}_T$ is the epoch at which $S/2$ trials are successes. It is common (e.g. Jacobs, 1987; Kruschke and Movellan, 1991; Veitch and Holmes, 1991) to report the mean and standard deviation along with the success rate $\lambda_T = S/N$, but the results are strongly dependent on the choice of T as shown by Fahlman (1988). The problem is to characterise training performance independent of T.

Tesauro and Janssens (1988) use the harmonic mean $\bar{t}_H$ as the average learning rate.

$$\bar{t}_H = \frac{N}{\sum_{i=1}^{N} \frac{1}{t_i}}$$

This minimizes the contribution of large learning times, so changes in T will have little effect on $\bar{t}_H$. However, $\bar{t}_H$ is not an unbiased estimator of the mean, and is strongly influenced by the shortest learning times, so that training algorithms which produce greater variation in the learning times are preferred by this measure.

Fahlman (1988) allows the learning program to restart an unsuccessful trial, incorporating the failed training time in the total time for that trial. This method is realistic, since a failed trial would be restarted in a problem-solving situation. However, Fahlman's averages are still highly dependent upon the epoch limit T which is chosen beforehand as the restart point.

The present paper proposes new performance measures for feed-forward neural networks. In section 4, the optimal epoch limit T_E is defined. T_E is the optimal restart point for Fahlman's averages, and the efficiency e is the scaled reciprocal of the optimised Fahlman average. In sections 5 and 6, the asymptotic learning behaviour is modelled and the mean and median are corrected for the truncation effect of the epoch limit T. Some benchmark results are presented in section 7, and compared with previously published results.

2   Performance Measurement

For benchmark results to be useful, the parameters and techniques of measurement and training must be fully specified. Training parameters include the network structure, the learning rate η, the momentum term α and the range of the initial random weights $[-r, r]$.

For problems with binary output, the correctness of the network response is defined by a threshold τ_c—responses less than τ_c are considered equivalent to 0, while responses greater than $1 - \tau_c$ are considered equivalent to 1. For problems with analog output, the network response is considered correct if it lies within τ_c of the desired value. In the present paper, only binary problems are considered and the value $\tau_c = 0.4$ is used, as in (Fahlman 1988).

3   The Training Graph

The training graph displays the proportion of correct networks as a function of the epoch. Typically, the tail of the graph resembles a decay curve. It is evident in figure 1 that the

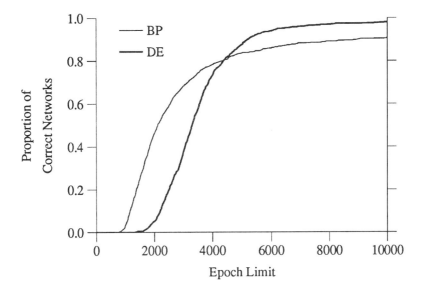

Figure 1: Typical Training Graphs: Back-Propagation ($\eta = 0.5, \alpha = 0$) and Descending Epsilon ($\eta = 0.5, \alpha = 0$) on Exclusive-Or (2–2–1 structure, $N = 1000, T = 10000$).

success rate for either algorithm may be significantly increased if the epoch limit was raised beyond 10000. The shape of the training graph varies depending upon the problem and the algorithm employed to solve it. Descending epsilon (Yu and Simmons, 1990) solves a higher proportion of the exclusive-or trials with $T = 10000$, but back-propagation would have a higher success rate if $T = 3000$. This exemplifies the dramatic effect that the choice of T can have on the comparison of training algorithms.

Two questions naturally arise from this discussion: "What is the optimal value for T?" and "What happens as $T \to \infty$?". These questions will be addressed in the following sections.

4   Efficiency and Optimal T.

Adjusting the epoch limit T in a learning algorithm affects both the yield of correct networks and the effort expended on unsuccessful trials. To capture the total yield for effort ratio, we define the efficiency $E(t)$ of epoch limit t as follows.

$$E(t) = 1000 \frac{\sum_{t_i < t} 1}{\sum_{i=1}^{N} \min(t, t_i)}$$

The efficiency graph plots the efficiency against of the epoch limit. The efficiency graph for back-propagation (figure 2) exhibits a strong peak with the efficiency reducing relatively quickly if the epoch limit is too large. In contrast, the efficiency graph for descending epsilon exhibits an extremely broad peak with only a slight drop as the epoch limit is increased. This occurs because the asymptotic success rate (λ in section 5) is close to

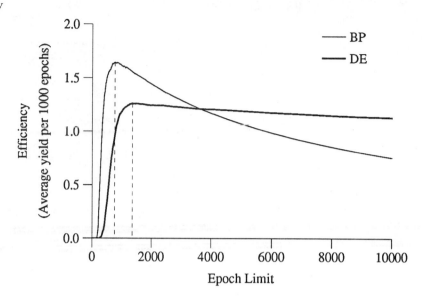

Figure 2: Efficiency Graphs: Back-Propagation ($\eta = 0.3, \alpha = 0.9$) and Descending Epsilon ($\eta = 0.3, \alpha = 0.9$) on Exclusive-Or (2–2–1 structure, $N = 1000, T = 10000$).

1.0; in such cases, the efficiency remains high over a wider range of epoch limits and near-optimal performance can be more easily achieved for novel problems.

The efficiency benchmark parameters are derived from the graph as shown in figure 3. The epoch limit T_E at which the peak efficiency occurs is the optimal epoch limit. The peak efficiency e is a good performance measure, independent of T when $T > T_E$. Unlike $\bar{t}_H$, it is not biased by the shortest learning times. The peak efficiency is the scaled reciprocal of Fahlman's (1988) average for optimal T, and incorporates the failed trials as a performance penalty. The optimisation of training parameters is suggested by Tesauro and Janssens (1988), but they do not optimise T. For comparison with other performance measures, the unscaled optimised Fahlman average $\bar{t}_E = 1000/e$ may be used instead of e.

The prediction of the optimal epoch limit T_E for novel problems would help reduce wasted computation. The range parameters T_{E1} and T_{E2} show how precisely T must be set to obtain efficiency within 50% of optimal—if two algorithms are otherwise similar in performance, the one with a wider range (T_{E1}, T_{E2}) would be preferred for novel problems.

5   Asymptotic Performance: $T \to \infty$

In the training graph, the proportion of trials that ultimately learn correctly can be estimated by the asymptote which the graph is approaching. I statistically model the tail of the graph by the distribution $F(t) = 1 - [a(t - T_0) + 1]^{-k}$ and thus estimate the asymptotic success rate λ. Figure 4 illustrates the model parameters. Since the early portions of the graph are dominated by initialisation effects, T_0, the point where the model commences to fit, is determined by applying the Kolmogorov-Smirnov goodness-of-fit test (Stephens 1974)

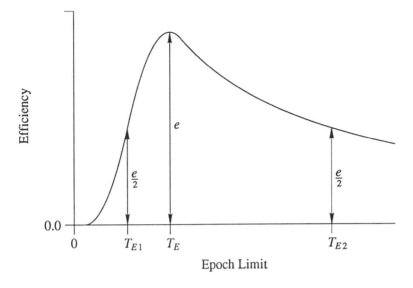

Figure 3: Efficiency Parameters in Relation to the Efficiency Graph.

for all possible values of T_0. The maximum likelihood estimates of a and k are found by using the simplex algorithm (Caceci and Cacheris, 1984) to directly maximise the following log-likelihood equation.

$$\mathcal{L}(t) = M \left[\ln a + \ln k - \ln \left(1 - \left(a(T - T_0) + 1 \right)^{-k} \right) \right] - $$
$$(k + 1) \sum_{T_0 < t_i < T} \ln \left(a(t_i - T_0) + 1 \right)$$

where M is the number of trials recording times in the range (T_0, T). The asymptotic success rate λ is then obtained as follows.

$$\lambda = \gamma + \frac{\lambda_T (1 - \gamma)}{F(T)}$$

In practice, the statistical model I have chosen is not suitable for all learning algorithms. For example, in preliminary investigations I have been unable to reliably model the descending epsilon algorithm (Yu and Simmons, 1990). Further study is needed to develop more widely applicable models.

6   Corrected Measures

The mean $\bar{t}_T$ and the median $\tilde{t}_T$ are based upon only those trials that succeeded in T epochs. The asymptotic learning model predicts additional success for $t > T$ epochs. Incorporating

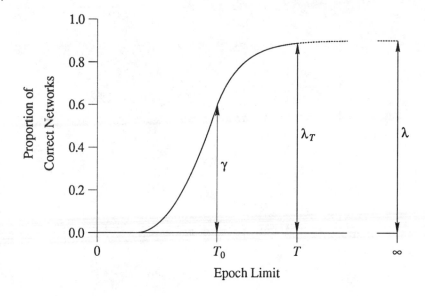

Figure 4: Parameters for the Model of Asymptotic Performance.

the predicted successes, the corrected mean $\bar{t}_C$ estimates the mean successful learning time as $T \to \infty$.

$$\bar{t}_C = \frac{\lambda_T \bar{t}_T + (\lambda - \lambda_T)\left(\frac{1}{a(k-1)} + T\right)}{\lambda}$$

The corrected median $\tilde{t}_C$ is the epoch for which $\lambda/2$ of the trials are successes. It estimates the median successful learning time as $T \to \infty$.

7   Benchmark Results for Back-Propagation

Table 1 presents optimised results for two popular benchmark problems: the 2–2–1 exclusive-or problem (Rumelhart, *et al.*, 1986, page 334), and the 10–5–10 encoder/decoder problem (Fahlman, 1988). Both problems employ three-layer networks with one hidden layer fully connected to the input and output units. The networks were trained with input and output values of 0 and 1. The weights were updated after each epoch of training; i.e. after each cycle through all the training patterns.

The characteristics of the learning for these two problems differs significantly. To accurately benchmark the exclusive-or problem, $N = 10000$ learning runs were needed to measure e accurate to ± 0.3. With $T = 200$, I searched the combinations of α, η and r. The optimal parameters were then used in a separate run with $N = 10000$ and $T = 2000$ to estimate the other benchmark parameters. In contrast, the encoder/decoder problem produced more stable efficiency values so that $N = 100$ learning runs produced estimates of e precise to ± 0.2. With $T = 600$, all the learning runs converged. The final benchmark values were

Table 1: Optimised Benchmark Results.

PROBLEM	r	α	η	e	T_E	T_{E1}	T_{E2}	$\bar{t}_E$
exclusive-or 2–2–1	1.4 ±0.2	0.65 ±0.05	7.0 ±0.5	17.1 ±0.3	49	26	235	59
encoder/decoder 10–5–10	1.1 ±0.2	0.00 ±0.10	1.7 ±0.1	8.1 ±0.2	∞	110	∞	124

PROBLEM	a	k	T_0	γ	λ	$\bar{t}_C$	λ_T	$\bar{t}_T$	$\bar{t}_H$
exclusive-or	0.1	0.5	54	0.66	0.93	409	0.76	50	40
encoder/decoder					1.00	124	1.00	124	114

determined with $N = 1000$. Confidence intervals for e were obtained by applying the jackknife procedure (Mosteller and Tukey, 1977, chapter 8); confidence intervals on the training parameters reflect the range of near-optimal efficiency results.

In the exclusive-or results, the four means vary from each other considerably. $\bar{t}_C$ is large because the asymptotic performance model predicts many successful learning runs with $T > 2000$. However, since the model is fitting only a small portion of the data (approximately 1000 cases), its predictions may not be highly reliable. $\bar{t}_T$ is low because the limit $T = 2000$ discards the longer training runs. $\bar{t}_H$ is also low because it is strongly biased by the shortest times. $\bar{t}_E$ measures the training effort required per trained network, including failure times, provided that $T = 49$. However, T_{E1} and T_{E2} show that T can lie within the range (26,235) and achieve performance no worse than 118 epochs effort per trained network.

The results for the encoder/decoder problem agree well with Fahlman (1988) who found $\alpha = 0$, $\eta = 1.7$ and $r = 1.0$ as optimal parameter values and obtained $\bar{t} = 129$ based upon $N = 25$. Equal performance is obtained with $\alpha = 0.1$ and $\eta = 1.6$, but momentum values in excess of 0.2 reduce the efficiency. Since all the learning runs are successful, $\bar{t}_E = \bar{t}_C = \bar{t}_T$ and $\lambda = \lambda_T = 1.0$. Both T_E and T_{E2} are infinite, indicating that there is no need to limit the training epochs to produce optimal learning performance. Because there were no failed runs, the asymptotic performance was not modelled.

8   Conclusion

The measurement of learning performance in artificial neural networks is of great importance. Existing performance measurements have employed measures that are either dependent on an arbitrarily chosen training epoch limit or are strongly biased by the shortest learning times. By optimising the training epoch limit, I have developed new performance measures, the efficiency e and the related mean $\bar{t}_E$, which are both independent of the training epoch limit and provide an unbiased measure of performance. The optimal training epoch limit T_E and the range over which near-optimal performance is achieved (T_{E1}, T_{E2}) may be useful for solving novel problems.

I have also shown how the random distribution of learning times can be statistically modelled, allowing prediction of the asymptotic success rate λ, and computation of corrected mean and median successful learning times, and I have demonstrated these new techniques on two popular benchmark problems. Further work is needed to extend the modelling to encompass a wider range of algorithms and to broaden the available base of benchmark results. In the process, it is believed that greater understanding of the learning processes of feed-forward artificial neural networks will result.

References

M. S. Caceci and W. P. Cacheris. Fitting curves to data: The simplex algorithm is the answer. *Byte*, pages 340–362, May 1984.

Scott E. Fahlman. An empirical study of learning speed in back-propagation networks. Technical Report CMU-CS-88-162, Computer Science Department, Carnegie Mellon University, Pittsburgh, PA, 1988.

Leonard G. C. Hamey. Benchmarking feed-forward neural networks: Models and measures. Macquarie Computing Report, Computing Discipline, Macquarie University, NSW 2109 Australia, 1992.

R. A. Jacobs. Increased rates of convergence through learning rate adaptation. COINS Technical Report 87-117, University of Massachusetts at Amherst, Dept. of Computer and Information Science, Amherst, MA, 1987.

John F. Kolen and Jordan B. Pollack. Back propagation is sensitive to initial conditions. *Complex Systems*, 4:269–280, 1990.

John K. Kruschke and Javier R. Movellan. Benefits of gain: Speeded learning and minimal hidden layers in back-propagation networks. *IEEE Trans. Systems, Man and Cybernetics*, 21(1):273–280, January 1991.

Frederick Mosteller and John W. Tukey. *Data Analysis and Regression*. Addison-Wesley, 1977.

D. E. Rumelhart, G. E. Hinton, and R. J. Williams. Learning internal representations by error propagation. In *Parallel Distributed Processing*, chapter 8, pages 318–362. MIT Press, 1986.

M. A. Stephens. EDF statistics for goodness of fit and some comparisons. *Journal of the American Statistical Association*, 69:730–737, September 1974.

G. Tesauro and B. Janssens. Scaling relationships in back-propagation learning. *Complex Systems*, 2:39–44, 1988.

A. C. Veitch and G. Holmes. Benchmarking and fast learning in neural networks: Results for back-propagation. In *Proceedings of the Second Australian Conference on Neural Networks*, pages 167–171, 1991.

Yeong-Ho Yu and Robert F. Simmons. Descending epsilon in back-propagation: A technique for better generalization. In *Proceedings of the International Joint Conference on Neural Networks 1990*, 1990.

Keyword Index

AUTHOR INDEX